MAMMALS OF COLORADO

SECOND EDITION

MAMMALS OF COLORADO

SECOND EDITION

David M. Armstrong, James P. Fitzgerald, and Carron A. Meaney

Denver Museum of Nature & Science and University Press of Colorado

Published by the University Press of Colorado
5589 Arapahoe Avenue, Suite 206C
Boulder, Colorado 80303

Printed in the United States of America

The University Press of Colorado is a proud member of
the Association of American University Presses.

The University Press of Colorado is a cooperative publishing enterprise supported, in part, by Adams State College, Colorado State University, Fort Lewis College, Mesa State College, Metropolitan State College of Denver, Regis University, University of Colorado, University of Northern Colorado, and Western State College of Colorado.

The paper used in this publication meets the minimum requirements of the American National Standard for Information Sciences—Permanence of Paper for Printed Library Materials. ANSI Z39.48-1992

Library of Congress Cataloging-in-Publication Data

Armstrong, David Michael, 1944–
Mammals of Colorado / David M. Armstrong, James P. Fitzgerald, and Carron A. Meaney. — 2nd ed.
p. cm.
Rev. ed. of: Mammals of Colorado / James P. Fitzgerald, Carron A. Meany, David M. Armstrong. 1994.
Includes bibliographical references and index.
ISBN 978-1-60732-047-0 (hardcover : alk. paper) — ISBN 978-1-60732-048-7 (e-book)
I. Fitzgerald, James P., 1940- II. Meaney, Carron A., 1950– III. Fitzgerald, James P., 1940– Mammals of Colorado. IV. Title.
QL719.C6F58 2011
599.09788—dc22

2011006206

Design by Daniel Pratt

20 19 18 17 16 15 14 13 12 11   10 9 8 7 6 5 4 3 2 1

Contents

CONTENTS

* Species of possible occurrence in Colorado.

* Species of possible occurrence in Colorado.

* Species of possible occurrence in Colorado.

* Species of possible occurrence in Colorado.

Introduction

This book has a single overriding purpose: to allow readers to increase their appreciation for Colorado's diverse fauna of native mammals. Our view is that the more we know about something, the more tenacious we are in protecting it. So we hope that this work will serve not only readers but also Colorado's native mammals (and their richly varied and beautiful habitats).

This book consists of 4 introductory chapters followed by chapters treating each of the 10 orders of mammals that are represented in the modern fauna of Colorado. The introductory chapters are intended to provide context and cover the environment, mammals in general, the history of the Coloradan fauna and the evolution of human understanding of that fauna, and the ongoing stewardship of Colorado's mammals (game and non-game) and their habitats.

Orders, families, and genera are treated in approximate phylogenetic order, following D. Wilson and Reeder (2005), the most recent comprehensive synopsis of mammalian species worldwide. Obviously, any summary and compilation of that sort is a progress report rather than the final word. Biological classification is a dynamic process, intended to reflect our best understanding of evolutionary relationships. The higher-level taxonomy of mammals is in an exciting state of flux; additional changes should be expected as the increasingly abundant fossil and molecular evidence is reported and synthesized.

Unlike ornithologists with their "American Ornithologists Union Checklist" of birds, mammalogists have not adopted an "official" list of common names. In this book, scientific names of species follow R. Baker, L. Bradley, et al. (2003), unless more recent published literature provides convincing reason to change (and such deviations are noted in text). The sequence of genera within families follows R. Baker, L. Bradley, et al. (2003) and species within genera are treated alphabetically. Common (vernacular) names of species generally follow R. Baker, L. Bradley, et al. (2003), unless traditional local usage favors a more familiar or appropriate name (and such exceptions are noted in text). We chose not to follow the comprehensive worldwide list of common names published by D. Wilson and Cole (2000) because that would have led to rather frequent deviation from familiar usage in Colorado and adjacent states.

Accounts are included for some 124 species of native mammals documented in Colorado since permanent Euro-American settlement in the mid-nineteenth century, of which 3 have been extirpated: the gray wolf, grizzly bear, and wolverine. (Interestingly, individuals of 2 of those species, the gray wolf and the wolverine, have wandered into Colorado from ongoing recovery efforts in northwestern Wyoming.) Additional accounts describe species introduced by humans (deliberately or not) and established in the wild. A number of additional species are included that may eventually be found to occur in Colorado (e.g., the banner-tailed kangaroo rat, Stephens' woodrat, and collared peccary). Note that these all are species that occur generally to the south or southwest of Colorado, species that may respond positively to ongoing climatic change. Our hope is that including such species in keys will help to document those mammals in Colorado should they eventually be found to occur here. Other southern species—such as the hispid cotton rat and nine-banded armadillo—appear to be expanding in the state, and perhaps we should include feral domestic hogs (*Sus scrofa*) on that list.

Accounts of species are organized under 4 subheadings. "Description" includes external and cranial measurements (mostly in metric units; see Appendix A) and occasional comparison with confusingly similar species. More detailed measurements and comparisons (by subspecies) are available in D. Armstrong (1972).

"Distribution" briefly summaries geographic and ecological distribution and lists Coloradan subspecies (where recognized). D. Armstrong (1972) reviewed Coloradan subspecies of native mammals to that date. Where more recent work has revised or questioned those subspecific designations, that is noted. Salient taxonomic remarks on species are also included in this section. Maps of North American distributions generally are based on E. Hall (1981), with permission of the publisher, John Wiley and Sons.

Range maps should be used with appropriate caution. Range maps are intended to present the approximate geographic range of a particular species. Maps of Coloradan distributions are based roughly on the "spot maps" in D. Armstrong (1972), which were documented by museum specimens and published records to that time and therefore summarize about a century of formal study of the fauna. Maps in this work try to capture more recent range expansions. Mapping species' ranges is not an easy matter, for a host of biological reasons. For thoughtful analyses of the problem, see Owen (2001) and Gaston (2009). Any published range map is necessarily crude, and the best of them would be out-of-date by the time it is printed because the range of a species is dynamic from moment to moment as individuals move in response to changing ecological opportunities and challenges at the levels of populations, communities, and ecosystems. Some have addressed this problem by abstracting predictive ranges, based on ecological niche modeling (A. T. Peterson 2001). The quality of that process depends, of course, on the quality and quantity of available data (see Lozier et al. 2009 for a cogent critique).

"Natural History" includes information on habitat, population ecology (e.g., density, dispersion, home range), predators and parasites, reproduction and development, behavior, food and foraging, and general status (including harvest by humans, where appropriate). Many species accounts point to gaps in our knowledge of particular species. Dedicated local naturalists have made remarkable contributions to our knowledge of Coloradan mammals over the past century and more. A great deal can be learned about mammals in the wild by simple, careful observation. Research on mammals that involves capture, collecting, or other intervention can be done only under permit from the Colorado Division of Wildlife. The American Society of Mammalogists promulgates strict guidelines for capture, handling, and use of wild mammals in research (Gannon et al. 2007).

Most of the information in this section is tied to citations to articles in the zoological literature (including wildlife management). Systematic review of literature continued through mid-October 2009, with a few items inserted thereafter. This literature review was by no means comprehensive, but we have attempted to cite the major studies of mammals in Colorado, studies of a particular species in areas adjacent to Colorado, and important and readily available general reviews. Interested readers are encouraged to pursue those sources for additional information. In particular, we note that to date (December 2010), some 90 percent of Coloradan mammals are the subject of accounts in the series *Mammalian Species*, published by the American Society of Mammalogists. All accounts are available gratis on-line (http://www.science.smith.edu/departments/Biology/VHAYSSEN/ msi/default.html).

We include photographs, line drawings, and maps to aid in identification and to encourage readers to make their own observations on the geographic and ecological distribution and habits of Coloradan mammals. In light of ongoing environmental change, new distributional records of Coloradan mammals are of particular interest and any of the authors would be glad to receive notes on readers' observations. Photographic documentation of animals or their sign is particularly valuable.

For each of the states near or adjacent to Colorado, there are comprehensive, technical taxonomic and distributional studies of mammals (or formal checklists of species): Arizona (Cockrum 1960; Hoffmeister 1986), Kansas (Cockrum 1952), Nebraska (J. K. Jones 1964), New Mexico (Findley et al. 1975; J. Frey 2004), Texas (W. Manning and Jones 1998), Utah (Durrant 1952), and Wyoming (Long 1965).

In a number of cases more general reviews of state and regional mammalian faunas are available, including for Kansas (Bee et al. 1981), Nebraska and the Dakotas (J. K. Jones, Armstrong, et al. 1983; J. K. Jones, Armstrong, and Choate 1985), New Mexico (Findley 1987), Oklahoma (Caire et al. 1989), Texas (Schmidly 1977, 1983; W. B. Davis and Schmidly 1994), southeastern Utah (Armstrong 1984), and Wyoming (T. Clark and Stromberg 1987).

Halfpenny (1986) provided an invaluable primer on tracking mammals and a field guide (2001) to sign of Rocky Mountain mammals. Elbroch (2003) published a richly illustrated guide to tracks and sign of mammals of North America generally. J. Russell et al. (2009) raised the prospect of computer-assisted tracking using image analysis. The field guide to Coloradan mammals by Tekiela (2007) included excellent photographs of many species.

Acknowledgments. Line art in keys and accounts of species is from the first edition of this work, with thanks to Dave Carlson of BioGraphics and Tim McCracken and students in the Biological Illustration Program of Colorado State University. Barry Syler donated his exquisite drawings for the chapter headings. Additional drawings were prepared by Marge Leggitt of the Denver Museum of Nature and Science (formerly the Denver Museum of Natural History). Maps of North American ranges were drafted by Lisa McGuire of DMNS based on maps in E. Hall (1981), with permission of John Wiley and Sons. Maps of distributional ranges in Colorado were drafted for this edition by Christine Fairbanks of the Department of Ecology and Evolutionary Biology, University of Colorado at Boulder (with guidance from the authors).

Photographs are credited individually in respective legends. Here we recognize all of these photo-naturalists generally, and with deep appreciation, for their skill and generosity and for their contributions to understanding and communicating the richness and beauty of Colorado's mammalian fauna.

Like any such project, this one demanded much of family, friends, and colleagues. We all thank the late Robert B. Finley of the US Fish and Wildlife Service for collegial conversation and inspiration over the years.

In additional to dozens of inspiring students over nearly four decades at the University of Colorado at Boulder (several of whom are recognized by citations throughout this volume), Armstrong gives special thanks to his partner, Susan Jessup, who tolerated his long hours over many months in front of the computer and negotiated precarious stacks of books, papers, and manuscript in the East Wing. Further, he celebrates her tenacious stewardship of Sylvan Dale Guest Ranch, at the mouth of the Big Thompson Canyon, where perpetual conservation easements protect panoramic views and diverse foothills backcountry for future generations—of Mexican woodrats, Townsend's big-eared bats, and northern rock mice.

Fitzgerald thanks again his wife, Jody, for her patience with his writing and for her love and appreciation of wild mammals, from her favorite pikas to the red squirrels, deer, and chipmunks of their backyard in Idaho. He also thanks Rick Kahn, Tom Beck, Bruce Gill, and all of the other personnel of the Colorado Division of Wildlife who have strived throughout their careers to move their agency toward a more holistic appreciation and respect for all wild mammals. Last, this is a book dedicated to the mammals themselves, from the grizzly and wolf that roam the wilds where he now lives to the prairie dogs, badgers, bats, shrews, voles, and ground squirrels of Greeley and South Park, Colorado, where his family spent many memorable years.

Meaney wishes to thank her daughter, Mara, for being a wonderful and loving inspiration in her life. A number of colleagues have provided much support and ongoing conversations about mammals; these include Marc Bekoff, Rick Adams, and numerous people at the Colorado Division of Wildlife and US Fish and Wildlife Service. A shared enthusiasm about all things wild with these folks and co-workers Scott Severs and Jenny Gerson, as well as many others, brings fresh energy to days spent in the field. Always, the glimpse of a wild mammal brings a special touch to any moment, whether it is a pika on Niwot Ridge, a quick glimpse of a vole diving for cover, a long-tailed weasel cavorting by the roadside, or a wolf hightailing away on ranchland in Wyoming. Here is to many more opportunities to see mammals when our paths cross.

MAMMALS OF COLORADO

SECOND EDITION

1

Environments of Colorado

Mammals are a familiar and important component of Earth's biodiversity. Biodiversity is the kinds of organisms and their genetic and ecological relationships—an evolutionary and ecological phenomenon in space and time (E. Wilson 1992). The mammalian fauna of Colorado is a fascinating piece of that whole. To understand the diversity of mammals we need to have a perspective of the ecosphere more generally. Such a perspective is the purpose of this chapter, with a focus on environments of Colorado.

Colorado is known for its scenic beauty—from majestic mountain peaks and rushing white rivers tumbling down dark canyons, to red-rock deserts and ceaselessly shifting sand dunes, to the expansive sweep of the shortgrass prairie. Grandeur is wherever we stop to appreciate it, at every scale, from canyons carved in crystalline rocks 2 billion years old, to bold peaks sculpted by the glaciers of the last Ice Age, to last night's furtive trail of a mouse across the snow. We humans appreciate ecological patterns and processes as beautiful or intriguing; to the rest of the mammalian fauna the evolving landscape represents opportunity, and native mammals respond accordingly. Thus, to understand the distribution and abundance of mammals and the details of their daily lives we must first understand the resource base, the mosaic of Colorado's environments in space and time.

Geography

From the standpoint of political geography, Colorado is simple: it is roughly rectangular (if we neglect some minor old surveyors' errors and the fact that Earth is spherical), measuring approximately 607 km by 444 km (377 by 276 mi.) and encompassing some 270,000 km^2 (104,000 sq. mi.). Colorado lies between approximately 102° and 109° west longitude and 37° and 41° north latitude, and is subdivided into 64 counties (Map 1-1). A few of the counties are nearly natural, ecological units (e.g., Jackson, Grand, and Park counties encompass North, Middle, and South parks, respectively), but most are simply political artifacts with rectilinear boundaries.

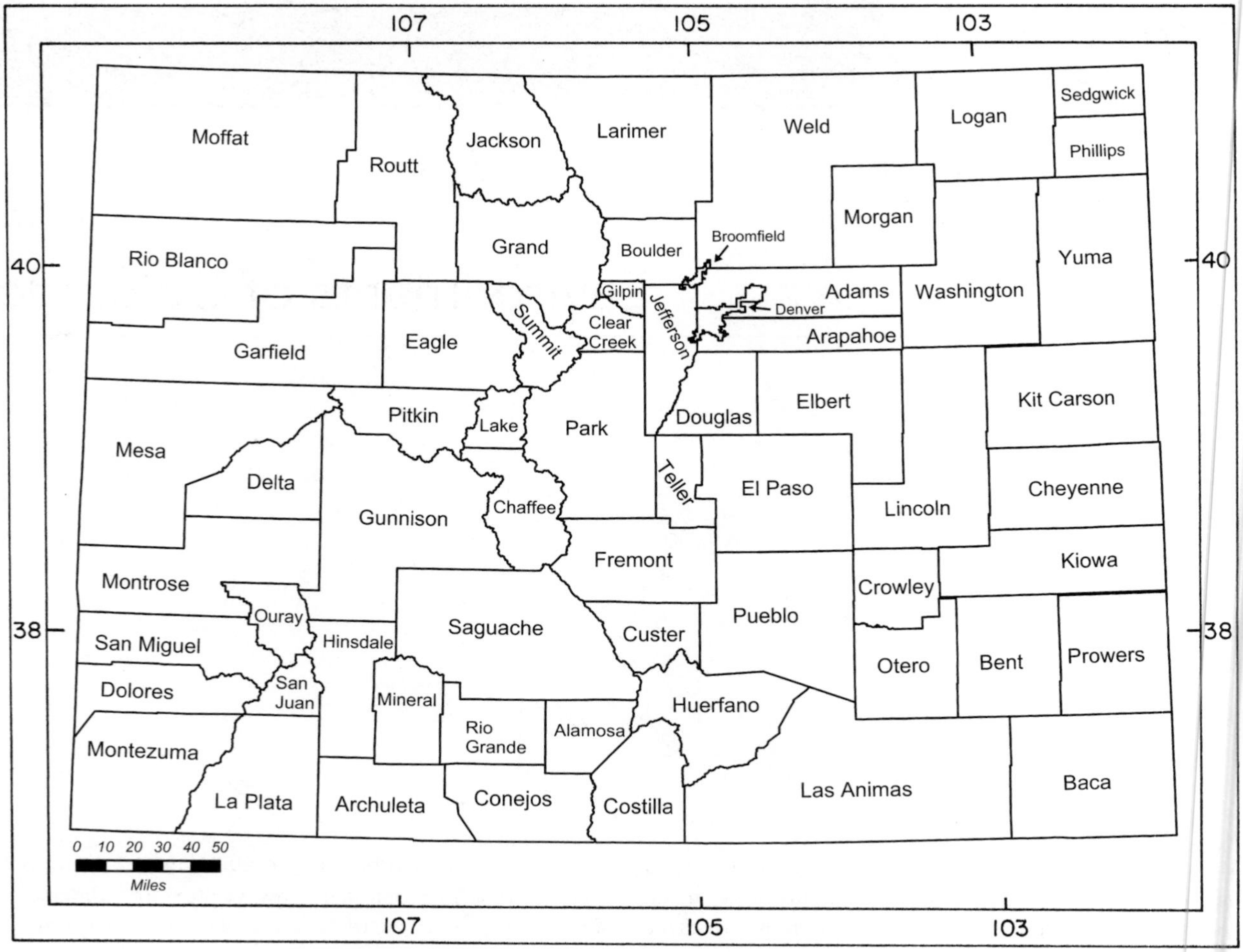

MAP 1-1. Counties of Colorado.

From the standpoints of physical and biological geography, Colorado is anything but simple. The marvelous complexity of the scenery is the subject of this chapter, which describes environments of Colorado from several interrelated points of view. Geologic history and materials underlie environmental patterns. Physiography is the shape of the land, reflecting hundreds of millions of years of landscape evolution. Patterns of drainage reflect and produce the landforms. Vegetation integrates climate and geologic parent material in the development of soils. Plants and animals, fungi and microbes interact as biotic communities, integrated by symbioses, and they interact with the physical environment in ceaseless cycles of materials powered by a flow of solar energy. We observe—and seek to understand—an ecological whole of extraordinary complexity. But let us begin simply, with a little history.

Geology and Landforms

Colorado straddles the "backbone" of North America, the Rocky Mountains. From the mountain front, the Great Plains extend eastward toward the Missouri River. To the west lie canyons and plateaus of the Colorado Plateau and the Wyoming Basin. The juxtaposition of these major physiographic regions affects temperature, precipitation, wind patterns, and drainage.

Colorado is the highest of the United States, with a mean elevation of 2,070 m (6,800 ft.). The lowest point is 1,021 m (3,350 ft.), east of Holly, Prowers County, where the Arkansas River exits the state, and the highest point is 4,399 m (14,433 ft.), the summit of Mount Elbert, Lake County, at the top of the Arkansas watershed. Because of these varied conditions, species richness is high.

Physiographers divide most of Colorado among three "provinces" (see Fenneman 1931): the Southern Rocky Mountains, the Great Plains, and the Colorado Plateau. Northwestern Colorado is on the periphery of two additional provinces: the Middle Rocky Mountains and the Wyoming Basin. For an excellent summary of Colorado's landforms and their development, see A. Benedict (2008).

The present-day Southern Rocky Mountains arose in a long-term event called the Laramide Orogeny, beginning some 72 million years ago, in the Late Cretaceous Period. Prior to that time (during the Mesozoic Era, the "Age of Reptiles") Colorado occupied a low-lying area, alternately covered by shallow seas or exposed as deserts and floodplains. With the rise of the Rockies, Mesozoic and older sediments were broken, bent, and tilted on end, resulting in the familiar hogback ridges and such features as Boulder's Flatirons, the spectacular Garden of the Gods, Loveland's Devil's Backbone, and the Grand Hogback. Streams heading in the newly uplifted mountains eroded the rocks, spreading the bits out in a deep "mantle" eastward across the mid-continent.

In Miocene to Pliocene times, about 5 million years ago, broad, domal regional uplift occurred, "raising the roof of the Rockies" by nearly a mile. Mountain ranges were exhumed from their mantle of Tertiary debris and today's "Fourteeners" reached their greatest elevations, only to face the inexorable processes of weathering we see today—the daily destructive march of rain and snow, wind and calm, freeze and thaw.

There is nothing simple about the Southern Rockies of Colorado (see Map 1-2), but we may think of the basic structure as two great ridges of granitic rocks arrayed in parallel lines oriented roughly north-south. The eastern series begins north of the Cache la Poudre River as the lower eastern Laramie Range and the higher western Medicine Bow Range. The Front Range extends from the Poudre to the Arkansas, ending in the Rampart Range (which includes Pikes Peak). The Wet Mountains are an independent range south of the Arkansas River.

A western chain of granitic mountains begins in southern Wyoming as the Sierra Madre (called the Park Range in Colorado); continues south as the Gore, Ten Mile, Mosquito, and Sawatch ranges; and then jogs a bit to the east to continue south into New Mexico as the spectacular ridge of the Sangre de Cristos. Between the granitic ridges are structural basins. North and Middle parks occupy a single structural basin, subdivided by the volcanic Rabbit Ears Mountains. South Park occupies a separate basin. West of the Park Range, the Wyoming Basin is continuous with much of southwestern Wyoming.

The San Luis Valley lies west of the main ranges of the Southern Rockies proper, but it looks like one of the parks, because it is surrounded by mountains, the Sangre de Cristos to the east and the younger, volcanic San Juans to the west. A range of volcanic hills marks the southern border of the San Luis Valley, roughly the southern border of Colorado. On the east side of the San Luis Valley is the spectacular Great Sand Dunes National Park and Preserve. *Valley of the Dunes* (Rozinski et al. 2005) provides a moving appreciation of *El Valle* in visual images and compelling prose. Every corner of Colorado deserves such treatment.

The main ranges of the Rockies represent uplifted Precambrian rocks and folded Paleozoic and Mesozoic sediments. Adjacent ranges like the San Juans were produced by Cenozoic volcanic activity. Features like the White River and Uncompahgre plateaus are independent uplifts. Grand and Battlement mesas are built of sedimentary rocks, protected by caps of resistant lava. J. Chronic and Chronic (1972), Matthews et al. (2003), and H. Chronic and Williams (2002) provided accessible introductions to the geology of Colorado; A. Benedict (2008) described the mountains in intimate detail; and Cairns et al. (2002) described the Rockies in the context of the ongoing human transformation of the region.

The eastern two-fifths of Colorado lies in the Great Plains Physiographic Province. When the Rockies rose, erosion and sedimentation clothed the area to the east with the pieces. For millions of years, this alluvium covered nearly all of eastern Colorado. In the Pliocene, and especially during the Pleistocene ice ages (with their high precipitation), the "Tertiary mantle" was largely eroded away and carried out of the state. Today it is preserved mostly on the High Plains, a nearly flat landscape interrupted occasionally by sandhills and eroded along stream courses to form canyons, cliffs, and escarpments. Between the High Plains and the mountain front lies the Colorado Piedmont. There the Tertiary mantle has been largely removed, exposing Mesozoic shales, limestones, and sandstones as hogbacks, low rolling hills, and canyons. Remnants of the Tertiary formations can be seen along the northern border of eastern Colorado. The dramatic Pawnee Buttes and

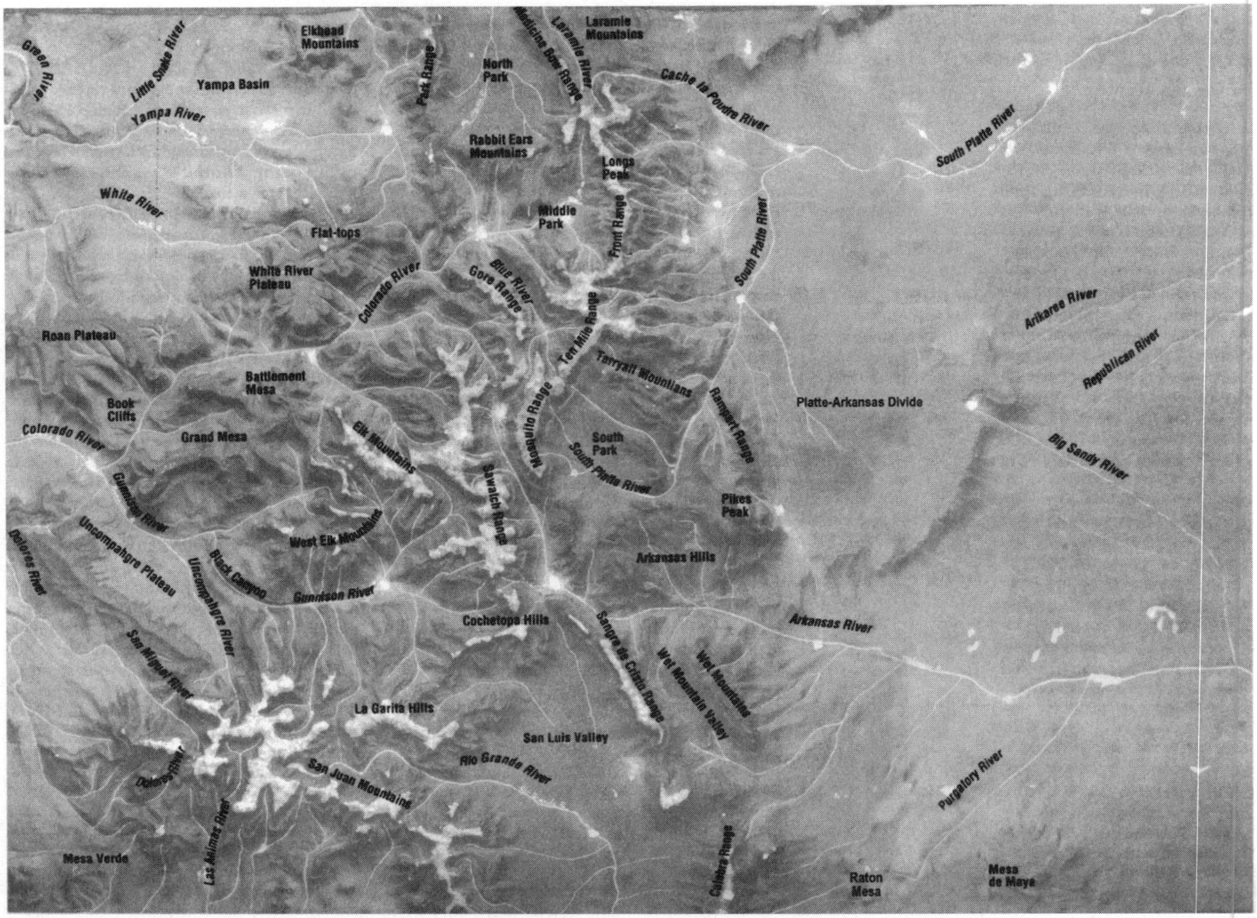

MAP 1-2. Some physiographic features of Colorado.

the escarpment of the Peetz Table suggest just how much material has been removed from the Colorado Piedmont. The divide between the Platte and Arkansas rivers is a remnant upland, providing an eastward extension of ecosystems of the foothills. The generally forested divide imposes a filter-barrier to north-south movement of many smaller mammals between the valleys of the master streams of the plains (D. Armstrong 1972, 1996).

At the foot of the mountains, sedimentary units generally dip steeply eastward, forming a great debris-filled trough, the Denver Basin. The southern rim of the basin is marked by roughlands south of the Arkansas River, which greatly complicate the ecology of southeastern Colorado, providing habitat for a number of species of Mexican affinities. Indeed, the very name of the physiographic region, the Raton Section, bespeaks its distinctive mammalian fauna, which includes several species of *"ratones,"* woodrats, whose dens are conspicuous features of the landscape.

The Colorado Plateau is a world-renowned showplace for the effects of erosion on flat-lying sedimentary rocks. Add to that the complications of a history of volcanism nearby, and the result is a landscape of remarkable ecological diversity. The country is typified by mesas and plateaus dissected by canyons. These include the Book and Roan plateaus, the Piceance Basin, and lava-capped Grand and Battlement mesas. Farther south, the uplifted Uncompahgre Plateau and isolated peaks like Ute Mountain are conspicuous. Mesa Verde is a major highland near the southern boundary of the state.

The boundaries between physiographic provinces are often visible in ecological patterns. The transition from the Great Plains to the Southern Rockies on the Eastern

Slope is especially dramatic, with the Front and Rampart ranges rising 2,400 m (nearly 8,000 ft.) in less than 30 km (18 mi.). Further, spectacular river canyons often mark gateways from the Rockies to adjacent physiographic provinces: Northgate Canyon on the North Platte, Glenwood Canyon on the Colorado, South Platte Canyon, the Royal Gorge of the Arkansas, the Black Canyon of the Gunnison, and the Big Thompson and Poudre canyons. These and numerous lesser canyons and gulches provide corridors for movements of the biota, their south-facing slopes providing microclimates especially favorable for southwestern species.

Watersheds

Rivers carve landscapes and support moist corridors of opportunity for living things. The influences of rivers are especially striking in the semiarid West. We cannot appreciate natural landscapes of Colorado—or much of human history—without knowing something of the patterns of drainage, the hydrography, of the state.

Colorado lies astride the Continental Divide. Water that falls to the west of the Divide ends up in the Sea of Cortez (Gulf of California). Waters of the Eastern Slope are destined for the Gulf of Mexico, via the Missouri-Mississippi system. The San Luis Valley is partly an internal drainage basin, but the Rio Grande flows through the southern part of the valley on its way to the Gulf of Mexico, having gathered its headwaters in the high San Juans.

The Continental Divide is a fundamental geographic fact in Colorado. The main ridge of the Rockies intercepts moisture coming from the Pacific Ocean. Air is forced up, hence cooled, and its water vapor condenses, falling in the mountains as rain or snow. The Eastern Slope is, therefore, in a "rain shadow." The Western Slope has about one-third of the land area of Colorado but receives more than two-thirds of the precipitation. However, because only about 11 percent of the state's human population lives on the Western Slope, ambitious efforts have been made for more than a century to move water—the lifeblood of agriculture and urban and industrial development—to the Eastern Slope, the center of Colorado's human population. The actual amount of diversion varies from one year to the next and the pattern is complex, but as an example, the amount of Western Slope water diverted annually to northeastern Colorado typically supplements the native flow of the South Platte River by about one-quarter.

Transmountain water diversion has greatly modified environments of Colorado. The South Platte and Arkansas valleys, which nineteenth-century explorer Stephen Long called the "Great American Desert," have been transformed into rich agricultural regions, expanding habitat for a number of species of mammals, including relative newcomers like fox squirrels, raccoons, and opossums. Also, the tunnels through which diverted water flows sometimes provide roosting habitat for bats.

Several of the major rivers of western interior North America originate in the Colorado Rockies. Indeed, the only sizable river that flows into the state is the Green, which heads in the Wind River Mountains of western Wyoming. The master stream of the Western Slope is the Colorado River. The Yampa and White rivers drain northwestern Colorado before they join the Green. The mainstem Colorado—once called the Grand River—drains Middle Park and the western side of Rocky Mountain National Park and then joins the Gunnison at Grand Junction, flowing thence westward into Utah where it is joined by the Green en route to the Grand Canyon in Arizona. Southwestern Colorado is drained by several tributaries of the Colorado, namely the San Miguel, Dolores, and San Juan rivers and their tributaries, all born as mountain snow in the San Juans and destined for a muddy end in Mexico's Sea of Cortez.

The North Platte River heads in North Park and drains much of eastern Wyoming before joining the South Platte in Nebraska. The South Platte and its tributaries drain the Front Range and South Park. The Arkansas River heads in the Rampart, Sawatch, and Mosquito ranges. The High Plains of eastern Colorado give rise to the Republican and Arikaree rivers. The Cimarron heads in New Mexico and drains extreme southeastern Colorado.

Climates and Climate Change

Mammals are endotherms; that is, they maintain a high and constant body temperature by elegantly controlled production and retention of metabolic heat. Endothermy partially liberates mammals from the direct influence of climate, but climate still is an important influence on mammals, affecting individual lives, populations, and broad patterns of the distribution of species.

Weather in Colorado is highly variable from place to place, season to season, and moment to moment, all part of a broader changing climate. We can sketch only the broadest outlines of the pattern of climate. The Southern

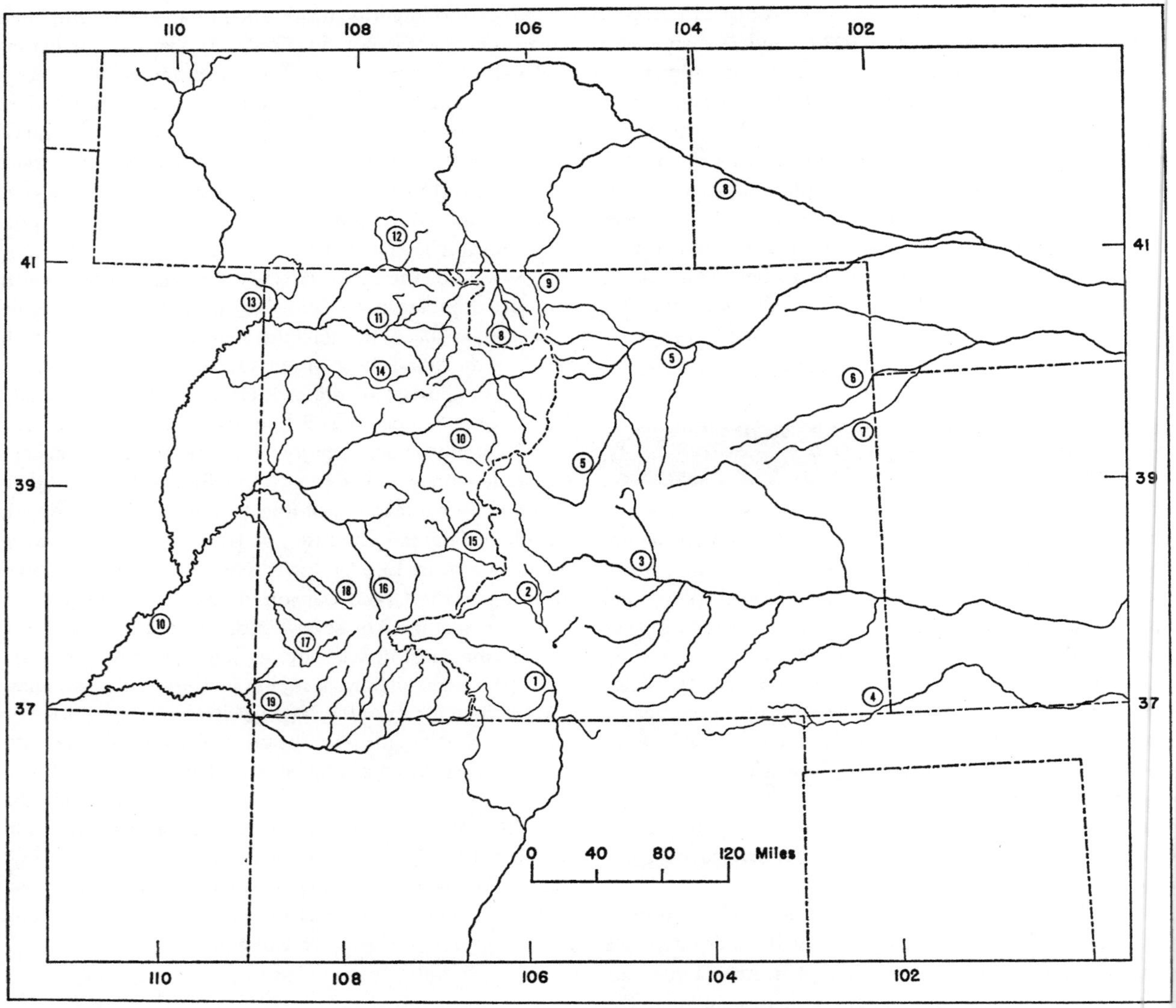

MAP 1-3. Watersheds of Colorado and parts of adjacent states; irregular, dashed north-south line is Continental Divide. Key: (1) Rio Grande; (2) northern San Luis Valley ("Closed Basin"); (3) Arkansas; (4) Cimarron; (5) South Platte; (6) Arikaree; (7) Republican; (8) North Platte; (9) Laramie; (10) Colorado; (11) Yampa; (12) Little Snake; (13) Green; (14) White; (15) Gunnison; (16) Uncompahgre; (17) Dolores; (18) San Miguel; (19) Mancos (from Armstrong 1972).

Rockies are the dominant influence. Other important factors are latitude, elevation, exposure, local topography, and location relative to storm tracks and prevailing winds. Far from the moderating effects of oceans (roughly 1,100 km [690 mi.] from the Gulf Coast, 1,600 km [994 mi.] from the West Coast, and 3,200 km [1,988 mi.] from the East Coast), the state has a "continental climate." Colorado's climate is temperate and semiarid overall, with low relative humidity and temperatures that show wide variation at all elevations. For example, annual precipitation ranges from more than 100 cm (39.4 in.) in some parts of the San Juan Mountains to less than 25 cm (9.8 in.) in parts of the San Luis Valley, just 80 km (about 50 mi.) away. The frost-free season in the Grand Valley averages 189 days; at Silverton it averages 14 days. The difference in mean annual temperature between Lamar and the summit of Pikes Peak (only 200 km [124 mi.]

to the west but 3,200 m [10,500 ft.] higher in elevation) is about 20°C (approximately 35°F).

The Great Plains are typified by low precipitation, high winds, and low humidity. Summer daytime temperatures, although frequently hot, only occasionally and locally exceed 38°C (100°F). Winters have relatively warm periods interrupted by Arctic air masses sweeping down from Canada. Precipitation declines along an east-west gradient from an annual mean of about 45 cm (18 in.) along the Kansas and Nebraska borders to about 30–35 cm (12–14 in.) at the foot of the mountains.

Winters near the foothills are milder than on the plains or in the mountains, and the Front Range corridor, from Fort Collins south to Pueblo, supports more than 80 percent of the state's human population. Denver, at an elevation of about 1,610 m (5,280 ft.), has a mean annual precipitation of about 35 cm (13.8 in.) and a mean annual temperature of 10°C (50°F).

In the mountains, temperature decreases with increasing elevation, at roughly 1.7°C (3°F) per 300 m (985 ft.). Above about 2,750 m (about 9,000 ft.), frost is possible any night of the year, particularly in valleys, into which heavier cold air drains. Winter and spring snowfall can be quite heavy in the mountains, but local differences are extreme. In the western mountains more precipitation falls as winter snow than as summer rain. By contrast, winter and summer precipitation are about equivalent on the Eastern Slope. Warm winter winds, or chinooks, melt or evaporate much of the snow on the Eastern Slope. In spring, rapid snowmelt causes peak flows of rivers that head in the mountains. Groundwater from snowmelt contributes to summer streamflow. The enclosed mountain parks and valleys are cooler and drier than the surrounding mountains. They lie in the rain shadow of the mountains and also trap sinking cold air masses for relatively long periods.

Western Colorado has a diversity of climates driven in large part by topography. The high plateaus are similar to the mountains, but the lowlands and river valleys are warmer and drier. Winds generally are less intense than on the Eastern Slope. Stable high-pressure systems often form in winter, resulting in long periods of clear weather with warm days and cool nights. Southwestern Colorado typically has monsoonal, or summer, rains. This increase in moisture during the warm season is in contrast to the pattern for the rest of the Western Slope, where the greatest moisture occurs during winter. Erickson and Smith (1985) summarized a vast amount of information on physical environments of Colorado, including climate. A. Benedict (2008) provided an invaluable account of mountain climates.

There is no question that climatic patterns are changing at present, in part because of the industrial enrichment of Earth's atmosphere with "greenhouse gases," including carbon dioxide released from burning fossil fuels. Colorado, with its high topographic relief and consequent ecological complexity, may expect marked local and regional effects from such changes. Ongoing climate change (which is at least partly anthropogenic) has profound implications for management and conservation of Coloradan mammals; *Season's End* (Wildlife Management Institute 2008) is a sobering assessment of impacts of human-influenced climate change on the wildlife populations upon which recreational hunting depends. S. Saunders and Maxwell (2005) summarized likely change in the climate of the West under the theme "less snow, less water." Summary predictions, all interrelated, were more heat, less snowfall, diminished snowpack, earlier snowmelt, and more wildfires. S. Saunders and Easley (2006) and Saunders et al. (2009) discussed possible impacts of climate change on western national parks, highlighting possible conditions in Colorado's Mesa Verde and Rocky Mountain national parks. S. Saunders et al. (2008) discussed climate change in the American West more generally. Chapin et al. (2000) discussed changes in biodiversity in the context of ecosystem services. K. McDonald and Brown (1992) discussed montane mammals as a model system for predicting extinction as a result of climate change.

Of course, climate change has been a feature of Earth for billions of years. The record of the rocks suggests repeated changes in the climate of Colorado and worldwide over eons. Mammals of Colorado have been influenced by those changes for nearly a quarter of a billion years. There is abundant evidence of strong, natural climatic change in the recent geological past (Kittell et al. 2002; Whitlock et al. 2002). Only 15,000 years ago valley glaciers of the Pleistocene Ice Age retreated to their cirques. Some Coloradan mammals are relicts of glacial times, occurring now on the forested "island" of the Southern Rockies, surrounded by an impassable "sea" of grasslands and shrublands. A geologically "mere" 4,000 to 7,000 years ago, a "Hypsithermal Interval" warmer and drier than the present allowed access to parts of Colorado by a number of species of southwestern affinities—species like Mexican woodrats, rock mice, and a variety of bats that are now restricted to particularly warm, dry locations in the foothills, canyons, and other roughlands of the state (D. Armstrong 1972, 1996).

Clearly, climatic change is nothing new. What is remarkable about ongoing change is its rate (as rapid as any change revealed by fossil evidence except the change at the Cretaceous/Tertiary boundary—which appears to have been almost instantaneous—and maybe the change at the Permian/Triassic boundary) (Hallam 2004; Erwin 2006). Further, what is surely unique about present climate change is its principal cause: our industrial (fossil-fueled) selves.

Climate change is the central environmental issue of our time. In research and management institutions and agencies worldwide, human-influenced climate change has been observed and understood, at least in broad outline, for decades. Depending on the observation point, global mean surface temperatures have increased 0.6°F to 1.2°F since 1890, and the rate of increase is itself increasing. The fact that humans are influencing this change, mostly by augmenting the heat-trapping capacity of the atmosphere through liberation of CO_2 from fossil fuels, also has been known for decades (see, e.g., National Assessment Synthesis Team 2000). Popular interest and understanding of the matter has come much later (perhaps spurred by the 2006 film *An Inconvenient Truth* and the subsequent award of the 2007 Nobel Peace Prize to former vice president Al Gore and the Intergovernmental Panel on Climate Change), and now political discourse and legislative action are beginning to grapple with the challenge. The extent of the challenge and its impacts on many aspects of society can be seen locally in the list of sponsors of the Rocky Mountain Climate Organization, which includes a coalition of municipal water utilities, environmental organizations, industry (especially brewers and the ski industry), and agricultural organizations, among many others.

One of the difficulties of public (hence political) appreciation of climate change is that the climate system of Earth is huge, complex, and variable over the planet and over time. Even the fastest supercomputers are not yet able to model climate in detail sufficient to make local predictions. We speak casually of "global warming," but that is a serious distortion of the likely future. Over the globe—epitomized by a complex place like Colorado—the best guess is that there will be climate change. Some places will be warmer, but some will be cooler; some places will be drier, some wetter. Some places will change a little; others will change dramatically. Earth's rapidly changing polar ice caps have provided some of the most vivid and poignant illustrations of rapid, ongoing change, and a mammal, the polar bear (*Ursus maritimus*)—a recently derived Arctic-endemic Ice Age cousin of the brown or grizzly bear (*U. arctos*)—has become a poster child for climate change.

Coloradans are likely better informed about climate change than are Americans in some other parts of the country. First, much of the basic research on climate change has been conducted at the National Center for Atmospheric Research in Boulder. Second, climate change is already making an obvious difference where we Coloradans live. Some ski seasons have been abbreviated. Agricultural water users have seen their allocations decline. Forest fires have increased in frequency and severity, and the fire season is longer (A. Hansen et al. 2001; Keane et al. 2002). Dramatic outbreaks of some forest insects may be related to milder winters and water-stressed summers.

S. Schneider and Root (2001), T. Root and Schneider (2002), T. Root et al. (2003), T. Root and Hughes (2005), Parmesan (2006), and Janetos et al. (2008) reviewed impacts of climate change on biodiversity in general and focused on several topics of interest in the context of Coloradan mammals: changes in distributions and phenology (seasonal events), changes in pests and pathogens, changes in particularly sensitive ecosystems, and concerns about the adequacy of monitoring systems. Computer models of climate change predict elevated extinction risk by 18–35 percent, with local endemic species (endemism implying narrow ecological tolerance, small geographic range, and small population sizes) being most vulnerable (C. Thomas et al. 2004).

Geographic distributions of species are changing, as detailed in accounts of the Virginia opossum, hispid cotton rat, eastern pipistrelle, and white-backed hog-nosed skunk, for example. See R. Davis and Callahan (1992) for general comments on northward movements of southern mammals. Other changes are expected, as noted in such accounts as that of the nine-banded armadillo. Phenology is the study of seasonal changes, like the flowering of plants, emergence of butterflies, and arrival of migrant birds. At Gothic, above Crested Butte, yellow-bellied marmots have emerged earlier by approximately 1 day per year from 1976 to 1999 (D. Inouye et al. 2000). Barnosky et al. (2003) provided historical perspective, reviewing mammalian response to global warming over the past 4 million years and concluding that present, ongoing climate change may be unprecedented in rate and degree in the history of the class Mammalia.

Comments on impacts of climate change on particular kinds of mammals are included in respective accounts of species, to the extent that they are known. As for changes in pests and pathogens, climatic correlates of some emerging diseases are still poorly understood, but it may not be coincidence that the appearance of hantavirus (see Chapter 4 and the account of the deer mouse in Chapter 8) and chronic wasting disease (see account of the mule deer in Chapter

14) have occurred mostly in the past decade. The explosive expansion of mountain pine beetle appears to be related to climate change, at least indirectly. For a general review of impacts of climate change on forests—and hence on forest-dwelling mammals—see Joyce and Birdsey (2000).

As regional climates change, impacts likely will be most intense at highest elevations, if only because highest elevation bands have the smallest areas. (Imagine climbing a cone; the higher you climb, the less surface area there is per vertical distance.) The impact of mountains on community-level diversity of mammals is complex, involving not only area but also local climate and overall community diversity (C. McCain 2005, 2007). Mountain environments were identified by Janetos et al. (2008) as particularly sensitive to climate change for the obvious reason that many species are tied to particular elevational zones, which tend to be zones with particular climatic conditions. As climates change, those zones are moving. The higher up the mountain they move, the less area there is to occupy, the smaller the populations that can be supported, and the inexorable consequence will likely be local extinction in some cases.

In a sense, mountaintops are "islands" in a "sea" of lower-elevation habitats. Therefore, the principles of island biogeography (R. H. MacArthur and Wilson 1967; Newmark 1986, 1987, 1995) apply. The basic principles are simple enough. The smaller an island, the fewer species it can support. Further, the farther a particular island is from another island or a mainland source of potential colonizing species, the fewer species can reach that island. Principles of area and isolation, of colonization and extinction, underpin much of modern thinking in conservation ecology and the management of Earth's remaining natural landscapes.

Of course, alpine ecosystems and their characteristic mammals, like the American pika and yellow-bellied marmot (species adapted to "life in the cold" [C. Carey et al. 1993]), will be influenced most directly because they already are on mountaintops, so they have nowhere to go. Guralnick (2006a) came to such a conclusion based on statistical modeling of the geographic ranges of 20 mammalian species (most of which occur in Colorado) in the context of regional climate and elevational gradients. However, because the topographic diversity of mountains produces local diversity of habitats, mountain-dwelling species may be able to respond to climate change more effectively than "flatland" species, whose habitats may be extensive but monotonous and so may change over large areas, most of which will not be adjacent to newly suitable habitats (Guralnick 2006b).

For these impacts and others, monitoring—or routine observation of any sort—is woefully inadequate for most mammalian species over most of Colorado. Exceptions are game species, where harvest reports are mandated by regulation, and species under long-term study at particular places, such as work on yellow-bellied marmots at Rocky Mountain Biological Laboratory over several decades by Professor Kenneth B. Armitage of the University of Kansas, studies of bats on Boulder Mountain Parks and adjacent public open space by Professor Rick A. Adams of the University of Northern Colorado, and study of a number of species over more than half a century on Niwot Ridge at the University of Colorado's Mountain Research Station (D. Armstrong et al. 2001). Other long-term, continuous studies of particular species or particular places are strongly encouraged; careful monitoring is essential to understanding change in the short term (years to decades) and planning for the longer term.

The Wildlife Management Institute (2008) edited an excellent volume focused on impacts of ongoing anthropogenic (fossil-fueled) climate change on wildlife and fisheries on a national scale. They visualized decreases in food resources for many species with climate change, accompanied by increasing disease, invasive species, and wildfire. If we remember that sport fish and game mammals and birds provide an "umbrella" that covers terrestrial and aquatic ecosystems generally, this is an important volume. The Colorado Division of Wildlife and Colorado Wildlife Federation (2008) hosted a "Colorado Wildlife Summit" in October 2008 at Keystone. A principal focus of the summit was climate change and its ramifications. Literature in this general field is developing rapidly and much of it is being issued on-line. We recommend periodic searches of the extensive Internet resources of the Environmental Protection Agency, the Colorado Division of Wildlife, and the Rocky Mountain Climate Organization—all excellent points of entry into this emerging literature.

Soils

Soils are the product of interaction over time among geologic parent material, topography, climate, vegetation, and animal activity. As one would expect, the pattern of soils in Colorado is complex. This is reflected in (and influenced by) distributions of biotic communities. The composition, texture, depth, and moisture of soils can influence mammals indirectly through influence on the vegetation of an area. Further, local distribution of burrowing mammals, which usually depend on specific soil characteristics for their activities, is affected directly. Kangaroo rats, for example, occur only in sandy soils. In general, soils of Colorado differ from those of more humid regions by being lower in organic matter and higher in inorganic nutrients. Soils of Colorado were summarized broadly by Erickson and Smith (1985) and have been mapped extensively and in detail in county soil surveys by the Natural Resources Conservation Service (formerly the Soil Conservation Service) of the US Department of Agriculture.

Humans in the Landscape

Human activity has strongly influenced opportunities for native mammals. Prior to permanent settlement, subsistence populations—first of Native Americans and then of Euro-Americans—relied on the native fauna for food and fiber. They influenced local populations of game mammals and furbearers but seldom modified physical environments permanently. The first permanent European settlers came for mineral wealth. The "Colorado Mineral Belt" extends from Jamestown, Ward, and Gold Hill in the Colorado Front Range southwest to Silverton and Rico in the San Juans. Beginning with the discovery of gold in Cherry Creek in 1859, much of mountainous Colorado was transformed. Mountains were turned inside out, changing the topography and hence the environment for many species, many negatively, a few positively. Roosting habitat for bats, for example, was greatly augmented by mining activities, as were the rubbly slopes favored by pikas and bushy-tailed woodrats (and hence their predators, such as long-tailed weasels).

Agricultural settlement of the eastern plains and the western valleys came a little later. Wholesale changes in habitats for mammals resulted from irrigated agriculture, impoundment of rivers in reservoirs and transmountain diversion of water, control of floods and prairie fires, and extirpation of the keystone species of the prairie, the bison. Early ranching activities often involved predator control (and even eradication, as with the gray wolf and grizzly bear) and overgrazing, expanding opportunities for species like the Wyoming ground squirrel and the black-tailed jackrabbit. Urbanization has had profound effects on the fauna of the state, obliterating habitat for some species but increasing it for several others, like white-tailed deer, fox squirrels, and raccoons (and, of course, introduced Norway rats and house mice).

Ecosystems of Colorado

To this point we have described aspects of the physical environments of Colorado that provide opportunities for the native fauna. Geology underlies environmental pattern. Physiography describes the broad shape of the land. Climatic patterns describe the distribution and periodicity of precipitation and temperature. Vegetation clothes the landforms, moderates climate, and uses solar energy to power the integration of air, water, and minerals into the chemical molecules of life. Soils are the dynamic result of the interaction of climate, vegetation, and geologic parent material over time. All of these pieces contribute to the pattern of landscapes that we describe as ecosystems. An ecosystem is an arbitrary volume of Earth's environment, with living organisms (the biotic community) and their physical (abiotic) habitat exchanging materials, the whole system powered by a flow of energy.

For purposes of this book, Coloradan environments are described in terms of eight ecosystem types. This is not the only way to describe the environment, of course. Cary (1911) described environments of Colorado in terms of the classical life-zone concept pioneered by C. Hart Merriam and the US Bureau of Biological Survey. Pattern in the environment was described as a series of elevational bands, ranging from Upper Sonoran Zone grasslands and shrublands, through a Transition Zone typified by ponderosa pine or sagebrush, to a Canadian Zone forest of spruce and fir, through a narrow band of Krummholz or elfin timber (the Hudsonian Zone) at upper tree line, to an Alpine Zone atop the higher mountains. This system describes in broad terms an ecological pattern readily seen in Colorado and elsewhere in the West where environmental change is rapid along steep gradients of elevation. Despite its simplicity, Cary's life-zone map of Colorado still is a valuable tool for the ecologist.

D. Armstrong (1972) tabulated distribution of Coloradan mammals in 14 ecological community types, Gregg (1963) used 31 vegetation types to describe ecological distribution of ants, and Erickson and Smith (1985) mapped 11 vegetation types. Marr (1967) detailed vegetation and climate of a transect from foothills to tundra in Boulder County. (By the way, Marr's original plots were re-sampled and reanalyzed by Korb and Ranker [2001], who noted significant decreases in species richness in aspen woodlands, along with major changes in species composition.) Greenland et al. (1985) quantified zonation of the Colorado Front Range in bioclimatic terms, comparing several pre-

TABLE 1-1. Summary of some physical and biotic characteristics of ecosystems of Colorado

Ecosystem	*Typical Plants*	*Elevation*	*Mean Annual Precipitation*	*Mean Annual Temperature*	*Typical Mammals*
Grassland	grasses, prickly-pear, yucca, fringed sage	1,220–3,050 m (4,000–10,000 ft.)	36 (25–46) cm; 14 (10–18) in.	11°C (52°F)	pronghorn, jackrabbits, pocket gophers, pocket mice
Semidesert shrubland	sagebrush, greasewood, rabbitbrush	1,220–2,440 m (4,000–8,000 ft.)	25 (15–38) cm; 10 (6–15) in.	6°C (43°F)	jackrabbits, ground squirrels, kangaroo rat, mule deer, pronghorn, coyote
Piñon-juniper woodland	piñon pine, juniper, bunchgrasses	1,680–2,440 m (5500–8000 ft.)	36 (25–46) cm; 14 (10–18) in.	10°C (50°F)	cottontails, bats, piñon mice, woodrats, gray fox
Montane shrublands	Gambel oak, mountain mahogany, skunkbush sumac, chokecherry	1,675–2,600 m (5,500–8,500 ft.)	38 (33–43) cm; 15 (13–17) in.	7°C (45°F)	rock squirrel, brush mouse, rock mouse, woodrats, coyote
Montane forest and woodland	ponderosa pine, Douglas-fir	1,700–2,750 m (5,600–9,000 ft.)	51 (38–63) cm; 20 (15–25) in.	7°C (45°F)	mule deer, cottontails, black bear, bobcat
Subalpine forest	spruce, fir, lodgepole pine, aspen, heaths	2,740–3,470 m (9,000–11,400 ft.)	76 (51–102) cm; 30 (20–40) in.	2°C (36°F)	pine squirrel, pine marten, snowshoe hare, elk, lynx
Alpine tundra	cushion plants, willow shrub	above 3,470 m (11,400 ft.)	76 (60–120) cm; 30 (24–49) in.	–3°C (27°F)	American pika, yellow-bellied marmot, elk (summer), northern pocket gopher, coyote
Riparian and wetland systems	cottonwoods, willow trees and shrubs, cattails, rushes, sedges	1,220–3,350 m (4,000–11,000 ft.)	variable; comparable to adjacent uplands	variable, but lower than adjacent uplands	shrews, bats, voles, beaver, cottontails, deer, raccoon, red fox

vious attempts to describe zonation. R. Bailey (1978, following Küchler 1964) mapped 14 types of potential natural vegetation within six ecoregions in Colorado. Ricketts et al. (1999) provided a conservation assessment of North America (including the status of mammals) at the level of ecoregions, four of which were mapped in Colorado: Colorado Rockies Forest, Western Short Grass, Colorado Plateau Shrublands, and Wyoming Basin Shrub Steppe. Mutel and Emerick (1992) described the Coloradan environment in a framework of 15 kinds of ecosystems, and A. Benedict (2008) utilized a hierarchy of 16 ecosystems across 5 zones to describe the landscapes of the Southern Rockies.

This diversity of alternative classification schemes should not be troublesome to the reader who keeps are mind a simple fact: naming and classifying ecosystems are human activities, done for human purposes. Our particular purpose is to describe the pattern of environmental opportunities for mammals, so we use a simple array of categories consistent with the scheme used in the "Explore Colorado" exhibit at the Denver Museum of Nature and Science (Kruger et al. 1995).

An ecosystem is a functioning volume of environment, involving interaction of living organisms (the biotic community) and non-living (abiotic) factors in continual cycles of materials powered by a ceaseless flow of solar energy. Ecosystems are arbitrary units, delineated for the convenience of people (naturalists, students, or managers, for example). An ecosystem might be as small as a pond, a field, or even an aquarium. It could be as large as the Great Plains. Indeed, one could argue that Earth has just one ecosystem—a single integrated, global ecological whole—the ecosphere. We abstract smaller ecosystems from the whole simply to have something manageable to study and, we hope, to understand.

The geography of the 8 broad ecosystems by which we describe environments of Colorado is sketched in Map 1-4. They are recognizable at a glance by their different biotic communities, the most visible component of the landscape. These 8 ecosystems readily lend themselves to subdivision for further, sometimes necessary, refinement. Estimates of percentage of the state covered by each ecosystem type are rough (determined by tallying townships by ecosystem type from the map, Major Land Resource

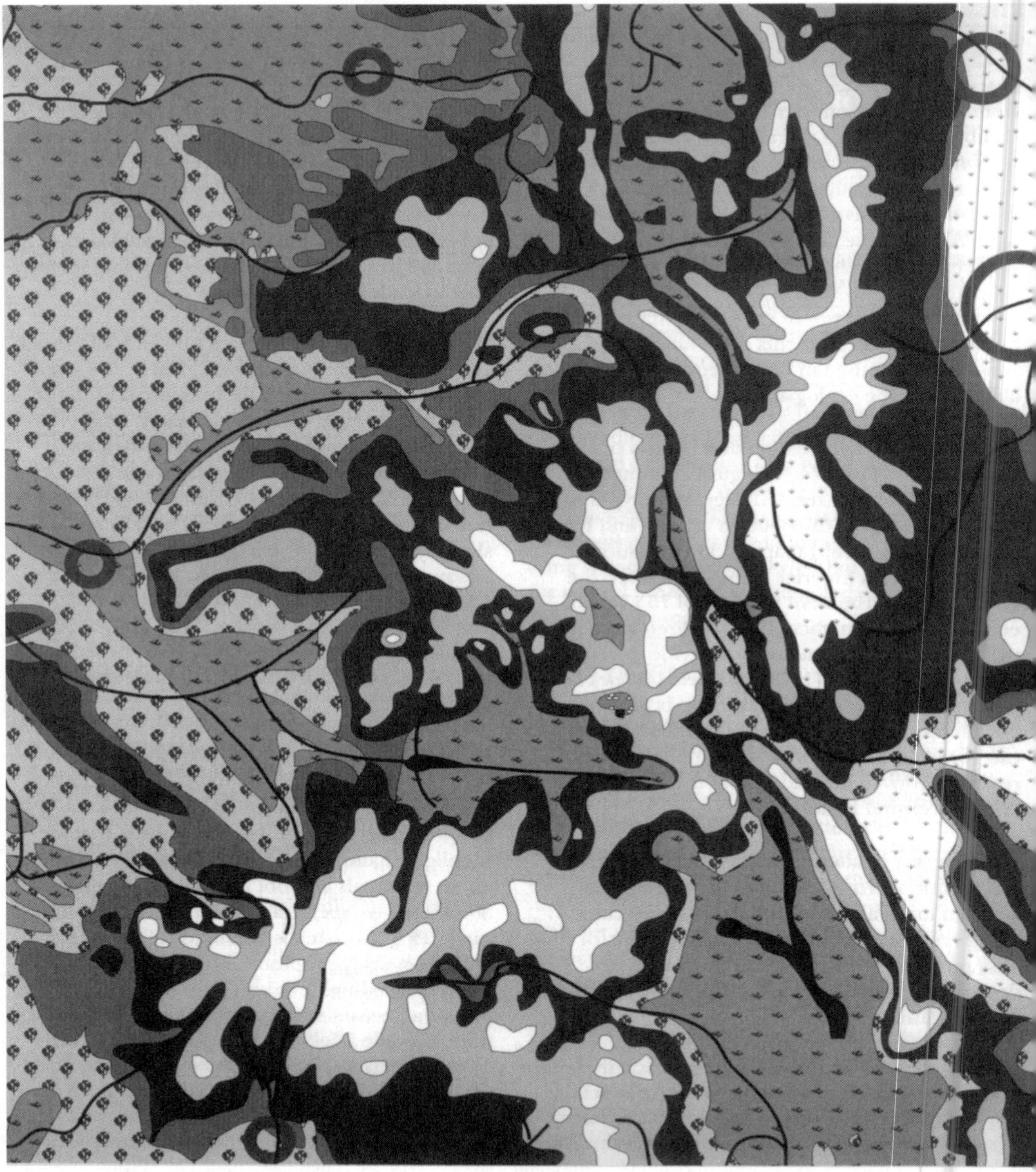

MAP 1-4. Ecosystems of Colorado.

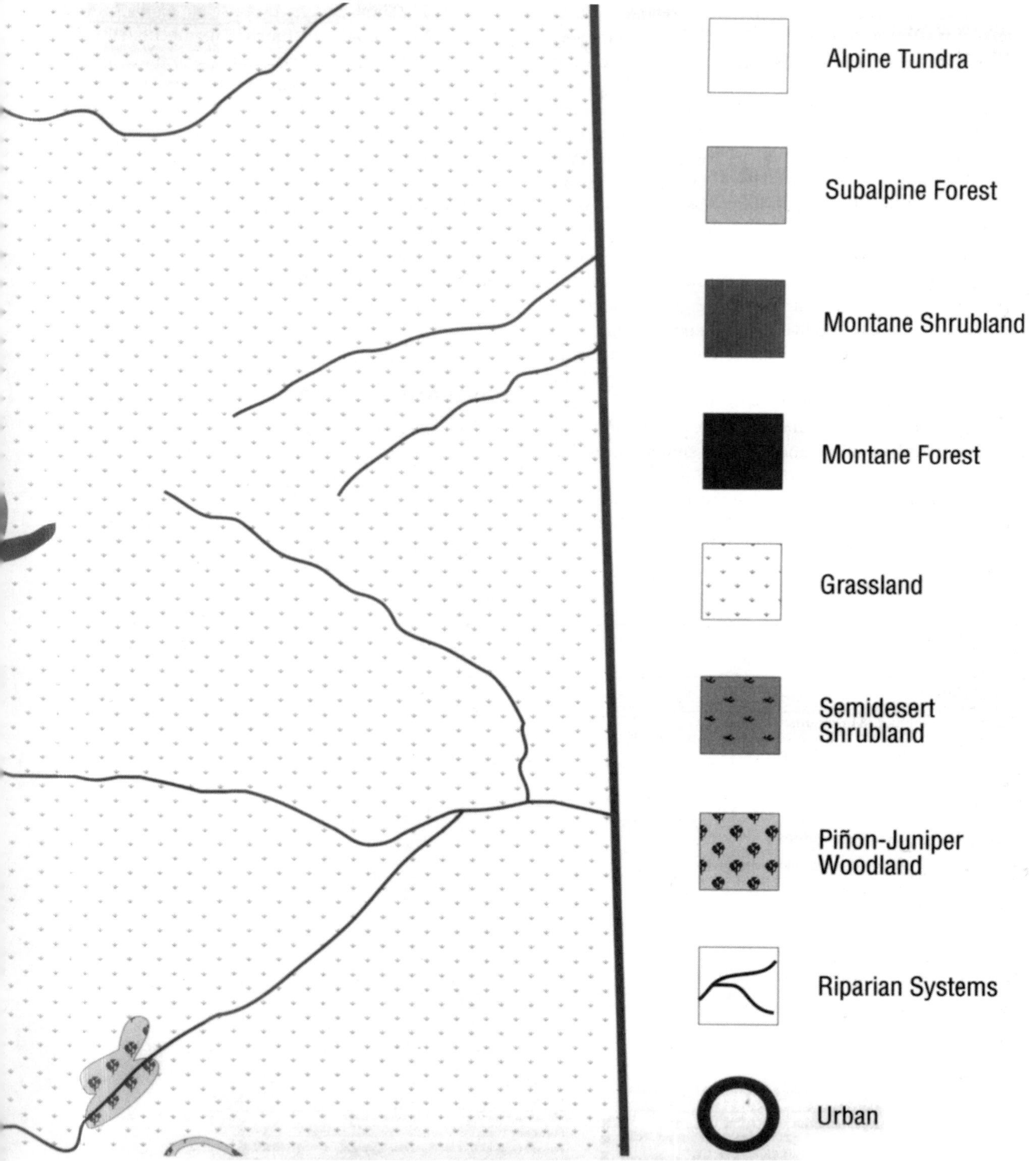
Alpine Tundra
Subalpine Forest
Montane Shrubland
Montane Forest
Grassland
Semidesert Shrubland
Piñon-Juniper Woodland
Riparian Systems
Urban

Area and Generalized Land Use Map, Colorado, produced by the Soil Conservation Service, USDA, Portland, 1965, approximate scale: 1:2,000,000). Botanical nomenclature mostly follows Weber (1976).

Some physical and biotic information on the ecosystem types is presented in Table 1-1. For each ecosystem type, we provide a brief sketch of the mammalian fauna. We highlight mammals only because this is a book about mammals and not about wildlife more generally. Sometimes we speak of a "mammalian community." This is perhaps convenient, but at best it is ecologically simplistic, and at worst actually misleading. A biotic community is the living part of an ecosystem: animals, plants, fungi, and microbes. We might reasonably subdivide the community into two functional components: (1) *producers* (the green plants and photosynthetic microbes that have the genetic know-how to use solar energy to assemble parts of water and air into chemical bonds of biological molecules); and (2) *consumers* (which includes mammals and all other animals as well as fungi and many microbial groups).

Table 1-2 is a checklist of Coloradan mammals indicating their general distribution across Colorado's ecosystem types. The species in a community that exploit similar resources in similar ways comprise an ecological *guild*. Visualizing communities of functional guilds often makes more ecological sense than visualizing a community organized taxonomically. For example, we can think of the guilds of primary consumers (grazers, browsers, seedeaters) and secondary consumers (predators, parasites) regardless of taxonomy. This ecological view focuses attention where the action is. In semidesert shrublands, for example, seed-eating kangaroo rats and pocket mice may compete directly with ants for seed resources, and they compete less with other kinds of mammals. On shortgrass prairie, grazing mammals (like bison and prairie dogs) compete with grazing grasshoppers, not with insectivorous grasshopper mice.

GRASSLANDS

Dominant plants. Blue grama (*Bouteloua gracilis*), buffalograss (*Buchloë dactyloides*), western wheatgrass (*Agropyron smithii*), sand sagebrush (*Artemisia filifolia*), yucca (*Yucca glauca*), prickly-pear cactus (*Opuntia* spp.), needle-and-thread (*Stipa comata*), sand bluestem (*Andropogon hallii*), sand dropseed (*Sporobolus cryptandrus*).

TABLE 1-2. Ecological distribution of native, recent mammals in Colorado

	1	*2*	*3*	*4*	*5*	*6*	*7*	*8*
MARSUPICARNIVORA								
Family Didelphidae: Opossums								
Virginia Opossum—*Didelphis virginiana*								X
CINGULATA								
Family Dasypodidae: Armadillos								
Nine-banded Armadillo—*Dasypus novemcinctus*								X
PRIMATES								
Family Hominidae: Humans and Kin								
Humans—*Homo sapiens*	X	X	X	X	X	X	X	X
RODENTIA								
Family Sciuridae: Squirrels								
Cliff Chipmunk—*Neotamias dorsalis*		X	X					
Least Chipmunk—*Neotamias minimus*		X	X	X	X	X	X	
Colorado Chipmunk—*Neotamias quadrivittatus*			X	X	X			
Hopi Chipmunk—*Neotamias rufus*		X	X	X				

TABLE 1-2. Ecological distribution of native, recent mammals in Colorado—*continued*

	1	*2*	*3*	*4*	*5*	*6*	*7*	*8*
Uinta Chipmunk—*Neotamias umbrinus*		X	X	X	X	X	X	X
Yellow-bellied Marmot—*Marmota flaviventris*				X	X	X	X	X
White-tailed Antelope Squirrel—*Ammospermophilus leucurus*		X						
Rock Squirrel—*Otospermophilus variegatus*			X	X	X			X
Golden-mantled Ground Squirrel—*Callospermophilus lateralis*		X	X	X	X	X	X	X
13-lined Ground Squirrel—*Ictidomys tridecemlineatus*	X	X						
Spotted Ground Squirrel—*Xerospermophilus spilosoma*	X	X						
Wyoming Ground Squirrel—*Urocitellus elegans*	X	X		X	X		X	
Gunnison's Prairie Dog—*Cynomys gunnisoni*	X	X		X				
White-tailed Prairie Dog—*Cynomys leucurus*	X	X		X				
Black-tailed Prairie Dog—*Cynomys ludovicianus*	X	X						
Abert's Squirrel—*Sciurus aberti*					X			
Fox Squirrel—*Sciurus niger*								X
Pine Squirrel, or Chickaree—*Tamiasciurus hudsonicus*					X	X		
Family Castoridae: Beaver								
Beaver—*Castor canadensis*								X
Family Heteromyidae: Pocket Mice and Kin								
Olive-backed Pocket Mouse—*Perognathus fasciatus*	X	X						
Plains Pocket Mouse—*Perognathus flavescens*	X	X	X					
Silky Pocket Mouse—*Perognathus flavus*	X	X	X					
Great Basin Pocket Mouse—*Perognathus parvus*	X	X	X					
Hispid Pocket Mouse—*Chaetodipus hispidus*	X	X						
Ord's Kangaroo Rat—*Dipodomys ordii*	X	X	X					
Family Geomyidae: Pocket Gophers								
Botta's Pocket Gopher—*Thomomys bottae*	X	X	X	X	X			
Northern Pocket Gopher—*Thomomys talpoides*	X	X		X	X	X	X	
Plains Pocket Gopher—*Geomys bursarius*	X							
Yellow-faced Pocket Gopher—*Cratogeomys castanops*	X	X		X				
Family Dipodidae: Jumping Mice and Kin								
Meadow Jumping Mouse—*Zapus hudsonicus*					X			X
Western Jumping Mouse—*Zapus princeps*					X			X
Family Cricetidae: Cricetid Rats and Mice								
Southern Red-backed Vole—*Myodes gapperi*					X	X		
Heather Vole—*Phenacomys intermedius*					X	X	X	
Long-tailed Vole—*Microtus longicaudus*				X	X	X	X	X
Mexican Vole—*Microtus mogollonensis*			X	X	X			X
Montane Vole—*Microtus montanus*				X	X	X	X	X
Prairie Vole—*Microtus ochrogaster*	X							X
Meadow Vole—*Microtus pennsylvanicus*	X							X

continued on next page

TABLE 1-2. Ecological distribution of native, recent mammals in Colorado—*continued*

	1	2	3	4	5	6	7	8
Sagebrush Vole—*Lemmiscus curtatus*		X		X				
Muskrat—*Ondatra zibethicus*								X
Western Harvest Mouse—*Reithrodontomys megalotis*	X	X						X
Plains Harvest Mouse—*Reithrodontomys montanus*	X							
Brush Mouse—*Peromyscus boylii*			X	X				X
Canyon Mouse—*Peromyscus crinitus*		X	X					
White-footed Mouse—*Peromyscus leucopus*								X
Deer Mouse—*Peromyscus maniculatus*	X	X	X	X	X	X	X	X
Northern Rock Mouse—*Peromyscus nasutus*			X	X	X			
Piñon Mouse—*Peromyscus truei*		X	X	X				
Northern Grasshopper Mouse—*Onychomys leucogaster*	X	X						
White-throated Woodrat—*Neotoma albigula*			X	X				
Bushy-tailed Woodrat—*Neotoma cinerea*			X	X	X	X	X	
Eastern Woodrat—*Neotoma floridana*								X
Desert Woodrat—*Neotoma lepida*		X	X					
Mexican Woodrat—*Neotoma mexicana*			X	X	X			X
Southern Plains Woodrat—*Neotoma micropus*	X	X						
Hispid Cotton Rat—*Sigmodon hispidus*	X							X
Family Erethizontidae: New World Porcupines								
Porcupine—*Erethizon dorsatum*			X	X	X	X	X	X
LAGOMORPHA								
Family Ochotonidae: Pikas								
Pika—*Ochotona princeps*						X	X	
Family Leporidae: Rabbits and Hares								
Desert Cottontail—*Sylvilagus audubonii*	X	X	X	X				X
Eastern Cottontail—*Sylvilagus floridanus*								X
Nuttall's Cottontail—*Sylvilagus nuttallii*				X	X	X		X
Snowshoe Hare—*Lepus americanus*						X		X
White-tailed Jackrabbit—*Lepus townsendii*	X	X	X	X	X		X	
Black-tailed Jackrabbit—*Lepus californicus*	X	X						
SORICOMORPHA								
Family Soricidae: Shrews								
Masked Shrew—*Sorex cinereus*					X	X	X	X
Pygmy Shrew—*Sorex hoyi*						X		X
Merriam's Shrew—*Sorex merriami*	X	X	X	X	X			
Montane Shrew—*Sorex monticolus*					X	X	X	X
Dwarf Shrew—*Sorex nanus*				X	X	X	X	X
Water Shrew—*Sorex palustris*								X

TABLE 1-2. Ecological distribution of native, recent mammals in Colorado—*continued*

	1	*2*	*3*	*4*	*5*	*6*	*7*	*8*
Preble's Shrew—*Sorex preblei* (?)				X				
Elliot's Short-tailed Shrew—*Blarina hylophaga*								X
Least Shrew—*Cryptotis parva*	X		X	X				X
Desert Shrew—*Notiosorex crawfordi*		X						
Family Talpidae: Moles								
Eastern Mole—*Scalopus aquaticus*	X							
CHIROPTERA								
Family Molossidae: Free-tailed Bats								
Mexican Free-tailed Bat—*Tadarida brasiliensis*	X	X	X	X				
Big Free-tailed Bat—*Nyctinomops macrotis*	X							
Family Vespertilionidae: Common Bats								
California Myotis—*Myotis californicus*		X	X					
Western Small-footed Myotis—*Myotis ciliolabrum*	X	X	X	X	X			X
Long-eared Myotis—*Myotis evotis*			X	X	X			
Little Brown Bat—*Myotis lucifugus*					X	X		X
Fringed Myotis—*Myotis thysanodes*			X	X	X			
Long-legged Myotis—*Myotis volans*			X	X	X	X		
Yuma Myotis—*Myotis yumanensis*		X	X	X	X			X
Red Bat—*Lasiurus borealis*								X
Hoary Bat—*Lasiurus cinereus*		X	X		X	X		X
Silver-haired Bat—*Lasionycteris noctivagans*		X			X	X		X
Western Pipistrelle—*Parastrellus hesperus*	X	X	X		X			X
Eastern Pipistrellus—*Perimyotis subflavus*								X
Big Brown Bat—*Eptesicus fuscus*		X	X	X	X	X		X
Spotted Bat—*Euderma maculatum*		X	X	X				X
Townsend's Big-eared Bat—*Corynorhinus townsendii*	X	X	X	X	X			
Pallid Bat—*Antrozous pallidus*	X	X	X	X				X
CARNIVORA								
Family Felidae: Cats								
Mountain Lion—*Puma concolor*		X	X	X	X	X	X	X
Lynx—*Lynx lynx*						X	X	
Bobcat—*Lynx rufus*		X	X	X	X	X		X
Family Canidae: Dogs and Kin								
Coyote—*Canis latrans*	X	X	X	X	X	X	X	X
Gray Wolf—*Canis lupus**	X	X	X	X	X	X	X	X
Kit Fox—*Vulpes macrotis*	X	X						
Swift Fox—*Vulpes velox*	X							

continued on next page

TABLE 1-2. Ecological distribution of native, recent mammals in Colorado—*continued*

	1	2	3	4	5	6	7	8
Red Fox—*Vulpes vulpes*				X	X	X	X	X
Gray Fox—*Urocyon cinereoargenteus*		X	X	X	X			X
Family Ursidae: Bears								
Black Bear—*Ursus americanus*				X	X	X		X
Grizzly Bear—*Ursus arctos**	X	X	X	X	X	X	X	X
Family Procyonidae: Raccoons and Kin								
Raccoon—*Procyon lotor*								X
Ringtail—*Bassariscus astutus*		X	X	X	X			X
Family Mustelidae: Weasels and Kin								
American Marten—*Martes americana*					X	X	X	
Ermine—*Mustela erminea*	X				X	X	X	X
Long-tailed Weasel—*Mustela frenata*	X	X	X	X	X	X	X	X
Black-footed Ferret—*Mustela nigripes*	X	X						
Mink—*Neovison vison*								X
Wolverine—*Gulo gulo*						X	X	
American Badger—*Taxidea taxus*	X	X	X	X			X	
Northern River Otter—*Lontra canadensis*†								X
Family Mephitidae: Skunks and Kin								
Western Spotted Skunk—*Spilogale gracilis*		X	X	X	X			
Eastern Spotted Skunk—*Spilogale putorius*								X
Striped Skunk—*Mephitis mephitis*	X	X	X	X	X	X	X	X
White-backed Hog-nosed Skunk—*Conepatus leuconotus*	X	X	X	X	X			
ARTIODACTYLA								
Family Cervidae: Deer								
Elk, or Wapiti—*Cervus elaphus*	X	X	X	X	X	X	X	X
Mule Deer—*Odocoileus hemionus*	X	X	X	X	X	X	X	X
White-tailed Deer—*Odocoileus virginianus*								X
Moose—*Alces alces*‡						X		X
Family Antilocapridae: Pronghorn and Kin								
Pronghorn—*Antilocapra americana*	X	X						
Family Bovidae: Cattle, Goats, Sheep and Kin								
Bison—*Bison bison**	X	X					X	
Mountain Goat—*Oreamnos americanus*‡						X	X	
Bighorn Sheep—*Ovis canadensis*					X	X	X	

Key: 1 = grassland; 2 = semidesert shrubland; 3 = piñon-juniper woodland; 4 = montane shrubland; 5 = montane woodland and forest; 6 = subalpine forest; 7 = alpine tundra; 8 = riparian and wetland systems.

Notes: This checklist does not include adventive species (e.g., Old World rats and mice, feral dogs, cats, pigs, llamas, horses), except deliberate introductions naturalized in the state. Used in conjunction with range maps in accounts of individual species, this list should allow construction of a provisional, hypothetical list of the potential natural mammalian fauna of native ecosystems at any locality in the state. Annotations of ecological distribution generally follow D. Armstrong (1972) and Meaney (1990a); * = extirpated within historic time; † = extirpated but restored; ‡ = deliberate introduction of non-native species; (?) = of questionable occurrence.

PHOTOGRAPH 1-1. Grassland, Pawnee National Grassland, Weld County. © 1993 Wendy Shattil / Bob Rozinski.

Grasslands occur over the Great Plains and in intermountain parks such as South Park and the Wet Mountain Valley. Prior to permanent settlement and cultivation, grasslands were the single most extensive ecosystem type in Colorado, covering 35 to 40 percent of the state. In Colorado, as generally around the globe, grasslands also are the most extensively modified biome (R. White et al. 2000). For review of the conservation challenges, see T. Weaver et al. (1996). Roughly half of Colorado's primeval grassland is now under cultivation, and about a quarter of that cropland is irrigated. Grasslands of the Great Plains and the mountain parks differ in species composition. Generally, grasslands cover a gently rolling topography of fine, deep soils. Winters are dry and most of the precipitation falls during spring and summer. Seastedt (2002) reviewed the history of grasslands of the Rocky Mountain region, emphasizing their deliberate and inadvertent transformation by humans. Over broad areas this ecosystem is a shortgrass prairie of blue grama and buffalograss. Where soil moisture is greater, western wheatgrass (*Agropyron smithii*), needle-and-thread, bluestems (*Andropogon*), reedgrass (*Calamogrostis* spp.), and dropseed interspersed with short grasses form mixed-grass prairies. Areas of low rolling sand hills are typified by sand sagebrush, Indian ricegrass (*Oryzopsis hymenoides*), bluestems, and reedgrass. In southeastern Colorado this ecosystem is characterized by lower precipitation and the presence of the candelabra cactus, or "cholla" (*Opuntia imbricata*).

Grasslands evolved in the presence of fire and with grazing by large and small mammals. Historically, bison, wolves, and black-tailed prairie dogs were a significant component. However, favorable topography and soils have led to such extensive human use that there are no known undisturbed tracts of native grassland in Colorado. About half of the state (some 32 million acres, about 13 million hectares) is devoted to agriculture, including extensive irrigated and dryland crops and grazing. In many areas, even where never plowed, the prolonged effects of livestock grazing have resulted in alteration of the floristic composition (Costello 1954; Adler and Lauenroth 2000) and animal assemblages (Milchunas et al. 1998). Vavra et al. (1994) reviewed ecological impacts of livestock on western grasslands generally, and Rowley (1985) provided historical perspective, particularly for grasslands managed by the US Forest Service. All of Colorado's natural environments are subject to habitat alteration by invasive, exotic plants, but such weed problems probably are most severe on grazing lands and fallow fields, hence grasslands generally. The challenges already are exacerbated by ongoing climate change (B. Bradley et al. 2009), which makes management of native ecosystems a moving target. Asner et al. (2004) reviewed impacts of grazing systems—including grasslands, shrublands, and woodlands—on ecosystem processes on a global scale, emphasizing process of desertification and encroachment of woody plants in response to grazing pressure.

Additional thousands of hectares have been converted to urban, suburban, and exurban landscapes (W. Travis et al. 2002; W. Travis 2007). Efforts to restore grassland and riparian ecosystems have used original land surveys to reconstruct pre-settlement landscapes (Galatowitsch 1990), and historical photographs are also useful for understanding human impacts (McGinnies et al. 1991). The shortgrass steppe of the High Plains of eastern Colorado was the heart of the Dust Bowl of the 1930s. Cooke (1936) provided a classic, contemporary account of the ecology of the area, which deserves wide rereading in the context of changing climates and mammalian habitats.

Mammals. One of two general "adaptive syndromes" characterize mammals of open grasslands: an ability to move rapidly (to escape predators or inclement weather) or an ability to live underground. The pronghorn and the white-tailed jackrabbit epitomize mammals of open grasslands, where their keen peripheral vision and great speed evolved. Most smaller mammals spend some or most of their lives belowground. Soil type determines the distribution of many small mammals of the grasslands. Plains pocket gophers may be abundant in deep sandy soils, Ord's kangaroo rats excavate dunes and sandy banks of ephemeral streams (or roadside borrow pits), and plains pocket mice occur in shrubby areas of sand sagebrush and yucca. In contrast to other pocket mice, the hispid pocket mouse is not limited to sandy soils but prefers open areas with a light cover of bunchgrasses. Prairie voles occur in mixed-grass prairie adjacent to riparian areas in eastern Colorado. Northern grasshopper mice are widespread in both grasslands and semidesert shrublands, and they seem to prefer loamy soils because they are obligate dust-bathers. Thirteen-lined ground squirrels prefer short bunchgrasses on friable sandy loams where they can dig their burrows. Swift foxes prefer sandy loams or loams where they dig dens for shelter year-round. Badgers are wide-ranging in open habitats with abundant burrowing rodents.

Recently, human disturbance has played a key role on the plains. Black-tailed jackrabbits successfully occupy areas disturbed by human activities, taking cover in and feeding on introduced grasses and weedy forbs; white-tailed jackrabbits do not respond as well to disturbed vegetation and are increasingly restricted to more open areas and the mountain parks. Desert cottontails may prefer brushlands and woodland-edge situations, but they occur throughout the open grasslands, where they use burrows excavated by other mammals. Black-tailed prairie dogs are scattered across the eastern plains in both short- and mid-length grasslands, often reaching high densities in unused open lands within urbanized areas, especially areas abandoned by agriculture but not yet permanently modified by residential, commercial, or industrial development.

Coloradan grasslands received intensive study beginning in the 1960s when the Grassland Biome component of the International Biological Program (IBP) was headquartered at Colorado State University, and the Central Plains Experimental Range and Pawnee National Grassland served as principal research sites (e.g., N. French 1971; Flake 1973; N. French et al. 1976; Abramsky 1978; Abramsky and Van Dyne 1980). Ecological work in the area continues as a Long-Term Ecological Research (LTER) site, funded by the National Science Foundation, as documented by numerous studies cited elsewhere in this book. Stapp et al. (2008) provided a thorough review of that literature. In North American grasslands, latitude and moisture gradients underlie broad patterns of community structure, and temporal variability in community composition occurs in all grassland types (Grant and Birney 1979).

Lovell et al. (1985) described successional patterns caused by development of a dam and canal, agriculture, and irrigation around Barr Lake. Changes in species composition occurred as opportunists (raccoons, least shrews, porcupines) moved in and sensitive species disappeared, while other more resilient species persisted. A number of studies have focused on the impact of grazing. Moulton et al. (1981a) found small mammals to be adaptable to habitat perturbation, more responsive to vegetational structure than to plant species composition. Other large Coloradan grassland sites where studies of mammals have occurred include the US Army's Piñon Canyon Maneuver Site southeast of Pueblo, Rocky Mountain Arsenal National Wildlife Refuge northeast of Denver, and a number of Nature Conservancy preserves. R. Benedict et al. (1996) reviewed grassland mammals from a conservation perspective. Recent reviews of the general ecology (natural and human) of the Great Plains include Licht (1997), Seastedt (2002), and Johnsgard (2005).

PHOTOGRAPH 1-2. **Semidesert shrubland, along Rio Grande, San Luis Valley, Costilla County. © 1993 Wendy Shattil / Bob Rozinski.**

SEMIDESERT SHRUBLANDS

Dominant plants. Big sagebrush (*Artemisia tridentata*), mountain sagebrush (*A. vaseyanum*), greasewood (*Sarcobatus vermiculatus*), shadscale (*Atriplex confertifolia*), four-winged saltbush (*A. canescens*), rabbitbrush (*Chrysothamnus nauseosus*), balsamroot (*Balsamorhiza sagittata*).

Often grayish green in general color, semidesert shrublands cover arid regions at lower elevations in western Colorado and the San Luis Valley, occupying about 15 percent of the state. This is a cold desert ecosystem, occurring at the eastern edge of the Colorado Plateau and the Wyoming Basin. Semidesert shrublands follow the canyon bottomlands of western Colorado, extend up onto mesas and plateaus, and penetrate deep into the mountains along the Yampa, Colorado, and Gunnison rivers. Semidesert shrublands are dominated by shrubs over a sparse understory of grasses and forbs or even bare ground where nutrient-poor, alkaline soils and drought prevail. Most of the moisture falls during winter. Early summer drought is common, and June is the driest month in western Colorado (whereas it is one of the wetter months in eastern Colorado).

Greasewood is often well developed on alkaline soils and extends over considerable areas in the San Luis Valley, the Grand Valley, and other arid areas of western Colorado. Herbaceous understory is sparse. Rabbitbrush or sagebrush may border greasewood stands, and where soils are less alkaline these species form mixed stands with the greasewood. White-tailed antelope squirrels burrow under rocks and shrubs in such ecosystems in southwestern Colorado.

Saltbush is widespread at lower elevations on soils that are well drained and less alkaline than those dominated by greasewood. Extensive stands are present in western Moffat, Mesa, Garfield, and Rio Blanco counties and in Delta County between Hotchkiss and the eastern slopes of the West Elk Mountains. Typically, saltbush plants are widely scattered and often are cushion- or mat-like in appearance. There is little herbaceous understory.

Sagebrush covers many thousands of hectares in western Colorado. In North Park and the upper Colorado River drainage (Middle Park, Gunnison Basin, and Blue River Valley), mountain sagebrush predominates, whereas in the northwestern corner of the state big sagebrush prevails. Grass and forb cover is often well developed. At their lower limits sagebrush stands often merge with either saltbush or greasewood. At the upper limits the transition may be with montane shrubland, montane forest, or subalpine forest. The most significant human use of semidesert shrublands has been for grazing, although large portions of the San Luis Valley and the Grand Valley have been converted to irrigated croplands. Shrublands and piñon-juniper woodlands are particularly subject to degradation by ongoing oil and gas development (Morton et al. 2004). A detailed conservation assessment of sagebrush habitats in Colorado was prepared for the Colorado Division of Wildlife by Boyle and Reeder (2005).

Mammals. Herbivores of this ecosystem must contend with foliage of low palatability and low summer moisture. Desert cottontails feed on sagebrush and rabbitbrush in winter. Black-tailed jackrabbits feed on the forb understory and turn to shrubs such as winterfat (*Ceratoides lanata*), shadscale, and sagebrush in late fall and winter. Wyoming ground squirrels feed on pasture sagebrush (*Artemisia frigida*), milk vetches (*Astragalus* spp.), and locoweeds (*Oxytropis* spp.). The Wyoming Basin is home to the white-tailed prairie dog, which favors xeric sites with a mix of shrubs and grasses. Ord's kangaroo rats exploit the rich seed resources of the shrublands. Canyon mice and ringtails favor warm, dry, rocky canyons in semidesert shrublands. Moderately friable sandy loams are favored by northern grasshopper mice. Sagebrush voles feed on the leaves of sagebrush, rabbitbrush, and other aridland shrubs in areas where they are mixed with grasses. Merriam's shrew and the desert shrew occur locally. The Yuma myotis and pallid bat occur in the canyon country of western and southeastern Colorado. Published studies of mammalian communities of Colorado's semidesert shrublands are few, but studies from adjacent Utah (D. Armstrong 1979, 1982) are pertinent.

PHOTOGRAPH 1-3. Piñon-juniper woodland, Colorado National Monument, Mesa County. Photograph by C. A. Meaney.

PIÑON-JUNIPER WOODLAND

Dominant plants. Piñon pine (*Pinus edulis*), one-seed juniper (*Juniperus monosperma*), Utah juniper (*J. osteosperma*) in western Colorado, red cedar (*J. scopulorum*), blue grama (*Bouteloua gracilis*), junegrass (*Koeleria macrantha*), Indian ricegrass (*Oryzopsis hymenoides*), prickly-pear (*Opuntia* spp.), fescues (*Festuca* spp.), muhley (*Muhlenbergia* spp.), bluegrass (*Poa* spp.).

Piñon-juniper woodlands form open stands on warm, well-drained sites, mostly in western and southern Colorado, covering 10 to 15 percent of the state. In southeastern Colorado, they are situated above grasslands and below montane shrublands. Western Colorado presents a more complex pattern. There, piñon-juniper woodlands are bounded below and sometimes also above by semidesert shrublands where the woodlands also interweave with montane shrublands. Piñon-juniper woodlands are found extensively on slopes in western and central Colorado and in the roughlands of the southeastern part of the state. An isolated grove of about 4,500 ha (11,120 acres) is located at Owl Canyon, north of Fort Collins. Soils are variable in composition, although generally coarse and shallow. Junipers are more drought-tolerant and thus dominate on the lower periphery, whereas piñons are more cold-tolerant and dominate the upper extreme. Grasses, cacti, and a variety of annual and perennial composites form much of the sparse ground cover. Many large mammals and birds use this ecosystem seasonally to avoid the rigors of higher elevations. Others are year-round residents. Species diversity in piñon-juniper woodlands is high, in Colorado second only to riparian systems. Native Americans harvested piñon nuts, which are produced by an individual tree only every 3 to 7 years, and they made extensive use of piñon wood and pitch. Early European settlers also used these resources and initiated cattle and sheep grazing, which continues today. The woodlands of Mesa Verde are exemplary and well studied (Floyd et al. 2003). Like semidesert shrublands, piñon-juniper woodlands are being degraded over wide areas by oil and gas development, particularly in western Colorado (Morton et al. 2004).

Mammals. During years of major cone production (sometimes called "mast years"), mammals feed on the rich resource of piñon "nuts." Many use the understory of grasses and forbs also. Townsend's big-eared bats and fringed myotis pick insects off the trees. The long-eared myotis roosts in tree cavities and under loose bark. Desert cottontails feed on the understory of grasses and forbs. Nuttall's cottontail turns to junipers in winter. Rock squirrels occupy areas of broken rock. Piñon-juniper woodlands in Colorado are home to as many as four species of *Peromyscus*. The piñon mouse occurs in areas with large rocks where the woodland is well developed. The canyon mouse inhabits the warm, dry canyons of western Colorado. The brush mouse occurs in piñon-juniper woodlands of both the Eastern and Western slopes, especially in the ecotone with oakbrush. The well-named rock mouse occurs only on the Eastern Slope, extending well northward in rocky foothills beyond the general range of piñon. Piñon-juniper woodland is a favored habitat of the Mexican woodrat, which reaches its northern limit in Colorado. Ringtails frequent rocky canyon country, often in association with channels of ephemeral streams. Gray foxes, mountain lions, and mule deer are common in this ecosystem. The few records of white-backed hog-nosed skunks in Colorado are from piñon-juniper woodlands and adjacent grasslands in the southeastern portion of the state.

PHOTOGRAPH 1-4. Montane shrubland, Black Canyon of the Gunnison, Montrose County. Photograph by David J. Cooper.

Peyton (2008) described small mammals of piñon-juniper woodlands (and adjacent shrub and grassland habitats) on chalk barrens on Fort Carson Military Reservation, Pueblo County. Somers et al. (2003) reviewed some aspects of the ecology of terrestrial mammals of Mesa Verde, focused on interactions with old-growth piñon-juniper woodland. Small mammals of piñon-juniper woodlands often segregate by extent of canopy cover, herbaceous cover, and tree dispersion (Ribble and Samson 1987). Haufler and Nagy (1984) concluded that competition was avoided by selection of different foods. For comparative studies from woodlands in adjacent Utah, see D. Armstrong (1979, 1982) and Sureda and Morrison (1999).

MONTANE SHRUBLANDS

Dominant plants. Gambel oak (*Quercus gambelii*), mountain mahogany (*Cercocarpus montanus*), serviceberry (*Amelanchier alnifolia*), skunkbush (*Rhus trilobata*), smooth sumac (*R. glabra*), wax currant (*Ribes cereum*), wild rose (*Rosa woodsier*), needle-and-thread (*Stipa comata*), blue grama (*Bouteloua gracilis*), western wheatgrass (*Agropyron smithii*), side-oats grama (*Bouteloua curtipendula*), mountain muhley (*Muhlenbergia montana*), rabbitbrush (*Chrysothamnus nauseosus*), chokecherry (*Prunus virginiana*).

Montane shrublands generally occur at higher elevations than either grasslands or piñon-juniper woodlands in eastern Colorado, and in western Colorado they occur upslope from semidesert shrublands or piñon-juniper woodlands and below montane forests. On the Eastern Slope of the Front Range, these shrublands form a distinctive and often quite narrow belt at the mountain front, often in association with sedimentary hogback ridges and other "foothills." West of the mountains, extensive Gambel oak communities often intermingle with piñon-juniper, and mixed stands of serviceberry, snowberry, and rabbitbrush cover extensive areas of northwestern Colorado. All told, such shrublands cover 5 to 10 percent of the state. The topographic setting is rocky, broken country; soils are coarse and well drained. Temperatures are less extreme than in adjacent ecosystems: warmer in winter than ecosystems above and cooler in summer than those lower in elevation. Gambel oak and serviceberry dominate throughout, except for the foothills west of Denver, where Gambel oak reaches its northern limit and is replaced by mountain mahogany. Montane shrublands form a rich and diverse ecosystem that supports plants and animals more typical of adjacent ecosystems, and they serve as winter refuge for some species. Montane shrublands are often areas of intensive human residential use, and they are quite colorful in fall.

Mammals. Many mammals favor the rocky outcrops and hogbacks common to montane shrublands. Abundant fruits, twigs, and foliage of shrubs provide forage, as does the understory of grasses. Rock squirrels prefer areas that have large rocks and can often be found basking on them or feeding on berries and grass seeds. Brush mice, piñon mice, and rock mice frequent montane shrublands, as does the ubiquitous deer mouse. Although four of Colorado's six species of woodrats can be found in montane shrublands, the Mexican woodrat is the most characteristic. Ringtails, western spotted skunks, and gray foxes feed on a broad variety of small mammals, reptiles, arthropods, and fruits. The western small-footed myotis frequents rocky areas where they forage and roost in rock crevices and among, or under, rocks on the ground. They winter in tunnels here and in montane forests. D. Armstrong et al. (1973) described species turnover in assemblages at different elevations, focused strongly on small mammals of montane shrublands.

PHOTOGRAPH 1-5. Montane woodland, City of Boulder Open Space, Boulder County. Photograph by David J. Cooper.

MONTANE WOODLANDS AND FORESTS

Dominant plants. Ponderosa pine (*Pinus ponderosa*), Douglas-fir (*Pseudotsuga menziesii*), quaking aspen (*Populus tremuloides*), white fir (*Abies concolor*), limber pine (*Pinus flexilis*), Colorado blue spruce (*Picea pungens*), lodgepole pine (*Pinus contorta*), wax currant (*Ribes cereum*), Arizona fescue (*Festuca arizonica*), sulphur flower (*Eriogonum umbellatum*), kinnikinnik (*Arctostaphylos uva-ursi*), mountain maple (*Acer glabrum*).

Montane forests range from open ponderosa pine parklands to dense Douglas-fir forests and clothe about 10 percent of Colorado. Bounded below by foothills shrublands, piñon-juniper woodlands, or grasslands, they grade into subalpine forests above. Most precipitation falls as snow in winter and spring, although summer showers are also important. Open ponderosa pine woodlands occur on well-drained sites in the Front Range and eastward on the Platte-Arkansas Divide, in the southern and southwestern mountains to Mesa Verde, and on parts of the Uncompahgre Plateau. Douglas-fir predominates in other mountainous regions and generally on moister, steeper slopes at higher elevation, whereas ponderosa pine occupies drier south-facing slopes. In some areas they intergrade along with quaking aspen or lodgepole pine, which will colonize sites after a disturbance, especially fire. This ecosystem has been exploited extensively for timber and also used for mining, grazing, historic and current human settlement, and recreation. Due to fire suppression over most of the past century, many ponderosa pine stands in Colorado are much denser than they would have been pre-settlement and as a consequence are prone to wildfire and insect damage (Cisla 2010).

Mammals. Many mammals in both montane and subalpine forests use the dominant conifers for food and shelter. A number of kinds feed on inner bark (cambium) and

PHOTOGRAPH 1-6. Subalpine forest, Rio Grande County. © 1993 Wendy Shattil / Bob Rozinski.

stems and make their nests or roost in the trees. Both the long-eared and long-legged myotis roost in tree cavities and under loose bark on standing dead snags. Nuttall's cottontails avoid dense forests but can be found at the edge of clearings. Least and Colorado chipmunks feed on fruits, nuts, berries, seeds, leaves, and stems; the Uinta chipmunk also occurs in montane forests but is restricted to higher areas, where it often is sympatric with the least chipmunk. Abert's squirrels make nests in ponderosa pine trees and feed on the twigs and seeds, whereas pine squirrels prefer more dense Douglas-fir or lodgepole pine stands. Porcupines feed on cambium, buds, and twigs of conifers, especially pines. American martens feed on small rodents and are excellent climbers. Numerous studies of Colorado's montane mammals are cited in respective accounts of species. Synecological studies have been remarkably few. Stinson (1978) contrasted communities on north- and south-facing slopes, and many of the observations of D. Armstrong (1993, 2008) pertain to this ecosystem type. Ecology of wildlife diseases in the montane forests of Rocky Mountain National Park was reported by A. Carey et al. (1980), G. Bowen et al. (1981), and McLean et al. (1981). Finch and Ruggiero (1993) emphasized the importance of montane and subalpine forests to wildlife conservation.

SUBALPINE FOREST

Dominant plants. Engelmann spruce (*Picea engelmannii*), subalpine fir (*Abies lasiocarpa*), quaking aspen (*Populus tremuloides*), bristlecone pine (*Pinus aristata*), limber pine (*P. flexilis*), lodgepole pine (*P. contorta*), myrtle blueberry (*Vaccinium myrtillus*), broom huckleberry (*V. scoparium*), heart-leaved arnica (*Arnica cordifolia*), Jacob's ladder (*Polemonium delicatum*).

This is a relatively homogeneous, dense coniferous forest ecosystem, often occurring on steep slopes. It is the highest-elevation forested ecosystem in Colorado and occupies about 15 percent of the land area of the state. Soils are shallow. High winter precipitation, in the form of snow, is augmented by windblown snow from the alpine tundra above. The trees are effective snow fences and cold temperatures prevent significant melting until late spring. "Freak" storms may have significant, local impacts on small mammals (Ehrlich et al. 1972). These factors create high snow accumulations. At their upper reaches, subalpine forests become low-growing stands of elfin woodland, or Krummholz (Mutel and Emerick 1992; A. Benedict 2008). Limber pine and bristlecone pine dominate on windy, exposed sites with rocky soils. Fire or other disturbance may lead to colonization by lodgepole pine or aspen. Spruce and fir seedlings are shade-tolerant, allowing them to invade stands of shade-intolerant lodgepole pine and aspen. Regeneration of a spruce-fir forest after disturbance is relatively slow because of the short growing season. In contrast to lodgepole pine and mature spruce fir, aspen stands typically have a luxuriant and diverse understory of forbs and grasses, so they provide important opportunities for mammals (V. Scott and Crouch 1988). Huckaby and Moir (1998) detailed forest communities on the Fraser Experimental Forest in the St. Louis Creek watershed of Grand County. Subalpine forests are used extensively for recreation year-round and provide cover for the watersheds so important to metropolitan areas. Human influences and general ecology of Colorado's forests were reviewed by Elias (2002), Stohlgren et al. (2002), and Tomback and Kendall (2002) and summarized by J. Baron (2002). Elias et al. (1986) studied subfossil pollen and insect remains from Rocky Mountain National Park and concluded that the subalpine forests of today had assembled by about 3,500 years ago; in the interval 6,800 to 3,500 ybp (years before present), pines were more prevalent in high-elevation forests. Schoennagel et al. (2007) discussed occurrence of wildfire in the context of multi-decadal climatic variability; fires should be expected to increase with ongoing warming and drying. W. Baker (2009) emphasized fire as an important and natural influence on forests in the Rocky Mountains, urging the importance of management rather than mere prevention or suppression.

Forests of Colorado are under obvious stress. Sudden Aspen Decline (SAD) is a poorly understood die-off of aspen groves that more than doubled in extent from 217 sq. mi. (approximately 560 km^2) in 2006 to 522 sq. mi. (about 1,350 km^2) in 2007 (Colorado State Forest Service 2007). Ungulates (especially elk) are often implicated in decline of aspen stands. On long-term exclosures in national forests of south-central Utah (Kay and Bartos 2000), aspen subjected to browsing (by mule deer and/or livestock, especially cattle) failed to regenerate or regenerated significantly less than on total exclusion plots. Ungulate herbivory also influenced understory plants. Utilization by deer alone tended to reduce shrubs and tall, palatable forbs while promoting growth of native grasses. Adding livestock to the mix, however, reduced native grasses and promoted introduced species and bare soil.

Aspen decline is not homogeneous across the broad landscape, and—judging from studies in the northern Colorado Front Range—a diversity of factors is involved, including damage by mammalian herbivores (especially elk; see W. Baker et al. 1997), depending on the local site (C. White et al. 1998; Kashian et al. 2007). Dr. Erin Lehmer and students from Fort Lewis College, Durango, are studying possible interaction among SAD, the abundance of deer mice, and the incidence of hantavirus (E. Lehmer, personal communication). For a general review of the ecology of aspen, see DeByle and Winokur (1985).

Mountain pine beetle is killing the older trees in mature lodgepole pine forests at a remarkable rate, with nearly a million acres (over 1,500 sq. mi.) in the high country affected (Colorado State Forest Service 2007). These changes doubtless will impact local mammalian populations. The changes compound deliberate and direct impacts of humans on subalpine ecosystems: mining, road and railroad building, and logging in earlier times, and development of winter resorts and high-speed highways more recently. Colorado's montane and subalpine forests appear to be under increasing stress from a complex combination of insect pests, changing climate, and human-influenced fire regimes and age structure (Romme et al. 2006; van Mantgem et al. 2009; Pennisi 2009). The Colorado State Forest Service reports annually on the status of Colorado's forested ecosystems (see Ciesla 2010).

In forests and other native ecosystems, exurban residential development is a major driver of habitat fragmentation in Colorado, and this has cumulative, negative impacts on native mammals (Theobald et al. 1997; R. Knight et al. 2000). Clustered development may prevent some of these impacts, as spatial pattern of houses was a more important factor in disturbance than was density of homes. Local initiatives like the Southern Rockies Ecosystem Project have been leading the effort to understand and then slow and even reverse the long-term trend toward anthropogenic fragmentation of Colorado's mountain landscapes (Shinneman et al. 2000; B. Miller et al. 2003).

Mammals. A number of mammalian species inhabit subalpine forests. Adaptations to winter include hibernation (yellow-bellied marmots, ground squirrels), seasonal color change (long- and short-tailed weasels, snowshoe hares), and use of runways beneath the snow (mice and shrews). Some species, such as least chipmunks and golden-mantled ground squirrels, prefer forest-edge situations to dense timber. Snowshoe hares select subalpine forests with a well-developed undergrowth of shrubs and forbs where they rest, hidden, during the day. They feed on the leaves and needles, twigs, and bark of the trees and shrubs. Yellow-bellied marmots inhabit rock piles in subalpine clearings, where they bask in the sun and make their hibernacula. Pine squirrels, or chickarees, prefer dense stands of lodgepole pines, spruce and fir, and Douglas-fir, where their chattering calls can often be heard before the squirrels themselves are seen. Southern red-backed voles prefer relatively dense coniferous forests, where they nest under logs, roots, and rocks. They are preyed upon by American martens, as are montane and long-tailed voles. Canada lynx (and wolverines, which may or may not persist in Colorado) are boreal forest predators, largely restricted in Colorado to this ecosystem. Lynx feed almost exclusively on snowshoe hares, whereas wolverines are omnivorous. Elk bed down in these forests during the warmer months.

Mammalian communities of the subalpine forest probably have received more attention than those of any other ecosystem type. D. Armstrong (1977a) reviewed some of the extensive older literature. Raphael (1987) reviewed non-game wildlife of subalpine forests, focused on Colorado and Wyoming. Vaughan (1974) studied differences in feeding strategies of four species of subalpine rodents. The northern pocket gopher (*Thomomys talpoides*) and the montane vole (*Microtus montanus*) were entirely herbivorous but preferred different plants of different sizes and foraged in different microenvironments. Least chipmunks (*Tamias minimus*) and deer mice (*Peromyscus maniculatus*) both ate seeds and arthropods but fed at different times. Roppe and Hein (1978) found species diversity in a subalpine burn to be higher than in adjacent forest. Stinson (1977a) described three periods of high mortality among subalpine small mammals: during spring thaw because of flooding, during summer because of higher physiological demands and predation, and during fall because of freezes. Merritt and Merritt (1978b) emphasized the importance of winter snow to population dynamics of small mammals. In the Upper Williams Fork Basin of Grand County, small mammals generally selected habitat according to structural features of the habitat (D. Armstrong 1977a). Work by D. C. Andersen, MacMahon, and Wolfe (1980) on small mammals in aspen, fir, and spruce forests and adjacent meadows in the Wasatch Mountains of northern Utah is generally relevant to the situation in Colorado, as is that by Nordyke and Buskirk (1988) and Raphael (1988) in the Medicine Bow Range of southeastern Wyoming. Lawlor (2003) provided a general review of ecology and biogeography of mammals in coniferous forests of western North America, and Halfpenny et al. (1986) published a thorough bibliography on the subalpine zone of the Colorado Front Range to that date. Troendle et al. (1987) provided a variety of review papers on important aspects of management, with special attention to the Fraser Experimental Forest in Grand County. Forest dynamics were reviewed by D. Knight (1994).

ALPINE TUNDRA

Dominant plants. Elk sedge (*Kobresia myosuroides*), alpine avens (*Acomastylis rossii*), Arctic willow (*Salix arctica*), tufted hairgrass (*Deschampsia caespitosa*), sedges (*Carex* spp.), American bistort (*Bistorta bistortoides*), alpine sandwort (*Arenaria obtusiloba*), marsh-marigold (*Caltha leptosepala*), old-man-of-the-mountain (*Rydbergia grandiflora*).

Alpine tundra occurs above subalpine forest. The ecotone between them is recognized as timberline (G. Stevens and Fox 1991). Tundra is distributed in Colorado as discontinuous "islands" of habitat and occupies less than 5 percent of the state. High winter winds lead to a dry environment characterized by sedges, grasses, low-growing willows, and low-growing perennials, which develop as cushion plants. Talus, rock outcrops, and areas of exposed, coarse, poorly weathered rock are common. The density of plant cover varies widely with microclimatic conditions, soil development, and moisture regime. Less precipitation falls on the tundra than on the adjacent forest because storm systems tend to move through mountain passes. Furthermore, the snow that does fall on the high peaks tends to be redistributed by wind, forming snowbeds interspersed with snow-free areas; some of the snow blows down into subalpine forests. Soils are subject to freeze-thaw action in spring and fall. This may lead to polygons of sorted ground as rocks are moved differentially according to their size. Much of this patterned ground effect was formed during glacial episodes of the Pleistocene. Because of its severe climate and inaccessibility, alpine tundra generally has less human activity than most other ecosystems, aside from mining and summer recreationists, including backpackers and off-road vehicle traffic. This ecosystem is fragile and highly susceptible to disturbance. Once disturbed, vegetation may take centuries to recover because of the dry, cold climate; short growing season; and slow formation of new soil (Zwinger and Willard 1972). For a review of alpine ecology focused on the National Science Foundation–sponsored Long-Term Ecological Research site on Niwot Ridge above Boulder, see Bowman and Seastedt (2001); the bibliography compiled by Halfpenny et al. (1986) provides access to the rich background literature. Bowman et al. (2002) provided a general appraisal of the ecology of tundra, including human disturbance. For an accessible introduction to Pleistocene environments of the Rockies, see Elias (1996).

PHOTOGRAPH 1-7. Alpine tundra, Rocky Mountain National Park, Larimer County. © 1993 Wendy Shattil / Bob Rozinski.

Mammals. Alpine tundra is a relatively inhospitable environment year-round but especially during winter. Adaptations include deep hibernation (yellow-bellied marmots), use of runways under the snow (mice, voles, and shrews), migration to lower elevations (elk, mountain sheep), and use of windswept, snow-free ridges (introduced mountain goats). In lieu of hibernation, pikas "make hay," accumulating large quantities of alpine grasses and forbs, which become critical in the event of a late snowmelt. Talus slopes provide cover and protection from predators. Northern pocket gophers feed on roots of perennial tundra plants, and their tunnels aerate the soil, contributing to the slow downward slumping of mountainsides. Montane and long-tailed voles range into the alpine tundra, where they are prey for coyotes and long-tailed weasels. Elk feed on tundra grasses and forbs on summer nights and move down to the forest edge during the day. Mountain sheep are well-known for their preference for remote, rugged areas and are found on the tundra during summer. I. Blake and Blake (1969) reported on alpine mammals of Mount Lincoln. Numerous autecological studies have been conducted on the tundra above Rocky Mountain Biological Laboratory at Gothic, Gunnison County. The tundra on Niwot Ridge west of Boulder has been the site of numerous autecological and community studies of mammals (summarized by D. Armstrong et al. 2001). Halfpenny and Southwick (1982) reviewed research on herbivorous small mammals of Niwot Ridge.

PHOTOGRAPH 1-8. Riparian communities, Conejos County. © 1993 Wendy Shattil / Bob Rozinski.

RIPARIAN AND WETLAND SYSTEMS

Dominant plants. Plains cottonwood (*Populus sargentii*), narrowleaf cottonwood (*P. angustifolia*), mountain willow (*Salix monticola*), Geyer willow (*S. geyeriana*), peach-leaved willow (*S. amygdaloides*), sandbar willow (*S. exigua*), broad-leaved cattail (*Typha latifolia*), bulrush (*Scirpus lacustris*), field horsetail (*Equisetum arvense*), saltgrass (*Distichlis spicata*), sand dropseed (*Sporobolus cryptandrus*), alder (*Alnus tenuifolia*), river birch (*Betula fontinalis*), rushes (*Juncus* spp.), water sedge (*Carex aquatilis*), beaked sedge (*C. utriculata*).

Riparian ecosystems occur locally throughout Colorado as corridors along rivers and streams (well-watered ribbons threading through other ecosystems at all elevations) and as islands of habitat adjacent to standing water, including ponds, lakes, and marshes. At lower elevations, riparian cottonwoods and willows contrast dramatically with adjacent treeless grasslands and shrublands. Riparian soils are variable. Prior to intensive hydrologic management, many riparian areas, especially at middle to low elevations, were subject to seasonal flooding (during times of intense rainfall or rapid snowmelt), with frequent overbank deposition of alluvial material.

At higher elevations, willows, alders, and sedges predominate adjacent to streams or other wetlands. This ecosystem is extremely rich in fauna because of the resources it offers: abundant food and water, cover, and travel routes. Riparian systems have the highest species richness of all major ecosystem types in Colorado, but they have the smallest areal extent, covering only 1 to 2 percent of the state. As favored sites for human residential, commercial, and industrial development, riparian lands have been extensively altered by introductions and invasions of non-native species (e.g., tamarisk or salt-cedar [*Tamarix gallica*] and Russian-olive [*Eleagnus angustifolia*]) and by livestock grazing, which significantly alters the structure of streambanks and can lead to substantial problems with erosion. Even greater changes result from dams and water-diversion projects. Knopf (1986) described "cosmopolitanism" of the avifauna along the South Platte near Crook, Logan County, since Euro-American settlement. No such dramatic change has occurred with the mammalian fauna, although there certainly must have been changes in species populations and local distributions. Knopf and Scott (1990) described historical changes in vegetation along the North and South Platte rivers. A thorough environmental history of Colorado's riparian ecosystems would be of great interest; rephotography holds great promise for such an effort (G. Williams 1978). D. Koehler and Thomas (2000) provided an extensive bibliography on riparian communities in the West.

Mammals. Riparian ecosystems of eastern Colorado are home to midwestern and eastern species (such as eastern cottontails, fox squirrels, and white-tailed deer) that have moved westward along these moist corridors with their abundant food and cover. Statewide, beaver, muskrats, and mink are dependent on waterways for shelter and food. Meadow voles are excellent swimmers and prefer moist, boggy areas, and jumping mice occupy riparian thickets. In western Colorado, riparian corridors carry some mountain species (montane and long-tailed voles, montane shrews, western jumping mice) to quite low elevations. Falck et al. (2003) studied small mammals of the regulated Green and unregulated Yampa rivers in Brown's Park, Moffat County, in the periods surrounding spring flooding.

Grazing can have substantial impact on habitat for native mammals, both game species and non-game species. Shultz and Leininger (1991) found differences in the mammalian assemblage between riparian areas grazed by livestock and those excluded from grazing along Sheep Creek, northwest of Fort Collins, at an elevation of 2,500 m (8,125 ft.). Deer mice were more abundant on grazed plots, but western jumping mice were more abundant in exclosures. Moulton et al. (1981b) found that grazing affected mammalian assemblages in riparian woodland more than in shortgrass prairie, and small mammals of grazed sand sagebrush were more similar to those in shortgrass prairie than to those of ungrazed sand sagebrush. Moulton (1978) found higher overall species richness in grazed (8 species) than in ungrazed (4 species) cottonwood riparian woodlands, although the prairie vole (*Microtus ochrogaster*) was negatively impacted by grazing. By contrast, F. Samson et al. (1988) found no difference in small mammal communities from grazing on a floodplain at the South Platte State Wildlife Area near Crook, Logan County. Contrary to the situation found in birds, mammalian species richness on upland shortgrass prairie is higher than that in nearby riparian communities (Olson and Knopf 1988).

Needless to say, dividing a place as complex and dynamic as Colorado into discrete ecosystems is a gross simplification of an almost incomprehensibly complex reality. Minimally, we should note that on their margins, Colorado's various ecosystems overlap or grade into each other. Ecologists term these zones of contact or overlap "ecotones" (from *tonus*, Latin for "tension"). Because of the complexity of the Coloradan fauna, ecotones clearly are high priorities for conservation. With ongoing climate change, such conservation areas need to be large enough to accommodate changes in the distribution of species. The Nature Conservancy of Colorado pioneered concrete action at significant scale with its Laramie Foothills Project, a complex of nature preserves and conservation easements in northeastern Colorado that eventually will provide a nearly continuous protected corridor from the Pawnee Buttes on the east to the Laramie Mountains on the west. A similarly large and dynamic landscape is being protected in a "Peaks to Prairie" project in the area east of Colorado Springs (for updates, see http://www.nature.org wherewework/northamerica/states/Colorado). Military lands (such as Fort Carson and the US Air Force Academy) protect substantial tracts of land in that same general area. Increasingly they are being managed with biodiversity as an important component of success. In a Ranching for Wildlife program, the Colorado Division of Wildlife partners with private landowners to ensure appropriate habitat management and to control access (Colorado Division of Wildlife 2009b). Each of these efforts eventually will contribute to the National Conservation System, now in a preliminary conceptual stage (Dunkel 2008), emerging from a growing consensus that wildlife require protected wildlands for persistence in changing times. *Colorado's Comprehensive Wildlife Conservation Strategy* (Colorado Division of Wildlife 2006a) was a first step toward wildlife habitat conservation on this visionary scale.

Biogeography: Patterns of Mammalian Distribution

Biogeography is the study of the patterns of distribution of organisms: Which species occur where? Why do they occur there? A mammal's presence in a particular place is a consequence of history, geology, physiography, climate, ecological relationships with plants and other animals, and the species' population dynamics. Geologic events have shaped the landscape. Physiography influences the occurrence of plant communities, which create past and present barriers and corridors to movement. Climate can restrict a species at its limit of tolerance. Chance may play a role, as in the documented movement of small rodents as stowaways aboard ships, trains, or hay trucks. Ecological relationships influence how species assemble into communities, a result of symbiotic interactions (competition, predation, and so forth).

Species diversity is a phenomenon of great interest to biogeographers. Two aspects of diversity are often recognized: *species richness*, the number of species in an area, and *species evenness*, which considers not only numbers of species but their relative abundance and is expressed by a variety of different indices (Magurran 1988). Species evenness varies widely over time and space and is too complex to generalize here, except that within a particular community type, species evenness is likely to be lower in disturbed areas than in undisturbed patches (D. Armstrong 1993). Species richness varies greatly with taxonomic group. Within historic times, Colorado has been home to some 130 species of mammals (4 of which have been introduced: 2 of them deliberately, 2 of them inadvertently), 428 species of birds, 50,000 to 100,000 insects, and 3,000 kinds of plants. For comparison, the approximate number of mammals in adjacent states is, for Wyoming, 115 (Long 1965; T. Clark and Stromberg 1987); Nebraska, 85 (J. K. Jones 1964; J. K. Jones, Armstrong, et al. 1983); Kansas, 84 (Cockrum 1952; E. Hall 1955; Bee et al. 1981); Oklahoma, 108 (Caire et al. 1989; L. Choate and Jones 1998); New Mexico, 151 (Findley et al. 1975; J. Frey and Yates 1996; Findley 1987; J. Frey 2004); Arizona, 138 (Cockrum 1960; Hoffmeister 1986); Utah, 126 (Durrant 1952; D. Armstrong 1977a). As a general rule, the more heterogeneous the landscape in a given area, the higher the species richness.

Individual organisms have genetic information in the nuclei of their cells that tells them how to make a living: how to survive and how to reproduce. No species has genetic information adequate to provide the know-how to operate in all environments. Because they have finite information, species reach distributional limits in the landscape. The limit at a particular time and place may be biotic or physical or some combination of factors. Often we do not know why a particular organism occurs one place but not another, although sometimes we can speculate. The range of tolerance of most species is fairly restricted. Brush mice (*Peromyscus boylii*) in Colorado live almost exclusively under the cover of oakbrush, whereas piñon mice (*Peromyscus truei*) are strongly associated with juniper trees. On the Eastern Slope, north of the Palmer Divide (between Colorado Springs and Castle Rock), both oakbrush and juniper trees occur, but neither of these mice is found. Perhaps they cannot (and could not) get to the suitable habitat because of the intervening ponderosa pine woodland on the Palmer Divide. Perhaps the seemingly suitable habitat is not really suitable at all because it is too cold. We simply do not know.

A few species (such as coyotes, striped skunks, and mule deer) are notorious for being broadly tolerant of a wide range of habitats. The deer mouse (*Peromyscus maniculatus*) is another species that occurs just about everywhere. However, the deer mouse may be scarce or absent where one or more of its larger, more specialized relatives occurs. Further, on closer analysis, it seems that deer mice do particularly well in disturbed areas. The disturbance may be of human origin (a highway margin, a vacant lot, or an overgrazed pasture) or it may be a natural disturbance (e.g., a floodplain or an avalanche chute). Any kind of disturbance seems to favor deer mice.

Because all species reach limits, it is possible to map (at least crudely) distributions of species. Biogeographers can then analyze distribution maps to reveal patterns. Patterns may indicate the history of the system or they may suggest physical factors controlling the distribution of organisms. Biogeographers frequently describe large-scale patterns of distribution in terms of biotic provinces (Dice 1943). D. Armstrong (1972) analyzed Colorado's mammals in an analogous way, identifying three major faunal areas (provinces), each subdivisible into smaller units, termed "faunal districts."

Not surprisingly, faunal areas correspond with physiographic units. The Great Plains Faunal Area is subdivisible north-south by the divide between the South Platte and Arkansas rivers, forming faunal districts marked by different subspecies within a number of mammalian species and by the presence of some species only in one watershed or the other. The Colorado-Wyoming border (Northern High Plains Faunal District) and southeastern Colorado (Raton Faunal District) both are distinctive. The latter area is strongly enriched with species of southwestern affinities, species that also extend northward along the foothills of the Eastern Slope; the northern high plains carry some foothills and mountain species eastward.

The Rocky Mountains are a coherent faunal unit, although dissected by valleys and canyons of the master streams. Major valleys of the Western Slope are distinctive from the Rockies as well as from each other. The Grand Valley and Dolores–San Juan faunal districts exhibit strong resemblance to areas downstream on the Colorado Drainage—the Four Corners area generally (see D. Armstrong 1972). The San Luis Valley, a high, cold desert, is unique in Colorado, but it has strong faunal affinities with both southwestern and southeastern parts of the state, indirectly through the Rio Grande Valley of New Mexico. The Wyoming Basin shows faunal affinities to the northwest, to adjacent Utah and Wyoming and beyond. Generally, environmental change is rapid in Colorado, and faunal turnover is more than 80 percent along particularly dramatic boundaries, such as the abrupt transition from the Great Plains to the Rocky Mountains along the Front Range.

Spector (2002: 1481) defined "biogeographic crossroads" as "regions where biogeographic assemblages intersect." Because the mammalian fauna of Colorado is complex and includes species with a spectrum of biogeographic affinities, the state has been called a "crossroads," but that is perhaps too simple a metaphor. Some three-fourths of Colorado's mammalian species do not cross the state—they simply stop here. For a quarter of the state's species, the Southern Rocky Mountains represent a sort of "remote parking lot," where species from the north or the mountainous West occupy an island of suitable habitat surrounded by an impassable "sea" of grasslands and sagebrush. Another quarter of Colorado's mammals are stuck in "dead ends" of brush-covered roughlands along the foothills of the Eastern Slope, in western valleys, or in the semidesert San Luis Valley. Remember, species occur where they do because they could get there, and once there, they could make a living—maintain homeostasis and reproduce.

Ecology is about patterns in space, and patterns imply processes in time. The ecological patterns that we discern today are but an interim report on processes as old as the planet. Chapter 3 includes a brief account of some episodes in the ongoing history of mammals in Colorado, a story already a quarter of a billion years long (and a story that is now strongly influenced by humans).

2

Mammals in General

Mammalian Origins

It is well-known that mammals arose from reptiles. Indeed, mammals *are* reptiles, of a sort. The term "reptile" as we usually hear it is imprecise, connoting lizards, snakes, crocodiles, turtles, and the strange "living fossil" tuataras of New Zealand. However, zoologists realize that not just reptiles but also birds and mammals all share a common ancestor. That common ancestor produced high-class embryos protected in a fluid-filled sac, the amnion. Hence, such animals are called amniotes. The eggs of most amniotes have shells. In this book, we mostly avoid the familiar term "reptile" in favor of the inclusive and evolutionarily precise term "amniote."

Amniotes arose from non-amniote tetrapods—familiarly known as "amphibians"—late in the Devonian Period, some 360 million years ago (Pough et al. 2009). Long before the origin of dinosaurs, indeed, just barely (in a geologic sense) after the origin of amniotes, a branch of the early amniotes embarked on a path that led eventually to the mammals. Those were the synapsids, which arose in Carboniferous times, some 350 million years ago. (Among early synapsids were the familiar sail-backed pelycosaurs, like *Dimetrodon*.) A branch of the synapsids was the therapsids—or "mammal-like reptiles"—which arose in the early Permian Period, nearly 300 million years ago. One of several lineages of therapsids gave rise to the earliest mammals, in the late Triassic Period, about 210 million years ago. Some highlights in the evolutionary story of mammals are described in Chapter 3.

For the moment, we need to recognize that about two-thirds of mammalian evolution occurred in the Mesozoic Era—the "Age of Reptiles." For some 150 million years, early mammals scuttled around in the imposing shadows of the "ruling reptiles," or archosaurs. Early mammals were mostly small (to about rat-sized) and rather shrew-shaped. As archosaurs got larger, proliferated in diversity, and evolved an increasingly broad spectrum of ecological niches, mammals stood by, remaining mostly small and rather unspecialized. When the Age of Reptiles had run its course, the descendants of therapsids stood poised on an "evolutionary threshold," eventually to assume the dominance that the archosaurs abdicated, ready to stage one of the most dramatic adaptive radiations ever seen on Earth. The mammalian radiation eventually produced a clever, bipedal species that presumed to name itself *Homo sapiens*, "wise self," and tries to comprehend the cosmos, assuming only that it is comprehensible.

Mammalian Characteristics

Two particularly significant trends stand out in mammalian evolution. One is the evolution of milk-producing glands, the mammae, whence the name Mammalia is taken. The mammary glands allow a long-term nutritional and social bond between mother and young. The second is the development of an enlarged brain, especially the neopallium (cerebral cortex), derived from the ancestral olfactory lobes, the smelling part of the brain. This gives mammals an intelligence unparalleled on Earth. Because of longer interaction between mother and offspring and a large brain capacity, mammals can learn much of their adult behavior rather than relying on "hard-wired" innate behaviors. Complex mental processes and interactions among individuals are then possible. Our own species may represent the zenith of these capacities.

A number of characteristics are unique to mammals, among them hair, sebaceous and sweat glands, mammary glands, a single bone in the lower jaw articulating with a single bone of the skull, three middle ear ossicles, a single left aortic arch, non-nucleated biconcave red blood cells, a muscular diaphragm separating the thoracic and abdominal cavities, and a highly developed cerebral cortex. These characteristics did not arise from nothing, of course; they have antecedents in structures of the "reptilian" ancestors of mammals.

Modern mammals differ from other extant amniotes in numerous ways. Mammalian traits evolved at different rates over tens of millions of years. Given this mosaic pattern of evolution, to state just when the transition was made from "mammal-like reptile" to "reptile-like mammal" is somewhat arbitrary. To avoid undue rancor and speculation, paleontologists generally have agreed on a single character complex—one that fossilizes rather well—as the critical feature defining mammals: the jaw-ear complex.

JAW-EAR COMPLEX

The ancestral reptilian jaw consists of three bones (dentary, prearticular, articular); the articular bone articulates with the quadrate bone on the skull to form the jaw joint. Among some more highly derived diapsid reptiles, this complex jaw arrangement is put to good use. In snakes, for example, the jaw can be essentially disassembled and the animals can swallow prey larger around than themselves. In the middle ear of reptiles is a single bone, the columella ("little column").

In mammals, the jaw has been simplified and strengthened. The lower jaw is a single paired bone, the dentary, or mandible. The dentary articulates directly with the squamosal bone of the skull. So radical a simplification obviously leaves some bones left over. French Nobel laureate François Jacob (1984) characterized evolution as "tinkering"; American wildlife biologist and conservationist Aldo Leopold (1949) pointed out the "First Law of Tinkering": never throw away any of the pieces. Evolution has tended to follow that rule. Thus, the spare jaw parts were "recycled." The articular became the hammer bone (malleus) of the middle ear and the quadrate became the anvil (incus). The columella remains in place to become the stirrup bone (stapes). The ancestral reptilian jaw had three bones, the ear just one; the mammalian ear has three bones, the jaw just one.

The mammalian jaw-ear complex was a net gain for assertive organisms. What was lost in jaw mobility was more than compensated in the strength of the jaw joint and increased effectiveness of the ear. The increased strength of the jaw was important to full exploitation of another mammalian specialty, fancy teeth.

TEETH

Mammalian teeth have three peculiarities, based on trends laid down by their therapsid progenitors: the toothrow is differentiated front to rear (*heterodont*); the teeth are set firmly in sockets (*thecodont*); and the teeth are present in two and only two sets (*diphyodont*), the deciduous (temporary) "milk teeth" and the permanent teeth. The milk teeth ("baby teeth") are lost as the permanent teeth develop in the jaws. These conditions contrast with those in ancestral vertebrates (and most living diapsid reptiles that have teeth) where the teeth are all the same size and shape (*homodont*), are perched atop the jaw bones (*acrodont*), and are mostly replaced as needed throughout life (*polyphyodont*).

In ancestral mammals and many species alive today, the socketed teeth are of four kinds: *incisors* (for nipping); *canines* (or "eye-teeth"), used for piercing and grasping prey; and two kinds of *cheekteeth*, *premolars* ("bicuspids" in humans) and *molars*, used for shearing or grinding the food.

The incisors are usually unicuspid, with a single root. In eutherians (placental mammals) the maximal number of incisors is three per quadrant of the jaw. (For description, teeth often are described per quadrant: upper right, upper left, lower right, lower left.) Canines are generally elongate, conical, unicuspid teeth, attached by a single root. Canines never number more than one per quadrant and they frequently are absent in herbivores. Evolutionary loss of teeth can lead to the formation of a gap in the toothrow, a *diastema*. Premolars and molars are distinguished by their development: by definition, molars are present only in the permanent dentition. This distinction may not be reflected in adult morphological features. This causes difficulty in distinguishing between molars and premolars, so they frequently are referred to collectively as cheekteeth. Complex in crown structure, cheekteeth have several roots anchoring them to the jaw. The ancestral condition for teeth in placental mammals is three incisors, one canine, four premolars, and three molars per quadrant. Many mammals have experienced evolutionary loss of teeth. Premolars are lost from front to rear. Thus, if there are fewer than four premolars, it is the anterior premolars that have been lost. Molars, however, are lost from back to front.

Teeth are made of dense, bony material. The *crown* projects above the gumline; the portion of the tooth set in the socket (*alveolus*) in the jaw is the root. Crowns of most teeth are covered by *enamel*, the hardest substance in the vertebrate body. This enamel surface is incomplete in many species, exposing the somewhat less dense *dentine*. Dentine forms the core of the tooth. In many species, normal aging and wear result in loss of enamel and exposure of dentine.

The outer surface of the root of the tooth is covered with a bony material, *cementum*, which interfaces with the *periodontal membrane*, the fibrous connective tissue that bonds the cementum to the bone of the alveolar wall. In the central core of the dentine a *pulp cavity* contains nerves and a blood supply connected by root canals. In most species, when the tooth reaches maturity the opening of the root canal constricts and growth ceases. Such teeth are termed rooted. In other mammals, especially rodents and other herbivores with a fibrous, coarse diet, root canals remain open and the tooth continues to grow throughout life, producing teeth termed rootless or ever-growing.

The topography of the *occlusal*, or biting, surface of teeth differs greatly among taxa. Teeth provide clues to diet and evidence of evolutionary relationships. Teeth are readily fossilizable; indeed, many extinct mammals are known only from their teeth and fragments of their jaws. Ancestral mammals had sharp-cusped, *sectorial* (cutting) cheekteeth. Most insectivores and bats, as well as some primates, largely retain these ancestral cheekteeth. Round-cusped, *bunodont* teeth are found in omnivores (e.g., bears, pigs, and humans); these function in grinding. Herbivores often exhibit expanded grinding surfaces. *Lophodont* teeth (as in horses) have expanded cusps; *selenodont* teeth (as in deer) show elongate, crescent-shaped ridges linking cusps. Often in development the enamel of the crown wears through, exposing the softer dentine. This establishes an occlusal surface of differential hardness, allowing continual sharpening as the teeth process grass and other abrasive foods. Such a surface accompanied by continual growth results in a remarkably effective grinding mechanism. The pattern of alternating dentine and enamel may be important in diagnosis of a taxon.

Teeth with particularly high crowns are termed *hypsodont*, whereas those with low crowns are called *brachydont*. Grazers tend to have higher-crowned teeth than carnivores, as the silicates in grasses cause great wear. The *lingual* side of a tooth is the side closer to the tongue, and the *labial* side is the side closer to the cheeks. Complex evolution necessitates a complex descriptive nomenclature. For an extensive discussion of teeth in their remarkable adaptive variety, see R. E. Martin et al. (2001).

The evolutionary plasticity of mammalian teeth has been tremendous, as teeth have been greatly modified within various groups to deal with different specialized diets. The typical deviation from the ancestral condition has been to lose teeth. Herbivores, like rodents, rabbits, and the even-toed hoofed mammals, have lost the canines and simplified the incisors. Carnivores have sacrificed grinding teeth. Anteaters of several lineages and the baleen whales have given up teeth altogether. The toothed whales, by contrast, have proliferated teeth; some have more than 200. Groups that retain fairly ancestral-looking dentition include bats, soricomorphs, carnivores, and primates. Tusks of elephants, walruses, narwhal, and warthog are highly derived teeth turned to tasks other than food processing.

The dental formula of a mammal indicates the number of teeth of each kind for one quadrant of the jaw. The number of upper teeth is indicated above a line and the number of lower teeth is indicated below the line. For example, the ancestral placental mammal had a total of 44 teeth arranged according to the dental formula: incisors 3/3, canines 1/1, premolars 4/4, molars 3/3, total = 44. This is conventionally abbreviated to 3/3, 1/1, 4/4, 3/3 = 44. For example, the dental formula of the deer mouse, *Peromyscus maniculatus*, is written: 1/1, 0/0, 0/0, 3/3 = 16. Usually dental formulae are the same for the species within a genus, although occasionally they differ even among individuals within a single species. Some black bears, for example, are missing an upper premolar. Table 2-1 lists dental formulae for Coloradan mammals.

Diverse and often specialized teeth are one of a number of mammalian features associated with an active lifestyle. Specialization within the toothrow allows thorough and efficient processing of food. In the gut, food comes into contact with digestive chemicals in small bits, with a large ratio of surface to volume. Therefore, digestion can take place rapidly, and the energy-demanding mammalian "engine" can run (or at least "idle") continually, well fueled and ready to spring into action at a moment's notice, regardless of the temperature of the environment.

Teeth and the structure of the ear region provide readily fossilizable evidence of the mammalian grade of organization. While these features were changing, major adjustments were occurring in the soft anatomy as well. In particular, a suite of traits was evolving that keeps mammals warm and active. Central to those adaptations was hair.

HAIR

Many of the fundamental features of the mammalian grade of organization are associated with hair. Hairs are specialized structures of the *epidermis* (the outer layers of skin). Hairs develop from roots in a *follicle*, which is an inpocketing of the epidermis into a depression in the *dermis* (the lower layer of the skin). Hair seems to have evolved independent of the scales seen in diapsid reptiles, as insulation between scales. This pattern can be seen today on the nearly naked, scaly tails of some rats and the Virginia opossum. Hairs are multicellular and are composed of three layers, the inner *medulla*, the *cortex*, and the outer *cuticle*. The portion of the hair exposed above the skin (the shaft) is composed of dead cells. Hair color results from the presence or absence of pigments, structural arrangements of air spaces, hair texture, hair thickness, or combinations of these features. The medulla is made of shrunken cells that may be pigmented and have air spaces. In the smallest and thinnest hairs the medulla may be absent, whereas in the largest hairs the medulla typically is well developed, with air spaces improving insulating quality, as in the hollow hairs of artiodactyls. The cortex makes up the bulk of the hair; it may or may not be pigmented. The cuticle is not pigmented and consists of a thin outer layer of cells arranged as scales. The scale pattern of the cuticle is frequently distinctive at the level of genera or even species (T. Moore et al. 1974).

The principal function of hair clearly is insulation. However, hair has been highly modified to serve other functions. In porcupines, some hairs have become protective quills. Most mammals have facial bristles (*vibrissae*) that serve a tactile function. In many species, hair is colored in a meaningful pattern. In most it provides concealment by cryptic coloration or by countershading, in which the dorsum typically is darker than the venter. Others (like skunks) signal a warning or reminder. Color patterns can serve in communication, such as a white-tailed deer or pronghorn flashing the white rump patch to signal danger. The mane of the male lion increases the apparent size of the head and may be associated with asserting and maintaining social dominance.

Pelage is the collective term for the total hair covering. The pelage is made up of two general types of hair, *guard hairs* and *underhairs*. Guard hairs are the most conspicuous, longest, and coarsest hairs. They protect the underhair and the skin from mechanical injury, screen out dirt and other debris, and shield it from damaging light radiation. Most guard hairs have a *definitive growth* pattern: they reach a certain length, cease growing, are shed, and then are replaced. Some guard hairs—such as the mane of a lion or the mane and tail of a horse—exhibit *angora* growth; the hair continues to grow without replacement. Guard hairs have been modified in some mammals to form stiff, thickened quills. Underhairs usually are dense and soft and function as insulation. In the fur trade a "sheared" pelt is one on which the guard hairs have been cut to the level of the underhair.

The root of the hair has attached to it a tiny muscle, the *arrector pili* ("hair raiser"). In typical mammals, this muscle can raise the hair to trap an insulating layer of air warmed by the animal. In humans, with our minimal body hair, the result is not so much protection from cold but a frequent sign of cold, "goose bumps."

Associated with skin and hair are glands. Many mammals have *sweat* (sudoriferous) *glands*. Sweat is evaporated from the hair and skin, making the surface cooler. Sweat glands are restricted to the soles of the feet of carnivores, whereas humans and many ungulates have sweat glands over much of the body. Most marine mammals, a number of fossorial groups (including moles), and rodents lack sweat glands altogether. (Mammals with few sweat glands, such as cats, often lick the fur to promote evaporative cooling; by contrast, members of the dog family pant, cooling

TABLE 2-1. Dental formulae of genera of mammals of Colorado (including genera of possible occurrence and domestic animals)

Incisors	*Canine*	*Premolars*	*Molars*	*Total*	*Genus*
5/4	1/1	3/3	4/4	50	*Didelphis*
3/3	1/1	4/4	3/3	44	*Sus*
3/3	1/1	4/4	2/3	42	*Canis, Urocyon, Ursus,* Vulpes*
3/3	1/1	4/4	2/2	40	*Bassariscus, Procyon*
2/3	1/1	3/3	3/3	38	*Myotis, Pecari*
3/3	1/1	4/4	1/2	38	*Gulo, Martes*
3/3	0–1/0–1	3–3	3/3	36–40	*Equus*
2/3	1/1	2/3	3/3	36	*Lasionycteris, Plecotus*
3/2	1/0	3/3	3/3	36	*Scalopus*
3/3	1/1	4/3	1/2	36	*Lontra*
2/3	1/1	2/2	3/3	34	*Euderma, Parastrellus, Perimyotis*
0/0	0/0	7–9/7–9†		28–36	*Dasypus*
3/3	1/1	3/3	1/2	34	*Mephitis, Mustela, Neovison, Spilogale, Taxidea*
0/3	1/1	3/3	3/3	34	*Cervus*
2/2	1/1	2/2	3/3	32	*Homo*
3/3	1/1	2/3	1/2	32	*Conepatus*
2/3	1/1	1/2	3/3	32	*Eptesicus*
3/1	1/1	3/1	3/3	32	*Sorex*
1/3	1/1	2/2	3/3	32	*Lasiurus*
4/2	1/0	2/1	3/3	32	*Blarina*
0/3	0/1	3/3	3/3	32	*Alces, Antilocapra, Bison, Bos, Odocoileus, Oreamnos, Ovis*
1/2–3	1/1	2/2	3/3	30 or 32	*Nyctinomops, Tadarida*
1/3	1/1	2/1	3/3	30	*Lama*
3/3	1/1	3/2	1/1	30	*Felis, Puma*
3/2	1/0	2/1	3/3	30	*Cryptotis*
3/3	1/1	2/2	1/1	28	*Lynx*
3/2	1/0	1/1	3/3	28	*Notiosorex*
1/2	1/1	1/2	3/3	28	*Antrozous*
2/1	0/0	3/2	3/3	28	*Lepus, Sylvilagus*
2/1	0/0	2/2	3/3	26	*Ochotona*
1/1	0/0	2/1	3/3	22	*Ammospermophilus, Callospermophilus, Cynomys, Glaucomys,* Ictidomys, Marmota, Neotamias, Otospermophilus, Sciurus,* Tamiasciurus,* Urocitellus, Xerospermophilus*
1/1	0/0	1/1	3/3	20	*Castor, Chaetodipus, Cratogeomys, Dipodomys, Erethizon, Geomys, Perognathus, Thomomys*
1/1	0/0	1/0	3/3	18	*Zapus*
1/1	0/0	0/0	3/3	16	*Lemmiscus, Microtus, Mus, Myodes, Neotoma, Ondatra, Onychomys, Peromyscus, Phenacomys, Reithrodontomys, Sigmodon, Rattus*

Notes: * One upper premolar may be absent; † Homologies with cheekteeth of other mammals uncertain.

by evaporation from the tongue.) Perspiration consists of water, salts, and some other compounds, including urea (so the skin is an excretory organ).

Each hair has an associated *sebaceous gland* that secretes an oily substance (*sebum*) into the follicle that lubricates and weatherproofs the hair. Both sweat and sebaceous glands have been modified into odor-producing scent glands. Most mammals have at least a few scent glands somewhere on the skin. Tarsal glands occur on the legs of deer, anal glands are found in most carnivores, ventral glands are found on American martens, flank glands on shrews, cheek glands on pikas and yellow-bellied marmots, and preorbital glands on deer, elk, and mountain sheep.

By the way, these scent glands are part of an extensive array of adaptations for olfactory communication. Scent marking is the general name given to behaviors that distribute or place odorous secretions in the environment. In addition to secretions of scent glands, urine and feces are handy and frequently used in scent marking. Scent marks may provide information on the identity, status, sex, or reproductive condition of the individual depositing them. Scent marking, not yet thoroughly understood by scientists, serves functions in reproduction, individual spacing and social integration, alarm, and defense.

MAMMARY GLANDS

In the history of mammals, the evolution of the mammary glands surely was the most profoundly significant modification of hair glands. The importance of the milk glands cannot be overstated. The name Mammalia refers to those glands and rightly so: mammary glands are central to the mammalian way of life and its success. Milk from the mammary glands—a highly refined concoction of water, carbohydrates, fats, proteins, and salts closely tuned to a particular species' developmental needs—provides newborn mammals a nutritional head start. Further, nursing makes of young mammals a captive audience and offers a period of interaction with the mother (and often with siblings) that allows training and socialization. Until recently it was thought that milk production (lactation) was limited to females except under experimental or pathological conditions. In recent years, lactation by both females and males has been reported in two Old World fruit bats (Pteropodidae): the Dayak fruit bat (*Dyacopterus spadeicus*) of Malaysia (Francis et al. 1994) and the masked flying fox (*Pteropus capistratus*) of Papua New Guinea (Bonaccorso 1998). The evolutionary ecology of this rare phenomenon was reviewed by Kunz and Hosken (2008).

HEART AND CIRCULATION

Like birds, mammals have an efficient, four-chambered (double pump) heart, with separate circuits for oxygen-poor and oxygen-rich blood. This circulatory system allows the efficient delivery of oxygen (and removal of carbon dioxide) that high activity demands. Evidence from comparative anatomy and embryology indicates that the four-chambered hearts of mammals and birds evolved independently. The common ancestor of birds and mammals was an ancient "stem reptile" (cotylosaur) that probably had a three-chambered heart.

The efficient mammalian circulatory system, coupled with insulative hair, allows *endothermy* ("warm-bloodedness"), the capacity to maintain a relatively constant body temperature despite changes in the external environment. The constant body temperature of both birds and mammals is fairly high, far closer to the upper limit of environmental conditions than to the lower limit. One explanation for this is that heating is less costly—in terms of water loss—than is cooling. Animal cooling systems mostly are based on evaporation (perspiration, panting, mud-bathing, and so forth). Water loss is expensive (or even destructive) to animals on dry land—animals that already are struggling hard to maintain the homeostasis of those tiny bags of seawater that we call cells.

Mature red blood cells of mammals lack a nucleus, thus maximizing their oxygen-carrying capacity, and they are biconcave in shape, thus maximizing the exchange surface. The body cavity of mammals is subdivided into thoracic and abdominal cavities by the *diaphragm*, a complex muscle that functions in ventilation.

BRAIN

Another factor in the success of early mammals was their behavior. Early mammals were small, probably nocturnal, and surely secretive (as individuals of most groups still are). The land and the shallow waters of the Mesozoic Earth were dominated by a great variety of diapsid reptiles. The sophisticated brains of early mammals must have been critical to their survival alongside their sometimes extravagantly large and successful contemporaries.

The mammalian brain shows several advances over that of ancestral amniotes. The *neopallium* of the forebrain is substantially enlarged, and development of the corpora quadrigemina of the midbrain serves as auditory and visual reflex centers. With this expansion of brain capacity, mammals have come to rely much more on learning and other cognitive processes than do other vertebrates.

The most dim-witted of mammals is wittier than the brightest bird, lizard, or fish. Please do not misunderstand this assertion. Bird brains are perfectly adequate for birds and birds' behavior, and bird behavior can be wonderfully complicated. (Have you tried to fly home to Tierra del Fuego in the dark recently?) But generally bird behavior is not what one would term "creative" (the fabulous vocal mimicry of some species notwithstanding). The same can be said of most non-mammalian reptiles, amphibians, and fish. Their behavior is not as individually variable or flexible as that of mammals and not as responsive to novel environmental opportunity. Mammals are more dependent on learned behavior than are any other animals. Lacking built-in solutions to many of the challenges they face, individual mammals must piece together effective solutions based on their individual experiences. That takes a brain adapted to such work. The mammalian brain differs from that of other amniotes in degree, not in kind. The basic pieces of the mammalian brain are present in other amniotes and even fish and "amphibians" (non-amniote tetrapods). What mammals have done is to elaborate parts of the brain, especially those parts involved with memory and integration, enabling complex, learned behavior accumulated with experience.

REPRODUCTION

The reproductive tract of female eutherians includes paired *ovaries* and *oviducts* and a *uterus*, *cervix*, and *vagina* of variable structure. In the *duplex* system, typical of lagomorphs and most rodents, there are two uteri, two cervices, and a single vagina. In a *bipartite* tract there are two uteri with a single vagina and cervix. Most carnivores and the pigs show this type. In soricomorphs, most ungulates, bats, and some primates the reproductive system is *bicornuate*, with the lower half of the uteri fused and the upper portion of the uteri remaining separate as horns, or cornua. The *simplex* uterus found in higher primates and xenarthrans has a single uterus, cervix, and vagina. The external genitalia of female mammals are termed the *vulva*. In many species, seasonal or cyclic swelling of the vulva indicates the period of sexual receptivity. The female reproductive tract of marsupials lacks a true vagina. Paired oviducts lead to paired uteri, which in turn connect to two lateral vaginal canals (pseudovaginae), which receive the forked penis of the male.

Environments often exhibit seasonal variation in the availability of resources. Reproduction is an expensive process, so it usually is cued to seasonal rhythms of the environment so that young are produced at optimal times for their survival. In most female mammals there is a fixed period of time termed *estrus*, or "heat," during which she will receive the male. This period of receptivity is part of a generalized *estrous cycle*. Mammals in which the female has a single reproductive cycle during the breeding season are termed *monestrous*. Those that exhibit recurrent cycles of estrus are termed *polyestrous*. The timing and frequency of reproduction are dictated by environmental conditions such as availability of food, stability of the environment, and weather. The white-footed mouse, deer mouse, and hispid cotton rat have restricted breeding seasons in northern parts of their ranges (including Colorado) but may breed throughout the year in more equable climes. Ovulation—the release of eggs from the ovary—may occur spontaneously, usually toward the end of estrus (*spontaneous ovulation*), or ovulation may result from the stimulus of copulation (termed *induced ovulation*).

Humans exhibit a distinctive reproductive cycle—the *menstrual cycle*. Some features typical of the menstrual cycle (such as menstrual bleeding, which represents sloughing of the uterine lining) are found in other Old World primates, but the situation in human females—involving more or less continual sexual receptivity, no obvious point of estrus, cryptic ovulation, and menstruation approximately on a lunar-monthly cycle—is a human specialty, an evolutionary descendent of the typical mammalian estrous cycle.

In males of most mammals paired *testes* are contained in an external pouch, the *scrotum*, at least during the breeding season. The high temperatures of the mammalian body cavity are deleterious to sperm-cell production; the scrotum maintains the testes at cooler temperatures. In some groups, including primates, artiodactyls (even-toed ungulates), and most perissodactyls (odd-toed ungulates), testes of adults are permanently scrotal. In other mammals (including many carnivores and most rodents) the testes remain in the abdominal cavity until the actual breeding season, at which time they migrate to the scrotum and begin to function. Whales, soricomorphs, and bats lack a scrotum and the testes remain in the body cavity permanently. Ducts carry sperm from the testes, mixed with seminal products from the accessory sex glands, to the *penis*, the copulatory organ.

Males of many species of carnivores, bats, and most rodents have a supportive bone, the *os penis* or *baculum*, in the penis. The shape of the baculum frequently differs among closely related species and thus has value as a taxonomic character. Speculation has been that the bone functions in species isolation, maintenance of prolonged copulation, and/or induction of ovulation, but the question is far from settled (Larivière and Ferguson 2002). The *os clitoridis*, or *baubellum*, is the homologous bone in females. Male primates and bats have a pendulous penis (and many of them have a baculum); the phallus of most mammals is not pendulous, however, but rather is withdrawn into a penile sheath when not in use.

The reproductive cycle in both sexes is closely controlled by hormones of the pituitary gland and the gonads. Estrogenic hormones of the ovaries and androgenic hormones of the testes regulate development of secondary sexual characters of females and males, respectively.

DEVELOPMENT

Except for the peculiar monotremes (platypus, echidnas) of Australia and New Guinea, mammals do not lay eggs. Rather, the embryo develops to some degree within the mother and then is given birth rather than hatched. In mammals other than marsupials (the pouched mammals of the Americas and Australia), some sort of intimate relationship develops between the mother and the embryos. The mediator of this relationship is the *placenta*, a remarkable cooperative structure built of maternal and embryonic tissues.

The embryonic contribution to the placenta is built from membranes first seen in the land egg of early amniotes. The *amnion* retains its ancestral function as a fluid-filled, shock-absorbing bag. The *chorion*, too, remains as a tough, protective sack that provides the surface for gaseous exchange. However, the ancestral *allantois* and *yolk sac* no longer are needed. In diapsid reptiles, the yolk sac stores food; embryonic eutherian mammals derive their nutrients from the mother's bloodstream. The ancestral allantois is a receptacle for embryonic wastes; embryonic placental mammals pass their wastes to the maternal circulation.

A handy fact about the yolk sac and the allantois is that they have blood vessels leading to and from the embryo. In placental mammals the ancestral "reptilian" structures have been recycled, the blood vessels "repurposed" to participate in the *umbilicus*, which connects the embryo to the placenta. The ancestral membranes of the yolk sac and the allantois lend physical strength to the umbilicus.

The maternal contribution to the placenta is the uterine lining, or *endometrium*. Across the placenta the embryo receives oxygen, food molecules—carbohydrates and fats for energy and amino acids for "building materials"—and also antibodies to fight infection. From the embryo, wastes—urea and carbon dioxide—diffuse back to the mother. Increased maternal mobility coupled with optimal maternal care and the advanced stage of development at birth have contributed to the success and diversity of placental mammals.

An almost solid mass of blood vessels, the placenta creates a large surface area that promotes efficient diffusion between the maternal and embryonic circulatory systems. *Villi*—fingerlike projections of the chorion into the wall of the uterus—further increase the area of contact and exchange, enhancing this function.

In most mammals the placenta is deciduous, tearing away from the uterine wall at birth. The result is *uterine scars*, which may be used to estimate numbers of young a particular female has produced. A so-called *nulliparous* (literally, "never-birthed") female has not produced young and shows no evidence of scarring. A *parous* female is pregnant or shows placental scars. A multiparous female shows several series of different-aged placental scars.

The placenta is remarkable enough when we appreciate its structure and its function. But there is more to the story than just remodeling a "reptilian" egg. Obviously keeping embryos inside the mother is a valuable adaptation. The embryos are protected, nourished, and—stored as they are within a warm body—incubated. But before this "big idea" would work, there was a serious problem to solve: the mother's immune response.

At the level of molecules, animal cells are able to recognize "self" and "not-self." There are mechanisms at various levels to destroy all that is "not-self": foreign organisms, toxins, and alien proteins, for example. From the mother's standpoint, the embryo is, of course, partly "not-self," because about half of its genetic information (and hence something like half of its proteins) came from the father. Before the embryo can implant in the uterine wall and establish the placenta, it must, therefore, overcome the maternal immune system. Just how this works is still poorly understood (see Feldhamer et al. 2007). However, solving the problem of immunologic incompatibility between the mammalian mother and her half-alien embryos allowed the extended period of internal development that is the hallmark of placental mammals.

Timing of reproduction and development frequently is tied to particularly favorable seasons. In some species (especially bats that hibernate in the temperate zone), *delayed fertilization* occurs. Individuals mate in late summer or early fall while gathering at the hibernation site. Sperm are stored over the winter in the uterus or vagina. Actual fertilization occurs in late winter or spring. A somewhat similar condition, *delayed implantation*, occurs in many of the mustelids, bears, armadillos, seals, and some deer. Fertilization occurs at the time of mating but the resulting zygote does not implant in the uterine lining for up to several months, remaining instead in a state of suspended animation in the upper regions of the uterine cavity. Both phenomena appear to have evolved as mechanisms to allow mating during peaks of activity in late summer or fall, while delaying development and parturition to coincide with favorable environmental conditions.

The *gestation period* is the length of time from fertilization until birth (*parturition*) of the young. Gestation lasts only 16 to 17 days in some rodents and up to 22 months in the African elephant. Length of gestation generally increases with increasing body size, but there are exceptions. For instance, the porcupine has a much longer gestation period (nearly 7 months) than one would predict from body size, giving birth to well-developed young.

Litter size is the number of young born at any one time, ranging from one to a dozen or more. Smaller mammals tend to have larger litters than do larger mammals. Bats are a major exception to the rule. Some bats are among the smallest of mammals, but females of most species have only one young per year. Most species of mammals bear *altricial* young, born at an early stage of development. In many mammals, neonates have the eyes unopened, little hair, and poorly developed limbs and are capable of little more movement than wriggling. Altricial young usually are reared in a nest. *Precocial* young, by contrast, are born furred, with eyes open, and are capable of walking shortly after birth.

SKELETON

The mammalian skeleton is frequently subdivided into *cranial* (head) and *postcranial* (everything else) anatomy. Mammalogists tend to emphasize cranial features because they are so useful in identification. Cranial adaptations often are concerned with dietary habits and with sensing the environment; the postcranial skeleton is adapted to locomotion.

Another frequent subdivision of the skeleton is *axial* versus *appendicular*. The axial skeleton is the skull and the vertebral column; it protects the central nervous system. The appendicular skeleton is the limbs and their points of attachment, the *pectoral* (or shoulder) and *pelvic* (or hip) *limb girdles*. These subdivisions are, of course, simply for descriptive and interpretive convenience: organisms function as integrated wholes.

Skull. Mammals are the epitome and the apogee of a general evolutionary trend that commenced with the flatworms: *cephalization*, the tendency to concentrate structures and functions in a *head*, that end of the organism that meets the environment. Heads are organized and adapted to deal with environmental resources and perils. In the head are the major organs of sensation: transducers for light, sound, and chemical (olfaction, gustation) inputs. The skull houses the brain, the centerpiece of the central nervous system, and it incorporates the front ends of the digestive and ventilatory ("respiratory") systems. The head is the "business end" of a mammal; the skull is its bony infrastructure.

Although the mammalian skull is a rather complicated affair, it is much simpler than its reptilian precursor. Many reptilian bones have been lost or rearranged. Adapted to a vast array of lifestyles, mammalian skulls are diverse. The skull can therefore be used effectively to classify and identify orders, families, genera, and sometimes even individual species. Taxonomic keys rely heavily on observation of cranial and dental characters. The skull, or *cranium*, is commonly divided into two major regions: the *braincase* and the *rostrum*. The braincase is the portion of the cranium containing the brain. Compared with other vertebrates, it is particularly well developed in mammals. The rostrum is the bony part of the snout or muzzle. The *mandible* is simply the lower jaw. Figures 2-1 and 2-2 illustrate major bones and regions of the skull of a coyote, including *foramina* (openings), *processes* (projections), *fossae* (depressions), and *condyles* (prominences that provide articular surfaces with other bones). The figures can be used to identify bones of the skull of most other mammals.

The braincase surrounds the brain and serves as the attachment point for jaw muscles and the *auditory bullae*, bony capsules in which the delicate structures of the middle and inner ear are housed. At the back of the braincase, two prominent *occipital condyles* surround the base of the *foramen magnum*, the large opening allowing for passage of the spinal cord. These condyles serve as articular surfaces with the first cervical vertebra, the *atlas*. The posterior wall of the braincase is the *occipital bone*, which bounds the foramen magnum and is composed of four fused elements: a dorsal *supraoccipital*, two lateral *exoccipitals*, and a ventral *basioccipital*. In most adult mammals sutures between these bones are fused, making them difficult or impossible to distinguish. In many species (such as pocket gophers; see Figure 8-5), a small *interparietal* bone lies between the posterior border of the *parietals* and the *supraoccipital*.

The rostrum extends forward from the anterior margin of the *orbits*, or eye sockets. At its anterior end are two large *external nares*, the openings of the nasal chambers. The nasal

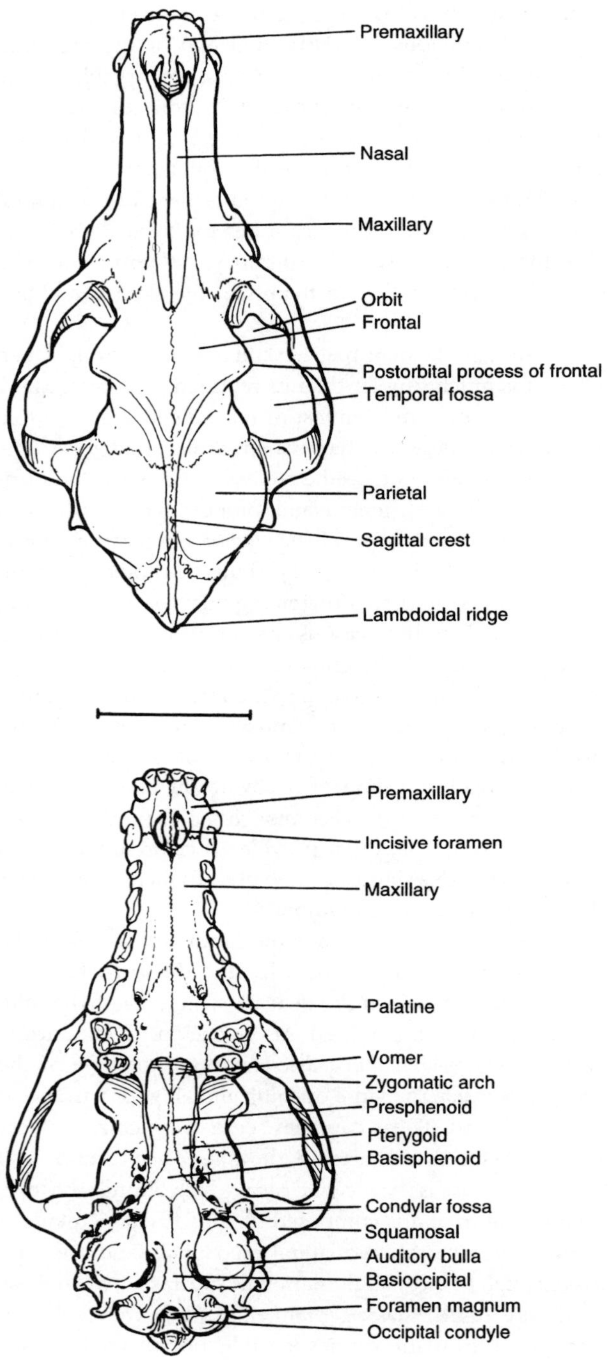

FIGURE 2-1. Dorsal and ventral views of the skull of a coyote (*Canis latrans*). Scale = 5 cm.

septum that separates the chambers is made of cartilage anteriorly and merges posteriorly into a bone, the *vomer*.

Each *zygomatic arch*, or cheekbone, is formed by a posterior extension of the *maxillary* bone, a *jugal* (malar) bone, and the forward-projecting zygomatic process of the *squamosal* bone. Each orbit, which houses an eyeball and the external eye muscles, is bounded posteriorly by *postorbital processes* of the frontal and jugal bones. In some mammals, like deer, these processes fuse to form a *postorbital bar* separating the orbit from the *temporal fossa*. In primates, there is a solid *postorbital plate* in this position. The temporal muscles, used in mastication, fill the temporal fossae.

Elevated ridges on the skull form points of attachment for muscles of the head and neck. Generally these increase in size with age, attesting to the fact that bone is a dynamic tissue, continually remodeling itself in response to the stresses of living. A prominent *sagittal crest* arises on the frontals near the postorbital processes and extends posteriorly along the medial sutures of the skull. A *lambdoidal ridge*, formed along the posterior border of the cranium from the dorsal surface of one auditory bulla to the other, may intersect the posterior edge of the sagittal crest.

The paired *premaxillary bones* bear the incisors, form the anterior portion of the hard *palate* (the bony shelf separating the oral cavity from the nasal chambers), and send wings dorsally along the nasal bones. The paired *maxillary bones* form the sides of the rostrum and most of the hard palate and bear the canines, premolars, and molars. The smaller, paired *palatine bones* form the posterior margins of the palate. This extensive palate is another feature associated with the active mammalian lifestyle. The palate separates the air passage from the food passage and thus allows breathing and chewing at the same time. Animals without such a palate (e.g., lizards, snakes, and salamanders) must bolt their food or suffocate. If they do bolt the food, the meal arrives at the stomach largely intact, poorly prepared for efficient chemical dismantling by the digestive organs. Obviously, such a system would not meet the needs of active, endothermic animals. In addition, the bony palate allows the young to suckle and breathe at the same time.

The *mandible* (Figure 2-2) consists of a single bone on either side, the *dentary*. The dentaries are fused at the *mandibular symphysis*, on the anterior midline. In rodents and most artiodactyls the symphysis is flexible and allows for considerable disarticulation, whereas in most other mammals the symphysis is fused and immobile. (Artiodactyl mandibles in museum collections are frequently disarticulated.) The *ramus* is the tooth-bearing horizontal portion of the dentary. The *coronoid process* extends up into the tem-

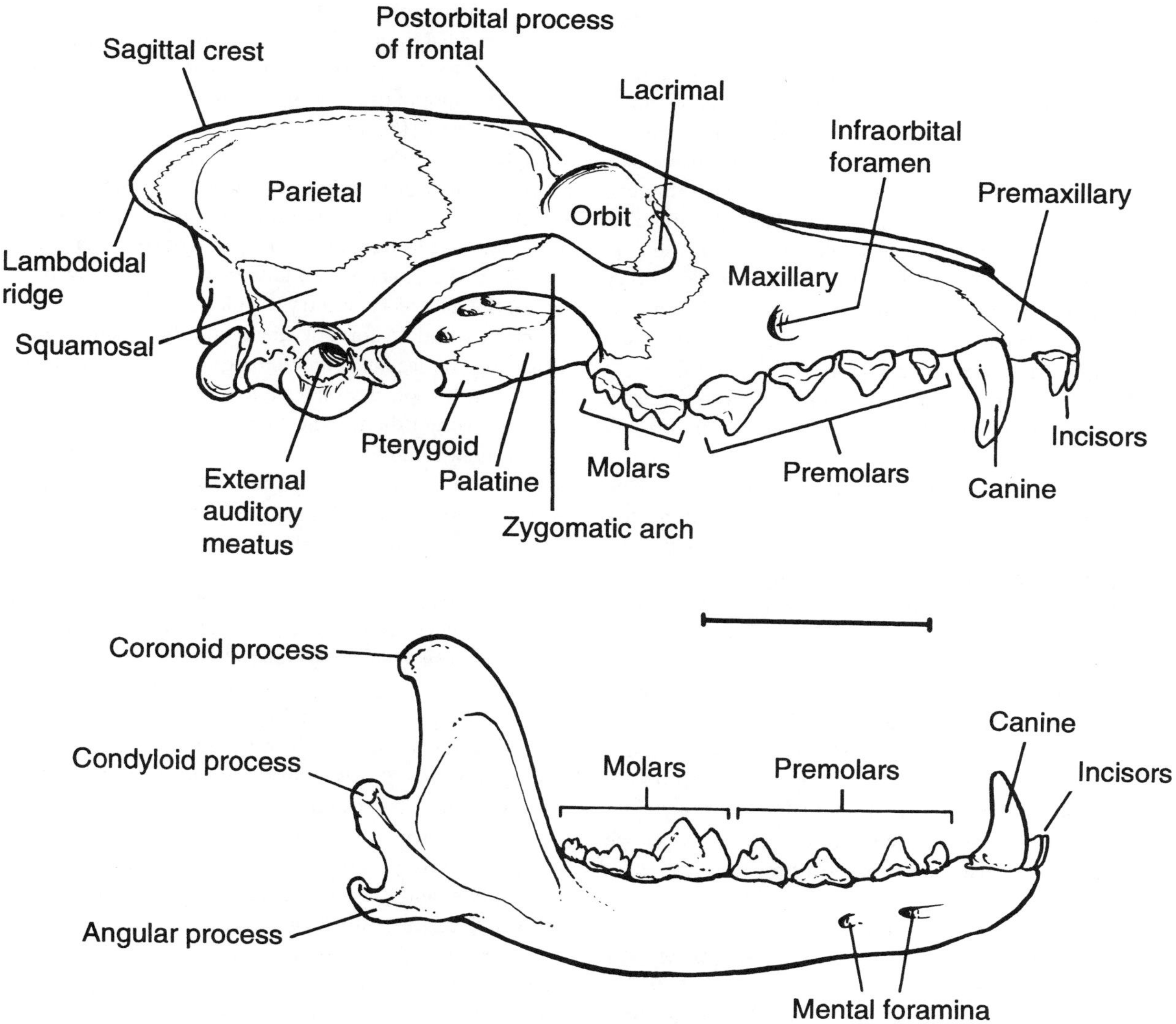

FIGURE 2-2. Lateral views of the skull and mandible of a coyote (*Canis latrans*). Scale = 5 cm.

poral fossa when the jaws are shut. The *mandibular condyle* (condylar process) articulates with the mandibular fossa of the cranium. In many mammals, including most rodents and lagomorphs, the mandibular condyle and fossa are rounded, allowing for lateral movement, rather than elongated transversely as they are in the coyote. The numerous foramina that penetrate the skull provide passage for blood vessels and nerves.

Postcranial skeleton. Mammal-like reptiles from the later Permian and Triassic exhibited not only mammalian cranial features but also advances in postcranial structure. They stood more erect than other amniotes, the elbows pointed backward, the knees forward.

The shoulder or *pectoral girdle* of most mammals is composed of two elements, the *scapula* and the *clavicle* (collarbone). Mammals that run on hard ground often have a reduced clavicle or none at all, lacking a bony connection between pectoral and axial parts of their skeletons. The shock of the running body striking the ground is absorbed by the soft tissues around the scapula rather than by bony joints.

The pectoral limb itself consists of three major parts: a proximal *humerus* and distal *ulna* and *radius*. The ulna and radius usually can rotate around each other, enhancing mobility of the forefoot. The hand (*manus*) includes three different sets of bones. The first, proximal group forms the *carpus*, or wrist; individual elements are *carpals*. The carpals are followed by the *metacarpals*, one for each *digit* (finger). The most distal series of bones is the *phalanges* (singular, *phalanx*). In the ancestral (the reader's) pattern, the first digit of the forelimb, or *pollex*, has two phalanges; other digits have three. Hence, the ancestral *phalangeal formula* is 2-3-3-3-3, a simplification of the general reptilian formula (as seen in modern lizards): 2-3-4-5-3.

The hip, or *pelvic girdle*, is composed of two symmetrical halves, the *innominate bones*, which form a ring through which products of the reproductive, urinary, and digestive tracts leave the body. The pelvic limb is similar to the front limb. The proximal bone (corresponding to the humerus) is the *femur*. The middle segment of the hind limb includes the larger *tibia* and narrower *fibula*. These two bones are often partly fused. Many mammals have a *patella* or kneecap. This bone is formed independently from the other leg bones and is unique to the Mammalia; it protects the knee joint. The hindfoot, or *pes*, consists of three series of bones. The most proximal are the *tarsals* (ankle bones), followed by *metatarsals*, and as in the manus, distal *phalanges*. The number of phalanges is the same as in corresponding digits of the forefoot. The first digit (the "big toe") is the *hallux*. Carpals and tarsals are often referred to collectively as *podials*; metacarpals and metatarsals together are called *metapodials*.

The basic mammalian stock was four-footed (*quadrupedal*) and each of those feet had five toes (*pentadactyl*). This is the same arrangement of toes found in ancestral quadrupeds of 400 million years ago. (Humans retain the ancestral arrangement, modified in detail, of course, to allow our peculiar bipedal gait.) Mammals have pushed the basic plan in myriad ways, showing diverse adaptations in both *stance* and *locomotion*.

Stance and locomotion (gait) are easy to confuse but they are different phenomena. Stance describes the way an animal stands; locomotion, or gait, describes how an animal moves. (Whales move but they do not stand.) Some species change their stance as they change their mode of locomotion. For example, human runners stand and walk on the soles of their feet (a *plantigrade* stance). Leaving the starting blocks, they run on their toes—that is, they become *digitigrade*. Loping along in full stride, they may again become plantigrade.

Some mammals—the ungulates—stand only on the longest, medial digits. The side toes were reduced, the remaining digits strengthened and elongated. Claws increased in size to support the toes and eventually surrounded the entire structure. Eventually, these *hooves* (ungules) became the only parts of the feet in contact with the ground. Members of two living orders show this *unguligrade* stance—most artiodactyls and the family Equidae, order Perissodactyla. Most artiodactyls have two principal digits of equal size on each foot, the *paraxonic* condition, the toes being beside (para-) the axis of symmetry. Metacarpals and metatarsals are often fused to form a single so-called cannon bone, increasing the legs' stability. Horses have only the medial digit in each foot, a *mesaxonic* foot, its axis of symmetry passing through the middle (meso-). In many artiodactyls and in horses, ulna and radius are fused as are the fibula and tibia, resulting in a single bone in the middle segment of each limb. The trend toward longer, simpler limbs specialized for high speed is generally accompanied by reduced lateral mobility.

In *saltatory* locomotion, as in rabbits, the stronger and longer hindlegs leave the ground last, and the front legs touch down first when the animal lands. Hind limbs provide the major part of the thrust. In contrast, kangaroo rats, like kangaroos proper, are bipedal; the front feet are not used for locomotion. The hindfeet are elongate and the strong, long tail provides support and counterbalance in such *ricochetal* locomotion.

Some heavy terrestrial mammals like elephants have *graviportal* limbs. The leg bones are arranged in a straight, vertical line, and the feet are large and broad, distributing the weight of the animal over a great area.

Many mammals are capable of digging, and most smaller mammals dig at least sporadically. Specialized burrowers have evolved in a number of lineages. Prairie dogs, marmots, and other *semifossorial* species—which often have small external ears (pinnae) and especially strong limbs and claws—dig elaborate burrows and use them as permanent homes, but they gather food outside their retreats. Semifossorial prey animals often have keen senses of sight and hearing and an ability to move quickly to the protection of the burrow.

The seemingly small step to a truly *fossorial* habit is accompanied by major anatomical specializations. Fossorial mammals usually have sturdy, compact bodies; short necks and tails; keen tactile and olfactory senses; reduced pinnae; small and sometimes completely non-functional eyes; and fur with no direction of lay. Both true moles (Soricomorpha: Talpidae) and the marsupial "mole" (*Notoryctes*) have front limbs with large, shovel-like hands, strong claws, and powerful shoulder muscles. Fossorial rodents (pocket gophers, mole rats) use strong, procumbent incisors for digging.

Mammals without obvious adaptations for climbing are often seen to take to the trees to reach food or safe, elevated places to rest. Many smaller rodents with unspecialized limbs are excellent climbers and forage in trees and shrubs. Among carnivores, most cats, martens, raccoons, bears, and even foxes spend time in trees. Tree squirrels have a basically terrestrial structure. Specializations are limited to sharp, curved claws and bushy tails that aid in balance. They tend to nest in trees, but in part they forage on the ground. Tree squirrels exhibit *scansorial* ("scampering") locomotion. Mammals like monkeys are specialized for more exclusive *arboreal* locomotion, with grasping ability provided by opposable digits or prehensile tails, or both. The "flying" squirrels have flaps of skin that extend between hind and front legs to greatly increase the surface area of the body, giving the animal the properties of a glider. Such *glissant* animals can travel great distances in one leap and often can maneuver well. However, no glissant mammal really flies; that is, none can gain altitude by their own power. Bats are the only mammals exhibiting true flight. These *volant* mammals are enormously successful and represent the second most diverse mammalian order, after the Rodentia.

When pressed, most mammals can swim, but some kinds are specialized for swimming (*natatorial* locomotion). Amphibious mammals like the water shrew, muskrat, and beaver have webbed feet or strong hairs growing at the edges of their toes. The tail may be flattened as a rudder or propeller. Their bodies are more streamlined than those of terrestrial relatives. However, amphibious mammals are well equipped to travel on dry land. A few mammalian groups, including some carnivores (seals, sea lions, walruses), the dugongs and manatees, and the whales, are so strongly specialized for life in the water that they have little or no capacity for movement on land.

The Diversity of Mammals

The several distinctive traits of mammals evolved through the long millennia of the Age of Reptiles. With the demise of the "ruling reptiles" (archosaurs) in the Cretaceous, mammals were "ready and waiting" to undergo a profound adaptive radiation in the Cenozoic, the most recent 70 million years. It is with good reason that the Cenozoic is called the "Age of Mammals."

Most living mammals are either placentals (the Eutheria, which build a placenta and carry the embryos inside) or marsupials (Metatheria, which carry "embryos" in an external pouch). The common ancestor of both placentals and marsupials was a rat- to opossum-sized mammal, quadrupedal, omnivorous, and basically terrestrial, that lived in the Cretaceous Period toward the end of the Age of Reptiles. The ancestral marsupial looked much like the living opossum. From those arose the insectivores (the order that includes modern shrews and moles), the basal placental stock. From those beginnings there quickly evolved forms as diverse as bats, whales, hoofed herbivores, and specialized carnivores. Most existing orders of mammals had appeared by the Eocene, some 60 million years ago.

Mammals are not the most numerous of vertebrates; there are some 4,629 living mammalian species (D. Wilson and Reeder 2005), compared to about 9,000 kinds of birds, nearly 8,000 species of "reptiles," 5,500 species of amphibians, and 27,000 species of bony fishes (Pough et al. 2009). However, mammals are by far the most diverse in body form and general "lifestyle," and earlier in the Age of Mammals, some 20 to 30 million years ago, our class was even more diverse than it is today.

The variety of mammals is truly remarkable. Existing mammals differ in weight by a factor of 10 million, from 3-gram shrews (the weight of a US penny) and tiny bats and mice to 190-ton whales (the mass of three full railway freight cars). They differ in length by a factor of 10,000, from bats shorter than your little finger (50 mm) to whales the length of a gymnasium (35 m).

Of the numerous fine references on mammals in general, we mention only a brief selection. Standard textbooks of mammalogy are T. Vaughan et al. (2011) and Feldhamer et al. (2007). Eisenberg (1981) provided an advanced analysis of the diversity of mammals that still is useful. A widely used laboratory manual by R. E. Martin et al. (2001) provided keys to families of mammals of the world, a vast amount of descriptive information, and a summary of field techniques. Elbroch (2006) presented a thorough but accessible review of animal skulls, focused mostly on mammals, including annotated photographs of many Coloradan species. Of several field guides to mammals, Kays and Wilson (2009) is recommended. R. Savage and Long (1986) and A. Turner (2004) provided accessible evolutionary accounts of mammals, and Kurtén (1971) published the classic, semi-technical synopsis of the Age of

Mammals; also see Chapter 3 in this volume. D. Wilson and Reeder (2005) outlined mammalian species of the world, Nowak (1999) provided brief accounts of all Recent genera, and S. Anderson and Jones (1984) detailed orders and families. Phylogenetic relationships among mammalian orders are by no means settled. At the present time, traditional classification (based mostly on morphology of fossil and living forms) and emerging molecular-based phylogenies have yet to be reconciled. The most comprehensive available review of higher classification is by McKenna and Bell (1997). Recent encyclopedic treatments of mammals (such as Attenborough 2002; D. W. Macdonald 2006, 2009) provide useful context for the local fauna, and works on animals generally (see Burnie and Wilson 2001) place mammals in a broad zoological perspective.

Orders of Mammals

Mammals are classified in 30 to 40 orders (depending on how finely one chooses to subdivide such groups as marsupials and insectivores), of which 20 to 25 are alive today. Extinct orders mostly were large-sized, hoofed beasts or the archaic forerunners of existing orders (e.g., the creodont ancestors of carnivores and the condylarth ancestors of ungulates). Native Coloradan mammals represent nine orders. The approximate percentage of worldwide mammalian diversity (by order) indigenous to Colorado is Didelphimorpha, 1.1; Cingulata, 4.8; Primates, 0.3; Rodentia, 2.6; Lagomorpha, 7.6; Soricomorpha, 2.3; Chiroptera, 1.6; Carnivora, 8.7; Artiodactyla, 3.3; in total, Colorado is the natural home of about 131 of some 4,629 mammalian species, or about 2.8 percent of extant mammalian diversity. By the way, that fraction of mammalian diversity occurs on Colorado's mere 0.2 percent of Earth's land surface. Colorado is home to more than its share of mammalian diversity because of its remarkable ecological diversity (see Chapter 1).

Key to the Orders of Mammals in Colorado

1. First toe on hindfoot thumblike, apposable; marsupium (pouch) present in females; incisors 5/4 . . . . Marsupialia

1' First toe on hindfoot not thumblike or apposable; marsupium (pouch) absent; incisors never more than 3/3 2

2. Forelimbs modified for flight; canines prominent; greatest length of skull less than 35 mm . . . . Chiroptera

2' Forelimbs not modified for flight; if canines prominent, then greatest length of skull greater than 35 mm. 3

3. Stance bipedal, plantigrade; body thinly haired, without bony plates; thumb completely apposable; digits with nails . . . . Primates

3' Stance quadrupedal; body well furred, or if thinly haired, then dorsum covered with bony plates; thumb (if present) not apposable or incompletely so, digits with claws or hooves 4

4. Cheekteeth peg-like, lacking enamel; dorsum covered with bony plates . . . . Xenarthra

4' Cheekteeth not peg-like, bearing enamel; dorsum covered with fur 5

5. Feet with hooves; upper incisors absent, or if present, then toothrow either not continuous or teeth bunodont 6

5' Feet with claws; upper incisors present 7

6. Hooves even-toed; upper incisors absent, or if present, then cheekteeth bunodont (e.g., Suidae) . . . . Artiodactyla

6' Hoof single; upper incisors present . . . . . Perissodactyla

7. Toothrow continuous (without conspicuous diastema); canines present 8

7' Toothrow with conspicuous diastema between incisors and cheekteeth; canines absent 9

8. Canines approximately equal in height to adjacent teeth; total length less than 200 mm . . . . Soricomorpha

8' Canines conspicuously longer than adjacent teeth; total length greater than 200 mm . . . . Carnivora

9. Ear flaps (pinnae) approximately same length or longer than tail; incisors 2/1 . . . . Lagomorpha

9' Ear flaps (pinnae) much shorter than tail; incisors 1/1 . . . . Rodentia

3

History of Mammals and Mammalogy in Colorado

Mammals—like the rest of biodiversity—are not just something to identify or memorize but something to appreciate deeply. Biodiversity is "the variety of life and its processes; the variety of living organisms, the genetic differences among them, and the communities and ecosystems in which they occur" (Keystone Center 1991). Biodiversity is not a mere list of species; it is life in its near-infinite variety, at all scales of time and space. Biodiversity is not an object but a phenomenon, a "happening," a progress report on evolutionary and ecological processes. Mammals are merely a part of—and presently a dominant participant in—an ancient, dynamic, and fascinating whole.

Mammals make no real sense when abstracted from their deeper and broader connections in space and time. Mammals over space we can imagine, perhaps: Coloradan mammals are different from East African mammals, for example. A deep appreciation of mammals as a phenomenon in time, however, is a serious exercise of the imagination. But it is an exercise that is worthwhile and one that can be disciplined and informed by the hard data from the geologic record of organisms and ecosystems of the past.

It is probably impossible to grasp the immensity of geologic time without a metaphor, a model. We humans use metaphors well when the need arises. To help us imagine scales of space beyond our field of view, our usual mental trick is a scale model. That is, we draw a map, and we understand intuitively that the map is merely a grossly simplified conceptual model of real spaces of our surroundings. My wall map of Colorado measures about 35 by 46 inches. A map has a scale (the ratio of model to reality). The scale of my map is 1:500,000, so 1 inch equals about 8 miles. A "real" mile equals 63,360 inches, so my map is a gross abstraction, but one that we all interpret readily. We need a similarly transparent mental trick to deal with time.

For many, an effective metaphor is to scale geologic time—the duration of Earth's history (some 4.5 to 5.0 billion years)—to a single year. Table 3-1 outlines such a model. On that timescale, we see that life arose on Earth about 3.8 billion years ago, April 19 on our scale model of Earth's duration. Eukaryotic cells—our kinds of cells, with their membrane-bound organelles and genetic information packaged in a nucleus—are known first from about

TABLE 3-1. A model of deep time: History of Earth scaled to a calendar year (assume Earth is about 4.8 billion years old, so a "day" is about 13 million years long). Geologic dates mostly from Geologic Names Committee, USGS (2007); mya = millions of years ago.

Era	*Period*	*Epoch*	*Time mya*	*Evolutionary Events during Interval*	*Calendar Date*
	Quaternary	Holocene	0.01	Dominance of *Homo sapiens*	
		Pleistocene	2.58*	Recurrent ice ages	
	Tertiary	Pliocene	5.3	Diversification of Hominidae	December 31
		Miocene	23.0	First extensive grasslands	December 30
		Oligocene	33.9	First apes, modern grazers	December 29
		Eocene	55.8	High point of mammalian diversity; first anthropoid primates	December 27
		Paleocene	65.5	Diversification of mammals	December 26
Cenozoic—"Age of Mammals"				XXXXX†—K/T boundary: extinction of archosaurs other than birds and crocodiles	December 22
				Diversification of angiosperms	
	Cretaceous		146		December 20
				First placental mammals, continents moving toward present positions	
				First known birds; height of dinosaur diversity	
	Jurassic		200	XXXXX	December 16
				Origin of angiosperms	
			220	Breakup of Gondwanaland	December 15
				First bona fide mammals; origin of dinosaurs	December 13
				Gymnosperms dominant	
				Separation of North America from Eurasia	
Mesozoic—"Age of Reptiles"	Triassic		251	XXXXX—"Great Extinction"	December 12
Paleozoic	Permian		299	Origin of therapsids—the "mammal-like reptiles"	December 8
				Breakup of Pangaea	
				Origin of synapsids	December 5
				Widespread glaciation	
				Extinction of trilobites	
"Age of Amphibians"	Carboniferous		360	Origin of "land egg" (amniote egg)	December 3
				Diversification of tetrapods; first seed plants	
				First terrestrial vertebrates (tetrapods)	
				Diversification of fishes	
"Age of Fishes"	Devonian		416	XXXXX	November 30
				First trees	
	Silurian		444	Life invades the land: origin of vascular plants, first terrestrial arthropods	November 28
				First vertebrates	
	Ordovician		488	XXXXX	November 23

TABLE 3-1. A model of deep time: History of Earth scaled to a calendar year (assume Earth is about 4.8 billion years old, so a "day" is about 13 million years long). Geologic dates mostly from Geologic Names Committee, USGS (2007); mya = millions of years ago.

Era	*Period*	*Epoch*	*Time mya*	*Evolutionary Events during Interval*	*Calendar Date*
				First corals	
"Age of Trilobites"	Cambrian		542		
			~600	First appearance of multicellular animals, "Cambrian Explosion"	November 17
				Origin of tissues?	
				Origin of meiosis? sexuality?	
			~1300	Oldest eukaryotic fossils	September 12
			~2000?	Origin of mitosis?	July 20
			~2700?	Origin of photosynthesis?	May 28
Proterozoic			~3200?	Oldest fossil "bacteria"	April 19
			~3800?	Oldest exposed rocks on Earth	March 4
			~4200?	First non-molten crust	February 1
Archeozoic			4600–5000	Origin of Earth—Happy New Year!	January 1

Notes: * See Gibbard et al. (2010); † XXXXX = major extinction event.

September 12, and multicellular animal life appears just before Thanksgiving, about November 17. Vertebrates appear in the fossil record in late November, and amniotes (vertebrates like ourselves, with embryos floating in amniotic fluid) begin to diversify in the Permian Period, about December 8.

Mammalian Evolution in Colorado: The Record in the Rocks

Early in the adaptive radiation of amniotes, a lineage that we call synapsids diverged from the "mainline" of amniote evolution (the line that led eventually to dinosaurs—including birds—and also to living crocodiles, lizards, and snakes). A branch of the synapsids that we call the therapsids ("mammal-like reptiles") gave rise to the mammals. The first record of bona fide mammals is from the Triassic Period, some 210 million years ago, about December 13 in our calendar year. The first evidence of mammals in Colorado is nearly that old, in the form of trackways found in the vicinity of Grand Junction.

Now glance up the calendar and note a few other highlights. The origin of placental mammals like ourselves occurred about December 20. The Cretaceous-Tertiary boundary, marked by the demise of the last of the non-avian dinosaurs, was on December 22; by that time the order Primates already had branched off on its storied journey to us. Anthropoid primates arose on December 27, and our family, the Hominidae, diverged and diversified on New Year's Eve.

Our direct knowledge of mammals of the past derives from careful "reading" of the fossil record. By geologic good fortune, several important chapters in the story of mammalian evolution are "written" in rocks exposed in Colorado. A brief review will help put the modern fauna (and its ongoing evolution) in perspective. The "punch line" is that the extant mammals of Colorado, as the mammalian fauna of any place, represent a progress report on genetic and ecological processes (variation and natural selection, population growth and decline, geographic range expansion and contraction, the evolution of symbioses) in a lineage of mammal-like reptiles nearly a quarter of a billion years old.

As we have noted, mammalian evolution began deep in the "Age of Reptiles," in the Triassic Period, when one group of mammal-like reptiles, the cynodont therapsids, achieved the fundamental hallmark of the mammalian condition, the dentary-squamosal jaw articulation. This not only strengthened the jaw joint, but it also freed old reptilian jaw elements (the articular and quadrate bones) to become mammalian ear ossicles, the malleus (or hammer bone) and the incus (or anvil bone), respectively. Earliest mammals were rather small (rat-sized) and their complex dentition suggests that they were insectivorous or carnivorous. Almost certainly, earliest mammals were hairy and endothermic, and judging from the presence of an extensive secondary palate separating the mouth cavity from the airway, which would allow breathing and chewing or suckling at the same time, there is every reason to suspect that they had mammary glands and nursed their young. Indeed, these traits—fossil hints at physiology and behavior—began to appear in therapsids back in the Permian Period, perhaps 250 million years ago.

The topographic grandeur of the Rockies draws attention to Earth processes and deep time, so the geology of Colorado has been described in a number of readily available, semi-technical books (e.g., Chronic and Williams 2002; Matthews et al. 2003). K. R. Johnson and Stucky (1995) provided an extended gallery guide to accompany "Prehistoric Journey," the extraordinary exhibit of the fossil riches of Colorado at the Denver Museum of Nature and Science. *The Eternal Frontier* (Flannery 2001) places the ecological history of Colorado in the wider, deeper context of the ecological evolution of North America. For a panoramic view of time and geologic change, *Annals of the Former World* (McPhee 1998) is without peer or parallel and much of the narrative applies directly to the evolution of Colorado. D. Wallace (2004) provided an insightful literary appreciation of early mammals and the paleontologists who have helped to unpack their story.

Knowledge of Mesozoic mammals has increased dramatically in the last half century (Kielan-Jaworowska et al. 2004) and much significant information is being derived from research in Colorado and adjacent states (see Table 3-2 for a broad summary), although much remains to be learned. When mammals arose from mammal-like reptiles in the Triassic Period (an interval of time between about 250 and 200 mya [million years ago]; see Table 3-1), the chunk of Earth's crust that we now know as Colorado was located near the equator and not on North America (which had yet to become a separate continent) but on the "world continent," Pangaea. Triassic rocks in Colorado are widely exposed and prominent as part of the spectacular "red beds" of the foothills of the Front Range and major valleys of the Western Slope. These rocks are remnants of a widespread Sahara-like desert. Fossil bones and teeth of Triassic mammals are rare in Colorado, but trackways of mammals (or perhaps mammal-like reptiles) are present (Lockley 1998). These are particularly well-known from the vicinity of Gateway, southwest of Grand Junction (Gaston et al. 2003; Lockley et al. 2004).

In the Jurassic Period (roughly 145 to 200 mya) our part of North America detached from Gondwanaland and drifted to the north and west. In Late Jurassic times, Earth was warmer than it is today; there apparently were no polar ice caps. What is now Colorado and surrounding areas were covered by a swampy lowland with stream channels and dunes, and the remains of their inhabitants are abundantly preserved today in the greenish to purplish shales of the Morrison Formation, exposed at such familiar sites in Colorado as Dinosaur Ridge near Morrison, Garden Park near Cañon City, and Dinosaur National Monument (see Kuntz et al. 1989; Nudds and Selden 2008). This real "Jurassic Park" is justly famous for its dinosaurs, but mammals also were there in the shadows, and they left abundant evidence of their presence as teeth and tracks. Occasionally, larger remains of archaic and extinct mammals have been found, such as shrew-like triconodonts and rodent-like multituberculates—an extinct but once immensely successful group of herbivorous mammals with gnawing incisors and curious serrated lower premolars (Rasmussen and Callison 1981).

Among mammals of Morrison times in Colorado was a peculiar form called *Fruitafossor*, described from a specimen from near Fruita and surely one of the most distinctive of known Jurassic mammals (Luo and Wible 2005). Skeletal adaptations suggest that it was a burrower (hence the root *fossor*, Greek for ditchdigger). Dental adaptations (tubular, ever-growing cheekteeth convergent with those of a modern armadillo) suggest a diet of social insects, such as termites. So peculiar was the newly discovered species that the authors were hesitant to place it within any known group of mammals, extinct or extant.

Colorado was subtropical during the Cretaceous Period (145 to 65 mya). For most of this chapter in Earth history, Colorado was beside or beneath an immense seaway that connected an ancient Gulf of Mexico from the southeast with an ancient Arctic Ocean from the north. The Dakota sandstone, often conspicuous in Colorado as a prominent "hogback" ridge at the western edge of the Great Plains, represents beach sands of the advancing seaway. Toward the end of the Cretaceous, uplift of the modern Rocky Mountains began and the stage was set for new levels of environmental complexity and a rich mammalian fauna throughout the ensuing Age of Mammals. Lowland swamps supported luxuriant vegetation that eventually became the coal deposits of the region. Trackways in the Cretaceous

TABLE 3-2. Traces through time: Some fossil mammals in Colorado (for details see text)

Time Interval	*Important Paleomammal Deposits (formations and/or representative localities)*	*Typical Habitats*	*Characteristic Mammals*
Mesozoic Era—"Age of Reptiles"			
Triassic Period	Wingate sandstone (Gateway)	Sahara-like desert	Ichnofossils ("trace fossils") of trackways of mammals or mammal-like reptiles of uncertain affinities
Jurassic Period	Dinosaur National Monument; Dinosaur Ridge (Morrison); Garden Park (Cañon City)	Lowland swamps and dunes	Triconodonts, multituberculates
Cretaceous Period		Exposed land near epicontinental seaway; uplift of Rockies toward end of period	Multituberculates, triconodonts, earliest therians?
Cenozoic Era—"Age of Mammals"			
Paleocene Epoch	Denver Basin; Debeque Formation (Piceance Basin)	Subtropical rainforests	Multituberculates, rodents, condylarths, insectivorans, marsupials
Eocene Epoch	Green River shales; Florissant Fossil Beds National Monument	Subtropical rainforests	Earliest known bats, "eohippus," tapirs, rodents, carnivores, lemur-like primates, shrew-mole, rabbits, rodents, ruminants
Oligocene Epoch	White River Formation (Pawnee Buttes, Weld County)	Temperate savannah and steppes	Horses, camels, hippos, titanotheres, creodonts, pangolins
Miocene Epoch	Pawnee Buttes, Weld County	Renewed uplift of Rockies; temperate rain-shadow grasslands	Camels, rhinos, chalicotheres, elephants
Pliocene Epoch		Canyon cutting in Rockies; habitats poorly known (erosional environment thanks to rejuvenated Rockies)	Mammals of modern genera present, although some (rhinos, hedgehogs, camels) now absent from North America
Quaternary Period			
Pleistocene Epoch	Record mostly fragmentary but statewide; Porcupine Cave, Park County; Haystack Cave, Gunnison County	Recurring alpine glacial episodes with periglacial steppe and forests; intervening interglacials with more moderate ("modern") climates	Arrival of *Homo sapiens* and coincident (or consequent?) megafaunal extinctions: mastodons, mammoths, giant ground sloths
Holocene Epoch	Statewide	more-or-less modern natural and cultural landscapes, local distribution of habitats dynamic	Increasing influence of humans

Laramie Formation near Golden probably represent marsupials or multituberculates, the predominant mammals of the time (Lockley and Foster 2003). Diversification of placental mammals began in the Cretaceous, as several modern orders diverged from a common ancestor (K. Rose and Archibald 2005; Bininda-Emonds et al. 2007).

From the standpoint of mammalian evolution, the boundary between the Cretaceous and Tertiary periods (the K/T boundary) appears to have been one of the most important events in Earth history. In a geologic "instant," evolutionary opportunities changed as an asteroid passed through Earth's atmosphere, producing the 90-mile-wide

Chicxulub Crater just offshore of the Yucatan Peninsula. Impact Day is marked indelibly in the rocks of South Table Mountain near Golden. There, in the 1940s, paleontologists first recognized the K/T boundary in terrestrial rocks of the Denver Formation, with dinosaur bones predominant below and mammalian bones predominant above. Eventually, detailed studies of rocks along Raton Pass in southern Colorado showed the telltale chemical signs of the impact, with sooty white clay and a record-high concentration of the rare element iridium. The iridium layer is thought to represent extraterrestrial fallout from the asteroid impact at Chicxulub.

The end of the Cretaceous marks the end of the Mesozoic Era, the so-called Age of Reptiles. Mammals appeared deep in the Mesozoic, when "ruling reptiles" were diverse and dominant. Beyond the K/T boundary, diversification of mammals was remarkable. The ensuing Cenozoic Era, the self-styled "Age of Mammals," was named by us mammals for ourselves—perhaps rightfully (and who makes the rules, after all?). Stucky (1990), J. Archibald and Rose (2005), and K. Rose (2006) provided authoritative reviews of diversification of mammals in the Cenozoic, focused on the rapidly expanding fossil evidence. J. Archibald (2003) integrated molecular and fossil evidence for the chronology and biogeography of the early branching of the eutherian family tree. Bininda-Emonds et al. (2007) provided a fascinating "supertree" of extant mammalian orders focused on branching sequence and divergence times of the groups.

Mammals are unquestionably the most influential animals on Earth at the present geologic moment; only mammals use fossil fuels and build nuclear warheads. However, we mammals are by no means the only evolutionary success story in the Cenozoic. The last 65 million years might also be called the "Age of Fancy Insects," because beetles, butterflies, true flies, and social insects—the ants, bees, and wasps—appear to be at or near their evolutionary zenith in these times. So too are flowering plants, so perhaps the Cenozoic should be called the "Age of Angiosperms." Better still, we might think of the Cenozoic as the "Age of Coevolution," because all of those dominant groups—mammals, insects, flowering plants—have been involved in an evolutionary positive feedback system, the success of each group building on the success of the others. And we humans are a part of that story, because our mammalian order, the Primates, is fundamentally dependent on the flowering plants for success. Prothero (2006) published a thorough and authoritative, yet accessible, review of the "Age of Mammals"; A. Turner (2004) published a popular-style summary; and D. Savage and Russell (1983) and S. Webb (1989) provided summaries and analyses of Cenozoic faunas of North America.

To date, the Cenozoic Era has lasted only about 65 million years (roughly a quarter the length of the Mesozoic Era—only about five days on our metaphorical calendar). The first 63 million years of the Cenozoic are termed the Tertiary ("3rd") Period, with five distinctive epochs (Paleocene, Eocene, Oligocene, Miocene, Pliocene—memorized by generations of geology students with the mnemonic "Put Eggs On My Plate"). Present times, the Quaternary ("4th") Period—which comprises the Pleistocene Epoch (known for its recurring "ice ages") and the Holocene Epoch or "Recent"—so far spans less than 2 million years, a mere 3 percent of the Age of Mammals and less than 1 percent of the duration of the class Mammalia. However, the Quaternary Period has been an important "eye-blink" of geologic time because one mammalian species (ourselves) has become increasingly influential in the future evolution of not only mammals but the entire ecosphere.

Mountain building that began in the Late Cretaceous—the so-called Laramide Revolution—continued through the first third of the Tertiary, heaving up the broad outlines of Colorado's dramatic scenery and thus its remarkable diversity of ecological opportunities. As the mountains rose they were eroded and sediments were carried downstream across the Great Plains, forming a deep "Tertiary mantle." Long intervals of volcanism covered much of the state with lava. Since the renewed uplift of the Rockies in the latest Miocene and Pliocene, erosion has removed the Tertiary mantle from much of the western Great Plains, but it remains along Colorado's northern border, familiar as the Pawnee Buttes and related uplands and cliffs, where it has proved a rich storehouse of mammalian fossils (and where nooks and crannies in the cliffs provide abundant habitat for a diverse array of bats and rodents today).

As we travel in our imaginations through Tertiary times, we watch the mammalian fauna change gradually from mostly archaic, "bizarre" (from our viewpoint, not theirs!), and unfamiliar forms to the fauna of modern times. The Paleocene of Colorado is represented by the Denver Formation of the Denver Basin. Colorado in the Paleocene was a land of rainforests; mammals mostly were of small to medium size, from shrew-like forms and marsupials to condylarths (precursors of modern ungulates) the size of small dogs (K. R. Johnson and Stucky 1995; K. R. Johnson and Raynolds 2006). Middleton (1983) reported six kinds of multituberculates, a marsupial, three kinds of insect-eating cimolestans, and at least a dozen kinds of condylarths from the Denver Formation. Eberle (2003) reported a multituberculate and 11 ungulates from a range of localities in the Denver Formation, scattered from Denver south to Colorado Springs and eastward on the plains past Kiowa in Elbert County. In western Colorado, the late Paleocene Fort Union Formation of the Piceance Basin has produced a variety of condylarths in addition to rodents, primates, perissodactyls, and artiodactyls (Burger and Honey 2008).

In the Eocene, Colorado supported subtropical rainforests. The Green River shales of northwestern Colorado and adjacent Wyoming and Utah represent a complex of Late Paleocene–Early Eocene lake beds, one of the best-preserved sequences of early Cenozoic lake deposits known anywhere in the world (Nudds and Selden 2008). Two of the earliest known bats—*Icaronycteris index* (Jepsen 1966) and *Onchonycteris feeneyi* (N. B. Simmons et al. 2008)—were discovered in the Green River shales of southwestern Wyoming and surely occurred in Colorado as well. Other "Green River" mammals included *Hyracotherium* (sometimes called "eohippus," the "dawn horse") and early tapirs, squirrel-like rodents, and a hyena-like carnivore. Lemur-like primates were diverse and abundant. Elsewhere, the Eocene fauna included rhinoceros-sized titanotheres and the hippo-like *Coryphodon* (a pantodont). Indeed, the Eocene saw the greatest number of mammalian orders of any chapter in the history of North America, perhaps a consequence of widespread warm climate (Woodburne et al. 2009a, 2009b). Most of the extant orders of mammals were present in the Eocene, along with perhaps a dozen more, now extinct.

Florissant Fossil Beds National Monument, west of Colorado Springs in Teller County, protects and interprets deposits from the latest Eocene that represent a temperate rainforest that some have compared to today's Muir Woods, north of San Francisco, California. The Florissant beds are widely known for their world-class plant and insect fossils (Elias 2002; Nudds and Selden 2008), but there were mammals there as well and recently they have become better known (Worley-Georg and Eberle 2006; K. Lloyd et al. 2008; K. Lloyd and Eberle 2008). The fauna unearthed to date includes an opossum, two kinds of shrew-like mammals and a burrowing shrew-mole, two kinds of rabbits, and several kinds of rodents, including relatives of the living sewellel ("mountain beaver") of the Pacific Northwest as well as true beavers, squirrels, and mice (in the broadest sense). Two kinds of deer-like ruminants were reported, along with an oreodont, a horse (*Mesohippus*), and a brontothere (*Megacerops*).

We can observe vestiges of the Oligocene in the White River Formation, deposited some 32 mya and exposed in the chalk cliffs and badlands of northeastern Colorado along the Wyoming state line. The rock itself represents outwash from erosion of the initial uplift of the Rocky Mountains. The temperate rainforests of the Eocene had been replaced by savannahs and steppes, so herding animals were plentiful, including not only early horses and camels but also hippos, rhinos, and car-sized titanotheres. Imagine dog-like creodonts (carnivorous mammals but not true carnivores because the shearing carnassial teeth were not of the modern P^4/M_1 pattern) preying on three-toed horses and sheep-sized oreodonts. There were a variety of rodents and even a pangolin (odd termite-eaters that now occur only in Africa and South Asia). In short, many of the mammals of the Oligocene might strike us as familiar enough from the zoo but quite out of place "in the wild" in Colorado.

At the level of families, the Miocene Epoch represents the global high point of mammalian diversity generally and doubtless in Colorado as well. In the Miocene there were some 175 families of mammals worldwide; today there are about 140. The Miocene fauna had a more modern look than that of the Oligocene, and Colorado was inhabited by strangely familiar mammals, representatives of modern families (several of them now gone from North America) but not quite familiar genera: for example, gazelle-like camels and 2-horned grazing rhinos. There also were archaic mammals, like giant chalicotheres (distant relatives of horses), whose claw-like hooves may have been used to excavate roots and tubers. Elephants arrived in North America in the Miocene and diversified here.

In the Late Miocene and Pliocene, renewed uplift of the Southern Rockies promoted canyon cutting by the major headwaters streams, including the dramatic gorges of the Colorado (Glenwood Canyon), Gunnison (Black Canyon), Arkansas (Royal Gorge), Clear Creek and Boulder Creek, the Big Thompson, and the Cache la Poudre. Today these canyons provide a rich diversity of habitats and complicate the distribution of species, their sunny south-facing slopes supporting a variety of southwestern mammals. The Pliocene record in Colorado is generally rather poor, as these were erosional times (thanks to the elevation of the rejuvenated Southern Rockies), but it is excellent downstream in Nebraska and Kansas, where outwash sands and gravels came to rest. Many Pliocene mammals would appear familiar to us; there were a variety of pronghorns, for example, and there still were a number of families in North America that no longer occur here, such as camels and hedgehogs and the last American rhinos (see Kurtén 1971).

Most of us probably think of the Pleistocene Epoch as the "Ice Age," which is partly true, but misleading. To be sure, there were repeated glacial episodes during the Pleistocene, and those glaciers sculpted the detail of Colorado's modern mountain landscape: freeze-thaw dynamics built the talus slopes that today support pikas, outwash streams scoured habitat for western jumping mice and water shrews, and well-drained glacial moraines support subalpine coniferous forests with their diverse fauna. But there were other ice ages in past times, and a Holocene Ice Age continues as the ice sheets of Greenland and Antarctica. Even in Colorado, glacial remnants of a "Little Ice Age" of just 200 to 800 years ago persist at the heads of some high mountain valleys. It is, of course, a matter for concern that climatic warming of the past few decades has accelerated the demise of Colorado's remaining glaciers, a not-so-subtle local reminder of the global impact of fossil-fueled industrial civilization (see Chapter 1).

Pleistocene Ice Age conditions were not limited to the mountains, of course. The Great Plains and the Colorado Plateau had Pleistocene climates very different from those of today. Winds off the mountain front carried sand and silt eastward, forming the sand hills of the eastern plains, dune fields in North Park, and the spectacular Great Sand Dunes of the San Luis Valley. Pleistocene deposits of loess (windblown silt) are eroded into badlands along Colorado's northeastern borders. Each of these features has its own influence on the local distribution of mammals. Pleistocene sand hills are home for today's kangaroo rats and plains pocket mice, for example. Pleistocene processes built modern habitats.

Over much of North America, the fauna of the Pleistocene is known from an abundant fossil record (Kurtén and Anderson 1980; R. Graham and Lundelius 1994). Entire skeletons of elephants weather out of streambanks in Nebraska; at Rancho La Brea, California, complete communities of animals are preserved in tar pits (Nudds and Selden 2008). No such deposits are known from Colorado and none should be expected. After all, Colorado is at high elevation, a headwaters state; water flows downhill from here. As it flows it carries with it the remains of whatever perishes upstream. Would-be fossil skeletons are carried downhill and broken on their descent, mostly gone to rest as undetectable bits downstream. Still, there are a few fossil remains from particular places that give us a glimpse at the life of the past. For example, in 2002, construction crews unearthed a mammoth tusk at a new subdivision in Parker (R. W. Graham, personal communication; R. L. Stucky, personal communication). Professional and amateur paleontologists from the Denver Museum of Nature and Science (then called the Denver Museum of Natural History) salvaged the material for research, education, and inspiration.

The mid-Pleistocene of the Colorado Rockies is represented by an extraordinary deposit at Porcupine Cave, in the southwestern corner of South Park (Barnosky 2004). Excavations began in 1985, involving professional and amateur paleontologists from the Denver Museum of Nature and Science, the Carnegie Museum of Pittsburgh, and the University of California (Berkeley) Museum of Paleontology. The deposit spans two glacial/interglacial transitions, from about 1 million to perhaps 600,000 years ago. The cave apparently was inaccessible to deposition or disturbance from about 300,000 years ago to late in the 1800s, when it was opened by human miners. Once the cave was opened, accumulation resumed by processes similar to those that prevailed a million years ago, among them collection and deposition of bones, raptor pellets, and carnivore scat by woodrats (*Neotoma*); carnivores using the cave as shelter so that their remains and the remains of their prey are present; and accidental occurrences, probably animals that fell into the cave through sinkholes. Add to that the movement of materials within the cave by untold generations of woodrats ("bioturbation") and occasional visits by miners and ranchhands, and the result is a remarkably complex record to sort and interpret. Of some 26 different fossil localities that have been worked within the cave, 16 are of unknown age and 4 are of mixed ages. Still, the deposit provides a remarkable picture of the Pleistocene fauna of South Park (including insights into past climate change; D. Wood and Barnosky 1994). The many thousands of specimens from Porcupine Cave represent the best record of the middle part of the Pleistocene known from anywhere in the Rocky Mountain West.

Primary consumers (vegetarians) preserved in Porcupine Cave include rabbits and hares, chipmunks, ground squirrels, a prairie dog, a marmot, a variety of voles (some representing genera now extinct), porcupines, deer, pronghorn, and mountain sheep—populations perhaps directly ancestral to those still present in South Park—plus an extinct species of mountain goat (*Oreamnos harringtoni*), perhaps three species of horses, a muskox, and two kinds of camels (*Hemiauchenia* and *Camelops*). Specimens of many genera have not been identified to species, but at least five species of woodrats (*Neotoma*) were identified (in an area that has just one species today). Secondary consumers included a shrew, weasels (including the now-endangered black-footed ferret), river otter, badger, spotted skunk, an extinct short-faced skunk (*Brachyprotoma*), and an extinct cheetah (*Miracinonyx*).

Haystack Cave, in Gunnison County, represents the end of the Pleistocene (12,000–15,000 years ago—contemporaneous with the famous fauna of the La Brea tar pits in Los Angeles). Haystack Cave preserved some two dozen mammalian species, including two lagomorphs (a cottontail and a hare), at least eight kinds of rodents, nine carnivores (including the extinct cheetah known also from Porcupine Cave), and five ungulates—among them a native horse, an extinct muskox (*Bootherium*), and an extinct kind of deer (*Euceratherium*) (Emslie 1986). Discoveries of skeletal remains of mammoth, mastodons, and ground sloth near Snowmass Village, Pitkin County, in October 2010 have stimulated much popular interest in the Pleistocene of Colorado and may prove to be one of the most significant deposits to date. The site is being excavated by personnel of the Denver Museum of Nature and Science (I. Miller 2010). Updates on the work are available online at http://www.dmns.org/museum-news/snowmass-mammoth-excavation. L. Martin and Hoffmann (1987) discussed the Pleistocene of the Central Great Plains, comments pertinent to eastern Colorado.

Fossils are the direct evidence of life of the past, and for the native fauna of any particular place "past is prologue" to the present. FAUNMAP (R. Graham and Lundelius 1994) is a rich source of information on Quaternary mammals of the United States. The project was conceived as an interactive, digital database of the fossil record of Pleistocene mammals. Eventually, the intent is to encompass the entire Pleistocene, although to date (November 2010), only information on the Late Quaternary (roughly the past 40,000 years) is available on-line. FAUNMAP tallied 75 species from Late Quaternary deposits in or adjacent to Colorado. Of those species, 89.3 percent occur in Colorado today.

Not surprisingly, the fossil record is incomplete (again, the headwaters are an erosional environment, not a depositional one) and apparently it also is biased. Specifically, "charismatic megamammals" are better represented in the fossil record than are smaller animals. Larger animals have larger parts and so are more obvious to the casual observers who usually are the first to stumble on new fossil localities. Further, predators are more likely to eat small mammals whole, leaving little recognizable to fossilize. Because there is a size bias, there is a concomitant taxonomic bias. Rodents, bats, and insectivores mostly are small in size; hence they are underrepresented; ungulates and larger carnivores, being larger in size, are overrepresented.

Further, there seems to be a geographical bias in the Late Pleistocene record. Species now typical of the Southwest—species that tend to reach their northern limits in Colorado today—seem to be underrepresented in the Late Quaternary record. That may not be a sampling bias, however; it may reflect history. D. Armstrong (1972, 1996) hypothesized that a number of southwestern species may be relative newcomers in Colorado, a hypothesis that now may be testable with modern molecular phylogeographic analysis. Waltari et al. (2007) used computer-based niche modeling to hypothesize location of Pleistocene refugia for several mammalian species, including three that occur in Colorado now or until recently: the short-tailed shrew (*Blarina brevicauda*—listed in this book as *B. hylophaga*), the southern red-backed vole (*Myodes gapperi*), and the American marten (*Martes americana*).

Of 8 species in the Late Quaternary fauna of Colorado (or immediately adjacent to Colorado) that no longer occur in the state, 6 are extinct: *Glossotherium harlani* (Harlan's ground sloth), *Mammuthus columbi* (Columbian mammoth), *Equus conversidens* (Mexican horse), *Platygonus compressus* (flat-headed peccary), *Camelops hesternus* (yesterday's camel), and *Bootherium bombifrons* (Harlan's muskox). One species (*Panthera leo*, now known as the "African lion") no longer occurs in the wild in North America, and one species (Franklin's ground squirrel, *Spermophilus franklinii*) lives as near Colorado as the vicinity of North Platte, Nebraska.

Development of the Modern Fauna

The only constant in life is change. The mammalian fauna of a place and time is not simply a static product of evolution. Rather, it is a progress report on ongoing processes of evolution and ecology—the evolution of species and the assembly of biotic communities. As we write this chapter a widespread and reasonable concern about environmental change is dawning (see Chapter 1). Environmental change is nothing new, of course. Change is the way things are. What is novel about the present are rates of change and causes of change. Rates of change seem to be rapid relative to typical rates over much of geologic time. Causes of change are unique in the history of the biosphere. Change is no longer merely cosmic (like the asteroid collision at Chicxulub that appears to have marked the Cretaceous-Tertiary boundary) or geophysical (like the recurrent ice ages of the Pleistocene). Rather, change today is largely cultural—change as a matter of human choice, our choices powered mostly by fossil fuels.

Table 3-3 is intended to place the recent history of the mammalian fauna of Colorado (the past 12,000 to 15,000

TABLE 3-3. Hypothetical timeline of major events in the Holocene history of the mammalian fauna of Colorado

Ybp	*Event/Process*
>13,000	Access to Southern Rockies by mammalian species of boreal forest and western mountains (eventually to include tool- and fire-using humans (subsistence hunters)
~12,000	Recession of Pinedale ice; beginnings of human study of Coloradan mammals; human-influenced (?) extinction of Pleistocene megafauna
4,500–6,000	Hypsithermal Interval; access to foothills for species of southwestern and Mexican affinities; humans increasingly influential in mammalian communities
200	Arrival of occasional, itinerant, Euro-American, market-driven hunters; near-extirpation of beaver
150	Permanent pre-industrial (wood-fueled) Euro-American settlement; beginnings of formal scientific study of Coloradan mammals; establishment of extractive, market-driven exploitation of native species and substrates; creation of artificial habitat for bats and other cavernicolous species; replacement of native grazers (bison, elk, pronghorn) with domestic cattle, sheep, horses
100	Permanent, industrial, fossil-fueled urban settlement; transmountain water diversion; export-market-driven, industrial-scale mining and irrigated agriculture; suppression of wildfire; deliberate eradication of keystone species (bison, grizzly bear, gray wolf); seasonal amenity-driven migration (summer visitors); founding of Colorado Division of Wildlife
60	Post–World War II re-invention of skiing; suburban and exurban development: seasonal and permanent amenity-driven settlement at wildland interface

Source: Based on D. Armstrong (1972).

years or so) in perspective. (The most recent episodes in this history are sketched in Chapter 4.) The take-home lessons of the table are simple enough. Humans have been a dominant force in the evolution of Colorado's ecosystems for at least 12,000 to 14,000 years. Industrial civilization here represents less than 1 percent of the duration of human occupation and influence. Our present time is but an eyeblink in history. A choice remains whether our influence will be a net positive or negative for the mammalian fauna of Colorado. This is an ethical and political choice (see Chapter 4), not a scientific one.

Patterns of mammalian distribution reflect history. Today, the Southern Rocky Mountains are a forested "island" surrounded by a "sea" of semidesert shrublands and grasslands (see Lomolino et al. 1989). Boreal species like the Canada lynx, pygmy shrew, pine squirrel, and snowshoe hare are isolated today from populations to the north. A mere 15,000 to 18,000 years ago, however, there probably was nearly continuous forest (at least along watercourses) from the Southern Rockies to the Uinta Mountains of Utah (Findley and Anderson 1956). Species of forested habitats could move back and forth freely, but the forest would constitute a barrier to mammals of steppe habitats.

We have noted that direct evidence for Pleistocene distribution of Colorado's mammals is meager. In the absence of a complete fossil record, analysis of existing distributional patterns can hint at the history of the fauna (D. Armstrong 1972, 1996; Patterson 1995). Distributional patterns that we see today must have been established since the last full glacial interval (the Pinedale), because climatic changes during that interval would have blurred or erased evidence of distributional patterns in previous episodes.

Based on examination of maps of continental distributions of species, D. Armstrong (1972) identified several "faunal elements" in the mammalian fauna of Colorado. About a quarter of Coloradan mammals are widespread in North America and so have no particular geographic affinity. So-called Cordilleran species—such as pikas and yellow-bellied marmots—are restricted to the Mountain West. Boreo-Cordilleran species like pine squirrels and pine martens are mammals of boreal forests of the northern United States and adjacent Canada but also occur in the Rocky Mountains and the Sierra Nevada and sometimes in the Appalachian Mountains as well. The Pleistocene of Colorado was marked by valley glaciers, not ice sheets. There were plenty of habitats here for mammals. Most species of Widespread, Cordilleran, and Boreo-Cordilleran faunal elements probably occurred in what is now Colorado even at the height of the last glacial episode, when forest and periglacial tundra linked the Southern Rockies with the Middle Rocky Mountains of Utah and Wyoming across what is now the sagebrush steppe of the Wyoming Basin. R. Graham (1987) reviewed Late Pleistocene mammalian faunas of eastern Colorado, including the Lindenmeier, Chimney Rock, Animal Trap, Jones-Miller, Selby-Dutton, and Lamb Spring sites.

Among Boreo-Cordilleran species of the late Pleistocene of Colorado was a curious, bipedal primate, *Homo sapiens*, fairly recently arrived from Asia via Beringia (G. Stuart 2001). The prehistoric record of humans in Colorado is fairly extensive but it is fragmentary, mostly mere hints across the millennia. What is known from numerous studies (see Stanford and Day 1992) is that by 11,000 to 10,500 years ago, humans ranged rather widely over what is now Colorado. An important Clovis-age Paleoindian site near Kanorado, Sherman County, Kansas, just east of the Colorado border (currently under study by personnel of the University of Kansas, the Kansas Geological Survey, and the Denver Museum of Nature and Science), may be 11,000 to 12,000 years old (Mandel et al. 2004). Clearly, earliest human Coloradans were gatherers and hunters, so we may assume that they were quite capable botanists and zoologists, hence serious, practical students of animal behavior. Because of their knowledge and technical skill they were able to exploit bison and probably also killed (or at least scavenged) mammoths and other large mammals. Large mammals provided food and also materials for clothing and shelter. For readable introductions to the rich prehistory of Colorado, see Stanford and Day (1992), J. Benedict (1992, 1999, 2005), Cassells (1997), and Stiger (2001). Late Quaternary paleoenvironments were reviewed by Elias (2001).

There is considerable circumstantial evidence that newly arrived humans caused or at least contributed to the extinction of much of the Pleistocene megafauna of Colorado, including antique bison (*Bison antiquus*), mammoth (*Mammuthus*), ground sloth (*Glossotherium*), camel (*Camelops*), llama (*Hemiauchenia*), and native horse (*Equus*). In the summer of 2008, in the course of a landscaping project a homeowner in Boulder discovered a cache of several dozen Clovis-age tools about 13,000 years old. Analysis of blood on blades led University of Colorado–Boulder archaeologist Douglas Bamforth to conclude that the tools had been used to butcher extinct horse and camel (Dell'Amore 2009). Gray (1993) reviewed the paleoanthropology of wildlife-human interactions. M. Waters and Stafford (2007) reviewed dates for the age of the Clovis culture, suggesting that the rapid spread of Clovis tools in the Americas hinted that human occupation was widespread in the Americas when Clovis technology arose about 10,500 years ago. P. Martin (2005) provided a provocative review of Late Pleistocene overkill on a global scale.

Because Paleolithic humans have been implicated in the demise of the rich late Pleistocene fauna of North America, some conservation biologists have suggested that postindustrial humans could "re-wild" the continent, restoring lions, cheetahs, horses, and other species to what were once their native ecosystems (Donlan et al. 2005). We might even introduce surrogates for species now extinct, modern elephants for extinct mammoths and mastodons, camels for the extinct *Camelops*, and so forth. This would not only contribute to restoration of the integrity of North American ecosystems but could compensate for losses of habitat and species in East Africa, the last refugium of these lineages.

Salvage archaeological work ahead of (and even alongside) the ongoing massive oil and gas development in the Wyoming Basin of southwestern Wyoming has yielded uniquely large sample data to illuminate postglacial hunter-gatherer lifeways and to allow empirical testing of theoretical ideas about foraging dynamics (D. Byers et al. 2005). Specifically, archaeologists have demonstrated what had mostly been theorized previously: that cool, moist periods allow production of larger populations of large game mammals (bison, bighorn sheep, pronghorn, elk, mule deer) and so allow greater harvest (relative to the harvest of lagomorphs and rodents). Predictably, climatic drying and warming decreased the so-called artiodactyl index: $\sum$ artiodactyls / [$\sum$ artiodactyls + $\sum$ lagomorphs + $\sum$ rodents].

With glacial recession, habitats opened in Colorado for species of adjacent regions. Great Basin species (like the Great Basin pocket mouse, the white-tailed jackrabbit, and the white-tailed prairie dog) and eastern species (like red bats, eastern moles, and eastern cottontails) moved in from the northwest and east, respectively. A suite of Campestrian (plains) species—black-tailed prairie dogs, northern grasshopper mice, and 13-lined ground squirrels, for example—may have been present on the savannas of eastern Colorado throughout the later Pleistocene, but warming and drying with glacial recession surely have increased opportunities for them.

Beginning about 6,500 or 7,000 years ago, there was a period of some 20 centuries or more that was warmer and perhaps drier than the present (Antevs 1948, 1954; J. Benedict 1979; Elias 2001). During that so-called Altithermal (or Hypsithermal) Interval, Chihuahuan species (D. Armstrong 1972)—mammals typical of northern Mexico and southwestern United States—may have moved into Colorado from the south and southwest, northward along either side of the mountains and also into the San Luis Valley. Several of these species (such as the Mexican woodrat, northern rock mouse, and Abert's squirrel) range northward along the foothills and in the canyons of the Eastern Slope today, reaching northern limits near the Wyoming boundary (D. Armstrong 1972). Many other Chihuahuan species occur mostly in southern Colorado, generally south of the Palmer Divide on the Eastern Slope (D. Armstrong 1996) and south of the Roan Plateau and Book Cliffs in the West. Among them are the desert shrew, white-tailed antelope squirrel, brush mouse, white-throated woodrat, white-backed hog-nosed skunk, and kit fox.

The FAUNMAP Working Group (1996) emphasized the fact that no two species of mammals have precisely the same geographic range and that species respond to changing climates individualistically. Lyons (2003) reviewed changes in geographic ranges through the later Quaternary (based on R. Graham and Lundelius 1994) and concluded that species responded individualistically but that there were some species that responded similarly to climatic change. Therefore, there were patterns and at least some mammalian assemblages remained together. She did not explicitly address the construct of "faunal elements," however. J. Frey (1992) did couch her observations of the generally concordant expansion of ranges in the central Great Plains of four species of "boreal mammals" within a framework of faunal elements.

Change is the nature of things. Opportunities change and species respond. Humans have watched faunal change in Colorado for at least 13,000 years. Further, organisms have major impacts on one another, sometimes in complex or improbable ways. Who would have guessed that the arrival of the plague bacillus with rodent stowaways from Asia to San Francisco around 1900 eventually would impact ground squirrels and prairie dogs in Colorado? Fleas from infected Norway rats on arriving ships spread the disease to local rodents, which in turn infected local ground squirrels. Plague then spread eastward, eventually reaching Colorado. Sylvatic plague showed up in Coloradan marmots and rock squirrels in 1941 (Ecke and Johnson 1952). In the late 1940s the outbreak largely eliminated Gunnison's prairie dogs from South Park and adjacent areas. Subsequently, Wyoming ground squirrels, lacking significant physical barriers and relieved of competition from prairie dogs, invaded South Park and are abundant today.

Much of the change in mammalian distributions that we witness today probably results from human influence, direct or indirect. Expanding our previous example, the Wyoming ground squirrel has moved southward over the twentieth century, responding in part to overgrazing (see R. Hansen 1962) and perhaps in part to the decimation of Gunnison's prairie dog by plague in areas like South Park. Eastern species like the fox squirrel and the raccoon have responded positively to urban plantings and stabilization of riparian corridors by flood control and fire suppression. Raccoons range nearly statewide in suitable habitat and fox squirrels probably are not far behind (although present distribution has not been detailed). A similar predominance of human-influenced changes in mammalian distributions is evident in Nebraska (R. Benedict et al. 2000).

Some of the deliberately introduced exotic species (e.g., moose, mountain goat) have prospered, but some have not. General William Palmer introduced European hedgehogs (*Erinaceus europaeus*) to his Glen Eyrie estate in the Garden of the Gods near Colorado Springs in the belief that they would control rattlesnakes. The experiment was unsuccessful. However, some inadvertent introductions have prospered (such as the house mouse and the Norway rat) and others have not become established. A curious example is the brief residence in Colorado of the Neotropical mouse opossum (*Marmosa canescens*—a species of southwestern Mexico and Central America), which probably arrived in Denver with shipments of bananas (see Warren 1942).

Species move continually. Some movements are rapid and obvious, like the ongoing expansion of fox squirrels in the foothills of the Front Range; others are slower and more subtle. But even if a species expands each generation by only the distance that the young disperse from their natal burrow, movements of hundreds of kilometers are possible in only a few hundred generations, only a few hundred years for an average, mouse-sized mammal.

The diverse Coloradan landscape, with its range of elevations, vegetation types, moisture regimes, and waterways, presents some species of mammals with significant barriers to movement and provides propitious corridors for the movement of others. The river that is an impassable barrier to a fossorial pocket gopher provides a corridor for the aquatic beaver or a riparian specialist like the raccoon.

Known distributions of some Coloradan mammals have changed over the past couple of decades. Meaney (1990a) combined records of museum specimens from a number of institutions and compared them with distributions mapped by D. Armstrong (1972). Data were included from annual reports to the Division of Wildlife from holders of scientific collecting permits, as were sight records tabulated for the Mammal Latilong Distribution Study (Bissell and Dillon 1982; Meaney 1991). In the 20-year period covered by the survey, 75 species were newly reported for 254 counties. (An unknown number of those reports were simply a matter of new data and thus represent expansions in knowledge rather than actual changes in distribution.) Of 254 new county records, 55 filled in former gaps within species' documented geographic ranges. Eliminating that group and ignoring deliberate introductions, 56 species showed possible expansion of ranges. These were sorted by direction of apparent "expansion." Twenty-four species had expanded northward, 13 westward, 12 eastward, and 7 southward. A number of species apparently are moving westward along irrigated corridors and riparian systems that have been stabilized by flood control. The southward movement is largely a movement southwestward from the Arkansas and Platte rivers, along irrigated corridors. Such changes are a natural phenomenon, augmented by human activities.

The most common directions of change were northward and westward. These may reflect slow Holocene (postglacial) readjustment. There is every reason to imagine that this trend continues, now augmented by the increasing pace of anthropogenic climatic warming. Perhaps these are the most significant changes to monitor, because they reflect—in a very real sense—human lifestyle choices. Climatic change and concomitant changes in mammalian distributions are nothing new, of course. What is novel is not change per se, or even the magnitude of change, but rather the causes of change (cultural, fossil-fueled) and the rapid pace of change—perhaps too rapid, in some cases, for mammals to cope. Understanding the dynamics of biogeography is critical to management and conservation and it demands careful observation and reporting. These are activities in which all knowledgeable naturalists can participate.

History of Coloradan Mammalogy

So much for the history of Coloradan mammals. What of the history of Coloradan mammalogy, the scientific study of mammals? That actually is a difficult question, because it begs a definition of "scientific." Some would date the beginnings of science to ancient Greeks like Archimedes or Thales, and the beginnings of biology to Aristotle or even Charles Darwin (and both of those luminaries did study mammals and they did it well). But if science is a process of asking honest, open-minded questions in nature and then posing plausible, testable answers, science is a whole lot older than these heroes, mere centuries or millennia old.

Certainly Paleolithic hunters in Colorado knew a great deal about mammals. Direct evidence is scant, but circumstantial evidence is immense. Bison jumps on the Great Plains and game walls on the alpine tundra (J. Benedict 1996) attest to people with deep knowledge of animal behavior. Rock art from the Southwest (S. Cole 2008)—and to a lesser extent from southeastern Colorado (Crum 2009)—conveys ancient but rich knowledge of mammalian structure and the "key characters" by which various species are recognized. A culture cannot depend on mammals for food and fiber and not come to know them "scientifically." After all, science is a self-correcting process. Incorrect ideas lead to unsuccessful actions. Unsuccessful actions lead to unsuccessful families. To paraphrase "Darwin's Bulldog," Thomas Henry Huxley, science is organized common sense, a natural way of working of the human mind. And if science is about adding up observations and making generalizations and predictions, then we might even argue that science is older than humans. Mammals are particularly adept at learning from experience, but many birds are as well, as are some other vertebrates and even invertebrates like octopi and squid.

Science typically is thought of—by scientists and "nonscientists" alike—as a huge array of information, an encyclopedic and expanding collection of data, in short, a lot of answers. It is more useful, however, to think of science not as a set of answers but as a mode of asking questions. Science is a process for searching for regularities in the seemingly chaotic diversity of phenomena in the world around us. Science is a process; scientific understanding is its product.

Where does our natural, scientific behavior come from? Humans (in common with other fancy animals) have sensory receptors and a remembering and abstracting brain. We build up sums of experience from which we generalize patterns of cause and effect. We use those patterns to make predictions. These predictions then guide our behaviors. As we behave on the basis of our predictions we test those predictions against further experience. If a prediction "holds up," we are likely to make it a piece of what we believe, at least tentatively. If the prediction does not hold up, we are likely to modify it or discard it altogether. We may not think about this process much, but the fact that we do it without thinking about it actually reinforces T. H. Huxley's point—science is a natural part of the way we work.

There is a most important fact about science implicit in our broad definition. Science is "evolution-tested" (to borrow a phrase from late, great paleomammalogist George Gaylord Simpson). Cast your imagination back 4 or 5 million years. Imagine a protohuman primate hiking down a savanna path in brightest Africa, looking for lunch. Our ancestor spies a ripe piece of fruit in a tree, a fruit that experience tells her (or him: obviously both sexes have this common sense we are calling science) is tasty and satisfying (that is, nutritious—after all, taste buds are evolution-tested too). She naturally predicts that what was a good lunch previously will be so again.

However, she also sees in the tree a large, if lethargic, leopard. She recalls stories of large leopards eating protohumans and she has heard that even small leopards can inflict serious damage. She considers her own experience and the experiences related by others, the size of the leopard, and the apparent depth of its sleep. She assesses the probabilities in a quick, natural cost-benefit analysis. She decides that some things in life are more important than any single lunch. Because of her scientific attitude—her innate faith in the predictable relationship between cause and effect—she returns home and eventually passes on her scientific good sense to another generation of protohumans, genetically, culturally, or both. All of us are heirs to her legacy of common sense.

In this broad definition of science, mammalogy—the scientific study of mammals—may be as old as mammals. Indeed, it probably is older. Imagine back over 200 million years ago to the Triassic deserts of what is now western Colorado. Imagine an ancient mammal eyeing a nestling dinosaur, sizing it up, making a scientific judgment of whether that dinosaur is predator or prey based on integration of its individual experiences with animal shapes, sizes, and behaviors. That is what science is about: integrating experience to make predictions. If that early Coloradan protomammal makes the sensible choice—the workable, adaptive choice—it lives to hunt another day. If it fails because of inexperience or misjudgment, it is selected against. Members of its species that make better judgments, judgments based on more thorough and accurate weighing of the evidence, are naturally selected: they are the parents of the next generation. Evolutionary success (Darwinian fitness) is measured as relative success in becoming a grandparent.

It should be obvious that humans have interacted from time immemorial with the rest of the native Coloradan mammalian fauna: studying, exploiting, and coping with other Coloradan mammals. Over the past 13,000 years or more, these interactions have changed significantly. Indeed, we may consider the interactions in three broad historical phases: several thousand years of subsistence use by native peoples, a century of largely unregulated exploitation by increasing numbers of Euro-American visitors and settlers, and a century of increasingly sensitive and scientific stewardship of wildlife. Let us look at each of these phases in turn, with special focus on changing views of wildlife in the last quarter of the twentieth century.

MILLENNIA OF SUBSISTENCE

Just when humans first came to what is now Colorado is a matter for debate. It was at least 13,000 years ago, and it may have been considerably earlier (Cassells 1997; Meltzer 2009). Whenever it was, this much we know: prehistoric peoples in Colorado depended on native mammals for subsistence and therefore they knew the fauna well. Paleoindians left numerous clues to the fundamental importance of mammals in their lives. Clovis people used stone tools to butcher mammoths (and perhaps to hunt them). Opportunistic omnivores, these Paleoindians also hunted and scavenged camels, native horses, and numerous smaller mammals. Somewhat later, Folsom people at the Lindenmeier Site (on the City of Fort Collins Soapstone Natural Area near the Wyoming state line) preyed on pronghorn, rabbits, fox, and coyote 10,900 years ago (Elias 2002). Already, the most significant game species was the bison, which continued in a central role for later Native Americans and then for early European settlers. Bison meat, fat, and bone marrow were eaten. Bison skin provided clothing, sleeping mats, and eventually tipi covers. Containers were made from horns, stomach, and scrotum, and tools were fashioned from bone. Even the brain was used to tan the hides. (The spring 2007 issue of *Colorado Heritage*, the magazine of the Colorado Historical Society, was devoted entirely to the indigenous peoples of Colorado, from earliest arrivals to the present day.)

Ten millennia ago, nomadic people already ranged into the high San Juans, above 10,000 feet (Elias 2002). Paleoindians developed techniques for driving herds of large mammals into natural traps. Major bison kill sites have been described from the plains in Yuma (Stanford 1974, 1975) and Kit Carson (Wheat 1967) counties, for example. High in the Front Range, rock walls were built to funnel game into traps. A game-drive system for mountain sheep and elk on Arapahoe Pass is 1.2 km long, with the most recent construction phase dated at just 800 years ago (J. Benedict 1985). A nearby site on Mount Albion was used by communal hunters to drive mountain sheep for 5,800 years—more than 200 human generations (J. Benedict and Olson 1978).

As noted previously, the Pleistocene fauna of Colorado included many mammals that no longer occur here: archaic camels and llamas, native horses, the short-faced bear, and even an American (now African) lion. There is considerable evidence that early human populations in the Americas hunted much of the Ice Age megafauna to extinction, or at least helped to push over the brink a fauna already stressed by global climatic change (P. Martin and Klein 1984). In a thorough analysis and synthesis, Faith and Surovell (2009) argued that the apparently synchronous extinctions of at least 16 genera of Pleistocene mammals in an interval about 13,800 to 11,400 years ago point to an abrupt and instantaneous event (presumably a geophysical mechanism rather than overkill by newly arrived humans). Koch and Barnosky (2006) concluded that the increase in Late Quaternary megafaunal extinctions was due to an intersection of climate change and initial human contact.

Later Native Americans in Colorado were entirely dependent on local ecosystems for food, clothing, and shelter. Not only were bison used for food but deer, elk, and mountain sheep also were taken, as was smaller game, including rabbits, hares, and a variety of rodents. Carnivores provided decorative skins for clothing and ritual objects. Mammals figured prominently in ceremony and religion, as symbols, totems, and characters in tribal stories. There clearly were situations in which subsistence hunters slaughtered animals that were not fully used, but mostly theirs appears to have been a sustainable, long-term relationship with the plants and animals upon which they depended. Hunting traditions of Native Americans reflect a deep knowledge of the ecology and behavior of mammals.

Apparently not all game taken in Colorado in pre-Columbian times was used locally. Scheiber (2006, 2007, 2008) and Scheiber and Reher (2007) discussed the role of bison hunting in Late Prehistoric indigenous peoples of the High Plains (AD 1000–1300), based in part on detailed work at the Donovan Site, a game-processing camp near Peetz, Logan County. Bison harvesting appeared to be seasonal, hunters working from temporary camps, and part of the game (including hides, pemmican, and even scapulae for hoe blades) was transported to the Republican River Valley of central Kansas and Nebraska, where it supplemented an agrarian culture based mostly on corn.

Some would attribute the apparent equilibrium between human predators and their prey to the hunters' respect for—or even spiritual connection with—the hunted. However, this belief may (at least in part) confuse virtue with necessity. Both predator and prey were migratory, following shifting resources and leaving behind disturbed areas with time to recover. Habitat alteration sometimes did occur on a massive scale, as when game was driven by prairie or forest fires, although on the longer timescales that ecologists must use, these are lesser disturbances than today's fossil-fueled cities and airports, or the diversion of western Colorado's rivers through tunnels into concrete-lined irrigation canals on the Eastern Slope. Mann (2006) provided a broad and readable review of pre-Columbian human impacts on the ecology of North America. Archaeological studies are critical to understanding the evolution of modern environments (J. Briggs et al. 2006).

THE NINETEENTH CENTURY: EXPLORATION AND EXPLOITATION

European exploration opened a new era of interaction between wildlife and people. Recorded European encounters with Coloradan mammals began in 1776 with the explorations of two Franciscan priests, Francisco Atanasio Dominguez and Silvestre Velez de Escalante, on the Colorado Plateau (W. Briggs 1976; T. Warner 1976). However, formal scientific study of mammals of Colorado began in the early nineteenth century, as explorers from the newly established United States began to venture west. Colorado lay north of the Santa Fe Trail and far south of the route of the Lewis and Clark Expedition, so it was left to Zebulon K. Pike—under orders from President Jefferson—to begin formal exploration of our hostile and unpromising corner of "Louisiana" in 1806–1807. Pike returned to the East with reports of an inhospitable landscape largely unsuited to civilization.

That negative description in itself may have been enough to lure the first wave of commercial exploiters, the storied mountain men. The young United States of America was at war with Great Britain in 1812 when Ezekiel Williams led the first band of Euro-American trappers to Colorado's mountain parks from the Bighorn Mountains of Wyoming. The real frenzy began after William Ashley's Rocky Mountain Fur Company encouraged trappers to travel to northern Colorado in 1822. Their quarry was beaver, whose underfur was made into hatters' felt. At the peak of the boom, 100,000 beaver pelts a year flowed downstream from the West, many from Colorado, gathered by legendary characters with names like Bridger, Smith, Carson, and Maxwell and traded at Fort Davy Crockett in Brown's Hole; Antoine Robidoux's Fort Uncompahgre (near the modern town of Delta); Forts St. Vrain, Vasquez, Lupton, and Jackson on the South Platte; Bent's Fort on the Arkansas; and other wilderness outposts. A shift of fashion from beaver-felt top hats to silk may have saved the beaver from extermination from the Rockies; it also led to the extinction of the legendary Mountain Men by about 1840.

Formal mammalogy in Colorado may be said to begin with Thomas Say, zoologist of the Long Expedition and namesake of a familiar Coloradan flycatcher, Say's phoebe (*Sayornis sayi*). Stephen H. Long explored eastern Colorado in 1820, entering the area along the South Platte, exploring the foothills of the Front Range to the Arkansas River (with a brief diversion so that part of the party could climb Pikes Peak), thence upstream to the Royal Gorge, and then backtracking to Rocky Ford before heading south into New Mexico at a point south of today's town of Branson. Thomas Say collected and named a number of new kinds of mammals: a tiny myotis bat (*Myotis subulatus*, now considered a synonym of *Myotis ciliolabrum*), Colorado chipmunk (*Neotamias quadrivittatus*), golden-mantled ground squirrel (*Callospermophilus lateralis*), rock squirrel (*Otospermophilus variegatus*), and swift fox (*Vulpes velox*). Despite zoological success, Long returned home with discouraging reports of a "Great American Desert" uninhabitable by civilized people—reports that only military necessity and the lure of gold eventually would overcome.

Colorado and its wildlife largely avoided the impacts of human migration to Oregon in the 1840s and the rush in the 1850s to the goldfields of California. Until about 1870, most mammalogical exploration was conducted incidental to military surveying expeditions. Expeditions led by John C. Frémont and later expeditions headed by Howard Stansbury and then John Gunnison all found Colorado generally impassable for the trails and rails of Manifest Destiny. However, from a mammalogical standpoint these expeditions contributed to a growing formal knowledge of Colorado. For example, Frémont's party collected a Coloradan pine squirrel in 1849 that John James Audubon and John Bachman named (in 1853) as *Sciurus fremonti* (now known as *Tamiasciurus hudsonicus fremonti*). In 1852 the Stansbury Expedition to the Great Salt Lake obtained the holotype (the specimen to which the name of a new species or subspecies is attached) of *Cratogeomys castanops* near Bent's Fort in what is now Bent County.

The most productive of these expeditions was the tragic journey of Captain John Williams Gunnison, whose surveys for a possible route for a transcontinental railroad along the 38th parallel led him across southern Colorado in 1853. Gunnison's expedition was attacked in Utah by Paiutes (or perhaps by Mormon insurgents disguised as Indians), and Gunnison and 7 members of the 12-man expedition were killed. Still, the expedition had collected a number of mammals new to science, including Gunnison's prairie dog (*Cynomys gunnisoni*), the San Luis Valley subspecies of both Ord's kangaroo rat (*Dipodomys ordii montanus*) and the meadow vole (*Microtus pennsylvanicus modestus*), and the plains harvest mouse (*Reithrodontomys montanus*). (For a summary of the still-puzzling history of the latter specimen, see D. Armstrong 1972.)

Much of the zoological material obtained by the various military and topographical expeditions was returned to the fledgling Smithsonian Institution and published by Spencer Fullerton Baird (1855), the second secretary of the Smithsonian Institution (Dall 1915; Rivinus and Youssef 1992), and summarized in his monumental *Mammals of North America* (Baird 1858). Many of the specimens from later expeditions were reported by Coues and Yarrow (1875) and Coues and Allen (1877).

In 1858, gold was discovered on Cherry Creek near what is now downtown Denver, and Colorado's environment has yet to recover. With the influx of settlers, the principal harvest was no longer furbearers but game mammals, and subsistence hunting soon shifted to commercial exploitation. Hunters supplied the mountain mining camps and the settlements along the mountain front. The great herds of bison, elk, deer, and pronghorn that had dominated the mountain parks and the Great Plains were slaughtered in a few short years. At first they supplied the local market, but when General Palmer's Denver Pacific Railroad linked Denver to the outside world via the Union Pacific at Cheyenne, markets expanded to the Midwest and even to the East Coast.

Native wildlife populations that had supported nomadic subsistence economies for millennia were no match for a settled human population with modern firearms and industrial-scale transportation. Elk were becoming rare in South Park by the early 1870s and were nearly extirpated from Colorado by 1910, reduced to a herd of 500 to 1,000 animals in the Upper White River watershed. Cary (1911) reported that he had neither seen mule deer nor heard reports of them in Boulder and Larimer counties in 1906. Bison had been removed from the Denver area by about 1875, the last native bison in eastern Colorado was killed at Springfield in 1889, the end of the bison in northwestern Colorado came in 1884, and the last wild bison in the state were slaughtered in South Park in 1897 (D. Armstrong 1972). Pronghorn were so heavily impacted by hunting that seasons were closed by 1893, not to reopen until 1945. As settlement expanded, mountain sheep retreated to the high mountains from the foothills, where they once had been abundant. To allow recovery from their slaughter for market, the hunting season remained closed from 1885 to 1953 (Barrows and Holmes 1990). Beidleman et al. (2000) provided a remarkable bibliography of the scattered literature on early zoological exploration in Colorado.

Since settlement, perhaps 7 species of native mammals have been extirpated from Colorado. Mammals present in the nineteenth or early twentieth century but absent by the mid-twentieth century include the American bison (*Bison bison*) and 6 carnivores—the gray wolf (*Canis lupus*), grizzly bear (*Ursus arctos*), black-footed ferret (*Mustela nigripes*), wolverine (*Gulo gulo*), river otter (*Lontra canadensis*), and Canada lynx (*Lynx canadensis*). Three of those species—the black-footed ferret, river otter, and Canada lynx—are being actively restored to the state (and individuals of two others—the gray wolf and the wolverine—have wandered into Colorado from the north). The bison has been reestablished as livestock. Details are provided in accounts of individual species. Newmark (1995) analyzed history of extinction (extirpation) of species in western US national parks, among them Colorado's Rocky Mountain National Park. One to 6 species have disappeared since establishment from 11 of 14 national parks studied, but none has been extirpated from Rocky Mountain National Park, perhaps because of its geographic and administrative context—an "island" of national park nearly surrounded by a much larger landscape of multiple-use national forest lands.

As domestic livestock replaced native species on Coloradan rangelands, competitors (alleged and real) with human enterprise—from grizzly bears and wolves to jackrabbits, prairie dogs, and pocket gophers—were shot, poisoned, or simply rounded up and clubbed to death. The recent history of these mammals is detailed in individual accounts of species.

SCIENTIFIC STUDY OF COLORADAN MAMMALS

As discussed previously, informal scientific mammalogy is as old as humankind or older, depending on how we agree to define "science." Study of the native mammalian fauna by humans doubtless began as the first waves of immigrants from Asia expanded across the Americas during the last Ice Age, relying on some mammalian species for food and fiber and avoiding becoming prey for some other species. From those days forward, the most insightful knowledge of the fauna of a particular area often is to be found not in books but in the stories of native peoples, ranchers, farmers, hunters, trappers, and other natural resource managers, who frequently get beyond merely exploiting the fauna to enjoy, admire, and understand it as well. D. Wilson and Eisenberg (1990) provided a broad outline of the history of North American mammalogy, and Gray (1993) published an overview of the anthropology of human knowledge of wildlife (especially mammals).

Unlike the folk science of the earliest Americans, formal science is peer-reviewed and published (and often supported by voucher specimens and archived field notes). From 1820 until about 1870, most formal mammalogical exploration was incidental to federal surveys and military expeditions, as sketched above. During the 1870s, non-governmental expeditions to Colorado provided new insights, including work by Brewer (1871), Trippe (1874), and J. Allen (1874) in the Colorado mountains.

The first local Coloradan naturalist of note was Martha Maxwell (1831–1881), a hunter and taxidermist who settled in Boulder in 1868 (M. Benson 1986). Her remarkable collection was exhibited in 1876 in a pioneering naturalistic diorama, first at the Centennial Exposition in Philadelphia, and then in Washington, DC (as detailed by Coues in Dartt 1879). Unfortunately, her collections were dispersed and eventually lost (M. Benson 1986).

Edwin Carter (1812–1900), "the log cabin naturalist" of Breckenridge, also developed renown for his taxidermic specimens, which shortly after his death became the founding collections of what is now the Denver Museum of Nature and Science. Although never published, Carter did maintain extensive records of observations on small slips of paper strung up around his small cabin in Breckenridge. The cabin has been restored and is now open to the public.

The 1880s and 1890s saw a new impetus for federally funded mammalian systematics and natural history, under the leadership of C. Hart Merriam. Merriam was trained as a physician but was lured from medical practice to the study of natural history by his experiences as a teenager on the Hayden Expedition to the Yellowstone region in 1871 (Sterling 1974). Merriam promoted the idea that one could judge appropriate land use from an understanding of the natural distribution of organisms, a useful lesson that still is little understood in some circles. Merriam developed the notion of life zones (which he also called "crop zones"). To extend his ideas he organized the Bureau of Biological Survey within the US Department of Agriculture to conduct field research, especially in the West. In Colorado, this effort, led by Merritt Cary, was conducted intensively from 1905 to 1909, resulting in invaluable collections for the National Museum of Natural History (Smithsonian Institution) and *A Biological Survey of Colorado* (Cary 1911), a work that still is useful to systematists and field naturalists. The Bureau of Biological Survey eventually evolved into the US Fish and Wildlife Service, which (along with the US Geological Survey) continues important mammalogical research in Colorado from offices in Fort Collins.

In the 1890s, "homegrown" natural history began to mature. E. R. Warren (1865–1942) was a mining engineer.

He was introduced to the wildlife of Colorado by observations around the mining camps in northern Gunnison County: Crested Butte, Ruby, Gothic, and Irwin. Retiring to Colorado Springs, he met W. L. Sclater, son of an officer of the London Zoological Society and son-in-law of General W. J. Palmer, railroad builder and a founder of Colorado Springs. Sclater had intended to prepare a book on Coloradan mammals but found that he had challenges enough with birds, so Warren took over the mammals, becoming the most prolific of Coloradan mammalogists, publishing 3 books (Warren 1910, 1927, 1942) and some 40 papers (see D. Armstrong 1986) on mammals. Warren's history of Coloradan mammalogy (1911) provided details on the research of several earlier workers. The revised version of his *Mammals of Colorado* appeared posthumously (in 1942), as Warren died shortly after reviewing the first proofs. His widow, Maude Baird Warren, saw the book through to completion. Warren's specimens and accompanying field notes and photographs (now in the University of Colorado Museum of Natural History) remain an invaluable research resource, the enduring legacy of a peerless field naturalist (D. Armstrong 1986).

World famous naturalists were attracted to the Coloradan fauna around the turn of the twentieth century. Theodore Roosevelt wrote popular articles on his hunts for mountain lion and bear, and Ernest Thompson Seton published articles on large mammals in *Scribner's Magazine* in 1906 and 1907. Enos Mills—the celebrated "Father of Rocky Mountain National Park"—achieved national prominence with his writing on Coloradan wildlife (E. Mills 1913, 1915, 1919, 1922). For a recent appreciation of Mills, see Drummond (1995).

ACADEMIC MAMMALOGY

Since the days of Cary, Warren, and Mills, much of the mammalogical work in Colorado has been conducted through universities and colleges. T.D.A. Cockerell, of the University of Colorado, was a wide-ranging taxonomist (see Weber 1965), studied mammals of Boulder County, and wrote generally on zoology in Colorado (T. Cockerell 1927). The late Professor Olwen Williams and a number of students conducted research on small mammals from the 1950s through the 1970s, mostly in Boulder County. W. L. Burnett, state entomologist at Colorado A&M College (now Colorado State University), was involved in mammalian pest control. However, he published numerous papers on the natural history of rodents, the eastern mole, and jackrabbits from 1913 to 1926. During the 1960s, when basic distributional inventory and taxonomic work were well under way, academic research shifted toward studies of behavior and ecology. R. M. Hansen and T. A. Vaughan both were active (along with a number of students) in the state during that decade, concentrating on pocket gophers and other rodents and on jackrabbits. R. R. Lechleitner, also of Colorado State University, focused his field efforts on the ecology of prairie dogs. His *Wild Mammals of Colorado* (1969) was a thorough and up-to-date treatment of abundance, distribution, and habits. Although not an academic institution, the Denver Museum of Nature and Science fostered early and continuing contributions, commencing with the work of F. W. Miller, J. D. Figgins, R. J. Niedrach, and their colleagues. In recent decades, professional mammalogists (including C. A. Meaney, C. A. Jones, and John Demboski) have curated the collections and used them as a basis for research.

Not only Coloradan institutions have been involved in research in the state. Significant contributions to the research literature and the specimen record have been made over several decades by faculty and students from the Universities of Kansas, Utah, and New Mexico and most recently from Fort Hays State University, Kansas, under the able direction of the late Professor Jerry R. Choate. Additional major collections of Coloradan mammals are in the American Museum of Natural History in New York City and the Carnegie Museum in Pittsburgh, as well as the National Museum of Natural History (Smithsonian Institution).

The Colorado Division of Wildlife has made important contributions not only to wildlife management but to basic mammalogy as well. Much of the earlier research was on harvested species: big game, small game, and commercial furbearers (Barrows and Holmes 1990). However, since the 1970s, there has been increasing emphasis on nongame species, stemming from statutory recognition that wildlife has value even when it is not exploited for human pleasure or profit. The diverse values that humans place on Coloradan mammals are the subject of Chapter 4.

The pattern of discovery and reporting of the fauna summarizes the history of mammalogy in Colorado. Of about 124 species of mammals native to Colorado at the time of permanent Euro-American settlement in the 1850s, some 90 percent had been reported by 1925 and 95 percent by 1955. In the past half century only about a half dozen species have been added to the state list. Beginning with the 1820s, when about 10 percent of the fauna had been reported, the decades of greatest increase in scientific knowledge of mammalian biodiversity were the 1870s (a decade when local faunal lists began to be published), the

1890s (with initiation of formal biological survey), and the 1900s (marked by intensive efforts by Merritt Cary and by E. R. Warren). Of course, some species are more difficult to document than others. On average, species of artiodactyls were first reported by 1835, lagomorphs by 1873, and carnivores by 1875. By contrast, average date of first reporting of species of rodents was about 1885, of bats about 1900, and of shrews about 1925.

We have seen that the nineteenth century was mostly an age of unregulated exploitation and extermination of native wildlife, excesses that eventually forced the development of new concepts of wildlife ethics and management. The foundations of scientific natural history emerged alongside the excesses of the frontier, however. The twentieth century was a time of deepened knowledge of Coloradan wildlife and ecosystems, a time of diversification of the values that people place on wildlife, and an era of fundamental shifts in public attitudes. Over the past several decades—especially since the National Environmental Policy Act of 1970 helped to discourage indiscriminate poisoning of mammals on public lands—the trend has been toward stewardship in an increasingly complex cultural and political environment. The complexity stems from the fact that some values of wildlife and attitudes about wildlife are in potential or actual conflict. In Chapter 4 we examine the diversity of these values and attitudes in some detail and explore some avenues for wildlife and its management in the rapidly changing human culture of Colorado in a new millennium.

4

People and Wildlife

Stewardship of Wild Mammals in Colorado

Colorado has a diverse and abundant mammalian fauna that is valued and enjoyed in numerous ways by residents and visitors alike. People are fascinated by wild mammals and find in them a range of recreational opportunities—from aesthetic and educational to consumptive. The US Fish and Wildlife Service estimated that in 2006 alone 87.5 million Americans spent $122 billion nationwide on wildlife-related recreational pursuits (US Fish and Wildlife Service and US Bureau of Census 2006). Between 1996 and 2006, the number of adults in the United States who participated in non-consumptive wildlife activities increased by 13 percent. This upward trend is expected to continue over the next several years, in large part because of a steadily increasing retired population, individuals with the leisure time to pursue their interests. By contrast, Bowker et al. (1999) predicted a nationwide decline in hunting of 11 percent over the period 1995–2050. Participation in hunting declined by 4.4 percent from 1990 to 2005 (White House Council on Environmental Quality 2008). These countervailing trends are having major impacts on Coloradan mammals and their management. Despite the reduction in the number of hunters, fees from hunting and fishing licenses and excise taxes on hunting and fishing equipment still provide about 70–85 percent of the funds for state wildlife agencies (see, e.g., Colorado Division of Wildlife 2007a).

Wild mammals enrich our lives in numerous ways, and for many of us their value increases as Earth is increasingly dominated by people. With technical developments like satellite mapping, radiotelemetry, and computer-based habitat models, the sophistication of our insights into the lives of wild mammals has increased dramatically, yet many of us still feel the same age-old wonder at the grace of a bounding deer, the stealth and strength of a mountain lion, the astonishing agility of a bat harvesting insects from the gathering darkness, or the stubborn industry of a pocket gopher or a beaver.

In Chapter 3 we emphasized how humans have interacted with the rest of the native Coloradan mammalian fauna from time immemorial. Over the past 12,000 to 15,000 years or more these interactions have changed significantly, and change has occurred at accelerating rates. We considered human-wildlife interactions in three broad historical phases: several thousand years of subsistence use by indigenous peoples; a century of largely unregulated (and increasingly efficient, hence often destructive and unsustainable) exploitation, mostly by Euro-Americans and often for commercial purposes; and a little over a century of increasingly sophisticated, scientific, and hopefully sustainable stewardship of wildlife. We now consider changes in human attitudes toward wildlife over the past few decades and the ongoing evolution of those views.

Recreational Values

All native mammals in Colorado are protected by law, as are two species introduced deliberately as game animals—the moose and the mountain goat. (Two Old World rodents, the house mouse and the Norway rat, have no protection under the law.) The management status of Coloradan mammals in indicated in Table 4-1. This classification was revised in 2008 and it is a work in progress at the Colorado Division of Wildlife. It is under continual scrutiny by the interested public, who bring their diverse wildlife values to the debate. The Colorado Wildlife Commission is responsible for making policy and the Colorado Division of Wildlife is responsible for professional administration and enforcement of those policies. For timely updates on management status of Coloradan wildlife species, the extensive website of the Colorado Division of Wildlife has current official information.

Generally, game species (Table 4-1) are those harvested for meat, fur, trophies, or simply "sport." Big game species mostly are ungulates, plus the black bear and the mountain lion. Small game mammals include a variety of lagomorphs and rodents. Pocket gophers are considered small game mammals, although few if any people pursue the animals for sport.

All Coloradan mammals have fur, of course, but under Colorado wildlife regulations, "'furbearers' means those species with fur having commercial value and which provide

TABLE 4-1. Management status of mammals in Colorado (see text for explanation of categories; for updates, see Colorado Division of Wildlife on-line; for consistency with usage elsewhere in this book, a few names have been changed from those used in CDOW publications)

	Management Designation	*Source*	*Notes*
DIDELPHIMORPHS			
Virginia Opossum (*Didelphis virginiana*)	Furbearer	CDOW 2009f	
XENARTHRANS			
Nine-banded Armadillo (*Dasypus novemcinctus*)	Non-game	CDOW 2009c	
RODENTS			
Cliff Chipmunk (*Neotamias dorsalis*)	Non-game	CDOW 2009c	
Least Chipmunk (*Neotamias minimus*)	Non-game	CDOW 2009c	
Colorado Chipmunk (*Neotamias quadrivittatus*)	Non-game	CDOW 2009c	
Uinta Chipmunk (*Neotamias umbrinus*)	Non-game	CDOW 2009c	
Yellow-bellied Marmot (*Marmota flaviventris*)	Small game	CDOW 2009f	
White-tailed Antelope Squirrel (*Ammospermophilus leucurus*)	Non-game	CDOW 2009c	
Rock Squirrel (*Otospermophilus variegatus*)	Small game	CDOW 2009f	*
Golden-mantled Ground Squirrel (*Callospermophilus lateralis*)	Non-game	CDOW 2009c	
13-lined Ground Squirrel (*Ictidomys tridecemlineatus*)	Small game	CDOW 2009f	
Spotted Ground Squirrel (*Xerospermophilus spilosoma*)	Non-game	CDOW 2009c	
Wyoming Ground Squirrel (*Urocitellus elegans*)	Small game	CDOW 2009f	* Listed as "Richardson's ground squirrel"

TABLE 4-1—*continued*

	Management Designation	*Source*	*Notes*
Gunnison's Prairie Dog (*Cynomys gunnisoni*)	Small game	CDOW 2009f	* Species not explicit
White-tailed Prairie Dog (*Cynomys leucurus*)	Small game	CDOW 2009f	* Species not explicit
Black-tailed Prairie Dog (*Cynomys ludovicianus*)	Small game	CDOW 2009f	* Species not explicit
Abert's Squirrel (*Sciurus aberti*)	Small game	CDOW 2009f	
Fox Squirrel (*Sciurus niger*)	Small game	CDOW 2009f	
Pine Squirrel, Chickaree, or Red Squirrel (*Tamiasciurus hudsonicus*)	Small game	CDOW 2009f	
Botta's Pocket Gopher (*Thomomys bottae*)	Non-game	CDOW 2009c	* Species not explicit; *T. b. rubidus* taxon of state concern (CDOW 2007g)
Northern Pocket Gopher (*Thomomys talpoides*)	Non-game	CDOW 2009c	* *T. t. macrotis* taxon of state concern (CDOW 2007g)
Plains Pocket Gopher (*Geomys bursarius*)	Small game	CDOW 2009f	* Species not explicit
Yellow-faced Pocket Gopher (*Cratogeomys castanops*)	Small game	CDOW 2009f	* Species not explicit
Olive-backed Pocket Mouse (*Perognathus fasciatus*)	Non-game	CDOW 2009c	
Plains Pocket Mouse (*Perognathus flavescens*)	Non-game	CDOW 2009c	
Silky Pocket Mouse (*Perognathus flavus*)	Non-game	CDOW 2009c	
Great Basin Pocket Mouse (*Perognathus parvus*)	Non-game	CDOW 2009c	
Hispid Pocket Mouse (*Chaetodipus hispidus*)	Non-game	CDOW 2009c	
Ord's Kangaroo Rat (*Dipodomys ordii*)	Non-game	CDOW 2009c	
Beaver (*Castor canadensis*)	Furbearer	CDOW 2009f	*
Western Harvest Mouse (*Reithrodontomys megalotis*)	Non-game	CDOW 2009c	
Plains Harvest Mouse (*Reithrodontomys montanus*)	Non-game	CDOW 2009c	
Brush Mouse (*Peromyscus boylii*)	Non-game	CDOW 2009c	
Canyon Mouse (*Peromyscus crinitus*)	Non-game	CDOW 2009c	
White-footed Mouse (*Peromyscus leucopus*)	Non-game	CDOW 2009c	
Deer Mouse (*Peromyscus maniculatus*)	Non-game	CDOW 2009c	
Northern Rock Mouse (*Peromyscus nasutus*)	Non-game	CDOW 2009c	
Piñon Mouse (*Peromyscus truei*)	Non-game	CDOW 2009c	
Northern Grasshopper Mouse (*Onychomys leucogaster*)	Non-game	CDOW 2009c	
Hispid Cotton Rat (*Sigmodon hispidus*)	Non-game	CDOW 2009c	
White-throated Woodrat (*Neotoma albigula*)	Non-game	CDOW 2009c	
Bushy-tailed Woodrat (*Neotoma cinerea*)	Non-game	CDOW 2009c	
Eastern Woodrat (*Neotoma floridana*)	Non-game	CDOW 2009c	
Desert Woodrat (*Neotoma lepida*)	Non-game	CDOW 2009c	
Mexican Woodrat (*Neotoma mexicana*)	Non-game	CDOW 2009c	
Southern Plains Woodrat (*Neotoma micropus*)	Non-game	CDOW 2009c	

continued on next page

TABLE 4-1—*continued*

	Management Designation	*Source*	*Notes*
Southern Red-backed Vole (*Myodes gapperi*)	Non-game	CDOW 2009c	
Western Heather Vole (*Phenacomys intermedius*)	Non-game	CDOW 2009c	
Long-tailed Vole (*Microtus longicaudus*)	Non-game	CDOW 2009c	
Mogollon Vole (*Microtus mogollonensis*)	Non-game	CDOW 2009c	
Montane Vole (*Microtus montanus*)	Non-game	CDOW 2009c	
Prairie Vole (*Microtus ochrogaster*)	Non-game	CDOW 2009c	
Meadow Vole (*Microtus pennsylvanicus*)	Non-game	CDOW 2009c	
Sagebrush Vole (*Lemmiscus curtatus*)	Non-game	CDOW 2009c	
Muskrat (*Ondatra zibethicus*)	Furbearer	CDOW 2009f	*
Norway Rat (*Rattus norvegicus*)	Non-native		Not protected as wildlife
House Mouse (*Mus musculus*)	Non-native		Not protected as wildlife
Meadow Jumping Mouse (*Zapus hudsonius*)	Non-game	CDOW 2009c	*Z. h. preblei* state endangered (CDOW 2007g); US threatened (USF&WS 2008b)
Western Jumping Mouse (*Zapus princeps*)	Non-game	CDOW 2009c	
Porcupine (*Erethizon dorsatum*)	Non-game	CDOW 2009c	
LAGOMORPHS			
American Pika (*Ochotona princeps*)	Non-game	CDOW 2009c	
Desert Cottontail (*Sylvilagus audubonii*)	Small game	CDOW 2009f	
Eastern Cottontail (*Sylvilagus floridanus*)	Small game	CDOW 2009f	
Mountain, or Nuttall's, Cottontail (*Sylvilagus nuttallii*)	Small game	CDOW 2009f	
Snowshoe Hare (*Lepus americanus*)	Small game	CDOW 2009f	
Black-tailed Jackrabbit (*Lepus californicus*)	Small game	CDOW 2009f	
White-tailed Jackrabbit (*Lepus townsendii*)	Small game	CDOW 2009f	
SORICOMORPHS			
Masked Shrew (*Sorex cinereus*)	Non-game	CDOW 2009c	
Pygmy Shrew (*Sorex hoyi*)	Non-game	CDOW 2009c	
Merriam's Shrew (*Sorex merriami*)	Non-game	CDOW 2009c	
Dusky or Montane Shrew (*Sorex monticolus*)	Non-game	CDOW 2009c	
Dwarf Shrew (*Sorex nanus*)	Non-game	CDOW 2009c	
Water Shrew (*Sorex palustris*)	Non-game	CDOW 2009c	
Preble's Shrew (*Sorex preblei*)			Not listed by CDOW 2009c
Elliot's Short-tailed Shrew (*Blarina hylophaga*)	Non-game	CDOW 2009c	
Least Shrew (*Cryptotis parva*)	Non-game	CDOW 2009c	
Desert Shrew (*Notiosorex crawfordi*)	Non-game	CDOW 2009c	
Eastern Mole (*Scalopus aquaticus*)	Non-game	CDOW 2009c	
BATS			
Brazilian Free-tailed Bat (*Tadarida brasiliensis*)	Non-game	CDOW 2009c	

TABLE 4-1—*continued*

	Management Designation	*Source*	*Notes*
Big Free-tailed Bat (*Nyctinomops macrotis*)	Non-game	CDOW 2009c	
California Myotis (*Myotis californicus*)	Non-game	CDOW 2009c	
Western Small-footed Myotis (*Myotis ciliolabrum*)	Non-game	CDOW 2009c	
Long-eared Myotis (*Myotis evotis*)	Non-game	CDOW 2009c	
Little Brown Myotis (*Myotis lucifugus*)	Non-game	CDOW 2009c	
Fringed Myotis (*Myotis thysanodes*)	Non-game	CDOW 2009c	
Long-legged Myotis (*Myotis volans*)	Non-game	CDOW 2009c	
Yuma Myotis (*Myotis yumanensis*)	Non-game	CDOW 2009c	
Eastern Red Bat (*Lasiurus borealis*)	Non-game	CDOW 2009c	
Hoary Bat (*Lasiurus cinereus*)	Non-game	CDOW 2009c	
Silver-haired Bat (*Lasionycteris noctivagans*)	Non-game	CDOW 2009c	
Western Pipistrelle (*Parastrellus hesperus*)	Non-game	CDOW 2009c	
Eastern Pipistrelle (*Perimyotis subflavus*)	Non-game	CDOW 2009c	
Big Brown Bat (*Eptesicus fuscus*)	Non-game	CDOW 2009c	
Spotted Bat (*Euderma maculatum*)	Non-game	CDOW 2009c	
Townsend's Big-eared Bat (*Corynorhinus townsendii*)	Non-game	CDOW 2009c	*C. t. pallescens* taxon of state concern (CDOW 2007g)
Allen's Big-eared Bat (*Idionycteris phyllotis*)	Non-game		First reported by M. Hayes et al. (2009); not yet listed by CDOW
Pallid Bat (*Antrozous pallidus*)	Non-game	CDOW 2009c	
CARNIVORES			
Coyote (*Canis latrans*)	Furbearer	CDOW 2009f	*
Gray Wolf (*Canis lupus*)	Non-game	CDOW 2009c	Colorado (CDOW 2007g) and US endangered (USF&WS 2008)
Kit Fox (*Vulpes macrotis*)	Non-game	CDOW 2009c	Colorado endangered (CDOW 2007g)
Swift Fox (*Vulpes velox*)	Non-game	CDOW 2009c	Colorado concern (CDOW 2007g)
Red Fox (*Vulpes vulpes*)	Furbearer	CDOW 2009f	*
Common Gray Fox (*Urocyon cinereoargenteus*)	Non-game	CDOW 2009c	
American Black Bear (*Ursus americanus*)	Big Game	CDOW 2009g	
Grizzly or Brown Bear (*Ursus arctos*)	Extirpated from Colorado; non-game	CDOW 2009c	Colorado endangered (CDOW 2007g); US threatened (USF&WS 2008b)
Ringtail (*Bassariscus astutus*)	Furbearer	CDOW 2009f	
Northern Raccoon (*Procyon lotor*)	Furbearer	CDOW 2009f	*
American Marten (*Martes americana*)	Furbearer	CDOW 2009f	
Ermine, or Short-tailed Weasel (*Mustela erminea*)	Furbearer	CDOW 2009f	
Long-tailed Weasel (*Mustela frenata*)	Furbearer	CDOW 2009f	
Black-footed Ferret (*Mustela nigripes*)	Non-game	CDOW 2009c	Colorado endangered (CDOW 2007g); federal endangered (USF&WS 2008b)
American Mink (*Mustela vison*)	Furbearer	CDOW 2009f	Also small game and furbearer (CDOW 2008b)

continued on next page

TABLE 4-1—*continued*

	Management Designation	*Source*	*Notes*
Wolverine (*Gulo gulo*)	Non-game	CDOW 2009c	Colorado endangered (CDOW 2007g)
American Badger (*Taxidea taxus*)	Furbearer	CDOW 2009f	*
River Otter (*Lutra canadensis*)	Non-game	CDOW 2009c	Colorado threatened (CDOW 2007g)
Mountain Lion, or Puma (*Puma concolor*)	Big Game	CDOW 2009g	
Lynx (*Lynx lynx*)	Non-game	CDOW 2009c	Colorado endangered (CDOW 2007); US threatened (USF&WS 2008b)
Bobcat (*Lynx rufus*)	Furbearer	CDOW 2009f	*
Western Spotted Skunk (*Spilogale gracilis*)	Non-game	CDOW 2009c	* Species not explicit (CDOW 2009f)
Eastern Spotted Skunk (*Spilogale putorius*)	Non-game	CDOW 2009c	* Species not explicit (CDOW 2009f)
Striped Skunk (*Mephitis mephitis*)	Furbearer	CDOW 2009f	* Species not explicit (CDOW 2009f)
White-backed Hog-nosed Skunk (*Conepatus leuconotus*)	Non-game	CDOW 2009c	* Species not explicit (CDOW 2009f)
PERISSODACTYLS			
Feral Horse—*Equus caballus*			Not managed as wildlife
ARTIODACTYLS			
Elk or Wapiti (*Cervus canadensis*)	Big Game	CDOW 2009g	
Mule Deer (*Odocoileus hemionus*)	Big Game	CDOW 2009g	
White-tailed Deer (*Odocoileus virginianus*)	Big Game	CDOW 2009g	
Moose (*Alces americanus*)	Big Game, introduced	CDOW 2009g	
Pronghorn (*Antilocapra americana*)	Big Game	CDOW 2009g	
Bison (*Bison bison*)	Extirpated		Restored as livestock; under authority of Colorado Department of Agriculture
Mountain Goat (*Oreamnos americanus*)	Big Game, introduced	CDOW 2009g	
Mountain Sheep (*Ovis canadensis*)	Big Game	CDOW 2009g	

Note: * Species may be taken without license or limit to protect private property (Colorado Division of Wildlife 2009f).

opportunities for sport harvest including mink, pine marten, badger, red fox, striped skunk, beaver, muskrat, coyote, bobcat and raccoon" (CDOW 2009c).

Non-game species (Table 4-1) are species that are not regulated as large game, small game, or furbearers (CDOW 2009c). This includes the majority of species because it includes all shrews and bats and most rodents. Non-game species cannot be harassed, killed, or taken into captivity except under a few specified circumstances, such as licensed scientific research or wildlife rehabilitation. Some take of "nuisance" non-game species is allowed by regulation: "Bats, mice except Preble's meadow jumping mouse (*Zapus hudsonius preblei*), opossums, voles, rats, and ground squirrels may be captured or killed when creating a nuisance or causing property damage" (CDOW 2009c:3).

Several mammalian species are subject to special regulations in Colorado when they present a threat to private property. "Badger, muskrat, beaver, red fox, bobcat, skunk [unspecified], coyote, raccoon, prairie dog, pocket gopher, rock squirrel and Richardson's [= Wyoming] and 13-lined ground squirrel . . . may be taken year-round as necessary to protect private property" (CDOW 2009c:23). When these animals are killed in the context of protecting private property, no license is required.

Probably the most obvious values of wildlife in Colorado are recreational, values that are both measurable and immeasurable. Many of us enjoy simply seeing native mammals. We may be amused by their antics or inspired by their strength or speed or their ability to make a living off a challenging land. To increase these opportunities, we create national parks, wilderness areas, open space, and corridors for wildlife and recreation. Tourism is a $9 billion business in Colorado (Colorado Tourism Office 2008), and about one-quarter of the state's tourist income is associated with wildlife, of which about $70 million is attributable to hunting and fishing license fees (Colorado Division of Wildlife 2007a). Pickton and Sikorowski (2004) reported that hunting and fishing provided 10.1 million activity-days in Colorado in 2002, of which more than two-thirds were by Colorado residents. Hunters and anglers spent nearly $800 million on expenses and equipment, and resident sportsmen accounted for about 58 percent of the total. Not surprisingly, nonresident hunters and anglers spent more per day ($300 vs. $35 per day) than did resident sportsmen. The Colorado Division of Wildlife (2007a) spent an additional $49 million on operations in support of hunting and fishing. Rocky Mountain National Park and the Denver Museum of Nature and Science—with its extensive and iconic wildlife dioramas—are the two most popular tourist attractions in Colorado. Rocky Mountain Arsenal National Wildlife Refuge doubtless will become a major attraction as well, as may the Rocky Flats National Wildlife Refuge, authorized in 2001 but as yet (November 2010) not open to the general public.

Many people enjoy a range of different recreational values from mammals, both consumptive and non-consumptive, and the distinction between consumptive and non-consumptive is hardly absolute. Consumptive uses remove individual organisms from the population. Hunting, trapping, catch-and-keep fishing, butterfly collecting, and berry picking all are consumptive uses of nature. Non-consumptive uses of wild species do not remove individuals from a population. Bird-watching, hiking, rafting, and wildlife photography are examples. The distinction between consumptive and non-consumptive uses raises questions of values, to which we return later in this chapter. Some non-consumptive users feel that consumptive use is inappropriate or even immoral. Others may argue that any deliberate use of wildlife—consumptive or not—is unethical (for a general review, see Mighetto 1991).

Hunting and trapping have been important activities throughout Colorado's human history (Chapter 3), providing subsistence for indigenous peoples and later encouraging Euro-American exploration and then helping to support permanent settlement. The wanton excesses of the nineteenth century began to be curbed when the State Fish Commissioner became the State Game and Fish Warden in 1891. The Colorado Department of Forest, Game and Fish was established in 1897. Laws were passed to help preserve the fledgling state's rich wildlife resources. However, enforcement was difficult initially, because of chronic understaffing and widespread ignorance of the law. The first hunting licenses were issued in 1903 and cost $1.00 for Colorado residents. Deer were the only game mammals that could be hunted legally in 1907. Eventually, Colorado developed scientific management strategies to protect and enhance the state's wildlife resources. Barrows and Holmes (1990) detailed the history of the Division of Wildlife, and a special issue of *Colorado Outdoors Magazine* (March 1997) celebrated the centenary of the division.

The Colorado Wildlife Commission was established by the legislature in 1937. Upon establishment, the Wildlife Commission took on the tasks of issuing hunting regulations and setting seasons, acquiring land, appointing the Director of the Department of Game and Fish, and establishing overall organization. By the late 1930s, game had again become abundant as a result of long-closed hunting seasons (e.g., the elk season was closed for 26 years) and better law enforcement with strict bag limits and larger fines. During the 1940s, hunting seasons expanded. Since that time, the general trend has been increased game populations and annual harvest, especially for elk and deer. It is likely that human harvest—especially modern human sport harvest, with its bias toward adults and especially trophy-sized animals—has driven a shift in selective pressures from an earlier time when non-human predators probably selected the easiest quarry: the young, the infirm, or the incapacitated. Where the phenomenon of human predation and trait evolution has been studied, differences from "natural predation" sometimes have been dramatic (Darimont et al. 2009).

In 1973, the Colorado Department of Game and Fish was renamed the Colorado Division of Wildlife, and its mission was broadened greatly, to include responsibility for management of the vast majority of native vertebrates (and also mollusks and crustaceans) that are not game animals and to focus on wildlife species as components of ecosystems. The commission is now an 11-member board appointed by the governor. There are 9 voting members and 2 nonvoting ex officio members, namely the Executive Director of the Department of Natural Resources and the State Agriculture Commissioner.

The Nongame Wildlife Program was established in 1973. Now mammals are categorized as big game, small game, furbearers, or non-game (see Table 4-1). (Note that there is some overlap between small game and furbearers in state regulations; see Colorado Division of Wildlife 2008b.) A majority of Coloradan mammals are non-game species, of course.

The Nongame Wildlife Cash Fund receives proceeds from voluntary contributions, much of which comes from a checkoff from individual state income tax refunds. This mode of voluntary funding originated with the Division of Wildlife's Nongame Advisory Council. From 1977 to 2001 the checkoff program generated some $11 million (Ragan 2002) and now generates roughly $500,000 annually. By the way, this mechanism of encouraging donations by a checkoff against state income tax refunds originated in Colorado. Today all of the 40 states with a state income tax have one or more checkoff options for taxpayers, and 90 percent of those states include wildlife (usually threatened and endangered or non-game wildlife) as a beneficiary (Keen 2008).

The Nongame Wildlife Program also is involved with Colorado's threatened and endangered species. The ongoing restoration of the river otter and lynx to Colorado are two of the more visible success stories of the Nongame Wildlife Program. Two Coloradan mammals—the gray wolf and the black-footed ferret—are listed by the US Fish and Wildlife Service (2008) as endangered under the Endangered Species Act (ESA) of 1973, and three taxa are listed as threatened: the grizzly bear (which, like the gray wolf, has no known population in Colorado at this time), the Canada lynx (which, like the black-footed ferret, is the beneficiary of an ongoing, active restoration program), and *Zapus hudsonius preblei* (Preble's meadow jumping mouse). M. Schwartz et al. (2008) provided an appraisal of the effectiveness of the ESA.

The state of Colorado also designates species as endangered, threatened, or "species of concern." Designation of the above-mentioned species generally parallels those under federal law (see Table 4-1), except the kit fox (*Vulpes macrotis*) is considered by Colorado as endangered, as are the wolverine (*Gulo gulo*) and lynx (*Lynx canadensis*). The lynx is being actively restored in the state (Colorado Division of Wildlife 2008d). There is no restoration program for wolverine at this time, but feasibility is being explored. A young male wolverine radio-collared in Grand Teton National Park, in northwestern Wyoming, was located by its radio signal in north-central Colorado in June 2009 (Colorado Division of Wildlife 2010); might the next wanderer be a pregnant female? The river otter (*Lontra canadensis*), listed as "threatened" in Colorado, also is being restored, with notable success. In addition, Coloradan populations of 5 other mammals are listed (Colorado Division of Wildlife 2007g) as being of state "concern": Townsend's big-eared bat (*Corynorhinus townsendii pallescens*), the black-tailed prairie dog (*Cynomys ludovicianus*), *Thomomys bottae rubidus* (a local endemic population of Botta's pocket gopher in the vicinity of Cañon City), *Thomomys talpoides macrotis* (a local subspecies of northern pocket gopher in northeastern Douglas County and adjacent areas), and the swift fox (*Vulpes velox*). Details on status and conservation of these taxa are included in respective accounts of species. For further information on the status of individual mammalian species worldwide, see NatureServe (http://www.natureserve.org/)—a broad-based, non-adversarial consortium of non-governmental research and conservation organizations, research institutions and researchers, and US and international governmental agencies—and the International Union for the Conservation of Nature (http://www.iucnredlist.org/), which maintains the well-known "Red List of Threatened Species." Patterns in species endangerment in the United States were reviewed by Flather et al. (1994).

Wildlife is big business in Colorado. Direct expenditures for hunting in 2002 were $338 million and total economic impact (including multiplier effects in businesses and households) was $695 million, supporting some 10,000 jobs. Total hunting days for Colorado residents were 1,475,000 and for nonresidents 618,000 (Pickton and Sikorowski 2004). The statewide impact of wildlife watching (including birding) in 2001 was estimated at $940 million (Pickton and Sikorowski 2004).

Despite its importance to the economy, hunting is declining in Colorado and nationwide. That translates into declining license revenue or increased license fees to offset the shrinking number of licensed hunters. To date the Colorado Division of Wildlife has been reasonably successful in maintaining revenues (Table 4-2), largely by recruiting nonresident elk hunters. However, recognizing that license revenues were inadequate to manage Colorado's diverse wildlife responsibly, the Colorado Wildlife Heritage Foundation (http://www.cwhf.info/) was founded in 1989 as a nonprofit, fund-raising adjunct of the Colorado Division of Wildlife. As of mid-2009, the foundation had raised more than $2 million to support wildlife conservation in Colorado (W. S. Daley, Executive Director, in litt.). Often their work is targeted at specific management or educational projects, such as the ongoing effort to restore the Canada lynx (Colorado Wildlife Heritage Foundation 2008). The foundation also supports visionary planning exercises, such as the 2008 Colorado Conservation Summit, "Colorado Wildlife at a Crossroads." For preliminary results

TABLE 4-2. Estimated number of hunters, harvest of big game mammals, and license revenues, 1995, 2000, 2005, 2006, 2007

	1995		*2000*		*2005*		*2006*		*2007*	
Species	*Hunters*	*Harvest*	*Hunters*	*Harvest*	*Hunters*	*Harvest*	*Hunters*	*Harvest*	*Hunters*	*Harvest*
Mountain Lion	905	317	1,501	315	1,617	238	2,919*	481*	1,425	295
Black Bear	8,305	553	14,207	818	9,182	450	8,023	454	8,464	615
Elk	219,852	36,171	246,778	60,120	246,521	56,462	236,518	56,933	227,262	49,012
Deer†	173,086	51,899	84,335	37,908	91,757	41,665	97,826	44,784	98,283	45,026
Moose	128	104	85	64	165	135	177	135	178	143
Pronghorn	13,690	9,538	12,057	7,564	9,314	6,229	11,445	7,300	12,647	8,492
Mountain Goat	114	94	210	192	203	174	194	147	212	174
Bighorn Sheep†	351	159	339	200	247	133	274	155	265	131
Big game licenses		441,670		395,030		390,155		386,606		382,554
Big game license $		$40,722,918		$40,318,279		$53,716,596		$56,447,022		$55,529,865
Total CDOW revenue		$54,282,366		$54,605,323		$65,291,639		$75,524,134		$75,494,528

Notes: *Mountain lion hunt in 2006 had split spring and fall hunts with roughly double the usual number of hunters; † future data-gathering will separate mule and white-tailed deer and also Rocky Mountain and desert bighorn sheep. (See species account for comment on that distinction.)
Source: Compiled by JPF using data provided by P. Lukacs and H. Turner, Colorado Division of Wildlife, personal communication.

of that conference, see http://coloradowildlife.org/news/colorado-conservation-summit-executive-summary.html.

Volunteer labor also augments the Division of Wildlife's ability to address its mission. In 2007, volunteers contributed more than 65,000 hours, the equivalent of some 31 full-time employees, with an estimated value in excess of $900,000 (Colorado Division of Wildlife 2007b).

HUNTING AND TRAPPING

Consumptive use of wildlife is critical to the stewardship of both non-game and game mammals, because the Colorado Division of Wildlife is charged by law with management of all of Colorado's wildlife species, and funding for the work that the division does on mammals is mostly from license fees and excise taxes on firearms and ammunition (so-called Pittman-Robertson dollars).

Beattie and Pierson (1977a) surveyed several hundred Colorado resident hunters who responded to a survey in *Colorado Outdoors*. Results suggested that hunter satisfaction derived from experiencing nature, escape from everyday activities, practicing and utilizing hunting skills (e.g., tracking), companionship, shooting, and harvest, in descending order of importance (Beattie and Pierson 1977b). For many people the annual hunting trip is an unparalleled recreational opportunity. Hunting may involve not only experiential values but measurable monetary values, putting food on the hunter's table (or donation to the needy) and cash in the tills of sporting goods dealers and the hospitality industry in numerous, usually rural, "gateway communities" across the state.

Comments on particular game mammals are included in accounts of species. In this chapter we consider consumptive use of Coloradan mammals in general. Sport hunting in Colorado attracts large numbers of both residents and nonresidents and is big business. In 2005, an estimated 541,962 individual mammals of more than 30 species were harvested under some 390,000 hunting licenses (Tables 4-2 and 4-3). (Harvest of prairie dogs was estimated as the mean of 5 earlier reporting years.) Steinert et al. (1994) found that harvest estimates for elk and mule deer were substantially similar whether based on check station interviews or telephone surveys; there was some error over time in reported details such as game management unit and date of kill. Rabe et al. (2002) compared methods of determining harvest across the western states. One should not overemphasize harvest estimates per se. It is clear that the outcome of the hunt is not the only criterion of the success of the hunting experience (Langenau et al. 1981; Hammitt et al. 1990). Being out-of-doors in an uncrowded environment and the hunting success of partners are often more important than individual harvest success in determining hunter satisfaction.

Nationwide, participation in hunting declined by 4.4 percent from 1990 to 2005 (White House Council on Environmental Quality 2008). From 1996 to 2006 the number of hunters in Colorado declined by 43 percent, hunter-days declined by 45 percent, and in-state expenditures declined by some 48 percent (US Fish and Wildlife Service and US Bureau of Census 2007). Factors contributing to the relative decrease in hunting in Colorado and nationally include urbanization, an increase in single-parent households, competition with myriad other recreational activities, and the development of organized anti-hunting movements. Among the responses to the decline in numbers of hunters has been an effort to encourage hunting by women and youth. From 2003 to 2007, overall sales of big game licenses declined by 1 percent, but sales to women increased 1 percent and sales to youth (ages 12–17) increased by 46 percent (Colorado Division of Wildlife 2008a). A drop in consumptive use of wildlife means a drop in the license revenue, which supports all of wildlife management, game and non-game species alike, so wildlife agencies across the country are involved in efforts to retain and recruit hunters (Responsive Management 2008).

Not only wildlife recreation is declining. There are signs of a more general decline in outdoor recreation in natural environments. Per capita visits to US national parks have declined since 1987, after a 50-year period of increasing visitation. There have been similar declines nationwide in hunting, fishing, and other nature-based activities (Pergams and Zaradic 2008). Kareiva (2008) labeled this trend "ominous" and suggested that it might have implications for support for conservation of biodiversity and natural lands (also see Zaradic et al. 2009). People tend to value what they know, and youthful experiences in natural settings are a predominant influence on individuals who appreciate and support nature for its intrinsic values. When youth lack experiences in nature—whether because of "videophilia," the narrowing of curricula in schools (teaching to the test, not to the natural world), or a lack of parental encouragement—they are less likely to value nature as adults. Louv (2005) characterized the general malady as "nature-deficit disorder."

On balance, herds of game mammals have been managed well since the turn of the twentieth century, and Colorado usually offers excellent hunting opportunities. In fact, elk populations in some areas of the state are near all-time highs, and hunting is presently an essential management tool. Overall, hunting licenses provided 78 percent of the Division of Wildlife's total revenue in 2007. An overall increase in hunting revenue to Colorado is attributable largely to nonresident elk hunters. Nonresident hunters provided about 62 percent of the division's total revenue in 2007 (H. Turner, personal communication).

Big game generates about 95 percent of the hunting license revenue (H. Turner, personal communication) and gets much of the management attention, but game mammals as defined by the Wildlife Commission also include small game and furbearers. Small game species (see Table 4-1) are smaller mammals (especially lagomorphs and rodents) that may be hunted, whereas furbearers are species whose pelts may have commercial value and provide sport harvest opportunities. Unlike big game species, most small game mammals and furbearers are not managed intensively. Some data on harvest are available from telephone surveys, however (Table 4-3). (Third-party estimates of capture of several kinds of mammals are available on-line from the Animal and Plant Health Inspection Service (http://www.aphis.usda.gov/ wildlife_damage/annual%20tables/97table11.rtf), the Colorado Trappers Association (http://www.coloradotrapper.com/), and Born Free, an anti-trapping organization (http://www.bancruel traps.com/). Landholt and Genoways (2000) provided an analysis of population trends of furbearers in Nebraska, by county, for the period 1941–1997. Unfortunately, data maintained by the Colorado Division of Wildlife appear not to allow that level of detail or precision. J. Fitzgerald (1993b) provided a thorough review of management of furbearers in Colorado with observations and recommendations on biological, economic, and sociological issues as well as organizational issues within the Division of Wildlife.

Many young hunters develop their skills on rabbits and squirrels and then turn to other game mammals as their skills and interests change. Hunters are not a homogeneous group, and those who hunt small game are the most difficult to characterize. Small game licenses permit year-round hunting opportunities. Small game licenses provide more recreation days, more animals harvested, and a wider variety of species than do big game licenses (Tables 4-2, 4-3).

Fur-trapping is the only legal consumptive use of Coloradan wildlife where the catch can be sold commercially. Annual fur harvest is highly variable, in terms of numbers of individuals of particular species taken and dollar value. Historically, beaver have been the most significant furbearers in Colorado. Beaver lured Euro-American trappers to Colorado originally, have served as a valuable fur resource, and can profoundly alter the riparian environment, even becoming a nuisance under some circumstances. Driven by unpredictable fashion, demand has been erratic. The market for beaver skins was strong in the early 1800s, the 1920s, and the 1940s. When demand for long-haired furs rises, sales of coyote pelts outnumber those of beaver (Barrows and Holmes 1990). Fur auction results for February 2009 showed 90 beaver pelts sold for an average price of $18.09 and 876 coyote pelts sold for an average of

TABLE 4-3. Colorado small game harvest by year, hunter numbers, and harvest

	1995/1996		*2000/2001*		*2001/2002*		*2002/2003*		*2003/2004*		*2004/2005*	
Species	*Hunters*	*Harvest*	*Hunters*	*Harvest*	*Hunters*	*Harvest*	*Hunters*	*Harvest*	*Hunters*	*Harvest*	*Hunters*	*Harvest*
Cottontail	16,985	76,670	9,914	46,571	10,029	45,633	9,907	39,629	9,263	52,415	10,938	58,057
Jackrabbit	3,347	11,145	1,247	2,430	1,852	7,187	1,438	4,176	1,633	5,520	2,049	6,621
Snowshoe Hare	544	1,622	405	810	733	12,980	827	768	780	1,532	750	969
Pine Squirrel	n/a	n/a	583	2,786	752	2,915	571	3,112	520	1,532	677	2,652
Fox Squirrel	n/a	n/a	567	1,555	477	807	295	768	390	1,113	329	969
Marmot	867	3,668	146	178	272	477	256	2,423	462	1,575	329	457
Prairie Dog	6,546	383,127	3,369	229,502	3,703	452,772	4,176	303,878	5,088	328,926	n/a	n/a
Ground Squirrel	n/a	n/a	97	4,276	n/a	n/a	453	34,449	390	38,990	512	32,888
Beaver	n/a	n/a	130	713	293	4033	158	1,576	303	896	91	238
Muskrat	n/a	n/a	146	405	110	1,870	98	1,300	72	87	91	439
Badger	n/a	n/a	113	65	128	697	98	158	217	159	110	110
Striped Skunk	n/a	n/a	130	437	220	1,668	217	2,482	289	896	183	274
Raccoon	621	1,355	211	373	238	3,703	335	2,777	376	2,153	183	293
Red Fox	580	875	356	340	495	1,540	473	1,517	607	997	567	457
Coyote	8,531	21,840	5,475	21,058	7,700	34,413	7,504	39,610	9,581	45,912	9,658	38,211
Bobcat*		567		461		644		766		796		1,261

Note: *Tabulated data for bobcat are for calendar years 1996, 2001, 2002, 2003, 2004, and 2005 (see text for explanation).
Source: Compiled by JPF from data furnished by Colorado Division of Wildlife, E. Gorman, personal communication.

$18.46 (http://www.coloradotrapper.com/10.htm). When demand for beaver fur (hence trapping effort) is low, populations have tended to increase, allowing the animals to become nuisances locally, plugging canals and culverts and thus flooding fields and roads. Both public and private funds have been spent on attempts to control them. Ironically, in the 1930s, ranchers bought live beavers and restored them on their lands to help steward scarce water resources, after having spent much effort on beaver control in previous years (Barrows and Holmes 1990). With increasing aridity in the West, beaver likely will once again come to be appreciated as an important natural solution to decreased late-season streamflows on Colorado's natural lands (K. Taylor 2009).

Harvest of furbearers in the United States has been a matter of contention for decades (J. Armstrong and Rossi 2000) and Colorado sometimes has been at the center of the heated controversy. Andelt et al. (1999) reviewed the debate on both its biological and human dimensions, including a thorough review of trapping methods and their efficacy. Among American trappers an important stimulus for reform stemmed from a partial ban by the European Economic Community on import of furs captured by what it considered inhumane methods. In Colorado, major players in recent decades have been the Colorado Trappers Association (founded in 1975) and Sinapu (founded in 1991). In 2008, Sinapu merged with Forest Guardians to form WildEarth Guardians, dedicated to protecting wildlands and wildlife in the interior West.

Protecting furbearers from inhumane capture was the intent of a public initiative, Amendment 14, passed in 1996 by a 52.4 percent majority and now Section 13 of Article XVIII of the Colorado Constitution. (For an excellent analysis of the motivation of activists and their successful strategies, see S. Cockerell 1999.) Amendment 14 includes the following statement: "It shall be unlawful to take wildlife with any leghold trap, any instant kill body-gripping design trap, or by poison or snare in the state of Colorado." Explicitly excepted from the amendment were "wild or domestic rodents, except for beaver or muskrat." The Division of Wildlife took that language to mean that furbearers could be trapped humanely and then killed for personal use or sale on the commercial fur market. To challenge that interpretation, Sinapu and Forest Guardians filed a lawsuit in 2006, arguing that the voters' intent in 1996 was to ban commercial and recreational trapping as well as inhumane methods of capture. That lawsuit was denied in April 2008, so legal fur harvest continues in Colorado.

Beginning in 2008, furbearers could be taken with either a furbearer or small game license. According to 2008 small game regulations, furbearers can be taken only with live traps. Once captured legally, individual furbearers may be released or killed by any legal means. Small game and furbearer hunters must register for the Harvest Information Program, a national initiative to gather data on harvest of small game mammals and migratory birds through survey of licensed hunters, the intent being to provide a basis for setting seasons and limits as necessary. For further information, consult the Colorado Division of Wildlife on-line: http://wildlife.state.co.us/Hunting/HarvestInformationProgram/. To complicate ethical and management issues further, Colorado law involves the state Department of Agriculture in management of "nuisance animals." A review of pertinent statutes is available on-line (http://www.dcsheriff.net/documents/ColoradoDivisionofWildlife.doc). For comparison of Colorado's trapping regulations with those of other states, see Batcheller at al. (2007).

The past few decades have seen major changes in recreational uses of mammals. Historically, the focus (and funding source) for the Colorado Division of Wildlife has been hunting and fishing. There is now a measurable move toward non-consumptive uses. This change is related to demographic and cultural changes in Colorado's human population, which is becoming more urbanized, less agrarian, more "white-collar," older, more broadly multicultural, and less male-dominated. An increasingly vocal constituency of wildlife enthusiasts is evolving who are non-hunters or even anti-hunters. In some cases this has led to conflict, as indicated by a debate over spring bear hunting, which resulted in a successful referendum on the general election ballot in 1992 that banned the activity, and probably contributed to expanded bear populations in various localities.

Aesthetic Values

"When the Grizzly is gone we shall have lost the most sublime specimen of wild life that exalts the western wilderness." These words by John A. McGuire, founder of *Outdoor Life* magazine, are inscribed on the famous bronze statue of a grizzly bear that graces the west entrance of the Denver Museum of Nature and Science. They express a sentiment that assigns aesthetic value to a species' mere presence. Something invaluable is lost with the extirpation of a species. There are many people who hold no hope that they will ever actually see a black-footed ferret but who still are deeply enriched by the simple knowledge that black-footed ferrets still exist, that in some places the integrity of prairie dog–dominated systems is being restored.

Other people find aesthetic value in actively seeking and seeing wildlife, perhaps in wilderness areas or in state or national parks. Even a fleeting glimpse of a large carnivore in the wild is exciting, as is the sight of a herd of elk or a band of mountain sheep. Sometimes a high point is reached by a more uncommon sighting of a common species, such as a long-tailed weasel "inchworming" through a meadow hunting voles or an American marten "hiking" from tree to tree, paralleling the trail of backpackers through the subalpine forest. Nature's beauty is an intangible but important resource for those who find comfort in the fact that Earth has wild animals in wild places, even if the animal might be as commonplace and close to home as a muskrat on a pond in a neighborhood park or a big brown bat coursing insects at twilight in our own backyard. Difficult to articulate and impossible to measure, this value reaches to the core of many of us. The aesthetic values of wildlife are expressed in graphic arts as well as in literary and scholarly writing (Mealy and Friederici 1992).

The Colorado Division of Wildlife has recognized people's desire to view wild animals. The Watchable Wildlife Program was established in 1988. The purpose of the program is to enhance people's enjoyment of wildlife by providing opportunities and tools for them to observe, photograph, and learn. The opportunities include use of developed viewing sites, such as the mountain sheep viewing station near Georgetown and sites on the Arkansas River between Salida and Cañon City. Watchable Wildlife is a broadly cooperative effort, variously involving schools, city and county governments, federal agencies, non-governmental organizations, and private landowners. The tools include interpretive signage and brochures, attractive and authoritative books (including Rennicke 1990; Shattil and Rozinsky 1990; M. Young 2000), and volunteer programs. A recent survey (US Fish and Wildlife Service and US Bureau of Census 2007) reported that 40 percent of Coloradans participated in wildlife-watching activities; the national average was 31 percent. Annual expenditures for wildlife watching in Colorado totaled nearly $33 million.

Scientific Values

Wildlife has immense scientific value. This value is complex and obviously is interrelated with other values, including aesthetic, recreational, and educational values. Scientists study the natural world for two broad reasons. Simply put, basic science asks, how do things work? Many human cultures give scientific knowledge an implicit value for its own sake. Other science is meant to be applied, asking not how the system works but how can we make the system work for human benefit? Of course, basic and applied sciences are related and they merge into each other. For example, ecologists study populations and communities of species to unravel the complex interrelationships in natural systems. This knowledge can then serve as a basis for enhancing species and their habitats. Enhanced populations have both practical and aesthetic values.

A number of features of Coloradan mammals are of scientific interest. Biological diversity is not merely an issue in tropical rainforests, it is an issue in Colorado as well. The importance of ecological diversity (the number of species in a biotic community and their relative abundances) to the stability and healthy functioning of ecosystems has become apparent in recent years. Yet there are threats to Colorado's biological heritage, both chronic and acute. For example, water is a critical resource in the West, and numerous plans to divert, pump, dam, or otherwise relocate water in Colorado may have tremendous impacts on mammalian populations. Wildlife concentrates at sources of water, and research on mammalian communities in riparian ecosystems and wetlands is critical to their survival.

Some scientific studies of wild mammals have practical value. Humans are mammals, so comparative study of non-human mammals is critical to biomedical progress. Laboratory studies of native mammals have contributed to our understanding of genetics, physiology, behavior, and disease. Studies of circadian rhythms in wild mammals have been applied to studies of human productivity and even jet lag. Knowledge of hibernation in black bears and ground squirrels may be applied to research on impacts of reduced metabolic activity in humans. From mammalian models we have learned the importance of control and predictability in our ability to cope with stress. Mammalian models have also revealed the significance of the social environment on the function of the reproductive and immune systems. The development of sonar—which has both military and medical applications—was both inspired and facilitated by studying echolocation in bats.

Coloradan mammals and wildlife biologists have teamed up to contribute much to the knowledge base of wildlife management. Specifically, much published research on such game species as mule deer, elk, and bighorn sheep has been conducted in Colorado, often involving cooperative work by the Colorado Division of Wildlife, faculty and students of Colorado State University and other educational institutions, and the US Fish and Wildlife Service.

Mammalian species may also be indicators of habitat quality. For example, the presence of the meadow jumping mouse (*Zapus hudsonius*) on the Colorado Piedmont may indicate intact stands of relict tallgrass prairie. The presence of non-native house mice (*Mus musculus*) is a sure sign of human disturbance and is strongly associated with the absence of the meadow jumping mouse (Clippinger 2002). Sagebrush voles occur mostly on well-managed sagebrush stands with an understory of grasses. American martens and southern red-backed voles are mammalian indicators of old-growth conditions in some subalpine forest types. The Colorado Division of Wildlife and the US Forest Service have cooperated on efforts to improve forest management by considering many of these indicator species and their habitat needs (Hoover and Wills 1987).

Other scientific values are less practical and more philosophical. As the natural sciences study non-human mammals, they teach us more about ourselves, perhaps allowing us to move beyond mere anthropocentrism. They provide a sense of perspective. Learning about the remarkable adaptations of non-human mammals to their environments can illuminate human physiological, ecological, and social adaptations.

Educational Values

Wild mammals offer educational benefits. Perhaps the greatest educational values of mammals are informal, in simple observations of mammals in their native haunts: hearing a beaver slap its warning at dusk with its paddle-shaped tail; watching mule deer bucks size each other up as they spar on a carpet of fresh snow; counting the trips a pika makes to collect its haypile; walking in the foothills at dawn and glimpsing a gray fox foraging for fruit in a tree; being momentarily alarmed by the snarling challenge of a badger with young in her den; watching a little brown bat flying earnest circles in the twilight sky, deviating only for the instant needed to capture an insect snack. These examples represent mammalian form and function in their natural contexts.

We also educate students and ourselves by observing and unpacking the connections in the natural world. Project WILD, one of a number of educational programs sponsored by the Colorado Division of Wildlife, reaches 12,000 teachers annually who work with some 300,000 to 400,000 students in Colorado's schools, helping to put people and wildlife in context (T. Kinion, personal communication; Colorado Division of Wildlife, personal communication). Observing wild mammals and letting them teach us, as we develop an understanding of their world, enrich all who have the humility and patience to watch and wonder.

The Colorado Division of Wildlife maintains a large and diverse website with information on regulations, licenses, and harvest and also information for schoolchildren and teachers, volunteer opportunities, and a color-illustrated series of mammalian species profiles (based in part on D. Armstrong 2006).

Wildlife habitat is often a justification for preserving open lands. The Colorado Natural Areas Program (now a part of the Division of Parks and Outdoor Recreation) was one of the first such programs in the West. Often, remnant natural areas protect not only distinctive vegetation and geology (Weston 2008) but also the wildlife species that depend on intact habitats. Designated "natural areas" are only the tip of the habitat protection "iceberg." As of 2003 some 10 percent of the area of Colorado had been dedicated to conservation (D. Armstrong 2009), of which about half is designated federal wilderness, a quarter state parks and wildlife areas, 16 percent private lands under perpetual conservation easements, 8 percent national parks, and 2 percent municipal and county open lands. This trend toward increased protection of wildlife habitat continues and in recent years has been monitored by the Colorado Conservation Trust (whose website [http://www.coloradoconservationtrust.org/] is a comprehensive source of current information). Conservation easements are a powerful means of protecting wildlife habitat on private lands. As with any other kind of easement, a conservation easement is a legally binding, mutually agreed restriction on the use of a piece of property. Like a utility or road easement, a conservation easement is a restriction on a deed. It removes some rights from the bundle of rights associated with private property. In particular, most conservation easements restrict residential or commercial building. G. Wallace et al. (2008) evaluated the value of private lands conservation.

Conservation easements are deeded to a public agency or non-governmental, nonprofit organization (some kind of land trust). The duty of the easement holder is to enforce the conditions of the deed of conservation easement. For additional information on conservation easements in general, see E. Byers and Ponte (2005) or Rissman et al. (2007). Pritchett et al. (2007) reviewed the importance of Colorado's ranchlands to conservation.

Urban Wildlife Values

In the nineteenth century, direct exploitation of particular species was the greatest human impact on wild mammals. In the twentieth century and beyond, indirect human effects on wildlife—especially habitat change—are surely much more important. Urban and suburban landscapes are the most rapidly expanding habitats in Colorado, as elsewhere in the United States (see Riebsame and Robb 1997; D. Armstrong 2009).

As Colorado's habitats and human population become increasingly urban, the ways that people interact with wildlife are changing. In 2008, for the first time in history, a majority of Earth's 6.7 billion humans lived in urban areas (Population Reference Bureau 2009). More than 80 percent of Colorado's human population lives along the Front Range corridor between Pueblo and Fort Collins (Colorado Office of Economic Development and International Trade 2007). Fortunately, in that region urban and suburban areas provide rich opportunities to see free-roaming mammals "close to home" (Rennicke 1990; Shattil and Rozinsky 1990; E. Webb 1990; E. Webb and Foster 1991). A number of Front Range cities, including Boulder and Fort Collins, and several counties and municipalities in Metropolitan Denver consider wildlife as central to planning for parks and open space.

How do non-human mammals respond to our expanding human "footprint"? Some species respond positively to habitats created by human activities, among them noxious invaders like the Norway rat and the house mouse, both of which were introduced to North America from Eurasia. But other, more benign species—such as the red fox, raccoon, fox squirrel, and striped skunk—also have become more widespread and abundant (and perhaps more detrimental) as a consequence of human activities.

Fox squirrels entered Colorado within historic times, initially along the riparian corridors of the South Platte and Republican rivers. Human activities—including deliberate introductions, the planting of deciduous trees, irrigation, and control of flooding and prairie fires—have encouraged these animals to the point that they are now abundant in areas where they did not even occur a century ago. With suburbanization of the foothills the expansion continues—subsidized by artificial feeding (which often involves pilfering from birdfeeders) and transplants by wildlife rehabilitators and others.

Striped skunks and raccoons are increasingly common in many areas. Both are species of riparian woodland on the eastern plains, and both have responded positively to human intervention in the landscape. With the development of suburbs in the foothills of the Front Range, raccoons have expanded their elevational range, taking advantage of new food resources such as domestic tree fruits, garden crops, and garbage. Red foxes also respond to expanded deciduous woodland and irrigated cropland and they are quite tolerant of human proximity and so often are observed even in urban environments.

Muskrats and beavers are also tolerant of civilization and may become nuisances. Sometimes chain-link or sheet-metal guards must be installed to protect valued trees from beavers. Mule deer have become pests to many a gardener in foothills subdivisions and even in major cities, and mountain lions, habituated to people, have wandered in to feed on the deer and an occasional domestic dog or cat. Lions that range too close to people often are captured and relocated by Colorado Division of Wildlife personnel.

Species that succeed in the urban environment often are habitat generalists whose diets are somewhat opportunistic (see C. A. Jones et al. 2003). In Colorado, these frequently are eastern species of riparian ecosystems: fox squirrel, raccoon, opossum. They have expanded in Colorado because human settlement has brought irrigation (both to croplands and to urban landscaping) and deciduous trees to the semiarid Great Plains. Thus, urban wildlife communities usually have different species composition and structure than do the native ecosystems that the city replaced.

Unintended Human Impacts on Wildlife

Many kinds of wildlife respond to indirect impacts of human recreational activity, not only motorized sports but also hiking and backpacking, climbing, and other seemingly benign activities; see R. Knight and Gutzwiller (1995) for a thorough review. Among unintended human impacts on native wildlife are harassment and predation by "subsidized predators," especially domestic cats and dogs. Although cats appear to be particularly important to populations of birds (Coleman and Temple 1993), they also influence populations of small mammals. Studies on City of Boulder Open Space found that native rodents were more abundant in the interior of patches of grassland (prairie voles in tallgrass meadows and hayfields, deer mice and hispid pocket mice in mixed grasslands) than on edges. Subsidized predators were suspected of contributing to this pattern (Bock et al. 2002). Domestic dogs (*Canis familiaris*) take a toll on small mammals but may be particularly detrimental to the welfare of larger mammals.

Dynamics of interaction between dogs and wildlife may be direct or subtle. Much of our knowledge of these interactions is based on work on the extensive public open space managed by the City of Boulder and Boulder County. In brief, dogs matter. On leash or off, dogs influence the behavior and distribution of native mammals. The activity of mule deer (*Odocoileus hemionus*) and rabbits (*Sylvilagus* sp.) decreased significantly where dogs were allowed on trails off leash (under "voice and sight control") and densities of black-tailed prairie dogs (*Cynomys ludovicianus*) were lower within 25 m of trails where dogs were allowed (see Lenth et al. 2008 for review of the literature). However, Bekoff and Meaney (1997) concluded that dogs off leash but under owners' control rarely chased wildlife on open lands in and near Boulder.

Some pets actually become feral—living in the wild without direct subsidy from humans. Many pets continue to be maintained by their owners but range into natural environments occasionally to harass or prey on native species. The degree to which this occurs in Colorado has not been surveyed systematically or quantified. It is important to note that, in Colorado, domestic dogs—feral or not—can be killed if they are harassing wildlife (Colorado Revised Statues, Title 33, Article 3-106, revised May 2003); domestic cats are not mentioned in that context. County and municipal laws and regulations sometimes are pertinent to management of pets at large.

Residents' attitudes about impacts of their free-ranging pets (especially cats) have been studied in Wisconsin (see Coleman and Temple 1993). Because of differences in patterns of landownership and productivity and perhaps other factors, the situation in Colorado may be quite different and deserves explicit attention. A comprehensive review of cat predation spanning 4 continents and 50 years indicated that small mammals represented about 70 percent of cats' prey (B. Fitzgerald and Turner 1988). Of course, some unknown number of those prey animals are introduced mice or rats living as "commensals" in the vicinity of human habitation and agricultural operations, but the remainder are native small mammals (shrews, rodents, and sometimes bats). Cats are known to compete with native predators under some circumstances, and cats' predilection for hunting is not suppressed even when they are well fed by humans (for review, see Coleman et al. 1997).

Wildlife and Public Health

Wild mammals of Colorado host a variety of endo- or ectoparasites and they may be infected with pathogenic organisms capable of infecting humans or our pets and livestock. E. Thorne et al. (1982) provided an excellent survey of more than 50 important diseases of wild mammals in Wyoming, and their insights are generally relevant in Colorado. Endoparasites include a variety of roundworms, flatworms, and protists, many of which have complicated life cycles that involve more than one host species (W. Samuel et al. 2001); for a thorough overview of wildlife diseases, see E. Williams and Barker (2001). Accidental infection of humans or domestic mammals can occur from eating raw or improperly cooked meat, handling and cleaning wild game, feeding on contaminated vegetation, or drinking from contaminated waters, leading to infection with tapeworm or hookworm, lungworm, or giardia. Depending on the severity of infection, many of these organisms can affect the general health and condition of the host and in severe instances can cause death. Ectoparasites include fleas, ticks, lice, mites, and true bugs (Hemiptera). Such animals can cause skin irritation and general discomfort or may transmit microbial diseases such as plague, tularemia, tick fever, Lyme disease, or spotted fever.

Zoonotic diseases are wildlife diseases transmissible to humans. The August 1995 issue of *Journal of Mammalogy* included a special section on zoonoses (Childs 1995). Because many people in Colorado engage in outdoor activities that place them close to wild animals and their diseases, a number of zoonoses are of importance to human health. There appears to have been an increase in numbers and severity of zoonotic diseases in recent decades (McLean 2008). Table 4-4 compares a few important zoonotic diseases. Rabies, plague, and hantavirus are of particular importance because they are life-threatening.

RABIES

Rabies is a virus (associated mostly with bats and carnivores) transmitted through the saliva of infected mammals. Infection typically occurs as saliva passes into a bite wound. Although human exposure usually is caused by the bite of a carnivore or bat, rabies can infect and kill any mammalian species, and animals ranging from squirrels to elephants are known to have passed the disease. Any person whose skin is broken by the bite of a wild or domestic mammal whose history is unknown should consult a physician as soon as possible. Individuals who routinely work with wild mammals should consider preventive vaccination.

The incubation period for rabies is highly variable, but in most species symptoms usually show within 2 to 8 weeks. (Dogs that bite people usually are quarantined for 10 days.) Once symptoms manifest themselves the disease is untreatable and death invariably results. At present, the only way to determine the presence of infection is to kill the animal and inspect brain tissue for the virus.

Biologists have identified a number of strains of the rabies virus that are host-specific (and especially virulent) for particular terrestrial mammals such as skunks, raccoons, and foxes (MacInnes 1987). Other strains are found in bats. Most regular and recurring epizootics (an outbreak in a population of wild animals) of rabies in terrestrial carnivores occur east of the 105th meridian (roughly the alignment of Interstate Highway 25), so a major part of Colorado lies just west of such outbreaks, and rabies in wild carnivores in the state is episodic and rare. By contrast with rabies in carnivores, most reports of rabies in bats are from the West (MacInnes 1987). North America seems to have the world's highest incidence of bat rabies.

The Colorado Department of Public Health and Environment (http://www.cdphe.state.co.usdc/zoonosis/rabies/Comp-08.pdf) reported an average of about 51 records of rabies-positive mammals per year from 1998 to 2007. Nearly 99 percent of those records were bats, with 60 percent of the observations being from just 4 counties along the Front Range urban corridor: Larimer, Boulder, Weld, and El Paso, in descending order of occurrence. Other than bats, the most recent records of rabies-positive individuals in Colorado are human, in 1931; domestic cat, 1985; raccoon, 1993; bobcat, 2002; domestic dog, 2003; fox (unspecified) and domestic cow, 2005; and skunk (species unspecified) and coyote, 2007.

It is very difficult to determine the incidence of infection of rabies (and most other wildlife diseases) in wild populations because diseases can spread rapidly, infected individuals may be difficult to observe, and it would be prohibitively expensive to maintain monitoring systems. Therefore, data on infection rates should be viewed with caution unless they are specific to a given area and have been

TABLE 4-4. Important microbial diseases of wild mammals in Colorado

Disease	*Typical Hosts*	*Transmission*	*Host Mortality*
PRION DISEASES			
Chronic wasting disease (CWD)	Cervids: deer, elk, moose	Contact via saliva, blood	Medium to high
VIRAL DISEASES			
Contagious ecthyma	Bighorn sheep, mountain goat	Direct contact	Low
Blue tongue	Elk, deer, pronghorn, bighorn sheep	Gnats	May be high
Canine distemper	Canids, mustelids, raccoon	Direct contact	May be high
Parvoviruses	Most canids, felids	Low	
Rabies*	All mammals, especially carnivores and bats	Bites, rarely via aerosol	High
BACTERIAL DISEASES			
Brucellosis	Elk, moose, bison, cattle	Ingestion of contaminated vegetation	Low
Leptospirosis*	Rodents, carnivores, ungulates	Ingestion of water or soil contaminated by urine of infected animals	Low
Tularemia*	Lagomorphs and rodents	Ticks; blood-blood contact; eating infected meat	High
Plague*	Rodents	Fleas	High
Pasteurellosis	Most ruminants, especially bighorn sheep and pronghorn	Droplet infection; ingestion	High
Hantavirus pulmonary syndrome, Sin Nombre virus*	Rodents, especially deer mice	Infected rodent feces and urine	High

Note: * Zoonotic disease; known to be transmissible from wild mammals to humans.
Source: Updated from E. Thorne et al. (1982).

obtained over long periods. However, it has been estimated that infection rates in wild bat populations are less than 0.1 percent, and less than 1 percent of these infected bats ever attack another animal. Most simply become paralyzed and die. Sick or injured bats are often obvious in their behavior and frequently are taken to the Colorado Department of Health and Environment for testing. A relatively high number of these test positive for rabies. Of course, this is a highly biased sample of the whole population.

Although rabies is uncommon, care should always be taken with a bat or other wild mammal that appears to be unhealthy or acts abnormally. By the way, canine distemper, a disease that does not infect humans, is not uncommon in raccoons and wild canids and mustelids in Colorado. Symptoms are almost identical to those of rabies, including apparent disorientation, lack of fear, and extreme aggressiveness. J. W. Krebs et al. (1995) summarized the biology of rabies, with special emphasis on issues important to mammalogists. For information on rabies, websites of the Colorado Department of Health and Environment, Bat Conservation International, and the Colorado Bat Society are updated frequently and so are recommended.

PLAGUE

Known as the "Black Death" in the Middle Ages, plague is caused by a bacterium (*Yersinia pestis*). The bacterium lives in the gut of a flea (the intermediate host), where it reproduces. The pathogen is then regurgitated into the saliva and enters the definitive host—a mammal—when the flea takes a blood meal. This leads to infection. The disease can also be transmitted by eating or handling infected carcasses if cuts or abrasions allow entry to the bloodstream. Because of the potential for human cases to become pneumonic (transmissible by aerosol), the disease is monitored closely by the US Public Health Service and is subject to quarantine. If misdiagnosed (initial symptoms are much like those of flu) and left untreated, the disease typically is fatal. From

1925 to 1964, plague cases in the western United States averaged two per year, most of them in California. Since then the annual number of cases in humans has increased steadily (averaging 16 per year since 1975), with the greatest number of reports from New Mexico (Barnes 1993). Plague may produce infections in cottontails or even carnivores and human infection occurs as hunters or trappers skin infected animals. Dogs and cats are sometimes implicated in human cases of the disease, especially in the Southwest.

Plague has been known in North America since 1900, probably introduced to West Coast ports on commensal rodents and then spreading over most of the western United States by 1960 (Eisen et al. 2007). For a review of the ecology of plague, see Gage et al. (1995). Plague was first documented in Colorado in 1941 (Ecke and Johnson 1952). By contrast with carnivore rabies, plague is a western disease not maintained in the wild much east of the 101st meridian—about the longitude of North Platte, Nebraska, and Garden City, Kansas. In Colorado, plague is most often associated with prairie dogs in the public mind, because nearly every summer the news media report dramatic die-offs (mortality often is close to 100 percent) of these rodents from the disease. Only about 3 percent of human plague cases are attributable to contact with prairie dogs, however (Barnes 1993). Practically any rodent in the state, from grasshopper mice and voles to woodrats, tree squirrels, chipmunks, and ground squirrels, can harbor infected fleas, although such populations usually do not exhibit major die-offs. In our area, the mammal most often implicated with transmission of sylvatic plague to humans is the rock squirrel, which may occur close to homes and whose fleas readily bite humans and their pets. Use of insecticidal powder at burrows or bait stations is an effective control.

As a bacterial disease, plague in humans is readily treatable with antibiotics if detected early in its course. Of 49 cases of plague in humans reported from 1975 to 2005, 7 were fatal, which averages about 0.23 fatalities per year (http://www.cdphe.state.co.us/dc/zoonosis/plague/plague_human_05.pdf); that is only about one-seventh the human mortality attributed to hantavirus pulmonary syndrome. For convenient review of plague in Colorado see Cranshaw and Wilson (2004). Salkeld and Stapp (2006) reviewed the possible importance of carnivores in moving rodent fleas (and hence the plague bacillus) through biotic communities. They found plague antibodies most prevalent in mustelids; intermediate in bears, cats, and canids; and lowest in raccoons; and they observed that this might reflect differences in exposure rates because of different dietary habits, active predators being more likely than scavengers to come in contact with plague bacilli. For further details on plague in Colorado, see accounts of species of *Cynomys* in Chapter 8, in particular the account for the black-tailed prairie dog, *C. ludovicianus*.

TULAREMIA

Also known as "rabbit fever," tularemia is caused by a bacterium (*Francisella tularensis*) that produces chills or fever in infected humans. In the wild, the pathogen is associated with a wide range of mammals, from lagomorphs (especially cottontails), muskrat, and beaver to ground squirrels and mice. Two major strains exist. Type A tularemia is associated with terrestrial rodents and rabbits and causes most human infection. Type B tularemia is associated with wetlands and aquatic environments and is carried by water or aquatic rodents. Tularemia is usually contracted by people skinning infected rabbits or beaver, but it also can be contracted by eating undercooked rabbit meat, drinking contaminated water, or inhaling contaminated dust. Flies and ticks also carry and transmit the disease. Reported human cases in Colorado are rather few, ranging from 0 to 19 per year from 1975 to 2006, with an average of 4.8 annually (http://www.cdphe.state.co.us/dc/zoonosis/tularemia /Colorado_tularemia.pdf). Treatment with a broad-spectrum antibiotic is effective if the disease is detected early in its course (Gage et al. 1995). Addison et al. (1987) and E. Thorne et al. (1982) provided useful summaries of the biology of tularemia.

OTHER TICK-BORNE DISEASES

During spring and summer, people active outdoors may be exposed to three different tick-borne diseases in addition to tularemia: Colorado tick fever (caused by a virus; G. Bowen et al. 1981), Rocky Mountain spotted fever (caused by a rickettsia, *Rickettsia rickettsii*), and perhaps Lyme disease (caused by a spirochete bacterium, *Borellia burgdorferi*). All three diseases are transmitted by tick bites and the respective species of ticks require small to medium-sized mammals to complete their life cycles. The diseases appear similar in humans, including cold or flu-like symptoms, chills, fever, and headache. Although recovery may take time, these diseases usually are not fatal. Although first described from our region, Rocky Mountain spotted fever actually is much more prevalent in the Southeast. Lyme disease is rather common in the Northeast (associated with ticks of white-tailed deer and white-footed mice), and no cases are known to have originated in Colorado (Cranshaw and Peairs 2000). According to the American Lyme Disease

Foundation (http://www.aldf.com/), the disease is known from eastern Kansas and Oklahoma, however, and also the West Desert of Utah, so there is every reason to believe it eventually will be detected in Colorado.

The spirochaete that causes Lyme disease has been found in Mexican woodrats (*Neotoma mexicana*)—and in the ticks (*Ixodes spinipalpis*) that feed on the woodrats—from three sites in Larimer County: the CSU Foothills Campus (west of Fort Collins), Carter Lake (west of Berthoud), and Owl Canyon (near Livermore) (Maupin et al. 1994). The ticks involved are restricted to woodrat dens and so are not likely to contact people. The tick is widespread in the West but seldom reported from people. *B. burgdorferi* is not known to be carried by the common Coloradan "wood tick," *Dermacentor andersoni*.

Some Coloradan squirrels (the least chipmunk and the golden-mantled ground squirrel) also have tested positive for the rickettsial agent of human granulocytic ehrlichiosis (DeNatale et al. 2002). Prairie voles from the vicinity of Fort Collins have been found to carry the protist *Babesia microti* (more recently assigned to the genus *Theilaria*), the causative agent of a malaria-like disease (Burkot et al. 2000). We caution that this focus on zoonotic diseases in north-central Colorado should merely alert field naturalists, not frighten them. It seems likely that these emerging diseases are quite widespread and occur where one looks for them. It just happens that one of the major research laboratories in the world for research on such diseases—the National Center for Zoonotic, Vector-Borne, and Enteric Diseases—is located on the Foothills Campus of Colorado State University in Fort Collins.

HANTAVIRUS

Hantavirus pulmonary syndrome is an emerging disease, apparently moving from reservoirs in the wild to people (see Childs et al. 1994 and McLean 2008 for general reviews). In the United States it was first recognized in the spring of 1993 in the Four Corners region (where Colorado, Utah, Arizona, and New Mexico meet), especially in the Navajo Nation (Stone 1993; Hughes et al. 1993). The causative agent eventually was identified as Sin Nombre virus, one of several hantaviruses. This is a disease most often associated with rodents, deer mice (*Peromyscus maniculatus*) in particular. It has been contracted most frequently by people working in areas where rodent feces and urine have accumulated, such as mouse-infested buildings and woodrat dens. From 1993 to 2008, 25 deaths in Colorado were attributed to hantavirus pulmonary syndrome, about 1.6 fatalities per year on average (http://www.cdphe.state.co.us/dc/zoonosis/hanta/Hanta_stats.pdf), about 7 times more frequent than deaths from plague. Details of disease prevention were reviewed by Mills et al. (1995) and are presented in the ordinal account of rodents (Chapter 8) and the account of the deer mouse, *Peromyscus maniculatus*.

The study and treatment of zoonotic disease is a dynamic field, so the Internet is often the best source of current information. Interested readers should consult the Colorado Department of Health and Environment on-line: http://www.cdphe.state.co.us/dc/zoonosis/index.html. That site has links to the Centers for Disease Control and Prevention of the US Department of Health and Human Services. Chronic wasting disease (CWD) of deer and elk is not yet known in humans, so is not presently considered a zoonotic disease. Information on CWD is presented in the accounts of affected game mammals: elk and deer (Chapter 14).

Problem Mammals

Mammals have impacts on people's livelihood and property in a number of different ways. Skunks, raccoons, and beaver can be annoyances or problems in urban neighborhoods; rodents, lagomorphs, and native ungulates feed on field crops and tame pastures; and predators sometimes harass or kill livestock. Nearly $17 million in damage by prairie dogs, pocket gophers, and ground squirrels was reported in Colorado for 1989 (Colorado Department of Agriculture 1990); no surveys of this kind have been conducted since 1990 (M. Threlkeld, Colorado Department of Agriculture, personal communication, 2009). Over two decades, 1987 to 2007, claims paid by the Colorado Division of Wildlife for damage by deer, elk, pronghorn, bear, and mountain lion ranged from a low of less than $200,000 in 1987 to a high of nearly $900,000 in 2001. In 15 of 20 years, claims were more than $500,000 (Colorado Division of Wildlife 2008g). Much of Colorado's human population lives in the Front Range urban corridor and may be largely unaware of these problems, but some ranchers and farmers face them on a daily basis, sometimes feeling direct and significant financial impact, and so have legitimate concerns. K. Wagner et al. (1997) surveyed compensation programs for wildlife damage in North America. Nineteen states and 7 Canadian provinces have compensation programs for wildlife damage to standing crops and stored forage and/or predation on domestic livestock. Thirty-four states and 7 provinces provide damage-prevention materials (fencing and the like). Inadequate data are a chronic challenge in understanding the costs of wildlife to people in the United States (Conover et al. 1995). Available data tend to be restricted to one or a few species or particular kinds of damage (e.g., predation on sheep) and are local or regional in scope.

Prairie dogs, pocket gophers, ground squirrels, and beavers are frequent subjects of damage complaints. On Colorado's rangelands, ranchers often feel the greatest impact from prairie dogs. Their concerns are that prairie dogs compete with cattle for forage and alter plant species composition, generally causing deterioration of rangeland, which translates to more acres of range needed per head of livestock. Many people believe that horses and cattle can be injured by stepping into prairie dog burrows (although, to our knowledge, an instance of such injury never has been formally documented), and burrows can divert increasingly scarce and valuable irrigation water. Some people are concerned about plague in prairie dog populations. At airports, prairie dogs may even violate federal regulations, which prohibit holes greater than two inches in diameter near runways! Hundreds of thousands of acres of private land in Colorado are inhabited by prairie dogs. Affected landowners sometimes feel that they are carrying the public burden of hosting prairie dogs and are frustrated by the cost of control. Reduced funds for rodent control from the Colorado Department of Agriculture and increasing emphasis on education have reduced control efforts in recent years.

Pocket gophers may damage rangeland as plants are killed in the vicinity of tunnels and species composition is altered as new seedbeds are formed by their diggings. They may disturb stands of alfalfa and other crops. Gopher mounds can even damage farm machinery, dulling or breaking sickle knives, for example. Pocket gophers also chew on underground cables and irrigation pipes, and irrigation water is lost to their burrow systems. In various parts of the state, 13-lined and Wyoming ground squirrels, rock squirrels, and marmots compete with livestock for forage, destroy food crops, invade pastures and hayfields, and eat newly planted seeds and seedlings. Methods for controlling pocket gophers and ground squirrels include mechanical traps as well as burrow fumigants and other poisons (Andelt and Case 1995).

Beavers can be a nuisance in both rural and urban environments by felling desirable trees, building dams in irrigation ditches or culverts, burrowing into ditch banks, and flooding hay meadows. Urban examples include Confluence Park along the South Platte River in Denver, where trees have metal guards to protect them from beavers. An unusual problem occurred in the 1930s when beavers dammed tunnels two miles underground at the Bonanza gold and silver mine in Saguache County (Barrows and Holmes 1990).

The establishment of commercial cattle and sheep operations in the western United States in the nineteenth century helped to create today's predator and rodent control problems. Young livestock provide an attractive food source for some predators. In Colorado, bounties were first set on wolves and coyotes in 1876 (Barrows and Holmes 1990). Subsequently, wolves were extirpated from Colorado and much of the West and, perhaps as a consequence, coyotes expanded in number and geographic range. Coyotes cause the heaviest damage losses to sheep and, to a much lesser extent, to calves. A number of nonlethal methods for coyote control are being developed and implemented to varying degrees. Black bears occasionally prey on livestock but probably do more damage by raiding apiaries and orchards. Each situation is unique, and relief from predation may require experimenting with different combinations of techniques (Andelt 1987).

Raccoons and striped skunks can be a nuisance around homes and sometimes prey on poultry. Skunks get under homes and outbuildings, causing legitimate concern (olfactory if not safety) to homeowners. Raccoons may climb into chimneys, enter houses and yards, and topple garbage cans in search of food. Especially bold raccoons have been observed to remove used charcoal from a patio grill and rinse it in a nearby wading pool before licking it for tasty barbecue drippings.

Deer and elk feed on irrigated hay meadows and alfalfa, especially in spring. In severe winters, they may exploit haystacks that are not protected by fencing. In particularly severe winters, public sentiment may even motivate the Division of Wildlife to supply alfalfa and deer pellets to avoid massive winter kill. This winter feeding activity is contentious; some view it as a short-term solution. When die-offs are a function of insufficient winter range, supplemental feeding may only exacerbate problems (Gill and Carpenter 1985).

A few other species deserve mention for the problems they may cause. Kangaroo rats have become a concern recently as large tracts of sandy soils (their preferred habitat) have been developed for sprinkler-irrigated corn and alfalfa production. The rats feed on newly planted seeds and emerging seedlings. Hispid cotton rats feed on crops, especially melons and sugar beets. These animals apparently have expanded their range in southeastern Colorado because of irrigation and climatic warming. Exotic house mice and Norway rats contaminate food and carry disease.

Although house mice may not consume large quantities of food, they do chew through packaging and foul the contents with their feces and urine. Rats can substantially impact stores of livestock feed and are common residents of feedlots. Voles and porcupines damage orchards, landscape plantings, and forests by girdling seedlings, branches, and ornamentals, especially in fall and winter.

A cooperative approach has been taken by the various agencies charged with handling these problems. Generally, the State Department of Agriculture advises on rodent problems and oversees a cooperative agreement for predator control by the Animal Damage Control Unit of the Animal and Plant Health Inspection Service (APHIS) of the US Department of Agriculture. The Cooperative Extension Service, a branch of Colorado State University in Fort Collins, has county extension agents statewide who provide information to the public on nuisance mammals and develop outreach programs, educational materials, and programs for landowners. The Colorado Division of Wildlife responds to big-game problems and damage claims. Lashnits (2008) described the Habitat Partnership Program, in which landowners and the Division of Wildlife cooperate to prevent or reduce wildlife damage through a wide variety of means, including fencing, water development, and habitat improvement.

Colorado is fortunate to be the location of several federal wildlife research agencies. The National Ecology Research Center in Fort Collins, a unit of the US Geological Survey, is involved in studies of ecosystems and regional landscapes, including long-term studies of grassland mammals. The National Wildlife Research Center in Fort Collins, a unit of the Animal and Plant Health Inspection Service of the US Department of Agriculture, is actively involved in research on new and progressive ways to handle animal damage problems. The wide range of ongoing projects includes developing protective collars for livestock, intended to impact only offending coyotes, and research on appropriate diameter and hardness of utility cables to resist rodent chewing. These efforts are important to the native fauna because effective solutions to nuisance and damage problems enhance positive public regard for wildlife.

Futures of Wildlife Management: The Human Dimension

Management of wildlife resources has changed over the years. As we have noted, the nineteenth century was an era of exploitation with decades of active and uncontrolled harvest. The early twentieth century ushered in intensive management of selected game species, sometimes with successful results. A generation ago, influential wildlife manager R. H. Giles Jr. characterized wildlife management as "the science and art of making decisions and taking actions to manipulate the structure, dynamics, and relations of wild animal populations, habitat, and man to achieve specific human benefits" (Beattie and Pierson 1977a). Biological (and sometimes political) factors influenced management schemes, and often results could be measured with plain economics. Dollars spent by hunters (directly or indirectly) were the measure of the value of the resource.

With the passage of time, increased knowledge and ongoing cultural changes have made this an oversimplification, however. People appreciate wildlife well beyond hunting. No fee is levied for non-consumptive use. It is difficult to compile data on the value per "head" of golden-mantled ground squirrels seen and appreciated. Both game and nongame mammals have significant value that can be measured only indirectly, such as by the flow of tourist dollars.

The urbanization (and perhaps the relative feminization) of our society has had a major impact on the way wildlife is viewed and valued by the public and is beginning to influence approaches to resource management. Most Americans value wildlife for one reason or another. However, only about 5 percent of Americans hunt (US Fish and Wildlife Service 2006). About 9 out of 10 hunters are men and only 1 percent of American women hunt (US Fish and Wildlife Service 2006). Thus, most people value wildlife in a non-hunting context and increasingly their voices are being heard in the political arena. Urbanites, who often have grown up with little contact with wild animals, hold different views and values of wildlife and hunting than do people from rural backgrounds. Furthermore, interest in wildlife has broadened in recent years. We no longer have a homogeneous view of the non-human animals among whom we live, and our differing views sometimes are in conflict.

A growing body of knowledge has developed on the human dimensions of wildlife management. Theory has often developed in universities, whereas applications research generally has been carried out by wildlife agencies, which increasingly recognize the "people factor" in management decisions. This approach links wildlife management with the social sciences to meet societal needs (Decker 1989). Examples of the human dimension in wildlife management are hunter and non-hunter attitudes toward particular programs, public preferences for methods and extent of game and non-game management, and farmers' and ranchers' attitudes toward damage by wildlife to crops and livestock. Gibbons (1988) argued for improving the management of non-game species, including improvements in public perception of this important component of biotic communities. The importance of the human factor in wildlife management is underscored by the selection by the Wildlife Society of *Wildlife and Society: The Science of Human Dimensions* (Manfredo et al. 2009) for the 2009 Wildlife Publication Award for outstanding edited book.

How we manage wildlife is largely a function of how, and to what extent, we value it. Research on human dimensions is a maturing field of growing importance. Humans have interacted with wildlife in various ways since the dawn of our species. Clearly "human dimensions" in wildlife management are nothing new; what is new is a scientific approach to due consideration of the human dimensions. Gray (1993) provided a general review of wildlife-human interactions in prehistoric times, including the likely role of humans in extinction of Late Pleistocene megafauna.

Traditionally, wildlife management was simply applied wildlife biology, but the field is now integrating studies of dynamic wildlife populations and their changing habitats with relevant studies of human behavior—the human dimensions of wildlife management (Bath 1998). This is a burgeoning, interdisciplinary field, reflecting and responding to societal changes and concerns, including changes in human valuing of wildlife and its environments and a growing recognition of "nature deficit" in children (Louv 2005). Aldo Leopold, iconic founder of scientific wildlife management and pioneer environmentalist, foresaw the importance of human dimensions in wildlife management: "The public problem will not be so much to conserve deer; but to so regulate the crowd as to keep deer hunting safe and enjoyable" (Flader 1974:126).

The value that we place on mammals is a function of our knowledge, attitudes, and perceptions about them. Once the manager's view of the public was simple: there were hunters and non-hunters. Over the past few decades, a body of knowledge has developed on the diverse values that people place on wildlife and the relationship of human behavior to these values (Decker and Goff 1987). In early studies, Kellert (1977, 1980) outlined a number of basic human attitudes toward animals. People exhibiting a *naturalistic* attitude have an interest in and affection for wildlife and the outdoors. The *ecologistic* attitude has primary concern for the environment as a system, for interrelationships between wildlife species and their natural habitats. A *humanistic* attitude expresses a primary interest in and strong affection for individual animals, especially pets. People with a *moralistic* attitude show primary concern for right and wrong treatment of animals and strong opposition to exploitation of and cruelty toward animals. The *scientistic* attitude has its primary interest in understanding the physical attributes and biological functioning of animals. People with a predominantly *aesthetic* attitude place their primary interest in the artistic and symbolic characteristics of animals. Those with a *utilitarian* attitude focus concern on the practical and material value of animals. A *dominionistic* attitude derives primary satisfaction from mastery and control over animals, typically in sporting situations. People with *negativistic* attitudes toward wildlife actively avoid animals because of dislike or even fear. Finally, those with a *neutralistic* attitude exhibit passive avoidance of animals, indifference, and a general lack of interest. Obviously, there is a possibility for conflict among people with these different attitudes, some of them diametrically opposed. Although few people would hold one or another of these attitudes exclusively, a focus on primary attitudes reveals interesting and important trends.

Through personal interviews with more than 3,000 randomly selected persons, Kellert (1980) found that the most common attitudes toward animals in the United States were humanistic, moralistic, utilitarian, and negativistic. The humanistic attitude characterizes some members of animal welfare organizations, which often work against activities that cause animals to suffer or die. The moralistic attitude is consistent with the beliefs of some animal rights advocates, who sometimes oppose any and all exploitative uses of animals. The utilitarian attitude, by contrast, embraces hunting as a valuable and positive (or even necessary) use of animals. The clash between these attitudes is a cause of much controversy. Overall, gender emerges as the most significant factor affecting attitudes toward animals (Kellert and Berry 1987). Addressing these different views and attitudes can lead to strategies for education and management as we attempt to ensure that wild mammals remain an integral component of Colorado's living landscape. Manfredo et al. (2003) found that increasing affluence, education, mobility, and urbanization influence value orientation toward wildlife, predicting a move from utilitarian to protectionist values. Duda, Bissell, and Young (1998) and Duda, Jones, and Criscione (2010) provided thorough, authoritative reviews of public perceptions, opinions, and attitudes toward wildlife in the context of responsive wildlife management. S. J. Riley et al. (2002, 2003) recommended integration of human dimensions and ecological insights in a process of adaptive management, to include situational analysis, systems models, identification and evaluation of management alternatives, actual management interventions, monitoring of intermediate outcomes, and then refinement of models and interventions. Jacobson and McDuff (1998) urged extension of human dimensions research beyond wildlife management to encompass conservation biology more generally.

Human dimensions research concerns human behavior (attitudes and actions) relative to wildlife but also can be broadened to consider the behavior of individual animals and wildlife populations in response to humans (Whittaker and Knight 1998). Although it is far too simple for actual prediction, the concept of carrying capacity traditionally has been an important tool for understanding the biological relationship between wildlife populations and habitats in ecological and management contexts. To expand beyond this, Decker and Purdy (1988:53) developed a new concept to account for the relationship between human beliefs and preferences and decisions of wildlife management. Wildlife acceptance capacity (WAC) is the "maximum wildlife population level in an area that is acceptable to people." The index recognizes the importance of public opinion. It incorporates numerous negative elements, such as tolerable amounts of damage and nuisance, competition with other species, and disease transmission, and weighs them against the aesthetic, educational, ecological, and scientific value of the species in question. Obviously, WAC is dynamic and will differ geographically over time among various segments of the public and among species. Different constituencies, with different fundamental attitudes toward wildlife, have different WACs. Educational programs and good communication with these constituencies can go far toward maintaining wildlife populations that integrate the values of the various constituencies. For example, gray wolves are reestablishing themselves in parts of Montana, Idaho, and Wyoming. To allay stockgrowers' concerns about the situation, it has been important to listen respectfully to their concerns, inform them about pertinent aspects of wolf biology, and provide a fair and effective program to compensate private individuals for depredation by the public's wildlife.

CONFLICTING VIEWS

Because humans have strong feelings about animals, both negative and positive, it is inevitable that conflict will arise. For example, "it will seem ridiculous to a sportsman to say that snail darters and louseworts have more recreational value than the reservoir behind a dam full of fish; while a naturalist will find extermination of a rare life-form in trade for yet another place to water-ski an obscenity" (Rolston 1986:79). Conflicts also arise in determining how best to handle problem species. What means of control are effective and acceptable? How much damage is tolerable?

Populations of mule deer and mountain lion along the foothills of the Colorado Front Range are subjects of controversy. Because of a combination of factors, including successful management programs, city or county ordinances banning harvest or control in populated areas, the palatability of ornamental plantings, and the lack of wildlife management tools to regulate populations without killing, urban and suburban deer are at very high population levels. Mountain lions apparently have become both more abundant and more habituated to people. On a given street, one family may enjoy seeing deer in their neighborhood, whereas a neighbor may resent their browsing on carefully tended shrubbery. One person may feel that mountain lions are a welcome attraction and that people are the intruders, but another person may be fearful of harm to family or pets. Where management calls for population reduction, the difficulty of culling operations in suburban neighborhoods is apparent. Nonlethal approaches, such as immunocontraception for the deer and aversive conditioning or tranquilization and removal for lions, may offer solutions to overabundance where more traditional population control methods (such as natural predation and hunting) are inappropriate or unacceptable.

Consumptive and non-consumptive uses sometimes come into conflict. This happens most frequently in areas of high human activity. On Mount Evans, people expecting to enjoy non-consumptive wildlife recreation have observed bighorn sheep and mountain goat hunters stalking and killing animals. It may be painful to non-hunters to see hunters in action, especially if illegal behavior is involved, such as poaching or shooting from the road. Surveys have shown that 18 percent of the population of Colorado disapproves of hunting, whereas 72 percent of Coloradans strongly disapprove of the use of steel-jaw traps for taking wild mammals (R. Gill 1991).

Heated wildlife issues are legion: Should we poison or shoot nuisance species like prairie dogs or should we leave them alone? How about the use of leg-hold traps, the spring bear hunt, hunting with bait and dogs, and the use of furs for coats? These conflicts cannot be eliminated. They are rooted in deeply held beliefs, values, and attitudes. We humans can, however, recognize different points of view, educate ourselves and others about biology and the decision-making process, develop new techniques, and—when needed—face head-on the hard decisions about what can or cannot be done both for managing wildlife and for facilitating public involvement.

WILDLIFE ETHICS

Holmes Rolston (1986:74), Distinguished Professor of Philosophy Emeritus at Colorado State University, wrote, "[T]o ask about values in nature is . . . to form a misleading question, for values are only in people, created by their decisions." We readily discuss how we *do* value nature and the spectrum of differing and sometimes conflicting views, and some thinkers have begun to ask how we *should* value nature. We can readily value things to which we ascribe some extrinsic, or monetary, value. If we ascribe intrinsic value to wildlife, value simply for the sake of its being there, have we perhaps reached a higher level of understanding? Is nature a resource to be used simply for our benefit, or is nature an entity to be treated with respect for its own sake and allowed to flourish?

There are two levels of environmental ethics. The first is anthropocentric: we should preserve nature because nature benefits humans, actually or potentially. This is often the most effective argument to justify preservation of natural resources. We are told to preserve tropical rainforests because yet undiscovered medicines and food plants abound that eventually will benefit us. An alternative environmental ethic can be termed naturalistic (Rolston 1986). This view, based on a belief in the unity of Earth with all its inhabitants and respect for its integrity, is held by a growing number of people. A naturalistic ethic values and preserves both resources and non-resources (Ehrenfeld 1974; also see Bekoff and Bexell 2010). Pioneer conservationist Aldo Leopold (1949:258) foresaw such thinking when he observed that "a system of conservation based solely on economic self-interest is hopelessly lopsided."

Currently, there is a thrust to encourage a stewardship approach toward natural systems. Dasmann (1966) wrote on the "old conservation," which emphasized the quantity of resources; in Colorado, that has often meant mule deer, elk, and trophy bighorn rams. The "new conservation," by contrast, sees things whole. It is about quality, not just quantity—the quality of ecosystems and hence of human life. In wildlife management, such ideas are traceable in part to Aldo Leopold, ideas epitomized in his essay titled "The Land Ethic." Leopold (1949:224–225) admonished us to "quit thinking about decent land-use as solely an economic problem. Examine each question in terms of what is ethically and aesthetically right, as well as what is economically expedient. A thing is right when it tends to preserve the integrity, stability, and beauty of the biotic community. It is wrong when it tends otherwise." Responsible decisions are beneficial to people and also to the resource. The notion of stewardship does, of course, make a subtle separation between humans and nature, implying that we humans know better and must be the responsible guardians of a landscape that needs our care. From a management point of view this probably is necessary, although some would urge that we approach the landscape as students rather than simply stewards, recognizing that we are a part of the system that we manage (Kellert 1987).

We noted in Chapter 3 that human interactions with other Coloradan native mammals have passed through a long-term phase of subsistence and a short-term phase of commercial exploitation. We are now in the midst of a third phase, sustainable use, typified by new forms of stewardship and a diversity of values and attitudes, in a state where wildlife economics and politics are connected in complex ways. Where present trends will lead and how generations hence will evaluate our times we cannot know.

Given the changes in society and science that can lead to a new relationship between humans and the other native mammals of Colorado, what are some outstanding questions that deserve discussion? We suggest the following merely as a starting point (also see Winternitz and Crumpacker 1985).

- How do we maintain the integrity of the distinctive mammalian faunas in intensively managed ecosystems, such as riparian systems (not only on the eastern plains but also on the Western Slope) and grasslands?
- How should decisions about introduction of exotic species be weighed against the integrity of native ecosystems? Moose and mountain goats prosper in parts of Colorado today, thanks to human intervention, although neither species managed to establish a population in Colorado on its own, despite the dramatic ecological changes that characterized the late Pleistocene. What are the ecological and aesthetic costs of these introductions, and how do these costs balance with the benefits?
- That the state of Colorado can manage wildlife resources for consumptive use is beyond question. But what is our appropriate relationship with the "non-resources" such as non-game mammals? Public interest is amply demonstrated by response to initiatives like the Colorado Bat Society and the Bats / Inactive Mines Project of the Colorado Division of Wildlife and the Office of Mined Land Reclamation. Should

we be establishing preserves for species like meadow jumping mice and olive-backed pocket mice—species whose habitats are being overrun by urbanization of the Front Range corridor?

Doubtless the future will bring new challenges to Colorado and its wild mammals, such as human population growth, continued and expanded human impact on native ecosystems, losses of biodiversity, maybe development of oil shale and certainly development of flow-limited energy resources (such as solar and wind power), local effects of global climatic change, and myriad others as yet unforeseen.

We can speculate but we cannot predict. Still, we do know a few things. Biologist Sir Julian Huxley (1953:132) was right: we humans are "no longer insignificant in relation to the cosmos," for we find ourselves "in the unexpected position of business manager for the cosmic process of evolution." Pioneer American conservationist John Muir (1911) was also right: everything *is* hitched to everything else. And ecologist Garrett Hardin (1972) was right: we can't do nothing. Not to choose is a strong choice.

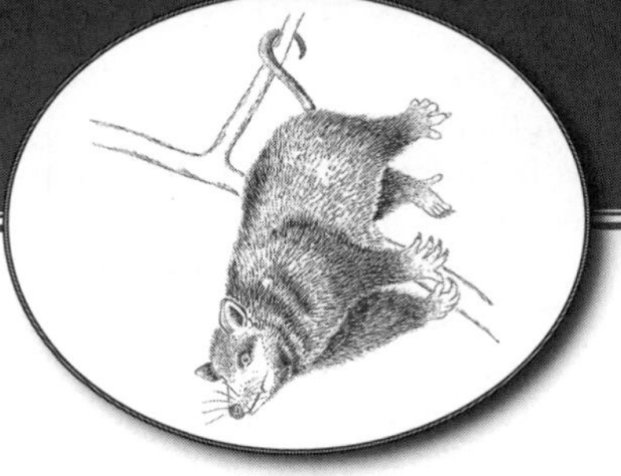

5

Order Didelphimorphia

Opossums and Kin

Zoologists traditionally considered an infraclass Metatheria to contain a single living order, the Marsupialia, a group including mammals as diverse as opossums, wombats, marsupial "moles," koalas, and kangaroos (G. Simpson 1945). More recent workers (Ride 1964, 1970; Kirsch 1977; Kirsch and Calaby 1977; McKenna and Bell 1997) have recognized 3 or more orders within this diverse group. Depending on the author, there are 8 (G. Simpson 1945), 14 (McKenna and Bell 1997), 16 (Kirsch 1977), or 20 (D. Wilson and Reeder 2005) families of marsupials, containing about 90 genera and more than 330 species (D. Wilson and Reeder 2005). Three families, Didelphidae, Caenolestidae, and Microbiotheriidae—totaling some 21 genera and 94 species—live in the Americas, but only 1 species, *Didelphis virginiana*, the Virginia opossum, occurs in the United States (Gardner 2005b). K. Rose (2006) reviewed the extensive fossil record of the marsupials.

Debate about their classification aside, marsupials have a suite of distinctive characteristics in common. Females give birth to young at a very immature stage of development and nourish them with milk for a relatively long period. The mammary glands usually are contained within an abdominal skinfold or pouch, the marsupium. The basic metatherian dental formula is 5/4, 1/1, 3/3, 4/4 = 50 (thus differing from placentals in having a greater total number of teeth, more incisors, with numbers of incisors different in the lower and upper jaw, and more molars than premolars). The palate is poorly ossified with many openings (fenestrae or vacuities). Auditory bullae are incompletely developed or lacking. The jugal bone is large and joins with the squamosal to form the glenoid fossa for articulation of the lower jaw. The horizontal ramus of the mandible is turned inward (inflected) at the angle of the dentary, a distinctive feature. Two small epipubic bones project forward from the anterior rim of the pelvic girdle. Females have a double reproductive tract with two ovaries, two oviducts, two uteri, and two lateral vaginae. In males the penis typically is forked at the tip and the testes are located in a scrotum anterior to the penis. The brain is relatively small, with poorly convoluted cerebral hemispheres, no corpus callosum, and large olfactory lobes.

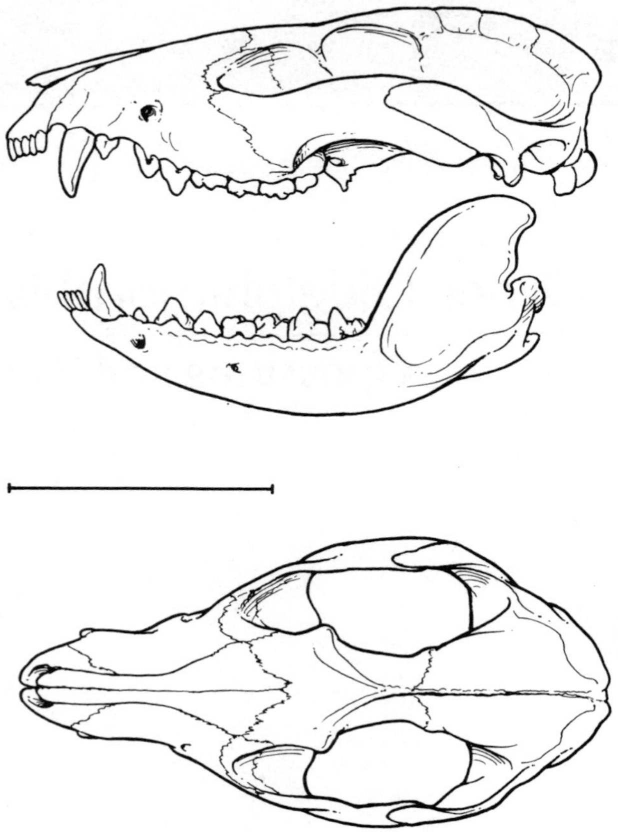

FIGURE 5-1. **Dorsal and lateral views of the skull of the Virginia opossum (*Didelphis virginiana*). Note the constricted cranium and the flared posterior ends of the nasal bones. Scale = 5 cm.**

There is a widespread, but mistaken, tendency to dismiss marsupials as "primitive" mammals, somehow inferior to placentals. It is true that marsupials have tended to fare rather poorly when faced with competition from ecologically equivalent placentals—such as occurred with successive invasions of South America from North America through the Cenozoic and with introduction of non-native placentals to Australia by successive waves of humans. Mostly, however, it probably is more accurate to view marsupials as "different" rather than inferior. Marsupials are a highly successful and diverse group, and the range of their adaptations is nearly as broad as that of placentals. Only bats and whales among placentals lack some analogous group among the marsupials, and that fact probably is the result of the nature of marsupial development. Both aerial and marine habitats would be awkward or impossible for pouch-young and their mothers.

Placental mammals have emphasized internal development, investing in an efficient mechanism for resource exchange, the placenta. In marsupials, however, internal development is limited. A rudimentary yolk sac placenta forms in most groups, but it is transitory. Maternal care emphasizes lactation. In mammals the duration of maternal care (gestation plus lactation) tends to be directly proportional to body size. Interestingly, the total period of maternal dependence in marsupials and placentals is essentially the same (Eisenberg 1981). The difference between the groups is not the duration of care but the timing of birth during the period of maternal care. Marsupial young are born early in the period of maternal care, placentals late. That is, maternal care in marsupials mostly is invested after parturition.

Family Didelphidae—Opossums

Didelphids are confined to the Americas, with the greatest diversity being in South America. In many ways didelphids resemble ancestral marsupials from the Cretaceous Period and hence have been called "living fossils." The teeth are rooted and heterodont, and all species have the ancestral metatherian dental formula, 5/4, 1/1, 3/3, 4/4 = 50. The snout is pointed and the tail is more or less prehensile and partly naked. The hallux, or big toe, is clawless and apposable to the other toes. The marsupium is well developed in *Didelphis* but completely lacking in some other genera. There are 11 genera and 75 species in the family; A. Gardner (2005b) provided a taxonomic synopsis. The genus *Didelphis* includes 3 species, of which 1, the Virginia opossum (*D. virginiana*), occurs in Colorado. Older references use the name *Didelphis marsupialis* for this species.

Didelphis virginiana

VIRGINIA OPOSSUM

Description

About the size of house cats, opossums have pointed snouts; naked, rounded ears; and long, scantily haired, prehensile tails. The fur is long, with coarse guard hairs and dark-tipped underfur. The color usually is gray with a

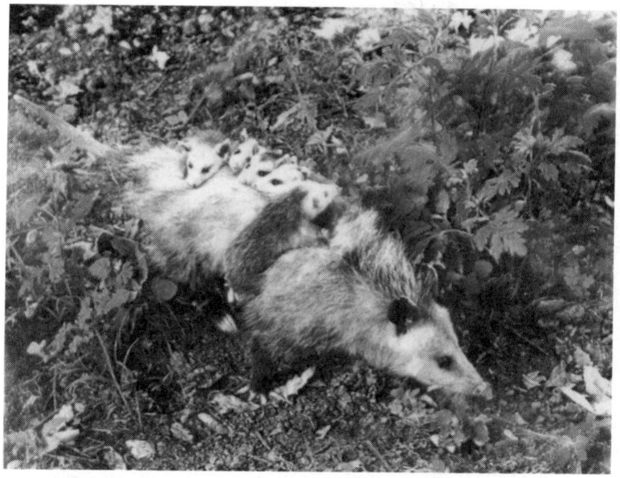

PHOTOGRAPH 5-1. Virginia opossum (*Didelphis virginiana*). Photograph by Joseph Van Wormer.

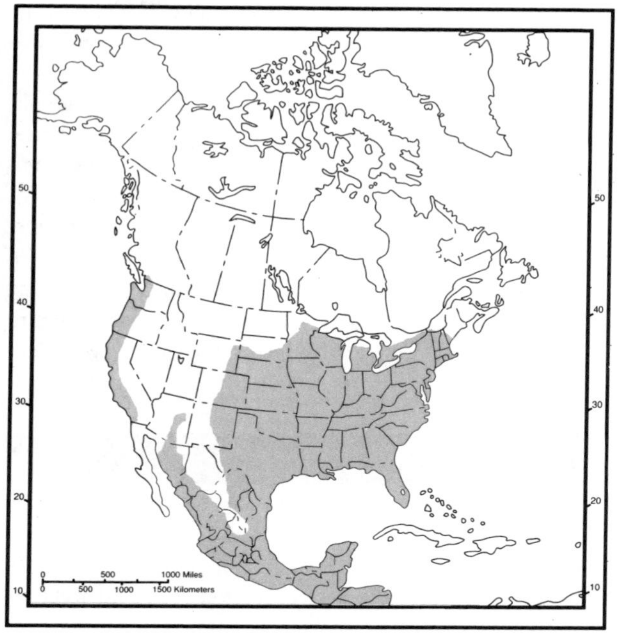

MAP 5-1. Distribution of the Virginia opossum (*Didelphis virginiana*) in North America.

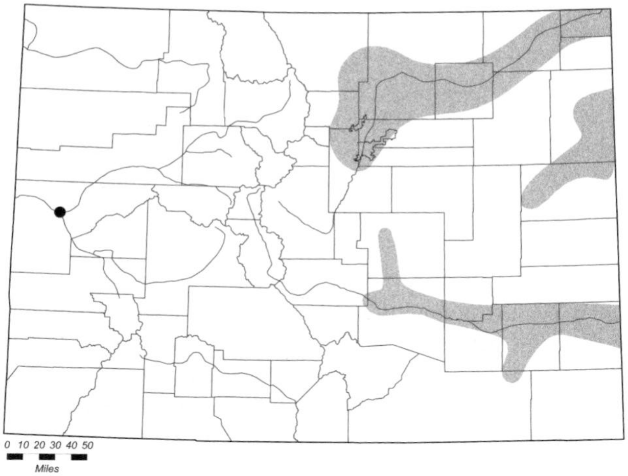

MAP 5-2. Distribution of the Virginia opossum (*Didelphis virginiana*) in Colorado. Solid circles represent introductions.

paler facial area but varies considerably among individuals, from nearly black to quite pale. The nosepad is pink, the eyes dark, and the tail dark at the base but becoming paler toward the tip. Measurements are: total length 650–1,020 mm; length of tail 250–400 mm; length of hindfoot 50–80 mm; length of ear 50–53 mm; weight 2–7 kg. The sexes are similar in appearance, although males usually are heavier than females. Testes are permanently descended in a scrotum located anterior to the penis. The feet are plantigrade with naked soles. The nasal bones are expanded at their posterior ends. The palate has several large vacuities. Skulls of older animals have prominent sagittal crests and lambdoidal (occipital) ridges. The cranium is relatively small and the skull is constricted posterior to the postorbital process. The auditory bullae are incomplete.

Distribution

The opossum is a Neotropical mammal, but since Pleistocene times it has become firmly established in the United States (Ride 1964). The animals have been introduced in the Pacific Coast states. In recent years the opossum has expanded its range to the north and west in the central United States, and continued expansion may be expected with ongoing climate change.

In Colorado, opossums are most abundant in riparian situations bordering agricultural lands on the eastern plains (Gruchy 1950; Beidleman 1952; Lechleitner 1969; D. Armstrong 1972). However, the species is extremely adaptable and can survive in marshes, forests, grasslands, urban areas, and wooded or brushy canyon country. Although museum specimens from Colorado are few, viable populations exist along the South Platte, Republican, and Arikaree rivers, and the animals may occur throughout the state east of the mountain front. There is a report from the Oklahoma Panhandle along the Cimarron River (Dalquest et al. 1990). Opossums are officially considered to be "accidental" in Wyoming (http://gf.state.wy.us/wildlife/nongame/SpeciesList/), but they apparently are resident in the southeastern part of the state (Crowe 1986).

In Colorado, reports of opossum sightings, roadkills, and captures by trappers have increased in recent years, even in several mountainous areas of the state. Opossums are not uncommon in Denver and suburbs. The status of the animal in the Arkansas drainage is poorly documented. Opossums in the Grand Junction area are the result of introductions made in 1920, 1930, and 1940 (D. Armstrong 1972). That population does not appear to be expanding its range. The subspecies in Colorado is *Didelphis virginiana virginiana*.

Natural History

Opossums generally are secretive and nocturnal, and their presence may go undetected even in areas where they are fairly abundant. They use a variety of temporary shelters: rock piles, brush, hollow trees, woodpiles, and burrows abandoned by other animals. Opossums do not dig their own dens and dens may be shared with other species. Radio-tracking and live-trapping studies indicate that opossums are highly transient. Except for females with litters of young, they rarely spend more than a few days in one particular den (Fitch and Sandidge 1953; Fitch and Shirer 1970). Opossums may construct a nest of grass. Nesting materials are carried wrapped in the prehensile tail (L. Smith 1941).

Omnivorous and opportunistic, opossums eat almost any organic matter available. Insects, other invertebrates, and carrion appear to provide most of the animal protein in the diet (Lay 1942; Sandidge 1953). Amphibians, reptiles, birds, and small mammals are eaten, but some of these are taken as carrion. Opossums are resistant to venom of pit vipers (rattlesnakes, copperheads, and water moccasins—Family Crotalidae) and can feed on them with impunity (Werner and Vick 1977). Berries, apples, cherries, and grapes and corn and other grains may be eaten in considerable quantities when available.

Opossums are active at all times of the year, but in the northern portions of the range (including Colorado) activity is reduced during colder periods and they may not emerge from the den for several days at a time. In cold weather some foraging occurs during the day. Because of transience, home ranges are highly variable and have been estimated from 5 to about 320 ha (A. Gardner and Sunquist 2003), depending on sex, age, locality of study, and method of calculation (A. Holmes and Sanderson 1965; Gillette 1980). Nightly foraging activities rarely exceed 500–700 m from the den site (Fitch and Shirer 1970; A. Gardner 1982). Density estimates ranged from 1/8 ha to 1/42 ha in the Midwest (A. Gardner and Sunquist 2003).

Opossums are generally solitary except during the breeding season or when females are rearing young. Most encounters between adults are agonistic, marked by hisses, growls, or screeches and fierce fighting. During the breeding season the female normally remains aggressive toward the male except for the brief periods when she is in estrus (H. C. Reynolds 1952; McManus 1970). Response of an opossum to being cornered varies from docility to bared teeth and profuse salivation. Opossums will bite if provoked and their large canines can be very effective. When pressed, the animals will often "play 'possum," rolling over on the side, with tongue protruding and eyes closed. The profound physiological changes of this catatonic period may last from less than a minute up to six hours (Wiedorn 1954). An effective defense against some predators, this behavior is maladaptive when the danger is a speeding vehicle, so opossums are traffic casualties in disproportionate numbers.

Opossums breed in late winter, spring, and summer in the southeastern United States, where two general peaks of breeding occur, one early in the season and a later, longer period (A. Gardner 1982). The breeding season in Colorado has not been studied but may be shorter. Females are polyestrous and 5 or 6 cycles can occur during the breeding season. The estrous cycle averages 29 days, with estrus limited to about 36 hr (H. C. Reynolds 1952). Females breed the first season following their birth and produce two litters a year in warmer parts of their range. The young, numbering up to 25 (average 6 to 9), are born after a gestation period of 12 to 13 days (H. C. Reynolds 1952). At birth, young average less than 1 g in weight and are about 20 mm in length. The relatively well-developed forelimbs drag the otherwise fetal newborn to the pouch. There it attaches to a teat where it remains for the next 50 to 65 days. The number of teats averages 13, so many of the offspring perish from lack of nourishment. By 80 days after birth the young can leave the pouch and cling to the mother's fur while she forages. By about 100 days they become independent of her and disperse (Seidensticker et al. 1987).

A variety of animals (including coyotes, dogs, bobcats, and great-horned owls) can capture opossums, but the species is not commonly reported in their diets. Population studies (reviewed by Seidensticker et al. 1987) indicate that very few animals live beyond 1 year of age, and a population turnover period of less than 3 years is to be expected. The opossum has been managed as a furbearer in Colorado (see Table 4-1) and as a small game mammal, but it was not mentioned in "2008 Colorado Small Game" (Colorado Division of Wildlife 2008b). Hunters and trappers have taken opossums for both food and fur, although the pelt is of low value and very few have been reported harvested in Colorado. Opossums are not seriously detrimental to humans despite an occasional raid on poultry pens and consumption of some cultivated crops and fruits. The animals support high parasite loads and may carry a number of infectious diseases, including leptospirosis and tularemia; experimental infection with rabies is difficult (A. Gardner and Sunquist 2003).

McManus (1974), A. Gardner (1982), Seidensticker et al. (1987), and A. Gardner and Sunquist (2003) provided thorough reviews of natural history.

6

Order Cingulata

Armadillos

Armadillos are familiar and distinctive mammals. Until recently they have been included in an order, Xenarthra (formerly called Edentata), with 3 superficially very different infraorders, the armadillos, the sloths, and the anteaters (or vermilinguas). Xenarthra now is considered a magnorder (see McKenna and Bell 1997) or a superorder (D. W. Macdonald 2006) with two living orders, Cingulata (armadillos) and Pilosa (the latter with two suborders, Vermilingua, or anteaters, and Phyllophaga, the sloths). Sloths were listed as Folivora by A. Gardner (2005a).

Despite their obvious morphological divergence, xenarthrans do share a number of similarities. Usually the forefeet have 2 or 3 of the digits enlarged and equipped with long, curved claws. (The hindfoot typically has 5 toes.) In all living forms the vessel that returns systemic blood to the heart (the posterior vena cava) is double. The clavicle is usually well developed. The dentition is generally reduced, and in anteaters it is absent entirely. Incisors and canines are absent; the cheekteeth are usually homodont and often lack an enamel covering. Further, all xenarthrans have extra articulations (points of contact called xenarthrous processes) between the lumbar vertebrae. In females, the urinary and genital tracts share a common urogenital sinus. In males, testes are abdominal. Differences are seen among species in diets, dentition, and preferred habitats. The only Coloradan xenarthran, the nine-banded armadillo, is a semi-fossorial omnivore.

The magnorder Xenarthra is strictly a New World group, with a fossil record dating to the Late Paleocene Epoch, 55–60 million years ago (McKenna and Bell 1997). The earliest adaptive radiation occurred in South America (K. Rose et al. 2005; K. Rose 2006), but some species eventually entered Central and North America, including Pleistocene forms, the giant ground sloths (Phyllophaga or Folivora) of the American Southwest and glyptodonts (Cingulata) of the southern United States, some of which were 3 m in length (Kurtén and Anderson 1980). There is a single living family in the order Cingulata.

Family Dasypodidae—Armadillos

Living armadillos are small to medium-sized mammals, ranging in weight from less than 1 kg up to 60 kg. The body is protected by bony plates covered with cornified (horn-like) epidermis. At the junctions of the plates are areas of thinner skin that allow for considerable flexibility and movement. The word *armadillo* is Spanish, referring to the armor-like "shell." The limbs are protected by smaller cornified plates and can be partly withdrawn into spaces shielded by the dorsal and lateral body plates. The head and tail are also covered with ossified plates or rings. The belly and medial margins of the legs have haired skin and are not protected by these plates. The forefeet have 3- to 5-clawed digits. The tibia and fibula are fused at their proximal and distal ends, contributing to a general skeletal rigidity consistent with passive protection and a burrowing habit.

The ears are of modest size, either rounded or pointed at their tips. Armadillos appear to have good visual, auditory, and olfactory senses. The muzzle is elongated and the tongue is long and extensible. Incisors and canines are absent and the cheekteeth are peg-like and ever-growing, and may number 40 or more.

Females usually have a pair of pectoral mammae and members of some genera have inguinal mammae as well. The simplex uterus passes into a combined urogenital tract that transports urine and serves as the birth canal. Delayed implantation is common. Litter size ranges from 1 to 12. Males lack a scrotum and no baculum is present.

Armadillos are terrestrial mammals. They are excellent burrowers and usually seek security underground during periods of inactivity. Various species may be diurnal, nocturnal, or crepuscular. Generally solitary, most live in relatively open habitats such as grasslands, brushlands, and open woodland. Their broad diets range from insectivory and carrion-feeding to omnivory. There are 9 genera and 21 species in the family (D. Wilson and Reeder 2005), one of which occurs in the United States. A. Gardner (2005a) presented a synopsis of the family.

Dasypus novemcinctus

NINE-BANDED ARMADILLO

Description

With their bony carapace, nine-banded armadillos are unique among Coloradan mammals. About the size of a large house cat, males are larger than females. The body is well protected by the carapace of bone and cornified skin, with the scutes extending onto the head, tail, and lateral margins of the legs. "Nine-banded" is a reference to the 8 to 11 rows of scutes lying between the much larger scapular and pelvic shields. Sparse, stiff hairs may be present at junctions between scutes and on the face. The belly and inner legs are covered with long, coarse hair. The dorsal color is a mottled dark to grayish to pinkish ivory with the sides typically paler in color. The belly is whitish to yellow. The ears are relatively long and conspicuous. Measurements are: total length 600–800 mm; length of tail 240–370 mm; length of hindfoot 75–110 mm; length of ear 40 mm; weight 3–7 kg. The skull is dorsoventrally flattened with an elongate, narrow rostrum. The zygomatic arch is complete. Auditory bullae, incisors, and canines are lacking. Cheekteeth are peg-like and ever-growing, and lack enamel in adults. The tooth count varies from 28 to 32, the latter being the mode. The limbs are short with 5 toes on the hindfeet and 4 toes on the forefeet. The digits are equipped with long, stout claws. Both sexes have well-developed anal scent glands that produce a strong musky odor.

PHOTOGRAPH 6-1. Nine-banded armadillo (*Dasypus novemcinctus*). © 1993 Wendy Shattil / Bob Rozinski.

Distribution

The nine-banded armadillo has the broadest geographic range of any xenarthran. They were introduced to Florida, and expansion of that population as well as natural population expansion in the central Gulf States has firmly entrenched the species in the United States. For the history of this range expansion see Humphrey (1974) and McBee and Baker (1982).

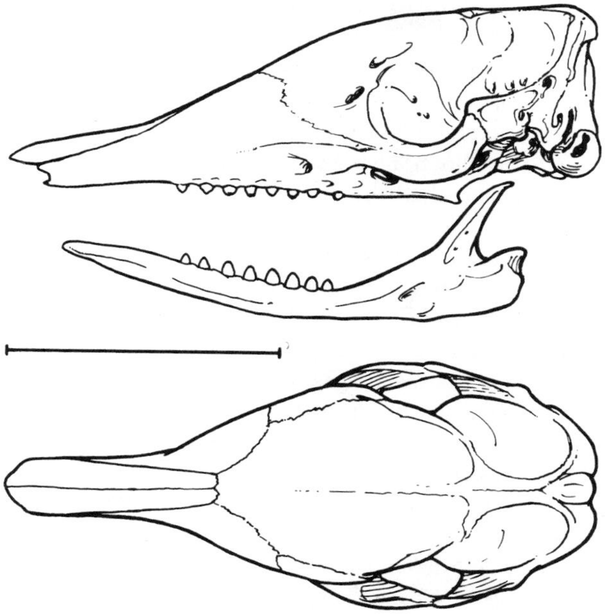

FIGURE 6-1. Lateral and dorsal views of the skull of a nine-banded armadillo (*Dasypus novemcinctus*). Scale = 5 cm.

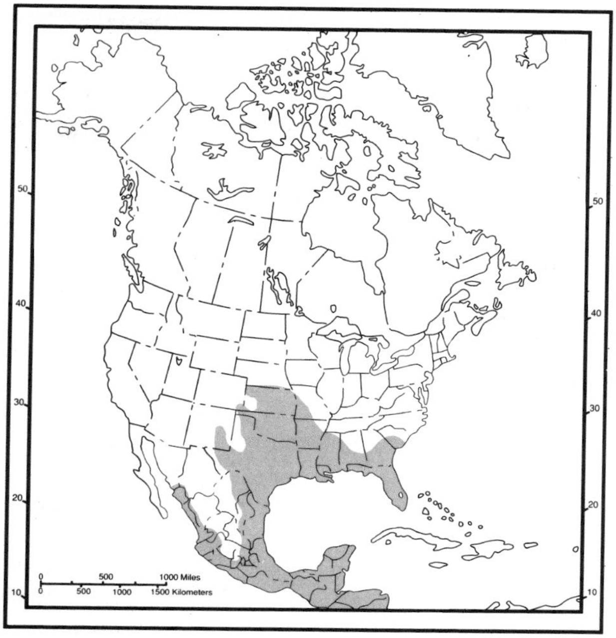

MAP 6-1. Distribution of the nine-banded armadillo (*Dasypus novemcinctus*) in North America.

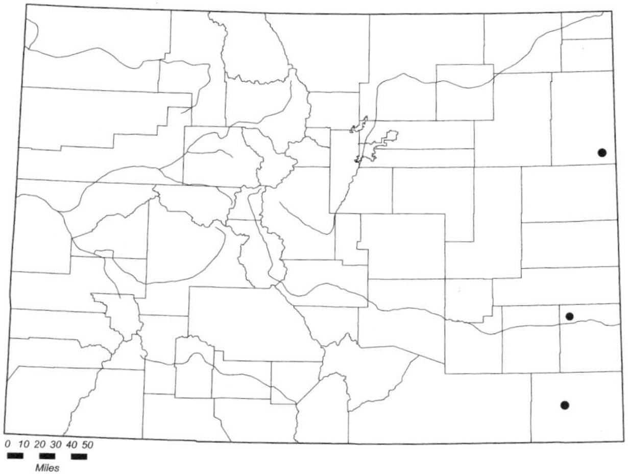

MAP 6-2. Distribution of the nine-banded armadillo (*Dasypus novemcinctus*) in Colorado. Solid circles represent localities mentioned in text.

The status of armadillos in Colorado is uncertain. There are no early records, but a few specimens have been reported in recent decades along the eastern boundary of the state, from Baca (Hahn 1966), Prowers (Meaney et al. 1987), and Yuma (J. Choate and Pinkham 1988) counties. Colorado mostly provides marginal habitat for the species and no actual breeding populations have been reported. However, more observations should be expected in southeastern and eastern parts of the state, because armadillos are known from adjacent states. They are documented in southwestern Nebraska by a sighting at a place 1 mi northeast of Champion, Chase County, and a specimen from Benkelman, Dundy County (P. Freeman and Genoways 1998). Both of these localities are in the Republican River watershed, about 6 and 25 miles from Colorado, respectively. Armadillos also are known from Stevens County, in southwestern Kansas (Bee et al. 1981). They are not yet reported from the Oklahoma Panhandle (Caire et al. 1989; Dalquest et al. 1990), but they are known from the northern tier of counties in the Texas Panhandle (J. K. Jones, Manning et al. 1988) and from northeastern New Mexico, within about 50 miles of the Colorado state line (J. Stuart et al. 2007). Certainly, irrigated agriculture, stabilization of riparian woodland due to flood control (by impoundment of spring runoff in irrigation reservoirs), and ongoing climatic warming all predict expansion of the *D. novemcinctus* in Colorado. The armadillo is considered a non-game mammal in Colorado (Table 4-1) and thus is protected by statute. *Dasypus novemcinctus mexicanus* is the only subspecies recognized in the United States.

Natural History

Nine-banded armadillos thrive in a variety of habitats, as suggested by their broad (and apparently expanding) distributional range. Although found in semiarid regions, they are intolerant of arid conditions and reach highest densities in habitats with rather heavy ground cover and high humidity. In the Plains states they are most commonly associated with wooded river-bottoms rather than upland prairie. Some authors have attributed range limitations to lack of deep moist soils and rotting litter, with their typically rich resources of arthropod prey (Galbreath 1982). Humphrey (1974) considered 38 cm of precipitation to be minimal to support viable populations in the United States. Taulman and Robbins (1996) concluded that the armadillo requires mean minimum January temperatures of –2°C or greater and mean annual precipitation of 38 cm or more. Extreme eastern and southeastern Colorado barely meets this requirement at present, and cold winters probably impose limitations on long-term survival of enough animals to form a viable population. Environments are not static, of course, and environmental change continues (much of it apparently anthropogenic). Winter temperatures are rising but the moisture regime of the area is less predictable. Further, irrigated acreage is being cut back in some areas as water levels in aquifers fall and surface water is redirected to municipal and industrial uses.

Animal matter constitutes about 93 percent of the diet, of which 54–100 percent is insects (Kalmbach 1943; Layne 2003), especially scarabaeid beetles and a variety of Hymenoptera (ants, bees, and wasps), Lepidoptera (butterflies and moths), and Orthoptera (grasshoppers, crickets). Other invertebrate prey includes earthworms, centipedes, and snails. Vertebrate prey and carrion are also eaten, including cottontails, birds, bird eggs, lizards, snakes, frogs, and salamanders. Plant matter in the diet includes berries, fruits, and seeds. Free water is necessary for survival.

Armadillos are generally reclusive, solitary animals, except when females are caring for young or during the breeding season, when transitory pair-bonding may occur. Most activity is either nocturnal or crepuscular, although some authors believe temperature is more critical to activity than is light. While foraging, armadillos "follow their noses" in seemingly erratic movements. The animals are not territorial and several individuals may use the same general foraging area. Armadillos seek shelter in "haystack" nests aboveground, in nests in burrows, or in rocky outcrops. Burrows may be more than a meter deep and up to 4 or 5 m in length. They may have multiple entrances and 1 chamber typically is modified as a nest, and they may use several different burrows over a short period of time. Armadillos bring leaves, twigs, and grasses to the nest tucked against the belly with the forelegs, and then they back into the burrow (W. K. Clark 1951). When alarmed aboveground, armadillos attempt to reach the security of a burrow, where they anchor the feet against the burrow wall with the carapace protecting the entrance. In this defensive position they are almost impossible to extract.

Data on home ranges and population densities are scanty. Layne (2003) summarized ecological studies from 8 states, reporting home ranges of 0.6–9.2 ha (mean, 4.1 ha). Home ranges of males and females appear to be similar and animals in more humid habitats have smaller home ranges. Home ranges are stable in size and those of near neighbors usually overlap. Density estimates range from 0.2 to 145.0 per 100 ha, depending on habitat and human impacts. Males appear to outnumber females in all age classes (Layne 2003). Although they are not territorial, competition has been reported for preferred open areas (Galbreath 1982).

Armadillos are capable of breeding at 2 years of age and exhibit delayed implantation (Galbreath 1982). Ovulation occurs during July and August (Hayssen et al. 1993). Development of the blastocyst is suspended for 5–7 days following fertilization, and the developing embryos are retained in the uterus until late October, November, or early December, when implantation occurs. Polyembryony is the rule, with 4 genetically identical offspring developing from one fertilized egg. A few authors have reported triplets, twins, and sextuplets (McBee and Baker 1982). Litters of males tend to be born before litters of females (Layne 2003). In Texas, young are born in March and April, suggesting a post-implantation gestation period of about 120 days, long for a mammal of this size (A. Enders 1966). The precocial young are born with eyes open and the carapace fully developed although not hardened. At birth the animals weigh about 85 g. They are weaned by about 3 months of age.

Armadillos are well protected by their "armor" and their burrowing habit and so have few habitual, natural predators, although they have been documented in the diets of coyotes, mountain lions, bobcats, raccoons, black bears, and domestic dogs (Layne 2003). Untold thousands of them are killed annually on highways in the South, where they are frequently the most common vertebrate roadkill. Some people hunt them for food (Fannin and Fannin 1982).

Longevity may exceed 8 years in captivity, although most wild animals probably do not survive that long (Galbreath 1982). The animals have been a subject of research interest because of their peculiar pattern of development and their morphology, and also because they provide a useful "model organism" for studies of leprosy, a bacterial infection known to afflict only armadillos and humans. Galbreath (1982) and Layne (2003) provided thorough reviews of the literature.

7

Order Primates

Monkeys, Apes, and Kin

The primates are a group of rather generalized mammals descended from an early insectivorous or omnivorous eutherian stock in the Paleocene or Cretaceous (Bininda-Emonds et al. 2007), at least 60 million years ago. Early in their history, competition with rodents may have been keen, but primates adapted to life in the trees, whereas most early rodents were terrestrial.

It actually is rather difficult to define the primates, but their distinctive traits and adaptive tendencies mostly are specializations that adapt them to arboreal life: grasping hands and feet; retention of the collarbone (allowing a wide range of movements in the shoulder); reduction of the snout (which allows the eyes to move toward the midline so the fields of vision of the eyes overlap, permitting stereoscopic vision and thus eye-hand coordination); small litter size per body size; and prolonged maternal dependence. Most primates are social to some extent and many species are highly vocal; the associative cortex of the brain is relatively large in monkeys and apes. The dentition is rather generalized, adapted to a frugivorous (fruit-eating) or omnivorous diet.

Recent primates are arranged in 15 families and 69 genera, including some 376 species (Groves 2005), mostly tropical or subtropical in distribution. Many primates depend on moist tropical forests for habitat, and these are areas of high human impact, whether the indirect impact of forest clearance or the direct impact of hunting for "bush-meat" or the illicit pet trade. About half of the species of primates are threatened or endangered (Baillie et al. 2004), the highest proportion of any of the large orders (i.e., those with more than 100 species) of mammals.

The physical similarity of humans to other primates has been recognized since antiquity. That recognition was formalized in 1758 by the great Swedish naturalist Carolus Linnaeus. In the foundational work of modern zoological taxonomy *Systema Naturae*, 10th Edition, Linnaeus included 4 genera in the order Primates: *Homo* (humans), *Simia* (non-human apes and monkeys), *Lemur* (lemurs and their kin), and *Vespertilio* (bats). In a contemporary English synopsis and appreciation of Linnaeus's work, Pulteney (1781:63) defined primates as "[a]nimals furnished with foreteeth, or cutting teeth: four above; parallel. Two pectoral teats" (hence the inclusion of bats among the primates). Pulteney went on to describe our human place among primates in terms that challenged the spirit of his time and can inform evolutionary discussions of ourselves today: "Howsoever the pride of man may be offended at the idea of being ranked among the beasts . . . , he nevertheless stands as an animal, in the system of nature. . . . But man is not left by Linnaeus to contemplate himself merely as such, but is led to the consideration of what he ought to be, as an intelligent [*sapiens*] and moral being, in a comment on the Grecian Sage's dictate, know thyself" (p. 64).

The bats have long since been moved to an order of their own, of course, and over the past 2 centuries zoologists have subdivided the Linnaean order Primates in a variety of ways (although the fundamental evolutionary integrity of the group has never been in doubt). Groves (2001, 2005) arranged *Homo* (including a single living species, *H. sapiens*) in a family, Hominidae, along with the genera *Gorilla* (with 2 species: *G. beringei* and *G. gorilla*, the eastern and western gorillas, respectively), *Pan* (composed of two species: the bonobo, or pygmy chimpanzee, *P. paniscus*, and the common chimpanzee, *P. troglodytes*), and *Pongo* (with two species: *P. abelii*, the Sumatran orangutan, and *P. pygmaeus*, the Bornean orangutan). The acrobatic gibbons of eastern India, Southeast Asia, and Indonesia were treated in their own family, Hylobatidae, which was included along with the Hominidae in a superfamily, Hominoidea. Groves (2001) provided a thorough review of primate taxonomy (and a concise summary of principles of systematic biology more generally).

Superficial similarities of humans and the great apes have been recognized for centuries (and doubtless for millennia in those parts of the Old World tropics where humans and other hominids are sympatric), but the development of molecular genetics has allowed a deeper appreciation of this evolutionary proximity (A. Wilson and Sarich 1969; M. King and Wilson 1975). Recent estimates of divergence of human and chimpanzee DNA range from about 1.5 percent to 5.0 percent, depending on techniques and assumptions of a particular study (Britten 2002).

In a sense, this entire book is a commentary on the importance of 1 industrial primate to the lives and prospects of local non-primate mammals, their environments, and the ecosphere as a whole. Chapter 3 is focused explicitly on the history of human understanding of the mammalian fauna, and Chapter 4 describes human stewardship of Coloradan mammals and their environments.

Family Hominidae—Humans and Kin

The family Hominidae has been variously defined but increasingly is construed to include the great apes (chimpanzees, gorilla, orangutan) as well as humans (Groves 2005). Previously, the family was restricted to a single living member, humans, and a number of extinct lineages; in that arrangement the great apes were grouped in a family, Pongidae. *Homo sapiens* is the most widespread mammalian species, permanently inhabiting all continents save Antarctica and occasionally moving briefly beyond Earth into space. Indeed, humans are among the most widespread of biological species; our obligatory microbial symbionts are coextensive with us, but no species has a wider distribution. The family dates to the Miocene, some 20 million years ago; the genus *Homo* is about 2 million years old (Pough et al. 2008), although the human lineage diverged from the branch that led to chimpanzees about 6 million years ago (Glazko and Nei 2003; Kumar et al. 2005).

Homo sapiens

HUMANKIND

Humans need no description, and perhaps objective description is impossible. Still, all of us recognize each other as representing a single species, highly variable biologically and culturally. So why mention us at all? There is a single compelling reason: humans are a part of the native mammalian fauna, probably established in Colorado as long as most other native species, and longer than many (see Table 3-3). Further, the extraordinary impacts of industrial humans on Coloradan environments (and Earth more broadly) are a product of mammalian evolution. Human minds represent an adaptation comparable to the adaptations of any of the other species discussed in this book. Humans have a "natural history" just as any species does. In addition, of course, humans have a unique cultural history, and that makes all the difference in the world.

Nearly everyone knows, of course, that we people are mammals, peculiarly "naked apes." But too often our evolutionary and ecological kinship to the rest of the fauna is forgotten. Our overwhelming dominance of native ecosystems (upon which we are utterly dependent for survival, of course) is poorly understood and underappreciated. We allow our unique (and fairly young, geologically speaking)

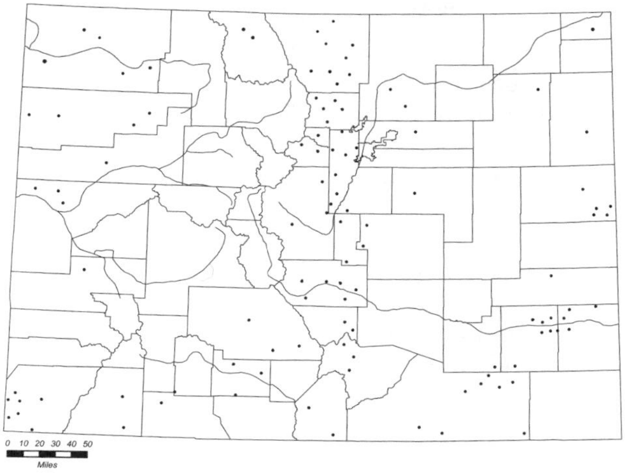

MAP 7-1. Estimated human population in Colorado, ca. 1500. One dot represents 60 individuals (after Erickson and Smith 1985).

humanity to obscure our ancient, fundamental "animality." Recognizing our zoological roots makes us no less unique—each biological species is unique. It does, however, reemphasize an important and immutable fact—we humans are a part of nature, not apart from it.

Humans occur statewide in Colorado, at least seasonally. Settlement is most dense along the ecotone between the Southern Rocky Mountains and the Great Plains, specifically the Colorado Piedmont and adjacent foothills. The distribution of humans is not mapped as those of other species are, but Figure 7-1 and Map 7-1 are intended as "pictures worth 10,000 words," to convey the impact of humans on the habitats of the rest of the native mammalian fauna and to illustrate the extraordinary suddenness with which this impact has been imposed.

When human beings first came to Colorado is not known with certainty. Paleoindians were here at least by the end of the last glacial interval, 10 millennia ago. Indigenous cultures left their dim marks on the landscape—fire scars, camp circles, artifacts, and the scraps remaining from their construction—but the long-term effects of early humans here are far less obvious in modern ecosystems than those of beaver or bison, let alone bark beetles or budworms. For more than 10,000 years, people lived in Colorado as nomadic, opportunistic omnivores, emphasizing hunting. Local

FIGURE 7-1. Satellite image of conterminous United States and surrounding area at night, June 17, 1996 (from US National Oceanic and Atmospheric Administration).

populations certainly were small, adjusted to the resources of the region. Imports and exports of materials and energy were minimal. Settled agriculture in Colorado is only about 1,000 years old, as preserved in magnificent textbook clarity at Mesa Verde and Hovenweep national monuments.

The first Europeans to visit what is now Colorado were transitory. In the eighteenth century it was occasional travelers from the missions of New Mexico, seeking a safe trail to the missions of California (W. Briggs 1976; Warner 1976; Kessler 1998). In the early nineteenth century it was fur trappers, the legendary "mountain men," and military explorers, especially the Long Expedition of 1820. Later it was miners and then (to provision the miners) ranchers and farmers. Some details of this history are outlined in Chapter 3, where we discuss the development of human knowledge of Colorado's mammals. The ongoing maturation of human stewardship of Colorado's mammals and their habitats is the subject of Chapter 4.

If information on the Internet is to be believed, a second kind of primate (apparently a hominid) ranges fairly widely in Colorado, especially in mountainous areas. An Internet search on "Sasquatch Colorado" will provide entertaining and imaginative text and video. The insights of Lozier et al. (2009) for the Sierra Nevada probably are relevant to the situation in the Southern Rockies. Based on comparative ecological niche modeling for the cryptozoid "Bigfoot" and the black bear, *Ursus americanus*, they suggest that observations of Sasquatch may represent mistaken identity.

8

Order Rodentia

Rodents

Rodents are the most numerous of mammals—both as species and as individuals—in Colorado and worldwide. More than 40 percent of Coloradan mammalian species are rodents, and there doubtless are more individual rodents in Colorado than there are individuals of all other mammals combined, humans included. Because of their great abundance and diversity, rodents are a significant component of the structure and function of terrestrial and aquatic ecosystems, and they have been the subject of much research. Rosenzweig (1989) reviewed the contributions of studies of rodents to developing theory in community ecology. J. Brown (1987) and J. Brown and Kurzius (1989) highlighted the spatial variability of community structure in the guild of granivorous desert rodents in the Southwest (including a site in west-central Colorado).

Rodents are important to people. On one hand, some rodents are beneficial as sources of food or fur, and many species—beaver and a number of kinds of squirrels, for example—are eminently "watchable wildlife," enriching our lives by providing non-consumptive recreational opportunities. Further, some rodents are especially important to science as laboratory animals and as indicators of environmental quality. On the other hand, some rodents are regarded as pests because of their burrowing habits, their sometimes annoying or even destructive occupation of human habitations, and their competition for crops, rangeland, and stored food. And, of course, attitudes toward some rodents, such as prairie dogs and beaver, are both positive and negative, depending on whom you ask, and when.

Several species of rodents carry diseases communicable to humans. Specifically, in recent years there has been public health concern in Colorado about plague and hantavirus pulmonary syndrome (HPS). Plague is considered in accounts of prairie dogs (especially the black-tailed prairie dog, *Cynomys ludovicianus*), and HPS is discussed in the account of the deer mouse (*Peromyscus maniculatus*).

Rodents date from the Late Paleocene, 65 million years ago. Origins and fossil history were reviewed by Meng and Wyss (2005) and K. Rose (2006). Worldwide, more than 40 percent of living mammalian species are rodents; some 2,277 species have been described (D. Wilson and Reeder

2005). These species are classified in 481 genera in 33 families (D. Wilson and Reeder 2005). Rodents are native to all major landmasses except Antarctica. The conservation status of North American rodents was reviewed in detail by D. Hafner et al. (1998a, 1998b).

Rodents range in size from the capybara (*Hydrochaeris hydrochaeris*) of South America (up to a meter long and weighing more than 45 kg) to minute mice like *Baiomys* and *Micromys*, which weigh only 5–6 grams, the mass of a US quarter. There has been an extraordinary diversification in locomotion, from primitive walking to the extreme bipedalism of kangaroo rats, the fossoriality of pocket gophers, the specialized swimming of beavers and muskrats, and through the arboreal scampering of squirrels to the remarkable gliding of "flying" squirrels. With habitats that range from wetlands to desert, from subterranean burrows to treetops, from open prairie to dense forest to open tundra, no Coloradan environment is without them. In Colorado, there are at least 55 species of native rodents representing 30 genera in 8 families.

Rodents are gnawing mammals, and many are strict vegetarians (although insectivory has evolved in a number of branches of the phylogenetic tree of rodents). They have a pair of chisel-shaped incisors in both the upper and lower jaws. Enamel covers the anterior face of the tooth, with softer dentine making up the rest of the exposed incisor. Differential hardness of enamel and dentine allows the ever-growing incisors to be sharpened by continual honing of the upper teeth against the lower teeth. The faces of the upper incisors of many rodents are reddish to yellowish brown in color. This is due to the presence of iron bound to hydroxyapatite crystals (Selvig and Halse 1975), which apparently makes the faces more resistant to wear (Halse 2007) and so may contribute to the self-sharpening of upper incisors by lower incisors. Injury to the incisors that precludes proper opposition of upper and lower teeth may lead to formation of anomalous tusk-like structures that prevent normal feeding. A wide diastema is present, the consequence of the absence of canines and loss of a variable number of premolars. The maximal dental formula for North American rodents is 1/1, 0/0, 2/1, 3/3 = 22; the minimum is 1/1, 0/0, 0/0, 2/2 = 12. Cheekteeth may be either ever-growing or rooted (definitive growth). The diverse patterning of enamel on the occlusal surface of the teeth, presence or absence of strong cusps, and the arrangement of cusps are all useful clues to relationships among rodents. The lower jaw articulates loosely with the skull, allowing both lateral and anterior-posterior chewing motions.

The clavicle is usually well developed. Radius and ulna are separate and the elbow joint permits free rotation of the forearm. Tibia and fibula are usually separate as well, and the fibula does not articulate with the calcaneum. A baculum is typically present in males (Ramm 2007), and a homologous structure, the os clitoridis, may be present in females. Females have a duplex uterus.

For many years, until the early twentieth century, rodents and lagomorphs were often grouped together in an order, Glires, because of similarities of their gnawing dentition, but they were distinguished as suborders Simplicidentata (the rodents proper) and Duplicidentata (for the rabbits and kin, with their two upper incisors per quadrant). There followed several decades when rodents and lagomorphs were thought to have no especially strong evolutionary connection. In recent years, however, a close relationship has been reasserted, and McKenna and Bell (1997) included rodents, lagomorphs, and also elephant shrews (order Macroscelidea) in a single grandorder, Anagalida. More recently, molecular evidence has suggested that not only rodents and lagomorphs but primates, tree shrews (Scandentia), and colugos, or "flying lemurs" (Dermoptera), are close relatives on the evolutionary tree and so should be considered members of a single superorder, Euarchontoglires (D. W. Macdonald 2006).

There is no real consensus on a proper classification of rodents at any taxonomic level. In the mid-nineteenth century, biologists subdivided rodents into 3 suborders—sciuromorphs, myomorphs, and hystricomorphs—based on whether the structure and function of the infraorbital foramen and associated jaw musculature are squirrel-like, mouse-like, or porcupine-like. Although widely used as informal descriptions, these groups have generally been conceded to be artificial (although there has been no agreement on an alternative arrangement that better reflects evolutionary relationships). G. Simpson (1945) provided a masterful appreciation of the inherent difficulties of rodent systematics. McKenna and Bell (1997) revived formal use of 3 suborders of rodents, whereas D. Wilson and Reeder (2005) arrayed rodents in 5 suborders. Carleton (1984) provided a thorough and cogent review of the complex history of rodent taxonomy to that date, and Honeycutt et al. (2007) reviewed the evolution of rodents in the general context of sociobiology.

In addition to the native and exotic species discussed beyond, the nutria (*Myocastor coypu*) was raised in captivity in Colorado in the 1930s as a furbearer. Some individuals escaped captivity (Presnall 1958; D. Armstrong 1972), but we have no evidence that a population ever was established in the wild.

Key to the Families of the Order Rodentia in Colorado

1. Body covered with stiff quills intermixed with softer hairs; infraorbital foramen as large as foramen magnum . . . . Family Erethizontidae, p. 225
1' Body not covered with stiff quills; infraorbital foramen smaller than foramen magnum 2

2. Infraorbital foramen small to minute, not providing passage for masseter muscle; mandibular cheekteeth four on a side 3
2' Infraorbital foramen medium-sized, V-shaped, oval, or round, providing some passage for masseter muscle; mandibular cheekteeth three on a side 6

3. Postorbital processes of frontal bone prominent and sharply pointed . . . . Family Sciuridae, p. 109
3' Postorbital processes of frontal bone absent to small and blunt 4

4. External, fur-lined cheek pouches present; tail variable but not flat or scaly 5
4' External, fur-lined external cheek pouches absent; tail dorsoventrally flattened and scaly . . . . Family Castoridae, p. 159

5. Forelimbs as large or larger than hind limbs; tail short, covered with short tactile hairs; infraorbital foramen small, never completely perforating nasal septum; skull heavy and angular, auditory bullae not strongly inflated . . . . Family Geomyidae, p. 177
5' Forelimbs usually smaller than hind limbs; tail long, usually well haired; infraorbital foramen medium-sized, completely perforating nasal septum; skull light, not angular, auditory bullae strongly inflated . . . . Family Heteromyidae, p. 163

6. Infraorbital foramen somewhat oval; total teeth 18; hindfoot and tail remarkably elongate . . . . Family Dipodidae, p. 188
6' Infraorbital foramen not oval; total teeth 16; hindfoot and tail not notably elongate . . . . . Superfamily Muroidea, 7

7. Cheekteeth all cusped, upper molars with cusps arranged in 3 longitudinal rows; tail scaly, round in cross section, and sparsely haired. . . . . Family Muridae, p. 252
7' Cheekteeth either cusped or prismatic, if upper molars with cusps, then cusps not in 3 rows; tail variable. . . . . Family Cricetidae, p. 194

Family Sciuridae—Squirrels

The squirrels are a diverse group of rodents ranging from fossorial ground squirrels, to scansorial chipmunks, to highly arboreal tree squirrels. Mostly colorful and mostly diurnal, they are among our most watchable smaller wildlife. They inhabit practically all habitats, from rainforest to tundra. The cheekteeth are cusped, rooted, and complex. The dental formula is 1/1, 0/0, 1–2/1, 3/3 = 20 or 22, depending on the presence or absence of a small upper premolar shed in some species as they become adults. The postorbital process is well developed and sharply pointed. The infraorbital foramen is small to minute and does not provide passage for any of the masseter muscle. The zygomatic arch is typically stout and well developed. There are 4 well-developed digits on the front foot (prairie dogs have 5 clawed front digits) and 5 on the rear, and all usually are clawed. The tail is well haired but varies greatly in length. Sciurid rodents date from the Oligocene, 40 million years ago. There are some 51 genera and 278 species, distributed worldwide except in parts of the Neotropics, on Madagascar, Australia, Antarctica, and in the High Arctic (D. Wilson and Reeder 2005). Eleven genera and 17 species are known to be present in Colorado, and 2 additional species (including possibly an eighth genus, *Glaucomys*, the flying squirrels) may eventually be found to occur here. W. Smith et al. (2003) discussed conservation of tree squirrels and other arboreal rodents in northwestern forests.

Coloradan squirrels represent 2 distinctive subfamilies, the tree squirrels (Sciurinae) and the ground squirrels (Xerinae) (Thorington and Hoffmann 2005). Relationships among ground squirrels remain something of a puzzle (see Blumstein and Armitage 1998a) but do seem to represent a natural group of closely related lineages "scaled" in 4 size groups: small (chipmunks), medium (so-called ground squirrels), large (prairie dogs), and extra-large (marmots).

Some squirrels are not easy to identify. Chipmunks are notoriously difficult, for example, and some people even confuse the golden-mantled ground squirrel and white-tailed antelope squirrel with the chipmunks. The following key may be inadequate to separate the various chipmunks (genus *Neotamias*) in some localities of sympatry. Sutton (1953), D. Armstrong (1972), Telleen (1976), and Bergstrom and Hoffmann (1991) presented more detailed descriptions of Coloradan species.

Key to the Species of the Family Sciuridae in Colorado

1. Tail generally less than one-third total length; condylobasal length 60 mm or greater 2
1' Tail usually greater than one-third total length; condylobasal length less than 60 mm 5

2. Maxillary toothrows parallel; forefeet with 4 clawed digits, pollex (thumb) with flat nail; total length greater than 450 mm . . . . Yellow-bellied Marmot—*Marmota flaviventris*, p. 120
2' Maxillary toothrows converging posteriorly; forefeet with all 5 clawed digits; total length less than 400 mm . . . . *Cynomys*, 3

3. Tail black-tipped . . . . Black-tailed Prairie Dog—*Cynomys ludovicianus*, p. 143
3' Tail gray- or white-tipped 4

4. Tip of tail whitish, without gray center . . . . White-tailed Prairie Dog—*Cynomys leucurus*, p. 140
4' Tip of tail whitish, with gray center . . . . Gunnison's Prairie Dog—*Cynomys gunnisoni*, p. 138

5. Loose fold of skin between forelimbs and hind limbs; infraorbital region narrow, deeply notched . . . . Northern Flying Squirrel—*Glaucomys sabrinus*,* p. 158
5' No loose fold of skin between forelimbs and hind limbs; infraorbital region broad, not deeply notched 6

6. Zygomatic arches nearly parallel; jugal oriented vertically 7
6' Zygomatic arches convergent anteriorly; jugal portion of zygoma twisted toward horizontal plane 9

7. Size small, less than 350 mm; greatest length of skull less than 50 mm; anterio-ventral border of orbit opposite last premolar; P^3 vestigial or absent . . . . *Tamiasciurus hudsonicus*, p. 155
7' Size large, more than 350 mm; greatest length of skull more than 50 mm; anterio-ventral border of orbit opposite first molar; P^3 usually well developed . . . . *Sciurus*, 8

8. Ears markedly tufted . . . . Abert's Squirrel—*Sciurus aberti*, p. 149
8' Ears not markedly tufted . . . . Fox Squirrel—*Sciurus niger*, p. 152

9. Sides of head with stripes; posterior border of zygomatic process of maxillary opposite P^3 . . . *Neotamias*, 10
9' Sides of head without stripes; posterior border of zygomatic process of maxillary opposite M^1 14

10. Dorsal stripes (especially lateral ones) obscure; general colors of upperparts grayish; edges of tail often whitish . . . . Cliff Chipmunk—*Neotamias dorsalis*, p. 111
10' Dorsal stripes distinct; general color of upperparts brownish; edges of tail buffy 11

11. Size smaller; greatest length of skull less than 34 mm; length of hindfoot less than 33 mm . . . . Least Chipmunk—*Neotamias minimus*, p. 113
11' Size larger; greatest length of skull more than 34 mm; length of hindfoot more than 33 mm 12

12. Dorsal stripes dark brownish, usually 3 in number; ground color of pelage brownish to grayish; zygomatic arch weak . . . . Uinta Chipmunk—*Neotamias umbrinus*, p. 118
12' Dorsal stripes black or tawny, usually 5 in number; zygomatic arch strong 13

13. Dorsal stripes black, ground color yellowish to brown . . . . . . Colorado Chipmunk—*Neotamias quadrivittatus*, p. 114
13' Dorsal stripes tawny, ground color orange to reddish orange . . . . . . Hopi Chipmunk—*Neotamias rufus*, p. 116

14. Infraorbital foramen a narrow oval; small masseteric tubercle directly ventral to infraorbital foramen; underside of tail with white median area . . . . White-tailed Antelope Squirrel—*Ammospermophilus leucurus*, p. 123
14' Infraorbital foramen oval or subtriangular; medium to large masseteric tubercle ventral and slightly lateral to infraorbital foramen; underside of tail without white median area . . . . Ground Squirrels, 15

15. Upperparts rather uniformly grayish or brownish gray; not predominantly dappled with black or buff . . . . Wyoming Ground Squirrel—*Urocitellus elegans*, p. 134
15' Upperparts notably dappled or striped 16

* Species of possible occurrence in Colorado.

16. Upperparts striped 17
16' Upperparts dappled 18

17. Upperparts with 2 broad white stripes bordered by darker areas; stripes not alternating with rows of spots . . . . Golden-mantled Ground Squirrel—*Callospermophilus lateralis*, p. 127
17' Upperparts with alternating rows of narrow white or buffy stripes and rows of spots . . . . 13-lined Ground Squirrel—*Ictidomys tridecemlineatus*, p. 129

18. Total length less than 350 mm; tail not especially bushy, shorter than 135; greatest length of skull less than 50 mm . . . . Spotted Ground Squirrel—*Xerospermophilus spilosoma*, p. 132
18' Total length greater than 350 mm; tail bushy, longer than 135 mm; greatest length of skull more than 50 mm 19

19. P^3 simple, less than one-fourth size of P^4; dappling of dorsal surface usually most pronounced in shoulder area; habitat in rocky areas or brushy habitats, not in tallgrass prairie . . . . Rock Squirrel—*Otospermophilus variegatus*, p. 125
19' P^3 bicuspid, with functional cutting edge, greater than one-fourth size of P^4; dappling on dorsal surface usually conspicuous to rump; habitat in mid- to tallgrass prairie, not in rocky areas . . . . Franklin's Ground Squirrel—*Poliocitellus franklinii*,* p. 132

Genus *Neotamias*—Western Chipmunks

The genus *Neotamias* includes some 23 species, of which 5 occur in Colorado. Our use of the generic *Neotamias* follows R. Baker, L. Bradley, et al. (2003), whose usage was based on Jameson (1999). There is no consensus on generic definitions and diagnoses in the chipmunks (Levenson 1985; Patterson and Heaney 1987; Thorington and Hoffmann 2005). For summaries of generic-level taxonomy, see Jameson (1999), Piaggio and Spicer (2001), and Thorington and Hoffmann (2005). Coloradan chipmunks have been treated in a genus *Eutamias* or lumped with eastern chipmunks and Siberian chipmunks in a broader genus, *Tamias* (as used in the previous edition of this work).

One or more species of chipmunks occur throughout most of Colorado except the grasslands and shrub-steppe of the Great Plains. Chipmunks sometimes are difficult to distinguish, particularly in the field. Frequently a larger-bodied species (such as the Colorado, cliff, Hopi, or Uinta chipmunk) is sympatric with the smaller, widespread least chipmunk. However, geographic and ecological ranges of larger chipmunks tend not to overlap with each other. Therefore, the field naturalist is well advised to look at size as a first clue at identification and then to consider the geographic and ecological setting. With museum specimens, the baculum (os penis) is a useful aid to identification. J. White (1953b) and Lechleitner (1969) provided drawings of the bacula of Coloradan chipmunks. Coloradan chipmunks are non-game mammals.

Neotamias dorsalis
CLIFF CHIPMUNK

Description

The cliff chipmunk is a fairly large chipmunk with obscure dorsal stripes and grayish dorsal color. The venter is whitish and the feet are brownish gray. Measurements are: total length 200–225 mm; length of tail 80–100 mm; length of hindfoot 32–35 mm; length of ear 23–26 mm; weight 50–70 g. Condylobasal length is 32–33 mm. The baculum has

PHOTOGRAPH 8-1. Cliff chipmunk (*Neotamias dorsalis*). Photograph by Andrew Langford.

* Species of possible occurrence in Colorado.

a thin shaft and is slightly compressed laterally. The keel of the baculum is about one-fifth the length of the tip (J. White 1953b).

Distribution

Cliff chipmunks are restricted to northwestern Moffat County, north of the Yampa River and mostly west of the Little Snake. Despite this restricted range they are not uncommon in suitable habitat. T. Clark and Stromberg (1987) considered them rare in adjacent Wyoming because of habitat destruction. One subspecies, *Neotamias dorsalis utahensis*, occurs in Colorado.

Natural History

The cliff chipmunk is appropriately named, being largely restricted to rocky outcrops and cliff areas in piñon-juniper and ponderosa pine woodlands in extreme northwestern Colorado. No detailed studies have been made on this species in Colorado, although Warren (1908) and Cary (1911) described habitats and made general behavioral observations.

Cliff chipmunks are retiring, and their drab color allows them to blend with their surroundings. They seldom venture far from dens located under rocks or in fissures and crevices of cliff faces (E. Hart 1971, 1976). Most foraging takes place early to mid-morning and late afternoon. The cliff chipmunk is opportunistic, eating a wide variety of seeds, stems, and flower heads, depending on the phenology of the plants and their proximity to dens. In Utah, mountain maple, serviceberry, balsamroot, bitterbrush, bluegrass, salsify, thistle, and wild carrot are important foods, and animal matter is not consumed (E. Hart 1971). Food caching occurred from June to October. Cliff chipmunks are excellent climbers and often forage in the tops of junipers, whose "berries" (actually cones) are a favored food (Cary 1911).

Cliff chipmunks enter dormancy during the colder months in Utah (E. Hart 1976) and Arizona (Dunford 1974; Hoffmeister 1986), and probably also in Colorado. They are not known to make significant weight gains before entering dormancy and probably arouse periodically to feed from caches in the den.

The animals become reproductively active upon emergence in spring, and mating probably occurs in late April and May. Gestation period is not known but probably is about 1 month, with only a single litter produced. About 30 percent of females studied in Arizona did not breed (Dunford 1974). Young are thought to remain belowground for 35 to 45 days. J. Fitzgerald observed young cliff chipmunks playing in rocks in mid-June in the Gates of Ladore area of Dinosaur National Monument, and in Utah young have been seen as early as mid-April (E. Hart 1976). Dunford and Davis (1975) described vocalizations.

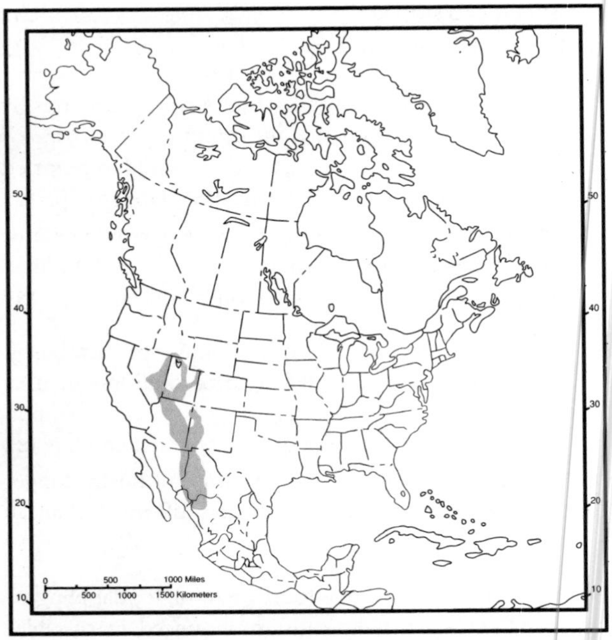

MAP 8-1. Distribution of the cliff chipmunk (*Neotamias dorsalis*) in North America.

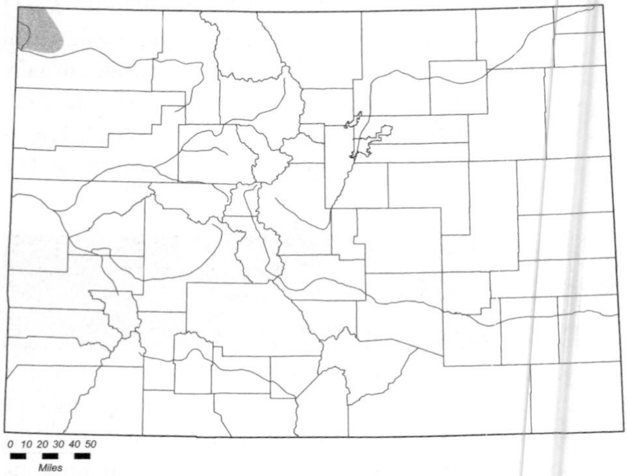

MAP 8-2. Distribution of the cliff chipmunk (*Neotamias dorsalis*) in Colorado.

Neotamias minimus

LEAST CHIPMUNK

Description

The least chipmunk is the smallest chipmunk in Colorado. Considerable geographic variation occurs in color and details of pattern. The least chipmunk usually has 5 dark dorsal stripes alternating with 4 paler stripes. Typically the lateral blackish stripes are darker than those of other Coloradan chipmunks. The dark center stripe extends from head to tail. Two pale stripes are present on the face. Measurements are: total length 185–218 mm; length of tail 75–100 mm; length of hindfoot 28–31 mm; weight 25–60 g. Condylobasal length is less than 31 mm, and the greatest length of the skull is less than 33 mm. The baculum has a relatively long shaft and a tip that is less than 29 percent of the shaft (see J. White 1953b).

PHOTOGRAPH 8-2. Least chipmunk (*Neotamias minimus*). Photograph by William E. Ervin.

Distribution

The least chipmunk is found throughout the western two-thirds of Colorado to elevations above treeline. It is a common mammal over most of its range in Colorado and is highly variable geographically, both in external appearance (D. Armstrong 1972) and physiology (Willems and Armitage 1975a, 1975b, 1975c). *Neotamias minimus caryi* is restricted to the San Luis Valley; *N. m. consobrinus* occurs over most of northwestern Colorado; *N. m. minimus* is restricted to extreme northwestern Colorado, north of the Yampa River and east of the Green River in Moffat County; *N. m. operarius* has the broadest distribution, occupying the

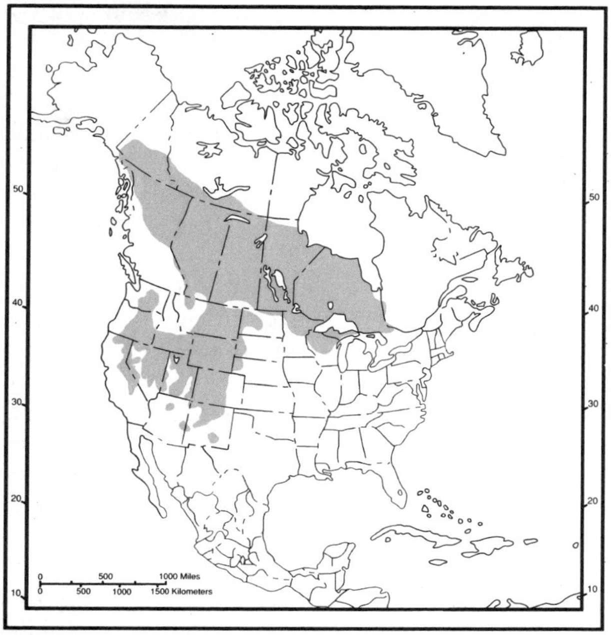

MAP 8-3. Distribution of the least chipmunk (*Neotamias minimus*) in North America.

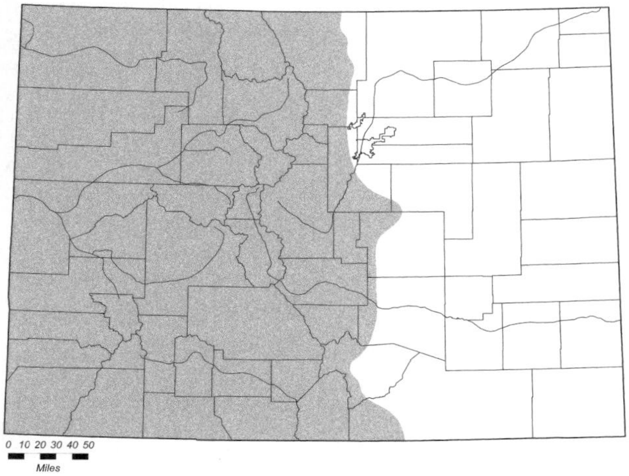

MAP 8-4. Distribution of the least chipmunk (*Neotamias minimus*) in Colorado.

Front Range and mountainous central and southwestern Colorado. Thorough ecological and evolutionary comparisons among some of these populations were reported by R. Sullivan (1985) and R. Sullivan and Peterson (1988), using color, cranial and bacular morphology, and molecular characters. Those studies did not suggest changes in subspecific designation of Coloradan populations.

Natural History

Least chipmunks range over a wider area and in more different habitat types than any other chipmunk in the state. They occur from low-elevation semidesert shrublands, through montane shrublands and woodlands, to forest edge, to alpine tundra. Within these diverse ecosystems, they typically occupy relatively open, sunny areas on the edge of escape cover.

Least chipmunks eat a variety of fruits, berries, flowers, seeds, leaves, and stems, and also insects and carrion (Carleton 1966; Tomberlin 1969). Plant material constitutes 77 to 94 percent of the diet, and seeds make up 50 percent of the total. The diet changes from flowering plants in spring to seeds and arthropods in early summer and seeds and berries in late summer and fall. Flowers of alpine parsley, dandelion, and Indian paintbrush and berries of *Vaccinium* and strawberry are favored (T. Vaughan 1974). Sedges, bitterroot, gilia, evening primrose, geranium, and violet are other important sources of seeds. Grass seed, currants, fungi, Douglas-fir seeds, and insects were important in Rio Grande County (Tomberlin 1969). In more xeric conditions in northwestern Colorado, a higher use of arthropods (more than 70 percent of the diet), especially lepidopteran larvae, was seen (Haufler and Nagy 1984). Use of prickly-pear, thistle, and fleabane was also noted. Large aggregations of least chipmunks may occur at sites where humans feed them. R. J. Smith (1995) demonstrated experimentally that *N. minimus* forages more efficiently closer to cover than does the golden-mantled ground squirrel, whereas the latter species is more efficient in riskier, open habitats.

These animals are diurnal, active during the warmer months of the year and dormant during winter. Winter dormancy is broken periodically when the animals arouse to use food stored in the den. When aboveground, least chipmunks dash about searching for food with short, rapid bursts of speed. In fact, its small size and notably nervous actions help to distinguish it from Colorado's other chipmunks. Large amounts of time are spent searching for, consuming, collecting, or transporting food in the capacious internal cheek pouches.

Least chipmunks excavate burrows beneath tree roots, fallen logs, and rocks and bushes, and also use these features for feeding platforms and observation posts (T. Vaughan 1974; Telleen 1978). The tunnel system includes a nest lined with grasses, leaves, and other materials. In sagebrush steppe in southeastern Idaho, burrows averaged 21.4 cm in maximum depth and 1.7 m in length (Laundré 1989). Home ranges were 1.5–1.8 ha in Montana (Martinsen 1968) and 1.4–5.4 ha in Colorado (Bergstrom 1988), although Friedrichsen (1977) calculated minimum home range of 0.2 ha and densities of 54.3 animals per hectare in a provisioned population in Rocky Mountain National Park. In Alberta, maximum distances between captures ranged from 143 to 413 m (Meredith 1974).

Least chipmunks are monoestrous. The breeding season varies with elevation and snow conditions. Vigorous mating chases occur soon after the animals emerge from hibernation. Most probably breed from late March to early July in Colorado (T. Vaughan 1969; Skryja 1974). Females enter estrus within 1 week of emergence. A significant number of females do not breed, possibly because of insufficient weight when entering hibernation the previous fall. Gestation takes 4 weeks (Criddle 1943). Litter size ranges from about 4 to 6. Young are blind and naked at birth. They are furred and the eyes open at about 2 weeks of age. Least chipmunks are weaned and emerge from the natal den at about 1 month of age. Hayssen (2008b) provided a comparative review of reproduction within ground squirrels generally (i.e., chipmunks, ground squirrels proper, and marmots), concluding that body size is a fundamental driver of patterns of development, with chipmunks having relatively larger litters, a single litter per year, and rapid rates of development.

Weasels, martens, hawks, foxes, coyotes, and bobcats are important predators. Along with golden-mantled ground squirrels, least chipmunks are important hosts of the virus that causes Colorado tick fever, and they are the source of the virus that is transmitted to immature ticks, *Dermacentor andersoni* (G. Bowen et al. 1981). Least chipmunks (and also chickarees) appear to be involved in dispersal of seeds of dwarf mistletoe (*Arceuthobium vaginatum*—an important forest parasite) on the Fraser Experimental Forest in Grand County (Nicholls et al. 1984). Despite its abundance, the biology of the least chipmunk is rather poorly known in Colorado, perhaps in part because it is difficult to distinguish from other chipmunks. Literature on the species over its wide range was reviewed by Verts and Carraway (2001).

Neotamias quadrivittatus

COLORADO CHIPMUNK

Description

The Colorado chipmunk is large, similar in size to the Uinta chipmunk. The central dorsal stripe is black and very distinct, whereas the dark lateral stripes are more reddish

PHOTOGRAPH 8-3. Colorado chipmunk (*Neotamias quadrivittatus*). Photograph by R. B. Forbes.

brown. White lateral stripes are also usually well defined. In animals with recently molted pelage the dorsal background color is bright reddish brown paling to orange-buff on the sides. The ventral color is pale gray. Measurements are: total length 200–245 mm; length of tail 90–110 mm; length of hindfoot 31–37 mm; length of ear 20–23 mm; weight 45–90 g. Condylobasal length is 31–35 mm. The width of the base of the baculum is less than one-fourth the length of the shaft and the keel height is one-fourth the length of the tip. For comparisons with similar species, see descriptions of the Uinta, Hopi, and least chipmunks.

Distribution

A fairly common species over most of its range, the Colorado chipmunk occurs in southern Colorado, where it reaches elevations of 3,200 m (10,500 feet). Its northern and eastern limits are in the Front Range, where it is restricted to the foothills along with the rock squirrel, Mexican woodrat, and northern rock mouse (D. Armstrong 1987). Along the Front Range, the Colorado chipmunk seems to occur mostly below the 2,130 m (7,000 ft.) contour, whereas the Uinta chipmunk occurs mostly above that elevation (Bergstrom and Hoffmann 1991).

Bergstrom (1992) hypothesized that this parapatric distribution might be driven by a balance between the dominance of *N. umbrinus* in interspecific territorial encounters counterbalanced by the greater tolerance of *N. quadrivittatus* for parasitism by botflies (Cuterebridae). As a southwestern species (D. Armstrong 1972), *N. quadrivittatus* may have a longer history with botflies than does the Uinta chipmunk, a Cordilleran species (D. Armstrong 1972) with a geographic range centered on the Middle Rocky Mountains. One subspecies, *Neotamias quadrivittatus quadrivittatus*, occurs in Colorado. Previously, the Hopi chipmunk (now known as *N. rufus*) was considered a subspecies

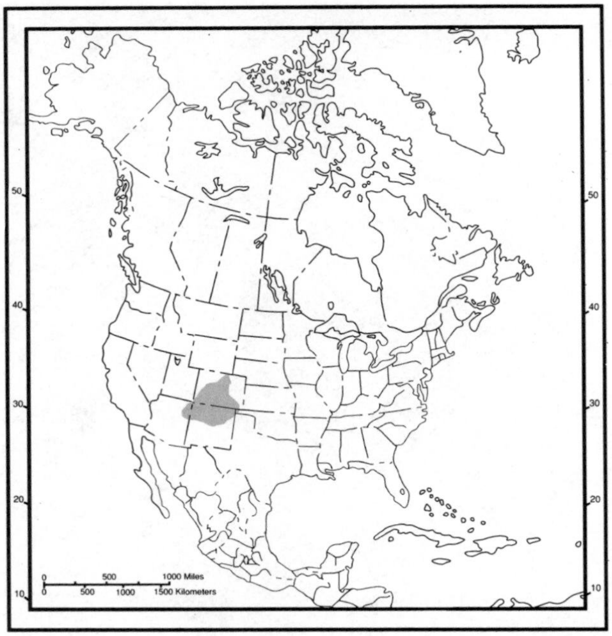

MAP 8-5. Distribution of the Colorado chipmunk (*Neotamias quadrivittatus*) in North America.

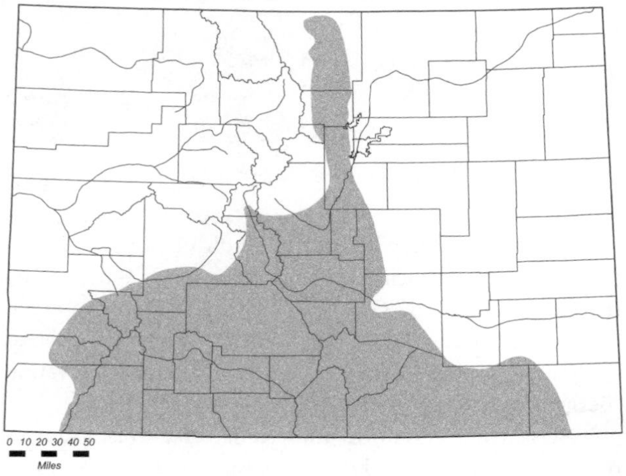

MAP 8-6. Distribution of the Colorado chipmunk (*Neotamias quadrivittatus*) in Colorado.

of the Colorado chipmunk (*N. q. hopiensis*), but this population is now recognized as a distinct species (Patterson 1984). Older accounts of studies at lower elevations in western Colorado and eastern Utah attributed to the Colorado chipmunk probably apply instead to the Hopi chipmunk.

Natural History

The Colorado chipmunk has not been studied extensively despite its relatively large range and local abundance. Colorado chipmunks occupy rocky, broken terrain in open woodlands and shrublands, mostly in foothills and canyons. At lower elevations they occur in piñon-juniper woodlands and montane shrublands, and at higher elevations they are found in montane forests.

Colorado chipmunks feed on seeds, berries, flowers, and herbage of a variety of plants. Common foods include mountain mahogany, prickly-pear, juniper "berries," currants, wild cherry, and snowberry (Cary 1911). The diet is undoubtedly supplemented by insects and carrion as available. All chipmunks are agile climbers, and it is not surprising to see the animals foraging high in trees and shrubs or on cliff faces. Some food materials are stored in the burrow for consumption during periods of belowground activity. In Arizona the animals depend on free water, although they also obtain water from plant material (Hoffmeister 1986).

Radio-tracking studies found home ranges in Colorado to be 3–7 ha, whereas trapping indicated home ranges of less than 1 ha (Bergstrom 1986, 1988). As with the other chipmunks, the species is not active aboveground during winter but probably does arouse periodically to eat. Activity peaks during early morning and late afternoon (Cary 1911).

Colorado chipmunks are monoestrous with a 30- to 33-day gestation period. Most breeding occurs in April or May. A single litter of about 5 young is born, furless except for vibrissae. Young are weaned at 6 to 7 weeks of age (D. Armstrong 1987).

Neotamias rufus
HOPI CHIPMUNK

Description

From the Colorado chipmunk this species is distinguished by somewhat smaller average size and a dorsal pelage that generally lacks significant amounts of black in the stripes, resulting in a more orange-red to buff pelage. Measurements are: total length 190–221 mm; length of tail 83–95 mm; length of hindfoot 31–35 mm; length of ear 15–22 mm. Condylobasal length is 31–34 mm. The auditory bullae are generally larger (especially in length) whereas the nasals are shorter and the interorbital region more narrowed than in the Colorado chipmunk. The baculum is also typically smaller than that of the Colorado chipmunk, with a shorter tip (Patterson 1984).

Distribution

The Hopi chipmunk occurs in western Colorado from the Yampa River south. It ranges eastward along the Colorado River to Eagle County and along the Gunnison to the western end of the Black Canyon. Patterson (1984) presented convincing evidence that the Hopi chipmunk is a distinct, monotypic species, as recognized here. Coloradan populations have been called *Eutamias quadrivittatus hopiensis* (see D. Armstrong 1972 for synonymy) and *E. q. rufus* (see Hoffmeister and Ellis 1979).

PHOTOGRAPH 8-4. Hopi chipmunk (*Neotamias rufus*). Photograph by David Behmer.

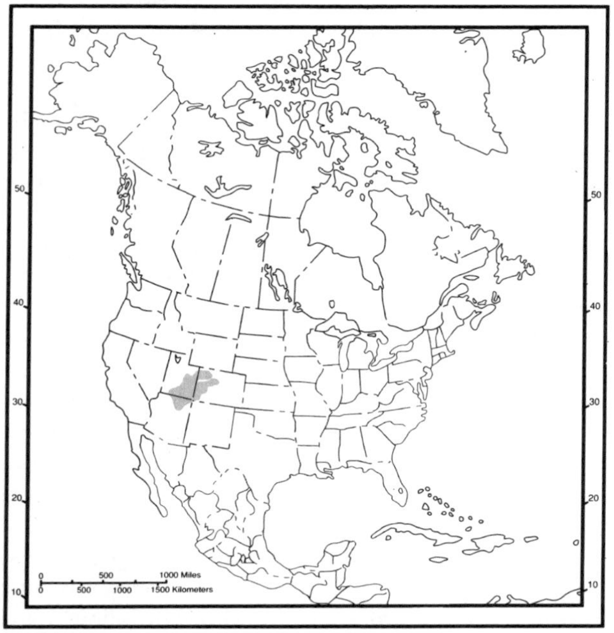

MAP 8-7. Distribution of the Hopi chipmunk (*Neotamias rufus*) in North America.

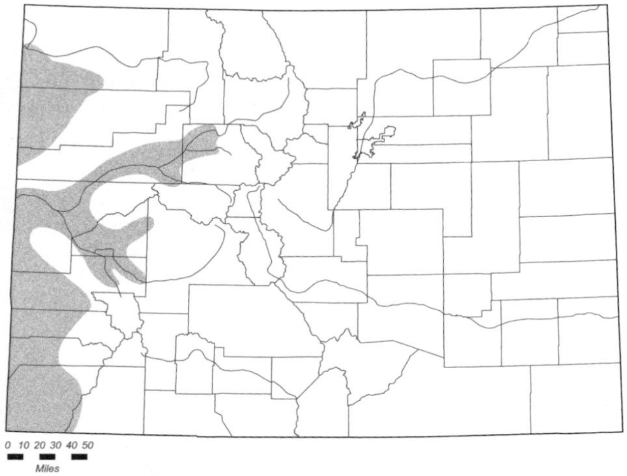

MAP 8-8. Distribution of the Hopi chipmunk (*Neotamias rufus*) in Colorado.

Natural History

This is the common chipmunk of the canyons and slickrock piñon-juniper country in western Colorado. Population densities appear to be highest in areas with an abundance of broken rock or rubble at the base of cliff faces or in rock formations with deep fissures and crevices suitable for den sites. Hopi chipmunks typically do not stray far from these rocky areas, although Cary (1911) thought them equally represented in extensive piñon-juniper stands on mesa tops. Some habitat manipulation, including chaining of piñon-juniper woodland and burning, benefit this species in some areas because the downed wood increases edge and cover.

Diet in southeastern Utah was about 60 percent seeds, 32 percent flowers, and 7 percent insects (D. Armstrong 1982). Seeds of Indian ricegrass and penstemon are eagerly sought, as are seeds of junipers, piñon, oak, skunkbush, and other shrubs. As with other chipmunks, food is gathered rapidly and stored in cheek pouches for transport to feeding sites (usually atop a rock or log from which visibility is good) or food caches. Individuals probably drink free water from depressions when available.

Home ranges have been estimated at about 0.5–1.0 ha based on dye-marked animals in Utah (Wadsworth 1969, 1972). Chipmunks, including this species, are diurnal, with activity cycles starting shortly after sunrise and often not ending until nearly dark. During the heat of summer they typically are inactive at midday. Winter dormancy is shorter than for other Coloradan chipmunks, with most animals not belowground until early December and arousing in late February or early March (Wadsworth 1972).

Chipmunks frequently exhibit aggression between species and this may promote habitat segregation. In an area of sympatry with the least chipmunk in Mesa County, Colorado, *N. rufus* was typically associated with trees in the juniper-piñon woodland. When *N. rufus* was abundant, *N. minimus* occurred mostly in sagebrush. When *N. rufus* was scarce or absent, however, the smaller *N. minimus* was more consistently associated with trees (J. Root, Calisher, and Beaty 2001).

In Colorado most breeding probably occurs in March or early April, with a gestation period of about 1 month. Individuals in southeastern Utah breed in late February and early March (Wadsworth 1969). Litter size ranges from 2 to 6, with only 1 litter per year. Young are blind and naked at birth. Eyes open at about 1 month of age, and the young leave the nest at about 5 weeks old. Weaning occurs when the young are 6 to 7 weeks old. Males and females reach sexual maturity at about 11 months of age. Literature on the Hopi chipmunk was reviewed by Burt and Best (1994).

PHOTOGRAPH 8-5. Uinta chipmunk (*Neotamias umbrinus*). Photograph by Joseph G. Hall.

Neotamias umbrinus

UINTA CHIPMUNK

Description

The Uinta chipmunk is larger than the least chipmunk and similar in size to the Colorado chipmunk. This chipmunk is often mistaken for the Colorado chipmunk, and older museum specimens are often mislabeled. Uinta, Colorado, and least chipmunks all occur in north-central Colorado. Most specimens of the Uinta chipmunk are not as brightly colored as the least and Colorado chipmunks. The lateral stripes are somewhat indistinct and the flanks are grayish in color. Overall dorsal coloration tends toward brownish, whereas in the other 2 species it is more reddish yellow. The dorsal stripes are generally more distinct than those of the cliff chipmunk. Measurements are: total length 215–235 mm; length of tail 88–110 mm; length of hindfoot 33–35 mm; length of ear 16–19 mm; weight 60–70 g. Condylobasal length is 31–34 mm. The Uinta chipmunk has a longer, narrower skull and a narrower jugal bone than does the Colorado chipmunk (D. Armstrong 1972). The baculum of the Uinta chipmunk has the distal half of the shaft laterally compressed, with the width of the base more than one-fourth the length of the tip. It has a distinctive bend lacking in the straighter baculum of the Colorado chipmunk (J. White 1953a, 1953b). Behavioral and elevational differences discussed below assist in separation of these very similar species. Because *N. umbrinus* and *N. quadrivittatus* are difficult to distinguish in the field, museum specimens should be prepared as vouchers of ecological work and deposited in a permanent, public museum collection (Bortolus 2008).

Distribution

The Uinta chipmunk has a complicated distribution across the western United States, probably reflecting expansion of forest during glacial periods and contraction during interglacial intervals. At the present postglacial (or perhaps interglacial) time, Coloradan populations are isolated from those to the north and west. In Colorado they occur along the Front Range, west to Routt and Rio Blanco counties

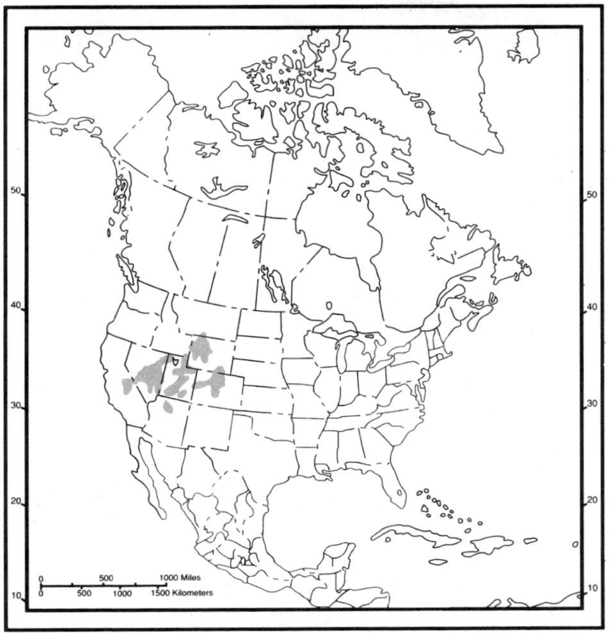

MAP 8-9. Distribution of the Uinta chipmunk (*Neotamias umbrinus*) in North America.

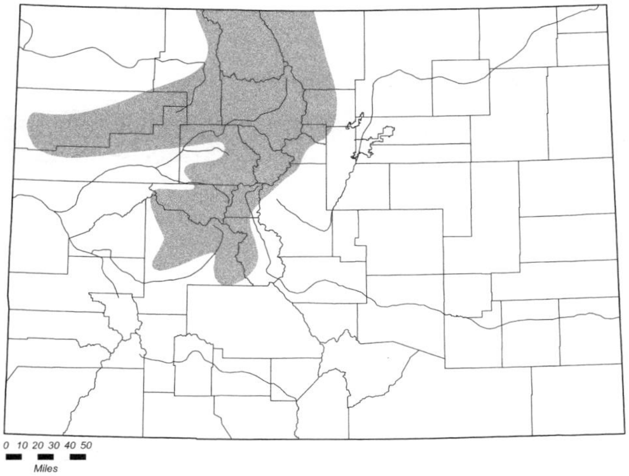

MAP 8-10. Distribution of the Uinta chipmunk (*Neotamias umbrinus*) in Colorado.

and south to Gunnison County. Ranges of the Colorado and Uinta chipmunks are mostly parapatric in Colorado (J. White 1953a; Long and Cronkite 1970; D. Armstrong 1972; Bergstrom and Hoffmann 1991), although this needs clarification in some areas on the Western Slope. Uinta chipmunks are often sympatric with least chipmunks and golden-mantled ground squirrels (Stinson 1978; Bergstrom and Hoffmann 1991). The Uinta chipmunk ranges from as low as 1,980 m (6,500 feet) to about 3,660 m (12,000 feet). One subspecies, *Neotamias umbrinus montanus*, occurs in Colorado.

Natural History

Because of the difficulty with identification, little information is available on the natural history of the Uinta chipmunk, although they occupy a variety of habitats in Colorado. In northwestern Colorado they occupy piñon-juniper woodlands and montane shrublands, where they were considered uncommon (R. Finley et al. 1976). Along the Taylor River in Gunnison County they were reported from cottonwood-willow river-bottoms (Long and Cronkite 1970). More commonly, they occur in higher-elevation forest-edge situations in montane and subalpine forests (especially lodgepole pine on rubbly moraines), and they sometimes range into the alpine. Like the Colorado chipmunk, the Uinta chipmunk favors rocky areas when available and is frequently common on talus slopes. Perault et al. (1997) described the importance of ecological distribution to patterns of gene flow in Uinta and least chipmunks in the Uinta Mountains of northeastern Utah.

The diet is similar to that of other chipmunks, consisting of a variety of berries, fruits, and seeds as well as new terminal growth, supplemented with insects and other animal matter, including carrion. As other species of chipmunks and ground squirrels, they often congregate in campgrounds, where they take practically any food offered them.

Telemetry studies in the Front Range found home ranges of 2–5 ha (Bergstrom 1988). The animals appear to make greater use of closed understory habitats than do least chipmunks. Good climbers, they forage on branches of conifers and shrubs. Uinta chipmunks excavate burrows under logs, rocks, shrubs, and similar surface features. On the basis of habitat, behavioral observations by K. Gordon (1943) probably pertain to this species.

Most individuals enter winter dens by early November. The animals are assumed to be dormant during much of the winter but probably arouse periodically to feed on stored food. Breeding occurs shortly after arousal in the spring. Gestation probably takes about 30 days, with 1 litter of 3 to 5 young produced per season.

Marmota flaviventris

YELLOW-BELLIED MARMOT

Description

Yellow-bellied marmots are large, stout-bodied ground squirrels, also known locally as "rockchucks" and "whistle-pigs" and sometimes mistakenly called woodchucks. Their tails are short (generally less than one-third the total length) and normally bushy. The pelage consists of long, coarse outer hairs and shorter, woolly underfur. Individuals vary widely in color, from yellow-brown to tawny, frequently with a heavily frosted appearance because of pale tips and darker bands on some of the guard hairs. There usually is a whitish band across the nose, and the sides of the neck are typically buffy. Ventrally the fur is somewhat sparse, pale brown to yellowish in color. Some Colorado marmots tend toward melanism (Warren 1942; Armitage 1961), and an albino marmot was observed in Rocky Mountain National Park in 2006 (F. Drumm, personal communication).

Measurements are: total length 470–680 mm; length of tail 130–210 mm; length of hindfoot 70–90 mm; length of ear 18–22 mm; weight 1.6–5.2 kg. Males are generally larger than females. The skull is broad and flat with a narrow interorbital region and well-developed postorbital processes that project posteriorly. The suture among the frontal, premaxillary, and nasal bones forms a distinct arch across the rostrum. Females have 10 mammae: 2 pectoral, 2 abdominal, and 1 inguinal pair. A baculum is present in males.

PHOTOGRAPH 8-6. Yellow-bellied marmot (*Marmota flaviventris*). © 1993 Wendy Shattil / Bob Rozinski.

Distribution

Yellow-bellied marmots occur mostly at higher elevations over the western two-thirds of the state, from as low as 1,650 m (5,400 feet) to over 4,270 m (14,000 feet). *Marmota flaviventris luteola* occurs throughout most of the occupied range in Colorado; *M. f. notioros* is found only in the Wet Mountains; *M. f. obscura* occurs in the Sangre de Cristo Range. Based on studies of the shape of lower third molars, Polly (2003) concluded that marmots in mid-Pleistocene deposits from Porcupine Cave, Park County, Colorado, were more closely related to modern woodchucks (*M. monax*) than to yellow-bellied marmots. This suggests that the yellow-bellied marmot may be a fairly recent arrival in Colorado.

Natural History

The biology of Coloradan marmots is well-known, especially from studies near Gothic, north of Crested Butte, Gunnison County, where Professor Kenneth B. Armitage (University of Kansas) and his co-workers at Rocky Mountain Biological Laboratory have studied them since 1962 (Armitage 1961, 1973, 1974, 1979, 1991, 1998, 1999, 2003; Armitage and Downhower 1974; Svendsen 1974; D. C. An-

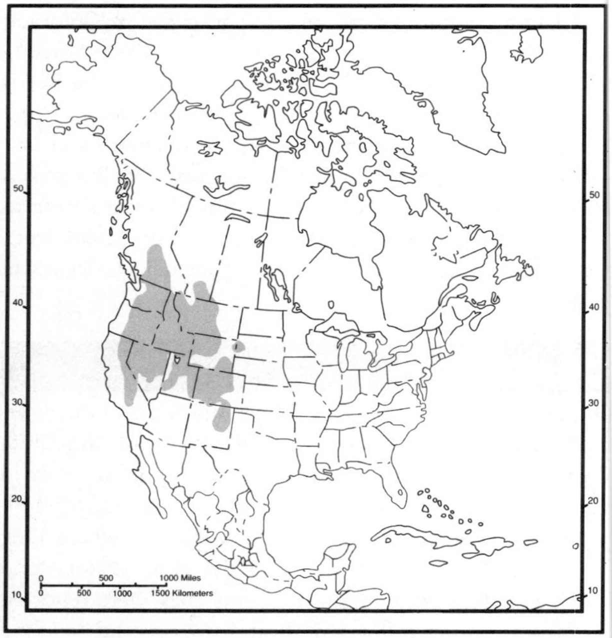

MAP 8-11. Distribution of the yellow-bellied marmot (*Marmota flaviventris*) in North America.

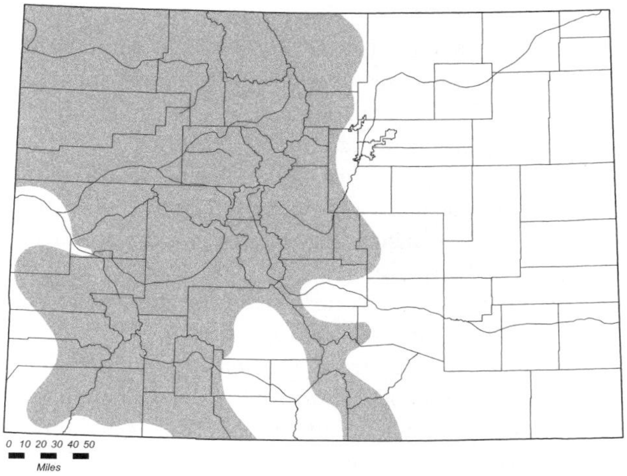

MAP 8-12. **Distribution of the yellow-bellied marmot (*Marmota flaviventris*) in Colorado.**

dersen, Armitage, and Hoffmann 1976; Armitage, Downhower, and Svendsen 1976; Armitage, Johns, and Andersen 1979; Van Vuren and Armitage 1994a, 1994b; Armitage and Schwartz 2000; Oli and Armitage 2003, 2008; Runyan and Blumstein 2004). Ozgul et al. (2010) analyzed the long-term record of research on marmots at Gothic to demonstrate a relationship between body mass at hibernation and population growth in response to earlier spring warming and snowmelt. Few studies exist on populations at lower elevations, and such studies are to be encouraged. There are a number of records from the foothills of the Front Range (D. Armstrong 1972), down to elevations of about 5,000 ft.; the lower-elevation limits might be expected to move upslope with ongoing climatic warming.

Yellow-bellied marmots occupy various habitats, being most common at elevations above 2,440 m (8,000 ft.) in alpine tundra and subalpine and montane meadows. They also range down into the foothills and canyon country on either side of the mountains where rock outcrops or boulders exist along with suitably productive and succulent vegetation.

Marmots eat a variety of forbs. Less than 6.5 percent of available net primary production was consumed in 1 Colorado study, at least partially because of selective foraging (Kilgore and Armitage 1978). Preferred food species include dandelions, cow parsnip, chiming bells, cinquefoil, and brome grass. Although marmots will eat flowers of potentially toxic species such as columbine, lupine, and larkspur, they tend to avoid plant parts where such chemicals concentrate. When foraging in lush vegetation, marmots often crawl on their bellies, forming conspicuous beaten-down paths (Armitage 1962). Seeds are consumed in late summer. Marmots are thought not to be food limited over their range, although duration of snow cover affects food availability in spring and early summer, which, in turn, affects reproductive success of females (Van Vuren and Armitage 1991). Some evidence suggests that moderate grazing by livestock favors marmots by enhancing forb production (Frase and Hoffmann 1980). Cannibalism has been reported (Armitage, Johns, and Andersen 1979).

Marmots are semi-fossorial, digging burrows under large rocks, buildings, bridge abutments, and other protective features. An estimated 80 percent of a marmot's life is spent in its burrow, with about 60 percent of that time in hibernation. Most home burrows are built on slopes oriented toward the northeast or southwest. Rock outcrops or boulders are usually close to the burrow entrance and serve as sites for sunning and observation (Svendsen 1976b). Trails develop between burrows.

Like other ground squirrels, marmots are diurnal, with peaks of activity in early morning and late afternoon. Although some individuals are solitary and transient, most are social, living in relatively stable colonies that consist of a dominant male, several females (usually related—mother, daughters, sisters—a "matriline"), and their offspring. Within a colony, social organization is maintained through a variety of behaviors, including play, grooming, sniffing of cheek glands, and agonistic behaviors such as threat postures, chases, and fights. Males defend territories that are usually less than 1 ha in area. Territorial behaviors include tail flagging and patrolling of boundaries (Armitage 1962). Sociality in marmots may be a response to a short growing season, which slows development and thus delays dispersal but increases survivorship (Armitage 1991, 2007). Subordinate adults may contribute to social thermoregulation (Armitage 1999, 2007).

Communication is auditory, visual, and olfactory. A variety of whistles function as alert, alarm, or threat signals. Pikas and golden-mantled ground squirrels also respond to these whistles. An undulating scream is a response to fear or excitement, and a tooth chatter signals aggression (Waring 1966). Some naturalists have thought that marmot calls differ in response to different predators, but experimental studies (Blumstein and Armitage 1997a, 1997b, 1998b) demonstrated that not to be the case. Marmots do seem to have some ability to discriminate predators (coyotes, wolves, eagles) acoustically (Blumstein, Cooley, et al. 2008); the fact that marmots appeared to discriminate wolf from coyote suggests an innate component to the behavior, as wolves have not occurred in their study area in Gunnison County for at least 75 years. Marmot pups have a distinctive call, a protracted scream (Blumstein, Richardson et al. 2008). Blumstein and Armitage (1997a, 1998a, 1998b) and Blumstein, Steinmetz, et al. (1997) attributed calling in marmots to kin selection. Marmots scent-mark with cheek glands, a behavior observed in conflict situations that probably expresses dominance (Armitage 1974).

Home ranges of males at Gothic vary greatly in size (Salsbury and Armitage 1994), from less than 0.1 to 47.5 ha (median, 1.02 ha), influenced by the distribution of females and the density of males. Territories increase or decrease in size in relation to the numbers of adult males in the colony (Armitage 1974). Territorial behavior and aggressive conflicts lead to development of relatively stable central colonies and peripheral "satellite" populations. Both males and females are recruited into colonies by immigration. Satellite populations tend to be less stable and may have lower reproductive success than central colonies. Lack of suitable burrowing sites may limit distribution. Home range size has been estimated at 0.13–1.98 ha (Armitage 1975).

Mating systems of marmots range from monogamous pairs to harems of one male with many females (Downhower and Armitage 1971; Armitage and Johns 1982; Armitage 1998). As other western marmots (but unlike the woodchuck, *M. monax*), *M. flaviventris* has a complex social structure (Blumstein and Armitage 1998a; Armitage 2007). Mating probably occurs within the first 2 weeks following emergence from hibernation. Yearling females do not reproduce in Colorado, and as many as 75 percent of 2-year-olds may not breed (Armitage and Downhower 1974; O. Schwartz et al. 1998). A single litter is produced per year (Howell 1915).

Gestation and lactation probably total about 7 to 8 weeks, and litter size ranges from 3 to 8. Average litter size in Colorado is about 4. Little is known about the development of the neonates, which occurs belowground. In mountainous regions of Colorado, young emerge from the natal den in late June and July, with weaning occurring by mid-July (Armitage et al. 1976), but this probably varies greatly with elevation. Based on work at Gothic, Colorado, O. Schwartz et al. (1998) developed a life history table for a cohort of more than 1,500 marmots of known age. Mean life expectancy at birth was 1.4 years for males and 1.9 years for females; the oldest male in the sample was 9 years of age and the oldest female was 15. Yellow-bellied marmots exhibit a "Type II" survivorship curve, the probability of death being about the same at any age, regardless of gender (O. Schwartz and Armitage 2003).

Survival of dispersing marmots (0.73) was only 16 percent lower than survival of philopatric marmots (0.87). The cost-benefit analysis suggested that survival cost of dispersal may be lower than some aspects of philopatry, so dispersal may be a tactic promoting individual fitness (Van Vuren and Armitage 1994a). Dispersal is nearly obligatory for males, but facultative for females. Costs of philopatry for females include inbreeding depression and reproductive inhibition, perhaps postponing first reproduction until the third year. Males that do not disperse seldom reproduce and face the possibility of fatal aggression.

Marmots are the largest true hibernators (Armitage 2007). Hibernation lasts 7 to 8 months, depending on local conditions, especially late summer food supply and timing of spring snowmelt. Some mortality occurs in hibernation. Lenihan and Van Vuren (1996) showed heavier juveniles were more likely to survive hibernation. Mass at entry into hibernation was more important to overwinter survival than was severity of the winter. Food is not stored; overwinter survival is fueled by energy from stored fat (Armitage 2003). Some animals tend to hibernate singly, although littermates or siblings of different ages (matrilines) may den together, as may dominant males and one or more females (Armitage 2003; Blumstein et al. 2004). Date of first emergence of marmots from hibernation at Gothic advanced by approximately 1 day per year from 1976 to 1999 (Inouye et al. 2000). Blumstein (2009) found that variation in emergence date was related to social structure of hibernating groups. Armitage (2007) argued that sociality in marmots is a correlate and consequence of hibernation in strongly seasonal environments. Marmots den with littermates at least their first winter and typically disperse as yearlings. Yellow-bellied marmots are important to laboratory studies of hibernation (see, e.g., Florant and Greenwood 1986; Florant et al. 2004; Hoehn et al. 2004).

Marmots are regular and frequent prey of coyotes. Other mortality is caused by badgers, eagles, hawks (Blumstein 1989), human hunters, and diseases (including plague). A little more than 10 percent of a marmot's time is spent in vigilance for predators. This increases when alarm calls are heard and decreases when marmots are in groups, have good visibility, and have burrows that are nearby and plentiful (H. Carey and Moore 1986). Survival of male marmots varies among sites in the vicinity of Gothic, Gunnison County (Borrego et al. 2008), apparently in response to local conditions, including the presence of other marmots. Blumstein, Barrow, and Luterra (2008) found that Coloradan marmots could distinguish the scent of potential predators (coyote, wolf, mountain lion) from that of non-predators (elk, moose). The fact that they could distinguish predators and herbivores with which they had no experience (wolf and moose, respectively) suggested that this olfactory discrimination is innate.

Frase and Hoffmann (1980) summarized the general literature on the yellow-bellied marmot; Armitage (1991) provided a thorough synthesis of 3 decades of research at Gothic, north of Crested Butte; and Armitage (2003) published a thorough, comparative review of literature on North American marmots generally. The marmot is classified as a small game species in Colorado (Table 4-1). Seasons and limits are set annually; in recent years there has been a brief season (August to October) with a possession limit of 4 (see Colorado Division of Wildlife 2009f).

Marmota is a Holarctic genus comprising some 14 species, 4 of which occur in North America. The monograph by Bezuidenhout and Evans (2005) on the anatomy of the woodchuck (*Marmota monax*) is largely pertinent to other marmots. The genus *Marmota* has provided a fascinating system in which to answer questions about the evolution of sociality and adaptation to rigorous, seasonal environments. Indeed, the study of marmot anti-predator behavior has even stimulated thinking about national security policy (Blumstein 2008). "The Marmot Burrow" is an international Internet clearinghouse for information on marmots, maintained by Professor Dan Blumstein of the University of California–Los Angeles (http://www.marmotburrow.ucla.edu/).

Ground Squirrels

Ground squirrels are a Holarctic radiation. Some 41 species (Thorington and Hoffmann 2005) formerly were included in a genus, *Spermophilus*. A majority of species are North American, ranging from the Arctic to the Mexican states of Michoacán and Jalisco and also Distrito Federal. One species, the Arctic ground squirrel (*S. parryi*), is amphi-Beringean (occurring on both sides of the Bering Strait). Helgen et al. (2009) presented a thorough revision of *Spermophilus*. They noted that recent molecular phylogenies have suggested that both the prairie dogs (*Cynomys*) and marmots (*Marmota*) are nested within *Spermophilus*, and thus *Spermophilus* as traditionally construed is a paraphyletic group (i.e., a group containing some but not all of the descendants of a common ancestor). Based on a thorough analysis of morphological data and review of the recent molecular genetic evidence, Helgen et al. (2009) proposed elevating a number of subgenera of *Spermophilus* to generic status, and that arrangement is followed here.

There are 6 species of ground squirrels in Colorado (and a seventh species, Franklin's ground squirrel, occurs near enough to the state to be considered of possible occurrence). Antelope ground squirrels (*Ammospermophilus*) are superficially similar to the mantled ground squirrels (*Callospermophilus*) but are generally conceded to represent an independent lineage (R. G. Harrison et al. 2003).

Coloradan ground squirrels are eminently "watchable wildlife," distinctive in external appearance and usually rather distinctive in habitat preferences as well. In fact, casual observers more frequently confuse golden-mantled ground squirrels with chipmunks (and rock squirrels with tree squirrels) than they confuse species of ground squirrels with each other.

Ammospermophilus leucurus

WHITE-TAILED ANTELOPE SQUIRREL

Description

White-tailed antelope squirrels are characterized by having single white lateral stripes that run from behind the shoulder to the hip. Striping is absent from the head. The dorsum is reddish brown to ash gray, and the venter is somewhat paler. The slightly bushy tail is whitish below and black to dark gray dorsally. While running, the animals carry the tail curved over the rump, revealing the flashy white undersurface and leading to the common name "antelope squirrel."

PHOTOGRAPH 8-7. White-tailed antelope squirrel (*Ammospermophilus leucurus*). Photograph by J. Perley Fitzgerald.

Measurements are: total length 190–240 mm; length of tail 55–90 mm; length of hindfoot 35–45 mm; length of ear 9–11 mm; weight 80–110 g. A small masseteric tubercle lies directly below the oval infraorbital foramen. Males have a baculum. Although chipmunks and golden-mantled ground squirrels resemble this species superficially, they are readily distinguished by having more dorsal stripes, the pale stripes being bordered by black stripes.

Distribution

The white-tailed antelope squirrel occurs in the western third of the state to about 2,100 m (7,000 ft.) in elevation. Cary (1911) reported it as common at a number of sites. R. Finley et al. (1976) attempted to secure specimens from some of the same sites in northwestern Colorado sampled by Cary (1911) some 70 years previously and concluded that the species is becoming uncommon, perhaps as a result of human encroachment or unknown environmental changes. *Ammospermophilus leucurus cinnamomeus* occurs south of the Colorado River drainage in the southwestern corner of the state; *A. l. pennipes* occurs in the Colorado and Gunnison drainages and along the White River in Rio Blanco County. McCoy and Miller (1964) discussed the ecological distribution of the subspecies.

Natural History

The biology of white-tailed antelope squirrels is poorly known in Colorado, the northeastern limits of their range. They inhabit semidesert shrublands, piñon-juniper woodlands, and lower montane shrublands and occasionally are found in lowland riparian communities. They occupy burrows dug by other animals, such as kangaroo rats or smaller ground squirrels, and also dig their own burrows under bushes, clumps of grasses, or at the bases of trees, often in sandy soils near rock outcrops. White-tailed antelope squirrels appear "nervous," seldom remaining still, but rather racing furtively to gather food or nest material and then retreating to the burrow. The tail is invariably held erect, curving over the body when the animals are moving.

No studies of food habits of this species have been made in Colorado. Farther west they are omnivorous, with flowers, fruits, and seeds making up about one-half to three-quarters of their diet (W. Bradley 1968; D. Armstrong 1982). These foods are supplemented with green matter, insects, small lizards, rodents, and carrion. They may capture and feed on pocket mice (Morgart 1985). Remains of insects may be conspicuous at the entrance of burrows (W. Bradley 1967). Some food is transported in the internal cheek pouches to be stored in the burrow. They do not need free water for drinking.

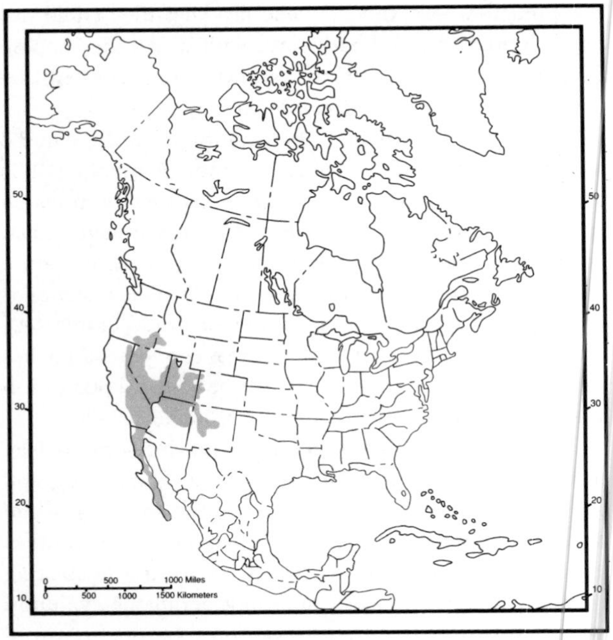

MAP 8-13. Distribution of the white-tailed antelope squirrel (*Ammospermophilus leucurus*) in North America.

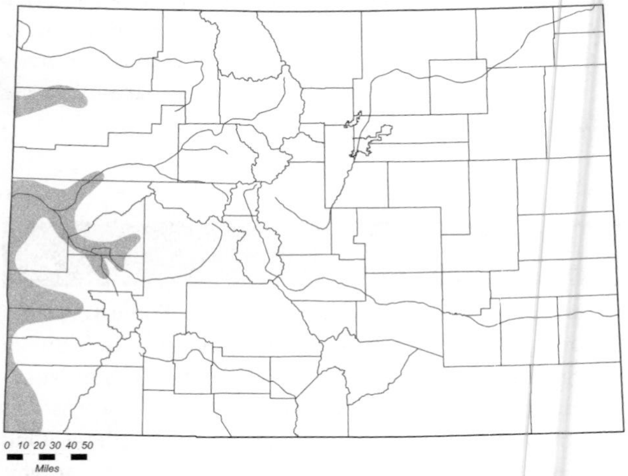

MAP 8-14. Distribution of the white-tailed antelope squirrel (*Ammospermophilus leucurus*) in Colorado.

White-tailed antelope squirrels are diurnal, with peaks of activity in morning and late afternoon; in extremely hot weather they may virtually disappear from aboveground, a behavioral strategy for avoiding heat stress (W.

Bradley 1967; Kavanau and Rischer 1972). Physiologically they show increased tolerance to dehydration, salivate (to increase evaporative cooling), and tolerate hyperthermia for short periods of time (Bartholomew and Hudson 1959; J. Hudson 1962). Antelope squirrels avoid cold weather by retreating to burrows but are not reported to hibernate.

Home ranges cover as much as 6 ha, with daily movements often encompassing 1.6 ha (W. Bradley 1967). Little is known about social behavior. In Utah, the species dominated Hopi chipmunks where home ranges overlapped (D. Armstrong 1982). They seem to be uncommon in Colorado, with only 1 or a few individuals observed in any particular area.

Breeding probably occurs from February to April, with most litters born in March and April (D. Armstrong 1982). Antelope squirrels are monoestrous. In Nevada, gestation takes 30 to 35 days, and litter sizes ranged from 5 to 11 (averaging 7.8) (H. Smith and Jorgensen 1975). Energy investment in reproduction is higher than in most squirrels (Hayssen 2008b). Mortality may be as much as 80 percent during the first year of life (W. Bradley 1967). Belk and Smith (1991) reviewed the literature.

Otospermophilus variegatus

ROCK SQUIRREL

Description

The rock squirrel is the largest of Coloradan ground squirrels. They may even be confused with fox squirrels, unless attention is paid to the variegated markings, less bushy tail, and grayer (less reddish) color. The color is grayish to blackish gray, with the dorsal surface showing pale dappling. The shoulders are darker than the rump, and the flanks are brownish. The venter is a pale grayish brown. Some individuals are quite pale in overall color. The bushy tail is about the same length as the head and body. Measurements are: total length 440–530 mm; length of tail 160–230 mm; length of hindfoot 53–63 mm; length of ear 17–27 mm; weight 650–1,000 g. The skull is large and robust, averaging 55–60 mm in condylobasal length. The masseteric tubercle lies ventral to the oval infraorbital foramen. Rock squirrels are more closely related to the golden-mantled ground squirrel than to other Coloradan ground squirrels (Gerber and Birney 1968; Helgen et al. 2009). For comment on use of the generic name *Otospermophilus*, see the general account of ground squirrels above.

PHOTOGRAPH 8-8. Rock squirrel (*Otospermophilus variegatus*). Photograph by Joseph G. Hall.

Distribution

Rock squirrels are found in foothills and valleys below 2,530 m (8,300 ft.). They occur in a band along the Front Range north nearly to the Wyoming border, up the Arkansas Valley, and eastward in southeastern Colorado to Baca County. They also occur in roughlands at lower elevations in western Colorado north to Dinosaur National Monument (R.

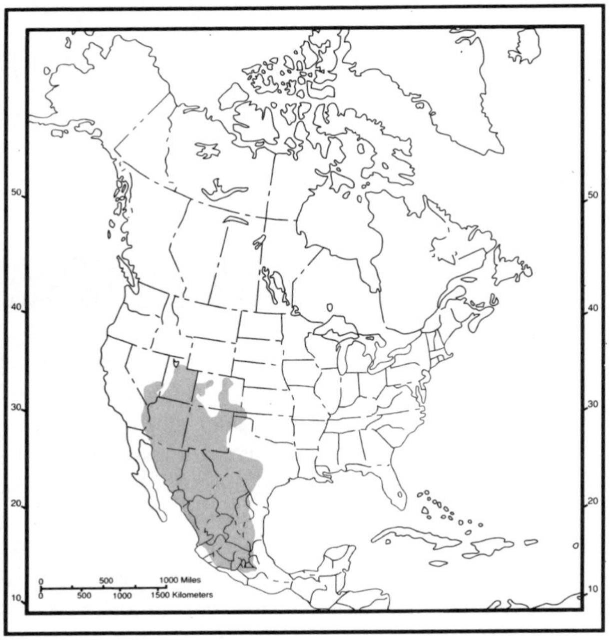

MAP 8-15. Distribution of the rock squirrel (*Otospermophilus variegatus*) in North America.

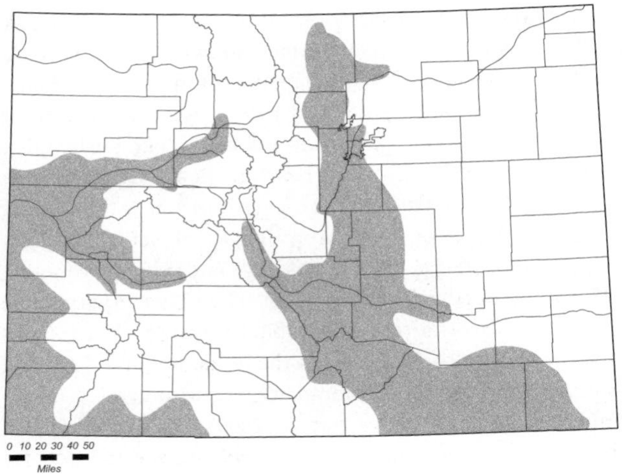

MAP 8-16. Distribution of the rock squirrel (*Otospermophilus variegatus*) in Colorado.

Finley and Bogan 1995). Small colonies have been making significant range extensions along riparian woodland corridors on the northeastern plains of Colorado. Populations are now well entrenched in Fort Collins (Quinones 1988) and they are spreading eastward along the Cache la Poudre River. In Greeley, several animals established a small colony in 1989 in riprap along the Poudre. Similar populations have existed near Windsor since the early 1980s. These pioneering populations are almost exclusively associated with rock, concrete, abandoned autos, and similar materials used to stabilize riverbanks (J. P. Fitzgerald, unpublished observations). These populations represent eastward extension of the range of some 50 km. One subspecies, *Otospermophilus variegatus grammurus*, occurs in Colorado.

Natural History

In Colorado, this is probably the least-known ground squirrel; no detailed studies have been done on its ecology in the state, where they are not generally abundant. The rock squirrel is a mammal of rocky hillsides, rimrock, and canyons, requiring boulders, talus, or tangles of dense vegetation under which to burrow (Cary 1911; D. Armstrong 1972; Steiner 1975). Piñon-juniper woodlands and montane shrublands are the ecosystems in which they are most likely to be found, but they also occur in montane forest, riparian woodlands, and orchards and increasingly in rock outcrops in cultivated and suburban areas. Such extensions are possible because of the plasticity of the species in adapting to novel denning sites, including piles of scrap tires, dumps, auto junkyards, riprap, construction debris, and woodpiles (Quinones 1988). In Utah they readily colonize abandoned woodrat dens (Juelson 1970).

Rock squirrels are opportunistic feeders, especially during times of low food availability. They are expert climbers and often feed in trees and bushes, and they also bury food—traits that may cause the casual observer to mistake them for fox squirrels. During the growing season, diet tends toward green material and flowering parts. In New Mexico, flowers of skunkbush, gooseberry, and oak were especially important (Stalheim 1965). Later in the season, seeds, fruits, and acorns are often eaten. Piñon nuts, acorns, and juniper "berries" are important foods in Colorado (Cary 1911). Damage to orchards and other crops has been reported in some areas. As with most other sciurids, carrion and insects are eaten. Cannibalism and predation on cottontails and nestling birds and eggs occur. Large internal cheek pouches aid in transport of seeds and other food items. Rock squirrels do not seem to store food regularly in the den, relying instead on fat accumulation for winter survival (Oaks et al. 1987). Rock squirrels and other rodents may be responsible for dispersal of Gambel oak (*Quercus gambelii*) at its northeastern limits in central Colorado (J. Reynolds et al. 2006).

Rock squirrels are usually colonial, with dominant males defending colony boundaries during the breeding season. Mature dominant females apparently control prime burrow sites as subordinate males are forced to peripheral habitats. Home ranges frequently overlap among adult males and 1 or more females. Densities probably average about 5 or 6 individuals per hectare but can vary from about 2 to 13, depending on habitat quality and season. During the non-breeding season, adults occupy individual home ranges separate from members of the opposite sex (Juelson 1970; K. Johnson 1979, 1981). In a New Mexico population, density of adults was low (fewer than 2 animals per hectare), and individual home ranges were large (3.8 and 7.9 ha for females and males, respectively), overlapping for all sex and age classes (Shriner and Stacey 1991). Ortega (1990a) described seasonal change in home range size in southeastern Arizona, with that of males being significantly larger during the breeding season. The animals were only moderately social and adults did not interact outside the breeding season.

Rock squirrels are diurnal, with 1 or 2 activity peaks, depending on temperature. They seek refuge at extreme temperatures. Communication is by postures, vocalizations, and scent marking. Familiar squirrels approach each other head-on and make nasal contact. Unfamiliar animals approach one another at an angle and use threat displays to assert dominance. Vocalizations are mostly warning calls given by colonial females (Krenz 1977). Rock squirrels have dorsal skin glands, which males rub against rocks during the breeding season (Juelson 1970), and cheek glands, which both sexes rub against rocks and sniff during intraspecific encounters (K. Johnson 1979). They also use specific sites for urination and defecation, suggesting scent mounds. The function of these behaviors is not known.

Rock squirrels dig extensive burrow systems beneath objects. Burrow systems usually are shallow but may reach close to 6 m in length. Side tunnels often are associated with the main tunnel, and as with most ground-dwelling sciurids, feces are typically deposited in tunnels outside the nest (Stalheim 1965; Juelson 1970). Tree bark frequently is stripped for nesting material, and leaves and grass are used also (R. M. Bradley 1929; Steiner 1975).

Males reportedly take several weeks to reach reproductive condition following emergence in the spring. (In most other ground squirrels, males are already in breeding condition at emergence.) Breeding occurs within 1 to 2 weeks after males come into season. Based on studies in Utah (Juelson 1970) and Texas (K. Johnson 1979), most breeding in our area probably occurs between late March and early June, depending on elevation. In Arizona, mating occurred from mid-April to early July, lasting 9 weeks in any 1 year, and this timing was closely associated with heavy summer rains (Ortega 1990b). The gestation period is unknown but is presumably about a month. Contrary to some earlier reports (see Oaks et al. 1987), Ortega (1990b) found rock squirrels to be monoestrous, having a single litter per year. Embryo counts range from 3 to 9 with an average of 5. Average aboveground litter size is 4.8 in Arizona. In Utah, mean embryo counts were 6.1. Four weaned pups are the average. Studies in Utah and elsewhere suggest that young stay in the burrow until 8 to 10 weeks of age, an unusually prolonged time belowground for a ground squirrel (Stalheim 1965; Juelson 1970). By 2 months postemergence, young approximate 90 percent of adult length but they may take 2 years to reach full weight. Juvenile animals may disperse in late summer, fall, or the following spring. In New Mexico, apparently only yearling males dispersed, yearling females remaining near their natal site (Shriner and Stacey 1991).

In colder parts of the range, rock squirrels hibernate. Little time was spent in dormancy at Colorado National Monument (P. Miller 1964). As with other ground squirrels the species shows diurnal activity patterns, with most activity occurring in the middle of the day during the colder months but taking on a bimodal pattern during the warm season. During extremely hot weather the animals aestivate (Juelson 1970; K. Johnson 1979).

Rock squirrels are important in plague epizootics over much of their range, with mortality reaching 40 to 60 percent (Barnes 1982; Quinones 1988). During 1974–1985, slightly more than 40 percent of human plague cases were associated with rock squirrels. Life span may exceed 3 years in wild populations. Most larger diurnal raptorial and ground-dwelling predators will prey on this species. The rock squirrel is considered a small game mammal in Colorado (Table 4-1), although harvest data are not gathered consistently. Oaks et al. (1987) reviewed the literature.

Callospermophilus lateralis

GOLDEN-MANTLED GROUND SQUIRREL

Description

Medium-sized, the golden-mantled ground squirrel has a distinctive reddish brown "mantle" on the head and shoulders. Two white stripes bordered by black extend from the shoulder onto the back. The eye is surrounded by a whitish ring; unlike chipmunks, there are no white stripes on the head. The belly is a pale buffy brown to creamy white. The tail is reddish brown to yellowish brown and not particularly bushy. Measurements are: total length 240–300 mm; length of tail 70–120 mm; length of hindfoot 38–45 mm; length of ear 16–23 mm; weight 170–290 g. Condylobasal length of the skull is about 40 mm.

PHOTOGRAPH 8-9. Golden-mantled ground squirrel (*Callospermophilus lateralis*). Photograph by J. Perley Fitzgerald.

Distribution

Golden-mantled ground squirrels are common over much of the western two-thirds of the state at elevations from 1,600 m to 3,800 m (5,200–12,500 ft.). *Callospermophilus lateralis lateralis* occurs over most of that area; the pale-colored *C. l. wortmani* is known only from along the Little Snake River in Moffat County, being mostly an animal of adjacent southwestern Wyoming. No Coloradan ground squirrels are thought to be threatened or endangered (Van Horne 2007). However, *C. l. wortmani* was highlighted by D. Hafner et al. (1998b) as being of conservation concern based on an absence of recent information. This species is treated in a genus, *Callospermophilus*, following Helgen et al. (2009); previously that name was used mostly at the subgeneric level (see E. Hall 1981).

Natural History

This is one of the more ubiquitous and easily observed small mammals in Colorado, comparable to the deer mouse and the least chipmunk in its tolerance for humans. Although the golden-mantled ground squirrel has a very broad distribution in the West and is often abundant in suitable habitat, surprisingly little work has been done on its life history. Yensen and Sherman (2003) reviewed the extensive literature on North American ground squirrels

Golden-mantled ground squirrels are animals of open woodlands, shrublands, mountain meadows, and forest-edge habitat. They usually are not present in heavily wooded areas, favoring sites with good sunlight over more shaded areas (Cary 1911; D. Armstrong 1972). In Colorado the species occurs in alpine tundra, montane and subalpine forests, semidesert shrublands, montane shrublands, and riparian woodlands. It is frequently found in association with different species of chipmunks, other ground squirrels, and woodrats. In western Montana, golden-mantled ground squirrels were favored by fuel-management programs that opened ponderosa pine stands while maintaining mature trees (Shick et al. 2006). Although Wyoming ground squirrels (*Urocitellus elegans*) are reported to displace *C. lateralis* (R. Hansen 1962; A. Carey et al. 1980), it in turn appears to dominate most *Neotamias* species for both den sites and food in areas of sympatry. For the most part, species of ground squirrels in Colorado are separated by habitat preferences (which may reflect present or past competition, of course).

The diet is rather diverse; green vegetation, fungi, and seeds are consumed in quantity (Tevis 1952; McKeever 1964; Carleton 1966). Near Gothic, Gunnison County, these squirrels preferred dandelion stems but also were observed to feed on aster, sunflower, larkspur, clover, vetch, monkshood, and groundsel as well as sagebrush leaves and grass seed. Animal matter eaten includes insects, carrion, eggs, and nestling birds. Larger size and greater speed allow the animals

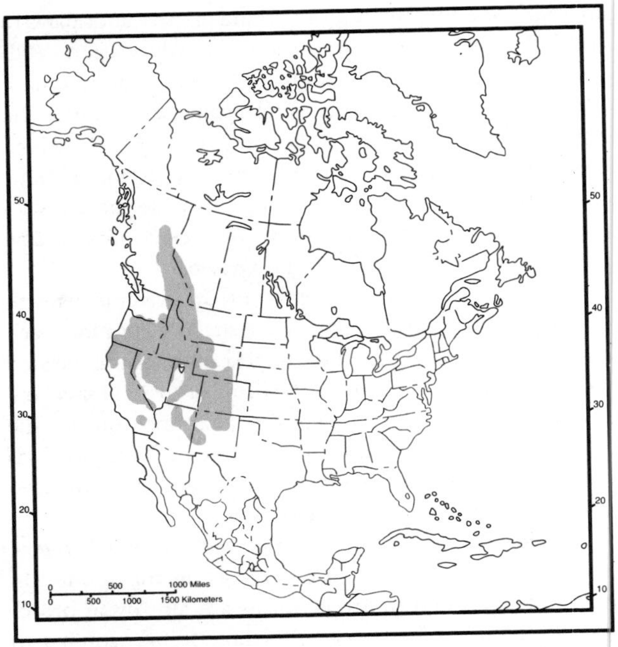

MAP 8-17. Distribution of the golden-mantled ground squirrel (*Callospermophilus lateralis*) in North America.

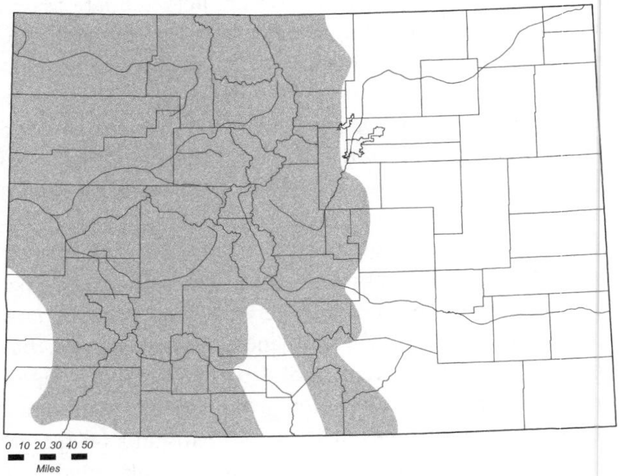

MAP 8-18. Distribution of the golden-mantled ground squirrel (*Callospermophilus lateralis*) in Colorado.

to forage more efficiently and safely in open meadow habitats than do sympatric least chipmunks (R. J. Smith 1995). Golden-mantled ground squirrels burrow beneath rocks, trees, and buildings. Burrow systems may be extensive, up to 8 m in length, with side tunnels and chambers and usually several entrances. Depth is usually not more than 20–30 cm. A nest is constructed from grasses and leaves.

Golden-mantled squirrels are monoestrous, with mating occurring within a few weeks following emergence in the spring. Gestation is probably 28 to 30 days. A single litter of altricial young is produced annually. Litter size ranges from 2 to 8 with an average of 5. As with most other ground squirrels, animals first breed at 1 year of age. Young are about 90 percent of adult size at 2.5 months of age (Tevis 1955; McKeever 1964; Skryja and Clark 1970).

Golden-mantled ground squirrels are mostly solitary and demonstrate territorial behavior near their dens. However, they may congregate in large numbers at artificial feeding sites in campgrounds and heavily used tourist areas. In such areas, dominance hierarchies form, determining access to provisioned resources. Diurnal activities begin soon after sunrise and give way to midday inactivity on hot days. Home ranges vary from 1 to 12 ha, depending on season and habitat; a density of 5 animals per hectare was found in a meadow along the Cache la Poudre River (K. Gordon 1938), and Friedrichsen (1977) found 8.8 individuals per hectare in a provisioned population in Rocky Mountain National Park.

In Colorado most golden-mantled ground squirrels are in hibernation by mid-October, several weeks ahead of chipmunks at the same elevation. They emerge in March, April, or May, depending on elevation. Females typically emerge several weeks later than males. Hibernating squirrels aroused about every 5 days when entering and coming out of hibernation, but periods of inactivity lasted as long as 14 days during the peak of dormancy (Jameson 1964). Males stored more fat than females prior to hibernation and animals from 2,900 m (9,500 ft.) had larger body sizes and fat stores than animals from lower elevations (B. Blake 1972). At room temperatures, animals from higher elevations also entered torpor more frequently than those from lower elevations. In California, emergence of females was related to snow cover of less than 50 percent (Bronson 1980). Like several other Coloradan ground squirrels, *C. lateralis* has been important to laboratory studies of the physiology of hibernation; see, for example, Pulawa and Florant (2000).

Most individuals probably do not survive more than 2 or 3 years in the wild. A variety of mortality factors contribute to population turnover, including predation by small and medium-sized carnivores, death during hibernation, and disease, including sylvatic plague (A. Carey et al. 1980). According to studies in Rocky Mountain National Park, *C. lateralis* and least chipmunks are important hosts for the virus that causes Colorado tick fever and the source of the virus for immature ticks, *Dermacentor andersoni* (G. Bowen et al. 1981). Bartels and Thompson (1993) provided a thorough review of the literature.

Ictidomys tridecemlineatus

THIRTEEN-LINED GROUND SQUIRREL

Description

Thirteen-lined ground squirrels are small and have a conspicuous series of alternating dark and light stripes on the back and head. The dark stripes each are marked by a series of nearly square white spots, and the general background color is buffy yellow, although variation is apparent (D. Armstrong 1971). The venter is buffy to yellowish. Measurements are: total length 170–297 mm; length of tail 60–132 mm; length of hindfoot 27–41 mm; weight 100–250 g. The skull is 23–38 mm in condylobasal length, with postorbital breadth averaging 10.5–11.5 mm.

PHOTOGRAPH 8-10. Thirteen-lined ground squirrel (*Ictidomys tridecemlineatus*). Photograph by J. W. Jackson. All rights reserved, Photo Archives, Denver Museum of Nature and Science.

Distribution

Thirteen-lined ground squirrels are found across much of the eastern third of Colorado. They also occupy some of the high mountain valleys, including the San Luis Valley, South Park, the Little Snake drainage in Moffat County, and the White River Plateau in Garfield County. Populations seem to have decreased in some of these mountain parklands. During 14 years of small mammal trapping in South Park in the 1960s and 1970s, J. Fitzgerald (1993a) captured no specimens, although a decade earlier Ecke and Johnson (1952) captured them frequently during plague surveys. Thirteen-lined ground squirrels may be affected adversely by Wyoming ground squirrels (which entered South Park only within the past century; R. Hansen 1962); several authors have commented on the apparent competitive superiority of *Urocitellus elegans*, including an ability to exclude *Callospermophilus lateralis* where sympatric (R. Hansen 1962; Zegers 1984).

Ictidomys tridecemlineatus arenicola occurs in the southeastern part of the state from the Wet Mountains east and south of the Palmer Divide; *I. t. pallidus* occurs in South Park and North Park and throughout northeastern Colorado; *I. t. parvus* is the subspecies of the northwestern corner of the state, north of the Roan Plateau and Colorado River. *I. t. blanca* probably is restricted to the San Luis Valley; E. Hall (1981) mapped a puzzling extension of the range of the subspecies to western New Mexico, apparently based on a misunderstanding of comments by D. Armstrong (1971). The conservation status of *I. t. blanca* probably is worthy of investigation, in light of intensive irrigated agriculture in large parts of the San Luis Valley. For comment on use of the generic name *Ictidomys*, see the general account of ground squirrels above.

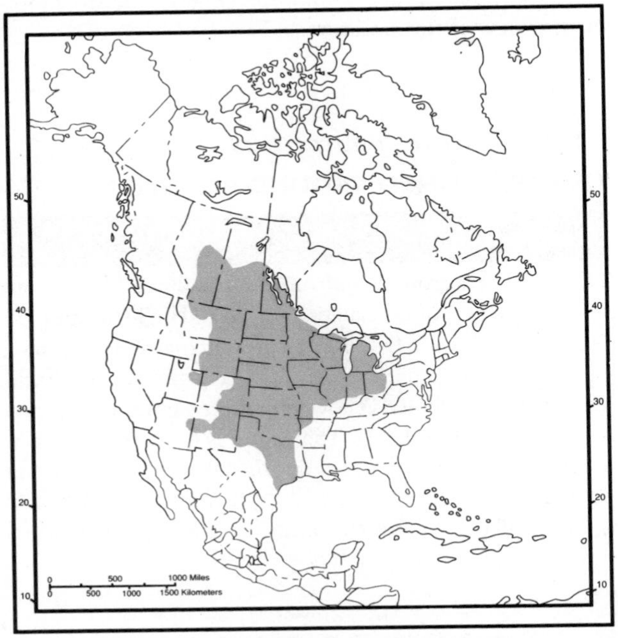

MAP 8-19. Distribution of the 13-lined ground squirrel (*Ictidomys tridecemlineatus*) in North America.

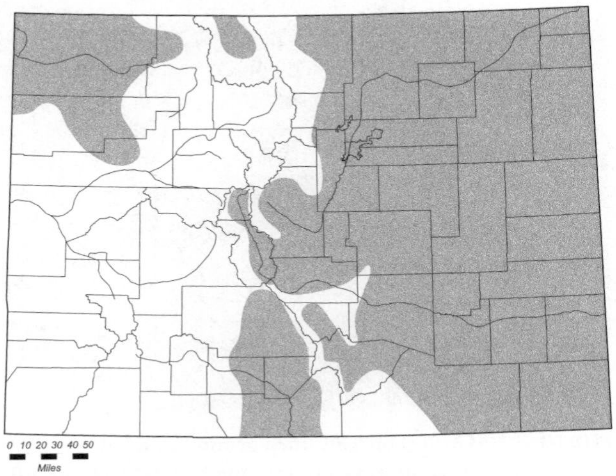

MAP 8-20. Distribution of the 13-lined ground squirrel (*Ictidomys tridecemlineatus*) in Colorado.

Natural History

Thirteen-lined ground squirrels are typical of grasslands of short- and midgrasses, and they utilize other habitats that are heavily grazed, mowed, or otherwise modified (Grant 1972; Moulton, Choate, and Bissell 1981; Moulton, Choate, et al. 1981; Lovell et al. 1985), including prairie dog towns. The species is frequently associated with heavier soils, including clays, loams, and sandy loams, and is less common on sandier soils in Colorado and southeastern Wyoming (Maxell and Brown 1968; R. Mitchell 1972; Flake 1974; Streubel 1975), which are usually occupied by *Xerospermophilus spilosoma* (D. Armstrong 1972; Tubbs 1977). At the Central Plains Experimental Range in Weld County, best predictors of presence of 13-lined ground squirrels were density of small shrubs and abundance of crickets and beetles (Higgins and Stapp 1997).

The diet includes both plant and animal matter. Various grasses, forbs, shrubs, fungi, lichens, and mosses are consumed; seeds are unimportant relative to other plant parts (Flake 1973). The diet contains nearly 50 percent animal matter (G. Johnson 1917); insect remains constitute 30 to

70 percent of stomach contents (Flake 1973; Streubel and Fitzgerald 1978b). Heavy consumption of lepidopteran larvae was observed in Morgan County (Streubel 1975), as were flowers and seeds of six-weeks fescue and saltgrass in May and June. On Pawnee National Grassland, adult and larval beetles, lepidopteran larvae, and grasshoppers were most important (Flake 1973). These squirrels are not averse to eating other vertebrates, including young cottontails, lizards, snakes, and birds. Prior to hibernation, 13-lined ground squirrels gain weight at a rate of about 4 g per day and may show a 30 to 40 percent increase in weight as they prepare for hibernation (Hohn 1966).

Thirteen-lined ground squirrels dig burrow systems that include relatively few deep "frost-free" nesting burrows, as well as a larger number (75 to 80 percent) of shallower "retreat" burrows (Desha 1966). Burrows generally have only 1 entrance. Little soil is deposited around the burrow entrance, making them difficult to locate visually.

Thirteen-lined ground squirrels are active throughout the warmer months of the year, spending the winter in hibernation. Percentages of time spent during spring-summer and fall, respectively, in captivity were as follows: burrowing (19 and 5 percent), aboveground activity (36 and 19 percent), and resting or eating in the burrow (45 and 76 percent) (Scheck and Fleharty 1980). Of aboveground time, foraging and feeding occupied 70 percent, alert behaviors 12 percent, and maintenance behaviors 8 percent (Streubel 1975). General investigative and nesting behaviors occupied most of the remaining time aboveground. Depending on season and temperature the animals may show either a bimodal or unimodal diurnal cycle. In hot weather, activity ceases during the hottest part of the day. When alarmed the animals typically race to their burrows and often give a trilling alarm call as they dive belowground.

The animals enter hibernation between July and October, with young of the year staying aboveground longest. Lechleitner (1969) reported the species as commonly seen into late October or early November near Fort Collins, but such late activity is unusual. Prior to hibernation animals become aggressive and intolerant of each other, reduce their home range, and become relatively inactive. Fatter animals typically enter hibernation before thinner ones (McCarley 1966; Streubel 1975). Hibernating animals plug their burrow entrances and heart rate drops from about 200 to only 4 beats per minute. Body temperature during hibernation approaches within 1 to 3°C of the ambient air temperature in the burrow. Brief periods of arousal occur about every 10 to 26 days during hibernation (Fitzpatrick 1925; G. Johnson 1928). Emergence dates in Colorado are early April or May. The seasonal activity period for adult males is only 100 to 120 days a year. The animals are frequent laboratory subjects for studies of hibernation (see Harder 2007).

Thirteen-lined ground squirrels generally are solitary and non-territorial, although parts of the home range may be defended from intruders. Home ranges vary from 1.4 to 12.0 ha, larger for males than for females, especially during the breeding season. Population estimates on shortgrass prairie in Colorado ranged from 18 animals per hectare on grazed prairie (R. Mitchell 1972) to 4.5 per hectare on ungrazed prairie (Grant 1972). As would be expected, highest numbers are associated with emergence of the young of the year.

Mating occurs soon after emergence from hibernation in mid-April or early May. Females are induced ovulators and copulation may last several minutes (G. Johnson et al. 1933). Six to 9 (and occasionally as many as 12) young are born. Mean litter sizes of 8.1 and 6.2 were reported for Weld and Morgan counties, respectively (Flake 1974; Streubel 1975). The gestation period is 27 to 28 days, with the young born in an altricial state (Bridgewater 1966). Eyes open at about 21 days and the young are weaned at about 28 days. Weaning typically coincides with the emergence of the young from their natal burrows. Ground squirrels mostly are monoestrous. In some parts of their range, 13-lined squirrels are reported to have 2 litters, but there is no evidence of this in Colorado.

Annual mortality has been estimated at close to 80 percent in Wisconsin (Rongstad 1965) and Texas (McCarley 1966), with juvenile males generally showing the highest losses. Most mortality occurs prior to hibernation, although few direct observations of predation have been reported. Among documented predators are bull snakes, roadrunners, swift fox, and several kinds of raptors. J. P. Fitzgerald (unpublished) observed a rattlesnake eating a 13-lined squirrel and found the animals in food caches made by swift fox on the Pawnee National Grassland. Streubel and Fitzgerald (1978b) reviewed the literature on the species. The 13-lined ground squirrel is classified as a small game mammal in Colorado (Table 4-1), although data are not gathered on harvest.

Poliocitellus franklinii

FRANKLIN'S GROUND SQUIRREL

Description

Franklin's ground squirrel is a long, slender ground squirrel, larger in size than the 13-lined ground squirrel, which may occupy similar habitat. When he watched the squirrel moving about, E. Hall (1955) was reminded of a long-tailed weasel. Others have described its long, gray bushy tail as suggestive of the eastern gray squirrel, *Sciurus carolinensis* (J. K. Jones, Armstrong, et al. 1983). Color of the dorsum is olive-gray to buff-gray, becoming paler on the sides, with the underparts yellowish white to olive-gray. Faint dappling is noticeable along the back and sides. The head tends to be grayer than the body. The tail is blackish mixed with paler buff and bordered in white. Measurements are: total length 360 to 412 mm; length of tail 123–160 mm; length of hindfoot 42–56; length of ear 13–18; and weight 375–540 g. The skull is long and narrow with little apparent inflation of the cranium.

Distribution

Franklin's ground squirrel is not known from Colorado, but specimens have been taken from 2 nearby sites in Nebraska: along the North Platte River near Lisco, Garden County, about 50 km north of the Colorado border, and near Curtis, Frontier County, in the South Platte drainage about 130 km east of the boundary (E. Hall 1981). In Kansas the species has been taken in Trego County (E. Hall 1955) about 160 miles east of the Colorado border. J. K. Jones (1964) suggested that the range of Franklin's ground squirrel has been expanding westward and it is possible that it will eventually appear in northeastern Colorado. *Poliocitellus franklinii* is monotypic; subspecies are not recognized (E. Hall 1981). For comment on use of the generic name *Poliocitellus*, see the general account of ground squirrels above.

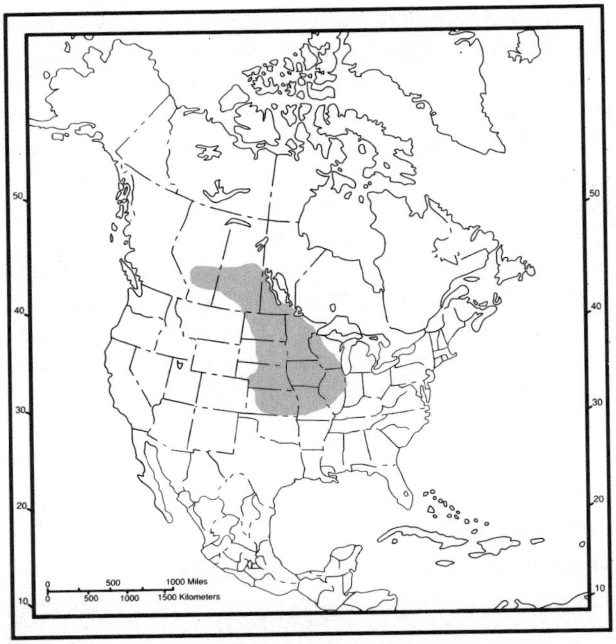

MAP 8-21. Distribution of Franklin's ground squirrel (*Poliocitellus franklinii*) in North America.

Natural History

Franklin's ground squirrel is an animal of tall- and mixed-grass prairie, tending to favor heavy, dense cover of grasses and associated forbs. It also invades openings in forest edge, including margins of riparian woodland. Biology of the species is better known in the Midwest than in the Great Plains states bordering Colorado. The animals are more solitary than most other ground squirrels, usually occurring in colonies of no more than a dozen individuals (J. K. Jones, Armstrong, et al. 1983). Burrows are generally constructed on sloping ground with 1 or 2 entrances bordered by conspicuous dirt mounds. The diet is omnivorous, with up to 30 percent animal matter when insects and nestling mammals are available. Breeding occurs in April or May, with females giving birth in May or June to 6–9 young. Aboveground activity may not begin until as late as May and most animals have entered hibernation by late August. Ostroff and Finck (2003) reviewed the literature on the species.

Xerospermophilus spilosoma

SPOTTED GROUND SQUIRREL

Description

This is a small, grayish brown ground squirrel dappled with indistinct buffy spots on the dorsal surface. The ventral color is paler. The tail is brown and usually tipped with black. Measurements are: total length 200–245 mm; length of tail 50–80 mm; length of hindfoot 28–35 mm; length of ear 6–8 mm; weight 100–200 g. The skull is similar to that of the 13-lined ground squirrel but tends to be broader at the postorbital constriction (13–15 mm) with larger auditory bullae. Condylobasal length is 34–40 mm.

Distribution

Spotted ground squirrels are widely distributed over Colorado's eastern plains, mostly in areas of sandy soils. In suitable habitat the animals can be quite abundant, but

PHOTOGRAPH 8-11. Spotted ground squirrel (*Xerospermophilus spilosoma*). Photograph by J. Perley Fitzgerald.

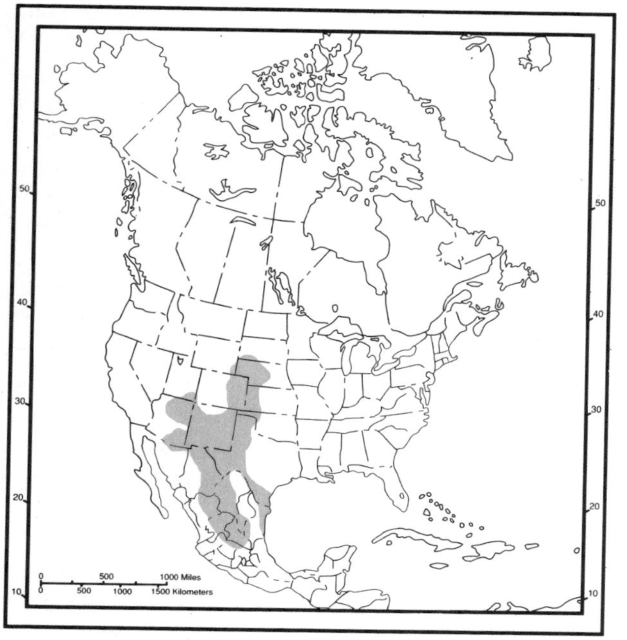

MAP 8-22. Distribution of the spotted ground squirrel (*Xerospermophilus spilosoma*) in North America.

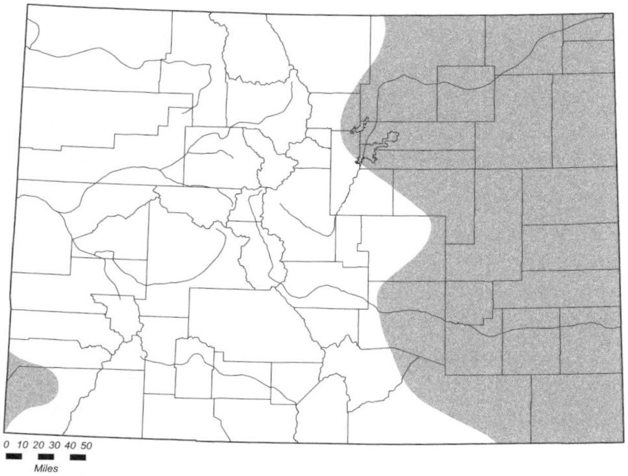

MAP 8-23. Distribution of the spotted ground squirrel (*Xerospermophilus spilosoma*) in Colorado.

the overall distribution is rather sparse. They are most abundant in the sandhills of the northeastern part of the state and along the Arkansas River. A considerable portion of this range has been lost to irrigated agriculture. They also occur in the extreme southwestern portion of the state, in Montezuma County, where their status is uncertain. *Xeropermophilus spilosoma cryptospilotus* occurs in extreme southwestern Colorado; *X. s. obsoletus* occurs in northeastern Colorado, generally in the South Platte River drainage; *X. s. marginatus* occurs over the remainder of the eastern plains. For comment on use of the generic name *Xerospermophilus*, see the general account of ground squirrels above.

Natural History

Although several studies have been conducted in Colorado, spotted ground squirrels have not been researched intensively. A species of semiarid grasslands, they are not as common on the eastern plains as 13-lined ground squirrels; rather, spotted ground squirrels occur more locally in suitable habitat. They prefer deep sandy soils with sparse vegetation, including areas of overgrazed sandhills vegetation and lightly grazed mixed-grass prairie with bunchgrasses and sand sage (Maxell and Brown 1968; N. Green 1969; D. Armstrong 1972; Streubel 1975; Tubbs 1977; Mohamed 1989).

The diet of the spotted ground squirrel seems to be somewhat less omnivorous than that of the 13-lined ground squirrel. A variety of grasses and forbs were consumed in northeastern Colorado, most notably needle-and-thread, six-weeks fescue, annual sunflower, *Mentzelia*, and croton (Streubel 1975). Plants were also the most important dietary item in a New Mexico study (Sumrell 1949). At the Sevilleta National Wildlife Refuge Long-Term Ecology Research (LTER) site in Socorro County, New Mexico, Hope and Parmenter (2007) found the diet to be roughly equal proportions of seeds, green vegetation, and arthropods. Spotted ground squirrels also feed on kangaroo rats, insects, and lizards.

Population densities of 3.8 animals per hectare in Morgan County (Streubel 1975) and 5.3–7.1 animals per hectare in Weld County (Tubbs 1977) have been reported, with highest populations in May and June. In the latter population, yearling adults constituted the largest cohort, with survivorship greater in males. Adults older than 2 years of age were not present. Tubbs (1977) reported more females than males, whereas Streubel (1975) had more males than females. Home ranges in Colorado range from 0.5 to 4.8 ha. Males have larger home ranges than females. Burrows of spotted ground squirrels typically have 2 or 3 entrances at the bases of shrubs, often sand sage. These squirrels build several separate burrow systems and establish definitive surface runways between them (Streubel 1975; Tubbs 1977).

Seasonal activity patterns are similar to those of 13-lined ground squirrels. Spotted ground squirrels emerge from hibernation in early to mid-April in northeastern Colorado. Yearlings emerge first, followed by adult males, which precede adult females by 1 to 2 weeks. Annual aboveground activity averaged 115 to 135 days for males and 95 to 125 days for females in Morgan County (Streubel 1975). Adult males usually entered hibernation by late July or early August, with females staying active slightly longer. By late September and early October only a few juveniles remained aboveground. Although this broad seasonal activity pattern is similar to that of the sympatric 13-lined ground squirrel, competition probably is minimal because of temporal differences with annual cycles (Streubel 1975). Emergence from hibernation, breeding, and emergence of young occurred 2 to 4 weeks earlier in *Ictidomys tridecemlineatus* than in *Xerospermophilus spilosoma*.

In Colorado, spotted ground squirrels were most active between 1100 and 1600 hours, even on the hottest days (Tubbs 1977). In New Mexico, Sumrell (1949) observed a bimodal activity pattern with little activity during the heat of the day. Time aboveground is typically spent foraging and feeding (66 percent), vigilance (15 percent), investigative behavior (6 percent), and maintenance behaviors such as sand-bathing, grooming, and sunning (8 percent). Sexual and agonistic behaviors occupied less than 2 percent of aboveground activity, increasing to only 7 percent during the breeding season (Streubel 1975).

Reproductive patterns are similar to those of 13-lined ground squirrels. Breeding occurs in April or May soon after emergence from hibernation. Pregnant females may be found in Colorado from early May to late July (Streubel 1975; Tubbs 1977). Litter size varies from 5 to 12 with an average of about 7. Juveniles weigh 40 to 50 g at first emergence from the natal burrow. Gestation is probably the same as in 13-lined ground squirrels, 27 to 28 days.

Scant information is available on predation. Bull snakes and possibly red-tailed hawks have been reported as predators. Streubel and Fitzgerald (1978a) reviewed the literature. The spotted ground squirrel in Colorado is a nongame species (Table 4-1).

Urocitellus elegans
WYOMING GROUND SQUIRREL

Description

This is a medium-sized ground squirrel with a fairly long tail. The upperparts are drab buffy gray. A few individuals may show a slight dappling of blackish hairs. The underparts are buff to grayish. The tail is grayish to pale brown beneath and has a border of white or buff. Measurements are: total length 250–335 mm; length of tail 65–100 mm; length of hindfoot 39–49 mm; weight 300–500 g. The skull is similar to that of other ground squirrels in this genus, with a somewhat narrow braincase and interorbital region. The wide zygomatic arches are not parallel and the upper surface of the jugal lacks an angular process. The infraorbital foramen is oval or subtriangular, with a large masseteric tubercle ventral to the foramen. Males have a baculum and the testes are scrotal during the breeding season. At times individuals of this species are confused with prairie dogs, especially Gunnison's prairie dog, from which it can

PHOTOGRAPH 8-12. Wyoming ground squirrel (*Urocitellus elegans*). **Photograph by J. Perley Fitzgerald.**

be distinguished by its smaller size, longer tail, relatively uniform color, and lack of facial markings.

Distribution

Wyoming ground squirrels are found in northwestern and central Colorado between 1,830 and 3,660 m (6,000–12,000 ft.) in elevation. R. Hansen (1962) reported on the dispersal of the species southward into Colorado and suggested that the rate of movement approached 2.4 km per year since 1930. At that time he speculated that their dispersal "is a natural consequence of past geologic events and not caused by modern man." This conclusion, however, may not sufficiently weigh the impacts of livestock grazing and reduction of prairie dogs through intensive poisoning campaigns. These human impacts, and differences between prairie dogs and Wyoming ground squirrels in resistance to plague, may in fact account for some of the rapid spread of this species in Colorado. Wyoming ground squirrels have moved over Poncha Pass and arrived in the San Luis Valley in recent years (P. B. Robertson, personal communication).

For use of the generic name *Urocitellus*, see the general account of ground squirrels above. Previously, this species in Colorado was known as Richardson's ground squirrel (*Spermophilus richardsoni*). Nadler et al. (1971), J. Robinson and Hoffmann (1975), and Fagerstone (1982) presented data on a number of criteria that justified separation of *U. elegans* from *S. richardsoni*, the latter being a species of the Northern Great Plains. One subspecies, *Urocitellus elegans elegans*, occurs in Colorado.

Natural History

Wyoming ground squirrels occupy grasslands and semidesert shrublands. The diet consists mostly of grasses and forbs, with the latter most often consumed (House 1964; T. Clark 1968), although a study in Larimer County found no preferred food plants (R. Hansen and Johnson 1976).

Wyoming ground squirrels live in groups, but these colonies appear to be little more than aggregations of individuals in favorable habitats. However, males may defend territories during the breeding season and females may maintain territories around natal burrows (Fagerstone 1982). In suitable habitat on the plains, densities may reach up to 44 animals per hectare (House 1964). In mountain meadows in Colorado, numbers ranged from 14 (May) to 48 animals per hectare (June) (Zegers 1977; Zegers and Williams 1979). Because their burrows undermine pastures and they may compete with livestock for forage, Wyoming ground squirrels have long been considered pests (Burnett 1931). A variety of control practices (including the controversial poison "1080," sodium monofluoroacetate) have been used to eliminate the species on pasture and agricultural lands.

Wyoming ground squirrels mate soon after emergence from hibernation. Females typically show behavioral estrus

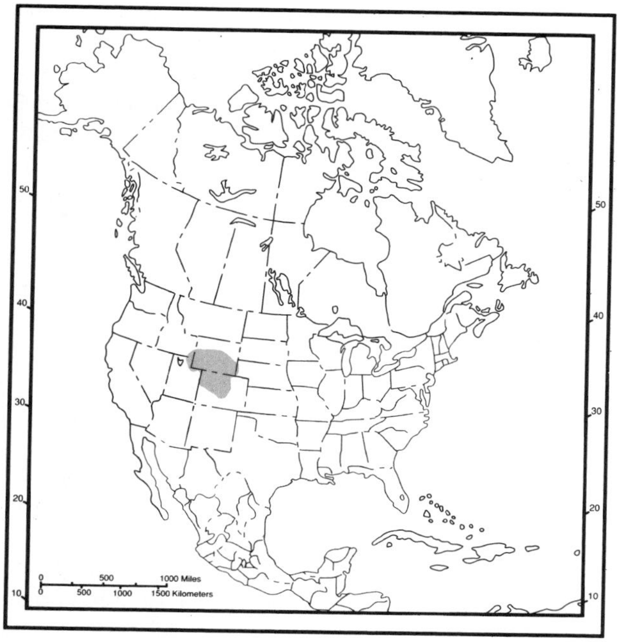

MAP 8-24. Distribution of the Wyoming ground squirrel (*Urocitellus elegans*) in North America.

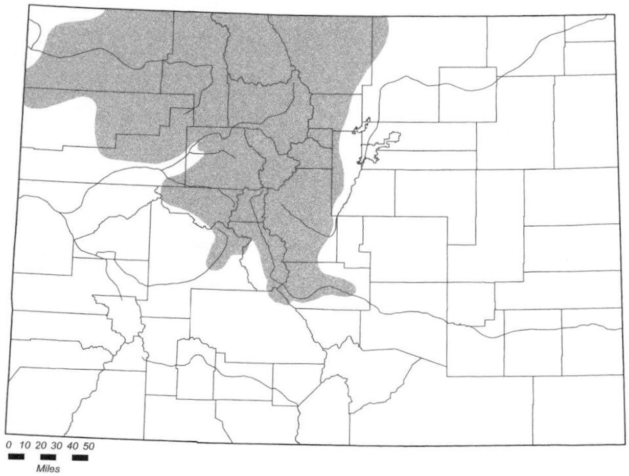

MAP 8-25. Distribution of the Wyoming ground squirrel (*Urocitellus elegans*) in Colorado.

and mate within 5 days of emergence. Gestation probably averages 22 to 23 days. Females have only 1 estrous cycle and 1 litter of 3 to 11 young annually, with an average of 4 to 5. Males and females can both breed following their first hibernation cycle but apparently breeding success of yearling females is influenced by environmental conditions. Neonates are blind and naked, with hair first appearing at 10 days of age, tooth eruption at 13 days, and eyes opening at 21 to 24 days. Young remain belowground for about a month after birth. The animals are weaned by the fifth or sixth week. Within 100 days of birth young reach adult size (R. M. Denniston 1957; T. Clark 1970; Zegers 1977; Fagerstone 1982, 1988).

As is true of most sciurids, Wyoming ground squirrels are strictly diurnal, emerging from burrows soon after sunrise and retreating before sunset. Peak activity is generally in early morning with a lesser peak in late afternoon. Behaviors include fighting, running, chasing, feeding, alert posturing, digging, hay-gathering, and tail-flicking. The animals frequently spend time aboveground in alert upright positions (T. Clark and Denniston 1970). This has led to one of their common names, "picket pin," for their resemblance to a stake driven into the ground to tether a horse. When alarmed the animals have a high-pitched alarm call, a twittering trill given as they dive into the burrow (Fagerstone 1987a). Up to 40 percent of aboveground activity is spent feeding, 36 percent in alert postures, and less than 5 percent in chasing and fighting (Zegers 1981).

Animals begin to hibernate as early as late July, with most animals belowground by mid-September. On the Laramie Plains of Wyoming they first appeared from hibernation in early April (T. Clark 1970), but in Middle Park, Colorado, they emerged in mid-March (Fagerstone 1988). Males typically emerge 1 to 2 weeks before females. Average weight losses during hibernation range from 0.7 to 0.8 g per day, with juveniles showing slightly lower daily losses than adults (R. Hansen and Reed 1969). Hibernation is believed to be triggered mostly by reduced food consumption, whereas arousal and emergence are under exogenous controls such as snow cover and air temperature. Harlow and Menkens (1986) found that Wyoming ground squirrels and white-tailed prairie dogs in the laboratory entered torpor at 7°C.

Generally survival rates are quite high during the winter, but a considerable population loss to predation occurs during summer (T. Clark 1970; Zegers and Williams 1979; Fagerstone 1982, 1988). A large number of predators feed on Wyoming ground squirrels, including raptors, badgers, coyotes, bobcats, weasels, and rattlesnakes. Red-tailed hawks and goshawks had a 17 percent kill efficiency when hunting these squirrels (Pfeifer 1980). Sylvatic plague may be a factor influencing densities of Wyoming ground squirrels in some areas (J. Fitzgerald and Lechleitner 1969; J. Fitzgerald 1970). The Wyoming ground squirrel is categorized as a small game species in Colorado (Table 4-1). The animals may be harvested by licensed hunters year-round without limit (Colorado Division of Wildlife 2009f). Table 4-3 suggests that data on harvest are incomplete but some years is nearly 40,000 individuals. Wyoming ground squirrels also are quite frequent traffic casualties. Zegers (1984) reviewed the literature on *U. elegans*.

Genus *Cynomys*—Prairie Dogs

Prairie dogs are uniquely North American squirrels, generally coextensive with steppe and shrub-steppe habitats of the Great Plains and parts of the Colorado Plateau and the eastern Great Basin, so ranging from southern Canada to northern Mexico. They are not dogs, of course, but large ground squirrels, misnamed *petit chien*—"little dog"—by early European explorers of the Great Plains for their somewhat doglike "barking." The phylogenetic sister group of prairie dogs is *Spermophilus*. The genus includes 5 species, of which 3 occur in Colorado. The genus was reviewed by Hollister (1916) and Pizzimenti (1975).

The genus *Cynomys* arose in the Late Pliocene, so it is about 2 million years old. Goodwin (1995) reviewed the biogeographic history of prairie dogs, based on the fossil record. The extant species are largely parapatric in distribution; that is, their ranges tend to meet but generally do not overlap. There are 3 well-marked species: white-tailed and Gunnison's prairie dogs (placed together in a subgenus, *Leucocrossuromys*) and black-tailed prairie dogs. Utah prairie dogs (*C. parvidens*) are closely related to white-tailed, and Mexican prairie dogs (*C. mexicanus*) are closely related to black-tailed prairie dogs. The black-tailed prairie dog is the best-studied species, perhaps because it has the widest geographic range and it is considered by some to have the most complex social behavior. Studies of prairie dogs are a cornerstone of the sociobiology of mammals (Hoogland 1995, 2003b).

Prairie dogs often are considered to be a "keystone species" (or "keystone engineer"; Bangert and Slobodchikoff 2000) in shortgrass prairie and some shrub-steppe communities. There is no doubt that the animals are profoundly important in driving plant succession (although the pattern is not always predictable). By bringing subsoil to the surface, prairie dogs influence soil structure, soil chemistry, and microtopography. Their burrows provide a third habitat dimension in a largely 2-dimensional environment; hence, they provide habitat to 150–200 vertebrate symbionts (obligatory or opportunistic)—predators, competitors, commensals, and so forth (Kotliar et al. 1999; R. R. Cook et al. 2003). Interaction between pocket gophers and prairie dogs in Colorado has not been investigated but studies of possible competition or commensalism are to be encouraged. All Coloradan prairie dogs are sympatric with pocket gophers in Colorado, and both black-tailed and Gunnison's prairie dogs are sympatric with more than 1 species of pocket gopher.

Scientific discussion of the "keystone" role of prairie dogs often hinges on the semantics of "keystone" (B. Miller, Ceballos, and Reading 1994; Power et al. 1996; Stapp 1998; B. Miller, Reading, et al. 2000). This technical debate should not be allowed to diminish appreciation of the importance of prairie dogs in their native habitat. In a sense, prairie dogs are a remnant of a nearly extinct ecosystem that once was dominated by bison and other large ungulates. Cattle and domestic horses, confined behind barbed wire, are a pale surrogate for the grazers of millennia past that shaped the vast interior grasslands of North America to which prairie dogs are uniquely adapted (Johnsgard 2005).

Being diurnal, of medium size, and fairly tolerant of human presence—at least at a respectful distance (see R. Adams et al. 1987), prairie dogs are eminently "watchable wildlife." They thrive in disturbed areas—disturbance that once was created by migrating bison and now is generated mostly by people. That means that prairie dogs tend to be particularly abundant and conspicuous at the expanding edges of human settlements. Hence, casual observers are likely to have an exaggerated impression of their abundance.

Monitoring populations of prairie dogs is notoriously difficult. Distinguishing active colonies in aerial surveys is sometimes challenging. Occupancy of individual colonies often is ephemeral, particularly when plague is active in a locality. Remote surveillance of white-tailed and Gunnison's prairie dogs is even more challenging, because shrublands (rather than shortgrass steppe) are typical habitat. Andelt, White, et al. (2009) published a sophisticated statistical analysis of random plots to conclude that direct observation of occupancy was necessary to monitor status and trends in these animals.

Human response to prairie dogs tends to be strong. As is typical of human-wildlife interaction, response depends on a complex (often subconscious) process of economic and aesthetic valuation, sometimes in the presence of prejudice and in the absence of hard data. Urban people may see "cute and cuddly" animals with a complex social behavior, but farmers and ranchers may see stiff competition as prairie dogs take field crops or forage intended for livestock, "degrade" rangeland by cropping grass and driving succession toward weedy forbs, and undermine pastures and fields with burrows. These strongly disparate attitudes toward prairie dogs were quantified in a study conducted in the vicinity of Fort Collins (Zinn and Andelt 1999).

For a variety of reasons, prairie dogs also have been a focal point of debates about endangered species and their conservation (S. Miller and Cully 2001; L. McCain 2008). Because of the confluence of direct control (by poisoning and shooting), habitat conversion (from native habitats to dryland or irrigated agriculture or to residential, commercial, or industrial development), and an ongoing epidemic of sylvatic plague (see Barnes 1993; Cully 1993; J. Fitzgerald 1993a; Cully and Williams 2001), all species of prairie dogs declined dramatically in abundance and extent of distribution over the twentieth century, with estimates of decline ranging from 90 percent to more than 99 percent (Lomolino and Smith 2004; S. Miller and Cully 2001). As prairie dogs have declined toward extinction, so too have some of their symbionts, most notably their highly specialized predator, the black-footed ferret (*Mustela nigripes*). The *Journal of Mammalogy* devoted a special feature to prairie dogs (S. Miller and Cully 2001). More recently, Hoogland (2007b) reviewed the conservation of prairie dogs. Strategies and techniques for management of plague by vaccinating prairie dogs are under active research (Rocke et al. 2008).

Despite concern by preservationists, prairie dogs are considered small game in Colorado, and there is an open season on all species of *Cynomys* from June 15 through February (Colorado Division of Wildlife 2009f). There is no bag or possession limit. Estimated harvest in some recent years is shown in Table 4-3, indicating that prairie dogs are by far the most harvested small game, with more than 300,000 individuals killed most years by upwards of 5,000 hunters.

Cynomys gunnisoni

GUNNISON'S PRAIRIE DOG

Description

Gunnison's prairie dog is the smallest of Colorado's prairie dogs. Dorsal color is yellowish buff to cinnamon with

PHOTOGRAPH 8-13. Gunnison's prairie dog (*Cynomys gunnisoni*). Photograph by J. Perley Fitzgerald.

numerous interspersed black hairs. The ventral color is slightly paler. The top of the head, cheeks, and superciliary line above the eyes are darker than the rest of the body, albeit less strikingly so than in the white-tailed prairie dog. The terminal third of the tail is gray to dirty white in color. Measurements are: total length 300–390 mm; length of tail 40–64 mm; length of hindfoot 53–61 mm; weight 450–1,350 g. Males are heavier than females by as much as 30 percent early in the breeding season (Hoogland 2003a).

Overall, the animals are darker and less strikingly patterned than the white-tailed prairie dog. Because of its dark color and relatively small size, Gunnison's prairie dog is sometimes mistaken for the Wyoming ground squirrel, from which it is distinguished by its larger size, relatively shorter tail, stockier build, and distinctive vocalizations. The skull of Gunnison's prairie dog differs from that of the white-tailed prairie dog in having a more broadly spreading zygomatic process of the maxillary, smaller and more oblique mastoids, and smaller auditory bullae. Females have 10 mammae.

Distribution

Gunnison's prairie dogs are restricted to southwestern and south-central Colorado. They range in elevation from 1,830 to 3,660 m (6,000–12,000 feet). Plague and poisoning have had major impacts on the distribution of this species in Colorado (Ecke and Johnson 1952; Lechleitner et al. 1962, 1968; J. Fitzgerald 1970, 1993a; Pizzimenti 1981; Raynor 1985a) and adjacent states (Cully et al. 1997). An epizootic in the 1940s greatly reduced numbers of prairie dog in South Park (Ecke and Johnson 1952), and J. Fitzgerald (1970) reported that most colonies were gone from the area, having been replaced by Wyoming ground squirrels. Pizzimenti and Hoffmann (1973) reviewed general literature on the species.

Cynomys gunnisoni gunnisoni occurs in the Gunnison River drainage, the upper Arkansas and South Platte drainages, and the San Luis Valley. This subspecies has been

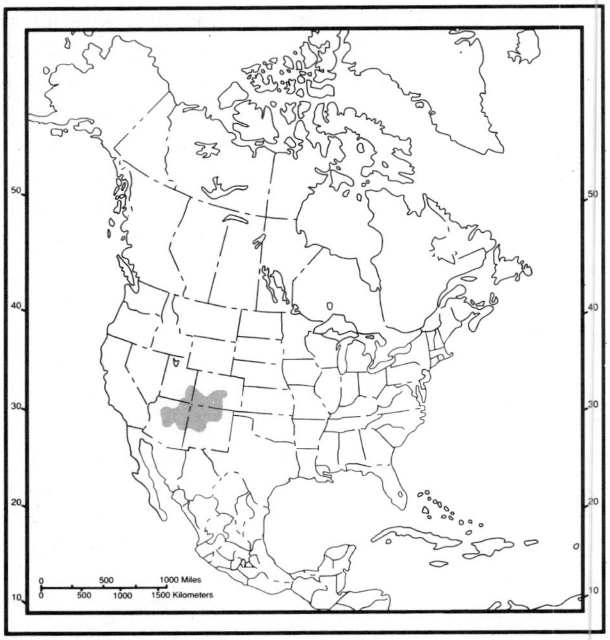

MAP 8-26. Distribution of Gunnison's prairie dog (*Cynomys gunnisoni*) in North America.

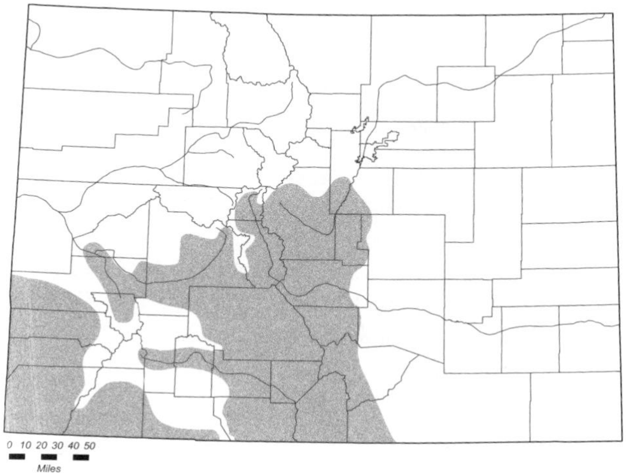

MAP 8-27. Distribution of Gunnison's prairie dog (*Cynomys gunnisoni*) in Colorado.

extirpated over much of its former range, although in 1991, R. B. Finley (personal communication) found small colonies in several areas of south-central Colorado. *C. g. zuniensis* occurs at lower elevations in southwestern Colorado in Montezuma, La Plata, Dolores, San Miguel, and Montrose counties.

Natural History

Gunnison's prairie dogs frequently are called "keystone species" (or "keystone engineers"; Bangert and Slobodchikoff 2000) in shrub-steppe communities within their range. Restoration of *C. gunnisoni* on the Sevilleta National Wildlife Refuge in west-central New Mexico had only minor impact on species richness of small mammals and plants during the first year, although banner-tailed kangaroo rats were more abundant on restoration sites than off (Davidson et al. 1999). Impacts of prairie dogs on biotic communities may be as subtle as improving locomotor efficiency for beetles (Bangert and Slobodchikoff 2004).

Studies in northern Arizona (Gallie and Drickamer 2008) indicated potential competition between two "ecosystem engineers," *C. gunnisoni* and valley pocket gophers (*Thomomys bottae*). Specifically, presence of prairie dogs seemed to have a negative influence on presence of pocket gophers, and density of prairie dog burrows was twice as high when pocket gophers were present. The authors speculated that pocket gopher mounds may favor the broad-leafed plants preferred by prairie dogs. Where Gunnison's prairie dogs were killed by plague in northern New Mexico, declines were noted in some raptors, especially ferruginous hawks (*Buteo regalis*) (Cully 1991).

Gunnison's prairie dogs inhabit grasslands and semi-desert and montane shrublands. Their diet consists mostly of grasses and sedges. In Costilla County, grasses constituted 81 percent of the diet (Longhurst 1944); other foods included borages, goosefoot, pigweed, lupine, dandelions, and mustards. In South Park, fescues, June grass, muhley, sedges, rushes, Indian paintbrush, *Senecio*, chiming bells, prairie sage, big sage, and rabbitbrush were commonly used (J. Fitzgerald and Lechleitner 1974). Flowers and other succulent parts of forbs and shrubs are also consumed but the animals do little digging for roots and tubers. About 60 percent of the time aboveground is spent foraging and feeding (Tileston and Lechleitner 1966). Clipping of non-food vegetation, so characteristic of black-tailed prairie dogs, has not been documented. As with all species of prairie dogs and most ground squirrels, Gunnison's prairie dogs gather grasses and forbs for nesting materials, especially in late summer. Free water is not required.

Reproduction occurs shortly after emergence from hibernation. Mating was observed in South Park in late April and May. Most copulation occurs belowground (Hoogland 1998). In an Arizona study of microsatellite DNA, 77 percent of litters had multiple sires (Haynie et al. 2003). Length of gestation is estimated at about 29 days (Hoogland 1997). Pups remain belowground for 4 to 5 weeks after birth, suggesting the duration of lactation (Hoogland 1997). Lactating females were noted in South Park in May and June, with first appearance of pups in the first week of July. Females have 1 litter per year. In northeastern Arizona, average litter size was 3.77 young (range, 2 to 7; Hoogland 2001). Sex ratios favor males at birth, with adult populations slightly favoring females. Such unequal sex ratios have been reported in black-tailed prairie dogs and are attributed to increased chance for mortality in young males. Cully (1997) reported that following a severe outbreak of plague (more than 99% decline in population) in northern New Mexico, populations showed greater survival to weaning, greater interyear survival, and breeding by yearling females, with populations tripling annually.

Gunnison's prairie dogs hibernate. In central Colorado at elevations around 3,500 m (10,000 ft.) individuals entered burrows by October and emerged in mid-April. Hibernation periods at lower elevations are shorter and some individuals may even appear aboveground during the winter months (Raynor et al. 1987).

The animals are diurnal, with bimodal peaks of activity typical during warmer times of the year. Although brief showers do not interrupt activity, periods of prolonged rain or snow cause the animals to retreat to their burrows. Prairie dogs are considerably more cautious in their behaviors on cloudy, overcast days than on days with bright sunshine. Alarm calls are used in response to predators, and all individuals within hearing range probably benefit. Interestingly, their alarm calls appear to have semantic properties; in an experimental situation, Gunnison's prairie dogs appeared to distinguish between (and announce information about) individual "predators" (in this case, researchers clothed in different ways) (Slobodchikoff, Kiriazis, et al. 1991), and their alarm calls show regional differences ("dialects"; Slobodchikoff, Ackers et al. 1998) in the Southwest.

Gunnison's prairie dogs are considerably less social than black-tailed prairie dogs, so colony organization is more similar to that of the less social ground squirrels (Scheffer 1947). aggregate in "clans" similar to those of white-tailed prairie dogs. Clans include 1 to 19 (mean, 5.3) individuals (Hoogland 1999). Females and young are tied more closely to particular locations within the colony than are males. Most agonistic behavior is between clans, related to disputes over feeding areas or specific burrow clusters rather than discrete territorial boundaries such as those of the coterie boundaries observed in black-tailed prairie dogs.

Densities of Gunnison's prairie dogs range from 5 or 6 to more than 57 animals per hectare in especially favorable habitat (Burnett and McCampbell 1926; Lechleitner et al. 1962; J. Fitzgerald and Lechleitner 1974; Raynor 1985b). Burrow systems and mound construction are less well developed than within black-tailed prairie dogs. In South Park only 13 percent of burrows had well-developed mounds, and 77 percent showed little or no excavated soil. Predators include badgers, golden eagles, coyotes, bobcats, and red-tailed hawks. Infanticide is rare or absent (Hoogland 1999).

Like all Coloradan prairie dogs, *C. gunnisoni* is listed as a small game animal (Table 4-1). Seasons are set annually and in recent years hunting has been more restricted on public land than on private land. There is no bag limit, but the season is closed from March through mid-June (Colorado Division of Wildlife 2009f) to reduce the chance of killing lactating females with dependent young in the den. For comments on harvest by humans, see the generic account of *Cynomys* above. C. Knowles (2002) reviewed the conservation status of *C. gunnisoni* across its range.

The literature on Gunnison's prairie dog was reviewed by Hoogland (2003b). The extensive work on Gunnison's prairie dog by Conrad Slobodchikoff and colleagues in northeastern Arizona probably is generally pertinent to the species in southwestern Colorado, including research on diet (Shalaway and Slobodchikoff 1988), habitat (Slobodchikoff, Robinson, and Schaack 1988), vocalizations (Slobodchikoff, Kiriazis, et al. 1991; S. Travis et al. 1996; Slobodchikoff, Ackers, and Van Ert 1998; Ackers and Slobodchikoff 1999; Placer and Slobodchikoff 2000; Perla and Slobodchikoff 2002; Slobodchikoff 2002; Frederiksen and Slobodchikoff 2007; Kiriazis et al. 2006; Slobodchikoff and Placer 2006), social systems (S. Travis and Slobodchikoff 1993; S. Travis et al. 1995, 1996), genetics (S. Travis et al. 1997), and community ecology (Slobodchikoff, Vaughan, and Warner, 1987; Bangert and Slobodchikoff 2000, 2004, 2006; Verdolin and Slobodchikoff 2002).

Cynomys leucurus

WHITE-TAILED PRAIRIE DOG

Description

White-tailed prairie dogs can be distinguished from other prairie dogs in Colorado by the presence of a short, white to grayish white tip on the tail; whitish gray to yellowish buff body color; and distinctive dark facial markings consisting of black to dark brown cheek patches that extend to above the eye (most prominent in summer pelage). The ventral color is slightly paler than the dorsum. Measurements are: total length 315–400 mm; length of tail 40–65 mm; length of hindfoot 60–65 mm, length of ear 8–14 mm; weight 650–1,700 g. Males are typically larger than females. White-tailed and black-tailed prairie dogs are similar in total length, but the latter has a tail 30 percent longer. Male white-tailed prairie dogs on average are heavier than adult black-tailed prairie dogs. The skull of the white-tailed prairie dog is not as heavy as that of the black-tailed. Females usually have 10 mammae. *Cynomys leucurus* is monotypic; geographic variation in morphology across its range does not suggest the existence of subspecies.

Distribution

White-tailed prairie dogs inhabit northwestern and west-central Colorado, to elevations over 3,050 m (10,000 ft.) although most records are from below 2,600 m (8,500 ft.). Generalizing from recent black-footed ferret work in northwestern Colorado (Holmes 2008), populations of *C. leucurus* in Colorado appear to be stable, a recovery probably largely the result of termination of broad-scale poisoning campaigns in the late 1960s and early 1970s. Hoogland (2007b) reviewed the conservation biology of prairie dogs.

PHOTOGRAPH 8-14. White-tailed prairie dog (*Cynomys leucurus*). Photograph by J. Perley Fitzgerald.

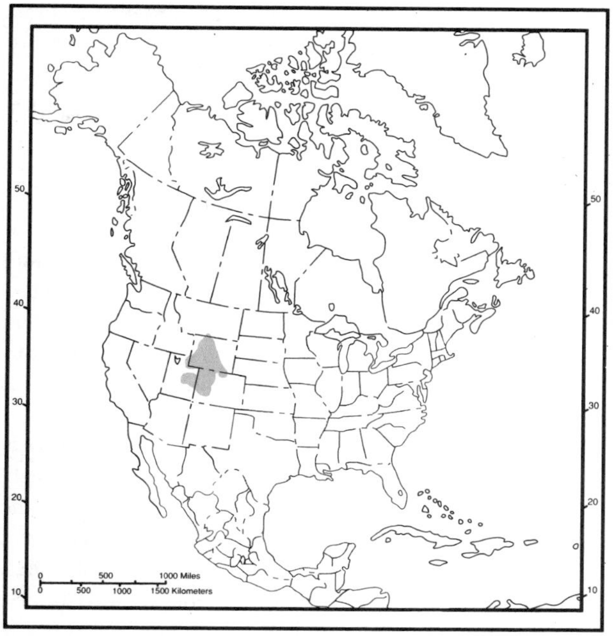

MAP 8-28. Distribution of the white-tailed prairie dog (*Cynomys leucurus*) in North America.

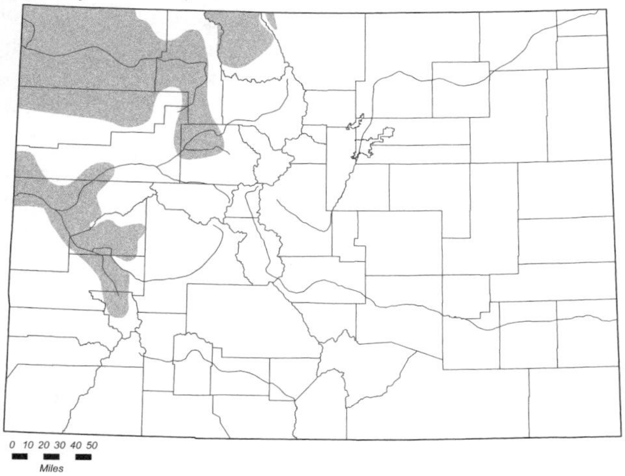

MAP 8-29. Distribution of the white-tailed prairie dog (*Cynomys leucurus*) in Colorado.

The last documented reports of the black-footed ferret (*Mustela nigripes*) in Colorado were from white-tailed prairie dog habitat near Craig in the early 1940s (D. Armstrong 1972). The last known wild population of black-footed ferrets throughout their range was associated with a white-tailed prairie dog colony near Meeteetse, Wyoming (T. Clark, Campbell, et al. 1988). After years of captive breeding, black-footed ferrets now are being restored at points throughout their original range. Restoration in northwestern Colorado began in 2001, and by late 2006 some 235 ferrets had been released. In 2005, a wild-born black-footed ferret was observed in Colorado for the first time in 60 years. With continued success of the black-footed ferret recovery program, the vast, lonely sage-covered hills of northwestern Colorado will be an ideal place to observe these fascinating weasels in the wild, providing that their prey base of white-tailed prairie dogs remains healthy.

Natural History

White-tailed prairie dogs are animals of open shrublands, semidesert grasslands, and mountain valleys. In Colorado, the species is most often encountered in semidesert shrublands. Occasionally they invade pastures and agricultural lands at lower elevations. Their colonies, like those of black-tailed prairie dogs, provide habitat for numerous vertebrate symbionts (T. M. Campbell and Clark 1981). In northeastern Utah, small mammals associated with occupied white-tailed prairie dog colonies included deer mice, piñon mice, and northern grasshopper mice; Ord's kangaroo rat was present on occupied colonies but more abundant on unoccupied colonies (Etchberger et al. 2006).

White-tailed prairie dogs feed on a wide range of grasses, forbs, and woody plants. They may prefer grasses and sedges when available (Tileston and Lechleitner 1966). Sage, saltbush, winterfat, rabbitbrush, goosefoot, and dandelions are consumed. Unlike black-tailed prairie dogs, they do not intentionally clip taller vegetation. Animal matter is not important in the diet.

White-tailed prairie dogs frequently occur in loosely organized colonies, termed "clans" by Tileston and Lechleitner (1966) and considered by Hoogland (1981) to be the equivalent of wards in black-tailed prairie dogs. Colonies may occupy hundreds of hectares on favorable sites. Sociality is not as pronounced as in black-tailed prairie dogs, sociality being restricted mostly to female-young and young-young interactions. Colony members benefit from group response to alarm calls, and their burrowing activities collectively favor development of broad-leafed herbaceous vegetation (Tileston and Lechleitner 1966; T. Clark 1977; Hoogland 1981).

Population densities are variable between years and sites, ranging from 0.8 to 12.6 animals per hectare in a 4-year study of 6 sites in Wyoming (Menkens and Anderson 1989). A density of 1.5 animals per hectare was estimated for North Park, Colorado, after emergence of young of the year (Tileston and Lechleitner 1966). Density in most colonies increases by 1.5 to 4.0 times with emergence of young of the year. Home ranges have been estimated at 5.9 to 6.9 ha, although typical movements are much more restricted and home ranges seldom exceed 1 ha in dense populations. Overgrazing by livestock may favor increases in density. Dispersal is important to establishment of new colonies (Tileston and Lechleitner 1966; T. Clark 1977).

White-tailed prairie dogs are diurnal, with a bimodal activity period during the warmer months of spring and summer and unimodal patterns in cooler weather. In Wyoming the animals have been shown to hibernate (Bakko and Nahorniak 1986), as long suspected. Harlow and Menkens (1986) contrasted hibernation of white-tailed prairie dogs with torpor in black-tailed prairie dogs. The period of hibernation varies from about 3 to 6 months, with many adults dormant by mid-August. However, that period may be shorter at lower elevations, as J. P. Fitzgerald (unpublished) has observed white-tailed prairie dogs active in December and early January near Rangely and Grand Junction. Hibernating animals probably emerge in late February or early March in most areas in Colorado. "Hibernation lines" are apparent on the lower incisors of those prairie dogs that are obligatory hibernators (*C. leucurus*, *C. gunnisoni*) but were observed in only 20 percent of specimens of *C. ludovicianus*, a facultative hibernator (Goodwin and Ryckman 2006). This pattern may allow paleontologists to determine whether extinct species of prairie dogs were hibernators.

White-tailed prairie dogs spend almost two-thirds of their lives in their burrows. These intensively used structures are laboriously constructed. A burrow re-excavated in Montana comprised 29 m of passages and contained a turning bay, sleeping quarters, 2 hibernacula, and a maternity area (J. A. Burns et al. 1989).

White-tailed prairie dogs are monoestrous, breeding in late March and April soon after they emerge from hibernation (Tileston and Lechleitner 1966). Gestation takes about 30 days (Bakko and Brown 1967), with young born in late April or early May. Litter sizes average 5.6 young. Pups do not appear aboveground until late May or June, when they are close to 1 month old.

Mortality is caused by a variety of predators, including eagles, hawks, badgers (Goodrich and Buskirk 1998), coyotes, black-footed ferrets, and rattlesnakes. Tileston and Lechleitner (1966) reported only 25 percent of marked animals present the following summer. Plague is an important disease over much of the species' range (T. Clark 1977; Ubico et al. 1988). Poisoning and habitat losses from agriculture and urbanization also contribute to population declines. However, their tendency to inhabit shrublands, have dispersed burrows, and maintain relatively low densities aids in their ability to survive plague epizootics and poisoning campaigns. In Wyoming, epizootics of plague were short-lived, with density and survival increasing within 1 to 2 years (Menkens and Anderson 1991); a complex mosaic of colonies near Meeteetse was differentially impacted by plague, some colonies recovering and some remaining unaffected (S. H. Anderson and Williams 1997). As in other species of prairie dogs, recreational shooting can be the major source of mortality in local populations (see generic account and Table 4-3), and the demographic impacts of this hunting are poorly understood (Reeve and Vosburgh 2006). Literature was reviewed by T. Clark, Hoffmann, and Nadler (1971); T. Clark (1977, 1986); Hoogland (2003b); and Pauli et al. (2006). T. Clark and others working on black-footed ferret recovery have conducted intensive and extensive studies of the species in Wyoming and adjacent areas (T. M. Campbell and Clark 1981; T. Clark, Campbell, et al. 1982; T. Clark, Bekoff, et al. 1989).

Cynomys ludovicianus

BLACK-TAILED PRAIRIE DOG

Description

Black-tailed prairie dogs are reddish cinnamon on the dorsum in summer and more reddish in winter. The venter is a paler buffy brown, yellow, or white. Albino individuals are not uncommon. The tail is long compared with that of other prairie dogs and is conspicuously tipped with black to brownish black hairs. As with many mammals in Colorado, the summer pelage is short and rather coarse. Winter pelage is longer and more lax. Measurements are: total length 336–410 mm; length of tail 60–93 mm; length of hindfoot 48–68 mm; length of ear 8–14 mm; weight 525–1,350 g. Females typically are slightly smaller than males. Magle (2008) reported no difference in seasonal weights of black-tailed prairie dogs along a gradient of urbanization in the Denver area. The skull is robust and the occipital region has an oval shape when viewed from behind. The jugal bone is thick and heavy, especially where it joins the rather stout zygomatic process of the maxillary. The cheekteeth are large, stout, and expanded laterally. Females have eight functional mammae. Molar attrition can be used to age live animals (Hoogland 1987).

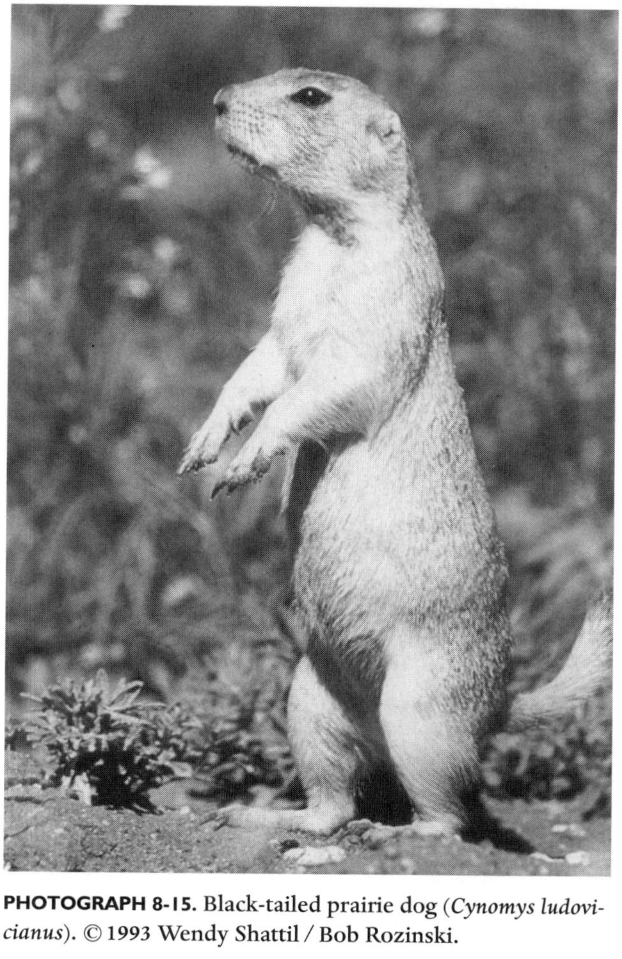

PHOTOGRAPH 8-15. Black-tailed prairie dog (*Cynomys ludovicianus*). © 1993 Wendy Shattil / Bob Rozinski.

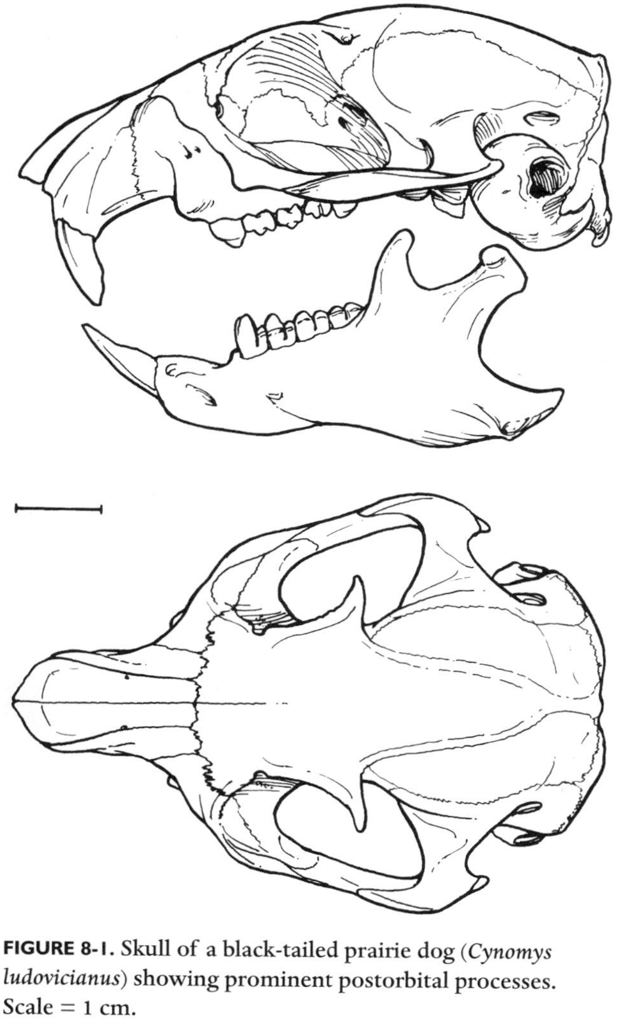

FIGURE 8-1. Skull of a black-tailed prairie dog (*Cynomys ludovicianus*) showing prominent postorbital processes. Scale = 1 cm.

Distribution

Black-tailed prairie dogs are present and sometimes common in most of the counties of the eastern plains, especially adjacent to the suburban fringe of the expanding Front Range corridor of the Colorado Piedmont. The greatest difference in distribution from the early 1900s is a decrease in size of colonies, with few now exceeding 40 ha and most being smaller than 20 ha (Lechleitner 1969). Because most of the eastern plains is in private ownership, it is likely that total numbers of prairie dogs will decline over time as development pressures continue. Based on aerial line-intercept sampling in 2001, G. White, Dennis, and Pusateri (2005) estimated that 1.94 percent of suitable habitat for black-tailed prairie dogs in eastern Colorado actually was occupied. On public lands such as the Pawnee National Grassland in Weld County and the Comanche National Grassland in Baca and Las Animas counties, political pressure from livestock interests keeps populations at low numbers. Prairie dogs occupy less than 0.5 percent of the 78,000 ha Pawnee National Grassland. Such low numbers and the dispersion of colonies have affected the distribution and ecology of some other species that depend on prairie dogs or their burrows, including burrowing owls, mountain plovers, and ferruginous hawks, as well as black-footed ferrets.

Although prairie dogs have been eliminated from millions of hectares of their former range, they are still abundant in many localities. Some of the highest densities presently found in Colorado are on lands being held by developers adjacent to or within urban areas such as Denver, Boulder, and Aurora. These holdings often were formerly farmed but no longer are used for agriculture, being left "idle" until economic conditions permit profitable subdivision and development. Black-tailed prairie dogs are able to colonize such disturbed areas with high success. One subspecies, *Cynomys ludovicianus ludovicianus*, occurs in Colorado.

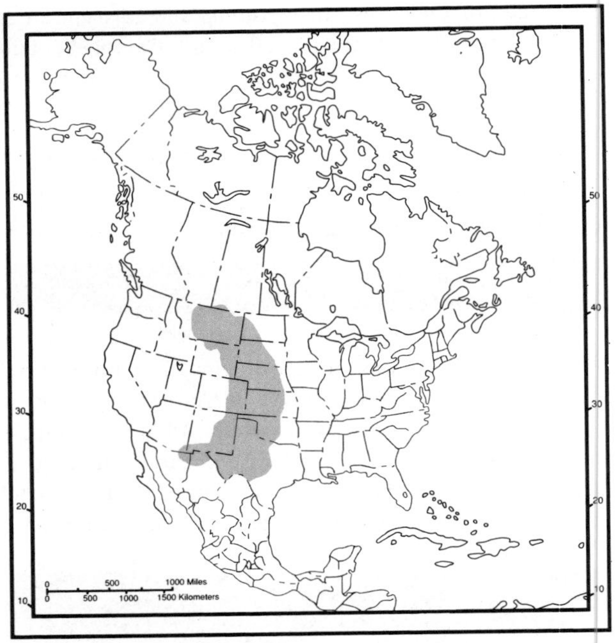

MAP 8-30. Distribution of the black-tailed prairie dog (*Cynomys ludovicianus*) in North America.

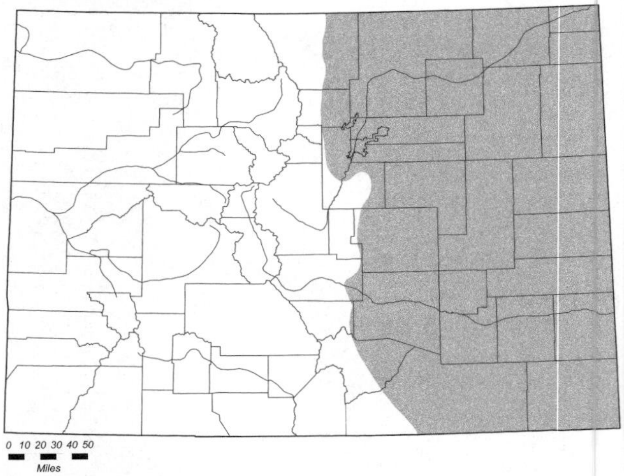

MAP 8-31. Distribution of the black-tailed prairie dog (*Cynomys ludovicianus*) in Colorado.

Natural History

Black-tailed prairie dogs are among the most intensively studied of rodents, because of their supposed negative impact on agriculture and also because of their complex and fascinating social behavior and diurnal habits. Further, the literature on the species in Colorado has expanded dramatically in recent years, partly because traditional debates between wildlife advocates and agricultural interests have been largely replaced by ecological debates about changing environments and alternative futures for the rapidly urbanizing Front Range corridor. Black-tailed prairie dogs create an environment that is inviting to other animals; some 200 species of vertebrates have been reported from prairie dog towns (B. Miller, Ceballos, and Reading 1994). Shipley and Reading (2006) and Shipley et al. (2008) found higher diversity of both "herptiles" (reptiles and lissamphibians) and small mammals on grasslands with black-tailed prairie dogs than on those without.

Black-tailed prairie dogs form their large colonies or "towns" in shortgrass or mixed prairie. Among North American mammals, prairie dogs, along with pocket gophers (Huntley and Inouye 1988) and beavers (Naiman 1988; Naiman et al. 1988), have had profound environmental impact (Whicker and Detling 1988). Historical estimates suggest that 20 percent of the shortgrass and mixed prairie may once have been inhabited by prairie dogs (Lauenroth 1979). Over much of that area they have been extirpated or severely controlled. Fleharty (1995) summarized observations of prairie dogs by early settlers in western Kansas.

Prairie dogs consume large quantities of annual forbs and native grasses (Klatt 1971; Bonham and Lerwick 1976; Gold 1976; R. Hansen and Gold 1977; Klatt and Hein 1978; Uresk 1984, 1987). Grasses and sedges are preferred. Western wheatgrass, buffalograss, grama, Russian-thistle, pigweed, and ragweed are common food items. During late fall, winter, and spring, prairie dogs frequently dig and eat roots of forbs and grasses. While foraging for these foods they sometimes select a small area, perhaps 1.5 to 4.5 m in diameter, and dig many circular pits 7.5 to 13.0 cm deep to access roots (Tileston and Lechleitner 1966). They also commonly cut vegetation that they do not eat, perhaps to keep cover down and thus allow ready detection of predators. Grass-dominated areas with prairie dogs typically lose 60–80 percent of annual net primary production because of consumption and clipping by prairie dogs and other herbivores (Whicker and Detling 1988). Their habits of clipping vegetation, consuming roots, and moving dirt for crater mounds lead over time to markedly different plant species composition than on areas surrounding the prairie dog town. In a 6-year study on the Central Plains Experimental Range in Weld County, Derner et al. (2006) reported that weight gain of cattle dropped by about 16 percent when the area occupied by prairie dogs increased from 0 to 60 percent. Although prairie dogs reduce the biomass of grasses and enhance production of forbs, they often increase the quality of remaining grasses because protein and digestibility are higher (Uresk 1987; Whicker and Detling 1993; Detling 2006). Based on studies on the Cimarron National Grasslands in southwestern Kansas, Van Nimwegen et al. (2008) determined that the most important "ecosystem engineering" impact of black-tailed prairie dogs was their burrowing and soil disturbance rather than their cropping of vegetation. Prairie dogs were a centerpiece of the review of rangeland rodents and lagomorphs by Fagerstone and Ramey (1996).

Black-tailed prairie dogs are highly social animals, more so than other prairie dogs. Using concepts from information theory, Blumstein and Armitage (1998a) calculated an index of "social complexity" for a number of species of ground-dwelling sciurids. By their metric, black-tailed prairie dogs are more social than yellow-bellied marmots, but *M. flaviventris* is more social than Gunnison's or white-tailed prairie dogs.

Prairie dog social systems are organized spatially around the burrow system. Black-tailed prairie dogs invest much of their time working on the burrows and the construction and repair of the associated mounds (J. King 1955; Sheets et al. 1971; Cincotta 1989). Burrows of black-tailed prairie dogs are deeper than those of *C. gunnisoni*, and burrows of Gunnison's and white-tailed prairie dogs have more entrances than do those of black-tailed prairie dogs (Verdolin et al. 2008). The animals dig complex burrow systems, the entrances marked by conspicuous mounds. Mounds may be dome- or crater-shaped. Dome-shaped mounds are gently rounded hummocks of subsoil brought up from the burrows. Crater-shaped mounds are conical, volcano-like, and constructed of a mixture of subsoils and surface soils. Prairie dogs mix about 220 kg of soil per burrow system (Whicker and Detling 1988). Burrow systems may number from 50 to 300 per hectare, so the total soil movement and mixing by a major colony can be tremendous (J. King 1955; O'Meilia et al. 1982; E. M. White and Carlson 1984; Archer et al. 1987). Burrows usually have 1 or 2 (but as many as 6) entrances (Hoogland 1995). Collection of surface soils for construction of typical crater mounds requires moving soil over a 1 m radius from the mound itself. This may be accomplished by digging trough- or trench-like furrows and pushing soil toward the mound with the front feet or throwing the dirt toward the mound using the rear feet. Crater mounds are formed when soils are moist; the animals push soil with their head, shoulders, and forelimbs and tamp the soil around the entrance with their noses. When the soils have dried, the impressions left by their noses are clearly visible in the adobe-like material. Craters with high rims pair with lower, dome-shaped mounds to facilitate ventilation (Hoogland 1995). The density of the burrow entrances varies greatly among towns. An average density of 104 entrances per hectare was reported for one town north of Fort Collins (Tileston and Lechleitner 1966). However, only about 12 percent of the entrances were used at any one time. Burrows and entrances may be used for several generations (Hoogland 1995). Prairie dogs can hasten soil formation by mixing materials from lower horizons with materials from the surface. This can increase or decrease plant productivity, depending on soil chemistry (Munn 1993).

Towns vary greatly in size, ranging from a few animals to thousands of individuals. Present-day colonies generally range from less than 10 ha to several hundred ha (Dahlsted et al. 1981; C. Knowles 1986), with populations of hundreds of animals. The larger towns are divided into smaller assemblages by topographic features or by social units and territorial defense. Such topographic subdivisions are called "wards," and smaller social units within wards are termed "coteries." Coteries are family units in the sense that females within coteries tend to be relatively closely related (Manno 2007). Winterrowd et al. (2009) discussed the importance of this social structure to conservation genetics. The number of wards and coteries within a town varies considerably from one town to another. Tileston and Lechleitner (1966) estimated 1 ward in their study to encompass 3 ha, the 8 included coteries averaging 0.21 ha each. Estimated density was about 6 animals per hectare when the population was at its peak following emergence of young of the year. In early spring the population was about one-third that size. Average densities ranging from 10 to 55 animals per hectare have been reported (O'Meilia et al. 1982; C. J. Knowles 1986; Archer et al. 1987). There is substantial gene flow between disjunct colonies in an area, suggesting that black-tailed prairie dogs can be understood as a metapopulation, with concentrations of individuals (colonies) linked by corridors. Travel between colonies apparently is mostly along seasonally dry drainages (Roach et al. 2001). Severson and Plumb (1998) contrasted methods for estimating populations. Facka et al. (2008) recommended a mark and re-sight method for assessing density for conservation purposes and reviewed the historical and present distribution of black-tailed prairie dogs.

Territory size for one coterie is usually a quarter hectare or less and is defended against members of other coteries. The activities of coterie members are usually confined to this territory. Each coterie is a well-knit social unit with a dominant male and a weakly developed dominance hierarchy. In general the majority of interactions among members of a coterie are cohesive, although infanticide by females of close kin has been observed (Hoogland 1985, 1995); this is particularly interesting because infanticide of related animals is quite rare in mammals. Increased size and complexity of colonies allow individuals to decrease time spent on alert and thus increase time available for other activities (Hoogland 1979a, 1979b; Devenport 1989).

Communication between prairie dogs involves tactile, visual, olfactory, and auditory stimuli. All species of prairie dogs have a variety of calls used for passing information from individual to individual or to the group as a whole. The distinctive "bark" or "alarm call" of black-tailed prairie dogs is familiar to anyone who has visited one of their towns. Different vocalizations function in different situations, including alert, threat, "pleasure," and warning (Waring 1970; Hoogland 1983).

Black-tailed prairie dogs are mostly diurnal and active aboveground year-round. However, during periods of inclement cold weather they may stay belowground for several days (A. H. Davis 1966). They do not hibernate but rather exhibit torpor during spells of especially cold weather. Major torpor involves a drop in body temperature to an average of 19°C (from the normal 37°C) and lasts an average of about 5 days; bouts of "minor torpor" last about 2, with body temperatures of about 30°C (Lehmer et al. 2001). Their eyes have only cones, and they are almost blind in dim light. The animals appear aboveground in the morning soon after sunrise and disappear in the late afternoon before sunset. Eads et al. (2010) observed nocturnal movements by black-tailed prairie dogs in black-footed ferret restoration areas in both South Dakota and New Mexico and suggested that this might reduce their vulnerability to predation by ferrets. Aboveground activity periods are bimodal in the warmer months, with peaks in early to mid-morning and again in mid- or late afternoon. Aboveground activity diminishes in winter by as much as 45 percent. In winter most aboveground activity occurs around midday when temperatures are highest. Most time aboveground, especially during the growing season, is spent foraging and feeding.

Contrary to popular lore, the reproductive output of prairie dogs is rather modest (Hoogland 2001). Black-tailed prairie dogs have only 1 estrous cycle and 1 litter of young per year. In Colorado, they breed from February to early March. The proportion of yearling females that contribute to breeding seems to vary widely with location, probably reflecting differences in nutrition, population structure, and social stress; in Colorado only about a third of yearlings reproduce. Based on studies in southwestern South Dakota on colonies treated and untreated with the biocide zinc phosphide, Cincotta et al. (1987) found that female immigrants to a colony may not breed (or failure to reproduce may stimulate dispersal by females).

The young, averaging about 3 per litter (range, 1 to 6), are born in late March and April. Gestation is estimated at 30 to 35 days. Young are blind, naked, and helpless at birth and remain in the burrow for 4 to 7 weeks. By 3 weeks of age hair covers the body and they begin to crawl. Eyes do not open until the animals are about 5 weeks old. The young are weaned when they come aboveground, in late May or early June, weighing 100 to 125 g. They gain weight readily, spending much of the summer and fall foraging, so that by late fall, weight approaches that of adults (G. Johnson 1927; Anthony and Foreman 1951; Koford 1958; Tileston and Lechleitner 1966; Stockrahm and Seabloom 1988).

At first emergence pups are wary and do not venture far from the burrow entrance. However, they gradually expand their travels and in a few weeks scurry about their own coteries, mixing and playing with other litters. Activities include chasing, mock fighting, and wrestling. Adults rarely show play behavior in the wild. Pups also spend considerable amounts of time soliciting attention from their mothers (R. E. Smith 1958). Adults show frequent contact behaviors, including mutual grooming, naso-nasal contact (wrongly interpreted as a "kiss"), anal sniffing, chasing, agonistic behavior, and use of vocalizations.

Many studies indicate clearly the integral role of prairie dog towns as a catalyst for biotic diversity in shortgrass prairie ecosystems (T. Clark, Campbell, et al. 1982; B. Miller, Ceballos, and Reading 1994). Species like black-footed ferrets (*Mustela nigripes*), western rattlesnakes (*Crotalus viridis*), and burrowing owls (*Athene cunicularia*; see Desmond et al. 2000; Winter and Cully 2007) are closely linked to prairie dog burrow systems for food and cover. Plumpton and Lutz (1993) found that burrowing owls usually selected areas at the Rocky Mountain Arsenal that had greater density of prairie dog burrows, less grass cover, and lower vegetation height than random sites. They made little use of elevated perches in the short vegetation of occupied towns and showed strong site fidelity to previously used colonies. In studies at the Plains Conservation Center in Arapahoe County, capture rates of amphibians and reptiles were similar on and off prairie dog colonies (Shipley et al. 2008). Bevers et al. (1997) modeled black-tailed prairie dog colonies at the landscape level to optimize habitat for black-footed ferret recovery. Kinlaw (1999) provided a general review of the importance of burrowing mammals in arid environments.

Prairie dogs feed badgers (Licht 2009), coyotes, black-footed ferrets, and ferruginous hawks (*Buteo regalis*) and other raptors, and prairie dogs clear ground for nesting by mountain plovers (*Charadrius montanus*). Nest predation on grassland birds may be higher in prairie dog towns than in adjacent areas (B. Baker et al. 2000), but that may be exacerbated by the fact that most prairie dog towns today are fragmented, presenting predators with easier access to nests. Experimental studies in South Dakota (Krueger 1986) demonstrated that bison and prairie dogs both favored edges of prairie dog towns for grazing, with bison improving range condition for prairie dogs.

In turn, prairie dog populations probably were influenced by great herds of bison, which "disturbed" the prairie, clipping the vegetation and facilitating colonization, although not all authors agree on this (see Slobodchikoff et al. 1988). Impact of prairie dogs on the biotic community needs to be considered at appropriate scales. At the landscape scale, over time, the biota of active prairie dog colonies differs from that of abandoned "towns" and from areas without prairie dogs (Stapp 2007). Prairie dog towns provided particularly good habitat for insectivorous northern grasshopper mice and omnivorous 13-lined ground squirrels. Sites without prairie dogs showed greater richness of species (such as the silky pocket mouse) that are typical of sandier soils or species that prefer taller or denser vegetation (such as western harvest mice). Black-tailed prairie dogs not only drive and maintain changes in vegetation and influence the mammalian community, but they influence the abundance and diversity (species richness) of fleas in the community of small mammals (Brinkerhoff, Ray et al. 2008).

The plague bacillus, *Yersinia pestis*, occurs widely in the western United States but is not co-extensive with prairie dogs (Cully and Williams 2001), as most records of plague are from west of the 100th meridian. All of Colorado is within the "plague zone," as are the westernmost counties of the Dakotas, Nebraska, and Kansas, as well as the Oklahoma and Texas panhandles and much of West Texas. Plague probably has spread through the range of prairie dogs only in the past century, having "jumped ship" on a rodent host in a West Coast port in the late nineteenth century (Biggins and Kosoy 2001). Mode of transmission of plague between colonies is poorly understood. Control of the flea vectors of plague has been demonstrated to improve survival of prairie dogs (Biggins et al. 2010, but see C. Webb et al. 2006).

A major study of landscape ecology of prairie dogs and plague is under way on City and County of Boulder Open Space lands (W. C. Johnson and Collinge 2004; Collinge et al. 2005). Plague transmission appears to be less effective in complex landscapes fragmented by roads, streams, and lakes. However, Stapp, Young, et al. (1994) analyzed 21 years of data from the Pawnee National Grasslands and found no predictable relationship between extinction probability and distance to next nearest colony; probability of extinction of colonies was linked to the warmer and sometimes wetter winters associated with El Niño events (also see Holmgren et al. 2006; Salkeld and Stapp 2008). Brinkerhoff, Markeson, et al. (2006) investigated the possibility of competition between species of fleas (*Oropsylla*) on their prairie dog hosts. *O. hirsuta* and *O. tuberculata* showed positive association, perhaps facilitation: the higher the population of 1 species present, the higher the population of the other. Bai et al. (2008) reported on infection of black-tailed prairie dogs in Boulder County with the bacterium *Bartonella*. The microbe is parasitic on red blood cells and cells of the capillary lining (endothelium). The potential importance of *Bartonella* in prairie dogs to human health is unknown.

For a general review of disease dynamics in prairie dogs and other social rodents, see Ostfeld and Mills (2007). Antolin et al. (2002) reviewed the landscape-level impacts on the intricate symbiosis of the plague, prairie dogs, and black-footed ferrets. Bevers et al. (1997) and Hof et al. (2002) discussed optimization of landscapes for recovery of prairie dogs (focused on South Dakota but relevant to Colorado).

Prairie dogs of all species are subject to high mortality from a variety of terrestrial and avian predators, including golden eagles, red-tailed and ferruginous hawks, coyotes, badgers, bobcats, foxes, black-footed ferrets, and rattlesnakes. Based on studies of spatial organization of occupied and unoccupied burrows in large prairie dog towns in South Dakota and Montana, Jachowski et al. (2008) concluded that managing spatial use of colonies by managing vegetation could have positive impacts for black-footed ferrets. Tileston and Lechleitner (1966) reported only 45 percent of marked animals recaptured the following year. In other studies mortality has ranged from 14 to 55 percent. Diseases include sylvatic plague, which can eliminate entire populations. Infanticide is the major non-human cause of juvenile mortality, affecting some 39 percent of litters (Hoogland 2007a). Infanticide is more common in *C. ludovicianus* than in other species of prairie dogs.

Humans are by far the most effective control agent, with millions of hectares of prairie dog towns eliminated by the intensive and extensive poisoning campaigns that have been waged since agriculture expanded into the range of the species. Prairie dogs may be as much a symptom of poor range management as they are a cause of degradation. Irrigation and careful range rotation can be effective controls on their populations in many situations (Fagerstone 1979). Control of nuisance prairie dogs is managed by the Colorado Department of Agriculture, especially through regulating application of pesticides. For details, see Andelt and Hopper (2000b) or the Colorado Department of Agriculture's website. As other species of prairie dogs, "black-tails" are considered small game under Colorado wildlife regulations (see Table 4-1). Seasons are set annually. Hunting of black-tailed prairie dogs is allowed year-round on private lands and from June 15 to the end of February on public lands (Colorado Division of Wildlife 2009f). There are no bag and possession limits. Comments on harvest are noted in the generic account of *Cynomys*.

Because of extensive loss of habitat during the twentieth century, the Rodent Survival Commission of the International Union for the Conservation of Nature (IUCN) declared black-tailed prairie dogs to be a species of "conservation concern" (D. Hafner et al. 1998b). In 1998, the National Wildlife Federation petitioned for listing of black-tailed prairie dogs as "threatened" under the Endangered Species Act of 1973, based on dramatic declines in populations and the fact that prairie dog towns provide essential habitat for a number of other species of the shortgrass steppe. The US Fish and Wildlife Service eventually concluded that listing was "warranted but precluded": warranted by the facts on the ground but precluded by competing priorities and a lack of funding. Principal threats to the species include habitat modification, diminution, destruction, overhunting, disease, and predation (B. Luce 2002; R. Luce 2002). A study conducted for the Colorado Department of Natural Resources estimated that there were just over 3,000 active black-tailed prairie dog colonies in Colorado, covering about 214,000 acres (EDAW 2000). Some 82 percent of existing colonies covered less than 100 acres, and more than half were less than 20 acres. Active towns represented less than 2 percent of potential short- and mixed-grass prairie habitat, much of which has been converted to agriculture. Pueblo and Weld counties had the highest active acreage (with more than 20,000 acres each), but in terms of occupied area per potential habitat, highest rates of occupancy were in Boulder and Denver counties. G. White, Dennis, and Pusateri (2005) found roughly similar numbers.

Appropriate agencies and organizations in the states within the historical range of *C. ludovicianus* cooperated in conservation assessment and planning (B. Luce 2002), in part to preclude federal listing of black-tailed prairie dogs as threatened or endangered under the Endangered Species Act. Based on aerial surveys in 2002, Colorado has more than 600,000 acres of black-tailed prairie dog towns, with 5.3 percent of suitable habitat occupied. This is a greater proportion than in any other state (B. Luce 2002). Within Colorado, proportion of suitable habitat occupied varies from less than 1 percent in Phillips and Sedgwick counties to nearly 80 percent in Boulder County (Colorado Division of Wildlife 2003b). The goal of grassland conservation in Colorado is "to ensure, at a minimum, the viability of the black-tailed prairie dog and associated species (mountain plover, burrowing owl, swift fox and ferruginous hawk) and provide mechanisms to manage for populations beyond minimum levels, where possible, while addressing the interests and rights of private landowners" (Colorado Division of Wildlife 2003b). Hoogland (2007b) considered the prospects for successful conservation of black-tailed prairie dogs to be "enormous."

Despite persecution, in some local areas prairie dogs have made a successful comeback and are abundant. In urban areas they become accustomed to humans (R. Adams et al. 1987; Bekoff and Ickes 1999) and are important "watchable wildlife" (B. Gill 2006), although animals in both rural and urban situations have been found to retreat more rapidly to their burrows after repeated approaches by humans (Magle et al. 2005). Magle et al. (2010) studied genetic structure of populations of *C. ludovicianus* in the southern part of the Denver metropolitan area. They found high levels of genetic differentiation among colonies, indicating less gene flow than in more natural habitats outside the urban area. There was enough movement of individuals to preclude inbreeding, however. Urban colonies can precipitate conflicts, because some people are concerned about public health and perceived nuisance problems, but others enjoy these interesting mammals as part of their shrinking natural world and want to retain them. A variety of organizations have been involved in relocating prairie dogs from where they are abundant but a perceived nuisance to suitable habitat elsewhere. K. Roe and Roe (2003) provided suggestions for habitat suitability for relocation of black-tailed prairie dogs, including considerations of soil, vegetation, slope, elevation, previous use by prairie dogs, proximity to extant colonies, opportunities for expansion, corridors for dispersal, and the welfare of prairie dogs and human neighbors. Based on experiments at the Rocky Mountain Arsenal on the effect of group size on relocation success, K. Robinette et al. (1995) suggested that transplants include a minimum of 60 individuals and that receiving areas have the potential for natural immigrants.

T. Clark (1971a, 1986) and Hoogland (1995, 1996a, 2003b) reviewed the extensive literature on the black-tailed prairie dog. A number of authors (see Licht 1997 and Johnsgard 2005 for reviews) have considered prairie dogs in the context of the broad natural and cultural history of the Great Plains. The US Fish and Wildlife Service (2009) is a good source of current information on conservation status as well as natural history.

Genus *Sciurus*—Tree Squirrels

The genus *Sciurus* includes some 28 species (Thorington and Hoffmann 2005), ranging in forested areas throughout most of North America and Eurasia (including Japan) and southward in the Western Hemisphere to Brazil and Bolivia. About half of the species in the genus occur in Mexico and Central America. Taxonomy of the subfamily Sciurinae was reviewed by J. Moore (1959). Colorado is home to 2 quite distinctive species of *Sciurus*. Both species are managed as small game mammals.

Sciurus aberti

ABERT'S SQUIRREL

Description

Also called "tassel-eared squirrel," Abert's squirrel, in its rich winter pelage, has to rank as one of Colorado's most beautiful mammals. A large tree squirrel, the species is polymorphic in coat color along the Front Range (Nash and Ramey 1970). The gray phase has a white belly and dark lateral stripes; other color phases are solid: jet black, dark brown, or pale brown. Proportional prevalence of various color phases varies with location, although all three color phases may occur in a single litter. The predominant color along the Front Range is black. Coat color polymorphism and geographic variation have been studied, and the former was found to be stable in populations since the turn of the century (C. Ramey and Nash 1976a, 1976b; Hoffmeister and

PHOTOGRAPH 8-16. Abert's squirrel (*Sciurus aberti*). Photograph by J. Perley Fitzgerald.

Diersing 1978; Hancock and Nash 1982). The ears have conspicuous tufts of hair, most noticeable in fresh winter pelage. In southwestern Colorado, almost all Abert's squirrels are salt-and-pepper gray, often marked with a broad dorsal patch of rust-red hairs. Measurements are: total length 450–580 mm; length of tail 200–300 mm; length of hindfoot 65–75 mm; length of ear 35–45 mm; weight 550–750 g. The skull resembles that of the fox squirrel but lacks the typical reddish tinge common in the latter species. The ventral anterior border of the orbit is opposite the first molar, and the third upper premolar is large and well developed.

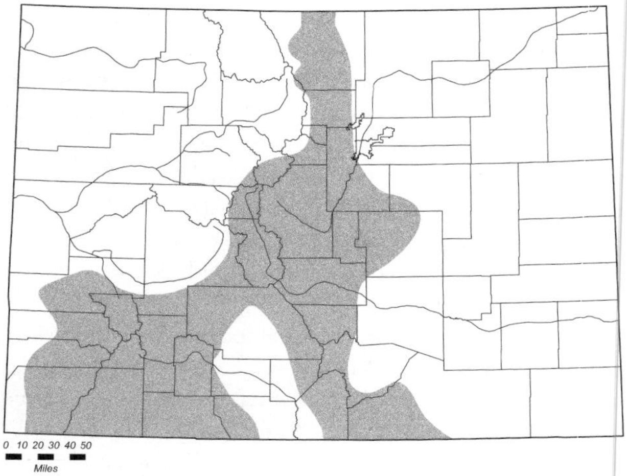

MAP 8-33. Distribution of Abert's squirrel (*Sciurus aberti*) in Colorado.

Distribution

Abert's squirrels are common in ponderosa pine forests in southern and central Colorado, and their distribution and pattern of color variation have generated interest (C. Ramey and Nash 1971). During the Late Pleistocene, Abert's squirrels apparently occurred only as far north as central Arizona and New Mexico, so their occurrence in Colorado is a result of post-Pleistocene dispersal (R. Davis and Brown 1989). Lamb et al. (1997) demonstrated the phylogeographic continuity of Abert's squirrels from Colorado's Eastern Slope with populations to the south in New Mexico. Extensions of the known range have occurred in recent years in southeastern (Mellott and Choate 1984) and western (R. Davis and Bissell 1989) Colorado. According to D. Armstrong (1972) and E. Hall (1981), *Sciurus aberti mimus* occurs in southwestern Colorado; *S. a. ferreus* occurs in the Front Range, Sangre de Cristos, and Wet Mountains. However, Hoffmeister and Diersing (1978) treated *S. a. mimus* as a junior synonym of *S. a. aberti*, as substantiated by genetic studies (Wettstein et al. 1995; Lamb et al. 1997). In the early twentieth century, the species was not common in Colorado but populations increased after closure of the hunting season (Wade 1935). At the present time, Abert's squirrel is classified as a small game mammal by the Colorado Division of Wildlife.

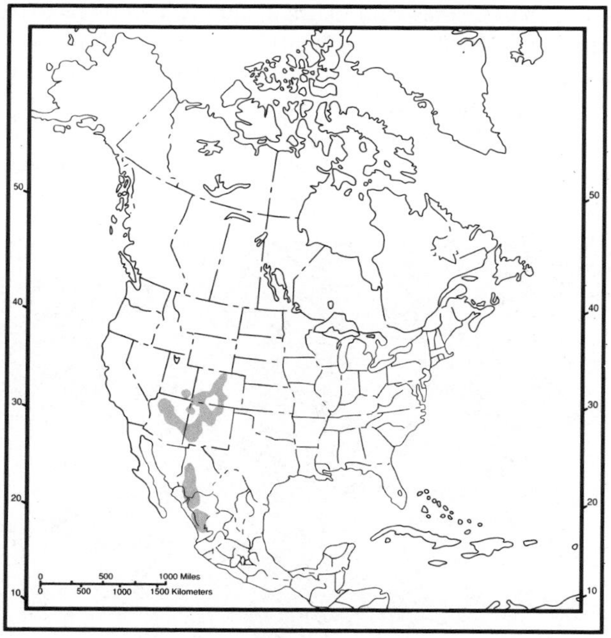

MAP 8-32. Distribution of Abert's squirrel (*Sciurus aberti*) in North America.

Natural History

Abert's squirrels are dependent on ponderosa pine for both nesting sites and food, and thus are restricted to open montane forests (J. Keith 1965; D. Patton 1977; M. Snyder 1992), although R. Forbes (1997) reported foraging on acorns beneath snow in the Sandia Mountains of New Mexico. Dodd et al. (2003) emphasized the importance for *S. aberti* in Arizona of larger trees and patches of trees with interlocking canopies. The squirrels feed on inner bark, seeds, twigs, buds, and young cones of ponderosa pines. Only about 10 percent of the weight of twigs cut is actually consumed. Abert's squirrels in northeastern Arizona were found to decrease the potential cone crop of individual trees by 20 percent. By direct predation on developing seeds, the squirrels reduced cone crop by an additional 25 percent over 2 years (Allred et al. 1994). Havlick (1984) studied Abert's squirrels in sympatry with fox squirrels (*S. niger*) and pine squirrels (*Tamiasciurus hudsonicus*) in the Boulder Mountain Parks. Fox squirrels mostly were observed in moist riparian systems, pine squirrels utilized mixed coniferous forests, and Abert's squirrel was observed only in ponderosa pine woodlands. Because fox squirrels are a relative newcomer to the foothills of the Colorado Front Range, long-term quantitative studies of populations and their interactions would be invaluable.

Abert's squirrels appear to select trees with low levels of certain monoterpenes and can reduce ponderosa pine cone production by up to 74 percent, depending on numbers of squirrels and the rate of cone production (Capretta et al. 1980). During winter, the squirrels feed almost exclusively on phloem (inner bark) of particular individual trees. This high-volume, low-quality diet is associated with a distinctively large gastrointestinal tract (Murphy and Linhart 1999). Target trees represent fewer than 10 percent of the trees in stands populated by Abert's squirrels along the Front Range, and they differ chemically and physiologically from non-target trees (M. Snyder 1992). The squirrels are probably important agents of natural selection in southwestern ponderosa pine woodlands, but not the only agents. M. Snyder (1998) noted that each of the other 3 major specialized consumers on *Pinus ponderosa*—North American porcupine (*Erethizon dorsatum*), western pine beetle (*Dendroctonus ponderosae*), and dwarf mistletoe (*Arceuthobium vaginatum*)—is biased toward trees with a different chemical signature, so the trees are caught in a complex system of diversifying selection. Abert's squirrels also eat fungi, both aboveground (epigeous) and belowground (hypogeous) forms. Fungal spores in the squirrel's feces may help spread mutualistic mycorrhizal associates of ponderosa pine (States and Wettstein 1998). Carrion also is eaten, and bones and antlers are often gnawed for their mineral content. Food caches are not established.

Abert's squirrels are diurnal and active year-round. Winter foraging focuses on terminal twigs in the tree crown. They gnaw through the base of a twig, strip the needle clusters, remove the outer bark, eat the inner bark, and drop the remaining part of the twig. These feeding sites are recognizable by the severed needle clusters and bare, discarded twigs at the base of trees (M. Snyder 1992). States et al. (1988) detailed seasonal patterns of foods and foraging by Abert's squirrels in northeastern Arizona.

At night and when inactive during the day, they retreat to tree nests. Occasionally animals of different ages and sexes share the same nest, especially in winter and spring. Nests are typically in ponderosa pine, with most nest trees having a diameter of more than 0.3 m. Nests are either constructed from pine twigs up to 60 cm in length and 2 cm in diameter or "excavated" in the mass of twigs that proliferates from dwarf mistletoe infestations. Nest chambers are lined with grass and other soft materials. Nests are 5–18 m aboveground. The nest is frequently located on the south side of the tree and near the trunk; such areas would receive early sun and be somewhat protected from wind. Abert's squirrels appear to do best in ponderosa pine stands with close to 60 percent canopy closure and over 220 stems per hectare (Farentinos 1972c; D. Patton 1977, 1984). Nest trees also differed in chemical composition from non-nesting trees (M. Snyder and Linhart 1994). In Arizona, Abert's squirrels nested preferentially in larger trees and nests tended to be on the south or east side of the bole. Where sympatric in the Pinaleño Mountains of Arizona, pine squirrels and Abert's squirrels used different kinds of nests. Pine squirrels mostly used tree holes (especially in quaking aspen), whereas Abert's squirrels built nests of branches and twigs in conifers, especially in Douglas-fir.

Although not territorial, Abert's squirrels are mostly solitary except during the breeding season. Home ranges in Colorado ranged from about 5 to 20 ha, depending on season and sex of the animal. Mean home range size for both sexes is about 8 ha. Males typically have larger home ranges, especially when breeding, although adult females may cover large distances in summer (Farentinos 1979).

Abert's squirrels show a variety of visual displays and have several vocalizations. Displays include tail-flaring, tail-flicking, and foot-stomping, all of which are associated with varying degrees of alarm. Calls include alarm barks, tooth chattering, screams, and clucks. Changes in position of the tail and ears and general body posture are used during agonistic displays in the mating season, communicating degrees of dominance or subordinance (Farentinos 1974).

As in other tree squirrels, courtship is marked by frantic chases, with males following estrous females up and down trees and over the forest floor. Such chases may continue for several hours and result in multiple copulations by the same or different males. Dominant males mate first, but in prolonged chases subordinate males may also have a chance to mate. Aggressive behaviors are typical during these chases, with the female attacking her male admirers or making vocalizations and threat displays. Males also engage in male-male aggressive behaviors during the chase (Rice 1957; Farentinos 1972b, 1980).

Most mating occurs in April or May in Colorado, with only 1 litter per year. (Winter breeding has been reported from Arizona, but its generality is not known; Pogany et al.

1998.) Gestation takes about 46 days. Litter size averages about 3 (range, 2 to 4; Farentinos 1972b). Young squirrels are naked at birth. The eyes are open and the pelage is well developed by about 6 weeks of age. Young animals may leave the nest at about 9 weeks of age but still rely on the female until about 2.5 months old.

Population dynamics of the species are poorly known. Sex ratios strongly favor males, 1.4:1.0 (J. Keith 1965; Farentinos 1972b). Population estimates range from 12 to 30 animals per square kilometer in the Black Forest of El Paso County, and from 82 to 114 animals per square kilometer near Boulder (Farentinos 1972a). Spring populations are lowest. Adults made up 53–65 percent of populations near Boulder. Annual mortality ranged from 22 to 65 percent in Arizona, with the speculation that severe snow conditions can lead to high mortality (R. Stephenson and Brown 1980). Drennan et al. (1998) successfully used track stations to index the abundance of Abert's squirrels, chipmunks, and ground squirrels in northeastern Arizona.

Information on predation is sparse. Hawks (especially northern goshawks) may be the most capable predators (Beier and Drennan 1997; Drennan and Beier 2003), as most terrestrial carnivores are not very successful at catching this arboreal species. Martens generally occur at higher elevations than do these squirrels. Food availability is probably important, as ponderosa pine seed crops are variable. A review of the biology of Abert's squirrel in comparison with other western tree squirrels was provided by W. Smith et al. (2003). Abert's squirrels are listed as small game mammals in Colorado (Table 4-1), with an open season from mid-November to mid-January, but data on harvest (Table 4-3) are unavailable. Nash and Seaman (1977) and J. Keith (2003) reviewed the literature on the species.

PHOTOGRAPH 8-17. Fox squirrel (*Sciurus niger*). Photograph by J. Perley Fitzgerald.

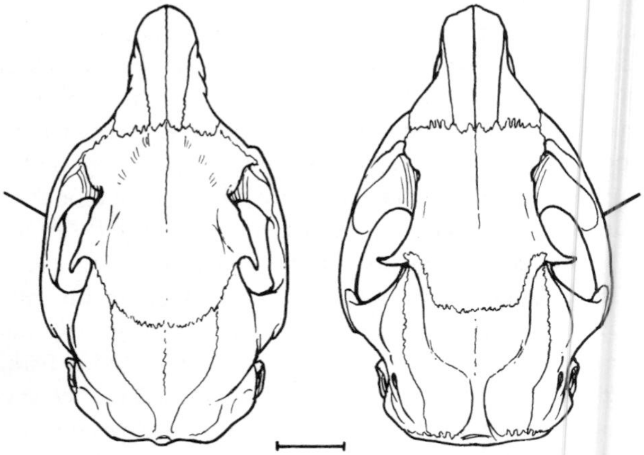

FIGURE 8-2. Dorsal views of skull of a fox squirrel (*Sciurus niger*; *left*), with relatively parallel and vertically oriented zygomatic arches, and that of a rock squirrel (*Otospermophilus variegatus*; *right*), with anteriorly convergent and more horizontally oriented zygomatic arches. Scale = 1 cm.

Sciurus niger

FOX SQUIRREL

Description

The fox squirrel is a large tree squirrel, gray-brown above and shading to reddish brown laterally. The belly is rufous, yellowish brown, or whitish. The tail is bushy, grayish red dorsally and red below. Measurements are: total length 450–600 mm; length of tail 170–300 mm; length of hindfoot 50–75 mm; length of ear 19–33 mm; weight 400–1,100 g. The skull is very similar to that of Abert's squirrel although it often has a reddish tinge. The skull of a fox squirrel will fluoresce red under ultraviolet light, a character unique to this mammal and caused by normal erythropoietic porphyria (Flyger and Levin 1977).

Distribution

Fox squirrels are common in riparian woodlands along the South Platte, Republican, and Arkansas rivers. They have extended their range along most tributaries of these rivers and are penetrating the foothills along riparian corridors as high as Evergreen and Rocky Mountain National Park, for example. Many populations are the result of deliberate introductions made in the early 1900s and more recently, but a natural invasion has also occurred as plains riparian habitats have been stabilized by control of floods and prairie fires, and as humans have created more favorable environments for fox squirrels by planting deciduous trees (Hoover and Yeager 1953; D. Armstrong 1972; K. Geluso 2004). Fox squirrels often are considered pests in urban areas because of their fondness for birdseed and so have been trapped and transported to "natural habitats" in the foothills (not the native habitat of fox squirrels). Further, injured urban fox squirrels frequently are treated in wildlife rehabilitation centers and then are released on public lands in the foothills (K. E. Taylor, personal communication). Fox squirrels may have a long-term negative impact on populations of Abert's squirrels in some areas, including the Black Forest between Denver and Colorado Springs. One subspecies, *Sciurus niger rufiventer*, occurs in Colorado. Fox squirrels are small game mammals (Table 4-1); seasons and limits are set annually.

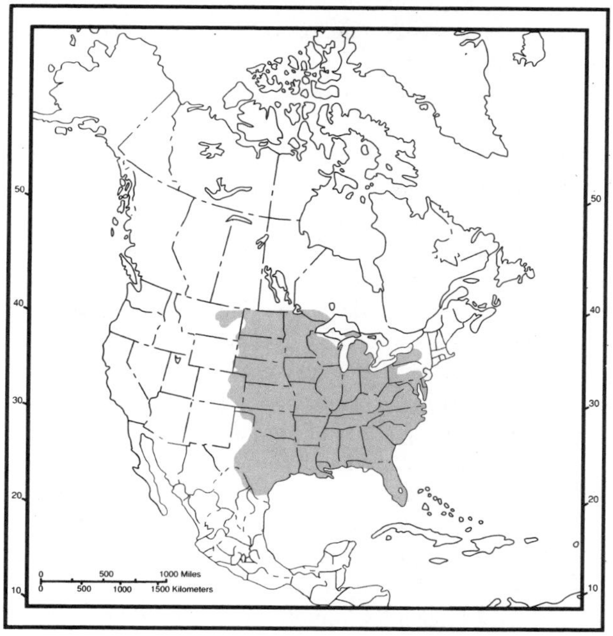

MAP 8-34. Distribution of the fox squirrel (*Sciurus niger*) in North America.

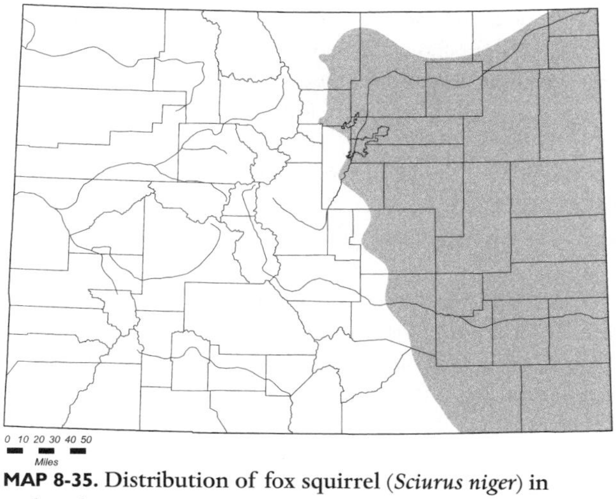

MAP 8-35. Distribution of fox squirrel (*Sciurus niger*) in Colorado.

Natural History

Despite its abundance and ubiquity along river-bottoms and in urban areas of the eastern plains, little research has been done on the biology of the fox squirrel in Colorado. Fox squirrels mostly inhabit open deciduous forest. In Colorado, the western margin of its range, it is associated with lowland shelterbelts and urban areas and riparian woodlands (Hoover and Yeager 1953). The creation of urban landscapes with mixed coniferous and deciduous trees has allowed the species to do well in many cities in the state (C. A. Jones et al. 2003), including extralimital populations at such seemingly unlikely places as Steamboat Springs (D. Armstrong, unpublished). Whether such populations represent natural expansion through suitable habitat or direct human introduction is not known. Eventually the species likely will be established statewide in "urban woodlands" and adjacent riparian communities.

The diet has been studied extensively in the eastern United States, where this is an important game species (Nixon et al. 1968; Korschgen 1981). Fox squirrels eat a variety of foods, including nuts, such as acorns and walnuts; twigs, buds, and tender leaves of many tree species, including cottonwood and elm; various berries, apples, Russian-olives, and other fleshy fruits; small grains; and corn (Yeager 1959). Fox squirrels also take food placed out for songbirds and feed on eggs of birds, nestlings, and other animal protein. Bones and antlers are also consumed, especially by pregnant and lactating females.

The animals are diurnal and active year-round. Individuals become active at or shortly after sunrise and exhibit morning and late afternoon activity peaks during the warmer months. In winter the animals are most active at midday (Hicks 1949; Bakken 1959). Fox squirrels have well-developed behaviors to reduce predation and defend resources. These include freezing in position, running to the opposite side of a tree trunk when approached, and vocalizing with warning and alarm barks when danger appears (Bakken 1959; Zelley 1971). Access to resources is determined by chases, with adult males being most aggressive.

Home ranges of fox squirrels are 0.4 to 16.4 ha, depending on habitat and population density (Flyger and Gates 1982). In Nebraska, home ranges averaged 7.5 ha for males and 3.5 ha for females, with yearlings having the largest home ranges (C. Adams 1976). In cottonwood river-bottoms near Greeley, squirrels ranged over 1 to 2 ha (S. Graham 1977). In late summer and early fall, young animals tend to disperse from their natal areas. Movements may exceed 3 km in some instances.

Fox squirrels live in nests that they construct or they utilize available tree cavities, birdhouses, and similar spaces. Cavities must have an opening of about 7 by 9 cm. The edges of such openings are gnawed and smoothed by the squirrels in their daily activity and movement (Baumgartner 1943). Nests are constructed from leaves, twigs, and bark of deciduous trees with layers of these materials built up into a compact, durable structure. The nest chamber is hollowed out as construction occurs and is lined with finer and softer materials, including shredded bark, grasses, and shredded leaves. Artificial materials are readily used. Nests are typically located close to the crotch of main limbs or near the top of the main trunk, usually at least 6 m above the ground (Stoddard 1920; Baumgartner 1940; R. Packard 1956). Although tree cavities are reported to provide more protection to fox squirrels in the winter months, in urban areas in Colorado the animals usually are forced to rely on leaf nests for their cover, because of urban forestry practices that prune out dead materials.

The fox squirrel has two breeding seasons per year. In Greeley, fox squirrels have their first season from mid- to late January to late March. The second season runs from late June through July. Breeding is characterized by mating chases similar to those described for Abert's squirrels (McCloskey and Shaw 1977). During the breeding season males tend to eat little and lose considerable weight. Females remain in estrus for about 10 days. Gestation takes 44–45 days, and the young are born naked and blind (Baumgartner 1940; L. G. Brown and Yeager 1945). Litter size probably averages a little below 3 in Colorado (J. P. Fitzgerald, unpublished), although a mean of 3.7 has been reported (Hoover and Yeager 1953). In Greeley, 2 is the average based on observations of females with young newly emerged from the nest. Pelage development and eruption of the incisors occurs at about 4 weeks. Ears open at 3 weeks and eyes at 5 weeks of age. Young are weaned by 10 weeks of age and are self-sustaining at 3 to 4 months (Baumgartner 1940; D. Allen 1942).

Individuals of both sexes can breed at 10 or 12 months of age. Yearling females have only 1 litter, but in subsequent years 2 litters are the rule. Males with scrotal testes can be observed during most months except late summer and fall. The review of reproductive biology of tree squirrels by Koprowski (2007) includes a great deal of information on the widespread fox squirrel. Hayssen (2008a) reviewed patterns of reproductive effort in squirrels generally, concluding that the principal constraint on reproduction and development is not the quantity of food and water resources per se but their seasonal availability.

Population biology is poorly understood. Adult fox squirrels can live more than 12 years in the wild (Koprowski et al. 1988). However, few survive more than 5 or 6 years. An urban, adult female in Greeley watched by James P. and J. Perley Fitzgerald (unpublished) lived more than 6.5 years. That female raised 2 litters of young each year of her adult life. Mortality in Colorado is caused mostly by hunting, traffic accidents, and predation by great horned owls, red-tailed hawks, domestic cats and dogs, foxes, and coyotes. Plague has been associated with urban populations in Denver and Greeley (B. Hudson et al. 1971). Fox squirrels in the Fort Collins area were found to be somewhat susceptible to West Nile Virus (J. Root, Hall et al. 2005; J. Root, Oesterle, Sullivan, et al. 2007), although under experimental conditions (J. Root, Oesterle, Nemeth, et al. 2006) obvious illness was rare and mortality was low (1 out of 18 animals infected).

Fox squirrels are considered small game in Colorado, but estimated harvest is modest (Table 4-3), with fewer than 1,000 individuals being taken most years. The extensive literature on fox squirrels was reviewed by Koprowski (1994) and J. Edwards et al. (2003), but the animals are rather poorly studied at the dynamic western boundary of their range.

Tamiasciurus hudsonicus

PINE SQUIRREL, CHICKAREE, OR "RED SQUIRREL"

Description

The pine squirrel is our smallest and noisiest tree squirrel, its mechanical chattering vocalizations as distinctive as its appearance. There is considerable color variation in this species throughout its wide range. In northern and central Colorado, little or no red is seen in the dorsal pelage. Squirrels from farther south may have somewhat brighter dorsal colors, but nowhere in Colorado does this species deserve the common name it bears elsewhere over its wide range, "red squirrel," so Coloradans tend to call them pine squirrels or chickarees (probably for their distinctive sound). The summer pelage is usually more reddish than the grayer winter pelage. The eyes have a conspicuous white eye ring, and the venter is white. The tail is dark, ranging from blackish gray to reddish brown, often fringed with white. The ears may show tufts, longer in winter pelage. Measurements are: total length 300–350 mm; length of tail 115–135 mm; length of hindfoot 45–55 mm; length of ear 19–30 mm; weight 190–260 g. The skull is more delicate than that of the other 2 tree squirrels, with the premolar being either reduced in size or absent. The antero-ventral border of the orbit is opposite the premolar. The male pine squirrel has an extremely small baculum compared with members of the genus *Sciurus*; females have a unique coiled vagina.

PHOTOGRAPH 8-18. Pine squirrel, or chickaree (*Tamiasciurus hudsonicus*). Photograph by J. Perley Fitzgerald.

Distribution

The pine squirrel is common in suitable forested habitat in Colorado at elevations from 1,830 to 3,660 m (6,000–12,000 feet). One subspecies, *Tamiasciurus hudsonicus fremonti*, occurs in the state. Evolutionary genetic studies (Arbogast et al. 2001) indicate that Coloradan chickarees differ from those of New Mexico and Arizona as a result of forest fragmentation during the Pleistocene.

Natural History

Pine squirrels are common throughout subalpine and montane forests in Colorado, except in stands of ponderosa

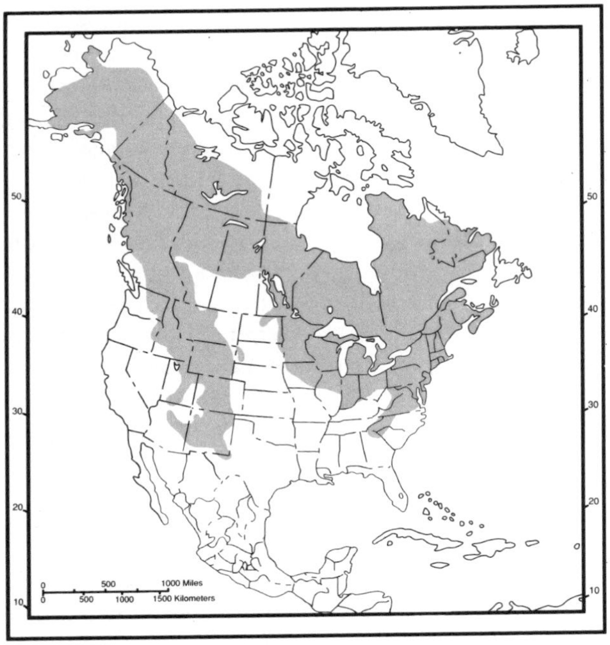

MAP 8-36. Distribution of the pine squirrel (*Tamiasciurus hudsonicus*) in North America.

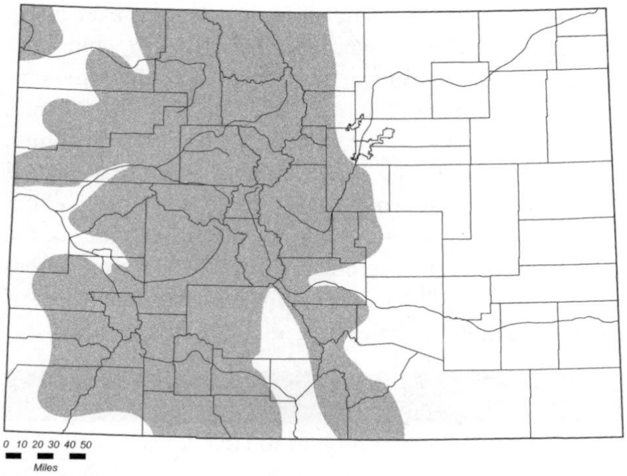

MAP 8-37. Distribution of the pine squirrel (*Tamiasciurus hudsonicus*) in Colorado.

pine occupied by Abert's squirrels. Where Abert's squirrels are absent from ponderosa pine, red squirrels can be expected at least in low numbers. They also occasionally use riparian cottonwood stands (Hatt 1943; R. Finley 1969; D. Armstrong 1972; Ferner 1974).

Chickarees eat a variety of foods, including buds, berries, and leaves of plants, although seeds of conifers and fleshy fungi are the staples (Obbard 1987). Pine squirrels have coevolved with the conifers upon which they feed (C. Smith 1970). Because most conifers, except the serotinous lodgepole pines, have cones that mature in the fall and release their seeds, squirrels must harvest "green" cones and store them in caches to prevent release of seeds. This demands a tremendous amount of activity at great energy expense. On a quiet late summer or early fall day one can hear the animals at work, clipping and dropping cones to the ground. Squirrels in productive trees can cut a cone every 2 or 3 seconds (D. Armstrong 1987). An Alaskan study indicated that one squirrel may cache up to 16,000 cones per year (C. Smith 1968). Cones may be cached in large central middens at the base of selected feeding trees or in satellite caches; cones stored in satellite caches were of lower quality (with significantly fewer seeds per cone) than those in the central cache (Elliott 1988). Middens may be as much as 9 m across and more than 0.5 m in depth, consisting of cone scales, cores of eaten cones, and stored uneaten cones. Large middens are the result of years of accumulated materials by generations of individual squirrels. As middens accumulate debris and increase in size, their function in holding moisture and maintaining cool temperatures for cone storage increases, resulting in added value in keeping seeds viable or available for food for several years. Such middens are an important source of seed for commercial sylviculture and reforestation (R. Finley 1969).

Seeds of limber pine (*Pinus flexilis*) often are harvested and dispersed by birds, especially Clark's nutcracker (*Nucifraga columbiana*). Where limber pine and Clark's nutcracker occur without pine squirrels, as on isolated mountain ranges in the Great Basin of Nevada, Benkman (1995) found that the trees allocate more than twice as much energy to production of kernels as to seed protection (cone, resin, seed coat) relative to trees growing in Colorado, where nutcrackers and pines co-occur with pine squirrels. Thus pine squirrels appear to exert a strong selective pressure on pines, driving resources from reproduction to protection.

In Colorado, nests in lodgepole pines are constructed of twigs, leaves, and grasses, 3–20 m (average, 5.3 m) above the ground, typically in interior trees within closed-canopy stands (Hatt 1943; Rothwell 1979). Occasionally, pine squirrels use sheds and attics as nesting sites. In other areas, use of tunnels in surface litter and hollow logs has been noted, but this is not common in the Southern Rockies (Obbard 1987). In Alaska and Canada the animals may burrow under the snow in search of food caches made during more hospitable times. In our area squirrels typically locate caches under dense tree canopy, thereby shielding their stores from significant snow accumulation.

Pine squirrels are active year-round, starting at dawn in warmer weather. Activity usually wanes during the middle of the day but picks up in late afternoon until dusk. During cold weather most activity occurs during midday. Thermoregulation is a problem for the animals and activity outside the nest generally ceases when air temperatures fall below –3.2°C. Temperatures in the nest during the winter may keep metabolic demand close to basal levels, whereas activity outside the nest may result in 2 to 4 times the basal energy needs. Food caches are usually located close to the nest tree, reducing time spent out of the nest in cold weather (Pauls 1978).

Chickarees are strongly territorial, linked to defense of food supplies and caches (Hatt 1943; C. Smith 1968, 1970, 1981; Kemp and Keith 1970; Gurnell 1984). The mechanical, chattering alarm call seems mostly to serve as a territorial announcement (and the common name "chickaree" may be someone's transcription of the call). Territories vary in size from about 0.4 to 2.0 ha per individual, depending on adequacy of cone crops and season. The degree of aggressive territorial behavior is related to the amount of available food in a given area (C. Smith 1968; Rusch and Reeder 1978). In Colorado, lodgepole pine has a relatively consistent cone crop while cone production in spruces and firs is much more variable. This variation in productivity influences sizes of territories. Territorial defense is reduced during years of abundant cone crops. Density estimates range from 50 to 250 animals per square kilometer in coniferous forests, similar to those found in Colorado (Obbard 1987). In the Yukon, one-third of mothers left their territory with juvenile offspring and established new territories (Berteaux and Boutin 2000); that phenomenon has not been observed in Colorado.

In Colorado, pine squirrels breed from mid-April through mid-June, with only 1 litter produced a year. Average litter size is just over 3 with a range of 2 to 5 (Dolbeer 1973). Females are sexually receptive for only 1 day and are spontaneous ovulators (Lair 1985a). Gestation is estimated to take 33–35 days (Lair 1985b), and most squirrels in Colorado are born in mid-May to mid-July. Young squirrels are able to leave the nest at about 40 days of age and start foraging and collecting food when about 1.5 months of age. Dispersal apparently is not sex-biased. In Alberta, males and females moved equally far from their natal territory (Larsen and Boutin 1998). However, following radio-telemetered squirrels in northern Minnesota, Sun (1997) found that some young animals exhibited a phase of exploratory behavior, in which they ranged away from the maternal territory during the day but returned at night. Eventually they established territories outside their natal territory. Other squirrels did not display exploration but established territories within their natal range. Pine squirrels may breed first as yearlings, although under nutritional stress, some females do not breed until they are 2 years old (Becker et al. 1998). Numbers of adult females breeding varied from 59 to 89 percent in Colorado (Dolbeer 1973). Reproductive biology of chickarees (and tree squirrels generally) was reviewed by Kaprowski (2007).

Chickarees have lived up to 9 years in captivity, but in the wild fewer than 5 percent live beyond their fifth year. Average annual mortality is estimated to be 67 percent in juveniles, 34 percent in yearlings, and 61 percent in adults (Obbard 1987). Most mortality is probably the result of weather and related fluctuations in cone production. Predators include martens, red fox, lynx, red-tailed hawks, goshawks, great horned owls, and eagles. Alarm calls may differ in response to aerial and terrestrial predators (Greene and Meagher 1998), aerial predators eliciting a short, high-pitched "seet," whereas terrestrial threats trigger the familiar chickaree chatter or "bark." Foresman and Pearson (1999) reported that American martens were active day or night, with no particular pattern, so that their activity overlapped that of their rodent prey, both diurnal pine squirrels and nocturnal voles. The pine squirrel is classified as small game in Colorado, and fall hunting seasons and limits are established annually (see Table 4-1). Annual harvest is estimated at 1,500 to 32,000 animals (see Table 4-3). Colorado is one of the few states that allow its harvest, but in Canada the red squirrel is an important furbearer, with up to 3 million animals taken annually for their pelts.

Some foresters have argued that pine squirrels damage coniferous trees by cutting cones and clipping shoots. However, Maser et al. (1978) concluded that these damages may be more than offset by the pine squirrels' dispersal of mycorrhizal-forming fungi, equally important to conifer success. The literature on the red squirrel was reviewed by Steele (1998), Flyger and Gates (1982), Obbard (1987), and Yahner (2003).

Glaucomys sabrinus

NORTHERN FLYING SQUIRREL

Description

The northern flying squirrel is a strikingly handsome animal, with long, velvet-soft, smoky gray-brown fur (paling to white below) and a broad, flattened tail. A broad flap of well-furred skin stretches from wrists to ankles and forms the gliding membrane (patagium). Measurements are: total length 310–340 mm; length of tail 145–160 mm; length of hindfoot 40–45 mm; length of ear 25–30 mm; weight up to 190 g. Females have 4 mammae and males have a well-developed baculum.

Distribution

Northern flying squirrels are not known to occur in Colorado, although Durrant (1952) reported them from extreme northeastern Utah; D. Rogers et al. (2000) reported a specimen taken in South Canyon, Uintah County, Utah—just 25 km from the Colorado border; and T. Clark and Stromberg (1987) noted a specimen from Sweetwater County, Wyoming, just north of the Colorado boundary. There is some unknown possibility that *Gaucomys sabrinus lucifugus* eventually will be discovered in extreme western Moffat County, west of the Green River, on Hoy Mountain and adjacent uplands (where a number of mammalogists

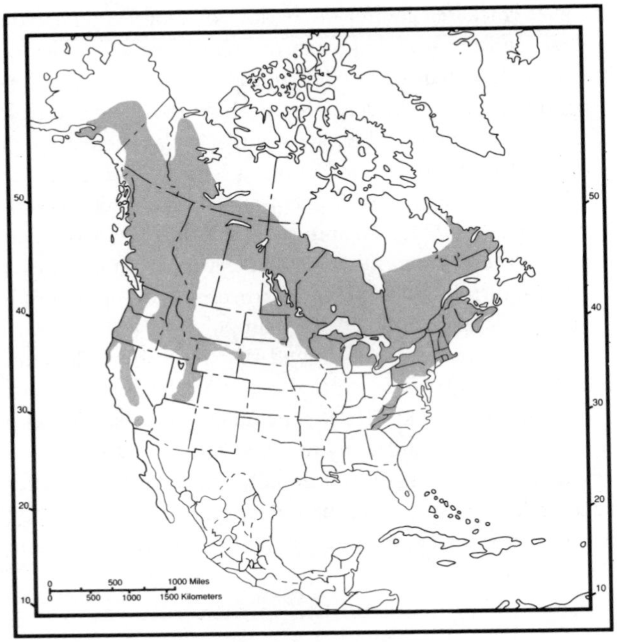

MAP 8-38. **Distribution of the northern flying squirrel (*Glaucomys sabrinus*) in North America.**

have searched for them over the years without success), or on the Roan Plateau, in the vicinity of Baxter Pass. A landowner on Roan Creek, northwest of DeBeque, reported to the Colorado Division of Wildlife an observation of a "sugar glider" (which is an Australian marsupial, *Petaurus breviceps*, rather popular in the exotic pet trade recently). CDOW personnel suspected this observation might, in fact, have been of a northern flying squirrel and searched for the animal to no avail (D. Neubaum, in litt.). The observation was in habitat similar to that from which Rogers et al. (2000) reported the species in Uintah County, Utah, roughly 90 km (55 mi.) to the west.

The northern flying squirrel is a species of the boreal forest, ranging from coast to coast across southern Canada and the Upper Midwest and extending southward through the Sierra Nevada, the Northern and Middle Rockies, and the Appalachians. Because of the importance of old-growth coniferous forests to the biology of *G. sabrinus*, the animals often are a target of conservation attention where they occur (W. Smith 2007).

Natural History

Flying squirrels do not fly, of course, but they are capable of magnificent glides, launching themselves from high in one tree and gliding gracefully or acrobatically to an adjacent tree 40 m or more away. The broad tail serves as a rudder and allows dramatic turns in midair. Further, a quick flick of the tail just before landing positions the squirrel to alight head-up, ready to scamper to the far side of the tree.

Habitat in the Uinta Mountains of Utah is dense spruce-fir or aspen forest. These are mostly cavity-nesters, building nests of grass and lichens in holes abandoned by woodpeckers or sapsuckers but occasionally remodeling a nest of a chickaree or a large bird. Much of the diet is fungi and lichens, and the animals are much less dependent on seeds than are most other tree squirrels. They do eat buds and staminate cones of conifers and a considerable amount of animal matter in season, including insects and nestling birds.

Females probably produce 1 litter of 3 to 6 (mode, 4) altricial young per year after a gestation period of 37–42 days (Wells-Gosling and Heaney 1984). Development is fairly rapid, and the young take their "maiden flight" at about the time of weaning, roughly 10 weeks of age. Wells-Gosling and Heaney (1984) reviewed the literature.

Family Castoridae—Beavers

The family Castoridae includes a single extant genus with 2 species, the European beaver (*Castor fiber*) and the American beaver (*C. canadensis*) (Helgen 2005). These are among the largest of living rodents, with some adults weighing more than 40 kg. Beavers are widely distributed across the Holarctic region. Both species are valued as furbearers. Populations in parts of Europe and North America have rebounded from overharvesting during the 1700s and 1800s, when felt hats made of beaver fur were a necessity of fashion (see Chapter 3). The geologic range of the family dates from the Oligocene, with some fossil forms reaching the size of modern black bears.

Castor canadensis

AMERICAN BEAVER

Description

This is the largest rodent in North America. Coloradan specimens not infrequently reach more than 24 kg (Denny 1952). Measurements are: total length 850–1,200 mm;

PHOTOGRAPH 8-19. American beaver (*Castor canadensis*). © 1993 Wendy Shattil / Bob Rozinski.

length of tail 200–350 mm; length of hindfoot 180–200 mm; length of ear 27–30 mm; weight 16–32 kg. Males are usually slightly larger than females. The pelage has long, shiny guard hairs and dense, softer underfur. Color varies from blackish to dark brown and chestnut, with kits having a darker pelage than adults. The long guard hairs may create a coarse appearance. The ears are short and rounded. The tail is flat, scaly, and sparsely haired. The legs are short and the hindfeet are webbed. The small forepaws are surprisingly dexterous. The medial toes of the hindfeet have split nails used to comb the fur. Other aquatic adaptations include valvular ears and nostrils and a nictitating membrane over the eyes. The skull is strongly built, with a small infraorbital foramen. The incisors are large and their enamel faces are orange-red. The anterior surface of each incisor usually is greater than 5 mm wide. The sexes are difficult to distinguish externally because the digestive and urogenital openings are enclosed in a common cloaca (which contributes to a streamlined, hydrodynamic shape). Palpation for the baculum is a reliable method for sex determination (Denny 1952). Both sexes have well-developed castor glands anterior to the cloacal opening (illustrated in Svendsen 1978).

Distribution

Beavers occur statewide in suitable habitat, marked by adequate supplies of water and food, whether in the alpine zone or on the eastern plains. One subspecies, *Castor canadensis concisor*, occurs in Colorado; the type locality of the subspecies is Monument Creek, southwest of Monument, El Paso County. (No modern study of phylogeography has been done to evaluate the validity of that subspecies.)

MAP 8-39. Distribution of the American beaver (*Castor canadensis*) in North America.

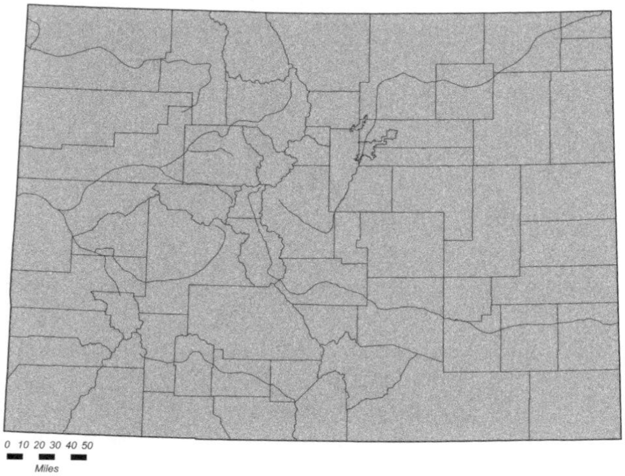

MAP 8-40. Distribution of the American beaver (*Castor canadensis*) in Colorado.

Natural History

Beavers are semiaquatic, constructing complex dams, lodges, and canal systems and thereby minimizing time spent on land foraging for food. Beavers are widespread over North America in a variety of habitats adjacent to water. In Colorado they are most common in areas with abundant willow, aspen, or cottonwood. They are most abundant in broad glacial valleys with low stream gradients and an abundance of deciduous trees and shrubs (Retzer et al. 1956; Rutherford 1964). Beavers can invade anthropogenic habitats, including reservoirs, canals, and irrigation ditches, as long as food resources are available. Beavers are fairly common, even in urban areas such as Denver (C. A. Jones et al. 2003), often causing localized destruction of tree plantings. Beavers fascinated Colorado's pioneer naturalists just as they do us today, and early accounts (such as Mills 1913 and Warren 1927) deserve rereading as sources of information and also as sources of enjoyment and inspiration. Earliest European exploration and exploitation of the area now known as Colorado focused on the beaver, whose dense fur makes a superlative hatter's felt. Indeed, one could argue that the beaver was saved from extinction in the mid-nineteenth century by a shift in the fickle winds of fashion, as Chinese silk replaced beaver felt as the material of choice for gentlemen's hats.

Beavers are "choosy generalists" in their food selection (S. Jenkins and Busher 1980). They eat a wide variety of plant parts and species but locally can be quite selective. The staple foods of beavers in Colorado are bark, buds, leaves, and twigs of quaking aspen, willows, and cottonwoods (Yeager and Rutherford 1957; Rutherford 1964; B. Baker and Cade 1995). These plants are especially important as winter food. Alder, river birch, oakbrush, and conifers are used much less frequently. The more varied spring and summer diet includes a variety of aquatic and terrestrial herbaceous plant material, and in North Park nonwoody plants were the main summer food (D. MacDonald 1956). Comparisons on the free-flowing Yampa River and the regulated Green River indicated that artificial flooding on the Green increased access of beavers to cottonwoods (Breck et al. 2003).

Beavers usually do not range more than a few hundred meters from water while foraging, and most food is taken within 100 m of water. Beaver are considered to be "hindgut digesters" and have microbial assistance processing their high-fiber diet. Both the cardiogastric gland in the stomach and the lobed cecum contain microflora that aid in digestion of woody material. The animals also are coprophagous, reingesting their feces generally during midday in the lodge (Buech 1984). About 33 percent of the cellulose from the woody plant materials consumed is actually digested, a level roughly equal to that of other non-ruminant mammals (A. Currier et al. 1960). Beaver intake of woody food ranges from 0.5 to 2.5 kg per day (Novak 1987). Beavers may "waste" 10 to 64 percent of trees cut for food, with greatest losses in large-diameter trees, which are felled for access to their smaller upper branches. The beaver's tail serves as an important fat storage depot (Aleksiuk 1970).

Beavers are excellent "engineers," building dams, lodges, bank burrows, and canals to provide shelter, regulate water levels, and provide waterways for floating food and construction materials to the main pond (Warren 1927). The pond provides safe passage beneath winter ice. Sticks, rocks, mud, and similar objects are used in construction, with many materials moved by holding them tucked to the chest with the forelimbs or carried in the mouth. Dams are constructed with materials embedded in the streambed and anchored by piling and interlacing other materials. Some dams may be as much as 2.0 to 2.5 m high and several hundred meters in length. Food supply and degree of siltation determine the longevity of lodges and ponds. In many cases water management by beaver is beneficial for fish and recovery of overgrazed, eroded streambanks (Call 1970; E. Hill 1982). Compared with reaches of stream above and below beaver dam complexes, beaver-influenced runoff contained 50–75 percent less suspended solids, 20–65 percent less total phosphorus and total Kjeldahl nitrogen, and 20–25 percent less nitrate (M. Parker 1986).

In areas where waterways freeze in winter, beavers typically store food in underwater caches, where it is available for use throughout the colder months. Food caches are started by constructing floating rafts of cuttings and placing other materials under the structure. Over time, waterlogging sinks the structure. Unpalatable or food remains (such as alder and peeled aspen logs) may be deliberately added to the cache, possibly to add weight for submergence (Slough 1978). Stored food consists of twigs, branches, and small trees. Caches may exceed 6.0 m in diameter and 3.6 m in height.

Beavers are crepuscular to nocturnal under most situations and do most of their tree cutting after dark (Tevis 1950), although those who fish quiet trout streams and beaver ponds know that it is not unusual to find animals out during the daytime. Most construction of dams occurs in spring after high runoff and in the fall in preparation for winter. Beavers can cut through a 12-cm-diameter willow in about 3 minutes, with the record felled tree having a diameter of 1.7 m and a height of more than 30 m (Rue 1964; Belovsky 1984). When constructing the winter food cache in the fall, a colony usually can harvest a mature aspen tree every other night.

Lodges may be conical or dome-shaped structures surrounded by water or built partially on land. On larger rivers they are generally of the latter type because of spring flooding and the general difficulty of building dams. Effects of flooding on a colony in northeastern Colorado were documented by Rutherford (1952). In some instances burrows are constructed in streambanks with little or no evidence of associated lodge construction. Studies of beaver in low-elevation riparian habitats in South Dakota suggested that lodge site selection is based in part on degree of cattle grazing and slope of the bank. They seemed to favor areas with lower grazing and with deep water close to steep banks (Dieter and McCabe 1989). The typical beaver lodge has an underwater entrance a meter or less below the water surface, which leads to a feeding chamber and an elevated, drier sleeping chamber. Internal chambers usually are about 1.3 m by 1.7 m and up to a meter high. The largest lodge ever recorded was more than 2 m high above the water and more than 12 m in diameter. Temperatures in beaver lodges in December are relatively stable, averaging about 1°C and fluctuating by less than 1°C (A. Stephenson 1969).

Beavers are highly social animals, living in family (or extended family) colonies. A colony typically consists of adults and their yearling and juvenile offspring. Beavers are monogamous, with pair-bonds lasting an average of 2.5 years. Death of a mate is likely the most important cause of mate turnover (Svendsen 1989). Average size of colonies in Colorado ranges from 4.5 to 7.8 animals (D. MacDonald 1956; Hay 1958; Rutherford 1964); the rule of thumb in field reconnaissance is that an active lodge or bank den represents 5 animals. The entire family unit defends the colony area from other beavers. However, the adult female is the dominant family member in many activities, including constructing and maintaining the lodge, building the food cache, and maintaining dams (Hodgdon and Larson 1973). Adult females tail-slap a warning twice as frequently as adult males, and their tail slaps are more effective in causing others to move to deep water. Adult males tend to inspect dams more closely and more regularly than females once the dam is built. Mounds of mud (scented with secretions of the castor glands) are constructed at strategic points around the colony to mark its boundaries (Aleksiuk 1968).

Young animals typically disperse from the colony at 2 years of age, at the time of birth of the new litter. Most movements of young are less than 16 km, with an average of about 7 km in Idaho (Leege 1968). Rutherford (1956) concluded that 2-year-old animals are considerably more susceptible to trapping than are yearlings because they are emigrants in unfamiliar surroundings. Serious fights may occur in late winter and spring when young animals are leaving the colony and seeking their own territories. Entire colonies of beaver may make much shorter movements up- or downstream as food supplies are exhausted (Neff 1957, 1959). Rutherford (1956) noted disproportionate sex ratios in trapped beavers, favoring females by 1.25:1.00, but he concluded that there was no reason to believe that actual sex ratios were other than about 1:1.

Beavers are monogamous (Svendsen 1989), generally mating in January, February, or early March. Gestation takes 104–111 days (Hediger 1970). In Colorado, average litter size was 2.7 for animals above 1,525 m (5,000 ft.) and 4.4 for females at lower elevations. These differences may be a response to lower nutritional levels at higher elevations because of the prolonged length of winter ice conditions (Rutherford 1955, 1956). A beaver from Weld County weighed 31 kg (69 pounds) and contained 8 fetuses, the largest number reported in the state (Hay 1957). Kits are born furred with their eyes partly open (Guenther 1948). They grow rapidly and are weaned by about 6 weeks of age. Most females have their first litter at 3 years of age, although in good habitat or in areas with low population density yearlings may reproduce (E. Hill 1982). In suitable habitats, most females 3 years or older can be expected to breed. Seventy-five percent of mature females were pregnant in a Colorado survey (Rutherford 1956).

Home range size is difficult to assess. Summaries of studies suggest that on streams, beavers may cover 0.8 to 0.9 km (Novak 1987), and others have found nearest-neighbor distances of 0.7 to 1.5 km. Territories of colonies range from 0.4 to 8.0 ha and average about 1.6 to 3.2 ha in Colorado, depending on such factors as valley and stream width, food availability, and stream gradient (Rutherford 1964). A number of studies, mostly focused on management, regulation, population estimation, and long-term effects on the landscape, have been conducted in Colorado (F. Packard 1947; Neff 1957, 1959; Yeager and Rutherford 1957; Harper 1968; and others cited in this account). Beaver were in better condition (larger body mass and tail size) and more dense (0.5–0.6 colonies per river-kilometer) on the regulated Green River than on the unregulated Yampa (0.35 colonies per river-kilometer). Breck et al. (2003) attributed the difference to the greater abundance of willow along the Green. Although beavers are associated with streams in mountainous areas, lowland reaches of all major drainages in the state also support large populations. C. A. Jones et al. (2003) documented beaver at various locations along the South Platte River in the city of Denver.

Predators include wolves, coyotes, bear, river otter, lynx, bobcat, and mountain lions. A young beaver kit in the collection at the University of Northern Colorado was taken from a coyote in South Park. The animal was severely wounded and died several hours later. Tularemia is an important epizootic disease, locally killing the animals. Other causes of mortality are starvation and drowning in spring floods (Rutherford 1952). Estimation of mortality in juvenile, yearling, and adult populations is problematic because of the difficulty in accurate aging and possible trap bias. That caveat aside, approximately 30 percent mortality is estimated for all age classes combined (Bergerud and Miller 1977).

Humans are by far the most important limiting factor; most states, including Colorado, have regular trapping seasons for their harvest. Beaver have a considerable economic impact, both positive and negative. Harvest for fur in North America averages more than a half million pelts per year, with a value of $10 to $20 per pelt. Beavers are managed as furbearers in Colorado. Following a ban on leg-hold traps in 1996, reported harvest has averaged fewer than 1,500 animals (Table 4-3), in contrast to some 6,000 annually in the 1980s and early 1990s (J. Fitzgerald 1993b). Beavers may respond to exploitation with changes in life-history patterns. In heavily harvested populations in Alaska, for example, females breed first at younger ages and smaller sizes and suffer higher mortality. As survival rates of adults decrease, sites are freed for dispersing young (Boyce 1981).

Beaver were scarce in Colorado in the late nineteenth and early twentieth centuries, recovering from exploitation by trappers. The period of low numbers sometimes is reflected in the topography of local watersheds, where modern beaver-regulated streams have a smaller, meandering channel within a broad, straighter channel carved by unregulated runoff in the second half of the nineteenth century (Harwood 1995).

Beavers have been called a "keystone species" because they drive species composition, function, and physical structure of ecosystems (Power et al. 1996). They also have been called "ecosystem engineers," because their activities control availability of resources for other species (R. Olson and Hubert 1994; B. Baker and Hill 2003; Müller-Schwarze and Sun 2003). In effect, beavers also are "farmers," slowing the flow of water-broadening riparian corridors and biasing plant succession toward their preferred phreatophytic food plants. Managing beaver is a fine example of the old adage, "You can never do just one thing." Obviously, management decisions on numbers and distribution of beaver (as with other important herbivores) influence ecosystem dynamics (Naiman 1988). Keith G. Hay (1957, 1958) studied Coloradan beaver in the 1950s with the Colorado Division of Wildlife. Since then he has revisited his study sites (in North Park) at approximately 5-year intervals, photo-documenting ecological change. This invaluable record is available at http://www.k6dd.org/BeaverStudy.htm and was summarized by Hay (2010).

Beavers manage watersheds, slowing spring runoff (hence reducing flooding) and raising the water table, often with net benefits in available water and forage for livestock. On the debit side of the ledger, they harvest landscape plantings and interfere with human engineers, plugging culverts and spillways and tunneling into canal banks, for example. On balance, most people would concur that beaver are among our most fascinating and watchable wildlife species. The extensive literature on the American beaver was reviewed by S. Jenkins and Busher (1979), Hodgdon and Larson (1973), E. Hill (1982), Novak (1987), and B. Baker and Hill (2003). Boyle and Owens (2007) provided a thorough review of the ecology of beaver in the Rocky Mountain region, in the context of conservation (including ongoing harvest and environmental degradation). The report includes an interesting "envirogram" for the beaver that integrates biotic and abiotic environmental factors and population parameters. For current strategies for dealing with "nuisance beaver," consult the Colorado Division of Wildlife on-line.

Family Heteromyidae—Pocket Mice and Kin

Heteromyids are small to medium-sized rodents, many of them adapted to arid and semiarid regions of western North America, Central America, and northwestern South America. The family exhibits a wide range of locomotor morphology, and living kinds exemplify evolutionary grades in the history of the Heteromyidae. The spiny pocket mice (*Liomys* and *Heteromys*) are not at all specialized for jumping. *Perognathus* and *Chaetodipus* (pocket mice) show moderate modification of limbs, moving by quadrupedal jumping (saltatory locomotion) when pursued. The kangaroo rats (*Dipodomys*) and kangaroo mice (*Microdipodops*) are bipedal, strongly modified for ricochetal locomotion with reduced forelimbs, greatly enlarged hind limbs and feet, and a long, well-haired tail for balance. Some authors (see McKenna and Bell 1997) place this group as a subfamily within the Geomyidae, but that arrangement is not widely accepted. J. Patton (2005a) reviewed the family Heteromyidae.

All members of the family have external fur-lined cheek pouches that open alongside the mouth, similar to those of the closely related pocket gophers. Food materials, typically seeds, are carried to the burrow in these pouches, where they are stored. Seed-hoarding by a number of species of heteromyids is important to plant succession, diminishing some favored species and encouraging others; see Fagerstone and Ramey (1996) for thorough review. Pouches can be turned inside out for cleaning and tucked back into place using the forepaws. Most heteromyids are competent burrowers, digging in loose, sandy soils despite the weak forelimbs of some species. The pelage ranges from coarse and harsh to soft and silky. The skull is thin and delicately built with inflated auditory bullae. The zygomatic arch is very thin (and easily damaged during specimen preparation or handling). The nasal bones project well beyond the upper incisors. The dental formula is 1/1, 0/0, 1/1, 3/3 = 20. The incisors are thin and ever-growing, and the uppers frequently show a longitudinal groove. All genera except *Dipodomys* have rooted cheekteeth. A baculum is present in males.

Except for the forest-dwelling *Heteromys* of northern South America and Central America, heteromyids are mostly inhabitants of desert shrublands and semiarid grasslands of the West. Fossils are known from the Oligocene, some 40 million years ago. The diversification of this family is generally associated with the development of drought-adapted vegetation over much of interior western North America in the Miocene Epoch in response to increasing aridity in the rain shadows of the Sierra Nevada and the Rockies. Phylogenetic studies of a number of species suggest that the regionally distinctive heteromyids and other rodents are the product of geological and ecological change in the Pliocene and Early Pleistocene (Riddle 1995). *Biology of the Heteromyidae* (Genoways and Brown 1993) is a collection of comparative reviews of various aspects of the biology of this diverse and interesting family; J. Patton (2005a) presented a taxonomic synopsis; and J. Hafner et al. (2007) provided a molecular systematic study of the group.

Most species live in sandy soils, digging burrows under shrubs, trees, or herbaceous cover. Most kinds occur in semiarid to desert landscapes. A. Reed et al. (2006) studied trends in rodent species richness along a continuum of increasingly xeric habitats from Iowa to Southern California. Diversity increased with aridity and diminished with primary productivity. Much of the increase in diversity was the result of increasing numbers of granivorous rodents, many of them heteromyids. They attributed the species richness of granivores in generally unproductive areas to a paucity of leaf litter.

Heteromyids typically are nocturnal, leaving the burrow only for short periods to forage. Burrow entrances are often located in concealed areas and frequently are plugged with soil during the day. The diet is largely seeds with high protein content, but green vegetation, insects, and other invertebrates also may be eaten. Many species are capable of meeting their water needs solely from the water produced as a by-product of the metabolism of fats in the diet. In colder areas, heteromyids undergo winter torpor. Even during favorable times of the year, aboveground activity appears to be minimized, perhaps to reduce predation and evaporative loss of water.

There are 6 genera and some 60 species of heteromyids (D. Wilson and Reeder 2005), about half of which occur in the western United States. Often several species of heteromyids are sympatric. That fact has led to numerous studies on the structure of communities, focused on niche structure, limiting similarity, and competition (J. Brown 1987; Findley 1989). J. Brown (1987) described several patterns of coexistence in the guild of granivorous rodents. Using extensive studies of museum records, DeBaca and Choate (2002) evaluated 2 of those patterns on the Central Great Plains and determined that sympatric granivores differ in body size and that more complex habitats support greater richness within the guild.

Colorado is home to 6 species of heteromyids in 3 genera, and a seventh species, the banner-tailed kangaroo rat (*Dipodomys spectabilis*), is possible in southwestern Colorado. All Coloradan members of the family are classified as non-game mammals (Table 4-1).

Key to the Species of the Family Heteromyidae in Colorado

1. Hindfeet greatly elongated, with soles of feet densely haired; face contrastingly marked; auditory bullae greatly inflated; cheekteeth ever-growing with simple crowns . . . . *Dipodomys*, 2

1' Hindfeet not greatly enlarged, soles of feet naked or sparsely haired; face not contrastingly marked; bullae only moderately inflated; cheekteeth rooted with more complex crown pattern 3

2. Four toes on hindfoot, total length greater than 300 mm; white tip of tail longer than 25 mm and preceded by black band . . . . Banner-tailed Kangaroo Rat—*Dipodomys spectabilis*,* p. 176

2' Five toes on hindfoot, total length less than 290 mm; white tip of tail less than 25 mm and preceded by bicolored band . . . . Ord's Kangaroo Rat—*Dipodomys ordii*, p. 173

3. Pelage harsh; soles of feet naked; total length greater than 190 mm; hindfoot longer than 24 mm; occipitonasal length 30 mm or more . . . . Hispid Pocket Mouse—*Chaetodipus hispidus*, p. 171

3' Pelage not harsh; soles of feet sparsely haired; total length less than 150 mm; hindfoot less than 24 mm; occipitonasal length less than 25 mm . . . . *Perognathus*, 4

4. Tail more than one-half total length; hindfoot longer than 20 mm; antitragus lobed . . . . Great Basin Pocket Mouse—*Perognathus parvus*, p. 170

4' Tail less than one-half total length; hindfoot shorter than 20 mm; antitragus not lobed 5

5. Fur markedly soft and silky; total length less than 120 mm; pale postauricular patch larger than ear . . . . Silky Pocket Mouse—*Perognathus flavus*, p. 168

5' Fur not markedly soft or silky; total length greater than 120 mm; postauricular patch smaller than ear or lacking 6

6. Upperparts olive-brown, usually heavily washed with black; auditory bullae generally do not meet at anterior ventral borders . . . . Olive-backed Pocket Mouse—*Perognathus fasciatus*, p. 164

6' Upperparts yellowish or reddish buff to pale brown, usually not heavily washed with black; auditory bullae usually meet at anterior borders . . . . Plains Pocket Mouse—*Perognathus flavescens*, p. 166

Genus *Perognathus*—Pocket Mice

There are some 9 species of pocket mice in the genus *Perognathus*, as the genus was restricted by J. Hafner and Hafner (1983). Formerly, the roughly 17 species of spiny pocket mice now included in the genus *Chaetodipus* were treated as species of *Perognathus*. In Colorado 4 species of *Perognathus* are known.

* Species of possible occurrence in Colorado.

Perognathus fasciatus

OLIVE-BACKED POCKET MOUSE

Description

The olive-backed pocket mouse has a dorsal pelage of olivaceous to buff, washed with black hairs. The darker hairs often form a distinct mid-dorsal band. This is the darkest-colored of our small pocket mice, although specimens from western Colorado are much paler in color. A conspicuous yellowish buff lateral line typically separates the darker dorsum from the usually white to pale buff belly. Measurements are: total length 125–145 mm; length of tail 55–75 mm; length of hindfoot 14–19 mm; length of ear 7–12 mm; weight 10–13 g. Greatest length of skull is 21.5–23.6 mm. The auditory bullae do not meet along their anterior margins. The interparietal bone is usually pentagonal and about equal in width to the interorbital breadth of the skull. The lower premolar is about the same length as the first lower molar. Females have 3 pairs of mammae.

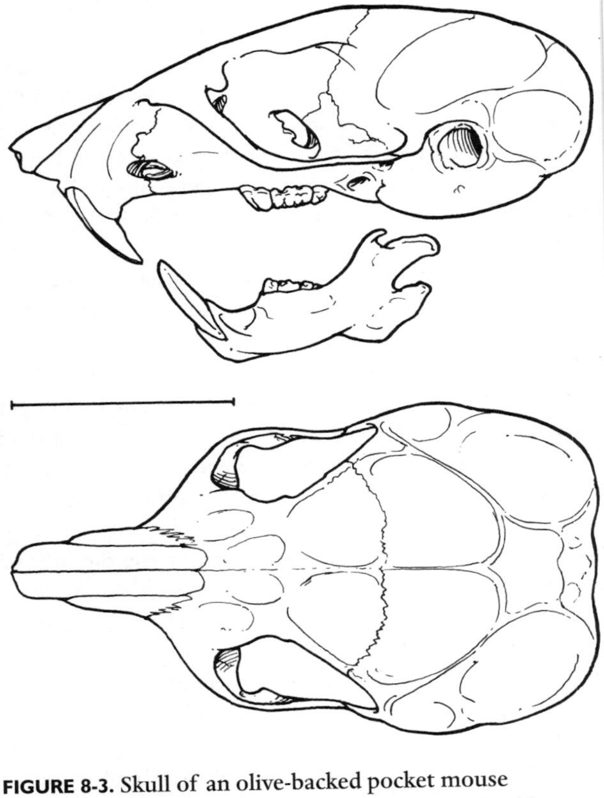

FIGURE 8-3. Skull of an olive-backed pocket mouse (*Perognathus fasciatus*) showing distinct interparietal bone. Scale = 1 cm.

PHOTOGRAPH 8-20. Olive-backed pocket mouse (*Perognathus fasciatus*). Photograph by David Gummer, Royal Alberta Museum (Mammalogy Program).

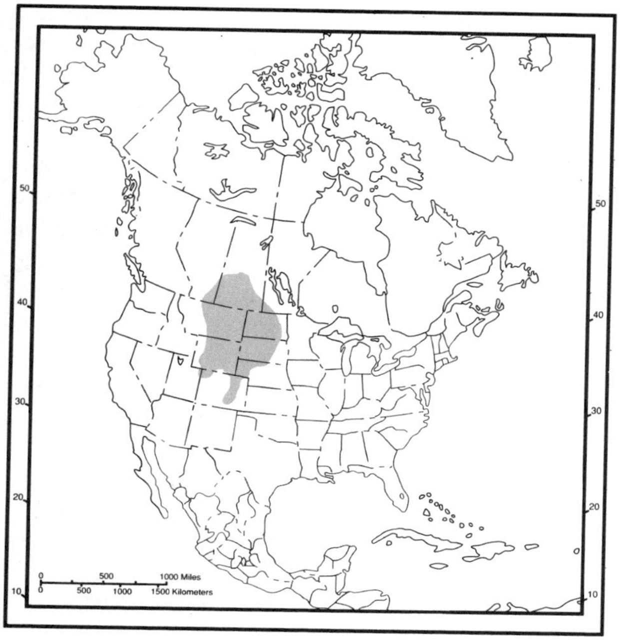

MAP 8-41. Distribution of the olive-backed pocket mouse (*Perognathus fasciatus*) in North America.

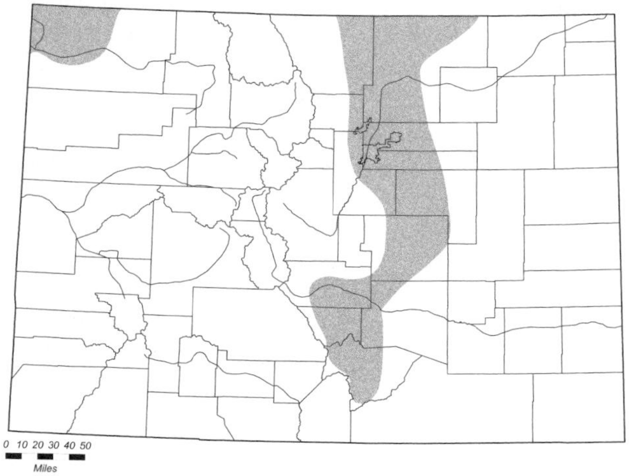

MAP 8-42. Distribution of the olive-backed pocket mouse (*Perognathus fasciatus*) in Colorado.

Distribution

Olive-backed pocket mice apparently are restricted to extreme northwestern Moffat County and to a narrow band along the Great Plains, at the foot of the Colorado Front Range, Rampart Range, and Wet Mountains, southward to northern Las Animas, Fremont, and Custer counties. The status of the species in Colorado is poorly known, but extensive residential and commercial development along the Front Range urban corridor probably has led to local extirpation of some populations and may threaten others. Recent captures are few, but Siemers et al. (2003) captured the animals at sites 3 mi. north of Deer Trail, Arapahoe County, and near the intersection of County Road 105 and Colorado Highway 86, Elbert County. Elevations of record in Colorado range from 1,525 to 2,135 m (5,000–7,000 ft.). *Perognathus fasciatus infraluteus* is the animal found on the Eastern Slope, along the foot of the Front Range; *P. f. callistus* apparently is restricted to the area north of the Yampa River in Moffat County. Systematics and geographic variation were reviewed by D. Williams and Genoways (1979).

Natural History

Little information exists on this species in Colorado. Records of occurrence are few and scattered, hinting that this is one of our rarest small mammals. The olive-backed pocket mouse is an animal of mixed prairie and shrub-steppe on the Northern Great Plains and Wyoming Basin. In Colorado they are restricted to grasslands along the western margin of the plains and to shrub-grasslands of the northwestern part of the state (D. Armstrong 1972). They have also been captured in ponderosa pine with an understory of yucca (J. K. Jones 1953). Low numbers were captured in blue grama–needlegrass communities in southeastern Wyoming (Maxell and Brown 1968). In northeastern Utah and northwestern Colorado, olive-backed pocket mice occur in sandy to gravel soils in semidesert shrublands

(C. Hayward and Killpack 1956). They seem to prefer sites with loamy sand to clay soils and low vegetative cover, often with substantial amounts of bare ground. Typical plant associations include blue grama, needlegrass, and wheatgrass.

As with other heteromyids, olive-backed pocket mice feed selectively on a variety of seeds of grasses and forbs. Seeds of weedy species, including croton, Russian-thistle, goosefoot, gaura, stipa, buckwheat, puccoon, and pigweed, are frequently eaten. A captive animal ate mealworms and it is likely that some insect matter is consumed in the wild (V. Bailey 1926; R. Turner and Bowles 1967).

Reproduction is poorly known. Females probably have 1 or 2 litters during the spring and early summer, with a cessation of reproduction during hot weather. From 2 to 9 embryos have been reported, with litters probably averaging 4 to 6. Gestation is about 1 month, with altricial young produced (R. Turner and Bowles 1967; Pefaur and Hoffmann 1974).

Olive-backed pocket mice dig burrow systems, usually at the base of grass, yucca, or shrub cover. Entrances are inconspicuous and may be plugged during the daytime. Tunnels may exceed 1.8 m in depth with side tunnels used for food storage (V. Bailey 1926). Individuals probably do not move much more than 100 m from their burrows when foraging. They are inactive aboveground in cold weather and probably exhibit periods of torpor. In Montana and North Dakota, densities have been estimated at 0.62 to 4.00 animals per hectare (Pefaur and Hoffmann 1975). In southeastern Wyoming, capture rates of 0.9 animals per 1,000 trap-nights indicate similarly low densities (Maxell and Brown 1968). Most small to medium-sized predators probably prey on the animals, although low densities doubtless preclude their being common fare for any predator. Literature on the species was summarized by R. Manning and Jones (1988).

Perognathus flavescens

PLAINS POCKET MOUSE

Description

The plains pocket mouse is pale buff to yellowish or reddish, with a variable dorsal wash of black hairs. The lateral line of buffy orange is generally less striking and the dorsal color usually is not as dark as that of the olive-backed pocket mouse. A buffy postauricular patch is often present.

PHOTOGRAPH 8-21. Plains pocket mouse (*Perognathus flavescens*). Photograph by Barbara L. Clausen.

This patch is never as large as in the silky pocket mouse, and the hair is coarser. Measurements are: total length 123–145 mm; length of tail 52–71 mm; length of hindfoot 16–19 mm; length of ear 6–8 mm; weight 7–12 g. The auditory bullae typically meet anteriorly. As with the olive-backed pocket mouse, the interparietal bone is about the same width as the interorbital breadth of the skull.

Distribution

Plains pocket mice are widespread across the eastern plains, with disjunct populations in the San Luis Valley and along the western margin of the state to Garfield and Mesa counties. In parts of the eastern plains they are abundant, especially in sandy prairie soils. Status of the species in western Colorado is less clear. Finley et al. (1976) did not find any specimens along the Colorado River near Rifle, an area where they were reported as common by Warren (1942), and in the late 1970s, D. Armstrong (unpublished) tried but failed to capture *Perognathus flavescens caryi* at its type locality, 8 mi. west of Rifle. However, they have been captured in the Piceance Basin (O'Meara et al. 1981).

Perognathus flavescens flavescens is the subspecies of the eastern plains (for review, see K. Reed and Choate 1986b); *P. f. relictus* is restricted to the San Luis Valley; *P. f. apache* occurs at lowest elevations in southwestern Colorado; and *P. f. caryi* occurs in the west-central valleys. The last 3 subspecies were formerly known as *P. apache*, the Apache pocket mouse. D. Williams (1978) concluded that *Perognathus flavescens* and *Perognathus apache* represent a single species. In Colorado, populations on the eastern plains are separated by the Southern Rocky Mountains from populations of the

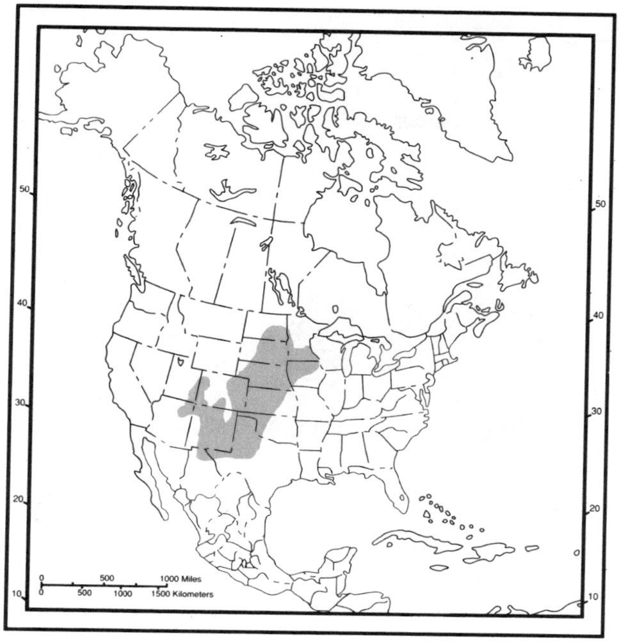

MAP 8-43. Distribution of the plains pocket mouse (*Perognathus flavescens*) in North America.

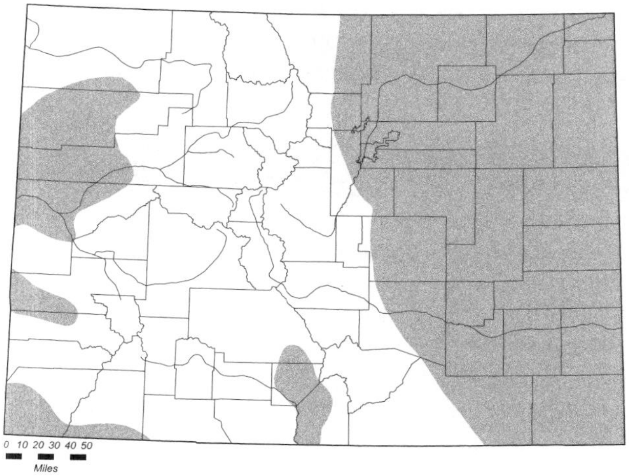

MAP 8-44. Distribution of the plains pocket mouse (*Perognathus flavescens*) in Colorado.

San Luis Valley and the Western Slope, although populations are generally continuous in New Mexico (Findley et al. 1975). Hoffmeister (1986) suspected that genetic continuity might not occur in Arizona and so maintained the usage of *P. apache* as a full species. This is not a question that can be answered in Colorado, so definitive resolution may await a molecular phylogeographic study of these forms.

Natural History

The plains pocket mouse is the most common species of *Perognathus* in grasslands on sandy to sandy loam soils in Colorado. On the eastern plains they favor sandy areas with moderate to good plant cover, although they can also tolerate a significant amount of bare ground (Maxell and Brown 1968; Mohamed 1989). Plant communities occupied usually include mid-grass species such as stipa, bluestem, ricegrass, and three-awn, as well as blue grama, often with sand sage (*Artemisia filifolius*) and yucca. Highest reported capture rates are from sand sage, where capture rates of 7 animals per 1,000 trap-nights have been reported (Moulton, Choate, and Bissell 1981). Margins of agricultural lands, including weedy fencerows, ditch banks, and margins of grain fields, are also used (Lovell et al. 1985). In Kansas, plains pocket mice are one of the most abundant mammals in agriculturally disturbed sand sage prairie (K. Reed and Choate 1986a), including the "waste corners" between center-pivot irrigation circles. In northwestern Colorado, highest numbers were captured in chained piñon-juniper stands 8 to 15 years after disturbance (O'Meara et al. 1981). Low numbers were captured in unchained piñon-juniper stands, where herbaceous vegetation was less well developed.

The diet of the plains pocket mouse is mostly seeds of grasses and forbs. Animals captured by Mohamed (1989) had seeds of spiderwort, ricegrass, needlegrass, lupine, scurfpea, three-awn, puccoon, bindweed, milkvetch, and *Cryptantha* in their cheek pouches. These plants are relatively common in the flora of the sand-sage prairie in eastern Colorado and suggest that the species is a generalist in its foraging for seeds. In Utah, seeds made up 81 percent of stomach contents, including several of the plants listed above (D. Armstrong 1982). Large seeds are stored for consumption in winter (K. Reed and Choate 1986a). Arthropods made up 59 percent of the diet in the Piceance Basin (Haufler and Nagy 1984). In Socorro County, New Mexico, Hope and Parmenter (2007) observed diets composed of 91 percent seeds (by volume) and 9 percent arthropods.

The plains pocket mouse is active aboveground during the warmer months. During 3 years of year-round trapping in Weld County, animals were captured from early March to early October (Mohamed 1989). In Kansas, they are active from March through October (K. Reed and Choate 1986a). The species, like others in the genus, probably enters periods of winter torpor with arousal from time to time to eat seeds stored in the burrow system (Beer 1961).

Burrows are typically constructed at the base of clumps of vegetation, and the entrances usually are plugged during the day. Of 3 burrows excavated, 2 were shallow, less than 30 cm long and 5 cm deep, and dug into the sides of old pocket gopher mounds (K. Reed and Choate 1986a). A third, whose entrance was beneath litter among sunflowers, was 2.4 m long and 0.5 m deep, the diameter of an index finger, and contained a food cache. Home ranges vary with sex and average 0.04 to 0.10 ha; average maximum distance moved between live captures was 22 m for males and 13 m for females (Mohamed 1989). In Kansas, average nightly movements were 20 to 30 m (K. Reed and Choate 1986a).

Reproduction is poorly known. In our area the animals breed from May through July. Females produce 1 or 2 litters, with litter size averaging 3 to 4. In Weld County, females were variously lactating, pregnant, or had uterine scars from mid-May through July, and then only uterine scars were seen in September. Males with scrotal testes were captured from late April to late June (Mohamed 1989). It may be that breeding ceases with the hot summer temperatures of late July and August.

Population dynamics are not well studied, and relative abundance is documented only in terms of trapping success. Although not typically abundant, plains pocket mice were the fourth commonest rodent in a study in Weld County (Mohamed 1989), averaging 1.2 animals per 1,000 trap-nights on both snaptrap and livetrap sites (after grasshopper mice, plains harvest mice, and deer mice). In eastern Colorado, they averaged 1.01 animals per 1,000 trap-nights (Moulton, Choate, and Bissell 1981). Of 13 species captured in that study, plains pocket mice were the sixth most common. In Wyoming, capture rates ranged from 2.7 to 7.1 animals per 1,000 trap-nights (Maxell and Brown 1968).

Information on predation is lacking. Probably snakes, grasshopper mice, and owls prey on the animals. Small size and generally low population density would predict that predation levels are low, resulting from opportunistic rather than systematic predation. Literature on the plains pocket mouse was reviewed by Monk and Jones (1996).

Perognathus flavus
SILKY POCKET MOUSE

Description

The silky pocket mouse is our smallest heteromyid. The hair is fine and silky, the pale buff to pinkish brown of the dorsum interspersed with black hairs. The overall darkness of the back varies geographically. The conspicuous buffy postauricular patch is generally almost twice as large as the ear. Measurements are: total length 95–118 mm; length of tail 41–58 mm; length of hindfoot 12–18 mm; length of ear 4–7 mm; weight 6–9 g. Small size, a relatively large ear patch, and remarkably soft fur should differentiate most specimens from adults of other small pocket mice. The interparietal bone is narrower than the interorbital breadth of the skull.

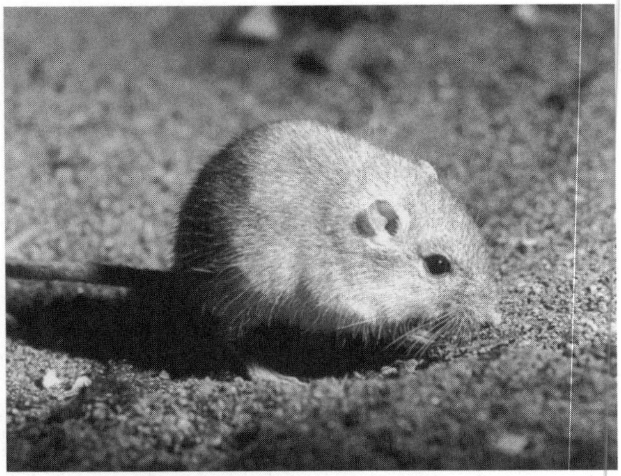

PHOTOGRAPH 8-22. Silky pocket mouse (*Perognathus flavus*). Photograph by Claude Steelman / Wildshots.

Distribution

Perognathus flavus bunkeri is the subspecies of most of the eastern plains, with populations extending up the Arkansas Valley to Salida; *P. f. hopiensis* occurs in extreme southwestern Colorado in Montezuma County; *P. f. sanluisi* is restricted to the San Luis Valley. Silky pocket mice appear to be relatively uncommon in northern Colorado but are apparently more common in southern parts of the state (Banta and Norris 1968; Moulton, Choate, and Bissell 1981; Moulton, Choate, et al. 1981; Ribble and Samson 1987). However, the status of the species is not clear; it is not known to be abundant in any location and is in need of further study. D. Wilson (1973) argued that *P. merriami* of the Southern Great Plains is a synonym of *P. flavus*, so literature on Merriam's pocket mouse from Texas and New Mexico may be pertinent to Coloradan silky pocket mice. Neiswenter and Riddle (2010) analyzed the evolution of the *Perognathus flavus* and *P. merriami* in the context of the evolution of desert and semidesert grasslands in western North America, including samples from two localities in Colorado

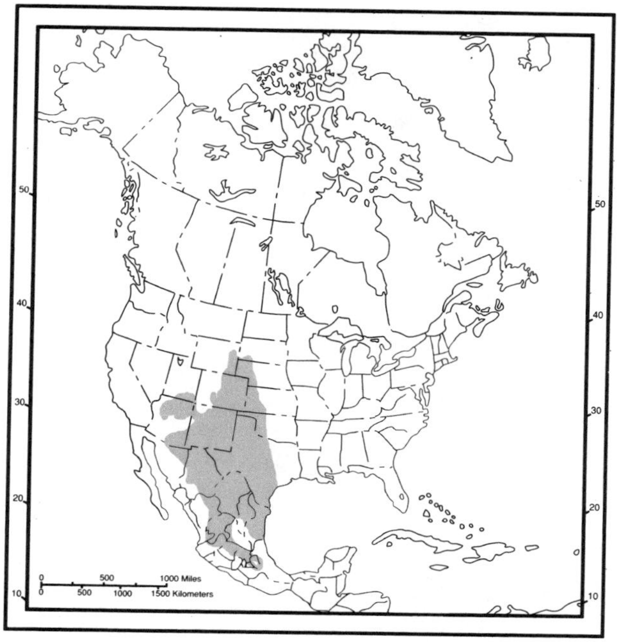

MAP 8-45. Distribution of the silky pocket mouse (*Perognathus flavus*) in North America.

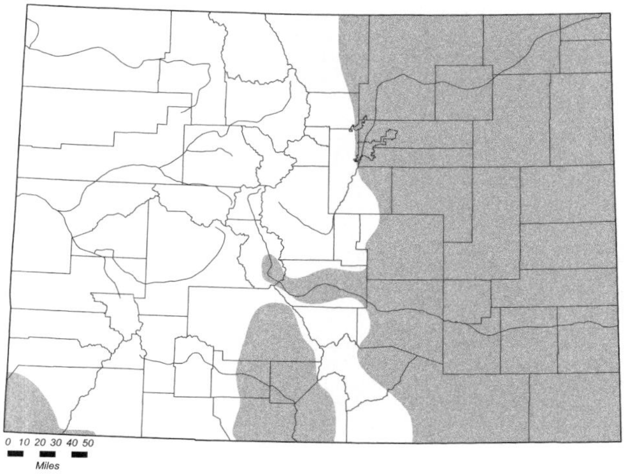

MAP 8-46. Distribution of the silky pocket mouse (*Perognathus flavus*) in Colorado.

(Fort Carson and Pawnee National Grasslands). Coyner et al. (2010) maintained the specific status of *P. merriami* and reported the animals from the Oklahoma Panhandle, in Beaver and Texas counties, so within about 15 miles of Baca County, Colorado. Research on *P. merriami* was reviewed by Best and Skupski (1994b).

Natural History

Relatively little is known about the silky pocket mice. The animals seem to require generally continuous short- to mid-grass prairie or herbaceous cover on loamy soils with low amounts of bare ground. They have been captured in low numbers on sand, loamy sand, and sandy loam soils. In southern Colorado their habitat is more varied and included piñon-juniper woodlands in Las Animas County (Ribble and Samson 1987). The apparent scarcity of the species over much of its range may result from competition with the plains pocket mouse, which appears to be more adaptable, or the silky pocket mouse may simply be less trappable.

Food habits are similar to those of other small pocket mice. Examination of 309 cheek pouches in New Mexico revealed seeds of pigweed, goosefoot, Russian-thistle, prickly-pear, globe mallow, and several grasses (R. Forbes 1961, 1964). In Texas, several of the same plants were used, as well as sandbur, phlox, gaura, and mustards (B. Chapman and Packard 1974). *Perognathus flavus* ate 93 percent seeds, 6 percent arthropods, and minimal green vegetation in a study in central New Mexico (Hope and Parmenter 2007). Silky pocket mice may feed on stored seeds during midday to prepare energetically for foraging in early evening (Wolff and Bateman 1978).

Burrows are constructed at the base of plants such as yucca, cactus, or shrubs. Two to 3 burrow entrances are typical, with the openings plugged during the day. Individual animals may maintain more than 1 burrow system. Burrow systems have blind side tunnels used for food storage and as defecation sites. Nests are constructed of fibrous plant materials (B. Chapman and Packard 1974). During winter the animals probably stay belowground with periods of torpor. The species is generally sedentary, with individuals usually not moving more than 40 to 60 m from the burrow.

In Texas, densities of *P. merriami* were 0.5 to 0.6 animals per hectare and home ranges were 0.77 to 2.40 ha (York 1949). Elsewhere, densities as high as 10 animals per hectare have been found (B. Chapman and Packard 1974). Highest densities were reported in southwestern New Mexico, where they reached 60 per hectare (Whitford 1976). In northern Colorado and southern Wyoming, densities are typically low and distribution seems patchy. Capture rates of 0.9 to 5.7 per 1,000 trap-nights have been reported (Maxwell and Brown 1968; Moulton, Choate, and Bissell 1981; Moulton, Choate, et al. 1981; Ribble and Samson 1987). Mohamed (1989) did not capture the animals in a study on loamy sand to sandy loam soils in Weld County.

Pregnant females have been found from March through October. The gestation period is about 28 days. One litter of 2 to 6 young per year is typical, with an occasional second litter in late summer. Juveniles become sexually active after their post-juvenile molt (Eisenberg and Isaac 1963; R. Forbes 1964). Best and Skupski (1994a) reviewed the literature.

Perognathus parvus

GREAT BASIN POCKET MOUSE

Description

This is a long-tailed, medium-sized pocket mouse with a sandy or grayish dorsal color. The underparts are white to buff and lateral stripes are indistinct or lacking. There are patches of pale fur behind the ears. The long tail is tufted and bicolored, dark above and paler below. Measurements are: total length 148–200 mm; length of tail 77–107 mm; length of hindfoot 19–27 mm; length of ear 7–10 mm; weight 16–30 g. The antitragus is lobed. Occipitonasal length of the skull is more than 24 mm.

PHOTOGRAPH 8-23. Great Basin pocket mouse (*Perognathus parvus*). Photograph by John Harris, Mammal Slide Library, American Society of Mammalogists.

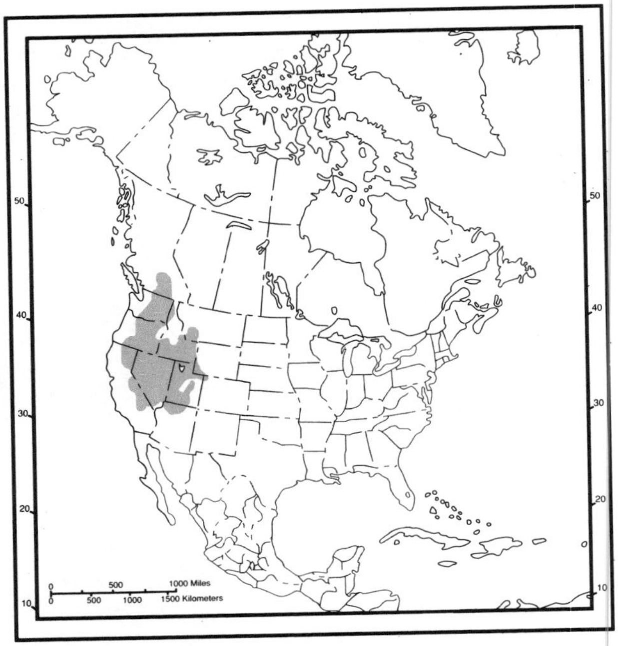

MAP 8-47. Distribution of the Great Basin pocket mouse (*Perognathus parvus*) in North America.

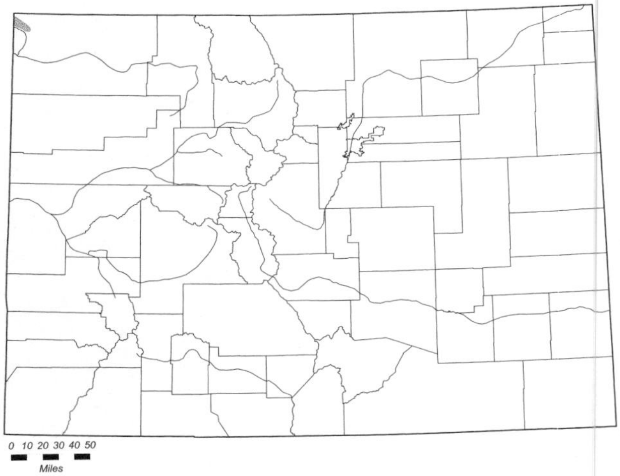

MAP 8-48. Distribution of the Great Basin pocket mouse (*Perognathus parvus*) in Colorado.

Distribution

The Great Basin pocket mouse is at the eastern margin of its range in Colorado and is known from only a few specimens collected in Browns Park in northern Moffat County (Bogan et al. 1988; R. Finley and Bogan 1995). T. Clark and Stromberg (1987) considered the species rare in Wyoming, attributing low numbers to overgrazing by livestock. One subspecies, *Perognathus parvus clarus*, occurs in Colorado.

Natural History

Great Basin pocket mice are most common in semidesert shrublands on sandy soils dominated by sagebrush, saltbush, and greasewood with an abundant understory of annual forbs (T. O'Farrell et al. 1975), and they are also found in grasslands and piñon-juniper woodlands. In grasslands they are associated with stands of Indian ricegrass, bromes, needlegrass, and legumes. They prefer areas of more than 40 percent ground cover (Feldhamer 1979). Little is known of this species in Colorado.

In Utah, seeds eaten included lupine, brome, milkvetch, scurfpea, ricegrass, and needlegrass (D. Armstrong 1982). In eastern Washington, Great Basin pocket mice used seasonal foods, including green plant material and insects, although seeds of annual grasses such as cheatgrass were also important in the diet (Kritzman 1974; T. O'Farrell et al. 1975).

Breeding begins soon after spring emergence from dormancy. Males typically are the first to appear aboveground, a trait common to many mammals that enter hibernation or undergo winter torpor. Females in southern Washington bred from April to September, and probably a similar breeding season occurs in northwestern Colorado. One litter per year is typical, with 2 litters possible in good years. Breeding success is tied to winter and spring precipitation, which affects production of annual plants. In years of poor food availability, 2 out of 3 females may not breed at all. Litter size is 3 to 4 (Kritzman 1974; T. O'Farrell et al. 1975; Dunigan et al. 1980).

Great Basin pocket mice can be abundant in suitable habitat. In the western Great Basin, they are often the predominant small mammal, with densities ranging from 28 to 82 animals per hectare (Verts and Kirkland 1988). Home ranges vary from 300 to 4,000 m^2, with males having larger ranges than females (Feldhamer 1979).

Burrows are similar to those of other small pocket mice, with entrances carefully plugged during the day. Great Basin pocket mice are inactive aboveground from late November to March, doubtless surviving on stored foods and undergoing periods of dormancy. Overwinter survival may be as high as 80 percent, with close to 20 percent of populations persisting for 2 years (T. O'Farrell et al. 1975). Verts and Kirkland (1988) reviewed the literature.

Chaetodipus hispidus
HISPID POCKET MOUSE

Description

The hispid pocket mouse is the largest pocket mouse in Colorado. Adult fur is somewhat harsh to the touch and

PHOTOGRAPH 8-24. Hispid pocket mouse (*Chaetodipus hispidus*). © 1993 Wendy Shattil / Bob Rozinski.

coarse in appearance relative to that of other pocket mice. Juveniles have much softer hair. Dorsal color is yellowish to reddish buff intermixed with black hairs. The sides are paler in color, shading to white on the venter. The scantily haired tail is dark above and pale below and lacks the conspicuous terminal tuft of kangaroo rats. Measurements are: total length 200–260 mm; length of tail 95–126 mm; length of hindfoot 25–29 mm; length of ear 11–13 mm; weight 40–70 g. The skull, although larger (condylobasal length usually more than 29 mm), is generally similar to that of other pocket mice. Incisors are conspicuously grooved.

Distribution

The hispid pocket mouse occurs on the eastern plains. The animals are common in suitable habitat. One subspecies, *Chaetodipus hispidus paradoxus*, occurs in Colorado. This species was formerly known as *Perognathus hispidus*. We follow J. Hafner and Hafner (1983) in according the hispid pocket mice generic rank as *Chaetodipus*.

Natural History

The hispid pocket mouse is an inhabitant of the central and Southern Great Plains. In Colorado and Wyoming the animals inhabit a variety of short- and mid-grass communities, including sand sage, yucca grass, and blue grama–needlegrass prairie and also rather disturbed sites like weedy ditch banks, hedgerows, and dry riparian areas. Sandy loam and loamy sand soils with 8 to 40 percent bare ground are favored. In general, they are most numerous in

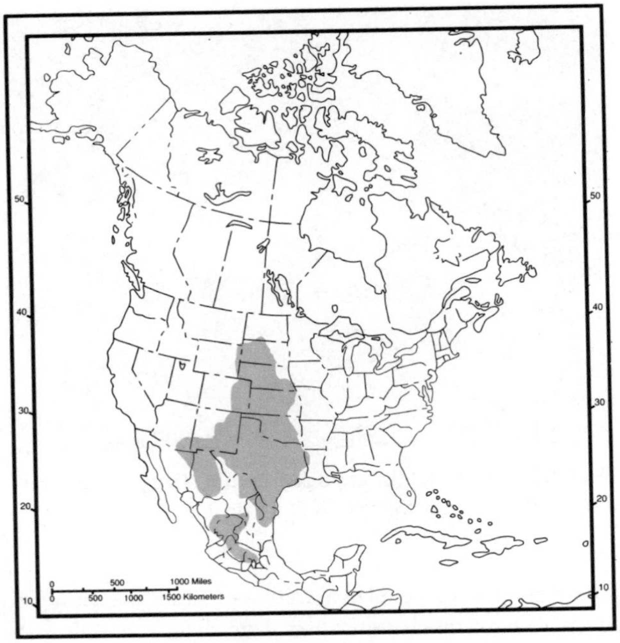

MAP 8-49. Distribution of the hispid pocket mouse (*Chaetodipus hispidus*) in North America.

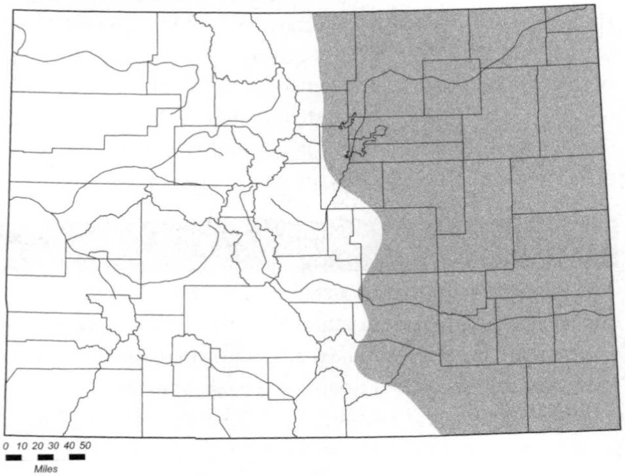

MAP 8-50. Distribution of the hispid pocket mouse (*Chaetodipus hispidus*) in Colorado.

sites also occupied by *P. flavescens*, the plains pocket mouse, although their numbers are usually lower (W. Archibald 1963; J. Fitzgerald 1978; Moulton, Choate, and Bissell 1981; Moulton, Choate, et al. 1981; Mohamed 1989).

Diet is similar to that of other heteromyids and consists of a variety of seeds, including sagebrush, prickly-pear, bluestem, annual sunflower, primrose, mallow, legumes, and switchgrass. L. A. Hoffmann et al. (1995) showed experimentally that Ord's kangaroo rats and hispid pocket mice preyed selectively on the larger seeds of buffalograss (*Buchloë dactyloides*) preferentially to the smaller seeds of blue grama (*Bouteloua gracilis*); thus—on a particular site—granivorous rodents may help to drive species composition of grasslands. Carabid beetles were an important food in Texas, especially during spring (Alcoze and Zimmerman 1973).

Hispid pocket mice reproduce during spring and summer in Colorado. Females have been captured with embryos in July and with uterine scars in mid-June, indicating spring litters. Males with scrotal testes were captured from mid-May to late September (Mohamed 1989). Other authors report similar breeding patterns, with litter size ranging from 2 to 9 and an average of 5 or 6. Two or more litters are produced (Bee et al. 1981; Hayssen et al. 1993). Young leave the nest at 1 month of age.

Abundance has been reported in terms of animals captured per trap-night in Colorado and southeastern Wyoming. The index ranged from 0.21 per 1,000 trap-nights in shortgrass prairie and grazed riparian habitats (Moulton, Choate, and Bissell 1981) to 4.1 per 1,000 trap-nights in a yucca-grass area on sandy loam (Maxell and Brown 1968).

Hispid pocket mice are mostly solitary, each individual constructing its own burrow complex, although in captivity several individuals may tolerate one another (P. Williams 1968). Burrow systems are usually at the base of a shrub, yucca, or bunchgrass. The number of entrances to such systems ranges from 1 to several, typically plugged during the day. Soil plugs resemble those of small pocket gopher mounds. Depths of burrows may be as much as 38 cm. Nests are rather large (about 4 by 3 cm) globes of grasses (Blair 1937; J. Thompson and Barrett 1969). In areas with high populations of kangaroo rats, hispid pocket mice may be in competition for seed resources.

In northeastern Colorado, earliest captures of hispid pocket mice were in mid-April and latest were in late September. The animals moved 10 to 23 m between livetrap captures. Home ranges were 0.24 to 0.34 ha. They retreated to burrow systems during winter. In such burrows they probably undergo intermittent periods of torpor, arousing from time to time to feed on stored seeds. Aboveground activity occurred when temperatures were as low as –10°C (Mohamed 1989). Predators include rattlesnakes and mammalian and avian carnivores, especially owls. Poulson (1988) provided a review of the literature.

Dipodomys ordii

ORD'S KANGAROO RAT

Description

Ord's kangaroo rat is a rather large heteromyid with a long, tufted tail; short forelimbs; and elongate hindfeet with 5 toes and densely haired soles. The upper parts are brownish yellow washed with black. The venter, legs, flanks, upper lips, and facial patterns are white. Black facial lines are present on the sides of the nose. The fur is sleek and silky. The tail is dark on its dorsal and ventral surfaces and white laterally. Measurements are: total length 240–280 mm; length of tail 133–163 mm; length of hindfoot 39–43 mm; length of ear 12–15 mm; weight 55–85 g. Males are larger than females. The skull has greatly inflated auditory bullae, and the zygomatic arches are fragile. The upper incisors are grooved.

The much larger banner-tailed kangaroo rat (*Dipodomys spectabilis*) may eventually be discovered at lowest elevations in La Plata and Montezuma counties but has not been reported to date. Oliver and Wright (2010) reported the animals from San Juan County, Utah, just 16.6 km (about 10.3 mi.) west of the Colorado boundary. Beidleman et al. (2000) implied that Bowers and Brown (1982) had mapped the distribution of *D. spectabilis* in Colorado, but their map was merely intended to represent the distribution mapped by E. Hall (1981) with a northern limit in San Juan County, New Mexico. The banner-tailed kangaroo rat differs from Ord's kangaroo rat in having 4 toes on the hindfeet and a striking white-tipped tail with a solid black band proximal to the white tip.

PHOTOGRAPH 8-25. Ord's kangaroo rat (*Dipodomys ordii*). Photograph by William E. Ervin.

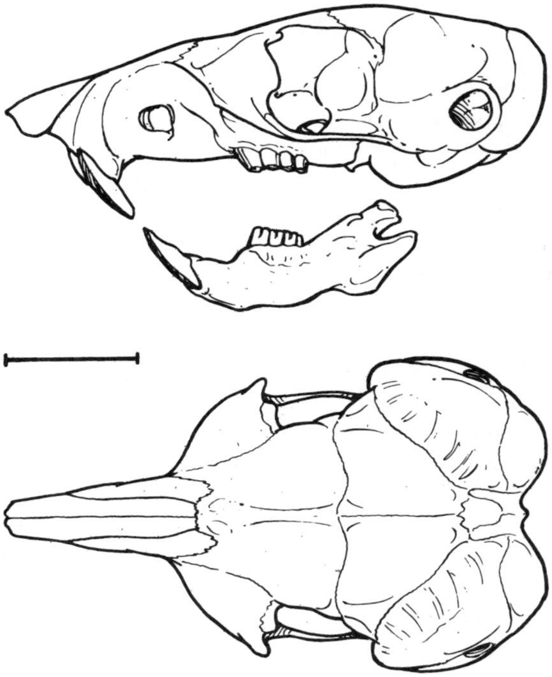

FIGURE 8-4. Skull of Ord's kangaroo rat (*Dipodomys ordii*) showing inflated auditory bullae and slender zygomatic arches. Scale = 1 cm.

Distribution

Ord's kangaroo rats are common small mammals in suitable habitat over their entire range. The animals are highly variable geographically, and 8 subspecies occur in Colorado. Two subspecies are rather widespread: *D. o. luteolus* occurs on the northeastern plains and *D. o. richardsoni* is known from the southeastern part of the state. Other subspecies are restricted to particular river valleys and separated by inhospitable uplands from adjacent populations. *D. o. evexus* occurs in the Arkansas Valley of Chaffee and Fremont counties, from Salida to Cañon City; *D. o. longipes* occurs in the San Juan watershed of extreme southwestern Montezuma County; *D. o. montanus* occurs in the San Luis Valley; *D. o. nexilis* occurs in the San Miguel and Dolores river valleys in southwestern Colorado; *D. o. priscus* inhabits the Yampa Valley in northwestern Colorado; *D. o. sanrafaeli* occurs in the Colorado River drainage in western Colorado.

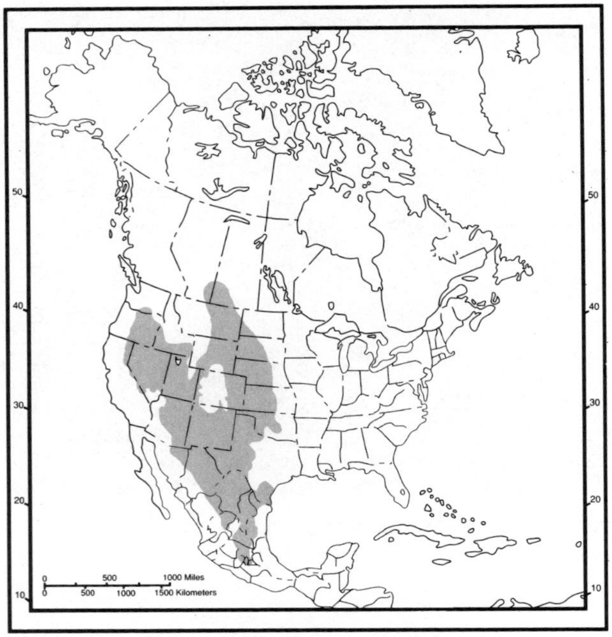

MAP 8-51. Distribution of Ord's kangaroo rat (*Dipodomys ordii*) in North America.

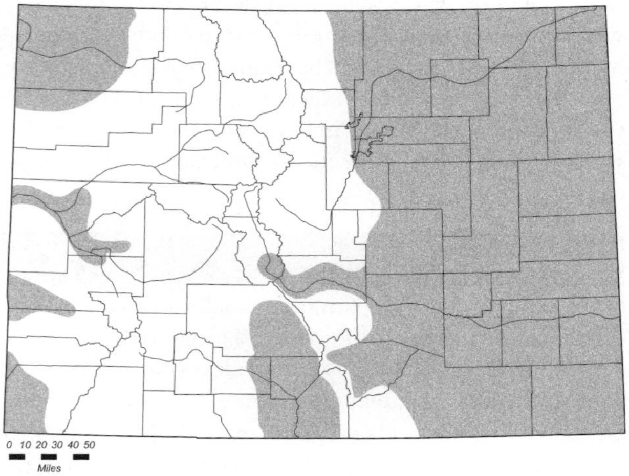

MAP 8-52. Distribution of Ord's kangaroo rat (*Dipodomys ordii*) in Colorado.

Natural History

This is the widest-ranging kangaroo rat, capable of occupying a variety of habitats, from semidesert shrublands and piñon-juniper woodlands to shortgrass, mixed, or sand sage prairie. It also invades dry, grazed riparian areas if vegetation is sparse (Moulton, Choate, and Bissell 1981; Moulton, Choate, et al. 1981). Ord's kangaroo rats are most common on sandy soils, which allow for easy digging and construction of burrow systems. Experimental studies on the Central Plains Experimental Range in northern Weld County indicated that kangaroo rats preferred to forage along roadsides, perhaps because of ease of burrowing, opportunities for dust-bathing, and higher soil seed banks (Stapp and Lundquist 2007). However, Ribble and Samson (1987) reported them in open areas with decreased canopy cover, increased shrub cover, and increased soil compaction. In suitable habitat they often are abundant and conspicuous. Based on survival rates, Schorr et al. (2007) modeled habitat quality for *D. ordii* in Pueblo County. Highest rates of survival were positively correlated with the extent of bare soil.

Kangaroo rats feed on a variety of seeds throughout the year, supplementing the diet with insects and flower parts. Up to 10 percent of the winter diet on Pawnee National Grassland is insects, especially larval beetles and moths, whereas seeds typically represent 85 to 95 percent of the diet (Flake 1973). Important seed sources include milkvetch, *Kochia*, Russian-thistle, spiderwort, grama, and sagebrush. In southeastern Utah, cheek pouch contents included seeds of mustards, Russian-thistle, brome, fescue, primrose, dock, lupine, and Indian ricegrass (D. Armstrong 1982). Hope and Parmenter (2007) reported a diet of 68 percent seeds, 25 percent green vegetation, and 7 percent arthropods in Socorro County, New Mexico. M. S. Miller et al. (2003) observed Ord's kangaroo rats in high densities in the lower floodplain of the Yampa River in Deerlodge Park, Dinosaur National Monument. They investigated factors that might draw fossorial rodents to a potentially dangerous habitat (see D. C. Andersen, Wilson, et al. 2000). Appropriate seed resources actually were more abundant higher on the floodplain. However, harvester ants (*Pogonomyrmex occidentalis*—an important competitor with kangaroo rats for seed resources) were less abundant and burrowing was less energetically expensive on the lower floodplain.

Seeds gleaned from the ground or harvested directly from plants are manipulated with the dainty forepaws and tucked into the cheek pouches for transport to the burrow system, where the pockets are turned inside out and the materials disgorged. As is often true of larger-bodied heteromyids, kangaroo rats are "larder hoarders," storing seeds in large quantities in a single location rather than "scatter-hoarding" in dispersed storage locations (S. Jenkins and Breck 1998). Those seed caches may be important in propagating particular plants.

Among several points of ecological interest about the Pawnee Buttes—prominent remnant Tertiary uplands in northern Weld County—is the presence of limber pine (*Pinus flexilis*). The principal disperser of limber pines seeds over most of the range of the tree is a jay (Clark's nutcracker, *Nucifraga columbiana*). Clark's nutcracker is only a rare visitor to Pawnee Buttes. There, deer mice and Ord's kangaroo rats appeared to be the important seed dispersers (Tomback et al. 2005).

Kangaroo rats, like other heteromyids, do not require free water but instead subsist on metabolic water produced as a by-product of oxidation of their foods. Many studies have been conducted on the physiological adaptations of kangaroo rats to life in stressful climatic conditions (Gettinger et al. 1986). When free water is available the animals use the forepaws to scoop water into the mouth (Allan 1946), and captives consume large amounts.

Well named, kangaroo rats typically move using bipedal, ricochetal locomotion, unlike pocket mice. The tail is used to maintain balance and facilitate quick changes in direction of movement. When chased, the animals can make quick, erratic escape movements (Bartholomew and Caswell 1951). They are nocturnal, with most activity occurring during the first few hours of night. Males are more active than females. Activity is reduced under full-moon conditions, at which time they are more secretive in their movements. Although kangaroo rats are active year-round, capture rates have been low in November, December, and January in Colorado (Flake 1973; Mohamed 1989). In Utah, animals were surface active about 1 hour per night with 95 percent of that time spent foraging (Langford 1983). Other aboveground activity includes digging, sand-bathing, and scent-marking around the burrow entrance. During activity, body temperature is raised 1.6° to 3.0° above resting temperatures of 37°C (B. Wunder 1974).

The breeding season and its length are variable, being regulated by the female's cycle, which is strongly affected by rainfall and appearance of green vegetation (Hoditschek and Best 1983). In Colorado, Ord's kangaroo rats breed from February through August, although testes start to show regression in July (Flake 1974). In southeastern Utah and probably western Colorado, breeding occurs from late March through July, with litters perhaps slightly larger than for eastern Colorado (D. Armstrong 1982). Mean embryo counts average 2.9 with a range of 2 to 4. Gestation is about 30 days (Duke 1944). Young are altricial. Hair develops in about 1 week, with the eyes opening at 2 weeks of age. By 5 to 6 weeks of age the young approach the size of adults. Young remain with the female for several months. Male siblings eventually become aggressive, which leads to a breakup of the family group (Eisenberg 1962). Sexual maturity is reached at about 83 days of age (W. Jones 1985), and individuals can reproduce as yearlings (Garner 1974).

Burrows are constructed under shrubs, yucca, or grass clumps or along exposed cutbanks and arroyos. The burrow systems have several entrances and a complex of tunnels (Warren 1942). A nest is constructed of convenient plant materials, including bark, yucca fibers, and dried grasses. Burrow entrances are typically plugged during the daytime. Burrows are dug primarily using the hind limbs, although the animals may gnaw through roots or use the teeth to loosen materials. Burrows of *D. ordii* averaged 40.9 cm deep in sagebrush steppe in southeastern Idaho (Laundré and Reynolds 1993).

Capture rates in Colorado are variable. Moulton, Choate, and Bissell (1981) and Moulton, Choate, et al. (1981) found them most abundant (4.49 captures per 1,000 trap-nights) in grazed sand sage and lowest in riparian woodland in Yuma County. In eastern Wyoming, Maxell and Brown (1968) found highest numbers in sand dunes (59.4), yucca grasslands (15.5), and sage grasslands (9.9). In Texas, average densities of 15.6 animals per hectare (range, 9.9–26.9) were calculated. Individual movement usually was less than 0.22 ha (Garner 1974). Lusby et al. (1971) captured kangaroo rats in Mesa County in only 5 of 10 years, with densities when present of only 0.04 animals per hectare. Kangaroo rats may be effective behavioral competitors with other species (Langford 1983); it is possible that densities of hispid pocket mice are kept low in areas with high densities of kangaroo rats. In laboratory studies, Ord's kangaroo rats were strongly dominant to deer mice (Falkenberg and Clarke 1998).

Although kangaroo rats may occur in high densities on suitable sites, they are agonistic toward each other in captivity (Eisenberg 1962). Intrusion results in chases and fighting bouts marked by kicking, biting, and wrestling. They also drum their feet and tooth-chatter during agonistic encounters. Maintenance behaviors include prolonged periods of washing and grooming and considerable time spent in sand-bathing, which consists of loosening sandy soil and then rolling and even submerging in it. The pelage of kangaroo rats deprived of the opportunity to sand-bathe is greasy. Sand-bathing sites are conspicuous in areas occupied by kangaroo rats, but other species such as spotted ground squirrels also make and use such depressions.

Many predators take kangaroo rats. Coyotes, swift foxes, and owls are proficient predators. They are important prey for the kit fox (*Vulpes macrotis*), a very rare carnivore in Colorado (Meaney et al. 2006). Captive kangaroo rats may live up to 5 years but in the wild most animals survive no longer than 2 or 3 years. Garrison and Best (1990) reviewed the extensive literature on Ord's kangaroo rat.

Dipodomys spectabilis

BANNER-TAILED KANGAROO RAT

Description

The banner-tailed kangaroo rat is a large rodent, similar in color to the much smaller Ord's kangaroo rat except that the tail, with its large white tip and proximal black band, is even more striking (hence the vernacular and scientific names). Measurements are: total length 310–350 mm; length of tail 180–210 mm; length of hindfoot 47–51 mm; weight 90–135 g. Only 4 toes are present on the hindfoot. The lateral tail stripes extend only about half the length of the tail.

Distribution

Occurrence in Colorado has not been documented, but banner-tailed kangaroo rats may eventually be found in southern La Plata or Montezuma county, especially on the Southern Ute Indian Reservation. The banner-tailed kangaroo rat is a species of the semiarid grasslands in New Mexico, West Texas, Mexico, northern Arizona, and extreme southeastern Utah. Overgrazing by livestock may prevent occupancy of much of this region by banner-tails, which seem to prefer well-developed grassland on clay soils (Findley et al. 1975; Hoffmeister 1986). *Dipodomys spectabilis clarencei* is known from northern San Juan County, New Mexico, including the areas around Fruitland and Blanco, less than 30 km from the Colorado border.

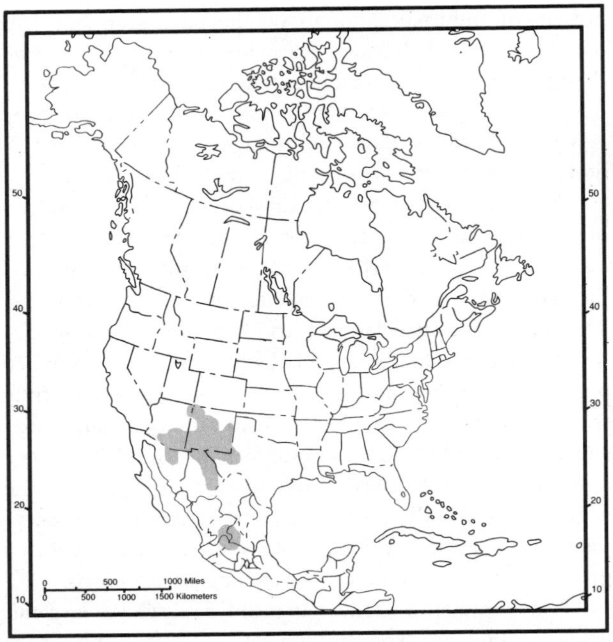

MAP 8-53. Distribution of the banner-tailed kangaroo rat (*Dipodomys spectabilis*) in North America.

Natural History

Banner-tailed kangaroo rats favor well-developed desert or semidesert grasslands with some exposed soil. Large mounds are excavated to form extensive burrow systems at the base of shrubs, yucca, or cactus. Over time such mounds can reach heights greater than 1 m and diameters in excess of 4.5 m. Multiple entrances with well-developed trails radiate from the mound (Holdenried 1957; Hoffmeister 1986). The animals are mostly nocturnal. Behaviors are similar to those of Ord's kangaroo rat, with food cached in the burrow system. Breeding probably occurs from late winter to August. Near Santa Fe, New Mexico, breeding started in December and ended in August, with up to 3 litters per year (Holdenried 1957). Gestation is estimated to be about 22 days. Best (1988) provided a thorough review of the literature.

Family Geomyidae—Pocket Gophers

Pocket gophers are fossorial, herbivorous rodents restricted to North and Middle America. Fossils are known from the Oligocene and Miocene. Periods of climatic change and glaciation have played major roles in the distribution pattern of the living species. Some 40 species in 6 genera are recognized (D. Wilson and Reeder 2005). Because of their relatively sedentary behavior and underground habits, pocket gophers have undergone much genetic isolation and microevolution, with close to 300 named subspecies for the 18 living species in the 3 genera found in the United States (E. Hall 1981). For the student of microevolution and systematics, pocket gophers offer much opportunity for study because populations inhabiting mountain valleys only a few kilometers apart may be genetically distinct. J. Patton (1990) provided a general review of these phenomena. Pocket gophers also are of biogeographic interest because species often show parapatric distributions, occurring adjacent to each other but not overlapping. This pattern usually has been attributed to competition (R. Miller 1964; T. Vaughan 1967b; but see Lovell et al. 2004 for critical review).

The common name "gopher" (from the French *gaufre*—"honeycomb"—in reference to the burrow systems of pocket gophers) is applied colloquially to a wide range of burrowing rodents, but the term is properly restricted to pocket gophers. Pocket gophers are named for the conspicuous, external, fur-lined cheek pouches that open on either side of the mouth. The family Heteromyidae (pocket mice and kangaroo rats) also has such external cheek pouches, but the cheek pouches of all other rodents are internal, opening inside the mouth cavity.

Pocket gophers are heavy-bodied, short-tailed mammals with powerful forelimbs equipped with stout claws for digging. They are specialized for a fossorial existence with sturdy skulls, small eyes, small ears, and relatively short fur that does not collect dirt and debris loosened during their tunneling activities. All members of the group dig complex burrow systems, periodically marked by piles of soil pushed to the surface. Pocket gophers are not gregarious but are strongly territorial in defense of burrow systems. They are active year-round, even under the severest of winter conditions.

The dental formula is 1/1, 0/0, 1/1, 3/3 = 20. The skull has a pronounced interorbital constriction and small auditory bullae. The cheekteeth are ever-growing, and enamel is reduced. The incisors are large with broad cutting surfaces. The presence or absence of grooves and the number of grooves on the upper incisors are of taxonomic importance. Males of all species have a baculum. Sexual dimorphism is pronounced, with males typically much larger than females, often by close to 40 percent of body weight.

Subterranean herbivores analogous in habits to pocket gophers have evolved in several lineages of rodents, including the naked mole rats of Africa (Bathyergidae), the tuco-tucos of South America (Ctenomyidae), and the mole rats of Asia and North Africa (Splacidae). These lineages are remarkably similar in morphology and physiology (see Nevo 1979), although only pocket gophers have "pockets," the external fur-lined cheek pouches unique to American geomyoids. Subterranean herbivores, whatever their phylogenetic origins, tend to have analogous influences on ecosystems, impacting soil structure, nutrient cycling, productivity, and plant succession (D. C. Andersen 1987; Huntley and Reichman 1994). Pocket gophers epitomize the definition of "ecosystem engineers," because their activities strongly influence the availability of resources for other species (Reichman and Seabloom 2002).

Literature on the family was reviewed by Chase et al. (1982), Teipner et al. (1983), and R. Baker, R. Bradley, and McAliley (2003). J. Patton (2005b) provided a taxonomic synopsis. A great deal of important research on pocket gophers was conducted in the 1960s and 1970s by the Colorado Cooperative Pocket Gopher Project, so much is known about these intriguing animals (and many fascinating questions remain unanswered). G. Turner et al. (1973) reviewed earlier literature and discussed pocket gophers of Colorado in detail. Their considerable and complex influences on rangeland were reviewed by Fagerstone and Ramey (1996). All pocket gophers in Colorado are classified as small game mammals (Table 4-1). Andelt and Case (1995) provided a thorough guide to management of pocket gophers, based on an understanding of the natural history of the animals.

Key to the Species of the Family Geomyidae in Colorado

1. Upper incisors without a longitudinal groove . . . . *Thomomys,* 2

1' Upper incisors with 1 or 2 longitudinal grooves 3

2. Sphenoidal fissure absent, incisive foramen opening anterior to infraorbital foramen, ear typically less than 6.9 mm. The interparietal is broader than long . . . . Northern Pocket Gopher—*Thomomys talpoides*, p. 180

2' Sphenoidal fissure present, incisive foramen opens posterior to anterior opening of infraorbital foramen, ear more than 6.9 mm, interparietal longer than broad . . . . Botta's Pocket Gopher—*Thomomys bottae*, p. 178

3. Upper incisor with 1 longitudinal groove, color dark with orange-yellow cheeks . . . . Yellow-faced Pocket Gopher—*Cratogeomys castanops*, p. 186

3' Upper incisor with 2 longitudinal grooves, color pale without conspicuous difference in cheek color . . . . Plains Pocket Gopher—*Geomys bursarius*, p. 183

Genus *Thomomys*—Pocket Gophers

The genus *Thomomys* has no distinctive vernacular name, probably because these and other pocket gophers are not commonly seen and their sign is superficially similar to the mounds of other kinds of pocket gophers. Taxonomy of *Thomomys* has been notoriously difficult, but J. Patton (2005b) listed 9 species, ranging from southwestern Canada throughout much of western United States and southward in Mexico to Veracruz and Puebla. Some species of *Thomomys* are rather restricted in distribution, but 2 of the most widespread species occur in Colorado.

Thomomys bottae

BOTTA'S POCKET GOPHER

Description

Botta's pocket gophers, also called valley pocket gophers, are small pocket gophers that vary widely in color and size; to describe this variation, 6 distinct subspecies are recognized in Colorado. They vary from yellowish in western Colorado to reddish brown in the southeast. The venter is slightly paler in color than the dorsum. Measurements are: total length 200–260 mm; length of tail 60–85 mm; length of hindfoot 28–33 mm; length of ear 5–7 mm; weight 110–215 g. Males are consistently larger than females.

PHOTOGRAPH 8-26. Botta's pocket gopher (*Thomomys bottae*). Photograph by R. B. Forbes.

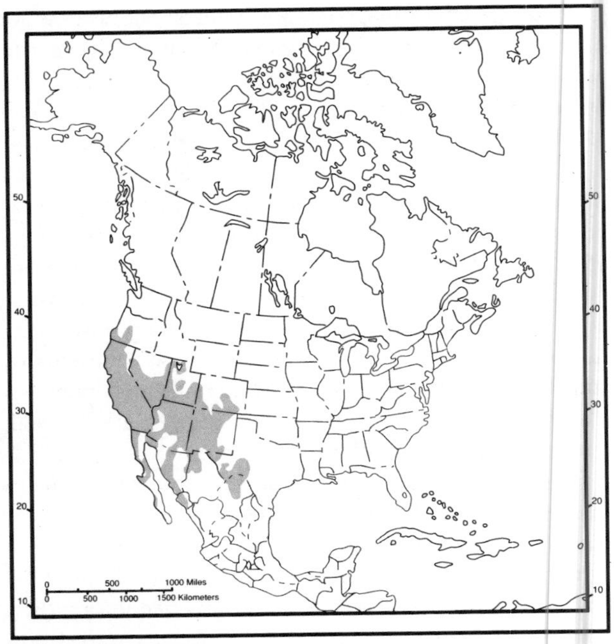

MAP 8-54. Distribution of Botta's pocket gopher (*Thomomys bottae*) in North America.

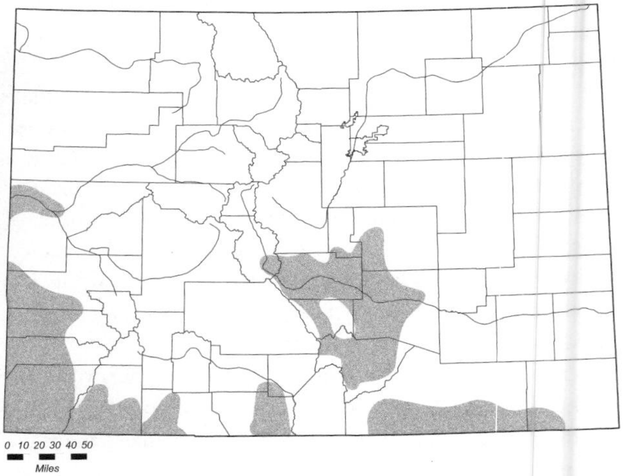

MAP 8-55. Distribution of Botta's pocket gopher (*Thomomys bottae*) in Colorado.

Distribution

Botta's pocket gophers occur in southern Colorado, where several local races have evolved. *Thomomys bottae aureus* occurs at lower elevations in southwestern Colorado, south of the Uncompahgre Plateau and southwest of the San Juan Mountains; *T. b. cultellus* occurs in the vicinity of Raton Pass; *T. b. howelli* occurs in the Grand Valley of the Colorado; *T. b. pervagus* occupies the floor of the San Luis Valley west of the Rio Grande. Microevolution within *T. bottae* in Colorado is worthy of molecular genetic study. Two subspecies are endemic to Colorado: *T. b. internatus* occupies the Arkansas Valley from Salida eastward to

Pueblo, except for a small area around Cañon City, Fremont County, where the local race *T. b. rubidus* occurs. For details of distribution of the 4 species of pocket gophers in southeastern Colorado, see Lovell et al. (2004). Thorough phylogenetic analysis of valley pocket gophers of Colorado and adjacent areas is to be encouraged. Patterns of microevolution need to be understood so that rational conservation attention can be given to evolutionarily significant units. M. Smith et al. (1983) described local differentiation and gene flow in valley pocket gophers in the Rio Grande Valley in New Mexico and found evidence of gene flow despite major karyologic and genetic differences between them. *T. bottae* was treated by E. Hall (1981) as inseparable from *T. umbrinus*, the southern pocket gopher. Most mammalogists recognize Botta's pocket gopher as a distinct species, however. A genetic analysis of relationships between the 2 forms was presented by M. F. Smith (1998).

Natural History

Botta's pocket gophers prefer sandy soils of valley bottom riparian areas but will use many other areas except soils high in clay or extremely coarse substrates (R. Miller 1964). On Mesa de Maya they are found in less favorable soils (Moulton, Choate, and Bissell 1979; Moulton, Choate, et al. 1983). They can be found in a variety of vegetation types, including agricultural land, grasslands, roadsides, open parklands, piñon-juniper woodlands, open montane forest, montane shrublands, and semidesert shrublands (Youngman 1958; C. L. Douglas 1969a; Moulton, Choate, et al. 1979, 1983). Their distribution has been linked to soil preferences (Best 1973) and to limiting competition with northern pocket gophers, plains pocket gophers, and yellow-faced pocket gophers, all of which appear capable of displacing the species on favored sites. T. Vaughan and Hansen (1964) located an area about 6 miles north of Cotopaxi, Fremont County, where the 2 Coloradan species of *Thomomys* occurred within a half mile of each other. Reciprocal transplants were made and both species were introduced into experimental sympatry in an unoccupied area. The northern pocket gopher was the better disperser and tolerated a wider range of environmental conditions and therefore reproduced more successfully in the experimental zone. Either species might be dominant in agonistic encounters. A. Baker (1974) found the northern pocket gopher to be behaviorally dominant in the laboratory. Moulton, Choate, et al. (1979) reported geographic overlap of *T. bottae* and *Cratogeomys castanops* on the Mesa de Maya by about 0.5 mi. at a place 9.5 mi. south and 14 mi. west of Kim, Las Animas County. Surface mounds of the 2 species were found about 20 m apart. Lovell et al. (2004) described a larger zone of sympatry, southeast of Walsenburg in Huerfano and Las Animas counties. East of Walsenburg, Huerfano Canyon appeared to be a barrier to the species, with *T. bottae* taken only west of the canyon and *C. castanops* only to the east.

The diet is similar to that of the northern pocket gopher. Seeds, tubers, roots, and green leaves and stems of a variety of forbs and grasses are eaten. Most food consists of aboveground plant parts. Succulent grasses, especially bromes, may constitute 40 to more than 80 percent of the diet. Forbs such as thistle, fleabane, and common sunflower generally make up the remainder. Insects make up less than 20 percent of stomach contents (T. Vaughan and Hansen 1964; Gottfried and Patton 1984). In Mesa Verde, piñon nuts, underground cactus parts, Indian ricegrass, rabbitbrush, and locoweed were eaten (C. L. Douglas 1969a). Food is stored in side tunnels of the burrow system. Coprophagy is practiced as a mechanism for maximizing nutrient uptake from ingested material.

Botta's pocket gophers, like other species of gophers, are thought to be polygynous because adult sex ratios sometimes favor females by almost 3 to 1. However, Daly and Patton (1986) raised questions regarding how effective male gophers can be in keeping other males from access to females because both sexes maintain exclusive territories. Breeding in Colorado probably occurs from March through July, based on work by Bandoli (1987) in New Mexico, where litter size ranged from 2 to 5 with an average of 2.6. Reproductively active females were found from February through April. Gestation takes about 19 days, with a single litter produced each year (Schramm 1961).

Botta's pocket gophers dig complex burrow systems in well-formed soils that include both shallow and deep tunnels. In California, nests were found in burrows about 38 cm below the surface, and shallower foraging burrows are about 10 cm belowground (Gettinger 1984). Where the animals live in relatively shallow soils, however, such as on Mesa de Maya in southern Colorado, burrow depths averaged 15 cm (Moulton, Choate, et al. 1979). Kinlaw (1999) provided a general review of burrowing mammals in arid environments, suggesting a number of directions for research. Curiously, pocket gophers were not included in the review, which focused on semi-fossorial vertebrates.

Botta's pocket gophers do not hibernate and are active at any time of the day or night. Radio-tracking studies in California found that animals spent 40 percent of their time away from the nest and tended to have bursts of activity in late afternoon (Gettinger 1984). A similar study in New Mexico found that only 19 percent of the time was spent away from the nest during the reproductive season (Bandoli 1987).

The animals are territorial, solitary, and aggressive toward other members of the species except when mating or when females are with young. Territories of males average 470 m² and contacted the territories of several females, whose territories average 290 m². The size of the burrow systems of males increases in winter and spring, apparently as they search for mates (Bandoli 1981). In California, burrow systems average 107 m², with 90 percent of activity occurring within 50 m of the nest (Gettinger 1984).

Densities of 10 animals per hectare are not unusual, and up to 153 per hectare were reported on a favorable site during a population peak in California (W. Howard 1961). Young pocket gophers disperse from the natal burrow in late summer or early fall. At this time they are especially vulnerable to a variety of predators, including coyotes, foxes, badgers, owls, and hawks. Significant mortality of young males is probably associated with male-male aggression and forced immigration. For thorough reviews of the literature see G. Turner et al. (1973); R. Baker, R. Bradley, and McAliley (2003); and C. A. Jones and Baxter (2004).

PHOTOGRAPH 8-27. Northern pocket gopher (*Thomomys talpoides*). Photograph by J. Perley Fitzgerald.

Thomomys talpoides

NORTHERN POCKET GOPHER

Description

The northern pocket gopher is a small gopher whose color varies geographically from dark brown or yellow-brown to pale, grayish yellow. Measurements are: total length 165–250 mm; length of tail 45–75; length of hindfoot 25–31; length of ear 5–7 mm; weight 100–150 g. The skull is robust, and the upper incisors lack a longitudinal groove. No sphenoidal fissure is present and the incisive foramina are anterior to the infraorbital foramen. LaVoie et al. (1971) reported albinism in the species.

Distribution

Northern pocket gophers are common in a variety of habitats above about 1,525 m (5,000 ft.) in elevation. Northern pocket gophers show wide geographic variation in color and size, and 9 subspecies are recognized in Colorado.

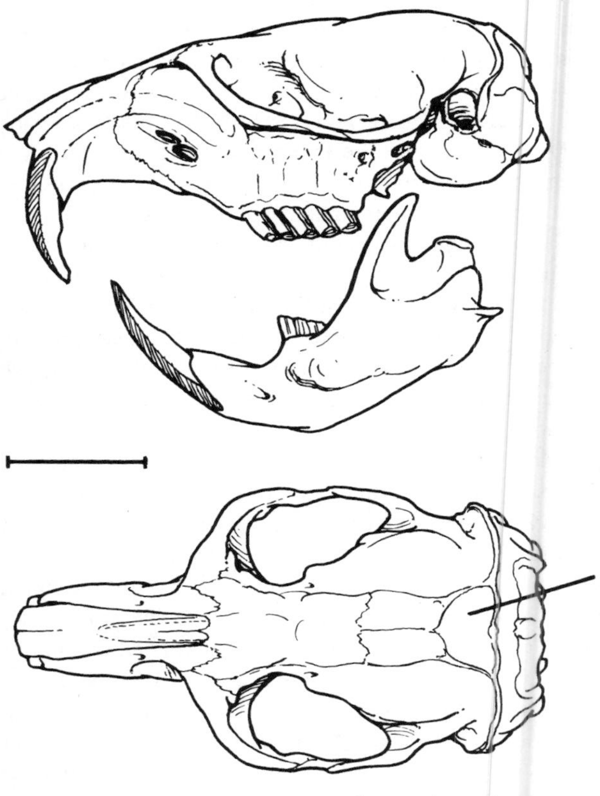

FIGURE 8-5. Skull of a northern pocket gopher (*Thomomys talpoides*), showing that the interparietal bone is broader than it is long. Scale = 1 cm.

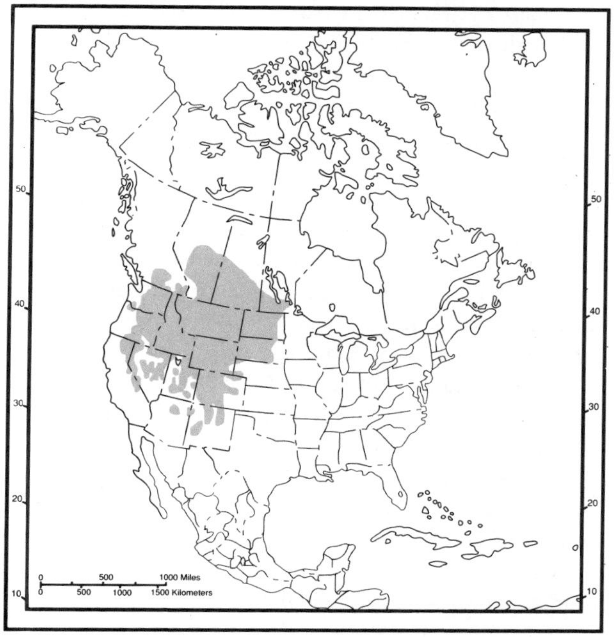

MAP 8-56. Distribution of the northern pocket gopher (*Thomomys talpoides*) in North America.

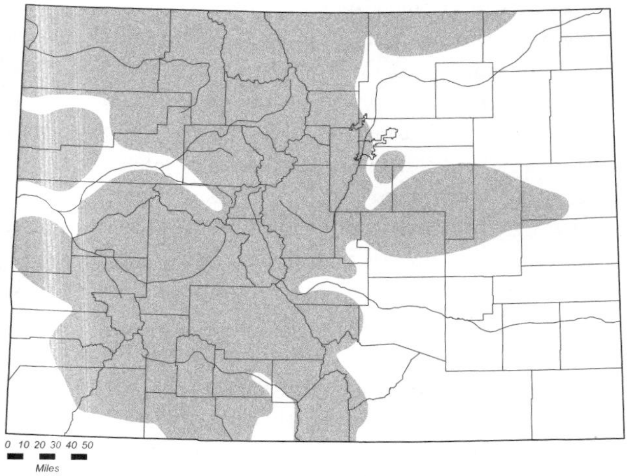

MAP 8-57. Distribution of the northern pocket gopher (*Thomomys talpoides*) in Colorado.

Thomomys talpoides agrestis occurs in the San Luis Valley north and east of the Rio Grande; *T. t. attenuatus* occurs along the High Plains escarpment in northern Larimer, Weld, and Logan counties; *T. t. durranti* occurs in the vicinity of the Roan Plateau in Rio Blanco, Garfield and Mesa counties; *T. t. fossor* occurs in the mountains of southwestern Colorado; *T. t. macrotis* is known only from Douglas County; *T. t. meritus* occurs in the mountains and parks of north-central Colorado, generally east of Moffat County and west of the Front Range; *T. t. ocius* occupies most of Moffat County; *T. t. retrorsus* occurs eastward on the eastern plains along the Platte-Arkansas Divide; *T. t. rostralis* occurs mostly in the Front Range. There is much to be learned about microevolution of pocket gophers in general, and northern pocket gophers in particular. Thaeler (1968) reported different chromosome numbers among several of the supposed subspecies of *Thomomys talpoides* in Colorado, suggesting that these populations might be specifically distinct. Based on analysis of mitochondrial DNA, R. Culver (2004) found that clades described by mitochondrial DNA corresponded better with karyotypes than with traditional subspecies (described mostly on the basis of size and color of pelage). The named subspecies should be used with caution until evolutionary processes in the species are better understood. However, managers do need to remain sensitive to the possibility that named kinds—and additional local populations not yet recognized taxonomically—represent evolutionarily distinctive and significant genetic units.

Natural History

Northern pocket gophers have been studied extensively in Colorado and elsewhere. They are the most broadly distributed of the gophers in the state and are found in many different habitat types, including agricultural and pasture lands, semidesert shrublands, and grasslands at lower elevations upward into alpine tundra (P. Miller 1964; D. Armstrong 1972; R. Hansen and Reid 1973). Soil development, drainage, and forage availability are factors that define their ecological limits. Grass-forb rangelands from 2,750 to 3,350 m (9,000–11,000 ft.) in elevation and with at least 50 cm of precipitation are the most productive native habitats in the state for this species (V. Reid 1973). Their broader environmental tolerance and higher vagility compared with Botta's pocket gopher, as well as possible behavioral dominance, give them a competitive and distributional advantage; however, the 2 species are also capable of coexistence under experimental conditions (T. Vaughan and Hansen 1964; A. Baker 1974).

Food habits of northern pocket gophers have been studied at several different localities in Colorado (J. Keith et al. 1959; Ward 1960; Ward and Keith 1962; R. Hansen and Ward 1966; T. Vaughan 1967a, 1974). Gophers use all parts of plants, and diets vary on a seasonal basis partly in response to availability and partly because of quality and succulence. Not surprisingly, roots and tubers provide most of the winter diet, whereas spring and summer diets are usually 60 to nearly 100 percent leaves and stems. Forbs, especially composites and legumes, are the most important foods. In some locations prickly-pear, mallows, saltbush, cinquefoil, and knotweeds are also important. Grasses are seasonally and locally significant and may constitute 8 to 50 percent of the diet, with highest consumption on shortgrass prairie (T. Vaughan 1967a). Locally and especially during the winter months, northern pocket gophers can do considerable damage to conifer seedlings, including lodgepole pine and Engelmann spruce (see Teipner et al. 1983). Food caches are stored in lateral tunnels usually plugged off from the main tunnel. Roots are often part of these stores, which may exceed 2 kg in weight. It appears that many caches are never used by the animals that stored them.

As in other species of *Thomomys*, northern pocket gophers use both teeth and claws in digging their extensive burrow systems (Lessa and Thaeler 1989). There are both deep and shallow tunnels (R. Hansen and Reid 1973). Deep burrows may be more than 40 cm below the surface whereas burrows used in foraging are typically 10–30 cm deep. Northern pocket gophers also form conspicuous earthen ridges (casts or "eskers") on the surface. These represent subsurface soils that were pushed into tunnels in the snow (see Stoecker 1976). As high-country snow melts in spring and early summer, these garlands of soil are lowered intact to the surface, patterning grasslands on the High Plains and also montane, subalpine, and alpine meadows, and influencing plant succession strongly. In northern Weld County, surface covered with gopher mounds ranged from 2.5 percent on lightly grazed sites to 8 percent on heavily grazed lands (Grant et al. 1980). Northern pocket gophers wintering in the alpine zone tend to occur in snowbed communities where an insulating blanket of snow prevents soils from freezing and thus permits burrowing through the winter (Dearing 2001). Density of aboveground vegetation on such sites is highest at the margins of mounds, where infiltration of rainfall is increased.

As ecological knowledge has increased, it has become apparent that burrowing by gophers over thousands of years has had a profound effect on soil development (L. Ellison 1946; Huntley and Inouye 1988). Estimating densities, home ranges, and soil movement is notoriously difficult and published estimates vary widely (Smallwood and Morrison 1999a, 1999b). A high population (74 animals per hectare) was estimated to move up to 400 metric tons of soil per hectare per year (Richens 1966). That scale of bioturbation (earth movement by living organisms) results in mixing and vertical cycling of soil components as organic material is incorporated into deeper layers and freshly developed parent material is exposed at the surface. Although mounds and casts may be vulnerable to erosion, the consensus has been that pocket gopher activity enhances soil formation and soil depth at lower elevations. However, Cortinas and Seastedt (1996) concluded that frequent disturbance by pocket gophers led to lower carbon content and fertility of alpine tundra; Litaor et al. (1996) reported lower carbon, nitrogen, and exchangeable calcium and potassium in gopher mounds; and Sherrod and Seastedt (2001) concluded that pocket gophers increase ecosystem heterogeneity. In the tundra, gophers are also significant geomorphic agents. Well-vegetated sites occupied by northern pocket gophers experience soil disturbance much greater than on the general tundra surface, with average surface lowering of 0.0037 cm per year, compared with 0.009 cm per year for freeze-thaw processes and 0.0001 cm per year for wind and water erosion (S. Burns 1979). Burrowing has also been correlated with the presence of alpine terracettes (Thorn 1978). For a broad review of animal influences on geomorphology, see D. Butler (1995).

Activity of gophers in localized areas can increase productivity of the plant community (L. Ellison and Aldous 1952), contribute to plant community structure and landscape-level pattern (Thorn 1982), drive predictable successional change (G. Turner 1973), and increase plant species richness (Sherrod et al. 2005). Common invaders are cheatgrass, other bromes, knotweed, gilia, and aspen fleabane. Interestingly, common dandelion, an aggressive invader, is suppressed in areas of high gopher activity, perhaps because it is consumed by them selectively. Lupines and pea vines are also typically suppressed in active gopher areas. By reducing surface litter, gopher activity may impact populations of other small rodents, such as voles, which are favored by a layer of thatch. Northern pocket gophers often reach very high population levels in irrigated alfalfa fields, where considerable crop damage can occur (T. Vaughan 1967a).

Northern pocket gophers in Colorado reproduce from mid-March through early summer; most breeding occurs in May and June right after snowmelt and varies with elevation. Forage availability and quality and factors such as irrigation may influence the length of the breeding season. Gestation takes about 18 or 19 days. Only 1 litter of 4 to 6 young is produced per year. Herbicide use in western Colorado decreased litter size in one study. Older females produce the earliest litters; yearling females do not have their litters until late spring or early summer (R. Hansen 1960; R. Hansen and Bear 1964; T. Vaughan 1969). The altricial young weigh about 3 g at birth. They grow rapidly and by 6 months of age have almost attained adult weight (D. C. Andersen 1978). Although differential sex ratios are reported for several other species of gophers, it approximates 1:1 for the northern pocket gopher.

Northern pocket gophers reach highest population levels in late summer and early fall with recruitment of young of the year. Populations then decline until the next breeding season. Juveniles constitute less than 40 percent of spring populations whereas in the fall they make up more than 43 percent of the population. Densities range from as low as 15 animals per hectare to more than 74 animals per hectare. Longevity is 1.5 to 2.5 years, with some individuals living more than 5 years in the wild. Complete population turnover thus occurs every 4 to 6 years. Populations typically show fluctuations when followed over a number of years (T. Vaughan 1969; V. Reid 1973). Although pocket gophers are territorial and generally seem to make exclusive use of burrow systems, all possible combinations of adults and young were taken from the same burrow systems in spring and summer months, suggesting that intraspecific tolerance may vary, especially during the reproductive season (R. Hansen and Miller 1959).

Terrestrial predators of northern pocket gophers include coyotes, red and gray foxes, bobcats, badgers, spotted and striped skunks, weasels, bullsnakes, and rattlesnakes. In the Yellowstone region, grizzly bears prey on pocket gophers and their stores of roots and tubers, accounting for about a quarter of all foraging activity just after snowmelt in April and May (D. Mattson 2004). Prior to their extirpation from Colorado in the early twentieth century, grizzlies may have been an important predator on gophers in Colorado. Red-tailed and Swainson's hawks, goshawks, and great-horned, long-eared, and barn owls are effective aerial predators. Ectoparasites were studied by R. Miller and Ward (1960). H. Pigage et al. (2005) reported 5 species of fleas from northern pocket gophers in Elbert County. Nearly 99 percent of individual fleas were *Foxella ignota*, the most frequent flea of pocket gophers in a number of other studies. S. Gardner and Schmidt (1986) described a new species of nematode from a northern pocket gopher taken in Huerfano County, Colorado. G. Turner et al. (1973) reviewed much of the vast literature on the biology of the northern pocket gopher in Colorado to that date, and Verts and Carraway (1999) provided a synopsis of the biology of the species throughout its wide range.

Geomys bursarius

PLAINS POCKET GOPHER

Description

Plains pocket gophers are pale brown to yellowish brown in color with a slightly paler ventral surface. By comparison, the similar-sized yellow-faced pocket gopher is much darker, a rich mahogany brown. Measurements are: total length 180–300 mm; length of tail 50–90; length of hindfoot 30–36; length of ear 3–5 mm; weight 170–330 g. The upper incisors have 2 longitudinal grooves, although the inner ones may be difficult to see on some specimens. Cranial asymmetry has been noted (T. Vaughan 1961b). Plains pocket gophers are the most strongly fossorial of pocket gophers in the state. Their limbs and claws are so modified for digging that they seem to have difficulty walking, moving on the sides of their feet in an awkward manner.

Distribution

Plains pocket gophers are common over most of eastern Colorado. Based on extensive field studies, Lovell et al. (2004) provided details of distribution of this and other species of pocket gophers in southeastern Colorado. Traditionally, 2 subspecies have been recognized in the state: *Geomys bursarius jugossicularis* in southeastern Colorado, south of the Platte-Arkansas Divide, and *G. b. lutescens* north of that divide (D. Armstrong 1972). Using karyotypic, morphologic, and electrophoretic methods, Sudman et al. (1987) described *G. b. halli* as a new subspecies, with a type locality in Ellis County, Kansas. They referred some of the specimens from eastern Colorado reported by D. Armstrong (1972) to the new subspecies on geographic grounds, but

PHOTOGRAPH 8-28. Plains pocket gopher (*Geomys bursarius*). © 1993 Wendy Shattil / Bob Rozinski.

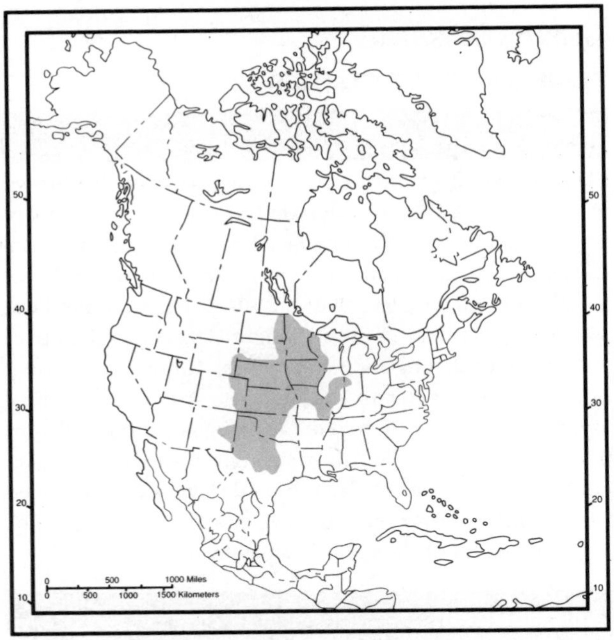

MAP 8-58. Distribution of the plains pocket gopher (*Geomys bursarius—sensu lato*) in North America.

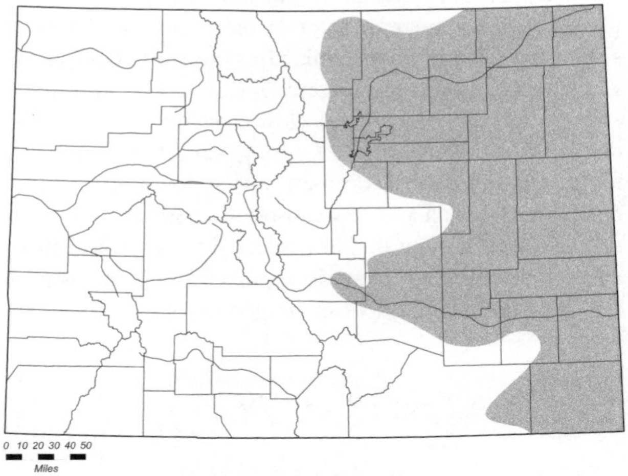

MAP 8-59. Distribution of the plains pocket gopher (*Geomys bursarius—sensu lato*) in Colorado.

the particular specimens so referred were not specified. Elrod et al. (2000) mapped 3 subspecies of *Geomys bursarius* in Colorado: *G. b. lutescens* in the northeast, *G. b. jugossicularis* in the southeast, and *G. b. halli* in the east-central part of the state. Their phylogenetic analysis based on the cytochrome-b gene showed that *G. b. halli* and *G. b. jugossicularis* form a natural group, closely allied to *G. b. lutescens*.

R. Russell (1968) and E. Hall (1981; see Map 8-58) considered plains pocket gophers as a single species, *Geomys bursarius*. In recent decades there have been considerable research and debate on systematics of plains pocket gophers in the region, based on a variety of molecular and other non-traditional characters. Based on cranial morphology, karyology, and ectoparasites (especially lice, Mallophaga; see Timm and Price 1980), Heaney and Timm (1983, 1985) allocated plains pocket gophers from eastern Colorado to *G. lutescens lutescens*, recognizing them as specifically distinct from *G. bursarius* but not recognizing *G. b. jugossicularis* as a separate subspecies. Heaney and Timm (2009) investigated a narrow hybrid zone between *G. lutescens* and *G. bursarius* in northeastern Nebraska. Sudman et al. (1987) recognized the 2 "chromosomal races." Jolley et al. (2000) also treated *Geomys bursarius* and *G. lutescens* as separate species. J. C. Burns et al. (1985); R. Baker, L. Bradley, et al. (2003); and D. Wilson and Reeder (2005) continued to recognize *G. bursarius* as a single species, including plains pocket gophers from eastern Colorado, and we follow that arrangement here, partly because we know of no way to distinguish the supposed species in the field, but with the caveat that consensus could shift in coming years as further studies of these pocket gophers are forthcoming.

Sudman et al. (2006) studied variation in the mitochondrial cytochrome-b locus from the 11 supposed species of *Geomys* recognized by Jolley et al. (2000). A sample from Fremont County, Colorado, was attributed to the subspecies *G. b. jugossicularis* in their Appendix I, but a map (their figure 1) shows southeastern Colorado in the range of *Geomys bursarius*, and their figures 2 and 3 are phylogenetic trees denoting *jugossicularis* as a subspecies of *G. bursarius*. Genoways, Hamilton, et al. (2008) studied genetic, molecular, and morphological variation in plains pocket gophers in Nebraska and identified a hybrid zone in Lincoln County between 2 groups that they considered full species, *Geomys jugossicularis* and *G. lutescens*. Their map (p. 828) indicated that *G. bursarius* (in their conservative sense) does not occur in Colorado. They ascribed to *G. lutescens* a range in Colorado north of the South Platte River and showed *G. jugossicularis* as extending over much of the eastern quarter of the state. Coloradan specimens were not included in their study, however. R. Chambers et al. (2009) evaluated phylogenetic relationships within the genus *Geomys* using DNA sequences from a nuclear gene and 2 mitochondrial genes. They concluded that 3 species of *Geomys* occur in eastern Colorado, *Geomys lutescens* in the northeast, *G. bursarius* in the southeast, and *G. jugossicularis* between them. The geography of these forms was not detailed, and morphological distinctions between them were not presented. In the absence of means by which field naturalists might distinguish these forms, we take the conservative course of treating plains pocket gophers as a single species.

Natural History

Plains pocket gophers occupy grasslands over the Great Plains as well as the margins of agricultural lands. They are adapted to a narrow range of conditions, requiring deep sandy to loamy soils that are well drained but moist. In Colorado they typically favor light soils of considerable depth, especially sand hills and other windblown soils. They appear, perhaps in part because of their larger size, to be less tolerant of harder and shallower soils than are species of *Thomomys* (Cary 1911; R. Miller 1964; Best 1973; Moulton, Choate, et al. 1983) and to be preadapted to colonize disturbed areas. Habitats include borrow pits, roadside edges, agrosystems, and lands with plant communities influenced by drought and reminiscent of the dustbowl conditions of the 1930s. In the sand hills of Nebraska, plains pocket gophers concentrated their activity in forb patches that were influenced by movements of bison (Steuter et al. 1995).

Plains pocket gophers show preferences for certain plant species at certain times of the year, not necessarily in proportion to species abundance. About 64 percent of the annual diet in Washington County consisted of grasses, especially stipa, wheatgrass, and blue grama, which together comprised 48 percent of the forage (G. Myers and Vaughan 1964). Significant amounts of cactus were eaten, and forbs were especially favored in spring and summer, important among them locoweed and globe mallow. Leaves and stems accounted for only 26 percent of the diet; most food was underground parts. Studies in western Nebraska (D. Luce et al. 1980) showed generally similar diets, with grasses contributing the greatest fraction. Underground and aboveground plant parts were 31 and 39 percent of the diet, respectively. Four species—needle-and-thread, scouring-rush, June grass, and Kentucky bluegrass—contributed 50 percent of the diet. Several studies indicate that plains pocket gophers can reduce production of alfalfa and forage production for livestock on native grasslands, in some cases by as much as 30–46 percent (M. Foster and Stubbendieck 1980; D. Luce and Stubbendieck 1981). Although pocket gophers may influence the plant communities dramatically, their overall quantitative impact usually is lower than that of herbivorous soil invertebrates, especially nematodes (Seastedt and Murray 2008).

Because of their impact on agricultural production, much effort has been spent on development of methods to control gophers, including toxicants and repellants. Much of that work has been conducted by researchers at the Denver Wildlife Research Center (Ward et al. 1967). Control per se may be shortsighted. In a broad "cost-benefit analysis" the value of pocket gophers in soil development and in altering plant succession must be considered. In the natural ecosystem, pocket gophers are neither "good" nor "bad"; only we humans can make such subjective judgments.

In suitable habitat, conspicuous mounds of earth indicate locations of underground tunnel systems. Surface mounds consist of fresh castings from tunnels, often added to older material from other tunnel systems adjacent to the one being dug. The burrow entrance is plugged with soil except when the animals are discharging soil or emerging briefly to forage. Shallow burrows (15–30 cm deep) interconnect with deeper tunnels that reach below the frost line. Side tunnels are constructed as food caches or latrines. As with other species of gophers, soil is loosened with the strong front feet and claws or by chewing with the incisors, which angle forward. Soil is pushed to the surface with the forelimbs, chest, and neck (Downhower and E. Hall 1966). In Texas, burrow temperatures ranged between 23°C and 33°C. Burrows typically have somewhat higher relative humidity levels than outside air and elevated carbon dioxide. Oxygen concentration may be 20 percent lower than in surface air. As in other burrow-dwelling mammals, elevated carbon dioxide and lower oxygen levels did not appear to impact the animals' physiology (Kennerly 1958, 1964).

Individuals are solitary, aggressive, and territorial. Once established, burrow systems are used throughout the life of an individual. There are equally spaced periods of activity day and night (T. Vaughan and Hansen 1961). Animals were active about 34 percent of the time, with bouts of activity averaging 0.5 hour and resting periods averaging 1 hour. Density estimates for the species are few. Schmidly (1983) reported estimates of 1 to 17 animals per hectare in central Texas. R. Beck and Hansen (1966) measured relative abundance of the species in dune sand and sandy loam habitats in Washington County, noting considerably higher activity in areas of sandy loam.

Males are polygamous and their territories may overlap those of females. Most reproduction in Colorado probably occurs during late winter and early spring. Most pregnant females were taken in April and May. The gestation period has been estimated at 30 days or more and may be as long as 51 days (Sudman et al. 1986). A single litter of 1 to 6 young (average, 3.5) is produced per year (T. Vaughan 1962). The young are altricial: small in size (5 g), hairless, with eyes, ears, and cheek pouches closed (Sudman et al. 1986).

A variety of terrestrial and avian predators prey on plains pocket gophers, particularly owls and burrowing predators such as badgers. The animals host a variety of ectoparasites, including lice, fleas, and ticks. S. Gardner and Schmidt (1988) described 2 new species of tapeworms from *G. bursarius* collected near Kersey, Weld County, and S. Gardner and Schmidt (1986) described a new species of filarial roundworm from a plains pocket gopher taken near LaSalle, also in Weld County. Probably few plains pocket gophers live longer than 5 years. Literature on the species was reviewed by Chase et al. (1982), Teipner et al. (1983), and G. Turner et al. (1973).

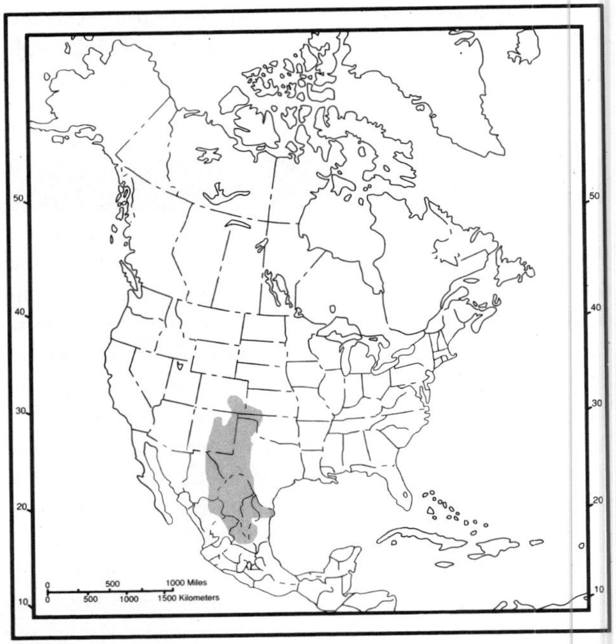

MAP 8-60. Distribution of the yellow-faced pocket gopher (*Cratogeomys castanops*) in North America.

Cratogeomys castanops

YELLOW-FACED POCKET GOPHER

Description

The yellow-faced pocket gopher is a large gopher, slightly larger in total length than other Coloradan gophers. Most specimens are reddish brown with a yellowish orange tinge on the cheeks and neck region. The underparts are buffy in color. Measurements are: total length 245–300 mm; length of tail 68–80 mm; length of hindfoot 34–40 mm; length of ear less than 7 mm; weight 160–350 g. The skull is heavy and the upper incisors have a single longitudinal groove.

Distribution

Yellow-faced pocket gophers occur widely in southeastern Colorado, in all counties south of the Arkansas River, and

PHOTOGRAPH 8-29. Yellow-faced pocket gopher (*Cratogeomys castanops*). Photograph by R. B. Forbes.

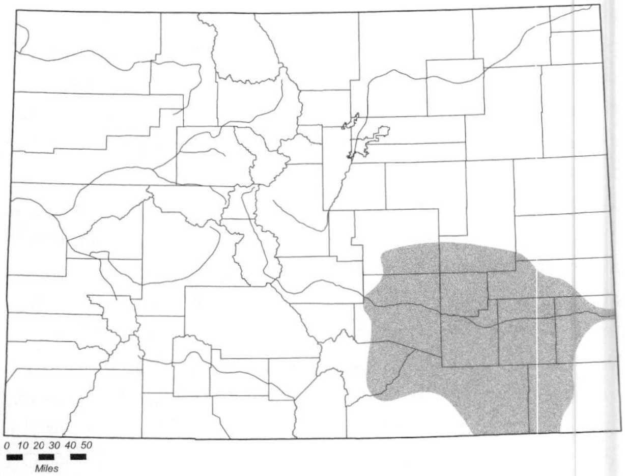

MAP 8-61. Distribution of the yellow-faced pocket gopher (*Cratogeomys castanops*) in Colorado.

northward to El Paso and Lincoln counties (Lovell et al. 2004). It is not uncommon in suitable habitat. One subspecies, *Cratogeomys castanops castanops*, occurs in Colorado (see Hollander 1990). The taxonomy of the species has been somewhat unstable; at times this species has been known as *Pappogeomys castanops* (see R. Russell 1968), but Honeycutt and Williams (1982) elevated *Cratogeomys* back to generic status, and that arrangement was followed by R. Baker, L. Bradley, et al. (2003). Hollander (1990) provided a biosystematic study of the species. Common names have included chestnut-faced pocket gopher and Mexican pocket gopher.

Natural History

Yellow-faced pocket gophers usually inhabit deep sandy or silty soils relatively free of rocks. However, they also occur in shallower, denser soils in some areas. In southeastern Colorado they are most often associated with grasslands but are also found in agricultural lands, roadside ditches, and montane shrublands and parklands (Cary 1911; R. Miller 1964; Moulton, Choate, and Bissell 1983). In parts of southeastern Colorado and northeastern New Mexico, the species is apparently being displaced by *Geomys*, perhaps because of increased disturbance of native habitats (Best 1973; Moulton, Choate, and Bissell 1983). In southwestern Texas, however, it is seemingly displacing *Geomys* in areas of increased aridity (Schmidly 1977).

Yellow-faced pocket gophers make earthen mounds at the entrance of their underground tunnels, but more frequently their surface activities result in formation of sunken plugs of soil not readily visible from a distance. Areas around such plugs are often disturbed, resulting in patches of annual or perennial forbs and grasses. Burrow depths range from 13 to 31 cm (Best 1973; Moulton, Choate, and Bissell 1983). In the same habitats *Thomomys* burrows were somewhat shallower. Moulton, Choate, and Bissell (1983) reported *T. bottae* and *C. castanops* in a zone of sympatry on Mesa de Maya, with burrow systems closely overlapping but at different depths, *T. bottae* occupying the shallower burrows. Burrow systems in Texas were 40 to more than 100 m in length with numerous side tunnels up to 3 m long (Hickman 1977). Usually burrow systems have a shallow foraging network of tunnels and a deeper system that contains the nest chamber and food stores.

Yellow-faced pocket gophers probably feed on a variety of green vegetation and root materials. Stomach contents favoring legumes and a large proportion of root materials have been described (V. Bailey 1932). Damage to crops is reported in some states. The animals harvest materials either from within the tunnel system by pulling plant roots and shoots down through the soil or by venturing aboveground to forage. When they forage aboveground, plant materials are quickly clipped off close to ground level and dragged into the burrow. Once food is in the burrow system, it is clipped into small pieces and carried in the cheek pouches to storage caches. Rhizomes are favored, and unused parts may be used to line the nest (Hickman 1975).

Breeding probably occurs from late March to August, with 1, 2, or possibly even 3 litters produced in a bimodal pattern, based on studies in Texas (Smolen et al. 1980), New Mexico (Hegdal et al. 1965), and Kansas (Birney, Jones, and Mortimer 1971). Most reproduction probably occurs from March to June in our area. Litter size ranges from 1 to 5 with an average of 2 or 3. Young are born blind and naked. Cheek pouches develop after birth and are apparent only as creases in neonates (Hickman 1975). Females carry their young by the loose skin of the belly. Adult sex ratios favored females by 4:1 in southeastern New Mexico (Hegdal et al. 1965), although other studies found ratios closer to 1:1 (Smolen et al. 1980).

Yellow-faced pocket gophers usually occupy exclusive burrow systems. Occasionally more than 1 individual will occur together, usually during the breeding season. Hegdal et al. (1965) reported multiple occupancy of burrows as common in southeastern New Mexico. These animals have relatively large home ranges and move around more than other species of gophers, probably also over land (S. Williams and Baker 1976). They do not swim very well and may be limited by aquatic barriers more than are other gophers. Both *C. castanops* and *Geomys bursarius* apparently were excluded from fields in western Kansas where the soil was tilled annually for crops such as corn, wheat, or grain sorghum (Hoffman et al. 2007). Moulton, Choate, and Bissell (1983) suggested that the plains pocket gopher might displace the yellow-faced pocket gopher in cultivated lands, but Hoffman and Choate (2008) found no evidence that *Geomys bursarius* was displacing *Cratogeomys castanops* in southwestern Kansas, where the yellow-faced pocket gopher is consider "a species of greatest conservation need."

The animals are rather short-lived. In Texas, males survived 7 months and most females survived 1 year, although a few survived almost 2 years (Smolen et al. 1980). Most small to medium-sized carnivores prey on the species, with owls being especially successful. The literature was reviewed by Davidow-Henry et al. (1989).

Family Dipodidae—Jumping Mice and Kin

This is a family of small to medium-sized rodents with long tails, long hindlegs, and hindfeet adapted for saltatory, or jumping, movement. Jumping mice (along with Old World birch mice) were considered in a separate family (Zapodidae) for many years (including the first edition of this work), although the animals were thought to be close relatives of the jerboas (family Dipodidae, Old World analogues of North American kangaroo rats). We treat jumping mice in the family Dipodidae, following the review by Holden and Musser (2005) and authorities cited by them. Jumping mice proper constitute the subfamily Zapodinae, which are known as fossils from the Miocene of North America and China. The skull has a large infraorbital foramen and the upper incisors are grooved on the anterior surface. The dental formula for Coloradan species is 1/1, 0/0, 1/0, 3/3 = 18, a tooth count unique among mammals in the state. Premolars are reduced in size. Molars are rooted and cusped. The enamel shows much infolding, with one lingual fold and four labial folds (Whitaker 1972).

Unlike the jerboas, which are mostly desert and semidesert mammals, zapodines typically inhabit areas of lush herbaceous vegetation. There are 3 genera and 6 species of zapodines in northern Eurasia and North America. One genus with 2 species occurs in Colorado. Krutzsch (1954) discussed the taxonomy and distribution of these mice in North America.

Key to the Species of the Family Dipodidae in Colorado

1. Skull relatively small and light with narrow braincase and small molars; palatal breadth at last molar usually less than 4.2 mm; incisive foramina usually less than 4.6 mm; maxillary toothrow 3.7 mm or less; anterior median toothfold on M_1 present. Tail distinctly bicolored, dark above and yellow to whitish below, ochraceous lateral line usually indistinct to lacking; mid-dorsal blackish patch poorly defined .... Meadow Jumping Mouse—*Zapus hudsonius*, p. 189

1' Skull relatively large and heavy with wider braincase and larger molars; palatal breadth at last molar usually greater than 4.4 mm; incisive foramina usually more than 4.6 mm; maxillary toothrow usually more than 3.7 mm; anterior median toothfold on M_1 absent. Tail less distinctly bicolored, ochraceous lateral line usually distinct; blackish mid-dorsal patch prominent .... Western Jumping Mouse—*Zapus princeps*, p. 192

Genus *Zapus*—Jumping Mice

The genus *Zapus* includes 3 species, Colorado's 2 kinds of jumping mice and the Pacific jumping mouse, *Z. trinotatus*. Closely related genera are the North American *Napaeozapus*, the woodland jumping mouse, and *Eozapus*, the Chinese jumping mouse. The latter 2 genera both are monotypic. Krutzsch (1954) reviewed North American jumping mice.

The Coloradan species—especially immature animals or adults with worn pelage and/or worn molars—are somewhat difficult to distinguish in the field or from skulls. Samples of hair or blood can provide voucher material for individuals captured and released in livetrapping studies (Bortolus 2008). Specimens from areas of potential co-occurrence along the foot of the Front Range should be examined by a mammalogist with access to comparative reference material. Discriminant function analysis may also be useful (M. Conner and Shenk 2003).

Zapus hudsonius

MEADOW JUMPING MOUSE

Description

The meadow jumping mouse is a small mouse with large hindlegs and feet and a long, sparsely haired tail that usually makes up at least 60 percent of the total length. The dorsal color is grayish to yellowish brown with the sides paler in color. The venter is white. The pelage is rather harsh in texture relative to that of most other small mice. Intermixed dark hairs in the dorsal area form an indistinct mid-dorsal

PHOTOGRAPH 8-30. Meadow jumping mouse (*Zapus hudsonius*). Photograph by Roger W. Barbour.

band or stripe, usually less pronounced than in the larger western jumping mouse.

Measurements are: total length 187–255 mm; length of tail 108–155 mm; length of hindfoot 28–35 mm; weight of adults seasonally variable, 16–28 g. The skull is small and light with a narrower braincase and smaller molars than in *Z. princeps*. The upper incisors have a distinct anterior groove and are orange in color. In younger age classes, an anterior median toothfold on M_3 is visible but becomes worn and obscure in older age classes (Klingener 1963). The baculum, usually less than 4.9 mm in length, is relatively simple, with a thin shaft curving slightly upward and tapering gradually from the base to near the tip. Females have 8 mammae. M. Conner and Shenk (2003, 2005) provided methods for distinguishing Coloradan jumping mice using repeated measurements and discriminant function analysis.

Distribution

The meadow jumping mouse is known in Colorado from Larimer, Weld, Boulder, Jefferson, Douglas, Elbert, El Paso, Adams, and Arapahoe counties and thus is present in both the South Platte and Arkansas river basins. It apparently is extirpated from Denver County. The animals also are known from southern Las Animas County, east of Raton

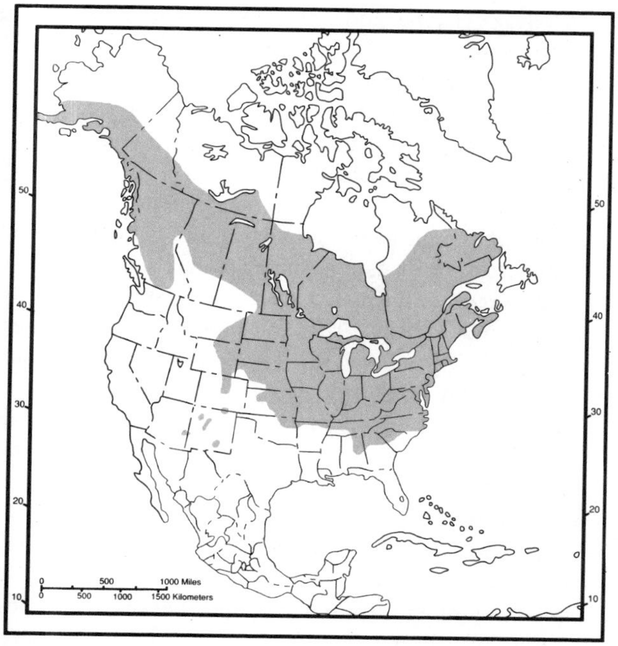

MAP 8-62. Distribution of the meadow jumping mouse (*Zapus hudsonius*) in North America.

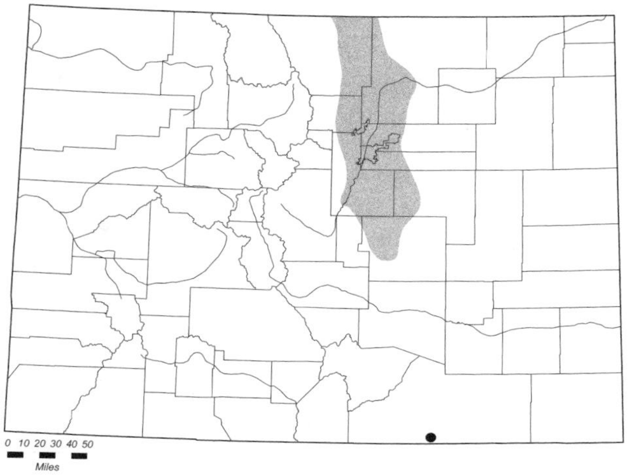

MAP 8-63. Distribution of the meadow jumping mouse (*Zapus hudsonius*) in Colorado.

Pass, at the Lake Dorothey State Wildlife Area, a population that apparently is disjunct from those to the north in the Front Range corridor (C. A. Jones 1999, 2002). A report of "*Zapus hudsonius/princeps*" from the Uncompahgre Plateau by Lomolino et al. (1989) may be confusing; only *Z. princeps* would be expected in that area.

Judging from its limited ecological and geographic distribution in Colorado, the meadow jumping mouse apparently is an Ice Age relict, perhaps once widespread in a tallgrass prairie across the eastern plains but now restricted to scattered localities on the Colorado Piedmont and similar situations (D. Armstrong 1972). Similarly relict populations are known from the White Mountains of Arizona and the Sacramento Mountains and Rio Grande Valley of New Mexico (D. Hafner et al. 1981). Doubtless such practices as gravel mining and converting natural wetlands into irrigation reservoirs over a century of agricultural, industrial, and residential development have had seriously negative impacts on populations. Ryon (1996) trapped 8 localities from which *Z. hudsonius* had been trapped prior to 1977; none of those localities supported *Z. hudsonius*. Habitat degradation is hardly limited to Colorado. J. Frey and Malaney (2009) surveyed for the mice and for suitable habitat within the historical range of the subspecies in the Jemez Mountains of northern New Mexico and concluded that *Z. h. luteus* was absent from 73 percent of historical localities. They attributed declines to habitat alteration, especially from livestock grazing, but also from drought, development, recreation, forest fire, and ecosystem alteration from loss of beaver from riparian systems. However, where large, undeveloped tracts of native grassland and riparian habitat persist along the boundary between the Colorado Piedmont and the Colorado Front Range, the animals often have been found. Not surprisingly, the largest such tracts are those protected from development in municipal open space (especially the City of Boulder and Boulder County; see Meaney, Ruggles, Clippinger, and Lubow [2002]; Meaney, Ruggles, Lubow, and Clippinger [2003]; and references cited by them) and federal lands (Rocky Flats Weapons Plant, now a national wildlife refuge) and the US Air Force Academy (Corn et al. 1995; Schorr 2001).

Because of the apparent rarity of this species and the difficulty of distinguishing individuals from *Zapus princeps*, caution in identification is encouraged. Two subspecies are known from Colorado. *Z. h. preblei* is the subspecies of the Colorado Piedmont, the so-called Front Range corridor, from about Colorado Springs northward to southeastern Wyoming. The type locality of the subspecies is Loveland (Krutzsch 1954). In recent years, a second subspecies (*Z. h. luteus*) was discovered to occur in Sugarite Canyon, Las Animas County, just north of the New Mexico state line (C. A. Jones 1999, 2002). Systematics of this geographic race are under study by Dr. Jennifer K. Frey of New Mexico State University (see Frey 2007; Frey and Schwenke 2007), who also has identified the form among specimens of jumping mice from the vicinity of Florida, La Plata County, Colorado (J. K. Frey, personal communication), specimens reported previously as *Z. princeps* (by Krutzsch [1954], D. Armstrong [1972], and others).

There has been debate as to whether *Z. h. preblei* is a subspecies distinct from *Z. h. campestris*, the subspecies of northeastern Wyoming and adjacent Montana and South Dakota (R. Ramey, Liu, et al. 2005; R. Ramey, Wehausen, et al. 2006; Vignieri et al. 2006). We follow T. King et al. (2006; but see R. Ramey, Wehausen, et al. 2007) and the most recent taxonomic revision of *Zapus hudsonius* (Krutzsch 1954) and recognize *Z. h. preblei* as taxonomically distinct. (Continuity of the distribution of the species across eastern Wyoming with the broader geographic range of *Z. hudsonius* in the Northern Great Plains and Upper Midwest has not been demonstrated.)

Perhaps because of its geographic range along the Colorado Piedmont—one of the nation's fastest-growing regions—the subspecies *Z. h. preblei* has been the object of considerable conservation controversy (T. King et al. 2006; Ramey, Wehausen, et al. 2007). Brosi and Biber (2009) used the tangled web of decisions on the status of *Z. h. preblei* as an example of the need to be cautious with the use of statistics and erring on the side of caution when the cost of error might be extinction. As of July 2008 the subspecies is designated as "threatened" in the segment of its range in Colorado but is not protected in adjacent Wyoming. For update on the status of conservation of the animals under the Endangered Species Act, consult the US Fish and Wildlife Service website: http://www.fws.gov/mountain-prairie/species/mammals/preble/. According to the International Union for the Conservation of Nature, both Coloradan subspecies of *Z. hudsonius* are "of concern" (D. Hafner et al. 1998b): *Z. h. luteus* was noted (p. 120) as "lower risk, near threatened," whereas *Z. h. preblei* was listed as "endangered."

Natural History

The meadow jumping mouse is a prairie species, occupying a variety of habitats, but is most common in heavy vegetation along watercourses or in herbaceous understories in wooded areas. Most specimens from Colorado appear to be from tallgrass habitats near water. The mice make extensive use of complex habitat structure that includes shrubs, grasses, and woody debris (Trainor et al. 2007). In a 3-year study in riparian habitats along South Boulder Creek, Meaney et al. (2002) found only weak evidence of impact of trails on small mammals, including meadow jumping mice. The species is often associated with coyote willow (*Salix exigua*). G. Jones and Jones (1985) reported the species from wetlands surrounded by sagebrush habitat in El Paso County. Meadow jumping mice used ledges within culverts to move beneath roads from one patch of suitable habitat to another, suggesting that man-made structures could be used to link fragmented prairie landscapes (Meaney, Bakeman, et al. 2007).

Diet of the meadow jumping mouse is mostly seeds and fruits, fungi, and insects. Animal matter is thought to be most important in the early part of the season, with seeds becoming important as particular plants mature in summer and early fall. The animals are not reported to cache food, but they do store body fat in preparation for hibernation.

Home ranges have been estimated at 0.08 to 0.35 ha, with males having slightly larger average home ranges (Quimby 1951). The species is reported to shift home ranges and wander, perhaps in response to loss of moist habitat in hot weather. In suitable habitat in the eastern United States, densities can approach 50 mice per ha, but seasonally numbers from 7 to 15 per hectare are probably more typical. In Colorado, linear densities are evaluated because the animals are restricted to riparian habitats in this semiarid region. Mark-recapture analysis of

352 marked individuals along South Boulder Creek and associated irrigation ditches resulted in densities of 23 to 86 animals per kilometer (Meaney, Ruggles, Lubow, and Clippinger 2003). However, linear densities are extremely variable over space and time, and lower linear densities are common.

Aboveground nests are used for daytime retreats. They are constructed from available vegetation and are 8–9 cm wide and 7–8 cm tall (Ryon 2001). Nests, typically several centimeters belowground, may be more substantial and are used for rearing young. The nest is constructed of grasses, leaves, or woody material. Nests are typically located in protected areas under logs, at the base of bushes, or in similar places. Bain and Shenk (2002) described a possible maternal nest 12 cm below the surface in a stand of bluegrass (*Poa pratensis*), brome (*Bromus* sp.), Canada thistle (*Cirsium arvense*), and willow (*Salix* sp.) in the Plum Creek watershed of Douglas County. A hibernation den was in a burrow 31 cm deep beneath cover of Gambel oak (*Quercus gambelii*), bluegrass, and poison-ivy (*Toxicodendron radicans*). Nest material was pliable, damp oak-leaf litter (95 percent) and shredded grass.

Because jumping mice live in rather tall, dense vegetation, when undisturbed they move by crawling or by short hops along the ground. When pressed, however, they can make prodigious leaps, changing course in midair by using the tail as a rudder. After a few such leaps they remain motionless in the shadows. They are good climbers, swimmers, and diggers; the digging behavior probably is used in the search for fungi. Although they often live in habitat occupied by voles and other runway-using rodents, jumping mice do not use such runs with any regularity. Instead they move along natural features of the terrain. Although generally nocturnal or crepuscular, it is not unusual for the animals to be active during daylight.

Meadow jumping mice are capable of breeding virtually throughout their period of aboveground activity, with most reproduction probably occurring between early June and mid-August. Most females seem to have 2 litters per year and some have 3. Litter size varies from 2 to 8 with an average of 4 to 5. The young are born after a gestation period of 17 to more than 21 days (Quimby 1951). The length of gestation is increased in lactating females. Young are naked at birth. The incisors erupt at about 13 days and the eyes open during the fourth week. The young reach minimum adult weight by about 2 months of age.

The animals are mostly solitary, but aggression between individuals does not occur when captives are housed together (Whitaker 1963). A number of sounds are reported, including chirping and clucking noises and, when excited, drumming with the tail (Whitaker 1963).

Jumping mice hibernate during the colder months; shorter day-length seems to stimulate fat deposition. Individuals studied in the laboratory were capable of weight gains of up to 2 g per day for brief periods. Individuals may gain more than 100 percent of their original body weight, with average daily gains of about 1 g. Body temperatures are variable and breathing is irregular during hibernation. They enter hibernation in September and October and emerge in May (Whitaker 1963; Meaney et al. 2003). Estimated overwinter survival in Colorado was 54 percent, summer survival was 16.2 percent, and the combined annual survival rate was 8.8 percent in Colorado (Meaney et al. 2003). The higher winter survival rate underscores the importance of hibernation and good hibernation sites for this species. Based on studies of animals live-trapped at the US Air Force Academy and equipped with passive integrated transponder (PIT) tags, Schorr et al. (2009) found that heavier animals of both sexes had better overwinter survival. During their aboveground cycle, meadow jumping mice are preyed on by a wide variety of terrestrial, aerial, and aquatic predators, including weasels, skunks, badgers, foxes, owls, hawks, snakes, and bullfrogs. Whitaker (1972) reviewed the literature on the species. Because the local subspecies, *Z. h. preblei*, is officially recognized as "threatened" under the US Endangered Species Act (ESA), the US Fish and Wildlife Service maintains a large archive of relevant references (http://www.fws.gov/mountain-prairie/species/mammals/preble/).

Zapus princeps

WESTERN JUMPING MOUSE

Description

The western jumping mouse strongly resembles the meadow jumping mouse. The dorsal surface is a yellowish gray and adults have a distinct blackish mid-dorsal patch. The venter is white and there is a pronounced yellowish to buffy lateral line. This species is somewhat larger in size than the meadow jumping mouse. Measurements are: total length 204–260 mm; length of tail 112–148 mm; length of hindfoot 27–33 mm; length of ear 13–17 mm; weight 19–37 g. The skull is larger and heavier and the molars are larger than those of *Zapus hudsonius*. The baculum resembles that of the meadow jumping mouse but is usually longer than 5.1 mm. For details on distinguishing Coloradan jumping mice, see M. Conner and Shenk (2003, 2005).

PHOTOGRAPH 8-31. Western jumping mouse (*Zapus princeps*). Photograph by Roger W. Barbour.

Distribution

The western jumping mouse occurs widely throughout the mountainous western two-thirds of the state, mostly along streams and in moist meadows from about 1,830 to 3,500 m (6,000 to 11,500 ft.). Because of potential co-occurrence with *Z. h. preblei* between 1,900 and 2,500 m elevation along the Front Range (R. A. Schorr, personal communication), care should be taken with identification. One subspecies, *Zapus princeps princeps*, occurs in Colorado. The type locality is Florida, La Plata County, Colorado.

Natural History

The western jumping mouse is an inhabitant of riparian communities at moderate to high elevations in Colorado, usually between 1,830 and 3,500 m (6,000 and 11,500 ft.). The species is most abundant in streamside alder, willow, and aspen stands with a well-developed understory of forbs and grasses (D. Armstrong 1977a, 1993). Montane riparian habitats protected from grazing supported higher populations of western jumping mice than did grazed areas (Schulz and Leininger 1991). Individuals also occur in bogs and marshes, and even occasionally on the fringes of dry meadows or sagebrush stands. Belk et al. (1988) studied habitat partitioning of montane habitats in Utah by deer mice, montane voles, red-backed voles, and western jumping mice and found significant differences in habitat, changes within season, and also between sexes within species, with females associated with more complex vegetation.

Because of their rather brief period of summer activity, these animals feed mostly on high-energy food sources that allow rapid deposition of fat in preparation for the

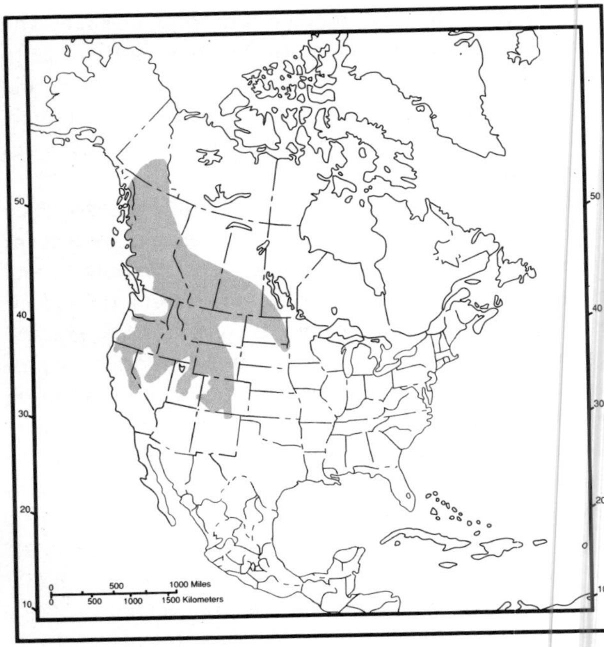

MAP 8-64. Distribution of the western jumping mouse (*Zapus princeps*) in North America.

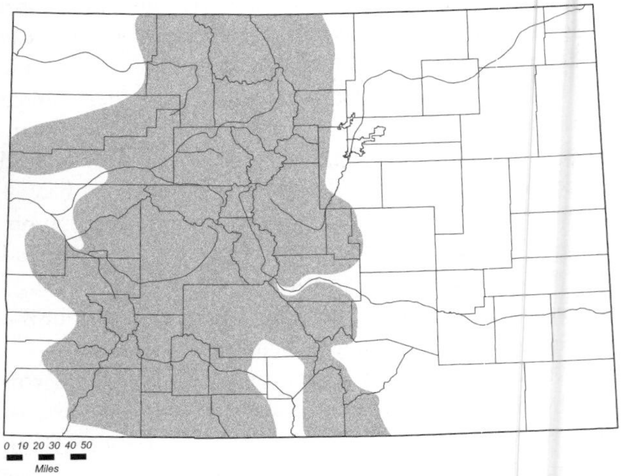

MAP 8-65. Distribution of the western jumping mouse (*Zapus princeps*) in Colorado.

next period of hibernation. Seeds and arthropods formed the bulk of the diet (40 and 33 percent, respectively) of animals on Rabbit Ears Pass, Colorado (T. Vaughan and Weil 1980), whereas 82 percent of the diet was seeds in Grand Teton National Park, Wyoming (T. Clark 1971b). Insects have sometimes been thought to be incidental food items. However, habitat conditions and competition with other vertebrates for seeds may affect optimal foraging and, at least locally, cause shifts toward increased consumption of insects (T. Vaughan and Weil 1980).

Western jumping mice breed during summer. Pregnant females have been captured in June and July, and lactating animals have been found into late August in southern Wyoming (L. N. Brown 1967a). The gestation period is about 18 days, with only 1 litter produced each year. Litter size ranges from 3 to 8 with an average of 5. A substantial proportion of females may not breed; L. N. Brown (1967a) reported that only 40 of 75 females examined showed signs of having bred in his study population in the Medicine Bow Mountains. Low fecundity may be a correlate of potentially great longevity. Perhaps because they are deep hibernators, western jumping mice are remarkably long-lived for small mammals, sometimes surviving 4 years or longer. Marked longevity is often associated with deep hibernation. A mammal that hibernates 8 or 9 months each year only "lives hard" about a quarter of its life.

Western jumping mice are most active at night but are occasionally seen in the daytime by anglers and others wandering along streambanks. Their season of aboveground activity is brief at high elevations, with estimates of 100 days on Rabbit Ears Pass (T. Vaughan and Weil 1980) and 87 days in the Wasatch Mountains of Utah (Cranford 1978). At lower elevations the animals may be aboveground an additional 30 or 40 days. Hibernacula used by the western jumping mouse in the Wasatch Mountains of Utah were typically 50 to 60 cm belowground where mean soil temperature was 4°C to 5°C. Nest chambers averaged 14 cm in diameter and were lined with dried plant materials, including bark, soft stems, leaves, and pine needles. The burrow entrance to such hibernacula was plugged with 15 to 30 cm of soil (Cranford 1978).

L. Myers (1969) reported an average home range of 3,075 m^2 for males and 2,350 m^2 for females at an elevation of 2,900 m (8,859 ft.) near Gothic, Gunnison County. Stinson (1977b) reported similar home ranges based on work in aspen forest at 2,900 m (9,650 ft.) in Boulder County. In that study, home ranges of males varied from about 300 to 3,300 m^2 and those of females were from 680 to 1,275 m^2. Females tended to exhibit more moderate territoriality and more uniform spacing than males. Population density estimates ranged from 28 to 35 per hectare in Boulder County (Stinson 1977b) to 3.2 animals per hectare in southeastern Wyoming (L. N. Brown 1970).

Contrary to studies of the meadow jumping mouse, Cranford (1978) found no correlation in Utah between increased fat deposition and either temperature or photoperiod; rather, fat deposition depended on availability of seeds. The onset of weight gain began about 1 month before the animals entered hibernation, and western jumping mice gained weight at an average rate of 0.65 g per day, with a maximum of 2.10 g per day. Up to two-thirds of the dry body weight can be in fat reserves, compared with one-half of the body weight for meadow jumping mice. Weight loss of hibernating western jumping mice averaged 0.07 g per day (Cranford 1978).

Annual mortality is probably very high as a result of both the rigor of hibernation and predation and disease. Data on predation are lacking but probably all terrestrial carnivores and most aerial ones are potential enemies.

Superfamily Muroidea—Rats, Mice, Lemmings, and Voles

The muroids are remarkably diverse, with some 1,518 species in 310 genera (D. Wilson and Reeder 2005). This is the largest superfamily of rodents and of mammals, including about two-thirds of all rodents and about a third of all extant mammals. The group encompasses a range of diets, dental adaptations, habits, habitats, locomotor modes, and reproductive patterns nearly as broad as the Rodentia as a whole. Muroids appear in the fossil record in the Late Eocene of China and the Early Oligocene North America. The dental formula is simple: 1/1, 0/0, 0/0, 3/3 = 16 teeth.

There is no consensus among systematists on the classification of this most diverse group of rodents. In the first edition of this work we included Coloradan species in 3 subfamilies within an inclusive family, Muridae (following Carleton and Musser 1984). For present purposes, we follow Musser and Carleton (2005) and arrange Coloradan rats and mice in 2 closely related families within the superfamily Muroidea. The native family Cricetidae includes some 25 Coloradan species of mice, rats, and voles. The Old World family Muridae is represented in Colorado by 2 introduced species, the Norway rat and the house mouse.

Family Cricetidae—Native Rats, Mice, and Voles

Cricetids are the largest family of New World rodents and the most important ecologically over most of North America. Because most species are primary consumers and many have high rates of reproduction, cricetids tend to be the most abundant mammals in Colorado's biotic communities, figuring prominently in energy flow. We discuss the 3 native subfamilies of Coloradan cricetids separately.

Key to Subfamilies of Cricetidae in Colorado

1. Skull with prominent supraorbital ridges; molars with sigmoidal lophs, dorsal fur harsh to the touch. . . . . .Subfamily Sigmodontinae: Hispid Cotton Rat—*Sigmodon hispidus*, p. 249

1' Skull without prominent supraorbital ridges; molars flat or cusped, but not as above; dorsal fur generally soft, not notably harsh. 2

2. Ears sparsely haired, usually conspicuous; skull not strongly constricted at level of rostrum (see Figure 8-8); body not notably stout, tail often as long or longer than head and body. . . . . Subfamily Neotominae, p. 216

2' Ears well haired but relatively inconspicuous; skull with braincase strongly constricted at level of rostrum (see Figure 8-6); body usually stout; tail shorter than head and body. . . . . Subfamily Arvicolinae, p. 195

Subfamily Arvicolinae: Voles, Meadow Mice, and Muskrat

Arvicolines are stocky, blunt-nosed, usually dark-colored rodents, mostly of small to medium size. The group includes about 151 species, arrayed in 28 genera (Musser and Carleton 2005). Previously, they were known as the Microtinae, or microtine rodents; many of the references cited herein will refer to them as such, and the informal name "microtine" doubtless will continue to be used for the group, especially by non-taxonomists. Our use of the name Arvicolinae follows Musser and Carleton (2005). Arvicolines are an important part of the vertebrate prey base and as such are important to energy flow in many biotic communities. A number of kinds of arvicolines experience pronounced population fluctuations and can reach high numbers in certain years. Arvicolines generally make a living at the interface of soil and vegetation, spending most of their time in runways and burrows. Unlike many neotomines, arvicolines are almost strictly herbivorous (except for the muskrat), feeding on green vegetation as long as it is available.

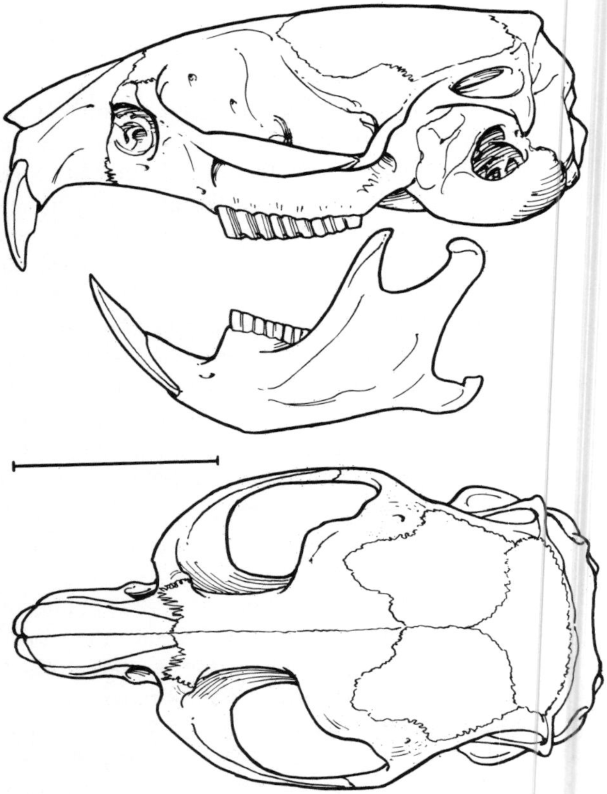

FIGURE 8-6. Skull of a representative arvicoline rodent (*Microtus pennsylvanicus*) showing the block appearance of the braincase. Scale = 1 cm.

Arvicolines have prismatic cheekteeth with deep infoldings of enamel and complex patterns of dentine. The skull is heavy and sharply angular with a stouter zygomatic arch than that of most neotomines. The braincase typically is constricted at the level of the rostrum, giving it a blocky appearance. The pinnae are typically small, well haired, but difficult to see because of the length of the general pelage. The tail is not as well haired as that of many neotomines and is often shorter than the length of the head and body. Five genera and 9 species of arvicolines live in Colorado. A sixth genus, *Synaptomys*, may eventually be discovered in the state. Coloradan arvicolines other than the muskrat are all categorized as non-game mammals (Table 4-1).

General biology of many of the voles occurring in Colorado was reviewed by M. L. Johnson and Johnson (1982), by Pugh et al. (2003), and in scholarly volumes edited by Merritt (1984) and Tamarin (1985). The latter 2 works include chapters on energetics and thermoregulation by Dr. Bruce A. Wunder (1984, 1985), a distinguished zoologist at Colorado State University who has spent many years working on the ecophysiology of various species of arvicoline rodents, often on Coloradan populations. Gaines (1985) summarized much of the work on the genetics of New World arvicolines.

Key to the Species of the Subfamily Arvicolinae in Colorado

1. Tail sparsely haired, scaly, laterally compressed; condylobasal length of skull more than 55 mm . . . . Common Muskrat—*Ondatra zibethicus*, p. 213

1' Tail haired, not scaly, round; condylobasal length of skull less than 35 mm 2

2. Cheekteeth rooted, height of crown decreases with wear 3

2' Cheekteeth ever-growing, height of crown maintained despite wear 4

3. Mid-dorsal fur reddish in color; palate terminates posteriorly as transverse shelf; inner reentrant angles of lower molars about equal in depth to outer reentrant angles . . . . Southern Red-backed Vole—*Myodes gapperi*, p. 196

3' Mid-dorsal fur grayish brown in color; palate with median spinous process, not terminating as transverse shelf; inner reentrant angles of lower molars deeper than outer reentrant angles . . . . Western Heather Vole—*Phenacomys intermedius*, p. 198

4. Tail short, as long as or slightly longer than hindfoot 5

4' Tail longer, obviously longer than hindfoot . . . . *Microtus*, 6

5. Tail slightly longer than hindfoot, sole of hindfoot densely haired; auditory bullae conspicuous dorsally; no obvious groove on face of upper incisor . . . . Sagebrush Vole—*Lemmiscus curtatus*, p. 211

5' Tail no longer than hindfoot, sole of hindfoot not densely haired; auditory bullae not conspicuous dorsally; well-developed groove on face of upper incisor . . . . . . Southern Bog Lemming—*Synaptomys cooperi*,* p. 215

6. Tail one-third or more total length . . . . Long-tailed Vole—*Microtus longicaudus*, p. 200

6' Tail less than one-third total length 7

7. Belly buff-colored; third upper molar with 4 dentine lakes (see Figure 8-7) . . . . Prairie Vole—*Microtus ochrogaster*, p. 206

7' Belly gray or whitish; third upper molar with 5 dentine lakes 8

8. Second upper molar with 4 dentine lakes and a rounded posterior loop (see Figure 8-7) . . . . Meadow Vole—*Microtus pennsylvanicus*, p. 209

8' Second upper molar with 4 dentine lakes but lacking a rounded posterior loop (see Figure 8-7) 9

9. Incisive foramina narrow and constricted posteriorly (see Figure 8-7); mammae 8; tail usually more than 36 mm . . . . . . Montane Vole—*Microtus montanus*, p. 204

9' Incisive foramina broad, short, truncated posteriorly (see Figure 8-7); mammae 4; tail usually less than 35 mm . . . Mogollon Vole—*Microtus mogollonensis*, p. 202

* Species of possible occurrence in Colorado.

Myodes gapperi

SOUTHERN RED-BACKED VOLE

Description

One of Colorado's most distinctive and attractive small mammals, the red-backed vole has a broad, reddish mid-dorsal stripe extending from forehead to tail. The background color is grayish brown. The belly is grayish with the bases of the hairs black. The bicolored tail is relatively long for an arvicoline but does not approach that of the long-tailed vole. The ears are short and partly hidden by the body fur. Measurements are: total length 125–152 mm; length of tail 33–44 mm; length of hindfoot 17–19 mm; length of ear 12–16 mm; weight 20–38 g. The skull resembles that of *Microtus*, with a blocky shape and prismatic cheekteeth, although the cheekteeth are different in that they are rooted (thus showing distinct patterns of wear), not rootless (hence ever-growing) as molars are in voles of the genus *Microtus*. The lower molars have inner and outer reentrant angles of about the same depth. The angles are generally opposite one another so that they nearly meet in the middle of the tooth. In *Microtus* and *Phenacomys*, by contrast, inner and outer reentrant angles of the lower molars

PHOTOGRAPH 8-32. Southern red-backed vole (*Myodes gapperi*). Photograph by Roger W. Barbour.

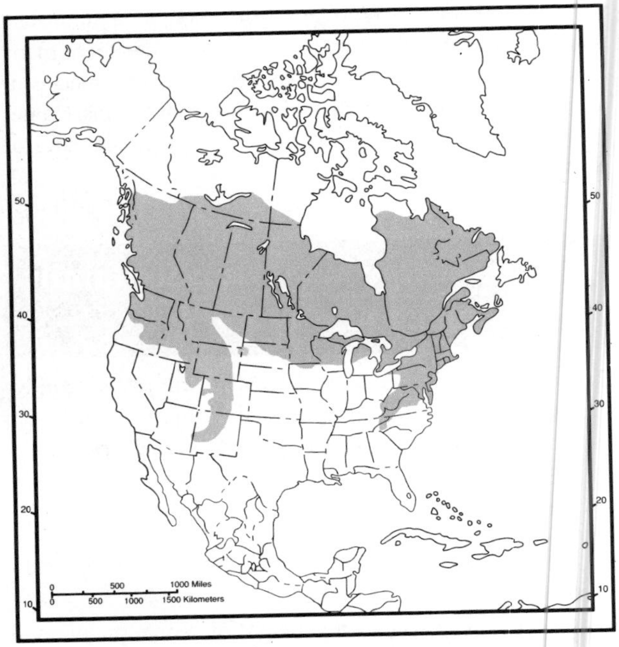

MAP 8-66. Distribution of the southern red-backed vole (*Myodes gapperi*) in North America.

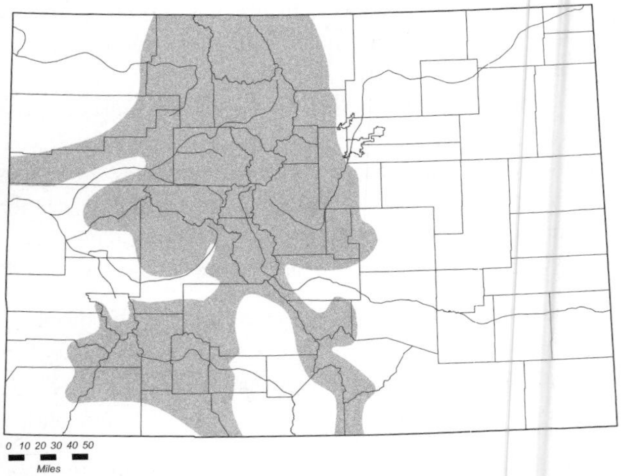

MAP 8-67. Distribution of the southern red-backed vole (*Myodes gapperi*) in Colorado.

are notably offset from each other. The palate ends at the level of M^3 in a simple transverse shelf with no posterior projection. Female have 4 pairs of mammae.

Generally we follow R. Baker, L. Bradley, et al. (2003) in matters of specific nomenclature, but Musser and Carleton (2005) argued convincingly that the traditional name for our red-backed vole, *Clethrionomys gapperi*, represents a long-standing nomenclatural error, and the proper generic name for these animals is *Myodes*. See Musser and Carleton (2005:1020) for details.

Distribution

Red-backed voles are found throughout the mountains of the state. *Myodes gapperi galei* is the subspecies of the central and northern mountains generally north of the upper Gunnison and Arkansas rivers; *M. g. gauti* is the subspecies in the mountains of the southern third of the state (Cockrum and Fitch 1952).

Natural History

Red-backed voles are mostly associated with mesic coniferous forests at middle elevations in Colorado, occurring in both upper montane and subalpine forests (O. Williams 1955a; D. Armstrong 1977b; Merritt and Merritt 1978a, 1978b). They are often common in mature lodgepole pine stands or in mixed spruce-fir forests with good cone production and an abundance of surface litter, including stumps, logs, and exposed roots of fallen trees. Nordyke and Buskirk (1988) found *M. gapperi* to be the best ecological indicator of old-growth conditions in spruce-fir stands in southeastern Wyoming. Red-backed voles were most abundant in old-growth spruce-fir forest with high understory coverage and downed timber in an advanced state of decay. Perhaps this relates to their dietary penchant for fungi. Condition of the voles in lodgepole forest was not as good as those living in spruce-fir timber (Nordyke and Buskirk 1991). In such habitats pine squirrels are often abundant and red-backed voles frequently use the middens of the squirrels for cover and as a source of fungi for food. Red-backed voles also are found in aspen woodlands, although such habitats are more often frequented by long-tailed and montane voles (D. Armstrong 1972, 1977b). Other habitats include subalpine meadows, riparian willow thickets, and krummholz.

Hadley and Wilson (2004b) found that red-backed voles were less dense on ski runs at Vail than on forested margins of ski runs; survival was greater on edges than in adjacent dense forest. Landscape-level studies (Keinath and Hayward 2003) of logged and adjacent undisturbed subalpine forests in the Medicine Bow Range of southeastern Wyoming showed that red-backed voles favored sites with greater overstory canopy and more coarse woody debris, and they avoided sites dominated by dwarf huckleberry (whortleberry—*Vaccinium scoparium*). Where disturbed (harvested) and undisturbed forests were paired, activity on disturbed plots was significantly lower. G. Hayward et al. (1999) showed that cutting patches (0.6–3.9 ha in size) did not have the detrimental effect that clear-cutting had on red-backed voles. The predilection of red-backed voles for forests with abundant coarse woody debris may be at odds with fire-prevention prescriptions that minimize such cover (Ucitel et al. 2003). If not considered in timber management plans, these population-level patterns could have significant community-level impacts on such forest predators as boreal owls (*Aeolius funereus*) and American martens.

Red-backed voles are opportunistic feeders, eating a variety of fungi, roots, bark, berries, other fruit, seeds, and leaves (O. Williams 1955c; Merritt and Merritt 1978a). Seed consumption increases in winter, and fungi are often favored in summer (O. Williams and Finney 1964). Red-backed voles drink more water than some other small rodents, and this may relate to their selection of mesic sites. Daily metabolism was calculated at 6.45 kilocalories (kcal)/day for voles averaging 19.1 g in body weight. Metabolic demand increases at a rate of 0.02 kcal/g/day for each degree below the thermoneutral point of 26°C (Merritt and Merritt 1978a).

Globular nests of grasses, mosses, and similar soft materials are constructed under suitable surface objects. Runways are not as well developed as in some other voles. Microhabitat studies (D. Armstrong 1977b; Belk et al. 1988; Wywialowski and Smith 1988) indicated strong affinity for situations with substantial ground cover or surface litter.

Red-backed voles are seasonally polyestrous with a postpartum estrus. The mating system is promiscuous. Gestation lasts about 18 days, with the length of the breeding season estimated to be about 7 months on Rabbit Ears Pass in Routt County (T. Vaughan 1969). On the Front Range the breeding season is at least 7.5 months. Animals begin to breed in late winter and continue to produce litters into late fall. Litter size ranges from 4 to 8, with an average of about 6 (T. Vaughan 1969; Merritt and Merritt 1978a). Females are reproductively mature at 3 to 4 months but most males do not breed until about 11 months of age. Young are naked, blind, and toothless at birth, weighing about 2 g. By day 4, skin pigmentation is developing rapidly and the animals have some sense of equilibrium. They are able to crawl by day 5. Body hair is developed by the end of the first week as the incisors erupt. Eyes open by 2 weeks of age, about the same time that they begin to eat solid food. Young usually are weaned by 3 weeks of age (Merritt 1981). Innes and Millar (1994) reviewed life history traits of *M. gapperi*.

Red-backed voles are active year-round, occupying home ranges of 0.01 to 0.50 ha. Density in Boulder County ranged from 2 to 48 animals per hectare, with highest numbers in late summer and early fall (Merritt and Merritt 1978a, 1978b; Merritt 1985). Fall freezes and spring thaws were times of greatest vulnerability. T. Vaughan (1969) estimated populations at fewer than 2.4 animals per hectare on Rabbit Ears Pass. The multi-year population cycles seen in several other arvicolines do not seem to occur in red-backed voles.

Red-backed voles are most active at dusk and at night during the warmer months. During winter the animals become more diurnal, as they are active under the snowpack (Merritt 1984). The animals reportedly are "shy" and "nervous" and individuals are not especially social. Some aggression is shown during male-male and female-female encounters but males and females get along well together and may share a nest. Females are sensitive when young are in the nest, and disturbance may result in cannibalism, abandonment, or movement of young. Longevity is usually 1 year or less, but some animals survive for up to 20 months (Merritt and Merritt 1978a).

Most mortality probably results from predation, fall freezes and spring thaws, and starvation during winter (Merritt 1984). A number of inconclusive and contradictory studies have been conducted on possible interspecific competition between this species and other small mammals, including the meadow vole and deer mouse (Merritt 1981). During the breeding season the red-backed vole may be able to displace other species from woodland habitats but in turn may be displaced from grassy areas. Merritt (1981) reviewed the literature on the species.

Phenacomys intermedius
WESTERN HEATHER VOLE

Description

The heather vole is a rather small vole with a tail only slightly longer than the hindfoot. The pelage is long and soft, almost shaggy, and dorsal color ranges from brown to grayish. The venter is silvery gray. The tail is bicolored, dark above and pale below, often with a sprinkling of white hairs over the dorsal surface. The feet are white to pale gray. Usually there are stiff, orangish brown hairs in the ears. Measurements are: total length 130–140 mm; length of tail 31–34 mm; length of hindfoot 16–19 mm; length of ear 13–17 mm; weight 30–50 g. The skull of adults is blocky with a square braincase and prominent supraorbital and lateral ridges. The palate does not end in a sharply transverse shelf as in *Myodes*. The cheekteeth are rooted and without cusps, similar in general occlusal appearance to the teeth of other voles. However, the molars of the lower jaw have inner (lingual) reentrant angles that are much deeper than the outer (buccal) reentrant angles, extending more than halfway across the tooth surface. The first lower molar has a variable number (3 to 7) of closed occlusal triangles (McAllister and Hoffmann 1988). Females have 4 pairs of mammae. Superficially the heather vole may closely resemble some smaller individuals of the montane vole, from which it can be separated by the rooted cheekteeth with their deep inner reentrant angles.

PHOTOGRAPH 8-33. Western heather vole (*Phenacomys intermedius*). Photograph by C. W. Schwartz / Animals Animals.

Distribution

The heather vole is known from scattered records throughout the higher mountains and plateaus of the state, but local distribution of the species is poorly known, perhaps because they are easily confused with more abundant arvi-

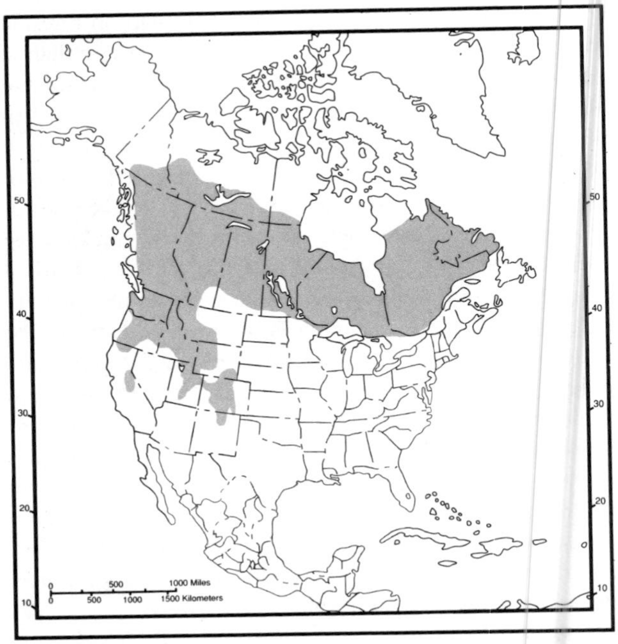

MAP 8-68. Distribution of the western heather vole (*Phenacomys intermedius*) in North America.

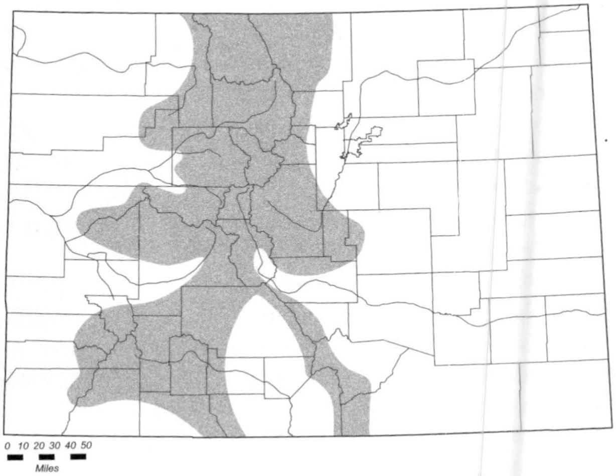

MAP 8-69. Distribution of the western heather vole (*Phenacomys intermedius*) in Colorado.

colines, such as the montane vole. Elevations of captured animals range from 2,130 m (7,000 ft.) to above timberline (D. Armstrong 1972). One subspecies, *Phenacomys intermedius intermedius*, occurs in Colorado.

Natural History

Although seemingly never particularly abundant, they are generally adaptable to a number of different habitats (Negus 1950). Heather voles occupy stands of spruce, fir, lodgepole, aspen, and ponderosa pine and grassy meadows in montane forests, subalpine forests, and alpine tundra. In Colorado they are most often associated with moist to seasonally dry areas close to water. D. Armstrong (1977b) found them most common in spruce and lodgepole forests with ground cover of heaths (such as huckleberry) such as frequently occur on glacial moraines.

Heather voles appear to be most active at night, foraging for green vegetation, bark of trees and shrubs, seeds, berries, and fungi (J. Foster 1961; O. Williams and Finney 1964). Their diet includes foliage and fruits of willows, myrtle blueberry, and snowberry; kinnikinnik (*Artcostaphylos uva-ursi*) may constitute the bulk of the diet locally. Bark of willow, birch, and blueberry; seeds; and lichens are important during fall, winter, and spring. The diet is broader than that of most *Microtus* and seems to include less abrasive plant materials. The animals store food (including fruits) in caches close to burrow entrances, which are used both summer and winter.

Heather voles are seasonally polyestrous. Most breeding occurs between May and September, with populations at higher elevations having a shorter season. Gestation is 19 to 24 days, and litter size is 2 to 9 with an average of 5 or 6. Overwintering females produce larger litters than do females having litters in their first summer. Halfpenny and Ingraham (1983) suggested that litters from Colorado are slightly larger than those of northern populations. Individual females probably do not have more than 3 litters per year. Young females are of breeding age in 4 to 6 weeks, with males not breeding until the following year. As with other mice, young are blind, naked, and helpless at birth. In Colorado, newborn animals gained on average 0.82 g per day. Incisors erupted at 1 week, eyes opened at about 15 days, and young walked at about 16 days of age (Halfpenny and Ingraham 1983).

Population biology of heather voles is poorly known. A number of authors have reported them as difficult to trap (O. Williams 1952; Pruitt 1954; S. Anderson 1959; T. Vaughan 1969), and livetrap mortality is high. Females show higher ratios of capture in traps than do males, although sex ratios at birth approximate 1:1. Density estimates from the Northern Rockies range from 0.5 to 10.0 animals per hectare, but such estimates may be affected by low trappability (McAllister and Hoffmann 1988).

Heather voles are active year-round. In summer they live in shallow burrow systems, usually less than 20 cm deep in the Northern Rockies (I. Cowan and Guiget 1956). Entrances usually are hidden by surface litter or overhanging vegetation. Nests are made of grasses and other dried vegetation, with a diameter of 10–15 cm. Winter nests reportedly have thicker walls and are better insulated. Winter nests under snow cover may be located on the surface of the ground in protected areas under shrubs, dead timber, or rock overhangs. Although most activity appears to be solitary, winter huddling by family groups is reported in Canada (Banfield 1974). Predators include American marten, long-tailed weasels (Quick 1951), and several species of owls and hawks. The literature on the species was reviewed by McAllister and Hoffmann (1988).

Genus *Microtus*—Voles

Five species of the Holarctic genus *Microtus* occur in Colorado. The genus is a perennial taxonomic challenge, in part because there appears to have been rapid speciation in the geologically recent past (in the Pleistocene, about 1.3 million years ago, according to Conroy and Cook 2000b), and many species are not strongly differentiated except by details of their cheekteeth. Further, there is no firm agreement on which closely related voles should be included as subgenera within *Microtus*, but the genus as construed by Musser and Carleton (2005) includes about 60 species, roughly a third of which are North American. Only 1 species (*M. oeconomus*, the tundra vole) occurs in both Eurasia and North America.

Not all Coloradan voles are in the genus *Microtus*; mice of 4 or 5 additional arvicoline genera also are called "voles." The common name "vole" is a shortening of volemouse, from the Norwegian *voll*, meaning "field." The generic name *Microtus* is derived from the Latin for "small ear," in reference to the fact that the pinnae are little if any longer than the dense, lax fur. Actually, the pinnae are not particularly short; rather, the hair is particularly long. These are, after all, mostly animals of northern forests, meadows, and tundra, habitats in which insulation against winter cold is at a premium.

General biology of many of the voles occurring in Colorado was reviewed by M. L. Johnson and Johnson (1982) and Pugh et al. (2003) and in scholarly volumes edited by Merritt (1984) and Tamarin (1985).

Microtus longicaudus

LONG-TAILED VOLE

Description

This is a fairly small-bodied, long-tailed vole, the tail greater than one-third the length of the head and body. Dorsal color is reddish brown to brownish gray interspersed with numerous black-tipped hairs. The ventral surface is gray to buff-gray. Measurements are: total length 174–196 mm; length of tail 53–68 mm; length of hindfoot 20–22 mm; length of ear 13–17 mm; weight 36–59 g. The skull is long and flattened with large, rounded auditory bullae. The first lower molar has a large anterior lake of dentine followed by 5 triangles and a crescent-shaped posterior prism. The second upper molar has 4 triangular prisms. By contrast, the meadow vole, which can approximate the size and even the tail length of the long-tailed vole, has 5 triangles on the second molar. Females have 4 pair of mammae. Judd and Cross (1980) described the karyotype of specimens from near Rustic, Larimer County.

Distribution

The long-tailed vole is a common mammal over the mountains and high plateaus of the western two-thirds of

PHOTOGRAPH 8-34. Long-tailed vole (*Microtus longicaudus*). Photograph by Roger W. Barbour.

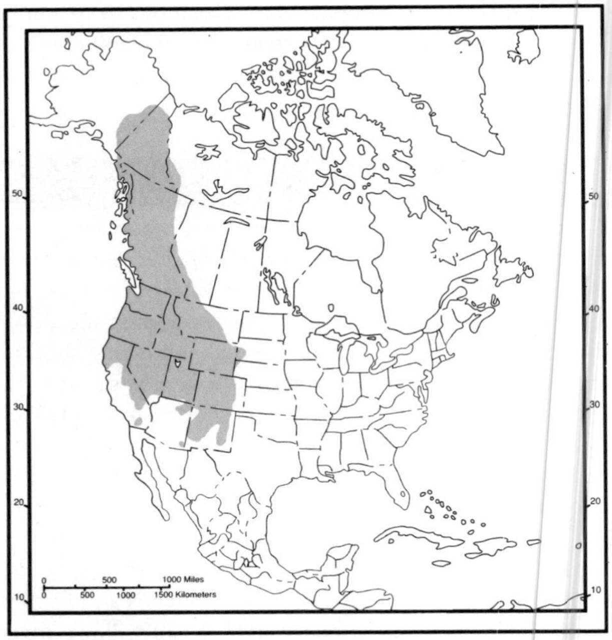

MAP 8-70. Distribution of the long-tailed vole (*Microtus longicaudus*) in North America.

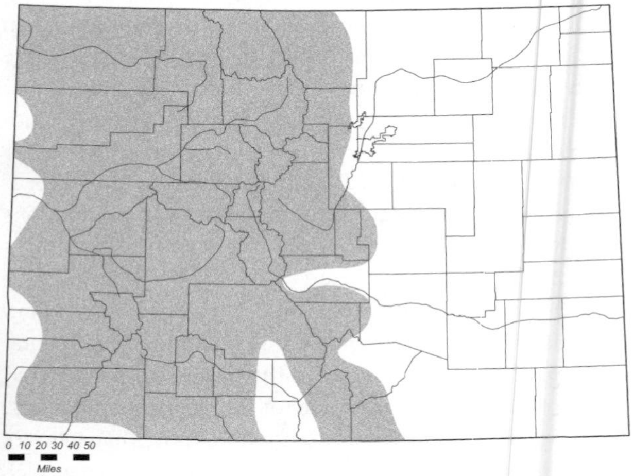

MAP 8-71. Distribution of the long-tailed vole (*Microtus longicaudus*) in Colorado.

Colorado. According to D. Armstrong (1972), one subspecies, *Microtus longicaudus longicaudus*, occurs in Colorado. However, Hoffmeister (1986) considered *M. l. mordax* to be the valid name for some populations from the Four Corners region (although Long [1965] considered *M. l. mordax* to be a synonym of *M. l. longicaudus*). R. Finley and Bogan (1995) suggested that subspecies of *M. longicaudus* are in need of review; a molecular phylogeographic study of the species would be of interest.

Natural History

Long-tailed voles are most often associated with marshy to dry grassy areas adjacent to water in the mountainous parts of the state. They seem to be especially abundant in aspen woodlands. They have a wide ecological tolerance (perhaps because they are poor competitors with other arvicolines, such as montane and meadow voles, or because they are not obligatory runway builders) and can be found in sedge-forb meadows on alpine tundra, subalpine meadows and forests, riparian willow and alder thickets, and even in grassy halophytic semidesert shrublands or beneath sagebrush in western Colorado. Fires or clear-cutting may favor this species, especially several years into succession (Van Horne 1982).

Long-tailed voles feed mostly on green vegetation, especially broad-leafed herbs, as well as on fruits and seeds. In winter, bark, buds, and twigs of most common trees and shrubs—including spruce, aspen, oakbrush, Oregon grape, and snowberry—are also consumed. Fescues, sedges, and yarrow are also commonly eaten. O. Williams and Finney (1964) reported the fungus *Endogone* in the diet in populations west of Boulder. Free water is probably utilized if available but does not appear to be required.

This vole breeds from mid-April or early May to October (Conley 1976). Most litters are born during late spring and summer. In the laboratory, mean litter size is about 5 and ranges from 1 to 7 (Colvin and Colvin 1970). Studies in Alaska suggest that few females have more than 2 litters in their lifetime and that most adults die in their first year of life (Van Horne 1982).

Long-tailed voles may be active both day and night and do not make well-defined runways. Nests of grass and stems of forbs are located underground or under surface litter. Greatest distance between captures (a rough index of home range) averaged 53 m in California. In Alaska, animals were mostly nocturnal and home ranges of males were larger than home ranges of females (Van Horne 1982). Long-tailed voles are less aggressive than montane and Mogollon voles. R. Finley et al. (1986), Randall and Johnson (1979), and others have suggested that long-tailed voles are displaced in the presence of more dominant species.

Densities of 5 and 120 animals per hectare have been reported in California (H. Jenkins 1948) and New Mexico (Conley 1976), respectively. Ten to 20 animals per hectare are probably typical for populations in good habitat when not undergoing major population fluctuations. Population dynamics have not been studied in detail, although both annual and possibly longer-term population cycles appear to occur in New Mexico (Conley 1976). Documentation of predation is poor, although several species of owls, prairie falcons (Marti and Braun 1975), weasels (C. Hayward 1949), and American martens are known predators. Literature on the long-tailed vole was reviewed by Smolen and Keller (1987).

Microtus mogollonensis

MOGOLLON VOLE

Description

This is a small, short-tailed vole with the tail less than 30 percent of the length of the head and body, usually less than 35 mm. The dorsal pelage is typically dark brown with the venter a buffy to ochraceous gray. The length of the hindfoot is usually less than 20 mm. Measurements are: total length 122–154 mm; length of tail 20–34 mm; length of hindfoot 16–21 mm; length of ear 13–16 mm; weight 28–32 g. The skull is short and broad with the zygomatic breadth usually greater than 60 percent of the condylobasal length. The last upper molar has 5 dentine lakes, similar to *Microtus pennsylvanicus* and *M. montanus*. Unlike *M. pennsylvanicus*, the second upper molar has only 4 dentine lakes

PHOTOGRAPH 8-35. Mogollon vole (*Microtus mogollonensis*). Photograph by R. B. Forbes.

with no posterior accessory loop. *M. mogollonensis* differs from *M. montanus* in having incisive foramina broad and rounded posteriorly rather than narrow or abruptly constricted posteriorly (see Figure 8-7). The jugal bone of the zygomatic arch is expanded and the posterior margin of the palate is notched or grooved. Females have only 2 pairs of mammae whereas other arvicolines in Colorado typically have 3 or more pairs. These animals can easily be confused with *Phenacomys intermedius* or *M. montanus* unless the skull is examined carefully.

Distribution

We follow J. Frey and Moore (1990) and J. Frey (2009) in recognizing the Mogollon vole as a species distinct from *M. mexicanus* (but see Musser and Carleton 2005:1006). Mogollon voles were first documented in Colorado (and reported as Mexican voles) at Mesa Verde (Rodeck and Anderson 1956). Reinterpretation of former collections (see discussion in the account of the montane vole) in the light of new collections (Mellott et al. 1987; C. Jones 2002) indicates that specimens of Mogollon voles have previously been misidentified and that the species may occur fairly regularly in southeastern Colorado (R. Finley et al. 1986) and rather widely in the southwestern part of the state as well (J. Frey et al. 2002). Mellott et al. (1987) reported the animals from the Spanish Peaks State Wildlife Area near Gulnare and Calisher. Mills et al. (2005) reported them (as *M. mexicanus*) on the US Army's Piñon Canyon Maneuver Site in Las Animas County. Studies in New Mexico (Findley et al. 1975) suggested that the species has made significant range expansions in recent times, and that may be the case in Colorado as well. The subspecies of Colorado is *M. m. mogollonensis*.

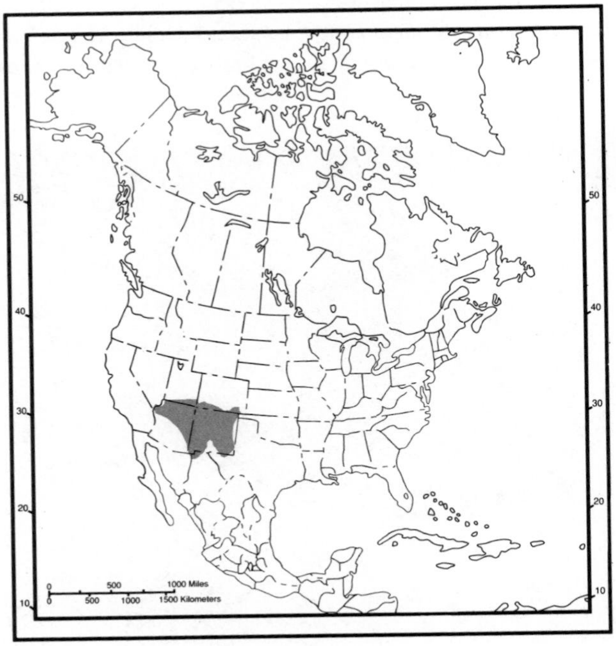

MAP 8-72. Distribution of the Mogollon vole (*Microtus mogollonensis*) in North America.

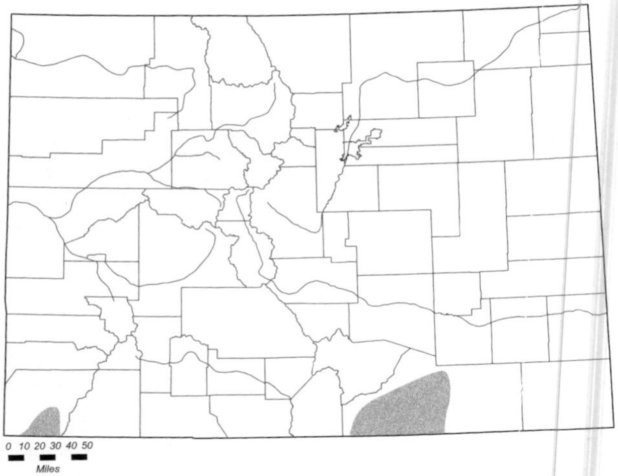

MAP 8-73. Distribution of the Mogollon vole (*Microtus mogollonensis*) in Colorado.

Natural History

This arvicoline is little studied in Colorado. The Mogollon vole appears to favor sites with abundant grass but drier than habitats of other Coloradan voles. It usually occurs in ponderosa pine woodland or savannah, piñon-juniper woodlands, or montane shrublands. However, observations in Colorado (R. Finley et al. 1986; J. Frey et al. 2002; C. A. Jones 2002), New Mexico (R. Finley et al. 1986), and Arizona (Hoffmeister 1986) suggest that it can survive in a wide variety of habitats, including dense mid-grasses, riparian areas, sagebrush, the lower margins of spruce-fir forests, and forest-meadow ecotones. Mellott et al. (1987) found the species in a wider range of habitats than meadow voles in the Spanish Peaks area, including meadows, riparian areas, and disturbed areas (beneath a woodpile in cleared forest and in grass under a mobile home). It apparently is not uncommon to have Mogollon, long-tailed, and meadow voles in the same general areas at higher elevations in southeastern

Colorado, with the long-tailed vole perhaps being displaced by the Mogollon vole (R. Finley et al. 1986). As estimated from stable isotope analysis of hair samples, the diet of Mogollon voles in northern Arizona was selective, the animals utilizing the more readily digestible C_3 ("cool season") grasses more than the more abundant, drought-adapted C_4 grasses (C. Chambers and Doucett 2008). R. Davis and Callahan (1992) argued that the present distribution of *M. mogollonensis* is in part a result of recent dispersal, not just Pleistocene vicariance.

Little is known about reproduction in the species. B. L. Keller (1985) listed it as a seasonal breeder. In New Mexico, Conley (1976) reported breeding from May through November. Data from Arizona suggest that females breed from April through August, with lower litter size than typical for most arvicolines (L. N. Brown 1968). Litter size ranges from 1 to 4 (mean, 2.2–2.5), in keeping with the small number of mammae. Mean embryo counts in northeastern Arizona (B. Hilton 1992) were 2.2, greater in summer (2.5) than in winter (2.0). Breeding was not observed under snow cover. J. Frey and Moore (1990) described morphologic variation by sex and age.

Annual fluctuations ranged from 15 to 50 animals per hectare in New Mexico, but the animals are thought not to exhibit cyclical populations. Mogollon voles in Arizona maintain 2 peaks of activity, one during the middle of the day and the other in early evening. Predators are probably similar to those of other voles and thus include snakes and most avian and mammalian carnivores.

Microtus montanus

MONTANE VOLE

Description

The montane vole is a medium-sized vole with a tail less than 40 percent of the length of the head and body. The dorsal color is grayish brown to brownish yellow. The venter is silver-gray with white-tipped, black hairs. The tail is indistinctly bicolored. Measurements are: total length 140–182 mm; length of tail 34–62 mm; length of hindfoot 17–22 mm; length of ear 11–18 mm; weight 35–60 g. The skull is stout with a square braincase. The last upper molar has 5 dentine lakes, the second molar has 4, and the incisive foramina are narrow and constricted posteriorly (see Figure 8-7). The posterior edge of the premaxillaries does not extend beyond the posterior margins of the nasals. Females have 4 pairs of mammae.

PHOTOGRAPH 8-36. Montane vole (*Microtus montanus*). Photograph by Roger W. Barbour.

Distribution

The montane vole is found throughout the mountains of Colorado and locally is quite common, from about 1,830 m (6,000 ft.) in elevation to well above tree line. Dalquest (1975) reported the species from Raton Pass, Las Animas County, and Mellott and Choate (1984) published new records from 32 km northwest of Trinidad. However, a review by R. Finley et al. (1986) corrected the identification of specimens from those studies, recognizing them as *M. mexicanus* (subsequently relegated to *M. mogollonensis*; see J. Frey and Moore 1990). Thus, to date, no records of montane voles are known from Colorado south of the Arkansas River and east of the Sangre de Cristo Range. *Microtus montanus fusus* occurs in the southwestern and south-central mountains, generally south of the Colorado River; *M. m. nanus* occurs in the mountainous northern portion of the state, generally north of a line from about Glenwood Springs to Pikes Peak (S. Anderson 1954).

Natural History

Montane voles generally occupy moist to wet habitats with thick grass or forb cover, including aspen stands. They also occur in drier grasslands with forbs and sagebrush, but usually in lower numbers (D. Armstrong 1977b). Typically they are found close to water, although in winter they may move farther away by using tunnels under the snow. *Microtus montanus* responded to spring flooding on the lower Yampa River in Dinosaur National Monument by moving to higher ground. That was not invariably to uplands, however, so the refuge sometimes was a temporary island that eventually was inundated (D. C. Andersen and Cooper 2000).

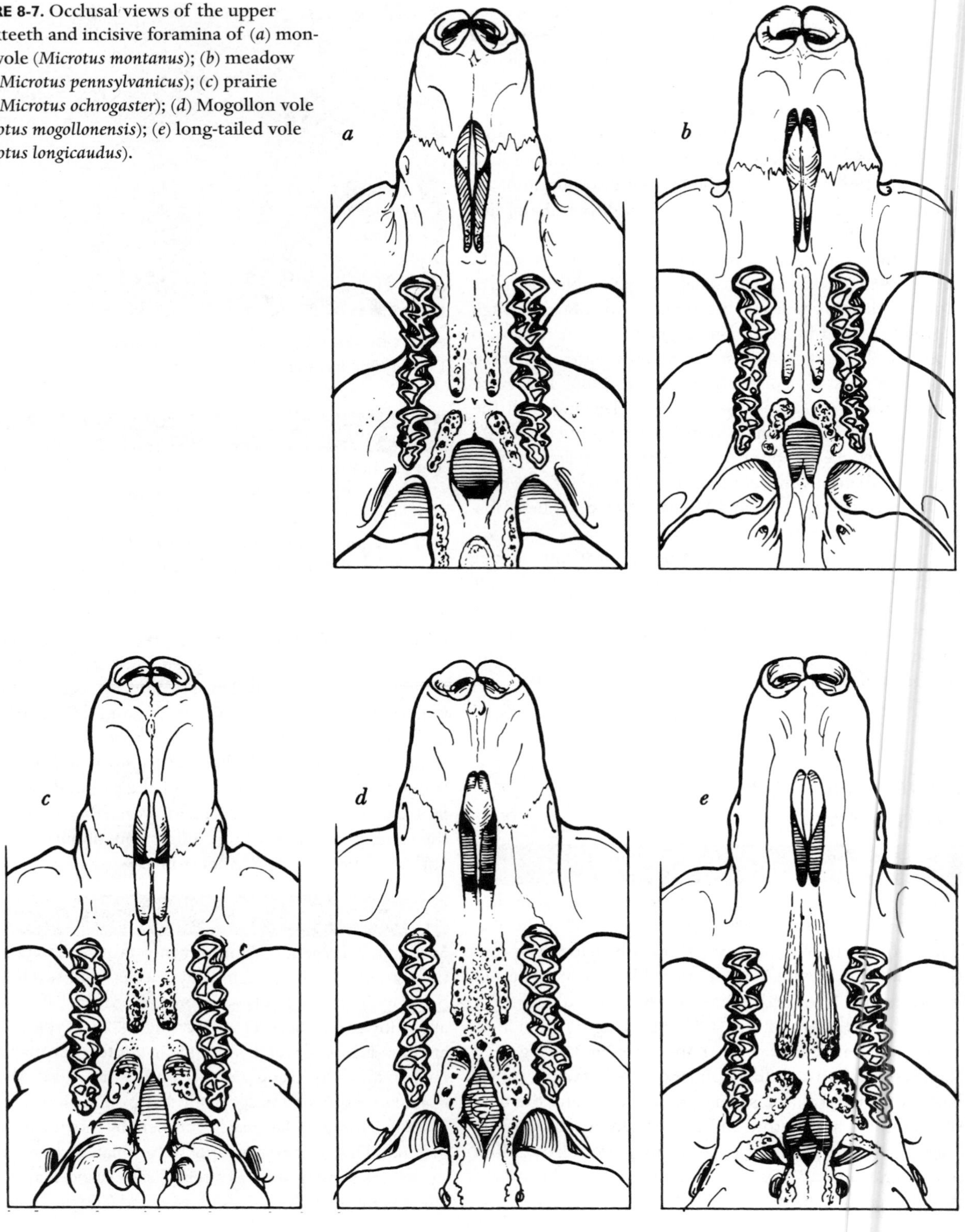

FIGURE 8-7. Occlusal views of the upper cheekteeth and incisive foramina of (*a*) montane vole (*Microtus montanus*); (*b*) meadow vole (*Microtus pennsylvanicus*); (*c*) prairie vole (*Microtus ochrogaster*); (*d*) Mogollon vole (*Microtus mogollonensis*); (*e*) long-tailed vole (*Microtus longicaudus*).

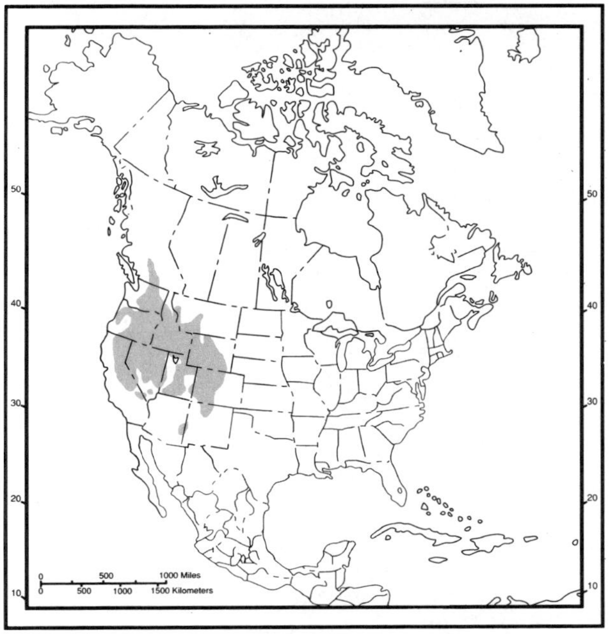

MAP 8-74. Distribution of the montane vole (*Microtus montanus*) in North America.

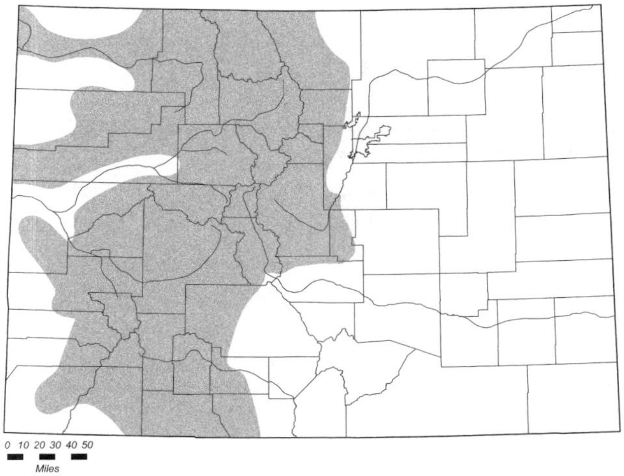

MAP 8-75. Distribution of the montane vole (*Microtus montanus*) in Colorado.

Montane voles are highly selective feeders; 5 plant species (*Oenothera minor*—evening primrose, *Vicia americana*—vetch, *Agoseris glauca*—false dandelion, *Collomia linearis*, and *Arnica* sp.—arnica) constituted nearly 70 percent of the diet. Summer food consists mostly of leaves of forbs (80 percent) but also includes grasses and sedges (9 percent) and fungi (3 percent) (T. Vaughan 1974). Grasses, bark, and twigs may become more important in winter after forbs have become less palatable. Foraging by *M. montanus* reduced survivorship of cottonwood (*Populus deltoides*) seedlings and saplings along the regulated Green River in Dinosaur National Monument but not on the nearby unregulated Yampa, where spring floods apparently preclude establishment of herbaceous understory and high populations of montane voles (D. C. Andersen and Cooper 2000). Seeds are not utilized to any extent (T. Vaughan 1974).

Montane voles construct well-developed runways and may be active at any time of day or night. They build a globular underground or surface nest of grass, about 13 cm in diameter, with 2 entrances, in a shallow burrow system (Jannett 1982). In sagebrush steppe in southeastern Idaho, burrows of *M. montanus* averaged 21.1 cm deep (Laundré and Reynolds 1993). Details of subnivean tunnels and food caches on the alpine tundra were provided by J. Benedict and Benedict (2001); some 887 tuberous roots of pygmy bitterroot (*Oreobroma pygmaea*) totaling 141 g were cached at 4 locations under snowpack.

Montane voles are polygynous except at low densities, when they may be monogamous by default. They do not form pair-bonds. Breeding montane voles are territorial, although male and female territories exhibit some overlap (Jannett 1980). They probably reproduce from April to October in Colorado. Breeding sometimes occurs in winter under the snow (Jannett 1980). Litter size averages about 6 with a range of 2 to 10. Females are polyestrous with a postpartum estrus. Ovulation is induced; gestation takes about 21 days (T. Vaughan 1969; B. L. Keller 1985). At low population densities, females abandon the brood nest when the young are about 15 days old. At high densities, females remain at the nest and are tolerant of the young, allowing offspring from at least 2 litters to nest with her. Adults maintain separate nests and paternal care of young is nonexistent under natural conditions (McGuire and Novak 1986).

Young montane voles breed first in the year of their birth. Survival rates of early summer litters, and their young produced at the end of the breeding season, are important in determining the size of populations in the fall (T. Vaughan 1969). Large litter size and relatively few litters per year are adaptations to the constraints of a short growing season. As with other arvicolines, populations can show large fluctuations, often in 3- to 4-year cycles. On Rabbit Ears Pass, variation in densities from less than 1 to more than 30 animals per hectare were found during a 3-year study (T. Vaughan 1974). However, studies in marshland adjacent to the Great

Salt Lake in Utah over a 9-year period showed no dramatic crashes (Negus et al. 1986).

Predators include coyotes, weasels, kestrels, Swainson's and red-tailed hawks, and great horned owls (Jannett 1984). In habitats optimal for meadow voles, montane voles were excluded, but the montane vole has broader ecological tolerances (Stoecker 1970). More research is needed on factors regulating the distributional patterns and interactions of Coloradan voles. A review of the literature on montane voles was provided by Sera and Early (2003).

Microtus ochrogaster

PRAIRIE VOLE

Description

This is a fairly large vole with a gray-brown to reddish brown dorsum and a pale buffy to grayish buff belly. The buffy venter separates it readily from other voles in Colorado, all of which have grayish or silvery gray bellies. Measurements are: total length 150–190 mm; length of tail 33–45 mm; length of hindfoot 20–23 mm; length of ear 11–15 mm; weight 50–75 g. The bicolored tail is short relative to that of other voles of eastern Colorado, typically less than 30 percent of the length of head and body. The skull is similar to others of the genus, although the third lower molar has 3 loops of dentine and no closed triangles (see Figure 8-7). The last upper molar has 4 dentine lakes somewhat similar to the pattern of the sagebrush vole, described below. The posterior margins of the premaxillary extend beyond the margins of the nasals. Females have 6 mammae.

PHOTOGRAPH 8-37. Prairie vole (*Microtus ochrogaster*). © 1993 Wendy Shattil / Bob Rozinski.

Distribution

The prairie vole is locally common in suitable habitat along the lower South Platte and Republican rivers. It has recently been reported also from several sites in southeastern Colorado (A. Carey 1978; M. Reed and Choate 1988) and adjacent states (McCaffrey et al. 2003). *Microtus ochro-*

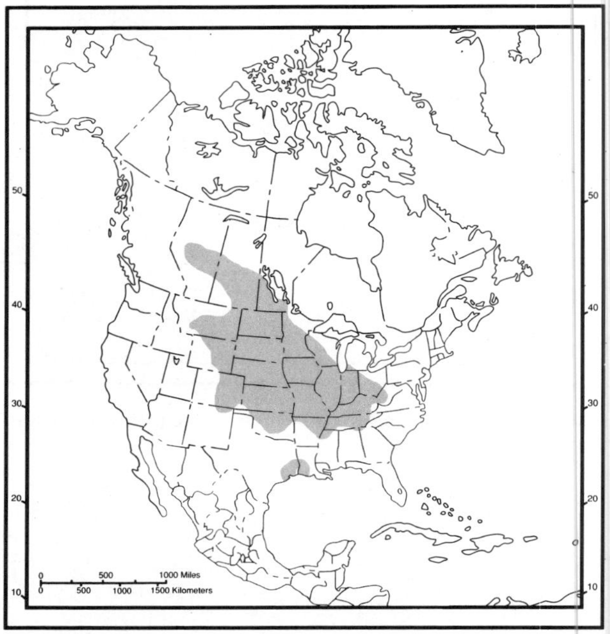

MAP 8-76. Distribution of the prairie vole (*Microtus ochrogaster*) in North America.

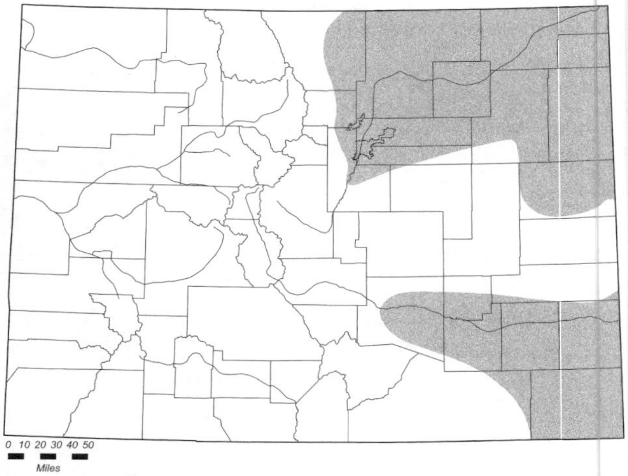

MAP 8-77. Distribution of the prairie vole (*Microtus ochrogaster*) in Colorado.

gaster haydenii may be the only subspecies in Colorado. *M. o. taylori* is a subspecies named from southwestern Kansas and known from within a few miles of the Colorado border near Holly. That subspecies has been reported as extirpated at the type locality (J. Choate and Williams 1978). Whether it now exists (or existed historically) in Colorado is not known.

Natural History

As the name implies, the prairie vole is adapted to the grasslands of interior North America. In northeastern Colorado it inhabits upland swales, grassy areas, edges of irrigation ditches and fencerows, and even the fringes of wooded riparian habitat consisting of open stands of willow and cottonwood (W. Archibald 1963; Cruzan 1968; R. Mitchell 1972; J. Fitzgerald 1978; Moulton, Choate, and Bissell 1981; Moulton, Choate, et al. 1981). In the foothills of north-central Colorado, the animals occupy patches of relict mixed and tallgrass prairie and the grassy understory of shrublands (D. Armstrong, unpublished). In southeastern Colorado the prairie vole has been reported from sage-grassland, grass-forb, and shrub-woodland communities (A. Carey 1978; K. Reed and Choate 1988). Prairie voles and meadow voles are broadly sympatric over a substantial area in northeastern Colorado; generally, prairie voles occupy mixed prairie on drier sites, whereas meadow voles occupy more mesic habitats. In Illinois, Tazik and Getz (2007) noted what they termed "interspecific territoriality" between the 2 species in sympatry in areas of habitat suitable for both species. Prairie voles were the most abundant small mammals on tallgrass plots and hayfields near Boulder (Bock et al. 2002); deer mice were more abundant than prairie voles on drier mixed grasslands.

In dense vegetation, well-developed, extensive runway systems are formed, but such trails are not always conspicuous on drier sites. The number of runways is positively correlated with vole density (D. Carroll and Getz 1976). The animals construct shallow (usually less than 10 cm) burrow systems in friable soils, using such burrows as shelters from which to make periodic foraging expeditions. Nests, constructed to 30 cm deep in the burrow system, are of grasses, shredded bark, and similar materials and may include large amounts of stored food, including seeds and roots. If vegetation is dense, the species will use surface grass nests located in depressions or sheltered by surface objects. Prairie voles are active at all times of the year and at any time of day, although most activity in the warm summer months occurs at dusk or at night.

Prairie voles feed on stems, leaves, and underground parts of a wide variety of plants. Grasses are common food items, but laboratory studies indicate that prairie voles cannot survive on a strict grass diet (Batzli and Cole 1979). They also feed on the bark of trees and shrubs. Arthropods can be important food items, especially in late summer. Food caches of seeds, cuttings, and roots are often stored in burrow systems.

Prairie voles are more social than most other species of *Microtus* (J. A. Thomas and Birney 1979; Getz et al. 1986; Getz et al. 2003). They are monogamous, noteworthy because only about 12 percent of mammalian species are monogamous (Eisenberg 1981). Social groups are formed by the addition of the offspring and other non-related adults (Getz and Carter 1980; Getz, Solomon, and Pizzuto 1990; Carter et al. 1995). Mates form strong pair-bonds and both parents assist in rearing young and in maintaining trails and burrows; both males and females tend to remain solitary if "widowed" (Getz and Carter 1996). In Illinois, prairie voles live in pairs from spring to early autumn, when snake predation is prevalent, but from autumn to early spring (when snakes are in hibernation) communal nests of 20 or more individuals are formed (Mankin and Getz 1994). Whether such seasonal change occurs in Colorado, at the western extreme of the species' geographic range, is unknown. Home ranges average about 0.10–0.25 ha, decreasing in size with increased population size and/or herb production. Home ranges of family units overlap and aggression associated with territoriality may be shown around the nesting burrows (Getz 1962). Home ranges of males were significantly larger than those of females in northeastern Kansas (Swihart and Slade 1989).

The animals are polyestrous, with breeding occurring throughout the year, although prevalence of pregnant females declines in the colder winter months. In the extremely hot, dry weather of mid-summer, breeding may also taper off. Peaks of breeding activity seem to coincide with increased precipitation during the growing season. Females must be near males to come into estrus. They exhibit postpartum estrus; induced ovulation occurs about 10 hours after copulation. Gestation takes about 21 days and the young are born naked and blind. Litters probably average 3 to 4 young with a range of 1 to 7. Infant mice of a number of species are known to produce ultrasonic distress calls when they are cooled. B. Blake (2002) compared ultrasonic calling in montane voles and prairie voles and found that infants of the latter species called much more. She attributed this to the monogamy of prairie voles and the fact that one of the parents tends to be nearby. Excessive calling by young of other species could be a disadvantage because the mother might be too far away to respond but predators could pick up the ultrasonic cue.

Young grow rapidly, gaining 0.6 to 0.8 g per day, and are weaned by about 4 weeks of age. Suppression of growth and reproductive maturity occurs as long as the young remain in the family group; dispersal is necessary for full maturation. Young female prairie voles can breed at about 5 weeks of age when two-thirds grown. Males reach sexual maturity 1 or 2 weeks later. The electronic Small Body Composition Analyzer is available commercially. Voltura and Wunder (1998) conducted studies to determine the efficacy of the device on prairie voles and found that it was useful for laboratory animals with moderate to high levels of body fat but inadequate for wild-caught animals with low levels of body fat.

The cyclic populations that typify several species of arvicolines have not been reported from Colorado, although populations do fluctuate widely in sites of known occurrence. Based on studies that included data on *M. ochrogaster* from the Pawnee Site of the International Biological Program (on the Central Plains Experimental Range northeast of Nunn, Weld County), Birney, Grant, and Baird (1976) suggested that a critical threshold of plant cover is necessary for vole cycles to occur and Coloradan grasslands do not meet that threshold under natural conditions. Long-term research in some areas suggests that prairie voles generally are not characterized by years of cyclical peaks and declines but rather have annual peaks of population highs and lows (Abramsky and Tracy 1979). In other studies, cycle intervals of 2 to 4 years have been noted. Reasons for population cycles are poorly understood but may be associated with disease, quality of foods, or physiological responses to subtle environmental changes. Survival of early juveniles and females were the best predictors of population growth in Kansas, where a 2-year cycle occurred during a 4-year study (Gaines and Rose 1976). Laboratory studies indicate that parental care by experienced mothers is more intensive and effective than that of primiparous (first-litter) females and that offspring of multiparous mothers developed more rapidly and had a higher survival rate. Experience of fathers showed no such effect (Wang and Novak 1994).

Prairie voles are short-lived, with mortality of adults during the breeding season ranging from 20 to 70 percent per month. Mortality in winter decreases to less than 50 percent. Captive voles have lived 16 months; in the wild few live more than 1 year. All of the small to medium-sized carnivores prey on these voles, with birds of prey being particularly effective. Stalling (1990) reviewed the literature on the species.

Microtus pennsylvanicus

MEADOW VOLE

Description

This is a fairly large, dark-colored vole with a gray to silvery belly. Dorsal color is usually dark gray-brown to chestnut. The tail is bicolored and scantily haired. The tail is longer than that of most prairie voles but relatively shorter than in the long-tailed vole. The ears are rounded and inconspicuous beneath the long fur of the head. Younger animals are typically darker in color than are older individuals. Measurements are: total length 155–192 mm; length of tail 35–67 mm; length of hindfoot 20–24 mm; length of ear 11–18 mm; weight 35–75 g. Females have 4 pairs of mammae. The skull is similar to that of other members of the genus, and identification is based on characters of the occlusal surface of the rootless cheekteeth. The second upper molar has 4 dentine lakes plus a rounded posterior loop. The last upper molar has 5 rounded dentine lakes (see Figure 8-7). The premaxillaries do not extend past the posterior margins of the nasals and the nasals are rounded posteriorly. The incisive foramina are long and relatively narrow, showing only slight expansion anteriorly.

Distribution

Meadow voles are locally common in favorable habitat. Their distribution in Colorado is discontinuous, perhaps a

PHOTOGRAPH 8-38. Meadow vole (*Microtus pennsylvanicus*). © 1993 Wendy Shattil / Bob Rozinski.

MAP 8-78. Distribution of the meadow vole (*Microtus pennsylvanicus*) in North America.

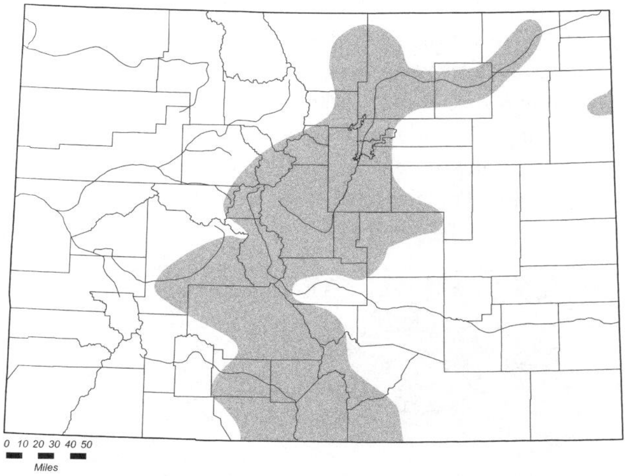

MAP 8-79. Distribution of the meadow vole (*Microtus pennsylvanicus*) in Colorado.

remnant of a more nearly continuous range in cooler, wetter glacial times just a few millennia past. *Microtus pennsylvanicus finitis* is restricted to the Republican watershed in Yuma County; *M. p. modestus* occurs in the mountains and parklands of south-central Colorado, including the wetlands of the San Luis Valley; *M. p. uligocola* occurs along the South Platte River to its headwaters in South Park (S. Anderson 1956).

Natural History

The meadow vole has the widest distribution of any species of *Microtus* and its biology has been studied extensively in eastern North America. The meadow vole is invariably associated with moist habitats. In mountainous areas it requires moist to wet meadows or bogs with dense cover of grasses, forbs, rushes, or sedges. On the eastern plains and along the foothills it is most common in marshy wetlands along riparian corridors. Ecology and competitive interactions between this and other *Microtus* species have been studied locally (Cruzan 1968) and more generally (Koplin and Hoffmann 1968). When found in association with other voles, the meadow vole typically occupies the wetter areas. The prairie vole replaces it in drier habitats of the eastern plains, whereas long-tailed and montane voles may replace it in drier montane habitats (Douglass 1976).

As with other voles, the food is largely green plant material during the warmer months. Clover, alfalfa, and dandelions are readily consumed. During winter, dried grass and herbaceous matter, bark, twigs, and buds are eaten. The animals build winter food caches. Meadow voles tend to eat more grasses and sedges than do other voles, in keeping with the moist environments they occupy.

Meadow voles are active year-round at any time of the day or night, with diurnal activity increasing under dense cover and during the winter when snow covers and protects the runway. Runways littered with grass clippings lead between nests and foraging areas. Nests are globular, built of grass and similar materials. The nest may be located in a protected area on the surface or contained within the burrow. Meadow voles swim readily, and in very wet areas they tend to build their nests on high points of ground or in well-drained clumps of grass.

Meadow voles can breed year-round but probably most success in Colorado occurs during the spring, summer, and early fall. Breeding males are attracted to estrous females and compete for mating opportunities. Females are polyestrous, with a postpartum estrus. Ovulation is induced by copulation and gestation takes 21 days. As with other arvicolines, the young are born naked, blind, and helpless. Litter size ranges from 1 to 11 with an average of 4 to 6 (B. L. Keller 1985). Females of large body size have the largest litters. Size of litters seems not to be correlated statistically with latitude or elevation, but summer litters are 10 to 14 percent larger than those produced at other seasons.

Young meadow voles grow rapidly, reaching weaning age by 2 weeks and breeding age by about 6 weeks.

Individuals are solitary and intolerant of conspecifics. Males are particularly aggressive when in reproductive condition or when populations are high (Getz 1960, 1962). Vocalizations often accompany aggressive threats (C. Krebs 1970). Home ranges vary from about 160 to 3,500 m^2, with home ranges of males being larger than those of females (Van Vleck 1969). Home ranges decrease in size when populations are high and during the winter. Individuals (especially males) often shift home ranges. Within the home range, actual territories (areas defended against conspecifics) are small, roughly 7 m in diameter (Getz 1961).

Populations cycle in numbers both seasonally and every 2 to 5 years. Densities during population peaks sometimes reach hundreds of individuals per hectare. At low points in the cycle, densities may be only a few animals per hectare. Cycles have been associated with a variety of causes, including food quality, predation, local climate, physiological stress, and genetically driven behaviors (C. Krebs and Myers 1974). Some individuals in populations disperse readily, perhaps an adaptation to environments where suitable habitat is limited and discontinuous. Dispersing individuals differ in genetics and behavior from sedentary voles (C. Krebs 1970). The general cycle of multi-annual cycles of abundance of various species of voles has been the subject of much research resulting in a vast and sometimes contentious literature. For example, based especially on studies of the California vole, *Microtus californicus*, Lidicker (1988) proposed a multi-factorial perspective on the "enigma" of microtine population cycles. Gaines et al. (1991) criticized that model on both zoological and epistemological grounds. Nearly 2 decades later, zoologists continue to puzzle over the mechanisms for the sometimes dramatic changes over time in many populations of voles.

Mortality is high with few animals living to 1 year of age and juvenile mortality often close to 90 percent. Mean survival time of adults averages about 8 to 10 weeks, with adult females surviving slightly longer than males. Most aerial or terrestrial predators—including owls, hawks, bitterns, snakes, coyotes, foxes, weasels, and even short-tailed shrews—prey on meadow voles, especially when populations of the rodents are high. Meadow voles were the most frequent of 26 species of mammals identified from food remains in nests of red-tailed hawks (*Buteo jamaicensis*) in Boulder County (Blumstein 1989). Reich (1981) reviewed the literature on the species. The abundant and dispersed literature on voles in general was reviewed by Pugh et al. (2003). Much of Tamarin's (1985) comprehensive, technical review volume on North American species of *Microtus* is devoted to the biology of the widespread and often abundant meadow vole.

Lemmiscus curtatus

SAGEBRUSH VOLE

Description

The sagebrush vole is a small, distinctly short-tailed vole with dense, long, soft pelage. The dorsal pelage is buff-gray to gray with the sides paler in color. The venter is buff to silver-gray and the tail is indistinctly bicolored. Hairs are dark gray at their bases. The tail is well haired but short, only about as long as the hindfoot. The ears are small, averaging slightly more than half the length of the hindfoot. The posterior soles of the feet are well haired. Measurements are: total length 100–142 mm; length of tail 16–30 mm; length of hindfoot 14–18 mm; length of ear 9–16 mm; weight 17–38 g. The skull is generally similar to that of other arvicolines but has well-developed auditory bullae that extend back beyond the occipital condyles and hence are readily visible from above. The last upper and lower molars typically have only 4 dentine lakes, compared with the 5 present in other arvicolines in Colorado. The pattern of the lakes consists of anterior and posterior loops separated by 2 more or less triangular-shaped prisms. The inner and outer reentrant angles are about equal in depth. The molars are ever-growing. Females have 4 pair of mammae.

PHOTOGRAPH 8-39. Sagebrush vole (*Lemmiscus curtatus*). Photograph by Andrew Langford.

Distribution

Sagebrush voles are associated with shrublands in northwestern and north-central Colorado. They do not seem to be common in any locality but this may be in part because of lack of information. One subspecies, *Lemmiscus curtatus levidensis*, occurs in Colorado. For a number of years this animal was considered to represent a Holarctic genus, *Lagurus*—the steppe vole—and *Lemmiscus* was considered a subgenus. We follow Carleton and Musser (1984) in use of the generic name *Lemmiscus* for the uniquely American sagebrush vole.

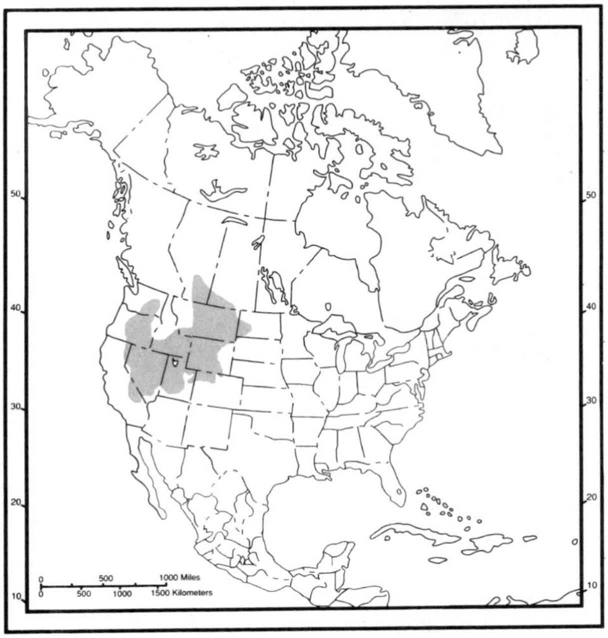

MAP 8-80. Distribution of the sagebrush vole (*Lemmiscus curtatus*) in North America.

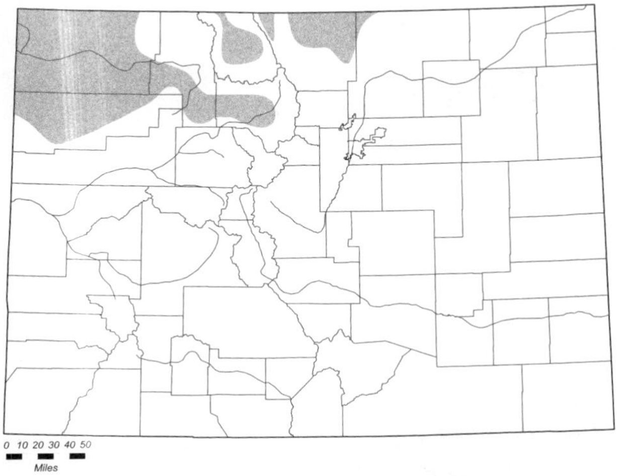

MAP 8-81. Distribution of the sagebrush vole (*Lemmiscus curtatus*) in Colorado.

Natural History

The species is aptly named; it is strongly tied with sagebrush and may be locally abundant on well-managed sagebrush-wheatgrass rangeland. It is also found in brushy canyon and hill country where sage, rabbitbrush, and wheatgrasses are common plant associates.

Sagebrush voles are strict herbivores, feeding on a variety of green vegetation, mostly grasses. Leaves and other softer tissues are consumed, but seeds (except for those of wheatgrass) are not typically eaten. Forbs and woody plants reported in the diet include greasewood, rabbitbrush, sage, winterfat, several species of mustard, lupine and other legumes, and several composites (F. Miller 1930; Maser et al. 1974). Legumes made up much of the stomach contents in a South Dakota study. Inflorescences, bark, and twigs of sagebrush are important in the winter months. Occasionally, sagebrush voles steal clippings accumulated by deer mice (Maser et al. 1974). Cut vegetation may be stored in loose piles near burrow entrances or along runways.

Sagebrush voles are active year-round at practically any time of the day. Most activity occurs during late afternoon and early nighttime hours. Activity also picks up around dawn. Runway systems are wider than those of *Microtus*, although typically not as distinct, because they are in areas with a sparser understory. The voles dig clusters of burrows with multiple entrances (range, 8 to 30), usually located at the base of shrubs, especially sagebrush. Burrow systems abandoned by pocket gophers are also utilized (F. Miller 1930; Warren 1942). Burrows, averaging about 45 mm in diameter, can go as deep as 46 cm and are littered with clippings of vegetation. Nest chambers are lined with leaves and stems of grasses and have multiple entrances (Deardon 1969). Snow tunnels are used in winter and are marked by cuttings of vegetation at irregular intervals. Fecal material is often deposited in scat piles along runway systems but not in the underground burrow system.

Sagebrush voles occur singly or in pairs. During the breeding season a mated pair shares a nest and continues to do so after young are born. However, the male does not participate actively in the care of the young (Mullican and Keller 1986; Hofmann et al. 1989).

Sagebrush voles are polyestrous and capable of breeding year-round, but most breeding occurs in the warmer spring and early summer months (W. James and Booth 1952; Maser et al. 1974). Breeding activity may be significantly reduced during extremely hot weather or periods of low precipitation. Probably 3 to 4 litters are produced annually in Colorado. The estrous cycle lasts about 20 days. Gestation takes about 25 days, and there is a postpartum estrus. Four to 6 altricial young are born. Young are weaned at about 3 weeks and capable of breeding at about 2 months of age. Embryo counts and trapping ratios tend to favor males slightly, but data may be skewed by trapping techniques or the behavior of males, especially during peaks in population cycles.

Numbers show extreme local variation. They may increase dramatically in years with mild winters or with increased summer and fall precipitation. In sagebrush habitat in Idaho, densities ranged from 4 to 16 animals per hectare (Mullican and Keller 1986).

A variety of predators probably feed on the sagebrush vole, with owls being particularly successful. Bobcats, foxes, coyotes, weasels, rattlesnakes, and bull snakes undoubtedly take their toll. The species is considered by public health experts to be one of the primary reservoirs of sylvatic plague in Washington. Literature on the sagebrush vole was reviewed by L. Carroll and Genoways (1980).

Ondatra zibethicus

COMMON MUSKRAT

Description

The muskrat is the largest and most specialized of arvicoline rodents. The body is stocky with a large, rounded head. The laterally flattened, scaly tail is about as long as the head and body. The hindfeet are enlarged and partially webbed with stiff hairs fringing the toes. The forefeet are small and dexterous. The lips close behind the incisors and the ears are valvular, both adaptations for their semiaquatic life. The eyes are relatively small and the ears are short, rounded, and barely visible above the surrounding fur. Most muskrats in Colorado have rich reddish brown to blackish brown pelage with slightly paler underparts. The gray-brown underfur is very soft, overlain by longer, coarser guard hairs. The dense underfur is nearly impervious to water. The winter pelage has a lustrous sheen. Measurements are: total length 450–550 mm; length of tail 200–250 mm; length of hindfoot 65–78 mm; length of ear 19–21 mm; weight 650–1,800 g. Females have 3 pairs of mammae and males have a well-developed baculum.

PHOTOGRAPH 8-40. Common muskrat (*Ondatra zibethicus*). © 1993 Wendy Shattil / Bob Rozinski.

The skull is typical of that of the arvicolines, stoutly built and angular, with an abrupt constriction at the anterior margin of the braincase. The incisive foramina are narrow and long. The ever-growing incisors are long and yellowish in color. The molars are rooted; the crown pattern consists of lakes of dentine and ridges of enamel.

Small muskrats might be confused with Norway rats, from which they differ by having a laterally compressed tail and webbed hindfeet. The cheekteeth of the Norway rat show rows of cusps and not lakes of dentine. From beavers, muskrats differ in their much smaller size and longer, laterally compressed tail (in contrast to the dorsoventrally flattened tail of the beaver).

Distribution

Muskrats occur statewide, wherever there is sufficient permanent water and a food supply, from the edges of alpine tarns to riparian wetlands on the plains and in semidesert valleys. They are often abundant locally. Frequently they occur as commensals of the beaver. *Ondatra zibethicus cinnamominus* is ascribed a range on the eastern plains, whereas *O. z. osoyoosensis* is the subspecies of the western two-thirds of the state. No modern revision of the subspecies of *Ondatra zibethicus* has been conducted.

Natural History

Because of its wide distribution and economic importance as a furbearer, the muskrat has been studied exten-

MAP 8-82. Distribution of the common muskrat (*Ondatra zibethicus*) in North America.

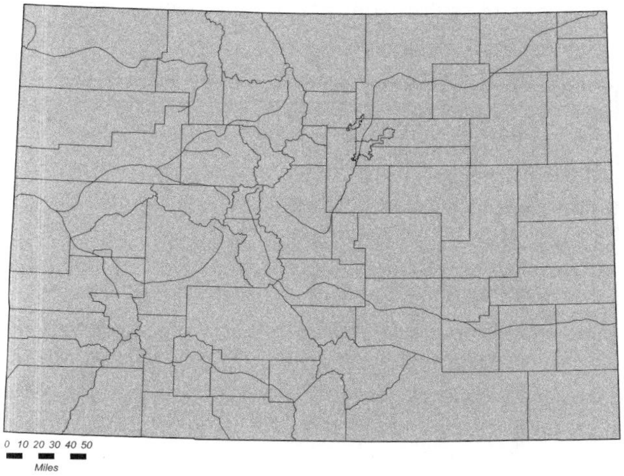

MAP 8-83. Distribution of the common muskrat (*Ondatra zibethicus*) in Colorado.

sively, although detailed studies of muskrat populations in Colorado have not been made. These are fascinating mammals, eminently "watchable" wildlife. Muskrats are semiaquatic animals occupying practically all aquatic habitats, from cattail marshes and ponds to lakes and rivers. In Colorado they range from the edges of the alpine tundra through all other ecosystems in the riparian zone. At highest elevations they are largely restricted to beaver ponds. In agricultural areas they frequently use irrigation ditches for movement between more permanent water sources. In marshes they may live in conical or dome-shaped houses built of leafy vegetation, especially cattails. Colorado has restricted areas of marshland, however, so most muskrats live in burrows in banks of ponds or slow-moving streams. Burrowing can damage earthen dams and unlined irrigation ditches and canals. McKinstry et al. (1997) reported use by muskrats of active beaver lodges in Carbon County, Wyoming.

Muskrats are mostly herbivorous but they will eat carrion, fish, crayfish, and mollusks, especially when plant materials are scarce or animal matter readily available. Obvious signs of muskrat activity are cut, floating strands of vegetation and feeding platforms located on floating, matted vegetation or on flattened areas on banks adjacent to water. Large numbers of muskrats in an area may destroy emergent vegetation, creating a situation termed "eat-out." This can affect nesting success of waterfowl adversely, so populations of muskrats are frequently controlled in waterfowl production areas.

Muskrat houses are built from the most common emergent aquatic vegetation in an area, including sedges, rushes, and cattails. Bank dens also are excavated. One to several nest chambers are hollowed out in the house or burrow and lined with plant material. The nest chambers are above the waterline and the den is accessible only through underwater tunnels. The size and development of houses vary with season, being larger and better insulated in winter. Small "feeding houses" may be constructed away from the main den. Most house-building activity occurs in spring, following ice breakup, or during late summer and early fall. Houses have a usable life span of 5 to 6 months. During the winter several individuals may huddle in the nest for warmth. Abandoned dens frequently are used by waterfowl as nesting platforms.

Both sexes are territorial and exhibit dominance hierarchies. Competition for breeding territories is intense. Females may be more aggressive than males and have been known to kill intruders (Errington 1963). Typically, juveniles and low-ranking animals are forced to occupy marginal habitat or migrate to new locations.

The mating structure is promiscuous or loosely monogamous (Errington 1963). Scent-marking with the perineal musk glands is frequent prior to breeding. Mating occurs while partially submerged. Muskrats are polyestrous with a cycle of about 30 days (Beer 1950). Muskrats in north-temperate areas (including Colorado) are seasonal breeders, the first litters typically born in late April or May. Probably 2 litters are typical in Colorado, with 3 being relatively uncommon. In the southeastern United States, up to 5 litters are produced. Gestation takes 25 to 30 days, with litter size ranging from 4 to 8. Newborn muskrats are naked and blind, with round tails. They are furred with the eyes open by about 2 weeks of age and weaned by 4 weeks. The tail becomes conspicuously compressed laterally during the second month of development. Muskrats generally reproduce first following their first winter, although precocial breeding by individuals from early litters has been reported (Errington 1963).

Muskrats are mostly crepuscular to nocturnal, with major activity peaks in late afternoon and near midnight, but in quiet, undisturbed areas they may be active during the daytime. Home ranges of individuals or family groups composed of females and young are typically small, and most activity occurs within about 15 m of the nest (R. A. MacArthur 1978). Males are very tolerant of the young and may participate in their care (Errington 1940).

Populations of muskrats are prone to fluctuations on 5- to 10-year cycles related to disease and other density-dependent regulatory mechanisms. In good habitat, populations can exceed 55 animals per hectare, although such numbers rapidly deplete food reserves (Willner et al. 1980). Dispersal occurs in spring with thawing and the increase in hormonal levels associated with breeding.

Muskrats, especially kits, are preyed on by a variety of species, especially mink and raccoons. Other terrestrial predators include foxes, coyotes, and dogs. Avian predators take relatively few muskrats. Zoonotic diseases include tularemia, hemorrhagic disease, and leptospirosis. Virgl and Messier (1996) showed that extreme fluctuations in water level during the ice-free period near Saskatoon, Saskatchewan, lowered population growth rate, influenced distribution of dens, and lowered juvenile and adult survival. Although prices and harvest fluctuate widely, muskrats are the most valuable semiaquatic furbearer in North America (Willner et al. 1980; Perry 1982), with a harvest of more than 5 million animals most years, valued at $10 million to $20 million. Populations in some parts of the United States are highly managed. Humans are the major population control, and up to 80 percent harvest can occur without depleting populations. Muskrats in Colorado are managed as furbearers, and licensed trapping or hunting is limited to the season when the fur is prime, November through February. There is no bag limit (Colorado Division of Wildlife 2009f). From 1982 to 1991, annual muskrat harvest averaged 19,600 animals (J. Fitzgerald 1993b). Since the 1996 ban on leg-hold traps, reported harvest has averaged fewer than 1,000 animals annually (Table 4-3). Willner et al. (1980), Perry (1982), Boutin and Birkenholz (1986), and Erb and Perry (2003) reviewed the extensive literature on the muskrat.

Synaptomys cooperi

SOUTHERN BOG LEMMING

Description

The southern bog lemming is a heavyset vole with a large head and a very short tail. The tail is about the same length as the hindfoot. The pelage is longer and coarser than that of other prairie-dwelling voles. Dorsal color varies from golden brown to brownish gray with a somewhat grizzled appearance. The flanks may show white hairs in the vicinity of glands, most pronounced in adult males. The venter is slate to silvery gray in color. Measurements are: total length 125–155 mm; length of tail 17–25 mm; length of hindfoot 17–26 mm; length of ear 10–14 mm; weight 35–55 g. The skull is robust and the upper incisors have

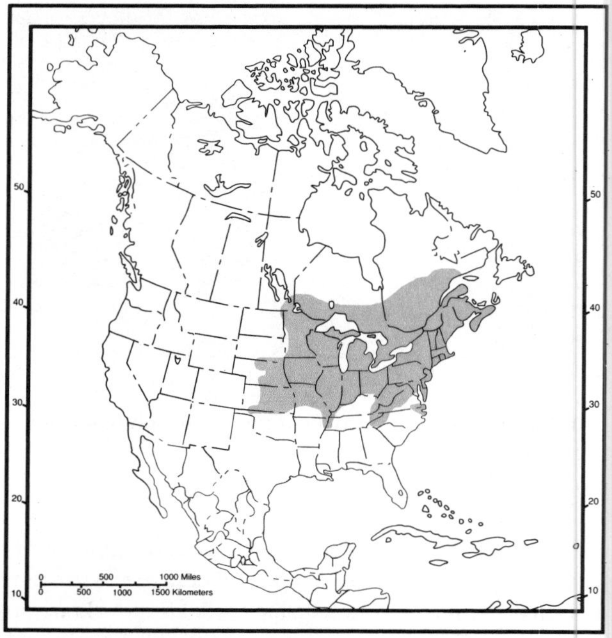

MAP 8-84. Distribution of the southern bog lemming (*Synaptomys cooperi*) in North America.

a shallow but conspicuous lateral groove on the anterior surface. That character, along with robust build and a very short tail, distinguishes it from other voles of northeastern Colorado.

Distribution

The southern bog lemming is mostly a species of the southern part of the boreal forest and the mixed deciduous forests of the northeastern United States and southern Canada, extending westward onto the edge of the Great Plains. It is not uncommon in eastern Nebraska and eastern Kansas, but J. K. Jones (1958) considered the species to be relict in western Nebraska. There are recent reports from Lincoln County, Nebraska, in the general vicinity of North Platte (R. A. Benedict et al. 2000; Huebschman et al. 2000). No specimens of the southern bog lemming are known from Colorado, but the animals are known in Dundy County, Nebraska (the type locality of the subspecies *S. c. relictus*), only about 25 km east of the boundary of Yuma County, Colorado (J. K. Jones 1958). G. Wilson and Choate (1997) noted that no specimens of *S. c. relictus* have been captured since 1968, and they noted that the taxon may be extinct, an opinion shared by D. Hafner et al. (1998b).

Natural History

The southern bog lemming has yet to be documented in Colorado but may be expected. The animals could possibly occur in Colorado in ungrazed riparian habitats along the Republican River, for example. These voles tolerate a variety of habitat types, ranging from upland grasslands to mesic grassland and sedge areas and riparian gallery forest with adequate ground cover (Linzey 1983). Habitats suitable for meadow voles, prairie voles, and short-tailed shrews support bog lemmings (D. Armstrong 1972), although the larger-bodied voles may exclude bog lemmings competitively (Linzey 1983).

Bog lemmings are active year-round, building runway systems and grass nests similar to those of other arvicolines. Studies summarized by J. K. Jones, Armstrong, et al. (1983) for the Northern Great Plains suggest that bog lemmings are often active during daylight hours. Grasses and sedges are preferred foods, and fecal material is reported to be large and bright green, as opposed to darker feces of other voles. Bog lemmings probably breed during the spring and summer on the western edge of their range, litter size averaging about 3. Linzey (1983) reviewed the literature on the species.

Subfamily Neotominae: New World Rats and Mice

The subfamily Neotominae consists of some 124 species of rats and mice in 16 genera. (Coloradan species were treated as sigmodontines in the first edition of this work and many readers will know this group as cricetines.) Neotomines come in various shades of gray and brown, and usually have prominent ears and eyes and well-furred tails. They typically make a living on the surface of the ground, not beneath the litter, and most are nocturnal. Colorado supports a fairly high diversity of neotomines, and their ecological and geographical relationships are of considerable interest.

These comments aside, neotomines are difficult to generalize. Many genera have prismatic cheekteeth with enamel ridges surrounding lakes of dentine. In genera with cusped teeth, the cusps of the upper molars are aligned in two parallel, longitudinal rows. The infraorbital foramen is medium-sized, and its dorsal border has a posteriorly directed notch. The incisive foramina are longer than the molar toothrow. The tail, unlike that of the many Old World rats and mice (Murinae), is usually well haired and not scaly. All Coloradan species are listed as non-game mammals (Table 4-1).

In the context of the following key, we note that hybridization has been reported among eastern, white-throated, and Southern Plains woodrats in southeastern Colorado and adjacent Oklahoma (R. Finley 1958; D. Spencer 1968; Huheey 1972; Birney 1973). Definitive identifications are not always possible without the aid of comparative specimens.

Key to the Species of the Subfamily Neotominae Known or Expected to Occur in Colorado

1. Occlusal surface of molars flat, a complicated pattern of exposed dentine lakes surrounded by enamel borders. . . . . *Neotoma,* 2

1' Occlusal surface of molars not flat, but with enameled cusps (cusps may be worn away exposing dentine, but patterns of dentine not as above) 9

2. Tail conspicuously bushy; soles of hindfeet well haired from heel to proximal tubercle . . . . Bushy-tailed Woodrat—*Neotoma cinerea*, p. 238

2' Tail not conspicuously bushy; soles of hindfoot naked or sparsely haired to heel 3

3. Nasal septum intact (when viewed through incisive foramina, vomer forms solid plate separating right and left nasal cavities) 4

3' Nasal septum with conspicuous notch on posterior margin (when viewed through incisive foramina, vomer separated posteriorly from maxillaries, creating notch) 5

4. Dorsal color of adults steel gray; anterior palatine spine not forked (when viewed through incisive foramina, anterior palatine spine rises from anterior margin of palatine and projects forward between foramina usually one-half to one-third length of foramina) . . . . Southern Plains Woodrat—*Neotoma micropus*, p. 247

4' Dorsal color buff washed with black; anterior palatine spine forked . . . . Eastern Woodrat—*Neotoma floridana*, p. 239

5. Anterior palatine spine blunt and stout . . . . Desert Woodrat—*Neotoma lepida*, p. 242

5' Anterior palatine spine sharply pointed 6

6. Antero-internal reentrant angle of first upper molar deep (extends more than halfway across crown) . . . . Mexican Woodrat—*Neotoma mexicana*, p. 245

6' Antero-internal reentrant angle of first upper molar shallow or not apparent 7

7. Hairs of throat lead gray at base; tail with moderately long hair, not sharply bicolored . . . . Stephens' Woodrat—*Neotoma stephensi*,* p. 249

7' Hairs of throat white at base; tail with very short hairs, sharply bicolored . . . . White-throated Woodrat, 8

8. Distributed in southwestern Colorado, north to Uncompahgre Plateau . . . . Western White-throated Woodrat—*Neotoma albigula*, p. 235

8' Distributed in southeastern Colorado, south of Arkansas River and east of Sangre de Cristo Mountains . . . . Eastern White-throated Woodrat—*Neotoma leucodon*, p. 243

9. Upper incisors with anterior longitudinal groove . . . . *Reithrodontomys*, 10

9' Upper incisors without longitudinal groove 11

10. Narrow, distinct dorsal stripe on tail; well-developed blackish mid-dorsal stripe; braincase breadth less than 9.7 mm . . . . Plains Harvest Mouse—*Reithrodontomys montanus*, p. 219

10' Wide, distinct dorsal stripe on tail; mid-dorsal stripe not well defined; braincase breadth more than 9.7 mm . . . . Western Harvest Mouse—*Reithrodontomys megalotis*, p. 218

11. Tail short, less than half length of head and body; coronoid process of dentary higher than condyloid process . . . . Northern Grasshopper Mouse—*Onychomys leucogaster*, p. 233

11' Tail long, more than half length of head and body; coronoid process no higher than condyloid process . . . . *Peromyscus*, 12

12. Tail obviously shorter than head and body 13

12' Tail about as long or longer than head and body 14

13. Tail sharply bicolored; hindfoot 21 mm or less; greatest length of skull less than 27 mm . . . . Deer Mouse—*Peromyscus maniculatus*, p. 226

13' Tail not sharply bicolored; hindfoot more than 21 mm; greatest length of skull more than 27 mm . . . . White-footed Mouse—*Peromyscus leucopus*, p. 224

14. Ear usually less than 20 mm . . . . Brush Mouse—*Peromyscus boylii*, p. 221

14' Ear 20 mm or longer 14

15. Ear usually more than 22 mm, longer than hindfoot; rostrum short; dorsal color dirty buff . . . . Piñon Mouse—*Peromyscus truei*, p. 231

15' Ear less than 22 mm, shorter or as long as hindfoot; rostrum relatively long; dorsal color more gray or brighter buff 16

16. Dorsal color bright buffy to orangish; tail well haired, almost bushy; first and second upper molars without well-developed accessory tubercle between primary outer cusps . . . . Canyon Mouse—*Peromyscus crinitus*, p. 223

16' Dorsal color grayish; tail not notably well haired; first and second upper molars with accessory tubercle between primary outer cusps . . . . Northern Rock Mouse—*Peromyscus nasutus*, p. 230

* Not documented from Colorado.

Genus *Reithrodontomys*—Harvest Mice

According to Musser and Carleton (2005), there are some 20 species of *Reithrodontomys*, 2 of which—both of them small mice—occur in Colorado. Harvest mice range from southern Canada to Panama, with the center of diversity being in Mexico (Hooper 1952).

Reithrodontomys megalotis

WESTERN HARVEST MOUSE

Description

The western harvest mouse is similar to the plains harvest mouse but larger in size. Color ranges from buffy to grayish brown. A poorly defined mid-dorsal blackish wash is typical. The tail is bicolored, the dorsal stripe being half the width of the tail. Measurements are: total length 113–160 mm; length of tail 48–74 mm; length of hindfoot 15–18 mm; length of ear 12–17 mm; weight 9–21 g. The skull usually is more than 21 mm in greatest length. For more detailed comparisons between Colorado's 2 harvest mice, see the account of the plains harvest mouse.

Distribution

The western harvest mouse occurs widely on the eastern plains, in the San Luis Valley, and in lower elevations of the Western Slope. It appears to be more common on the eastern plains than the plains harvest mouse, using riparian areas as well as drier upland sites. *Reithrodontomys megalotis aztecus* occurs in southwestern Colorado from the Colorado drainage southward, in the San Luis Valley, and in southeastern Colorado, south of the Arkansas-Platte Divide; *R. m. dychei* occurs across the northeastern and east-central plains; *R. m. megalotis* is the subspecies of extreme western Moffat and Rio Blanco counties.

Natural History

No detailed investigations have been done on the western harvest mouse in Colorado. On the eastern plains, it occurs in riparian communities, weedy disturbed areas, margins of wetlands, and relatively dense, tall stands of grasses. In western Colorado it may occupy drier habitats, including semidesert shrublands in washes and relatively dry riparian sites, as well as the margins of irrigated agricultural lands.

PHOTOGRAPH 8-41. Western harvest mouse (*Reithrodontomys megalotis*). Photograph by J. Perley Fitzgerald.

Western harvest mice are largely granivorous, feeding on seeds of grasses or forbs. Insects are frequently eaten and green vegetation is consumed to some extent, probably in part for its moisture content. In central New Mexico, food habits varied strongly across shortgrass prairie and shrubland habitats but overall averaged 60 percent seeds (by volume), 30 percent arthropods, and 10 percent green vegetation (Hope and Parmenter 2007). Harvest mice may use runways made by other species such as voles.

Home range estimates vary from 3,500 m^2 to a radius of 70–100 m from the burrow (Meserve 1977). Densities have been estimated to range from 4 to 11 animals per hectare to as high as 60 animals per hectare in New Mexico (Whitford 1976). Most activity occurs at night. They are gregarious and huddle together in the winter for mutual warmth. They are reported to hibernate in Nevada

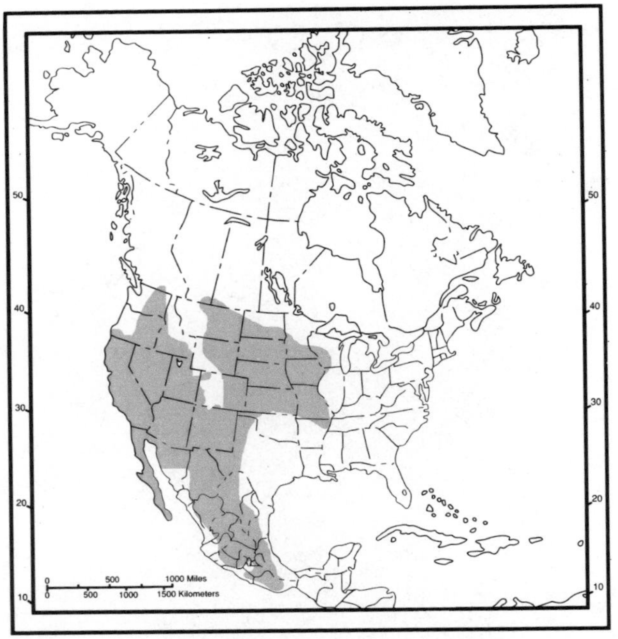

MAP 8-85. Distribution of the western harvest mouse (*Reithrodontomys megalotis*) in North America.

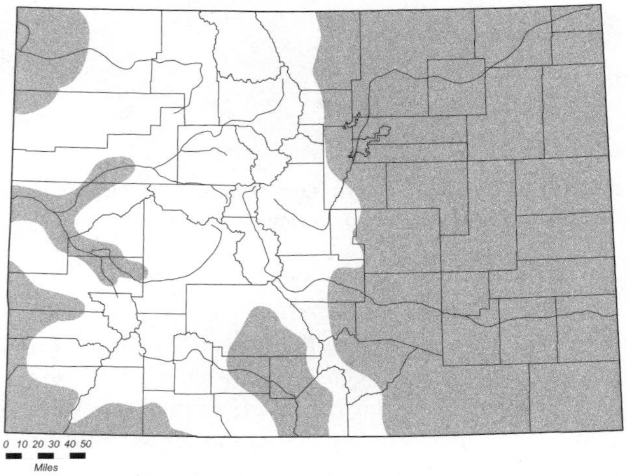

MAP 8-86. Distribution of the western harvest mouse (*Reithrodontomys megalotis*) in Colorado.

(J. O'Farrell 1974), and short periods of winter torpor probably occur in our area.

The western harvest mouse is polyestrous, and in Colorado breeding probably occurs from March through late fall. Males are polygamous with a dominance hierarchy. Baseball-sized nests are woven from grasses or other fibrous plant materials. The nest chamber is lined with soft, fluffy plant material, including milkweed and thistle down and cottonwood "cotton." Nests are located in depressions on the ground or above ground level in clumps of grass, low shrubs, or weeds. Cummins and Slade (2007) analyzed 13-years of livetrapping data on *R. megalotis* from northeastern Kansas and found that captures in traps at ground level decreased significantly during summer. Based on increased effectiveness of livetraps positioned on elevated platforms, they concluded that there was a seasonal increase in activity in the third dimension, with scansorial ("scampering") movement into tall grasses, forbs, and shrubs.

A postpartum estrus allows females to have from 2 to 5 litters per season in our area, although captive individuals have had up to 14 litters per year (Richins et al. 1974). Gestation takes about 18 days, and the weight of an average litter at birth is about half the weight of the mother. Litter size ranges from 3 to 7 with an average of 4. Sex ratios slightly favor males at birth. The young are altricial but grow rapidly, being weaned at about 3 weeks. Females reach breeding age in about 3 or 4 months.

Most long-lived individuals are females, but in general, populations turn over annually. The status of the species varies with location. In some areas populations can be relatively high. However, feral populations of the house mouse (*Mus musculus*) may displace and out-compete the western harvest mouse. Most small to medium-sized predators feed on the species when the opportunity presents itself. In southwestern Colorado the animals are (along with 3 species of *Peromyscus*) an important reservoir for hantavirus, specifically El Moro Canyon hantavirus (Calisher, Mills, et al. 2005; Calisher, Root, et al. 2005; J. Root, Wilson, et al. 2005). Webster and Jones (1982) reviewed the literature on the species.

Reithrodontomys montanus

PLAINS HARVEST MOUSE

Description

The plains harvest mouse is the smallest of Coloradan sigmodontines, a slender mouse that superficially resembles the deer mouse (*Peromyscus maniculatus*). Gray-brown in color, it has a distinctive darker mid-dorsal stripe. The venter and hindfeet are white. The tail is bicolored with a thin black dorsal stripe, only one-fourth the width of the tail.

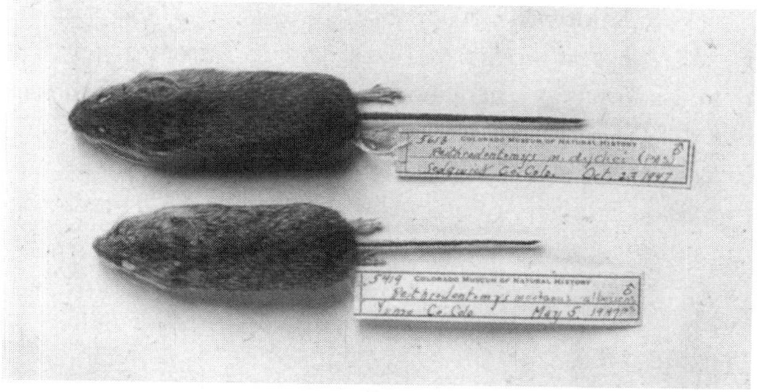

PHOTOGRAPH 8-42. Museum study skins of *Reithrodontomys megalotis* (*above*) and *Reithrodontomys montanus* (*below*). Note wider dorsal stripe on tail of *R. megalotis*. Rick Wicker, Denver Museum of Nature and Science, © DMNS 1993.

PHOTOGRAPH 8-43. Plains harvest mouse (*Reithrodontomys montanus*). Photograph by John Tveten.

Measurements are: total length 111–146 mm; length of tail 48–62 mm; length of hindfoot 15–17 mm; length of ear 12–16 mm; weight 10–14 g. Rather difficult to distinguish from the western harvest mouse, plains harvest mice are slightly smaller externally and cranially (greatest length of the skull is less than 21 mm, although the braincase is relatively broader), have a more pronounced mid-dorsal dark patch, and have a narrower tail stripe than the western harvest mouse. Generally the tail is equal to or shorter than the head and body in the plains harvest mouse and longer than the head and body in the western harvest mouse (see Photograph 8-42). Hoofer et al. (1999) distinguished troublesome specimens of *R. megalotis* and *R. montanus* by a combination of cranial measurements. From the deer mouse, both harvest mice are readily distinguished by their grooved upper incisors. The molars are rooted and cusped. Females have 3 pairs of mammae.

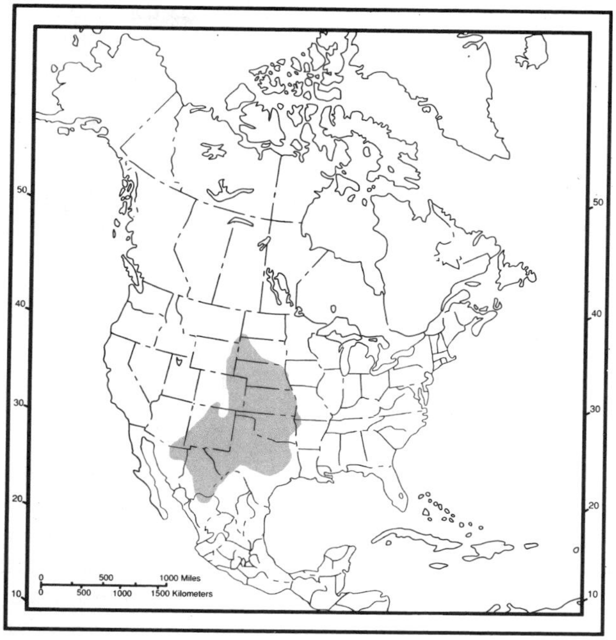

MAP 8-87. Distribution of the plains harvest mouse (*Reithrodontomys montanus*) in North America.

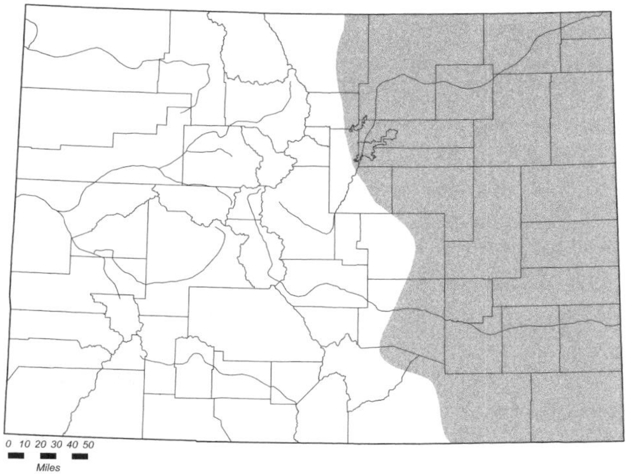

MAP 8-88. Distribution of the plains harvest mouse (*Reithrodontomys montanus*) in Colorado.

Distribution

The species is widely distributed across the eastern plains of Colorado. It does not appear to be particularly abundant, however, and populations may be affected by prolonged grazing of upland shortgrass steppe. *Reithrodontomys mon-*

tanus albescens is the subspecies of the eastern plains; *R. m. montanus* may occur in the San Luis Valley, based on a single problematic specimen captured by the Gunnison Expedition in 1853. For a synopsis of this taxonomic history, see D. Armstrong (1972).

Natural History

The plains harvest mouse is a species of semiarid grasslands in the Central and Southern Great Plains. It favors well-developed grass and forb cover of low or moderate height and pastures where scattered rocks provide cover. In eastern Colorado, Moulton, Choate, and Bissell (1981a) and Moulton, Choate, et al. (1981b) found the species in ungrazed and grazed grassland, in sand sage prairie, and in grazed riparian areas. Mohamed (1989) found it in moderately grazed yucca-grassland communities on sandy soils in Weld County. In southeastern Wyoming, it was more common on sites with less than 40 percent bare ground (Maxell and Brown 1968). This mouse is also found in margins of croplands along fencerows and in similar disturbed but productive weedy habitats, but it is not as common in such areas as the western harvest mouse.

The diet is similar to that of the western harvest mouse, consisting mostly of seeds supplemented by some green material, berries, fruits, and insects. Grasshoppers are important food items during the warmer months. Plains harvest mice may store foods underground for winter use.

Plains harvest mice are active year-round, with most foraging occurring at night. Home range estimates vary from 0.04 to 0.84 ha (Wilkins 1986). Mean home ranges in Oklahoma approximated 0.17 ha for males and 0.21 for females (Goertz 1963). Harvest mice are excellent climbers and locate their nests in low shrubs and weeds, suspended above the ground in taller grasses, inside objects such as tin cans, or under objects on the surface of the ground. The nest is similar to that of the western harvest mouse, consisting of grasses shaped into a small sphere (H. Brown 1946), roughly 6 by 10 cm.

Plains harvest mice probably reproduce in Colorado during all but the coldest winter months. Females are polyestrous, having several litters per year of 1 to 9 young, with an average litter size of 4. Gestation takes about 3 weeks. The altricial young develop more rapidly than those of the western harvest mouse, are weaned at about 2 weeks of age, and leave the nest at about 3.5 weeks of age (Lerass 1938). At 5 weeks old the young are the size of adults, and at 2 months of age they are capable of breeding.

Populations do not appear to be as dense as those of the western harvest mouse. In Texas, density estimates were less than 2 animals per hectare (Schmidly 1983), and in Kansas densities of up to 6.8 animals per hectare were reported (H. Brown 1946). Most individuals live less than 1 year. They are preyed on by a variety of small and medium-sized predators. Literature on the species was reviewed by Wilkins (1986).

Genus *Peromyscus*—White-footed Mice

This is a remarkably diverse and successful group of rodents, with some 56 species (Musser and Carleton 2005). The center of diversity is Mexico and middle America, but the genus ranges from subarctic Canada and southeastern Alaska to Panama. The importance of species of *Peromyscus* to understanding the ecology, behavior genetics, and evolution of mammals cannot be overestimated; Musser and Carleton (2005:1062) called them (humorously but aptly) "the *Drosophila* [fruit fly] of North American mammalogy"—that is, the "model mammal." Major reviews of the biology of the species include J. King (1968) and Kirkland and Layne (1989). The 6 Coloradan species of *Peromyscus* generally are fairly distinctive ecologically and morphologically, as they represent 5 different "species groups" (Carleton 1989); *P. nasutus* and *P. truei* both are in the "*Peromyscus truei* species group."

Peromyscus boylii

BRUSH MOUSE

Description

Brush mice are large, long-tailed, relatively short-eared, and gray-brown to buffy brown in color with a whitish gray venter. The sides are often brighter orange-brown. The feet are white but the ankles are gray or dusky. The indistinctly bicolored tail is longer than the length of the head and body. Hair on the tail is rather sparse, so scales are apparent. Measurements are: total length 180–220 mm; length of tail 80–115 mm; length of hindfoot 20–24 mm; length of ear 15–22 mm (usually less than 20 mm); weight 20–30 g. The hindfoot is usually longer than the ear. Molecular systematic research confirms that the brush mouse is closely related to the piñon mouse and the northern rock mouse (Durish et al. 2004).

PHOTOGRAPH 8-44. Brush mouse (*Peromyscus boylii*). Photograph by R. B. Forbes.

Distribution

The brush mouse occurs in the rough, broken country of southeastern Colorado from Salida to Colorado Springs and south and east onto the Mesa de Maya and the canyons of Baca County. In western Colorado the species occurs south and west of the San Juan Mountains northward to western Gunnison and Delta counties. Svoboda et al. (1988) captured specimens in the San Luis Valley, near Villa Grove, Saguache County. One subspecies, *Peromyscus boylii rowleyi*, occurs in Colorado.

Natural History

In Colorado, brush mice typically occur in montane shrublands—especially oakbrush and mountain mahogany—and in piñon-juniper woodlands. They usually favor areas of rough, broken terrain with boulders and heavy brush. They also occur in riparian cottonwood stands, willow thickets, or brushy tamarisk bottoms.

Brush mice are good climbers and frequently forage in trees and shrubs. Over most of their range, acorns are a staple of the diet. Juniper "berries," mistletoe, and prickly-pear are also important foods. Insects are eaten whenever possible, accounting for 30 to 50 percent of the diet in California and New Mexico (Jameson 1952; Smartt 1978). In Utah and Arizona, stomachs contained more than 80 percent seeds (Duran 1973; D. Armstrong 1982). In Socorro County, New Mexico, Hope and Parmenter (2007) found a diet of 51 percent seeds, 6 percent greens, and 43 percent arthropods averaged over the years.

The brush mouse probably breeds from late winter through early fall in Colorado, with a peak during the warmer spring months. Several litters are produced per year. Litter size ranges from 1 to 6 with an average of 3. Some animals may live more than 18 months in the wild but most die before 1 year of age. Nests, open on top and similar to those of goldfinches, are built in sheltered areas under rocks and debris or in crevices in cliff faces. Woodrat dens (even occupied dens) are used as cover by brush mice and other

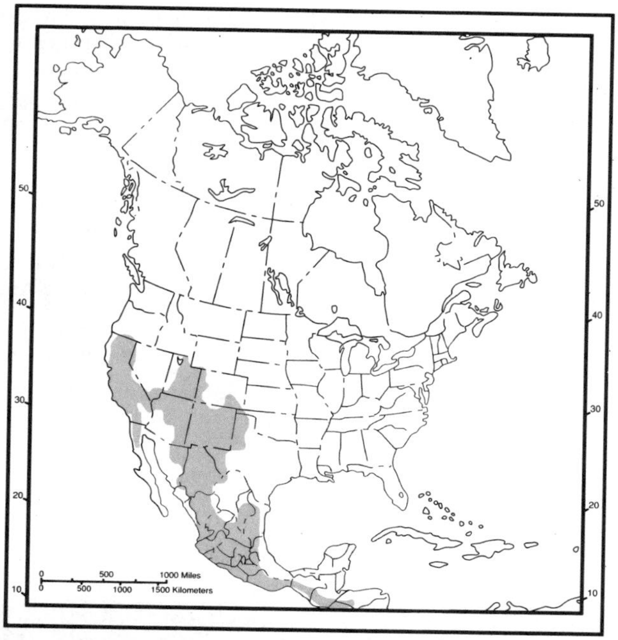

MAP 8-89. Distribution of the brush mouse (*Peromyscus boylii*) in North America.

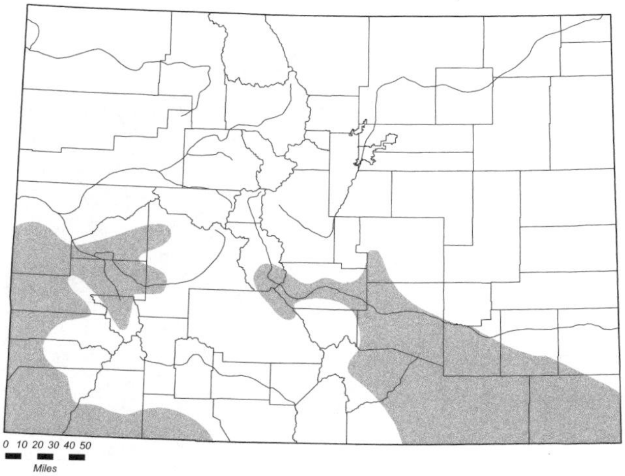

MAP 8-90. Distribution of the brush mouse (*Peromyscus boylii*) in Colorado.

rock-dwelling species of *Peromyscus*. K. N. Geluso (1971) found brush mice associated with white-throated woodrats in the canyon country in the Oklahoma Panhandle, and D. Armstrong (1979, 1982, 1984) documented their close association with several species of *Neotoma* in southeastern Utah.

Home ranges of brush mice are 0.09–0.35 ha. Densities were 0.48 to 0.56 animals per hectare in Texas (Garner 1967). A combination of data from radiotelemetry and trapping revealed home ranges of 0.64 ± 0.36 ha for male brush mice in northeastern New Mexico and 0.0032 ± 0.18 ha for females (Ribble et al. 2002). Ribble and Stanley (1998) studied *P. truei* and *P. boylii* in northeastern New Mexico. Males had larger home ranges than females. Females tended not to overlap with conspecifics. Males overlapped home ranges of multiple males and females. These data are consistent with a promiscuous mating system for both species. Brush mice are implicated as a reservoir for hantavirus, along with some other species of *Peromyscus* and also the western harvest mouse, *Reithrodontomys megalotis* (J. Root, Wilson, et al. 2005). Kalcounis-Rueppell and Spoon (2009) reviewed the literature on the brush mouse.

Peromyscus crinitus

CANYON MOUSE

Description

The canyon mouse is small to medium-sized with ears as long as the hindfoot. The tail is generally longer than the head and body. The fur is long and silky with the dorsal color a bright ochraceous buff. The bases of hairs are lead gray. The sides are even more brightly colored than the back. A yellow-orange to buff pectoral spot is generally present in Coloradan populations. The belly is white to gray and the feet are white. The bicolored tail, typically longer than the head and body, has a pronounced terminal tuft, and the

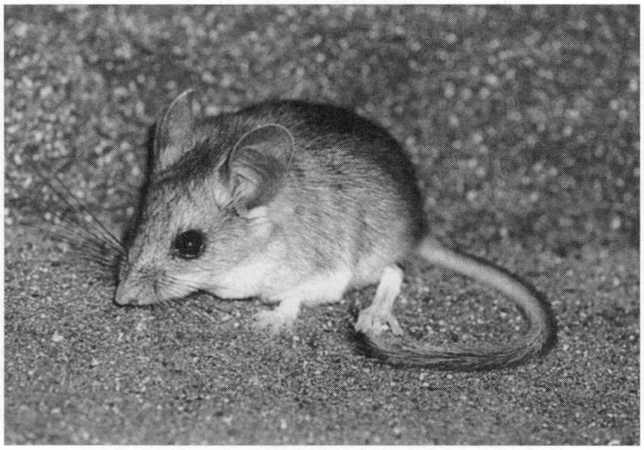

PHOTOGRAPH 8-45. Canyon mouse (*Peromyscus crinitus*). Photograph by Claude Steelman / Wildshots.

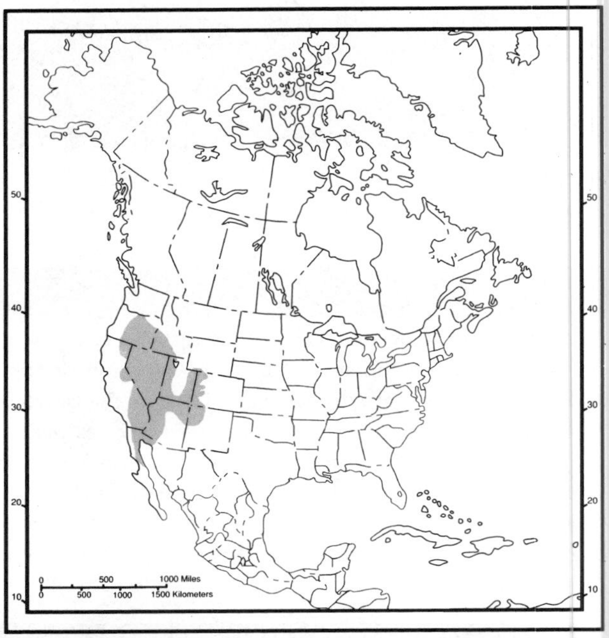

MAP 8-91. Distribution of the canyon mouse (*Peromyscus crinitus*) in North America.

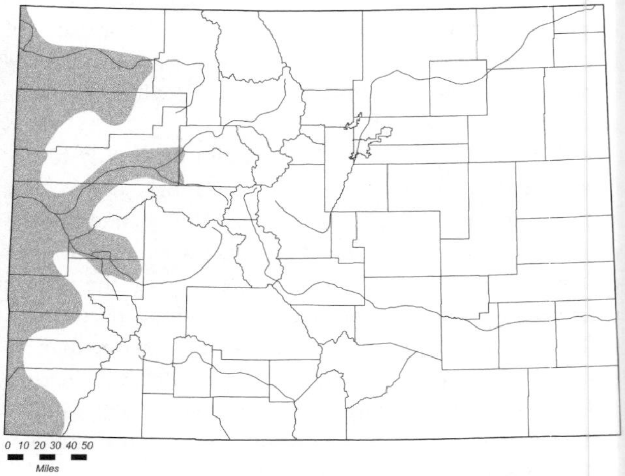

MAP 8-92. Distribution of the canyon mouse (*Peromyscus crinitus*) in Colorado.

scales are usually visible through the thin covering of hair. Measurements are: total length 160–190 mm; length of tail 82–110 mm, length of hindfoot 18–25 mm; length of ear 17–23 mm; weight 12–30 g. The maxillary toothrow is typically less than 4 mm long. The skull is fragile with a long, slender rostrum. Zygomatic breadth is only slightly greater than cranial breadth. The nasals are long, narrowing posteriorly. The premaxillary ends at about the level of the posterior margin of the nasals. Females are typically somewhat larger than males and have 4 inguinal mammae.

Distribution

The canyon mouse inhabits the canyonlands along the western border of Colorado from the southern half of Moffat County to Montezuma County. Little is known about its status in the state. One subspecies, *Peromyscus crinitus auripectus*, is known to occur in Colorado, but *P. c. doutti* may be present west of the Green River in extreme western Moffat County. Collections have not been made there.

Natural History

Canyon mice, as the name implies, are mostly animals of dry, rocky canyon country. Their distribution is somewhat patchy and often habitat that would seem to be suitable is not occupied. They often occur in talus and outwash rubble or eroded, exposed sandstone "slickrock" (D. Armstrong 1979). Vegetation occupied includes piñon-juniper woodlands and montane and semidesert shrublands. They seem to favor sunny south- and west-facing slopes in northwestern Colorado (R. Finley et al. 1976).

Canyon mice are omnivorous and feed on seeds, berries, fruits, fungi, and insects (D. Armstrong 1982). Seeds are more important in winter and insects may dominate the diet during the warmer months. Free water is not needed and efficiency of the kidneys is equal to or greater than that of the kangaroo rats (MacMillen 1983). When deprived of food and water in the laboratory, individuals enter torpor. This may be a mechanism for coping with the dry environments in which the mice live.

Egoscue (1964b) studied reproduction in this species under laboratory conditions in Utah. Canyon mice are seasonally polyestrous. Most breeding in Colorado probably occurs in spring, early summer, and fall, with reproductive activity ceasing during extremely hot or cold weather. An estrous cycle is completed in about 6 days. Gestation takes from 24 to 31 days, with an average of 3 young (range, 1 to 5) per litter. A postpartum estrus occurs with lactating females having a longer gestation. Number of litters per year probably varies depending on food availability and seasonal temperatures. In the lab, up to 8 litters per year were produced, but probably 2 or 3 are more typical of wild animals. Young, although blind and naked at birth, are slightly more precocial than newborn deer mice but have a longer period of postnatal development. Neonates are large, as seems to be typical of aridland *Peromyscus* (Layne 1968). The young open their eyes around 2 weeks of age and are weaned at 1 month. Females can begin to breed as early as 75 days of age but most actually do not begin to reproduce until 4 to 6 months old. Females have lived to almost 4 years of age in the laboratory.

In laboratory studies canyon mice were most active at night under conditions approximating full-moon intensities (Egoscue 1964b). In the wild they tend to forage primarily at night when light conditions are fairly dim and they are less conspicuous to predators. Individuals are tolerant of one another, and sites suitable for occupancy usually have good populations. Densities in southeastern Utah range from about 1 to 6 animals per hectare and up to 43 animals per hectare on the tops of isolated buttes that were inaccessible to other species (D. W. Johnson 1981). Home ranges averaged 0.36 ha in southeastern Utah (D. W. Johnson 1981). As with other *Peromyscus*, the species is vulnerable to predation by a variety of hawks, owls, snakes, and small to medium-sized mammals, including weasels, skunks, ringtails, foxes, and coyotes. D. W. Johnson and Armstrong (1987) reviewed the literature on the species.

Peromyscus leucopus

WHITE-FOOTED MOUSE

Description

The white-footed mouse closely resembles the deer mouse but is larger in size with a less distinctly bicolored tail. The tail is usually longer than that of the deer mouse, generally exceeding 65 mm in length. The color is pale gray-brown to buffy with white underparts and feet. Most individuals are grayer in overall color than deer mice of similar size. The white hairs of the belly are gray at their bases. Measurements are: total length 150–200 mm; length of tail 60–100 mm; length of hindfoot 19–24 mm; length of ear 13–16 mm; weight 20–36 g. Greatest length of the skull is usually more than 27 mm, and the hindfoot is usually longer than 21 mm. For additional comparisons with the deer mouse, see the account of that species. Females have 3 pairs of mammae.

PHOTOGRAPH 8-46. White-footed mouse (*Peromyscus leucopus*). Photograph by Roger W. Barbour.

Distribution

The white-footed mouse is known to occur only in the southeastern part of the state, throughout the Arkansas drainage east of the mountains, where it is common in suitable habitat. One subspecies, *Peromyscus leucopus tornillo*, is found in the state. A second subspecies, *P. l. aridulus*, is of possible occurrence in northeastern or east-central Colorado (see Stangl and Baker 1984). Mention of this species in the context of studies of hantavirus in southwestern Colorado (Calisher, Sweeney, et al. 1999) probably is an error of identification; *P. leucopus* is not documented by specimens from the Four Corners region (see D. Armstrong 1972; E. Hall 1981) and is not to be expected.

Natural History

Although this species is studied extensively in the eastern United States, a detailed study from our part of the range would be useful. White-footed mice range widely in eastern North America in habitats ranging from deciduous forest to brushy fields. In Colorado, white-footed mice are associated with rank, weedy vegetation, especially cottonwood riparian habitat or even stands of the exotic phreatophyte tamarisk ("salt-cedar," *Tamarix* spp.). They also occur in rocky canyon country in southeastern Colorado. The density of shrub cover appears to influence positively the presence of the animal in our part of the range. Studies by D. Wilson (1968) and Holbrook (1978) in New Mexico, K. N. Geluso (1971) in the Oklahoma Panhandle, and D. W. Kaufman and Fleharty (1974) in Kansas probably pertain to ecology and habitat preferences of white-footed mice in Colorado.

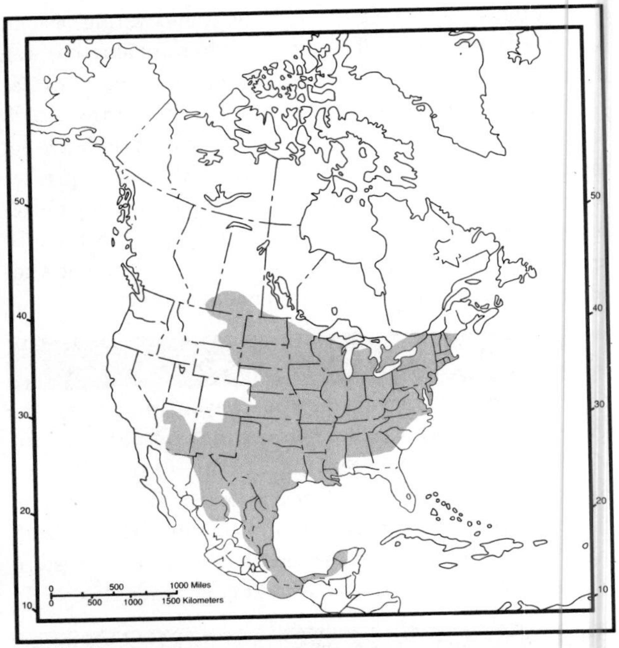

MAP 8-93. Distribution of the white-footed mouse (*Peromyscus leucopus*) in North America.

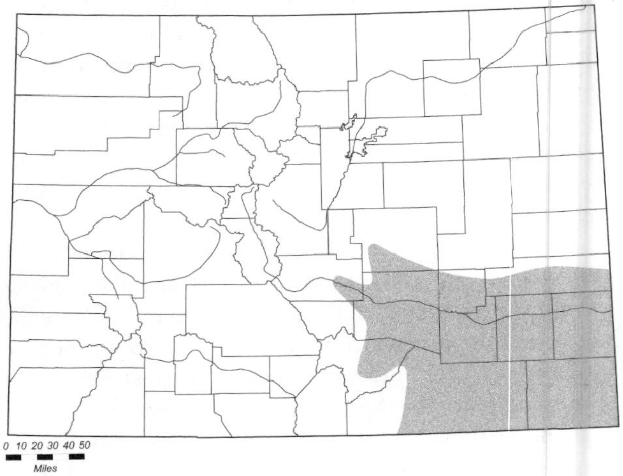

MAP 8-94. Distribution of the white-footed mouse (*Peromyscus leucopus*) in Colorado.

White-footed mice feed on a variety of plant and animal foods. Insects are often the most common item in stomach samples, followed by seeds of a variety of plants, and together these constitute more than 60 percent of the diet. In a quantitative study in central New Mexico, white-footed mice ate about half (45 percent) seeds and 5 percent green vegetation (Hope and Parmenter 2007). Caches of food probably are made, as such behavior is seen in the laboratory.

White-footed mice are semiarboreal, scampering easily among tree and shrub branches and climbing relatively smooth-barked trunks. The shorter-tailed deer mice, by comparison, are much more terrestrial in their habits. In areas with competition from even better climbers (rock mice, canyon mice, or piñon mice), white-footed mice tend to be more terrestrial (T. Thompson and Conley 1983). D. M. Kaufman and Kaufman (1992) noted that relative length of tail increased from east to west across Kansas and suggested that white-footed mice in the west may be more arboreal than those in eastern Kansas.

White-footed mice are polyestrous. In our area they probably breed during all but the coldest months. Ovulation is spontaneous and females typically exhibit postpartum estrus. Gestation ranges from 22 to more than 30 days, depending on whether females are nursing a previous litter (Svihla 1932). Lactating females require about 25 percent more energy intake than non-lactating females or males. The average number of young per litter is 4, with a range of 1 to 7. The young develop relatively rapidly, with eyes and ears open by 2 weeks of age. Young are weaned at about 1 month of age and attain adult size by about 6 weeks. Females generally are sexually mature at that time, although sexual maturity can be delayed by the presence of feces or urine of other white-footed mice (J. Rogers and Beauchamp 1976).

Nests are built from a variety of locally available plant materials, including shredded bark, leaves, grass stems, and down of milkweed, as well as feathers and hair, if available. Nests are used for resting, warmth, and protection of young, and nest-building increases during cold weather or when young are about to be born. Despite their climbing ability, white-footed mice frequently nest on the ground under sheltering objects, including rocks and fallen trees.

These animals are mostly nocturnal, with higher trappability under conditions of high humidity, high temperature, and cloud cover (Drickamer and Capone 1977). Some diurnal activity is reported during the winter months. Animals exhibit torpor, especially under conditions of food deprivation or low temperature. Such torpor may last 3 or more hours and does not necessarily occur every day. The frequency of torpor increases with colder temperatures (D. Snyder 1956).

Home ranges typically have been estimated at less than 0.10 ha, larger in the breeding season and smaller during winter (Stickel 1968); males have slightly larger home ranges than females. Few animals are thought to survive more than 1 year, suffering predation by nocturnal avian and mammalian carnivores as well as harsh environmental conditions. The extensive literature on the white-footed mouse was reviewed by Lackey et al. (1985).

Peromyscus maniculatus

DEER MOUSE

Description

This is a highly variable mouse, both morphologically (D. Armstrong 1972) and physiologically (Wasserman and Nash 1979). In Colorado, dorsal color ranges from grayish brown to rufous orange to pale buff. The underparts and feet are white. Juveniles are medium gray in color, darker than some adults. The ears are conspicuous but usually shorter than the hindfoot. The tail is distinctly bicolored and obviously shorter than the head and body. Measurements are: total length 135–180 mm; length of tail 57–78 mm; length of hindfoot 17–21 mm; length of ear 14–21 mm; weight 14–27 g. The maxillary toothrow is usually less than 4 mm long (that of the white-footed mouse is often more than 4 mm). Females have 6 mammae, 4 inguinal and 2 pectoral. The species is sometimes difficult to tell from the white-footed mouse but usually the deer mouse has a shorter skull (greatest length less than 27 mm) and a shorter hindfoot (less than 21 mm), and the tail is more distinctly bicolored.

PHOTOGRAPH 8-47. Deer mouse (*Peromyscus maniculatus*). Photograph by J. Perley Fitzgerald.

The zygomatic arches of the white-footed mouse show a slight but distinct bowing compared with the straighter arches in the deer mouse.

Distribution

The deer mouse is surely the most common mammal in Colorado, occupying most habitats at all elevations. *Peromyscus maniculatus nebrascensis* is the subspecies of northwestern Colorado and most of the eastern plains; *P. m. rufinus* occurs in southwestern and south-central Colorado and throughout the central and northern mountains; *P. m. luteus* occurs along the eastern margin of the state, mostly in the Republican and Arikaree drainages. Phylogeographic studies of deer mice (Dragoo et al. 2006) suggest that what we now know as *Peromyscus maniculatus* may actually represent more than one species. Eastern and western forms (and their hantaviruses) show deep genetic subdivisions. Storz and Dubach (2004; also see Storz 2002 and Storz and Nachman 2003) showed genetic divergence at the albumin locus along an elevational transect from the plains to the top of Mount Evans. They attributed differences to diversifying selection rather than to secondary contact between distinctive populations.

MAP 8-95. Distribution of the deer mouse (*Peromyscus maniculatus*) in North America.

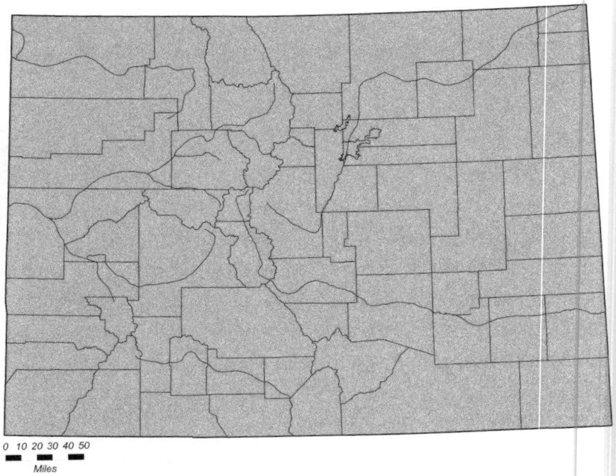

MAP 8-96. Distribution of the deer mouse (*Peromyscus maniculatus*) in Colorado.

Natural History

The deer mouse is the widest-ranging and commonest small mammal in North America, and it has been the subject of extensive research. So large is the "*Peromyscus* industry" that the on-line *Peromyscus Newsletter* is published twice a year to keep specialists in touch with one another (http: / / stkctr.biol.sc.edu / Peromyscus.Newsletter.htm). In Colorado, deer mice are found from the tops of the highest peaks to the lowest elevations, surviving practically anyplace where suitable cover occurs, including burrows of other animals, cracks and crevices in rocks, surface debris and litter, human structures, and virtually every native habitat except wetlands (O. Williams 1955a; Finney 1962; J. Fitzgerald 1978; Moulton 1978; Stinson 1978; Ribble and Samson 1987; Samson et al. 1988; Mohamed 1989). Deer mice may be thought of as mammalian "weeds," not in a pejorative sense but because—like weedy annual plants—they are adapted to exploit disturbed habitats. The disturbance may result from grazing (Lusby et al. 1971; Moulton, Choate, and Bissell 1981; Moulton, Choate, et al. 1981; F. Samson et al. 1988), land-clearing (O'Meara et al. 1981), artificial forest-thinning (Converse et al. 2006), mining, construction, avalanches, fire, flooding, or landslides (D. Armstrong 1977b). In short, anything that disturbs the habitat of specialists creates habitat for this quintessential generalist (D. Armstrong 1977b).

Deer mice were significantly more abundant in grazed than ungrazed riparian lands along Sheep Creek (elevation about 2,500 m) in Larimer County (Schulz and Leininger

1991). By contrast, western jumping mice (*Zapus princeps*) were almost never present on grazed riparian sites. Similarly, along South Boulder Creek, on City of Boulder Open Space, deer mice were more abundant where plant cover was reduced by grazing (Meaney et al. 2002). Deer mice were the first small mammals to colonize the barren alluvial fan produced by the 1982 Lawn Lake Flood in Rocky Mountain National Park (D. Armstrong 1993) and were by far the most abundant mammals, accounting for more than half of the biomass of small mammals in all 4 years of the study and in nearly all habitats. At Vail, deer mice (and least chipmunks) were more abundant on ski runs than in adjacent undisturbed forest (Hadley and Wilson 2004a). Although they are mostly terrestrial, deer mice responded to flooding by moving to higher ground or climbing into cottonwood saplings along the Yampa River in Deer Lodge Park, Dinosaur National Monument (D. C. Andersen, Wilson, et al. 2000).

In laboratory experiments under simulated moonlight, *P. maniculatus* decreased activity as light increased, but light levels did not influence the degree to which cover was used. Deer mice did increase their use of cover in the presence of Ord's kangaroo rats, however (Falkenberg and Clarke 1998).

Dieldrin is a fat-soluble cyclodiene insecticide. It is known to cause liver and kidney damage to laboratory animals. At the Rocky Mountain Arsenal National Wildlife Refuge increased levels of dieldrin were significantly associated with higher populations of deer mice (D. Allen and Otis 1998). The authors speculated that there may be natural selection for dieldrin resistance at the Arsenal.

Where specialized kinds of *Peromyscus* are present, deer mice may be scarce or absent locally (C. L. Douglas 1969b; D. Armstrong 1979). In removal experiments in shrub-steppe habitat on the Central Plains Experimental Range in northern Weld County (Stapp 1997a), *P. maniculatus* declined as grasshopper mice (*Onychomys leucogaster*) increased, and deer mice, Ord's kangaroo rats, and western harvest mice increased with removal of grasshopper mice. On the Central Plains Experimental Range in Weld County, Stapp and Van Horne (1997) found that deer mice used shrubby habitats selectively.

Deer mice eat practically anything, from insects and other small invertebrates to carrion, fungi (O. Williams 1955c; O. Williams and Finney 1964), bone, and various plant parts, particularly seeds (Jameson 1952). Leaves and bark are eaten when other materials are in short supply. Seeds accounted for 69–76 percent of the stomach contents of mice from Colorado and Wyoming, whereas insects accounted for 14–25 percent (O. Williams 1959). Sterner et al. (2003) found no direct impact of small mammals (deer mice, grasshopper mice, 13-lined ground squirrels) on dryland crops in a study near Briggsdale, although deer and jackrabbits were implicated in some clipping of soybeans.

Pregnant females have been captured from February through November in northeastern Colorado (Beidleman 1954; Flake 1974) and in January in north-central Colorado (E. Reed 1955), supporting the notion that deer mice breed almost year-round in the state. Variability is introduced by elevation and food availability. Differences between high- and low-elevation sites have been observed in reproductive strategy (A. Spencer and Steinhoff 1968; Halfpenny 1980). Generally speaking, litter size and age at weaning were greater at higher elevations; number of litters per year and birth weights were greater at lower elevation. In northeastern Colorado, litter size averaged 4.7 and ranged from 2 to 8 (Flake 1974). The gestation period is 24–28 days. Females may have several litters per year. Pups are weaned at about 25 days of age (Jameson 1953). Breeding begins at 7 to 8 weeks of age, allowing many young of the year to enter the pool of reproductive animals before the onset of winter. The gray juvenile pelage takes almost a month to replace, starting at 30 to 45 days of age, with a brown subadult pelage. The rich, brown adult pelage comes in at about 4 months of age and is then replaced in a pattern of spring (vernal) and fall (autumnal) molts.

Deer mice use the same trails repeatedly, and trails can get as wide as 30 cm as variations are added. There are a number of different nest sites within a given home range, and the animals move among them (Stickel 1968). The animals seek shelter beneath rocks, downed logs, and various opportunities provided by human settlement—woodpiles, stored materials, haystacks, buildings—wherever they can escape inclement weather and would-be predators. In sagebrush steppe in southeastern Idaho, burrows of *P. maniculatus* averaged 19.2 cm in depth (Laundré and Reynolds 1993). Active throughout the year, during winter deer mice use runways beneath the insulating blanket of snow.

Merritt and Merritt (1978b, 1980) compared home ranges during summer and winter at a subalpine forest site in the Front Range. They found that subnivean home ranges averaged 0.015 ha and summer home ranges averaged 0.026 ha; in both situations, males had larger home ranges than females, as was found by O. Williams (1955a). The reduction in size of winter home ranges, short-term torpor, and aggregate nesting are the combined strategies used by deer mice to mitigate energetic losses during cold temperatures and seasons of reduced food availability.

Densities of deer mice are variable, depending on season, habitat, food availability, predators, and presence of other small rodents (Catlett and Brown 1961; C. L. Douglas 1969b; Sleeper et al. 1976; Merritt and Merritt 1980; D. Armstrong 1993).

Deer mice that survive to adulthood probably do not live much past 1 year of age. Numerous predators feed on mice, including snakes, owls, hawks, coyotes, foxes, badgers, weasels, and grasshopper mice. Often the notoriously fecund deer mouse is the major prey item for predators; they were the principal prey of great horned owls on shortgrass prairie (G. Zimmerman et al. 1996). Papers edited by J. King (1968) provided a thorough synopsis of the earlier literature on this and other species of *Peromyscus*, and Kirkland and Layne (1989) edited an essential update. A recent molecular phylogeny of *Peromyscus* and related genera (R. D. Bradley et al. 2007) suggests that a revised concept of *Peromyscus* may become warranted as additional molecular data become available.

In the Rocky Mountain region, deer mice appear to be a natural reservoir of hantavirus, the causative agent of an "acute pulmonary syndrome" that was first recognized in the Four Corners area of the US Southwest—especially pronounced in the Navajo Nation (R. Stone 1993; Pottinger 2005)—but now is recognized rather widely in both North and South America (Mills et al. 1999; Monroe et al. 1999; Callisher et al. 2003; Calisher, Root, et al. 2005; J. Root, Hall, et al. 2005; Yates et al. 2002). The virus seems to have no detrimental impact on its rodent host. Research on hantavirus (especially Sin Nombre virus) in the Southwest is ongoing; G. Glass et al. (2006) provided a predictive model of hantavirus risk. Presence of stable populations of deer mice may provide an effective reservoir for hantavirus (Calisher, Mills, et al. 2001). Peixoto and Abramson (2006) provided a theoretical model suggesting the importance of competition between sympatric rodents in controlling the rate of infection. Studies of deer mice in southwestern and west-central Colorado showed that gene flow (hence, movement of individuals) generally is restricted and local, but some exceptions do occur, and those could spread hantavirus more widely (J. Root, Black, et al. 2003; J. Root, Wilson, et al. 2005). J. Root, Black, et al. (2004) showed in pair-wise comparisons that genetically related deer mice were more likely to share hantavirus infection than were less closely related mice. Langlois et al. (2001) showed that landscape structure—especially proximity to human habitation and suitable cover—was a better predictor of hantavirus infection in deer mice in Canada than were climate and season.

Precautions against hantavirus infection are urged for persons who have occasion to enter seasonal cabins, livestock barns, outbuildings, rock-shelters, or other closed, dark spaces where rodent dung and dust can accumulate. Naturalists working with small mammals in the field probably are at particular risk (Childs 1995; Mills et al. 1995). A prudent first step is to consult the website of the Centers for Disease Control of the US Department of Health and Human Services (http://www.cdc.gov/ncidod/diseases/hanta/hps/. Kelt et al. (2010) provided updated guidelines for protection of researchers against hantavirus pulmonary syndrome.

Childs et al. (1994) found that 29 percent of deer mice trapped in southwestern Colorado (Mesa, Montezuma, and La Plata counties) tested positive for antibodies to hantavirus antigens. Other species reported as positive for hantavirus antibodies in the Four Corners area were *Peromyscus truei* (but not *P. nasutus*, although we note that this species is not documented by specimens from southwestern Colorado), *P. boylii*, *Reithrodontomys megalotis*, *Neotoma albigula* (but no other woodrats), *Neotamias rufus*, *N. quadrivittatus*, *N. minimus*, *Otospermophilus variegatus* (but no other ground squirrels or prairie dogs), *Mus musculus*, and a cottontail, *Sylvilagus audubonii*. No heteromyid rodents showed sign of infection. Calisher et al. (2000) suggested that captures of 2 or more individuals in the same trap—particularly common with male deer mice—imply social foraging and might have implications for transmission of hantavirus. Ongoing studies near Mancos suggest that populations of deer mice (and the prevalence of hantavirus) increase with changes to aspen forests impacted by the poorly understood phenomenon of Sudden Aspen Decline (E. Lehmer, personal communication). Studies in western Montana indicated that programs of biological control for spotted knapweed by exotic gallflies (*Urophora* spp.) had the unintended consequence of subsidizing populations of deer mice (which preyed on gallfly larvae) and thereby increase the prevalence of hantavirus (D. Pearson and Calloway 2006).

Hantavirus is not the only emerging wildlife pathogen capable of spreading to humans. Lyme disease is widespread in the eastern United States and has been moving westward in recent years. Two species important in the ecology of the disease—white-footed mice and white-tailed deer—both are present in Colorado. As with so many other aspects of human-wildlife interaction, a combination of scientific understanding and vigilance is called for. McLean (2008) reviewed the general problem of emerging wildlife diseases in North America.

Peromyscus nasutus

NORTHERN ROCK MOUSE

Description

The northern rock mouse is a long-eared mouse, rather similar in appearance to the piñon mouse. However, the pelage is grayish brown, less buffy than that of the piñon mouse, with whitish to silver-gray underparts. Furthermore, the bicolored tail is usually slightly longer than the head and body, and the ears usually are less than 22 mm long, equal to or shorter than the hindfoot. Measurements are: total length 170–200 mm; length of tail 80–100 mm; length of hindfoot 22–25 mm; length of ear 21–24 mm; weight 25–30 g. *Peromyscus nasutus* is closely related to *P. truei* (E. Zimmerman et al. 1978; Janacek 1990), so great care should be taken in distinguishing the species where they are sympatric, as they are in southeastern Colorado. No definitive cranial characteristics easily distinguish the rock mouse from either the piñon mouse or the brush mouse, although the rostrum of the rock mouse usually is distinctively slender and long.

PHOTOGRAPH 8-48. Northern rock mouse (*Peromyscus nasutus*). © 1993 Wendy Shattil / Bob Rozinski.

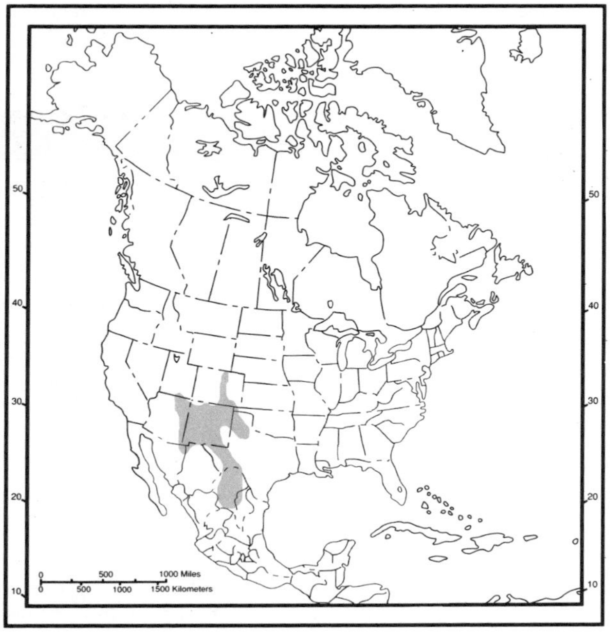

MAP 8-97. Distribution of the northern rock mouse (*Peromyscus nasutus*) in North America.

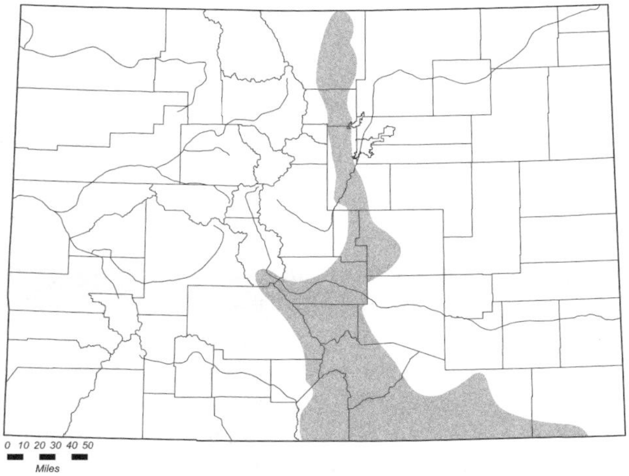

MAP 8-98. Distribution of the northern rock mouse (*Peromyscus nasutus*) in Colorado.

Distribution

The northern rock mouse has a restricted geographic range in Colorado, occurring northward along the foothills of the Sangre de Cristos and the Front Range to terminate abruptly near the Wyoming border. It extends eastward in the roughlands of the Raton Section to southwestern Baca County, and westward to the eastern part of the San Luis Valley. The rock mouse in Colorado was previously known as *Peromyscus difficilis*, but a number of authors (reviewed by Carleton 1989) have argued that northern populations warrant recognition as a full species. In a broad analysis of relationships within *Peromyscus* based on DNA from the mitochondrial cytochrome-b gene, Durish et al. (2004)

confirmed that conclusion. One subspecies, *Peromyscus nasutus nasutus* (named on the basis of a specimen from Estes Park), occurs in Colorado.

Natural History

As the name suggests, the northern rock mouse lives in rocky canyons, cliffs, cuestas, and exposed hogbacks that provide numerous cracks, fissures, and overhanging ledges. The animals occupy colluvial debris at the bases of such outcrops. The rock mouse is almost always captured under ledges or rocks and not in areas devoid of rock cover, where deer mice are more common.

Rock mice are associated with montane shrublands and piñon-juniper woodlands along the Eastern Slope. Skunkbush sumac, mountain mahogany, chokecherry, and bitterbrush are common woody species that provide cover and seeds for food. Other plant materials and insects are also consumed.

In northern Colorado, female rock mice breed from April through August, with a peak of activity in June; males enter breeding condition earlier, in March. October breeding has been noted (Cinq-Mars and Brown 1969; Kisiel 1971). (Late breeding in *Peromyscus* is associated frequently with relatively dry, warm conditions.) Litter size ranges from 2 to 6, with an average of 4. As with other *Peromyscus*, the species is polyestrous.

PHOTOGRAPH 8-49. Piñon mouse (*Peromyscus truei*). Photograph by Claude Steelman / Wildshots.

Peromyscus truei

PIÑON MOUSE

Description

This is a large, buff-colored, long-eared mouse with a tail slightly shorter than the head and body (based on specimens from our area). The distinctive ears are the longest of any species of *Peromyscus* in Colorado, usually exceeding 22 mm. The dorsal color is pale buff to rich grayish brown, with the tail distinctly bicolored. The venter is white but the hairs have gray bases. The hindfeet are either white or pale grayish. The fur is long and soft. The tail is covered with short hairs generally concealing the scales. Hairs at the tip of the tail are longer. Measurements are: total length 187–198 mm; length of tail 90–103 mm; length of hindfoot 23–25 mm; length of ear 23–30 mm; weight 20–28 g. The piñon mouse differs from the rock mouse and the brush mouse, the other two long-eared species of *Peromyscus* in Colorado, in having ears longer than the hindfoot and a tail usually no longer than the head and body. The skull is large, with large, inflated auditory bullae. Greatest length of skull is 28–29 mm, similar to that of the rock mouse but relatively broader and with a less elongate rostrum.

Distribution

Piñon mice occupy semiarid roughlands on both sides of the Continental Divide, a general range similar to that of the brush mouse, but unlike the brush mouse they are found north of the Colorado River Valley to southwestern Moffat County. Piñon mice often are abundant in suitable habitat. One subspecies, *Peromyscus truei truei*, occurs in Colorado.

Natural History

The piñon mouse is the characteristic mouse of piñon-juniper woodlands. Indeed, the animals seldom are taken from

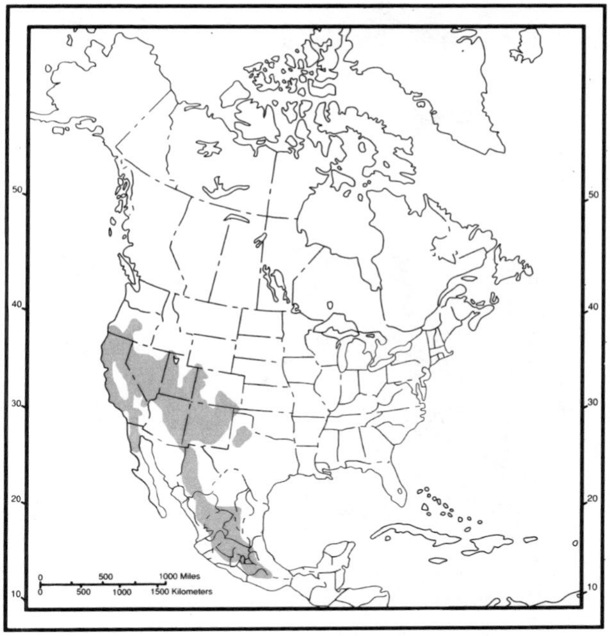

MAP 8-99. Distribution of the piñon mouse (*Peromyscus truei*) in North America.

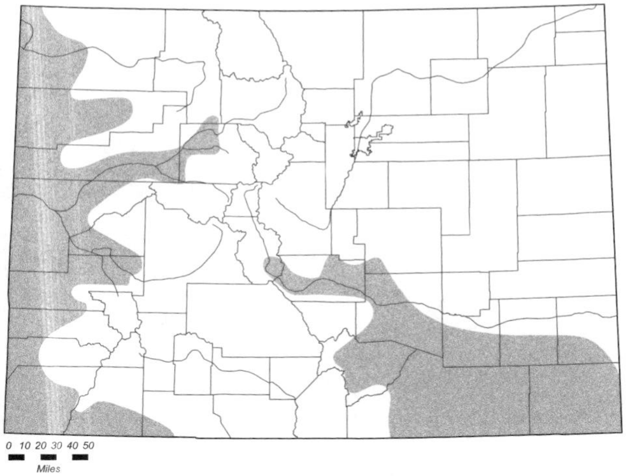

MAP 8-100. Distribution of the piñon mouse (*Peromyscus truei*) in Colorado.

areas lacking junipers, which are used for cover and food, although on occasion they do occur in sagebrush stands and Hoffmeister (1986) reported it from cottonwood river-bottoms in Arizona. Although frequently associated with rocky canyon country, in Mesa Verde the animals did not require rocky terrain but thrived in piñon-juniper stands on flat areas, although highest numbers were in rocky areas (C. L. Douglas 1969b). Chaining and overgrazing of piñon-juniper woodlands are detrimental to the species (O'Meara et al. 1981). The animals have been found to harbor hantavirus (see J. Root et al. 2005), but this probably is less an issue with piñon mice than with deer mice because piñon mice are much less likely to occupy human-built structures. In Nevada, male piñon mice showed seasonal shifts of habitat in response to reproductive condition of females, but females showed little change in habitat over the course of the year (Scheibe and O'Farrell 1995).

Piñon mice are opportunistic omnivores, but seeds and cones ("berries") of junipers are staples. Feeding sites in the crotch of a tree are marked with food debris and feces. Insects are eaten when available, as are fungi, staminate cones of pines and junipers, some flowers, and some carrion. Smartt (1978) reported usage of staminate cones of juniper, prickly-pear, mistletoe, and arthropods in addition to the pistillate cones ("berries") of juniper in New Mexico, and Hope and Parmenter (2007) noted that the annual diet was 59 percent seeds, 35 percent arthropods, and 6 percent green vegetation. In western Nevada, piñon mice (and also deer mice and larger pocket mice) appear to be important to local dispersal of piñon pine, gathering seeds from the ground and carrying them to scatter hoards up to 38 m from the source (Vander Wall 1997). Birds, by contrast, carried piñon seeds much farther, from 1 to more than 10 km. Piñon mice may be responsible for seed dispersal that fills stands and expands their margins, whereas birds (especially jays) may contribute to establishment of new stands (Vander Wall 1997). Under severe water deprivation piñon mice may become torpid.

Home ranges of piñon mice in southwestern Colorado were 0.8–1.4 ha (C. L. Douglas 1969b); home ranges of males were larger than those of females. The animals are tolerant of crowding and show little evidence of territorial behavior. Piñon mice are active year-round; most foraging is nocturnal.

The animals are seasonally polyestrous, and females exhibit postpartum estrus. Breeding occurred on Mesa Verde from April through September (C. L. Douglas 1969b). An average of 4 young (range, 3 to 6) are born following a gestation period of 25 to 27 days. Eyes open at 3 weeks of age. Young mice are weaned at about 5 weeks and females may start breeding when 2 months old. Population turnover is high, and probably only 2–3 percent of animals that breed as juveniles live to breed again the following spring (Svihla 1932; C. L. Douglas 1969b). Animals from the Four Corners area were reported to harbor hantavirus (Calisher et al. 1999). Hoffmeister (1981) reviewed the literature on the species.

Onychomys leucogaster

NORTHERN GRASSHOPPER MOUSE

Description

The northern grasshopper mouse is a stout-bodied, short-tailed mouse that superficially resembles a deer mouse. The dorsal color is gray in juveniles, molting to cinnamon-buff or reddish brown and becoming gray again in very old animals. The underparts and distal part of the tail are white. Measurements are: total length 128–158 mm; length of tail 34–52 mm; length of hindfoot 20–23 mm; length of ear 14–19 mm; weight 23–45 g. The skull is distinctly heavier than that of the deer mouse but otherwise similar, although the third upper molar is reduced in size and the coronoid process of the mandible is as high or higher than the condyloid process (Figure 8-8); the latter character distinguishes the species from any other mouse in Colorado.

Distribution

The northern grasshopper mouse is common over much of semiarid Colorado at lower elevations. *Onychomys leucogaster arcticeps* is the subspecies of northwestern Colorado, North Park, and the eastern plains; *O. l. pallescens* occurs in the San Luis Valley and in the valleys of the southwestern

PHOTOGRAPH 8-50. Northern grasshopper mouse (*Onychomys leucogaster*). © 1993 Wendy Shattil / Bob Rozinski.

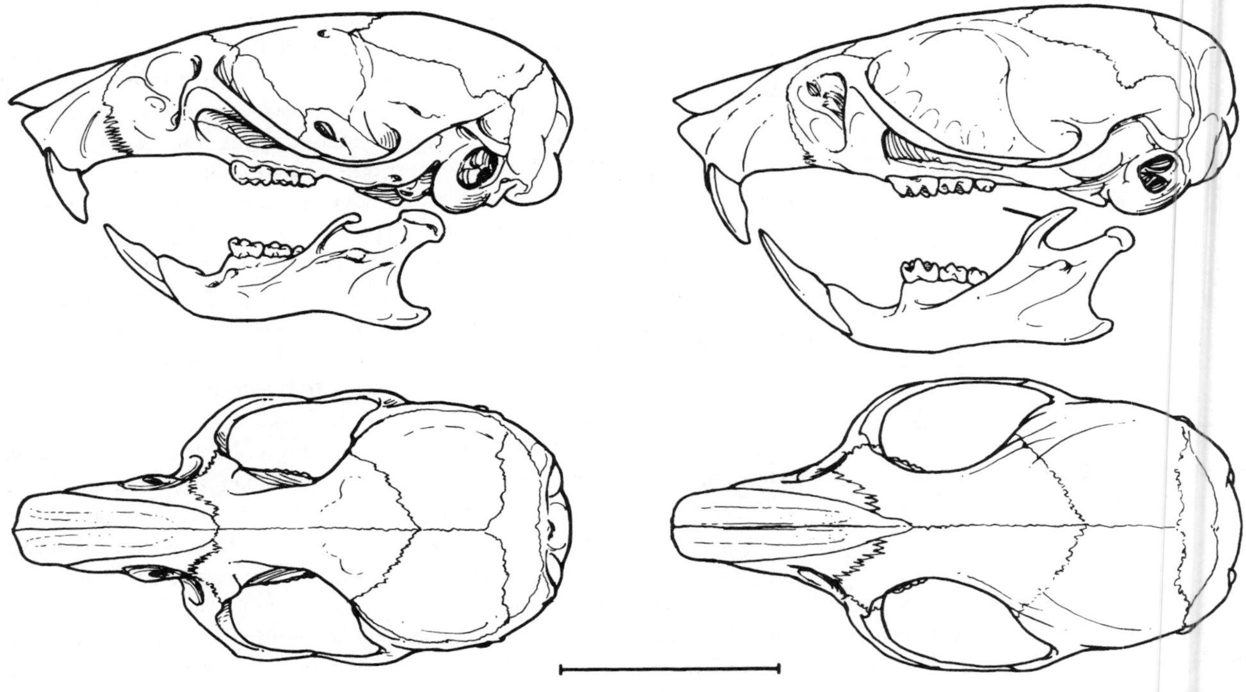

FIGURE 8-8. Skull of a deer mouse (*Peromyscus maniculatus, left*) and that of a northern grasshopper mouse (*Onychomys leucogaster, right*), showing the relatively high coronoid process of the latter. Scale = 1 cm.

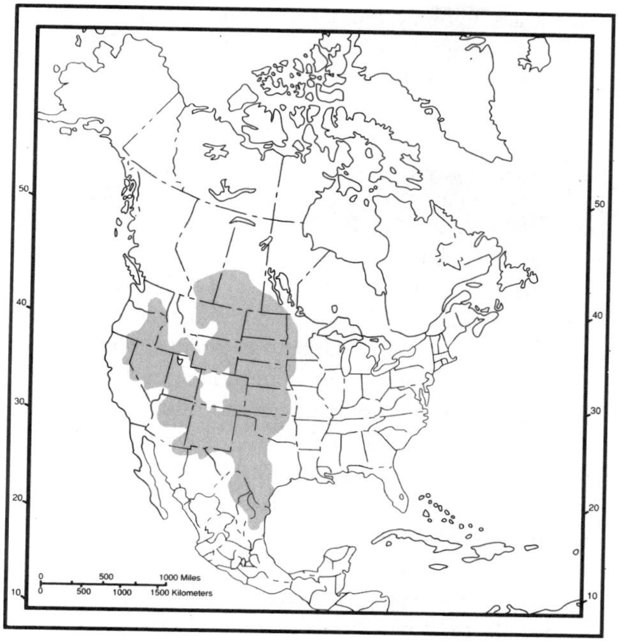

MAP 8-101. Distribution of the northern grasshopper mouse (*Onychomys leucogaster*) in North America.

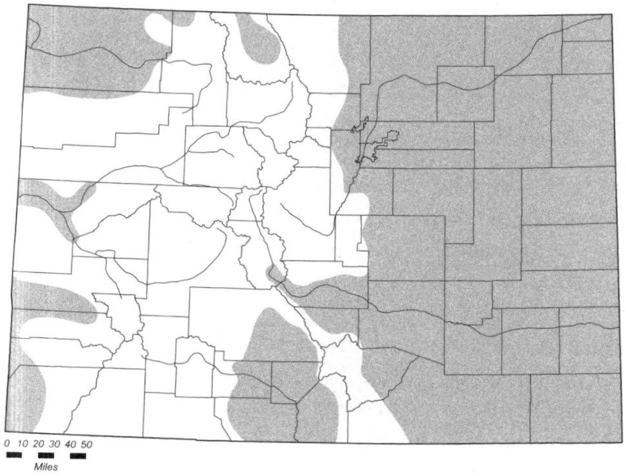

MAP 8-102. Distribution of the northern grasshopper mouse (*Onychomys leucogaster*) in Colorado.

and west-central parts of the state, from the Grand Valley southward. Phylogenetic studies of mitochondrial DNA led Riddle and Honeycutt (1990) to visualize repeated fragmentation and coalescence of semiarid grasslands through the Quaternary Period. Grasshopper mice of semidesert shrublands of the Colorado Plateau, Wyoming Basin, and Great Plains are genetically nearest neighbors, suggesting at least periodic continuity over the past 2 million years. Riddle (1995) reviewed the biogeography of aridland rodents and concluded that speciation leading to the present-day diversity of such genera as *Perognathus* and *Onychomys* predates the Pleistocene Epoch.

Natural History

Grasshopper mice occur in semiarid grasslands, sand hills, and open semidesert shrublands. They seem to reach highest densities on overgrazed rangelands, which typically have both high populations of insects and the sandy "blowouts" that provide soils loose enough for burrowing and for their seemingly obligatory dust-bathing. However, Mohamed (1989) found them to be the most abundant rodents on moderately grazed sand prairie, and Flake (1973) captured large numbers on shortgrass prairie in northeastern Colorado. In extensive studies of the mammalian assemblage on and near black-tailed prairie dog towns on the Central Plains Experimental Range in Weld County, northern grasshopper mice generally were more abundant on prairie dog towns than on control sites (Stapp 2007). The fine-scale distribution of grasshopper mice reflected the distribution of insect prey, which were particularly abundant around prairie dog mounds and burrows (Stapp 1997b). Home ranges of grasshopper mice are much larger than those of other rodents of similar size; those of 6 males in Weld County averaged 1.72 ha and overlapped home ranges of multiple females (Stapp 1999).

This is the most strongly carnivorous of North American mice, the bulk of the diet being composed of grasshoppers, crickets, and ground-dwelling beetles. Seeds are also eaten, especially in winter. Green vegetation seems not to be used. In studies in Colorado, R. Hansen (1975) reported a diet of 87 percent arthropods, 7 percent grasses and forbs, 4 percent seeds, and 1 percent mammal and reptile remains, whereas Flake (1973) reported 74 percent of the stomach volume to be animal matter, mostly insect larvae, beetles, grasshoppers, and small vertebrates. Plant matter averaged 25 percent by volume. In central New Mexico, arthropods constituted 35 percent of the winter diet (when seeds were 55 percent of the diet), 66 percent in spring, and 91 percent in summer. Grasshopper mice readily kill small mice and other vertebrates, but the importance of such animals in the diet is not well-known. In interspecific bouts in the laboratory, small mammals up to the size of hispid cotton rats and hispid pocket mice are readily killed by grasshopper mice (Ruffer 1968). Because of the animal protein in their diet, grasshopper mice have a strong acrid odor, probably in the urine, and can be identified by smell. Based on field data from the Pawnee National Grasslands and computer modeling, Salkeld et al. (2010) argued that grasshopper mice could be an effective intermediate host for fleas and the plague bacillus, capable of carrying the disease and its vector from one prairie dog colony to another.

Carnivory and insectivory have led to adaptive changes in behavior relative to other small sigmodontines. Similar to some carnivores, they are monogamous and both adults care for the young. They mark territories and have a well-developed repertoire of vocalizations (Hildebrand 1961; M. Hafner and Hafner 1979). In confined laboratory situations, dominant animals chase subordinates and usually kill them within 24 hours. Because they are active hunters, home ranges and territories are rather large, averaging 2.3 ha (Blair 1953), and population densities often are relatively low, although on suitable sites they can be one of the commoner small mammals (Flake 1973; Moulton, Choate, and Bissell 1981; Moulton, Choate, et al. 1981; Mohamed 1989). They are mostly nocturnal and are active year-round. Burrow openings are small and go almost straight down for several inches before angling off (Ruffer 1965a).

Grasshopper mice have young from March through September (Flake 1974), with a short postpartum estrus. Gestation is 26–37 days for non-lactating females (Egoscue 1960) and up to 47 days for lactating females (Svihla 1936). Litter size ranges from 1 to 6, with an average of 4. In Colorado probably 3 to 4 litters per year are produced. Young females can reproduce at 6 months of age. Newborn young are blind and hairless. Hair develops and incisors begin to erupt at a little over 1 week of age. Eyes are open by 20 days and young are weaned by about 25 days (Svihla 1936; Ruffer 1965b).

Mortality from predation is relatively low, and local populations probably are not regulated by predators (Egoscue 1960; R. McCarty 1978). Plague ecologists have suggested that the species may be an important reservoir for the disease in the western United States because of their carnivory and wide distribution (R. Thomas 1988; R. Thomas et al. 1989). Studies on the Central Plains Experimental Range in Weld County (Stapp, Salkeld, et al. 2008) suggested that grasshopper mice may be a short-term reservoir for *Yersinia pestis*, the plague bacillus. Nearly a quarter of grasshopper mice were plague-positive during the epizootics that eradicated black-tailed prairie dogs. However, no seropositive mice were captured 2 years after epizootics, so grasshopper mice apparently are not a long-term reservoir. In the wild most individual animals probably do not survive much more than 2 years; in captivity they have lived more than 4 years (Egoscue 1960). Riddle and Choate (1986) provided a thorough review of systematics, and R. McCarty (1978) reviewed the literature on the species.

Genus *Neotoma*—Woodrats

Woodrats, also called "pack rats" for their characteristic collecting behavior, comprise 22 species of the genus *Neotoma*. This is a distinctly North American group, ranging from the Yukon and southeastern Alaska to Nicaragua. Mexico is the center of diversification of these intriguing rodents. Four of the species listed by Musser and Carleton (2005) are endemic to single islands off Baja California. C. Edwards and Bradley (2002) investigated relationships within the genus based on mitochondrial genetics, and Matocq et al. (2007) provided a thorough phylogenetic study of male external genitalia, reviewing the rich earlier literature on those structures.

Colorado's diverse environments support 6 species of *Neotoma*. These populations were the subject of intensive investigation by the late Dr. Robert B. Finley (especially see R. Finley 1958). No other group of Coloradan mammals has had the benefit of that depth and extent of field study by a single individual.

Middens of woodrats are built by successive generations of rats, sometimes reaching back millennia. In addition to the rat's deliberate collection of debris, and a by-product of rat droppings, the viscous urine traps pollen and spores from the air. The ancient deposits can be dated radiometrically. All of this adds up to a treasure trove of information for paleoecologists in the US Southwest—a detailed record of the vegetation over tens of thousands of years. Such work was pioneered by P. Wells and Jorgensen (1964) and summarized by a number of authorities reviewed by Betancourt et al. (1990). T. Vaughan (1990) contributed a general review of the ecology of woodrats to Betancourt et al. (1990), and R. Finley (1990) wrote the chapter on behavior of woodrats. For a general review of woodrat dens as paleoenvironmental indicators, see Elias (1995).

Neotoma albigula

WESTERN WHITE-THROATED WOODRAT

Description

The western white-throated woodrat is a medium-sized, brownish rat with short, dense soft fur. The dorsal pel-

PHOTOGRAPH 8-51. Western white-throated woodrat (*Neotoma albigula*). Photograph by Claude Steelman / Wildshots.

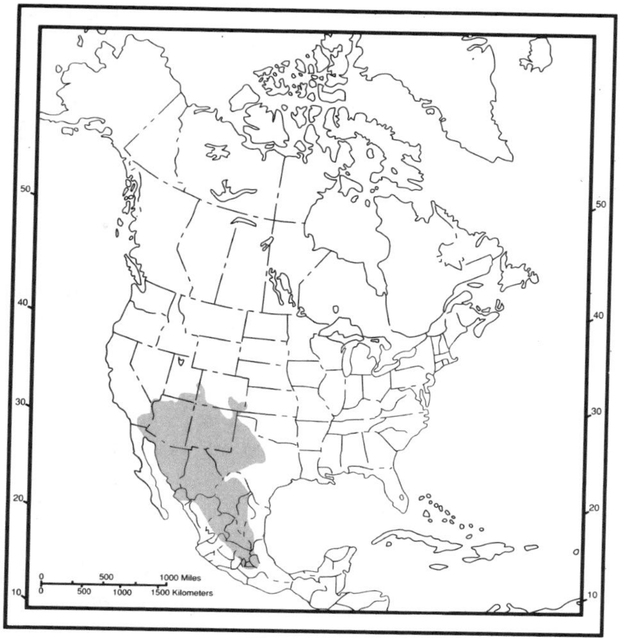

MAP 8-103. Distribution of the western white-throated woodrat (*Neotoma albigula*) and the eastern white-throated woodrat (*N. leucodon*) in North America. (The boundary between the species in New Mexico is the Rio Grande Valley; C. Edwards et al. 2001.)

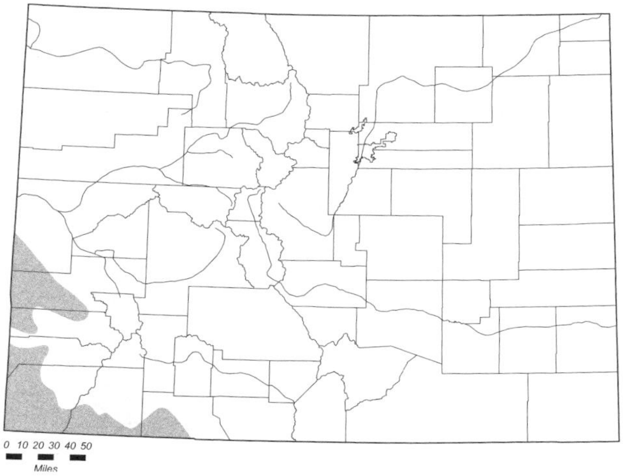

MAP 8-104. Distribution of the western white-throated woodrat (*Neotoma albigula*) in Colorado.

age is washed with black, whereas the throat and chest are white, individual hairs white to their bases. The tail is distinctly bicolored, dark brown above and whitish below. Measurements are: total length 310–340 mm; length of tail 130–150 mm; length of hindfoot 33–36 mm; length of ear 28–30 mm; weight 150–250 g. F. Smith et al. (1998) observed change toward smaller body mass with climatic warming on the Sevilleta National Wildlife Refuge in Socorro County, New Mexico.

The skull has a pointed anterior palatal spine. The posterior margin of the palate is concave, as is the dorsal margin of the foramen magnum. The interorbital region is only slightly arched. The antero-internal reentrant angle of M^1 is generally shallow. As in other woodrats, males have a pronounced mid-ventral scent gland.

Distribution

The western white-throated woodrat is found in southwestern Colorado on escarpments, mesas, and valley floors. Upper elevational limits are about 2,140 m (7,000 ft.). *Neotoma albigula laplataensis* occurs in the San Juan drainage and *N. a. brevicauda* occurs in the Dolores–San Miguel watershed (R. Finley 1958). The form now known as *Neotoma leucodon* once was considered to represent *N. albigula* (see J. Fitzgerald et al. 1994).

Natural History

The western white-throated woodrat is an animal of varied habitats, including piñon-juniper woodlands and semidesert shrublands. Although often associated with rocky canyon country, it also inhabits degraded pastures with prickly-pear well away from rocks. Occurrence, habitat use, and location of den sites of the white-throated woodrat appear to be influenced by sympatry of other species of woodrats (R. Finley 1958).

Cactus is the main food of this woodrat. Woodrats can metabolize the oxalic acid in cacti without ill effect, whereas it is often toxic to other mammals. The cactus diet is supplemented with juniper needles, yucca blades, and leaves, buds, and reproductive structures of other plants, including piñon, cottonwood, sagebrush, blackbrush, saltbush, mountain mahogany, winterfat, oakbrush, skunkbush, pigweed, ragweed, blue grama, cheatgrass, goosefoot, and milkweed (R. Finley 1958). In central New Mexico, diet was variable across habitats but the annual average was 66 percent vegetative plant parts, 24 percent seeds, and 10 percent arthropods (Hope and Parmenter 2007). As other woodrats, *N. albigula* is a hindgut digester, deriving substantial energy from fiber with the assistance of microbes (Justice and Smith 1992). Food caches are made in dens. The high water content in cacti satisfies water needs. On the Sevilleta National Wildlife Refuge in New Mexico, adult body size of white-throated woodrats decreased with increasing temperature over an 8-year period (F. Smith et al. 1998). Whether that was a direct or indirect impact of climate change was not determined.

In Colorado, away from rocky areas, dens of this species typically are constructed of cactus joints or juniper sticks and other materials, such as branches of juniper and sagebrush, cow chips, bones, pinecones, and trash, when available. The houses are often built at the base of cholla, juniper, or shrubs, with the nest chamber itself usually located below ground level at the base of the pile. Houses may be 2 m in diameter and a meter high, but most are considerably smaller. In rocky country, houses are typically constructed under overhanging rock or in piles of fallen rocks at ground level, not on actual cliff faces. Dens in rocky areas typically conform to the space available at the construction site. Houses and dens typically have a central chamber at or above ground level with several entrances. The domed nest is constructed of fine-fibered plant materials (especially shredded bark of juniper and yucca) or, less commonly, grasses. Nests range from about 15 to 25 cm in diameter. R. Finley (1958:458) provided an "architectural sketch" of a complex den near Gateway, Mesa County.

Western white-throated woodrats typically have 2 (occasionally 3) young per litter. Most breeding in our area probably occurs from late winter and spring until about mid-June. Females apparently have a postpartum estrus and may have 2 litters sharing a nest at the same time (R. Finley 1958). Newborn are large, weighing about 11 g. The eyes open at about 15–19 days and the young grow rapidly. Attempts are made to eat cactus as early as day 17 after birth and nest-building is attempted at a little over 1 month of age. Young females may reach sexual maturity in as little as 3 months, although most probably do not breed until closer to 10 months of age.

White-throated woodrats are solitary animals, with little social interaction between adults except for mating. Individual home ranges often overlap and animals may share foraging areas, although the den area is defended exclusively. Home ranges usually have been estimated as less than 500 m^2 (Boggs 1974). Density estimates, based on active den sites or trapping, range from 1 to 12 animals per hectare (Boggs 1974). With their dependence on pricklypear and cholla for both food and shelter, highest densities are often on heavily grazed rangeland (Vorhies and Taylor 1940).

Activity is mostly nocturnal, and the animals are active year-round (Macêdo and Mares 1988). Scent-marking with the mid-ventral scent gland occurs at a high rate during the breeding season and is associated with agonistic behavior. It is performed mostly by the dominant animal during paired encounters in captivity and may serve to delineate territories in the wild, especially during the breeding season (Howe 1977). Ventral rubbing is performed by males, as the gland is not well developed in females. Individuals of both sexes perform perineal drags, however, in which the animal deposits scent by lowering its hind end and slowly moving forward. Some scent may also be deposited while sand-bathing. The musty odor of woodrats is distinctive and one quickly learns to recognize when these animals have been about.

Parasites include mites and fleas, and most carnivorous vertebrates prey upon them, including weasels, badgers, coyotes, larger snakes, and owls—although surely their rock or cactus dens protect them from both predators and extremes of weather. Males have a higher rate of survival than do females, but few probably survive much beyond a year or so in the wild. Maximal longevity in captivity is about 5 years (Landstrom 1971). Macêdo and Mares (1988) reviewed the literature on white-throated woodrats (both western and eastern).

Neotoma cinerea

BUSHY-TAILED WOODRAT

Description

The bushy-tailed woodrat is a large woodrat with a bushy tail (especially pronounced in mature males). The ears are larger than those of other woodrats in Colorado. Although variable, color is typically ochraceous buff to gray often washed with black. The sides are buffy. The venter is white, with the hairs gray at their bases. White hairs of the chest and throat are usually white to their bases. The tail is dark gray above and whitish below. The feet are white. The soles of the hindfeet are fully furred from the proximal tubercle to the heel. Measurements are: total length 340–420 mm; length of tail 142–176 mm; length of hindfoot 40–46 mm; length of ear 30–33 mm; weight 270–299 g. The skull has a narrow, channeled interorbital region. The temporal ridges are separated by a narrow interparietal usually not much wider than long. The nasal septum has a maxillo-vomerine notch and the anterior palatine spine is slender and pointed. This is the most distinctive of Coloradan woodrats and usually is placed in its own subgenus, *Teonoma* (see E. Hall 1981).

Distribution

The bushy-tailed woodrat has the broadest range of any woodrat, generally occurring throughout the mountains and foothills and also eastward along the High Plains escarpment on the Wyoming-Nebraska-Colorado border. *Neotoma cinerea arizonae* is the subspecies of the canyons

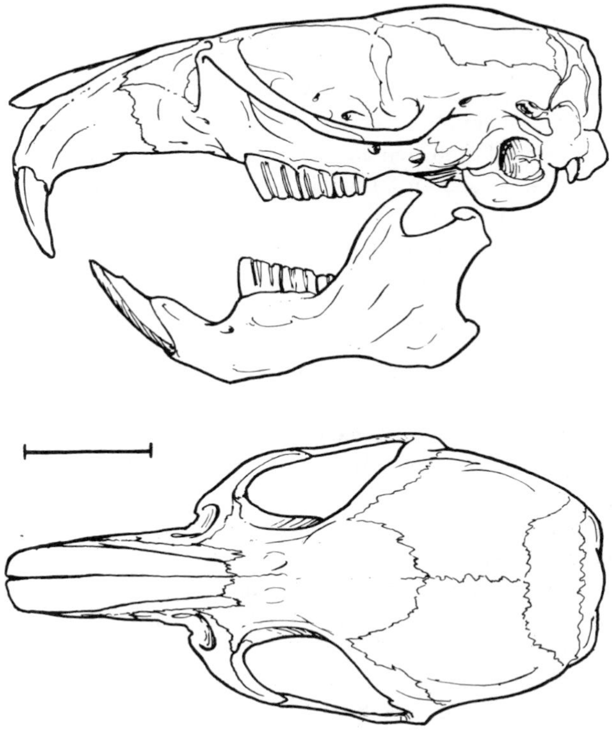

FIGURE 8-9. Lateral and dorsal views of the skull of a bushy-tailed woodrat (*Neotoma cinerea*). Scale = 1 cm.

PHOTOGRAPH 8-52. Bushy-tailed woodrat (*Neotoma cinerea*). Photograph by J. Perley Fitzgerald.

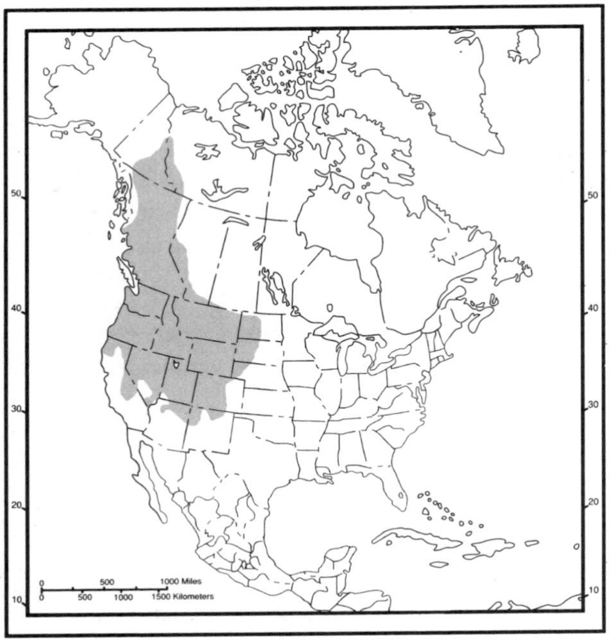

MAP 8-105. Distribution of the bushy-tailed woodrat (*Neotoma cinerea*) in North America.

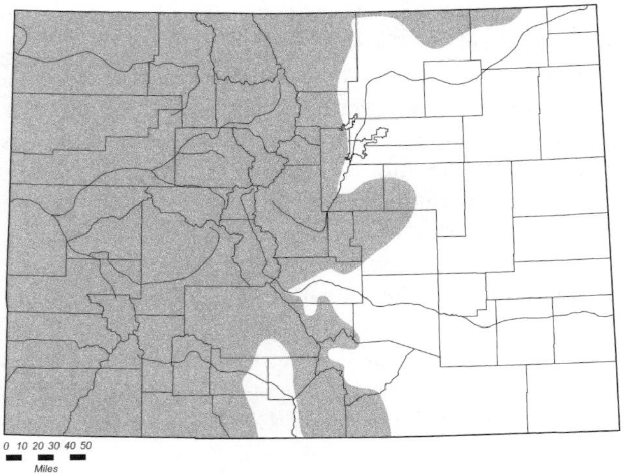

MAP 8-106. Distribution of the bushy-tailed woodrat (*Neotoma cinerea*) in Colorado.

and plateaus at lower elevations on the Western Slope; *N. c. orolestes* occurs throughout the central mountains; *N. c. rupicola* occurs on the High Plains escarpment of northern Weld and Logan counties.

Natural History

This is a species of mountains and roughlands of western North America, the northernmost of woodrats. In Colorado this is the woodrat of montane and subalpine forests—and especially Douglas-fir, ponderosa pine, and aspen communities—and alpine talus. The animals often are quite common around old mining camps and diggings at higher elevations. They also occur in lower-elevation canyon country in semidesert shrublands and piñon-juniper woodlands, typically in rimrock, rock outcrops, and similar physiographic features.

Over its broad geographic range, the animals generally conform with Bergmann's Rule, with larger body size in more northern or higher-elevation parts of the range. F. Smith et al. (1995) showed that body size of bushy-tailed woodrats varied with temperature during the last ice age, based on detailed measurements of subfossil droppings.

The bushy-tailed woodrat is an excellent climber and seems to favor vertical crevices high on cliff walls rather than sites at ground level or in horizontal crevices. However, in the absence of other kinds of woodrats, bushy-tailed woodrats use practically any available opening, including caves. They also construct houses at the base of trees, on or under partly fallen trees, in tree cavities close to the ground, and in abandoned or occupied buildings and mineshafts. In wooded areas the den is usually built from sticks, branches, bones, and similar debris. As with other woodrat species, a cup-shaped nest is constructed and lined with fine plant fibers. Although the nest is often within the den, in well-protected areas such as rafters or walls in an abandoned cabin or a shallow cave or mine, the nest may be completely exposed.

Bushy-tailed woodrats feed on a wide variety of plant materials. Leaves of forbs and shrubs are frequently used, as are needles of coniferous trees. Foods that are particularly important when available include juniper "berries," fungi, chokecherry, aspen, rose, snowberry, currant, goldenrod, mountain mahogany, saltbush, piñon pine, rabbitbrush, prickly-pear, skunkbush, Russian-thistle, and hackberry (R. Finley 1958). Additional foods include bristlecone pine needles and bark, goosefoot, mustards, and a wide variety of composites. Frase and Sera (1993) described clippings in dens of *N. cinerea* in Gunnison County. Virtually all woody plants within 30 m of the den were represented in the midden. Only 1 plant not found within 30 m of den was included. By contrast, less than 50 percent of herbaceous plants were represented.

Bushy-tailed woodrats are the characteristic "pack rats" of the high mountains and they frequently collect bones, dung, and old rags as well as bright objects, including bottle caps, pieces of aluminum foil, metal objects, buttons, cans, and silverware, and place them in their dens. Practically every abandoned cabin and mine building in the mountains of Colorado has a den of this rat and the characteristic black, tar-like varnish formed by years of urination and fecal deposition in established "toilets." Once one is familiar with the odor of the animals it is easy to detect their presence. Emslie et al. (2005) recorded dates on middens from about 3,450 to about 160 years old in the Upper Gunnison Basin and were able to discern changes in vegetation corresponding to climatic fluctuations.

Bushy-tailed woodrats probably breed in Colorado from April through August, depending on elevation, with a potential of 2 litters per year. Litter size ranges from 1 to 6, with an average of 3 to 4. In a study in the Canadian Rockies, DNA fingerprinting indicated that all offspring in a given litter were sired by the same male but individual males did not sire more than 1 litter from a particular female either within or between years (Topping and Millar 1998). Also in Alberta, Moses et al. (1995) found that sex ratios of offspring correlated strongly with pre-breeding body weight of mothers, with lower-weight yearling females raising fewer male pups.

Neotoma floridana

EASTERN WOODRAT

Description

The eastern woodrat is a rather large rat with a relatively short, sparsely haired tail that is not scaly. The fur is relatively long, soft, and fine. The color is brownish gray washed lightly with black, paler on the sides. Hairs of the belly are whitish with lead gray roots. The throat and chest are white with individual hairs white to their bases. The tail is bicolored, white below and blackish brown above. Measurements are: total length 340–380 mm; length of tail 139–159 mm; length of hindfoot 38–43 mm; length of ear 18–28 mm; weight 275–400 g. The skull is relatively long with a condylobasal length greater than 43 mm. The nasals are also long, usually more than 19 mm. The interorbital region is not strongly arched. The nasal septum is intact, lacking a maxillo-vomerine notch. The posterior margin of the palate is notched or concave. This is the only woodrat in Colorado with a forked anterior palatine spine. As with all woodrats, the cheekteeth are prismatic. Females have 4 mammae.

Some woodrats in Colorado can be difficult to identify. The eastern woodrat is sympatric in some areas with the Southern Plains, Mexican, or eastern white-throated woodrats. The eastern woodrat differs from the Southern Plains woodrat by having brownish gray rather than slate gray pelage (at least in adults), having a forked anterior palatine spine, and nasals that usually exceed 19 mm in length. From the Mexican woodrat, the eastern woodrat differs in having a paler dorsal pelage, throat hairs white (not gray) at their bases, an intact nasal septum, and a forked anterior palatine spine. From the white-throated woodrat, the eastern woodrat differs in its slightly larger size, more robust and arched skull, and intact nasal septum (no maxillo-vomerine notch).

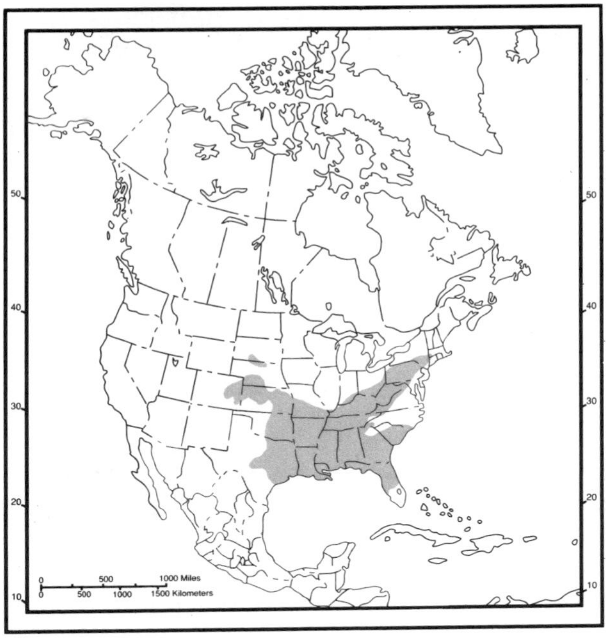

MAP 8-107. Distribution of the eastern woodrat (*Neotoma floridana*) in North America.

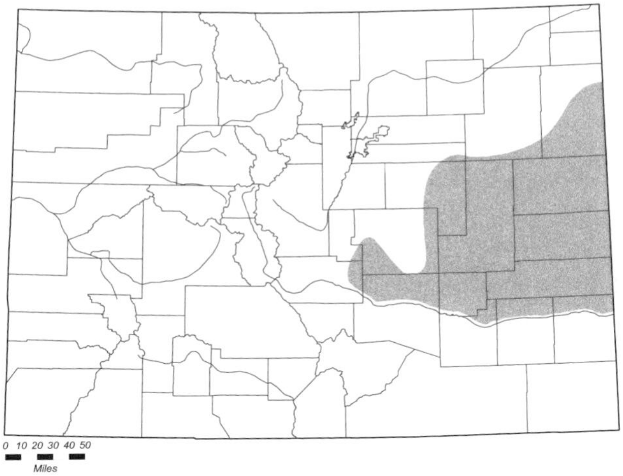

MAP 8-108. Distribution of the eastern woodrat (*Neotoma floridana*) in Colorado.

PHOTOGRAPH 8-53. Eastern woodrat (*Neotoma floridana*). Photograph by Roger W. Barbour.

Distribution

The eastern woodrat is a species of deciduous forests of the eastern and midwestern United States. Eastern Colorado represents the western limit of its distribution, the species occurring north of the Arkansas River to western El Paso County and north and east to Yuma County. Populations are localized in suitable habitat. Planz et al. (1996) provided a molecular phylogeny of the *"Neotoma floridana* species group," construed to include *N. albigula* (including *N. leucodon*), *N. floridana*, and *N. micropus*. In Oklahoma, *N. floridana* has hybridized with *N. micropus* (D. Spencer 1968). One subspecies, *Neotoma floridana campestris*, occurs in Colorado.

Natural History

Over most of its range the eastern woodrat inhabits deciduous forest, but in Colorado it occurs on the eastern plains, where it occupies rocky draws or riparian woodland and well-developed shrublands with yucca and cactus. Eastern woodrats in Colorado are marginal populations of the species. Its environment here is much drier—with greater extremes of temperature—than the habitat farther east in its extensive range. The eastern woodrat appears to have expanded its range in southwestern Nebraska in recent decades (Kugler and Geluso 2009), especially in the Republican River drainage.

In Colorado, eastern woodrats eat a variety of fruits, twigs, bark, and leaves from locally available plants, including cottonwood, saltbush, rabbitbrush, snakeweed, chokecherry, poison-ivy, skunkbush, currant, rose, greasewood, snowberry, cholla, prickly-pear, yucca, various grasses, pigweed, ragweed, gumweed, sunflower, evening star, Russian-thistle, and scurfpea (R. Finley 1958). Cactus joints and leaves of shrubs appear to be the most important food items. Bones are also consumed, probably as a source of calcium. Food is stored in the house, with increased storage activity occurring in fall and winter. Free water is not necessary; water needs are met from the diet.

Eastern woodrats are polyestrous with a gestation period of 32–38 days. Litter size averages 3 with a range of 1 to 6 (Rainey 1956; Birney 1973). The animals probably breed in our area from early spring through late summer. Each estrous cycle lasts 4 to 6 days. Two to 3 litters are possible because females typically have a postpartum estrus (Rainey 1956).

Young are blind and naked at birth and capable of only weak movements. However, even at this early stage of development the incisors have broken through the gumline. Young weigh about 12 g at birth. Their ears open by 10 days of age and the eyes are open by 15 days of age. Full adult weight is not reached until about 8 months of age (P. Pearson 1952; W. Hamilton 1953; Rainey 1956; D. Spencer 1968). Although females can breed at 5 or 6 months of age, in our area they probably do not have young until after their first winter.

Eastern woodrats are mostly nocturnal, solitary animals, active year-round. Greatest activity occurs from nightfall to about midnight, and especially between 2030 and 2230 hours. They are most active on dark nights with little or no moonlight, although juveniles may be active in late afternoon (R. Finley 1959; Wiley 1971).

As with other woodrats, eastern woodrats construct complex houses that provide cover and protection from predators and the physical environment. Houses are constructed from practically any movable materials, including sticks, stalks of herbaceous plants, cactus joints, and other vegetation, stones, dried fecal materials, bones, feathers, hides of dead animals, and human trash. Houses generally take on a conical shape, especially if constructed at the base of a tree or cactus. However, in rocky areas they conform to the shape of the overhangs, crevices, and rock outfall under which they are built. These homes may exceed a meter in height and diameter but are typically smaller than those of other species occupying the same general area. Eastern woodrats use less cactus in house construction than do white-throated or Southern Plains woodrats. Houses are augmented throughout the lifetime of the occupant. A path may surround the house, with the debris pushed to one side of the path, forming a conspicuous ridge. Side paths radiate into surrounding vegetation. Inside the house is a series of tunnels, passages, and chambers above- or sometimes belowground. Two or 3 cup-shaped nests, made of yucca fibers, soft grasses, fur, feathers, and shredded bark, are found in some of the chamber areas in the house (Fitch and Rainey 1956; Rainey 1956; R. Finley 1958).

The house is typically defended against other eastern woodrats. Such territorial defense is especially marked in females during the reproductive season. Severe fights occur, with the front paws held like boxing gloves while the animals jab with their front feet and slash with their incisors. Individuals grind their teeth and thump their feet during aggressive interactions. Foot thumping also occurs when the animals are nervous or excited, as when detained in a livetrap. Behavior was reviewed by Wiley (1980).

Woodrats tend to occupy linear habitats along rock outcrops or stream courses, so densities are difficult to estimate. Therefore, some authors have used counts of active houses to describe abundance. In habitats with favorable sites for houses, densities approximate 1 animal per hectare. Home ranges are associated with the area immediately around the house and are usually less than 0.25 ha (Goertz 1970). Home ranges overlap in favorable habitat.

Individuals can live up to 3 years but most probably survive less than 1 year in the wild. Great horned owls, skunks, and long-tailed weasels are effective predators. Wiley (1980) reviewed literature on the species, and Monty and Emerson (2003) reviewed the extensive literature on *Neotoma floridana* and other species of woodrats.

Neotoma lepida

DESERT WOODRAT

Description

The desert woodrat is a small yellow-buff to buffy gray woodrat. The tail is sharply bicolored and short-haired. The underparts are whitish to buff. White hairs on the chest are usually gray at their bases except for a small patch or mid-ventral strip with white base. Measurements are: total length 266–295 mm; length of tail 110–126 mm; length of hindfoot 31–33 mm; length of ear 28–30 mm; weight 100–140 g. The skull is not strongly arched in the interorbital region. A maxillo-vomerine notch is present in the nasal septum. The anterior palatal spine is stout and blunt. Small size, pale color, and generally naked soles of the hindfoot separate this species from *Neotoma cinerea*. From *N. mexicana* it differs in having a much less arched skull, some hairs on the chest white to their bases, and a blunt anterior palatal spine.

PHOTOGRAPH 8-54. Desert woodrat (*Neotoma lepida*). Photograph by Joseph Van Wormer. All rights reserved, Photo Archives, Denver Museum of Nature and Science.

Distribution

The desert woodrat is restricted in Colorado to the northwestern and west-central parts of the state, along the

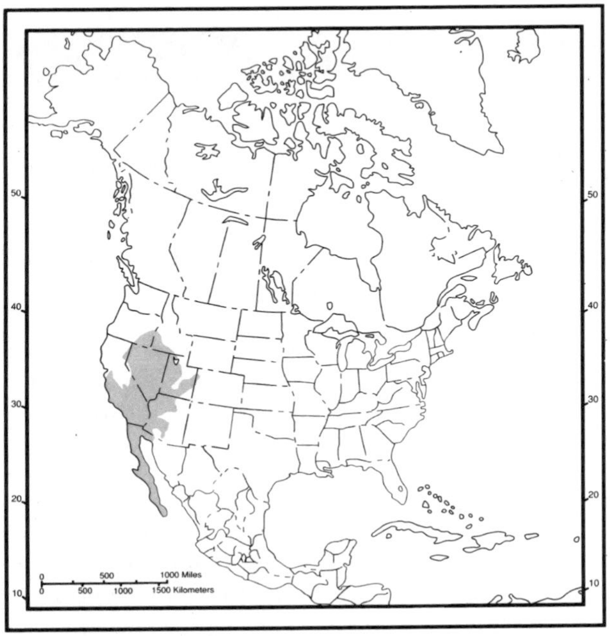

MAP 8-109. Distribution of the desert woodrat (*Neotoma lepida*) in North America.

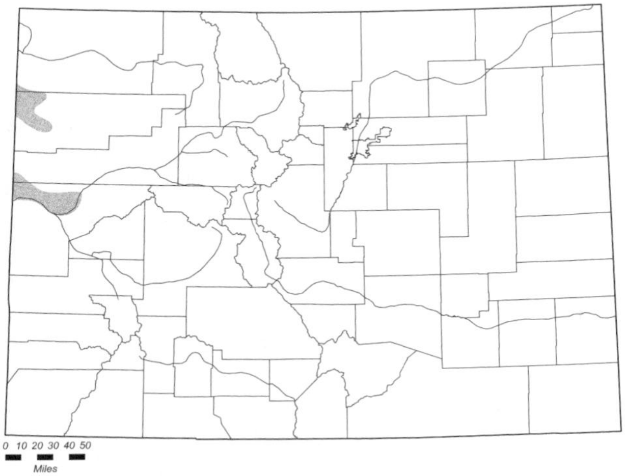

MAP 8-110. Distribution of the desert woodrat (*Neotoma lepida*) in Colorado.

Colorado and White rivers, north and south of the Roan Plateau. R. Finley (1958) and D. Armstrong (1972) considered Coloradan desert woodrats to represent the subspecies *Neotoma lepida sanrafaeli*. J. Patton et al. (2008) provided an exhaustive systematic review and taxonomic revision of the *Neotoma lepida* group of woodrats and considered *N. l. sanrafaeli* to be a junior synonym of *N. l. monstrabilis*, to which Coloradan desert woodrats were referred.

Natural History

The desert woodrat has not been studied as intensively as some other species of *Neotoma*. It is mainly a species of canyonlands and semiarid shrublands of the Great Basin (Llewellyn 1981), reaching eastern limits in northwestern and west-central Colorado. Desert woodrats tend to locate dens among fallen rock slabs and boulders, in ledges and crevices along rock faces, or occasionally in trees (especially juniper).

Desert woodrats apparently feed on a wider variety of food items than do Colorado's other woodrats. The animals are not as closely associated with cactus as other species are, and much less of the diet is cactus, although it is readily eaten if available. Other dietary items include stems, twigs, bark, berries, and seeds of locally common xerophytic shrubs and forbs. Saltbush, juniper, and Russian-thistle are frequently used as well as greasewood, snakeweed, sagebrush, and yucca. In Utah, 88 percent of the diet was shrubs and forbs. Juniper branches and leaves are important foods, especially in the winter months. The animals also eat Mormon tea (*Ephedra*) and piñon nuts. Food stores in the den consisted mainly of juniper leaves and "berries" in Utah (Stones and Hayward 1968).

Desert woodrats in Colorado do not appear to construct houses away from rocky areas to any significant extent (R. Finley 1958), although Cary (1911) discussed and illustrated a house made of cow dung and prickly-pear pads near Rangely. At that site he reported houses numerous enough to resemble "muskrat houses on a marsh." Improvement in livestock grazing practices on public lands since the 1930s may have shifted the amount of habitat away from rocky areas suitable for the species. In Utah, houses were most abundant in dense stands of juniper, and nests were located in juniper trees (Stones and Hayward 1968).

Dens in rock shelters are typically constructed of small sticks, plant stalks, and cacti, with fewer bones reported than in dens of bushy-tailed woodrat. Dens are rarely constructed in vertical crevices but typically are found in horizontal crevices and under boulders. Size of dens varies widely, with some being built in crevices that would not be used by larger woodrats; at other times the size of the den may equal that of one constructed by a bushy-tailed woodrat. This may be because in areas of sympatry dens are occupied serially by different species of woodrats (D. Armstrong 1982). An average den is constructed in 7 to 10 nights of activity (Bonaccorso and Brown 1972). As with other species of woodrat, dens have more than 1 entrance. The nest is usually a ball-shaped mass of finely shredded bark, grass, or similar material. In Utah, oval, circular, or gourd-shaped nests were made with shredded juniper bark (Stones and Hayward 1968). In a 3-year study in the Mojave Desert of Southern California, F. Smith (1995) demonstrated that both survivorship and the duration of occupancy of dens were greater in habitats dominated by (and hence in dens constructed of) cholla cactus than in those dominated by Mojave yucca.

The species is polyestrous, reproducing throughout the warmer months. Two litters are probably typical in Colorado, although up to 4 litters per year have been reported from farther southwest. The gestation period is 30–36 days, with litters ranging from 1 to 5 with an average of slightly more than 2 (Egoscue 1957, 1962b; Egoscue et al. 1970; G. Cameron 1973). Young are relatively precocial, with incisors erupted at birth. This allows pups to grip the nipples of the mother so tightly that suckling young are dragged as the mother scurries to deeper cover to escape perceived danger. Young grow rapidly, with their eyes opening at about 12 days. They are weaned at about 4 weeks of age. Females can reproduce at about 3 months of age.

The desert woodrat is mainly nocturnal, although there are several reports of their moving about in the daytime. The animals forage or collect materials for the nest within about 100 m of the den. Males are more active outside the den than are females.

In juniper and sage-juniper woodland in Utah, densities varied from 4.5 to 7.7 animals per hectare; these same sites contained 12 and 21 houses per hectare, respectively. Only about 37 percent of houses were occupied, usually by a single adult. Animals moved between houses readily, and young animals usually took up occupancy of existing (but unoccupied) houses (Stones and Hayward 1968). Hantavirus infection is known from woodrats in the Southwest, but prevalence is much lower than in deer mice and other species of *Peromyscus* (Dearing et al. 1998), despite the fact that several species of *Peromyscus* are known to inhabit woodrat dens (D. Armstrong 1982). The extensive literature on desert woodrats was reviewed by Verts and Carraway (2002).

PHOTOGRAPH 8-55. Eastern white-throated woodrat (*Neotoma leucodon*). Photograph by M. Patrikeer.

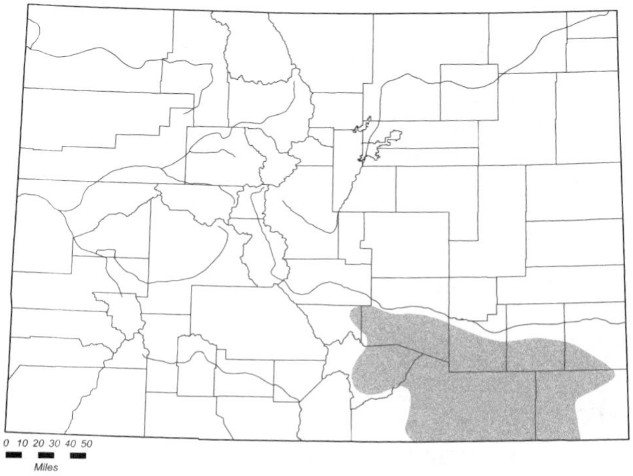

MAP 8-111. Distribution of the eastern white-throated woodrat (*Neotoma leucodon*) in Colorado; for North American distribution, see Map 8-103.

Neotoma leucodon

EASTERN WHITE-THROATED WOODRAT

Description

The eastern white-throated woodrat is of medium size for the genus, with a distinctly bicolored tail, dark brown above and white below. Hairs of the throat are white to their bases and there is no dark line around the mouth. The animals are somewhat variable in dorsal color, predominantly pale brownish but with a blackish "wash," provided by black-tipped hairs. Measurements are: total length 300–350 mm; length of tail 125–150 mm; length of hindfoot 33–37 mm; length of ear 26–30; weight 150–280 g.

Neotoma albigula and *N. leucodon* are distinctive genetically (C. Edwards et al. 2001), but no macroscopic characters are known to distinguish them reliably except by direct comparison, especially of museum specimens. R. Finley (1958: 299) noted that woodrats now known as *N. leucodon* differ from western white-throated woodrats in grayer dorsal color and "in more angular configuration of temporal ridges, narrow maxillo-vomerine notch, and deeper antero-internal enamel fold of M^1."

N. leucodon was listed with the vernacular name "white-toothed woodrat" by D. Wilson and Reeder (2005), but we use the name "eastern white-throated woodrat" (following R. Baker, L. Bradley, et al. 2003) because the species is white-throated and the name indicates the traditional understanding of relationships of this population with *Neotoma albigula*, the western white-throated woodrat. Literature on *Neotoma albigula* prior to 1981 may pertain to this species.

Distribution

The eastern white-throated woodrat occurs in southeastern Colorado, south of the Arkansas River and east of the Sangre de Cristo Range. Where *N. leucodon* and *N. micropus* are sympatric, the eastern white-throated woodrat typically dens in rocky outcrops, whereas the Southern Plains woodrat dens in more open situations, especially about the bases of cacti (R. Finley 1958).

Three species of woodrats in southeastern Colorado—*N. albigula* (*sensu lato*), *N. floridana*, and *N. micropus*—have been difficult to distinguish and are subjects of ongoing taxonomic research and dispute. R. Finley (1958) suspected hybridization in southeastern Colorado between *N. micropus* and *N. leucodon* (then known as *N. albigula warreni*). E. Zimmerman and Nejtek (1977) demonstrated the close genetic similarity among eastern, Southern Plains, and white-throated woodrats. The history of this taxonomic quandary was summarized briefly by C. Edwards et al. (2001). Birney (1973, 1976) suggested—based partly on work in southeastern Colorado—that *M. albigula*, *M. floridana*, and *N. micropus* were quite closely related and should be considered members of a single "*floridana* species group." E. Zimmerman and Nejtek (1977) characterized these 3 related woodrats as "semispecies." Planz et al. (1996) provided a molecular phylogeny of the "*Neotoma floridana* species group."

Based on sequence of the mitochondrial DNA cytochrome-b gene, C. Edwards et al. (2001) concluded that eastern and western white-throated woodrats are different species, *N. leucodon* and *N. albigula*, respectively. C.

Edwards et al. (2001) did not utilize specimens of western white-throated woodrats from Colorado in their analysis, but these 2 kinds of arid-adapted woodrats are separated in Colorado by the Southern Rocky Mountains, including the Sangre de Cristo Range and the San Juan massif. The animals are not known from the San Luis Valley. Consequently, observing the critical test of species—reproductive isolation—is not possible in Colorado. Rather, the genetics of woodrats in New Mexico tell the story. There the 2 kinds of white-throated woodrats appear to be separated by the Rio Grande Valley.

The closest relative of the eastern white-throated woodrat is *N. micropus*, the Southern Plains woodrat, whereas the closest relative of the western white-throated woodrat is the eastern woodrat (*N. floridana*). C. Edwards et al. (2001) hypothesized that the eastern white-tailed woodrat per se was "isolated geographically by reduction of suitable habitat brought about by changing climatic patterns that allowed formation of xeric communities soon after the end of the Late Wisconsin." That reduction would have been exacerbated by the Hypsithermal Interval of 4,500 to 6,000 years ago, which likely made the middle Rio Grande Valley of New Mexico even drier than it is today.

Macêdo and Mares (1988) and Monty and Emerson (2003) reviewed the literature on *Neotoma albigula* (*sensu lato*). Research based on animals from southeastern Colorado, New Mexico east of the Rio Grande, the Oklahoma Panhandle, West Texas, and central and eastern Mexico applies to the animals now known as *N. leucodon*.

Natural History

Ecology of the eastern white-throated woodrat was reported in detail (under the name *N. albigula warreni*) by R. Finley (1958). Except for differences driven by available food resources (e.g., cholla, or "tree cactus," does not occur in southwestern Colorado), there appear to be no salient differences between the ecology of *N. leucodon* and that of *N. albigula* in Colorado. Fortunately, R. Finley (1958) detailed the natural history of "white-throated woodrats" at the level of subspecies, so comments pertinent to the newly recognized *N. leucodon*, reported by R. Finley (1958) as *N. albigula warreni*, are distinguishable.

Dens are known from a variety of plant communities, including piñon-juniper woodland, juniper-sage, juniper-yucca, cottonwood-juniper-cholla, and shortgrass steppe with cholla, yucca, and scattered juniper (R. Finley 1958). Dens often are in rock-shelters but may also be built at the base of junipers. The most frequent situation is at the base of cholla, especially in areas where Southern Plains woodrats (*N. micropus*) are absent. R. Finley (1958) described a number of dens in rich detail. The most abundant building materials were sticks, cholla joints, prickly-pear pads, livestock dung, bones, small stones, and pinecones, but carnivore scat and a variety of human rubbish are also reported. Preferred food plants include cholla, juniper, yucca, skunkbush, and leaves of a variety of forbs. Cholla, juniper, and yucca were the most frequent stored foods (R. Finley 1958). The animals obtain needed water from cacti and other fleshy food items.

Ectoparasites include ticks, a number of species of mites, sucking lice, and fleas (R. Finley 1958). Tapeworms infest the animals internally. Predators include coyotes, gopher ("bull") snakes and western rattlesnakes, and owls. Calisher, Nabity, et al. (2001) reported antibodies to Whitewater Arroyo virus (a transmissible *Arenavirus* known to cause fatal infection in humans) in white-throated woodrats from the US Army's Piñon Canyon Maneuver Site in Las Animas County.

The animals breed through the warmer months. Three-quarters of females captured in late May and early June were pregnant or lactating (R. Finley 1958). Individual females probably have 2 or more litters per year. Young of early litters likely breed in their first year.

Neotoma mexicana

MEXICAN WOODRAT

Description

The Mexican woodrat is a medium-sized woodrat. Dorsal color of animals from the foothills of the Front Range is usually dark gray, often washed with black. Animals from southwestern Colorado are more grayish buff on the dorsum, whereas those from the San Luis Valley and southeastern Colorado are grayish yellow to gray-buff. The sides are a paler grayish buff. The underparts are whitish with all hairs gray at their bases. There is typically a dusky line or ring around the mouth. The short-haired tail is distinctly bicolored, blackish above and whitish gray below. The feet are white. Measurements are: total length 297–380 mm; length of tail 124–178 mm; length of hindfoot 29–38 mm; length of ear 26–28 mm; weight 149–255 g. The skull is robust and often somewhat arched in the interorbital region. A maxillo-vomerine notch divides the nasal septum. The anterior palatal spine has a sharp tip. In most

PHOTOGRAPH 8-56. Mexican woodrat (*Neotoma mexicana*). Photograph by R. B. Forbes.

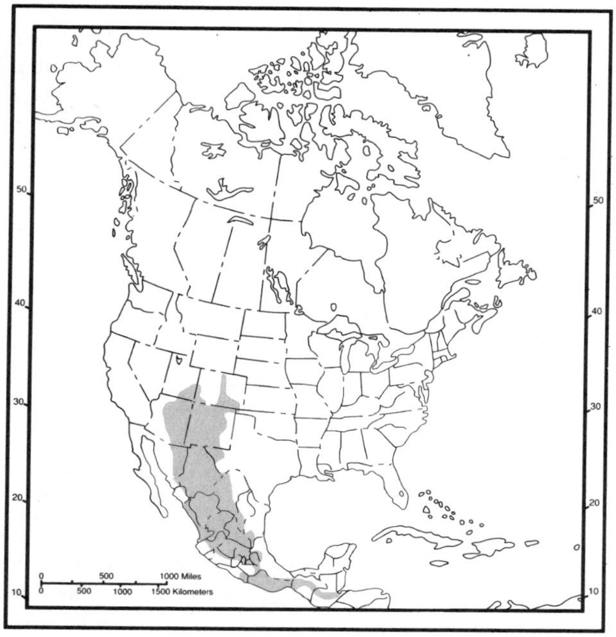

MAP 8-112. Distribution of the Mexican woodrat (*Neotoma mexicana*) in North America.

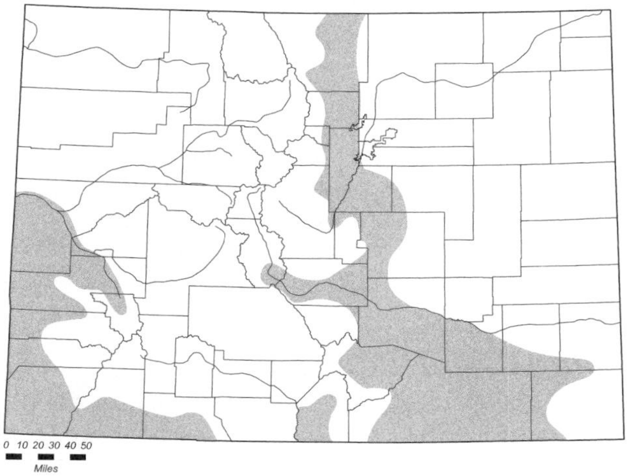

MAP 8-113. Distribution of the Mexican woodrat (*Neotoma mexicana*) in Colorado.

specimens the antero-internal fold of M^1 is deep, extending more than halfway across the crown.

Distribution

Like some other species of Mexican affinities (e.g., Abert's squirrel, rock squirrel, northern rock mouse, piñon mouse; see D. Armstrong, 1972, 1996), the Mexican woodrat is found in a narrow band along the Front Range and in southeastern Colorado, south of the Arkansas River. They also occur in the volcanic San Luis Hills and in the canyon country of southwestern Colorado. *Neotoma mexicana fallax* is the subspecies of the Front Range, from the Arkansas River northward nearly to the Wyoming border, and extending westward up the Arkansas Valley to about Salida; *N. m. inopinata* occurs in southwestern Colorado south of the Gunnison and Colorado rivers; *N. m. scopulorum* occurs in southeastern Colorado south of the Arkansas River and also in the San Luis Valley. C. Edwards and Bradley (2002) included a sample of *N. m. scopulorum* from Las Animas County, Colorado, in a molecular systematic study of some species of *Neotoma*. No nomenclatural changes were suggested by that work.

Natural History

The Mexican woodrat is a species of semiarid canyonlands, sedimentary foothills, and lower mountains, generally below about 2,600 m (8,500 ft.) in Colorado. It is usually associated with rocky slopes and cliffs in montane shrublands, piñon-juniper woodlands, and montane forests. In riparian woodlands in canyons and draws in the foothills, dens are constructed beneath shrubs and downed logs. They also utilize sheds and barns, including buildings in active use. As with all woodrats, the species is herbivorous; leaves comprise up to 90 percent of stomach contents (D. Armstrong 1982). Buds, flowers, and cones of a variety of species are also eaten. R. Finley (1958) reported the animals to be food generalists, eating practically any kind of plant available and especially oak, sagebrush, juniper, ponderosa pine, skunkbush, mountain mahogany, chokecherry, winterfat, snowberry, currant, rabbitbrush, and yucca. Cactus does not appear to be used much in Colorado. Acorns, piñon nuts, and juniper "berries" are important foods. The species cuts and caches large amounts of foliage. Greatest collecting activity occurs in the fall. The ability to concentrate urine is not as well developed as that of the white-throated woodrat, and the animals will take free water if available (Brownfield and Wunder 1976). In the laboratory, Mexican woodrats can tolerate large quantities of tannins if they are allowed to adjust gradually to the compounds (Voltura and Wunder 1994).

Mexican woodrats are active year-round, mostly at night. Unlike some other woodrats in Colorado, they do not build houses away from rocky areas (R. Finley 1958). Dens and nests typically are beneath ledges or in fissures of cliffs. Both horizontal and vertical crevices are used. They also use abandoned or seasonally occupied buildings or mine tunnels and will adopt houses constructed by other species of woodrats. Their dens are typically built of small and medium-sized sticks, twigs, and leaf cuttings. Much of the material probably also is used for food. Nests are either cup-shaped or ball-shaped masses of shredded bark from juniper or sage or yucca fibers. Woodrats are "pack rats," and other materials, including bones, feathers, and dung, are gathered to add to the house. Fecal material accumulates rapidly around active den sites, and this along with fresh clippings of vegetation makes it easy to determine their presence. Study of middens of Mexican woodrats at the Owl Canyon Piñon Grove suggests that the grove is only about 400 years old. There is no evidence of piñon in the ancient midden record, which includes materials gathered from 1,200 to 5,000 years before present (Livo 1992).

The tendency of the Mexican woodrat to occur at lower elevations reduces possible interaction with the bushy-tailed woodrat. In areas of sympatry the latter species often constructs its dens higher up on cliff faces, while the Mexican woodrat uses crevices closer to ground level. Where the species do not coexist, Mexican woodrats use the entire cliff face. In areas of sympatry with white-throated woodrats, such as in southeastern and southwestern Colorado, Mexican woodrats tend to make more use of the rocky, steep sides of canyons, whereas white-throated woodrats use the valley floor. In certain locations, dens of both species are found in the same rocky habitat. Populations of eastern and desert woodrats in Colorado are largely allopatric to the Mexican woodrat.

Mexican woodrats are seasonally polyestrous and breed from late March to mid-June in Colorado. A postpartum estrus occurs, and typically 2 litters are produced per year. Gestation takes 31 to 34 days, with an average of 3 young per litter and a range of 2 to 5. Females born in April and May can breed late in their first year and usually produce 2 young per litter (L. N. Brown 1969). Males typically do not breed until after their first winter. Maximal size of testes occurs in April. Howe (1978) reported considerable agonistic behavior associated with mating in the Mexican woodrat in the laboratory. During mating encounters males made wheezy, gasping sounds when approaching estrous females. Cornely and Baker (1986) reviewed literature on the species.

Neotoma micropus
SOUTHERN PLAINS WOODRAT

Description

Formerly called the gray woodrat, the Southern Plains woodrat is of medium size with a dense, soft slate to ash gray pelage. The tail is relatively short and sparsely haired, dusky gray above and paler whitish gray below. The venter is gray and the throat and chest are white. The feet are white. As with other woodrats the vibrissae are long and conspicuous. Measurements are: total length 310–411 mm; length of tail 130–175 mm; length of hindfoot 30–45 mm; length of ear 25–30 mm; weight 180–320 g. The skull has

PHOTOGRAPH 8-57. Southern Plains woodrat (*Neotoma micropus*). Photograph by Roger W. Barbour.

a strongly arched interorbital region, no maxillo-vomerine notch, and a short palatal bridge (usually with a posterior median spine). Females have 2 pair of mammae.

Distribution

The Southern Plains woodrat is largely restricted to the eastern plains south of the Arkansas River, with only a few specimens from Crowley and Bent counties north of the river. In localized areas in Colorado, *Neotoma micropus* has hybridized with *N. leucodon* (reported as *N. albigula warreni*; R. Finley 1958; Huheey 1972), and in Oklahoma with *N. floridana* (D. Spencer 1968). One subspecies, *Neotoma micropus canescens*, occurs in Colorado.

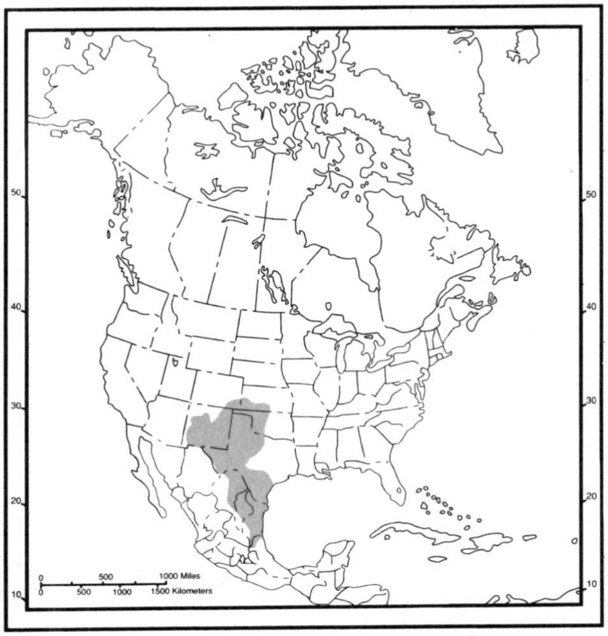

MAP 8-114. Distribution of the Southern Plains woodrat (*Neotoma micropus*) in North America.

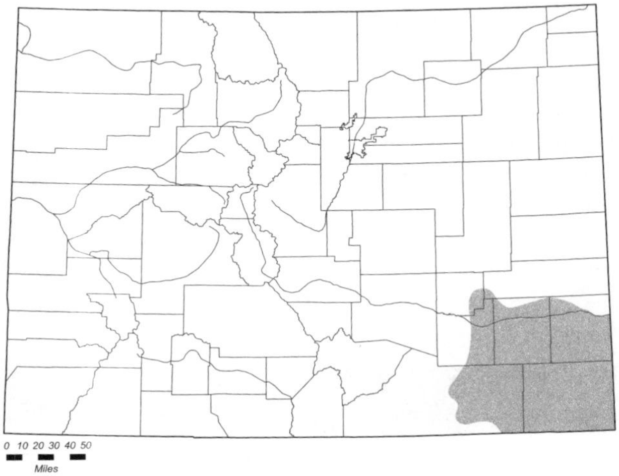

MAP 8-115. Distribution of the Southern Plains woodrat (*Neotoma micropus*) in Colorado.

Natural History

These animals are associated with a variety of semiarid and desert grassland environments, including shrub- and cactus-grasslands of the Southern Great Plains. In Colorado the species is largely restricted to grasslands with prickly-pear and candelabra cactus (cholla). A few individuals have also been captured in yucca-grass communities and on rocky outcrops in mixed shrub stands. Houses are built at the bases of cholla or yucca and sometimes under rockfalls and rocky overhangs (R. Finley 1958). In southwestern Oklahoma, prickly-pear cactus was the most common material added to houses except in spring, when sticks and cattle dung were the materials most frequently gathered (Thies et al. 1996). The animals are not as strongly associated with rocky areas as are Mexican and white-throated woodrats.

In Colorado the diet appears to be mostly joints of cholla. A wide variety of other plants are also consumed, including yucca, prickly-pear, juniper, currant, blue grama, milkweed, Russian-thistle, and copper mallow (R. Finley 1958). Although captive animals drink readily, free water is not needed, as cactus in the diet provides ample water in the wild.

A typical house is constructed at the base of a cholla and is built largely from the joints of the cactus, supplemented with other materials, including cow dung, small stones and sticks, prickly-pear pads, stalks of herbaceous plants, feathers, and bones. Houses are usually less than a meter in height and usually have a well-worn path around the outside. The house has several entrances usually bordered by cactus joints. Passages lead to a central chamber or to smaller side chambers. The ball-like nest is located in a side chamber and is constructed from softer, finer plant materials such as grass or yucca fibers. This species shows some preference for underground nest locations (R. Finley 1958).

A territory is defended around the house and individuals usually use the same den throughout their lives. As with other woodrats, a variety of small mammals (including desert shrews), lizards, and insects are commensals in houses of Southern Plains woodrats. The animals are largely nocturnal and solitary, with most activity occurring before midnight. Unlike the situation reported in other species, there does not seem to be any correlation between trapping success and intensity of moonlight or cloud cover (J. Braun and Mares 1989). Movement is usually limited to about 15 m or so from the den. Home ranges have been estimated at 258 m^2 to more than 1,300 m^2, with those of males being larger than those of females (J. Braun and Mares 1989).

Southern Plains woodrats in our area are probably capable of having 2 or 3 litters a year. Females may have a postpartum estrus. For most females gestation takes 33–35 days, although much variation has been reported (Birney 1973). Pregnant females show abdominal hair loss and enlargement and swelling of the mammae. Litter size averages 2 to 3. Growth of young animals is similar to that of the eastern woodrat, the eyes opening and juvenal pelage complete at about 2 weeks of age. By 3 months of age they have attained about 85 percent of adult weight (Wiley 1984).

Woodrats are seemingly nervous animals while active outside the den, ears in constant motion and whiskers twitching. They have excellent hearing and use it as a primary sensory mechanism to avoid predators. J. Braun and Mares (1989) reviewed the literature on the species.

MAP 8-116. Distribution of Stephens' woodrat (*Neotoma stephensi*) in North America.

Neotoma stephensi

STEPHENS' WOODRAT

Description

Stephens' woodrat is small and pale yellow to buff-gray in color. The belly and throat are white, the hairs of the throat gray at their bases. The tail is indistinctly bicolored, with the hairs relatively long and slightly bushy at the tip. Measurements are: total length 280–333 mm; length of tail 112–144 mm; length of hindfoot 30–33 mm; length of ear 27–30 mm. Any small, pale-colored woodrat from lower elevations in extreme southwestern Colorado (south of Durango and Cortez) should be examined by an expert for identification.

Distribution

Stephens' woodrat is undocumented in Colorado but is of probable occurrence. It ranges over much of northern and central Arizona and western New Mexico, barely extending into south-central Utah. It occurs within a few kilometers of Colorado's southern border, near Navajo Reservoir, and may be expected on the Southern Ute Reservation. *Neotoma stephensi relicta* is the subspecies to be expected in Colorado.

Natural History

In northern Arizona the species is typically associated with piñon-juniper woodlands, rock debris at the base of cliffs, and rocky outcrops. T. Vaughan (1990) reported that most nests near Flagstaff were located at the base of junipers. The diet is almost exclusively "berries" and leaves of juniper (T. Vaughan 1982; A. Green et al. 2004). Mormon tea (*Ephedra*) also is eaten. The animals probably breed from March to August, with 1 or 2 young per litter (range, 1 to 3). Probably 2 litters are produced per year. C. Jones and Hildreth (1989) reviewed the literature on *Neotoma stephensi*.

Subfamily Sigmodontinae

The Sigmodontinae is a diverse subfamily of about 377 species in 74 genera. Most are subtropical or tropical in distribution. A single species occurs in Colorado.

Sigmodon hispidus

HISPID COTTON RAT

Description

Hispid cotton rats have harsh, dark-colored pelage. Dorsal color is blackish brown interspersed with yellowish to buffy hairs. The underparts are paler in color, tending toward gray. The tail is sparsely haired, revealing the scales underneath. Length of the tail is less than that of the head and body. The ears are small but well haired. Measurements are: total length 224–265 mm; length of tail 81–166 mm; length of hindfoot 28–35 mm; length of ear 16–24 mm; weight 100–225 g. Males are typically slightly larger than females. Molars are rooted and high-crowned. Their occlusal surface has large, flattened cusps (sometimes described as "lozenge-shaped") arranged in a sigma-shaped pattern (hence the generic name). The skull is long, narrow, and stout with well-developed supraorbital (temporal) ridges. The infraorbital foramen is prominent, and the infraorbital plate of the zygomatic arch has a pronounced, blunt, spine-like, anterior projection unlike that of any other rodent in Colorado. Females typically have 5 pairs of mammae.

PHOTOGRAPH 8-58. Hispid cotton rat (*Sigmodon hispidus*). Photograph by Roger W. Barbour.

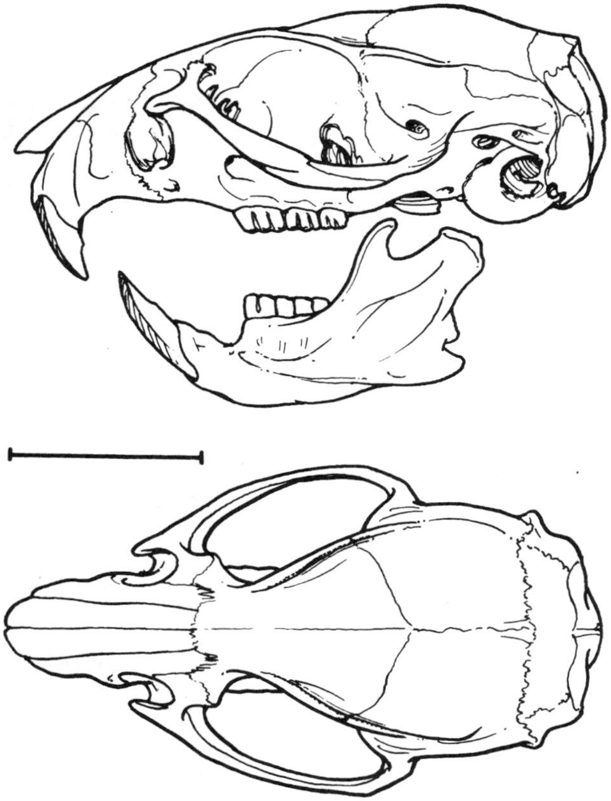

FIGURE 8-10. Lateral and dorsal views of the skull of a hispid cotton rat (*Sigmodon hispidus*). Note the prominent supraorbital ridges. Scale = 1 cm.

Distribution

First collected in Colorado in Baca County in 1946 (Goldman and Gardner 1947), the hispid cotton rat has now been reported from nearly all Coloradan counties in the Arkansas watershed, especially from irrigated country (R. Hansen 1963; D. Armstrong 1972; A. Carey 1978; Mellott and Fleharty 1986), where they often are common. When first discovered, Coloradan cotton rats were named by Goldman and Gardner (1947) as a new subspecies, *Sigmodon hispidus alfredi*, but D. Armstrong (1972) suggested that Coloradan cotton rats probably were not a peripheral isolate and predicted that this name eventually will be judged a junior synonym of *S. h. texianus*. No modern phylogeographic analysis or subspecific revision has been published, although R. D. Bradley et al. (2008) did provide a molecular systematic review of species in the *Sigmodon hispidus* complex.

Natural History

Little is known about the species in Colorado other than general observations on its rapid range expansion in the southeastern part of the state. The hispid cotton rat is an animal of grasslands, especially where forbs and shrubs are well developed (Fleharty and Mares 1973). In Colorado it is

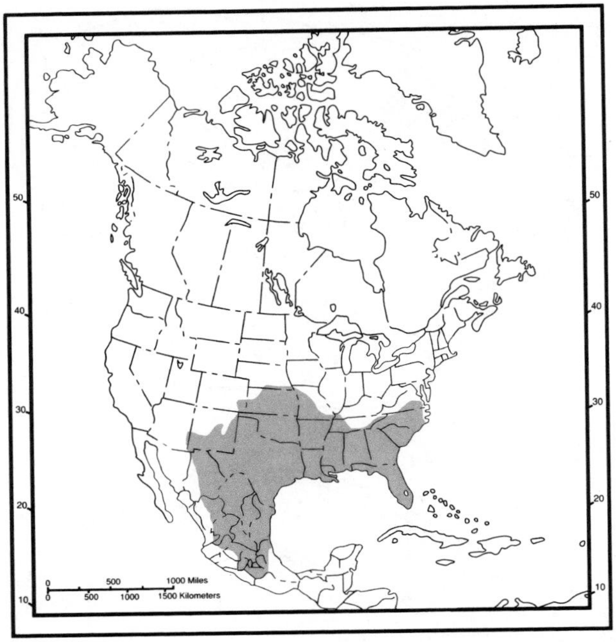

MAP 8-117. Distribution of the hispid cotton rat (*Sigmodon hispidus*) in North America.

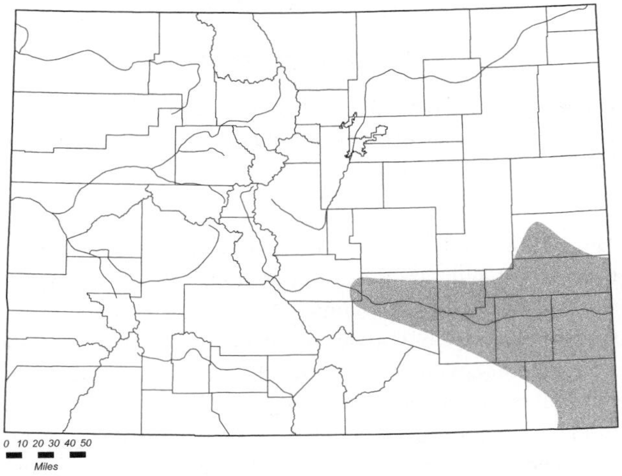

MAP 8-118. Distribution of the hispid cotton rat (*Sigmodon hispidus*) in Colorado.

associated usually with mid- and tallgrass prairie or weedy areas in riparian zones that provide good canopy cover. It is not found in wooded areas and appears to favor moist sites when available.

The diet is primarily grasses, with forbs and insects also consumed as available (Fleharty and Olson 1969). Cotton rats will clip and leave some vegetation during their foraging activities. In northern parts of their range, probably including Colorado, individuals gain significant weight during the fall to store as fat and metabolize during cold weather (Fleharty et al. 1972). Randolph et al. (1991) discovered that cotton rats on the Texas coastal prairie were selective in their diets, choosing plants high in soluble carbohydrates through the year. They also showed that some of the bias for grasses over broad-leafed plants was based on efficiency, as indicated by lower handling time for grasses.

Cotton rats may be active anytime of the day or night but are mostly nocturnal or crepuscular. They use burrow systems, especially during cold weather in northern parts of their range. Globular or cup-shaped nests of grasses may be located either under surface objects or in burrows (Shump 1978; Shump and Christian 1978).

Polyestrous, cotton rats are induced ovulators with a postpartum estrus. Gestation averages 27 days (Meyer and Meyer 1944). Litter size ranges from 1 to 15, with an average of 6 to 7 in northern parts of their range in Kansas (Kilgore 1970). Older females typically have the largest litters. Extrapolating from studies in adjacent Kansas (Kilgore 1970; Fleharty and Choate 1973), cotton rats probably breed during the warmer months in southeastern Colorado.

Newborn young are relatively precocial, weighing close to 7 g and having a coat of fine hair. They are capable of coordinated movements within hours after birth. The eyes open usually within 36 hours and growth is rapid for the first 40 days of life, averaging close to 2 g per day. Weaning occurs at about 2 weeks of age. Animals are essentially full-grown in 100 days (Svihla 1929; Meyer and Meyer 1944). Females have shown signs of estrus as early as 10 days of age, with pregnancy being recorded in females about 40 days old. Males typically have sperm in the epididymis by 3 months of age (Meyer and Meyer 1944; Fleharty and Choate 1973).

Cotton rats are extremely prolific and populations can grow rapidly; in southern parts of their range cyclic peaks and crashes in abundance are not uncommon. In northern areas population cycles are not well documented, but population crashes do occur. In Kansas, low population numbers (0.02 animals per hectare) occur in the spring, with peaks (20 animals per hectare) in the fall (Fleharty et al. 1972). Mean life expectancy is about 2 months, with few individuals living more than 10 months. Studies of population dynamics suggest that dominant animals are more susceptible to trapping than juveniles, making it difficult to make accurate density estimates. This appears to be the result of social structure and trap avoidance by subordinates of traps visited by dominant individuals (Summerlin and Wolfe 1973).

Home ranges average 0.2 to 0.4 ha. Males have larger home ranges than females, and adult home ranges are larger than those of subadults and juveniles. Females maintain exclusive home ranges and dominance systems develop in some populations (Fleharty and Mares 1973). Individuals of all ages and both sexes may disperse, the net effect of which is to reduce population pressures and local densities. A number of studies (summarized by G. Cameron and Spencer 1981) have suggested that high population densities of cotton rats may have a negative effect on populations of sympatric voles and harvest mice, some of which may result from a predilection of cotton rats for feeding on the young of these species. Hawks and owls prey heavily on cotton rats, as do mammalian carnivores such as foxes, coyotes, skunks, weasels, and domestic pets. G. Cameron and Spencer (1981) reviewed the rich literature on the species.

Family Muridae—Old World Rats and Mice

Murid rodents are native to Eurasia, Africa, Australia, and adjacent islands. Today—mostly from inadvertent introductions by people—the family occurs nearly worldwide (except Antarctica). There are about 730 species in some 150 genera (D. Wilson and Reeder 2005). Murid rodents typically have sparsely haired, scaly tails and cusped teeth. Cusps of the upper molars are arranged in 3 longitudinal rows. The palate terminates beyond the plane of the last molars.

Members of the group are highly adaptable and some are commensal or competitive with humans. In Colorado 2 genera and 2 species are present, house mice and Norway rats. Introduced Eurasian species, they both first reached North America with early European colonists but undoubtedly other individuals entered the United States later at major ports along both coasts. House mice have traveled with humans on ships, trains, and trucks to become established practically worldwide except polar areas. Similarly, Norway rats have been introduced to many parts of North America and reside in practically every major city on the continent. In Colorado they are more strongly restricted to urban areas or feedlots than are house mice. Murine rodents in Colorado are not listed as wildlife (Table 4-1) and receive no protection under state law; hence, they can be trapped or otherwise destroyed without license or limit.

Key to the Species of the Subfamily Murinae Known or Expected to Occur in Colorado

1. Length of skull less than 20 mm; total length less than 200 mm; first upper molar longer than combined length of second and third molars . . . . House Mouse—*Mus musculus*, p. 253

1' Length of skull more than 20 mm; total length more than 200 mm; first upper molar shorter than combined length of second and third molars 2

2. Tail shorter than head and body; M^1 without distinct outer notches on first row of cusps . . . . Norway Rat—*Rattus norvegicus*, p. 252

2' Tail longer than head and body; M^1 with distinct outer notches on first row of cusps . . . . Black Rat—*Rattus rattus**

Rattus norvegicus

NORWAY RAT

Description

The Norway rat is a large, heavy-bodied rat with a long, sparsely haired, scaly tail. The upperparts are usually brown to brownish black whereas the underparts are paler in color. Occasionally some individuals show a high degree of spotting or splotching with white. The pelage is somewhat coarse. The ears are conspicuous and covered with short hairs. Measurements are: total length 300–480 mm; length of tail 150–255 mm; length of hindfoot 30–44; length of ear 18–21 mm; weight 150–540 g. Anal scent glands produce a musky odor. Males have a baculum. Females have 6 pairs of mammae. The skull is long and narrow with conspicuous temporal ridges. The length of the first upper molar is lower than the combined length of molars 2 and 3. Although superficially similar in size and appearance, Norway rats can be distinguished from woodrats (*Neotoma*) by their naked tail, poorly haired ears, and relatively coarser hair. The cheekteeth of woodrats are prismatic whereas those of Norway rats have well-defined cusps arranged in 3

* Couplet after E. Hall (1981); populations not reported from the wild in Colorado.

PHOTOGRAPH 8-59. Norway rat (*Rattus norvegicus*). Photograph by Steve Shumake.

parallel rows. The black rat (or roof rat, *Rattus rattus*) is not known in the wild in Colorado.

Distribution

Norway rats are relatively common in Denver (C. A. Jones et al. 2003) and in most cities on the eastern plains and also in rural areas, especially where livestock and poultry are produced in confinement facilities. The distribution is not well documented by museum specimens and is not mapped. One subspecies, *Rattus norvegicus norvegicus*, occurs in Colorado.

Natural History

Norway rats typically live in close commensal or competitive associations with humans, occupying buildings, sewer systems, outbuildings around farms, rubble, and landfills. They can be found in tunnel systems on vacant lots and weedy agricultural lands, usually not far from urbanized areas. One of us (JPF) livetrapped rodents for the US Fish and Wildlife Service Wildlife Research Center while attending graduate school at Colorado State University in the mid- and late 1960s. Norway rats in many different color patterns—from nearly all white to spotted to the more typical brown pelage—were found along ditch banks and railroad rights-of-way several kilometers from Fort Collins and nearby towns. Feral laboratory rats are abundant from time to time on the University of Colorado at Boulder campus (D. Armstrong, unpublished). Roof rats (*Rattus rattus*) occur in the United States mostly in the Southeast (westward across much of Texas) and along the Pacific Coast. They have not been reported from the wild in Colorado, but continued vigilance is recommended.

Similar to house mice, Norway rats are omnivorous, eating practically any organic matter. When available, cereal grains and native seeds are heavily used. Rats will also kill birds (including domestic poultry), small mammals, young of larger mammals including baby pigs and lambs, snakes, and similar prey. Cannibalism is not uncommon, especially by large males and under crowded conditions. Adults typically require at least 20 to 30 g of food per day and can consume up to one-third of their body weight daily.

Nests of grasses, cloth, paper, and leaves are concealed under or in various objects on the surface of the ground. Well-developed colonies dig complex tunnel systems, which may be as much as half a meter below ground level. Such tunnels usually have a main entrance and several escape holes. Digging is done with the forefeet, with loosened soil pushed to the surface using the head, chest, and forefeet.

Norway rats are agile climbers and good swimmers. It is not unusual to see them swimming along the margins of irrigation ditches that pass through towns and cities on the plains, where they may be confused with muskrats. During spring and summer, rat populations expand into agricultural lands and weedy areas, but during the colder months the animals congregate again around farms and urban areas.

Norway rats are mostly nocturnal where they are subject to disturbance by humans. However, in areas with little disturbance or with plentiful food supplies, such as poorly managed refuse dumps, they may be active at any time. Most foraging occurs shortly after dark and again just before daylight. Rats live in colonies usually numbering about 12 to 15 individuals dominated by an older adult male. At extremely high population levels social pressures result in increased fighting, physiological stress, reduced breeding, and increased mortality. Male Norway rats can breed year-round but females are seasonally polyestrous, producing about 5 litters a year, mostly in spring and summer. The gestation period is 21 to 26 days. Litter size ranges from 2 to 22, with an average of 7 to 11 young. Pups are blind, naked, and helpless at birth. Eyes open at 2 weeks of age, with weaning completed at 3 weeks. Juveniles are sexually mature at about 3 months of age.

Most medium-sized to large carnivores prey on Norway rats. Weasels, foxes, skunks, large snakes, hawks, and owls probably are the most important predators. Humans wage extermination campaigns against the animals, using burrow fumigants, toxicants, and poisoned baits. Most Norway rats probably die in their first year of life and a rare individual survives to 2 or 3 years of age.

Norway rats are vectors for a variety of diseases dangerous to humans, including typhus, plague, tularemia, and occasionally rabies. Contamination of crops by urination and defecation and direct consumption of human food result in millions of dollars in losses annually in the United States alone. Their gnawing activity can also destroy underground utility cables as well as water pipes. On the positive side, domesticated laboratory rats have contributed to much beneficial research in medicine and pharmacology. Calhoun (1962) provided the most detailed study of this species in the United States, and W. Jackson (1982) reviewed its general biology.

Mus musculus

HOUSE MOUSE

Description

This is a small, slender, brown to blackish brown mouse with a sparsely haired, scaly tail. The underparts are slightly paler in color than the dorsum without any clear line of demarcation. The ears are relatively large and sparsely haired. Measurements are: total length 130–200 mm; length of tail 60–105 mm; length of hindfoot 14–21 mm; length of ear 11–18 mm; weight 18–23 g. The skull is flattened and has a short rostrum. Cusps of the molars are aligned in 3 longitudinal rows (Figure 8-11). The first upper molar is longer than the combined length of the second and third molars. Superficially this species might be confused with the harvest mouse (*Reithrodontomys*). However, harvest mice have grooves on the upper incisors, which are lacking in the house mouse. House mice also have a characteristic strong, musky odor produced by anal glands. Once acquainted with that odor, one can recognize the presence of a house mouse in a closed trap simply by the scent. Females have 5 pairs of mammae.

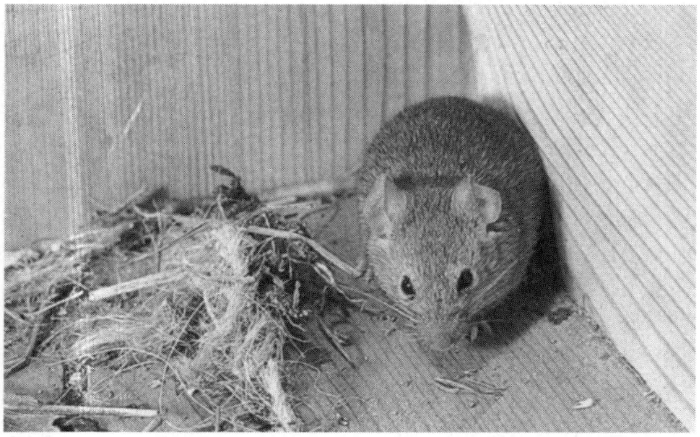

PHOTOGRAPH 8-60. House mouse (*Mus musculus*). Photograph by Roger W. Barbour.

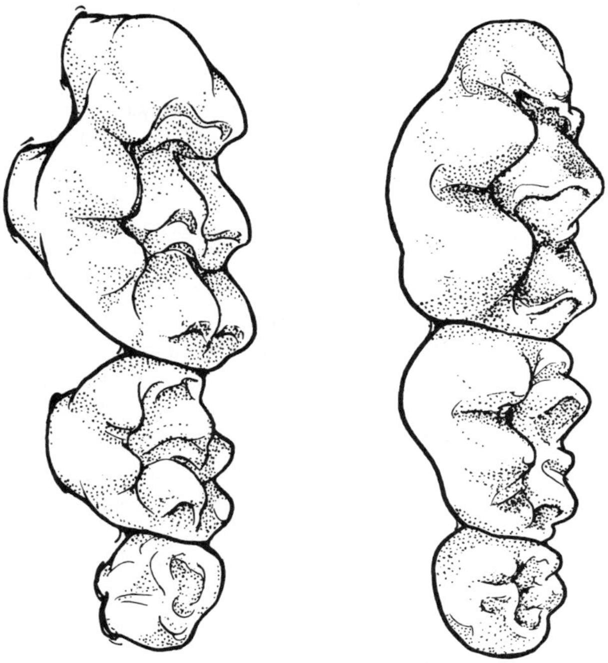

FIGURE 8-11. Comparison of occlusal patterns of upper molars: house mouse (*Mus musculus, left*), with cusps in 3 longitudinal rows, and deer mouse (*Peromyscus maniculatus, right*), with cups in 2 longitudinal rows.

Distribution

The status and distribution of house mice in Colorado have not been studied, and the distribution is not mapped. The house mouse thrives in occupied homes, urban and rural, and around agricultural areas, especially where grains are grown, stored, or fed. The animals probably live in all major cities and towns in Colorado as well as on adjacent farmlands, ranchlands, and "waste" areas. It can be locally abundant, even in apparently "natural" habitats. House mice can be serious pests. North American house mice represent the subspecies *M. m. domesticus* (L. Silver 1995).

Natural History

As the common name implies, house mice frequently live alongside humans in dwellings, grain bins, barns, warehouses, and other structures. House mice also survive as feral populations at lower elevations over much of Colorado, living along fencerows, ditch banks, rights-of-way, abandoned fields, and croplands. In north-central Kansas, house mice were rare in natural habitats, hayfields, wheat fields, and roadside ditches but were occasionally abundant in sorghum fields (D. W. Kaufman and Kaufman 1990). House mice frequently are termed "commensals" of people, but that is usually inaccurate. Commensalism is a symbiotic relationship in which one species benefits and a second is not affected, either positively or negatively. By that definition, house mice are not commensals but often are competitors of humans for growing and stored food and other resources.

House mice are active year-round, although in cold weather they may spend considerable amounts of time huddled together in communal nests. They are mostly nocturnal and secretive, traveling along or under objects at ground level or along baseboards and in crawlspaces beneath buildings. In the wild they use established runways, making rapid, furtive movements and pausing only briefly to gather or consume food. Nests are constructed from whatever materials are handy, including cloth and paper scraps, corn husks, grass, leaves, and feathers. Nests are hidden under or in objects such as furniture and old mattresses. In our region it is not unusual for house mice to invade houses in the fall and early winter and then to disperse into outdoor environments during the warmer months.

Opportunistic in their diet, house mice eat everything from grains and vegetable crops to insects, carrion, glue, and leather. Feeding, defecation, and urination on stored grains by house mice can cause tremendous losses of such crops. If food is plentiful, the animals cache the excess near the nest site. Free water is consumed if available but apparently is not required, the water needs being met from dew or the moisture in food.

House mice communicate by scent, vocalizations, and postures. They have a variety of chirps, squeaks, and "songs." Scent-marking involves urination and use of a preputial gland. House mice are polyestrous, with females coming into heat about every 5 days. Gestation takes about 19 days and litters of 2 to 13 (average, 4 to 7) young are produced. In Colorado probably 5 to 7 litters are produced annually, with most breeding occurring from late spring through early fall. The young are blind and naked at birth, but by 2 weeks of age they are well furred with the eyes open. They are weaned at about 3 weeks and are sexually mature by 6 weeks of age (Breakey 1963).

Prolific and often promiscuous, populations of house mice can increase rapidly. Very high densities can be attained when resources are effectively unlimited, as in poorly secured grain bins. Under natural conditions, stable family groups form with 1 male and 1 or more females (Crowcroft and Rowe 1963). These families maintain territories and expel other mice from the occupied area. Adult males are more aggressive than females and are most active in territorial maintenance. Levels of aggression in males increase with increases in population density. The family group shares a nest until one of the females becomes aggressive as a result of pregnancy. If 2 females become pregnant at the same time, they may make a communal nest, which they eventually will share with their offspring of a couple of generations. As young males mature, their aggression increases and eventually they are forced to leave the communal nest.

Individuals disperse into suitable adjacent habitats, including abandoned fields, ditch banks, and croplands, where they may displace small native rodents, such as harvest mice. Most house mice probably do not survive more than 6 or 7 months in the wild but they have lived up to 6 years in captivity.

A diversity of wild carnivores prey on house mice, including foxes, coyotes, weasels, hawks, owls, and snakes. Domestic pets also kill house mice but often do not eat them, perhaps because of their odor. In the wild, these animals are "indicators" of disturbance (Clippinger 2002) and most people consider them undesirable, but their contributions to human well-being—owing to their status as a "model" mammal in biomedical research—have been invaluable (J. Fox et al. 2006). W. Jackson (1982) provided a general review of the literature on the house mouse and the Norway rat.

Family Erethizontidae—New World Porcupines

This family of New World rodents is characterized by a robust build and modification of some of the guard hairs into sharp, barbed quills. The feet are plantigrade and modified for an arboreal life, with broad, scaly soles that assist in climbing and clinging to branches. The skull has a large infraorbital foramen, typically larger than the foramen magnum. The cheekteeth are rooted and have complex occlusal surfaces characterized by many infoldings of the enamel. The dental formula is 1/1, 0/0, 1/1, 3/3 = 20. The family evolved in South America, and fossils date from the Oligocene. Two genera (*Erethizon* and *Coendou*) invaded North America by the Late Pliocene, but only the genus *Erethizon* reached the United States and Canada. Five genera and 12 species are presently recognized in the family. Woods and Kilpatrick (2005) provided a taxonomic review of the infraorder Hystricognathi, which includes the porcupine family, Erethizontidae.

Erethizon dorsatum

NORTH AMERICAN PORCUPINE

Description

The porcupine is the second largest rodent in Colorado, outweighed only by the beaver. Porcupines have stout bodies, relatively short legs, and short, thick, heavy tails used as a brace while climbing or perching. Many of the guard hairs on the back and tail are modified into sharp, barbed quills. Measurements are: total length 640–930 mm; length of tail 150–300 mm; length of hindfoot 85–125 mm; length of ear 20–40 mm; weight 4–18 kg. The skull is stout and broad with heavy ridges forming in older animals. The infraorbital foramina are slightly larger than the foramen magnum. Incisors are stout and ever-growing. Cheekteeth are rooted and have deeply folded enamel on the outer edges. The occlusal surface of each cheektooth shows both dentine and enamel folds. Earle and Kramm (1980) provided techniques for determining age.

Younger animals are generally dark in color while older animals are more yellowish. Color variation is mostly the result of the color of the coarse, long, stiff guard hairs, which can exceed 10 cm in length. The underfur is long, soft, and dark. The quills are whitish yellow with dark tips. The venter lacks quills but has underfur and short guard hairs. There are 4 digits on the front feet and 5 on the hind. The soles of the feet are oval and covered with black scaly plates, which assist the animal in gaining traction while climbing. Females have 4 mammae and males have a distinctive baculum that is flattened dorsoventrally with a bulbous base.

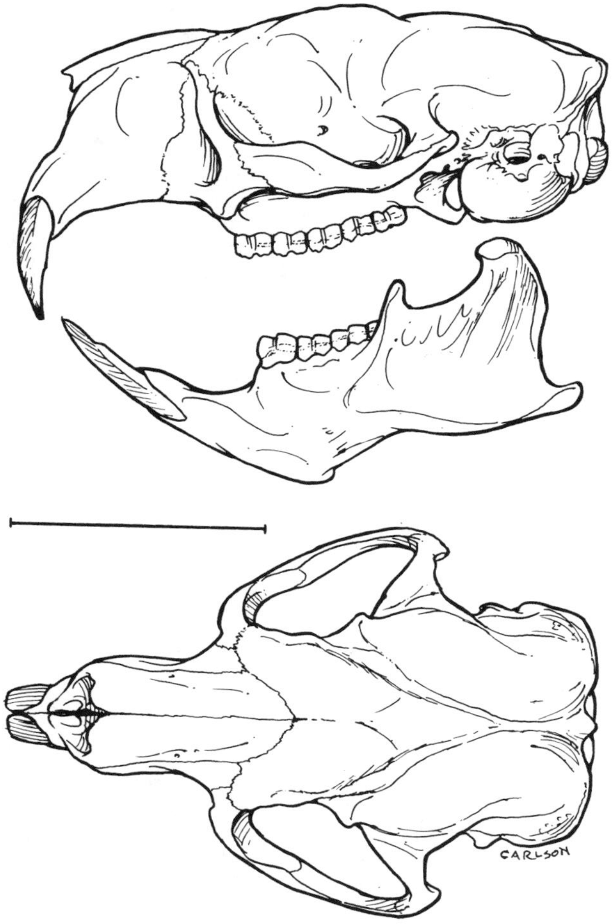

FIGURE 8-12. Lateral and dorsal views of the skull of a North American porcupine (*Erethizon dorsatum*). Scale = 5 cm.

PHOTOGRAPH 8-61. Common porcupine (*Erethizon dorsatum*). Photograph by Walker Van Riper and R. J. Niedrach.

Distribution

Porcupines occur throughout the state but are most common in forested regions, especially in mountainous areas with coniferous trees. It is not unusual, however, to find individuals in sagebrush flats or even on open prairie on the eastern plains. No modern taxonomic revision exists, but 3 subspecies have been ascribed ranges in Colorado (D. Armstrong 1972): *Erethizon dorsatum bruneri* along the

MAP 8-119. Distribution of the common porcupine (*Erethizon dorsatum*) in North America.

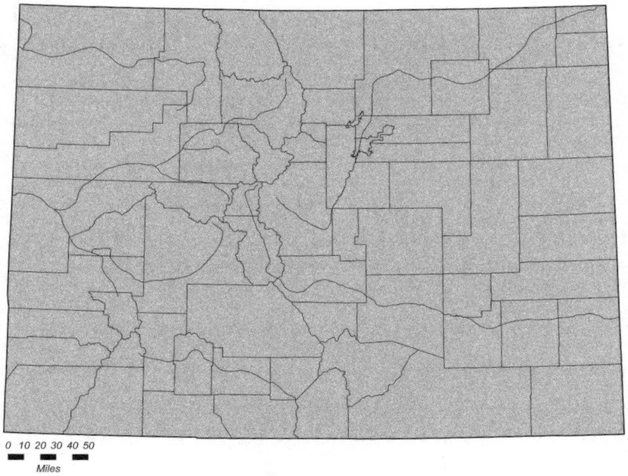

MAP 8-120. Distribution of the common porcupine (*Erethizon dorsatum*) in Colorado.

break of the High Plains in extreme northern Weld and northwestern Logan counties; *E. d. couesi* in the extreme southwestern part of the state; and *E. d. epixanthum* over most of the western two-thirds of Colorado and in the roughlands of the southeastern part of the state. Stangl et al. (1991) argued that *E. d. couesi* is a junior synonym of *E. d. epixanthum*. Their conclusion may be valid, but it was not based on study of the species throughout its range. Describing geographic variation in North American porcupines is complicated by cranial asymmetry (Stangl et al. 1991). Populations of porcupines appear to have declined substantially along the Front Range over recent decades. The extent and cause of this decline are unknown.

Natural History

Porcupines are mostly associated with conifers in montane and subalpine forests and piñon-juniper woodlands. In addition, they occupy cottonwood-willow forests in river-bottoms, aspen groves, and semidesert shrublands. Individuals are often observed above timberline and occasionally even on the open grasslands of eastern Colorado. Despite their abundance, there is a dearth of studies on porcupines from the Rocky Mountain region.

Cambium, phloem, buds, and foliage of shrubs, saplings, and trees are a mainstay of the porcupine's diet. They eat leaves, buds, and young shoots of grasses and forbs during the warmer months and concentrate on inner bark in winter. Cambium, buds, and needles of conifers—especially ponderosa pine, lodgepole pine, and Douglas-fir—are particularly important foods in Colorado. A porcupine found dead at the base of a tree in the foothills of Boulder County had a stomach filled with dwarf mistletoe (*Arceuthobium vaginatum*) (C. A. Meaney, unpublished). There is considerable variation in the amount of damage done to individual trees by foraging porcupines, with some trees in a stand showing extensive use while others remain untouched. M. Snyder and Linhart (1997) found that trees favored by porcupines had lower levels of the monoterpene limonene in the xylem than did non-target trees. The porcupine is consistently less selective in ponderosa pine woodlands than is the sympatric Abert's squirrel. In an investigation of this phenomenon in the Front Range, trees fed upon by porcupines were closer to steep, rocky outcrops (where dens might be located) and had more tannins in their phloem than trees not selected by porcupines (Habeck 1990). Occasionally, porcupines may invade alfalfa fields during the summer, causing considerable damage.

Porcupines are active year-round and may be observed moving at any time of the day or night, although they are usually considered nocturnal. During the day they typically seek refuge under rocks or ledges, in hollows, or in the crotch of a tree. These sites may be accompanied by fecal piles. Linear daily movements during summer ranged from

111 to 129 m, and home ranges averaged 14 ha (Marshall et al. 1962). Although they are not considered territorial, porcupines do defend particularly good feeding sites.

Porcupines are generally solitary, except for females with their young. During winter, however, individuals may concentrate in den sites such as caves, abandoned buildings, hollow trees, and brush piles. These denning sites are not defended. Densities differ widely from winter to summer and also as a consequence of food availability. Densities of 0.77 and 9.50 animals per square kilometer were reported from Arizona and Wisconsin, respectively (W. Taylor 1935; Kelker 1943). In Idaho shrub desert, home ranges were 0.07 ha in winter and 23.10 ha in spring and summer (Craig and Keller 1986). One male had a home range of 61.7 ha. These home ranges are smaller than have been reported from forested habitats in the western United States.

Vocalizations include subdued grunts and whines used by females with their young, and grunts, whines, and shrill screeches used by males during the breeding season. The latter cries may be confused with sounds made by wild felids (Dodge 1982). One of us (JPF) kept a young male porcupine (which had lost one of its hindlegs in a coyote trap) for almost a year. When approached, he would make a number of grunts and whines interpreted as greeting and care-soliciting sounds. Vision is poor, but hearing and olfaction are good. They stand on their hindlegs to assess a passing scent.

Porcupines are monoestrous or seasonally polyestrous, with most breeding taking place in fall or early winter. Sex ratios tend to favor females by as much as 100:30, but more typically 100:80 or 100:90 is to be expected in this polygamous species. Adults form only brief associations to breed and usually separate within 6 hours following copulation (Shadle et al. 1946; Shadle 1951). The gestation period is about 210 days (remarkably long for a rodent or for any mammal of its size), with young being born in the spring. A single young is typical, although twins have been reported. Young porcupines are precocial, are born well furred, and have soft quills that harden quickly after delivery. The young begin to take solid food when only a few days old and forage with the mother at 1 to 2 weeks of age. They are weaned at about 4 months of age. Males are sexually mature at about 16 months, and it is assumed that females reach sexual maturity at about the same age (Tyron 1947; Shadle 1952).

A porcupine's first alarm reaction is to remain still. When threatened, it typically assumes a hunched posture with quills erected. The animal moves in a circle, keeping its armament "pointed" toward the enemy, and thrashes or waves the well-muscled tail at the source of danger. Unfortunately this strategy assumes that predators are capable of learning from experience, so it is not an effective defense against motor vehicles.

Quills have microscopic, imbricate (overlapping, shingle-like) barbs. They are not ejected, but they are only loosely attached at their bases and so are readily shed and become embedded upon contact. Roze (2002) conducted laboratory experiments on quill release and found that individual erect quills were released with nearly 40 percent less tension ("pull") if the quill was first pushed into the follicle, mimicking the force of a predator's attack. Porcupines are adept at removing quills with their teeth and forefeet from their own bodies, as is necessary after an aggressive intraspecific encounter. Longevity in captivity may exceed 10 years, but in the wild they only survive 5 to 7 years. Tooth wear and malocclusion often become problems as individuals age (Dodge 1982).

To be quilled by a porcupine is a painful, educational experience. Every attempt should be made to remove all quills from the victim. If a quill breaks off in the wound, it may start an infection or continue to work its way into tissue, doing further damage. Quills should be pulled with pliers with a straight, even motion, gripping each quill as close to the skin as possible. Porcupines in Colorado probably have few effective natural enemies. Animals that become proficient in killing them attempt to get at the underbelly, which is devoid of quills. In mid-summer of 1975, J. P. Fitzgerald (unpublished) found the skin of an adult porcupine in an open meadow in South Park, 150 m from the nearest trees. The meat had been thoroughly eaten from the skin and the skin was opened from tail to throat along the belly. The predator could not be determined. Fishers are reported to kill and devour porcupines in the manner described above, but fishers are not known to occur in Colorado. Documented native predators of porcupines in the state include coyotes, lynx, bobcats, mountain lions, and black bears.

Humans are by far the most important enemy of porcupines from both deliberate control programs and road-kill. The porcupine is classified as a non-game mammal in Colorado (Table 4-1). Timber producers often seek control of porcupines because their feeding girdles trees, causing damage to commercial forests, although such damage is generally not extensive (Curtis 1941, 1944; Van Deusen and Myers 1962). At times they may damage crops and the quills may injure pets or livestock. Costello (1966), Woods (1973), Dodge (1982), Roze (1989), and Roze and Ilse (2003) reviewed the abundant but scattered literature on the American porcupine.

9

Order Lagomorpha

Pikas, Rabbits, and Hares

The order Lagomorpha contains small to medium-sized mammals that superficially resemble rodents. The order is old, dating from the Late Paleocene in Asia, approximately 60 million years ago. Our understanding of the phylogeny of the lagomorphs is in a state of flux. An affinity between lagomorphs and rodents has long been suspected and has been emphasized recently by several mammalogists and paleontologists (Eisenberg 1981; Li and Ting 1985; Novacek 1985, 1990; Meng and Wyss 2005; K. Rose 2006). The likelihood of a common ancestor in the Paleocene has led to placement of lagomorphs and rodents together in a grandorder or cohort, Glires (see Carleton and Musser 2005; Hoffmann and Smith 2005).

Lagomorphs are herbivorous mammals. There are 4 incisors above and 2 below; the second upper incisors are small, peg-like teeth located directly behind the larger front incisors. A longitudinal groove marks the face of the upper incisors. A transitory pair of third upper incisors is lost soon after birth. The cheekteeth are hypsodont, and both incisors and cheekteeth are rootless and ever-growing. Several teeth have been lost and a long diastema is present in both upper and lower jaws.

The skull tends to be light, often with numerous intricate perforations (fenestrae, Latin for "windows"). The palate is short, with large incisive foramina. Chewing movements are mostly lateral, facilitated by a small amount of surface contact at the articulation of the mandibular fossa and the condyloid process. The radius and ulna are distinct but the elbow prevents rotation of the forearm. The tibia and fibula are fused distally, and the latter bone articulates with the calcaneus. The forefeet are digitigrade and the hindfeet are plantigrade during walking and digitigrade during running. The tail is short or vestigial.

The cecum is very large and contains a spiral valve. Coprophagy, or reingestion of specialized fecal material, is common in this group (Lechleitner 1957). Bacteria in the cecum break down cellulose, rendering the specialized "soft feces" a nutrient-rich food source.

The uterus is duplex. Males lack a baculum and the testes are abdominal except during the breeding season. The scrotum, when it develops, is anterior to the penis.

The position of the genitalia and the lack of a scrotum in non-breeding males make it difficult to sex these animals externally.

There are 3 families, 13 genera, and about 92 species of lagomorphs (D. Wilson and Reeder 2005). Lagomorphs were absent from southern South America, west-central Africa, Australia, and New Zealand until European exploration and settlement spread the animals worldwide. Several species, particularly the European rabbit (*Oryctolagus cuniculus*), have been introduced widely, even onto remote islands, and they have become pests in many areas. Members of 2 families, 3 genera, and 7 species occur in Colorado.

Key to the Families of the Order Lagomorpha in Colorado

1\. Ears about as wide as long; tail not visible externally; 5 cheekteeth on one side of upper jaw; no supraorbital shield; jugal bone elongated and projecting far posterior of zygomatic process of squamosal . . . . Ochotonidae, p. 260

1' Ears longer than wide; tail short, visible externally; 6 cheekteeth on one side of upper jaw; supraorbital shield present; jugal not extending far posterior of zygomatic process of squamosal . . . . Leporidae, p. 263

Family Ochotonidae—Pikas

Pikas are small and short-eared with hind limbs only slightly longer than forelimbs. There are 5 digits on each foot and the soles of the feet are well haired. The tail is not visible externally. There is only 1 genus, *Ochotona*, with 14 species. Twelve species occur in Eurasia (including Japan) and 2 species occur in North America: the American pika, *O. princeps*, in mountain ranges of the western United States and southwestern Canada, and the collared pika, *O. collaris*, in Alaska and northwestern Canada. The range of the collared pika is disjunct in British Columbia from that of the American pika by about 800 km of seemingly suitable habitat, a curiosity that has yet to be explained.

Ochotona princeps

AMERICAN PIKA

Description

American pikas are small and grayish brown, with short rounded ears and no visible tail. The pelage is rather long, soft, and fine-textured. The ventral surface is paler than the dorsum and is usually washed with buff. The hind limbs are not elongated and are only slightly longer than the forelimbs. Pikas are sexually monomorphic, and the gender of a captured animal can be determined only by extrusion of the genitalia (Duke 1951). Pikas are sometimes called "little chief hares" or "rock rabbits." Locally in Colorado they are sometimes, but quite inappropriately, called "cony"—a name also used in the Bible for the hyrax, which is not a lagomorph but a "subungulate" (or a "paenungulate," in the sense of D. W. Macdonald 2006, or an "afrothere," in the sense of other authors [see Pough et al. 2009])—and so is a fairly close relative of manatees and elephants!

Measurements are: total length 162–216 mm; length of hindfoot 25–35 mm; length of ear 19–25 mm; weight 120–250 g. The skull is dorsoventrally flattened, lacks a supraorbital ridge, and has a long jugal bone forming a prominent projection from the posterior zygomatic arch (Figure 9-1). The maxillae have a single large fenestration rather than the numerous small fenestrae of the Leporidae.

PHOTOGRAPH 9-1. American pika (*Ochotona princeps*). © 1993 Wendy Shattil / Bob Rozinski.

Distribution

Pikas are distributed throughout the higher mountains on talus slopes, mostly above 3,000 m (10,000 ft.). According to Armstrong (1972), *Ochotona princeps figginsi* occurs in the

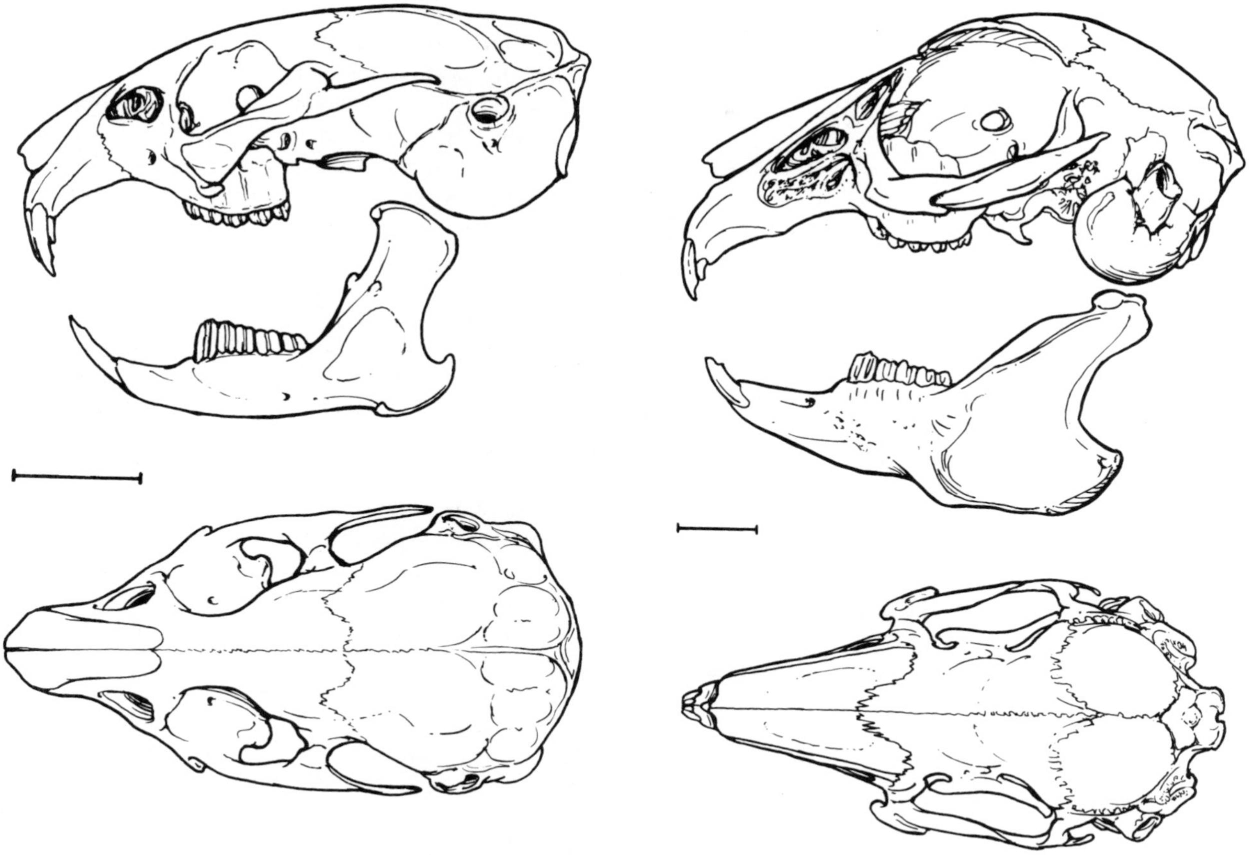

FIGURE 9-1. Lateral and dorsal views of the skulls of an American pika (*Ochotona princeps, left*) and a desert cottontail (*Sylvilagus audubonii, right*) to show comparative length of the jugal bones. Scale = 1 cm.

West Elk and Elk mountains and the Park Range; *O. p. incana* occurs in the Sangre de Cristo and Culebra ranges and the Spanish Peaks; and *O. p. saxitilis* occurs in the Front Range, Sawatch and nearby ranges, and the San Juan Mountains. D. Hafner and Sullivan (1995) concluded from geographic patterns of allozymes that pika of the Southern Rockies have been separated from those of the Middle Rockies of Wyoming for more than 120,000 years. D. Hafner and Smith (2010) revised subspecies of American pikas and referred specimens from most of Colorado, southeastern Utah, and New Mexico to *O. p. saxatilis*, whose type locality is Montgomery, Park County, Colorado. Specimens from the Park Range and the Flat Tops (Trappers Lake) were referred to *O. p. princeps*, the type locality of which is near Athabasca Pass, in the Canadian Rockies or Alberta. A molecular phylogeographic study of variation in the American pika throughout its range would be of great interest.

Natural History

Pikas inhabit talus slopes in the mountains of Colorado. They are restricted to talus rock in alpine tundra or subalpine forests in areas adjacent to alpine meadows of grasses, forbs, and sedges, which serve as their food. Occasionally, pikas use burrows or woodpiles for cover (Pruitt 1954). The range map (Map 9-2) provided here may be misleading. Range maps are necessarily crude approximations to the complex and dynamic situation in the field, because of both their small scale and the fact that they are static. For example, the map shows a continuous distribution of pikas along the "spine" of the Southern Rockies, but there are numerous passes along the chain that likely interrupt movements of pikas and hence gene flow. With a warming climate and upslope movement of "life zones," this fragmentation can only increase. The mountains of Colorado are an "archi-

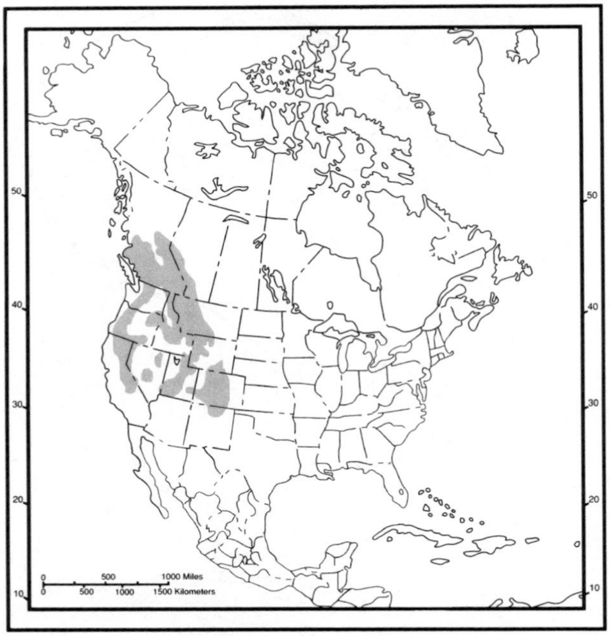

MAP 9-1. Distribution of the American pika (*Ochotona princeps*) in North America.

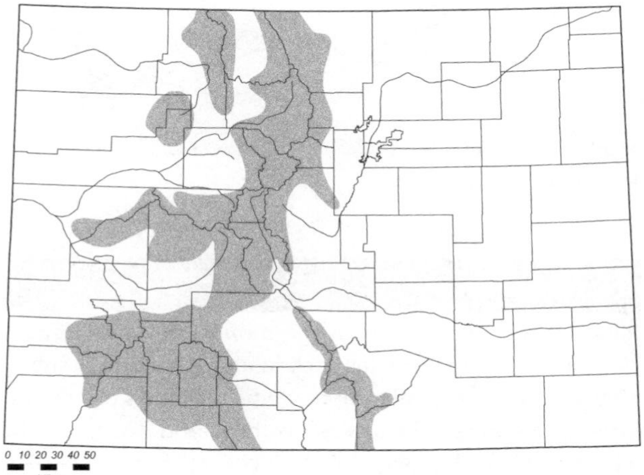

MAP 9-2. Distribution of the American pika (*Ochotona princeps*) in Colorado.

pelago" of alpine "islands," and as tree lines move upslope the area of the islands decreases and the distance between islands steadily increases. Working in the isolated mountain ranges of the Great Basin in Nevada and adjacent states, Beever et al. (2003) found that 7 of 25 populations surveyed appeared to have gone extinct over the previous century. Extent of talus habitat and elevation of the mountain range predicted the persistence of pikas. A. Smith et al. (1990) reviewed the conservation biology of ochotonids throughout their range, noting that several subspecies are imperiled but no species is in imminent danger of extinction. In May 2009, the US Fish and Wildlife Service announced that it would conduct a 12-month "status review" of the American pika, based on a petition from the Center for Biological Diversity. For current status, see http://www.fws.gov.mountain-prairie/species/mammals/americanpika.

Leaves and stems of forbs and shrubs constitute 78–87 percent of the diet, with alpine avens (*Acomastylis rossii*), clovers, and sedges as important components (D. R. Johnson 1967). Needles of conifers and bark of several woody species are also eaten. Starting in mid-July, pikas collect vegetation and store it in haypiles located under overhanging rocks and underground among the rocks. More correctly referred to as a haypile complex, these stashes may extend over an area of 100 square meters. Many haypiles contain significant "leftovers" after the winter. D. Conner (1983) concluded that haypiles are not the exclusive winter food source for this non-hibernating mammal; rather, they serve as insurance against an unusually harsh or prolonged winter. However, Dearing (1997c) estimated that haypiles of pikas on Niwot Ridge, west of Boulder, contained food sufficient for 350 days, more than enough to feed the animals through the winter, and collected over roughly a 10-week season. The average mass of haypiles on Niwot Ridge was 28 kg of fresh vegetation per individual pika (Dearing 2001). The volume of a haypile ranges from a bushel to bathtub-sized, and 30 species of plants may be found in one haypile (Beidleman and Weber 1958). Theft of hay from neighbors' haypiles has been reported, and its frequency differs strongly from one local population to another, with a high of 44.4 percent of individuals stealing on Niwot Ridge in 1989 (McKechnie et al. 1994).

Summer diets are different from winter diets (as represented by the haypiles). On Niwot Ridge, pikas are generalists in summer, but they eat leaves of Parry's clover (*Trifolium parryi*) preferentially, taking leaves of moss pink (*Silene acaulis*) and leaves and flowers of bistort (*Bistorta bistortoides*) in proportion to their abundance in the environment but eating graminoids and alpine avens less frequently than their abundance would predict (Dearing 2001). The winter diet of pikas is much more specialized. Leaves of alpine avens provide up to three-quarters of the winter diet, with bistort, Parry's clover, and grasses and sedges making up the rest. Dearing (1996, 1997a, 1997b, 1997c) found that phenolic compounds in alpine avens slowed microbial action and so preserved the plants through the winter. As the avens and other plants aged, levels of phenolic compounds decreased and the plants thus became more palatable.

Pikas are diurnal and have peaks of activity in the morning and in the late afternoon to early evening, although their calls can also be heard at night. In late fall and winter, activity decreases and the animals spend large portions of time in their dens. When snow covers the talus, they dig snow tunnels up to the surface where they forage.

Pikas are territorial and territories vary in size from 680 m^2 in June to 300 m^2 in September (Svendsen 1979; Meaney 1990b). Some overlap occurs in territorial boundaries. Home ranges vary from 860 to 2,100 m^2 (A. Smith and Ivins 1984) and considerable overlap occurs between males and females. It has been suggested that adjacent home ranges are occupied by members of the opposite sex (A. Smith and Weston 1990), although the data do not always support this claim (R. Brown et al. 1989).

Pikas are philopatric, tending to stay near their birthplace (A. Smith and Ivins 1983, 1984). Females are more likely to disperse as a result of unsuccessful competition with male siblings (Whitworth and Southwick 1984). Pikas have notably low levels of genetic heterozygosity for a mammal of broad distribution (Tolliver et al. 1985), perhaps a consequence of insular populations and philopatry. Dominance is influenced by age, sex, and resident status and is a key factor in the defense of territorial boundaries. Chases and short fights are frequent between animals involved in territorial disputes. Territorial behavior in late summer and fall centers on protection of haypiles (Kawamichi 1976).

Vocalizations and scent-marking are well developed in this species and are significant in maintenance of territorial boundaries (D. Conner 1984; Meaney 1990b). There are a number of different vocalizations (D. Conner 1985a) as well as geographic differences in dialects (Somers 1973; D. Conner 1982). Urine, feces, and secretions of cheek glands all are used in scent-marking. The cheek gland, located at the angle of the jaw, is perfunctorily rubbed against rocks. Pikas can discriminate individual differences in calls and cheek-gland secretions (D. Conner 1985b; Meaney 1987). Cheek-marking also serves to facilitate breeding, in that females are more likely to breed with males whose odors are familiar (Meaney 1986). Urine and feces are strategically placed by haypiles.

Pikas breed in April, May, and June. Females have a postpartum estrus and initiate 2 litters per season, although only 1 litter is produced. The gestation period is 30 days, with an average litter size of 3. Young are altricial but growth of neonates is rapid (Whitworth and Southwick 1980).

Population densities vary from 3.4 to 9.8 per hectare in Colorado (Southwick et al. 1986). They tend to be rather stable, perhaps as a consequence of their highly developed territoriality (Southwick et al. 1986). Pikas are relatively long-lived for a mammal of their size. A number of predators feed on them, including golden eagles, long-tailed weasels, short-tailed weasels (J. Dixon 1931), coyotes, and martens. The pika is a protected non-game mammal in Colorado (see Table 4-1). A. Smith and Weston (1990) reviewed the literature.

Family Leporidae—Rabbits and Hares

Leporids are medium-sized mammals with elongated hindlegs and feet and ears longer than wide. The tail is short. The skull is strongly arched and has well-developed supraorbital processes. The jugal bones are long but do not project much beyond the zygomatic process of the squamosals. There are 11 genera and 61 species of hares and rabbits in the world (D. Wilson and Reeder 2005). Colorado is home to 2 genera and 6 species.

Colorado's hares, species of the genus *Lepus*, are larger than rabbits, have longer ears and legs, give birth to precocial young (i.e., fully furred with their eyes open at birth), and do not dig or live in burrows. Colorado's rabbits, species of the genus *Sylvilagus*, are smaller than hares; have shorter ears and legs; give birth to altricial young that are naked, blind, and helpless; and often dig or use burrows for shelter. When leporids were given common names by early explorers, little heed was paid to these distinctions between hares and rabbits, leading to much confusion, especially in common parlance. Cottontails are true rabbits, but the snowshoe "rabbit" and the jackrabbits are hares. "Hare" versus "rabbit" is well defined by systematists, but much remains to be learned about affinities of the species within the respective genera. Ramos (1998, 1999) studied morphometric variation among some North American leporids (including all 6 Coloradan species) with an eye toward identifying specimens from fossil deposits. She concluded that mandibular characteristics distinguish species more reliably than do maxillary characters and that enamel patterns of the lower third premolar generally allow identification of fossil specimens of the modern species.

Leporids are important locally as food species or species with sport hunting value. The fur is sometimes used by the clothing industry but the skin is thin, easily torn, and does not wear well. Many members of the group are considered to be agricultural pests, competing with livestock for forage or raiding crops, including alfalfa and vegetables. In Colorado, all leporids are managed as small game mammals (Table 4-1).

Key to the Species of the Family Leporidae in Colorado

1. Hindfoot more than 105 mm in adults; interparietal not distinct, fused to parietals (Fig. 9-2) . . . . *Lepus*, 2

1' Hindfoot 105 mm or less in adults; interparietal distinct, not fused to parietals (Fig. 9-2) . . . . *Sylvilagus*, 4

2. Ear of adults less than 80 mm long; little or no development of anterior projection on supraorbital process . . . . Snowshoe Hare—*Lepus americanus*, p. 271

2' Ear of adults 80 mm or longer; well-developed anterior projection on supraorbital process 3

3. Dorsal surface of tail with prominent medial black stripe extending onto rump; skull relatively low and flattened; rostrum relatively long and shallow . . . . Black-tailed Jackrabbit—*Lepus californicus*, p. 274

3' Dorsal surface of tail white, sometimes with gray medial stripe, but not extending onto rump; skull relatively arched; rostrum relatively short and deep . . . . White-tailed Jackrabbit—*Lepus townsendii*, p. 276

4. Predominant dorsal color pale grayish; patch on throat and chest often orangish; auditory bullae large, nearly as long as basioccipital (as measured from anterior end of basioccipital to posterior plane of occipital condyles) . . . . Desert Cottontail—*Sylvilagus audubonii*, p. 264

4' Predominant dorsal color grayish but with many dark (reddish to blackish) hairs; patch on throat and chest rusty brown; auditory bullae smaller, usually shorter than basioccipital 5

5. Inside of ears densely furred; neck and chest patch dark rusty brownish; diameter of external auditory meatus greater than crown length of upper molars . . . . Mountain Cottontail—*Sylvilagus nuttallii*, p. 268

5' Inside of ears not densely furred; neck and chest patch bright rusty brown; diameter of external auditory meatus less than crown length of upper molars . . . . Eastern Cottontail—*Sylvilagus floridanus*, p. 266

Genus *Sylvilagus*—American Rabbits

There are some 17 species of *Sylvilagus*, a genus distributed in the temperate and tropical Americas, from southern Canada to southern Brazil and northern Argentina (Hoffmann and Smith 2005). The greatest diversity within the genus is in the southwestern United States and Mexico. There are 3 species in Colorado, more readily identifiable by cranial characters than by external differences. Cottontails are classified as small game in Colorado. Estimated harvest figures are presented in Table 4-3. Note that the number of rabbit hunters ranges around 10,000 annually and harvest is thought to be from 45,000 to nearly 60,000 individuals per year.

Sylvilagus audubonii

DESERT COTTONTAIL

Description

A small rabbit, the desert cottontail has relatively long hindlegs and long, sparsely furred ears. The dorsum is pale grayish brown with a few blackish hairs on the mid-dorsum. The sides are paler than the back. The underparts are white, except for an orangish brown spot on the throat extending to the chest between the front legs. Measurements are: total length 360–420 mm; length of tail 30–60 mm; length of hindfoot 70–90 mm; length of ear 60–90 mm; weight 700–1,200 g. The auditory bullae are greatly enlarged but are only roughly rounded with a rugose surface. The

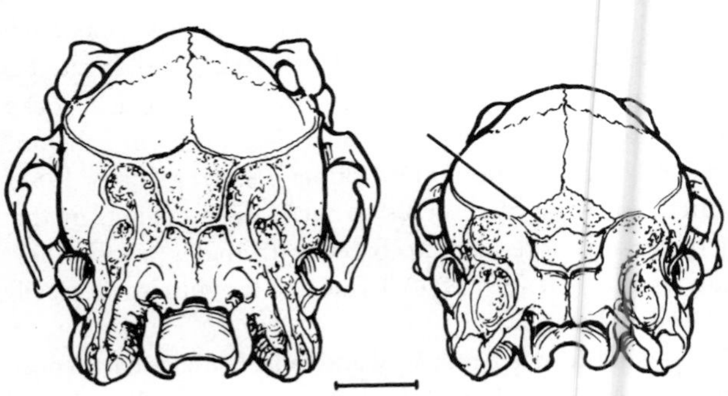

FIGURE 9-2. Posterior views of the skulls of a hare (*Lepus*, *left*) and a cottontail (*Sylvilagus*, *right*) to show the distinct interparietal bone in the latter. Scale = 1 cm.

PHOTOGRAPH 9-2. Desert cottontail (*Sylvilagus audubonii*). Photograph by Andrew Langford.

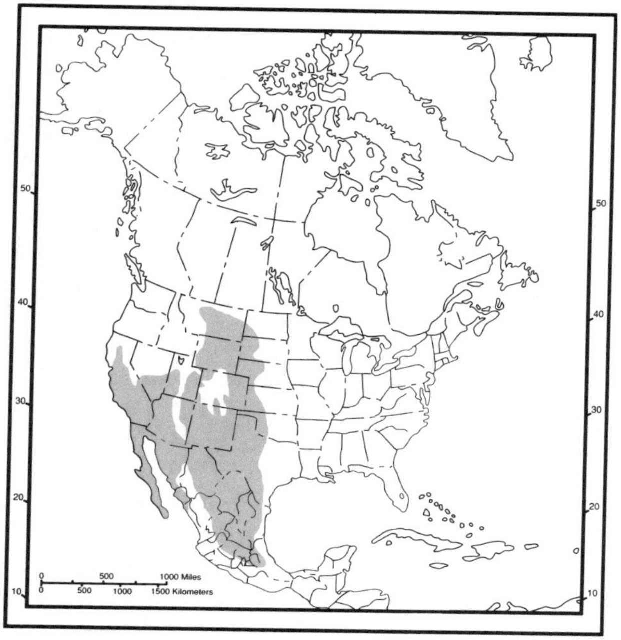

MAP 9-3. Distribution of the desert cottontail (*Sylvilagus audubonii*) in North America.

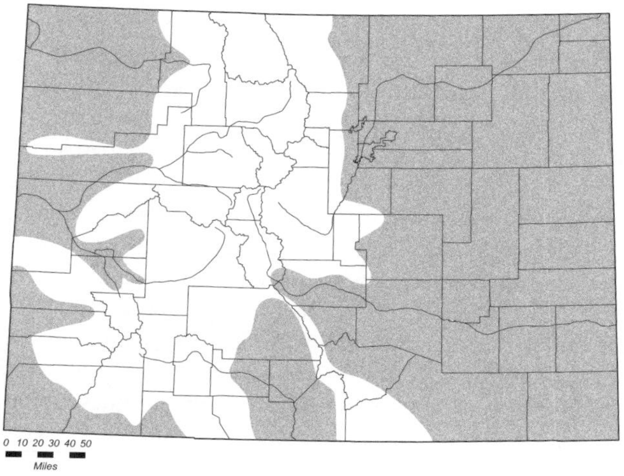

MAP 9-4. Distribution of the desert cottontail (*Sylvilagus audubonii*) in Colorado.

external auditory meatus is also very large (Figure 9-3). The supraorbital process is generally prominent, with an upward flair to the margin. Both the mandibular and maxillary toothrows are reportedly shorter than for the other 2 species (J. K. Jones, Armstrong, et al. 1983; Hoffmeister 1986). Differences among cottontails in Colorado are subtle, and it can be difficult to separate the 3 species by external characteristics alone. Hoffmeister and Lee (1963) revised the subspecies in the Southwest, including southwestern Colorado.

Distribution

Desert cottontails occur throughout eastern Colorado, up into the lower foothills of the Front Range. In western Colorado they are common in semidesert and montane shrublands, below about 2,135 m (7,000 ft.). The subspecies *Sylvilagus audubonii baileyi* occurs on the eastern plains and in northwestern Colorado, and *S. a. warreni* occurs in the San Luis Valley and in western Colorado.

Natural History

Although desert cottontails are widely distributed, their biology has not been studied thoroughly. They occur on grasslands on the eastern plains, especially in prairie dog colonies, where burrows provide excellent cover. The species inhabits a variety of other situations, including montane shrublands, riparian woodlands and thickets, semidesert shrublands, piñon-juniper woodlands, and various woodland-edge habitats. They can live in areas with minimal vegetation provided that adequate cover is present in the form of burrows, scattered trees and shrubs, or crevices and spaces under rocks. Studies in southern New Mexico indicated that chaining of piñon-juniper is detrimental to cottontails unless 70 to 90 living shrubs or downed trees are left per acre. High tree density reduces the density of desert cottontails by discouraging growth of shrubs (Kundaeli and Reynolds 1972).

Desert cottontails forage mostly on forbs and grasses, which constitute 80 percent of the diet. Shrubs are of relatively little importance except as cover (DeCalesta 1971; Turkowski 1975). Desert cottontails are mostly nocturnal or crepuscular and, like other leporids, are active throughout the year. They are able to swim and also clamber into low trees and brush piles.

Ovulation is induced by copulation. The gestation period is about 28 days, followed by postpartum estrus. Young of early litters may breed in their first year. In north-central Colorado, 3 to 5 litters are produced per season, with an average litter size of 4 (Wainwright 1968). The young are reared in sheltered nests lined with fur, grass, and weeds. Typical of lagomorphs, females often are "absentee mothers" and up to 30 hours may elapse between nursing bouts (Ingles 1941).

Desert cottontails are not territorial. Home ranges are from about 0.5 ha to 6.0 ha. Densities of 2 to 7 cottontails per hectare are typical, with highest densities (16 per hectare) reported in northeastern Colorado (Flinders and Hansen 1973). Moderate cattle grazing tends to promote increased cottontail densities by favoring broad-leafed herbs and shrub cover (Flinders and Hansen 1975). A wide variety of predators, including coyotes, foxes, badgers, weasels, eagles, hawks, owls, and snakes, prey on the desert cottontail. Desert cottontails and black-tailed jackrabbits (*Lepus californicus*) provided more than three-quarters of the diet of great horned owls (*Bubo virginianus*) on the Central Plains Experimental Range in Weld County (G. Zimmerman et al. 1996). Human hunters take desert cottontails, and hares and rabbits were important in the diets of indigenous peoples of Colorado. Indeed, zooarchaeologists have used the ratio between *Sylvilagus* and *Lepus* remains in midden sites to infer such cultural attributes as the degree of land clearance and hunting strategies (for review, see Driver and Woiderskia 2007).

Tularemia and plague are not uncommon, and large fluctuations in population numbers occur periodically. For notes on harvest, see the generic account of *Sylvilagus*, above. The literature was reviewed by J. Chapman and Willner (1978), J. Chapman et al. (1982), and J. Chapman and Litvaitis (2003).

Sylvilagus floridanus

EASTERN COTTONTAIL

Description

The eastern cottontail is generally larger and darker than the other 2 cottontails in Colorado, and its ears are shorter relative to body size. Measurements are: total length 380–490 mm; length of tail 40–70 mm; length of hindfoot 75–111 mm; length of ear 45–70 mm; weight 500–1,500 g.

PHOTOGRAPH 9-3. Eastern cottontail (*Sylvilagus floridanus*). Photograph by Bill Bevington.

Distribution

As the name suggests, the eastern cottontail is a mammal of eastern (and central) North America, although it has the broadest distribution of any cottontail. The animals

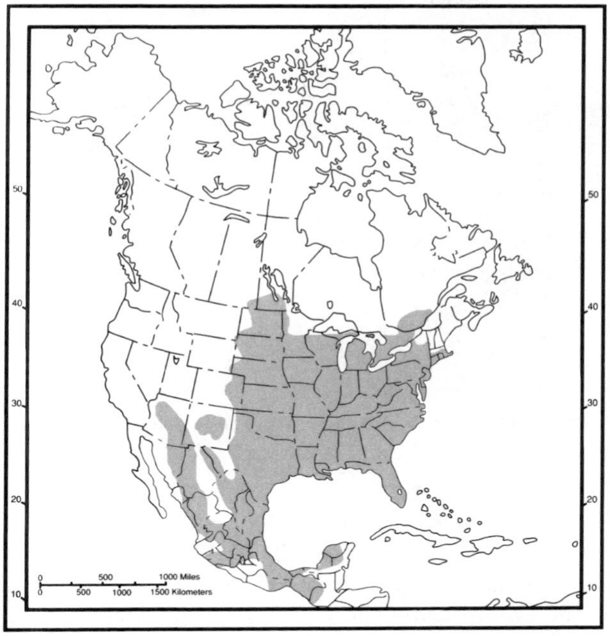

MAP 9-5. Distribution of the eastern cottontail (*Sylvilagus floridanus*) in North America.

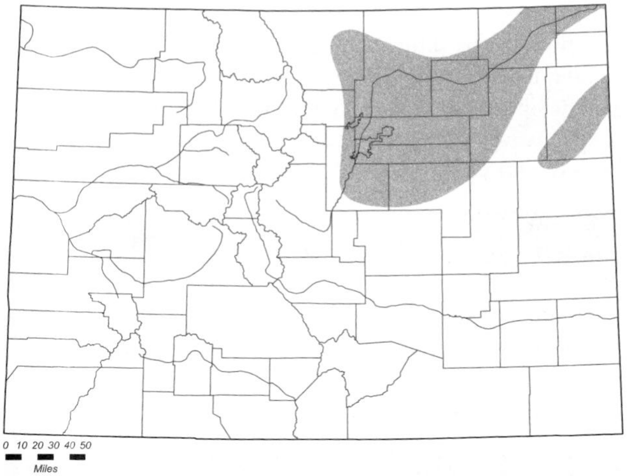

MAP 9-6. Distribution of the eastern cottontail (*Sylvilagus floridanus*) in Colorado.

have been introduced to Washington and Oregon (Verts and Carraway 1998; J. Chapman and Litvaitis 2003); these extralimital introductions are not shown on Map 9-5. In Colorado, eastern cottontails are found below about 1,980 m (6,500 ft). *Sylvilagus floridanus similis* is restricted to the eastern plains and foothills of the northeastern quarter of Colorado; *S. f. llanensis* has been ascribed a range in southeastern Colorado (D. Armstrong 1972).

Natural History

The eastern cottontail has been studied extensively in eastern North America, probably more than any other small game species. However, information about the ecology and biology of the species in the western portions of the range is scant. This cottontail occupies a wide variety of habitats and is common in brush, rank weeds, and grassy areas. In Colorado it inhabits riparian situations on the eastern plains and lower foothills. It is mostly nocturnal but can also be seen in early morning or late evening. Eastern cottontails eat a variety of grasses and forbs. In winter their diet shifts to woody plants and buds, bark, twigs, and shoots from shrubs and smaller trees. They are coprophagous, reingesting their soft feces in order to extract the maximal amount of nutrients.

The animals are mostly solitary except for the brief estrous period and when the female is rearing her young. Eastern cottontails breed during the warmer months, and in the southern part of their range they may breed year-round. Females of reproductive age achieve almost 100 percent pregnancy rates (Trethewey and Verts 1971; J. Chapman et al. 1977). In Colorado the breeding season is probably similar to that of the desert and mountain cottontails, beginning in February or March and ending in August, but firm data are lacking. Eastern cottontails are induced ovulators. The gestation period is 28 to 32 days, with a post-partum estrus. The number of litters ranges from 3 to 8 per year depending on latitude. Litter size varies from 2 to 7 with an average of 3 or 4. Sex ratios of young approximate 1:1; sex ratios of adults may slightly favor females (J. Chapman et al. 1982).

Young are blind, naked, and helpless at birth and are kept in a nest lined with fine grass and hair from the female's belly. The nest is usually in a thicket or dense stand of grass. Young grow rapidly and by 2 to 4 weeks of age are ready to leave the nest and forage on their own. Juveniles from early litters may become reproductively active by late summer.

Social behavior of the eastern cottontail is characterized by a dominance hierarchy established and maintained by postures, displacement, scent-marking, and occasional direct agonism. Dominant males paw-rake with the fore-paws and copulate with the majority of females. Eastern cottontails scent-mark by chinning (rubbing objects with a gland on the underside of the chin) and marking vegetation with the corner of the eye (Marsden and Holler 1964). During courtship, the male approaches the female, who adopts a threat posture. They face off; the male then makes a running dash by the female, she boxes him or jumps, and they face off again. This sequence is repeated and eventually the female becomes receptive to the male (Marsden and Holler 1964). As with other leporids, vocalizations include a shrill scream given when attacked. Cottontails communicate danger or threat by thumping their hindfeet, they emit squeals during copulation, and females use soft vocalizations with the young.

Densities in favorable habitat range from about 3 to 15 per hectare (J. Chapman et al. 1980, 1982). Home ranges have been estimated to be about 2 ha (Janes 1959), but seasonal, age, and sex differences result in much variation. The animals are not considered to be territorial (Trent and Rongstad 1974). Home ranges of adult females show little overlap during the breeding season, unlike other age and sex classes. Turnover of eastern cottontail populations is high. G. Rose (1977) estimated that annual mortality in Illinois averaged 79 to 81 percent. Individuals can live up to 10 years in captivity, but few survive past their second year in the wild.

Eastern cottontails are preyed upon by numerous medium-sized to large avian and mammalian carnivores, including bobcats, coyotes, foxes, owls, hawks, and eagles. Predation may be the major cause of death in cottontails. Cottontails are host to numerous internal and external parasites, and they are also susceptible to enzootic tularemia, which can destroy populations. Notes on harvest are included in the generic account of *Sylvilagus*, above. J. Chapman et al. (1980, 1982) and J. Chapman and Litvaitis (2003) reviewed the abundant literature.

Sylvilagus nuttallii

MOUNTAIN, OR NUTTALL'S, COTTONTAIL

Description

The mountain cottontail (also called Nuttall's cottontail) is similar in general appearance to both desert and eastern cottontails. It differs from the former in being darker with more blackish hairs dorsally and by having smaller ears and hindlegs. The auditory bullae are much smaller than in the desert cottontail. It is distinguished from the eastern cottontail by its paler dorsal color, a duller brownish shoulder patch, and more densely furred ears. The supraoccipital

PHOTOGRAPH 9-4. Mountain cottontail (*Sylvilagus nuttallii*). Photograph by Andrew Langford.

process is pointed posteriorly, the posterior extension of the supraorbital ridge is typically free from the braincase, and the external auditory meatus is slightly larger than in the eastern cottontail (Figure 9-3). Measurements are: total length 340–415 mm; length of tail 30–55 mm; length of hindfoot 90–110 mm; length of ear 56–65 mm; weight 900–1,100 g. In some parts of Colorado, this cottontail is sympatric with the other 2 species of cottontail, and identification can be difficult. In particular, *S. floridanus* and *S. nuttallii* can be troublesome to distinguish. Based on cytogenetic and molecular evidence, T. Robinson and Matthee (2005) arrayed them as "sister species," that is, each other's nearest relative.

Distribution

Mountain cottontails inhabit the mountainous western three-fifths of the state between 1,830 and 3,500 m (6,000–11,500 ft.). *Sylvilagus nuttallii grangeri* occurs in the White and Yampa river basins; *S. n. pinetis* occurs over the remainder of this species' distribution in the state.

Natural History

The mountain cottontail is mostly a species of the Intermountain West. In Colorado, it is found most frequently in montane and semidesert shrublands and in piñon-juniper woodlands as well as in edge habitats of montane and subalpine forests. It also inhabits open parklands with sufficient shrub, rock, or tree cover. In southern British Columbia, suitable habitat had at least 30 percent cover of sagebrush (T. Sullivan et al. 1989). The mountain cottontail does not construct its own burrow but uses bur-

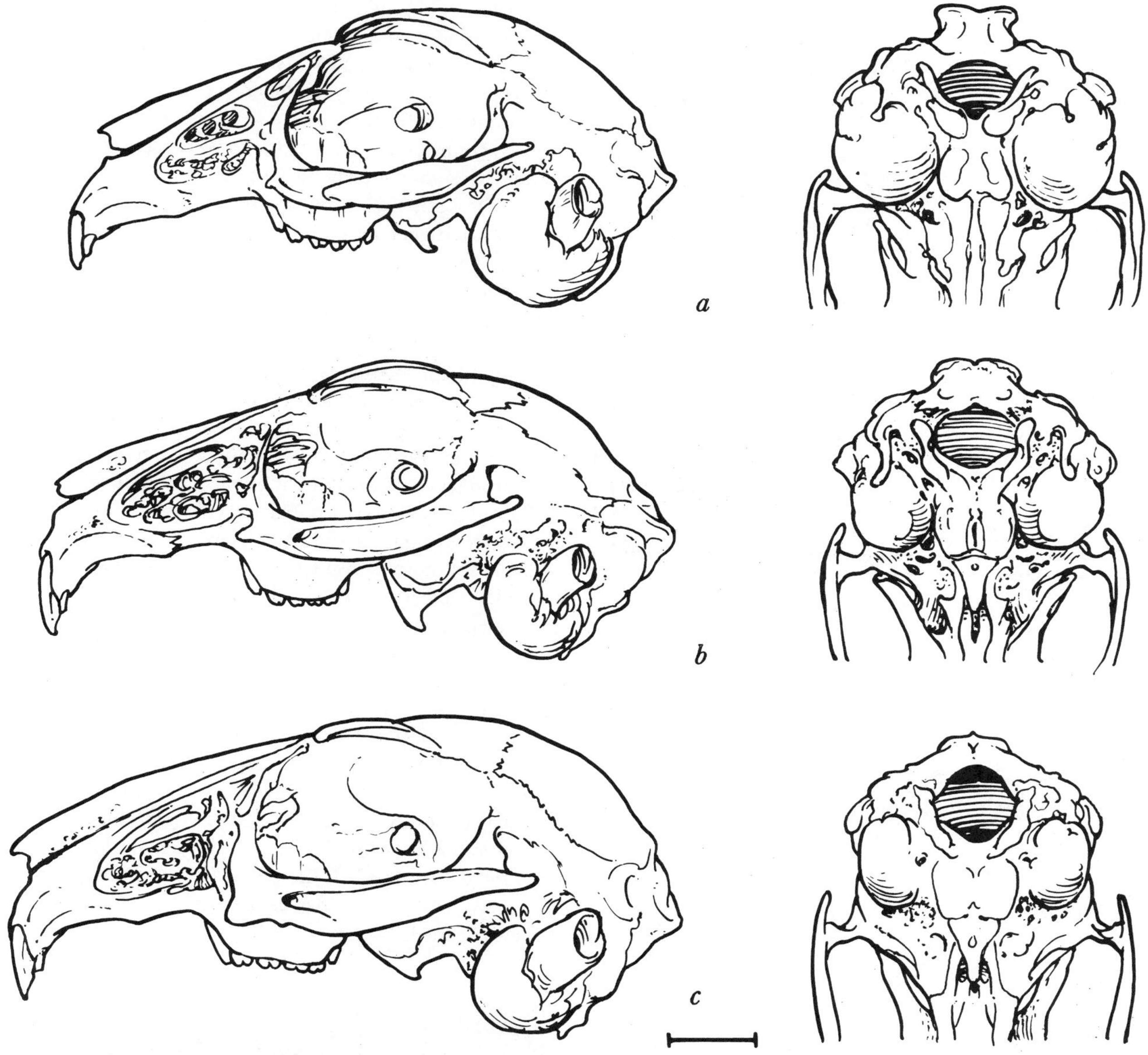

FIGURE 9-3. Lateral and ventral views of the skulls of 3 species of cottontails found in Colorado: (*a*) desert cottontail (*Sylvilagus audubonii*); (*b*) mountain cottontail (*Sylvilagus nuttallii*); (*c*) eastern cottontail (*Sylvilagus floridanus*). Note the relative diameter of the external auditory meatus ("ear canal") and the auditory bulla in the 3 species. Scale = 1 cm.

rows of other species. The animals tend to avoid dense riparian vegetation and heavy coniferous forest.

During warmer months, grasses and forbs are the mainstay of the diet. In southern Idaho several grasses, globe mallow, vetches, sage, winterfat, and prickly-pear were favored (M. K. Johnson and Hansen 1979). Sagebrush, rabbitbrush, and junipers are important in winter. Mountain cottontails are somewhat more crepuscular than other cottontails, often feeding early in the afternoon or from dawn to mid-morning if undisturbed. They are active

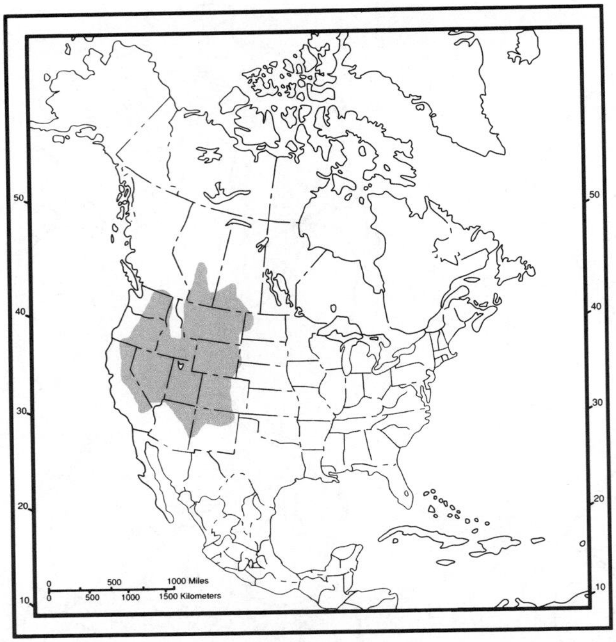

MAP 9-7. Distribution of the mountain cottontail (*Sylvilagus nuttallii*) in North America.

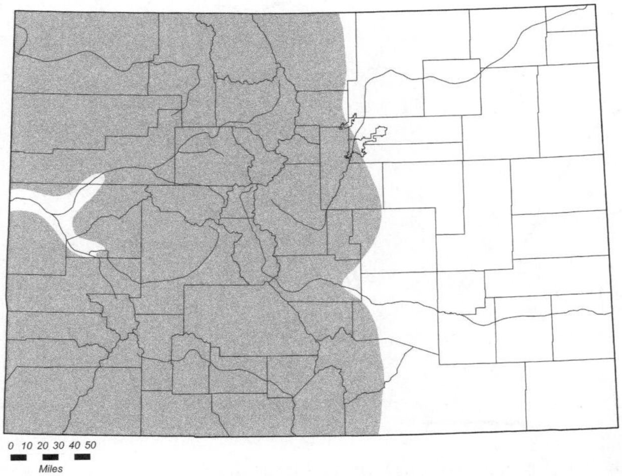

MAP 9-8. Distribution of the mountain cottontail (*Sylvilagus nuttallii*) in Colorado.

year-round, but temperature, precipitation, and wind may alter behavioral patterns. They retreat to cover during the middle of the day. When frightened they typically dash a short distance, stop, crouch, and face away from danger. If approached they repeat the process or retreat to heavy cover, a burrow, or similar shelter (J. Chapman 1975).

Data on reproduction in Colorado are lacking. In Oregon, mountain cottontails breed from late February to early July (Powers and Verts 1971). Juvenile females can breed but few apparently do. Juvenile males are non-breeding. Adult females have 4 litters a year, with an average embryo count of 4.3. A few females were reported to have 5 litters. Gestation is 28 to 30 days, followed by postpartum estrus. Drought-induced curtailment of plant production appears to trigger cessation of reproduction. Sex ratios approximate 1:1. The young are reared in a nest of dried grass lined with fur. Nests are typically covered with sticks, grass, or fur. Young are mobile when they weigh as little as 40 to 75 g (Orr 1940).

Population densities in juniper scrubland in Oregon ranged from about 2.5 per hectare in August to as low as 0.06 per hectare in November, December, and January (McKay and Verts 1978). Peaks in population coincided with production of the third litter. Most mortality occurred in fall and early winter; drought and cold temperatures contributed to juvenile mortality. At the northern limit of their range in southern British Columbia, densities were 0.2–0.4 individuals per hectare (T. Sullivan et al. 1989). Dispersal and mortality are key elements in control of local populations. Predators include bobcats, coyotes, badgers, eagles, goshawks (Drennan and Beier 2003), great horned owls, and humans.

The 3 species of cottontails are sympatric in Rist Canyon west of Bellvue (D. Armstrong 1972) and doubtless elsewhere along the Front Range. As with other cottontails, this species deserves more detailed ecological investigation in Colorado. Notes on harvest are present in the generic account of *Sylvilagus*. J. Chapman (1975), J. Chapman et al. (1982), and J. Chapman and Litvaitis (2003) provided reviews of the literature.

Genus *Lepus*—Hares and Jackrabbits

The genus *Lepus* is widespread, with some 33 species distributed throughout much of North America (south to Chiapas in southern Mexico), most of Eurasia (including Japan), and parts of Africa (R. Hoffmann and Smith 2005). Species of *Lepus* generally are called "hares," except in western North America, where several species are known as "jackrabbits." Hares mostly are animals of open country (steppe and savannah) and females give birth to precocial young.

Lepus americanus

SNOWSHOE HARE

Description

The snowshoe hare, sometimes termed "snowshoe rabbit" (a misnomer, as it is not a rabbit) or "varying hare," is a medium-sized hare with disproportionately large hindfeet and only moderately long ears. The summer pelage is rusty brownish to gray-brown above and white below. The tips of the ears are blackish, and frequently the animals show striking whitish gray stockings. During the fall the animals molt to a white winter pelage with only the tips of the ears remaining black. This pelage is shed in the spring. For a short time in spring and fall the animals are mottled brown and white. Measurements are: total length 365–525 mm; length of tail 25–55 mm; length of hindfoot 110–150 mm; length of ear 60–80 mm; weight 1.0–1.5 kg. Zahratka and Buskirk (2007) cautioned against using the size of fecal pellets to distinguish *Lepus americanus* from sympatric cottontails (in Colorado, *Sylvilagus nuttallii*). The interparietal bone is indistinct, entirely fused with the parietals. The supraorbital process is present but lacks the conspicuous anterior projection of jackrabbits (Figure 9-4).

In winter pelage, the species can be mistaken for the white-tailed jackrabbit, which also changes color, but the snowshoe hare has much shorter, black-tipped ears and relatively larger, more densely furred feet. The outsized "snowshoe" hindfeet seem to have real survival value in winter. During the snow-free period in central Wisconsin, survival of snowshoe hares and eastern cottontails is about equivalent, but in winter, survival of eastern cottontails dropped from 89 percent to 18 percent, whereas survival of snowshoe dropped only from 84 percent to 63 percent (L. Keith and Bloomer 1993).

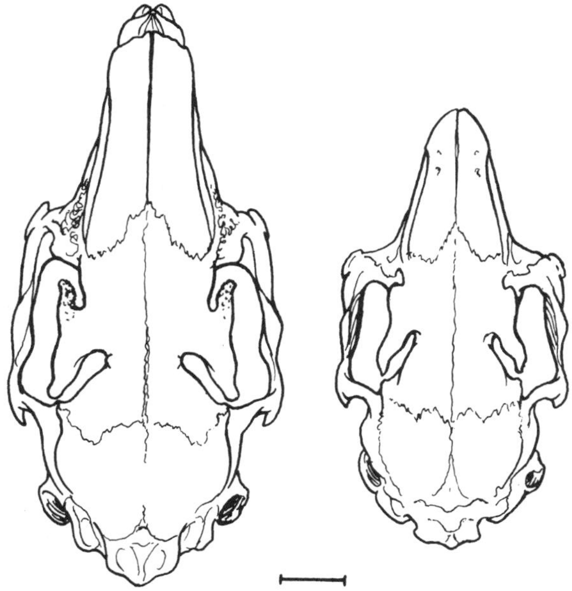

FIGURE 9-4. **Comparison of the development of the anterior projections of the supraorbital shield in the black-tailed jackrabbit (*Lepus californicus, left*) and snowshoe hare (*Lepus americanus, right*). Scale = 1 cm.**

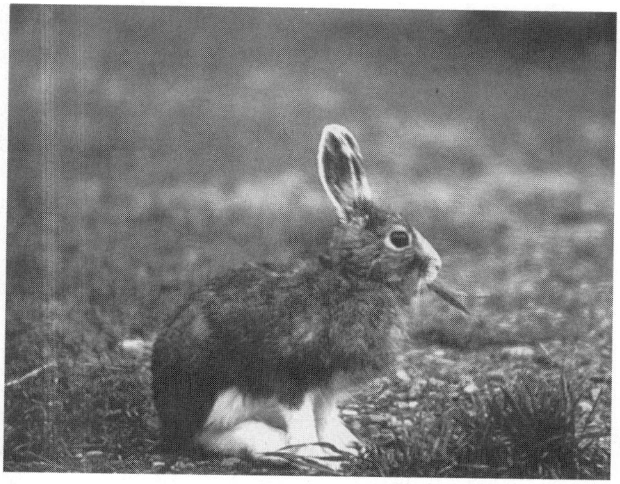

PHOTOGRAPH 9-5. **Snowshoe hare (*Lepus americanus*). Photograph by J. Perley Fitzgerald.**

Distribution

Snowshoe hares are Boreo-Cordilleran mammals (D. Armstrong 1972), ranging through the coniferous forests of North America from Alaska to Newfoundland and southward along the Sierras, Rockies, and Appalachians. They are rather common over most of mountainous Colorado. Elevational distribution usually ranges from about 2,440 to 3,500 m (8,000–11,500 ft.). The lowest record is 1,980 m (6,500 ft.) from Gunnison County (Warren 1942). The westernmost specimen is from Anvil Points, near Rifle, Garfield County (R. Finley et al. 1976). A single subspecies, *Lepus americanus bairdii*, occurs in the state.

Natural History

Ecological information on snowshoe hares in the Southern Rocky Mountains is scant. Several of the recent studies in

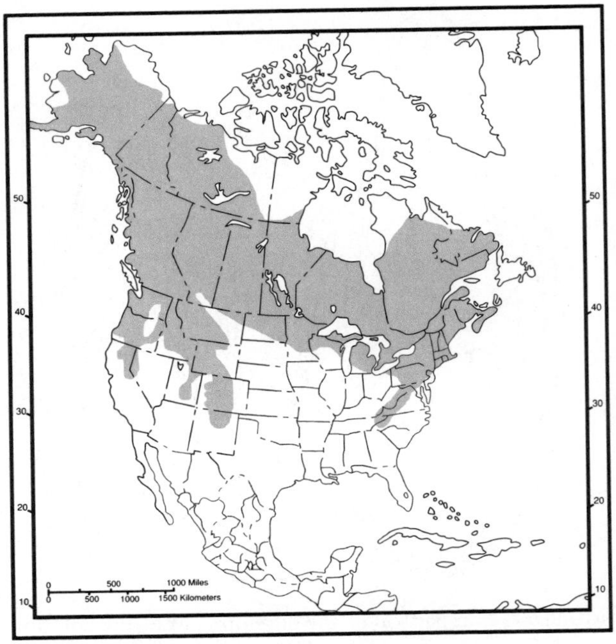

MAP 9-9. Distribution of the snowshoe hare (*Lepus americanus*) in North America.

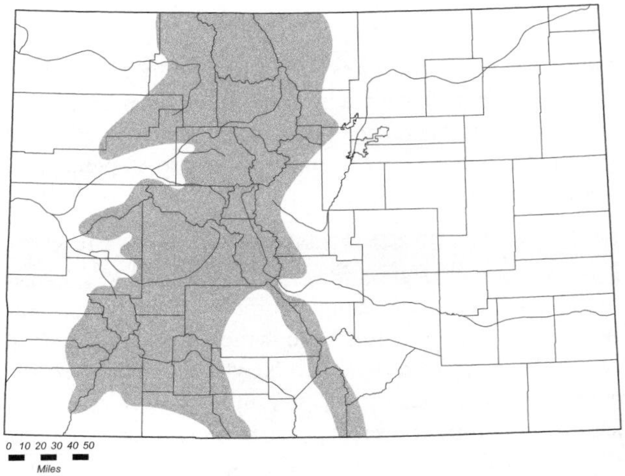

MAP 9-10. Distribution of the snowshoe hare (*Lepus americanus*) in Colorado.

Colorado have been done in the context of Canada lynx restoration (see, e.g., Zahratka 2004; Ivan 2008; Zahratka and Shenk 2008). In Colorado the snowshoe hare is restricted to the higher mountains, most commonly in or near dense stands of subalpine forest and alpine tundra near tree line. J. Frey and Malaney (2006) found the animals mostly restricted to subalpine coniferous forests in New Mexico, and Zahratka and Shenk (2008) found in Colorado that spruce forests supported the highest densities and lodgepole pine forests the lowest.

The animals are most abundant under cover of thickets where forbs and shrubs are dense. Forests impacted by wildfires, windfall, or logging provide excellent habitat, once sufficient succession has occurred. Dense cover within 2.5 m of the ground, which could be widely spreading branches of conifers, for example, appears to be more important to habitat suitability than are shrubs per se (Malaney and Frey 2006). Preliminary work by Ivan (2008) using livetrapped, radio-collared hares in the Taylor Park / Pitkin area of Gunnison County suggested that hare density is highest in the summer in stands of small-diameter (2.5 to 12.7 cm dbh [diameter breast height]) lodgepole that are regenerating from clear-cuts 20 to 40 years old. Lower numbers were observed in spruce/fir and older-growth lodgepole. In winter, density differences between small-diameter and older lodgepole forests were not apparent, with hares apparently able to use the older forest for forage and cover as snow levels accumulated. Hare densities recorded to date are low, less than 0.7 per hectare compared to the numbers that Hodges (2000a, 2000b) summarized from other studies, which indicated a range of less than 1–2 hares per hectare as typical for southern populations. Such densities correspond to the low end of cyclical hare populations in more northern habitats (1–16 hares per hectare).

Their diet consists of foliage, twigs, and bark of deciduous and evergreen trees and shrubs, as well as a variety of grasses and forbs when available (R. Hansen and Flinders 1969). Snowshoe hares need to ingest 91 to 122 kcal/kg of body weight to meet energy demands of minimal activity (Holter et al. 1974). On ad libitum diets the animals ate about 6.4 percent of their body weight per day. Liquid water and snow are both consumed. Green succulent plants, including clovers, sedges, and grasses, are important in late spring and summer. During winter the diet consists mostly of needles, browse, and bark of coniferous trees, especially Douglas-fir, subalpine fir, and spruce. Aspen, willow, birch, and even oakbrush are also acceptable winter foods. When the animals turn to a dry, high-fiber diet of browse, they typically show an enlargement of the cecum (R. L. Smith et al. 1980). Locally the animals may cause some damage to tree plantings and seedlings from browsing. Favored browse generally has a diameter of 4 mm or less. Browsing effects of snowshoe hares may reach heights of 2 m in deep snow conditions. In Canada, M. Ferguson and Merriam (1978) reported considerable consumption by snowshoe hares of twigs cut and dropped by porcupines. On the Clearwater National Forest in Idaho, Wirsing and Murray (2002) found that food quality, not quantity, may limit production of *L. americanus*. Available browse was 10 times that needed for forage, but levels of protein and some minerals were low and that may depress reproductive rates. This differed from the species in Canada, where at high densities hare populations may be limited by the quantity of suitable browse or by chemical defenses of browse plants.

Snowshoe hares do not appear to venture more than 60 to 120 m into clearings, so large openings created by burning may not be used effectively (Roppe and Hein 1978). The hares are mostly nocturnal, spending the day concealed in scrapes or "forms" in protected areas, such as a dense tangle of shrubs or young conifers. Unless flushed, snowshoe hares remain quiescent during the day. At night they leave the resting place and forage, usually traveling on well-used runways. Densities in southwestern Colorado ranged from 0.1 to 1.3 individuals per hectare (Zahratka and Shenk 2008).

Snowshoe hares are solitary and males and females have overlapping home ranges (Boutin 1979). In addition to territorial aggression, these hares show dominance interactions. Males are generally dominant in winter, whereas females are dominant during the breeding season (Graf 1985). Home ranges were estimated to be about 8 ha in subalpine forests in Colorado, with juveniles forced to utilize marginal areas (Dolbeer and Clark 1975). In prime habitat, densities of adults reach 46 to 73 per square kilometer (Dolbeer and Clark 1975).

During the breeding season males fight frequently; unless in estrus, females repel advances by males. Breeding starts in mid- to late April in Colorado and typically is over by late August or early September. Females have 2 or 3 litters of 1 to 7 young (average, 3 or 4). The abundance of winter food supply influences the timing of reproduction and the numbers of young produced per year. Average natality per female per year was estimated at 8 to 11 young in Colorado and Utah. The gestation period is 37 to 40 days and females have a postpartum estrus. Pregnancy rates for females are 94 to 100 percent for the first 2 litters and about 38 percent for third litters (Dolbeer and Clark 1975). Females rarely breed as juveniles. The young are precocial and huddle in the form for their first few days. They are weaned at about 1 month and reach adult size by 5 months of age.

In the northern portions of their range, snowshoe hares are noted for dramatic 10-year population cycles, which in turn affect predator populations. A number of hypotheses have been presented to account for the cycles, including behavioral interactions, endocrine responses, food shortages, and interactions of food and predators (L. Keith 1974; L. Keith and Windberg 1978; M. Vaughan and Keith 1981; Graf 1985; Boutin et al. 1985). In Colorado little is known of their population dynamics. The discontinuous nature of suitable habitat, the tendency to force juveniles to suboptimal open habitats, and sustained pressure by facultative predators may act to dampen population fluctuations (L. Keith 1990).

Adult survival averages 45 percent, with an estimated 15 percent survival in juveniles. Juveniles living in more open, less favorable habitat have the highest mortality. An estimated 16 percent of juveniles need to survive to maintain stability of populations in Colorado (Dolbeer and Clark 1975). A variety of predators, including coyotes, bobcats, lynx, weasels, marten, golden eagles, hawks, and great horned owls, feed on snowshoe hares (T. Williams 1957); coyotes were the principal predator in central Wisconsin (L. Keith and Bloomer 1993). In Montana, American martens were active both day and night and thus able to prey on both diurnal pine squirrels and nocturnal voles and snowshoe hares. In appropriate habitat, snowshoe hares provide a significant component of the predator food base. In a study in Idaho, snowshoe hares were taken irrespective of body condition (Wirsing et al. 2002).

Presence of snowshoe hares usually is considered an essential component of habitat for the lynx (*Lynx lynx*) in Colorado, so careful management of hares may be critical to managing lynx. McKelvey et al. (2002) provided guidance on using pellet density to monitor populations, and Zahratka (2004), J. Frey and Malaney (2006), and Zahratka and Buskirk (2007) urged caution in use of pellet surveys where mountain cottontails are sympatric. Snowshoe hares are subject to internal and external parasites. Epizootics of tularemia seem to have little impact. Recent cytogenetic and molecular studies (T. Robinson and Matthee 2005) suggested that *L. americanus* and *L. californicus* are more closely related to each other than either is to *L. townsendii*.

The Colorado Division of Wildlife (2009f) has a liberal hunting season on snowshoe hares during fall and winter, with a daily bag limit of 10 animals and a possession limit of 20. Table 4-3 provides some estimates of annual harvest; take most years is modest, fewer than 2,000 individuals. Unfortunately, little is known of population fluctuations in Colorado and how hunting impacts them. The literature was reviewed by Bittner and Rongstad (1982), Hodges (2000a, 2000b), and D. Murray (2003). Ellsworth and Reynolds (2006) prepared a Technical Conservation Assessment of the species for the USDA Forest Service.

Lepus californicus

BLACK-TAILED JACKRABBIT

Description

The black-tailed jackrabbit is medium to large in size with a grayish black dorsum and white venter. A black dorsal stripe extends from the tail onto the rump. The ears are dark on the outer tips. The young have a pronounced white spot on the forehead. Winter pelage is paler than summer pelage but never approaches white. Measurements are: total length 470–630 mm; length of tail 50–112 mm; length of hindfoot 110–145 mm; length of ear 100–130 mm; weight 1.3–3.2 kg, slightly less than the white-tailed jackrabbit. The supraorbital process may be somewhat concave in profile, with the projections never denticulate. The interparietal is indistinct. The skulls of some individuals of Colorado's 2 species of jackrabbit are virtually impossible to differentiate.

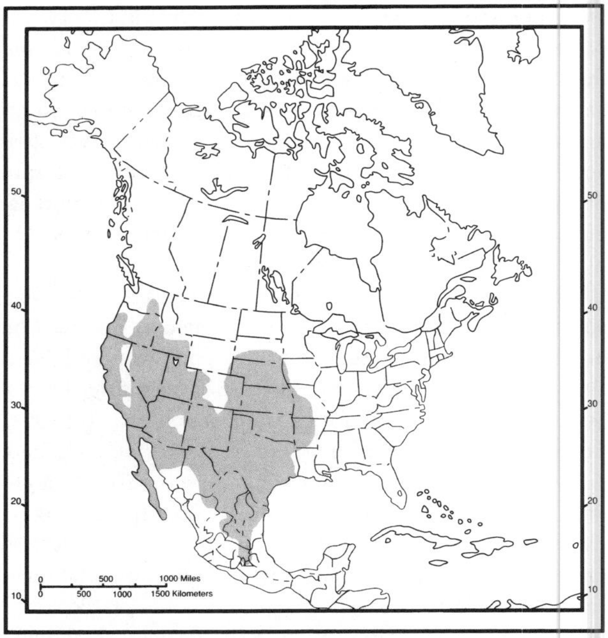

MAP 9-11. Distribution of the black-tailed jackrabbit (*Lepus californicus*) in North America.

PHOTOGRAPH 9-6. Black-tailed jackrabbit (*Lepus californicus*). Photograph by William E. Ervin.

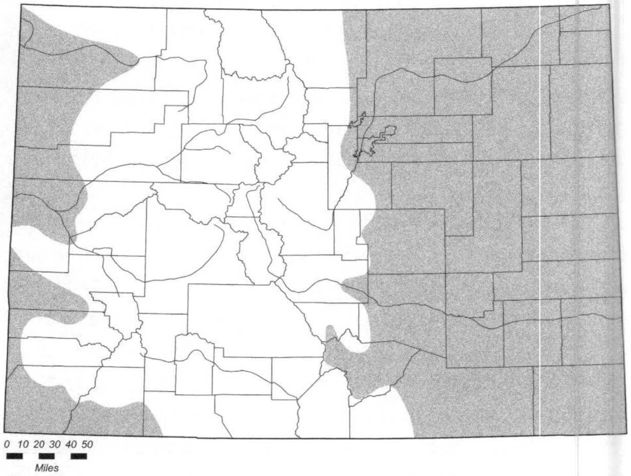

MAP 9-12. Distribution of the black-tailed jackrabbit (*Lepus californicus*) in Colorado.

Distribution

The black-tailed jackrabbit is of more southerly distribution than the white-tailed jackrabbit. Black-tailed jackrabbits are restricted to areas below 2,150 m (7,000 ft.) in Colorado, where they are associated with semidesert shrublands and grasslands. They are often found on the margins of cultivated lands. Density of black-tailed jackrabbits is directly proportional to shrub density in northeastern Colorado, whereas white-tailed jackrabbit density is inversely proportional to shrub density (Donoho 1972). With permanent settlement and the development of irrigated agriculture in eastern Colorado, black-tailed jackrabbits increased their range at the expense of white-tailed jackrabbits (Burnett 1925; Flinders and Hansen 1972). Prior to 1972, there was no documented evidence in western Colorado of black-tailed jackrabbits north of the Colorado River. Records from Rio Blanco County (R. Finley and Bogan 1995) and

Moffat County (Meaney 1991) suggest that they may be spreading northward into what was formerly white-tailed jackrabbit habitat in extreme northwestern Colorado. Despite this expansion, white-tailed jackrabbits do not appear to be declining in Dinosaur National Monument (R. Finley and Bogan 1995). *Lepus californicus melanotis* occurs on the grasslands of the eastern third of the state; *L. c. texianus* occurs in the western portion of the state.

Natural History

The black-tailed jackrabbit is a common resident of grasslands and semidesert shrublands of the western United States. The species has been studied in a variety of situations, in part because of their foraging on crops and supposed competition with livestock (Tiemeier 1965; Currie and Goodwin 1966; R. Hansen 1972; Westoby and Wagner 1973; Fagerstone et al. 1980) and partly because they may constitute the primary food base for a number of predators, especially coyotes (T. Clark 1972; F. Wagner and Stoddart 1972; Stoddart 1985). Because of a tendency of large populations to further degrade poorly managed rangeland, black-tailed jackrabbits have sometimes become serious pests in parts of eastern Colorado. From 1893 to 1895, 32,000 jackrabbits were killed in Las Animas and Prowers counties in organized hunts (Warren 1942). However, populations of jackrabbits are not monitored over much of their range. Flinders and Chapman (2003:139) noted that "as we continue to lose essential habitat to human development, agriculture, and exotic plant-dominated landscapes, the 'rabbit problem' of the future may well be cascading loss of historical jackrabbit populations and their dependent predators." Those authors urged better monitoring and mapping of populations, and that certainly is to be encouraged in Colorado, especially in the context of conservation concern in the face of energy development (and consequent fragmentation) on Colorado's sagebrush and other shrubland habitats.

The diet consists of a variety of grasses, sedges, forbs, and shrubs. Diet is closely linked with seasonal changes in palatability and availability of forage and may vary from year to year, depending on local conditions. In northeastern Colorado, 65 percent of the diet consisted of western wheatgrass, alfalfa, kochia (burning-bush), winter wheat, crested wheatgrass, rabbitbrush, and sun sedge (Flinders and Hansen 1972). In eastern Colorado, grasses were eaten in early spring and summer, forbs were mostly consumed during summer and fall, and shrubs were eaten in fall and winter (D. R. Sparks 1968). Studies in Arizona and Utah also indicated preference for grasses and forbs, with shrubs important in the winter months. In Utah, sagebrush, greasewood, and saltbush were important browse species (F. Wagner and Stoddart 1972). Black-tailed jackrabbits, like other lagomorphs, practice coprophagy, the reingestion of specialized feces. This enables them to assimilate the nutrients synthesized by bacteria in the cecum (Lechleitner 1957).

Jackrabbits can have economic impact. Studies in Arizona and Utah suggested that forage consumption of 5.8 to 30.0 jackrabbits equals that of 1 domestic sheep, and 74 jackrabbits equal 1 cow. Depending on season and condition of range, competition may occur between sheep and jackrabbits. R. Hansen (1972) estimated that consumption of forage by jackrabbits cost ranchers about $9.35 per hectare in the sandhills country of northeastern Colorado. C. Cook (1972) estimated that adult jackrabbits consumed an average of 0.54 pound (0.24 kg) of food per day. He also reported them to be 1.82 times as efficient as domestic cattle and sheep at converting food to biomass. Modeling, based mostly on data from northern Utah, suggested that populations are not food-limited (W. Clark and Innes 1982). In the high desert of eastern Oregon, black-tailed jackrabbits avoided experimental plantings of certain cultivars of basin wild rye and Russian wild rye. This suggests that such plantings might be useful in controlling competition with livestock or jackrabbits as traffic hazards. Attractive cultivars might be used to lure jackrabbits away from crops or valuable forages (Ganskopp et al. 1993).

In southeastern Colorado, black-tailed jackrabbits breed from February to July (Esch et al. 1959). The reproductive cycle, from conception through gestation and postpartum estrus to the next conception, takes 40 days. Up to 5 litters are produced per year, with ranges in mean litter size from 1.9 for late litters to 6.4 for litters in the middle of the breeding season. The young are precocial and are raised in fur-lined nests under dense vegetation. An estimated 27 percent of juvenile females are born early enough in the year to breed (John Gross et al. 1974). In California, young jackrabbits were capable of breeding at 8 months of age (Lechleitner 1959). The sex ratio approximates 1:1.

Black-tailed jackrabbits are mostly nocturnal or crepuscular. They may forage in open areas at night but typically move to denser vegetation during the day. They are most active on well-lit nights and least active during high winds (G. Smith 1990). They usually spend the day in a form—a shallow depression under a shrub—and occasionally use badger dens or prairie dog burrows for cover and protection from predation. In winter they become more social, sometimes congregating in groups of 30 or more animals. Density estimates range from 0.1 to 34.6 jackrabbits per hectare, with home ranges of 16 to 183 hectares (Lechleitner 1958; Tiemeier 1965; Flinders and Hansen 1973). Home ranges often overlap.

In semidesert shrublands in northern Utah, populations fluctuated by a factor of 9. Average mortality ranged from 45 to 62 percent depending on year. Juvenile mortality ranged between 55 and 70 percent (John Gross et al. 1974). In California, the distribution of age classes was as follows: 35 percent 2–9 months old, 38 percent 7–12 months old, and 27 percent older than 1 year. This indicates a population turnover within about 5 years (Lechleitner 1959).

Most medium-sized and large avian and mammalian predators—including coyotes, foxes, badgers, and eagles—take jackrabbits. Coyotes are closely tied to jackrabbit populations over much of the western United States, and there is evidence that this interaction impacts numbers of both species (T. Clark 1972; F. Wagner and Stoddart 1972). Predation by coyotes on livestock and rodents increases with a decrease in jackrabbit density. Black-tailed jackrabbits and desert cottontails (*Sylvilagus audubonii*) contributed more than three-quarters of the diet of great horned owls (*Bubo virginianus*) on the Central Plains Experimental Range in Weld County (Zimmerman et al. 1996). Diseases include tularemia (see Chapter 4), which, although it can infect jackrabbits, does not appear to cause cyclical epizootics. This is a small game mammal (Table 4-1). Estimates of harvest (Table 4-3) do not distinguish species of jackrabbits, but given the apparent scarcity of white-tailed jackrabbits over much of their former range, one would suspect that much of the harvest represents *L. californicus*. Harvest usually is modest, around 5,000 individuals annually. Dunn et al. (1982) reviewed the abundant literature on the species, as did Best (1996) and Flinders and Chapman (2003).

Lepus townsendii

WHITE-TAILED JACKRABBIT

Description

This is a large jackrabbit with a white rump and tail. In summer the upperparts are pale grayish brown except for the rump and tail, which are white. There may be a pale grayish to blackish band of hairs on the dorsal side of the tail, but this stripe does not extend onto the rump. In the northern portions of the range and at higher elevations, the fall molt results in winter pelage that is almost totally white. In southern Colorado the winter pelage tends to be somewhat brownish dorsally and only slightly paler than the summer pelage (R. Hansen and Bear 1963). The ears are tipped with black as in the snowshoe hare but the species in winter is readily recognizable by its much longer ears. Measurements are: total length 560–660 mm; length of tail 66–112 mm; length of hindfoot 145–175 mm; length of ear 100–115 mm; weight 2.5–5.0 kg.

PHOTOGRAPH 9-7. White-tailed jackrabbit (*Lepus townsendii*). Photograph by Dawn Reeder.

The skull has a well-developed supraorbital process (sometimes referred to as a shield) with bony anterior and posterior projections. These processes are slightly bulged dorsally and give the skull a convex appearance, and the margins of the shield are often denticulate. The interparietal is indistinct. The skull of this species is virtually identical to that of the black-tailed jackrabbit; dental details mentioned in the key are not absolutely reliable.

Distribution

The white-tailed jackrabbit is widely distributed throughout the state except in the extreme southeastern and southwestern corners. It ranges from elevations of about 1,200 m (4,000 ft.) to over 4,240 m (14,000 ft.) (Hoeman 1964; C. Braun and Streeter 1968). Intrusion of the black-tailed jackrabbit into white-tailed jackrabbit habitat on the eastern plains probably started with habitat changes (overgrazing, plowing) around the turn of the twentieth century (Burnett 1925; H. Brown 1947) and apparently has led to a

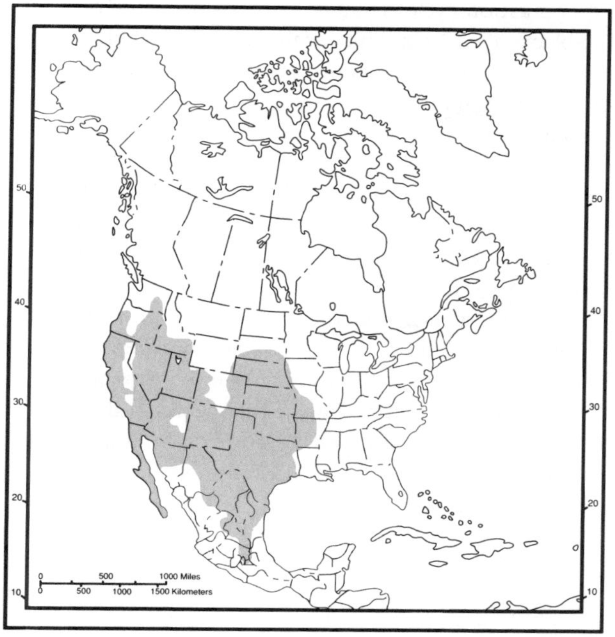

MAP 9-13. Distribution of the white-tailed jackrabbit (*Lepus townsendii*) in North America.

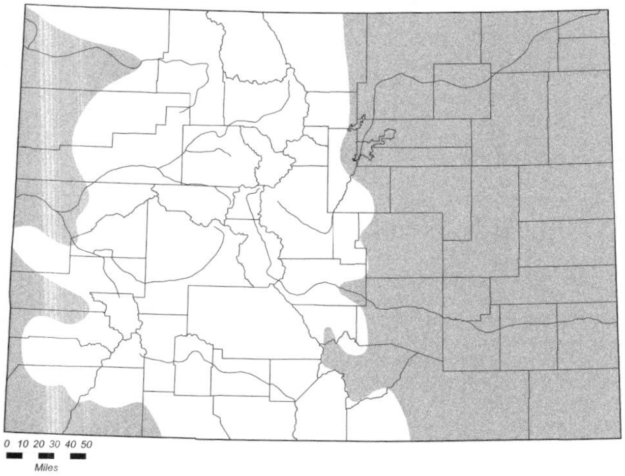

MAP 9-14. Distribution of the white-tailed jackrabbit (*Lepus townsendii*) in Colorado.

decline in populations of white-tailed jackrabbits. The species appears to have disappeared from western Kansas (Bee et al. 1981) and parts of Nebraska (R. Benedict et al. 2000). *Lepus townsendii campanius* is the subspecies of the eastern two-fifths of the state and *L. t. townsendii* occurs west of the Continental Divide.

Natural History

This is mostly a species of open country: prairie, open parkland, and alpine tundra. In western Colorado the species is found in semidesert shrublands and may migrate to such areas in winter. On the Pawnee National Grassland in northeastern Colorado, white-tailed jackrabbits predominated on blue grama–buffalograss prairie, whereas black-tails predominated in stands of four-wing saltbush. They were equally prevalent on a saltbush and grass mixture (Donoho 1972). In general, white-tailed jackrabbits are less tolerant of losses of native vegetation than are black-tailed jackrabbits.

The diet has been studied in a variety of habitats in Colorado. In the mountain parks, Bear and Hansen (1966) found rabbitbrush and fringed sage to be important, as were clover, dandelion, sedges, and paintbrush. In spring, summer, and early fall, grasses and sedges are favored, but in colder months forbs and shrubs become more important. On the plains, winter wheat was consumed in spring and early summer, along with western wheatgrass, summer cypress, legumes, sun sedge, rabbitbrush, and crested wheatgrass (Flinders and Hansen 1972). As in other lagomorphs, specialized soft fecal pellets are reingested for additional nutrition.

White-tailed jackrabbits are mostly nocturnal (Rogowitz 1997) but can occasionally be observed moving about on cloudy days or in late afternoon, or when disturbed from their form, a minimal shelter scraped out at the base of larger plants. They also frequent burrows and may even have their young in underground nests, an unusual occurrence for true hares. Mostly they rely on speed for escape.

The sex ratio is about 1:1 (Rogowitz and Wolfe 1991). The breeding season is March through late August in south-central Colorado (Bear and Hansen 1966). Females in estrus are often followed by several males. Breeding is promiscuous. A single litter is typical in the mountains of southern Colorado, although a postpartum estrus occurs and more than 1 litter is possible. Litter size ranges from 1 to 11 with a mean of about 5. In North Dakota and Wyoming, breeding occurs from February to mid-July, with 1 to 9 young per litter (average, 4.5) and 3 or 4 litters per year (T. James and Seabloom 1969; Rogowitz 1992). Populations on the eastern plains of Colorado may also show a higher reproductive potential than the mountain populations. Unlike black-tailed jackrabbits, juvenile female white-tailed jackrabbits are not reported to breed (T. James and Seabloom 1969; Rogowitz 1992). At birth the young weigh 85 to 115 g and are fully furred with eyes open. They move about soon after birth and grow rapidly. In southwestern Wyoming, growth rates between days 20 and 80 were about 30 g per day (Rogowitz and Wolfe 1991), but they do not reach adult weight until about December.

Home range size and behavior are poorly known. Rogowitz and Wolfe (1991) estimated densities at 7 per square kilometer; Flinders and Hansen (1972) estimated densities of 2.2 animals per square kilometer in winter, generally a lower density than is observed for black-tailed jackrabbits. Animals from southwestern Wyoming in captivity in northern Utah showed thicker pelage, lower thermal conductance, and lowered critical temperature in winter, so that they expended minimal energy for thermoregulation at usual ambient temperatures in their rigorous environment (Rogowitz 1990).

A large number of predators—including foxes, coyotes, eagles, and humans—harvest these animals, and natural population cycles recur at 8- to 10-year intervals. Like the black-tailed jackrabbit, white-tailed jackrabbits are not looked on favorably by some agricultural producers in Colorado. The hunting season is from October 1 until the end of February (Colorado Division of Wildlife 2009f). Total harvest of jackrabbits is rather modest, around 5,000 per year. Estimates of harvest (Table 4-3) do not distinguish white- versus black-tailed jackrabbits, but given the apparent scarcity of white-tailed jackrabbits over much of their former range in Colorado, we suspect that much of the harvest represents *L. californicus*. A careful study of the status of white-tailed jackrabbits in Colorado would be of interest. Berger (2008a, 2008b) discussed the possible importance of the apparent decline of the species in the Greater Yellowstone Ecosystem. The literature on *L. townsendii* was reviewed by Dunn et al. (1982), Lim (1987), and Flinders and J. Chapman (2003).

10

Order Soricomorpha

Shrews, Moles, and Kin

Shrews and moles were included traditionally in an order, Insectivora. However, it has long been recognized that Insectivora is a taxonomic grab bag, including a number of groups that are only distantly related. McKenna and Bell (1997) placed some groups of the former order Insectivora into a grandorder, Lipotyphla, recognizing orders Erinaceomorpha, Chrysochloroidea, and Soricomorpha for the hedgehogs, the African Cape golden "moles," and the shrews and moles, respectively. Hutterer (2005) used a similar arrangement, and that is followed here.

Once considered among Insectivora, both elephant shrews and tree shrews now are placed in their own separate orders, the Macroscelidea and Scandentia, respectively. A number of groups that formerly were included in the order Insectivora have been placed in a superorder, Afrotheria. Those include the tenrecs of Madagascar and Cape golden moles (order Afrosoricida) and "elephant shrews" or sengis (order Macroscelidea). Some of the forms once known as "subungulates" are now considered afrotherians as well, including the aardvark (order Tubulidenta) and the hyraxes and manatees (order Paenungulata) (D. W. Macdonald 2006).

D. W. Macdonald (2006) placed shrews in an order, Eulipotyphla, within a superorder, Laurasiatheria, along with the bats (Chiroptera), carnivores, the pangolin (Pholidota), perissodactyls (horses and kin), and the Cetartiodactyla (including even-toed ungulates and whales). Asher (2005) and K. Rose (2006) reviewed the fossil history of soricomorphs.

Most soricomorphs are small, ranging from the pygmy and dwarf shrews (*Sorex hoyi* and *S. nanus*—both of which occur in Colorado), which measure 80–90 mm in length and weigh 2–3 g, to about 500 mm in total length for the largest solenodons (unique insectivorous mammals of Cuba and Hispaniola). North American soricomorphs have small brains; specialized dentition; reduced eyes; a long, pointed, flexible snout; poorly developed auditory bullae; and a jugal bone that is reduced or absent, resulting in a weak or incomplete zygomatic arch. Guard hairs are absent, so all hairs of the pelage are of the same type. Each foot has 5 clawed digits, and the feet are plantigrade. The testes usually are abdominal or inguinal and a baculum has been reported in only a few taxa. The uterus is bicornuate with a single cervix and vagina. Soricomorphs have large olfactory bulbs and a well-developed sense of smell. A vomeronasal organ is present, as are a variety of scent-producing glands. Glandular secretions vary seasonally and may serve as signposts and as a means to facilitate encounters between solitary individuals (Holst 1985).

The order Soricomorpha includes about 45 genera and 428 species in four families (D. Wilson and Reeder 2005). Soricomorphs are present in Eurasia, Africa, North America, Central America, northern South America, and the West Indies. Two families, 5 genera, and 9 species are known with certainty in Colorado (and at least 1 additional shrew, *Sorex preblei*, may be present). All Coloradan soricomorphs are listed as non-game species (see Table 4-1 and Colorado Division of Wildlife 2009c).

Key to the Families of the Soricomorphs in Colorado

1. Forefeet not spade-like; zygomatic arch absent; total teeth fewer than 36; teeth mostly with brown tips . . . . Family Soricidae, p. 280

1' Forefeet spade-like; zygomatic arch weak but present; total teeth 36; teeth without brown tips . . . . Family Talpidae, p. 298

Family Soricidae—Shrews

Most shrews are very small mammals. None of the species in Colorado exceeds 175 mm in total length or 30 g in weight. Shrews are somewhat mouse-like in appearance but their snouts are longer and pointed (hence their German name, *Spitzmaus*, "sharp mouse"). The eyes are small and vision is poor. The olfactory sense is strong and hearing is acute, especially for high-frequency sounds. Shrews produce high-pitched twittering vocalizations and some may echolocate. Facial vibrissae are prominent and the tactile sense apparently is well developed. Flank glands, located anterior to the hind limbs, have been found in all species investigated (Holst 1985). These glands produce a dark, moist-looking oval on the fur of the flanks. The glands are present in both sexes and glandular activity seems to correlate with reproductive activity, although patterns are not always clear.

The fur is short and dense with a velvety texture. Colors vary from gray through brown to almost black, and in most species there is little difference between the dorsal and ventral color; that is, countershading may not be obvious. The feet have 5 clawed digits. The tail—variable in length—is always haired. Skulls are relatively long and narrow without a zygomatic arch or auditory bullae.

The teeth are tubercular and sectorial, well suited to a diet of small invertebrates. Homologies of teeth with those of other placentals are poorly understood. The first tooth on each side of the upper jaw is bicuspid, with a variable number of unicuspid teeth immediately behind. Unicuspid teeth are followed in turn by a variable number of teeth with 3 or more cusps. Teeth are rooted, and the bicuspids and unicuspids of Coloradan species have reddish brown tips. The extent of pigmentation varies from one individual to another (and from one tooth to another). The pigment results from iron-containing molecules in the enamel, which may make the teeth more resistant to abrasion and perhaps to acidic chemicals (Kozawa et al. 1988; Strait and Smith 2006).

Coloradan shrews are terrestrial. They typically live in shallow tunnels or form runways in the litter on the surface of the soil. Some species use the tunnels or runways of other mammals such as moles or voles. Shrews seldom live much longer than 1 year. Shrews are active animals with high metabolic rates, so the animals must forage almost constantly, consuming 1 to 2 times their body weight in food every 24 hours. Their prodigious appetites cause them to take practically any available animal matter, including small mammals, but mostly they rely on insects and other small invertebrates. Foraging periods are brief, averaging 55 minutes in the European common shrew *Sorex araneus*, and are followed by periods of sleep that average 64 minutes. Foraging bouts are interrupted by rest periods of 5–10 minutes, which occur when the gut is full. During these brief rest periods, the shrew stands, moving its muzzle from side to side (Saariko and Hanski 1990). McNab (1991) reviewed energetics of shrews. Hallett et al. (2003) summarized the variety of complex symbiotic relationships of terrestrial small mammals (especially shrews and rodents) in western coniferous forests.

There are about 26 genera and 376 species of shrews (D. Wilson and Reeder 2005) distributed on all continents except Australia. Four genera and 9 species are known with certainty in Colorado. Innes (1994) reviewed data on life histories of shrews, highlighting the extraordinary diversity within the group.

Key to the Species of the Family Soricidae in Colorado

1. Total teeth 28 with 3 unicuspid teeth in each side of the upper jaw . . . . Crawford's Desert Shrew—*Notiosorex crawfordi*, p. 296

1' Total teeth more than 28 with more than 3 unicuspid teeth in each side of the upper jaw 2

2. Total teeth 30 with 4 unicuspid teeth in each side of the upper jaw (the last upper unicuspid is tiny, not visible from the side but visible ventrally) . . . . Least Shrew—*Cryptotis parva*, p. 294

2' Total teeth 32 with 5 unicuspid teeth in each side of the upper jaw (one or more of the unicuspid teeth may be tiny and difficult to see without use of hand lens or microscope) 3

3. Tail less than one-third of body length, body stout . . . . Elliot's Short-tailed Shrew—*Blarina hylophaga*, p. 292

3' Tail greater than one-third of body length; body rather slender . . . . *Sorex*, 4

4. Third and fifth unicuspid teeth tiny and barely or not at all visible from side . . . . Pygmy Shrew—*Sorex hoyi*, p. 283

4' Third unicuspid tooth not especially tiny so 4 unicuspid teeth are visible from side 5

5. Size large for a shrew, total length over 130 mm; upperparts blackish gray; underparts pale to dark gray; hindfoot with conspicuous fringe of stiff hairs . . . . Water Shrew—*Sorex palustris*, p. 290

5' Size small; total length less than 130 mm; upperparts brownish, never blackish gray; hindfoot without fringe of stiff hairs 6

6. Third unicuspid conspicuously smaller than fourth (Fig. 10-1) 7

6' Third unicuspid not conspicuously smaller than the fourth (Fig. 10-1) 8

7. Braincase with convex profile; foramen magnum relatively ventral, extending more into basioccipital than supraoccipital; occiput with rounded appearance when viewed from behind; hindfoot generally more than 11 mm; greatest length of skull generally more than 15 mm; total body length usually more than 100 mm . . . . Montane Shrew—*Sorex monticolus*, p. 287

7' Braincase with flattened profile; foramen magnum not relatively ventral, extending more dorsally into supraoccipital; occiput with shield-shaped profile when viewed from behind; hindfoot less than 11 mm; greatest length of skull usually less than 15 mm; total length generally less than 100 mm . . . . Dwarf Shrew—*Sorex nanus*, p. 288

8. Feet and underparts whitish; skull with relatively short, broad rostrum abruptly truncated anteriorly; maxillary breadth usually greater than 4.8 mm; teeth stout, molars as broad as long . . . . Merriam's Shrew—*Sorex merriami*, p. 285

8' Feet and underparts not whitish, only slightly paler than dorsum; skull with relatively long, narrow rostrum not abruptly truncated anteriorly 9

9. Condylobasal length 14.7 mm or more; unicuspid toothrow 2.05 mm or more . . . . Masked Shrew—*Sorex cinereus*, p. 282

9' Condylobasal length 14.6 mm or less; unicuspid toothrow 2.05 mm or less . . . . Preble's Shrew—*Sorex preblei*, p. 292*

Genus *Sorex*

The genus *Sorex* is Holarctic in distribution, with some 77 species ranging from the Arctic southward in North America to Chiapas, Mexico, and in Asia to Kashmir and Sichuan (Hutterer 2005). In some parts of the Coloradan mountains as many as 5 species of *Sorex* occur at a single locality. Identification of long-tailed shrews (*Sorex* and kin) is difficult at best. The annotated key developed by Junge and Hoffmann (1981) may be of help. Occasionally—as when identifying remains of shrews from owl pellets—one has only lower jaws (dentaries) by which to identify shrews to species; under those circumstances, the key by Carraway (1995) is unique and invaluable. The evolution, systematics, and biogeography of the genus *Sorex* were detailed by S. George (1986b, 1988).

* Not known with certainty from Colorado; see species account.

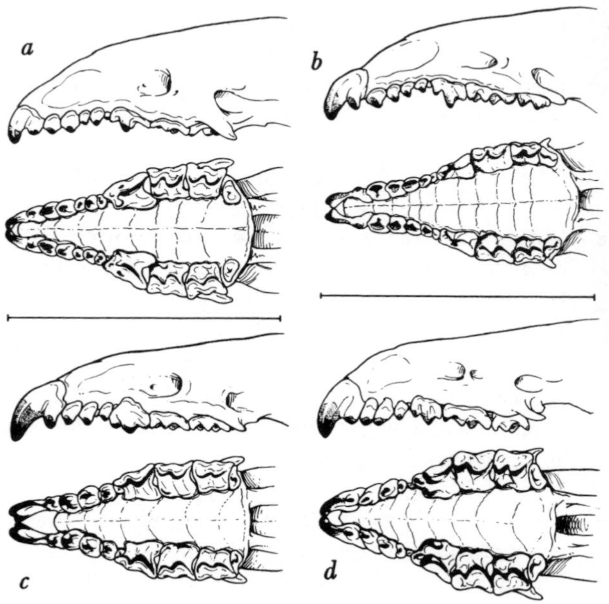

FIGURE 10-1. Ventral and lateral views of upper jaws of shrews showing relative size and position of unicuspid teeth: (*a*) montane shrew (*Sorex monticolus*); (*b*) masked shrew (*Sorex cinereus*); (*c*) pygmy shrew (*Sorex hoyi*); (*d*) least shrew (*Cryptotis parva*). Scale = 1 cm.

Sorex cinereus

MASKED SHREW

Description

The masked shrew is medium grayish to brownish in color, slightly paler on the ventral surface. The tail is indistinctly bicolored. Pelage is slightly paler in winter than in summer. Measurements are: total length 80–109 mm; length of tail 35–46 mm; length of hindfoot 11–12 mm; weight 3–6 g. Greatest length of skull is 14–16 mm. The third unicuspid is as large as or larger than the fourth. This species is difficult to distinguish from the montane shrew without careful examination of the teeth.

Distribution

The masked shrew occurs over much of the central mountains, westward on the Roan plateau, and eastward onto the Colorado Piedmont (Beidleman 1950). The elevational range is 1,500–3,350 m (5,000–11,000 ft.). A single subspecies, *Sorex cinereus cinereus*, occurs in Colorado. The masked shrew was

PHOTOGRAPH 10-1. Masked shrew (*Sorex cinereus*). Photograph by Roger W. Barbour.

reported from Tamarack Ranch in Logan County (Samson et al. 1988). Specimens of long-tailed shrews from that area should be examined with great care and with the benefit of comparative material, as they may represent the closely related Hayden's shrew (*Sorex haydeni*), sometimes treated as a subspecies of *S. cinereus*. J. K. Jones (1964) reported *S. c. haydeni* from near North Platte, Nebraska, about 75 mi. from Colorado; in Wyoming, Hayden's shrew apparently is restricted to the Black Hills (T. Clark and Stromberg 1987). Junge and Hoffmann (1981) provided illustrated keys to distinguish the species. Van Zyll de Jong (1991) and Demboski and Cook (2003) discussed diversification of *Sorex cinereus* and kin based on morphology and genetics, respectively.

Natural History

Often the most abundant shrew at localities in Colorado's central mountains, the masked shrew occurs in moist habitats in montane and subalpine forests, especially in willow thickets and moist meadows. It extends eastward onto the plains in situations with lush vegetation and suitable moisture, such as cattail marshes and cottonwood river-bottoms. The ecology of the masked shrew over much of its range is similar to that of the montane shrew (A. Spencer and Pettus 1966; T. Clark 1973) and they frequently are taken in the same habitat, although the montane shrew has a more restricted geographic range than does *S. cinereus*. Masked shrews seem to be more abundant on the Eastern Slope and montane shrews are more abundant on the Western Slope (D. Armstrong 1972). Crawford (2003) tested the hypothesis of character displacement where the 2 species are sympatric and found no evidence for it. The masked shrew is active at any time of day but leaves little sign of its presence. Masked

MAP 10-1. Distribution of the masked shrew (*Sorex cinereus*) in North America.

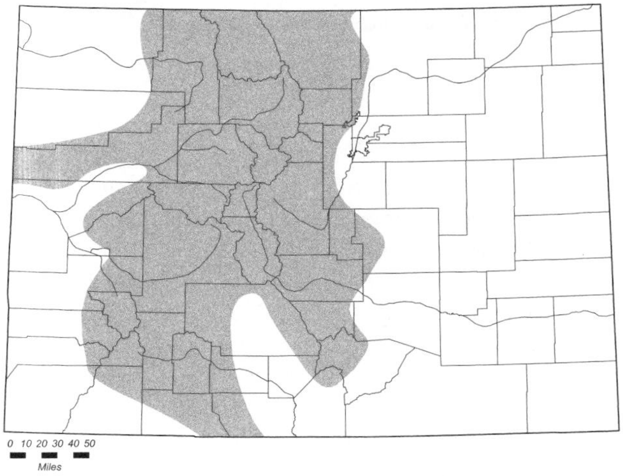

MAP 10-2. Distribution of the masked shrew (*Sorex cinereus*) in Colorado.

shrews hunt aboveground, among leaf litter, in burrows of their own making, and in those dug by other animals. Plant cover greater than 75 percent is preferred, and they rarely are found away from standing water (T. Clark 1973). They are active year-round, favoring the subnivean (under-snow) environment in winter. They survive cold weather because of a suite of physiological adaptations, including non-shivering thermogenesis (using stored brown fat as fuel) and an elevated metabolic rate (Merritt 1995). Aggregation behavior, as noted in a variety of species of shrews (including *S. cinereus* in the eastern United States; Maier and Doyle 2006), has not been reported from Colorado.

Food is mostly small invertebrates, especially insects. A captive individual readily ate grubs, mealworms, grasshoppers, and earthworms (Pokropus and Banta 1966). The masked shrew apparently reproduces throughout the warmer months. An individual female may have several litters during the summer, with 4 to 10 young per litter. The young are self-sufficient by about 4 weeks of age (Forsyth 1976). In Wyoming, litter size averaged 4.6 (range, 3–7) (T. Clark 1973). Whitaker (2004) summarized knowledge of the species.

Sorex hoyi

PYGMY SHREW

Description

Well named, the pygmy shrew is very small, even by shrew standards. The pelage of Coloradan specimens is dark brown, shading to slightly paler on the venter. In other populations, color varies from reddish brown to gray-brown. The tail is indistinctly bicolored and relatively short. Measurements of specimens from Colorado and Wyoming (L. N. Brown 1966; D. Armstrong 1972) are: total length 70–90 mm; length of tail 25–31 mm; length of hindfoot 9–11 mm; weight 2–5 g. Greatest length of skull is under 16 mm for these Rocky Mountain specimens. The skull is narrow and flattened, similar to other small species of *Sorex*. The third unicuspid tooth has a flattened disclike shape, and the fifth unicuspid is minute; both are barely or not at all visible from the side but may be seen in occlusal view. The distinctive dentition of *S. hoyi*, its small size, shorter tail, and normally darker color help to distinguish it from the montane shrew. A number of authors have treated this species in a genus, *Microsorex*; however, Diersing (1980) placed the species in the genus *Sorex*, as it was originally described by Baird (1858).

Distribution

Until 1961 this shrew was not known in the Rocky Mountains south of Montana. In that year the first specimens from

PHOTOGRAPH 10-2. Pygmy shrew (*Sorex hoyi*). Photograph by Rob Simpson, Simpson's Nature Photography.

Colorado were taken around the edge of a small sphagnum bog in coniferous forest at 2,950 m (9,700 ft.) near Cameron Pass, west of Fort Collins (Pettus and Lechleitner 1963). The pygmy shrew has since been captured on Rabbit Ears Pass in western Grand County (T. Vaughan 1969) and near Gothic in northern Gunnison County (DeMott and Lindsey 1975), extending the known range of the species some 145 km to the south. In 2009, J. L. Siemers of the Colorado Natural Heritage Program at Colorado State University captured pygmy shrews in pitfall traps in Summit, Eagle, and Pitkin counties (personal communication). It is possible that the pygmy shrew occupies suitable habitat throughout the mountains of central Colorado. Populations may be discontinuous relicts of Pleistocene glacial times. Most captures have been at elevations above 2,900 m (9,600 ft.). One subspecies, *Sorex hoyi montanus*, occurs in Colorado.

Natural History

The pygmy shrew is poorly known in the West but apparently it is able to live under a variety of ecological conditions. It has been captured in subalpine forests (spruce, fir, and lodgepole pine), clear-cut and selectively logged forests, forest-meadow edges, bogs and moist meadows, willow thickets, aspen-fir forests, and subalpine parklands (Pettus and Lechleitner 1963; A. Spencer and Pettus 1966; T. Vaughan 1969; DeMott and Lindsey 1975). In northern and eastern parts of its range this shrew has been reported from sandy areas and even cultivated fields (Feldhamer et al. 1993). In Wisconsin, pygmy shrews move from wet marshy areas to peripheral, drier areas as populations increase in late summer (Long 1972).

Behavior of the pygmy shrew is poorly known. It builds runways under stumps, fallen logs, and litter and has been observed in captivity to build nests. The animals are active both day and night, and like other shrews, they prey on a variety of small invertebrates and carrion of vertebrates, including mice and other shrews. One captive shrew ate 11 g of food over a 2-day period. As other members of the genus, the pygmy shrew probably eats 1 to 2 times its weight daily, with alternating periods of foraging and sleeping.

MAP 10-3. Distribution of the pygmy shrew (*Sorex hoyi*) in North America.

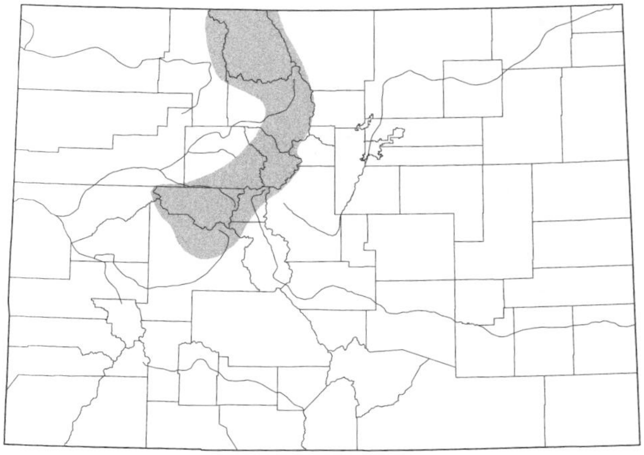

MAP 10-4. Distribution of the pygmy shrew (*Sorex hoyi*) in Colorado.

Pygmy shrews breed in the warmer months, with up to 8 young reported from a Colorado specimen (DeMott and Lindsey 1975). There are no reports of more than 1 litter per year. Low reproductive rate combined with difficulty of capture may help to explain the lack of information on the animals (Long 1974). Data on populations are scarce. Manville (1949) estimated 0.52 animals per hectare in Michigan. A. Spencer and Pettus (1966) captured more than 40 individuals over a 4-year period from their 25-hectare study area in western Larimer County, Colorado. Literature on the species was reviewed by Long (1974) and Beauvais and McCumber (2006).

Sorex merriami

MERRIAM'S SHREW

Description

Merriam's shrew is medium-sized and grayish in color with whitish feet and underparts. The tail is conspicuously bicolored and sparsely haired. Measurements are: total length 88–107 mm; length of tail 33–42 mm; length of hindfoot 11–13 mm; weight 4–7 g. Greatest length of skull is 16–18 mm. The skull has a short, broad rostrum, abruptly truncated anteriorly, with the braincase flattened and not much higher than the rostrum. The dentition is stout, with the second unicuspid the largest and the third unicuspid larger than the fourth.

PHOTOGRAPH 10-3. Merriam's shrew (*Sorex merriami*). Photograph by Claude Steelman / Wildshots.

Distribution

Specimens of Merriam's shrew in Colorado have generally come from elevations between 1,370 and 2,920 m (4,500 and 9,600 ft.), as summarized by D. Armstrong (1972), with subsequent specimens reported for El Paso, Gunnison, Rio Blanco, and Garfield counties (A. Spencer 1975; Finley et al. 1976; Diersing and Hoffmeister 1977). These data suggest a broad distribution over much of the lower foothills and mountains of the state. A record from Sierra Grande (southwest of Des Moines), Union County, New Mexico (S. George 1990), hints that *Sorex merriami* may occur in adjacent Las Animas County, Colorado. Further, reports of Merriam's shrew from Taos County, New Mexico (D. Hafner and Stahlecker 2002), would lead one to imagine that the animals may occur in the San Luis Valley of Colorado, and a report of the species from Rio Chama Wildlife Management Area, northeast of El Vado, Rio Arriba County, New Mexico (D. Hafner and Stahlecker 2002), suggests that the animals may occur more widely in southwestern Colorado than in Mesa Verde, whence the species has been reported (Rodeck and Anderson 1956; Hoffmeister 1967). Additionally, records from eastern Wyoming (T. Clark and Stromberg 1987) and western Nebraska (P. Freeman et al. 1993) hint that the animals may even occur on the High Plains of northeastern Colorado—on the Pawnee Buttes and adjacent uplands. Indeed, as with several other shrew species, Merriam's shrew probably is more common and widespread in Colorado than has been thought.

This shrew was named for C. Hart Merriam, who served as first chief of the US Bureau of Biological Survey (now the US Fish and Wildlife Service), was the first president of the American Society of Mammalogists and was instrumental in the establishment of The Wildlife Society. Based on examination of specimens from throughout its range, Diersing and Hoffmeister (1977) considered *Sorex merriami* to be monotypic; that is, subspecies were not recognized. However, E. Hall (1981) continued earlier usage, which recognized 2 subspecies, one of which (*S. m. leucogenys*) was ascribed a range in Colorado.

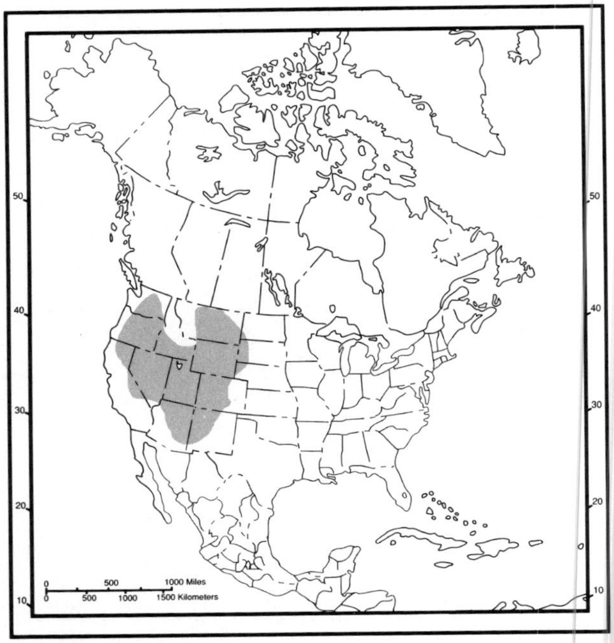

MAP 10-5. Distribution of Merriam's shrew (*Sorex merriami*) in North America.

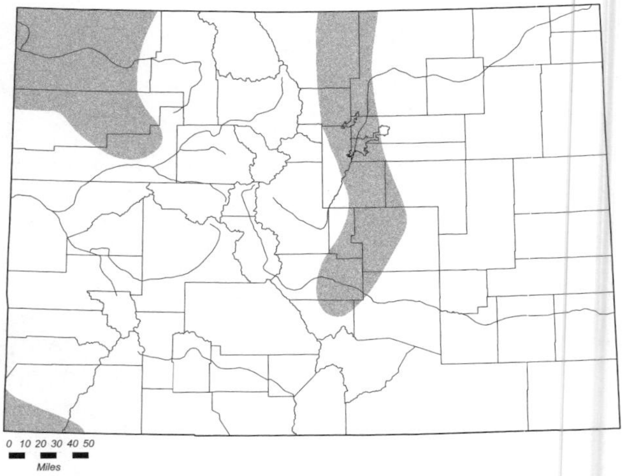

MAP 10-6. Distribution of Merriam's shrew (*Sorex merriami*) in Colorado.

Natural History

Little is known of the habits of this shrew anywhere in its range and virtually nothing is known of them in Colorado. *Sorex merriami* occupies drier habitats than other shrews in the state, particularly sagebrush or other semidesert shrublands. The species has also been captured in montane shrublands, piñon-juniper woodlands, mixed montane and subalpine forests, and grasslands. The largest numbers of captures of this species in Colorado were in montane shrublands in the Arkansas River drainage of Fremont and Custer counties (D. Armstrong et al. 1973).

Merriam's shrews frequently use burrows and runways of other mammals, especially sagebrush voles (*Lemmiscus*) and other arvicoline rodents (D. Armstrong and Jones 1971). Diet includes spiders, beetles, caterpillars, and other small invertebrates. Flank glands are prominent on the males during the breeding season and are thought to be associated with mate attraction. Breeding occurs during the spring and early summer, and females have 5 to 7 young. It is not known whether the species has 1 or 2 litters a year (M. L.

Johnson and Clanton 1954). Literature on Merriam's shrew was reviewed by D. Armstrong and Jones (1971).

Sorex monticolus

MONTANE, OR DUSKY, SHREW

Description

The montane shrew is a stout-bodied brown shrew with a relatively long tail. It is the largest of the brown-colored shrews (*Sorex monticolus*, *S. cinereus*, *S. nanus*, *S. hoyi*, and perhaps *S. preblei*) of the mountainous areas of the state, although only slightly larger than the masked shrew (*S. cinereus*). Dorsal color is medium to dark brown, becoming slightly paler on the venter. The tail is bicolored but not conspicuously so. Measurements are: total length 90–125 mm; length of tail 35–50 mm; length of hindfoot 10–14 mm; weight 4–7 g. The skull varies in total length from 15 to 17 mm. The braincase is rounded or convex in profile, and the foramen magnum extends farther into the basioccipital than into the supraoccipital. The third unicuspid is smaller than the fourth, as in the smaller, slimmer dwarf shrew (*S. nanus*). The teeth are more robust than in the latter species. In Colorado this shrew can also be confused with the masked shrew, which it strongly resembles in color and general size. However, the teeth of the masked shrew are characterized by a third unicuspid as large as the fourth. Flank glands are apparent, especially in males, from January through the breeding season. Darker winter pelage and paler summer pelage result from spring and fall molts (Clothier 1955).

Distribution

The montane shrew is found over much of western North America in coniferous forests and mountainous areas. In Colorado the species has been taken in a variety of habitats throughout the foothills, plateaus, and mountains at elevations from 1,620 to 3,500 m (5,300–11,500 ft.), eastward in Las Animas County at least to the James John State Wildlife Area, east of Raton Pass (C. A. Jones 2002). One subspecies, *Sorex monticolus obscurus*, occurs in Colorado. There has been considerable confusion regarding the taxonomy of this species. Because of great similarities between *Sorex vagrans* and *Sorex obscurus*, Findley (1955) lumped them together as *Sorex vagrans*. However, Hennings and Hoffmann (1977) showed that these shrews are specifically distinct and that *obscurus* is a subspecies of *S. monticolus*. Coloradan montane shrews, *S. monticolus obscurus*, may be referred to in earlier literature as *S. obscurus* or *S. vagrans*, under the common names "wandering" or "vagrant shrew."

PHOTOGRAPH 10-4. Montane shrew (*Sorex monticolus*). Photograph by Lloyd Ingles, California Academy of Sciences.

Natural History

Scientific knowledge of the montane shrew was reviewed by M. E. Smith and Belk (1996). The montane shrew is most frequently associated with the mesic habitats of aspen stands, willow thickets, moist openings in subalpine forests, and riparian communities. Marshy and clear-cut areas in the subalpine forest are also used, as is the case for the ecologically similar and sympatric masked shrew (A. Spencer and Pettus 1966). In South Park, this species and *S. cinereus* are commonly taken around beaver ponds and similarly flooded lowlands and boggy areas at the margin of ponderosa-bristlecone pine forest (J. P. Fitzgerald, unpublished). No strong habitat segregation was observed between *Sorex cinereus* and *S. monticolus* in a study in subalpine habitats in southeastern Grand County, although *S. monticolus* was less often associated with willows than was *S. cinereus*, and more often associated with lodgepole pine and spruce forests (D. Armstrong 1977b). The montane shrew has also been collected in relatively dry subalpine meadow and coniferous forest edge (T. Vaughan 1969), in streamside communities (O. Williams 1955a), and in alpine rockslide areas and alpine bogs (L. N. Brown 1967b). In moist forested areas the animal lives in or beneath leaf litter or under downed and rotting timber. Montane shrews are greatly affected by temporal variation in ground cover. Dense herbaceous ground cover or woody ground cover such as logs and shrubs is

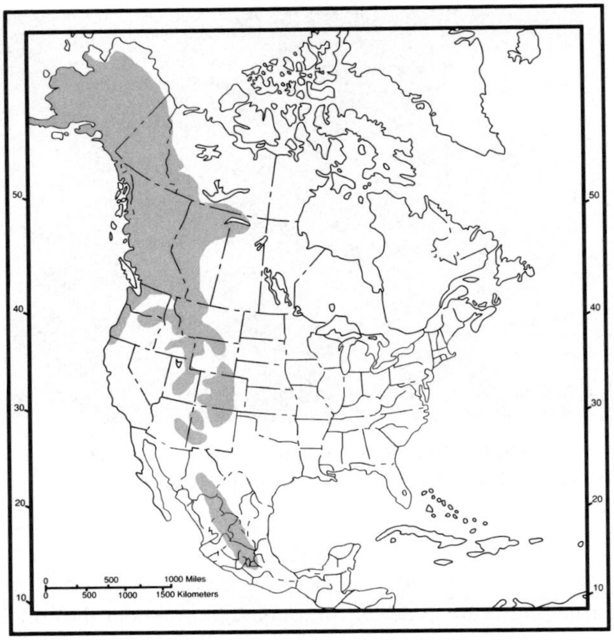

MAP 10-7. Distribution of the montane shrew (*Sorex monticolus*) in North America.

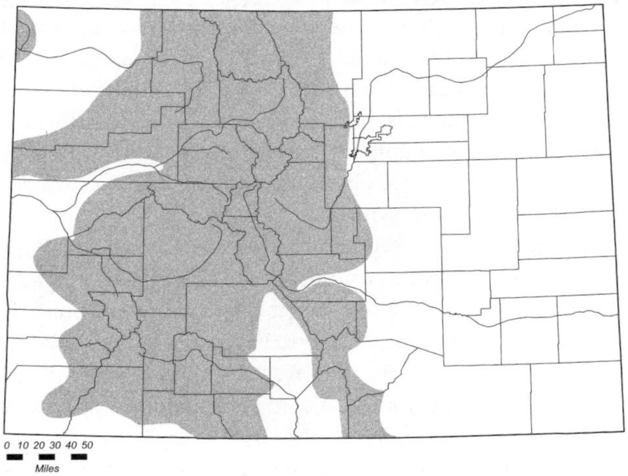

MAP 10-8. Distribution of the montane shrew (*Sorex monticolus*) in Colorado.

preferred (Belk et al. 1990). When herbaceous growth declines at the end of summer, these animals move to more mesic, adjacent aspen stands where dense cover persists. In mesic habitats along streams the species has been taken at elevations as low as 2,075 m (6,800 ft.) in the Arkansas River drainage (D. Armstrong et al. 1973).

Montane shrews are active year-round. During the winter months they forage under snow cover. Stomach contents consist mostly of insects (both adult and larvae), earthworms, other invertebrates, and some plant material (Clothier 1955). As with other shrews, alternating hour-long bouts of foraging and sleeping probably occur. Shorter rest periods interspersed with activity apparently serve to allow passage of food through the digestive tract (Saarikko and Hanski 1990). The montane shrew does not construct elaborate tunnels or burrows but utilizes runs of other small mammals. It constructs a nest of grasses and leaves. In captivity the animals are solitary and tend to avoid one another. Intruders elicit agonistic behavior and nest defense (Eisenberg 1964). The species has a high level of activity both day and night (Ingles 1960) but seems to fare well in captivity.

Montane shrews breed from April through August in the Rocky Mountains, with more than 1 litter reported in Montana. In Wyoming, pregnant females were first seen in mid-June (T. Clark 1973). Gestation lasts 20 to 22 days and the young are born blind and naked. Litter size averages about 6 young, with a range of 2 to 9. A nest in Montana consisted of a ball of dried grass about 10 cm in diameter with no definite nest cavity (Clothier 1955). Although the young develop rapidly, females apparently do not breed until the summer after their birth.

In a given area the montane shrew may be abundant one year but scarce in a subsequent year. A. Spencer and Pettus (1966) indicated that populations of montane and masked shrews varied synchronously in an area west of Fort Collins, suggesting that the species were being affected either by similar environmental conditions or by each other. In California, home ranges were 260–6,758 m^2, with the longest axis 14–59 m (Ingles 1961). The size and shape of the home range seem to vary with season and age; mature animals have larger home ranges than do immatures.

Sorex nanus

DWARF SHREW

Description

Colorado's smallest-bodied mammal, the dwarf shrew, is a delicate animal with a relatively long tail. Although total length of the pygmy shrew is shorter, its body length is greater. The color is generally medium brown dorsally merging to a grayer color ventrally. The tail is indistinctly

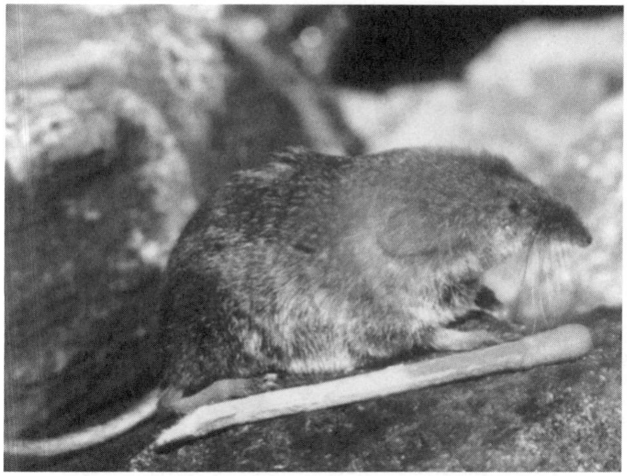

PHOTOGRAPH 10-5. Dwarf shrew (*Sorex nanus*). (Paper match for scale.) Photograph by Donald L. Pattie.

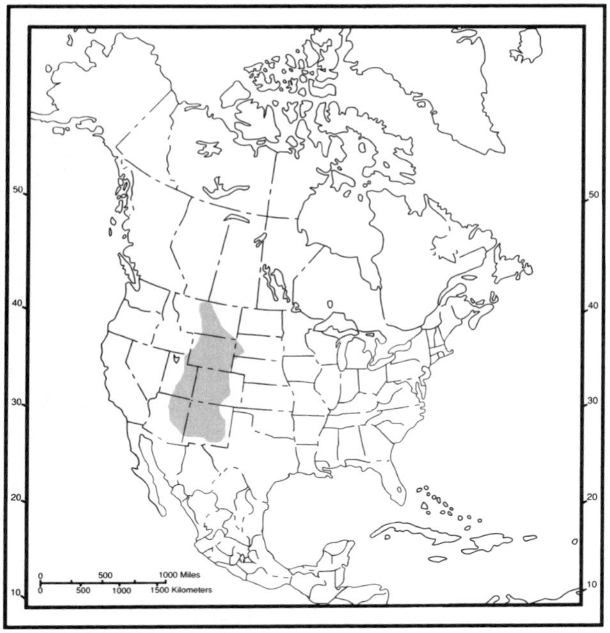

MAP 10-9. Distribution of the dwarf shrew (*Sorex nanus*) in North America.

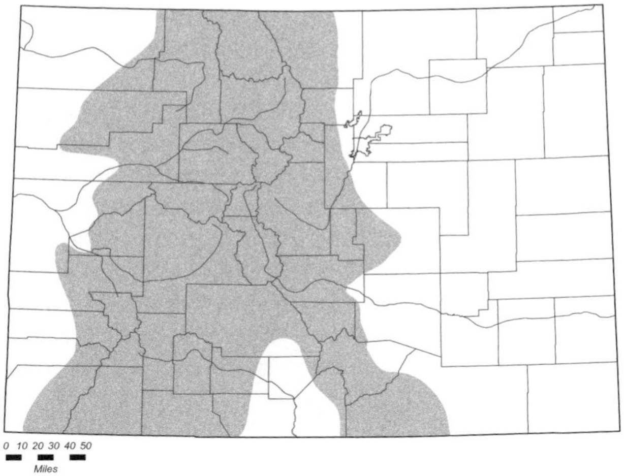

MAP 10-10. Distribution of the dwarf shrew (*Sorex nanus*) in Colorado.

bicolored. Winter pelage is paler and grayer. Measurements are: total length 82–105 mm; length of tail 27–45 mm; length of hindfoot 10–11 mm; weight 1.8–3.2 g. The skull is slim and delicate, with a braincase that appears flattened when viewed from the side. The foramen magnum extends farther into the supraoccipital than into the basioccipital. The condylobasal length is less than 15 mm. The third unicuspid is smaller than the fourth but is visible from the side. The fifth unicuspid is also small. A diagnostic dental measurement for the dwarf shrew is that the distance from the posterior border of the alveolus of the fifth unicuspid to the anterior margin of the alveolus of the incisor ranges between 1.8 and 2.4 mm (A. Spencer 1966). This measurement and the size of the third unicuspid allow distinction of the dwarf shrew from similar species.

Distribution

The dwarf shrew is known from the Southern Rocky Mountains at elevations above 1,680 m (5,500 ft.). Two collections from Colorado represent some of the greatest numbers of these animals ever captured. D. Armstrong et al. (1973) reported a total of 81 dwarf shrews collected in pitfalls at elevations of 1,600–3,050 m (5,300–10,000 ft.) in the Arkansas River drainage. A. Spencer and Pettus (1966) captured more than 2 dozen specimens in pitfalls at their study area in Larimer County. In south-central Wyoming, L. N. Brown (1967b) captured 25 of the animals in subalpine and alpine areas of the Medicine Bow Mountains. These reports indicate that in suitable locations, when searched for using suitable techniques, this tiny mammal may be found to be fairly abundant.

Hoffmeister (1967) and A. Spencer (1975) captured the dwarf shrew at Mesa Verde and Durango, respectively. A report of the species from Rio Chama Wildlife Management Area (northeast of El Vado, Rio Arriba County, New Mexico;

D. Hafner and Stahlecker 2002) would predict that the species may be more widespread in southwestern Colorado than is documented at present. Further, a specimen from Sierra Grande, southwest of Des Moines, Union County, New Mexico (S. George 1990), suggests the possible occurrence of the animals on Fisher Peak and Mesa de Maya, east of Trinidad, Colorado. The dwarf shrew is monotypic; that is, subspecies are not recognized.

Natural History

The type specimen of the dwarf shrew is from Estes Park, Colorado, but we know very little about the ecology, behavior, or reproductive cycles of this species in the state. The animal has been taken from a variety of habitats in the Southern Rocky Mountains, ranging from the edges of alpine and subalpine rockslides to spruce-fir bogs, coniferous forest, sedge marsh, open woodland, and dry, brushy hillsides at elevations to nearly 3,400 m (Muths 1999). In Colorado the species usually has not been captured at low elevations on either side of the mountains, but in South Dakota it has been found in grasslands (Cinq-Mars et al. 1979). The dwarf shrew apparently can tolerate arid to semiarid conditions as captures have been made up to a half mile from water sources. The wide diversity of habitats occupied suggests that the animal is probably more widely distributed than records indicate.

In Montana, breeding occurs in June and July in alpine and subalpine areas (R. Hoffmann and Owen 1980), and probably earlier at lower elevations. A number of pregnant, lactating females have been taken, indicating that second litters are common at least in some areas. The average number of embryos varies from 4 to 8. Juvenile males may reach breeding age their first year, but there is no evidence for such early sexual maturity in females. A. Spencer and Pettus (1966) observed captive dwarf shrews feeding on carrion of vertebrates as well as insects and spiders. Literature on the species was reviewed by R. Hoffmann and Owen (1980).

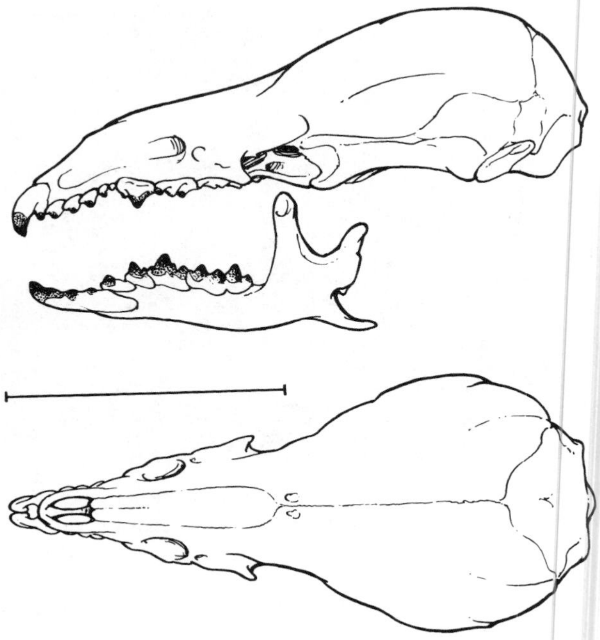

FIGURE 10-2. Dorsal and lateral views of the skull of an American water shrew (*Sorex palustris*). Scale = 1 cm.

PHOTOGRAPH 10-6. American water shrew (*Sorex palustris*). Photograph by J. Perley Fitzgerald.

Sorex palustris

AMERICAN WATER SHREW

Description

The water shrew is a beautiful, distinctive mammal, a large dark shrew with a long tail. The color is blackish gray above and silvery gray below. The tail is distinctly bicolored and about the same length as the body. There is a conspicuous fringe of stiff hairs along the toes and margin of the relatively large hindfeet. The sexes are similar in size and coloration, although mature males generally weigh more than females. There are 2 molts per year, but little difference in color or texture between them. Measurements are: total length 140–175 mm; length of tail 63–80 mm; length of

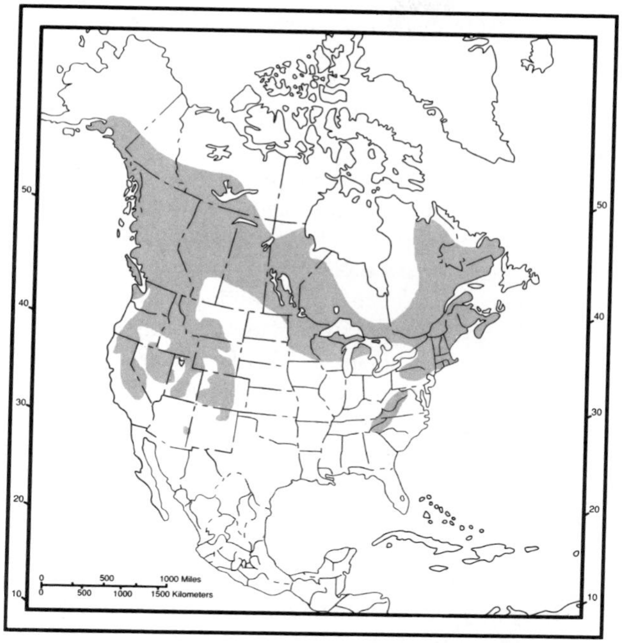

MAP 10-11. Distribution of the American water shrew (*Sorex palustris*) in North America.

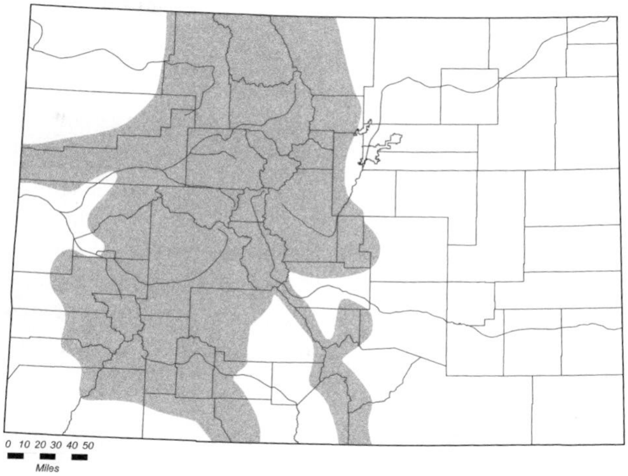

MAP 10-12. Distribution of the American water shrew (*Sorex palustris*) in Colorado.

hindfoot 18–21 mm; weight 13–19 g. This shrew is 4 times the size of the diminutive pygmy shrew. The skull (Figure 10-2) is stout and long for a shrew of the genus *Sorex*, with greatest length up to 22 mm. There are 5 unicuspid teeth in each side of the upper jaw, with the fifth much smaller than the others but still visible in a lateral view. The third unicuspid is smaller than the fourth, as in *S. nanus* (Figure 10-1) and *S. monticolus*.

Distribution

In Colorado the water shrew is found in mountainous areas in the western two-thirds of the state from 1,800 to 3,050 m (6,000–10,000 ft.) in elevation (D. Armstrong 1972). *Sorex palustris navigator* is the subspecies in the state.

Natural History

Restricted to riparian ecosystems, this is one of the better studied soricids (Beneski and Stinson 1987). Still, a study by Conaway (1952) in Montana remains the most detailed field investigation of the species to date. The American water shrew has several morphological adaptations to semi-aquatic life and it is seldom seen or captured far from water. The animals are not uncommon along the banks of rivers and streams (especially in the tangle of roots under cut-banks), beside ponds and lakes, and in marshes in forested areas. They swim well both on top of and under the water. Underwater, tiny air bubbles become trapped in their short, velvety fur, giving it a silvery appearance while keeping the animal dry. Reports by anglers of a silvery, mouse-like animal swimming under the water are undoubtedly sightings of this shrew. The stiff hairs on the hindfeet allow the animal to race across the water surface for short distances without breaking the surface.

The water shrew feeds mainly on aquatic insects, but other insects, small fish, and other animal matter may be eaten. Green plant material is also consumed (T. Clark 1973). The water shrew remains active all winter and forages along streambanks under the protective cover of ice and snow (Conaway 1952).

Water shrews have 2 periods of intense activity, 1 between sunset and 2300 hours and another shortly before sunrise. Captive animals dig short tunnels and make nests from available materials. Nests average 8 cm in diameter. Excess food is cached under logs. Individual water shrews in captive colonies are solitary and aggressive toward other individuals of the species (Sorenson 1962).

The animals reproduce from January through August in Montana and females have several litters per year (Conaway 1952). The number of young varies from about 5 to 7. Ovulation is thought to be induced by copulation. The gestation period is about 3 weeks. Males apparently are not sexually active during the year of their birth, but a few females may breed in their first year.

Sorex preblei

PREBLE'S SHREW

Description

This is a tiny shrew, generally similar to the masked shrew, but smaller. External measurements from across the species' range are: total length 77–95 mm; length of tail 28–38 mm; length of hindfoot 7–11 mm. Published weights range from 2.8 to 4.1 g; condylobasal length from 13.8 to 15.1 mm; and maxillary toothrow from 4.8 to 5.3 mm long (Cornely et al. 1992).

Distribution

Preble's shrew is poorly known, and its occurrence in Colorado is questionable. The species was first described from eastern Oregon and has been captured fairly broadly in the Great Basin and adjacent mountains (from northeastern California, eastern Oregon, and southeastern Washington across northern Nevada to northern Utah) and also on the Northern Great Plains (and adjacent mountains) of Montana. The habitat most often reported is brushlands (especially sagebrush) and bunchgrass steppe, but they also are known from marshy areas and wet habitats in coniferous forests (Cornely et al. 1992).

Sorex preblei has been recovered from Pleistocene cave deposits from southern New Mexico (Harris and Carraway 1993). Kirkland and Findley (1996) reported Preble's shrew from northern New Mexico, southwest of Los Alamos, specifically in the Jemez Mountains of Sandoval County, 3.5 km north and 16.4 km east of Jemez Springs. The habitat of capture was ponderosa pine with an understory of Gambel oak, a habitat that is generally continuous from that area into southern Colorado. Other mammals taken in pitfalls at that locality were montane and masked shrews, deer mice (*Peromyscus maniculatus*), and northern rock mice (*P. nasutus*). Kirkland et al. (1997) reported *S. preblei* from sagebrush steppe near Kemmerer, Wyoming, the least abundant in an assemblage of 5 species of shrews. In Utah, Preble's shrew is known from Timpie Springs Waterfowl Management Area, Tooele County, on the south shore of the Great Salt Lake (Tomasi and Hoffmann 1984).

Based on continuity of suitable habitat with adjacent states, Preble's shrew may occur in Colorado, but its presence is not yet settled. Long and Hoffmann (1992) reported *S. preblei* from the South Rim of the Black Canyon of the Gunnison, but that identification is open to question (M. Wunder, personal communication). A report from San Juan County (Siemers and Schorr 2007a) has yet to be confirmed by direct comparisons (C. Ramotnik, personal communication). A mandible of a Late Pleistocene shrew from Cement Creek Cave, near Crested Butte, Gunnison County, was tentatively referred to as *S. preblei* by Emslie (2002). Any tiny, long-tailed shrew from Colorado with the third unicuspid tooth obviously larger than the fourth should be submitted for identification to a museum-based specialist with access to comparative specimens.

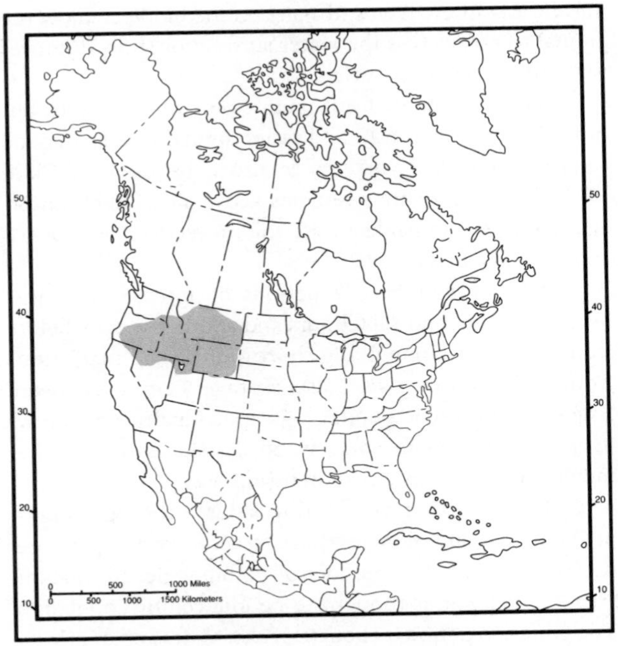

MAP 10-13. Distribution of Preble's shrew (*Sorex preblei*) in North America.

Blarina hylophaga

ELLIOT'S SHORT-TAILED SHREW

Description

This is a stout-bodied, mouse-sized shrew with a tail less than one-third the length of the body. The color varies from silvery gray through brown to almost black and lacks significant countershading. Ear openings are large but hidden by fur. The tiny eyes are apparently of little use. The vibrissae on the snout are well developed. The paired flank glands are well concealed by fur, unlike the conspicuous

PHOTOGRAPH 10-7. Elliot's short-tailed shrew (*Blarina hylophaga*). Photograph by R. B. Forbes.

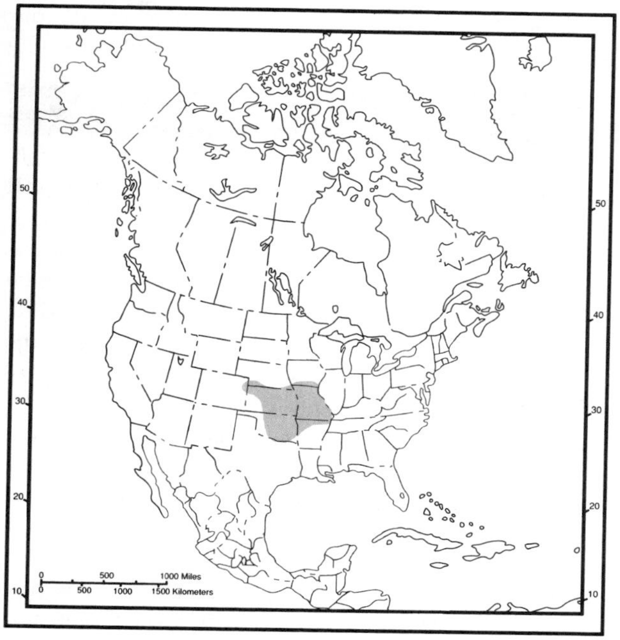

MAP 10-14. Distribution of Elliot's short-tailed shrew (*Blarina hylophaga*) in North America.

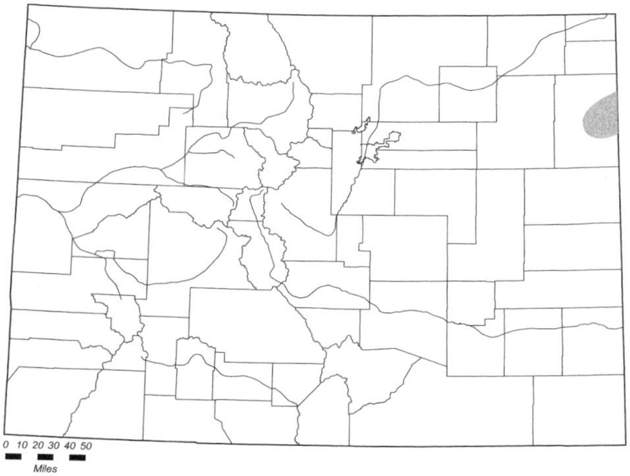

MAP 10-15. Distribution of Elliot's short-tailed shrew (*Blarina hylophaga*) in Colorado.

scent glands of the desert shrews (*Notiosorex*). In addition to flank glands, short-tailed shrews have large ventral glands on the midline of the abdomen (O. Pearson 1946). Males are heavier than females and have better developed scent glands. The animal's range in Colorado overlaps that of the least shrew, but *Blarina* is readily distinguished from *Cryptotis* by its heavy build, larger size, and lack of significant countershading. Measurements are: total length 95–135 mm; length of tail 17–30 mm; length of hindfoot 11–17 mm; weight 15–30 g. The skull is quite stout and angular for a shrew and varies from 18 to 25 mm in length. The teeth are robust with dark brown tips, but as the animal ages the brown tips may be worn away. There are 5 unicuspid teeth in each side of the upper jaw. The fifth is smaller than the others but readily visible from the side.

Distribution

Elliot's short-tailed shrew occurs on the Southern Great Plains from southern Nebraska and southern Iowa through Oklahoma and Kansas and into Missouri and northwestern Arkansas. The species is known in Colorado only from specimens taken by J. K. Jones and Loomis (1954) along the Republican River 1 mi. east of Laird in Yuma County. More recent work in apparently suitable habitat in that general area (at the Fox Ranch Preserve of The Nature Conservancy of Colorado, on the Arikaree River) has not resulted in captures of short-tailed shrews (D. M. Armstrong, unpublished). The subspecies in Colorado is *Blarina hylophaga hylophaga*.

The short-tailed shrew in Colorado formerly was called *Blarina brevicauda*. A number of morphological (Genoways and Choate 1972) and genetic (Genoways et al. 1977; S. George et al. 1981, 1982) studies have demonstrated that what was considered a single species actually is several. Now 3 species are recognized: *B. hylophaga* at midlatitudes in the Midwest; *B. brevicauda* in the Upper Midwest, the Northeast, and southern Canada; and *B. carolinensis* in the

Southeast. For comparative discussion of these species, consult accounts by S. George in D. Wilson and Ruff (1999).

Natural History

Considerable information exists on the life history of *B. brevicauda* (O. Pearson 1942, 1944; Pruitt 1953; Randolph 1973; Tomasi 1978, 1979; I. Martin 1980, 1981, 1983; S. George et al. 1986). Except for studies of diet and ectoparasites (Ritzli et al. 2005), there is a dearth of information on the relatively recently recognized *B. hylophaga*. Therefore, we draw on the literature on *B. brevicauda*, although the extent to which the details of these studies characterize Elliot's short-tailed shrew is not known.

Short-tailed shrews are most common in mesic forests (indeed, the specific epithet *hylophaga* derives from the Greek for "feeding in the woods") and moist brushy areas, being less common in fields, meadows, and marshes. In the eastern portion of its range it may be found in both coniferous and deciduous forests, but on the Great Plains it is most common in riparian situations with cottonwoods or in rank grasses and weeds along roadsides and irrigation ditches. *B. hylophaga* may be more dependent on mesic environments with mulch for burrowing than is the least shrew (*Cryptotis parva*), which tolerates more arid environments and shallower soils (J. Choate and Fleharty 1973). Scarcity of short-tailed shrews in Colorado may be linked to aridity and meager herbaceous cover in bottomlands of the South Platte and Republican river systems because of grazing by livestock.

The diet consists mostly of insects, snails, earthworms, and other small invertebrates but is known to include vertebrates (salamanders, snakes, birds, and small rodents). Ritzli et al. (2005) found that Elliot's short-tailed shrew ate more beetles and fewer earthworms and fungi than did other species of *Blarina*. Short-tailed shrews are aided in killing relatively large prey by a toxic secretion from the submaxillary glands that enters the wounds made by its initial bites (Tomasi 1978). Humans who have been bitten by short-tailed shrews have reported intense pain and swelling at the site of the bite (O. Pearson 1942). Biochemically, the venom resembles that of elapid snakes (cobras and coral snakes).

Short-tailed shrews either dig their own tunnels under surface litter or in loose soil or utilize burrows of other mammals. Runways may be as much as 50 cm below the ground's surface. The animal makes a nest from shredded grasses, leaves, other plant material, or even the fur of voles. The nest has several openings. Nests are most often under decaying logs, old hay bales, or similar surface structures or in deeper burrow systems. Studies of behavior of captive *B. brevicauda* indicate that they are solitary and highly territorial (I. Martin 1981). Territories range in size from 300 to more than 4,000 m^2, depending on habitat. Some 7–31 percent of daily activity is outside the nest. Total daily activity is highly correlated with mean ambient temperature (I. Martin 1983). The animals shake or shiver upon awakening, probably helping to raise body temperature. The animals are inactive on hottest summer days and coldest winter nights.

The breeding season is from late February to October. Adult females have 1 or 2 litters of 3 to 10 young (average, 5 to 7). The gestation period is about 22 days (W. Hamilton 1929; O. Pearson 1944). Young leave the nest by about 30 days of age, and maturity is reached in 3 months. In Nebraska, *B. brevicauda* breeds once in spring and once in fall (J. K. Jones 1964).

Although other shrews have been reported to eat their weight in food daily, the larger *Blarina*, with its relatively large size and more favorable surface/volume ratio, typically eats about half that amount. Periods of higher activity are interspersed with periods of lower metabolic output (Martinsen 1969; Randolph 1973). Known predators include owls, hawks, house cats, foxes, reptiles, and fish. Known ectoparasites include fleas, mites, and ticks (Ritzli et al. 2005).

Cryptotis parva

LEAST SHREW

Description

The least shrew is a tiny mammal with a long, pointed snout and a short tail. Color varies from brown to grayish brown, often slightly darker on the back than on the belly. The ear openings are large but hidden by fur. The limbs and feet are small. Measurements are: total length 70–100 mm; length of tail 12–22 mm; length of hindfoot 9–13 mm; weight 3–5 g. The skull is delicate but higher and broader than in *Sorex*. Greatest length of skull ranges from 14 to 16 mm. The teeth are brown-tipped. There are 4 unicuspid teeth on each side of the upper jaw, each of them slightly smaller than the one in front. The last unicuspid is minute and rarely visible from the side. Students sometimes mistake the skull of this shrew for that of *Notiosorex crawfordi*, failing to notice the last small unicuspid tooth. Externally the 2 species may also be confused unless one looks for

PHOTOGRAPH 10-8. Least shrew (*Cryptotis parva*). Photograph by Roger W. Barbour.

the conspicuous ears, heavier tail, and grayish (rather than brownish) color of the desert shrew.

Distribution

Colorado marks the western limit of the distribution of the least shrew. They occur along the South Platte and Republican drainages in northeastern Colorado and are not rare on the Colorado Piedmont from Denver to Fort Collins. The species was reported more recently from southeastern Colorado, being taken in riparian habitat along the Cimarron River in extreme southeastern Baca County (J. Choate and Reed 1988). Specimens were first reported from the Arkansas drainage by Siemers et al. (2006), from localities along Fountain Creek east of Fort Carson, south of Colorado Springs, and south of Fountain. Other individuals were captured in 1999 on the Pueblo Chemical Depot, Pueblo County. A single subspecies, *Cryptotis parva parva*, occurs in Colorado.

A glance at the overall range of this species suggests that it is basically an eastern and midwestern species. The least shrew probably is a fairly recent arrival in Colorado. It was first reported in Colorado from Yuma County (F. Miller 1924). First records from along the mountain front were in the 1950s (see Lechleitner 1964), although that area had been sampled rather intensively by students from Colorado State University and the University of Colorado beginning in the 1920s. It seems reasonable to imagine that the current distribution of the least shrew in Colorado is largely

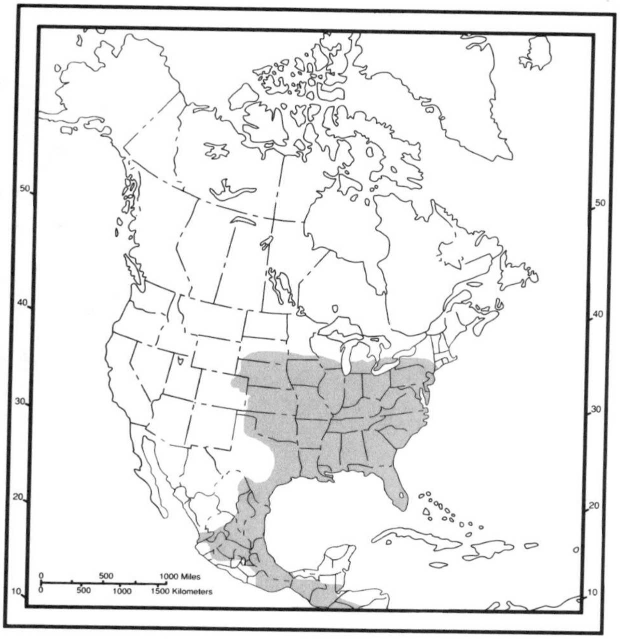

MAP 10-16. Distribution of the least shrew (*Cryptotis parva*) in North America.

anthropogenic, a consequence of perennially moist habitats provided by irrigation and the stability of riparian vegetation provided by flood control (D. Armstrong 1972). D. Hafner and Shuster (1996) discussed westward expansion of *C. parva* from Texas into New Mexico.

Natural History

The least shrew inhabits a variety of habitats but seems to occur most often in grassy, weedy, or brushy areas that sometimes are quite dry. In Colorado, the species has been taken in shortgrass prairie (Marti 1972), old field communities (Williams and McArthur 1972), marshy areas (Beidleman and Remington 1955; Lechleitner 1964; O. Williams and McArthur 1972), and riparian woodland (J. Choate and Reed 1988; J. P. Fitzgerald, unpublished). Occasionally they are taken from beehives, window wells, basements, and garages in suburban areas. The animals may construct burrows and runways in leaf litter or along the soil surface or utilize runways of other animals. When digging, least shrews root with the nose while using the front and hindfeet to remove dirt. Nests are made of loosely piled grass or leaves and are 8 to 15 cm around. Latrines are frequently located near nests. Least shrews are relatively gregarious,

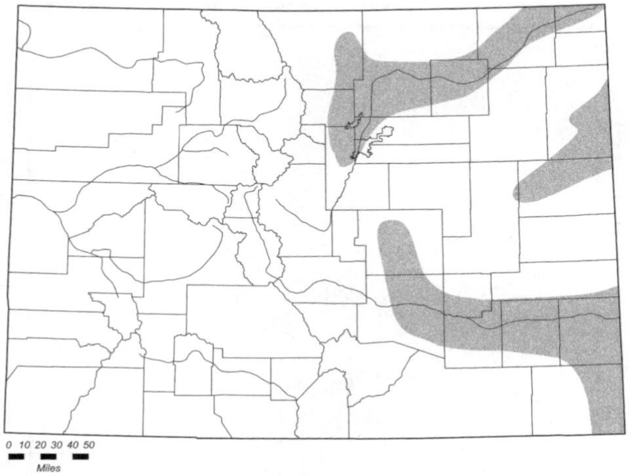

MAP 10-17. Distribution of the least shrew (*Cryptotis parva*) in Colorado.

with up to 31 individuals reported in communal nests (McCarley 1959). Such behavior serves to conserve heat. The least shrew is most active at night but may forage at any time. When fed they may sleep for considerable periods of time.

Females have an aural gland, located in front of and below the ear, which seems to inform males of their reproductive condition (Kivett and Mock 1980). Least shrews appear to be induced ovulators. Mating pairs form a "lock" or "tie" and copulation may last up to 40 minutes (Kivett and Mock 1980). J. Choate (1970) suggested that most breeding was in spring and summer. More than 1 litter may be born per year, with litter size ranging from 3 to 7. Gestation takes 21 to 23 days. Young are born blind and hairless. By day 14 the eyes open; young are close to adult size by 30 days of age. Weaning apparently occurs about 21 to 23 days postpartum.

Food habits are similar to those of other shrews and include insects, other arthropods, and earthworms. In captivity the animals have been reported to kill and eat leopard frogs. Food-hoarding behavior, especially by females, is well documented (Formanowicz et al. 1989). Owls, skunks, foxes, and snakes of several species prey on least shrews. Remains of least shrews found in long-eared and barn owl pellets documented the first record for Weld County (Marti 1972). Few detailed studies have been made on this species and its biology is poorly understood in Colorado. Whitaker (1974) summarized the general literature on the least shrew.

Notiosorex crawfordi

CRAWFORD'S DESERT SHREW

Description

This is a small, slender shrew with a tail less than one-third the total length. The pinnae are quite conspicuous in contrast to those of many other soricids. Color varies from silvery gray to a darker brownish gray, with the undersides slightly paler. Juveniles are often paler in color than adults. Measurements are: total length 77–93 mm; length of tail 24–32 mm; length of hindfoot 9–11 mm; length of ear 7–8 mm; weight 4–6 g. The skull is relatively long and narrow, with the greatest length generally exceeding 16 mm. The cranium is flattened, with the braincase only slightly elevated from the rostrum. Flank glands are conspicuous, especially in mature males. The glands are usually marked by a halolike ring of hair or thinned pelage.

PHOTOGRAPH 10-9. Crawford's desert shrew (*Notiosorex crawfordi*). Photograph by Roger W. Barbour.

Distribution

Crawford's desert shrew (mostly called simply desert shrew or gray shrew, locally) has been documented from southeastern, southwestern, and west-central Colorado. The northernmost record of the species is of an animal captured in a pitfall in juniper woodland near Rifle (Caire and Finley 1977). A single specimen has been reported from Mesa Verde National Park, Montezuma County (C. L. Douglas 1967). In southeastern Colorado, desert shrews have been collected from the following counties: Otero (Finley 1954; Gionfriddo et al. 2002), Baca and Huerfano (D. Armstrong 1972), Fremont (D. Armstrong et al. 1973), and Las Animas (Saldaña-DeLeon and Jones 1998). Elevations of capture

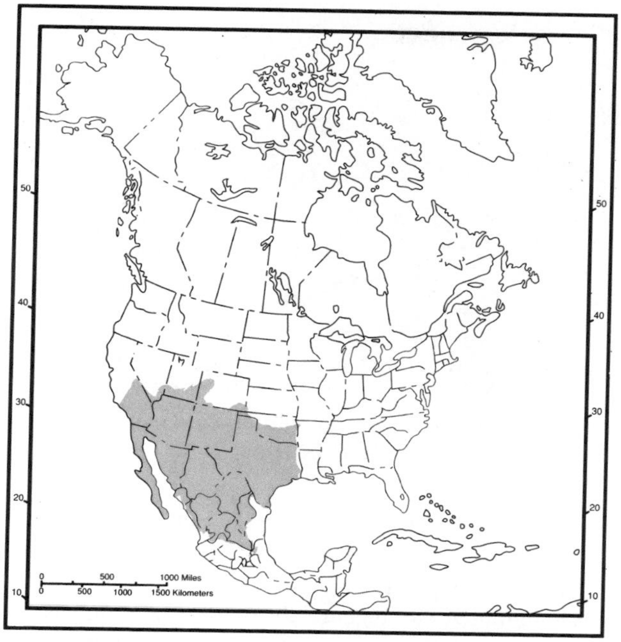

MAP 10-18. Distribution of Crawford's desert shrew (*Notiosorex crawfordi*) in North America.

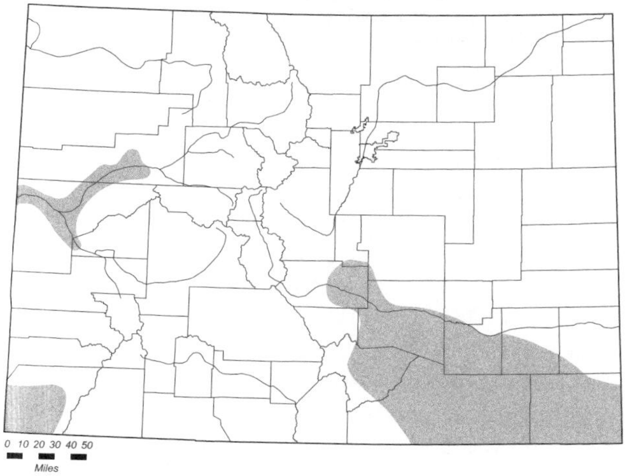

MAP 10-19. Distribution of Crawford's desert shrew (*Notiosorex crawfordi*) in Colorado.

range from 1,280 m (4,200 ft.) in Otero County to 2,075 m (6,800 ft.) in Fremont County. The species is apparently not as rare as once suspected and populations probably exist at moderate elevations on either side of the mountains northward to the Grand Valley in western Colorado and at least as far north as Monument Divide on the Eastern Slope. One subspecies, *Notiosorex crawfordi crawfordi*, occurs in Colorado.

Natural History

Crawford's desert shrew occupies various habitats often in arid and semiarid regions of the southwestern United States and Mexico. Most often they occur in semidesert shrublands, but they have also been reported from riparian woodland, grasslands, piñon-juniper woodlands, piñon-ponderosa pine stands, and dry, rocky areas.

Desert shrews construct nests of leaves, bark, or grass under surface debris such as plant litter, building materials, trash, or car bodies. Nests are variable in size, ranging from 50 to more than 150 mm in diameter. The species has been reported to occupy woodrat dens, including those of *Neotoma micropus*, *N. albigula*, and *N. leucodon* (Hoffmeister and Goodpaster 1962; Preston and Martin 1963; Brach 1969).

There are conflicting data on the degree of burrowing activity shown by these shrews. In certain situations they may use fissures and cracks in the ground for cover and passageways. D. Armstrong (1972) noted that behavioral observations reported by Pokropus and Banta (1966) for *Cryptotis parva* actually apply to the desert shrew. Movements appear erratic and nervous, and while foraging, they may utilize runways of other small animals. Desert shrews apparently are not as agonistic toward conspecifics as are some other soricids, and if food is abundant they can be maintained together in captivity without much conflict.

Reproduction occurs as early as April in Arizona (Turkowski and Brown 1969) and as late as mid-November in Oklahoma (R. Baker and Spencer 1965) and varies with locality. Gestation period and number of litters per year are unknown. Litter size ranges from 3 to 5. Young are naked and blind at birth. By 3 days they have a fine covering of hair and by 11 days are completely furred. The animals reach adult size in less than 3 months (Hoffmeister and Goodpaster 1962).

Foods eaten by captives included juvenile and adult insects of various kinds such as moths, beetles, crickets, grasshoppers, cockroaches, and carrion or fresh-killed mammals, birds, and reptiles, but not live rodents, scorpions, or earthworms (Hoffmeister and Goodpaster 1962). The animals apparently can survive without free water but will drink when water is available. Fecal material is deposited at regularly used defecation stations, often on objects elevated from their surroundings, such as dead leaves. The significance of such apparent marking behavior is not known.

No data exist on population dynamics of the species, but it is unlikely that individuals live much more than 1 year. Barn owls and great horned owls prey on desert shrews. D. Armstrong and Jones (1972) reviewed the literature on the species. Since that time, Carraway and Timm (2000) recognized populations from the northeastern Mexican state of Tamaulipas as a new species (*Notiosorex villai*) and shrews from western Mexico formerly known as *N. crawfordi evotis* were elevated to specific status as *N. evotis*. Based on molecular evidence, R. Baker, L. Bradley, et al. (2003) described *Notiosorex cockrumi* from southern Arizona and adjacent Sonora. Carraway (2007) reviewed these species and provided morphological characters by which the newly recognized species can be distinguished. McAliley et al. (2007) recognized further genetic subdivision within *Notiosorex crawfordi* in Baja California. None of those studies impact nomenclature of Coloradan desert shrews.

Family Talpidae—Moles

Moles are stocky animals strongly adapted to digging and a fossorial existence. There are about 39 species of moles in the world in 17 genera, of which 9 are monotypic (Hutterer 2005). The family is distributed widely in Eurasia and in North America from southern Canada to northern Mexico. In North America there are 5 genera and 7 species (Hartman and Yates 2003). Only the eastern mole, *Scalopus aquaticus*, is found in Colorado.

Scalopus aquaticus

EASTERN MOLE

Description

The eastern mole has a stocky body and large, muscular feet. The front feet are spade-like, the palms wider than long. The toes on all 4 limbs are webbed. The snout is pointed with a naked tip. The eyes are vestigial and are not detectable externally. Pinnae are lacking and the ear openings are tiny holes. The fur is dense, short, and soft, ranging from pale gray or silver to nearly black in color. The tail is scantily haired and short, less than one-fourth of the total length of the animal. Measurements are: total length 133–190 mm; length of tail 19–36 mm; length of hindfoot 17–24 mm; weight 65–100 g. The forelimbs and pectoral girdle

PHOTOGRAPH 10-10. Eastern mole (*Scalopus aquaticus*). Photograph by Roger W. Barbour.

are highly modified, with a greatly shortened and flattened humerus and a keeled sternum. These modifications allow for attachment points and maximal development of the forelimb muscles for digging. Males are significantly larger than females in most external and cranial measurements (F. Davis and Choate 1993).

Distribution

The eastern mole reaches its western distributional limits in Colorado and Wyoming. The species appears to be limited to well-developed, well-drained soils of floodplains and sand hills in northeastern and extreme southeastern Colorado. Although seemingly suitable habitat exists along much of the South Platte River and other drainages on the plains, the species does not appear to be expanding its range in the state. Casual observers frequently report damage to lawns by "moles" along the mountain front or from the mountains. These reports doubtless represent misidentified pocket gophers or their sign. The subspecies *Scalopus aquaticus caryi* occurs in Morgan, Logan, Sedgwick, Phillips, Yuma, and Washington counties; *S. a. intermedius* is known from a single record in Baca County (T. Vaughan 1961a).

Natural History

The eastern mole is a fossorial mammal, spending an estimated 99 percent of its life belowground. Despite being abundant over much of the eastern United States, the species has been the subject of little long-term ecological research, doubtless because their subterranean habits make them difficult to study. Moles are active all year-round. They construct both deep and shallow burrow systems. The

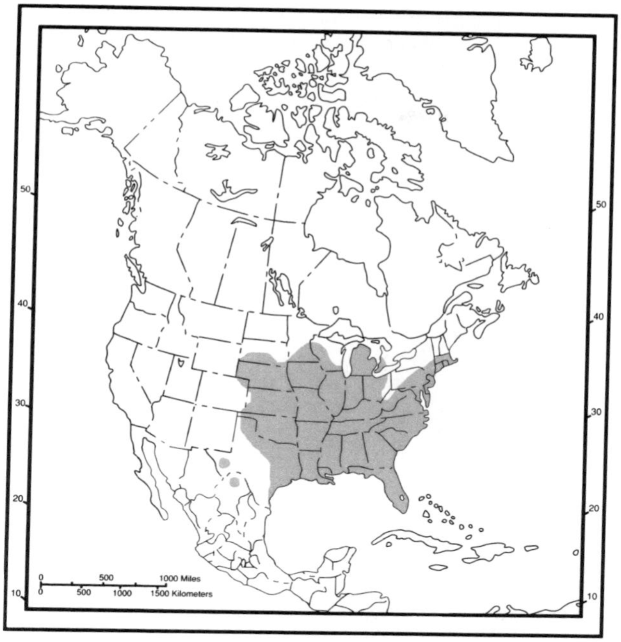

MAP 10-20. Distribution of the eastern mole (*Scalopus aquaticus*) in North America.

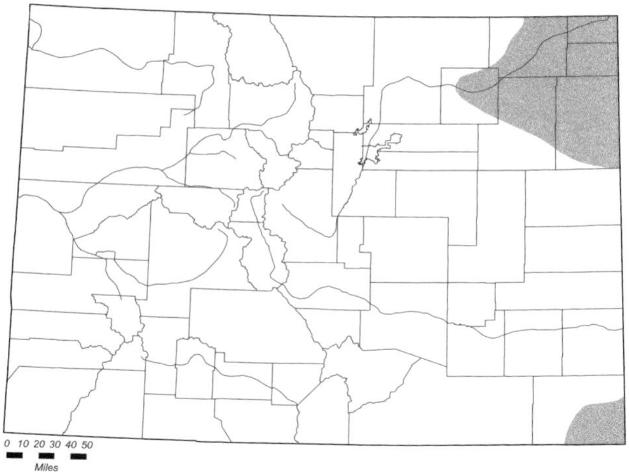

MAP 10-21. Distribution of the eastern mole (*Scalopus aquaticus*) in Colorado.

shallow tunnels consist of runs several centimeters below the ground surface, resulting in the characteristic surface ridges that can annoy lawn owners in the eastern states (J. Silver and Moore 1941). Such tunnels are used mostly for foraging. Deeper tunnels, 10–50 cm below the surface, are used for nesting and for access to shallower runs. Although new runs may be constructed at any time of the year, most activity seems to occur when soils are moist and not frozen, in the spring or following precipitation (Harvey 1976). Shallow tunnels of moles can be confused with those of pocket gophers, but moles do not typically leave the large accumulated mounds of soil so characteristic of pocket gopher activity. Moles are most numerous in loose, loamy, or sandy soils that are sufficiently moist to allow tunneling. The animals usually are not found in heavy clay, stony, or gravel soils (H. Jackson 1915).

Moles feed mostly on invertebrates, especially earthworms and insects. In captivity the animals have also eaten dead mice and small birds. Some vegetable matter is consumed. Several researchers have reported that moles consume food equal to 25 to 100 percent of their body weight daily (Arlton 1936; W. B. Davis 1942).

Moles construct nests of dried grass or leaves in the deeper runways of their tunnel system and appear to utilize only 1 nest at a time, although they may move to new nests and abandon old ones. Moles tracked with radioisotopes (Harvey 1976) did not move more than 280 m from their nests during a foraging period. About 35 to 40 percent of a mole's time is spent in the nest, sometimes for periods of more than 6 hours at a time. Activity peaks are bimodal, between 0800 and 1600 hours and between 2300 and 0400 hours. The home range of males averaged 1.9 ha, whereas that of females averaged 0.28 ha. The size of home ranges of males exceeds that reported for a number of fossorial rodents, such as the plains pocket gopher (*Geomys bursarius*) and the valley pocket gopher (*Thomomys bottae*), animals considerably larger in size than eastern moles. This difference in home range size may relate to the fact that moles feed higher in the food web; moles are secondary consumers, whereas gophers are primary consumers—herbivores (Harvey 1976).

Little is known about reproduction and development in the eastern mole. The species is reported to have only 1 litter per year with 2 to 5 young (H. Jackson 1915). The gestation period is estimated to be 28 to 45 days (Arlton 1936; Conaway 1959). Most breeding apparently occurs in March or April in northern portions of its range, including Colorado. The young are naked and blind at birth but develop a covering of grayish fur in about 10 days (H. Jackson 1915). They become independent of the female in about 1 month.

Moles may live more than 3 years in the wild (Harvey 1976; F. Davis and Choate 1993), although there are no data on population dynamics and turnover rates. Moles appear to have few natural enemies other than humans. Skunks, cats, dogs, and other predators capture them on occasion, as do snakes. In their rare appearances aboveground, they may be taken by owls. Floods may be the most important natural control on populations. Although moles may create unsightly mounds on lawns, their activities mostly are beneficial because they eat insect larvae (some of which would be detrimental to human interests) and they aerate the soil. Yates and Schmidly (1978), Yates and Pedersen (1982), and Hartman and Yates (2003) reviewed the literature on eastern moles.

11

Order Chiroptera

Bats

Bats are the only mammals capable of true flight. They have numerous anatomical and physiological specializations in support of their unique locomotion. Bats are delicately built; their long bones are slender and filled with large amounts of marrow. The forelimbs and elongated digits support a flexible, usually leathery, membrane—the patagium—which extends from the shoulders to the hind limbs. Another membrane, the uropatagium (or interfemoral membrane), connects the hind limbs and includes part or all of the tail. The humerus is short, the radius long, and the ulna rudimentary. The wrist has 6 carpals, and the hand has 5 metacarpals and 5 digits. The thumb is free from the flight membrane, very short, and usually clawed. In the Megachiroptera ("flying foxes"), one of the 2 suborders of bats, the second digit ("index finger") is also clawed and free of the flight membrane. The pectoral girdle of bats has a stout scapula and a well-developed clavicle. The sternum is usually keeled, increasing the surface area for attachment of flight muscles. In contrast to the shoulder, the pelvic girdle is relatively weak and the hind limbs do not rotate forward during development, so the knees are directed outward and backward. The femur is long and the tibia stout. The fibula may be rudimentary. There are 5 clawed digits on each hindfoot. For excellent discussions of the origin, mechanics, physiology, and anatomy of flight, and adaptations in wing shape, see Fenton et al. (1987).

For general accounts of the biology of bats, see Kunz (1982b), Fenton (1983), Graham and Reid (1994), J. Hill and Smith (1984), Nowak (1994), D. Wilson (1997), Kunz and Racey (1998), Neuweiler (2000), Kunz and Fenton (2003), Zubaid et al. (2006), Lacki et al. (2007), Kunz (2008), Kunz and Parsons (2009), and references cited in those excellent works.

Bats date back to the Eocene Epoch, 50 to 60 million years ago. The order Chiroptera apparently is derived from an arboreal insectivorous stock. The order is divided into 2 suborders, the Megachiroptera and the Microchiroptera. The Megachiroptera are the large Old World fruit bats, or "flying foxes" (the largest of which weigh more than a kilogram and have wingspans well in excess of 1 m); the Microchiroptera are generally smaller in size and sense their surroundings mostly with echolocation. Because the organization of the innervation of the eye in the Megachiroptera is similar to that in primates, some have suggested that the "megabats" are more closely related to primates than to Microchiropterans (Pettigrew 1986). If that were true, however, wings must have evolved independently in the 2 groups of bats. The bulk of morphological and molecular evidence indicates that the neurological similarity between Megachiropterans and primates is the result of convergent evolution (R. D. Martin 1986). The fossil record was reviewed and synthesized by N. B. Simmons (2005a) and K. Rose (2006).

Bats are remarkable mammals, and they lead lives very different from most other mammals (including us diurnal primates). Bats fly; we walk. Bats are nocturnal; we are basically diurnal. Bats listen for their food; we look and smell for ours. Surely these profound differences have influenced the depth of our scientific knowledge of bats and also have led to much of the speculation and superstition that we see in folklore and popular perceptions. Several references on bats' biology correct the many misconceptions (Fenton 1983; Tuttle 1988), as does R. Adams's (2003) authoritative guide to bats of the Rocky Mountain West.

In recent years research on the behavior and ecology of bats has expanded greatly, thanks in part to major developments in research techniques, including ultrasonic detection. Echolocation is a form of sonar, used by most Microchiropterans. The use of sound for orientation in bats was first studied and reported in the eighteenth century. However, it was not until the 1930s that scientists began to understand bats' echolocation in biophysical terms (Griffin 1958). Microchiropterans investigate their surroundings and navigate by emitting a series of ultrasonic pulses through the nose or mouth and then detecting the echoes that return to their ears (Fenton 1985). The brain then integrates the echoes into a 3-dimensional "picture" of the environment.

Many species of birds, frogs, and insects make distinctive calls as well, used to help members of a species recognize each other, as potential mates for example; Bohn et al. (2009) characterized some distinctive, stereotyped calls of Brazilian free-tailed bats as "songs." Calls of bats differ in function from those of other noisy animals and are usually more complex. The sonar pulses are emitted through the mouth (or the nose—as in phyllostomid fruit bats) and bounce off objects in the environment, producing echoes that are processed mentally, allowing the bats to form dynamic images of their environments (Griffin 1958). Information contained in the echoes may concern food resources (such as individual insects), the structure of vegetation, or the layout of the physical environment (e.g., potential dangers or potential roosting sites). To appreciate the sophistication of chiropteran sonar, simply watch bats over a woodland pond, coming home to roost in an attic or bat house, or flying circuits around a neighborhood streetlight. Clearly there is a lot more to a bat's calls than the robin's simple, amorous "Hello—I'm a male robin and I'd like to show you my territory."

Different species of bats emit distinctive ultrasounds, and sometimes calls of free-flying bats can be used to identify local species (Fenton and Bell 1981). R. Adams (2003) presented sonograms of Coloradan bats. As technology expands for recording bat ultrasound, "libraries" of calls recorded from hand-released bats or tethered bats flown on a "zip line" are being assembled at a number of institutions (D. Waters and Gannon 2004). A search on-line for "Bat Call Library" should provide links to current resources. Although bat sonar calls are species specific, there is much overlap in call structure among closely related species, so Barclay (1999), Sherwin, Gannon, and Haymond (2000), and Gannon et al. (2003) cautioned against extending electronic studies of echolocation without appropriate consideration of the assumptions involved. Betts (1998a) investigated individual differences among individual big brown bats and silver-haired bats and also differences between the 2 species and found that skilled human observers were less accurate in determining species than was multivariate analysis.

Not all bat calls are ultrasonic. For example, spotted bats, pallid bats, and big free-tailed bats have social calls that are audible to humans. For an accessible review of the physics and biology of echolocation, see R. Adams (2003); Gannon et al. (2003) provided important methodological caveats for studies of acoustic ecology of bats. Analyses of a fossil found recently in Wyoming suggested that flight evolved in bats prior to the evolution of echolocation, at least echolocation using the sophisticated sonar observed in bats today (N. B. Simmons et al. 2008).

"Blind as a bat" is not quite blind. Most microchiropterans have small but well-developed eyes, at least capable of distinguishing light and dark, and perhaps more detail than that. The "flying foxes" (Megachiroptera) have large eyes used in navigation and hunting. There is even increasing evidence that some bats have a degree of color vision; ultraviolet-sensitive cones have been identified in the retinas of some phyllostomid (leaf-nosed) bats (Müller et al. 2009).

The pinnae ("ear flaps") of many species are large and conspicuous and they often have a projecting central lobe, the tragus. A flap-like lobe, the antitragus, may be present on the lower edge of the outer margin of the pinnae. The degree of development of these structures is of value in identification. Many microchiropterans have distinctive, conspicuous facial protuberances, flaps, or folds that give their faces a grotesque appearance (by human standards). These structures (along with the well-developed pinnae) are thought to function as deflectors or funnels for echolocatory pulses, allowing them to locate targets at angles above the horizontal. Facial vibrissae are present in many species and sensory hairs are also located on the flight membranes and on the feet.

The dentition of most insectivorous bats is simple and fairly close to the basal placental condition but with a reduced number of incisors and premolars. The front teeth are sectorial, with bladelike cutting edges that shear against another tooth. Molars and premolars have sharp cutting edges as well, allowing rapid dissection of prey. The cerebrum is small with few convolutions. In most species males and females are of similar size (monomorphic), but males have a readily visible, pendant penis. A baculum is present except in New World leaf-nosed bats (Phyllostomidae), fishing bats (Noctilionidae), and species in a few other families (Hosken et al. 2001). The testes may be abdominal, descending into a scrotum during the breeding season. Microchiropterans show all 4 uterine types—bicornuate, bipartite, simplex, and duplex—according to J. Hill and Smith (1984). Often only the right ovary is functional. The placenta is usually discoidal and hemochorial. The 2 mammae are thoracic. Females typically give birth to 1 young per year, although a few species are known to twin or even give birth to 4–5 young per year. Survivorship of young, once they leave the nursery colony (where maternal care is indulgent), may be as low as 10 percent.

Diets of bats show a complex adaptive radiation. Ancestral bats doubtless were insectivorous, and about 70 percent of living species still feed on insects, but others are specialized to prey on fish, frogs, lizards, birds, and small mammals, including other bats. Vampire bats (of which there are 3 species in a single subfamily, the Desmodontinae, within the leaf-nosed bats, Phyllostomatidae) are specialized to feed on the blood of mammals or birds, and other bats have become specialized to feed on fruits, pollen, and nectar. This dietary divergence has allowed for tremendous evolutionary success. Almost a quarter of mammalian species are bats, with more than 1,100 species worldwide.

Despite their generally small size, many bats are surprisingly long-lived. The present longevity record for any bat is 41 years, for Brandt's myotis (*M. brandti*) in Siberia (Podlutsky et al. 2005), and individuals of many species routinely live 10 years. (By contrast, a mouse or shrew of similar body mass might be old at 10 months.) It has been speculated that the longevity of bats might have something to do with daily and seasonal torpor. Many kinds of bats spend much of their lives asleep, their physiology regulated to a minimum. Perhaps bats live a long time because "they don't live very often." Recently, Salmon et al. (2009) reported evidence from the Mexican free-tailed bat (*Tadarida brasiliensis*) and the cave myotis (*Myotis velifer*) that longevity may be enhanced at the level of the homeostasis of individual protein molecules.

Despite greatly expanded research efforts in recent decades, many species of bats still are poorly understood. Bats typically emerge from a day roost about a half hour after sunset, forage for several hours into the night, and then enter night roosts, usually open-air overhangs, where they spend several hours resting before an early morning foraging bout. Then they return to the day roost. Some species are crepuscular and a few may even fly on cloudy days. Coloradan bats tend to be especially active during the first few hours after sunset (G. Freeman 1984). This may be because of rapid cooling during the night in Colorado's semiarid climate. Cooler temperatures increase the energetic expense of flight and reduce insect activity.

Upon leaving day roosts that have been baking in the sun all day, females and their young immediately visit nearby water sources to drink. The order in which different species visit is predictable (R. Adams and Thibault 2006). Lactating females visited water sources to drink 13 times more often than did non-reproductive females (R. Adams and Hayes 2008). Females and young are also known to visit preferentially those water sources that are high in dissolved calcium, apparently to help facilitate skeletal health of the mother and skeletal growth of the young (R. Adams et al. 2003).

Some species make long-distance migrations, traveling southward to areas where insect prey is abundant year-round. Others undergo short, local migrations, usually to higher elevation, to hibernate in abandoned mines and caves. Roosting behavior differs widely among species. Some bats form colonies that number in the thousands or even millions of individuals. Others are solitary, roosting in trees, under bark, in cracks and crevices of rock faces, or in other similar sites. Some species use caves, mines, tunnels, or buildings (abandoned or occupied) for roosts. For some Coloradan species, females and their young have been located roosting under rocks on the ground or in talus slopes, as well as within crevices of boulders. L. E. Ellison (2008) reviewed bat-banding programs in the United States, especially those facilitated by the US Fish and Wildlife Service, and made recommendations for future studies. With new and safer methods for marking individual bats (such as passive integrated transponders—"PIT tags") and the possibility of digital information management, effective methods for tracking bats are emerging. No systematic banding has taken place in Colorado, although a few banded bats have been recovered (Navo et al. 2002).

Humphrey (1975) analyzed Nearctic bat assemblages, highlighting the importance of roosting sites to species richness and conservation of bats. Hoffmeister (1970) argued persuasively for better range maps for bats based on seasonal presence but noted that data to produce such maps are lacking for many species. This is still true, unfortunately, illustrating the extent to which our knowledge of bats often is more casual and circumstantial than comprehensive.

Habitat of bats in Colorado is diverse. The big brown bat and the little brown bat can be found in almost all ecosystems, including urban environments, but other species are much more particular. For example, the red bat is restricted to deciduous riparian woodlands. Most Coloradan bats are associated to one degree or another with forested habitats for roosts or foraging or both. A recent detailed synthesis of the ecology of bats in forests is available (Lacki et al. 2007), as is a review of the ecology of bats in western coniferous forests (J. Hayes 2003). In the Rocky Mountain region, the 2 biotic community types used by the most species of bats are piñon-juniper and sagebrush (R. Adams 1990). An estimated 10–15 percent of Colorado is covered in piñon-juniper woodland, but 86 percent of bat species use this habitat. This is likely a consequence of high insect activity in the woodlands, the frequent association of "P-J" with Gambel oak brushlands (which also support high insect diversity), the open structure of the woodland, rocky and broken substrate, and mild temperatures relative to ecosystems at both lower and higher elevations. Chung-MacCoubrey and Bogan (2003) reviewed bats of piñon-juniper woodlands with particular emphasis on Mesa Verde National Park, an area where most Coloradan bats occur in sympatry.

In recent decades there has been growing concern about the status of bat populations (Bogan et al. 1996; R. Adams 2003; R. Adams and Hayes 2008). A number of characteristics contribute to the vulnerability of bats. They have low reproductive rates; females of most species produce a single young per year. Most bats lead fragile little lives. Some bats are unable to tolerate the energetic stress of disturbance during hibernation, disturbance that often is human-caused. Many are demonstrably susceptible to chemical pesticides and to long-term reduction of environmental water sources resulting from regional climate change.

The loss or reduction of forest stands by clear-cutting and the federal Forest Health Initiative (with its emphasis on forest-thinning) have had significant impacts on bat populations, affecting foraging areas and roost site availability (Wigley et al. 2007). Bats may be impacted in large numbers when people explore old mines or caves and unintentionally disturb the animals to the point that they abandon their roosts. Many caves, tunnels, abandoned mines, and abandoned buildings in Colorado are visited so frequently by people that they no longer offer safe, secure habitat for bats. As a safety measure, large numbers of abandoned mines are being closed in the western United States, including some 600 per year in Colorado (Tuttle and Taylor 1994; Bogan 2001); summer roosts are lost as old buildings are demolished or modernized (and thereby bat-proofed, deliberately or not). Emphasis in management of bats often is on day, night, and nursery roost sites; Ball (2002) and Duchamp et al. (2007) suggested a broader, landscape-level approach to description of habitats and planning for conservation of bats.

L. E. Ellison et al. (2003) prepared the Colorado Bat Conservation Plan, focused on mines and mining, caves and crevices (and recreational impacts on them), forest and rangeland management practices, and urban development. All Coloradan bats are protected as non-game mammals (Table 4-1), and the Colorado Division of Wildlife (CDOW) is charged with their management. Colorado's Bats / Inactive Mines Project, pioneered by CDOW wildlife biologist Kirk Navo, is a nationally recognized model for conservation of bat habitats (Lewandowski 2007; Bonewell and Hayes 2009). Navo and Krabacher (2005) reviewed the project to that time. The effort began in 1990, and as of 2005, 330 gates had been installed on 295 mines. Bats continued to use 91 percent of mines after gating; 8 species of bats are known to use gated mines. R. King (2005) quantified microclimatic effects of closing abandoned trench-portal mines with culvert bat gates. He concluded that negative impacts were minor and surmountable by bats.

None of Colorado's bats is listed as "endangered" under the federal Endangered Species Act (ESA), but a number of species or subspecies known or likely to occur in Colorado have been identified for special conservation consideration by the Colorado Division of Wildlife, the Bureau of Land Management, the Colorado Natural Heritage Program, the US Forest Service, and the Western Bat Working Group. Among taxa of concern are Townsend's big-eared bat (*Corynorhinus townsendii pallescens*), spotted bat (*Euderma maculatum*), Allen's big-eared bat (*Idionycteris phyllotis*), western small-footed myotis (*Myotis ciliolabrum*), little brown bat (in particular, *M. lucifugus occultus*—but see the account of that species for comments on systematics), fringed myotis (*M. thysanodes*), cave myotis (*M. velifer*), long-legged myotis (*M. volans*), Yuma myotis (*M. yumanensis*), and big free-tailed bat (*Nyctinomops macrotis*) (O'Shea and Bogan 2003b). Monitoring bat populations is a key to recognizing trends that could indicate direct or indirect human impacts on species and point to needed intervention (O'Shea et al. 2003). The US Geological Survey maintains a "Bat Population Database," focused especially on species that frequent caves, abandoned mines, and buildings (L. E. Ellison et al. 2003).

Bats pose problems for management under the ESA for several reasons. First, as we have noted, bats are notoriously difficult to study. They are nocturnal, aerial, and acoustically biased (rather than diurnal, terrestrial, and visually biased as we are). Some difficulties are being overcome with some modern research methods, such as ultrasonic monitoring. Also, because most species are difficult to observe closely or to identify, involving amateur naturalists in studies of most species has been difficult. Bat biologists can only envy the National Audubon Society's Christmas Bird Count; a "Fourth of July Bat Count" has yet to catch on, although the city of Boulder Open Space and Mountain Parks Department has conducted a volunteer bat-watch program annually since 1996, with 50–60 volunteers tallying bat activity.

Until the past couple of decades bats have not had the popular appeal of such accessible groups as birds, "herps," and butterflies, although that is changing thanks to the excellent public education work of such organizations as the Colorado Bat Society (www.coloradobats.org) and Bat Conservational International (www.batcon.org). Many homeowners have been led to an interest in bats as agents of inexpensive, organic insect control. That has led to the construction of large numbers of bat houses, with mixed results. For information on bat houses, consult the websites of the Colorado Bat Society or Bat Conservation International. Tuttle (2004) provided guidance on construction and siting of bat houses in a variety of environments, and E. P. White (2004) evaluated efficacy of bat houses in Colorado, concluding that the houses were most effective when bats were already present at a site (as when a bat house was placed beside a traditional entrance to an attic or other day roost). The biology of most species of bats is rather poorly known and their public image is often negative (perhaps mostly because they are so different from us and other mammals in structure, function, and behavior). Public education and conservation efforts are to be encouraged to improve this situation. For current status of this work, consult Bat Conservation International and the Colorado Bat Society on-line. Untrained individuals should not attempt to keep bats in captivity; however, bats rather frequently are received at wildlife rehabilitation centers. Barnard (1995) provided a standard reference on care of bats by professional wildlife rehabilitators.

Surveys of public knowledge and attitudes in conjunction with the Fort Collins Bat Project (Sexton and Stewart 2007) discovered that residents were familiar with bats but not particularly knowledgeable about them. General attitudes toward bats were neutral to positive as respondents recognized the importance of bats to ecosystems and their value in insect control and they perceived the risk of negative encounters with bats to be low.

In recent years there has been redoubled interest in the ecology of bats because of the rapid development of technologies for harnessing wind energy for electrical power generation. Preliminary data suggest that both the ecological context of wind farms and the structure of the local bat fauna influence the potential for conflict (Tuttle 2005). A number of studies (especially in the eastern United States) have documented serious impacts of wind farms on bats, especially facilities in forested areas where the greatest impact tends to be on migratory tree-roosting species such as the hoary bat, eastern red bat, and silver-haired bat (Kunz et al. 2007a, 2007b; Arnett et al. 2008). Initial concern was about injury and death from collisions with blades. However, the impact of wind turbines on bats has been something of a mystery because carcasses of many bats found dead on and near wind farms show no external injuries. Recent studies in Canada (Baerwald et al. 2008) recognized that 90 percent of dead bats showed internal bleeding, traceable to "exploded lungs"—barotrauma caused by the vortex of low-pressure air at the tips of windmill blades. At their annual meeting in June 2008, members of the American Society of Mammalogists unanimously passed a resolution urging care in siting, construction, and operation of wind-power facilities to avoid harmful impacts on populations of bats (American Society of Mammalogists 2008).

The field test site of the National Wind Technology Center of the National Renewable Energy Laboratory is located just north of the Rocky Flats National Wildlife Refuge, south of Boulder in northern Jefferson County. Studies there (E. Schmidt et al. 2003) indicated little bat activity on the test site itself, although bats were frequent and diverse on adjacent public open space. As wind energy development continues in Colorado, protection of bats must be a high priority.

Recently there has been considerable concern about an emerging disease of bats, so-called white-nose syndrome (WNS), characterized by a mildew-like white growth on muzzles, ears, and/or wings. First noticed in hibernacula in New York in 2006, by the winter of 2010/2011 it had been documented from Quebec and Ontario southward to North Carolina and west to eastern Missouri. An apparently isolated report of suspected WNS from western Oklahoma in 2009/2010 suggests the possibility that the disease occurs in Colorado. Affected bats include the little brown bat, northern myotis (*M. septentrionalis*), Indiana myotis (*M. sodalis*), big brown bat, eastern small-footed myotis (*M. leibii*), and eastern pipistrelle—in short, all of the species known to hibernate in the Northeast (Veilleux 2008). Some colonies have shown mortality estimated at 95–99 percent.

The fungal growth is due to a species newly described by Gargas et al. (2009), *Geomyces destructans*, a member of a genus peculiar to cold environments, including Antarctica (Blehert et al. 2008). The occurrence and scientific understanding of WNS are dynamic. For the current status of this disease and updates on efforts to contain its spread and to eradicate it, interested readers should consult the US Fish and Wildlife Service, Fort Collins Service Center (www.fort.usgs.gov/WNS/), Bat Conservation International (www.batcon.org), or the Colorado Bat Society (http://www.coloradobats.org/).

The Fort Collins Bat Project has studied the potential for bats as vectors of other emerging diseases such as the virus that causes SARS (Dominguez et al. 2007). For updates on threats to bats worldwide—and threats to humans of bat-borne diseases—consult Bat Conservation International on-line. The website of the Colorado Bat Society also provides information on conservation of bats, focused on Colorado and the West.

Bats and rabies are often linked in public perception. As in many other mammals, bats can harbor rabies. Most bats attempt to bite if handled. Rabid bats are more likely to bite than non-rabid bats. People should be cautious of bats found on the ground, roosting in exposed areas, or captured by pets. Such bats may be unable to act normally because of rabies. Children should always be cautioned not to handle wild mammals, and bats are no exception. The word to the wise is "If you can catch a bat, don't."

This threat of bat rabies is real but should not be overemphasized. Over the past half century, confirmed human deaths from bat rabies average less than one per year in the United States and there has been no case of human rabies in Colorado since 1931 (Pape et al. 1999). The importance of rabies in bats has been difficult to evaluate. Bats accounted for 98 percent of reported animal rabies cases in Colorado from 1977 to 1996 (Pape et al. 1999). Bats appear to develop some tolerance of the rabies virus. Rabies was diagnosed in 15 percent of 4,470 bats tested by the Colorado Department of Health and Environment over that period. Three species of bats (big brown bat, hoary bat, silver-haired bat) accounted for nearly 75 percent of the bats submitted for testing, 70 percent of bats involved in bite incidents, and 84 percent of rabies-positive specimens.

When evaluating these numbers, it is essential to note that the bats tested were those that had encountered humans—bats brought home by house cats, fallen from trees, captured in houses or workplaces, and so forth. These all are odd circumstances for bats. It is almost certainly true that these individual bats are not a random sample of the species that they represent. (Indeed, it is analogous to studying the incidence of human disease by sampling only people who are hospitalized.) Genetic analyses of rabies viruses (Shankar et al. 2005) suggested that there is some exchange of viruses among species of bats and also transmission from bats to other wildlife as well as domestic animals. A long-term study of rabies in bats in and near Fort Collins is a national model for studies of enzootic disease in native mammals in an urban environment (Shankar et al. 2004). For details on rabies in bats, consult Bat Conservation International, the US Centers for Disease Control, the Colorado Bat Society, or the Colorado Division of Wildlife on-line or the US Fish and Wildlife Service's Fort Collins Bat Project.

In summary, rabies in bats is rather rare, and fear of rabies certainly is not a reasonable ground for persecution of bats (R. Adams 2003). Overall, bats are quite beneficial to the interests of humans because of their consumption of immense numbers of insects (although on occasion they invade attics and walls of older buildings where they may cause noise and odor problems).

The order Chiroptera is second only to the Rodentia in terms of extant diversity. There are about 160 genera and some 930 species in 17 families in the Microchiroptera (the suborder that includes all New World bats) and there are some 42 genera and about 186 species in the Pteropodidae, the sole family of the suborder Megachiroptera—the Old World "megabats," including the so-called flying foxes (D. Wilson and Reeder 2005). The diversity of bats is greatest in the tropics (Willig and Selcer 1989), but for a place in the North Temperate Zone, Colorado has a rich bat fauna because of the diversity of roosting and foraging habitats.

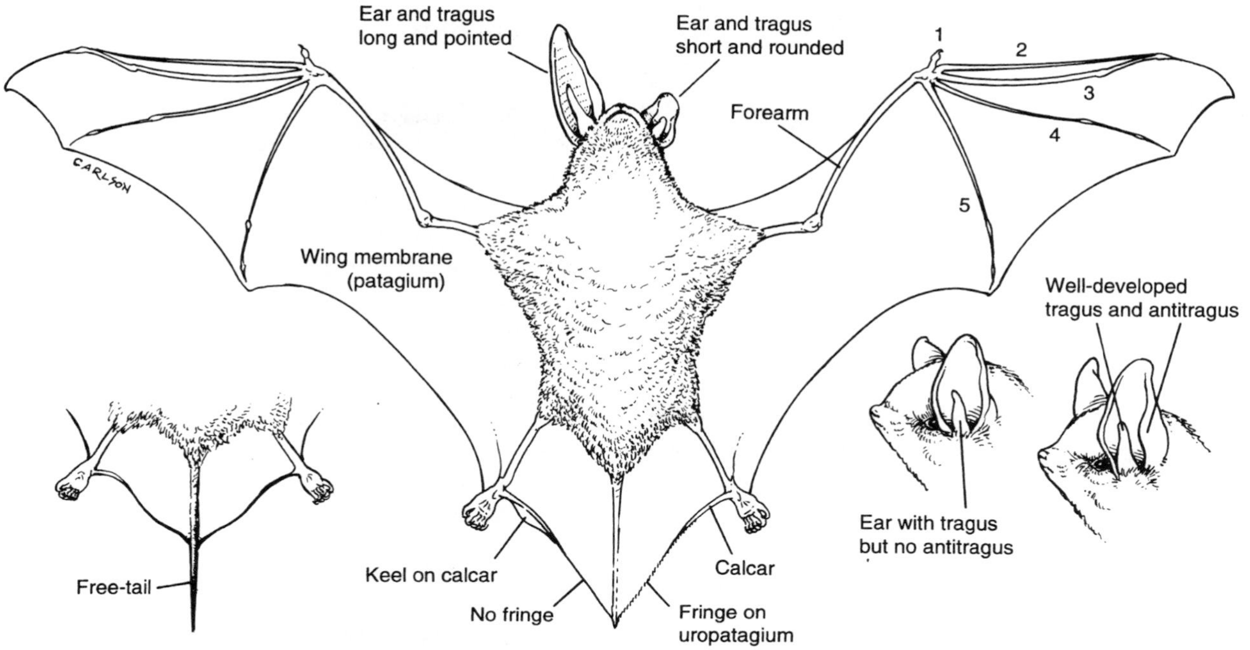

FIGURE 11-1. Composite, generalized bat showing features of diagnostic importance.

Coloradan bats represent 2 families, 10 genera, and at least 18 species. Most of these species reach distributional limits in Colorado (D. Armstrong 1972; G. Freeman 1984; D. Armstrong et al. 1994), emphasizing the fidelity of many species to particular environmental conditions. As climate warms (and as research on bats continues) we may find several more species in the state, especially those known from Arizona or New Mexico but not observed in Colorado. All Coloradan bats eat insects; roost during the day in a variety of situations, such as trees, buildings, caves, and crevices; and emerge to forage in the evening or at night. In the colder months, bats hibernate or migrate. Details of winter distribution and activity of several Coloradan species are poorly known.

Because bats are difficult to study, much of our knowledge of their lives in Colorado has been pieced together from chance encounters and short-term studies. Notable exceptions include studies of niche structure of an assemblage of bats near Elk Springs, Moffat County, by Dr. G. E. "Jerry" Freeman (see D. Armstrong et al. 1994); detailed and extensive studies of bats in Mesa Verde National Park, one of the richest habitats for bats in Colorado (O'Shea et al. 2011); and long-term studies by Dr. Rick A. Adams of bats of the foothills near Boulder (see, e.g., R. Adams and Simmons 2002; R. Adams 2003; R. Adams et al. 2003; R. Adams and Thibault 2006). Based on those intensive, long-term studies of ecology of bats in Boulder County, R. A. Adams (2010) modeled predictable declines in populations of several species with ongoing climatic warming and drying. The US Fish and Wildlife Service has studied bats at Rocky Mountain Arsenal National Wildlife Refuge, near Denver (Everette et al. 2001), including impacts on bats of remnant chemical residues on this Superfund site (O'Shea et al. 2001). Work of the Fort Collins Bat Project (2001–2005) has provided extraordinary insight into urban populations of bats; salient results are reviewed in appropriate accounts of species, especially that of the big brown bat, *Eptesicus fuscus*. Kunz and Parsons (2009) reviewed techniques for the study of bat ecology and behavior. Amman et al. (2002) provided descriptions and scanning electron micrographs of cuticular patterns of hairs of Coloradan bats, as well as a dichotomous key to bats of the state based on traits of individual dorsal hairs. Bats of Wyoming were reviewed by B. Luce (1998) and Bogan and Cryan (2000). Noel and Johnson (1993) provided an illustrated account of the diverse chiropteran fauna of Arizona, Sparks and Choate (2000) reviewed the distribution of bats of Kansas, and P. Freeman et al. (1997) did the same for bats of Nebraska. For a general review of literature on North American bats, see Gannon (2003).

Key to the Families of the Order Chiroptera in Colorado

1. Tail free from interfemoral membrane for approximately one third its length; fibula well developed, about one-half diameter of tibia . . . . Family Molossidae, p. 308
1' Tail contained within interfemoral membrane; fibula slender or rudimentary . . . . Family Vespertilionidae, p. 312

Family Molossidae—Free-tailed Bats

Molossid bats are called "free-tailed" because the tail extends about two-thirds of its length beyond the narrow uropatagium. The tragus is small and the antitragus is large. The well-developed fibula is bowed outward from the tibia. The second digit has only 1 rudimentary phalanx. The wings are narrow with thick, leathery membranes. The ears vary in size and often are joined at their bases. The animals are insectivorous, and most are highly colonial. There are 16 genera and about 100 species of molossids (also called mastiff bats, because of the foreshortened, "bulldog" shape of the muzzle), most of them in the warmer temperate and tropical areas of the world (D. Wilson and Reeder 2005). Two species in 2 different genera occur in Colorado.

Key to the Species of the Family Molossidae in Colorado

1. Greatest length of skull less than 22 mm; length of forearm less than 54 mm; ears not united at bases and relatively short, not extending much beyond nose when laid forward; second phalanx of fourth digit more than 5 mm; anterior rostral breadth much greater than interorbital breadth . . . . Brazilian Free-tailed Bat—*Tadarida brasiliensis*
1' Greatest length of skull greater than 22 mm; length of forearm greater than 54 mm; ears united at bases, relatively long, extending well beyond the nose when laid forward; second phalanx of fourth digit less than 5 mm; anterior rostral breadth only slightly greater than interorbital breadth . . . . Big Free-tailed Bat—*Nyctinomops macrotis*

Tadarida brasiliensis

BRAZILIAN FREE-TAILED BAT

Description

The Brazilian free-tailed bat is a chunky, dark-colored bat. The dorsum is grayish brown and the venter is slightly paler. The ears and flight membranes are thick, leathery, and dull black. There usually are several thickened papillae on the anterior rim of the ears. The rounded ears are not united at their bases. Prominent vertical wrinkles or grooves are present on the upper lip. The calcar is not keeled. The tail projects beyond the margin of the interfemoral membrane for more than one-third its length. Measurements are: total length 90–105 mm; length of tail 32–40 mm; length of hindfoot 10–11 mm; length of ear 11–14 mm; length of forearm 36–46 mm; wingspan 30–35 cm (R. Adams 2003); weight 8–12 g. In North America, this widespread species is sometimes called the Mexican free-tailed bat.

PHOTOGRAPH 11-1. Brazilian free-tailed bat (*Tadarida brasiliensis*). Photograph by Merlin D. Tuttle, Bat Conservation International.

Distribution

The widespread Brazilian free-tailed bat has been recorded in Colorado from Garfield, Mesa, Gunnison, Montezuma, Rio Grande, Saguache, Las Animas, and Baca counties. The late Dr. Joseph G. Hall described a maternity colony of about 200 *Tadarida brasiliensis* in a historic hotel in downtown Grand Junction, the only maternity colony

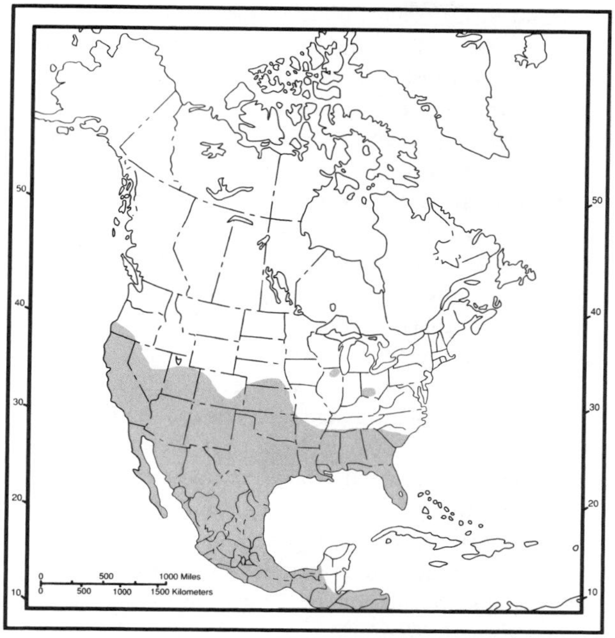

MAP 11-1. Distribution of the Brazilian free-tailed bat (*Tadarida brasiliensis*) in North America.

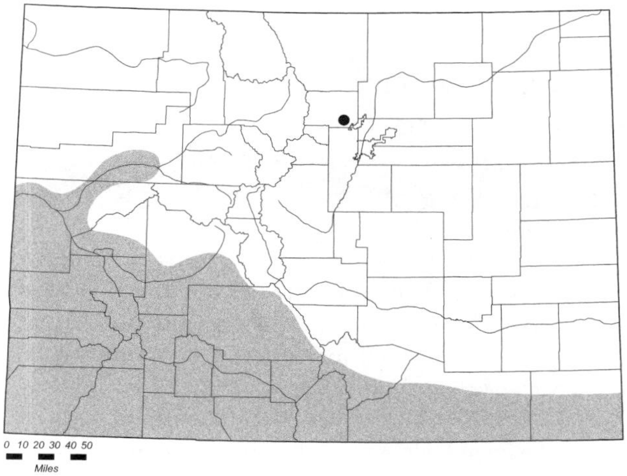

MAP 11-2. Distribution of the Brazilian free-tailed bat (*Tadarida brasiliensis*) in Colorado.

reported in the state (J. Hall 1997; R. Adams 2003). This bat is widely documented in western Colorado, but R. Adams and Thibault (1999) reported *Tadarida brasiliensis* from the foothills (6,150 ft., about 1,875 m) immediately southwest of Boulder. The lack of specimens from southeastern Colorado is surprising, as the species is not uncommon in nearby Oklahoma, Kansas, and northeastern New Mexico. Coloradan populations represent the subspecies *Tadarida brasiliensis mexicana*.

Natural History

In the southwestern United States, the Brazilian free-tailed bat occurs at lower elevations, in piñon-juniper woodlands, arid grasslands, and semidesert shrublands. The animals typically roost in caves, mines, rock fissures, or buildings. Instances of roosting under bridges have also been reported. In the southeastern United States the Brazilian free-tailed bat lives mostly in buildings.

These bats are gregarious, known to form colonies of as many as 5 to 10 million individuals. Most summer colonies in the United States are in Texas, Oklahoma, New Mexico, and Arizona (McCracken 2003). This is the bat responsible for the famous, spectacular summer exit flights from Carlsbad Caverns, New Mexico, and the Congress Avenue Bridge in Austin, Texas. One of the largest known summer concentrations of male Brazilian free-tailed bats is located at the Orient Mine above Villa Grove, Saguache County, Colorado, first reported by Meacham (1971, 1974). Numbers per year were summarized by L. E. Ellison et al. (2003) as follows: 1967, 9,000; 1978, 50,000; 1979, 75,000; 1980, 100,000; 1981, 86,000; 1982, 88,771; 1983, 107,240 (also see Svoboda and Choate 1987 and G. Freeman and Wunder 1988; the former authors reported some females and young). A population of approximately 230,000 animals was estimated in 1989 (R. Adams 2003). Populations of Brazilian free-tailed bats are limited and patchy in their distribution because of their need for large, secure, well-ventilated roosts. At roosts, the bats literally cover the walls and ceiling and make constant noise late at night and early in the morning. Communication by "songs" has been described (Bohn et al. 2009). The animals are quiescent in early afternoon and arouse shortly before sunset to forage.

Evening foraging starts shortly after sunset and the animals may feed up to 50 km from the roost. Flight speed can exceed 40 km per hour. The animals forage almost exclusively on small moths taken on the wing. They forage 6–15 m above the ground and may reach altitudes of 3,000 m (9,840 ft.) when traveling from the roost to distant foraging areas (R. B. Davis et al. 1962). Brazilian free-tailed bats do not appear to use night roosts and simply return to the day roost after feeding. Average foraging time is about 4 hours. At the Orient Mine, there are 3 separate out-flights of bats, each lasting about 20 minutes and separated by about a half hour. The bats then return individually to the roost throughout the night, and a few stragglers arrive only at sunrise.

The sexes are together during the winter but typically segregate in the warmer months when females are rearing young. Breeding occurs from February to April with no delayed fertilization. Gestation takes 77–100 days and usually a single young is born, in June or early July, although up to 3 young have been reported. Pups may reach densities of 5,000 individuals per square meter on the wall of the nursery (Loughry and McCracken 1991). Yearling females can produce young, unlike many vespertilionid bats, which do not mate first until they are yearlings. The young are born feet-first, in the breech position, as is common in bats. While giving birth the female remains suspended head-down. Young are left in large nursery groups while the females leave to forage. Although hundreds or thousands of young are present in some roosts, females identify and nurse their own offspring, mostly by smell (McCracken 1984; Gustin and McCracken 1987). The source and character of individual odor are not yet known. Females also can discriminate, and show preference for, the calls of their own pups (Balcombe 1990). Young can fly at about 5 weeks of age. The population in Colorado's Orient Mine is mostly males, but a few females and young have been captured in July, August, and September, suggesting that the animals do reproduce in Colorado.

Seasonal migrations typically occur from summer to winter range, with only a few reports of animals overwintering in the West. Populations in the Southeast appear to be more sedentary. Migrations of nearly 1,900 km are common in the bats from Oklahoma and New Mexico that winter in Mexico (Wilkins 1989; R. Adams 2003). Such migrations take about 2 months to complete. In Colorado, bats begin to appear at the Orient Mine in mid-June and reach highest numbers from July to early September. By late September, numbers are reduced to a few hundred individuals (G. Freeman and Wunder 1988). Where Colorado's Brazilian free-tailed bats hibernate is not known.

Longevity is about 7 to 8 years in the wild, with some individuals living up to 15 years. This is one of several species of bats seriously impacted by widespread use of insecticides in this country and in Mexico. For example, the population at Carlsbad Caverns, New Mexico, dropped from an estimated 8 to 9 million in the 1930s to about 200,000 individuals in 1973 (http://www.nps.gov/archive/cave/bat-count.htm).

Negative impacts of artificial chemical insecticides on bats are something of a cruel irony, as bats are themselves remarkable biological insecticides. The value to agricultural interests of colonial bats like *T. brasiliensis* can be immense. Cleveland et al. (2006) modeled pest control by bats in southern Texas, where an estimated 100 million Brazilian free-tailed bats roost in caves and beneath bridges. Foraging bats consume some two-thirds of their body weight in insects each night, especially beetles, true bugs, and moths (Whitaker, Neefus, and Kunz 1996). The diet includes vast numbers of the moths whose larvae are corn earworms (also known as cotton bollworms) (McCracken 1996). The value of this natural pest control has been estimated at \$0.7–\$1.7 million annually. The population in Colorado's Orient Mine apparently has low levels of pesticide contamination (G. Freeman and Wunder 1988).

Brazilian free-tailed bats are preyed on by a variety of raptors and by cave-dwelling mammals and reptiles, including raccoons, skunks, opossums, and several species of snakes (Sparks et al. 2000). Rabies occurs in Brazilian free-tailed bats, although not in concentrations any higher than in less colonial species. Histoplasmosis is commonly associated with cavernicolous populations in the Southwest. Experimental inoculation of *T. brasiliensis* and also big brown bats with West Nile Virus (A. Davis et al. 2005) suggested that these bats were unlikely vectors of the pathogen. Wilkins (1989) reviewed the literature on the species.

Nyctinomops macrotis

BIG FREE-TAILED BAT

Description

The big free-tailed bat is the largest bat in Colorado. The dorsal surface is pale reddish to dark brown and the ventral surface is slightly paler. Hairs are bicolored with the bases nearly white. The tail extends about one-fourth its length beyond the interfemoral membrane. The tail membrane has a well-developed pocket at the angle of the tibia and the femur. The ears are united at their bases and when laid forward extend well beyond the nose. Measurements are: total length 125–140 mm; length of tail 48–54 mm; length of hindfoot 14–16 mm; length of ear 9–11 mm; length of forearm 58–64 mm; weight 12–18 g. The wingspan is 42–46 cm, compared with 34–41 cm for the hoary bat (R. Adams 2003), Colorado's largest vespertilionid bat.

Distribution

Scattered records for the big free-tailed bat, a species of the Southwest and Mexico, exist from only 8 counties in Colorado: Rio Grande, Mesa, Otero, El Paso, Gunnison, Las

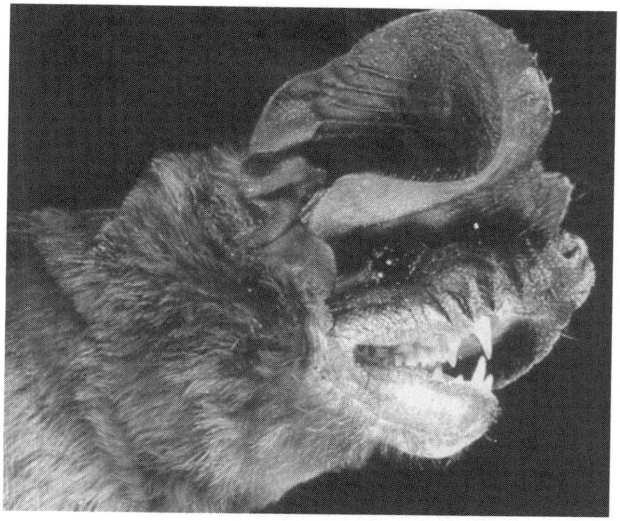

PHOTOGRAPH 11-2. Big free-tailed bat (*Nyctinomops macrotis*). Photograph by J. Scott Altenbach.

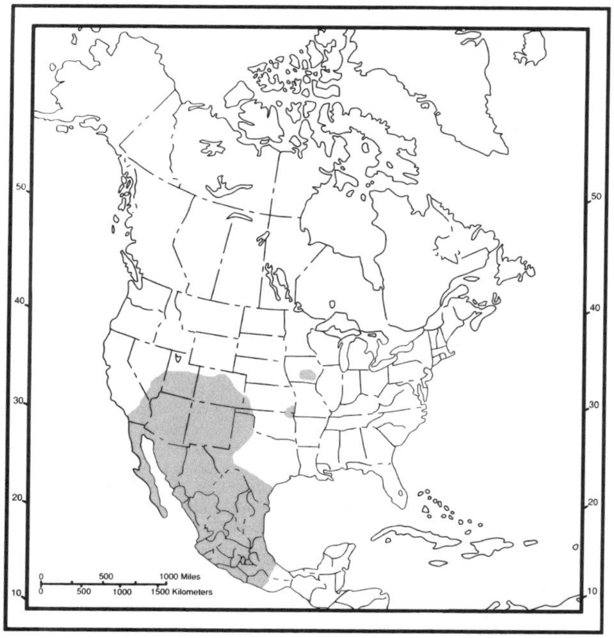

MAP 11-3. Distribution of the big free-tailed bat (*Nyctinomops macrotis*) in North America.

Animas, Lincoln, and Weld, with the northernmost record being from Greeley (J. Fitzgerald et al. 1989; D. Armstrong et al. 1994; Shankar et al. 2005). Big free-tailed bats should

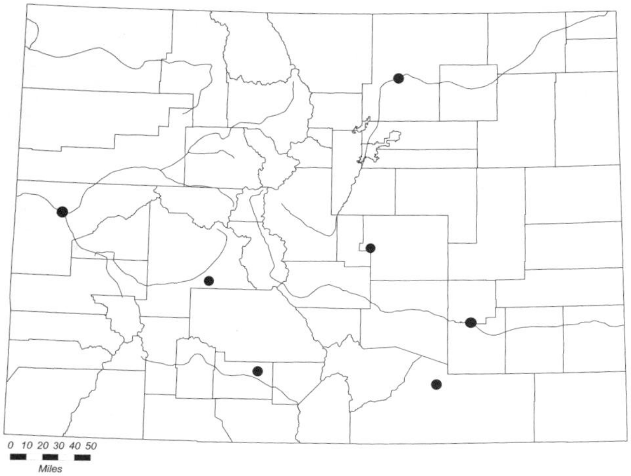

MAP 11-4. Distribution of the big free-tailed bat (*Nyctinomops macrotis*) in Colorado.

be expected in southeastern Colorado, as they are documented from Morton County, Kansas, in the southwestern corner of that state (Sparks and Choate 2000), and from Cimarron County, Oklahoma, in the Panhandle, adjacent to Baca County, Colorado (Dalquest et al. 1990; J. K. Jones and Manning 1990). Individual wanderers may be expected over most of the state, but probably no breeding population exists in Colorado. *Nyctinomops macrotis* is monotypic; that is, geographic variation is minimal and subspecies have not been recognized.

Natural History

The big free-tailed bat occupies habitat similar to the Brazilian free-tailed bat but does not reach the densities of the latter species. The animals roost in crevices on cliff faces or in buildings, but little is known of their natural history. Big free-tailed bats generally leave the roost after dark and forage mostly on large moths. When foraging, both *N. macrotis* and *T. brasiliensis* make loud, piercing calls that can be discriminated by observers familiar with both species.

Females congregate into small nursery colonies during the summer months and give birth to single young in late June or July (Hasenyager 1980). Lactating females have been reported in August and mid-September in New Mexico (Findley et al. 1975). No breeding records exist for Colorado. The literature was reviewed by Milner et al. (1990), and Hasenyager (1980) presented information on the animals in Utah that may be particularly useful to Coloradan workers.

Family Vespertilionidae—Vesper Bats

This is a family of small to medium-sized bats. The muzzle and lips are simple. The ears are usually separate from each other at their bases and exhibit well-developed tragi. Both the ulna and fibula are vestigial (T. Vaughan 1959). The second digit consists of a metacarpal and a single small phalanx. The interfemoral membrane is well developed and includes the tail. This is the largest family of bats, and nearly all species are insect feeders. In most species, females are slightly larger than males (D. Williams and Findley 1979). Ranges of many species extend well into the North Temperate Zone. The family includes 48 genera and 407 species (D. Wilson and Reeder 2005), of which 8 genera and 16 species are known in Colorado, and others may be expected.

Findley (1993) reviewed community-level studies of bats worldwide, with an emphasis on the southwestern United States. Chung-MacCoubrey and Bogan (2003) summarized work on bats in the old-growth piñon-juniper woodlands of the Mesa Verde country. The vespertilionid bats of the western United States constitute a guild of nocturnal, aerial insectivores (C. Jones 1965; M. O'Farrell et al. 1967; M. O'Farrell and Bradley 1970; C. Jones and Suttkus 1972; Black 1974; Ellinwood 1978; Ruffner et al. 1979; G. Freeman 1984). Within that guild, certain aspects of morphology are predictive of habitat utilization and different foraging modes such as gleaning, aerial capture with the interfemoral membrane, filter feeding, and terrestrial foraging. Interestingly, there seems to be little or no competition in present-day communities, because food resources do not appear to be limiting (D. Armstrong et al. 1994).

Key to the Species of the Family Vespertilionidae Known or Expected to Occur in Colorado

1. Ears long, greater than 26 mm; teeth fewer than 38 2

1' Ears shorter, generally less than 25 mm; if ears approach 25 mm then dentition totals 38 teeth 5

2. Dorsal color black with 3 large white spots; total teeth 34, cheekteeth 5/5 . . . . Spotted Bat—*Euderma maculatum*, p. 339

2' Dorsal color pale yellowish to brownish, or if black then lacking white spots; total teeth 36 or 28; cheekteeth 5/6 or 4/6 3

3. Ears usually less than half length of forearm, not joined at bases; color pale yellowish, almost white in some individuals; total teeth 28, cheekteeth 4/6 . . . . Pallid Bat—*Antrozous pallidus*, p. 343

3' Ears longer, usually more than half length of forearm, joined at bases; color usually brown; total teeth 36, cheekteeth 5/6 4

4. Accessory basal lobe of ears forming 2 prominent leaf-like lappets projecting over forehead; calcar keeled; breadth of braincase more than half greatest length of skull . . . . Allen's Big-eared Bat—*Idionycteris phyllotis*,* p. 342

4' Leaf-like structures not obvious over forehead; calcar not keeled; breadth of braincase less than half greatest length of skull . . . . Townsend's Big-eared Bat—*Corynorhinus townsendii*, p. 340

5. Incisors 1/3 6

5' Incisors 2/3 or 1/2 8

6. Upper surface of uropatagium naked or nearly so . . . . Evening Bat—*Nycticeius humeralis*,* p. 338

6' Upper surface of uropatagium densely furred . . . . *Lasiurus*, 7

7. Dorsal color brown with many hairs white-tipped, giving a frosted appearance; ears with black rim; greatest length of skull more than 16 mm . . . . Hoary Bat—*Lasiurus cinereus*, p. 328

7' Dorsal color brick red to yellowish red with only a few white-tipped hairs; ears without black rim; greatest length of skull less than 15 mm . . . . Eastern Red Bat—*Lasiurus borealis*, p. 327

8. Dorsal color blackish, some hairs white-tipped; ears relatively short and rounded; interfemoral membrane densely furred on proximal half of dorsal surface . . . . Silver-haired Bat—*Lasionycteris noctivagans*, p. 330

8' Dorsal color not blackish; hairs not white-tipped 9

9. Total teeth 34 or 32; cheekteeth not 6/6 10

* Species of possible occurrence in Colorado.

9' Total teeth 38; cheekteeth 6/6 . . . . *Myotis,* 12

10. Total teeth 32; size large, forearm longer than 40 mm; color not yellowish gray, generally brown . . . . Big Brown Bat—*Eptesicus fuscus*, p. 335

10' Total teeth 34; size small; forearm shorter than 36 mm 11

11. Dorsal hairs distinctly tricolored, dark at tips and base and paler in middle . . . . Eastern Pipistrelle, or Tricolored Bat—*Perimyotis subflavus*, p. 353

11' Dorsal hairs not distinctly tricolored . . . . Western Pipistrelle, or Canyon Bat—*Parastrellus hesperus*, p. 332

12. Calcar with well-developed keel 13

12' Calcar without noticeable keel 15

13. Underside of wing furred to level of elbow or beyond; foot usually longer than 8.5 mm; forearm usually longer than 35 mm; rostrum noticeably short . . . . Long-legged Myotis—*Myotis volans*, p. 323

13' Underside of wing not furred to level of elbow; foot shorter than 8.5 mm; forearm usually shorter than 35 mm; rostrum not noticeably short 14

14. Braincase rising abruptly from rostrum, skull with steep profile when viewed from side; third metacarpal as long or longer than forearm; hair on back dull, lacking burnished tips . . . . California Myotis—*Myotis californicus*, p. 314

14' Braincase sloping gently from rostrum, skull with flattened appearance when viewed from side; third metacarpal not as long as forearm; hair on back shiny, with burnished tips . . . . Western Small-footed Myotis—*Myotis ciliolabrum*, p. 315

15. Conspicuous fringe of stiff, short hairs along trailing edge of uropatagium . . . . Fringed Myotis—*Myotis thysanodes*, p. 321

15' No conspicuous fringe of stiff, short hairs along trailing edge of uropatagium 16

16. Ears longer, usually 21–24 mm, extending well beyond nose when laid forward . . . . Long-eared Myotis—*Myotis evotis*, p. 317

16' Ears shorter, usually less than 16 mm, not extending beyond nose when laid forward 17

17. Hairs short, somewhat coarse; condylobasal length greater than 16 mm; sagittal crest well developed in adult; forearm usually greater than 44 mm . . . . Cave Myotis—*Myotis velifer*,* p. 323

17' Hair not especially short and coarse; condylobasal length less than 16 mm; sagittal crest not well developed; forearm usually less than 44 mm 18

18. Dorsal hairs glossy, with burnished tips; greatest length of skull usually greater than 14.2 mm; mastoid breadth 7.5 mm or more . . . . Little Brown Myotis—*Myotis lucifugus*,* p. 318

18' Dorsal hairs not glossy, without burnished tips; greatest length of skull less than 14.2 mm; mastoid breadth 7.4 mm or less . . . . Yuma Myotis—*Myotis yumanensis*, p. 325

Genus *Myotis*

The genus *Myotis* (the "mouse-eared bats") includes more than 100 species, distributed in temperate and tropical regions worldwide (N. B. Simmons 2005b). In Colorado at least 7 species occur, and here as elsewhere, several species of *Myotis* may be sympatric at a particular locality. The species are sometimes difficult to distinguish, even in hand. R. Adams (2003) provided keys to species, photographs, and also sonograms of echolocatory calls. D. Armstrong et al. (1995) also provided color photographs of the species; parts of that publication are available on-line from the Colorado Division of Wildlife. Studies of assemblages of species of *Myotis* are of interest, because the species often subdivide resource space in subtle ways. G. Freeman (1984, reviewed by D. Armstrong et al. 1994) described the ecology of 11 species of sympatric bats at Elk Springs, Moffat County, of which 6 were species of *Myotis.* He found that the assemblage of bats was structured by food habits, with different species of bats selecting prey that differed in size and hardness. Foraging habits differed as well, with some species foraging in the open and others gleaning insects directly from leaves.

G. Miller and Allen (1928) reviewed the systematics of North American *Myotis*. No comprehensive modern revision of the genus has been done, although there have been some molecular phylogenetic studies of phylogenetic

* Including *Myotis occultus* of some authors.

or geographic subsets of species. Ruedi and Mayer (2001) published a molecular systematic analysis of 30 species of *Myotis* and concluded that subgenera described on the basis of morphological characters likely are not monophyletic groups. Rather American species may form a distinctive clade, members of which have converged with Old World species in response to environmental opportunities.

Myotis californicus

CALIFORNIA MYOTIS

Description

The California myotis is a small, usually yellowish brown bat (although individuals range in color from pale tan to deep brown). The pelage is typically dull and the hairs lack burnished tips. The calcar is distinctly keeled. Hair on the ventral side of the patagium does not extend to the level of the elbow. Measurements are: total length 70–84 mm; length of tail 30–40 mm; length of hindfoot 5.5–8.2 mm; length of ear 11–15 mm; length of forearm 29–36 mm; wingspan 22–26 cm (R. Adams 2003); weight 3–5 g. This species needs careful comparison with *Myotis ciliolabrum*. Even in hand, these 2 species can be confused. The greatest length of the small, fragile skull is less than 13.5 mm in most specimens (Findley et al. 1975). The braincase has an abruptly rising profile whose height is equal to or greater than 32 percent of the greatest length of the skull in three-fourths of specimens examined (Findley et al. 1975). Height of the skull in *M. ciliolabrum* is typically less than 32 percent of the greatest length. Rostral breadth does not exceed 5.0 mm in *M. californicus*, and in *M. ciliolabrum* it exceeds 5.2 mm (Bogan 1974). The ears of the California myotis are relatively long, extending beyond the nose when laid forward. Differences between *M. ciliolabrum* and *M. californicus* in size and shape of pinnae correlate with differences in echolocatory calls, with lower-frequency calls associated with larger pinnae (Gannon et al. 2003). It may be possible to distinguish living or fluid-preserved specimens of *M. californicus* and *M. ciliolabrum* by the fact that the tail of the latter projects 1.5 to 2.5 mm beyond the uropatagium, whereas that of *M. californicus* does not (Constantine 1998). This character generally is not discernible in standard dry museum specimens and it has not been confirmed in Coloradan animals. Analysis of mitochondrial DNA of these 2 species (Rodriguez and Ammerman 2004) did not reflect the usual morphological distinctions, suggesting that the 2 kinds have either diverged quite recently or that they represent one phenotypically variable species.

PHOTOGRAPH 11-3. California myotis (*Myotis californicus*). Photograph by Claude Steelman / Wildshots.

Distribution

The California myotis occurs in dry canyon and mesa country of the western United States. It is most common in semidesert shrublands and piñon-juniper woodlands up to

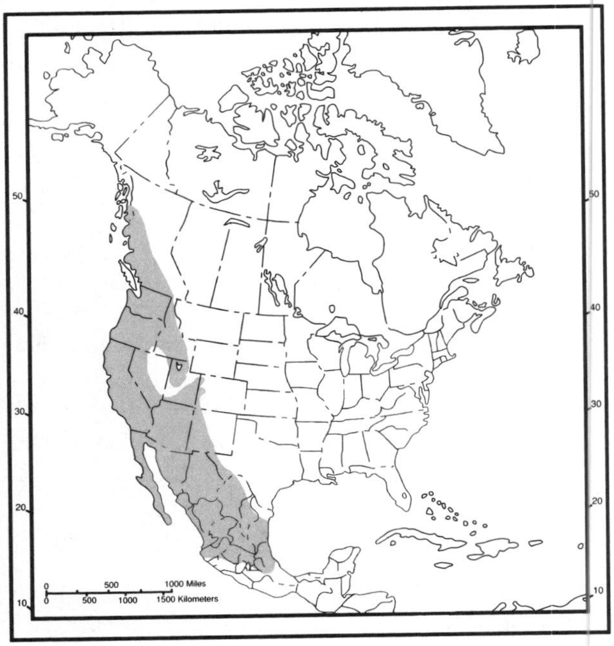

MAP 11-5. Distribution of the California myotis (*Myotis californicus*) in North America.

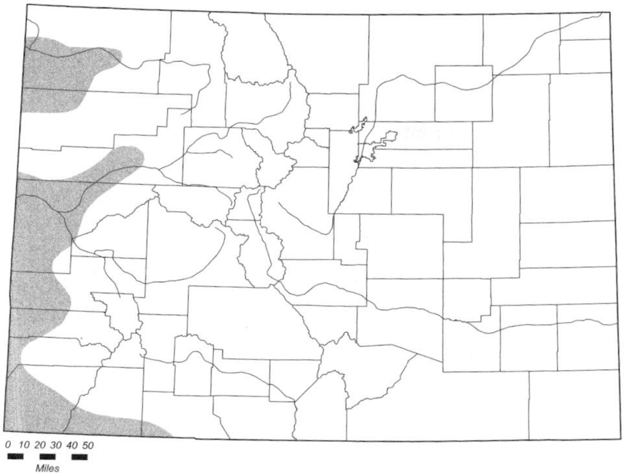

MAP 11-6. **Distribution of the California myotis (*Myotis californicus*) in Colorado.**

elevations of about 2,290 m (7,500 ft.). The species has been captured all along Colorado's western boundary except in San Miguel and Dolores counties, where it will likely be found eventually. One subspecies, *Myotis californicus stephensi*, occurs in Colorado.

Natural History

The biology of the California myotis is poorly known, and it does not appear to be abundant in Colorado. During a 3-year study in Moffat County, G. Freeman (1984) captured only 44 individuals. The California myotis uses abandoned structures, mines, caves, and cracks and crevices in cliff faces for night roosts. Day roosts are similar and include hollow trees and the space beneath loose tree bark. They occur in piñon-juniper woodlands and semidesert shrublands at lower elevations in the canyons and valleys of western Colorado, a habitat similar to that of the western pipistrelle (R. Finley et al. 1976).

The California myotis starts to forage early in the evening, shortly after western pipistrelles emerge. They usually fly 2–3 m above the ground in search of prey, largely moths, small beetles, and lacewings (G. Freeman 1984). Foraging occurs over stock tanks, riparian canyons, arroyos, open areas, and along cliff faces (G. Freeman 1984). The animals may be somewhat transient, not spending much time in any particular roost, although frequenting the same general roosting area. Breeding occurs in the fall. In Colorado, young are probably born in May and June, although pregnant females have been captured in June and July and lactating females in August (R. Adams 1988; Chung-MacCoubrey and Bogan 2003), suggesting that at least some females give birth later. Although the gestation period is not known, it likely is 50–60 days. Females give birth to a single young annually.

The winter range of Coloradan California myotis is not known, and information on migration is unavailable. The animals may emigrate from Colorado to winter, although hibernation records in mines, caves, and stone buildings are common in many of the western states. M. Simpson (1993) reviewed the literature on the California myotis.

Myotis ciliolabrum

WESTERN SMALL-FOOTED MYOTIS

Description

This is 1 of the 3 species of Colorado *Myotis* with a keeled calcar (the other 2 being *M. californicus* and *M. volans*). *M. ciliolabrum* is smaller than *M. volans* and slightly larger than *M. californicus*. Coloration of *M. ciliolabrum* varies geographically in Colorado. Specimens from eastern Colorado (*M. c. ciliolabrum*) are paler than the rich reddish brown of the western subspecies (*M. c. melanorhinus*), although the latter shows clinal variation in color and is paler in northwestern Colorado than in the Four Corners region (D. Armstrong 1972). The pelage often has a pronounced sheen because of the burnished tips of the hairs. A dark facial mask is present on some individuals. Measurements are: total length 75–88 mm; length of tail 33–42 mm; length of hindfoot 5–8 mm; length of ear 12–16 mm; length of forearm 30–35 mm; wingspan 21–25 cm (R. Adams 2003); weight 3.5–5.5 g. The skull of *M. ciliolabrum* is relatively flat in lateral view. When laid forward the ears barely extend beyond the muzzle. The tail of *M. ciliolabrum* extends about 4 mm beyond the posterior border of the uropatagium, and this character is absent in *M. californicus* (Constantine 1998). However, genetic analysis of mitochondrial cytochrome b did not reveal distinctions between these 2 species, indicating a recent divergence (Rodriguez and Ammerman 2004). For other differences from the very similar *M. californicus*, see the account of that species.

Distribution

A bat of western North America, *M. ciliolabrum* is not uncommon in Colorado at elevations below about 2,600 m (8,500 ft.) where roosting and foraging habitat is available.

PHOTOGRAPH 11-4. Western small-footed myotis (*Myotis ciliolabrum*). Photograph by William E. Ervin.

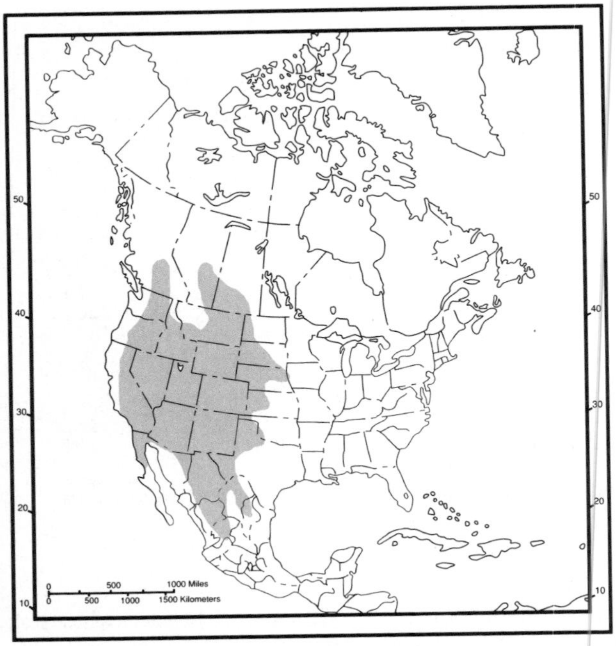

MAP 11-7. Distribution of the western small-footed myotis (*Myotis ciliolabrum*) in North America.

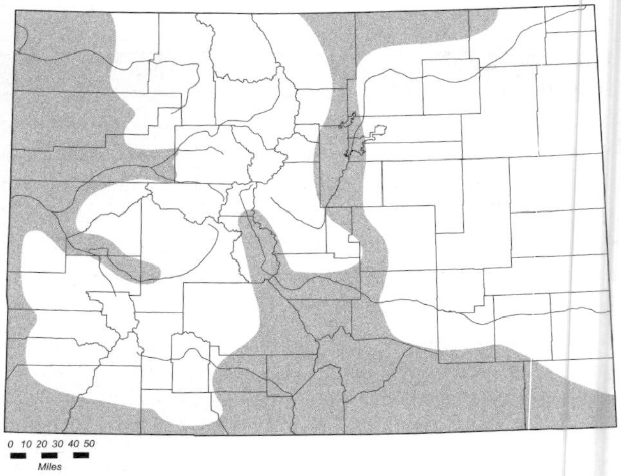

MAP 11-8. Distribution of the western small-footed myotis (*Myotis ciliolabrum*) in Colorado.

It probably is absent from most of the eastern plains where suitable roosting habitat is scarce; records there are restricted to the rocky, eroded terrain, especially north of the South Platte River and south of the Arkansas River. Hibernation occurs as high as 2,895 m (9,500 ft.—D. Armstrong et al. 1994).

Systematics and nomenclature of this species have long been problematic (D. Armstrong 1972; E. Hall 1981). Van Zyll de Jong (1984) revised the small-footed myotis, recognizing 2 distinct species, *Myotis leibii*, the eastern small-footed myotis, and *M. ciliolabrum*, the western small-footed myotis. Previously the forms were treated together as *M. leibii*; in older literature this bat was called *Myotis subulatus*. Coloradan subspecies are *M. c. melanorhinus* in western Colorado and the San Luis Valley and *M. c. ciliolabrum* in the eastern part of the state.

Natural History

The western small-footed myotis is widely distributed in the western United States in a variety of habitats. In summer it has been found roosting in rock crevices, caves, dwellings, and burrows; among rocks; under bark; and even beneath rocks scattered on the ground. Along the Rockies and adjacent plains, the bat is generally found in the broken terrain of canyons and foothills, commonly in places with cover of trees or shrubs. Unlike cavernicolous bats, this and other cavity-roosting species are notoriously difficult to census and monitor (Bogan et al. 2003).

The western small-footed myotis forages only a meter or so above the ground and flies with an erratic butterfly-like pattern. Half of the foraging time is spent near rocks and cliffs (G. Freeman 1984), and the remainder is spent over open areas, arroyos, and forest canopy. As with other small Coloradan bats (western pipistrelle, California myotis), the western small-footed myotis tends to fly early in the evening. That behavior may help reduce predation by larger sympatric bats such as the hoary bat. In northern Weld County the species is not uncommon along the High Plains escarpment but is difficult to capture at cattle tanks (the principal water supply) because of its ability to detect and avoid mist nets. The western small-footed myotis was relatively abundant at a study site in Moffat County (G. Freeman 1984).

The diet of the small-footed myotis has not been studied in detail but is known to include moths, flies, and spiders (D. Armstrong et al. 1994). Small beetles and ants are also eaten. Highly maneuverable in flight, the animals forage among rocks, shrubs, and trees.

The reproductive cycle is poorly known. Apparently most females give birth to 1 young, although twins have been reported. Parturition apparently occurs from June to September in Colorado (R. Adams 2003). Aside from forming small nursery colonies of 10 to 20 individuals, these bats generally are thought to be solitary.

The animals overwinter in caves and rock crevices in Colorado (Warren 1942; D. Armstrong 1972), often in locations with temperatures near freezing, low humidity, and significant air circulation. Such hibernacula are atypical for bats, as most species select more protected, humid sites with somewhat higher temperatures. The literature on the western small-footed myotis was reviewed by Holloway and Barclay (2001).

Myotis evotis

LONG-EARED MYOTIS

Description

The long-eared myotis is a medium brown bat with notably long ears. Black patagia and ears contrast markedly with the paler pelage. There is a pale, inconspicuous fringe of hairs on the posterior margin of the interfemoral membrane. The underside is paler than the dorsum. Measurements are: total length 88–92 mm; length of tail 41–46 mm; length of hindfoot 8–10 mm; length of ear 18–23 mm; length of forearm 35–41 mm; wingspan 25–30 cm (R. Adams 2003); weight 5–7 g. Greatest length of skull is 16.0–16.8 mm, similar to that of *Myotis thysanodes* but lacking the well-developed sagittal crest. The braincase rises gradually from the rostrum. Long ears, coupled with relatively small size and lack of a conspicuous fringe of hair on the trailing edge of the uropatagium, distinguish *M. evotis* from other Colorado bats.

PHOTOGRAPH 11-5. Long-eared myotis (*Myotis evotis*). Photograph by Joseph G. Hall.

Distribution

A western species and an inhabitant of ponderosa pine forests in Colorado, the long-eared myotis has been taken from scattered areas in the western two-thirds of the state, mostly at elevations between 1,830 and 2,750 m (6,000 and 9,000 ft.). Observations of swarming in September at Groaning Cave, Garfield County (Navo et al. 2002), suggest that *M. evotis* may hibernate in Colorado. This was the species of bat most commonly captured in studies in Mesa Verde National Park (Chung-MacCoubrey and Bogan 2003). *M. e. chrysonotus* is the subspecies of Colorado and much of the interior West north and west of Colorado (Manning 1993).

Natural History

The long-eared myotis occurs in coniferous forests at moderate elevations (to 3,100 m near Gothic, Gunnison County;

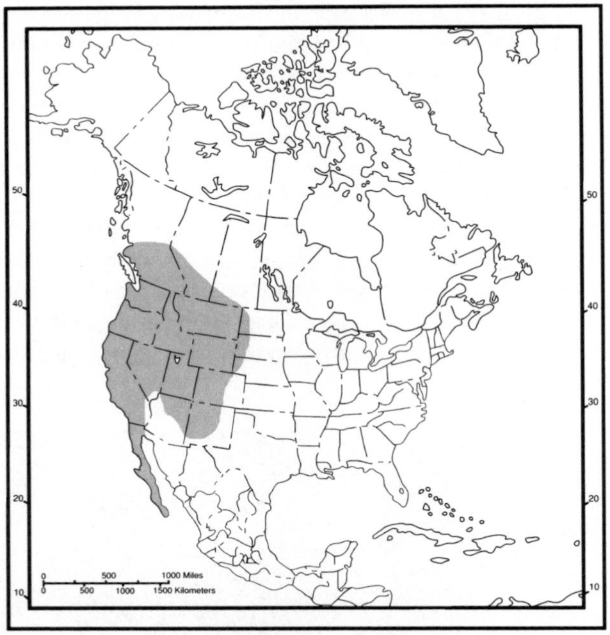

MAP 11-9. Distribution of the long-eared myotis (*Myotis evotis*) in North America.

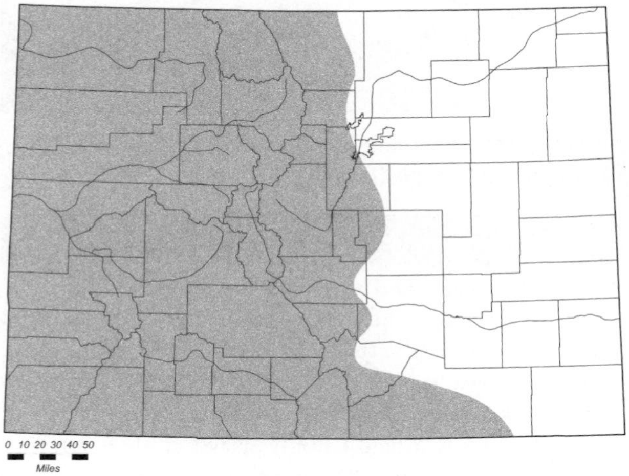

MAP 11-10. Distribution of the long-eared myotis (*Myotis evotis*) in Colorado.

Storz and Williams 1996). It probably is most common in ponderosa pine woodlands but is also found in piñon-juniper woodlands, subalpine forests, and riparian habitats (Schorr 2006). The animals roost by day in tree cavities, under loose bark, and in buildings. In Oregon, snags were used in older forests, whereas rotting stumps were used in previously clear-cut forests (Waldien et al. 2000). Trees and buildings, as well as caves and mines, are used as night roosts.

The long-eared myotis feeds over water and along the margins of vegetation. A gleaner, it picks individual insects from leaves (G. Freeman 1984; R. Adams 2003). The long ears probably facilitate auditory sensitivity to allow this behavior. The animals have been classified as beetle strategists (Black 1974), but they also feed on moths and other insects, including caddisflies (G. Freeman 1984). The long-eared myotis tends to emerge to forage late in the evening.

Maternity colonies contain up to 20 individuals. G. Miller and Allen (1928) reported a small nursery colony in an abandoned ranch building near Dolores, Montezuma County. Birth of a single young probably occurs in June and July. Four females captured in Mesa Verde National Park between July 4 and July 9 were pregnant (Chung-MacCoubrey and Bogan 2003). In Colorado, lactating females have been taken in June, July, and August, with greatest numbers in August (Finley et al. 1983; G. Freeman 1984; R. Adams 1988). Males are scrotal in July, August, and September, and mating probably occurs in fall, with fertilization delayed until spring. Manning and Jones (1989) reviewed the literature on the species.

Myotis lucifugus

LITTLE BROWN MYOTIS

Description

The little brown myotis (or even less distinctively, "little brown bat") is pale to dark brown above with somewhat paler undersides. The hairs are relatively long, with burnished tips lending a definite sheen to the pelage. There usually are long hairs on the toes that extend beyond the tips of the claws. Measurements are: total length 90–100 mm; length of tail 36–47 mm; length of hindfoot 8–10 mm; length of ear 11–15 mm; length of forearm 33–41 mm (but usually in the 39–41 mm range); wingspan 22–27 cm (R. Adams 2003); weight 4.5–5.5 g. Females are slightly larger than males. The ears of *Myotis lucifugus* barely reach the tip of the nose when laid forward. The greatest length of the skull is 14.0–15.9 mm. The little brown myotis can be confused with several other species of *Myotis*. Probably the most productive approach for identification is to search for the characters that distinguish other, more distinctive species known to occur in the area. The most similar Coloradan species is the Yuma myotis, from which the little brown bat differs in having a greater mastoid breadth (greater than 7.5 mm vs. less than 7.4 mm) and glossy, darker pelage (Findley et al. 1975).

PHOTOGRAPH 11-6. Little brown myotis (*Myotis lucifugus*). Photograph by Merlin D. Tuttle, Bat Conservation International.

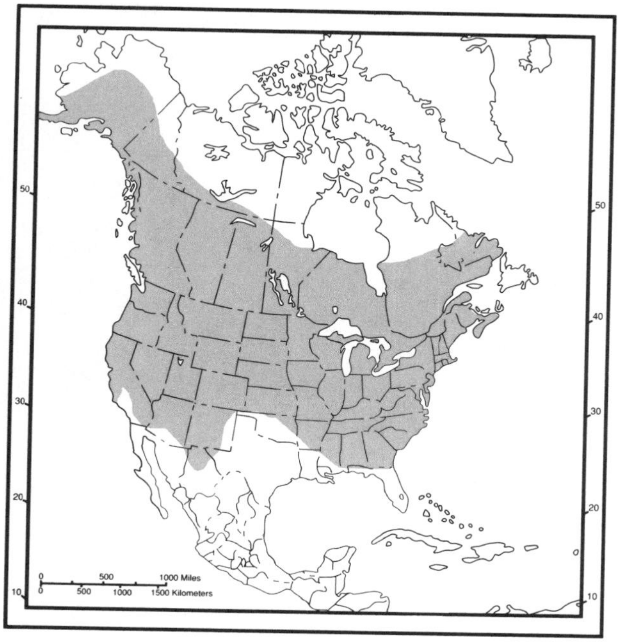

MAP 11-11. Distribution of the little brown myotis (*Myotis lucifugus*) in North America.

Distribution

The most widespread of North American species of *Myotis*, the little brown myotis is common in wooded areas of the western two-thirds of the state at elevations of 1,530 to 3,700 m (5,000 to above 12,100 ft.; see Storz and Williams, 1996). It is also found in riparian woodlands, piñon-juniper woodlands, and montane shrublands (D. Armstrong 1972; Ellinwood 1978; G. Freeman 1984).

Most authors have identified Coloradan little brown bats with the subspecies *Myotis lucifugus carissima* (see D. Armstrong 1972 and D. Armstrong et al. 1994), although Lausen et al. (2008; see also Lausen 2009) suggested that *M. l. carissima* is indistinguishable from *M. l. lucifugus*, based on studies of nuclear gene flow in southern Alberta and north-central Montana.

A second subspecies (*M. l. occultus*) may occur in the southern part of the state, but the taxonomic status of that form is uncertain. *Myotis occultus* was named by Hollister (1909) with a type locality on the Lower Colorado River 10 mi. above Needles, California. G. Miller and Allen (1928) revised the genus *Myotis* and recognized *M. occultus* as a distinct species. Findley and Jones (1967) reviewed the status of the species; noted apparent intergradation between *M. lucifugus* and *M. occultus* in specimens from Alamosa County, Colorado; and concluded that the bats were only subspecifically distinct. Barbour and Davis (1969:75) suggested that animals from southern Colorado might be hybrids between species, not intergrades between subspecies. Later, Barbour and Davis (1970) concluded that intergradation best explained the available evidence. However, Findley (1972) raised questions about the status and affinities of *M. occultus*. This stimulated Hoffmeister (1986) to review *M. occultus* in Arizona in detail, including quantitative analysis of 25 cranial characters. Principal components analysis indicated that specimens from Arizona were distinct from samples from the San Luis Valley of Colorado. He concluded that specimens from Arizona represented *M. occultus*, as distinct from *M. lucifugus*. K. N. Geluso (1975, 1978) and Bassett and Wiebers (1979) found in laboratory studies that individuals of *M. l. occultus* had a greater ability to concentrate urine (hence greater tolerance of low humidity in the roost) than did individuals of *M. l. lucifugus*. Chung-Macoubrey and Bogan (2003) noted that little brown bats from piñon-juniper woodlands of southwestern Colorado might be found to represent *M. occultus*.

Recent molecular studies have pointed to conflicting conclusions about the taxonomic status of *M. occultus*. E. Valdez et al. (1999) used data from electrophoresis of proteins to conclude that *M. occultus* and *M. lucifugus* are not specifically distinct. D. Wilson and Cole (2000) did not list *Myotis occultus* as a species. However, Piaggio, Valdez, et al.

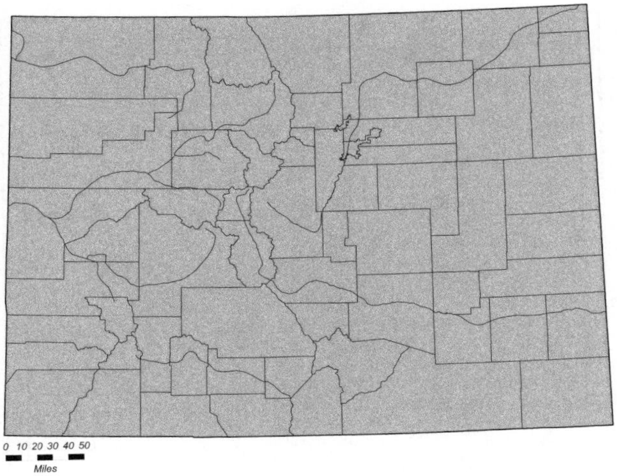

MAP 11-12. Distribution of the little brown myotis (*Myotis lucifugus*) in Colorado.

(2002) concluded from analysis of mitochondrial DNA that the 2 populations are indeed specifically distinguishable, and on the authority of that study R. Baker, L. Bradley, et al. (2003) and D. Wilson and Reeder (2005) listed *M. occultus* as a full species. In text, R. Adams (2003:185) treated *occultus* as a subspecies of *M. lucifugus* but labeled a photograph (p. 184) as *Myotis occultus*. In studies of part of the mitochondrial cytochrome-b gene from little brown bats and other species of *Myotis* across their wide range, Dewey (2006) tested the hypothesis "that *Myotis lucifugus* is a single, monophyletic lineage and that morphologically recognized subspecies correspond to patterns of genetic variation." She concluded that *Myotis occultus* is not a distinct species. We do not treat the "occult myotis" as separate from *M. lucifugus*, but it probably is fair to say that much remains to be learned about the evolution of these bats in western North America.

Natural History

Relative to other bats, the biology of the little brown myotis is well studied; there are more publications on this species than any other North American bat (Humphrey and Cope 1976; Fenton and Barclay 1980; Fenton et al. 1987). It inhabits most of North America, roosting by day under bark and rocks; in trees, woodpiles, buildings, and other structures; and less frequently in caves and mines. Similar areas are used for night roosts. If the same site is used for both day and night roosts, different locations within the roost are utilized. Because of a lack of food resources, little brown bats must hibernate in winter. Caves, mines, and buildings are typical hibernacula, but little is known about wintering habits of the little brown bat in Colorado or elsewhere in the western United States.

Nursery colonies form in summer, numbering up to 800 individuals in the eastern United States. In Colorado, nursery colonies typically contain fewer than 100 adult females and have invariably been found in buildings, usually in warm attics. Females and young are tolerant of extremely high temperatures (Studier and O'Farrell 1972). A nursery colony near Stonewall, Las Animas County, was located behind 15- to 25-cm-wide ponderosa pine slab siding on a rustic lodge (Ellinwood 1978). In early August 1977 it contained an estimated 180 to 200 bats, most of which were the little brown myotis. Seventy-three of 89 little brown myotis captured were juveniles that had only recently begun to fly. A site in an attic at Red Feather Lakes, Larimer County, contained an estimated 250 bats on July 20. The young, probably about 2 weeks old, were only half the size of the females and were not yet volant (S. Ellinwood and J. P. Fitzgerald, unpublished). Unfortunately, the colony was exterminated before the young reached maturity. Another nursery colony, on the Colorado State University campus, shared their roost for part of the year with big brown bats (L. Wunder and Nash 1981; L. Wunder 1987). M. O'Farrell and Studier (1973) discussed maternity roosts of *M. lucifugus* in northeastern New Mexico.

Little brown bats mate in late fall and winter while the animals are in the vicinity of their hibernacula. Copulation may occur with both sexes alert, or the male may copulate with torpid females (D. Thomas et al. 1979). Both species are promiscuous and mate more than once. Ovulation occurs 1 or 2 days after arousal from hibernation (Buchanan 1987). Sperm are stored and fertilization occurs when females leave the hibernaculum. The gestation period is 50 to 60 days. Little brown bats give birth in late May or early June (early for Coloradan bats), and lactation is terminated by about the end of June (R. Adams 1988). Delivery is remarkable because the female reverses her normal head-down roosting posture and hangs head-up from her thumb claws, capturing the newborn bat in her interfemoral membrane as it is expelled. Other species of bats often give birth in the head-down position.

Young are born with fine, silky hair, and their eyes and ears open 2 to 3 days after birth. Occasionally, the young are carried attached to the female's nipples while she forages, but usually they are left in the roost. They develop rapidly, fly by about 3 weeks of age, and reach adult weight in about 1 month. R. Adams (1996, 1997, 2000) reported spatial segregation in foraging between newly volant juveniles and adults at Fort Laramie National Historic Site in southeastern Wyoming.

The little brown myotis emerges at dusk to drink and feed and generally forages over water or in clearings, in seemingly erratic, "zigzag" flight. In intensive studies near Boulder, R. Adams and Thibault (2006) showed temporal segregation in drinking sites between *M. lucifugus* and 2 sympatric bats of roughly similar body size (*M. volans* and *M. thysanodes*); the smaller *M. ciliolabrum* overlapped with *M. lucifugus*. Little brown bats forage 3–6 m aboveground. Insect prey are struck with a wing tip, caught in the uropatagium, lifted to the mouth with an upward curl of tail, and consumed in flight. During this remarkably rapid procedure, the animals appear to tumble briefly in the air. Known as moth specialists, they also take many other prey items, including mosquitoes. In fact a single individual can capture up to 600 mosquitoes per hour (Tuttle 1988). A colony of these bats can thus have a substantial impact on insect populations, hence the use of bat houses to attract and accommodate little brown bats as an organic pest-control service.

These bats feed periodically through the night, rapidly fill their stomachs, then rest and eliminate undigested food for an hour or so, and then resume their foraging activities. Females at maternity colonies show seasonal selectivity in foraging and diet (Aldridge 1976). The exoskeleton of insects is composed of the mucopolysaccharide chitin. The enzyme that digests chitin is chitinase, which has been identified in guts of a number of kinds of bats, including *M. lucifugus*. Whitaker, Dannelly, and Prentice (2004) demonstrated that this chitinase is produced not by the bats themselves but by several kinds of symbiotic bacteria. Digestion of chitin in bat guts is incomplete so fecal pellets of bats usually include identifiable remains of their insect prey.

Little brown bats—like a number of other kinds of bats—exhibit remarkable longevity for small mammals. Oldest reported age is over 30 years (Fenton and Barclay 1980) and many survive more than 10 years. Mortality is highest in the first year, occurring mostly as the young learn to fly or during their hibernation. Foraging skills must develop, so the young are not as adept as adults. Based on a study of specimens (reported as *M. occultus*) from New Mexico and southern Colorado, ectoparasites include a wide variety of mites and also fleas, bat bugs (Cimicidae), and bat flies (Nycteribiidae) (E. Valdez et al. 2009), A variety of predators feed on these bats, including snakes, passerine birds, birds of prey, domestic pets, and other small carnivores. Documented predators of the little brown myotis include fish, snakes, owls and other birds, and house cats (Sparks et al. 2000). Rabies appears to be rare.

Myotis thysanodes

FRINGED MYOTIS

Description

The fringed myotis is yellowish brown to reddish brown, with the ventral color similar to the dorsum. The ears are quite large, extending 3–5 mm beyond the nose when laid forward. The free edge of the interfemoral membrane has an obvious fringe of stiff hairs, hence the common name. This feature most readily distinguishes this bat from others in Colorado. Measurements are: total length 77–100 mm; length of tail 34–45; length of hindfoot 9–11 mm; length of ear 16–21 mm; length of forearm 39–46 mm; wingspan 27–32 cm (R. Adams 2003); weight 6–7 g. The skull is relatively large, slender, and fragile; greatest length of skull is 16.0–17.2 mm. A well-developed sagittal crest is present.

PHOTOGRAPH 11-7. Fringed myotis (*Myotis thysanodes*). Photograph by Roger W. Barbour.

Distribution

A western species, the fringed myotis is an animal of coniferous woodlands and shrublands at elevations to 2,290 m (7,500 ft.). The few Coloradan records are widely scattered both east and west of the Continental Divide (J. Fitzgerald et al. 1989). D. Armstrong (1972) reported a specimen from Wooton, near Raton Pass, but the species probably occurs farther east along the New Mexico boundary, as Dalquest et al. (1990) reported the animals from the northeastern corner of Union County, New Mexico, adjacent to Baca County, Colorado. One subspecies, *Myotis thysanodes thysanodes*, occurs in Colorado.

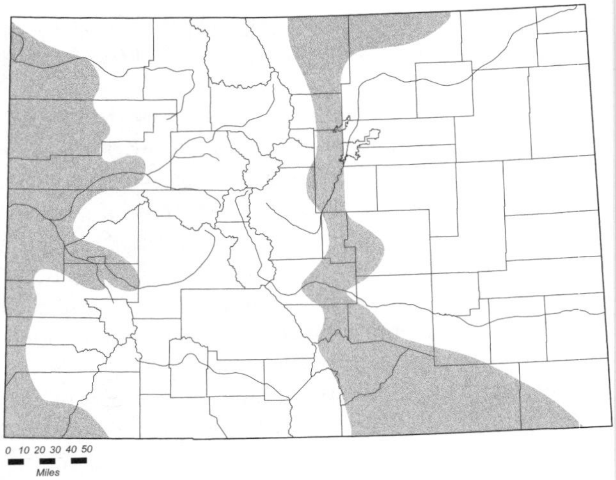

MAP 11-14. **Distribution of the fringed myotis (*Myotis thysanodes*) in Colorado.**

Natural History

The fringed myotis apparently is not particularly abundant in Colorado. It is found in ponderosa pine woodlands, greasewood, oakbrush, and saltbush shrublands. In the Pacific Northwest 93 percent of day roosts were in ponderosa pine; "snag" trees were used infrequently (only 5 percent of roosts located; Lacki and Baker 2007). However, in northern California, Douglas-fir snags in early to medium states of decay were used frequently, accommodating up to 88 individuals (Weller and Zabel 2001). In the Black Hills of South Dakota, the fringed myotis roosted in rock crevices as well as trees (Cryan et al. 2001). These bats may begin to forage shortly after sunset, although most of their activity occurs within 2 hours after dark. As with some other bats, moderate precipitation does not much influence activity. Gleaners, they forage close to the canopy, where they pick prey insects off the vegetation during a slow maneuverable flight. The fringed myotis has a relatively broad diet, feeding on moths, beetles, caddisflies, hymenopterans (ants, bees, and wasps), and other insects (G. Freeman 1984).

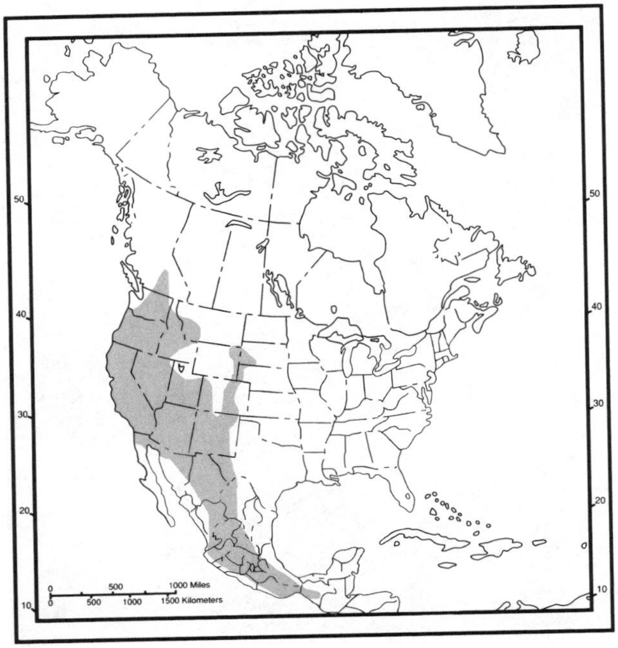

MAP 11-13. **Distribution of the fringed myotis (*Myotis thysanodes*) in North America.**

Females mate in the fall and store sperm over winter, with ovulation and fertilization occurring in late April and May. The gestation period is 50–60 days, with 1 young produced annually. Barbour and Davis (1969) captured pregnant fringed myotis near Colorado Springs in mid-June. Young are capable of flight by 2.5 weeks of age and by 3 weeks young are indistinguishable in size from adults.

Nursery colonies of several hundred fringed myotis have been reported in other areas but records on distribution, behavior, and ecology of this species in Colorado are scarce. Caves, mines, and buildings are used as both day and night roosts. M. O'Farrell and Studier (1973) discussed maternity roosts of *M. thysanodes* in northeastern New Mexico. Localized migrations are thought to occur, but firm data are lacking. Hibernation sites include caves and buildings. R. Adams and Hayes (2008) found that lactating fringed myotis visited waterholes 13 times more often than did non-lactating females. From their data they built a model that predicted serious impacts on these bats from a warming and drying climate. The literature on the fringed myotis was reviewed by M. O'Farrell and Studier (1980) and Keinath (2004).

Myotis velifer
CAVE MYOTIS

Description

The cave myotis, a species of possible occurrence in Colorado, is large for the genus, with pale brown dorsal pelage and a somewhat paler venter. The hair is of moderate length and coarse, has no sheen, and is often described as "woolly." This species may be confused with *Myotis lucifugus* or *M. yumanensis* and is best distinguished by having a forearm longer than 41 mm, a condylobasal length greater than 16 mm, and a well-developed sagittal crest on the skull.

Distribution

The cave myotis has not been documented in Colorado, but it is likely to be found. It occurs at lower elevations in the Southwest (north and east to south-central Kansas) and Mexico. Individuals of the Great Plains subspecies *Myotis velifer grandis* may occasionally enter southeastern Colorado. Caire et al. (1989) and Dalquest et al. (1990) reported captures in Cimarron County, Oklahoma, in the Panhandle within about 25 km of Colorado, and the westernmost record from Kansas (J. K. Jones, Fleharty, and Dunnigan 1967) is 140 km from the Colorado border. By contrast, the southwestern subspecies, *M. v. velifer*, is known from southern New Mexico, about 400 km from Colorado (Findley et al. 1975).

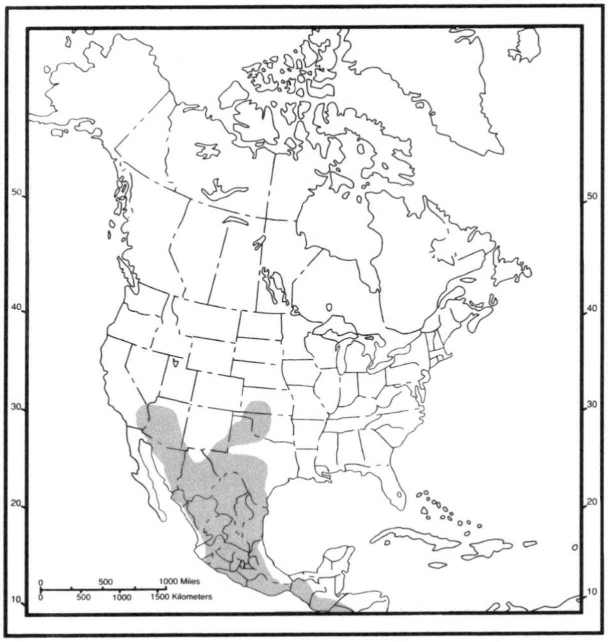

MAP 11-15. Distribution of the cave myotis (*Myotis velifer*) in North America.

Natural History

As the vernacular name implies, the cave myotis is mostly a cave-roosting species that forms large colonies in caves, mines, and sometimes buildings. They leave the roost a few minutes after sunset and generally forage 4–6 m over open water. The flight is strong and not as erratic as that of some other species of *Myotis*.

Myotis volans
LONG-LEGGED MYOTIS

Description

The long-legged myotis is a large-sized representative of the genus. Color is reddish or orangish brown to dark brown, with paler undersides. The pelage is relatively long and soft. The underside of the patagium is furred to the level of the elbow or beyond. The ears are relatively short, barely reaching the nose when laid forward. The calcar is long and conspicuously keeled. Measurements are: total length 95–108 mm; length of tail 40–43 mm; length of hindfoot 8–9 mm; length of ear 11–14 mm; length of forearm 35–41 mm; wingspan 25–30 (R. Adams 2003); weight 8–10 g. Greatest length of the skull is 12–15 mm. The rostrum is short and the braincase rises abruptly. This animal can be confused with *Myotis lucifugus*, frequently found in the same area. The little brown bat lacks a keel on the calcar and has a glossier pelage.

Distribution

Generally distributed in the West, the long-legged myotis is known from numerous locations in the western two-thirds of Colorado. It would not be surprising to find them in the chalk bluffs of northern Weld and Logan counties, the Black Forest in Elbert and El Paso counties, or the roughlands of

PHOTOGRAPH 11-8. Long-legged myotis (*Myotis volans*). Photograph by Roger W. Barbour.

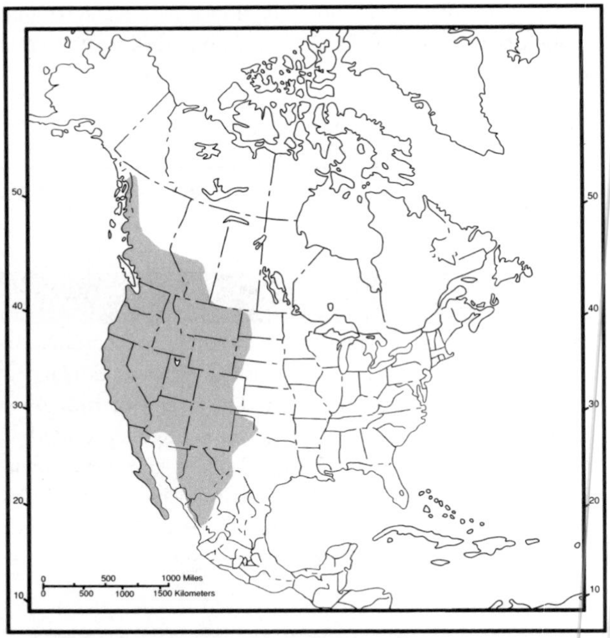

MAP 11-16. Distribution of the long-legged myotis (*Myotis volans*) in North America.

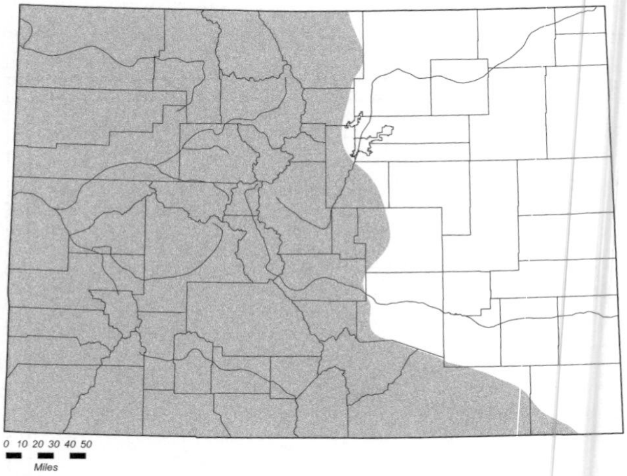

MAP 11-17. Distribution of the long-legged myotis (*Myotis volans*) in Colorado.

Baca County. *M. volans* occupies montane forests, piñon-juniper woodlands, montane shrublands, and subalpine forests to about 3,700 m (to over 12,400 ft.; see Storz and Williams 1996). This is perhaps Colorado's highest-elevation bat. In July 1999 an individual was found dead on the wall of the ruins of the Summit House (Crest House) on Mount Evans, Clear Creek County, elevation ca. 14,130 ft. (4307 m; Kevin J. Cook, personal communication); by a considerable margin that is the highest elevation record for any bat in Colorado and the highest elevation reported for *M. volans* across its broad geographic range. One subspecies, *Myotis volans interior*, occurs in Colorado.

Natural History

A western bat, the long-legged myotis is relatively common in ponderosa pine forests, piñon-juniper woodlands, and also riparian areas in sagebrush country (Schorr 2006). This bat roosts in a variety of sites, including trees, buildings, crevices in rock faces, and even fissures in the ground in severely eroded areas. Tall, large-diameter conifers may be preferred roosting sites (Chung-MacCoubrey and Bogan 2003). Caves and mines do not appear to be important as day roosts but are used as night roosts if available. Animals roost in small groups or alone. Hibernacula have not yet been found in Colorado, but the animals probably hibernate locally or make only short migrations (Schowalter 1980). Probably they hibernate singly in mines and caves.

The long-legged myotis emerges at early dusk and forages over openings in forested areas or over water (Storz and Williams 1996), usually at a height of 3–5 m. Rapid, direct fliers, they are capable of long-distance pursuit of prey (Fenton and Bell 1979; Fenton et al. 1980). They forage singly and feed on large numbers of moths (G. Freeman 1984). Typical of vespertilionids, as they approach their flying prey the rate of echolocatory clicks increases to a "feeding buzz."

The reproductive biology of the long-legged myotis is poorly known. Large nursery colonies are formed. Forty-five females were banded in the Conejos County Courthouse in the San Luis Valley (W. H. Davis and Barbour 1970). The animals breed in late June, July, and August in our area. In Mesa Verde (Chung-MacCoubrey and Bogan 2003), as elsewhere in Colorado, pregnant females have been captured from June to August, and lactating females have been captured in August (W. H. Davis and Barbour 1970; R. Adams 1988). A single young is produced annually.

These bats are believed to migrate but little is known of their movements or wintering areas. Both little brown myotis and long-legged myotis were captured at a nursery colony behind pine siding on a building near Stonewall, Las Animas County (Ellinwood 1978). Males may become reproductively active their first year (Schowalter 1980). In the Black Hills of South Dakota, pregnant female *M. volans* (and those of several other species) were captured at significantly lower elevations than were males and nonreproductive females (Cryan et al. 2000). The speculation was that reproductive females are constrained by the compounding energy demands of foraging, gestation, and lactation and so are limited to more favorable microhabitats. Literature on the long-legged myotis was reviewed by R. Warner and Czaplewski (1984).

Myotis yumanensis

YUMA MYOTIS

Description

The Yuma myotis is a pale, tawny to buff-colored bat with undersides somewhat paler than the dorsum. The animal is similar in size to the little brown myotis. Measurements are: total length 78–90 mm; length of tail 32–37 mm; length of hindfoot 7–9 mm; length of ear 12.5–14.0 mm; length of forearm 32–38 mm; wingspan 22–26 cm (R. Adams 2003); weight 3.5–5.0 g. The braincase rises steeply from the rostrum and there is no sagittal crest. The calcar is not keeled. The animal can be confused with the little brown myotis, from which it differs by having a duller and paler pelage, paler-colored ears, a steeply sloping forehead, and a mastoid breadth of 7.4 mm or less (Harris 1974).

PHOTOGRAPH 11-9. Yuma myotis (*Myotis yumanensis*). Photograph by Roger W. Barbour.

Distribution

A western species, the Yuma myotis is frequently associated with semiarid canyonlands and mesas at lower elevations in southern and western Colorado, but ranges into mixed coniferous forests where suitable roosts are present. Siemers

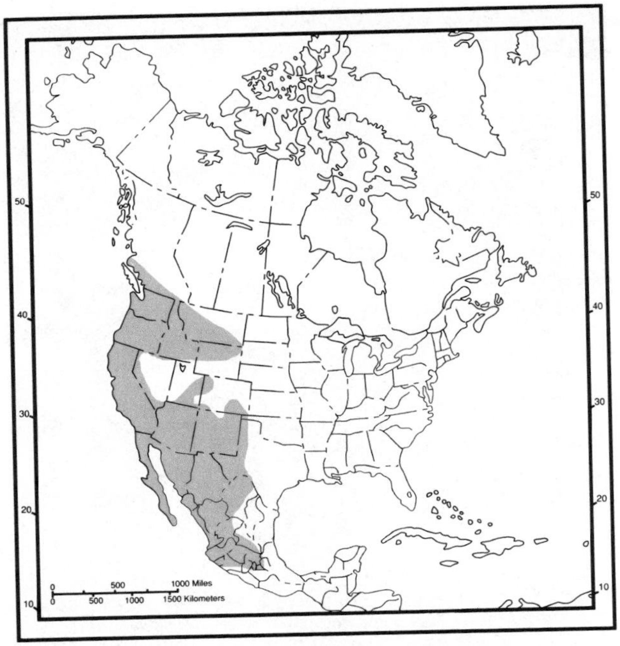

MAP 11-18. Distribution of the Yuma myotis (*Myotis yumanensis*) in North America.

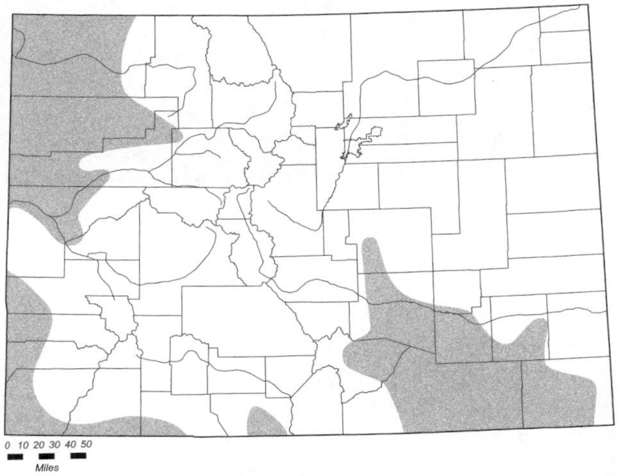

MAP 11-19. Distribution of the Yuma myotis (*Myotis yumanensis*) in Colorado.

(2002) reported the animals in Groaning and Honkey caves, Garfield County (the latter at an elevation of 9,890 ft. [3,014 m]). The Yuma myotis is not uncommon in suitable habitat in the western third of the state and in southeastern Colorado and is represented in both areas by one subspecies, *Myotis yumanensis yumanensis*.

Natural History

The Yuma myotis is associated with riparian habitats in otherwise dry and shrubby landscapes over much of the semiarid western United States, ranging from western Mexico northward to southern British Columbia. They roost by day in rock crevices, buildings, caves, and mines and are known to utilize swallows' nests. Night roosts typically are in buildings, under ledges, or in similar shelters. Nursery colonies usually are in buildings or caves and may contain a large number of individuals.

This bat forages early, often before dark in shadowy canyons. A shorter feeding period may occur in the morning (Ellinwood 1978). The animals typically forage rather low over water, often just a few centimeters above the surface. The diet is not well studied, but probably aquatic insects make up much of it. Moths, flies, and beetles are taken, as are a number of other insects, including grasshoppers. House cats and bobcats are reported to prey on the Yuma myotis (Sparks et al. 2000).

Reproduction in this species also is not well-known. The animals breed in autumn; females store sperm over the winter and give birth to a single young, generally between late May and July. Lactating females have been captured in early and mid-July in Colorado (W. H. Davis and Barbour 1970; Ellinwood 1978), which suggests that the young were born in June and early July. Wintering habits of the species are poorly documented, but they may hibernate near their summer range. Navo et al. (2002) reported swarming in September at Groaning Cave, on the White River Plateau in Garfield County (elevation 3,048 m [about 10,000 ft.]), raising the possibility that the species hibernates in Colorado. Dalquest (1947) published a thorough study of this species in California.

Genus *Lasiurus*—"Shaggy-Tailed" Bats

The generic name *Lasiurus* is derived from Greek roots meaning "shaggy tail," a reference to the heavily furred uropatagium. There are some 17 species in the genus, ranging from Arctic Canada to southern Argentina and Chile and westward to Hawai'i and the Galapagos. Two species are known from Colorado, and a third (the western red bat, *Lasiurus blossevillii*) is of possible occurrence. E. Hall (1981) listed species of *Lasiurus* in a genus, *Nycteris*.

Lasiurus borealis
EASTERN RED BAT

Description

This is a medium-sized reddish to yellowish red bat with some of the dorsal hairs tipped white. Males generally are brighter and redder in color than females. The shoulders may have paler buffy spots, and the ventral surface is paler than the dorsum. The white-tipped hairs have a reddish band below the white, then a brown band, and then a black basal band. The ears are short, rounded, and lack a black rim. The interfemoral membrane is densely furred above and sparsely furred below. Measurements are: total length 107–128 mm; length of tail 40–60 mm; length of hindfoot 11 mm; length of ear 8–13 mm; length of forearm 35–46 mm; wingspan 28–33 cm (R. Adams 2003); weight 7–16 g. The skull is short and robust but smaller than that of the hoary bat. The rostrum is nearly as broad as the braincase. Greatest length of skull usually is less than 15 mm. As with the hoary bat, a tiny peg-like first premolar is present.

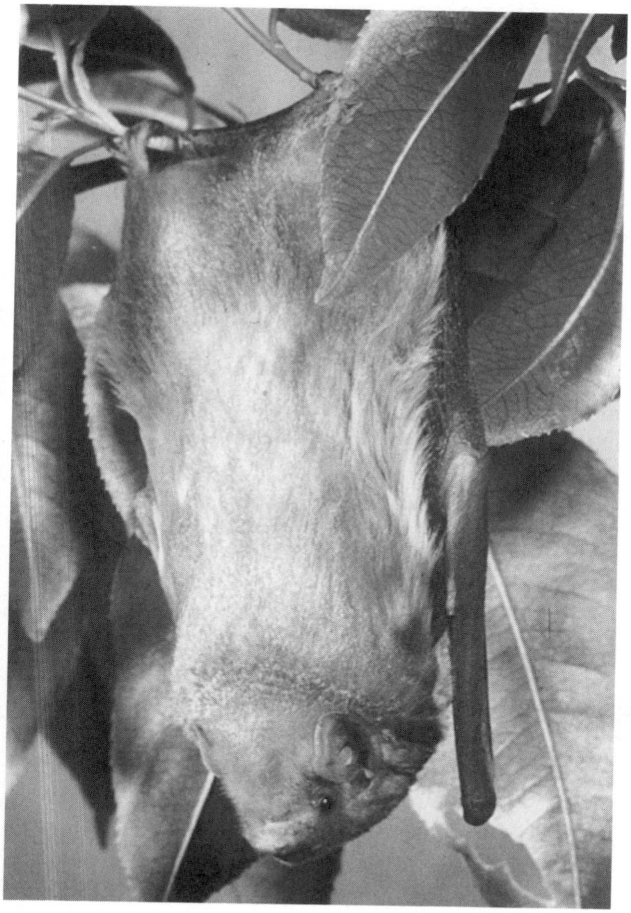

PHOTOGRAPH 11-10. Eastern red bat (*Lasiurus borealis*). Photograph by Roger W. Barbour.

Distribution

Abundant in the Midwest, only a handful of specimens were known in Colorado prior to the 1980s, collected in riparian woodlands on the eastern plains in Weld, Arapahoe, Yuma, Otero, and Baca counties (D. Armstrong 1972; Ellinwood 1978). In 1985 a red bat was found on the University of Colorado campus in Boulder, and in 1990 one was found dead in Las Animas County, impaled on barbed wire (David Leatherman, personal communication). R. A. Adams (personal communication) reported an eastern red bat found dead on the grounds of the Denver Zoo in 2006, and in July 2007 he netted one in Bear Creek Canyon above Boulder. Everette et al. (2001) identified the species acoustically at Rocky Mountain Arsenal National Wildlife Refuge, Adams County. Two animals were mist-netted in Fort Collins—on Spring Creek and near the Poudre River (D. Neubaum 2005). Four records from Greeley, dating back to 1898, suggest that the species was not uncommon in the early days of that city. Colorado now has more extensive woody vegetation on the eastern plains (both riparian and urban woodlands) than existed a century ago. These changes are directly related to irrigation and seem to have increased available habitat for the red bat. With more sampling we may find that red bats are not unusual at certain times of year in Colorado. The subspecies *Lasiurus borealis borealis* occurs in the state.

It is possible that a second species of red bat, the western red bat (*Lasiurus blossevillii*), eventually will be found to occur in southwestern Colorado. That is the red bat of the desert Southwest, including the Grand Canyon and southwestern and central Utah (R. Baker et al. 1988; R. Adams 1993).

Natural History

The eastern red bat is a solitary, tree-roosting species. On occasion red bats have been taken in or on the sides of buildings. Although apparently rare in Colorado, red bats are common in the Midwest and east-central states, where they roost in deciduous trees (Constantine 1966). Suspended from small twigs or branches, from a distance they may look like dead leaves. Like the hoary bat, red bats appear to favor trees located on the edge of clearings or

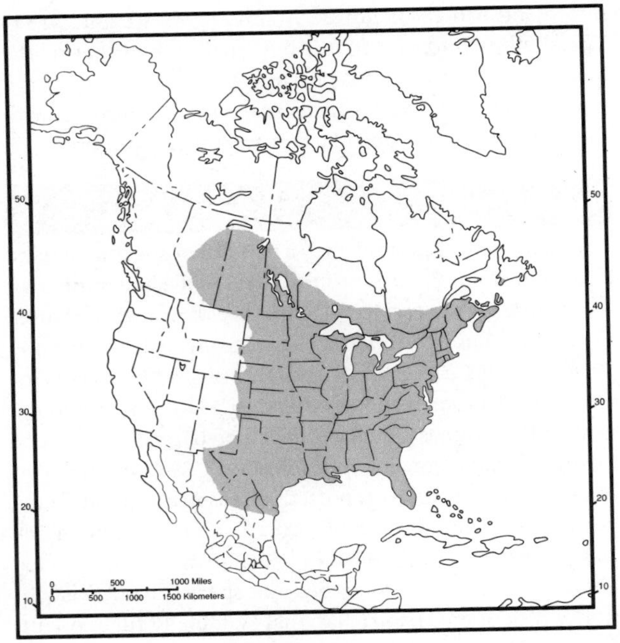

MAP 11-20. Distribution of the eastern red bat (*Lasiurus borealis*) in North America.

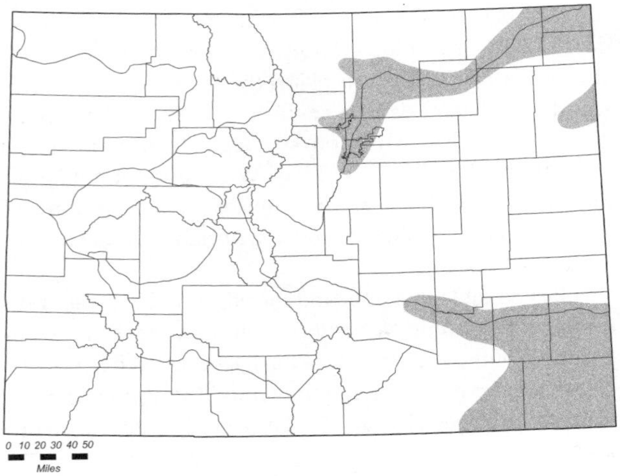

MAP 11-21. Distribution of the eastern red bat (*Lasiurus borealis*) in Colorado.

along fencerows, generally roosting on the south and east sides of such trees. The roost area is protected from the sides and from above, with a clear flight path below. Roost height ranges from 1.5 to 4.0 m aboveground.

The eastern red bat emerges to feed relatively early in the evening but typically after other bats have begun to fly. Some of the early flight behavior is erratic at altitudes well above the treetops. Most foraging occurs within the first few hours after dark, although some foraging occurs throughout the night (Mumford 1973).

The animals feed from the treetops down to within a meter of the ground. Foraging flight is swift and straight, a series of broad, sweeping arcs. Red bats appear to be relatively sedentary, foraging over the same areas night after night and frequently close to the day roost. The varied diet consists of moths, flies, beetles, and crickets. The animals are often attracted to insects congregating around artificial lights and will forage at such sites with little apparent fear. They also land on the ground and forage for crickets, beetles, and other insects. Eastern red bats are reportedly preyed upon by frogs, snakes, owls, hawks and other birds, and opossums (Sparks et al. 2000). In short, predation on red bats is opportunistic and one might speculate that females burdened by nursing young are especially vulnerable.

Eastern red bats probably mate in August and September over most of their range, and females store sperm in the oviducts until about February or March. B. Glass (1966) reported that copulation was initiated in flight. Gestation is 80 to 90 days, with 2 to 5 young (average, 2 to 3) born from late May to early July (R. Hamilton and Stallings 1972). This is an unusually high number of young for a bat. The young are usually left at the roost while the female forages. The young bats reach flight age by about 4 weeks and are weaned at about 5 weeks of age.

Eastern red bats are thought to undertake long-distance migrations at least in their northern ranges. Spring migrations occur in May and early June and fall movements in September, October, and November (LaVal and LaVal 1979). Perhaps Coloradan individuals migrate eastward and southward but data are lacking. Shump and Shump (1982b) reviewed the literature.

Lasiurus cinereus

HOARY BAT

Description

The hoary bat is Colorado's largest vespertilionid. Quite handsome, its white-tipped dorsal hairs lend a "frosted" (hoary) appearance. The venter is yellowish in the neck area, brown on the chest, and almost white on the belly. The dorsal hairs are black at the base, followed by a yellow band, a brown band, and a white tip. The ears are short

PHOTOGRAPH 11-11. Hoary bat (*Lasiurus cinereus*). Photo Archives, Denver Museum of Nature and Science.

MAP 11-22. Distribution of the hoary bat (*Lasiurus cinereus*) in North America.

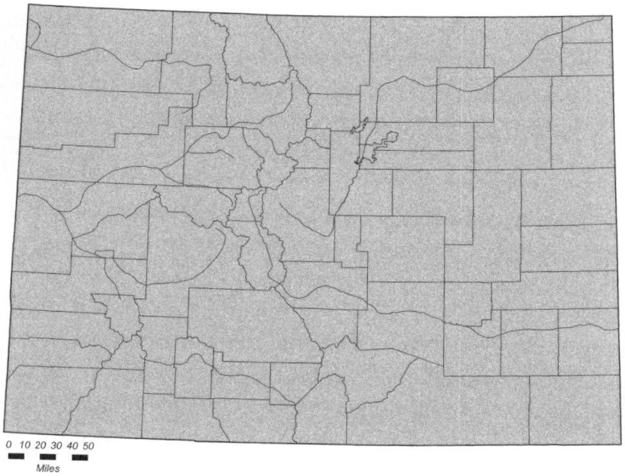

MAP 11-23. Distribution of the hoary bat (*Lasiurus cinereus*) in Colorado.

and rounded, with conspicuous black rims. The wings are long and pointed, spanning 380–410 mm. The uropatagium is heavily furred on its dorsal surface. Measurements are: total length 120–145 mm; length of tail 49–60 mm; length of hindfoot 9.0–11.8 mm; length of ear 12.5–18.0 mm; length of forearm 46–56 mm; weight 18–32 g. The skull is large (greatest length, 17.0–18.5 mm) and robust, and the upper first premolar is very small.

Distribution

A widespread species, the hoary bat probably occurs throughout Colorado in suitable habitat, from the eastern plains to elevations of about 3,100 m (nearly 10,200 ft.) in the mountains (see Storz and Williams 1996). Males are more common in Colorado in summer than are females, which tend to occur mostly in the eastern United States (Cryan 2003). D. Armstrong (1972) suggested that only migrants were to be expected on the plains of Colorado, but early summer-taken specimens (a female and young) from Greeley in the collection at the University of Northern Colorado

(J. P. Fitzgerald, unpublished) suggest that females may give birth on the eastern plains under some circumstances. Hoary bats accounted for nearly 10 percent of bats captured at Rocky Mountain Arsenal National Wildlife Refuge near Denver (Everette et al. 2001). One subspecies, *Lasiurus cinereus cinereus*, occurs throughout North America.

Natural History

Hoary bats are solitary and wide-ranging (the only land mammal native to Hawai'i, Earth's most remote archipelago). It uses a variety of trees as roost sites. The animals appear to favor deciduous trees for roosts in the eastern United States, but in the mountains of Colorado hoary bats are taken frequently in ponderosa pine forests where large deciduous trees are lacking (D. Armstrong 1972; Ellinwood 1978). Finley et al. (1983) reported the animals from Douglas-fir–cottonwood forest, and G. Freeman (1984) reported them from piñon-juniper woodland. Roosts are located 4–5 m aboveground, protected from above with good leaf cover and branches but allowing a clear flight path below. Such trees are frequently associated with the margins of clearings, windbreaks, or the narrow fringe of deciduous cottonwoods and willows along irrigation canals on the plains. The species seldom seems to be abundant in any area and most observations are of single individuals unless small groups are encountered in migration. Males and females are segregated in summer, males tending to stay in Colorado while females continue north to bear and rear the young.

Hoary bats emerge well after dark, although migrants are known to emerge shortly after nightfall. Flight is straight and rapid. These bats make a distinctly audible chatter during flight, enabling researchers to detect their presence with relative ease. The diet is mostly moths (93 percent by volume in north-central New Mexico; E. Valdez and Cryan 2009), although other insects—including beetles, true bugs, flies, and wasps—also are taken (Black 1974; G. Freeman 1984; E. Valdez and Cryan 2009). Owls and hawks are known to prey on hoary bats, and hoary bats, in turn, are reported to prey upon *Eptesicus fuscus*, *Lasionycteris noctivagans*, pipistrelles (*Parastrellus hesperus* and *Perimyotis subflavus*), and *Tadarida brasiliensis* (Sparks et al. 2000).

The reproductive biology of hoary bats is rather poorly known. Mating is thought to occur on the winter range, although males with scrotal testes have been captured in Colorado in July and August. Pregnant females have been collected in June, July, and August (R. Adams 1988). Unusual for a microchiropteran, twins are typical and single births are rare (Bogan 1972). The young are capable of flight by 34 days of age. Most young are born in the northern and eastern parts of North America (Findley and Jones 1964).

The species apparently migrates north and south in distinct waves, with northward movement occurring mostly in May and June, whereas southward movement occurs in late August or early September. Females migrate north about a month earlier than males (E. Valdez and Cryan 2009). Winter range of Coloradan animals is not known, although it probably is in Mexico (Cryan 2003). Stable isotope analysis of hair may eventually provide an efficient method to track movements of hoary bats (Cryan et al. 2004); preliminary work suggests individual movements in excess of 2,000 km (greater than 1,200 mi.). Shump and Shump (1982a) reviewed the literature on *L. cinereus*.

Lasionycteris noctivagans

SILVER-HAIRED BAT

Description

The silver-haired bat is a medium-sized, blackish colored bat with a variable wash of white-tipped dorsal hairs that give the animals a distinctive silvery appearance. The black ears are relatively short, naked, and rounded. The interfemoral membrane has fur on its dorsal surface. Measurements are: total length 90–112 mm; length of tail 35–48 mm; length of hindfoot 8–11 mm; length of ear 13–16 mm; length of forearm 37–44 mm; wingspan 27–32 cm (R. Adams 2003); weight 7–15 g. The skull is somewhat flattened and the rostrum is broad. This is the only short-eared bat in Colorado with a total of 36 teeth. That, coupled with the presence of white-tipped hairs on the dorsum, separates this species from any of the darker-colored species of *Myotis*.

Distribution

Widespread in North America, the silver-haired bat probably occurs statewide at elevations of 1,370–2,900 m (4,500–9,500 ft.), at least during migration. Most records are from along the mountains on either side of the Continental Divide at elevations of 2,100–2,700 m (7,000–8,900 ft.). Nowhere in Colorado does it appear to be abundant, but neither is it an unusual species, especially during spring and fall. *Lasionycteris noctivagans* is monotypic; that is, geographic variation is insignificant and subspecies have not been recognized.

PHOTOGRAPH 11-12. Silver-haired bat (*Lasionycteris noctivagans*). Photograph by Merlin D. Tuttle, Bat Conservation International.

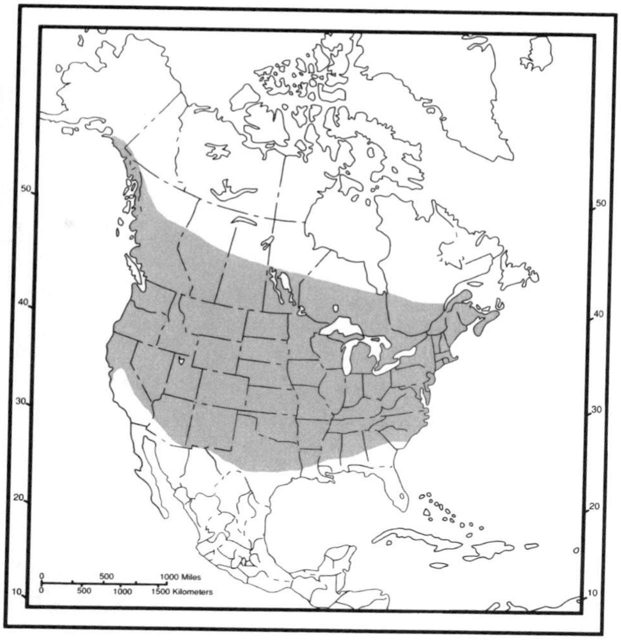

MAP 11-24. Distribution of the silver-haired bat (*Lasionycteris noctivagans*) in North America.

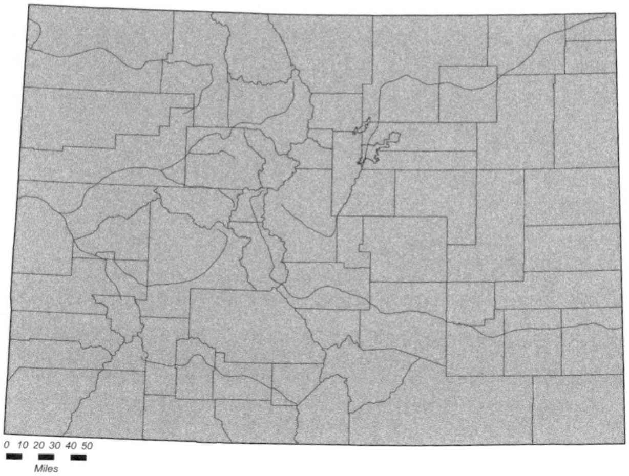

MAP 11-25. Distribution of the silver-haired bat (*Lasionycteris noctivagans*) in Colorado.

Natural History

Despite its solitary habits this is one of the more common bats of North America. Silver-haired bats roost in trees, including aspen and conifers. They often roost in tree "snags" but not all trees are created equal. Working in northeastern Oregon, Betts (1998b) showed that female silver-haired bats selected as maternity roosts trees that were taller, in earlier stages of decay, and farther from other tall trees than were "control" trees. He speculated that such trees would have favorable thermal properties and would be more conspicuous in the auditory and visual landscape. Similar results were found by L. Campbell et al. (1996) in northeastern Washington. Crampton and Barclay (1998) demonstrated the importance of mature aspen stands to silver-haired bats (and little brown bats) in Alberta. In the Black Hills of South Dakota, roosts mostly were in ponderosa pines (T. Mattson et al. 1996). The animals seem to prefer forest edges and are most frequently seen foraging over open areas or over streams and ponds. They have been found in buildings, caves, and woodpiles during migration or hibernation.

The silver-haired bat has been reported as a late flyer (Kunz 1973) and as an early flyer (Whitaker, Maser, and Keller 1977). When foraging, flight is slow and methodical, often close to the ground, but occasionally up to 6 m high. At times the animals feed on the ground. They may form small foraging groups of 3 or 4 animals. Silver-haired bats feed on a variety of insects, including moths, beetles, flies, wasps, mayflies, and isopterans, but moths probably are the most important food (Black 1974; G. Freeman 1981). Predation by owls and skunks is documented for silver-haired bats (Sparks et al. 2000).

Silver-haired bats migrate in spring and fall. In summer, males tend to stay at higher elevations in the Rocky Mountains while females move farther north to rear their young. Wintering grounds are not well-known, but speculation is that the animals overwinter in the Southwest (Cryan 2003). In Colorado they usually have been captured from March through early October (D. Armstrong 1972); an individual was observed roosting in Greeley on the wall of a building at the University of Northern Colorado on December 3, 2006 (R. A. Adams, personal communication).

Two young are born from June to mid-July (Druecker 1972). Males examined in Colorado were scrotal in July, August, and September (R. Adams 1988). Mating occurs in late summer and fall, and sperm overwinter in the female reproductive tract. Kunz (1982a) reviewed the literature on silver-haired bats.

PHOTOGRAPH 11-13. Western pipistrelle (*Parastrellus hesperus*). Photograph by Roger W. Barbour.

Parastrellus hesperus

WESTERN PIPISTRELLE, OR CANYON BAT

Description

Colorado's smallest bat, the western pipistrelle or canyon bat, has pale yellowish gray fur contrasting with the dark, sparsely haired membranes of the ears, muzzle, wings, and uropatagium. Wing venation is conspicuous, forming a delicate pattern. The tragus is blunt and club-shaped, and the calcar is keeled. Measurements are: total length 60–86 mm; length of tail 25–36 mm; length of hindfoot 5.5–7.1 mm; length of ear 12–14 mm; length of forearm 27–33 mm; wingspan 19–23 cm (R. Adams 2003); weight 4–6 g. The skull is delicate and flattened, with virtually no rise between the rostrum and cranium. The first upper premolar is tiny and peg-like, and the inner upper incisor is unicuspid.

Distribution

Mostly a species of the Southwest and Great Basin, western pipistrelles have been treated in the genus *Pipistrellus*. Until recently, *Pipistrellus* was construed to include some 70 species distributed nearly worldwide. It has long been recognized that there was a "*Pipistrellus* problem," meaning that the genus is not a natural "branch" of the evolutionary tree of vespertilionid bats. Molecular analysis is throwing new light on the problem (see Hoofer et al. 2006); we follow those authorities in use of the generic name *Parastrellus*. *Parastrellus hesperus hesperus* occurs in the western quarter of Colorado, and *P. h. maximus* is known from a few specimens from the southeast (D. Armstrong 1972; Ellinwood 1978; G. Freeman 1981).

Natural History

The western pipistrelle is one of the more common bats in the canyon and desert country of the southwestern United States (Barbour and Davis 1969). The animals roost under loose rocks, in crevices or caves, and occasionally in buildings. They will also use the burrows of animals in open desert scrub communities.

These bats fly very early in the evening or even in late afternoon, when canyon walls shade them from the setting sun. The flight pattern is weak and erratic, somewhat butterfly-like. Fluttering flight and small size generally restrict activity to calm weather. On windy evenings they remain in their roosts. In Colorado, as elsewhere, 2 peaks of feeding activity occur, one early in the evening and a second, lesser

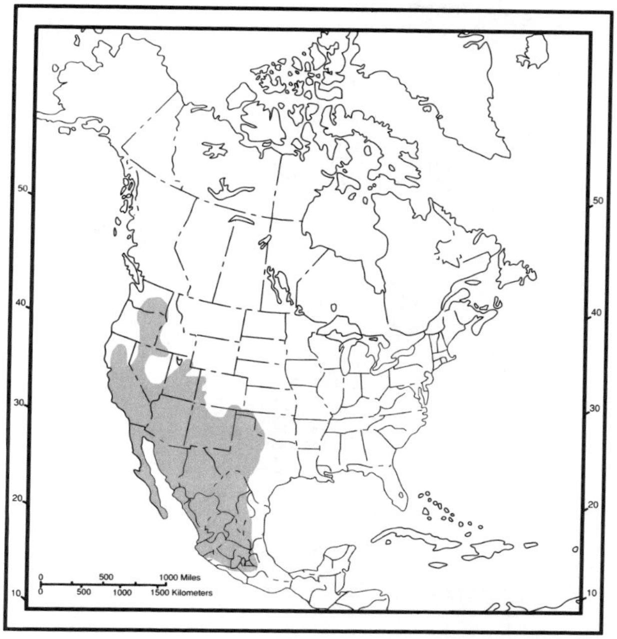

MAP 11-26. Distribution of the western pipistrelle (*Parastrellus hesperus*) in North America.

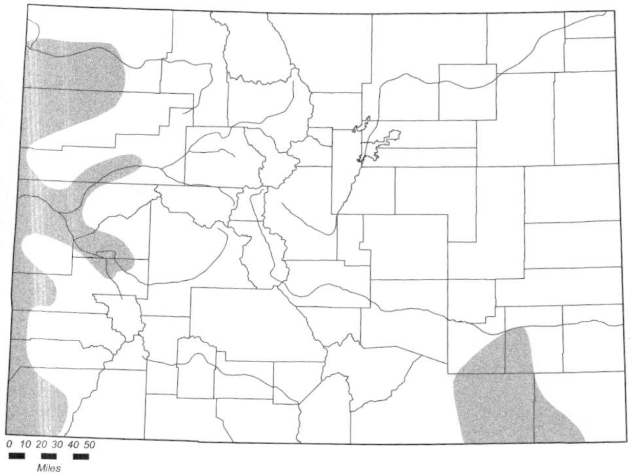

MAP 11-27. Distribution of the western pipistrelle (*Parastrellus hesperus*) in Colorado.

peak at dawn (Ellinwood 1978). Their early foraging may result in some competition with swallows or other diurnal insectivorous birds, but insects are an abundant resource and neither competition nor competitive exclusion has been documented. Reported predators of *P. hesperus* include fish and owls (Sparks et al. 2000).

The western pipistrelle appears to be a rather sedentary bat that roosts and hibernates close to its summer range. In some areas, including Nevada (M. O'Farrell et al. 1967) and Utah (Ruffner et al. 1979), the animals are active even in colder months at temperatures close to 1–2°C (34–36°F). In Colorado National Monument they are active in all months except December, January, and February (P. Miller 1964). D. Armstrong et al. (1994) reported hibernation at 9,500 ft. (2,895 m) in the La Plata Mountains above Mancos.

Populations probably occur in suitable habitat along the entire western margin of Colorado and in extreme southeastern parts of the state. The animals may be observed flying about mist nets, but very few individuals are captured because they readily avoid the nets with their slow, deliberate flight (Barbour and Davis 1969). Future studies may show them to be more widespread than current records indicate.

Young are born in June or July (Krutzsch 1975); twinning apparently is the rule (R. Adams 2003). Small nursery colonies have been reported, as have solitary females with young (Ellinwood 1978).

Perimyotis subflavus

EASTERN PIPISTRELLE, OR TRICOLORED BAT

Description

This is one of the smallest of bats in the United States, only slightly larger than the western pipistrelle. It has distinctly tricolored dorsal hairs, the dark bases and tips being separated by a relatively broad band of paler yellow, and so is called the tricolored bat. The general color of the fur varies from brownish to yellowish gray on the dorsum, with the venter slightly paler. Wing venation is not as pronounced as in the western pipistrelle. The ears are rounded at their tips and of moderate length, barely reaching beyond the tip of the nose if bent forward. The tragus is straight and tapered. Measurements are: total length 70–90 mm; length of tail 32–42 mm; length of hindfoot 8–11 mm; length of ear 12–14 mm; length of forearm 30–35 mm; wingspan 21–26 cm (R. Adams 2003); weight 4.5–8.0 g. The inner upper incisor is bicuspid. The calcar is not keeled.

Distribution

Mostly a species of the Midwest and eastern United States, the eastern pipistrelle was first observed in Colorado in

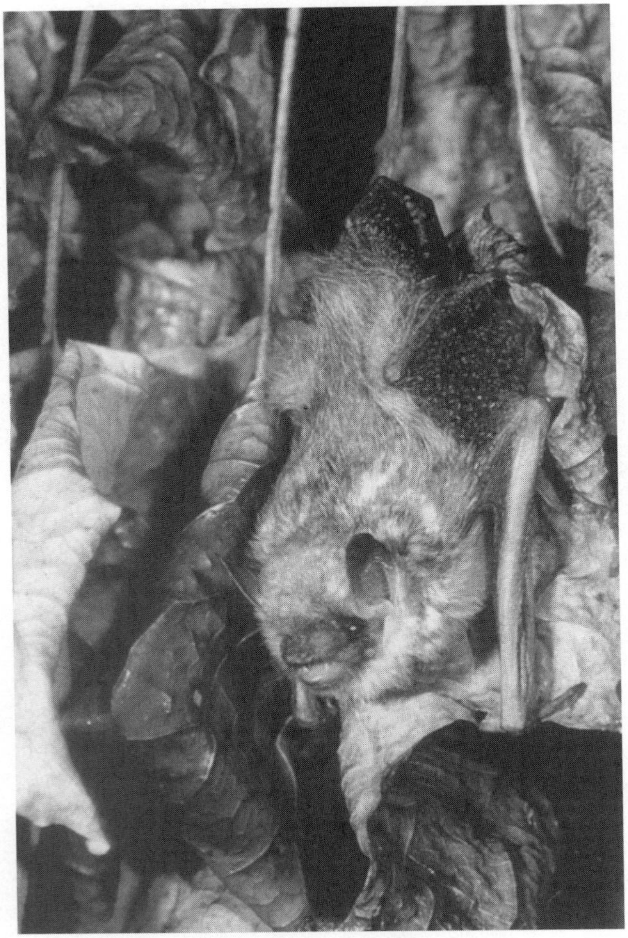

PHOTOGRAPH 11-14. Eastern pipistrelle (*Perimyotis subflavus*). Photograph by Merlin D. Tuttle, Bat Conservation International.

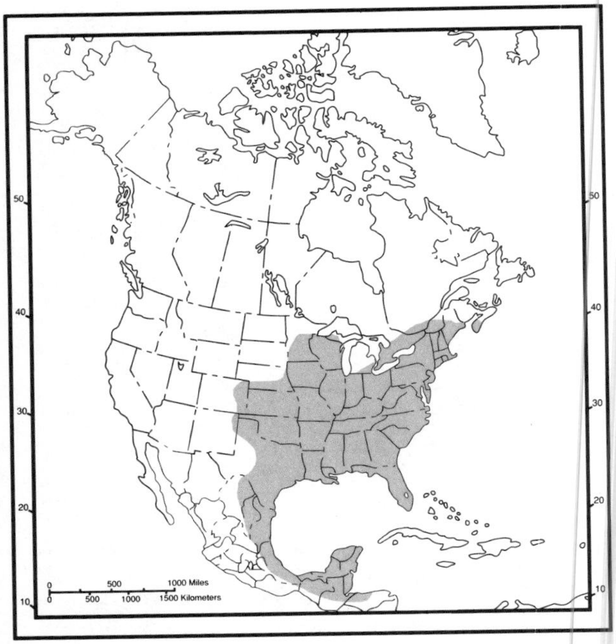

MAP 11-28. Distribution of the eastern pipistrelle (*Perimyotis subflavus*) in North America.

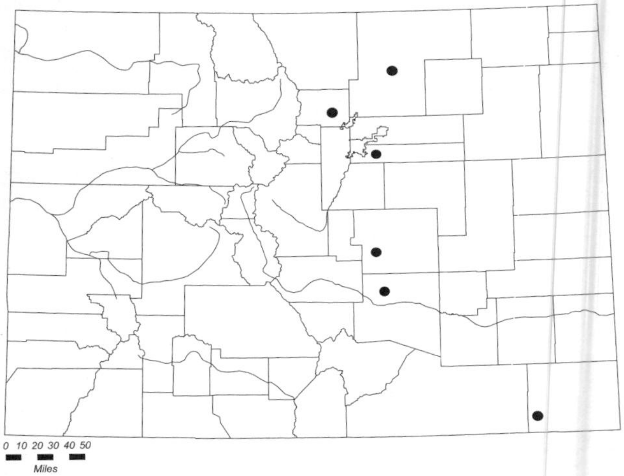

MAP 11-29. Distribution of the eastern pipistrelle (*Perimyotis subflavus*) in Colorado.

early September 1987, when a single adult female was collected on the side of a house in Greeley (J. Fitzgerald et al. 1989). That specimen was reasonably considered as "accidental" or "erratic," rather than marking an expanded geographic range. The site of capture was approximately 480 km northwest of its then-known range in central Kansas. The individual appeared to be in good condition with considerable body fat and no evidence of disease.

D. Armstrong et al. (2006) reported a female obtained in late March 2004 in Boulder. They also noted a previously unpublished record of a female captured in Arapahoe County (locality not specified), probably in late summer or fall 1996, and submitted to the Colorado Department of Health and Environment for rabies testing. Again, these records might have been accidentals, although a specimen from early spring does suggest a resident animal recently emerged from hibernation, reinforcing a suspicion that these animals should now be considered not "accidentals" but part of the fauna of Colorado. Wostl et al. (2009) reported capture of a female in September 2007 in Cottonwood Canyon, western Baca County, and a male in April 2008 on Fort Carson Military Reservation in Pueblo County. Both individuals were documented by photographs and released. The apparently good condition of the animals and their capture early and late in the warmer season of the year suggested to the authors that the eastern pipistrelle is resident in eastern Colorado. K. Geluso et al. (2005) reported new records of eastern pipistrelles from South Dakota, Texas, and New Mexico and concluded that the specimens represented actual expansions of the range of the species rather than accidental records or previously undetected populations.

Use of the generic name *Perimyotis* for the eastern pipistrelle follows Hoofer and Van Den Bussche (2003), who summarized the taxonomic history of this species, the sole member of the genus. Coloradan eastern pipistrelles are assigned on geographic grounds to *P. subflavus subflavus*, the subspecies of the Northern Great Plains.

Natural History

Although the wastern pipestrelle is a common bat over much of the eastern United States, its ecology is not well-known. It is thought to be mostly a bat of open woodlands, typically foraging over water or along the edges of openings. It is an early flier, and its movements are erratic, similar to those of the western pipistrelle. In summer the animals are thought to roost in trees, using foliage for diurnal cover, similar to the behavior of red bats. They seem to be more tolerant of exposure to light than are most other vespertilionids, and they may roost in full (albeit indirect) daylight under porch roofs and similar overhangs. Except for small maternity colonies, the animals are not often found in buildings (Barbour and Davis 1969). Mines, rock crevices, and caves are typical hibernation sites and are often used as summer night roosts as well. Hibernation sites are often in locations warmer than those chosen by other species (R. Raesly and Gates 1987). The bats generally are solitary during summer but considerable numbers may congregate at hibernacula. Swarming may occur in late summer around caves in suitable wintering areas (Barbour and Davis 1969). Moths are a principal food source.

Although reproductive biology is poorly known, adults can be found in breeding condition from November to April in the southeastern U.S. Young are born in late June or early July in the East, with a typical litter size of 2. Mortality is highest in the first several years of life. Females may live to 10 years and some males to 15 years. Eastern pipistrelles are not strongly migratory and they generally seem to stay within 60 to 100 km of hibernacula. Frogs are reported to prey on eastern pipistrelles (Sparks et al 2000), and any opportunistic predator with access to the animals might be expected to take them. Fujita and Kunz (1984) reviewed the literature on the species.

Eptesicus fuscus

BIG BROWN BAT

Description

The big brown bat is a large bat with dorsal color ranging from pale to dark brown. The venter is somewhat paler than the dorsum. Ears, muzzle, and flight membranes are

PHOTOGRAPH 11-15. Big brown bat (*Eptesicus fuscus*). © 1993 Wendy Shattil / Bob Rozinski.

dark. The ears are relatively small and the tragus is broad and rounded. The interfemoral membrane may be sparsely haired. Measurements are: total length 90–138 mm; length of tail 34–56 mm; length of hindfoot 11–13 mm; length of ear 14–18 mm; length of forearm 39–54 mm; wingspan 32–40 cm (R. Adams 2003); weight 12–20 g. The calcar is keeled. The skull (Figure 11-2) is rather large and robust (greatest length, 15–23 mm). To the novice, young individuals of *Eptesicus fuscus* could be confused with some of the *Myotis* species, but the dental formula is different. (*Eptesicus* has only 32 teeth whereas all species of *Myotis* have 38 teeth.) Only *M. volans*, *M. californicus*, and *M. ciliolabrum* have keeled calcars, but the latter 2 species are smaller and generally paler in color than the big brown bat.

Distribution

The big brown bat is one of the most common bats in North America and the species most frequently observed in urban areas. These bats probably occur throughout Colorado in all habitats to elevations as high as 3,800 m (12,500 ft.; R. Adams 2003). Roosting areas on the eastern plains are now available because of human settlement, which provides abandoned buildings and similar cover.

MAP 11-30. Distribution of the big brown bat (*Eptesicus fuscus*) in North America.

Coloradan big brown bats have been allocated to the subspecies *Eptesicus fuscus pallidus* (the type locality of which is Boulder; R. Young 1908), based on pelage color and the fact that litter size is almost always 1 (J. Howard 1967). Recent molecular studies suggest a more interesting and complex evolutionary pattern than is expressed by current subspecific nomenclature. M. Neubaum et al. (2007) studied big brown bats from Colorado's Eastern Slope eastward to Morgan County and south to Pueblo County, with intensive study in the vicinity of Fort Collins. Based on studies of mitochondrial DNA, they detected eastern and western "lineages" that showed 10.3 percent sequence divergence, indicating long-term segregation. Individuals of both lineages were found in 19 or 20 maternity colonies studied. The lineages did not differ in forearm length (a proxy for overall size), color, or litter size (which usually was one). The authors concluded that big brown bats in the region represent populations only recently merged, after a substantial period of segregation during the Late Pleistocene. Specifically, they speculated that urbanization and irrigation beginning in the mid-nineteenth century allowed expansion of eastern populations westward.

Natural History

This bat is found in almost every habitat in the United States. Unlike many bats, the big brown bat is common in urban areas (Tuttle 1988) and frequents occupied buildings as roost sites. The animals also use other man-made structures, hollow trees, rock crevices, caves, bridges, and practi-

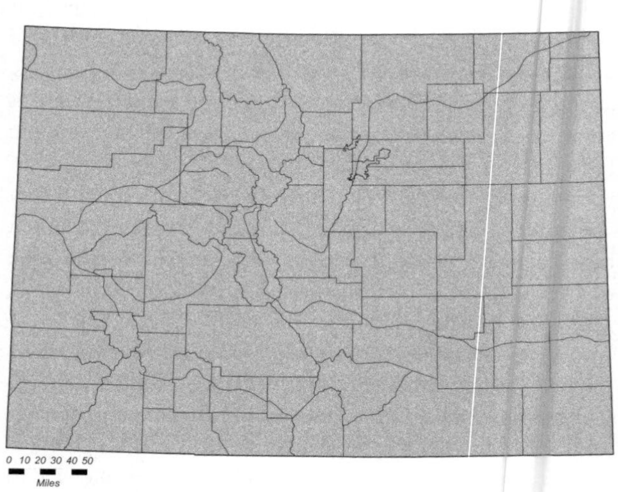

MAP 11-31. Distribution of the big brown bat (*Eptesicus fuscus*) in Colorado.

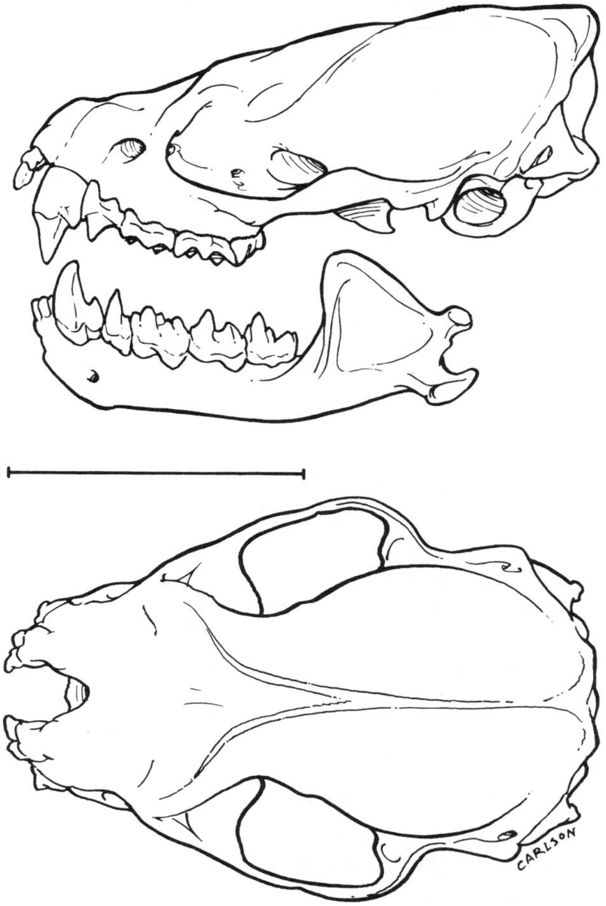

FIGURE 11-2. Lateral and dorsal views of the skull of a big brown bat (*Eptesicus fuscus*). Scale = 1 cm.

cally any other location that offers concealment and cover from the elements. Kunz and Reynolds (2003) stressed the importance of buildings to bats and bat conservation. Ultrasonic vocalizations of big brown bats may be sexually dimorphic, depending on context. Specifically, Grilliot et al. (2009) found sexual dimorphism in calls recorded in an enclosed, anechoic chamber but calls were not dimorphic when bats were flying on tethers in the open.

Big brown bats generally emerge from the day roost at dusk (Gillis 1968) and fly with a steady, straight flight. Foraging generally occurs at altitudes of 7–10 m. Foraging habitat is frequently a considerable distance away from the roost. Big brown bats commuted as far as 20 km from urban roosting areas in and near Denver to forage at Rocky Mountain Arsenal National Wildlife Refuge (Everette et al. 2001). Individuals tend to patrol the same feeding areas night after night (Goehring 1972). The diet consists mostly of beetles (G. L. Phillips 1966); moths are less important to this species than they are to many other bats (Black 1974; G. Freeman 1981). Corcoran et al. (2009) discovered that a species of tiger moth (*Bertholdia trigona*) produces ultrasonic clicks that "jam" the sonar system of big brown bats (and may defend against predation by other bats as well). Big brown bats are efficient foragers and may fill their stomachs in an hour or less. They use feeding stations or perches where they rest between foraging bouts or they return to the day roost. Guano and food debris—such as moths' wings or beetle-wing covers (elytrae)—on a doorstep or porch are signs of such a resting station. *E. fuscus* is also known to prey on smaller bats (Sparks et al. 2000).

D. Neubaum et al. (2005, 2006) reported on a 3-year study of movements of big brown bats from summer habitat in buildings in Fort Collins to hibernacula in rock crevices in the Upper Poudre River watershed to the northwest. Sites selected were deep enough to maintain temperatures near but above freezing and had north to northwest exposure, thus precluding direct solar gain. Hibernacula ranged to 2,876 m (nearly 9,450 ft.) in elevation. During summer females were more abundant than males at lower elevations. Sex ratios were equal at higher elevations in late summer and fall, however, when breeding probably occurred.

Beyond that study, little is known about the location of hibernacula in Colorado. Big brown bats have been reported wintering in mines and tunnels in the state (D. Armstrong 1972), and occasionally a few are discovered in an attic or inside the walls of a building being demolished or remodeled. The numbers thus encountered in no way compare to the densities observed in summer, when nursery colonies may exceed 300 bats.

Mating occurs in fall and winter and spermatozoa are stored in the female's reproductive tract until spring. Testes are scrotal in August and yearlings do not reproduce. D. Neubaum et al. (2007) studied selection of maternity roost sites in buildings in Fort Collins. Buildings selected had larger exit points located higher from the ground and had warmer average temperatures than did a random sample of buildings. Further, roosts were in areas of lower building density, higher street density, and lower traffic count. Because of this selectivity, the authors cautioned that closing buildings to roosting could be detrimental to bat populations because suitable alternative roosts might be unavailable. Female big brown bats in maternity colonies in Fort Collins moved within or between buildings in response to high summer temperatures (>90°F [>32°C]) (L. E. Ellison et al. 2007).

Parturition occurs about 60 days after fertilization. Lactating females have been collected from June to September, but highest numbers are found in July (R. Adams 1988). Young are born naked and helpless, weighing about 3.5 g, but begin to fly at 3 to 5 weeks of age (Kunz 1974; R. Adams 2003). The usual litter size in the eastern United States is 2, but a single young is the mode in the West (Cockrum 1955; Christian 1956; D. Neubaum et al. 2007).

As with many other bats, the big brown bat forms nursery colonies during the summer months, and males are segregated from females and young. Nursery colonies may be as large as a couple of hundred individuals but average 1 or 2 dozen. O'Shea et al. (2010) detailed recruitment of big brown bats in Fort Collins. In Maryland, young were apparently born weighing 2.5 g in maternity colonies in hollow trees (Christian 1956). In late June or July, the colony moved to cover behind window shutters, where they remained until October. Considerable shifting occurs, and males and females roost together in July. Females first give birth at 1 year of age.

A number of predators have been reported to capture big brown bats, including frogs, snakes, owls, diurnal raptors, weasels, raccoons, and house cats (Sparks et al. 2000). Ectoparasites include mites and chiggers, ticks, bat flies, bat bugs (closely related to—and frequently confused with—bedbugs), and fleas (Pearce and O'Shea 2007). Much of the focus of the Fort Collins Bat Project has been on *E. fuscus*. For detailed information see Shankar et al. (2004), Wimsatt et al. 2005), and L. E. Ellison et al. (2006).

Nycticeius humeralis

EVENING BAT

Description

Nycticeius humeralis is a small bat (forearm 34–38 mm) with grayish brown fur and pronounced facial glands. Adults have a single upper incisor on either side of the upper jaw and only 30 total teeth, the fewest of any bat in western North America.

Distribution

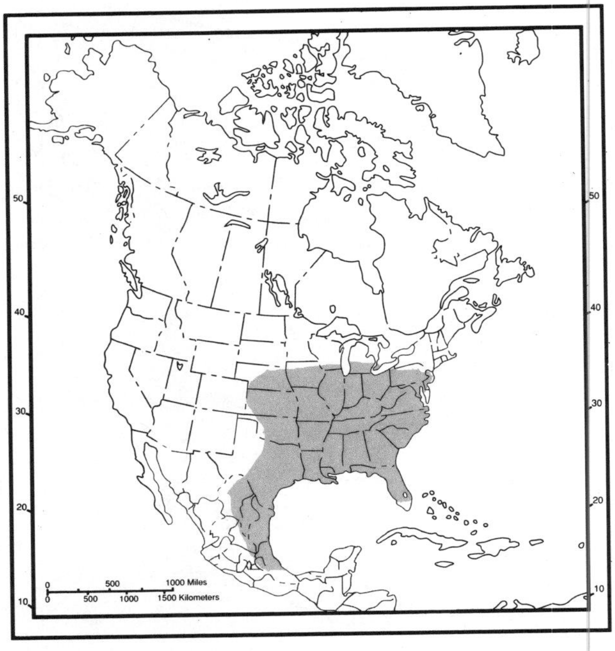

MAP 11-32. Distribution of the evening bat (*Nycticeius humeralis*) in North America.

The evening bat has yet to be reported in Colorado but is expected, as there are reports from nearby in Kansas and Nebraska. Phelps et al. (2008) reported a male evening bat from Stanton County, Kansas, about 2 km east of the Baca County, Colorado, border. More recently, Serbousek and Geluso (2009) reported lactating female and newly volant young evening bats (*Nycticeius humeralis*) from southwestern Nebraska, in the Republican River watershed of Hitchcock County, within about 60 mi. (about 100 km) of the Colorado border. In short, the animals may eventually be found to occur in riparian woodlands of the Republican watershed in northeastern Colorado (which includes the Arikaree River) and the Arkansas and Cimarron watersheds of southeastern Colorado.

Natural History

Few adult males have been reported from the northern part of the range (from Nebraska and Kansas eastward to the Atlantic seaboard). The breeding range of the animals is not known. This is a tree-roosting bat that also inhabits buildings but seldom utilizes caves. The animals probably are migratory, with winter records mostly from the southern United States, from Texas to Florida. Watkins (1972) reviewed the literature on the species.

Euderma maculatum

SPOTTED BAT

Description

The spotted bat is a beautiful and unmistakable animal: a medium-sized bat with enormous ears and a distinctive black dorsum with 3 large white spots. The venter has a frosted appearance because the hairs have black bases and white tips. The ears are pink to gray-brown. White hairs are usually present at the posterior base of each ear. Measurements are: total length 107–119 mm; length of ear 37–47 mm; length of forearm 48–52 mm; wingspan 34–38 cm (R. Adams 2003); weight 13–14 g. The skull measures 18–19 mm in greatest length. The braincase is elongate and the zygomatic arches are stout and expanded near their

PHOTOGRAPH 11-16. Spotted bat (*Euderma maculatum*). Photograph by Roger W. Barbour.

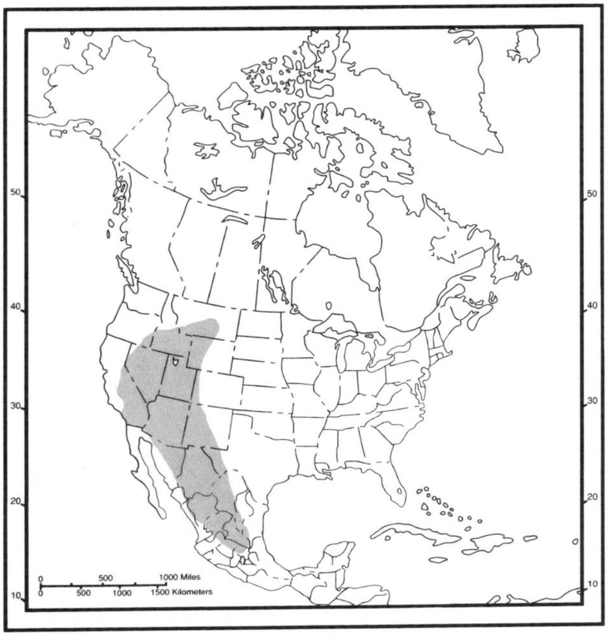

MAP 11-33. Distribution of the spotted bat (*Euderma maculatum*) in North America.

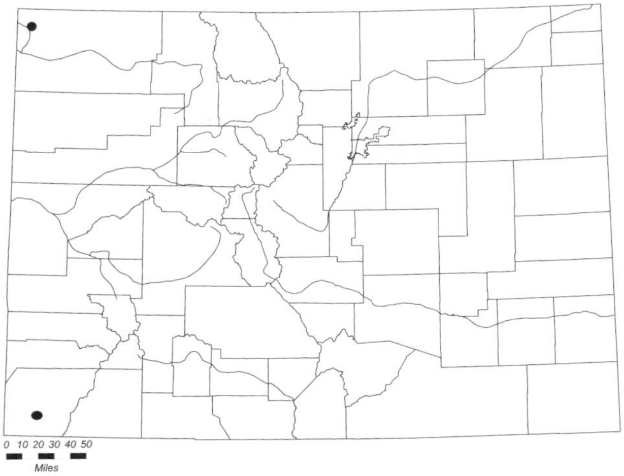

MAP 11-34. Distribution of the spotted bat (*Euderma maculatum*) in Colorado.

midpoints. The auditory bullae are elliptical and enlarged. The lower canine is somewhat reduced in size.

Distribution

The spotted bat is a species of the interior West. Finley and Creasy (1982) reported the first record from Colorado, an individual from Brown's Park, Moffat County; Storz (1995) studied the animals in that area both visually and acoustically, and Siemers and Schorr (2006) reported additional captures nearby. In surveys in Mesa Verde National Park, a spotted bat was heard in Morfield Canyon, and skulls of 3 individuals were recovered from pellets of spotted owls in Navajo Canyon (Chung-MacCoubrey and Bogan 2003). The species likely will be captured elsewhere in suitable habitat in western and south-central Colorado. Observations of the species range in elevation from below sea level in Southern California to 3,230 m (10,600 ft.) in New Mexico. *Euderma maculatum* is monotypic; that is, no appreciable geographic variation and subspecies have been recognized.

Natural History

The ecology and distribution of the spotted bat have been poorly understood until recent years. The most extensive studies are from Utah (Poché and Bailey 1974) and Texas (Easterla and Whitaker 1972; Easterla 1973). In Colorado, the animal has been captured (or monitored acoustically; Navo et al. 1992; Storz 1995; Siemers and Schorr 2006) in ponderosa pine woodlands or montane forests, piñon-juniper woodlands, and riparian vegetation; over sand and gravel bars; and in open semidesert shrublands. Rocky cliffs are necessary to provide suitable cracks and crevices for roosting, as is access to water. The animals also roost in and on buildings (Sherwin and Gannon 2005). The animals show apparent seasonal change in habitat, seemingly occupying ponderosa pine woodlands in the reproductive season and lower elevations at other times of the year.

Individual spotted bats forage alone in open habitat, flying 5–10 m aboveground. Foraging usually begins shortly after dark (Navo et al. 1992; Storz 1995) and continues throughout the night, mostly over open areas (Storz 1995). The diet appears to consist of moths, with only the abdomens eaten, but grasshoppers, beetles, katydids, and perhaps smaller insects may also be taken. Their calls (which are audible to humans, thus facilitating their detection) apparently help individuals space themselves in suitable habitat (M. Leonard and Fenton 1984). Peregrine falcons are known to prey on spotted bats (Sparks et al. 2000).

Little is known of reproduction in spotted bats, although lactating females have been captured from June until mid-July in various areas of the range. Litter size is thought to be 1. Watkins (1977) and R. Luce and Keinath (2007) reviewed the literature on the species.

Corynorhinus townsendii

TOWNSEND'S BIG-EARED BAT

Description

Townsend's big-eared bat is of medium size. The color is brown to grayish brown and the ventral surface is slightly paler in color than the dorsal surface. There is a pair of protruding glandular masses between the eyes and the nostrils. The hairs are usually brown at the tips and grayish at their bases. The markedly long ears have conspicuous transverse ridges. The tragus is well developed. Measurements are: total length 90–112 mm; length of tail 35–54 mm; length of hindfoot 9–12 mm; length of ear 30–38 mm; length of forearm 39–48 mm; wingspan 30–34 cm (R. Adams 2003); weight 9–14 g. The skull is slender, the rostrum is rather short, and the auditory bullae are large. The greatest length of the skull is 15–17 mm. The calcar is not keeled as it is in Allen's big-eared bat (*Idionycteris phyllotis*), which it greatly resembles. *C. townsendii* also lacks the well-developed lappets that project over the forehead of *I. phyllotis*.

PHOTOGRAPH 11-17. Townsend's big-eared bat (*Corynorhinus townsendii*). Photograph by Merlin D. Tuttle, Bat Conservation International.

Distribution

A western species, Townsend's big-eared bat occurs over most of the western two-thirds of Colorado and in roughlands of the extreme southeastern part of the state to elevations of about 2,900 m (9,500 ft.). D. Armstrong (1972:73) mapped a single subspecies of *Corynorhinus townsendii* in Colorado, following Handley (1959). Molecular genetic analyses (Piaggio and Perkins 2005; Piaggio, Miller, et al. 2009; Piaggio, Navo, and Stihler 2009) have demonstrated that Coloradan bats represent 2 "phylogroups." Those authors suggested that Townsend's big-eared bats of lower elevations on the Western Slope appear to represent *C. t. townsendii* whereas *C. t. pallescens* is the subspecies of the central mountains and the foothills of the Eastern Slope of Colorado. Further, they noted that individuals of both "phylogroups" occur in Boulder County, a fact that they attributed hypothetically to secondary contact between formerly isolated populations. Work by S. Smith et al. (2008) in western Oklahoma augmented and corroborated major findings of Piaggio and Perkins (2005).

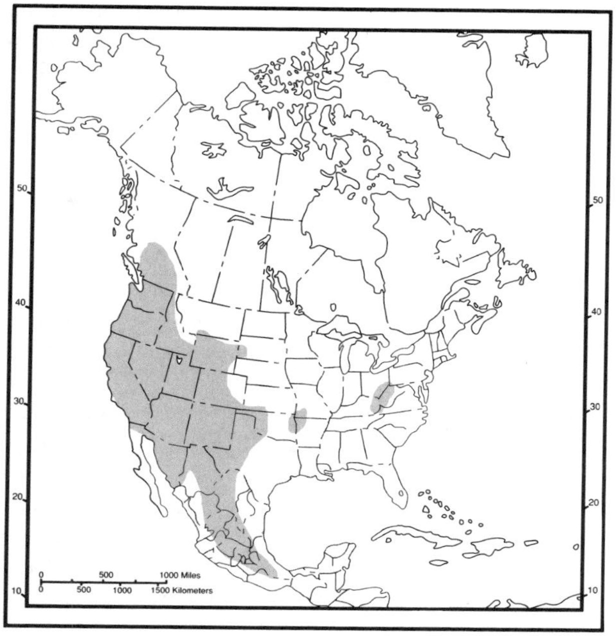

MAP 11-35. Distribution of Townsend's big-eared bat (*Corynorhinus townsendii*) in North America.

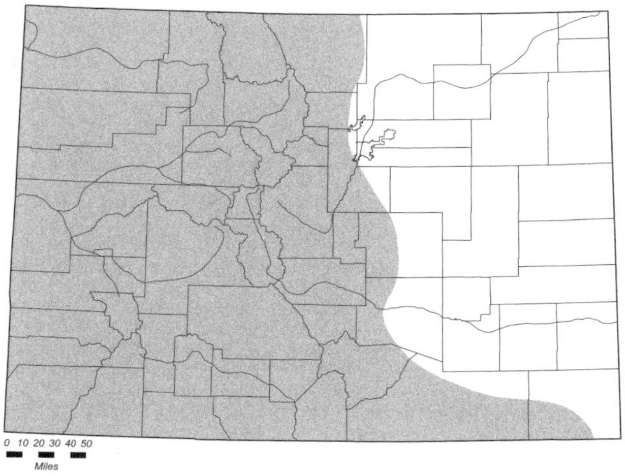

MAP 11-36. Distribution of Townsend's big-eared bat (*Corynorhinus townsendii*) in Colorado.

Natural History

Townsend's big-eared bat is a western species occupying semidesert shrublands, piñon-juniper woodlands, and open montane forests. Where the species does occur on the Great Plains, it is restricted to deciduous woodland near suitable caves and rocky outcrops. It is frequently associated with caves and abandoned mines for day roosts and hibernacula (Sherwin et al. 2000, 2003) but will also use abandoned buildings and crevices on rock cliffs for refuge in summer. One of us (DMA) has observed a single Townsend's big-eared bat over the course of several summers roosting by day between the ridgepole and the sheet-metal roof of a little-used bunkhouse at Sylvan Dale Guest Ranch's Cow Camp, above Cedar Cove, at an elevation of 6,240 ft. Several animals were captured in an abandoned mansion near Larkspur, Douglas County, in September 2010 (J. Fitzgerald et al. 1989). In January 1990 a hibernaculum was examined in an active gold mine at 9,500 ft. (2,895 m) in the La Plata Mountains near Mancos (D. Armstrong et al. 1994), and a survey in 2001 and 2002 found them in Honkey Cave, Garfield County, at 9,860 ft. (Siemers 2002). D. Armstrong (1972) reported use of water diversion tunnels by this and associated species (*M. ciliolabrum* and *E. fuscus*) of hibernating bats in the Laramie Foothills of northern Larimer County. R. Finley et al. (1983) reported a hibernaculum in a limestone cave in Rio Blanco County. Townsend's big-eared bats occupy caves and mines throughout the year. However, Ingersoll et al. (2010) demonstrated that microclimatic preferences of the bats differ between autumnal swarming roosts and winter hibernacula. Specifically, the warmer temperatures of swarming roosts allow more economical arousal from daily torpor, whereas the cooler temperatures of hibernacula suppress nocturnal arousal and conserve energy. Data were compiled from 1997 to 2002 by the Colorado Division of Wildlife's Bats / Inactive Mines Project. Townsend's big-eared bats are relatively sedentary. They do not move long distances from hibernacula to summer roosts, nor do they move far from their day roosts to forage.

Townsend's big-eared bats breed in late fall and winter while in their hibernacula. Females store sperm until spring. Gestation lasts 50–60 days and a single young is born in May or June. Lactating females were captured in Morfield Canyon, Mesa Verde National Park, in the first week of August (Chung-MacCoubrey and Bogan 2003). Females assemble into nursery colonies of a few to several hundred individuals, forming dense clusters, apparently to take advantage of shared metabolic heat. Warm nursery sites are essential for reproductive success (Humphrey and Kunz 1976). Females leave the young in the roost when they forage. Young develop rapidly, becoming volant at 3 to 4 weeks of age. Adult males are segregated from females at this time, either in the same cave or in separate roost sites. Males are usually found as solitary individuals or in small groups. At summer roosts individuals do not hide in cracks or crevices but may hang exposed from the roof or walls of the chamber, taking flight if disturbed.

These bats are late flyers, generally emerging from the roost well after dark. Caddisflies appear to be a staple of their diet (G. Freeman 1984), which also includes moths, flies, and other insects. They are gleaners, picking insects from leaves. Foraging usually is over water, along the margins of vegetation, or over sagebrush. Their late flight, reclusive habits, and capable avoidance of mist nets may allow this species to go undetected in an area unless roost sites are found.

During hibernation Townsend's big-eared bats coil their long ears back and fluff the fur to conserve heat. They are very sensitive to fluctuations in temperature and humidity and move in response to them. Hibernacula with the appropriate stable temperature and humidity appear to be a limiting resource for this bat. Both males and females lose half their body weight before spring, leading to the suggestion that winter mortality may be a prevailing factor limiting populations (Humphrey and Kunz 1976). Furthermore, they are easily disturbed and leave caves or mines where human harassment occurs, even though such disturbance may be unintentional. This sensitivity suggests that caves and mines should be closed or access strictly limited to protect the animals. The ecology and habits of this species were reviewed and summarized by Barbour and Davis (1969), Kunz and Martin (1982), and Gruver and Keinath (2006).

Idionycteris phyllotis

ALLEN'S BIG-EARED BAT

Description

Allen's big-eared bat is a medium-sized bat, tan to olive-brown to nearly black on the dorsum with the venter slightly paler. The bases of all hairs are black or brown. A blackish shoulder patch is usually present, as is a patch of white hair at the base of each ear. Measurements are: total length 103–121 mm; length of tail 46–55 mm; length of hindfoot 9–12 mm; length of ear 38–43 mm; length of forearm 43–49 mm; wingspan 31–34 cm (R. Adams 2003); weight 10–12 g. Greatest length of the skull is 17.5 mm, and the breadth of the braincase is more than half that. This bat has conspicuous accessory facial lappets, a pair of leaf-like structures that project from the bases of the ears over the forehead. These lappets distinguish this species immediately from any other bat in Colorado. The calcar is keeled.

PHOTOGRAPH 11-18. Allen's big-eared bat (*Idionycteris phyllotis*). Photo by J. Scott Altenbach.

Distribution

A species of Mexico and the Southwest, Allen's big-eared bat was first documented in Colorado by M. Hayes et al. (2009), from La Sal Creek, western Montrose County. Identification was based on analysis of the distinctive echolocatory call (see R. Adams 2003 for sonogram). The species had long been suspected to occur in Colorado, as it was known from the canyon country of southeastern Utah, from piñon-juniper woodlands close to the Colorado border (Black 1970; D. Armstrong 1974).

This bat formerly was known as *Plecotus phyllotis*, and the vernacular name "Mexican big-eared bat" has been ap-

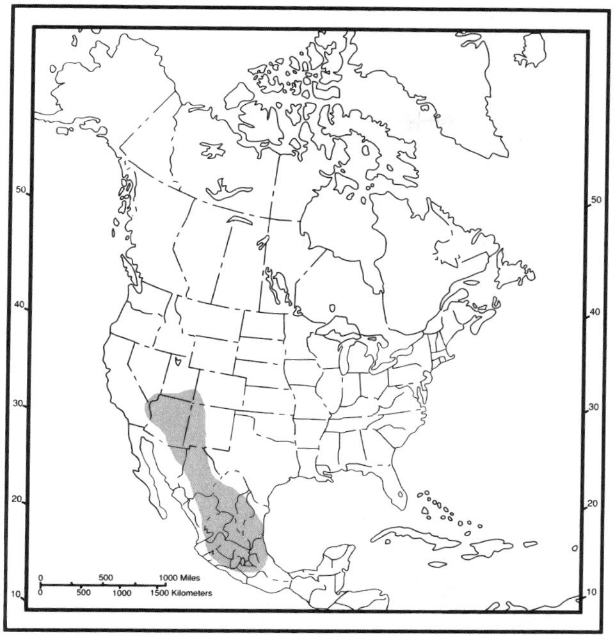

MAP 11-37. Distribution of Allen's big-eared bat (*Idionycteris phyllotis*) in North America.

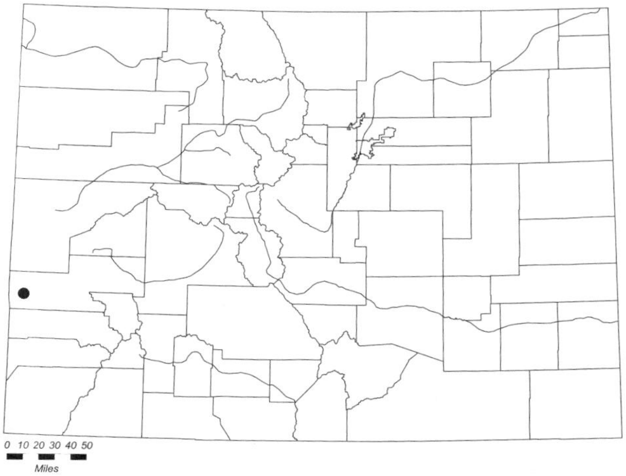

MAP 11-38. Distribution of Allen's big-eared bat (*Idionycteris phyllotis*) in Colorado.

plied to the animals. As now understood, the genus *Idionycteris* contains a single species. On geographic grounds, the subspecies in Colorado is *I. phyllotis hualapaiensis*, named from a type locality in Mojave County, west-central Arizona (Tumlison 1993).

Natural History

Allen's big-eared bat seems to be most typically associated with shrublands and ponderosa pine and piñon-juniper woodland. It also has been captured in riparian cottonwood stands in the Southwest. The recent recording of the bat in Colorado (M. Hayes et al. 2009) was made in riparian vegetation in the narrow canyon of La Sal Creek, in a landscape generally dominated by piñon-juniper woodland. Snag ponderosa pines were important as nursery roosts to this and other bats in northern Arizona (Rabe et al. 1998). Maternity roosts in southwestern Utah were in cracks in the top half of the northwest face of a cliff about 150 m high (Siders and Jolley 2009).

Similar to Townsend's big-eared bat, Allen's big-eared bat prefers caves, mines, and similar shelters for day roosts and also utilizes cracks and spaces between boulders and fallen rock. Roosts may be shared with other species, such as the fringed myotis and Townsend's big-eared bat. Known elevational range is from about 1,100 to 3,225 m (3,500–9,800 ft.); the La Sal Creek record (M. Hayes et al. 2009) was at an elevation of 1,715 m.

This bat seems to fly relatively late, at least several hours after dark; calls reported by M. Hayes et al. (2009) were recorded from 2100 to 0220 hours on August 18, 2006. Major foods of *I. phyllotis* include moths and beetles that are probably gleaned from the ground or vegetation. Reproductive biology is poorly known, but 1 young per year is reported. The literature was reviewed by Czaplewski (1983).

Antrozous pallidus

PALLID BAT

Description

The pallid bat is a large, pale yellowish gray bat with big ears. The eyes are large and the face has numerous sebaceous glands that resemble warts. Measurements are: total length 90–113 mm; length of tail 40–47 mm; length of hindfoot 10–12 mm; length of ear 23–37 mm; length of forearm 48–60 mm; wingspan 37–41 cm (R. Adams 2003); weight 14–17 g. The skull has a large braincase, large auditory bullae, and a relatively long rostrum. Large size, pale color, and dental formula distinguish this from other bats in Colorado.

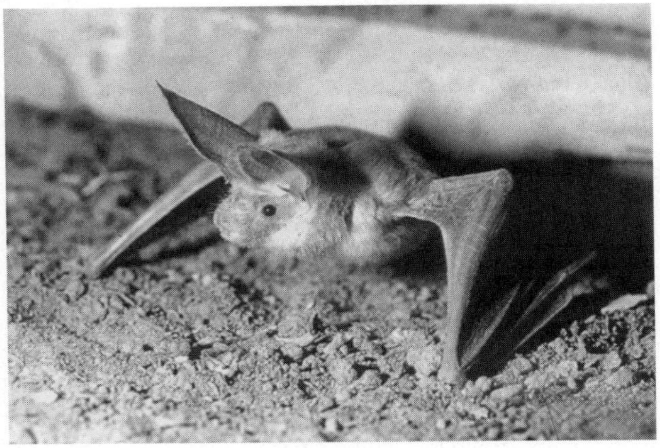

PHOTOGRAPH 11-19. Pallid bat (*Antrozous pallidus*). Photograph by Claude Steelman / Wildshots.

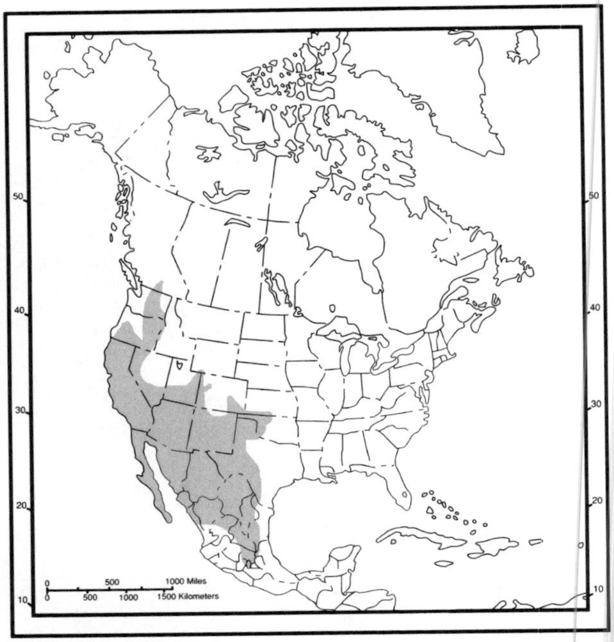

MAP 11-39. Distribution of the pallid bat (*Antrozous pallidus*) in North America.

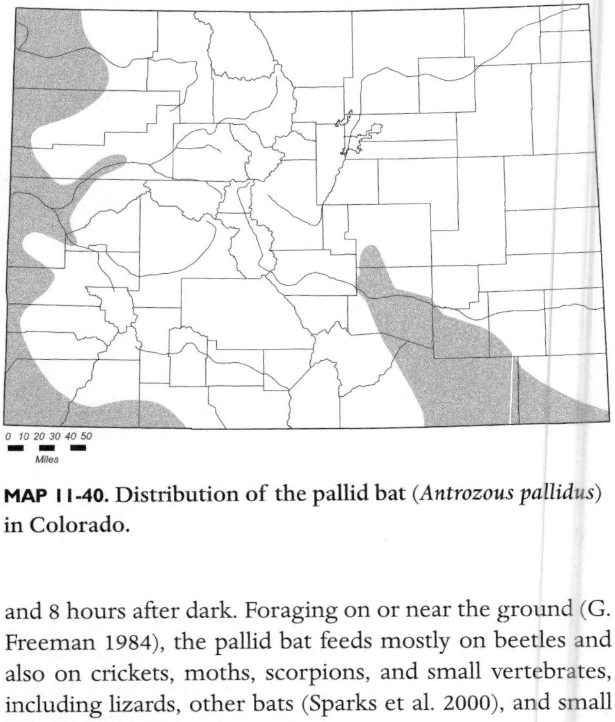

MAP 11-40. Distribution of the pallid bat (*Antrozous pallidus*) in Colorado.

Distribution

While the pallid bat is mostly a western species, one subspecies, *Antrozous pallidus pallidus*, is found in much of the semiarid canyon country of western Colorado and similar rocky habitat in the southeastern corner of the state. Stromberg (1982) reported the species from near Torrington, Wyoming, signaling its possible occurrence in northeastern Colorado. The roughlands along the Colorado-Wyoming border in northern Weld and Logan counties might provide suitable habitat.

Natural History

The pallid bat is found mostly in semidesert shrublands, montane shrublands, piñon-juniper woodlands, and riparian woodland in foothills and canyon country. Cliff faces with crevices and fissures, shallow caves, or human dwellings are used for day roosts (O'Shea and Vaughan 1977). Night roosts in the high desert of north-central Oregon were mostly in buildings (Lewis 1994); pallid bats switch roosts frequently (Lewis 1995). Males and females may segregate from one another at roosts or seasonally. Pallid bats are not thought to be highly migratory and it is likely that they hibernate in Colorado, although hibernacula have not been located.

The pallid bat generally begins to forage an hour or so after dark, later than most species of *Myotis*, western pipistrelles, and the big brown bat, all of which may forage in the same areas. Ellinwood (1978), however, observed pallid bats leaving roosts before dark in southeastern Colorado and also reported bimodal peaks of feeding, at about 2 and 8 hours after dark. Foraging on or near the ground (G. Freeman 1984), the pallid bat feeds mostly on beetles and also on crickets, moths, scorpions, and small vertebrates, including lizards, other bats (Sparks et al. 2000), and small mice. While foraging, pallid bats emit clicks audible to the human ear. Reported predators of pallid bats include frogs, snakes, owls, and diurnal raptors (D. W. Sparks et al. 2000). Torpor has been described in day-roosting pallid bats at the northern limits of their range in the Okanagan Valley of southern British Columbia (Rambaldini and Brigham 2008). We might expect similar behavior at the upper elevational limits of their range in Colorado.

Reproductive biology is poorly understood. Copulation probably occurs in fall and winter. Gestation is thought to take about 9 weeks. Females hang upright when giving birth and catch the young in the uropatagium. Two young, naked and blind at birth, are the mode. Eyes open by the ninth day and young are furred by day 24. Young pallid bats can fly by 6 weeks of age. Births in Colorado probably occur in June. Information on natural history was reviewed by Orr (1954) and Hermanson and O'Shea (1983).

12

Order Carnivora

Carnivores

The order Carnivora is a diverse group of mammals, including both terrestrial (fissiped) and marine (pinniped) species. Terrestrial forms range in size from the huge brown and polar bears, weighing more than 700 kg, to the diminutive least weasel, which weighs only 50 g. Marine carnivores include the true seals, the fur seals (or sea lions), and the walrus. Elephant seals are larger than any of the land carnivores; bulls weigh up to 3,600 kg.

Marine carnivores formerly were often treated as a separate order, the Pinnipedia (G. Simpson 1945; Ewer 1973; Lawlor 1979; Nowak 1999). Today pinnipeds usually are considered to be carnivores (McKenna and Bell 1997; Wozencraft 1989, 2005; Bininda-Emonds et al. 2007), but there is no firm agreement on whether the group is a natural (monophyletic) one. Some fossil evidence suggests a diphyletic origin for the pinnipeds: fur seals and walruses took to the Pacific Ocean possibly from ursid ancestors; true seals entered the Atlantic Ocean from otter-like ancestors around 25 million years ago (Tedford 1976). Other evidence, combining morphology and biochemistry or molecular genetics, suggests that the pinnipeds are monophyletic (Arnason and Widegren 1986; Wyss 1987, 1988, 1989; Bininda-Emonds et al. 2007). In any event, they belong in the Carnivora (Stucky and McKenna 1993). Flynn and Wesley-Hunt (2005) and K. Rose (2006) reviewed the fossil history of the order. The 2-volume set edited by Gittleman (1989, 1996) provides efficient entry into many aspects of the world of carnivores.

Within the terrestrial carnivores, there are 12 families, some 105 genera, and about 250 species. By comparison there are 3 families, 21 genera, and 36 species of pinnipeds (D. Wilson and Reeder 2005). The carnivores evolved in the Early Paleocene, probably from insectivore ancestors, or possibly from lineages closer to the primates and bats. The oldest known fossils, small arboreal viverrid-like miacids, are from the Eocene in western North America. Early in their evolution the carnivores split into 2 lineages (Bininda-Emonds 2007), usually treated as suborders (D. Wilson and Reeder 2005). Feliform ("cat-shaped") carnivores include cats, civets, mongooses, hyenas, and some less familiar families. Caniform ("dog-shaped") carnivores include not only the dogs but also bears, weasels, skunks, raccoons, and "pinnipeds." A recent "supertree" (Bininda-Emonds et al. 2007) suggests that these major branches of the family tree of carnivores may date back nearly to the Cretaceous/Tertiary boundary, some 65 million years ago. Agnarsson et al. (2009) provided a molecular phylogeny of the Carnivora, underscoring the subdivision of the group into feliforms and caniforms—cats and their kin versus dogs and their kin. The study included some 90 percent of species in the order.

Although there were numerous carnivorous marsupials, terrestrial members of the Carnivora were absent from the Australian region until the dingo (*Canis lupus*—sensu Wozencraft 2005) was introduced by humans. In part because of the commercial value for furs of fissiped carnivores, introductions have led to the establishment of populations of various fissiped carnivores worldwide except Antarctica.

The carnivores represent a broad adaptive radiation in size, locomotion, dentition and diet, behavior, and reproductive patterns. Terrestrial carnivores are plantigrade or digitigrade with 4 or 5 toes. All digits are clawed, and neither hallux nor pollex is apposable. As is typical of many cursorial mammals, the clavicle is reduced or absent. The radius is separate from the ulna, and the tibia is not fused to the fibula. The atlas has large winglike processes. The sacrum is well developed, usually consisting of 2 fused vertebrae. Dentition is variably modified for true carnivory, insectivory, or omnivory. The dental formula (3/3, 1/1, 2–4/2–4, 1–4/1–5) ranges from 26 teeth in the aardwolf to 50 teeth in the bat-eared fox, both extremes being insectivorous mammals. Two species, the insectivorous sloth bear and the sea otter (which feeds mostly on marine invertebrates), have lost 2 upper and 2 lower incisors, respectively. In many carnivores the last upper premolar and the first lower molar form powerful shearing teeth, the so-called carnassial pair. Among Coloradan carnivores, the carnassials are best developed in the canids and felids; moderately developed in the procyonids, mustelids, and mephitids; and least developed in the bears, which have bunodont, crushing teeth well suited to their generally omnivorous diet. The canines are typically enlarged, pointed, and curved, serving as piercing and stabbing weapons. The orbits communicate with the temporal fossae, and the zygomatic arch is strongly developed. The braincase is large and the brain has well-developed cerebral hemispheres.

Most land carnivores are solitary except during the breeding season, although some species pair (foxes) and others live in packs (wolves, dholes, Cape hunting dogs). The uterus is bicornuate or bipartite. The placenta is usually endotheliochorial in structure and zonary in shape. Males have a baculum (Ramm 2007). Females of most species have a single litter each year, although some species (e.g., bears) have young only every second or third year and a few species of viverrids and herpestids (civets, mongooses and kin) have 2 or more litters per year. Gestation periods range from about 50 to 250 days, the wide variation being related in part to body size but also to delayed implantation of the early embryo in a number of mustelids and ursids. Mead (1989), S. Ferguson et al. (1996), S. Ferguson and Larivière (2002), and Larivière and Ferguson (2002, 2003) provided insight into reproductive strategies (including delayed implantation) in the evolutionary ecology of carnivores. Litter size ranges from 1 in some ursids to 13 in some mustelids. Neonates are typically altricial but usually are haired. One or both parents are involved in rearing the young and learned behaviors are important in the development of hunting skills. For authoritative coverage of a range of topics in the biology of carnivores, see Gittleman (1989, 1996). Gittleman et al. (2008) provided a variety of perspectives on the conservation of carnivores. Conservation of carnivores is a major issue, not merely because a number of species are "charismatic" but because most species are high on the food chain so they necessarily have less biomass (which often translates to smaller populations) than the prey on which they depend. J. L. Weaver et al. (1996) reviewed the conservation of carnivores in the Rocky Mountain region.

Because of wide variation in size and details of food habits and habitats, a half dozen or more species of carnivores may be present at any given locality. Brinkerhoff, Collinge, et al. (2008) reported on diversity in an important aspect of a particular local carnivore assemblage. Specifically, they noted levels of plague antibodies in a variety of carnivores from eastern Boulder County. Overall prevalence was 2.4 percent, the highest incidence being in red foxes (1 of 3 individuals = 33.3 percent). The largest sample size was for striped skunks (*Mephitis mephitis*) with a 3.4 percent incidence, $n = 29$, and raccoons (*Procyon lotor*) with 0 percent, $n = 28$. The authors concluded that targeting carnivores for plague surveillance may not be appropriate, at least in the foothills and grassland habitats of north-central Colorado.

Many carnivores are valued as furbearers; Deems and Pursley (1983) summarized the legal status of furbearers in North America. In 1996, Colorado voters passed Amendment 14 (Colorado Revised Statute 33-6-203), making it "unlawful to take wildlife with any leghold trap, any instant kill body-gripping trap, or by poison or snare in the state of Colorado." That amendment has impacted management of carnivores by greatly reducing or eliminating sport harvest. A number of furbearing carnivores (coyote, red fox, raccoon, striped skunk, badger, mink, pine marten, bobcat) can be hunted or livetrapped with possession of a small game or furbearer license (Colorado Division of Wildlife 2009f). Livetrapped animals must be released or killed immediately if they are legally harvested species (Colorado Division of Wildlife 2009f). At present, kit fox, swift fox, gray fox, ringtail, ermine, long-tailed weasel, eastern spotted skunk, hog-nosed skunk, wolverine, river otter, and lynx are considered non-game species (Colorado Division of Wildlife 2009c) protected from sport harvest. However, under furbearer and small game regulations (Colorado Division of Wildlife 2009f), "skunks" (with no designation of species) are listed among mammals that can be taken without license or limit to prevent damage to private property.

The passage of Amendment 14 led to considerable controversy and commentary (Manfredo et al. 1997; Minnis 1998; Sikorowski et al. 1998; Andelt et al. 1999; Manfredo et al. 1999). Other states have faced the same issue, and debate over the need for (and the ethics of) using leg-hold traps continues. Muth et al. (2006) recently found that 46 percent of wildlife professionals favored outlawing leg-hold traps, whereas 39 percent were in favor of their continued use. Losses of sheep and lambs to predators (mostly carnivores) in Colorado were responsible for about 42.5 percent of total losses in 2004 versus 57.5 percent from all other factors (disease, weather, and the like) (Agricultural Statistics Board 2005). Amendment 14 does constrain options for predator control.

Key to the Families of the Order Carnivora in Colorado

1. Muzzle short and broad; total teeth 30 or less; claws retractile . . . . Family Felidae, p. 349
1' Muzzle usually not short and broad; total teeth more than 32; claws not retractile 2

2. Cheek teeth bunodont, lacking conspicuous cutting edges; tail either shorter than hindfoot or banded with hairs of contrasting color 3
2' Cheek teeth not totally bunodont, secondont teeth present; tail not as above 4

3. Tail shorter than hindfoot, not banded . . . . Family Ursidae, p. 386
3' Tail longer than hindfoot and conspicuously banded with hairs of contrasting color . . . . Family Procyonidae, p. 430

4. Hindfoot with 4 toes; total teeth 42. . . . . Family Canidae, p. 364
4' Hindfoot with 5 toes; total teeth fewer than 42 5

5. Dorsal color black with white spots or stripes; auditory bullae both small and flattened . . . . Family Mephitidae, p. 421
5' Dorsal color variable, usually brown, black, or buffy, if white only seasonally; auditory bullae not notably small and flattened . . . . Family Mustelidae, p. 394

Family Felidae—Cats

The felids are highly specialized carnivores, adapted both behaviorally and morphologically as extremely efficient predators. Felids are more carnivorous than most other members of the order and rarely, if ever, take vegetable matter. They kill their prey rapidly, usually with a strangulation hold on the neck or throat. This behavior, combined with their specialized dentition, makes them formidable predators. Their dentition is specialized in the reduction of the number of teeth, the sharpness of the canines, and the precision of the shearing carnassial pair (last upper premolar and first lower premolar). More than any other carnivores, the carnassials have a scissorlike action as the jaws close. In addition, the jaws can open to almost 90 degrees, allowing for a good hold on the throat of their prey. Felids have good visual and auditory senses, also used in hunting. Most species stalk their prey and follow up with a short rush and pounce. The cheetah is capable of longer endurance chases than other cats.

Most felids are solitary and crepuscular or nocturnal. Most are mobile, not regularly using denning or resting areas for prolonged periods of time, except for females rearing their altricial young. Their secretive nature has led researchers in recent years to devise new methods for detection, including use of infrared cameras, DNA analysis of scat, and even detector dogs (R. L. Harrison 2006; Heilbrun et al. 2006; McKelvey et al. 2006; M. Alldredge 2007). Females of most species are polyestrous but have only a single litter every 1 to 3 years. Size varies from the diminutive wildcats of Europe and Asia, weighing 3–8 kg, to the tiger, males of which may exceed 300 kg. The domestic cat (*Felis catus*) is thought to be descended from the wildcat, *Felis silvestris*, of the Mediterranean region. Large felids, including tigers, lions, and leopards, sometimes attack humans. Closer to home, the number of human–mountain lion encounters in North America has increased markedly in recent years as urbanized deer populations provide an attractive food resource for lions in close proximity to humans.

Felids mostly share a typical catlike build, with a short muzzle, large eyes, well-developed canine and carnassial teeth, and sharp, retractile claws. Length of tail and limb proportions vary, however, from shorter-legged arboreal forms to long-legged cursorial cheetahs. Cats are digitigrade, walking and running on their toes rather than on the soles of their feet. Front feet have 5 digits, with the pollex (thumb) reduced in size and elevated into a non-weight-bearing claw. There are 4 digits on the hindfoot. The tooth count is 28 or 30. The eyes are large and frontally placed, and the pupils close vertically.

Felids evolved in the Late Eocene. Fossil mountain lions (*Puma*) appeared about 300,000 years ago in North America (A. Turner 1997). *Lynx rufus* is represented in North American fossils in the Late Pleistocene about 2.5 million years ago, but *Lynx canadensis* is more recent, showing up as fossils about 200,000 years ago (Werdelin 1981). Modern species are found worldwide except in polar areas, on isolated oceanic islands, and in Australia. Considerable controversy exists over the classification of felids; Wozencraft (2005) listed 54 genera and 121 species. Many species are categorized as threatened or endangered, often because of overharvest for their pelage or loss of habitat. Two genera and 3 species occur in Colorado.

Key to the Species of the Family Felidae in Colorado

1. Tail more than 30 percent of length of head and body; 3 premolars on each side of upper jaw . . . . Mountain Lion—*Puma concolor*, p. 350

1' Tail less than 30 percent of length of head and body; 2 premolars on each side of upper jaw . . . . *Lynx*, 2

2. Tail more than one-half length of hindfoot; black tip on tail incomplete ventrally; hypoglossal foramen confluent with posterior lacerate foramen* . . . . Bobcat—*Lynx rufus*, p. 360

2' Tail less than one-half length of hindfoot; black tip on tail complete ventrally; hypoglossal foramen separate from posterior lacerate foramen* . . . . Canada Lynx—*Lynx canadensis*, p. 356

Puma concolor

MOUNTAIN LION, PUMA, OR COUGAR

Description

The mountain lion is the largest cat north of Mexico except for the jaguar (which only rarely enters the United States). Other names for this magnificent cat include puma, cougar, painter, and panther. Color is brownish to reddish brown with paler underparts. The tail is long, cylindrical, and black-tipped. The nosepad and backs of the ears are also black. Coloradan individuals are among the largest representatives of the species. Measurements are: total length 1,500–2,750 mm; length of tail 600–850 mm; length of hindfoot 225–300 mm; length of ear 50–115 mm; weight 36–103 kg. Males are larger than females throughout the species' geographic range (Gay and Best 1995). The forefeet are slightly larger than the hindfeet, and their naked heelpads may measure up to 7.6 cm across on large males; Halfpenny (2007b) described techniques for tracking cougars. Young mountain lions have spots that disappear at about 1 year of age. The skull is short (condylobasal length 160–220 mm), broad, and heavily built. Females have 8 mammae, of which only 6 are functional. Age can be determined by wear and appearance of teeth (M. Currier et al. 1977) and by gumline recession (Laundré et al. 2000). The Colorado Division of Wildlife has provided the on-line "Mountain Lion Education and Identification Course," which provides a practical summary of lion biology in the state (http://wildlife.state.co.us/NR/rdonlyres/60841375-CCC2-4C86-9DB5-7113A52670DF/0/MountainLionEducationAndIdentificationCourse.pdf).

Distribution

Mountain lions have the widest geographical range of any mammal in the New World, from the Yukon to Tierra del Fuego. They once were distributed over all of the conter-

* This character may not always distinguish these species in the Southern Rockies; for additional distinguishing traits, see accounts of species.

PHOTOGRAPH 12-1. Mountain lion (*Puma concolor*). Photograph by David Neils.

minous United States, but most populations have been extirpated in the East and over significant areas in the West as well. In Colorado, the species is still common in much of the western two-thirds of the state, and in recent years has been seen increasingly in rougher parts of the eastern plains, from which it had been largely eliminated. In recent years, they have become increasingly common in and near residential areas of the foothills of the Front Range, especially in the Boulder area. We follow Wozencraft (1993, 2005) and R. Baker, L. Bradley, et al. (2003) in use of the generic name *Puma* rather than the more inclusive *Felis*. That idea was supported by the work of C. Anderson et al. (2004). D. Armstrong (1972) listed Coloradan mountain lions as *Felis concolor hippolestes*, following Goldman (1946); however, it may be that only 1 subspecies of the mountain lion exists in the United States (see Pierce and Bleich 2003). For insights into mountain lion systematics, see M. Culver (2009).

Natural History

The Colorado Division of Wildlife has been actively engaged in mountain lion research for a number of years because of the importance of the species as a big game animal, its role in elk and deer mortality (A. Anderson et al. 1992; M. Alldredge et al. 2008), and its growing importance in human-wildlife interaction, especially in much of the urbanizing corridor along the Colorado Front Range (M. Alldredge 2007, 2008; M. Alldredge and Freddy 2008). Logan (2008) is involved in a 10-year study in southwestern Colorado that will allow some comparisons with the 7-year study of A. Anderson et al. (1992).

Mountain lions inhabit most ecosystems in Colorado, including the eastern plains, according to periodic reports. They are most common in rough, broken foothills and canyon country, often associated with montane forests, shrublands, and piñon-juniper woodlands. A habitat model

MAP 12-1. Distribution of the mountain lion, or puma (*Puma concolor*) in North America.

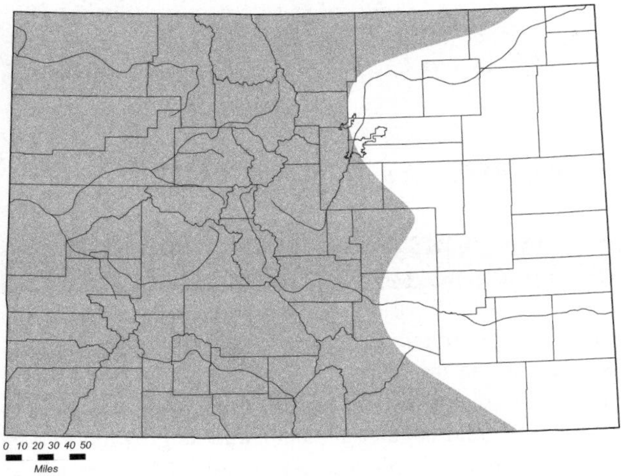

MAP 12-2. Distribution of the mountain lion, or puma (*Puma concolor*) in Colorado.

developed in south-central Utah found that slope and the height and type of overstory cover were most indicative for high-use habitat. Sixteen percent of telemetry locations of lions were in sandstone ledges, 15 percent in mixed ponderosa pine–Gambel oak forest, 13 percent in piñon-juniper areas, and 11 percent in spruce-fir forests (Laing and Lindzey 1991). Mountain lions may hunt during the day or at night, but most activity is crepuscular or nocturnal, especially if close to humans (Van Dyke et al. 1986). They require sufficient cover for stalking prey and most kills are reported from brushy, wooded, or rough terrain (S. Young and Goldman 1946; Hornocker 1970). They hunt by stealth rather than by chase, moving frequently and then waiting in ambush (Beier et al. 1995); the kill is accomplished with a final short rush and lunge. Mountain lions gorge when given the opportunity and well-fed mountain lions spend much of their time resting (Beier et al. 1995).

Mountain lions prey mainly on deer in North America, although they are capable of taking other large mammals, including elk, moose, feral (J. Turner et al. 1992) and domestic horses, cattle, sheep (wild and domestic), and feral pigs (A. Anderson 1983; Pierce and Bleich 2003). They can become important predators on bighorn sheep, especially in desert habitats (Kamler et al. 2002), in some situations pushing small herds toward extirpation (Wehausen 1996; Ross et al. 1997). A. Anderson et al. (1992) estimated mountain lions killed 8–12 percent of deer annually on the Uncompahgre Plateau. More recently M. Alldredge et al. (2008) reported about equal predation levels (22 to 24 percent) by mountain lion on adult deer, fawns, adult elk, and elk calves on the plateau, with most kill sites in mid-upper-elevation deer winter range where both prey species overlapped. The importance of elk in the diet of mountain lions ranges from as low as 2 percent in Nevada to as high as 24 percent in central Idaho (K. Dixon 1982). Elk are the primary prey of mountain lions in Yellowstone (Ruth 2004). In Idaho, deer and elk comprised 70 percent of winter scats. Of animals killed, 60 to 80 percent were fawns, yearlings, or over-mature individuals. Logan (2005) estimated ungulate use rates for adult lions to range from 25 to 53 animals per year, somewhat higher than in other studies. In that same study area M. Alldredge et al. (2008), using GPS location data from radio-collared lions, reported that the probability of a lion kill was high and approached certainty if a lion spent more than 2 or 3 days in the same general area. Hornocker (1970) estimated that an adult lion must kill a deer about every 2 weeks to survive the winter, with annual requirements of 5 to 7 elk or 14 to 20 deer. Pierce and Bleich (2003) estimated kill rates of 1 deer every 8 to 17 days. C. Anderson and Lindzey (2003) estimated kill intervals of 5.4 to 9.5 days, depending on age and social unit. Females with kittens usually have to kill more regularly than single animals (C. Anderson and Lindzey 2003; Ruth 2004).

Individual mountain lions may consume up to 4 or 5 kg of food at a meal. Free water is required, more so for females with cubs than for solitary males. In Idaho, a prey population of 200 ungulates was estimated to provide a sustainable yield of food to maintain one mountain lion (Hornocker 1970). Mountain lions on winter deer and elk ranges may be beneficial in keeping herds moving, breaking up concentrations, and reducing overbrowsing. Recent studies suggest that lions may not be selecting prey in poor condition (Kunkel et al. 1999; Pierce et al. 2000a). Large prey is often moved from the site of the kill and buried with snow or surface litter. When a cache is made, lions typically stay close to the site (Beier et al. 1995; Pierce et al. 1998). Caching surplus food may reduce competition from insects and microbes as well as mammalian scavengers and predators, including other cougars (Bischoff-Mattson and Mattson 2009). As with bear and wolf kills, mountain lion kills provide food for a large number of scavengers; 75 percent of lion kills are scavenged in Yellowstone, and wolves often displace mountain lions from their kills (Ruth 2004).

At times mountain lions use smaller prey, including mice, ground squirrels, beavers, lagomorphs, porcupines, and armadillos. Sweitzer et al. (1997) found mountain lion predation virtually eliminated a population of porcupines in a juniper woodland in Nevada. Other carnivores, including raccoons, skunks, bobcats, coyotes, and gray fox, also are eaten, as well as birds, fish, insects, and berries (Lindzey 1987). In southern Utah, increased consumption of jackrabbits and small carnivores occurred during winter (Ackerman et al. 1984). Cannibalism is not uncommon (Pierce and Bleich 2003). Carrion apparently is eaten rarely (K. Russell 1978). Sheep are the most frequent livestock prey, and they sometimes are killed more than one at a time; most cattle taken are calves (Lindzey 1987). Cougars were reported to be the third most important predator on domestic sheep and lambs in the United States, after coyotes and domestic dogs (Agricultural Statistics Board 2005), killing an estimated 12,700 animals in 2004, valued at about $1.1 million. In Colorado, some 300 sheep and lambs were taken. A study of lion predation of livestock in Colorado found that transient and old lions were mostly responsible (K. Dixon and Boyd 1967).

Mountain lions range widely and cover large areas in search of food. Distances of 8 to 12 km are easily traversed in a day, and transient individuals may move more than 500 km between points of capture (Lindzey 1987; Logan and Sweanor 2000). Average movements of dispersing young range from 29 to more than 160 km; young females move shorter distances than males (Lindzey 1987). In Colorado, 2 young males moved 247 and 260 km, which are among the longest reported distances moved by the species (Brent 1983). Physical barriers seldom seem to limit their movements. Preliminary results from microsatellite DNA sampling of female Colorado mountain lions support that assertion (M. Alldredge 2007)

Mountain lions mostly are solitary and do not associate with each other except for brief periods during the breeding season and when females are with cubs. Therefore, an observation by Tischendorf et al. (1995) is particularly noteworthy. They reported a chance encounter in September 1992 with a group of 10 or 11 pumas together along a canyon road south of Gypsum, Eagle County. They speculated that the group might have been 2 adult females each with 4 or 5 full-grown kittens. Social intolerance and avoidance—rather than active defense of territory—maintain spacing (Hornocker 1969; Seidensticker et al. 1973; Koloski 2002). Resident females typically outnumber resident males in a population (Henker et al. 1984). On the Southern Ute Reservation, Koloski (2002) estimated a total lion population of 55, with a male/female ratio of 1:1.29. Logan (2008) estimated a population of 33 mountain lions, including 16 adult females and 8 adult males on the Uncompahgre study area, from November 2007 to March 2008, an increase from 24 estimated the previous winter. In southern New Mexico, Logan et al. (1996) calculated a male/female ratio of 1.0:1.4, whereas Lindzey et al. (1994) found a ratio of 1:2 in southern Utah. Females with cubs are extremely intolerant of adult males, who are likely to kill the cubs.

Resident mountain lions maintain contiguous home ranges, whose size varies seasonally depending on prey density as well as a lion's sex, reproductive condition, and age. Male home ranges frequently overlap, with 1 or more females. In western states individual mountain lions often show distinct winter-spring and summer-fall home ranges that correspond to movements of their ungulate prey and local weather conditions (Seidensticker et al. 1973). In Colorado, much of the best mountain lion habitat is at mid-elevations, such as the foothills of the Front Range. In these habitats resident deer herds may be relatively sedentary and lions do not make significant seasonal shifts in home range. Sizes of home ranges vary from about 40 to more than 700 km^2 for females and from 120 to 830 km^2 for males (Lindzey 1987; Pierce and Bleich 2003). Average annual home ranges of 7 females on the Uncompahgre Plateau varied from 190 to 463 km^2 (A. Anderson et al. 1992); those of 3 males were 436 to 732 km^2 in the same area. Koloski (2002) found an average home range of 253 km^2 for males and 182 km^2 for females on the Southern Ute Reservation.

Mountain lions, especially adult males, make scrapes (collections of leaves, dirt, and debris formed by scratching with the hindfeet), often marked with urine and feces. Such signs are often located near the margins of home ranges (Seidensticker et al. 1973).

Densities of mountain lions under non-hunted conditions are thought to be maintained by internal population regulation rather than by their prey base. Behavioral intolerance, especially for individuals of the same sex, generally precludes high densities (Seidensticker et al. 1973; Lindzey et al. 1994). However, Logan and Sweanor (2001) and Pierce et al. (2000b) suggested that prey populations are the principal regulator of lion populations. Reported densities of mountain lions vary greatly, from 0.04 to 7.10 lions per 100 km^2 (A. Anderson 1983; Pierce and Bleich 2003). Near Cañon City, density was estimated at 1 lion per 36 to 60 km^2; taking behavioral intolerance into consideration, maximal mountain lion density was estimated to be 1 animal per 25 to 50 km^2 (M. Currier 1976; M. Currier et al. 1977). Near Rifle, densities were 1 lion per 28 to 30 km^2 (Brent 1983). Koloski (2002) estimated density of 0.92 to 2.70 lions per 100 km^2 near Ignacio. The Colorado Division of Wildlife uses density estimates of 2.0 to 4.6 lions per 100 km^2 in setting harvest quotas (Logan 2005). Density estimates are usually based on population studies in fair to good habitats and often include transients; thus densities are probably much lower over all occupied habitats. The proportion of resident animals is 47 to 82 percent (Lindzey 1987).

Mountain lions have no set breeding season; rather, females may come into estrus ("heat") at any time of the year. Because of the pattern of overlap of home ranges, males are surely polygynous, but females probably rarely breed with more than 1 male. Females are polyestrous, cycling about every 2 weeks until bred (S. Young and Goldman 1946; Rabb 1959). Females in estrus use vocal "caterwauling" to attract males (Rabb 1959; Beier et al. 1995). Gestation lasts about 92 days. Litters are more likely to be born in spring and summer in Colorado, Idaho, western Utah, and Nevada and in late summer or fall in southern Utah and Wyoming (Lindzey 1987; Koloski 2002). Logan et al. (1996) reported 73 percent of adult females in southern New Mexico had litters in January. Logan (2008) recorded births of 28 litters from 15 females from 2005 to 2008 on the Uncompahgre Plateau. Twenty-six of the litters were born between May 1 and September 30, with 19 litters born in May, June, and July. Average litter size was 2.8, with an average birth interval of about 18 months. About 65 percent of adult females produced cubs each year. Timing of parturition may coincide with prey abundance and the birth of primary prey (Logan and Sweanor 2000; Pierce et al. 2000a). Females do not prepare special natal dens for birthing. Litter size ranges from 1 to 6, with 2.6 the average (A. Anderson 1983).

Cubs are blind at birth, covered with fine fur with black spots. Eyes open in about 10 days, and weaning occurs at about 2 months. The female continues to hunt to provide food for her young during their long tutelage of 12 to 22 months. This lengthy dependence on the female keeps her reproductive potential low. Females average only 4 litters over a 10-year period (K. Russell 1978). Dispersal of young lions from the mother probably coincides with her coming back into reproductive condition. Females are sexually mature as early as 20 months but may be prevented socially from breeding until they are older (Seidensticker et al. 1973; Lindzey 1987).

Human exploitation can have a major impact on lion populations. In a marked and radio-tagged population of 41 lions on the Uncompahgre Plateau, 50 percent of individuals had died by 5½ years of age (A. Anderson et al. 1989). The animals were studied in an area closed to hunting, but 11 of the individuals were killed illegally by humans. An ongoing study on the Uncompahgre Plateau is also being conducted in an area closed to hunting, and no illegal kills were recorded in the first almost 4 years of research. Survivorship has been high for adult and subadult animals, with cub survival estimated at about 50 percent. Mortality is primarily caused by male cougars (Logan 2008). Twenty-two lions were captured and marked from 1981 to 1983 near Rifle and on the Uncompahgre Plateau: 14 were adults, 2 were yearlings, and 6 were kittens. Sixty percent of the animals were dead by the end of 1986. All known mortality was caused by humans, from legal and illegal harvest and accidental death in a coyote snare (Brent 1983). C. Anderson and Lindzey (2005) studied effects of intensive harvest pressure (reducing population of independent cougars from 58 to 20 from fall 1998 to spring 2000) on mountain lions in the Snowy Range of Wyoming. They concluded that it required about 3 years of light harvest to allow for population recovery. As intensive hunting pressure increased, the take of adult females also increased from 20 to 58 percent of the harvest, with resulting decline in the population.

Prenatal mortality is estimated at as high as 15 percent (W. Robinette et al. 1961). Mortality of cubs prior to dispersal averages 20 to 30 percent (Lindzey 1987), although Ruth (2004) estimated close to 50 percent cub mortality in Yellowstone, with production of young in a downward trend. Increased cub mortality may be from wolves killing cubs or stealing cougar kills from the cubs' parents; however, more research is needed. Koloski (2002) reported mean annual survival rates of 0.89 and 0.72 for males and females, respectively. That is close to the 0.88 reported by A. Anderson et al. (1992) and the 0.74 reported by Lindzey et al. (1994).

Humans are the chief cause of mountain lion mortality, through regulated harvest, poaching, and deliberate predator control for protection of livestock. Young animals dispersing from their mothers are especially vulnerable to harvest. Disease is probably not significant because of low densities and the solitary nature of the animals. Some, especially cubs, may die from porcupine quills (W. Robinette et al. 1959). Adult males occasionally kill each other; males may also kill and eat kittens. A few reports of adult females killing each other were also noted. Two of 11 mountain lions in Koloski's (2002) study were killed by other lions. Ruth (2004) summarized mountain lion studies in Yellowstone National Park, where interactions of bears, mountain lions, and more recently wolves have been under study since 1986. Wolves killed 7 mountain lions in Yellowstone and Glacier national parks. Lions killed at least 1 wolf and possibly 2 in that same period in Yellowstone (Ruth 2004). Accidents occur, including lethal falls during unsuccessful predation attempts. Starvation is likewise thought to be important, especially for individuals of advanced age with worn or broken teeth or for young cubs that the mother cannot maintain.

From 1929 until 1965, mountain lions were listed officially as "predators" in Colorado, and a bounty was paid. In 1965 the Wildlife Commission changed the status of mountain lions from predator to game mammal and no longer paid bounties. The present management status of the lion makes it a trophy animal. For the period 1980–2008, legal harvest of cougars in Colorado averaged 259.2 animals per year (range 81–439), ranking the state fourth in the country, after Idaho, Montana, and Utah (Hornocker and Negri 2009). An average of about 1,500 hunters have killed a few hundred mountain lions annually from 1999 to 2007 (see Table 4-2). In Washington, Cooley et al. (2009) found that a heavily hunted population showed increased immigration, reduced kitten survival, reduced growth in the female population, and an age structure biased toward young animals. By contrast, a slightly hunted population showed increase emigration, higher survival of kittens, increased female population growth, and an age structure dominated by older animals.

Mountain lions and their management evoke considerable debate (Manfredo et al. 1998). Some view lions as a species of great aesthetic value and a symbol of wilderness and argue against hunting. Livestock producers and wildlife managers sometimes believe regulated harvest and management are essential. Sweitzer et al. (1997) suggested that mountain lions are increasing in numbers and distribution in much of western North America, resulting in increasing influence on survival of small populations of prey species, possibly even influencing patterns of biodiversity. Packer et al. (2009) modeled the interaction of sport hunting and predator control in the demography of mountain lions.

The common perception that cougar populations are increasing may stem from an increase in reported human-cougar encounters (S. J. Riley and Malecki 2001). However, Lambert et al. (2006) presented evidence of a declining population despite increased human-lion encounters. With increased residential development of foothills environments, sometimes providing enhanced habitat for deer, human–mountain lion conflicts have increased. Beier (1991) summarized all human-lion encounters for which data were available from wildlife agencies in North America. From 1890 to 1990, 9 fatal attacks of mountain lions on 10 humans were recorded (in California, Washington, Montana, New Mexico, and British Columbia) and there were 41 non-fatal attacks, with the incidence of reported attacks increasing since 1970. M. Alldredge and Freddy (2008) indicated that since the work of Beier (1991), 7 fatal and 38 non-fatal mountain lion attacks on humans have occurred and they estimated that mountain lion attack rates on the Colorado Front Range are 1 per 2.2 million person-days. These statistics have led the Colorado Division of Wildlife to initiate research on mountain lion distribution and population structure along the Front Range as well as to investigate the development of aversive conditioning techniques for problem lions (M. Alldredge 2008). In January 1991 a jogger was killed by a mountain lion near Idaho Springs (D. Baron 2004; for commentary, see Keefover-Ring 2004a, 2004b; D. Baron 2005). This prompted the Colorado Division of Wildlife to host a symposium dealing with conflicts between humans and mountain lions (C. Braun 1993) and to develop policies to address such conflicts. Most (62 percent) attacks were on children. Etling (2004) provided a comprehensive account of cougar attacks on humans, including a chapter on encounters in Colorado. A carefully stratified public survey for the Colorado Division of Wildlife of about 1,300 Coloradans (Corona Research 2006) found generally positive opinions about lions and a fairly low level of concern about being attacked by a lion, although concern for pets was fairly high. A large majority of respondents believed it was important that lions exist in Colorado, even if they never get to see one (96 percent), and that future human generations will have lions in their environment (93 percent). Forty-seven percent of respondents supported regulated hunting of mountain lions and 41 percent opposed it. Keefover-Ring (2004a) reviewed management of mountain lions in the West in general and in Colorado in particular (Keefover-Ring 2004b). Zinn and Manfredo (1996) assessed public preferences toward mountain lion management on the Front Range.

The Colorado Division of Wildlife (2007e) provided helpful tips for preventing potentially dangerous encounters with mountain lions, as did S. Torres (2005). Halfpenny (2007b) provided a useful illustrated guide to tracking mountain lions. The Cougar Management Guidelines Working Group (2005) provided rationale and strategies for management, focused on the United States and Canada. Literature on mountain lions was reviewed by K. Dixon (1982), A. Anderson (1983), M. Currier (1983), Lindzey (1987), Logan and Sweanor (2000, 2001), and Pierce and Bleich (2003). *Cougar Ecology and Conservation* (Hornocker and Negri 2009) is an excellent review of biology and critical conservation issues. *Listening to Cougar* (Bekoff and Lowe 2007) includes essays and stories and mostly is focused on the human dimension of mountain lions in contemporary landscapes.

Genus *Lynx*

The taxonomy of the genus *Lynx* has been somewhat controversial. Wozencraft (2005) recognized 4 species, with the Canada lynx (*L. canadensis*) and Iberian lynx (*L. pardinus*) separate from the Eurasian lynx (*L. lynx*). Others have recognized just 2 species in the genus—a Holarctic lynx and the New World bobcat. McKenna and Bell (1997) and Nowak (1999) treated *Lynx* as a subgenus of *Felis*.

Lynx canadensis

CANADA LYNX

Description

The lynx is a medium-sized cat with long legs, large feet, and a short tail. The fur is long, dense, soft, and fine. The dorsal color is grizzled gray to reddish brown, often tinged with black. The legs, feet, and underparts are paler, buff to white. Although spotting may be present, it usually is more muted than in the bobcat. The ears have long, dark tufts and the face has a pronounced ruff of fur. The tail is short with a completely black tip. The hindlegs are slightly longer than the front legs. The paws are much larger than those of the bobcat and can support twice as much weight on snow. Measurements are: total length 670–1,067 mm; length of tail 95–125 mm; length of hindfoot 203–250 mm; weight 5–15 kg. Males are slightly larger than females. The skull is broad with a short muzzle. The skulls of lynx and bobcat are almost identical. In some lynx specimens the hypoglossal foramen and the posterior lacerate foramen, both adjacent to the auditory bullae, are separated (Banfield 1974); however, it is not clear whether this trait invariably distinguishes lynx and bobcat in southern populations such as ours. Females have only 4 mammae.

PHOTOGRAPH 12-2. Canada lynx (*Lynx canadensis*). Photograph by William E. Ervin.

Distribution

The southern boundary of lynx distribution in North America is roughly the northern boundary of the range of the bobcat, except for southward extensions of forested lynx habitat in the mountains (E. M. Anderson and Lovallo 2003). In the Rockies, lynx tend to occur at higher elevations than do bobcats. Historically, lynx occurred sparsely in areas of Colorado above 2,700 m (9,000 ft.) in the Park, Gore, San Juan, and La Plata mountains and the White River Plateau (D. Armstrong 1972). Denney (1975), Halfpenny and Miller (1981), Halfpenny, Bissell, et al. (1986), R. Thompson and Halfpenny (1989), and G. Byrne (1997) added more records. However, evidence of a viable lynx population was lacking. Squires and Laurion (2000) reported trappers taking 18 lynx in the early 1970s from the Wyoming Range of west-central

MAP 12-3. Distribution of the Canada lynx (*Lynx canadensis*) in North America.

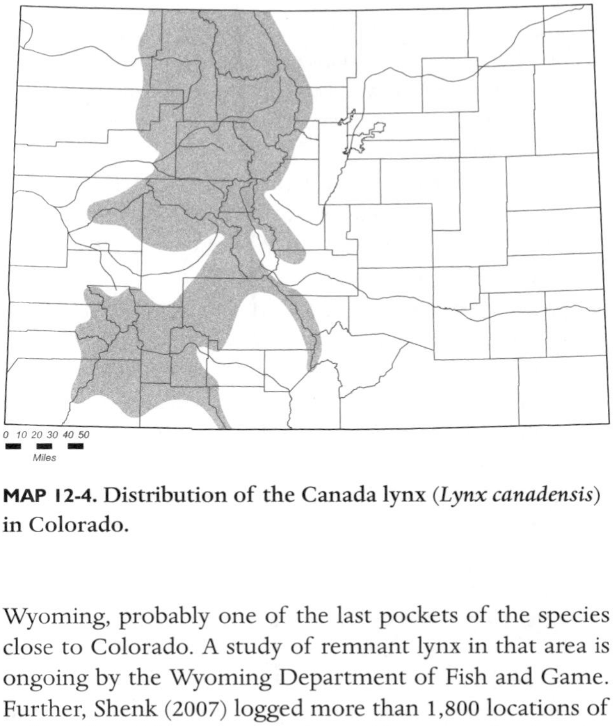

MAP 12-4. Distribution of the Canada lynx (*Lynx canadensis*) in Colorado.

Wyoming, probably one of the last pockets of the species close to Colorado. A study of remnant lynx in that area is ongoing by the Wyoming Department of Fish and Game. Further, Shenk (2007) logged more than 1,800 locations of radio-collared lynx in Wyoming, with most animals using the Medicine Bow National Forest or the Yellowstone–Grand Teton–Laramie Range corridor. Shenk (2007) has also recorded numerous lynx locations in Utah, primarily in the Uinta Mountains, and in New Mexico. J. Frey (2006) considered New Mexico to be within the natural range of the Canada lynx, based on ecological and biogeographic considerations. These records are of animals restored to Colorado, beginning in 1999. For details, see "Natural History" below.

The lynx is designated as federally threatened and state endangered. Taxonomy of the lynx has long been debated. The Nearctic lynx has been treated as *Lynx canadensis* (E. Hall 1981; Wozencraft 1993, 2005; E. M. Anderson and Lovallo 2003; R. Baker, L. Bradley, et al. 2003), suggesting a species distinct from the Palearctic lynx, *L. lynx*. However, J. K. Jones, Hoffmann, et al. (1992) considered the 2 to be conspecific, and J. Fitzgerald et al. (1994) did likewise. In this edition we follow R. Baker, L. Bradley, et al. (2003) and Wozencraft (2005) in use of the name *L. canadensis*. One subspecies, *Lynx canadensis canadensis*, is known from Colorado; indeed, that single subspecies ranges across northern and central North America; only the lynx of Newfoundland is considered to be subspecifically distinct (Hall 1981).

Natural History

Dense coniferous forests are the preferred habitat of the lynx over most of its range. Uneven-aged stands with relatively open canopies and well-developed understories, favorable habitat for snowshoe hares, are ideal (Quinn and Parker 1987). Squires and Laurion (2000) noted that knowledge of southern lynx populations was limited to 7 studies in Washington, Montana, and Minnesota. Information from the Colorado release program represents the only information existing from the Southern Rockies. Based on aerial tracking, Colorado lynx are primarily using 3 cover types, with Engelmann spruce–subalpine fir most important followed by Engelmann spruce–subalpine fir–aspen and various mixes of riparian habitats, with the latter type of most importance in summer and fall (Shenk 2008). Engelmann spruce–subalpine fir stands were the most commonly used habitat type in winter for all lynx activities, ranging from travel and kill sites to den locations (Shenk 2008). Use of riparian habitats seems to increase in summer and fall months. Coarse woody debris is often present. Lodgepole forests do not seem of much importance in Colorado, in part because lodgepole distribution is limited in southwestern Colorado (Buskirk and Zahratka 2002; Shenk 2002) and not enough lynx have moved into potential lodgepole habitats in northern parts of the state. G. Koehler (1990), G. Koehler and Brittell (1990), and G. Koehler and Aubry (1994) suggested that lynx in the Southern Rocky Mountains and the northern mountains of Washington need not only late successional forest for denning and rearing of kits but also early successional areas that tend to have higher populations of snowshoe hare and rodents. For example, G. Koehler (1990) found snowshoe hare numbers 4 to 9 times larger in 20-year-old lodgepole pine forests than in older (43- to 100-year) stands. Dense stands of aspen are not thought to provide good snowshoe hare habitat, but in early successional recovery from fire, aspen stands may provide hare cover (G. Koehler and Aubry 1994). Snowshoe hares in Utah (M. Wolfe et al. 1982) seldom used habitat with less than 40 percent visual obstruction in the understory, and it is likely that lynx would focus on good hare habitat.

In 1998 the Colorado Division of Wildlife drafted a conservation and restoration plan for lynx and wolverine (J. Seidel et al. 1998). Ninety-six lynx were restored to the San Juan Mountains in 1999–2002 using animals from Alaska, Manitoba, Quebec, British Columbia, and the Yukon. Since then, augmentations have increased the total to 218 animals (Shenk 2000, 2001, 2002, 2003, 2004, 2005, 2008). Since 1999 there have been 112 mortalities of adult released lynx. Humans likely caused 30 percent of the deaths. Starvation and disease, including plague (Wild et al. 2006), have accounted for about one-fifth of deaths. Almost 27 percent of mortality has occurred outside the state. Any human-caused mortality is thought to be additive in impacting populations (E. M. Anderson and Lovallo 2003). Over their wide range, lynx are known to be killed by gray wolves and wolverines, and adult male lynx occasionally kill kittens. In captivity lynx may live 26 years; in the wild few live past 16 years.

Most surviving lynx in Colorado have stayed in the lynx-release core area centered in the San Juan Mountains, with other individuals establishing a secondary core area centered on Taylor Park and the nearby Collegiate Range (Shenk 2008). A few individuals have wandered widely—to Utah, Wyoming, Nebraska (Hoffman and Genoways 2005), Montana (Shenk 2000, 2001, 2002, 2005), Kansas (C. Schmidt et al. 2008), and Iowa. The known lynx populations nearest to Colorado are located in northwestern Wyoming and in Montana (McKelvey et al. 2000; Squires and Laurion 2000). Reproduction has been documented from 2003 to 2006, with a total of 116 kittens reported (mean, 2.78 litter). However, no litters were found in 2007 and 2008 (Shenk 2008). In 2009, 10 lynx kittens were reported from 5 dens, 3 of them in the headwaters of the Rio Grande, 1 in Gunnison County, and 1 in Eagle County (Berwyn 2009). Despite these setbacks, the Colorado Division of Wildlife declared "success" of the lynx restoration program in 2010 (Lewis 2010), when at least 14 kittens were born in 5 separate dens, including 2 dens from Summit County (outside the core restoration area).

In Colorado most dens have been in late successional spruce-fir forests with large quantities of down timber at north-facing elevations of 3,117 to 3,586 m (10,227 to 11,766 ft.) (Shenk 2005). Bed sites, kill sites, and travel routes typically have been about 3,100 to 3,200 m (10,171 to 10,499 ft.) in elevation. Fire and logging of small, patchy clear-cuts may benefit the Canada lynx by enhancing snowshoe hare habitat (G. Koehler and Brittell 1990). Lynx may not be entirely intolerant of humans, as tracks were observed around garbage dumps at a central Colorado ski area. G. Koehler and Aubry (1994) suggested that populations of lynx and snowshoe hare in the southern limits of their ranges interact like northern populations do when snowshoe hare populations are at the low point of their cycle. Southern populations seem to have 3 factors operating to keep populations of hares, and therefore lynx, low: presence of relatively stable populations of several different hare predators (coyotes, bobcats, red fox, mountain lions, large owls, and hawks), an abundance of lower-quality suboptimal hare habitat that hares rarely populate, and possibly more competitors (cottontails, jackrabbits) with snowshoe hares for resources in marginal habitats.

The principal prey of North American lynx is the snowshoe hare, providing 35 to 100 percent of the diet (J. Saunders 1963b; Nellis et al. 1972; Brand et al. 1976; More 1976; G. Koehler 1990; E. M. Anderson and Lovallo 2003). Other prey species aer grouse, ptarmigan, mice, ground squirrels, beavers, and muskrats. When snowshoe hares are scarce, mice and voles may comprise up to 28 percent of the diet and pine squirrels up to 24 percent (G. Koehler and Aubry 1994). Ungulates, including deer, caribou, and moose, are rarely eaten and mostly as carrion or by killing fawns or calves. Most dietary diversity occurs in the warmer months.

To remain in good condition, a lynx requires about 4 snowshoe hares per week (170–200 per year). They kill and cache hares when they are plentiful. Estimates of dietary needs range from about 600 to 960 g/day (J. Saunders 1963b; Nellis and Keith 1968; Brand et al. 1976). The success rate for capturing snowshoe hares varies from 24 to 36 percent (G. Koehler and Aubry 1994). In Colorado, preliminary data on lynx kills (n = 548) indicated snowshoe hare were most important (55–91 percent of kills annually), with an annual mean of 74 percent. Red squirrels were the next most frequent kill item (Shenk 2008). Mice and other small mammals are probably supplementing their diets, but Shenk (2008) believed Colorado lynx are finding enough food for survival.

It may be difficult for lynx to survive if forced to switch to smaller prey. A grouse equals approximately 0.5 hares and a pine squirrel about 0.2 hares, so it might be difficult for lynx to capture either kind of prey in numbers sufficient to maintain condition (Nellis and Keith 1968). Preliminary work by Buskirk and Zahratka (2002), Zahratka (2004), Ivan (2008), and Zahratka and Shenk (2008) suggested that snowshoe hare populations are low in southwestern Colorado, ranging from 0.06 to 1.32 hares per hectare, with highest densities in Engelmann spruce–subalpine fir forests and lowest in lodgepole pine. The use of pellet surveys for estimating snowshoe hare population and distribution is made more difficult by the presence of mountain cottontails in some areas in the same habitat (Zahratka 2004; J. Frey and Malaney 2006). Studies in western Canada and the western United States have shown hare densities of 0.17 to 2.95 ha, depending on season and location (D. Murray 2003).

Lynxes are mostly solitary and nocturnal. However, they have also been observed traveling together (2 females and their 3 young) and hunting cooperatively for marmots, ground squirrels, and snowshoe hares (Barash 1971; Carbyn and Patriquin 1983; G. Parker et al. 1983). Lynx do not bury their scat; rather, they use dung and urine for scent-marking (J. Saunders 1963a). The animals hunt mostly on the ground but also can climb. Lynxes den or bed under ledges, trees, deadfalls, or occasionally in caves. In Washington, G. Koehler (1990) and G. Koehler and Brittell (1990) found most dens on north- and northeast-facing slopes with high densities of downed logs lying 1–4 feet above the ground surface. Such sites had to be relatively close to favorable snowshoe hare habitat and connected by cover corridors. In severe weather lynx may bed in thick evergreen cover. Lynx in Colorado seem to use similar habitats. Shenk (2008) found lynx to have a high degree of site fidelity in winter months, with more extensive movements in the summer months.

Shenk (2008) found reproductive females to have the smallest home ranges (mean, 75.2 km^2), followed by attending males (mean, 102.5 km^2). Non-reproductive lynx had average home ranges of 653.8 km^2. In areas with low snowshoe hare populations (similar to the Southern Rocky Mountains), average home ranges vary from 39 km^2 to 506 km^2 (Squires and Laurion 2000; E. M. Anderson and Lovallo 2003). In Washington, G. Koehler (1990) found average home ranges of 69 km^2 for males and 39 km^2 for females, with a density of 2.3 lynx per 100 km^2. Squires and Laurion (2000) reported averages of 220 km^2 for 6 Montana animals and 116 km^2 for a single male lynx from the Wyoming Range, with home ranges of females about half the size of males. G. Koehler (1990) attributed the large home ranges and low densities to marginal snowshoe hare habitat and low prey base. Mowat et al. (2000) found that when snowshoe hare density dropped to 0.5–1.0 hares per hectare, the size of lynx home ranges increased.

Average density for lynxes in areas with low snowshoe hare populations is 3 per 100 km^2 (E. M. Anderson and Lovallo 2003). The Colorado project is hoping to achieve a lynx density of approximately 13 lynx per 500 mi^2 (13 per 1,300 km^2) (Shenk 2003), a density approximately that of northern populations during the low point of the cycle. In lynx there seems to be considerable overlap of male and female home ranges, unlike the pattern seen in bobcats (G. Koehler and Aubry 1994; E. M. Anderson and Lovallo 2003). Variability in size of home ranges results from sex, age, reproductive status, transients in the population, and sometimes prey density (Brand et al. 1976). Site fidelity seems to be strong in lynx based on studies with radio-collared individuals (G. Koehler and Aubry 1994). One Colorado female has produced litters 3 years in a row in the same general area with the same mate (Shenk 2005).

In northern populations, lynx density fluctuates greatly with cycles of snowshoe hare populations, sometimes with lynx numbers reaching 30 to 45 animals per 100 km^2 (E. M. Anderson and Lovallo 2003). Fluctuations in the prey base in those areas involve a complex of interactions of the hares with their food supply and its quality, leading to roughly 10-year cycles of abundance and decline (Quinn and Parker 1987). Low hare populations may lead to reduced lynx reproduction and loss of young from starvation. Populations of snowshoe hares in Colorado do not appear to fluctuate cyclically (Dolbeer and Clark 1975), and this may make lynx populations here more stable, as G. Koehler and Aubry (1994) suggested. Plague—perhaps contracted from exposure to an infected prey animal—reportedly killed a female lynx and her 5-month-old cub (Wild et al. 2006).

Lynx are polygamous and females are believed to be seasonally polyestrous. Most lynx breed in March and April. The gestation period is about 9 weeks. The single annual litter contains 1 to 6 (average, 3) young (Quinn and Parker 1987; E. M. Anderson and Lovallo 2003). Females raise the litter alone, and the young disperse in the fall or the following spring. Females can apparently breed as yearlings, but breeding by such animals may be reduced or delayed if prey is scarce. Neonates are blind, and the ears are closed. They are well haired, even including some indication of the ear tufts to come (J. Saunders 1964; Nava 1970; Tumlison 1987).

The eventual success of restoration efforts in Colorado remains to be seen, of course. A failure of most females to reproduce in the first few years was attributed to insufficient numbers of potential breeding pairs, leading to subsequent releases in 2003–2005 for a total of 204 animals (Shenk 2005). A total of 126 lynx kittens are known to have been born in Colorado: 16 in 2003, 39 in 2004, 50 in 2005, 11 in 2006, and 10 in 2009; no lynx kittens were found in 2007 and 2008 (Colorado Division of Wildlife 2009a). In 1999 and 2005, collared lynx from Colorado's restoration program were taken in Nebraska, 2 in the North Platte drainage in Morrill County, and 1 near Ogallala, Keith County, in the South Platte drainage. One of the animals was returned unharmed to Colorado. The lynx restoration program is a highly visible activity of the Colorado Division of Wildlife, and frequent updates on status are available on-line (Colorado Division of Wildlife 2008f). Glick (2006) reviewed the Colorado lynx restoration program and provided excellent photographs of the animals, their habitats, and the restoration process.

McCord and Cardoza (1982), Quinn and Parker (1987), Tumlison (1987), G. Koehler and Aubry (1994), Ruggiero et al. (2000), and E. M. Anderson and Lovallo (2003) reviewed the vast and diffuse literature on the Canada lynx.

Lynx rufus

BOBCAT

Description

Bobcats are medium-sized cats, about twice the size of a domestic cat, with a bobbed tail and long legs. Dorsal color in winter pelage is a grayish buff, whereas summer pelages are more reddish; both are marked with variably conspicuous streaks or spots. Bobcats have one annual molt, in the fall. The summer coat is simply a worn winter pelage. A facial ruff of fur is most noticeable in winter pelage. The underside, also spotted, is white and the insides of the forelegs are marked with horizontal bands. Measurements are: total length 730–1,000 mm; length of tail 120–160 mm; length of hindfoot 143–200; length of ear 50–85 mm; weight 5–14 kg. Males are about one-third larger than females. The bobcat can be difficult to distinguish from the lynx but differs in having shorter fur, shorter dark ear-tufts, smaller feet, a longer tail, dark bands across the front legs, and more distinct spots overall than the lynx. Both species have a black-tipped tail, but the bobcat's tail is incompletely so—black above and white below. The skulls are very similar, as detailed in the account of the lynx. There are 28 teeth, compared with 30 teeth in domestic cats. Females have 6 mammae; males have a rudimentary baculum. Methods for aging bobcats were provided by Crowe (1975).

PHOTOGRAPH 12-3. Bobcat (*Lynx rufus*). Photograph by Joseph Van Wormer. All rights reserved. Photo Archives, Denver Museum of Nature and Science.

Distribution

The bobcat has the broadest distribution of wild felids in the conterminous United States. Bobcats occur widely in Colorado, most abundantly in the western two-thirds of the state and the roughlands of southeastern Colorado. Little is known about the status or ecology of the bobcat in Colorado outside of piñon-juniper woodlands and montane forests and shrublands.

In Colorado, *Lynx rufus baileyi* is the subspecies of southeastern and southwestern roughlands and the San Luis Valley; elsewhere in the mountains and the Western Slope, *L. r. pallescens* occurs; and where present in northeastern Colorado, *L. r. rufus* is the likely subspecies (D. Armstrong 1972). Twelve subspecies are recognized in North and Central America, but a thorough revision syn-

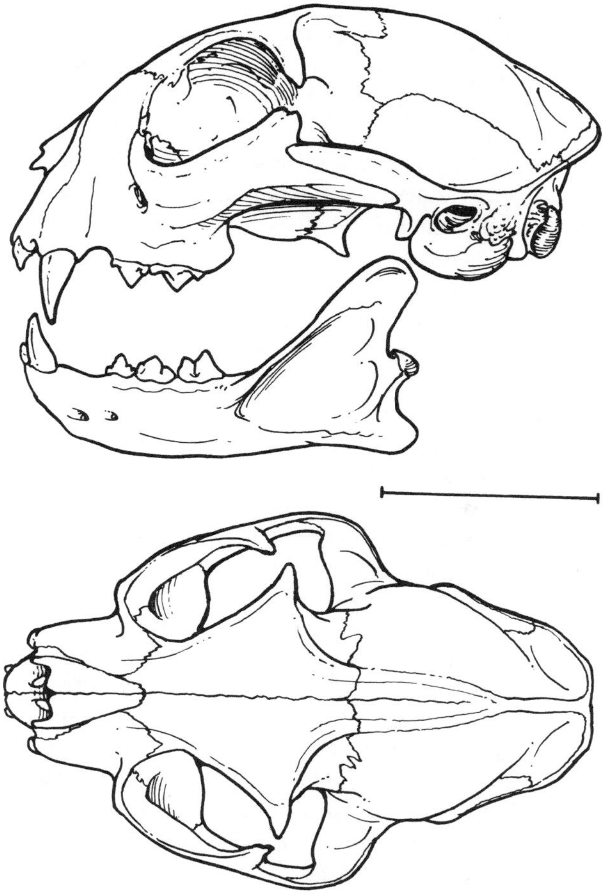

FIGURE 12-1. Lateral and dorsal views of the skull of a bobcat (*Lynx rufus*). Scale = 5 cm.

MAP 12-5. Distribution of the bobcat (*Lynx rufus*) in North America.

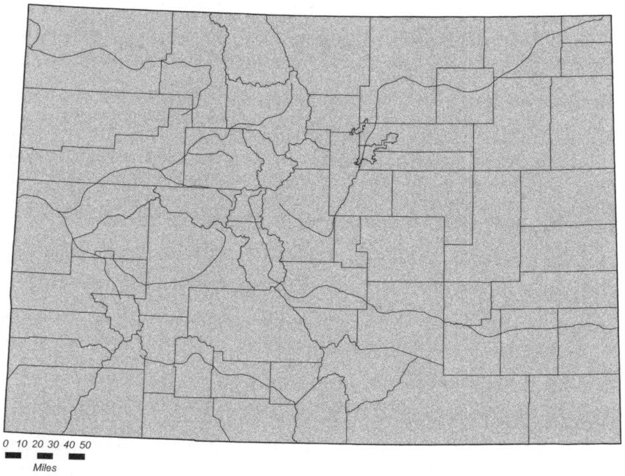

MAP 12-6. Distribution of the bobcat (*Lynx rufus*) in Colorado.

thesizing molecular genetics with morphological variation might reduce this number substantially (see Werdelin 1981).

Natural History

Bobcats in the western United States are most common in the rocky, broken terrain of foothills and canyonlands. Preferred habitats are piñon-juniper woodlands and montane forests, although they occupy most ecosystems in Colorado, including riparian woodland on the eastern plains. They avoid unbroken grasslands, agricultural land, and densely populated areas, although R. L. Harrison (1998) reported bobcats as frequent in residential areas in north-central New Mexico. Favored habitats provide resting and denning sites and good cover for hunting and stalking prey. Females are thought to be more selective of quality habitat than males. In Montana, bobcats favored sites with at least 52 percent vertical cover (P. Knowles 1985). In Colorado, bobcats chose diurnal loafing sites in steep-sloped, rocky areas with dense vertical cover (more than 70 percent) and little herbaceous ground cover (E. M. Anderson 1990).

Snow cover in excess of about 15 cm restricts their movements and may cause them to follow game trails, windblown areas, roads, or similar routes.

Bobcats hunt by stealth, either stalking prey or waiting in ambush, relying on surprise rather than on a lengthy chase. Bobcats and lynx are both reported to occasionally use "hunting beds," in which they lie in wait for prey in areas with high numbers of lagomorphs (E. M. Anderson and Lovallo 2003). Lagomorphs, cottontails in particular, are their specialty and comprise 20 to 70 percent of the diet in studies in western states; they switch prey when leporids are in short supply (Knick 1990; E. M. Anderson and Lovallo 2003). In south-central and southeastern Colorado, bobcats often fed on cottontails and woodrats (L. Jackson 1985; E. M. Anderson 1987b). Opportunistic, bobcats will feed on practically any other prey, including mice, chipmunks, tree squirrels, ground squirrels, prairie dogs, snowshoe hares, porcupines, small birds, deer, amphibians, and even crayfish (J. H. Jones and Smith 1979). They also kill young domestic sheep, goats, and poultry. Bobcats were implicated in the deaths of 11,100 sheep (especially lambs) in the United States in 2004 (Agricultural Statistics Board 2005). In Colorado, a reported 100 sheep were killed.

Deer remains were present in 34 percent of bobcat scats in Utah and Nevada (Gashwiler et al. 1960). Trainer (1975) considered bobcats an important predator on deer fawns in Oregon, and Beale and Smith (1973) reported bobcats to effectively kill antelope fawns in Utah. Adult deer usually are killed when bedded down, by means of bites to the neck and throat, which can be made in extremely rapid succession. Juveniles and adult females are more likely to feed on rodents than are males, if rabbits are available. Bobcats occasionally cache food. Biggins and Biggins (2006) described in detail a bobcat attack on a cottontail (*Sylvilagus* sp.) near Livermore. The bobcat stalked the rabbit for more than an hour and then culminated a 12-second chase covering 116 m (more than 20 mph). Two strides were measured at 5.2 m long, and the final leap was 5.5 m.

There is little dietary overlap between coyotes and bobcats in Rocky Mountain National Park, where bobcats preyed heavily on snowshoe hares and cottontails and coyotes fed on ungulates and rodents (Makar 1980). Like other felids, bobcats require a much higher protein diet than most other mammalian carnivores. Vegetable matter does not provide the animals with adequate nitrogen. Grass boluses are often reported in studies of food habits, but such materials probably function as a purgative and not as a food resource. Caged bobcats in Georgia averaged 138 kcal/kg/day in food intake, although they could maintain condition on half of that amount (Golley et al. 1965). Physiological studies and computer modeling in New York suggested that seasonal energetic demands are actually lower in February and March, despite cold weather, because animals metabolized stored fat and reduced daily activity. Males and females both required about 374 g of food daily per kilogram of body weight in March, whereas during peak seasonal activities males needed about 760 g/kg and females about 830 g/kg (Gustafson 1984).

Bobcats are generally solitary except during the breeding season and when females are rearing young. A number of authors have suggested bobcats have a "land tenure system" based on prior rights and residency that prevents much displacement (Lovallo and Anderson 1995, 1996; E. M. Anderson and Lovallo 2003; J. Benson et al. 2004). The degree of social tolerance depends on population density, prey availability, weather, and presence and distribution of suitable dens or shelters. Home ranges of males overlap with those of several females; home ranges of adult females are usually non-overlapping (E. M. Anderson 1987b). However, bobcats may share refuges during inclement weather. Home ranges in the West vary from 9 to more than 100 km^2 for adult males and 2 to 70 km^2 for adult females, with variation due to habitat quality, sex, and season of year (McCord and Cardoza 1982; Rolley 1987; G. Koehler and Hornocker 1989; E. M. Anderson and Lavallo 2003). Home ranges in southern Colorado averaged 42 to 46 km^2 for adult males and 17 to 22 km^2 for adult females (D. Jackson 1986; E. M. Anderson 1987b). Subadults are tolerated on adult home ranges in most situations although there are a few reports of intense fights between adults and juvenile males; a few instances of cannibalism have been reported (McCord and Cardoza 1982; Rolley 1987). Density estimates of bobcats in the western United States range from 5 to 77 per 100 km^2 (E. M. Anderson and Lavallo 2003)

Bobcats scent-mark with feces, urine, and anal gland secretions, which are rubbed on objects or discharged on the ground. These odorous deposits may be enhanced by scrapings with the feet, which add a visual component to the signal. Marking with these secretions occurs along trails and at scent posts. Feces may be covered or uncovered and placed on unprepared ground, or placed in a scrape made with the hindlegs. Females with kittens are responsible for most fecal marking. The use of such scent stations may serve to mark territories (T. Bailey 1974; McCord and Cardoza 1982).

Bobcats are active all year-round. Most hunting occurs at night or at dawn and dusk. On cloudy days in undisturbed areas, or during periods of extreme cold, they may hunt during the middle of the day. Daily movements averaged 1.8 km for males and 1.2 km for females in Idaho and 1 to 3 km in Colorado. Long-distance movements of up to 182 km by young males have been reported in a situation where lagomorph populations declined and local food resources became scarce. Juveniles dispersing from their natal areas may move 20 or 30 km (T. Bailey 1974; E. M. Anderson 1987b).

Female bobcats are seasonally polyestrous and ovulate spontaneously. Previously they were thought to be induced ovulators, as are domestic cats. Females may have up to 3 estrous cycles over a 4-month period if not bred. Although bobcats may breed at any time of the year, reproductive activity is highest in February and March in Wyoming, with most births occurring in April or May (Crowe 1975). In Utah, embryos are present in females from January to September, although mostly in March and April (Gashwiler et al. 1961). In Idaho, pregnancy rates of adult females dropped from 100 to 12 percent because of a decline in jackrabbits (Knick 1990). Gestation takes 60 to 70 days (E. M. Anderson 1987a). Females that lose a litter may be able to produce a second litter the same year. Average litter size was 2 to 3 (average, 2.9) in the Fort Carson area, south of Colorado Springs (D. Jackson 1986). In that study, 2 females each had 2 litters within a 9-month period. Most adult females only have 1 litter per year. Kittens are nursed for about 60 days and remain with the female into the fall. In Colorado most juveniles are 9 to 11 months of age when they disperse. Some breeding occurs in yearling females, who have smaller litters and lower pregnancy rates than older females. Otherwise, females are sexually mature in their second year, as are young males (E. M. Anderson 1987a).

Although most adults in a population are residents, a small but important component is transients. These individuals are quick to fill in territories left vacant by the death of the resident. Little is known about population dynamics of bobcats in Colorado; most of the data represent harvest trends, which are subject to vagaries of trapping and inconsistencies in reporting. Limited data from Fort Carson and Piñon Canyon studies suggest that predation and hunter harvest are the principal causes of death in bobcats, accounting for 29 and 46 percent of observed mortality, respectively (D. Jackson 1986; E. M. Anderson 1987b). Starvation and disease accounted for another 12 to 20 percent of known mortality. Annual survival rates were 76 percent for adult bobcats at Fort Carson. Studies in other western states summarized by E. M. Anderson and Lovallo (2003) showed annual survival rates ranging from 0.14 to 0.70, with human take and predation being the major causes of death. Most research suggests that harvest is additive to other sources of mortality and that populations are susceptible to overharvest when fur prices are high. Some local populations in Colorado probably were overexploited until the ban on leg-hold traps in 1997. From 1939 to 1982 an average of 1,042 pelts was sold annually in Colorado. From 1982 to 1991, trapper questionnaires showed an average annual harvest of 1,312 animals (J. Fitzgerald 1993b). Lipscomb et al. (1983) reported 61 percent of harvested bobcats were males, with adults making up 80 percent of the harvest. Sex ratio of adults at Fort Carson was 0.73:1.00 males to females. The overall sex ratio was 0.79:1.00. Juvenile/adult age ratio was 0.35:1 (D. Jackson 1986).

Mountain lions and coyotes have been implicated as predators on female bobcats, and bobcat populations may be suppressed in areas where coyote control is absent. Habitat suitability, status, and management of bobcats in Colorado were addressed by L. Alexander (1977) and Donoho (1977). Bobcats can be trapped as furbearers or hunted as small game in Colorado with a 4-month season. However, under provisions of the Convention on International Trade in Endangered Species, the US Fish and Wildlife Service regulates total harvest in the United States by issuing a limited number of tags to each state per calendar year. (Therefore, in Table 4-3, data on bobcat harvest are reported by calendar year and not by hunting/trapping season as other species are.) From 1995 to 2007 an average of 768 bobcat pelts were tagged annually (E. Gorman, Colorado Division of Wildlife, personal communication). Bobcats killed in Colorado (deliberately or inadvertently as roadkill) must be inspected and tagged by a representative of the Colorado Division of Wildlife.

Literature on bobcats was reviewed by McCord and Cardoza (1982), E. M. Anderson (1987a), Rolley (1987), Larivière and Walton (1997), E. M. Anderson and Lovallo (2003), and K. Hansen (2006).

Family Canidae—Dogs, Foxes, and Kin

Members of this family are typically doglike, with long legs; a long, usually bushy tail; long ears; and a pointed, sharp muzzle. Feet are digitigrade, with 4 toes on the hindfoot and 4 or 5 toes on the forefoot. Claws are non-retractile. The rostrum is long, and the auditory bullae are well developed. The dental formula for all Coloradan canids is 3/3, 1/1,

4/4, 2/3 = 42 teeth. The carnassial teeth are well developed, and the canines are long and conical. Most canids are excellent thermoregulators, and several species live in extremely cold climates. Other species are adapted for semiarid to arid conditions where salivation and panting are used as cooling mechanisms. Sweat glands are restricted to the pads of the feet. Canids are monoestrous, and Coloradan species generally breed in January, February, and March. Burrows or other dens are typically used as whelping sites, and litters usually range from 3 to 6 young. The baculum is well developed, and males are generally larger than females. In many areas 2 (e.g., kit fox–coyote) or 3 (e.g., wolf–coyote–red fox) species of canids are sympatric, leading to some degree of competition for either food or habitat (W. E. Johnson et al. 1996; Bekoff and Gese 2003; Cypher 2003; Paquet and Carbyn 2003). Canids generally are considered to be the living carnivores closest to the "root" of the family tree of carnivores. A recent "supertree" of carnivores based on molecular, morphological, and fossil evidence supports this contention (Bininda-Emonds 2007).

Some aspects of the taxonomy of the family are unresolved, for example species limits in North American wolves (Wozencraft 2005). The family contains about 13 genera and 35 species (D. Wilson and Reeder 2005) and is native to all land areas except Antarctica, the Australian region, and some oceanic islands. Since its domestication from wolves some 16,000 (Pang et al. 2009) to 33,000 or more years ago (Shipman 2009), the dog, *Canis familiaris* (also known as *Canis lupus familiaris*; see Wozencraft 2005), has been introduced to ecosystems worldwide and has diversified genetically to a remarkable degree (Ostrander 2007). The family itself dates from the Late Eocene (40–43 million years ago) to the Recent in North America, with early canids probably colonizing the New World from Asia. In Colorado there are 3 genera and 6 species of canids, of which 1, the gray wolf, was extirpated about 70 years ago (but may eventually restore itself).

Key to the Species of the Family Canidae in Colorado

1. Postorbital processes thin and concave 2

1' Postorbital processes thick and convex . . . . *Canis*, 5

2. Backs of ears red and cheeks reddish; tail with black dorsal mane and tip; skull with lyre-shaped temporal ridges (Fig. 12-2); mandible notched on posterior end of horizontal ramus . . . . Common Gray Fox—*Urocyon cinereoargenteus*, p. 384

2' Backs of ears not red; tail without dorsal mane; skull without conspicuous lyre-shaped temporal ridges (Fig. 12-2); mandible not notched on posterior end of horizontal ramus . . . . *Vulpes*, 3

3. Tip of tail white, ears with black tips, upper body reddish; length of maxillary toothrow greater than 55; condylobasal length greater than 125 . . . . Red Fox—*Vulpes vulpes*, p. 380

3' Tip of tail black, ears without black tips, upper body buffy gray to reddish gray; blackish spots on sides of muzzle; length of maxillary toothrow less than 55 mm; condylobasal length less than 125 mm 4

4. Ear longer, greater than 75 mm from notch; auditory bullae larger . . . . Kit Fox—*Vulpes macrotis*, p. 374

4' Ear shorter, 75 mm or less from notch; auditory bullae smaller . . . . Swift Fox—*Vulpes velox*, p. 377

5. Total length greater than 1,400 mm; greatest length of skull greater than 230 mm; condylobasal length greater than 200 mm; tips of upper canine teeth usually not extending below a line connecting mental foramina of mandible when jaws are closed; tail held high while running . . . . Gray Wolf—*Canis lupus*, p. 369

5' Total length less than 1,400 mm; greatest length of skull less than 230 mm; condylobasal length less than 200 mm; tips of upper canines extending below a line connecting anterior mental foramina of mandible; tail held low while running . . . . Coyote—*Canis latrans*, p. 365

Genus *Canis*—Wolves and Kin

Wozencraft (2005) asserted that the genus *Canis* includes 6 species—the Holarctic wolf, the North American coyote, and 4 Old World species: 3 species of jackals and the Ethiopian wolf. He listed the domestic dog and the Australian dingo as domestic forms derived from the wolf. The red wolf is considered by some to be a valid species (*C. rufus*), but others believe that the form is a hybrid between wolves and coyotes. The genus *Canis* probably originated in the Early to Middle Pliocene (Wayne et al. 1995).

Canis latrans
COYOTE

Description

The coyote is a slender canid about the size of a small German shepherd dog. The tail is bushy and usually held low. The ears are pointed and held erect. Color varies considerably depending on season and location. Dorsal color is tawny gray, and animals from desert areas or low elevations are usually paler than those from other habitats. The face, forelegs, and ears tend to be reddish to brownish buff. The tail sports a black tip, and often the neck and shoulder areas have black-tipped hairs forming a "saddle." The throat and belly are paler than the rest of the body. Measurements are: total length 1,050–1,400 mm; length of tail 300–400 mm; length of hindfoot 175–220 mm; length of ear 80–130 mm; and weight 9–16 kg, with a range for adult males of 8–20 kg and slightly smaller for adult females (7–18 kg). The largest reported coyote weighed almost 34 kg and was more than 1,600 mm in length. The skull is usually less than 220 mm long. Females have 8 mammae.

Coyotes can generally be differentiated from wolves on the basis of longer and more pointed ears, more pointed rostrum, smaller size (usually less than 20 kg), a smaller nosepad (about 25 mm in diameter), and a hindfoot pad with a diameter of 32 mm or less (compared with 38 mm or greater in the wolf). Skulls of some breeds of domestic dogs may be difficult to distinguish from either wolf or coyote. The ratio of palatal width (distance between inner margins of alveoli of first upper molars) to length of upper cheektooth row (from anterior alveolar margin of first premolar to posterior alveolar margin of the last molar) is about 95 percent accurate for distinguishing dogs and coyotes. If the toothrow is 3 times the palatal width or greater, it probably is a coyote. If the ratio is less than 2.8, the animal likely is a dog.

PHOTOGRAPH 12-4. Coyote (*Canis latrans*). Photograph by William E. Ervin.

Coyotes are adaptable and widespread and may hybridize with red wolves and domestic dogs, rendering positive identification of some specimens almost impossible unless multivariate analysis or genetic techniques are used. DNA can be used to differentiate coyote scat from that of other carnivores (Onorato et al. 2006), and even to identify sex of individual coyotes killing livestock (Blejwas et al. 2006). Tooth sections and tooth wear patterns can be used to age individuals (W. Bowen 1982).

Distribution

Coyotes are among the most widespread and adaptable of carnivores, ranging from Costa Rica to the North Slope of Alaska. Elimination of the gray wolf, human modification of the environment, and possible human translocation of coyotes have enabled the species to colonize the entire United States, including the interior of large cities (Voight and Berg 1987; Bekoff and Gese 2003). Prior to efforts to eliminate them in the late 1800s and 1900s, they probably reached their greatest numbers on the plains of North America (Gier 1975). The extirpation of the gray wolf appears to have removed competition and predation pressure on coyotes, allowing them to expand in abundance and distribution (Carbyn 1987; Crabtree and Sheldon 1999b; but see Gese, Ruff, and Crabtree 1996a, 1996b). There are 19 recognized subspecies of coyotes; given the mobility of the species, the usefulness of some of these nominal taxa is questionable (Nowak 1978). *Canis latrans latrans* has been ascribed a range on Colorado's eastern plains; *C. l. lestes* occurs in western Colorado except for the extreme southwest, where *C. l. mearnsi* occurs (D. Armstrong 1972).

Natural History

Coyotes are probably the best studied of all wild carnivores, largely because of long-term efforts to reduce populations. In Colorado, however, there also has been a great deal of basic and applied research on the animals, especially by Professor Marc Bekoff and students at the University of Colorado at Boulder (see Bekoff [2001] for partial bibliog-

MAP 12-7. Distribution of the coyote (*Canis latrans*) in North America.

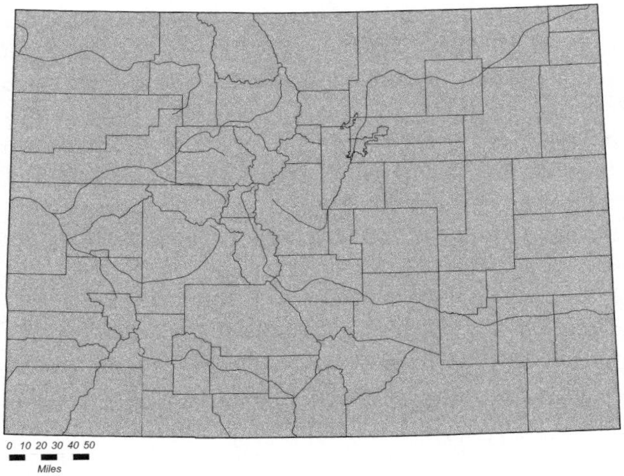

MAP 12-8. Distribution of the coyote (*Canis latrans*) in Colorado.

raphy) and Professors Eric M. Gese and William F. Andelt and students at Colorado State University. Coyotes are common statewide in all habitats and at all elevations, including suburban and even urban environments (C. A. Jones et al. 2003). They probably are least abundant in dense coniferous forests. In areas where they are subjected to intense human control efforts, they are often restricted to broken, rough country with abundant shrub cover and a good supply of lagomorphs or rodents. Churchill (2009) provided a useful review of the urban coyote situation in Colorado.

Coyotes are opportunistic consumers. Well over 100 studies have been conducted on coyote food habits since the early work by O. Murie (1935) and A. Murie (1940), yet their findings, in terms of range of diet and proportional contribution of food items, are little changed (Crabtree and Sheldon 1999a, 1999b). Coyotes prefer animal matter, which comprises roughly 90 percent of the diet (Bekoff 1977). Diet changes with availability of food. In much of the West and Midwest, jackrabbits, cottontail rabbits, and rodents make up the bulk of the prey (F. Clark 1972; Andrews and Boggess 1978; H. Hilton 1978; Van Vuren 1990), with rodents important summer prey and lagomorphs important in winter. Carrion of livestock and big game is also eaten (R. S. Cook et al. 1971; A. Todd and Keith 1983; Andelt 1987; Gese, Ruff, and Crabtree 1996b). Coyote predation on big game and livestock is usually targeted at younger animals; it is not clear whether they seek malnourished, diseased, or weaker individuals (Andelt 1987). Coyotes readily prey on fawns (G. White, Garrott, et al. 1987). They have greater difficulty taking adult wild ungulates, but in Colorado, coyotes do kill healthy adult deer (Dorrance 1965; Compton 1980; Gese, Rongstad, and Mytton 1988b). Social hunting and the accumulation of deep snow enhance the ability of coyotes to prey on adults (Gese and Grothe 1995). Coyotes feeding pups may switch to hunting larger prey. Plant material consumed generally consists of fruit, berries, and cultivated crops, including melons and carrots. In southeastern Colorado, juniper "berries" were a major component of the winter diet; rodents were important in spring; ungulate fawns in June and grasshoppers were eaten when available in summer (Gese, Rongstad, and Mytton 1988b). An adult coyote requires 600 g of meat per day (250 kg per year) and a lactating female requires half again as much (Gier 1975). Predatory behaviors in coyotes, including methods of stalking and capturing small mammals, have been described by Bekoff and Wells (1986) and Gese, Ruff, and Crabtree (1996b). Cooperative hunting by coyote packs was described by Bowyer (1987) and Gese and Grothe (1995).

Coyote social structure is centered on mated pairs and their pups and is based on a dominance system. Where winter-kill ungulates provide an important food resource, larger groups may form that include non-breeding adults. These additional group members ("helpers") are from previous years' litters and assist in the care of the young of the year. Extended family groups serve to defend better concentrated resources provided by ungulate carcasses (Camenzind 1974, 1978; Andelt et al. 1980; Bekoff and Wells 1980; Andelt 1985; Gese, Ruff, and Crabtree 1996b). Packs of coyotes defend territories but pairs or solitary animals generally do not (Bekoff and Wells 1980; Gese and Ruff 1997, 1998). Group size may decrease in fall, when pups disperse, and increase in winter as pairs come together for breeding. In Yellowstone National Park, large pack structure and behaviors greatly resemble those of wolves (Gese, Ruff, and Crabtree 1996a, 1996b, 1996c). Transient or lone coyotes tend to be young dispersing animals or older nonbreeding individuals displaced by younger animals. In Colorado, 78 percent of individuals in a population were residents and 22 percent were transients (Gese, Rongstad, and Mytton 1988b).

Visual communication (including a variety of facial and postural expressions; Bekoff 1974) and vocal communication (Lehner 1978a, 1978b) are frequent and ongoing among members of the group and are also used in intergroup communication. Vocalizations include yips, howls, and short doglike barks; social status may influence vocalization rates (Gese and Ruff 1998). Olfactory communication is also significant; scent-marking with both urine and feces may have a function in clearly delineating territorial boundaries, and the use of urine is especially important during courtship (M. Wells and Bekoff 1981; Gese and Ruff 1997; J. Allen et al. 1999).

Courtship activities start 2 to 3 months before actual mating (Bekoff and Diamond 1976; Bekoff and Wells 1982). Pairing between adults may persist for several years but need not be permanent. Coyotes are monoestrous, with females in breeding condition for about 5 days, usually from January to March (Kennelly and Johns 1976). Gestation takes about 63 days and litters average 5 or 6 young (Bekoff and Diamond 1976). Litter sizes may fluctuate by 1 or 2 young depending on the abundance of rodents and density of the coyote population (Gier 1968; Knowlton 1972). In years with good food supply yearling females often breed (Knowlton and Gese 1995); in most years 60 to 90 percent of adult females produce litters (Gese, Rongstad, and Mytton 1989a; Knowlton et al. 1999). Sex ratios approximate 1:1. Compensatory reproduction occurs in areas where coyotes are subjected to prolonged stringent control (Andelt 1987; Voigt and Berg 1987).

Natal dens are generally excavated in areas with heavy cover, including shrub thickets, downed timber, steep banks, or rocky areas. Young, blind and helpless at birth, may emerge from the den as early as the second or third week and are weaned at about 6 weeks of age. During this time, important developmental interactions occur during play with littermates. These play fights, with aggression, submission, and posturing, establish the groundwork for future dominance relationships. Dispersal, if it occurs, is usually at 6 to 9 months of age, but it may be slowed or halted when population densities are high (Voigt and Berg 1987).

Population density is variable and may be closely related to the density of jackrabbits, snowshoe hares, and rodents (F. Clark 1972; John Gross et al. 1974; A. Todd and Keith 1983). In Wyoming, densities were 0.5 animals per square kilometer before pups emerged from the den. Following whelping, densities increased almost threefold (Camenzind 1978). In sagebrush areas in Utah and Idaho, densities were 0.1–0.3 animals per square kilometer (F. Clark 1972). One denning pair per square kilometer was estimated as maximal for the rolling plains of eastern Colorado and Kansas, with up to 3 pairs per square kilometer in more eroded "badlands" environments (Gier 1975). Densities of 0.2 to 0.4 animals per square kilometer are probably representative over much of coyote range (Knowlton 1972; Bekoff and Gese 2003).

Coyotes may be active at any time, although most activity occurs in the early morning and evening; activity can vary with the amount of human disturbance (Gese, Rongstad, and Mytton 1989b; A. Kitchen, Gese, and Schauster 2000a). During winter months in snow country coyotes may spend more time resting, especially if carrion is available (Bekoff and Wells 1986; Gese, Ruff, and Crabtree 1996a). Buskirk et al. (2000), Crete and Larivière (2003), and Bunnell et al. (2006) suggested that coyotes following snowmobile trails can reduce energy expense and occupy habitats otherwise not readily accessible, possibly hampering lynx conservation and recovery. Home ranges vary widely, from 4 to 5 km^2 in Texas to as large as 143 km^2 in central Washington (Voigt and Berg 1987). In southeastern Colorado, the mean annual home range was 11.3 km^2 (range, 2.8–32.0 km^2) for residents and 106 km^2 (range, 61–185 km^2) for transients (Gese, Rongstad, and Mytton 1988a). Home range fidelity was high for coyotes in this area (A. Kitchen, Gese, and Schauster et al. 2000b). Home ranges of males and females are about equal in size in a given area, probably because they represent pairs on territories. Home ranges are often smaller for coyotes feeding on big game carrion than for those that have to hunt for smaller prey (Bekoff and Wells 1980).

Coyotes are ubiquitous and abundant in Colorado and sometimes cause problems for people and their pets and livestock. Predation by coyotes on livestock has been a concern of ranchers for more than a century. For much of this period, active control has been pursued, often with governmental subsidy. Nationwide, coyotes are the principal wildlife predator on sheep and lambs, making up about 60 percent of total predators and implicated in the deaths of some 135,600 animals in 2004, valued at some $10.7 million (Agricultural Statistics Board 2005). In Colorado, some 6,100 sheep and lambs were reportedly taken by coyotes, about 62.5 percent of all predation on livestock reported for the state. The Colorado Division of Wildlife (2007d) provided helpful suggestions for avoiding conflict. Predation on domestic sheep by coyotes (and also by black bears and mountain lions) can be reduced by use of guard dogs (especially Great Pyrenees, Akbash, and Komondors). In 1993, 125 sheepgrowers reported that 392 dogs prevented $891,440 in losses (Andelt and Hopper 2000a).

Controversy and emotions run high on issues of coyote control and on how serious losses are to livestock growers. Andelt (1996) reviewed aspects of coyote biology, as well as that of other potential predators, on western livestock ranges. Domestic sheep are often the target of coyotes on western rangelands, but some coyotes totally ignore them as prey (Shivik et al. 1996; Knowlton et al. 1999; Sacks et al. 1999). Blejwas et al. (2006) suggested that breeding male coyotes are responsible for most predation on sheep and urged targeting of such individuals explicitly. In Colorado, 5 percent losses of domestic sheep to coyotes were reported by Sterner and Shumake (1978). Studies summarized by Bekoff and Gese (2003) suggested losses of lambs range from 1 to 29 percent and for ewes from 0.1 to 8.0 percent, depending on levels of coyote control. Research has led to more effective and humane methods for coyote control, as well as techniques for decreasing losses without coyote removal, such as improved animal husbandry, fencing, and use of guard animals (Andelt 1987, 1996; Knowlton et al. 1999; Bekoff and Gese 2003). Management of carnivores harassing or preying upon domestic livestock is the responsibility of the Wildlife Services branch of the Animal and Plant Health Inspection Service of the US Department of Agriculture (Wildlife Services 2002); Keefover-Ring (2009) prepared an analysis of Wildlife Services and recommended its abolition.

Impacts of historical coyote control are poorly documented, although W. Robinson (1953) did compile some information, based on data from "1080 stations." (Compound 1080 is sodium fluoroacetate—also known as sodium monofluoroacetate—a chemical that was used widely for federal "animal damage control" until banned by an executive order in 1972.) For Colorado, Wyoming, and New Mexico, coyotes were a quarter as abundant in the 1950s as in the early 1940s, and at the same time populations of bobcats, skunks, badgers, and raccoons increased. W. Robinson (1953) speculated that the change might have been caused by a decline in commercial trapping, but it could also represent differential susceptibility of various carnivores to poisoned baits.

Coyotes may live 13 to 15 years (Knowlton 1972; Gese 1990) but such longevity is rare. Annual mortality is estimated at as high as 40 to 70 percent in juveniles and about 35 to 40 percent in animals over 1 year of age. Depending on location, human-caused mortality has been estimated to range from 38 to 90 percent (Voigt and Berg 1987). In Colorado, coyotes are classified as furbearers (Table 4-1) and can be hunted year-round statewide with no possession limits. Except for a low point during the 1950s, about 7,000 coyote pelts were sold annually from 1939 to 1982 (J. Fitzgerald 1993b). Reported harvest in recent years has increased to more than 30,000 per year (Table 4-3). Wolves and mountain lions frequently kill coyotes, especially in winter when more competition exists (G. Koehler and Hornocker 1991; Crabtree and Sheldon 1999a). Wilkinson and Douglass (2002) observed a group of mule deer killing a yearling coyote near Cody, Wyoming. Coyotes are susceptible to canine distemper, canine parvovirus, and canine hepatitis but rarely show evidence of rabies (Pence and Custer 1981; Gese, Schlutz, et al. 1991; Gese, Schlutz, et al. 1997).

Coyotes are well documented for interspecific killing of smaller canids, including red foxes (A. Sargeant and Allen 1989) and kit and swift foxes (P. White, Ralls, and Garrott 1994; Cypher and Spencer 1998; A. Kitchen 1999; A. Kitchen, Gese, and Schauster 1999). Kamler, Ballard, Gilliland, et al. (2003) suggested that suppression of coyotes might be warranted to increase swift fox populations in some areas in Texas. Henke and Bryant (1999) considered coyotes to be keystone predators in Texas. Coyotes may partially restrict populations of other small carnivores, including bobcats and possibly badgers, by direct predation or interspecific competition for food (Linhart and Robinson 1972; Gier 1975; Rathbun et al. 1980; A. Sargeant 1982; Crabtree and Sheldon 1999a). On the other hand, cooperative hunting with badgers may occur (Dobie 1961). The vast literature on coyotes was reviewed by Bekoff (1977, 1978, 1982), Voight and Berg (1987), and Bekoff and Gese (2003). Works by S. Young and Jackson (1951) and A. Murie (1940) are classics on the natural history of the species. For an anthology of literary appreciation of the coyote, see W. Bright (1993).

Canis lupus

GRAY WOLF

Description

The gray wolf is a large, powerful canid with a long bushy tail and erect ears, more rounded than those of the coyote. The legs are longer, the feet larger, and the chest narrower than on a comparable-sized dog. When the animal is running, the tail is held high, but it does not curl up onto the back. The fur is thick, long, and coarse. There is much individual variation in color, and not much geographic pattern. Most gray wolves are not actually pure gray in color. Dorsal color is more often a pale tan to cream mixed with darker and paler hairs. Darker-colored hairs often are concentrated on the dorsum whereas the extremities, lower body, and facial areas are paler. Adults almost invariably have white around the mouth. Cary (1911) noted that in Colorado, mountain-dwelling animals were darker than those from the plains. However, S. Young and Goldman (1944) indicated that pelage was relatively pale for both subspecies in Colorado and that there was wide variation in color even in littermates, citing a litter of 6 from near Pueblo in which 2 pups were almost white, 2 were intermediate, and 2 were gray-black to brownish black. Measurements are: total length 1,300–1,600 mm (although a few males may measure close to 1,800 mm); length of tail 360–500 mm; length of hindfoot 70–90 mm; weight 18–80 kg. Adults are about 700 mm tall at the shoulder. Males are usually slightly larger than females. The skull is 230–290 mm in greatest length with a zygomatic breadth of 120–150 mm. The sagittal crest is typically prominent. Females have 10 mammae. As with most canids, a well-developed pre-caudal or tail gland is located on the dorsal side of the tail near its base. Anal glands are also present. Hybrids between gray wolves, red wolves (*Canis rufus*), coyotes, and domestic dogs are not uncommon, and in many parts of the present ranges of gray and red wolves, hybridization is obscuring the original gene pools. J. Reed et al. (2004) presented methods for differentiation of wolf from coyote scats using DNA analysis. Pilgrim et al. (1998) and D. Boyd et al. (2001) discussed methods for detecting hybridization in coyotes and wolves and also dogs and wolves using DNA analysis of tissues.

PHOTOGRAPH 12-5. Gray wolf (*Canis lupus*). Photograph by William E. Ervin.

Distribution

The gray wolf is circumpolar in the Northern Hemisphere and historically it had one of the largest geographic ranges of any mammalian species. It had been thought that gray wolves were one of the few large predators to survive North America's dramatic extinction of megafauna in the Late Pleistocene, but that may not have been the case. Rather, extirpation may have occurred (more or less concurrent with the arrival of humans), with natural restoration from Eurasia (J. Leonard et al. 2007). In historic times, gray wolves formerly occupied most of western and central North America except for much of coastal California and the deserts of Baja California. Over much of their range in the United States, the animals were eradicated, partly at public expense, to eliminate their depredation (real and imagined) on livestock. M. J. Robinson (2005) reviewed governmental attempts to exterminate wolves, particularly in the West.

Some have argued that gray wolves of the northeastern states and much of Ontario and Quebec represent a separate species, the eastern timber wolf (*Canis lycaon*) (P. Wilson et al. 2000). The southeastern states and the Gulf Coast are the range of the red wolf (*Canis rufus*) (Nowak 2002). In the contiguous United States, wolf populations still exist in northern Minnesota, northern Wisconsin, Michigan's Upper Peninsula, and parts of Montana, Idaho, Washington, and Wyoming. Populations in central Idaho, southern Montana, and northwestern Wyoming are largely the result of restoration in Yellowstone National Park and Idaho in 1995–1996. A few wolves exist in southern Arizona and New Mexico and are part of the Mexican wolf (*C. l. baileyi*) recovery effort (Parsons 1998; Paquet et al. 2001). In theory, Colorado could eventually receive immigrating wolves from either or both restoration areas.

For administrative purposes, the US Fish and Wildlife Service (2003) declared that wolves encountered in Colorado north of Interstate 70 will be assumed to have

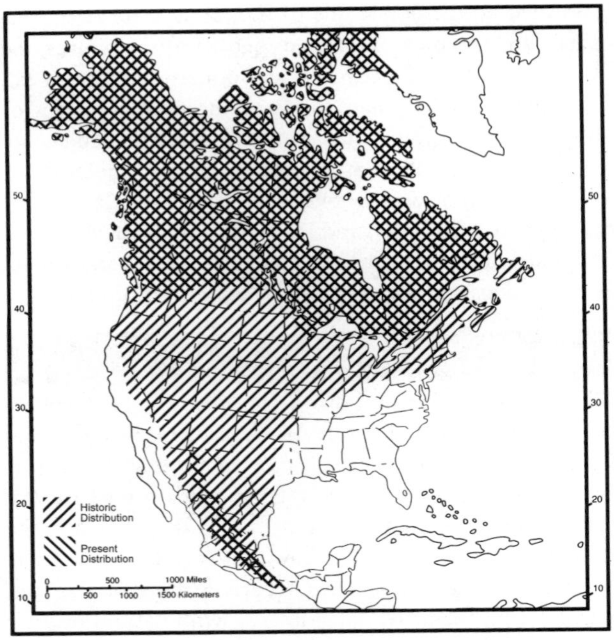

MAP 12-9. Historic and present distribution of the gray wolf (*Canis lupus*) in North America.

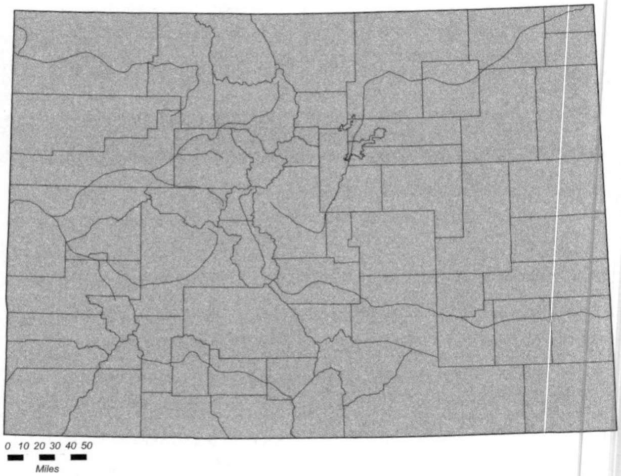

MAP 12-10. Historic distribution of the gray wolf (*Canis lupus*) in Colorado.

dispersed from the Yellowstone area, and so would be considered part of the Western Distinct Population Segment (DPS), whereas wolves observed south of I-70 will be assumed to have dispersed from the restoration area of the Mexican gray wolf in Arizona, the Southwestern DPS. This means that within Colorado, gray wolves would differ in degree of protection and details of management. By the way, these administrative distinct population segments do not correspond with the ranges of subspecies delineated by Goldman (1944), mapped by E. Hall (1981), or reviewed by Bogan and Mehlhop (1983). D. Armstrong (1972) did not attribute any Coloradan specimens to the Mexican gray wolf (*Canis lupus baileyi*). Nowak (1995) analyzed geographic variation in skulls of wolves and revised subspecies of North American wolves. Colorado was within the range of just one geographic race, *C. l. nubilus*. The Mexican wolf (*C. l. baileyi*) was ascribed a range in southeastern Arizona, southwestern New Mexico, Trans-Pecos Texas, and most of Mexico.

Historically, wolves occupied every county in Colorado; pressure from the livestock industry and public fear of the animals led to their persecution and eventual extirpation. Gipson and Ballard (1998) compiled and evaluated historical accounts of infamous wolves of the late nineteenth and early twentieth centuries, several of which ranged in Colorado, including Big Foot (Mesa County), the Greenhorn Wolf (Pueblo County), Old Clubfoot (Moffat County), Old Lefty (Eagle County), and Three Toes of the Apishapa (Las Animas County). Most of these storied animals were recognized by their tracks and renowned for their predilection for preying on livestock.

L. Bennett (1994) produced a thorough review of the feasibility of wolf recovery in Colorado. He identified 7 "potential wolf recovery areas" focused on national forests and scattered across the mountainous parts of the state: Grand Mesa–Uncompahgre–Gunnison, Rio Grande, Arapahoe-Roosevelt, Routt, Pike–San Isabel, San Juan, and White River. All of these areas support a prey base ample to support wolves. L. Bennett (1984) stressed the importance of restoring wolves from areas with topography, vegetation, and a prey base similar to those of Colorado and identified the Canadian Rockies of southwestern Alberta and adjacent British Columbia as an appropriate source area. D. Armstrong and Amoroso (2002) predicted that wolves eventually would disperse to Colorado from the restored population in the Yellowstone region.

Although there have been occasional reports (see, e.g., C. Foster 1976), no authenticated records of wolves in Colorado existed from 1935 (D. Armstrong 1972) until a marked wolf from the Yellowstone recovery area was found dead on I-70 in June 2004. *Comeback Wolves* (Wockner et al. 2005) is a collection of essays and poems by a wide range of writers all dedicated to the pioneer from Yellowstone,

"Wolf 293F." In March 2006 a wolf was observed and videotaped in North Park. Wolves may be present in Colorado, at least occasionally, and remain undetected. An 18-month-old female wolf from the "Mill Creek Pack," which ranges near Gardiner, Montana, was located by satellite in February 2009 (but not on the ground) in Eagle County, Colorado. GPS data indicated that she had wandered from Montana through Wyoming, southeastern Idaho, and northeastern Utah before arriving in Colorado (W. Lewis 2009).

It seems likely that wolves from release programs will continue to disperse to Colorado periodically. Whether that will eventually result in a breeding population is, of course, unknown. Gosnell (2009) discussed problems and prospects of wolf restoration in Colorado, in the general context of "rewilding" the Southern Rockies. D. W. Smith, Peterson, and Houston (2003) compared the ecological dynamics of wolves in Yellowstone with those in Isle Royale National Park, Michigan, where wolves reestablished themselves in the late 1940s, crossing Lake Superior on the ice. Isle Royale has a simpler predator assemblage and food web than does Yellowstone and so might have important lessons for the Southern Rockies.

Peek et al. (1991) stressed the importance of extensive public involvement in wolf restoration. Successful restoration demands matching biological needs of wolves with human needs and interests. Human dimensions were stressed by a workshop convened by the International Union for the Conservation of Nature (M. K. Phillips et al. 2000). In 2004, the Colorado Wildlife Commission adopted recommendations for the interim management of wolves that migrate to Colorado (Colorado Wolf Management Working Group 2004). If packs eventually form, new management practices will be established. The gray wolf in the conterminous United States is listed as endangered under the Endangered Species Act of 1973; it will probably be down-listed soon. In Colorado the wolf is listed as "state endangered." Current information on gray wolves in the state can be found on-line (Colorado Division of Wildlife 2008g), including links to "Guidelines for Response to Gray Wolf Reports in Colorado" and to the remarkable video of the wolf sighted north of Walden in 2006.

Goldman (1944) recognized 24 subspecies of wolves in North America. In Colorado, *Canis lupus nubilus* was ascribed a range east of the Continental Divide, with *C. l. youngi* ranging west of the Divide (D. Armstrong 1972). Nowak (1995) analyzed geographic variation in skulls of wolves and revised subspecies of North American wolves. Colorado was within the range of just one geographic race, *C. l. nubilus*. The Mexican wolf (*C. l. baileyi*) was ascribed a range in southeastern Arizona, southwestern New Mexico, Trans-Pecos Texas, and most of Mexico. Molecular research may eventually allow a modern revision and decrease the number of subspecies recognized. Wolf systematics have been studied by a number of workers, including Bogan and Mehlhop (1983) and Nowak (1995, 2002).

It has been thought that *C. lupus* was one of the few megafaunal species to survive the Late Pleistocene extinction event about 12,000 years ago. Genetic evidence from 12,000-year-old wolf remains preserved in Alaskan permafrost suggests, however, that North American wolves did not survive the extinction event in Beringia but rather recolonized North America from Eurasia more recently (J. Leonard et al. 2007).

Natural History

Wolves are not habitat specific; populations were apparently highest in habitats with plentiful large prey, principally ungulates (S. Young and Goldman 1944). Observations on wolf behavior in and around Glacier National Park (e.g., D. Boyd et al. 1994; D. Boyd and Pletscher 1999; Kunkel et al. 1999; Kunkel and Pletscher 1999) and Yellowstone National Park (e.g., Mech et al. 2001; D. W. Smith, Drummer, et al. 2004; D. W. Smith 2005) contribute to our understanding of how wolves probably behaved over much of Colorado. Gray wolves spend almost their entire active life hunting or eating. Most time is spent traveling in search of food, with an average of 36 km between kills in Michigan (Mech 1970). Wolves locate prey by direct scent, tracking, and chance. Wolves are specialized for a meat diet, and there are no accounts of them feeding on vegetation. Large mammals (beaver to ungulates) account for 56 to 96 percent of the wolf's diet, with deer, moose, bighorn sheep, and similar-sized species among the most frequent prey (Paradiso and Nowak 1982).

In Yellowstone and Glacier, elk are the main prey, although some packs in Yellowstone have become accomplished bison hunters. Predation on bighorn sheep and pronghorn in Yellowstone is negligible. An adult wolf can consume about 9 kg of food at one meal. A maintenance diet for an adult is 1.7 kg of food per day (Mech 1970), and they can consume up to 0.21 kg of prey per kilogram of wolf per day (Carbyn 1983). Kill rates vary with pack size and weather conditions (primarily snow cover) but usually range from 2.7 to 16 days between kills (Paquet and Carbyn 2003). In Yellowstone each wolf killed an average of 1.9 elk per 30 days in winter, with elk making up 90 percent of all documented winter ungulate kills ($n = 1{,}275$) over a 10-year period (D. W. Smith, Drummer, et al. 2004; D. W. Smith 2005). Wolves killed 38 percent calves, 26 percent bulls, and 36 percent cows, although cows were 60 percent of the elk population.

Conservation or restoration of top predators such as gray wolves frequently is promoted as critical to conservation at higher levels of integration—biotic communities, landscapes, ecosystems. Wolves clearly are important to maintaining species diversity and trophic structure of communities (Sergio et al. 2008). In Yellowstone, wolves appear to have had a marked effect on altering distributional patterns of elk, especially in the Lamar Valley, and may be driving a "trophic cascade," affecting features of the ecosystem beyond the prey species itself, ranging from an increase in nesting songbirds to recovery of woody vegetation from heavy browsing (C. White et al. 1998; Ripple and Larsen 2000; Ripple and Beschta 2004; Fortin et al. 2005; D. W. Smith 2005; but see Creel et al. 2009). Detailed studies of aspen growth and recruitment (M. J. Kauffman et al. 2010) raise questions about some details of the trophic cascade hypothesis in Yellowstone. Mexican wolves introduced into Arizona and New Mexico showed markedly similar food habits to coyotes, leading Carrera et al. (2008) to speculate that successful wolf colonization would have long-term negative impacts on coyote populations. B. Miller et al. (2001) provided a broad overview of the importance of top carnivores to ecosystem function, and F. Harrington and Paquet (1982) published authoritative papers on wolf behavior and ecology in the context of conservation.

During their long tenure in Colorado, wolves undoubtedly fed mostly on elk, mule deer, and bison. Unfortunately, the tendency of some individuals to harvest domestic livestock led to their demise. Restored wolf populations also locally conflict with livestock interests (Bangs et al. 1998, 2001); however, impacts of wolves on sheep and cattle in the Greater Yellowstone Ecosystem have been near predicted levels. It was estimated that 100 wolves would kill on average 19 cattle and 68 sheep per year. From 2000 to 2003 an average of 27 cows and 79 sheep were confirmed killed, with the wolf population ranging from 177 to 301 animals (P. White, Smith, et al. 2005). Duffield et al. (2008) estimated losses to livestock owners were about $63,000 per year from wolf predation for both 2004 and 2005 when the wolf population was at its highest level. They estimated the total economic impact from park visitors coming specifically to see and hear wolves was $35.5 million in 2005, a major economic plus.

Wolves are social animals that typically live in packs. A pack is normally composed of 2 to 8 animals, although packs of up to 37 animals have been reported in Alaska (R. A. Rausch 1967) and Yellowstone (D. W. Smith 2005). Generally, the larger the prey, the larger the pack; packs in Yellowstone that specialize in killing bison tend to have more than 15 wolves. Although variable, most packs consist of at least 1 pair of breeding adults, pups, and extra adults that may or may not breed (Carbyn 1987). Lack of breeding in subordinates is often the result of lack of copulation attempts rather than gonadal repression (J. Packard et al. 1983). Packs typically show linear dominance hierarchies that are separate for males and females. Dominant animals typically have first choice of food, bedding sites, and mates and often show leadership in hunting or moving from one hunting area to another (Mech 1970). The alpha male is the leader of the pack. The alpha female, although dominant over other females, may be submissive to other males for purposes of mating (Mech 1970). Alpha males may become less important in breeding once they take over pack leadership.

Wolves may exhibit territoriality, especially when high populations curtail the size of available hunting area (Peters and Mech 1975; F. Harrington and Mech 1983). Wolf densities are highest where prey biomass is the greatest. Presently, concerns exist about impacts of wolves on the Yellowstone elk herd (Mech et al. 2001; D. W. Smith, Drummer, et al. 2004; Barber et al. 2005; D. W. Smith 2005; P. White and Garrott 2005). The northern herd has declined from about 17,000 animals in 1995 (the year of the first restoration of wolves) to about 8,000 in 2005. With the decline in elk numbers, the ratio of wolves to elk has changed from about 3 wolves per 1,000 elk to almost 13 wolves per 1,000 elk. The overall decline in elk is probably due to a combination of interactions of predators (wolves, grizzlies, black bear, coyotes, mountain lion), weather (drought and snow conditions), and hunting outside the park boundaries. Hunters and wildlife biologists are also concerned about growing numbers of wolves and their impacts on elk in the Northern Rockies. G. Wright et al. (2006) reported that human hunters probably have a greater total reproductive impact on elk in the Yellowstone herds than wolves because hunters tended to select younger females of prime reproductive age, whereas wolves tended to take older females and calves. In any event, in wolf restoration areas, either hunting pressure or wolf numbers may have to be regulated to maintain herd levels.

Voicing concern over the eventual invasion of chronic wasting disease (CWD) into Yellowstone elk and deer herds, P. White and Davis (2007) expressed the hope that wolf and bear predation on diseased animals might slow or disrupt any spread of the disease. They cited Wild and Miller (2005) as suggesting that wolves could have "potent effects" in reducing the prevalence of chronic wasting disease in areas like Rocky Mountain National Park, based on model simulations. Yellowstone may soon serve as a test site for these hypotheses, as CWD is present in the Bighorn Basin, within 130 mi. of the park.

There is considerable variation in the size of wolf home ranges. Minimum home ranges vary from 94 km^2 for a pack of 2 animals to more than 3,400 km^2 for a pack in the Northern Rocky Mountains (Paquet and Carbyn 2003). It appears that, at a minimum, a single wolf requires 50 to 1,300 km^2 (Paradiso and Nowak 1982). Daily movements range from 1 to 19 km or more, depending on season and prey availability (Carbyn 1987). Habitat use is influenced by prey abundance, road density, livestock abundance and distribution, availability of protected lands, human disturbance, topography, and elevation. Wolves typically do not inhabit areas with high human population density or intensive agriculture (Paquet and Carbyn 2003). Oakleaf et al. (2006) found recolonizing wolves in Idaho and Montana had higher pack persistence in areas with increased forest cover, high elk density, low domestic sheep density, and low human population density. L. Bennett's (1994) review of the feasibility of wolf restoration in Colorado was generally favorable, but the linear pattern of human development in most Colorado mountain valleys might impede natural wolf colonization in the state. Rocky Mountain National Park (about 1,500 km^2 and now mostly designated wilderness) has been mentioned as a possible restoration site, and a large number of Coloradans favor restoration (Pate et al. 1996; Meadow et al. 2005). Whether deliberate restoration in the park would be either feasible or in the best interest of wolves has yet to be examined carefully.

Mated pairs of wolves may remain together for life but supportive data in the wild are lacking. Breeding occurs between January and April. Females are in estrus 5 to 7 days. Typically only the dominant pair in a pack breeds. In Colorado, wolves probably mated in late January and February. Copulation is typical of canids—the pair form a tie achieved by the vaginal sphincter muscle of the female locking around the bulbous base of the penis. A typical copulation lasts up to 30 minutes. The blind, helpless young are born in March, April, or May following a 63-day gestation. A den is usually used for the birthing site and may consist of a hole dug by the wolves, an enlarged burrow dug originally by another mammal, a shelter under a rock overhang, the interior of a beaver lodge, or the area under a stump or in a hollow log. Litter size ranges from 1 to 11, with an average of 6 (Mech 1974). Litter size and numbers of females bred may increase in populations experiencing high mortality. Eyes open at about 12 to 13 days; pups emerge from the den at about 3 weeks of age and are weaned at about 5 weeks (S. Young and Goldman 1944). Within a few weeks of emergence, pups are typically moved to one of several other home sites used while they mature. Pups normally do not travel and hunt with the pack until fall. Instead they are left at established rendezvous sites in the company of an adult wolf. A pack will often use the same natal den site and rendezvous sites year after year (Paquet and Carbyn 2003). The female is usually provisioned by the male or other pack members for 4 to 6 weeks following the birth of the pups. Wolves are most sedentary when females have pups in the den. The young are sexually mature at 2 years of age but often do not breed until 3 years (R. A. Rausch 1967; Mech 1970). From 1995 to 2007, wolf numbers in western Montana increased by about 13 percent annually (Hamlin and Cunningham 2009).

Other than humans and each other, wolves have no effective predators. Wolf-on-wolf mortality (21 deaths in 103 observed conflicts) and human-caused deaths are the major checks on populations in Yellowstone (D. W. Smith 2005). Wolves compete and interact, sometimes fatally, with grizzly and black bears, mountain lions, coyotes, red foxes, and wolverine (Paquet and Carbyn 2003; Ruth 2004; D. W. Smith 2005). Several grizzly bear cubs have been killed by wolves in Yellowstone since wolf restoration (D. W. Smith and Ferguson 2005). Disease (including parasites, parvovirus, and other zoonoses), malnutrition, and injuries and accidents take a toll but impacts of such mortality are poorly understood.

In addition to mortality, social behaviors—including territoriality between packs—probably regulate populations. The Yellowstone release demonstrates how rapidly wolf populations can grow. Starting from 58 animals in 1995–1996 the wolf population in 2005 was estimated at 169 animals, with most (85) residing on the northern elk range (D. W. Smith 2005). This represents a growth rate of 40–50 percent from 1995 to 2000, with a slower rate (10–15 percent) since then. Survival rates average 80 percent. In 2005–2006, mortality jumped, with the winter census yielding only about 118 animals, the lowest number since 2000. The decline is primarily attributed to death of pups from canine parvovirus or distemper. D. W. Smith and Almberg (2007) reported that Yellowstone wolves sampled between 1995 and 2005 tested 100 percent positive for parvovirus, with the graph of distemper over time showing variable peaks and valleys. Overall annual mortality rates of less than 35 percent probably result in stability.

The extensive literature was reviewed by Mech (1974), Paradiso and Nowak (1982), Carbyn (1987), and Paquet and Carbyn (2003). See Mech and Boitani (2003) for scholarly reviews of major aspects of wolf biology. S. Stone et al. (2008) prepared a useful guide for ranchers who must manage livestock and wolves and their interaction. Urbigkit (2008) provided a "neighbor's view" of some of the complex controversy surrounding restoration of wolves in Yellowstone. Halfpenny (2003) published a fascinating, well-illustrated account of the Yellowstone wolves, and Halfpenny and Thompson (1996) provided a "watcher's guide" to Yellowstone wolves that includes a useful summary of ecology and the history of restoration. D. W. Smith and Ferguson (2005) detailed the history of restoration of wolves to Yellowstone (a "firsthand look" as Smith led the Yellowstone Wolf Recovery Project). Meaney and Beauvais (2004) reviewed the literature on the gray wolf, particularly as pertinent to Wyoming. J. Murray (1987) reviewed the literature on Colorado's endangered and extirpated carnivores in general. Nie (2003) provided insight into the human dimensions of wolf recovery and subsequent management to that time. The saga continues, of course. Updates on wolf management in Colorado are available from the Division of Wildlife on-line (http://wildlife.state.co.us/species_cons/GrayWolf/).

Genus *Vulpes*—Foxes

There are some 12 species of foxes in the genus *Vulpes*, 3 of which occur in Colorado. The genus is quite widespread, one or another species occurring naturally throughout most of North America and Eurasia and also in Africa both north and south of the Sahara. The Holarctic red fox (*V. vulpes*) was introduced to Australia in the nineteenth century as a game species. It has since become Australia's most important predator and a major conservation challenge.

Vulpes macrotis

KIT FOX

Description

This is a dainty fox of the desert Southwest. It closely resembles the swift fox, *Vulpes velox*, in appearance but has larger ears and a generally more angular appearance.

PHOTOGRAPH 12-6. Kit fox (*Vulpes macrotis*). Photograph by Joseph Van Wormer. All rights reserved. Photo Archives, Denver Museum of Nature and Science.

See the account of the swift fox for distinction between the 2 aridland foxes. The dorsal color of the kit fox varies from yellowish gray to grizzled. The underfur is thick and harsh in texture. The underparts are usually paler yellow to white. The sides of the muzzle are dark, and the tail is black-tipped. Measurements are: total length 730–840 mm; length of tail 260–323 mm; length of hindfoot 113–137 mm; length of ear 78–94 mm; weight 1.5–2.5 kg. Females average 15 percent lighter in weight than males. Kit foxes are known to hybridize with swift foxes and red foxes, *Vulpes vulpes* (Thornton et al. 1971; Rohwer and Kilgore 1973). A number of authors (most recently Dragoo et al. 1990; Dragoo and Wayne 2003) have suggested that kit and swift foxes are conspecific; Mercure et al. (1993) suggested otherwise. Within Colorado the animals are strongly separated geographically by the Southern Rocky Mountains. Roell (1999) found significant differences in length of ear and tail and in weight between kit foxes and swift foxes captured in Colorado. Even if the genetic situation were unequivocal in the narrow zone of intergradation or hybridization in southern New Mexico, these aridland foxes in Colorado are reproductively isolated from one another and have distinctive ecological (and hence management) requirements.

Distribution

The kit fox ranges from southeastern Oregon and southwestern Idaho across much of Utah into extreme western Colorado and south into Mexico. Western Colorado represents the northeastern edge of the geographic range. No verified specimens have been taken in Colorado from north of the Grand Valley, although regular reports of an aridland fox are received from Moffat County (J. Fitzgerald 1996). Previous Coloradan records are limited to those of Egoscue (1964a), P. Miller (1964), and P. Miller and McCoy (1965). Link (1995) and J. Fitzgerald (1996) expanded the known range of the kit fox in western Colorado eastward by 96 km, but they were unable to confirm the presence of the species in the McElmo Canyon area (whence the kit fox was reported by Egoscue 1964a) or in Colorado National Monument (as reported by P. Miller 1964).

In 1994, the Colorado Wildlife Commission closed harvest on the kit fox and imposed trapping restrictions on parts of its range. Since passage of the 1996 trapping amendment it has been a protected species. The kit fox is listed as state endangered in Colorado, with its status precarious in the Grand Valley and in Montrose and Delta counties, and with fewer than 100 animals thought to exist (T. Beck 1999, 2000b). A specimen from McElmo Canyon, Montezuma County, was reported as *Vulpes macrotis neomexicana*, and those from Colorado National Monument were reported by P. Miller and McCoy (1965) as *V. m. arsipus*. Investigations of the status of the kit fox on Ute Indian lands in southwestern Colorado would be of interest. Reed-Eckert (2010) investigated the status of kit fox in the Grand and Gunnison valleys of western Colorado and along the Colorado River in adjacent Utah. She was unable to confirm the presence of the animals, despite exhaustive efforts with baited tracking stations. Based on historical distributions in the context of climatic variability, she concluded that the presence of kit fox in west-central Colorado, at the eastern limit of the species' range, may be erratic and dependent on climatic and perhaps stochastic factors.

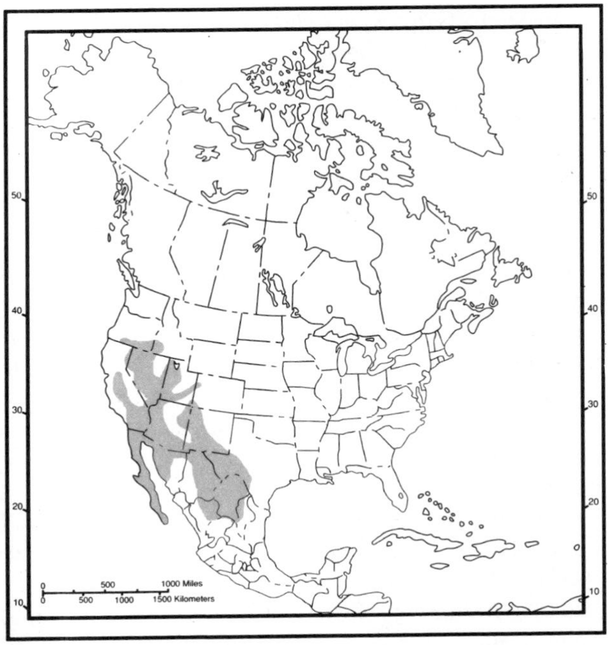

MAP 12-11. Distribution of the kit fox (*Vulpes macrotis*) in North America.

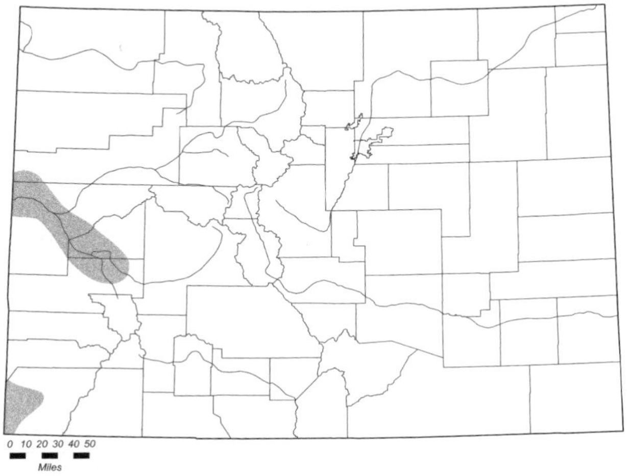

MAP 12-12. Distribution of the kit fox (*Vulpes macrotis*) in Colorado.

Natural History

The kit fox occupies semidesert shrubland and margins of piñon-juniper woodlands over much of the arid West. Saltbush, shadscale, sagebrush, and greasewood are woody plants typical of kit fox habitat. In Utah, the species preferred areas with less than 20 percent ground cover and with pale, loamy soils (McGrew 1977). Densities seem to be highest in relatively flat terrain (Warrick and Cypher 1998; Cypher et al. 2000). At Colorado National Monument, they were observed most frequently in mixed juniper-sagebrush communities and in rimrock (P. Miller 1964). All recent captures of kit fox in Colorado were made in areas of adobe soils, with saltbush, sagebrush, greasewood, or grassland habitats at elevations between about 1,460 and 1,829 m (4,865 and 6,000 ft.).

J. L. Nelson et al. (2007) found that kit foxes avoided exploitation competition with coyotes by selectively using grasslands while coyotes more frequently used shrublands. However, kit foxes did select kangaroo rat for prey and had to hunt them in shrublands. The authors suggested that management for heterogeneous landscapes to provide kit foxes with open areas would increase their predatory efficiency and decrease the foxes' vulnerability to predation by coyotes.

The kit fox appears to rely heavily on lagomorphs as prey in the cold desert regions of Utah, where 94 percent of the diet of a family of kit foxes consisted of black-tailed jackrabbits (Egoscue 1962a). O'Neal et al. (1986), working in the same area, also reported high use of jackrabbits. Kangaroo rats (*Dipodomys* sp.) are important prey in California (McGrew 1979; Cypher and Spencer 1998) and Utah (O'Neal et al. 1986). In California, Cypher et al. (2000) reported prey-switching between leporids and kangaroo rats as abundance of prey shifted. Some authors have suggested that the distribution of the kit fox is closely tied to the distribution of kangaroo rats (Cypher 2003). Others have suggested that kit foxes are reluctant to switch to alternative species of rodents (P. White, White, and Ralls 1996). However, Eussen (1999) found cricetid rodent remains most common (35–36 percent), followed by squirrels (18–25 percent) and lagomorphs (16–17 percent), in kit fox scats from two locations in western Colorado. If preferred prey is unavailable, the kit fox is opportunistic and will feed on ground-nesting birds (especially horned larks; O'Neal et al. 1986), reptiles, and insects; rarely is vegetable matter eaten. Cypher and Frost (1999) reported kit foxes in urban areas of Bakersfield, California, to be in better condition than foxes on the Elk Hills Naval Petroleum Reserve. They suggested that anthropogenic foods were advantageous to urban foxes. Coyotes compete for many of the same food resources (P. White, Ralls, and Garrott 1994; P. White, Ralls, and White 1995; Cypher and Spencer 1998).

The kit fox digs its own dens, which normally have multiple entrances (Egoscue 1962a). Link (1995) reported from 1 to 4 entrances at dens in Montrose County. Dens are clustered, not randomly distributed. The animals move from 1 den to another, especially during summer when pups are present. Foxes in Colorado used from 2 to 6 dens. In California, individual foxes used about 12 dens per year. Fewer dens were used during the breeding and pup-rearing season than during dispersal (Koopman et al. 1998). Mated pairs shared a den about 45 percent of the time.

Kit foxes are active year-round. Most foraging is done at night, and the animals normally do not move more than 3 km from their dens. J. Fitzgerald (1996) reported a number of foxes moved more than 10 km, with a 4-year-old female moving 40 km. O'Neal et al. (1986) and Koopman et al. (2000) also reported some dispersal in adult kit foxes. Home range estimates vary from 250 to 1,160 ha (Cypher 2003). In Colorado J. Fitzgerald (1996) estimated home ranges of 9 foxes to average 450 ha. The variation in estimated home range size may relate to differences in food availability (Zoellick et al. 2002) or to methods of calculation and duration of studies. Home ranges overlap and evidence of territoriality is lacking. Densities have been estimated to range from $0.1/km^2$ to $1.7/km^2$ (S. Morrell 1972; Egoscue 1979; P. White, White, and Ralls 1996; Cypher et al. 2000).

Kit foxes pair in late fall, when females select and clean out dens. Females are monoestrous, and breeding occurs in December, January, and February. J. Fitzgerald (1996) estimated that breeding in a Colorado population occurred in February, about a month later than for more southerly populations. Some females may breed as young as 10 months of age (T. O'Farrell 1987); however, a 16-year study in California suggests it is not common (Cypher et al. 2000). In that study, annual reproductive success averaged 61 percent for females older than 1 year. The gestation period is unknown but probably is similar to the 51 days reported for *V. velox*. Litters of 1 to 6 pups (average, 3.8) are born in February, March, or April, with a sex ratio usually close to 1:1. A bias toward males may occur when populations are growing (Cypher et al. 2000). Pups first emerge from the den at about 4 to 5 weeks of age and begin foraging with the parents when 3 to 4 months old. In Utah, dispersal occurs in October, with young of the year showing the longest movements (Egoscue 1956, 1962a).

The extent of monogamy in kit foxes is not clear; some pairs mate for life but others do not (Egoscue 1956). Ralls et al. (2001) reported instances of polygyny and that additional adults may be present to assist in caring for the young. Additional adults were offspring of one of the mated pair. Pair bonds last at least through 1 breeding season, but males sometimes sire 2 litters. Males provision the female for the first few weeks that she is nursing the young, as she stays with the pups. At weaning, both adults bring food items to the den for the first few months; they do not regurgitate food (Egoscue 1962a; Morrell 1972). When rearing the pups the parents may split up, with each tending some of the pups at separate dens. Pups stay with at least 1 of the parents for up to 18 months and sibling pups may stay together until 21 months old (Koopman et al. 1998).

Coyotes are the major predator on kit foxes, often causing half or more of observed mortality (O'Neal et al. 1986; T. O'Farrell 1987; Ralls and White 1995; Cypher et al. 2000). Agricultural conversion of native habitat, trapping, shooting, predator poisoning, and motor vehicle kills also have negative impacts on kit fox populations. Mean annual survival estimates range from 0.20 to 0.81 for adult foxes;

juvenile survivorship rarely exceeds 0.20 (Cypher 2003). J. Fitzgerald (1996) reported that of 47 kit foxes marked in western Colorado, 86 percent died or disappeared before reaching 36 months of age. A few animals reach 7 years of age in the wild. Reed-Eckert (2010) described intensive but unsuccessful efforts to document kit foxes in areas of Mesa and Delta counties, Colorado, from which the animals have been reported historically. Literature on the species was reviewed by S. Morrell (1975), McGrew (1979), T. O'Farrell (1987), and Cypher (2003). Development of a species recovery plan by the Colorado Division of Wildlife was halted in 2000 as a result of internal reorganization of resources and priorities for managing threatened and endangered species (T. Beck 2000b). Meaney, Reed-Eckert, and Beauvais (2006) wrote a conservation assessment including recommendations for recovery of the species in Region 2 of the USDA Forest Service. Conservation of the kit fox in the context of their sagebrush habitat was reviewed by Boyle and Reeder (2005). The Colorado Division of Wildlife (2007c) provides frequent updates on the status of the kit fox on-line, as is done for other endangered mammalian species.

Vulpes velox

SWIFT FOX

Description

The swift fox is small and slender. The dorsal pelage ranges from yellowish to a buffy gray, with the underfur tan and interspersed with multicolored guard hairs so that the overall dorsal color is fairly dark. The ventral pelage ranges from white to yellow. Conspicuous black marks are present on either side of the snout and the tail is always tipped with black. The black facial marks clearly separate the species from young coyotes. Measurements are: total length 700–880 mm; length of tail 240–350 mm; length of hindfoot 113–135 mm; length of ear 56–75 mm; weight 1.8–3.0 kg. Males average 8 percent heavier than females. Adults stand about 300 mm at the shoulder. The ears are typically shorter than those of the closely related kit fox, *Vulpes macrotis*. Swift foxes have rounded eyes, unlike the slit-like eyes of the kit fox, and a shorter, broader muzzle. Females have 8 mammae. In zones of contact, swift and kit foxes hybridize in western Texas and eastern New Mexico (Thornton et al. 1971; Rohwer and Kilgore 1973). R. L. Harrison et al. (2002, 2004) discussed methods for identifying individual swift fox using DNA analysis of scats and for separating swift fox scat from that of coyotes and other small carnivores.

PHOTOGRAPH 12-7. Swift fox (*Vulpes velox*). Photograph by Joseph Van Wormer. All rights reserved. Photo Archives, Denver Museum of Nature and Science.

Distribution

The swift fox, along with the black-tailed prairie dog and the white-tailed jackrabbit, is an animal of the grasslands. It once occupied short- and mid-grass prairies over most of the Great Plains, including eastern Colorado. Crowe (1986) mapped the species in northwestern Colorado, but there are no data to support that. D. D. Finley (1999) and D. Finley et al. (2005) found a strong relationship between the amount of shortgrass prairie and the presence of swift foxes on live-trapping grids scattered across eastern Colorado. The swift fox was extirpated in the late 1800s and early 1900s over much of its range in North America, probably because of its susceptibility to poisoning and trapping campaigns aimed at wolves and coyotes. Some populations in South Dakota, Wyoming, Nebraska, and Kansas have experienced recovery. In Montana, recovery is partially the result of restoration of the species in Canada. In response to a proposed listing of the swift fox under the Endangered Species Act, states in the historic range of the species wrote a conservation assessment and conservation strategy for swift fox in the United States (Kahn et al. 1997) with the intent of monitoring and/or recovering the species across its historic range.

In Colorado, the swift fox apparently never declined to the low numbers experienced elsewhere. Cary (1911) and Warren (1942) indicated that populations were low but present. Lechleitner (1969) remarked, "Nowhere are they presently abundant and I do not expect they will ever again become common on our plains." In fact in recent years the density of swift foxes in certain areas on the eastern

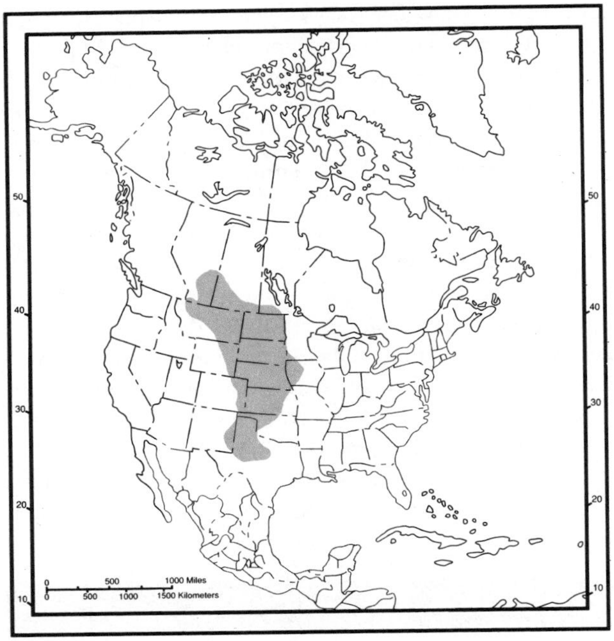

MAP 12-13. Distribution of the swift fox (*Vulpes velox*) in North America.

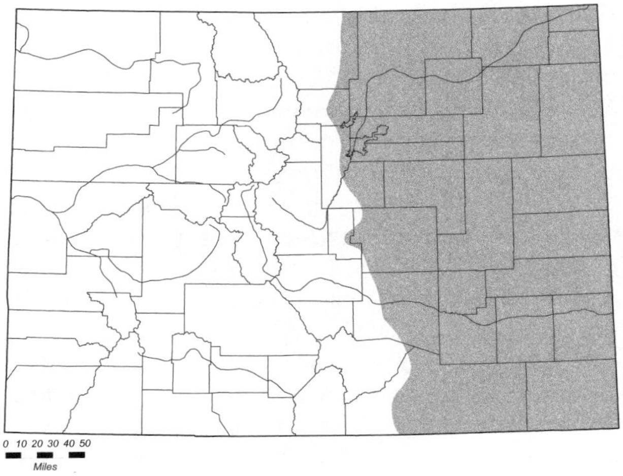

MAP 12-14. Distribution of the swift fox (*Vulpes velox*) in Colorado.

plains of Colorado has been rather high (Rongstad et al. 1989; Covell and Rongstad 1990; D. Finley 1999; Roell 1999; Schauster et al. 2002; D. Finley et al. 2005). D. Finley (1999) found them present in most areas with shortgrass prairie; highest numbers were in Weld, Lincoln, and Las Animas counties. Covell and Rongstad (1990) reported difficulty in finding swift foxes on the Comanche National Grassland and in areas of high coyote density. The swift fox is appropriately a focus of conservation planning by the Colorado Division of Wildlife (2003b). In Colorado, the swift fox can be expected from any county on the eastern plains where native shortgrass prairie remains intact. *Vulpes velox velox* was named on the basis of a specimen taken by the Long Expedition in northeastern Colorado in 1820. For comments on relationships with the kit fox, *V. macrotis*, see the account of that species.

Natural History

Over most of its range the swift fox appears to be most numerous in shortgrass prairie areas with relatively flat to gently rolling topography, and less common in terrain that is highly eroded with gullies, washes, and canyons (R. L. Harrison and Whitaker-Hoagland 2003). In Texas, Kamler (2002) and Kamler, Ballard, et al. (2003) believed fragmented areas with only remnants of shortgrass prairie resulted in poor success of swift fox populations and that the swift fox was much more specialized than other canids in habitat selection. In Colorado, habitat is mostly shortgrass prairie but also includes grassland ecotones with piñon-juniper woodlands and shrublands (Rongstad et al. 1989; D. Finley 1999; Schauster et al. 2002). In Kansas, swift foxes commonly use cropland, almost like red foxes (V. Jackson and Choate 2000; Matlack et al. 2000; Sovada et al. 2001). In Wyoming, sagebrush steppe–shortgrass prairie ecotones are used (T. L. Olson and Lindzey 2002a). In New Mexico, shortgrass prairie was utilized but foxes were not recorded on croplands or Conservation Reserve Program (CRP) lands (R. L. Harrison and Schmitt 2003). Based on studies of response to prescribed burning in the Comanche National Grassland, C. Thompson et al. (2008) recommended fire as an appropriate tool to maintain high-quality habitat for swift foxes.

Swift foxes are excellent diggers and excavate their own dens, which are typically located on flat areas or along slopes or ridges that afford a good visual field. More than 1 den is used at a time. Dens used for whelping typically have 3 to 6 entrances; dens used by solitary foxes usually have only 1 or 2 entrances. Dens excavated in Colorado were simple structures, with most tunnels located about 40 cm below the surface (Loy 1981). More complex dens have been found in Oklahoma and Texas (Cutter 1958a; Kilgore 1969). Scat and prey remains litter the tunnel floors.

In northern Colorado, dens are typically on sites dominated by blue grama or buffalograss. D. J. Martin et al. (2007) captured 136 swift foxes on 40 grids, with 71 percent of the captures on grids with more than 50 percent shortgrass prairie. Estimated occupancy of grids was 71.1 percent, with no evidence of any declines from the 1995–1997 surveys of D. Finley et al. (2005). The soil accumulated at the burrow entrance may be visible for several hundred meters, although typically not forming as large a mound as that from badger excavations (Loy 1981; M. Cameron 1984). Hillman and Sharps (1978), Hines and Case (1991), Kintigh (1999), V. Jackson and Choate (2000), and Gilin (2002) all reported that swift foxes often had dens close to roads. Several studies suggest that swift foxes regularly use roads as travel lanes and for foraging; disturbed areas along roads frequently have high plant productivity and hence higher small mammal densities than surrounding prairie (Kahn et al. 1996; Almasi-Klausz and Carbyn 1999; D. Finley 1999; R. L. Harrison and Whitaker-Hoagland 2003). Some authors have suggested that swift foxes den close to water (R. L. Harrison and Whitaker-Hoagland 2003), but if so, it may be because of increased hunting opportunities and not because they need free water (Flaherty and Plakke 1986). In southwestern South Dakota, vegetation was denser on denning sites than on random control sites (Uresk et al. 2003a).

Swift foxes are almost entirely carnivorous, preying on a variety of small rodents, lagomorphs, birds, insects, and similar quarry; however, Sovada et al. (2001) reported considerable use of sunflower seeds in Kansas. Studies indicate that jackrabbits and cottontails provide the bulk of the diet, supplemented by ground squirrels, prairie dogs, insects, and ground-nesting birds. In Kansas, mammals (especially rabbits) comprised 65 percent of the diet; the remainder was mostly birds and carrion (Zumbaugh et al. 1985). Use of lagomorphs, especially cottontails, also was high in southern Colorado (Rongstad et al. 1989). In northeastern Colorado M. Cameron (1984) found 66 percent of the biomass in swift fox scats was remains of lagomorphs, 11 percent from rodents, 10 percent from insects, and 4 percent from birds. Consumption of ground-nesting birds increased in spring and summer. Eussen (1999) found dietary differences between swift foxes on the Central Plains Experimental Range (CPER) and those on the Pawnee National Grassland (PNG). His PNG site included M. Cameron's study area. Eussen noted less total use, as percentage occurrence, of leporids on the CPER than on the PNG (8.2 percent vs. 14.6 percent), higher use of sciurids on the CPER site (33.0 percent vs. 8.2 percent), and lower use of murid rodents (10.2 percent vs. 26.0 percent) and insects (32.0 percent vs. 42.0 percent). The lower use of leporids in Eussen's study than in M. Cameron's may reflect lower populations of lagomorphs (especially jackrabbits) in recent years. When food is plentiful, swift foxes kill and cache excess prey in shallow, poorly covered holes. In Colorado, lagomorphs, prairie dogs, and 13-lined ground squirrels have been excavated from such caches (Loy 1981). Because they feed on rodents in prairie dog towns, swift foxes have been implicated as carriers of the plague bacillus. Some 24 percent of swift foxes on the Pawnee National Grassland had plague antibodies in their blood (Salkeld et al. 2007). The fleas (*Pulex simulans*) of those swift foxes, however, did not harbor the plague bacterium.

Kamler, Ballard, Gese, Harrison, Karki, and Mote (2004)—based on the studies by A. Kitchen, Gese, and Schauster (1999) in southeastern Colorado; Lemons (2001) in Texas; and R. L. Harrison (2003) in New Mexico—suggested that the swift fox is mostly insectivorous, especially in summer, and that this influences social structure during pup rearing. Food habit studies in northern parts of their range may not support this conclusion.

Swift foxes live in pairs and occasionally in trios of one male and two females. The seasonal pair-bond seems strong, and males assist in provisioning the young (Kilgore 1969; Loy 1981; Covell 1992). However, Kamler, Ballard, Gese, Harrison, and Karki (2004) suggested that swift foxes have a female-based social system and that males are not essential during the pup-rearing season. Swift foxes do not hibernate. The animals are most active at night; however, they may forage in late evening or early morning and also spend time sunning at the den entrance on favorable days. Studies of marked animals with infrared cameras showed they could travel as much as 2 mi. in a single night's foraging and up to 4 mi. over 2 or 3 nights. Individuals showed a consistent pattern of running fence lines or roads to visit such baited camera stations (Kahn et al. 1996). Uresk et al. (2003b) found in southwestern South Dakota that scent stations were more successful than spotlight counts at assessing presence of swift foxes; also see G. Sargeant, Johnson, and Berg (1998, 2003) and G. Sargeant, White, et al. (2003).

Swift foxes mate in late December, January, and February, at which time the animals become highly vocal (Avery 1989). Kamler et al. (2004) found that swift foxes were monogamous in areas of low density in Texas, but foxes in areas of high density exhibited polygyny and communal denning. Females are monoestrous. Pups are born in late March, April, or early May following a gestation period of 51 days. Litter size ranges from 1 to 8, with 4 to 5 young the average. The altricial pups develop rapidly. Their eyes and ears are open by the end of the second week and they first come aboveground at about 4 to 5 weeks of age (Kilgore

1969). Both parents assist in rearing the young, but during the pup-rearing season females are more closely tied to the core area of a family group home range than are males (A. Kitchen, Gese, et al. 2005). The young gradually learn their surroundings and hunt with the adults as they get older. They disperse in September–October or January–February; juvenile female dispersal peaked in September, males in February (Kamler, Ballard, Gese, Harrison, and Karki 2004). Females may breed in their first year (Kilgore 1969; Loy 1981). Covell (1992) reported that males dispersed an average of 9.4 km and females 2.1 km.

Rongstad et al. (1989) and A. Kitchen, Gese, and Schauster (1999) estimated home ranges of 20–30 km^2 and 760 ha (7.6 km^2), respectively, in studies in southeastern Colorado. In Nebraska, Hines (1980) estimated an average home range of 1,730 ha (17.29 km^2) and Hines and Case (1991) estimated 15.22 km^2. R. L. Harrison (2003) reported an average home range size of 1,495 ha in New Mexico. Olson and Lindzey (2002b) determined annual home range size averaged 18.6 km^2. Males had larger home ranges than females in the pup-rearing season. Home range overlap of pairs was high, averaging 70.8 percent. There was minimal home range overlap between adjacent pairs, suggesting territoriality. Covell and Rongstad (1990) suggested that coyotes and eagles are major regulators of numbers of swift foxes. Coyotes have since been recognized as the primary source of mortality (A. Kitchen, Gese, and Schauster 1999; Matlack et al. 2000; Schauster et al. 2002). McGee et al. (2006) reported artificial escape dens increased swift fox distribution in an area with high coyote depredation in Texas. Humans are also important causes of mortality, due to roadkill and deliberate harvest. Swift foxes are "naïve" and easy to trap. Locally, populations have been reduced or exterminated by overzealous hunting, trapping, and poisoning campaigns. In Colorado the swift fox is a species of special concern; no season is allowed for its take. D. Finley (1999), D. Finley et al. (2005), and D. J. Martin et al. (2007) suggested that populations on Colorado's eastern plains have not declined since 1998. Records from the Colorado Division of Wildlife show annual harvests between 2,000 and 3,300 from 1979 to 1982 when fur prices were high; more typically, fewer than 1,000 animals were taken annually (J. Fitzgerald 1993b).

On the US Army's Piñon Canyon Maneuver Site southeast of Pueblo, mortality of all sex and age classes was 44 percent, with pups showing 62 percent mortality (Covell and Rongstad 1990). Annual survival rates in Colorado range from 0.50 to 0.74 (Rongstad et al. 1989; Covell 1992; A. Kitchen, Gese, and Schauster 1999; Roell 1999). Olson and Lindzey (2002a) reported annual adult survival of 40 to 69 percent in Wyoming. R. L. Harrison (2003) reported survival of 0.41 to 0.64 for adults in New Mexico. Sovada et al. (1998) estimated mortality rates of 0.55 for adults and 0.67 for juveniles in Kansas. Density estimates range from 1 fox per 2.0 km^2 in Kansas (L. Fox and Roy 1995) to 1 fox per 4.0 to 14.3 km^2 in Colorado (Rongstad et al. 1989; Roell 1999). Dieni et al. 1996 estimated a density of 1.6 foxes per 10 km^2 in Wyoming. Few adults survive past their fourth year in the wild, although captive females have bred successfully until 6 years of age and 1 male bred until his tenth year.

The literature on the species was reviewed by Egoscue (1979), Scott-Brown et al. (1987), Cypher (2003), Marks (2005), and Stephens and Anderson (2005). Papers from a symposium on swift and kit foxes were published by Sovada and Carbyn (2003).

Vulpes vulpes

RED FOX

Description

The red fox is a slender, doglike mammal with a long, sharp-pointed muzzle and a long, bushy, white-tipped tail. Measurements are: total length 940–1,045 mm; length of tail 310–380 mm; length of hindfoot 145–160 mm; length of ear 80–89 mm; weight 3–7 kg, with females smaller than males (Storm et al. 1976). The tail is approximately 70 percent as long as the body. The ears are pointed and held erect; the feet, nose, and backs of the ears are typically black. Three color phases—red, cross, and silver—exist, with the red phase the most common in the wild. The typical red phase has a dorsal pelage of yellowish red, with the underparts yellow to white. The so-called cross fox has a yellowish dorsum with a dark cross of hairs extending over the shoulders and on the dorsal midline. The silver fox is black with silver tips on some or all of the dorsal guard hairs, lending the pelage a frosted or silvery appearance. Melanistic foxes, lacking these silver tips, are not uncommon in the foothills of the Front Range. In all color phases, the tip of the tail is white. The skull is relatively slender with a long, narrow rostrum. The sagittal crest is well developed, especially in older animals. The postorbital processes of the frontal bones are thin and concave. Females have 8 mammae. Males have a well-developed baculum with a long, broad urethral groove and a slightly expanded distal end.

PHOTOGRAPH 12-8. Red fox (*Vulpes vulpes*). Photograph by Bill Bevington.

Distribution

The red fox has the widest geographic distribution of any carnivore, occurring naturally over most of North America and Eurasia as well as North Africa. It has also been introduced to other areas, including Australia, either to be hunted or to help control pest mammals, such as rabbits. In the United States the species has been absent from much of the Southwest and Intermountain West. However, its range is expanding in north Texas and northeastern New Mexico (Kamler et al. 2005) and probably will continue to spread into southeastern Colorado. In Colorado the species occurs throughout the state, with the fewest records from the southern half of the eastern plains. They have been thought to be rather scarce in the Four Corners region, but they apparently are frequent in the Navajo Nation (Mikesic and LaRue 2003). For many years the North American red fox was known as *Vulpes fulva* and considered to be distinct from the Eurasian red fox, *V. vulpes*. Churcher (1959) determined that the populations are conspecific, so the older name, *V. vulpes*, applies.

One subspecies, *Vulpes vulpes macroura*, is currently recognized in Colorado (D. Armstrong 1972). However, subspecific assignment of red foxes in Colorado has been complicated by the expansion of foxes in the eastern part of the state, and also by foxes escaped (or freed) from fox farms. Whether red foxes on the eastern plains dispersed from the mountains (the range of *V. v. macroura*) or from the east (*V. v. regalis*) is unknown. Of some 10 North American subspecies of the red fox (E. Hall 1981), 3 (*V. v. cascadensis*, *V. v. necator*, and *V. v. macroura*) are generally agreed to be

MAP 12-15. Distribution of the red fox (*Vulpes vulpes*) in North America.

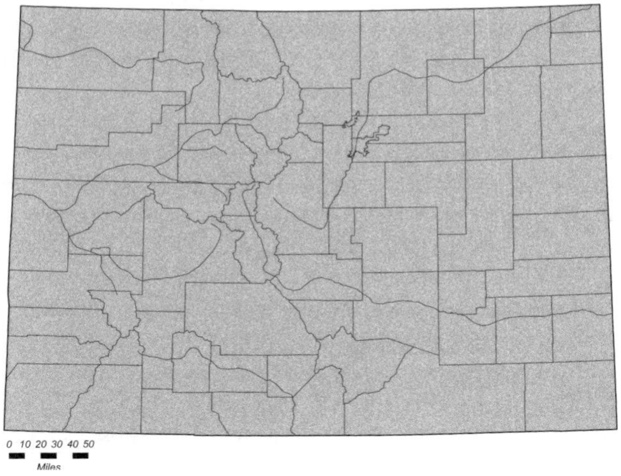

MAP 12-16. Distribution of the red fox (*Vulpes vulpes*) in Colorado.

high mountain specialists, isolated following glacial retreat in the Late Pleistocene (Kamler and Ballard 2002; Perrine 2005). In Washington (Aubry 1984) and California (Aubry 1997; Perrine 2005), studies of *V. v. cascadensis* and *V. v. necator*, respectively, described a degree of ecological separation and genetic differentiation from red foxes of lower elevations. Perrine (2005) studied haplotypes from 75 red fox specimens from California, Nevada, and Washington to compare genetic differences between his Mount Lassen population of *V. v. necator* and other "mountain foxes" (*V. v. cascadensis* and *V. v. macroura*) as well as introduced red foxes. His initial findings supported the recognition of the 3 mountain forms. A comparable study of Coloradan red foxes would be of interest.

Natural History

There have been no detailed ecological studies of the red fox in the Rocky Mountain region. A few studies in California and Washington have provided most of the available information about the ecology of the species in the Mountain West (Aubry 1983; Perrine 2005). Across North America the red fox is commonest in open woodlands, riparian ecosystems, pastures, and other agricultural lands. Red foxes also do well on the margins of urbanized areas and are common in open space and other undeveloped areas adjacent to cities along the Front Range corridor (C. A. Jones et al. 2003). They tend to favor areas with mosaics of vegetation types with good development of ground cover (Ables 1975). Intensive monoculture agriculture and clean farming resulting in reduced cover and reduced prey have negatively affected red foxes while urbanization have probably been favorable (Gosselink et al. 2003).

Red fox habitat selection, hunting strategy, and interactions with other predators (striped skunk, coyotes) have been studied for years in waterfowl nesting areas of the Prairie Region of North Dakota (e.g., A. Sargeant 1972, 1982; A. Sargeant and Allen 1989; M. L. Phillips et al. 2003, 2004). There, in areas with little grassland, foxes foraged on edges or in core areas of planted cover. In areas with more than 45 percent grassland they foraged more on the grasslands or on edges of grassland with planted cover. Foxes hunting in areas of patchy, high-quality habitat tended to make straighter, directed movements to those patches compared with randomized, searching movements in areas with more homogeneous habitat like large expanses of grasslands. On the Bear River Refuge in Utah, red foxes, raccoons, and striped skunks utilized levee banks and roadsides for dens and to increase access to wetland foraging areas (S. Frey and Conover 2006). In the mountains they occur in montane and subalpine meadows as well as on alpine and forest edges, usually near water.

Perrine (2005) studied red fox, pine marten, and coyote interactions on Mount Lassen, California. Red foxes were the least abundant species and found in fewer habitat types (typically coniferous forests) and usually at high elevations, moving to slightly lower elevations (average 440 m) in winter. This is a pattern not unusual for a number of other carnivores, including coyotes, mountain lions, and bobcats (G. Koehler and Hornocker 1991; Crabtree and Shelden 1999a), although G. Byrne (1998) found coyotes in the high country of Colorado common above 8,000 ft. (2,440 m) in winter. In the Cascades, Aubry (1983) found red fox in ponderosa pine and Douglas-fir forests but not in wetter coniferous forest types. Study of red foxes at high elevations in Colorado would be interesting to see if similar patterns of abundance and habitat use exist. Semidesert shrublands are not utilized to any great extent, unless adjoining riparian wetlands or irrigated agriculture. Some biologists believe the species is becoming more numerous on irrigated and urbanizing areas on the fringes of kit fox habitat in western Colorado and swift fox habitats in eastern Colorado. Van Etten et al. (2007) hypothesized that competition with coyotes constrained habitat selection by red foxes in Yellowstone National Park. R. L. Harrison and Schmitt (2003) and Ralls and White (1995) discussed this situation in the case of red foxes and swift foxes in New Mexico and red foxes and kit foxes in California.

Limited studies of food habits in Colorado indicate that red foxes are adept at taking ground-nesting birds and their eggs, including sage grouse, pheasants, and waterfowl, as well as jackrabbits, cottontails, and occasionally pocket gophers (Hogue 1958). Small rodents, including deer mice and voles; rabbits; birds; and insects are common dietary items (T. Scott 1943; Findley 1956; Korschgen 1959; Stanley 1963). Voles are often reported as the major prey (Voigt 1987; Cypher 2003). Fruits, nuts, and berries are also eaten (D. Samuel and Nelson 1982). Elias and Halfpenny (1991) reported a red fox scat from Niwot Ridge, Boulder County (3,475 m, about 11,400 ft.), that was composed almost entirely of exoskeletons of 2 kinds of carabid beetles, *Amara alpina* and *Carabus taedatus*. In mountain populations, pocket gophers (*Thomomys* sp.) were a staple along with voles (Aubry 1983; Perrine 2005). Snowshoe hares were important in Washington but not in Northern California, where mule deer were important in the diet. Perrine (2005) found over 50 percent overlap among diets of coyotes, martens, and red foxes, with the greatest similarity being between diets of red fox and marten. In southeastern Idaho, red foxes ate more rodents than did coyotes, and coyotes ate more rabbits than did red foxes (J. Green and Flinders 1981). In general, red foxes are opportunistic and eat whatever is available, including some carrion and domestic poultry. As with almost all canids, red fox hunting behaviors when pursuing small to medium-sized prey include "mousing" (pouncing), stalking, and chasing (Cypher 2003). To watch a red fox stop, leap high in the air, pounce, and come up with a mouse is a sight to behold.

Red foxes make efficient use of prey, having an average intake requirement of about 223 kcal/kg/day, with a mean assimilation efficiency of 91 percent (Vogtsberger and Barrett 1973). Foxes require 2.2 to 2.5 kg per individual per week. In the den, red fox pups consumed 1.3 to 1.9 kg per week on a diet of jackrabbits, ducks, and duck eggs (A. Sargeant 1978). Prey biomass required for a mated pair plus 5 young ranges from 18.5 to 20.4 kg/km^2 (assuming a territory size of 7.8 km^2).

The red fox is generally nocturnal or crepuscular in its hunting habits but in winter may sun outside the den or increase daytime foraging activity, perhaps as a result of difficulty finding food (Ables 1969). In Yellowstone National Park and on Mount Lassen, red foxes were more nocturnal than coyotes, perhaps a mechanism for reducing encounters (Crabtree and Sheldon 1999a; Perrine 2005). Red foxes use dens less regularly than do kit and swift foxes. However, the den is the focal point for rearing pups during the spring and summer months. Natal dens are built in late winter, usually in well-drained, loose soils surrounded by good vegetative cover. In good weather foxes simply curl up on the surface and do not utilize dens for protection. Perrine (2005) did not find any use of dirt dens or burrows by red foxes in California; animals rested under conifer branches or among boulders. Foxes in the Cascades did use dirt dens (Aubry 1983). Dens are usually in burrows previously excavated by other mammals, including badgers and marmots in our area, but they can dig their own dens if necessary. Most dens have at least 2 openings but some have 12 or more in areas of traditional use (Ables 1975).

Red foxes are often together in pairs or family groups, except during fall after dispersal of the young. Social units in red fox populations are families: a mated pair and their young, or occasionally 1 male and several females with kinship ties; usually only 1 of the females will have young. Polygyny is occasionally reported, with 1 male having 2 bred females in his home range. The pups from the 2 litters may even be raised together. This pattern seems to be more common in red foxes in Europe than in those studied in North America (Cypher 2003). Non-breeding females help rear young in such groups.

Red foxes are monoestrous. Estrus lasts 1 to 6 days and the gestation period is about 52 days (Hayssen et al. 1993). Females and males may breed as juveniles, depending on population size, mortality, and food availability. Mating in the central United States occurs in the winter months from December through March. Most matings in Colorado probably occur in January and February. Young are born in March or early April on the eastern plains. Litter size is usually 4 to 5 (Lloyd 1975) but is reported to range from 1 to 17 (Holcomb 1965). Larger litters are usually associated with populations that have high annual mortality (Voigt 1987). Both members of the pair provision the young (Voigt 1987). The young mature rapidly and their eyes open by 9 days of age. They remain in the den for the first month of their lives (Ables 1975). Sex ratios may slightly favor males over females (Storm et al. 1976). Pups are reported to be moved to different den sites 1 or more times.

Juveniles disperse in the fall. Considerable variation exists in distances moved, but an average of 29 to 30 km for males and 16 km for females is not unusual in the Midwest (R. Phillips et al. 1972). Actual dispersal distances may relate to the distance that places the disperser beyond home ranges of resident foxes (D. W. Macdonald and Bacon 1982). Daily movements of red foxes may exceed 10 km. Home ranges are exclusive (but undefended) areas whose borders are visited every 1 to 2 weeks (A. Sargeant 1972). Home ranges have been estimated to be as small as 57 ha in urban areas and more than 6,000 ha in less diverse habitats (Storm 1965; Ables 1969; Perrine 2005). In North Dakota, Ables (1969) and A. Sargeant et al. (1987) estimated home ranges of up to 11.9 km^2. S. Frey and Conover (2006) reported home ranges to average 3.5 km^2 in Utah marshlands. Males defend the territory of the mated pair during the breeding season. Scent-marking with urine and feces or scent from the anal sacs (P. White, Kreeger, et al. 1989) is commonly observed and it may be that the red fox is more territorial than are other species of *Vulpes* (Cypher 2003).

Humans are the principal source of mortality, accounting for 80 to 90 percent in the central United States, with hunting, trapping, and automobiles being the major agents. From 1974 to 1991, harvest of red foxes in Colorado ranged between 900 and 1,900 animals (J. Fitzgerald 1993b). The red fox is presently listed as a small game species in the state with a 4-month season. In recent years, estimated licensed harvest (Table 4-3) has averaged fewer than 1,000.

Coyotes, eagles, bobcats, and wolves may also kill red foxes (Storm et al. 1976; Cypher 2003). Red foxes may avoid areas with coyotes and coyotes also may negatively impact red fox populations by displacement and habitat partitioning (Gese, Stotts, and Grothe 1996; Gosselink et al. 2003; Randa and Yunger 2006). Rabies and mange may cause some mortality but do not seem to be common in Colorado. Red foxes can become a nuisance to people in

Colorado, especially when they prey on free-ranging (or inadequately housed) poultry. The Colorado Division of Wildlife (2007f) provided suggestions for accommodation. D. Samuel and Nelson (1982), Voigt (1987), Larivière and Pasitschniak-Arts (1996), and Cypher (2003) reviewed the literature. D. Henry (1986) published a general account of the species.

Urocyon cinereoargenteus

COMMON GRAY FOX

Description

The gray fox is a slender fox with a bushy, black-tipped tail. It is shorter and more robust than the red fox, an impression enhanced by the relatively short ears and muzzle. The dorsal color is grizzled gray. The ears, neck, and legs are reddish buff. The throat, upper chest, and belly are usually whitish. The dorsal surface of the tail is grayish with a blackish median mane that terminates in a black tip. Measurements are: total length 800–1,130 mm; length of tail 275–430 mm; length of hindfoot 100–150 mm; length of ear 65–70 mm; weight 3–7 kg, with males slightly heavier than females. The skull has distinctive, lyre-shaped temporal ridges rather than a sagittal crest (Figure 12-2). The dentary has a deep notch on the posterior end of the horizontal ramus. Females have 6 mammae. The baculum has a long urethral groove and a well-developed keel.

Distribution

The common gray fox is a species of the eastern deciduous forests of North America and semidesert shrublands of the southwestern United States and Mexico. In Colorado, gray foxes are widely distributed along the foothills of the Eastern Slope, in southeastern Colorado, and at lower elevations on the Western Slope. A skull was picked up at 10,000 ft. (3,050 m) in Gunnison County by D. R. Virchow of the Panhandle Research and Extension Center, Scottsbluff, Nebraska (T. Labedz, University of Nebraska State Museum, personal communication). Little is known of the abundance or population dynamics of the gray fox in Colorado. One subspecies, *Urocyon cinereoargenteus scottii*, occurs in the state.

Natural History

Except for limited research in Utah, New Mexico, California, Arizona, and Texas, little is known of the biology of the

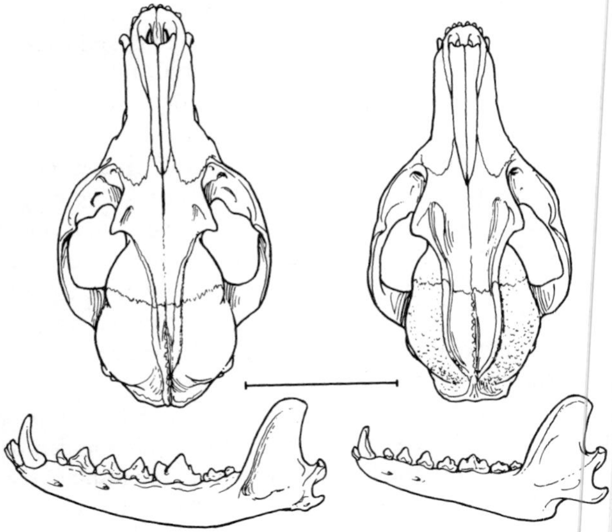

FIGURE 12-2. Dorsal views of the skulls and lateral views of mandibles of a red fox (*Vulpes vulpes, left*) and a common gray fox (*Urocyon cinereoargenteus, right*) to show the prominent lyre-shaped temporal rides and notch in the ramus of the mandible of the latter species. Scale = 5 cm.

PHOTOGRAPH 12-9. Common gray fox (*Urocyon cinereoargenteus*). Photograph by Joseph G. Hall.

gray fox in the West. In Colorado, gray fox habitat is usually rough broken terrain in semidesert shrublands, lower montane shrublands, piñon-juniper and riparian woodlands, orchards, and weedy margins of croplands. Gray foxes do not appear to occupy intensive agricultural lands or higher elevations in the mountains; they are negatively impacted by the clearing of piñon-juniper woodland in urbanizing

MAP 12-17. Distribution of the common gray fox (*Urocyon cinereoargenteus*) in North America.

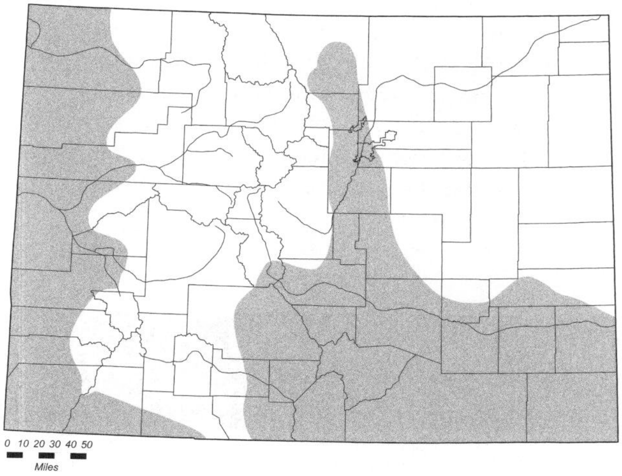

MAP 12-18. Distribution of the common gray fox (*Urocyon cinereoargenteus*) in Colorado.

areas of New Mexico (Harrison 1993). Competition with red foxes, swift foxes, or kit foxes may influence their distribution in many areas of the West, where they seem to occupy habitats in between those preferred by the other species. Gray foxes tolerate urbanized environments within their preferred habitats and have been studied in mixed residential-wildland areas in California (T. Fuller 1978; S. Riley 2001, 2006) and New Mexico (R. L. Harrison 1993, 1997).

Gray foxes are secretive and mostly nocturnal, and they may be more common in a given area than direct observations suggest (R. L. Harrison 1997). Like the red fox, gray foxes use dens primarily for pup rearing or temporary shelter. They den in rocky outcrops, brush piles, hollow trees, or burrows. Dens are commonly close to water in the East. The animals climb trees and rocky ledges with ease.

Gray foxes are more omnivorous than other Coloradan foxes. In Zion National Park, Utah, foods included fruits, arthropods, small mammals, some carrion, reptiles, and a few birds (Trapp and Hallberg 1975). Their diet in that area was more herbivorous and insectivorous than in eastern studies. In the Southwest, mammals were present in about 60 percent of stomachs examined, arthropods were found in 55 percent, and plants were found in 40 percent (Turkowski 1969). Studies in the East showed cottontail rabbits to be especially important prey, but rodents may be more important than lagomorphs over much of the gray fox's western range, with *Peromyscus*, *Microtus*, *Spermophilus*, *Neotoma*, and *Thomomys* identified as prey. Juniper cones and prickly-pear fruits are eaten, as are acorns (Turkowski 1969; Trapp and Hallberg 1975). In New Mexico, Harrison (1997) found much higher levels (95 percent occurrence) of plant material in scat samples of wildland foxes than in those living in residential areas (62 percent) and higher intake of mammalian prey (59 percent occurrence) in residential than in wildland areas (46 percent). Lagomorphs, *Peromyscus*, and *Neotoma* were among the most important mammalian prey, with grasshoppers being important insects. Various cultivated fruits were important foods, comprising more than 10 percent of the volume of food in scats of foxes in residential areas. S. Riley (2001) found *Microtus* the primary prey of gray foxes and bobcats at the Golden Gate National Recreation Area, California. Diets of urban and rural foxes and bobcats had 61 and 56 percent overlap in diets, respectively.

Reproductive biology is poorly known. Gray foxes are monoestrous. Mating occurs from January to March over much of their range (although data for the Rocky Mountain region are lacking). The gestation period is about 59 days. Litter size averages 3.8 and ranges from 1 to 7 young (Fritzell 1987). Dispersal occurs in fall or winter. Females reach sexual maturity at about 10 months and are capable of breeding their first year, but many may not breed as yearlings (J. Wood 1958). However, data summarized by Trapp and Hallberg (1975) suggested that populations of gray foxes appear to be composed mostly of juveniles (48 to 73 percent), suggesting that breeding by juvenile females is important to population success. However, in an unharvested population in South Carolina, foxes over 34 months of age made up 52.6 percent of the population compared with 37 percent juveniles (J. Weston and Brisbin 2003). Sex ratio probably is close to 1:1.

Home ranges were 30 to 200 ha for gray foxes in Utah (Trapp 1978) and California (T. Fuller 1978). In New Mexico, home ranges averaged 654 ha (R. L. Harrison 2002). S. Riley (2006) reported mean home ranges of 78–100 ha in Marin County, California, depending on whether they had primarily rural or urban distributions. In Mississippi, Chamberlain and Leopold (2000) reported home ranges of 165 ha (winter) to 352 ha (breeding season), with core areas being larger in the breeding season. Home ranges in other parts of the East are often larger, not infrequently more than 500 ha (Fritzell 1987). Gray foxes may be territorial, as exclusive areas of occupancy are established and scent-marking is common. Chamberlain and Leopold (2000) concluded that gray fox pairs were territorial, because they frequently traveled together in their home ranges and showed minimal area of overlap among family groups and mutual avoidance of neighbors. On the contrary, Hallberg and Trapp (1984) and K. Haroldson and Fritzell (1984) questioned whether gray foxes are territorial. Mean distances moved in foraging in Utah were 475 m for males and 600 m for females (Trapp 1978). Estimated densities ranged from 1 to 2 animals per square kilometer (Fritzell 1987).

Little is known of causes or rates of mortality, although attrition in the young probably is high. In Colorado, gray foxes were harvested as furbearers until closure of kill trapping in 1997. From 1974 to 1991, estimated harvest ranged from 1,400 (in 1984) to fewer than 200 (in 1990); several Division of Wildlife employees believed gray fox were decreasing in numbers in their management areas (J. Fitzgerald 1993b). There is no open season on the species at this time. Golden eagles, coyotes, mountain lions, and bobcats kill gray foxes (Fedriani et al. 2000; S. Riley 2001; Cypher 2003). R. L. Harrison (1993) found no evidence that gray foxes were affected by loose dogs in urban areas. Rabies outbreaks occur periodically in the eastern United States. The literature on the species was reviewed by Fritzell and Haroldson (1982), Fritzell (1987), and Cypher (2003).

Family Ursidae—Bears

The family Ursidae contains the largest of the living terrestrial carnivores, the polar bear (*Ursus maritimus*) and the brown bear (*Ursus arctos*); Alaskan brown bears weigh up to 700 kg. Bears have 5 digits on each foot with heavy, nonretractile claws. Front claws are longer than hind claws. The skull is stoutly built with the auditory bullae only moderately inflated. Incisors are unspecialized, and canines are large, conical, and somewhat curved. The dental formula is 2–3/3, 1/1, 4/4, 2/3 = 40 or 42 teeth. Premolars are typically poorly developed and may number from 1 to 4. The fourth premolar is almost always present but lacks the third or inner root. Premolars and molars are bunodont with low, rounded cusps; sectorial carnassial teeth are absent. The stomach is simple, and there is no cecum. Males have a well-developed baculum and typically average one-fourth to one-fifth larger than females.

Closely related to canids, the first ursids appeared relatively recently in the fossil record, during the Miocene Epoch, about 29 million years ago. By the Middle Pleistocene, ancestors of the modern black bear had reached North America from Asia (Kurtén and Anderson 1980; J. Craighead and Mitchell 1982). The grizzly bear probably originated in Europe in the mid-Pleistocene, expanding into North America by the Late Pleistocene. Wozencraft (2005) recognized 5 genera and 8 species of living bears, found in North America, Eurasia, and the Andes of South America. One species lived in the Atlas Mountains of North Africa into the nineteenth century, until it was exterminated by humans. One genus and 2 species are known from Colorado. Halfpenny (2007b) provided a beautifully illustrated introduction to Yellowstone's bears that may hint at the situation in Colorado before Euro-American settlement.

Key to the Species of the Family Ursidae in Colorado

1. Claws of front and hindfeet of about equal length; length of last upper molar less than 1.5 times length of first upper molar; length of maxillary toothrow less than 110 mm . . . . Black Bear—*Ursus americanus*, p. 387

1' Claws of front feet longer and larger than claws of hindfeet; length of last upper molar more than 1.5 times length of first upper molar; length of maxillary toothrow more than 110 mm . . . . Grizzly, or Brown, Bear—*Ursus arctos*, p. 391

Genus *Ursus*—Bears

Wozencraft (2005) recognized 4 species in the genus *Ursus*, the Holarctic brown bear (*U. arctos*), the American black bear (*U. americanus*), the polar bear (*U. maritimus*—the largest of terrestrial carnivores), and the Asian black bear (*U. thibetanus*).

Ursus americanus

AMERICAN BLACK BEAR

Description

A medium-sized bear, the black bear is Colorado's largest extant carnivore. Color varies greatly, from black to pale brown or (rarely) even blonde. In a Coloradan population, 83 percent of bears of both sexes were brown (T. Beck 1991), not unusual for black bears in mountainous regions of the West. Considerable seasonal color change occurs as a result of bleaching and fading of the pelage. Subadults may change color with age, usually going from brown to black, but the reverse also occurs. A white chest blaze is not uncommon for Coloradan animals. The muzzle is typically pale brownish yellow. Measurements are: total length 1,400–1,950 mm; length of tail 80–125 mm; length of hindfoot 190–280 mm; length of ear 60–80 mm; weight 90 kg, although some individuals weigh as much as 225 kg. In Colorado, weights of adult bears captured on Black Mesa, on the Uncompahgre Plateau, and in Middle Park ranged from 44 to 83 kg for females and from 68 to 138 kg for males (T. Beck 1996), with Middle Park animals weighing on average about 20 percent less than those from southwestern Colorado.

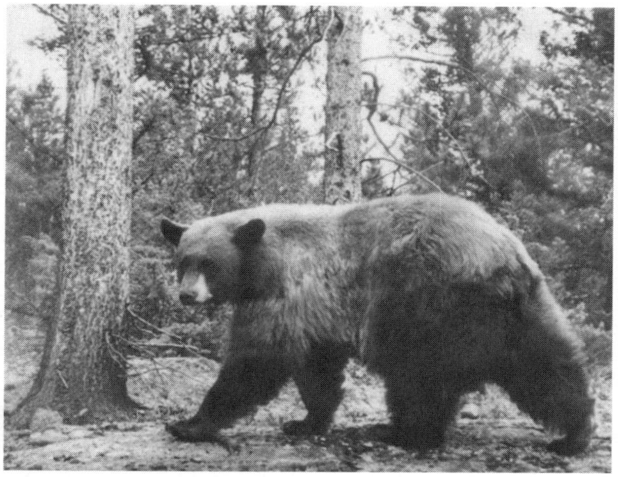

PHOTOGRAPH 12-10. American black bear (*Ursus americanus*). Photograph by Joseph Van Wormer. All rights reserved. Photo Archives, Denver Museum of Nature and Science.

Some adult black bears closely resemble brown bears, *Ursus arctos*, in color and can be misidentified in the field. The black bear generally lacks the mane of hairs present on the shoulders of the brown (or grizzly) bear, and the tips of the hairs are not grizzled as they are in many individuals of *U. arctos*. When standing, the rump usually appears as high or higher than the shoulder area whereas grizzlies usually appear slightly higher in the shoulder. There is considerable overlap between the size of footpads for Coloradan black bears and Yellowstone grizzly bears, and separation on the basis of tracks is not always possible (T. Beck 1991). In general, the claws on the front feet of black bears are not as strongly developed as on most individual grizzly bears and are not much larger than the rear claws. The skull typically has a straight profile while most grizzly bears have a shortened, dished face and slightly shorter ears. Females have 6 mammae.

Distribution

Black bears can survive in practically any habitat that offers sufficient food and cover, from the deserts of Arizona to the coniferous forests of northern Canada. Pelton and Vanmanen (1994) estimated that black bears still inhabit about 62 percent of their historical range. In Colorado, black bears are locally common in suitable habitats in the western two-thirds of the state. Highest population densities usually occur in the montane shrublands from Walsenburg and Trinidad west to the San Luis Valley, in the San Juan Mountains, and in the canyon country of west-central Colorado. In recent years the animals have become much more prevalent in the foothills of the Front Range, along the urban-wildland interface, and black bears frequently range into the western suburbs of the Front Range corridor. Based on presence of a possible breeding population of black bears in Cimarron County in the Oklahoma Panhandle, Kamler, Ballard, Fish, et al. (2003) predicted that the animals will continue to expand from southeastern Colorado back into their historical range in southwestern Kansas, Oklahoma, and the Texas Panhandle. *Ursus americanus amblyceps*, the subspecies of the Southern Rockies, once occurred statewide except in extreme northeastern

MAP 12-19. Distribution of the American black bear (*Ursus americanus*) in North America.

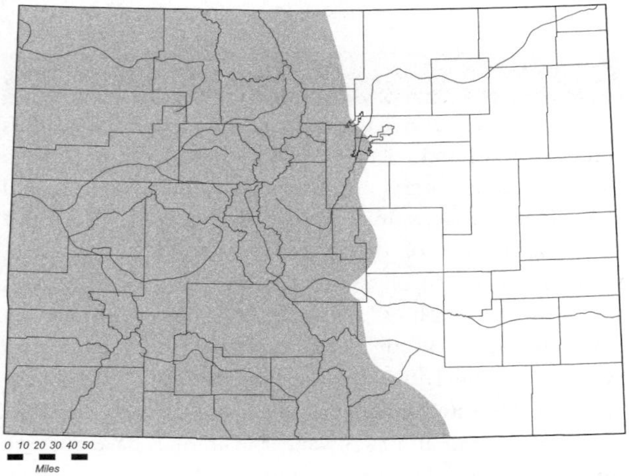

MAP 12-20. Distribution of the American black bear (*Ursus americanus*) in Colorado.

Colorado, where *U. a. americanus* may have occurred (D. Armstrong 1972).

Natural History

In Colorado the black bear is most common in montane shrublands and forests and subalpine forests at moderate elevations, especially in areas with well-developed stands of oakbrush or berry-producing shrubs such as serviceberry, native plum, and chokecherry. However, the animals also occupy habitats ranging from the edge of the alpine tundra to the lower foothills and canyon country. Extensive work on the species has been done by T. Beck (1991, 1996, 1997) in western Colorado and McCutchen (1987, 1989) in Rocky Mountain National Park. Black bears are mostly retiring and secretive, typically staying close to rough topography or dense vegetation that provides escape cover. Numbers are usually low in any particular locale, making it difficult to census and study the animals.

Detailed study of food habits of black bears has not been conducted in Colorado. However, black bears are omnivorous and their diet depends largely on which kinds of food are seasonally available, although their mainstay is vegetation. In spring, emerging grasses and succulent forbs are favored. In summer and early fall, bears take advantage of a variety of berries and other fruits. In late fall, preferences are for berries and mast (acorns) where available. When the opportunity is present, black bears eat a diversity of insects, including beetle larvae and social insects (ants, wasps, bees, termites, etc.), and they kill a variety of mammals, including rodents, rabbits, and young or unwary ungulates (R. Gill and Beck 1990). Carrion may be eaten at any time but is especially important in spring, a fact formerly exploited by spring bear hunters, who attracted the animals with bait. In some areas in Idaho, black bears were effective predators on elk calves, killing 37 percent of tagged young (Schlegal 1977). They also kill elk calves in Yellowstone National Park in spring and summer, but less frequently than do grizzly bears (Barber 2005; Barber-Meyer et al. 2008). The extent and significance of predation on wild ungulates in Colorado are unknown. Bears (species not reported) were responsible for killing an estimated 8,500 sheep and lambs in the United States in 2004 (Agricultural Statistics Board 2005). In Colorado, bears killed 600 adult sheep and 1,700 lambs. Black bears frequently raid apiaries and orchards. Bears can habituate to humans and their foods, leading to bear-human conflicts and sometimes substantial economic damage (Meadows et al. 1998). Ample food supplies are critical to black bear survival in spring, when they emerge from dormancy, and in the late summer and fall, when they are storing fat for winter.

There are 4 physiological phases in the annual cycle of black bears, closely tied to nutritional needs: hibernation, walking hibernation, normal activity, and hyperphagia (R. Gill and Beck 1990). Aspects of hibernation have been well studied in Colorado black bears (R. Nelson and Beck

1984; Tinker et al. 1998; Harlow et al. 2001, 2002, 2004). During hibernation, black bears may exist more than 200 days without eating, drinking, defecating, or urinating. A fecal plug blocks the intestinal tract until spring. During this period many individuals of both sexes shed the outer layers of their footpads. New pads develop and harden on emergence in the spring. Black bears normally lose 20 to 27 percent of their body weight during hibernation (R. Nelson et al. 1973). Hibernation is marked by a drop of 50 to 60 percent in metabolic and heart rates. The body temperature remains rather high, however, dropping only 7° or 8°C. Thus, bears can arouse fairly quickly when disturbed in their hibernacula. Energy is supplied from fat storage, and metabolized nutrients can be resynthesized into protein (R. Nelson and Beck 1984). The walking hibernation stage lasts for at least 2 to 3 weeks following emergence from the hibernation den. At that time, black bears are not inclined to feed or drink appreciably, and apparently urination rates are low. In Montana, bears continued to lose weight from April to as late as the end of July (Jonkel and Cowan 1971). By late July, they start to gain weight at an average of 0.7 kg per day. The normal activity phase is characterized by an increase in metabolic demand, and bears forage selectively for plant materials with high sugar and starch content and readily digestible animal protein. The hyperphagic phase is characterized by gorging during late summer and fall, with preferences shown for foods high in fat, sugar, and starch.

In Colorado, winter denning may begin as early as the first week in October and extend to late December. Peaks of denning activity occur in the third and fourth weeks of October for females and the second and third weeks of November for males (T. Beck 1991). R. Inman et al. (2007) reported similar differences in denning and emergence times for male and female bears in northern New Mexico, but animals from farther south did not show that pattern. On the east side of Rocky Mountain National Park, bears entered winter dens later during wetter years and when their home ranges had more use by humans. They emerged earlier in spring in areas where human use was greater. The suggested reason for this pattern was the availability of food in areas frequented by humans. In Colorado, black bears generally use rock-shelters (60 percent of dens examined) or excavations under shrubs and trees for den sites. Dens dug under serviceberry bushes were favored over other shrub types. In some instances the animals simply curl up under protective cover and sleep on the ground. Of dens examined, 53 percent had definitely been used in previous years, and most dens showed some degree of prior use (T. Beck 1991). Baldwin (2008) and Baldwin and Bender (2008a, 2009) studied demography and den site characteristics of black bears in Rocky Mountain National Park. In the course of the study (2003–2006), fewer than 25 black bears occurred in the park. Preferred den sites included steep slopes and greater snow depths. They believed that contemporary den sites indicated shifts closer to roads and perhaps increasing habituation to areas frequented by humans.

Black bears in Colorado probably breed from early June to perhaps mid-August, based on studies in Montana (Jonkel and Cowan 1971). Females remain in estrus until bred or until the ovarian follicles degenerate. Ovulation is induced by copulation. The gestation period is 7 to 8 months, with implantation delayed until November or December. Cubs are born in the den in late January or February, while the mother is in hibernation. Litter size is 2 or 3 (Kolenosky and Strathearn 1987). Typically, black bear populations in the western United States have lower productivity than those in the East. Bears in parts of Colorado have some of the higher success rates reported in the West (T. Beck 1991). Based on a small sample size, usual litter size in Colorado is 2, and occasionally 3 (T. Beck 1991). The age of adult females bearing their first litter averaged 5 years, with a range of 3 to 7. Frequencies of litters for females ranged from 1 to 4 years, with most females having a litter every other year.

At birth the cubs weigh only 225 to 250 g and are blind, naked, and helpless. Birth weight is only about 1/200th the weight of the mother, compared with about 1/20th for a newborn human. Cubs weighed in dens in Colorado averaged 1.5 kg in late February and early March, and 2.9 kg in late March (T. Beck 1991). The cubs grow rapidly and are weaned by September. They stay with the female during their first year of life. They disperse at the age of 1.5 years in spring or summer when the female comes into estrus again. Costello (2010) found that most male black bears in the Sangre de Cristo Mountains of northern New Mexico moved 22 to 62 km from their natal den, whereas most females ranged only 0 to 7 km from their birthplace.

Black bears are typically solitary, except for family groups (a sow and cubs) or aggregations at concentrated food resources, where bears may show a relatively high tolerance for each other. At such times the animals maintain temporal spacing through dominance behaviors such as threat displays. Bears may forage at any hour, but most activity tends to be diurnal or crepuscular. Larivière, Huot, and Samson (1994) found that female black bears become active about one-half hour after sunrise, with activity periods averaging 245 minutes followed by resting periods of about 1 hour. Most nocturnal behavior is observed in spring and fall or in animals raiding human food sources (Pelton 2003). T. Beck (1997) reported a peak of bear visits to camera units near nightfall, with nocturnal visits representing less than 16 percent of the total.

Signs of bear activity in an area include large piles of scat with readily recognizable food remains, rocks rolled and rotten logs ripped open to expose insect prey, and broken, bent, or stripped branches on fruiting bushes. Black bears can climb trees, and it is not unusual to see climbing scars on large aspen trunks. Black bears as well as grizzly bears also mark trees by biting and clawing the trunk about 1 to 2 m off the ground. Such marking behavior is thought to increase in mid-summer, possibly relating to the onset of the breeding season.

Black bear populations are difficult to estimate because individual bears wander widely. In Colorado, densities were estimated at 1 animal per 5.6 to 7.7 km^2 during early summer, with a considerable increase in numbers starting in mid-August when migrant animals moved into mast-producing areas. This is a very low density compared with populations in other parts of the country (T. Beck 1991). McCutchen (1987) estimated 1 bear per 26 to 31 km^2 in Rocky Mountain National Park and considered that area to represent some of the least productive bear habitat in Colorado. Using infrared camera units, T. Beck (1995, 1997) estimated black bear population densities in mixed oak–brush–aspen–dry meadow on the Uncompahgre Plateau and in montane coniferous forest in Middle Park. The Uncompahgre density estimate was 36 bears per 100 km^2, whereas that in Middle Park was 8.1 per 100 km^2. T. Beck (1997) considered bear habitat on the Uncompahgre Plateau as among the best in the state and the coniferous forests of Middle Park as some of the poorest. Grogan and Lindzey (1999) estimated densities of 1.8 to 3.7 (mean, 2.54) bears per 100 km^2, based on remote camera detections in the Snowy Range of southern Wyoming. These are the lowest densities reported for black bears in the Mountain West.

Beckmann and Berger (2003) studied effects of residential development on black bear behaviors and biology at the urban-wildland interface in the Lake Tahoe area along the California-Nevada border. Urbanized bears showed increased density (especially of males), increased reproductive years in females, increased body mass, reduced home range size, and delay in fall hibernation. However, females were less likely than males to be present near humans and their cubs had less chance of successful dispersal than did offspring of non-urban bears. A similar study of bear behavior would be interesting in urbanizing areas of Colorado's Front Range corridor.

Home range depends on topography, food availability, and the sex and age of the individual. In mountainous parts of Colorado, some individual bears show seasonal migrations of 13 to 36 km from summer foraging sites to areas where fall mast and berry production are high (T. Beck 1991). Adult males appear to have the largest home ranges, and non-breeding females have the smallest. Annual home ranges in Colorado ranged from 4 to 189 km^2, and home ranges for more than 1 year varied from 14 to 199 km^2 for resident adult females. For adult males, annual home range varied from 31 to 145 km^2, and total home ranges were 223 to 451 km^2 (T. Beck 1991). In Idaho (Amstrup and Beecham 1976) and Washington (G. Koehler and Pierce 2003), home ranges of adults varied from 16.6 to 130.3 km^2, with overlap of home ranges being common. Males tended to show larger daily movements (average, 1.7 km) than females (average, 1.4 km) in the Idaho study. In Arizona, home ranges were 13 km^2 for subadult females and 42 km^2 for subadult males (LeCount 1977). Little overlap was observed in home ranges in Montana (Jonkel and Cowan 1971), but home ranges of adult males overlapped in Arizona (LeCount 1977).

Black bears have low biotic potential because of the advanced age at which breeding starts, small litter size, and infrequency of litters, and there may even be some tendency for the bear population in Colorado to be cyclical (R. Gill and Beck 1990). T. Beck (1996) estimated proportion of adult females in trapped and hunted populations to range from 40 to 44 percent compared with an estimated 50 percent on his Black Mesa study area (T. Beck 1991), which was closed to legal hunting. He suggested the need to recalculate female survival rates for Colorado bears and to consider the overall impact of such lowered reproductive potential on populations. In many states improper management has led to significant population declines. In Colorado, annual survival rates in a population partly protected from hunting by boundary closures were 0.56 for cubs, 0.94 for yearlings, and 0.70 to 0.96 for adults and subadults combined. Male bears typically had higher mortality than females in Colorado (T. Beck 1991). In part this probably is related to behavioral differences, including having larger home ranges, traveling more, and being more aggressive (R. Gill and Beck 1990; G. Koehler and Pierce 2005). Survival beyond 6 months of age was mostly dependent on an individual's interactions with humans. On the Black Mesa, 26 percent of tagged animals were killed by humans, and about 85 percent of all subadult and adult mortality was human-caused (T. Beck 1991). G. Koehler and Pierce (2005) had adult survival rates of 0.73 for marked males and 0.93 for marked females in Washington, with no statistical difference in survival between the marked bears and animals taken by hunters. No evidence exists for compensatory reproductive success in hunted populations. Most black bears do not live more than 8 to 10 years in the wild, although one captured individual was about 14 years old (T. Beck 1981).

Black bears are big game mammals in Colorado. In 1990 the state enacted a black bear management plan (R. Gill and Beck 1990) to attempt to stabilize harvest at about 580 animals per year, while still accommodating about 4,600 hunters. However, in recent years numbers of hunters and kill have increased substantially above those goals, with total hunters averaging 10,253 from 1995 to 2007 and kill averaging 625 animals (T. Beck 2000a; also see Table 4-2). Biologists of the Colorado Division of Wildlife and several environmental groups had been concerned that overharvest of females was leading to decline of bear populations in a number of the game management units. In 1992, Colorado's voters passed a referendum outlawing spring bear hunting and banning the use of bait and dogs for hunting (Loker et al. 1994; Loker and Decker 1995).

In 1994 the Division of Wildlife also instituted its "two-strike" rule for so-called problem bears. If an animal caused problems leading to management action (i.e., it had to be trapped and relocated) twice, the third time the animal would be destroyed. Human–black bear interactions frequently occur at the interface of urbanizing areas and black bear habitat. Baruch-Mordo et al. (2008) examined bear conflicts in Colorado from 1985 to 2003 involving agricultural operations, human development conflicts (property damage, proximity to humans, aggressive actions by bears, etc.), and road-killed bears. Most incidents were in areas of foothill shrublands along the central and southern Front Range and in the southwest, near Durango, with numbers of conflicts increasing in recent years. Black bears occasionally attack and sometimes even kill humans. Most instances involve female bears with cubs or animals defending food, but in a few cases apparently predatory attacks occur (Herrero and Fleck 1990; Herrero 2005). The Colorado Division of Wildlife has records of 23 documented black bear attacks on humans since 1998. Masterson (2006) provided a useful and comprehensive book on how to live in bear country while minimizing conflicts.

The literature on black bears was reviewed by Pelton (1982, 2003), Kolenosky and Strathearn (1987), and Larivière (2001). Kunkel (2003) reviewed natural history and conservation status of black bears in the context of other large forest carnivores.

Ursus arctos

GRIZZLY, OR BROWN, BEAR

Description

The grizzly or brown bear is a large, brownish bear. Some individuals from western North America show a grizzled or silver-tipped appearance on their dorsal guard hairs. Other individuals are brown with a paler wash of yellowish on the shoulders and back. There is usually a pronounced mane of long hairs on the shoulders; the rest of the fur is dense, long, and coarse, at its finest in late fall and early spring. The shoulder region appears higher than the rump on most individuals because of a well-developed mass of muscle overlying the scapula. The claws on the front feet are very long and only slightly curved. The skull generally has a dished-in profile, with the rostrum sloping gradually from the forehead. Females have 6 mammae. Few records exist on actual sizes of grizzly bears. Measurements are: total length 1,700–2,800 mm; length of tail 70–80 mm; length of hindfoot 230–280 mm. An adult grizzly stands about 1,050 to 1,350 mm at the shoulder and most adults weigh 135 to 275 kg. The largest grizzly handled in the Greater Yellowstone Ecosystem weighed 509 kg (F. Craighead 1979). It appears that grizzlies in Colorado were somewhat smaller than those from farther north.

PHOTOGRAPH 12-11. Grizzly, or brown, bear (*Ursus arctos*). Photograph by Joseph Van Wormer. All rights reserved. Photo Archives, Denver Museum of Nature and Science.

Distribution

Although grizzlies once ranged throughout western North America, few now remain in the lower 48 states, mostly in and adjacent to Yellowstone and Glacier national parks. Other remnants may exist in northern Idaho and Washington. Servheen (1999) estimated that 800–1,020 grizzlies survived south of Canada. An estimated 57,000 brown bears remain in western Canada and Alaska (C. Schwartz et al. 2003). The grizzly population in the Greater Yellowstone Ecosystem has increased since the species was listed in 1975 as threatened under the Endangered Species Act. It has recently been recommended for delisting, with management responsibility shifting to the states of Idaho, Montana, and Wyoming (Gunther 2008).

Grizzly bears were once present throughout Colorado (Cary 1911; Warren 1942; D. Armstrong 1972) but appeared to have been extirpated by the mid-twentieth century, the last known grizzly having been killed on Rio Grande Pyramid, Hinsdale County, in 1952 (D. Armstrong 1972). Then in 1979, to the surprise of many, an adult female grizzly attacked hunting guide Ed Wiseman near Platoro Reservoir in the San Juan Mountains (Barrows and Holmes 1990). Wiseman was severely injured but recovered from the incident. The animal's skull, skeleton, and skin are housed in the Denver Museum of Nature and Science. That was the last specimen to be collected in Colorado, although periodic rumors of additional grizzlies continue to circulate. Popular books have chronicled reports and rumors of grizzlies in Colorado in recent decades (Bass 1995; D. Peterson 1998). The grizzly is listed as endangered by the state of Colorado but is thought to have been extirpated and likely will not be reestablished deliberately.

Because of great individual and geographic variations, the taxonomy of the large brown bears of North America remains a subject of controversy (C. Schwartz et al. 2003). Previously, 87 named kinds (species and subspecies) were recognized (as listed by E. Hall 1981). Most of those forms were named by C. Hart Merriam, first chief of the US Bureau of Biological Survey and a founder of the American Society of Mammalogists. Four kinds were named from Coloradan type localities (D. Armstrong 1972). R. L. Rausch (1953, 1963) recognized all of the brown and grizzly bears of North America as conspecific with the Eurasian brown bear, *Ursus arctos*. E. Hall (1984) revised systematics of American brown bears and recognized 9 subspecies in a single species. One subspecies, *Ursus arctos horribilis*, occurred in Colorado.

MAP 12-21. Historic and present distribution of the grizzly, or brown, bear (*Ursus arctos*) in North America.

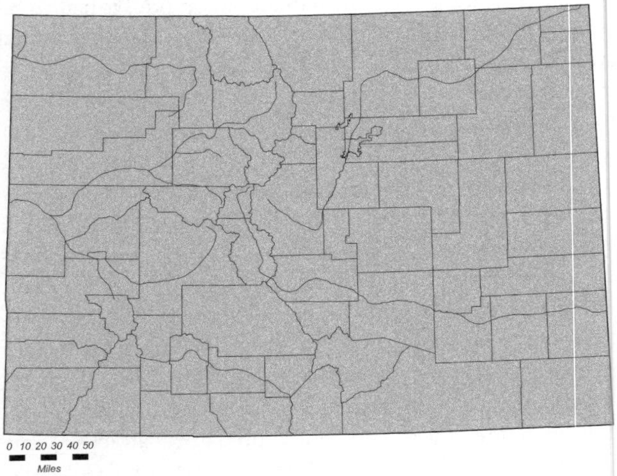

MAP 12-22. Historic distribution of the grizzly, or brown, bear (*Ursus arctos*) in Colorado.

Natural History

Grizzly bears are not limited to any particular habitat (D. Craighead 1998). Unlike the black bear, the grizzly does not usually climb trees; its activities are almost strictly terrestrial. The species is mostly crepuscular to nocturnal, especially in areas where it is threatened by humans. Coloradan specimens were taken from prairie grasslands to alpine tundra. Productive grizzly bear habitat provides a variety of locally abundant foods that can be used sequentially by season (Jonkel 1987). In northern Montana and southwestern Canada, McLellan and Hovey (2001) identified 2 distinct habitat selection strategies of bears coming out of hibernation. Some ("mountain residents") moved into avalanche chutes in the spring; others ("elevational migrating bears") moved down to lowland riparian habitats. In the summer both groups tended to move into 50- to 70-year-old burn areas. Bears in Colorado may have shown similar differences in behavior and movement in response to the seasons.

The grizzly is largely a vegetarian, with up to 90 percent of the diet composed of plant material. D. Mattson (2004) reported grizzly bear foraging in Yellowstone on food stores of pocket gophers and the gophers themselves, and D. Mattson and Reinhart (1997) reported them stealing caches built by pine squirrels. Based on research in the Greater Yellowstone Ecosystem (J. Craighead et al. 1969, 1995; F. Craighead 1979; Schullery 1986; S. French and French 1990; D. Mattson et al. 1991; S. French et al. 1994; G. Green et al. 1997; Tardiff and Stanford 1998), one can infer the ways in which Coloradan grizzlies once made their living. Depending on location, they probably fed on grasses, sedges, roots, and succulent forbs in alpine tundra and subalpine forests, supplemented by insects, smaller mammals (such as marmots, pocket gophers, and ground squirrels excavated from their dens), and the occasional large mammal or carrion. At lower elevations, the staple was probably grasses and succulent forbs supplemented with fruits such as chokecherries and currants. Colorado is not noted for the large crops of berries characteristic farther north, and availability was limited. However, following severe winters, carrion, including winter-killed deer, elk, and livestock, was plentiful.

In Yellowstone, grizzlies kill and eat several different ungulates, with many individuals becoming adept at killing elk calves (S. French and French 1990; Barber et al. 2005). Of Colorado's native ungulates, probably only bighorn sheep and pronghorn were relatively secure from periodic grizzly attacks because of their habitats and their speed and agility. Singer et al. (1997) estimated 23 percent of elk calf mortality in Yellowstone prior to wolf restoration was from bears. Since wolf restoration, bears account for 55 to 60 percent of calf mortality in their first 30 days of life, with wolves and coyotes accounting for 10 to 15 percent in that same time period (Barber et al. 2005). It appears that bears are more successful in finding young calves when they are most vulnerable. They are also skilled in taking over kills made by wolves or mountain lions (Ruth 2004; D. W. Smith 2005), and some evidence suggests that a number of bears leave Yellowstone in the fall to move out into areas where elk hunters leave gut piles (Ruth et al. 2003; M. Haroldson et al. 2004). Bears have been observed to work equally hard excavating talus slopes at high elevations, seeking adult miller moths (S. French et al. 1994). These are the same insects that appear in large numbers at lower elevations many springs and summers during migration in Colorado. D. White et al. (1998) estimated that a grizzly in Glacier National Park could eat 40,000 moths per day, securing up to 20,000 kcal.

Good habitat for grizzly bears frequently contains food supplies that are seasonally and elevationally restricted. In such situations, the animals may have distinct and well-defined seasonal home ranges connected by migration corridors (sometimes more than 65 km long). Home ranges in the Greater Yellowstone Ecosystem have been estimated at 57 km^2 for seasonal spring/summer ranges for females with cubs and up to 2,600 km^2 for annual ranges of adult males. Mean home range sizes in that area are 281 km^2 for females and 874 km^2 for males (C. Schwartz et al. 2003). This vast area is barely large enough to encompass the wanderings of some individuals and the spatial demands of a viable population (J. Craighead and Mitchell 1982). Individual animals have been reported to move up to 10 or 11 km daily in that area.

Grizzlies, like black bears, den in the winter months. They typically enter dens in late October or early November and emerge in late March to early May. In the den they exhibit physiological patterns similar to those described for the black bear. Dens typically are located on steep slopes at high elevations. Dens are excavated into the soil; natural shelters, like rock overhangs and caves, are not used much in the Yellowstone area (F. Craighead and Craighead 1972) but are used by bears in parts of Alaska (C. Schwartz et al. 2003).

Grizzly bears are polygamous and may mate as early as mid-May or as late as mid-July. Most breeding occurs in June. Estrus continues for up to 2 months (J. Craighead et al. 1969, 1995). Copulation may last from 10 to 60 minutes, depending on individuals, and females may mate more than once, even accepting more than 1 male on the same day. Delayed implantation occurs, and cubs are born in the den in late January (J. Craighead et al. 1976). Average litter size is 2 for Yellowstone, with an average reproductive cycle producing cubs every 2.9 years. Female grizzlies typically produce their first litters at 5.9 years of age and breed throughout their lifespan (J. Craighead and Mitchell 1982; J. Craighead et al. 1995; C. Schwartz et al. 2006). Thus, grizzly bears have considerably lower biotic potential than even the black bear. The oldest breeding female grizzly bear in Yellowstone was approximately 25 years of age (F. Craighead and Mitchell 1982).

Despite their low reproductive rate, the grizzly bear population in the Greater Yellowstone Area has increased from an estimated 136 bears in 1975 to some 571 in 2007. Interestingly, that increase coincided with the rapid growth of the wolf population. Population increase has led to bears becoming more visible and established in much of Grand Teton National Park as well as reclaiming portions of the Gros Ventre and Wind River ranges. This represents an expansion of grizzly bear range and distribution by nearly 50 percent since the 1970s (Servheen and Shoemaker 2008).

Sex ratios (at least in Yellowstone) may slightly favor males at birth (J. Craighead and Mitchell 1982) but may slightly favor females in the adult population (C. Schwartz et al. 2003). The age structure of the Yellowstone population was 19 percent cubs, 13 percent yearlings, 25 percent 2- to 4-year-olds, and 44 percent adults (J. Craighead and Mitchell 1982). Such age structure is probably essential for maintaining populations in other areas. Annual survivorship is usually high (0.90 or more) for adult females, slightly lower for subadult females, and lowest for subadult males (0.66 to 0.91), especially in hunted populations (C. Schwartz et al. 2003). Survival rates of cubs and yearlings both were negatively related to population size, suggesting density dependence in the Greater Yellowstone Ecosystem is highest outside Yellowstone National Park boundaries (C. Schwartz et al. 2006). Up to 90 percent of bear mortality is caused by humans even in non-hunted populations (McLellan et al. 1999; C. Schwartz et al. 2006).

Grizzly bears are large, efficient predators and encounters with humans are not uncommon in and around Yellowstone and Glacier national parks (Herrero 2005). E. Mills (1919) summarized observations of grizzly bears a century ago in the northern Colorado Front Range. That classic has been republished in several editions.

Literature on the species was reviewed by J. Craighead and Mitchell (1982), Jonkel (1987), Pasitschniak-Arts (1993), C. Schwartz et al. (2003), and Reed-Eckert et al. (2004). Halfpenny (2007a) presented a well-illustrated portrait of Yellowstone bears and Servheen et al. (1999) summarized the conservation status of bears worldwide.

Family Mustelidae—Weasels and Kin

The family Mustelidae is a diverse adaptive radiation of terrestrial, semi-fossorial, arboreal, aquatic, and marine mammals. Mustelids generally rely on dens for protection when not foraging and are crepuscular or nocturnal. Most have pelage of a uniform color that blends with their environment; a few species in northern climates may change color seasonally. Most mustelids seek vertebrate prey. In size, mustelids range from the smallest of carnivores, the diminutive least weasel (*Mustela nivalis*), measuring about 200 mm long and weighing about 50 g, to the giant otter (*Pteroneura brasiliensis*) of South America, which measures 2 m in length and weighs up to 34 kg. Mustelids are sexually dimorphic: typically males are about one-quarter larger than females. The legs of most species are short, and the body of most is elongate. The tail is usually long and often bushy. The feet are plantigrade, semi-plantigrade, or digitigrade. All feet have 5 digits with well-developed non-retractile claws. In a few species the feet are webbed. The ears are short and rounded. Anal musk glands that produce pungent secretions are well developed in most species.

The skull is stout and lacks an alisphenoid canal. The face is typically short and broad, and the braincase is flattened. The condylar process of the dentary locks tightly into the flanged glenoid (mandibular) fossa so that the jaws close tightly and do not disarticulate when gripping prey. The dental formula for Coloradan mustelids is 3/3, 1/1, 3–4/3–4, 1/2 = 34 to 38 teeth. Most commonly the dental formula is 3/3, 1/1, 3/3, 1/2 = 34 teeth. The carnassial pair (fourth upper premolar and first lower molar) is well developed in most species. The single upper molar is normally large and dumbbell-shaped or squarish. The upper toothrow may show an angle at the junction of the last premolar and first molar. The stomach is simple and lacks a cecum. Females are monoestrous and many species show induced ovulation and delayed implantation. Males have a well-developed baculum (see Baryshnikov et al. 2003; S. Ferguson and Larivière 2004).

The family is rather old, dating from the Oligocene Epoch, approximately 40 million years ago. In North America, mustelids appear as fossils in the Miocene (*Martes*—20 to 7 mya), Late Pliocene–Early Pleistocene (5–3 mya—*Mustela, Taxidea*), or mid- to Late Pleistocene (*Gulo, Lontra*—2 mya or less) (Kurtén and Anderson 1980). There are 22 genera and about 59 species of mustelids (D. Wilson and Reeder 2005) naturally distributed worldwide, except in the Australian region, the Antarctic, and most oceanic islands. Several species have been introduced into some of these areas. Many species are prized for their fur. In Colorado there are 5 genera and possibly 10 (or even 11) species of mustelids.

Key to the Species of the Family Mustelidae Known or Expected to Occur in Colorado

1. Premolars 4/4 2

1' Premolars 4/3 or 3/3 4

2. Dorsum dark brownish bordered dorsolaterally by two paler brown bands from shoulder to rump; length of tail about one-fourth total length; sagittal crest greatly enlarged and overhanging the occiput . . . . Wolverine—*Gulo gulo*, p. 412

2' Dorsum blackish, dark brownish, or yellowish brown, not bordered by paler lateral bands; length of tail usually more than one-third total length; sagittal crest neither greatly enlarged nor overhanging the occiput . . . . *Martes*, 3

3. Dorsum brown to yellowish brown; greatest length of skull 90 mm or less . . . . American Marten—*Martes americana*, p. 396

3' Dorsum grizzled black to dark brown; greatest length of skull greater than 90 mm . . . . Fisher—*Martes pennanti*,* p. 399

4. Premolars 4/3; hindfeet webbed . . . . Northern River Otter—*Lutra canadensis*, p. 417

4' Premolars 3/3; hindfeet not webbed 5

5. Front claws longer than 30 mm; white medial stripe on head and neck; greatest length of skull more than 90 mm . . . . American Badger—*Taxidea taxus*, p. 415

5' Front claws shorter than 30 mm; no medial white stripe on head; greatest length of skull less than 90 mm . . . . *Mustela*, 6

6. Hindfoot more than 55 mm; greatest length of upper toothrow more than 20 mm in males and 17.8 in females; greatest length of skull more than 60 mm 7

6' Hindfoot less than 50 mm; greatest length of upper toothrow less than 20 mm in males and less than 17.8 in females; greatest length of skull less than 55 mm 8

7. Dorsal color buffy to yellowish white with a black facial mask; legs, feet, and tip of tail also black; distance between canines greater than distance between medial margins of auditory bullae . . . . Black-footed Ferret—*Mustela nigripes*, p. 405

7' Dorsal color uniformly brown to dark brown, except for possible white throat or chest patch; distance between canines about equal to distance between medial margins of bullae . . . American Mink—*Neovison vison*, p. 409

8. Tail with conspicuous black tip 9

8' Tail without conspicuous black tip; at most a few black hairs . . . . Least Weasel—*Mustela nivalis*,* p. 408

9. Ventral color yellowish orange in summer pelage; tail more than 44 percent of length of body; greatest length of skull usually more than 44 mm; auditory bullae relatively short, shorter than maxillary toothrow; postglenoid length usually less than 46 percent of greatest length of skull . . . . Long-tailed Weasel—*Mustela frenata*, p. 402

9' Ventral color white in summer pelage; tail less than 44 percent of body length; greatest length of skull usually less than 44 mm; auditory bullae relatively long, about equal to maxillary toothrow; postglenoid length usually more than 46 percent of greatest length of skull . . . . Ermine—*Mustela erminea*, p. 400

* Species of possible occurrence in Colorado.

Martes americana

AMERICAN, OR PINE, MARTEN

Description

The American marten—often called pine marten or simply marten—is weasel-like, smaller than an average house cat, with a pointed face and conspicuous, rounded ears. The long, bushy tail accounts for about one-third of the animal's total length. The dorsal color is highly variable from dark brown to pale brownish yellow, with the ventral surface sometimes slightly darker except for an orange to yellow-orange chest or throat patch. The tail and legs are usually

* Species of possible occurrence in Colorado.

darker in color than the body. The borders of the ears are often paler than the rest of the body. This prized furbearer has long, glossy, relatively stiff guard hairs and dense, silky underfur. Measurements are: total length 460–750 mm; length of tail 170–250 mm; length of hindfoot 75–98 mm; length of ear 45–55 mm; weight 0.5–1.2 kg. Females have 8 mammae. Martens are digitigrade and equipped with semi-retractile claws. The hind limbs, like those of their tree squirrel prey, have excellent rotational ability, enabling them to climb rapidly and to descend trees headfirst. Aging and sexing techniques have been developed (Strickland and Douglas 1987).

PHOTOGRAPH 12-12. American, or pine, marten (*Martes americanus*). All rights reserved. Photo Archives, Denver Museum of Nature and Science.

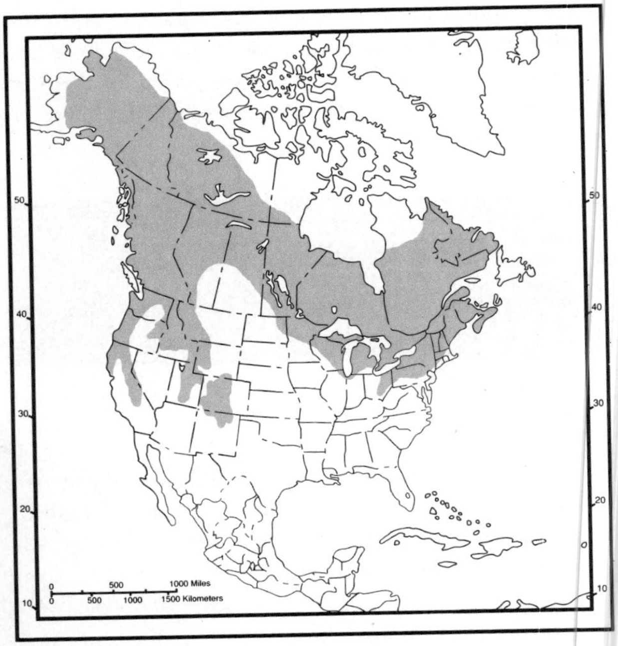

MAP 12-23. Distribution of the American marten (*Martes americanus*) in North America.

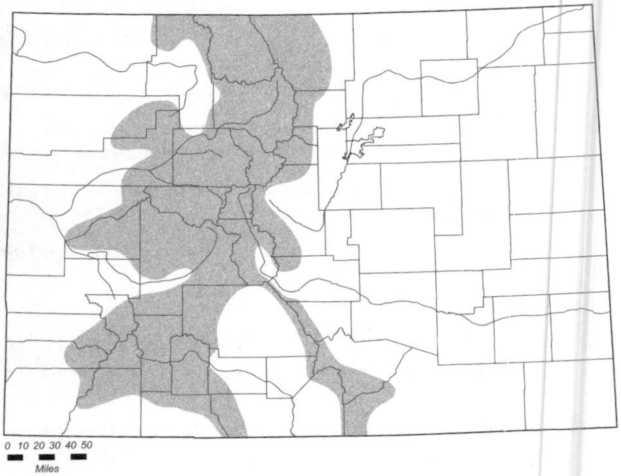

MAP 12-24. Distribution of the American marten (*Martes americanus*) in Colorado.

Distribution

The marten is widely distributed across boreal North America, with southward extensions in the Sierras to central California and along the Rocky Mountains to northern New Mexico. Wisz (1999) found that martens were not effective colonizers of outlying, isolated mountain ranges in Montana. They occur in most areas of coniferous forest in the higher mountains of Colorado. One subspecies, *Martes americana origenes*, occurs in the state. E. Anderson (1994) reviewed the evolution, distribution, and systematics of *Martes*, and Proulx et al. (2004) reviewed the conservation status of the 7 species of *Martes* over the Holarctic range of the genus.

Natural History

The marten is an inhabitant of subalpine spruce-fir and lodgepole pine forests, alpine tundra, and occasionally montane forests (Yeager and Remington 1956). It is generally associated with older growth or mixed-age stands of spruce-fir and lodgepole pine, especially in winter (Wilbert et al. 2000). Mesic forests are more important habitats than xeric forest types (J. W. Thomas et al. 1988). More than 30 percent canopy cover of coniferous trees is thought necessary for suitable marten habitat, with an optimum of 40 to 60 percent for resting and foraging (G. Koehler and Hornocker 1977; A. Allen 1982; W. Spencer et al. 1983). In studies with remote-sensing cameras in Rocky Mountain National Park, martens were more abundant on the Western Slope and associated with riparian–mixed coniferous forests and mixed conifer with patches of aspen (Baldwin and Bender 2008b). More xeric and open sites (most common on the east side of the park) were avoided. Juvenile animals use more different habitat types than do adults (Powell et al. 2003).

Moderate or light timber harvest may be favorable to martens by creating seral shrub and herb stages that enhance the prey base and berry crops. However, in Utah, Hargis et al. (1999) found fragmented forests associated with logging to reduce carrying capacity, with martens not tolerating more than 25 to 30 percent of their home ranges to be in open areas. Abundant physical structure is necessary close to ground level; overgrazing and regular, periodic fire reduce quality of habitat (Powell et al. 2003). Minta et al. (1999) considered the American marten to be an indicator species for ecosystem integrity at both microhabitat- and landscape-level scales. Clearly, perpetuation of old-growth forests is central to the maintenance of healthy marten populations. Habitat assessment for martens—and doubtless many other species—must consider the landscape context of habitat. Suitable habitat in a matrix of unsuitable habitat may be inaccessible and therefore useless (Schulz and Joyce 1992). Buskirk and Zielinski (2003) reviewed the comparative ecology of mesocarnivores in western coniferous forests. Of Coloradan carnivores, only marten and Canada lynx are forest specialists. Most other species (except the badger and the black-footed ferret) only utilize forested habitats to some degree.

Martens den in tree cavities, logs, rock piles, and burrows and frequently rest on tree limbs during the day. Large-diameter snags, large logs, and large live trees are important den sites in Wyoming (T. Clark and Campbell 1977; Ruggiero et al. 1998) and California (S. Martin and Barrett 1983). Objects on the forest floor, including logs, rock piles, stumps, wind-thrown trees, and slash, are important in providing den sites and access in winter to subnivean rodent populations (T. Clark and Campbell 1977; Hargis and McCullough 1984; Buskirk and Ruggiero 1994).

A variety of prey are taken; however, voles and other mice may constitute more than 60 to 88 percent of the diet. Buskirk and Ruggiero (1994) considered voles, especially *Microtus*, to be the dominant prey species over the entire range of the marten. However, Poole and Graf (1996) thought martens foraged more on hares and preferred such prey to smaller mammals when available. In Manitoba up to 53 percent of the diet was snowshoe hares (Strickland and Douglas 1987). Pine squirrels may be important food in some localities and martens often prey in and around squirrel middens (Sherburne and Bissonette 1993). Chipmunks, ground squirrels, cottontails, pikas, and shrews are also eaten. Winter food in Colorado is mostly voles (83 percent occurrence in samples), shrews, insects, and vegetable matter (C. Gordon 1986). Remains of snowshoe hare and beaver occurred in 7 percent of samples. Carrion is utilized, as are berries when available (S. Martin 1994). Birds are taken only rarely. Martens pursue prey on the ground as well as in the trees (T. Clark and Campbell 1977). Using remote cameras to detect marten activity in the Bitterroot National Forest, Montana, Foresman and Pearson (1999) found that the animals were active at random, day and night, thus overlapping the activity of a variety of rodent prey species, including various voles and squirrels. Martens cache food, often at a resting site (S. Henry et al. 1990). Adult martens require about 80 kcal/day of food for resting metabolism (Worthen and Kilgore 1981). This is roughly equivalent to 3 voles per day.

Usually crepuscular to nocturnal in habits, martens are active year-round. Diurnal activity may occur in summer in locations where ground squirrels are important prey or in very cold winter weather. I. Thompson and Colgan (1994) reported that martens were active less than 20 percent of the day in winter and close to 60 percent in summer. Martens seem to avoid traveling across open areas more than 100 to 250 m wide, although they have been observed in alpine boulder fields up to 3.2 km from timber (Streeter and Braun 1968). Travel routes are not used in any regular pattern. Coarse woody debris, such as is found in old-growth forests, provides access to subnivean resting sites, which are important to marten energetics in winter (Buskirk et al. 1989). Buskirk et al. (1988) and S. Taylor and Buskirk (1994) found martens to enter shallow daily torpor in winter and to thermoregulate behaviorally by changing position and even forest types to reduce heat loss.

Home ranges of martens vary depending on sex, season, location, and availability of food; the range is larger for eastern and northern animals than for animals farther south (Strickland and Douglas 1987). Powell and Zielinski (1994) concluded that martens consistently demonstrated intrasexual territoriality, calculating mean home ranges of 8.1 km^2 for males and 2.3 km^2 for females. They speculated that such territoriality was imposed on females by the larger, more dominant males. In Wyoming, average home ranges from telemetry studies were 2.0 to 3.2 km^2 for males and 0.8 km^2 for females (T. Clark and Campbell 1977; T. Clark et al. 1989). Home ranges of similar size were estimated from mark-recapture studies in Montana (V. Hawley and Newby 1957).

Populations within a given area can fluctuate widely because of variation in reproductive success and resident mortality as well as large numbers of highly mobile transient individuals. Some 65 percent of individuals in a Montana population were transients (on site no longer than 1 week) or temporary residents (on site less than 3 months) (V. Hawley and Newby 1957; Weckworth and Hawley 1962). In Wyoming, both males and females averaged 145 days for their length of stay on the study site (T. Clark et al. 1989). Population densities of 0.4 to 1.7 martens per km^2 have been reported (V. Hawley and Newby 1957; Powell et al. 2003). An apparent increase of martens occurred in the early 1950s in Colorado (Yeager and Remington 1956).

Martens communicate by scent-marking and vocalization. In addition to anal glands, both sexes have abdominal glands whose location is indicated by short hair (probably from wear) that is stained. The animals drag their bellies on logs and branches to deposit scent, especially during the breeding season. Vocalizations include huffs, growls, screams, and something akin to a chuckle, the last being used during the breeding season (Markley and Bassett 1942; Belan et al. 1978).

Most breeding occurs between late July and early September. Polygynous matings are common and females may be selectively polyandrous (Powell et al. 2003). Two periods of estrus may occur if breeding is not successful the first time (Markley and Bassett 1942). In captivity, males become increasingly aggressive during the breeding season, sometimes killing their female pen-mates. Female-to-female aggression also increased in the breeding season, marked by vicious fighting. Summaries of field studies and scarring of pelts of males suggest that fighting, especially among males, may also be common in the wild (Strickland and Douglas 1987). Induced ovulation is suspected, based on work summarized for various mustelids (Ewer 1973). Delayed implantation occurs. Gestation ranges from 230 to 275 days (Strickland and Douglas 1987); however, the actual developmental time from implantation to parturition is slightly less than 1 month (Jonkel and Weckwerth 1963). In northern populations, parturition dates range from mid-March to late April (Strickland et al. 1982). Martens have only 1 litter of 1 to 5 young (average, slightly less than 3) per year.

Both sexes become reproductively active at about 12 to 15 months of age (Strickland et al. 1982; Strickland and Douglas 1987). However, annual fecundity rates vary widely even within populations, making it difficult to estimate annual production. Some of this variance has been attributed to year-to-year fluctuations in the prey base. A 13-year study in Ontario reported an average of 80 percent conception in yearling females and 93 percent success in females older than 1.5 years (Strickland and Douglas 1987). One of the reproductive females was estimated to be about 14 years old. Sex ratios of young are about 1:1, but males usually outnumber females in surveys of trapped animals by as much as 3 to 1. Males may be more susceptible to trapping because of their much larger home ranges, a fact that was most noticeable in populations trapped during fall rather than winter (Yeager 1950).

Young are altricial but partly furred. Ears open at about 3 weeks, and eyes open at slightly over 1 month of age. By about 1.5 months they can leave the nest and are very active soon after that. Permanent dentition is complete by 18 weeks and the young approximate adult size at about 3 months. Males grow more rapidly than females (Brassard and Bernard 1939; Remington 1952).

In states and provinces allowing harvest, most mortality is probably due to trapping. The animals are relatively easy to capture, and unless monitored closely, populations can be overharvested (Strickland and Douglas 1987; Powell et al. 2003). In Colorado, harvest data, prior to the restrictions on trapping in 1997, showed increasing pressure on some populations in the mid- and late 1980s, with harvest climbing from 900 animals to more than 3,000, with Gunnison, Grand, Routt, and Mineral counties providing the highest take (J. Fitzgerald 1993b). The Colorado Division of Wildlife (2009f) lists the marten as a small game mammal or furbearer, with take again allowed after closure of seasons since 1996 with the passage of Amendment 14. The division will need to monitor populations carefully in the context of widespread die-off of subalpine conifers and renewed take by hunters and trappers. There are scattered reports of predation by coyotes, red foxes, lynx, mountain lions, eagles, and great horned owls. Forty-four percent of mortality in Oregon was from bobcats, and 22 percent was from other martens (Bull and Heater 1995, 2001). The mean annual probability of survival was 0.63. The literature on the species was reviewed by Strickland et al. (1982), T. Clark et al. (1987), Strickland and Douglas (1987), Buskirk and Ruggiero (1994), and Powell et al. (2003). Buskirk et al. (1994) provided an important collection of papers on marten and fisher.

Martes pennanti

FISHER

Description

The fisher is a large mustelid, similar in appearance to the marten. Unlike the marten, it lacks the orange to white chest or chin patch. Color is typically dark brown to blackish, with the legs, tail, and rump darker than the rest of the body. Late winter and summer pelage is often paler than that of late fall and early winter. The head and shoulders are often grizzled silvery gold, and white patches may be present around the genitals or between the forelegs. Males are about 20 percent longer than females and may weigh nearly twice as much. Measurements are: total length 830–1,030 mm; length of tail 340–420 mm; length of hindfoot 90–130 mm; length of ear 40–60 mm; weight 2.0–5.5 kg. The skull is similar to that of the marten but usually is more than 95 mm in length, with the outside length of the fourth upper molar more than 9.5 mm and the length of the first lower molar more than 11 mm.

Distribution

Fishers are distributed across much of northern North America, although the range has contracted since permanent European settlement (C. H. Douglas and Strickland 1987). The fisher is a highly doubtful species for the Southern Rockies. Specimens are known from the Yellowstone region (Long 1965; Crowe 1986) and the Bighorn Mountains (T. Clark and Stromberg 1987) of Wyoming. Durrant (1952) listed it from the Uinta Mountains of Utah based on photographs of a single set of tracks. E. Hall (1981) listed 1 record from Trial Lake, Utah. D. Armstrong (1972) discussed references to the fisher in Colorado but did not find them convincing. G. Byrne (1997 and personal communication) kept track of suspected fisher, wolverine, and lynx sightings but was unable to verify the presence of fisher, with 1 exception (noted later). Hoffmann et al. (1969) believed the southern limit of the range was in northwestern Wyoming and central Idaho. C. H. Douglas and Strickland (1987) mapped fisher range to include isolated patches in Wyoming, including the Colorado-Wyoming border, the Bighorn Mountains, and the Yellowstone area. Powell (1993), Maj and Garton (1994), and Powell and Zielinski (1994) dismissed reports of the species from the Rockies south of northern Wyoming. Powell et al. (2003) eliminated Wyoming entirely from a map of the species' range. The Wyoming Game and Fish Commission reported fisher sightings close to the Colorado-Wyoming border in the Snowy Range (Anonymous 1992), but observations were not verified. In 1992 the skull of an individual found south of Aspen, Pitkin County, was submitted to Colorado Division of Wildlife personnel. It was estimated by the late Dr. Elaine Anderson, of the Denver Museum of Nature and Science, to be about 6 years old. The general opinion was that it represented remains of a captive animal released unlawfully into the wild by a nature photographer. The near-

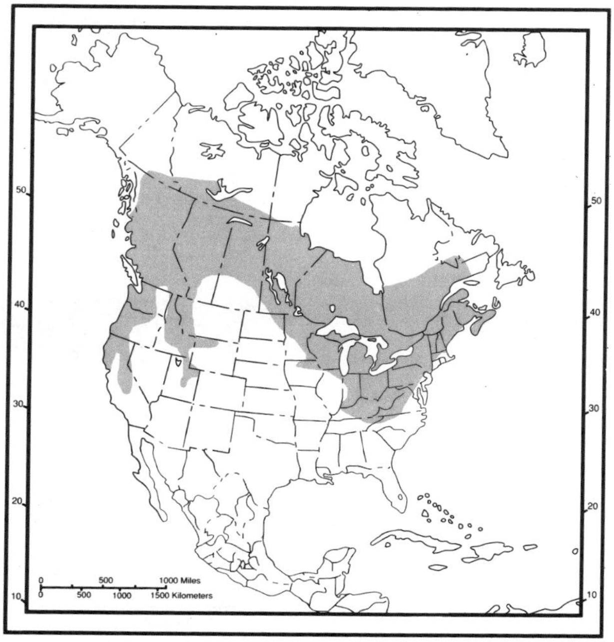

MAP 12-25. Distribution of the fisher (*Martes pennanti*) in North America.

est fossil record of the fisher is from late glacial times in Harlan County, Nebraska (Graham and Lundelius 1994). Based on the weight of presently available evidence, we believe it unlikely that the fisher ever existed in the wild in Colorado. The species is not listed by the Colorado Division of Wildlife as present in the state.

Natural History

Fishers are associated with dense mixed deciduous-evergreen forest over most of their range in North America. Optimal habitats probably have more than 50 percent canopy closure, trees more than 25 cm in diameter, and at least 2 stories of canopy cover (C. H. Douglas and Strickland 1987). Fishers are solitary, rarely together except for the breeding season. Home range estimates vary from 15 to 35 km^2, with extensive overlap of males and females. Daily movements average about 2 km, with animals using temporary sleeping sites in hollow trees, beaver lodges, or burrows or under logs, brush piles, or rockfalls. Natal dens are typically in hollow trees. Fishers mate from March to May, with delayed implantation contributing to a gestation period of about 11 months (Powell 1981). Parturition occurs from February to May, with an average litter size of 3.

Fishers are opportunistic carnivores, feeding on the most available species of mammals and birds. Although fairly adept climbers, most hunting takes place on the ground. Snowshoe hare, voles, tree squirrels, mice, and carrion of ungulates commonly show up in dietary studies. Porcupines are a favored prey species in many areas. Literature on the fisher was reviewed by Powell (1981), C. H. Douglas and Strickland (1987), and Powell et al. (2003).

Genus *Mustela*—Weasels and Kin

The genus *Mustela* has some 17 species (Wozencraft 2005), including weasels, polecats, and ferrets, mostly Holarctic in distribution (although there are species of weasels in Brazil, Amazonian Ecuador and Peru, Colombia, Southeast Asia, and Indonesia). The American mink was formerly included in this genus, but we list it as *Neovison vison*, consistent with Wozencraft (2005) and Kurose et al. (2008). Most species of *Mustela* are terrestrial or semi-arboreal predators on small mammals and birds. With their short limbs and elongate bodies, weasels are adapted to "follow their prey home" to burrows or dense vegetation.

Mustela erminea

ERMINE, OR SHORT-TAILED WEASEL

Description

Also called short-tailed weasel or stoat, the ermine is a small, short-legged, slender-bodied mustelid with a short, black-tipped tail. It is the smallest carnivore known to occur in Colorado (the least weasel, *Mustela nivalis*, is smaller but has not been recorded in Colorado). Color varies with season. In summer, the dorsal color is chocolate to pale brown, with a black tip on the tail. The venter is whitish to buff. In winter the animals are snow white except for the black tip on the tail. Measurements are: total length 190–245 mm; length of hindfoot 23–31 mm; length of ear 13–16 mm; length of tail 42–66 mm (usually less than 44 percent of the head and body); weight 30–200 g. Males are much larger than females. The soles of the feet are well haired. Seasonal color change involves an orderly molt and individuals are a mottled brown and white for periods in the fall and spring. The spring molt may be triggered by increasing photoperiod, but colder temperatures may slow the rate of change (Bissonette and Bailey 1944; Rust 1962). The anal glands produce a secretion with a strong odor. Females have 8 to 10 mammae.

PHOTOGRAPH 12-13. Ermine, or short-tailed weasel (*Mustela erminea*). Photograph by Bill Bevington.

Distribution

The short-tailed weasel is a Holarctic species, distributed widely in northern parts of Eurasia and North America. In North America it is probably most often associated with

MAP 12-26. Distribution of the ermine, or short-tailed weasel (*Mustela erminea*) in North America.

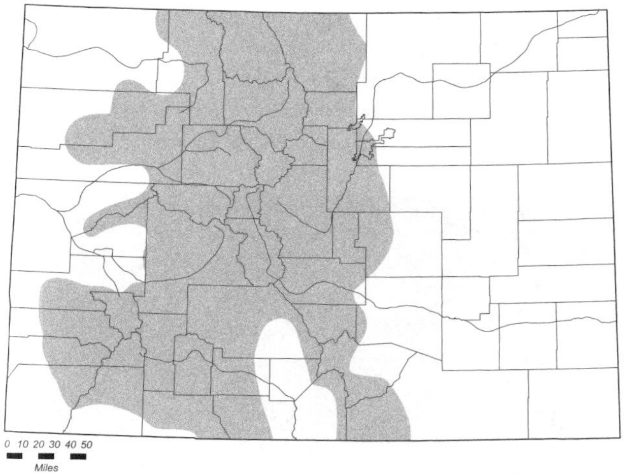

MAP 12-27. Distribution of the ermine, or short-tailed weasel (*Mustela erminea*) in Colorado.

tundra, boreal and montane forests, riparian zones, wetlands, and forest-edge situations. It ranges from extreme northern Alaska and Canada southward to Colorado and northern New Mexico (Fagerstone 1987b; Svendsen 2003). It occurs widely in mountainous areas of Colorado, where a single subspecies, *Mustela erminea muricus*, is known.

Natural History

Ecological requirements of the ermine in the Southern Rocky Mountains are poorly understood. Studies in California (B. Fitzgerald 1977) and Canada (Simms 1979a) suggested that moist areas in early successional stages are favored. Coloradan records are from above 1,830 m (6,000 ft.) in elevation, and observations of the animals have been made in alpine tundra (J. Dixon 1931) and subalpine forests (C. Hayward 1949). In South Park, where long-tailed weasels were relatively common, J. Fitzgerald (unpublished) captured only 2 ermines in 14 years of small mammal trapping. Both animals were from a moist hay meadow interspersed with willow stands in which long-tailed weasels were never captured. The latter were frequently seen and livetrapped on drier upland sites adjacent to the hay meadow and along banks of the stream running through the area. C. Samson and Raymond (1998) studied ermine in a mixed conifer-deciduous forest in Quebec. They considered early successional patches, such as logged areas, spruce plantations, and abandoned cultivated fields, as quality habitat, similar to findings by Simms (1979b) in Ontario. Brushwood piles, trails, and streamside edges were used as microhabitats. J. Frey and Schwenke (2007) captured an ermine in montane scrub habitat in Sugarite Canyon State Park, New Mexico, which is east of Raton Pass along the Colorado state line.

Ermines appear to be more nocturnal than long-tailed weasels and are active year-round (Erlinge 1979). Bouts of foraging activity lasting about 1 hour are followed by rest periods. The animals can climb to prey on small semi-arboreal rodents when necessary (Nams and Beare 1982). In Idaho, short-tailed weasels repeatedly followed the same hunting circuits without reliance on a home den (Musgrove 1951), although other reports indicate that weasels typically use a random search pattern while hunting.

No studies of food habits of ermines have been reported for Colorado, except for unsuccessful attempts to prey on pikas (J. Dixon 1931). In northern portions of the range, ermines prey on voles, other mice, and shrews (E. Hall 1951; Fagerstone 1987a). Mice occurred in 59 percent of stomachs in Minnesota (Aldous and Manweiler 1941). In New York, voles accounted for about 36 percent of remains in digestive tracts, and *Peromyscus* accounted for 11 percent (W. Hamilton 1933). In California, 54 percent of winter mortality in a montane vole population was attributed to predation by ermines (B. Fitzgerald 1977). Captive short-tailed weasels ate an average of 14 g of vole per day in the winter during that study. Shrews are also commonly eaten.

Carrion, insects, and remains of birds and fish are also part of the diet. It appears that there is some separation of feeding niches between sexes, females being more specialized (Raymond et al. 1990). The animals may be selective of prey; captive animals chose red-backed voles over deer mice (Nams 1981).

Ermines may exhibit marked population cycles, thought to correlate with fluctuations in arvicoline rodents (B. Bailey 1929; MacLean et al. 1974; B. Fitzgerald 1977). Population estimates of 4 to 11 animals per square kilometer (the latter in preferred habitat) have been made in Alberta (Soper 1919) and Ontario (Simms 1979b). Estimates of home range vary widely, males typically having home ranges 2 to 4 times larger than those of females. In California, home ranges were 3 to 7 ha during winter (B. Fitzgerald 1977). In Ontario, home ranges were 10 to 25 ha, with some animals moving more than 500 m per day in their hunting rounds (Simms 1979b). In summer in southern Quebec, home range of a radio-collared adult male was 35 ha, that of a female was about 16 ha, and that of a juvenile male was 9 ha (C. Samson and Raymond 1998).

Young are born in May, June, or July. Delayed implantation leads to a gestation period of about 270 days. Parturition occurs about 4 weeks after implantation of the blastocyst (W. Hamilton 1933, Svendsen 1982). Females become reproductively active soon after parturition, and most are bred by late summer. A single litter of 6 to 9 young is reared by the female (W. Hamilton 1933). Females are reproductively mature at about 2.5 months of age; some even breed prior to weaning. Males are thought to breed at about 1 year of age (W. Hamilton 1933). Young are raised in nest burrows, which are often remodeled from vole burrows or located under rock piles, tree roots, or similar structures (E. Hall 1951; B. Fitzgerald 1977). Teeth appear at about 3 weeks of age, and the eyes are open by 6 weeks. Animals about 6 to 7 weeks of age spend considerable time playing (W. Hamilton 1933).

Annual survival rates of short-tailed weasels are about 40 percent. Life expectancy is less than 2 years, although animals up to 7 years of age have been reported (summarized in Fagerstone 1987a). Most mortality is attributed to lack of food and to predation by a variety of terrestrial and avian predators. Harvest of the species usually is low in the United States, but some individuals are killed by automobiles. Until 1996 the ermine was considered a furbearer in Colorado, but only a few dozen to a few hundred were harvested annually (J. Fitzgerald 1993b). It is now a protected species. Svendsen (1982), C. King (1983), Fagerstone (1987a), and Svendsen (2003) reviewed the literature on the species. C. King and Powell (2006) provided a thorough review of literature on weasels in general.

Mustela frenata

LONG-TAILED WEASEL

Description

This is the largest of the 3 true weasels in North America. In summer the dorsal color varies from pale to rich brown, depending on the individual and the subspecies. Ventral color ranges from rusty orange to yellowish and some individuals may have white on the throat and chin. Some specimens from extreme southeastern Colorado may show conspicuous white facial markings and are often referred to as "bridled" or "masked" weasels (and sometimes are mistakenly identified as black-footed ferrets). In winter the color is white except for the black tip on the tail. Individuals are mottled brown and white for a period of weeks during fall and spring molts. A detailed discussion of molting patterns was provided by E. Hall (1951). The tail is long, typically more than 44 percent of the length of the head and body. Measurements are: total length 318–441 mm; length of tail 111–160 mm; length of hindfoot 38–50 mm; length of ear 16–26 mm; weight 110–300 g. As with many mustelids, males are larger than females. Condylobasal length is greater than 40 mm. Females have 8 mammae.

PHOTOGRAPH 12-14. Long-tailed weasel (*Mustela frenata*). Photograph by Robert E. Barber.

Distribution

The long-tailed weasel is a New World species, ranging from southern Canada and all but the driest desert areas of the

United States well into northern South America. The long-tailed weasel is distributed over all of Colorado, although it seems to be most abundant in the mountains at moderate to high elevations. According to D. Armstrong (1972; following E. Hall 1951), *Mustela frenata longicauda* occurs on the east-central and northeastern plains; *M. f. neomexicana* occurs in the roughlands of southeastern Colorado; *M. f. nevadensis* occurs throughout the mountainous western two-thirds of the state.

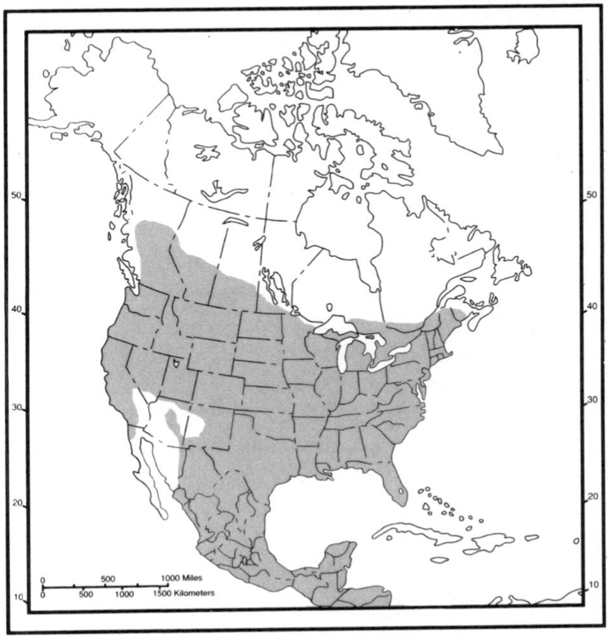

MAP 12-28. Distribution of the long-tailed weasel (*Mustela frenata*) in North America.

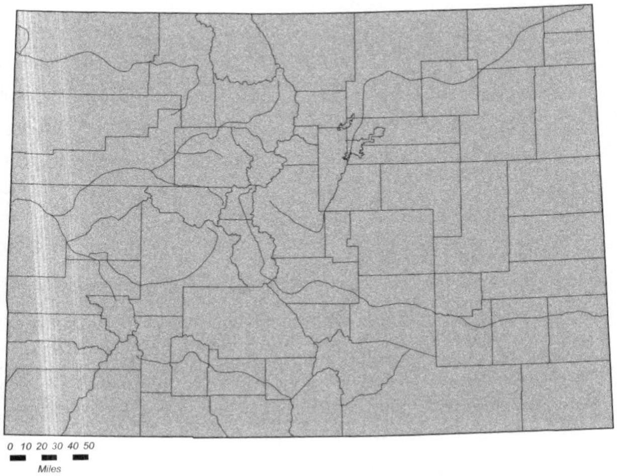

MAP 12-29. Distribution of the long-tailed weasel (*Mustela frenata*) in Colorado.

Natural History

Long-tailed weasels are common but seldom observed. They are present in all habitat types. Their distribution is probably more dependent on prey species availability in particular habitats than on vegetation or topography. Gehring and Swihart (2003) compared habitat and landscape-level patterns of use of 8 carnivores in agricultural lands in Indiana. They concluded that the occurrence of long-tailed weasels was more dependent than were other species on the presence of small and medium-sized mammal prey and complex habitat with patches and corridors of high ground cover and lower amounts of canopy cover. Weasels were more sensitive to local features than to landscape-level patterns but were more mobile than raccoons or opossums, probably because of their more carnivorous food habits. Long-tailed weasels are active year-round and day and night. In a study in central Colorado, they were most active in morning and late afternoon; 98 percent of captures were made in the daytime (Svendsen 1982). Activity periods are probably keyed to prey activity. While hunting, long-tailed weasels often carry the tail vertically above the body, especially when running or alarmed. The animals are seemingly curious, and when one is frightened into a hole it will often peer out for another look after a few minutes.

Voles, deer mice, other mice, chipmunks, shrews, pocket gophers, ground squirrels, prairie dogs, pikas, nestling rabbits, birds, and reptiles have been reported in the diet of long-tailed weasels. Small mammals comprise between 50 and 80 percent of the annual diet (Quick 1951; Svendsen 1982; Fagerstone 1987b). Weasels also prey on eggs of grouse and waterfowl. Egg predation is reported on introduced greater prairie chicken populations in northeastern Colorado (G. Beauprez, personal communication). A small amount of vegetable matter and berries is also eaten. In general, any prey species small enough to be subdued is potential food. Generally, weasels kill aboveground prey by hugging the animal with the 4 limbs and severing the spinal cord by biting at the nape of the neck. Prey captured in burrows are killed by grasping the throat and suffocating the animal (Glover 1943; A. Byrne et al. 1978).

The elongate body with its high surface-to-volume ratio has a high energetic cost to weasels. The estimated metabolic rate of the long-tailed weasel is about 50 percent higher than that of more compact mammals of equivalent weight (J. Brown and Lasiewski 1972). Long-tailed weasels consume between 20 and 40 percent of their body weight in food daily, and the young have higher metabolic needs than adults (Fagerstone 1987b). The increased metabolic demands caused by the elongated shape are probably compensated for by the additional underground foraging areas that can be accessed. Weasels can often simply "follow their prey home" in their burrows. Also, they kill prey underground with throat bites and suffocation, a procedure that may require less energy than the nape attack used aboveground (A. Byrne et al. 1978).

Home ranges estimated from tracking animals on snow near Gunnison were 83 to 125 ha (Quick 1951). Another study in Gunnison County found home ranges of 12 to 16 ha (Svendsen 1982). Home ranges of females were included within the larger home range of adult males. In Kentucky, home ranges of males were small (10–24 ha) in areas where food was abundant, and winter home ranges were smaller than summer ranges (Fagerstone 1987b). Animals in winter tended to make more frequent but shorter hunting forays from the den, perhaps as a strategy for reducing heat loss. In Indiana, Gehring and Swihart (2004) reported home ranges of 51 ha for females and 180 ha for males in fragmented agricultural lands. Weasels had faster mean hourly rates of movement in areas of cropped fields, and rate of movement was inverse to the presence of prey biomass.

Density of weasels was estimated to be 0.8 per square kilometer across all habitats in Gunnison County, ranging from aspen-sagebrush to alpine tundra (Quick 1951). Studies in the East (summarized by Fagerstone 1987b) reported densities of 0.4 to 38.0 animals per square kilometer. In many areas where long-tailed and short-tailed weasels are sympatric, the latter are more numerous. However, that does not seem to hold true for Colorado, based on numbers of animals in museum collections (D. Armstrong 1972) and general field observations.

Long-tailed weasels live in nests constructed inside burrows abandoned by other species, under fallen trees and rocks, in rotten logs, or in similar structures. Nests are made of grass and fur of small mammals. The animals communicate by odor and sound. Captive animals used one site for a latrine, whereas for wild animals latrines are located at the entrances of burrows, in side chambers in the burrow, and in some cases in nests. Scats are deposited on rocks along trails, at times with more than one scat on the same rock, suggesting repeated visits to the site (Polderboer et al. 1941; E. Hall 1951; Quick 1951). Anal glands are well developed and emit a pungent odor. Their function is not known, but they probably play a role in notifying conspecifics of an individual's presence. In addition to scent-marking, weasels communicate with vocalizations, including a trill (used in various behavioral contexts), a screech (used when surprised), and a squeal (produced under duress or pain) (Svendsen 1976a).

The social structure of long-tailed weasels is not well-known. They are generally solitary except during the breeding season. However, pairs of long-tailed weasels have been observed together at other times. Long-tailed weasels may have a variable social structure, being more social when resources are abundant and more solitary in less optimal habitat (Fagerstone 1987b). Resident animals of both sexes maintain territories, and they allow overlap only with individuals of the opposite sex; transients do not have territories (Svendsen 1982).

Most breeding occurs during July and August. A female mates with the adult male(s) whose home range encompasses hers. Males may form transitory pair-bonds with females for several weeks but leave before the young are born (W. Hamilton 1933). Delayed implantation occurs, with gestation taking 220 to 237 days. Parturition occurs about 27 days after implantation. Only 1 litter of young is reared per year, and most litters are born in April or May. Litter size averages about 7, with up to 9 young reported (P. Wright 1942, 1947, 1948a, 1948b).

The young are blind and sparsely haired at birth. Soft white fur develops quickly, to be replaced by pigmented hair within a few weeks. At 5 weeks of age the eyes open and tooth eruption is sufficient to allow eating meat. At 6 weeks scent glands are developed, and the young are weaned and begin to forage with the mother (W. Hamilton 1933). The young stay with the female until about 7 weeks old. Animals reach adult weight by about 3 months of age, at which time females are capable of breeding (P. Wright 1948a), which they are likely to do with the male whose home range encompasses their natal site. This male is not necessarily their father, because of high population turnover. Males reproduce at 15 months of age.

The long-tailed weasel is taken by a wide variety of predators, ranging from coyotes and foxes to snakes and owls (Svendsen 1982; Fagerstone 1987b). Mathematical models (Powell 1973) suggested that raptor predation could be sufficient to limit weasel populations. Terrestrial carnivores such as foxes may also act to limit weasel numbers. Long-tailed weasels are frequently killed by automobiles. The species is now protected in Colorado, but until 1997, trappers harvested a few hundred each year in the state (J. Fitzgerald 1993b). The literature was reviewed by Svendsen

(1982, 2003), Fagerstone (1987b), and Sheffield and Thomas (1997).

Mustela nigripes
BLACK-FOOTED FERRET

Description

The black-footed ferret is the largest member of the genus *Mustela* in Colorado and slightly larger than the mink (*Neovison*). The black-footed ferret has the elongate body shape and short legs typical of weasels but is distinguished by its black facial mask, feet, and legs. The moderately long tail is tipped with black. The general pelage color is yellow-buff, paler around the face, abdomen, and throat and darker brown down the top of the head and back. The fur, including the guard hairs, is relatively short and fine-textured. The ears are conspicuous and rounded.

Measurements are: total length 457–572 mm; length of tail 90–150 mm; length of hindfoot 57–73 mm; length of ear 29–31 mm; weight 530–1,300 g. Females are usually about 10 percent smaller than males. The skull greatly resembles that of the mink. However, in the mink the distance between the bases of the upper canines is less than the width of the basioccipital bone (measured at the level of the foramina located midway along the medial sides of the tympanic bullae); in the black-footed ferret the distance is equal to or greater than the width of the basioccipital (T. Clark et al. 1988). Females have 3 pairs of mammary glands.

The species is similar in appearance to the European polecat, or domestic ferret, *Mustela putorius*, which sometimes is released in the wild by irresponsible pet owners. The black-footed ferret may have evolved from an ancestral stock of Siberian ferrets (*M. eversmanni*) that successfully crossed the Bering land bridge in the Pleistocene (E. Anderson et al. 1986). Wisely, Statham, and Fleischer (2008) used DNA technology to examine the Holocene expansion of black-footed ferrets from Pleistocene refugia on the Great Plains.

Distribution

The original range of the black-footed ferret was roughly coextensive with the range of prairie dogs; a century of effort by agricultural interests to eliminate prairie dogs generally led to extirpation of ferrets as well. Elimination of prairie dog populations has reduced available black-footed

PHOTOGRAPH 12-15. Black-footed ferret (*Mustela nigripes*). Photograph by Kathleen A. Fagerstone.

ferret habitat to as little as 2 percent of former potential range. During the 1970s and 1980s, efforts were made by state and federal agencies to find black-footed ferrets in western Colorado and on the eastern plains. No ferrets were found, although several skulls were recovered. D. Armstrong (1972), J. Torres (1973), and E. Anderson et al. (1986) reviewed the status and historical records of the species; Roelle et al. (2006) provided a progress report on ongoing recovery efforts; and Gober (2009) summarized efforts more recently. *Mustela nigripes* is monotypic; that is, subspecies have not been recognized.

Natural History

Prior to the discovery in 1981 of black-footed ferrets living in colonies of white-tailed prairie dogs near Meeteetse, Wyoming, this was one of America's least understood carnivores. Since 1981, almost 200 articles and reports have been published on the animal, and its biology is now better known than that of most other mustelids. Black-footed ferrets have coevolved with prairie dogs; their ranges and habitats closely overlap (E. Hall 1981; Fagerstone 1987b). Black-footed ferrets have historically occupied areas ranging from the shortgrass and mid-grass prairie to semidesert shrublands.

Black-footed ferrets use prairie dog burrows for living quarters and as nursery dens to rear their young, and they prey on these animals as well (Hillman and Clark 1980). They will excavate dens in search of prey and in preparation of home dens. Their digging activity may result in the formation of characteristic "troughs" consisting of excavated subsoil thrown out in a relatively narrow, linear pattern with

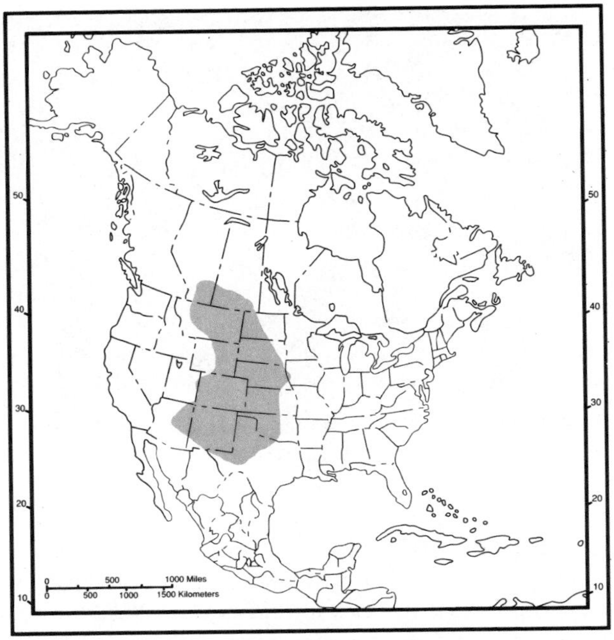

MAP 12-30. Historic distribution of the black-footed ferret (*Mustela nigripes*) in North America.

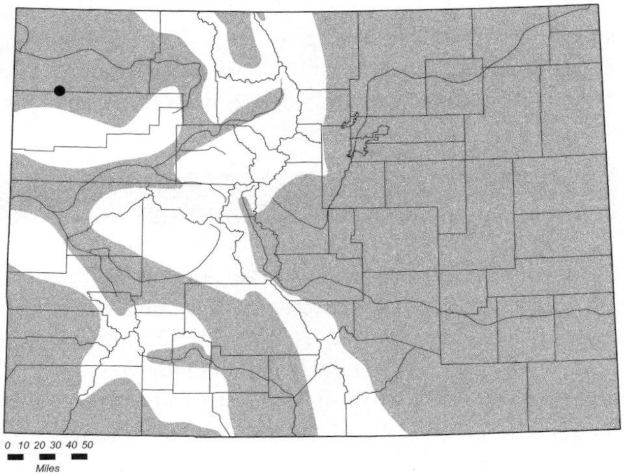

MAP 12-31. Historic and present distribution of the black-footed ferret (*Mustela nigripes*) in Colorado (closed circle indicates present restoration site).

a conspicuous medial trench (T. Clark et al. 1988; T. Clark 1989).

At the Meeteetse site, most digging activity occurred between October and January. Aboveground activity of black-footed ferrets increased over the winter months, probably corresponding with the onset of the reproductive season in February (Richardson et al. 1987; T. Clark 1989). Most aboveground activity was at night, between 0100 and 0400 hours, although bimodal peaks of nightly activity occurred in summer (Biggins et al. 1986; Fagerstone 1987b). Most daylight activity was limited to the first 5 hours after sunrise. Individuals, particularly juveniles, were mobile, frequently changing locations within the prairie dog town or moving between adjacent towns (Fagerstone 1987b; T. Clark 1989).

Prairie dog remains were present in more than 86 percent of scats examined (Sheets et al. 1972; T. M. Campbell et al. 1987). To a much lesser degree, mice, ground squirrels, lagomorphs, birds, reptiles, and insects are eaten. No data exist to indicate that the species can survive without prairie dogs as a food base; in fact, the distribution of ferrets suggests that they are entirely dependent on prairie dogs. Adult ferrets seem to require 1 prairie dog every 2 to 6 days on the average (Fagerstone 1987b). This intake requires that a ferret be able to access about 100 prairie dogs per year, or 19 to 38 ha of prairie dog habitat. Further research may indicate that the animals can survive with lesser demands on the prairie dog resource if supplemented with other dietary items.

The density of black-footed ferrets at Meeteetse ranged from 1 animal per 49 ha to 1 per 74 ha (T. Clark 1989). Estimated population numbers for July based on spotlight counts were 88, 129, and 56 for 1983, 1984, and 1986, respectively. Population estimates for September, based on livetrapping mark and recapture, were 125 and 30 animals for 1984 and 1985, respectively (Forrest et al. 1988). The smallest prairie dog colony in Meeteetse that supported a litter of black-footed ferrets was 49 ha. In South Dakota, 5 litters of ferrets were reported on black-tailed prairie dog towns smaller than 40 ha (Hillman et al. 1979).

Home range size for black-footed ferrets at Meeteetse averaged 40 to 60 ha (T. Clark 1989), although individual monthly ranges varied from 1.2 to 258.0 ha, depending on sex and season (Fagerstone 1987b). Juveniles typically stay close to the natal den, and even by late August their activity is contained within an area of 4 ha or less. However, during September and early October considerable dispersal of juveniles occurs, with movements of up to 7 km (Fagerstone 1987b). Individual ferrets may travel more than 10 km in 1 night when hunting with males, covering more ground than females.

The species is presumed to be polygynous, on the basis of home range size and the fact that home ranges of adult males usually encompass those of several females

(Fagerstone 1987b). Animals of the same sex are thought to be intolerant of each other. Data on reproductive biology are scant. Breeding activity probably occurred from mid-February through March at Meeteetse (T. Clark et al. 1986). Copulation in captive animals occurred in March and April. Early estrus has been induced in captive females by manipulation of the light cycle. Copulation lasts for up to 3 hours and is believed to induce ovulation. Delayed implantation does not occur, and gestation takes about 42 to 45 days. Most litters in the wild probably are born in May. Litter size averages 3.5, with a range of 1 to 5. Litters in South Dakota are slightly larger than those reported at Meeteetse. Only 1 litter is born per year. The young first appear aboveground in July when about three-quarters grown. By September or October they are capable of dispersal. Sexual maturity is reached at 1 year of age (Hillman 1968; Linder et al. 1972; Hillman and Linder 1973; J. Carpenter and Hillman 1978; Forrest et al. 1988).

A variety of predators kill ferrets, including great horned owls, golden eagles, coyotes, badgers, and domestic dogs. Canine distemper was responsible for elimination of many of the Meeteetse ferrets (E. Thorne and Williams 1988), a factor that prompted the capture of the survivors for maintenance in captivity. Black-footed ferrets from South Dakota also were susceptible to canine distemper, resulting in loss of a captive colony (J. Carpenter et al. 1976). Loss of the prey base to epizootics of plague impacts populations (Ubico et al. 1988; Barnes 1993; J. Fitzgerald 1993b), and black-footed ferrets themselves appear to be susceptible to plague (Matchett et al. 2009). Poisoning programs to control prairie dog or other rodent populations (Fagerstone 1987b; T. Clark 1989) can have an impact. Fully a quarter of all known museum specimens of black-footed ferrets were killed by predator or rodent control agents, mostly in the 1920s.

Capture of black-footed ferrets from 1985 to 1987 near Meeteetse, Wyoming, the last known population in the wild, led to establishment of captive breeding colonies in several states. Restoration of ferrets from the captive breeding programs has been made, with variable success in Montana (Charles M. Russell Wildlife Refuge, Fort Belknap Indian Reservation), South Dakota (Conata Basin in Badlands National Park and Buffalo Gap National Grassland), Wyoming (Shirley Basin), Colorado, Utah, Arizona (Aubry Valley), and Mexico. The successes of the captive breeding program and of ferret recovery results in the Conata Basin of South Dakota are the most promising signs for potential species recovery. However, significant numbers of both black-tailed prairie dogs and black-footed ferrets died from an extensive plague epizootic in the Conata Basin restoration area in 2008, leading to new concerns for the species' future. In 2001, black-footed ferret restoration was started on Bureau of Land Management lands in Coyote Basin on the Colorado-Utah border in Rio Blanco County and in the Wolf Creek Management Area in Moffat County. The recovery effort in Colorado included release of 126 black-footed ferrets in the initial efforts, supplemented by release in 2003 of additional wild-born ferrets from the Conata Basin. Ferrets have successfully reproduced at both sites in Colorado; the first black-footed ferret born in the wild in the restored population in Colorado was reported in 2005 (Anonymous 2006). The US Fish and Wildlife Service established the National Black-footed Ferret Conservation Center in 2005 near Carr, Weld County, Colorado. This is the largest captive breeding facility for the species, producing more than half the ferrets released each year.

B. Holmes (2008) provided authoritative and accessible comments on the black-footed ferret restoration program in northwestern Colorado, and Lewandowski (2006) reviewed progress to that date. The black-footed ferret has been a federally endangered species since 1967; it is a state-designated endangered species in Colorado.

Prospects for survival of the black-footed ferret are uncertain, depending on the success of restorations. The captive breeding program has been a success, with more than 240 captive breeders scattered in several zoos and recovery centers around the country, including zoos in Colorado Springs and Pueblo. Some animals are also bred at release sites, including the Moffat County site. In Colorado, releases are made in the fall to mimic normal dispersal patterns. Animals surplus to the breeding population are considered available for restoration. Animals, mostly kits, are preconditioned prior to release, learning to hunt prairie dogs and get familiar with prairie dog burrow systems. Captive ferrets have lived up to 11 years, and animals more than 1 year of age typically breed every year (Fagerstone 1987b). However, the potential loss of viability of black-footed ferret populations because of small population size and inbreeding effects is of concern (T. Clark 1989). Wisely, Santymire et al. (2008) analyzed genetic patterns and consequences of restoration history. D. Martin and Holmes (2007) provided a popular-style review of restoration efforts in Colorado.

The literature on the species was reviewed by Henderson et al. (1969), Hillman and Clark (1980), Casey et al. (1986), Fagerstone (1987b), T. Clark (1989), Seal et al. (1989), Reading and Clark (1990), and Svendsen (2003). For updates on restoration programs in Colorado, consult the Colorado Division of Wildlife (2007g).

Mustela nivalis

LEAST WEASEL

Description

The least weasel is the smallest carnivore in North America. It is similar in color to the ermine, in both summer and winter pelages. However, the tail is one-quarter or less the length of the head and body and lacks a conspicuous black tip, although a few sparse black hairs may be present. Total length is less than 250 mm in males and 225 mm in females (E. Hall 1951). Greatest length of the skull is usually less than 34 mm. Skulls of *Mustela nivalis* and *M. erminea* may be difficult to distinguish, but for many specimens the skull of *M. nivalis* is narrower and has a relatively greater height (J. K. Jones, Armstrong, et al. 1983). The ratio of the height at the anterior margin of the basioccipital to mastoid breadth in *M. nivalis* ranges from 0.64 to 0.76, whereas for *M. erminea* those values lie between 0.59 and 0.68.

Distribution

The least weasel has not been documented in Colorado but once ranged in Nebraska to within about 50 km of the Colorado border (Swenk 1926). Any small weasel from northeastern Colorado, especially if it lacks a black-tipped tail, should be examined carefully, and any specimen obtained should be submitted to an individual expert on weasels with access to comparative material for study.

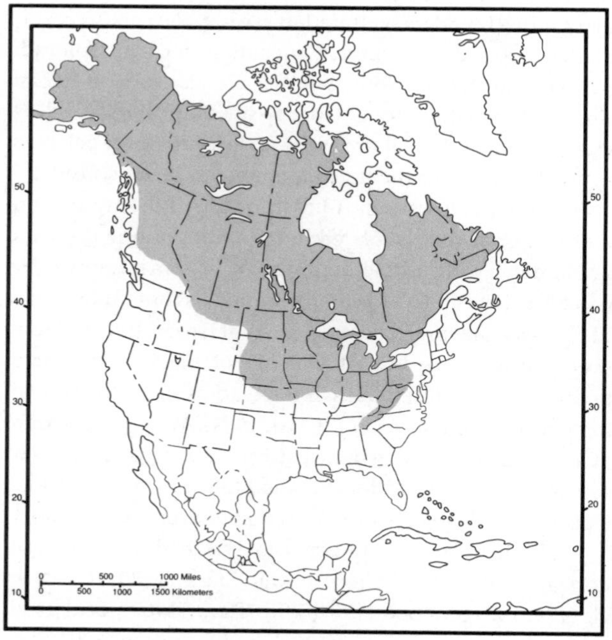

MAP 12-32. Distribution of the least weasel (*Mustela nivalis*) in North America.

Natural History

On the Northern Great Plains the least weasel occupies meadows, grasslands, and woodlands and is most commonly observed in marshy areas (J. K. Jones, Armstrong, et al. 1983). On the margins of its range the species tends to be associated with riparian areas. The behavior and diet are similar to those of the ermine. Unlike other weasels, least weasels do not show delayed implantation and females may produce several litters in 1 year. Litter size ranges from 1 to 10 and gestation lasts about 35 days (Fagerstone 1987b).

Neovison vison

AMERICAN MINK

Description

Mink are similar in general size and appearance to the American marten, although their ears are less conspicuous. Typical of many mustelids, the legs are short and the body is long and slender. The fur is soft and glossy with thick underfur and long guard hairs. Glands at the base of hairs produce water-repellent oils that prevent the hair from becoming waterlogged. Color varies from rich chestnut brown to blackish, with the venter slightly paler. Some individuals have white patches or spots on the throat, chest,

PHOTOGRAPH 12-16. American mink (*Neovison vison*). Photograph by Robert E. Barber.

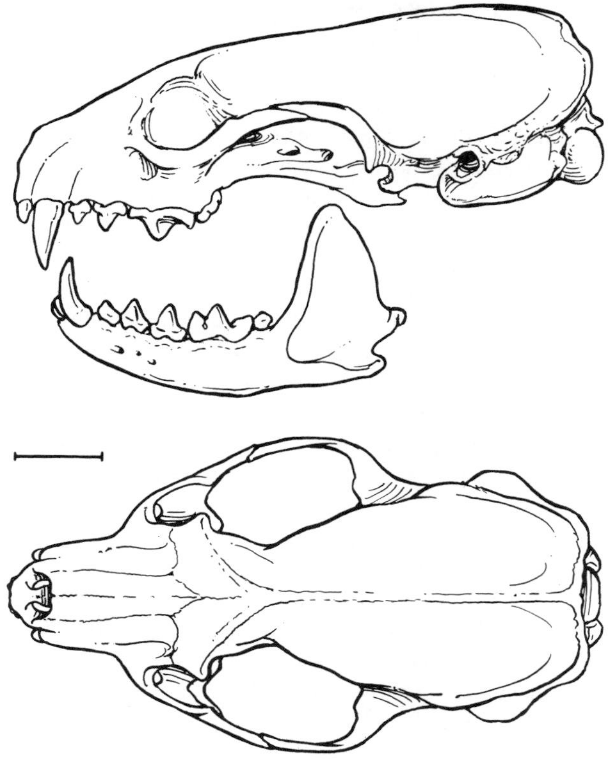

FIGURE 12-3. Lateral and dorsal views of the skull of the American mink (*Neovison vison*). Scale = 1 cm.

or abdomen. The tail is long and well furred, about one-third to one-half of the total length. The toes of the feet are partially webbed. Measurements are: total length 491–720 mm; length of tail 158–194 mm; length of hindfoot 57–75 mm; average weights from central Idaho are 780 and 525 g for males and females, respectively. Males are about 10 percent larger than females (and may be nearly double the weight) (Whitman 1981). The skull is stout, with the palate extending beyond the last molar. The auditory bullae are conspicuous. As with other mustelids, the upper molars are dumbbell-shaped. Females have 6 to 8 mammae. The testes are developed in both sexes. A variety of techniques, including skull measurements, development of the baculum, size and color of nipples, and evidence of penis scars on dried pelts, have been used to age and sex animals or their remains (Linscombe et al. 1982). Skulls of mink and black-footed ferret are very similar; for detailed comparison, see the account of the latter species. Use of the generic name *Neovison* follows Wozencraft (2005) and Kurose et al. (2008), who reviewed the cytogenetic and biochemical studies that detail differences between mink and weasels.

Distribution

Mink are widely distributed across North America from extreme northern Alaska and Canada southward through

MAP 12-33. Distribution of the American mink (*Neovison vison*) in North America.

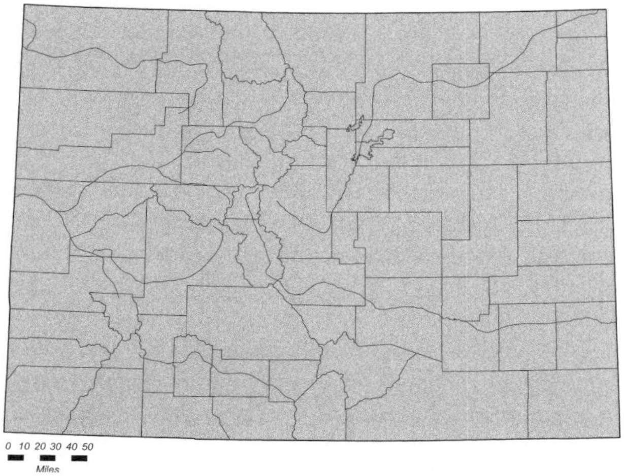

MAP 12-34. Distribution of the American mink (*Neovison vison*) in Colorado.

the southeastern states and westward to the fringes of the southwestern deserts of California, Arizona, New Mexico, and Texas. The mink has been introduced into most of northern Europe and Russia (Larivière 2003). Although widespread across Colorado, mink seem not to be abundant, and only a few hundred were trapped annually prior to the passage of Amendment 14 in 1996. Perhaps because of their commercial value, few museum specimens exist (D. Armstrong 1972). Portions of the Yampa and Eagle drainages, North Park, and the White River Plateau were important mink habitats historically. R. Finley et al. (1976) cited only one report in the Piceance Basin and White River area since pioneer times. Two subspecies are ascribed ranges in Colorado: *Neovison vison energumenos* in the central and western parts of the state and *N. v. letifera* on the eastern plains. R. T. Stevens and Kennedy (2006) analyzed complex geographic variation in body size of mink from throughout North America but did not propose changes in subspecific nomenclature.

Natural History

Despite its importance as a furbearer, relatively few intensive studies have been carried out on mink in the wild in North America and none has been done in the Southern Rocky Mountains. Many studies of the species have been made in Europe, where some aspects of their biology may differ (Eagle and Whitman 1987; Larivière 1999b, 2003). Although mink can be found in practically any habitat type, from boreal forests to saltwater marshes, they are obligate riparian animals, never found far from permanent streams, wetlands, or other surface water. In the Great Lakes region, research is ongoing to determine if mink can serve as environmental indicators of water quality and productivity (Loukmas and Halbrook 2001). A number of specific factors affect the presence and density of mink. Den sites, such as abandoned beaver lodges and muskrat dens, are very important (Schladweiler and Storm 1969). Other factors include permanence of water and abundance of wetland habitat (A. Allen 1986), development of shoreline vegetation including willow and emergent vegetation (Marshall 1936; Mason and MacDonald 1983), crayfish abundance (Burgess and Bider 1980), availability of logjams for fall and winter hunting sites (Melquist, Whitman, and Hornocker 1981), and abundance of muskrats (Errington 1943). Reaches of streams where banks have been degraded by livestock are avoided (L. E. Eberhardt and Sargeant 1977), as are ephemeral streams and streams of high gradient. Hence, mink are less abundant in Colorado than in the Upper Midwest.

Food habits of mink in Colorado are unknown, but thorough studies have been possible elsewhere because mink use habitual latrine sites, providing concentrated sources of scats for analysis. Data are also available from examination of intestinal tracts of trapper-killed mink. The animals are generalists, eating a variety of animal prey, including muskrats, cottontails, deer mice, voles, ground- and marsh-nesting birds and their eggs, frogs, snakes, fish, insects, and crayfish as well as small amounts of plant material. Mammalian prey, especially muskrats, mice, and voles, is most important (Eagle and Whitman 1987); however, during waterfowl nesting season, hens, eggs, and ducklings may be important prey (Arnold and Fritzell 1987a; Larivière 2003). Mink, like some other predators, apparently can hear ultrasounds produced by their rodent prey (Powell and Zielinski 1989). Fish enhancement projects that improve stream habitat may benefit mink by increasing aquatic food species. Game fishes such as trout are less regularly taken by mink than are slower-moving species such as carp, minnows, and suckers. Fish appear to become increasingly important during the winter months, apparently offsetting some dependence on birds and invertebrates during the warmer seasons. In waterfowl production areas, mink can be important predators on ducks, especially if nesting habitat is concentrated (Schladweiler and Tester 1972; Cowardin et al. 1985). Males appear to feed on larger prey than females. Surplus prey is cached. Mink frequently live in the same areas as river otters but relatively little competition existed for food in an Alberta study, with mink tending to forage less on aquatic prey and more on mammals and birds on drier sites (F. Gilbert and Nancekivell 1982).

Because of their importance in commercial fur farming, reproduction in mink has been studied extensively (Hansson 1947; R. K. Enders 1952; Venge 1959). Mink are polygamous. Both sexes mate with multiple partners; in fact, a given litter may have more than one father. No pair-bond is formed. The breeding season is late February to early April. Females are polyestrous throughout this period until they are bred, with cycles of 7 to 10 days. Ovulation is induced by copulation. Gestation period is highly variable, 40 to 74 days (average, 51), because delayed implantation occurs in females that breed early in the season whereas it seems not to occur in late-breeding females (Eagle and Whitman 1987). There is 1 litter of 1 to 8 (average, 5) young per year, born in late April or May.

The young are altricial, with eyes opening at about 3 weeks of age. By fall, they are close to adult weight. Males and females are reproductively mature at about 10 months of age and are reproductive for about 7 years. Young stay with the female until fall, and littermates may travel together when dispersing (Linscombe et al. 1982; Eagle and Whitman 1987).

Mink are active year-round, and much of their foraging occurs along or in the water. In winter they are mainly diurnal and occasionally active at night as well. Activity may be connected to that of their prey. The animals are inactive during cold periods after heavy snows (Marshall 1936). Mink are adept at tree climbing and may use trees as resting or escape sites (Larivière 1996). Except for brief periods of mating, mink are solitary. Mink den in burrows close to streambanks and often use abandoned muskrat dens and beaver lodges. Powell (1979) considered mink territorial, maintaining intrasexual territories with little or no overlap between individuals of the same sex; Larivière (2003) was not convinced. Whitman (1981) found in Idaho that they did not defend territories against other mink of the same sex. "Territories" are marked with the secretions of scent glands.

Home ranges vary in size with age and sex of the resident, social tolerance, and availability of food, including seasonal foods such as spawning fishes (Marshall 1936; McCabe 1949; J. Mitchell 1961; Melquist, Whitman, and Hornocker 1981). Also, mink seldom range far from water, a characteristic that constrains their movements along narrow, linear corridors. Home range estimates for radio-telemetered animals in Tennessee were linear, averaging 7.5 km (R. T. Stevens et al. 1997). In Manitoba, mink in prairie wetlands had home ranges averaging 7.7 km^2 (Arnold and Fritzell 1987b). In other studies, females have been estimated to occupy home ranges of 8 to 20 ha, whereas males may use areas up to 1,626 ha. Home ranges of females may overlap portions of the home range of adult males (Whitman 1981). Some of the increased size of home ranges of males may be attributable to breeding activities, but it is also likely that demand for food resources forces the larger males to have bigger home ranges. Yamaguchi and Macdonald (2003) estimated that a male consumed as much as 30 percent of his monthly food budget within the home range of a female. This may have forced females to maintain larger ranges as well, especially if pregnant or with dependent young.

Densities of mink are rarely high and vary with habitat, season, and abundance of prey. Furthermore, a variety of methods are used to estimate; estimates vary widely and may contain inaccuracies (Eagle and Whitman 1987). In Montana, riverine populations ranged from 8 to 22 mink per square mile (259 ha) (J. Mitchell 1961). In marsh habitat in Wisconsin, populations fluctuated from 7 to 24 mink on 445 ha over a 5-year period (McCabe 1949). Density was 0.6 females per square kilometer during the winter in Michigan (Marshall 1936). In northwestern Colorado, density was estimated at 1.7 mink per square mile (259 ha) (McKean and Burkhard 1978).

Mink are not thought to be heavily preyed upon, although they have been killed by great horned owls as well as a variety of carnivores, including wolves, bobcats, and fishers (Linscombe et al. 1982). Trapping is the greatest source of mortality in most areas. Mink were harvested as furbearers in Colorado until 1996. However, numbers trapped declined greatly after the mid-1940s from more than 1,000 to usually fewer than 300 from 1982 to 1991 (J. Fitzgerald 1993b). Since the ban on leg-hold traps by popular vote (Amendment 14) in 1996, mink are still listed as furbearers (or small game), but detailed records on harvest are not maintained. In trapped populations in Montana, juvenile to adult ratios of 4:1 have been found (Lechleitner 1954). Population turnover was about 3 years in Montana (J. Mitchell 1961). Mink are also very sensitive to water pollution by mercury and polychlorinated biphenyls (PCBs), although the degree to which they are impacted by these contaminants in the wild is not known. Linscombe et al. (1982), Eagle and Whitman (1987) and Larivière (1999b, 2003) reviewed the literature on the species.

Gulo gulo

WOLVERINE

Description

The wolverine is the largest terrestrial mustelid. Blocky and somewhat bear-like in appearance, it has a broad head and short heavy neck. Unlike that of bears, the tail is bushy and relatively long, about one-fourth the length of the body. The ears are short and rounded. The feet are large with semi-retractile claws. During the winter stiff hairs develop between the toes and on the soles of the feet, creating a snowshoe effect and a weight load of only 27–35 g/cm^2 (Pasitschniak-Arts and Larivière 1995). Coloration varies widely with individuals and is typically medium brown to dark brown with broad yellowish brown lateral stripes extending from the neck to the rump and joining at the base of the tail. A pale facial mask is often present. The venter is generally paler in color and there may be white to yellowish tan spots on the throat and chest. Measurements of males are: total length 900–1,125 mm; length of tail 190–260 mm; length of hindfoot 180–192 mm (E. Hall 1981). Males average 10 percent longer and 30 percent heavier than females. Weights range from 7 to 32 kg (Nowak 1999). The skull is massive, with a short muzzle, powerful jaws, and strong teeth. The auditory bullae are moderately inflated. Females have 4 mammae.

PHOTOGRAPH 12-17. Wolverine (*Gulo gulo*). Photograph by Claude Steelman/Wildshots.

MAP 12-35. Historic and present distribution of the wolverine (*Gulo gulo*) in North America (after D. Wilson 1982).

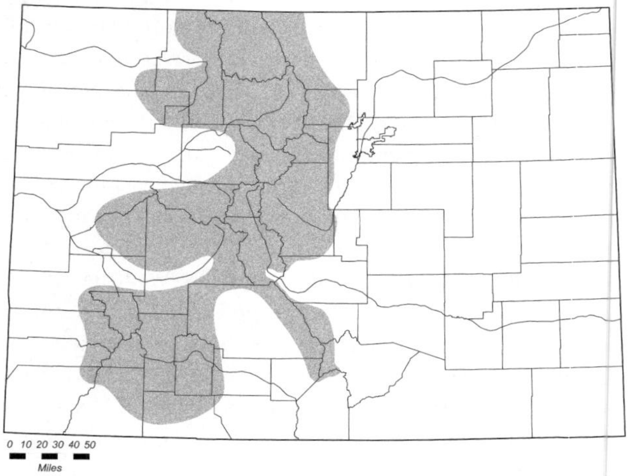

MAP 12-36. Historic distribution of the wolverine (*Gulo gulo*) in Colorado.

Distribution

The wolverine is a circumpolar species, occupying tundra, taiga, and boreal and montane coniferous forests. In North America it ranges across Alaska and northern Canada and southward along the Sierra Nevada and the Rocky Mountains (Copeland and Whitman 2003). Although there were several substantial records from Colorado in the nineteenth century (D. Armstrong 1972), populations apparently never were high. A specimen claimed to have been killed in eastern Utah (but probably taken in Rio Blanco or Garfield County, Colorado) was brought to the attention of wildlife officials in 1979 (J. Seidel et al. 1998). In 1996 a wolverine was trapped 18 mi. north of Cheyenne, Wyoming (G. Byrne and Copeland 1997). Nowak (1973), Field and Feltner (1974), Nead et al. (1984), Banci (1994), Maj and Garton (1994), G. Byrne (1997), and J. Seidel et al. (1998) summarized reports of the species in Colorado to those dates. Copeland and Whitman (2003) did not map Colorado as part of the current range. Copeland et al. (2010) explored the "bioclimatic envelope" of the wolverine on a circumpolar scale, based on the premise that wolverines are limited by the persistence of the spring snow cover necessary for successful nursery dens. An implication of their study is that Colorado may provide even less suitable habitat for wolverines in the future. Aubry et al. (2007) suggested that the most recent verifiable record for wolverine in Colorado was from 1919; however, records listed by D. Armstrong (1972) and unpublished reports maintained by G. Byrne of the Colorado Division of Wildlife suggest that at least occasionally individual wolverines have been present in the state. Nonetheless, any report of wolverines or other rare species should be accompanied by physical evidence (Aubry et al. 2007). On ecological and biographic grounds, J. Frey (2006) considered New Mexico to be within the natural range of the wolverine. Wolverines in the Teton Mountains of Wyoming probably represent the present-day population closest to Colorado (K. Inman et al. 2003). In June 2009 a young male wolverine radio-collared by the Wildlife Conservation Society near Grand Teton National Park was located in north-central Colorado, having moved more than 500 miles from the point at which it was collared (Pankratz 2009). The animal was photographed in Hidden Valley, Rocky Mountain National Park, by professional wildlife photographer Ray Rafiti (Blumhardt 2009; Rafiti 2009). As of December 2010, the animal still was being radio-tracked in the vicinity (J. Copeland, personal communication to J. P. Fitzgerald). A petition to list the wolverine as threatened in the conterminous United States was denied by the US Fish and Wildlife Service in 1995. Federal land management agencies consider it a "sensitive species." The wolverine is listed as endangered in Colorado. In July 2010, the Colorado Wildlife Commission granted the Colorado Division of Wildlife the authority to begin exploration of the possibility of restoring wolverines to Colorado (Colorado Division of Wildlife 2010). This likely will be a spirited discussion, in part because the wolverine has also been proposed for listing as "Threatened" under the Endangered Species Act and also because the potential natural habitat of wolverines is largely coextensive with Colorado's "Ski Country." One subspecies, *Gulo gulo luscus*, is ascribed a range in Colorado. Tomasik and Cook (2005) discussed phylogeography and conservation genetics of North American wolverines.

Natural History

Wolverines are animals of boreal forests and tundra. In Canada and Alaska, they prefer marshy areas such as lowland spruce forests that support extensive wetlands (D. Wilson 1982). However, wolverines in Idaho and Montana are associated with coniferous forest, primarily subalpine fir communities in Montana and mid-elevational conifers in Idaho in the winter; alpine tundra is used widely in summer (Hornocker and Hash 1981; Copeland 1996). Copeland (1996) believed that wolverines preferred slopes with northern aspects and that subadults were tolerant of a broader range of habitats than adults. Preliminary studies in the vicinity of Yellowstone (K. Inman et al. 2003) showed wolverines used a wide range of elevations, from 1,500 m to 3,599 m, going slightly lower in winter and higher in summer months. High elevations, steep slopes, and northwest- and north-facing slopes were important, as were Douglas-fir and subalpine fir forests. Large and diverse ungulate populations may also be an important component of wolverine habitat, primarily as a source of carrion (van Zyll de Jong 1975; Hornocker and Hash 1981; Copeland 1996; Copeland et al. 2007). Modeling suggests probable wolverine presence can be determined based on the amount and kind of habitat, road density, and human population density (Rowland et al. 2003). Aubry et al. (2007) presented detailed maps of wolverine occurrence records superimposed on potential natural vegetation types (Küchler 1964) and climatic life zones (Holdridge 1967) to present a clear picture of the species' habitat requirements.

Wolverines eat small rodents, rabbits, porcupines, ground squirrels, marmots, birds and eggs, fish, carrion, and plant material, especially roots and berries. In Europe, wolverines do attack large game, including moose and reindeer; there are no documented kills of big game in North America (Hornocker and Hash 1981; Pasitschniak-Arts and Larivière 1995). Ungulate remains in the diet are probably from carrion. In winter the diet is mostly carrion and mammalian prey, with more diversity at other times of the year. Wolverines fed on kills made by mountain lions in Montana (Hornocker and Hash 1981) and on deer and elk wounded by hunters in Idaho (Copeland 1996). Wolverines cache surplus food, marking the site with urine and scent (D. Wilson 1982; Hash 1987).

Wolverines are active year-round. Once thought to be mostly nocturnal, they may instead have regular 3- to 4-hour bouts of activity or sleep (D. Wilson 1982; Copeland 1996). When necessary, wolverines are good swimmers and agile tree climbers. They are typically solitary, with pairing occurring only during the brief mating season, although adult pairs occasionally travel together for brief periods in winter (Hash 1987). Young animals travel with the female in late summer and fall. Wolverines spend considerable time in marking behaviors, using their anal and ventral glands to mark objects. They also bite and claw trees in a manner similar to bears (G. Koehler et al. 1980; Hornocker and Hash 1981). Such behaviors may be used to mark territory or label food caches.

The extent to which wolverines are territorial in North America is not clear (Hash 1987). In Europe, intrasexual territories are maintained. Home ranges frequently overlapped in Montana. In Alaska and Montana they varied from 94 to 388 km^2 for females and from 422 to 666 km^2 for males (Hornocker and Hash 1981; Hash 1987). In Idaho, Copeland (1996) reported larger home ranges, averaging

400 km^2 for females and 1,500 km^2 for males. K. Inman et al. (2003) found home ranges of young to shift as they occupied areas previously held by adult animals. Home ranges varied in their study area from 429 to 910 km^2 for resident animals; a dispersing male ranged over 38,000 km^2 in 3 states, visiting 8 different mountain ranges (K. Inman et al. 2003). Lactating females typically have the smallest home ranges. The home range of a male may overlap that of several females. The size of home ranges is probably increased by movements of ungulate prey and heightened activity by males during the breeding season. Individual wolverines may move over 35 km in 1 night (D. Wilson 1982; Copeland 1996). Movements of dispersing juveniles seeking suitable habitat may exaggerate the size of "home ranges" reported in the literature. Copeland (1996) reported 3 2-year-old males to move more than 200 km. Wolverines have historically had one of the lowest densities of any carnivore. Copeland (1996) estimated 1 wolverine per 109 to 304 km^2 in Idaho. In Montana, Hornocker and Hash (1981) estimated 1 wolverine per 65 km^2.

Studies in Alaska and the Yukon and in captivity indicate that wolverines are polygamous and can breed from late spring until early fall (Rausch and Pearson 1972; Magoun and Valkenburg 1983; Mead et al. 1991). Ovulation is induced; delayed implantation results in blastocysts not implanting until January or February. Variation in the delay of implantation results in a variable gestation period of 214 to 272 days (Mehrer 1976; Mead 1981; Mead et al. 1991). Active gestation is about 30 to 40 days post-implantation. Fetal sex ratios approximate 1:1.

Two to 5 young (average, 2 or 3) are usually born in March or April. In Idaho, Copeland (1996) reported an average of 2 kits. The young are born in simple, unlined natal dens in logjams, under rocks and boulders, or under tree roots (Hash 1987; Copeland 1996; Magoun and Copeland 1998). Most dens usually have to be accessed by tunneling through several feet of snow. Females may use more than 1 den when rearing young, and repetitive human disturbance can lead to abandonment of the den (Magoun and Copeland 1998). Neonates are altricial but covered with fine white fur (Mehrer 1976); weaning occurs at 9–10 weeks of age (Copeland 1996). Reproductive success is low in wolverines, apparently in part because of loss of kits, lack of mating opportunity, and age at first litter (Hash 1987). Females are not reproductively mature until 12 months of age. Liskop et al. (1981) reported pregnancy rates of 85 percent in females 12 to 24 months old, and 88 percent in females older than 24 months. Males are sexually mature at about 2 years of age.

Most animals do not live more than 10 to 11 years in the wild and average 4 to 6 years for animals harvested in Montana, the only state in the Lower 48 that allows harvest (Hash 1987). J. Krebs et al. (2004) estimated annual mortality of 0.27 to 0.55 for trapped populations and 0.00 to 0.15 for protected populations. Squires et al. (2007) estimated annual survival was 0.80 when trapping was not a factor and 0.57 when such mortality was added. Other than humans and an occasional wolf or cougar kill, natural enemies are few (Copeland 1996). Some animals starved in Idaho and Montana studies; K. Inman et al. (2003) reported 1 animal killed in an avalanche and another by a black bear. The literature was reviewed by D. Wilson (1982), Hash (1987), Pasitschniak-Arts and Larivière (1995), and Copeland and Whitman (2003). Ruggiero et al. (2007) summarized a special section in the *Journal of Wildlife Management* on recent research on North American wolverines.

Taxidea taxus

AMERICAN BADGER

Description

Badgers are short, stout mustelids with thick necks and short legs specialized for digging. The legs are muscular, with strong claws on the front feet that may exceed 50 mm in length. The tail is short but bushy. The general dorsal color is silvery gray, sometimes tinged with brown, yellow,

PHOTOGRAPH 12-18. American badger (*Taxidea taxus*). © 1993 Wendy Shattil/Bob Rozinsky.

or buff and grizzled with black. The snout, top of the head, feet, parts of the legs, and areas around the ears are black. A narrow, white stripe runs from the nosepad onto the head, which also sports white facial marks. The ventral surface is paler than the dorsum. Long guard hairs give the appearance of shagginess and of greater size. Measurements are: total length 660–889 mm; length of tail 98–174 mm; length of hindfoot 88–155 mm; length of ear 50–53 mm; weight 6–14 kg. On the Northern Great Plains, weights averaged 8.4 kg for males and 6.4 kg for females (P. Wright 1969). The skull is triangular and stoutly built. Females have 8 mammae. Badgers are sexually dimorphic, males averaging larger than females.

Distribution

Badgers are found from the northern and central parts of the western provinces of Canada east to the Great Lakes states and southwest into Mexico. They are found throughout Colorado in all open habitats. Densities are highest in areas with abundant ground squirrels or prairie dogs. Data summarized by Messick (1987) suggest that the animal is expanding its range to the north and east in North America, but Long and Killingley (1983) presented some evidence that badgers were declining in parts of several western states. R. Finley et al. (1976) speculated that badger populations in northwestern Colorado might be lower now than in the past because of elimination of prairie dogs. *Taxidea taxus berlandieri* is the subspecies of extreme southwestern Colorado; *T. t. taxus* occurs on the eastern plains; *T. t. montana* occurs in the western and central portions of the state.

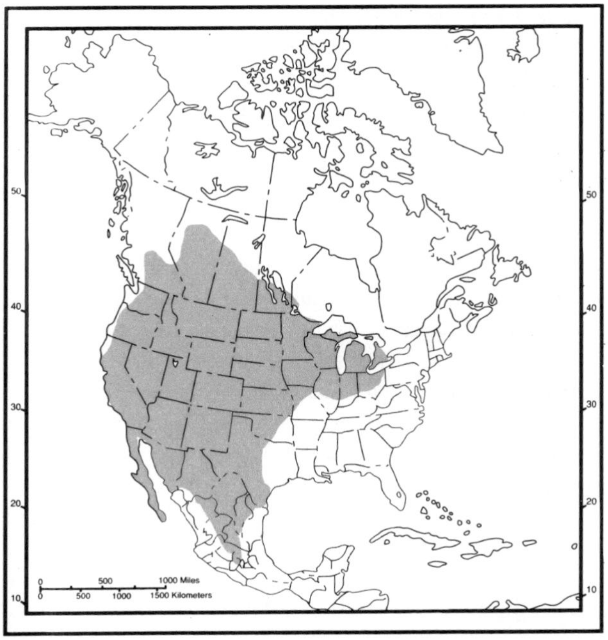

MAP 12-37. Distribution of the American badger (*Taxidea taxus*) in North America.

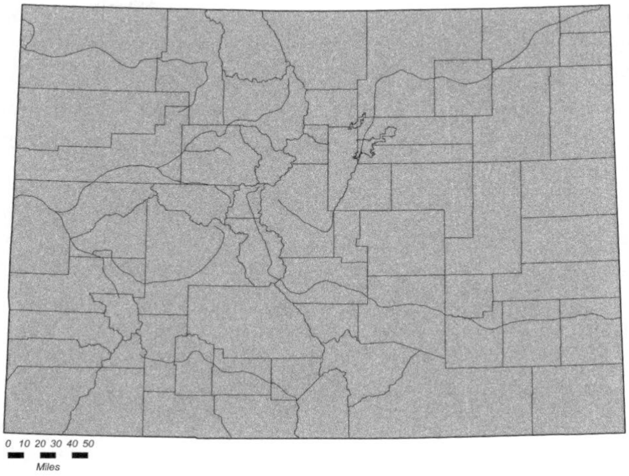

MAP 12-38. Distribution of the American badger (*Taxidea taxus*) in Colorado.

Natural History

Badgers occur in practically all habitat types in Colorado. They prefer open habitats and avoid densely wooded areas, although they will enter forest margins. Badgers occur in grasslands, meadows in subalpine and montane forests, alpine tundra, and semidesert shrublands. Badgers in South Park not infrequently hunted in stands of aspen and open stands of conifers (Hetlet 1968; J. Fitzgerald, unpublished observations). They are most common in areas with abundant populations of ground squirrels, prairie dogs, and pocket gophers (T. Clark et al. 1982).

Badgers are opportunistic predators, eating practically any fossorial or terrestrial prey they can capture. They are excellent diggers and can quickly excavate burrows of rodents to obtain prey. The diet includes prairie dogs, ground squirrels, gophers, mice, cottontails, jackrabbits, snakes, lizards, ground-nesting birds and their eggs, and insects. Lindzey (2003) credited R. P. Lampe with reports of considerable amounts of corn in stomachs of badgers in the fall in northwestern Iowa, but plant materials are not present in most reported dietary studies. The widest range of dietary items occurs during the warmer months (Lindzey 1982; Messick 1987). Hoff (1998) most frequently located badgers on the Rocky Mountain Arsenal in prairie dog colonies, and prairie dogs comprised 13 percent of badger scats (despite an estimated 90 percent loss of prairie dogs from epizootic plague in 1994 and 1995). The most prevalent remains in scats were voles (with 45 percent frequency). Eggs of such birds as sage grouse were important items in the diet of Coloradan badgers (Warren 1942; Hogue 1955). In South Park, badgers preyed on Gunnison's prairie dogs, Wyoming ground squirrels, and golden-mantled ground squirrels (Hetlet 1968; J. Fitzgerald and Lechleitner 1974). Badgers also prey on marmots in Colorado (D. Anderson and Johns 1977). Carrion is eaten, and food may be cached, either above- or belowground, when surplus prey is secured (Michener 2000; Lindzey 2003). Juveniles feed more heavily on insects and birds than do adults (Messick and Hornocker 1981). Individual badgers may improve their predatory success on prairie dogs over time, accommodating tactics to behavior of prey (e.g., speed, direction, and possible escape responses; Eads and Biggins 2008).

The reproductive biology of the American badger has not been studied as intensively as that of some other mustelids. Mating occurs from late June to August (P. Wright 1966; Messick and Hornocker 1981; T. M. Campbell and Clark 1983). M. Todd (1980) and Messick (1987) used swelling of the vulva as an indicator of estrus. Four adult badgers captured between mid-August and early September in South Park, Colorado, had conspicuously swollen vulvae, indicating breeding condition (J. Fitzgerald, unpublished). Badgers are induced ovulators (P. Wright 1966). Following breeding, implantation is delayed, with total gestation period being 7 to 8 months. Most females give birth in March or April (Messick 1987). Litter size ranges from 1 to 4, with 2 being the mode.

The young remain belowground for about 6 weeks after birth. They stay with the female through the summer and disperse in the fall. Some females breed their first autumn, but males do not breed until they are more than 1 year old (Messick 1987). Sex ratios approximate 1:1. Percentage of females producing young varied from 52 to 72 percent in Idaho (Messick et al. 1981), and 40 to 52 percent of females 12 months of age had young.

Badgers are generally solitary except during the mating season and when females are rearing their young. They dig holes in pursuit of prey and also dig conspicuous burrows for dens. In Idaho, Eldridge (2004) found densities of 790 badger mounds per hectare on the Snake River Plains and calculated that mounds and diggings occupied 5 to 8 percent of the landscape and resulted in movement of 26 tons per hectare of soil. A burrow is usually characterized by a mound of dirt fanning out at the entrance. Average dimensions of 112 badger burrows in South Park, Colorado, were 19 cm high by 21 cm wide (Hetlet 1968). Lengths of dirt mounds at the burrow entrance averaged 102 cm, and these "spoil piles" had a mean maximum depth of soil of about 13 cm. Of these burrows, 16 percent were being used by Wyoming ground squirrels or least chipmunks, and 5 percent were being used by badgers. With the exception of winter, 84 percent of badger dens dug by radio-tracked animals in Utah and Idaho were used only 1 day. Winter use of the same burrow is much more prolonged, up to 72 days. Of the burrows used by badgers, 85 percent had been previously excavated (Lindzey 1978; Messick et al. 1981). Badgers burrows are abundant in some areas. Many of these holes represent prospecting for prey or predation bouts (i.e., "meal stops" rather than residences).

Badgers may be active at any time, but in areas with considerable human disturbance they are most active at night. During 5 years of study in South Park, 44 badgers were observed or captured, of which 28 were in daylight hours (Hetlet 1968; J. Fitzgerald 1970 and unpublished). In cold areas the animals are inactive for long periods during the winter. Adaptations to prolonged periods without food include inactivity, torpor, and increased efficiency of food assimilation (Harlow 1981; Harlow and Seal 1981).

Badger populations are made up of 2 groups, resident adult animals and juveniles without permanent home ranges (Messick 1987). Home ranges of adults overlap, and males have larger areas than females. Average home ranges for adult females on the Rocky Mountain Arsenal varied over 3 years from 3.9 to 9.0 km^2 (Hoff 1998). Largest home ranges were those of females that doubled their usual home ranges because of scarcity of prairie dogs as prey. Adult male badgers in the same study area had average home ranges of 14–33 km^2. Hoff (1998) estimated that 26 to 45 badgers inhabited the 68 km^2 refuge in August 1996, an average of 0.49 badgers per square kilometer. In Idaho, Messick (1981) estimated home ranges of male and female adult badgers at 2.4 and 1.6 km^2, respectively, and a badger density of 5/km^2. Minta (1993) reported home ranges of males as 8.4 km^2 and those of females as 2.8 km^2 on his Teton study area. Badger density was estimated as 24 badgers on the 15 km^2 area (Minta and Mangel 1989). In Utah, Lindzey (1971) estimated home ranges of 5.8 and 2.4 km^2 for males and females, respectively, and a density of 1 badger per 2.6 km^2. In south-central Wyoming, on a site with low badger density (0.8–1.1/km^2), Goodrich and Buskirk (1998) reported home ranges of males during the breeding season of 11.1 km^2, and 5.4 km^2 when non-breeding. Females had home ranges of about 3.4 km^2. In South Park, an average of 9 badgers occupied a 16–26 km^2 site over 5 years (J. Fitzgerald 1970, 1993b). At the Rocky Mountain Arsenal in Adams County, minimum estimate of density of badgers was 0.27 per square kilometer (E. Hein and Andelt 1995). There is no evidence of territorial behavior. In parts of Idaho, seasonal crowding occurs because of agricultural practices, including burning, plowing, and cropping of fields. Such crowding leads to increased aggression among animals (Messick et al. 1981).

A summary of data from several different studies revealed that animals less than 1 year of age constituted 35 to 48 percent of badger populations (Messick 1987). Sixteen to 26 percent are 1 year of age; 11 to 22 percent are 2-year-olds, and 15 to 24 percent are from 3 to 7 years of age. The oldest animal of known age (capture-recapture) trapped in South Park was 3.5 years old (J. Fitzgerald 1993b). Individuals up to 14 years old may occur in some populations (Crowe and Strickland 1975; Messick et al. 1981). Because of their relatively sedentary habits and longevity, badgers have proven useful in detection and assessment of levels of sylvatic plague activity in rodent populations (J. Fitzgerald 1970, 1993a; Messick et al. 1983).

Badgers have few natural enemies other than humans, although golden eagles, coyotes, wolves, mountain lions, domestic dogs, and similar predators can kill juveniles (Messick et al. 1981; Lindzey 2003). Rathbun et al. (1980) reported cooperative hunting of a badger by coyotes. Hoff (1998) found significant levels of dieldrin in badgers on Rocky Mountain Arsenal more than 20 years after its disposal on the site, suggesting that some parts of the national wildlife refuge still harbor hazards for resident mammals. Badgers tend to face danger aggressively, and most mortality is caused by vehicles or deliberate killing by humans. In Idaho, 33 percent of known mortalities were caused by automobiles and 60 percent were directly caused by humans (Messick et al. 1981). In Colorado, the kill-trapping season on badgers was ended in 1997. From 1982 to 1992, annual harvest averaged about 800 animals (J. Fitzgerald 1993b). At present, there is a 4-month fall and winter season when badgers can be hunted or livetrapped (Colorado Division of Wildlife 2009f). Annual harvest in recent years has averaged roughly 300 animals (Table 4-3). Literature on the species was reviewed by Long (1973), Lindzey (1982, 2003), Long and Killingley (1983), and Messick (1987).

Lontra canadensis

NORTHERN RIVER OTTER

Description

River otters are elongate, robust mustelids with a thick, tapering tail. The head is relatively small and flattened with a shortened muzzle and small ears. The legs are short and the feet are large and webbed. The heels of the hindfeet have roughened pads for traction on steep, muddy streambanks. Webbed feet, a powerful tail, and short fur are all adaptations for an aquatic life. The short underfur is extremely dense and protected by longer, glossy guard hairs. Dorsal color ranges from dark brown to chestnut with ventral coloration pale brown to silvery. The chin and throat are sometimes whitish. Measurements are: total length 880–1,300 mm; length of tail 300–510 mm; length of hindfoot 100–150 mm; weight 5–14 kg. Males are slightly larger than females. The skull has a shortened rostrum and is flattened dorsoventrally with only slightly inflated bullae. Females have 4 mammae.

PHOTOGRAPH 12-19. Northern river otter (*Lontra canadensis*). Photograph by Joseph Van Wormer. All rights reserved. Photo Archives, Denver Museum of Nature and Science.

Distribution

The river otter occurred throughout Canada and the United States when North America was first settled by Europeans. Subsequently the species was extirpated over much of the southern parts of its range. In Colorado, historical records of river otters are almost statewide, except for the southeastern part of the state (P. Schnurr, Colorado Division of Wildlife, personal communication). Efforts to restore river

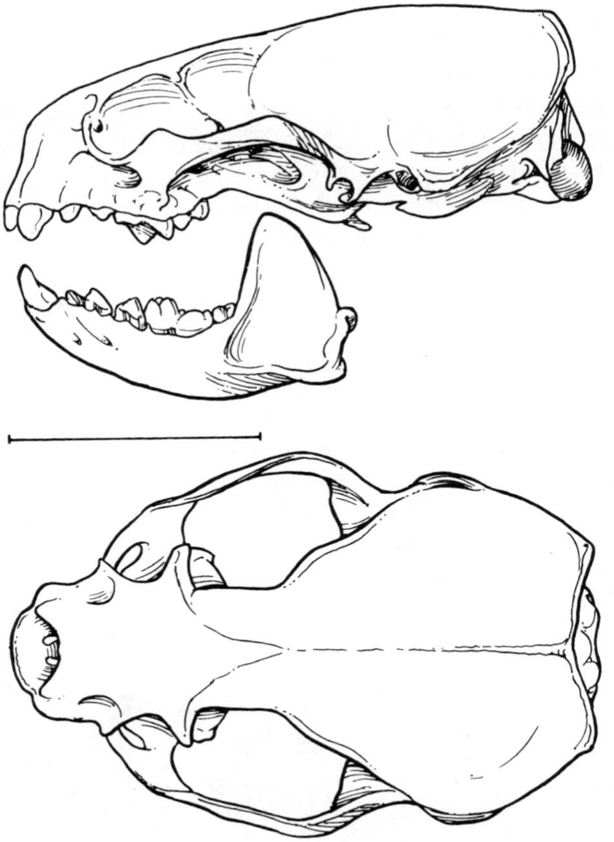

FIGURE 12-4. Lateral and dorsal views of the skull of a northern river otter (*Lontra canadensis*). Scale = 5 cm.

MAP 12-39. Distribution of the northern river otter (*Lontra canadensis*) in North America.

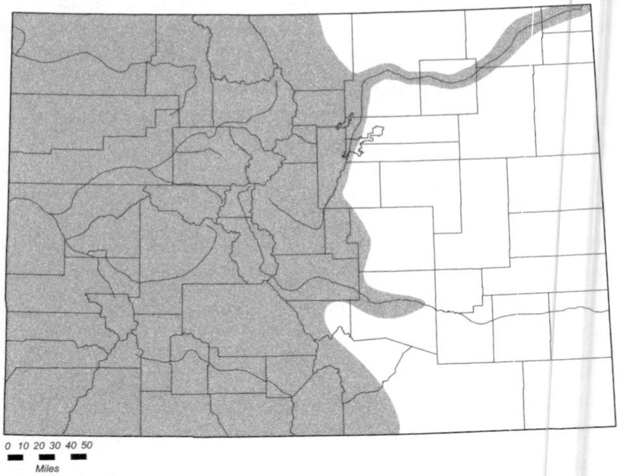

MAP 12-40. Distribution of the northern river otter (*Lontra canadensis*) in Colorado.

otters to Colorado began in the late 1970s (E. Raesly 2001). Melquist, Polechla, and Toweill (2003) mapped the results of those efforts. Colorado was the first state to translocate otters (Polechla 2002b). In 1976, Colorado initiated restoration efforts in several drainages and later increased the effort (Goodman 1984; Colorado Division of Wildlife 2003a). Transplants were made to the Colorado, Gunnison, Piedra, and Dolores rivers and (apparently unsuccessfully) at Cheesman Reservoir. Tracks and other sign of otters have also been found in the Cache la Poudre and Laramie drainages in Larimer County. These animals are thought to be either from the Upper Colorado River or escapees from Division of Wildlife facilities near Fort Collins (Malville 1988). Polechla (2002b) found otter sign on the Piedra River, suggesting a viable population. Evidence for otter populations on the Los Piños and San Juan rivers was inconclusive. River otters still are listed in Colorado as threatened. Studies attempting to estimate populations using DNA collected from hair-snag traps and latrine site selection are ongoing (DePue 2007; DePue and Ben-David 2007, 2010). DePue (2007) found little gene flow between study sites only 45 km apart.

The taxonomy of the river otter has undergone a number of revisions. We follow van Zyll de Jong (1987) and

Wozencraft (2005) in separating the New World (*Lontra*) and Old World (*Lutra*) otters. E. Hall (1981) mapped 3 subspecies in Colorado: *Lontra canadensis lataxina*, *L. c. pacifica*, and *L c. sonora*. However, the paucity of specimens makes it impossible to determine the validity of these supposed taxa or their historical ranges in the state (D. Armstrong 1972). Even if those named subspecies once were valid, their distribution may be unknowable, given recent restorations. Otters translocated to restore the species in Colorado have come from at least 6 different states or Canadian provinces (Goodman 1984), so considerable genetic mixing has occurred. As with other endangered species in Colorado, current status and conservation efforts for river otter are updated frequently on the Division of Wildlife's website. (Colorado Division of Wildlife 2008c).

Natural History

River otters inhabit riparian habitats that traverse ecosystems ranging from semidesert shrublands to montane and subalpine forests. Polechla (2002b) considered the otter to be an indicator species for water quality and quantity, although the population in the Dolores River tolerates heavy sediment loads, at least seasonally. Suitable habitat has an abundant prey base of fish or crustaceans. Minimum water flows are estimated at 10 cubic feet (0.28 cu. m) per second. Other habitat features that may be important include the presence of ice-free reaches of stream in winter, water depth, stream width, and suitable access to shoreline (Lytle et al. 1981; Goodman 1984). Most historical distributional records in Colorado (D. Armstrong 1972) are from relatively large rivers at low to moderate elevations. Restored animals occupy sites in low-elevation gravel ponds and irrigation reservoirs near Fort Collins (Malville 1988), mountain lakes and streams (Mack 1985), and canyon river systems at lower elevations (Malville 1990). Several authors have suggested a facultative commensal relationship between beaver and river otter (Melquist, Polechla, and Toweill 2003), with the beaver managing water supply, providing den sites, and enhancing fish habitat for the otter.

Diets of river otters have been studied in a number of states, but we know little about food habits in the Southern Rockies. Slow-moving fishes and those in greatest abundance are the principal prey. Fishes were found in 100 percent of scats examined in Grand County, Colorado (Mack 1985). Berg (1999) found that 36 percent of prey in that area were suckers, 34 percent crayfish, and 23 percent salmonids. Polechla (2003) found sculpins, stonefly nymphs, and salmonid fishes most numerous in studies on the Piedra–San Juan rivers. Crustaceans (especially crayfish) are also important food items in waters where they are abundant. Crayfish and suckers were important components of otter diets on the Dolores River (T. Beck 1989; Malville 1990) but were not as important in the Piedra–San Juan complex (Polechla 2003). Using an estimate of 1,394 kcal per animal-day, Mack (1985) calculated that prey availability exceeded demand by sixfold on his restoration site and that the area could support 5 reproductively active females. Insects are also frequently reported in studies of food habits. Mammals, amphibians, and birds are utilized less than the other items. In winter, in the Northern Rockies and the Pacific Northwest, fish may provide almost 100 percent of the diet (Greer 1955; Toweill 1974; Melquist, Whitman, and Hornocker 1981; Zackheim 1982; Melquist and Dronkert 1987). Otters process foods rapidly, with crayfish remains passing in as little as 1 hour (Liers 1951). Food transit time averaged about 200 minutes in captive otters and they required about 34 g of dry food per kilogram body weight per day (Melquist, Polechla, and Toweill 2003). Toweill (1974) found copious mucous production in the intestinal tract, perhaps facilitating food passage and protecting the gut from abrasive food debris. Most foraging seems to occur near water. About 50 percent of scats that Berg (1999) collected were found on boulders along the shoreline, although some were more than 30 feet inland. Scat accumulates in latrine sites, the location of which correlated with the presence of beaver activity, on prominent rocks adjacent to deep water shaded by cliffs or overhanging rocks (DePue 2007).

Because of the river otter's aquatic habits, many aspects of the species' behavior and ecology are not well studied. The animals do not hibernate and are active year-round. Otters in the Upper Colorado drainage were mostly diurnal in winter and more nocturnal in summer, with the least activity in late summer and early fall (Mack 1985). Most activity of animals in Idaho occurred near midnight and dawn (Melquist and Hornocker 1983).

Social organization of river otters appears to vary widely, from family groups composed mostly of females and their young to males either solitary or in "bachelor groups." Large congregations of 7 to 30 animals have been reported, and these groups doubtless include males (Melquist and Hornocker 1983). Intrasexual territoriality may be exhibited in females and not in males (Melquist and Hornocker 1983; Gorman et al. 2006).

River otters use both terrestrial resting sites and dens when not actively moving. Beaver bank dens are particularly favored sites. They were used in 31 percent of some 1,300 observations (Melquist and Hornocker 1983). Logjams, dense riparian vegetation, and snow and ice caves were also used. Less frequent use was made of brush piles, talus, muskrat dens, undercut banks, and beaver lodges.

A comparison of the ecology of mink and otters in Idaho revealed that the 2 species differed in diet, foraging strategy, and activity patterns (Melquist, Whitman, and Hornocker 1981). In Alberta, trenching through beaver dams by otters during the winter reduced water levels behind the dams. Otters appeared to do this to allow under-ice access to adjacent water, but it also may have improved access to air and it concentrated fish prey (D. Reid, Herrero, and Code 1988).

Reproductive biology of river otters is poorly known. Females mate immediately after the birth of the young, probably in March and April in Colorado. Estrus may last more than 40 days, during which time males follow scent trails of females. Some evidence suggests that females can have a second litter if the first one dies (Nowak 1999). Copulation takes 15 to 20 minutes and is accompanied by female vocalizations. Ovulation is thought to be induced by copulation. Controversy exists (Melquist and Dronkert 1987) over whether delayed implantation is obligatory, as some studies in southern populations suggest that it may not always occur. Total gestation period has been estimated at 290 to 375 days, with post-implantation development taking about 60 days (Liers 1951; W. Hamilton and Eadie 1964; Tabor 1974). Females retreat to secluded areas for parturition and rearing of the young, generally using abandoned dens of other aquatic mammals, especially beaver bank dens, and usually not using the same natal den more than once (Melquist and Hornocker 1983). Litter size ranges from 1 to 6 young, with an average of slightly less than 3 (Melquist and Dronkert 1987). Sex ratios approximate 1:1 but in adults harvest ratios are skewed toward males. Males are thought to be more vulnerable to trapping because of their larger home ranges and their tendency to form social groups (Chilelli et al. 1996; Melquist, Polechla, and Toweill 2003).

The altricial young are blind at birth but are fully furred and have open auditory canals. Young can leave the den on their own at 2 months, when they begin to eat solid food, and are weaned at about 3 months (Liers 1951). Young otters spend some time in play, but reports of sliding on snow and mud appear to be exaggerated (Beckel-Kratz 1977; Melquist and Hornocker 1983).

Young otters remain with the female for about 7 to 8 months, and siblings may stay together for more than a year (Melquist and Hornocker 1983). Young may disperse up to 200 km (Melquist and Hornocker 1983). Otters do not reach sexual maturity until 2 years of age, and males in some populations may not breed successfully until 5 years or older (Liers 1951, 1958). Breeding success of 2-year-old females ranges from 20 to 55 percent, and adult females may not breed every year (Toweill and Tabor 1982).

No long-term studies of population dynamics of river otter have been made, and turnover rates of populations are unknown. In Oregon, Tabor and Wight (1977) estimated annual survival ranged from 46 to 73 percent, depending on age class. Similarly, few estimates have been made on population densities, in part because no suitable census techniques exist. Density estimates based on radiotelemetry ranged from 1 otter per 3.85 km of waterway (Melquist and Hornocker 1983) to 1 otter per 5.8 km of waterway (Melquist, Polechla, and Toweill 2003). Home ranges reportedly vary from 2 to 78 km long (Melquist and Hornocker 1979, 1983), with a mean length of 32 km reported for 13 telemetered animals in Colorado (Mack 1985). Berg (1999) estimated a population of 16–17 otters in the general area studied by Mack (1985). In Alberta, D. Reid, Code, et al. (1994) found home ranges of some males to be more than 200 km^2 while females usually had ranges of about 70 km^2. In Wisconsin, home ranges varied from 9.5 to 30.3 km^2, with males having home ranges about 3 times those of females. Males tended to reuse home ranges and core areas from year to year more than did females (Gorman et al. 2006).

Adult river otters apparently have few natural predators, although individuals have been killed by bobcats, dogs, coyotes, and foxes (Toweill and Tabor 1982). Most mortality is thought to occur from trapping and roadkill. Habitat destruction and water pollution have an impact as well. Otters may live more than 14 years in the wild (Melquist and Dronkert 1987). The literature on the species was reviewed by Toweill and Tabor (1982), Melquist and Dronkert (1987), Larivière and Walton (1998), Polechla (2002a), and Melquist et al. (2003). Kruuk (2006) provided an appreciative review of otters in general.

Family Mephitidae—Skunks and Stink Badgers

The family Mephitidae includes 10 species in 3 genera in the New World and 1 genus (*Mydaus*) with 2 species of stink badgers in the Old World (Wozencraft 2005). The stink badgers are a poorly known group whose members have a skunk-like face and snout and black to brownish coloring with at least some white hairs or patches. Their anal scent glands greatly resemble those of the skunks.

Skunks are terrestrial omnivores, with animal matter the principal component of the diet. Spotted skunks weigh as little as 200 g whereas striped and hog-nosed skunks may top 5 kg. Males are usually about 10 percent larger than females. The feet are plantigrade with 5 digits equipped with sharp, non-retractile claws. The tail is long and bushy. Coloration is typically some pattern of black and white, varying considerably among species and even individuals within a species. All skunks have paired anal scent glands with a nipple. Well-developed sphincter muscles allow skunks to compress the glands and discharge an irritating, odoriferous musk in a cloud or stream up to several meters long. The ears are short and rounded. The skull is well built, with a short, broad rostrum and a fairly flattened braincase. The upper and lower jaws do not articulate ("lock") quite as tightly when the jaw is closed as do those of the Mustelidae. The dental formula for skunks is 3/3, 1/1, 2–3/3, 1/2 = 32 or 34 teeth. Carnassial teeth are well developed. Skunks are monoestrous; delayed implantation occurs in some species. Ovulation may be induced or spontaneous. A baculum is well developed in males.

Skunks are restricted to the New World, with species ranging from the southern Yukon and Northwest territories of Canada to Chile and Argentina. The stink badgers are restricted to the Philippines and Indonesia. Skunks have only recently been removed from the Mustelidae (Dragoo and Honeycutt 1997). Spotted skunks (*Spilogale*) show up in the fossil record in the United States in the Late Pliocene and Early Pleistocene. Striped skunks (*Mephitis*) appear in the fossil record in the Pleistocene (Kurtén and Anderson 1980).

Key to the Species of the Family Mephitidae in Colorado

1\. Premolars 2/3; tail completely white . . . . White-backed Hog-nosed Skunk—*Conepatus leuconotus*, p. 429

1' Premolars 3/3; tail with at least a few black hairs 2

2\. Upper body generally with 2 continuous, longitudinal white stripes merging anteriorly in the head and neck region (rarely all black, but never with broken white stripes or spots); skull arched, highest just behind the orbits; greatest length of skull more than 65 mm . . . . Striped Skunk—*Mephitis mephitis*, p. 426

2' Upper body generally with 4 or more broken white stripes, breaking into spots or blotches posteriorly; skull not highly arched, highest above posterior portion of bullae; greatest length of skull less than 65 mm . . . . *Spilogale*, 3

3\. Tip of tail white . . . . Western Spotted Skunk—*Spilogale gracilis*, p. 422

3' Tip of tail with at least some black hairs . . . . Eastern Spotted Skunk—*Spilogale putorius*, p. 424

Genus *Spilogale*

There are 4 species of *Spilogale*, according to Wozencraft (2005), ranging from North Dakota and Minnesota southward to Costa Rica. A thorough molecular systematic study of the group would help clarify evolutionary relationships among the nominal species.

Spilogale gracilis

WESTERN SPOTTED SKUNK

Description

The western spotted skunk is a small skunk, black to brownish in color, with a series of broad white stripes from the head to the base of the tail that are broken up into spots. There is also a white spot between the eyes. It is similar to the eastern spotted skunk, from which it is distinguished by being somewhat smaller, having broader white stripes that break into larger spots (see Photograph 12-20) and a tail with a white tip that extends to the underside of the tail for half its length. D. M. Armstrong (unpublished) examined a pure black individual livetrapped above Boulder Canyon near Nederland. Measurements are: total length 340–482 mm; length of tail 110–160 mm; length of hindfoot 35–50 mm; length of ear 15–23 mm; weight 400–700 g. The skull is similar to that of *Spilogale putorius* but can be distinguished by its smaller condylobasal length, 60 mm or less.

Distribution

The western spotted skunk ranges across much of Mexico and most of the western United States, giving way to the eastern species in the short- and mixed-grass prairies of the Great Plains. It is found in canyons and foothills areas at

PHOTOGRAPH 12-20. Museum study skins of western spotted skunk, *Spilogale gracilis* (*left*), and eastern spotted skunk, *S. putorius* (*right*). Note the white-tipped tail and larger white spots of the western spotted skunk. Photograph by Rick Wicker, Denver Museum of Nature and Science, © 1993 DMNS.

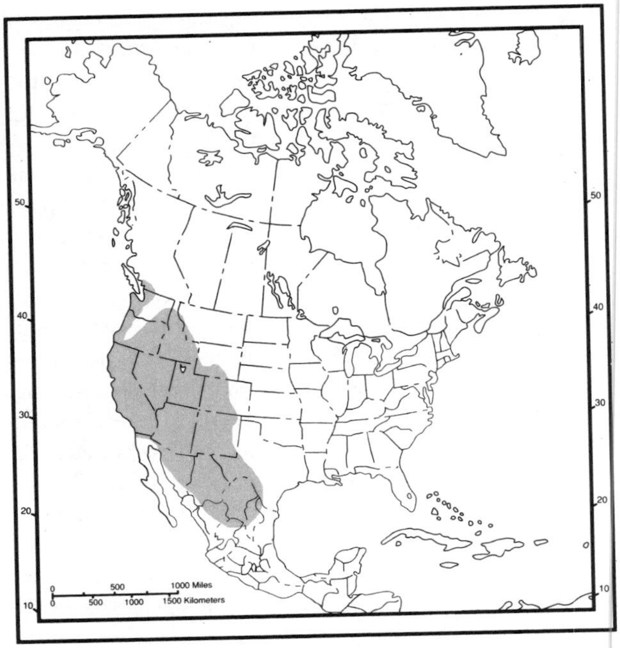

MAP 12-41. Distribution of the western spotted skunk (*Spilogale gracilis*) in North America.

PHOTOGRAPH 12-21. Western spotted skunk (*Spilogale gracilis*). Photograph by Ronald G. Altig.

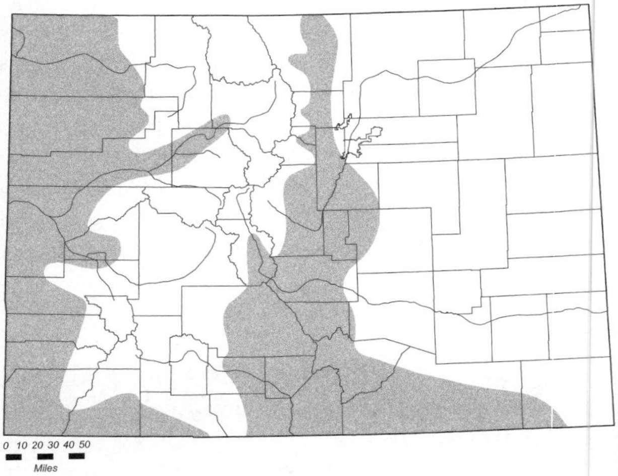

MAP 12-42. Distribution of the western spotted skunk (*Spilogale gracilis*) in Colorado.

elevations generally below 2,440 m (8,000 ft.) in Colorado (D. Armstrong 1972) on either side of the mountains. It extends northward along the foothills of the Front Range into southern Wyoming, eastward through the roughlands of southeastern Colorado, and throughout the semiarid canyon country at lower elevations on the Western Slope. R. Finley and Bogan (1995) added distributional records from in and near Dinosaur National Monument. The western spotted skunk does not appear to be common in most areas and may show fluctuations in populations, as has been noted for the eastern spotted skunk. One subspecies, *Spilogale gracilis gracilis*, occurs in the state.

Natural History

The biology of the western spotted skunk is poorly known. It is usually thought of as a species of the semiarid West, most common in shrubby habitats in broken country. It can be found in montane forest and shrubland, semidesert shrubland, and piñon-juniper woodlands. In Washington and Oregon the species is even found in old-growth coniferous forests (usually with good shrub understory) of the Coast Range and on the Olympic Peninsula as well as regularly inhabiting riparian habitats (A. Carey and Kershner 1996). It also frequents rocky habitats and is an agile climber. In the early 1900s the species was reported as far more common than the striped skunk in a number of areas on the Western Slope (Cary 1911).

Somewhat omnivorous, western spotted skunks eat a variety of foods but seem to concentrate on arthropods, small mammals, and birds. In Texas, western spotted skunks were mostly insectivorous and carnivorous, feeding on small rodents, including mice and kangaroo rats (R. Patton 1974). Bird eggs are also eaten. In Oregon, dietary items included fruit and berries, deer mice, lagomorphs, birds, and some arthropods (Maser et al. 1981). In Arizona, the skunks preyed on *Peromyscus* (Hoffmeister 1986).

Male western spotted skunks become reproductive as early as June. Females enter estrus in September, and the animals mate in September or October. Delayed implantation occurs, with the blastocyst implanting usually in April; total gestation takes 230 to 250 days. The post-implantation period is 1 month. The young are born in May or early June, with an average litter size of 4. Females may breed at 4 to 5 months of age. Thus most females, both adults and young of the year, breed in the fall. Some juvenile males are sexually mature in their first fall (Mead 1968b; Foresman and Mead 1973; Sinha and Mead 1976).

Little life history information has been published on the species. Adults apparently are solitary except during the mating season. The animals are strictly nocturnal and rarely seen. In Texas, they den on the surface of the ground or in rock crevices, woodpiles, burrows, tree cavities, and hollow logs as well as under human habitations and outbuildings (R. Patton 1974; K. Carroll 2000; Dowler et al. 2005). Dens were rarely used more than once; 22 percent of dens were in burrows, usually concealed by cactus or shrubs (Doty and Dowler 2006). Most commonly, both surface dens and burrows were under prickly-pear. Burrow dimensions averaged 10 by 19 cm with a depth of 1.23 m. Woodrat nests are also used for shelter (Verts and Carraway 1998). In Oregon, an individual den was found in a round hole in a sand dune area (Maser et al. 1981). An island population in California tended to avoid wetlands (Crooks 1994a; Crooks and Van Vuren 1995). In Oregon in forests ranging in age from 40 to more than 200 years, A. Carey and Kershner (1996) had capture rates of spotted skunks ranging from 0.2 to 1.2 per 1,000 trap-nights in traps set for flying squirrels. Maser et al. (1981) associated spotted skunks with riparian habitats. Neiswenter and Dowler (2007) found that spotted skunks foraged primarily in mesquite shrublands and generally avoided agricultural lands.

Doty and Dowler (2006) captured 16 western spotted skunks and 36 striped skunks on a 3,040 ha site in 4,755 trap-nights of effort for a trap success of 0.48 and 0.86 percent, respectively. Home range is probably not much larger than 50 to 60 ha, based on studies of eastern spotted skunks and a study on Santa Cruz Island, California (Crooks and Van Vuren 1995). In the latter population K. Jones et al. (2008) observed a marked increase in spotted skunks, to densities as high as 9–19 skunks per square kilometer. They attributed the increase to removal of livestock and decreasing populations of the endemic island gray fox (*Urocyon littoralis*). Colorado trapping records of spotted skunks from 1939 to 1991 suggest greater numbers up to the early 1940s, with harvest again increasing in the 1970s and 1980s (J. Fitzgerald 1993b). The western spotted skunk is classified as a non-game species in Colorado, with no open season on harvest. Literature on the species was reviewed by W. Howard and Marsh (1982), Rosatte (1987), Crooks (1999), Verts et al. (2001), and Rosatte and Larivière (2003).

Spilogale putorius

EASTERN SPOTTED SKUNK

Description

The eastern spotted skunk (sometimes called "civet" or even "civet cat") is a dainty black skunk with 4 to 6 white stripes on the dorsum that are broken into spots. Spotted skunks have long, glistening, dense black fur. The ears are rounded and partially hidden in the fur. The front claws are well developed, about twice the length of the hind claws. The forehead typically has a single large white spot. The eastern spotted skunk has a black-tipped tail whereas the western spotted skunk, *Spilogale gracilis*, has a white-tipped tail (see Photograph 12-20). The tail of spotted skunks is somewhat shorter than that of other genera of skunks, usually not exceeding 75 percent of the body length. Measurements

PHOTOGRAPH 12-22. Eastern spotted skunk (*Spilogale putorius*). Photograph by Roger W. Barbour.

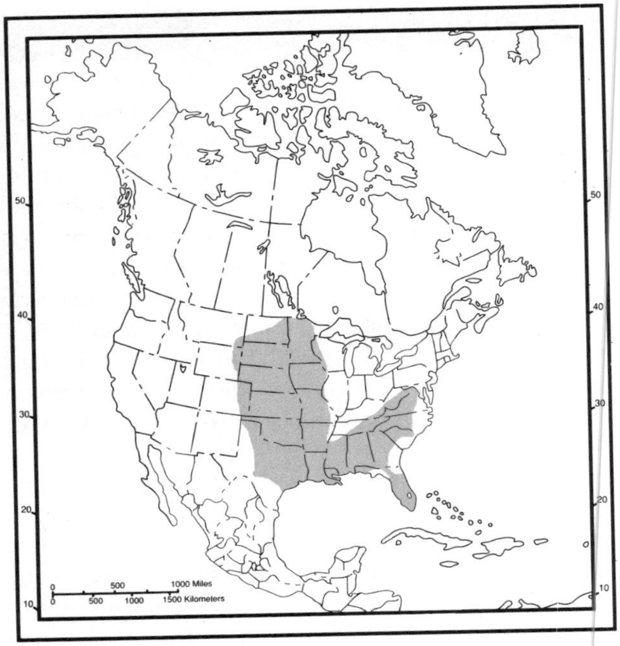

MAP 12-43. Distribution of the eastern spotted skunk (*Spilogale putorius*) in North America.

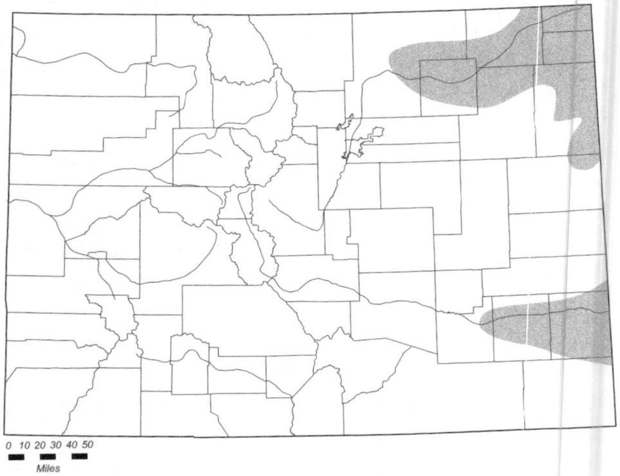

MAP 12-44. Distribution of the eastern spotted skunk (*Spilogale putorius*) in Colorado.

are: total length 410–585 mm; length of tail 138–280 mm; length of hindfoot 38–59 mm; weight 453–885 g. Males are about 10 percent larger than females. The skull is relatively flat with little arching over the orbits, and the condylobasal length is 62 mm or less. Anal glands are well developed and produce an extremely pungent odor. Females have 8 mammae. Aging techniques are available (Mead 1967).

Distribution

The eastern spotted skunk is mostly an animal of the grasslands and southeastern forests of the United States. In Colorado the eastern spotted skunk is known from only a few specimens collected along the eastern border of the state. Its status in Colorado is unclear. The species has expanded its range on the Northern Great Plains in recent decades, probably as a result of human activities (J. K. Jones, Armstrong, et al. 1983). One subspecies, *Spilogale putorius interrupta*, occurs in Colorado.

In earlier literature, *S. putorius* and *S. gracilis* were considered to be conspecific, arrayed as subspecies of *S. putorius* (Van Gelder 1959; E. Hall 1981). However, because *S. putorius* breeds in the spring and *S. gracilis* breeds in the fall (Mead 1968a, 1968b), the 2 forms are reproductively isolated and thus must be recognized as separate biological species.

Natural History

Relatively little is known of the ecology of the eastern spotted skunk; most of our knowledge is based on studies by Crabb (1941, 1944, 1948) and Selko (1937) in Iowa. In the Great Plains, the eastern spotted skunk appears to be most common in agricultural areas; in rough, broken country with abundant stands of brush; or in riparian woodlands. Their range may have expanded in some areas with agricultural expansion, including plantings of windbreaks and creation of fencerows. In the southeastern states it may prefer mixed deciduous forest to open grassland (C. McCullough and Fritzell 1984). Meta-analysis of trapping records suggested that eastern spotted skunks are much less abundant than they were in the first half of the twentieth century (Gompper and Hackett 2005). A variety of causes for decline have been suggested, including pesticide use, disease (particularly distemper and rabies), "clean-farming" practices—with decrease of complex hedgerows, and even changes in grain storage practices (e.g., changing from cribbed corn, with its high populations of rodent prey, to steel grain bins).

Eastern spotted skunks use a variety of dens, including abandoned burrows of other mustelids, ground squirrels, pocket gophers, woodchucks (in other parts of the country) and caves, rock overhangs, and similar features as well as buildings, culverts, woodpiles, and abandoned vehicles. In the Ouachita Mountains of western Arkansas, eastern spotted skunks almost always denned individually rather than communally. Dens were located in burrows excavated by other mammals, under decaying or burned tree roots, in rocky outcrops, in dens of eastern woodrats, or in tree cavities or hollow logs. The animals selected sites with high structural complexity. In Missouri, the species used tree cavities 1 to 7 m above the ground (C. McCullough and Fritzell 1984). A given den is used for 3 to 4 months and may be used sequentially by a number of individuals. Females with young protect the natal den. Underground dens typically have a nest chamber lined with grass, whereas aboveground resting sites do not contain nest materials. Dens are located close to suitable habitat or escape cover (Crabb 1948; Polder 1968; Henderson 1976).

In Iowa, insects comprised the bulk of the summer diet, and fruits and some cereal grains were used more in the fall. During winter, fall, and spring, small mammals (including voles, mice, and cottontails) were significant. Corn was an important component of the diet, especially in the winter (Selko 1937; Crabb 1941).

Eastern spotted skunks are active year-round. During cold weather their activity is restricted, and they may den communally at this time. Otherwise, they are solitary. Highly nocturnal, they rarely venture out during the daytime unless molested. They appear to be less tolerant of close contact with humans than are striped skunks. Eastern spotted skunks are agile climbers, a characteristic that serves them well for foraging (Crabb 1948). Spotted skunks exhibit a curious handstand posture when threatened, a prelude to spraying with the anal glands (C. Johnson 1921). The animals can sometimes be detected by the noise of their front feet patting the ground, apparently a warning behavior (Polder 1968).

Female eastern spotted skunks are polyestrous and enter estrus in late March. Spontaneous ovulators, they breed in April and give birth in June. Delayed implantation does not occur in this species, as in the western spotted skunk. Gestation takes about 55 to 65 days. Litter size averages 4 to 5 altricial young (Constantine 1961; Mead 1968a, 1968b). The young are born nearly naked, blind, and deaf yet even at birth they show black and white markings. Eyes open at about 30 to 35 days of age, and scent glands are functional by 45 days. The young develop rapidly and are full-grown at about 3 months of age (Crabb 1944).

Densities of eastern spotted skunks averaged about 2.2 animals per square kilometer in Iowa (Crabb 1948). Home ranges were 64 ha to more than 530 ha, depending on habitat and sex. Males typically had larger ranges. In Missouri, radio-collared male spotted skunks had home ranges averaging 1,420 ha, with a range of 40 to 4,360 ha (C. McCullough and Fritzell 1984). Long-term fluctuations in abundance of the species have been documented in Kansas, probably a consequence of human activities (J. Choate et al. 1974).

Humans are the chief cause of mortality, either directly via trapping and roadkill or indirectly through habitat alteration and destruction. Diseases, including rabies, also take a toll. In captivity, spotted skunks have lived to 10 years (Egoscue et al. 1970). There is no open season on the eastern spotted skunk in Colorado; it is classified as a nongame species. W. Howard and Marsh (1982), Rosatte (1987), Kinlaw (1995), and Rosatte and Larivière (2003) reviewed the literature on the species.

Mephitis mephitis
STRIPED SKUNK

Description

The striped skunk is a large skunk with a long bushy tail and a black background color. Most individuals have a single white dorsal stripe from the nose to the nape of the neck, where it splits into 2 white, lateral body stripes that converge near the base of the black and white tail. The ears are small and rounded. The underfur (which may be tinged deep reddish brown) is long, wavy, and dense, and the guard hairs are long and glossy. Measurements are: total length 580–770 mm; length of tail 190–350 mm; length of hindfoot 60–86 mm; weight 1,800–4,500 g. Considerable weight gain and loss occur seasonally. Females are smaller than

PHOTOGRAPH 12-23. Striped skunk (*Mephitis mephitis*).
© 1993 Wendy Shattil / Bob Rozinski.

males by up to 15 percent (E. Hall 1981). The legs are relatively short, with the soles of the feet nearly naked. Front claws are long, sometimes reaching 3 cm in length; hind claws are shorter. The skull is arched, deepest at the level of the frontals. The auditory bullae are barely inflated. The palate terminates close to the posterior border of the upper molars. Females have 10 to 14 functional mammae.

Distribution

The striped skunk ranges widely from the northern edge of the southern Canadian provinces southward into northern Mexico. It occurs throughout Colorado and is locally common at elevations to 3,050 m (10,000 ft.). *Mephitis mephitis estor* occurs in southwestern Colorado; *M. m. hudsonica* occurs in the northeastern, western, and central parts of the state; *M. m. varians* occurs on the southeastern plains and in the San Luis Valley.

Natural History

No intensive research has been conducted on the striped skunk in the Rocky Mountains, and information presented below draws primarily from studies in the northeastern United States and Canada, especially from the prairie regions, where skunks have been well studied because of predation on waterfowl nests (Rosatte and Larivière 2003). Striped skunks occur in most habitats in Colorado, except for alpine tundra. They appear to be most abundant at lower elevations, especially in and near cultivated fields and pastures and in the vicinity of farmsteads (D. Armstrong 1972).

Striped skunks are omnivorous and opportunistic. Arthropods, especially beetles, grasshoppers, and other insects, are a mainstay of the diet. Voles, mice, and ground-nesting birds and their eggs also are eaten. Plant material—including berries and other fruit, grains, and vegetables—comprises 20 percent or less of the diet. Insects (and to a lesser extent small mammals) are most important in the warmer months. In fall and winter there is increased use of vertebrates (including carrion) and plant foods. Both striped and spotted skunks reportedly can break open bird eggs by throwing them backward between the legs up against a hard surface. During the winter months, 14 to 65 percent of summer and fall weight is lost (Godin 1982; Wade-Smith and Verts 1982).

Like red foxes and mink, striped skunks have been implicated in the destruction of nests of ground-nesting birds, including waterfowl (T. Bailey 1971; Larivière and Messier 1998a; Rosatte and Larivière 2003) and pheasants (Kimball 1948). However, Larivière and Messier (1997a, 1998a) and Vickery et al. (1992) considered predation on nests to be incidental to skunks' foraging for small mammals and insects. In Saskatchewan, Larivière and Messier (2001a, 2001b) reported most skunk depredation on duck nests occurred at about 0208 hours, whereas red foxes and coyotes tended to forage earlier, preying on nests between 1800 and 2300 hours.

Foraging activity during the spring and summer months usually starts in early evening and continues through the night, with a resting period of about 80 minutes during the night (Larivière and Messier 1997b). The percentage of time reproductive females were active varied according to reproductive events, being lowest (34 percent) at pre-parturition and highest (66 percent) just prior to dispersal of

MAP 12-45. Distribution of the striped skunk (*Mephitis mephitis*) in North America.

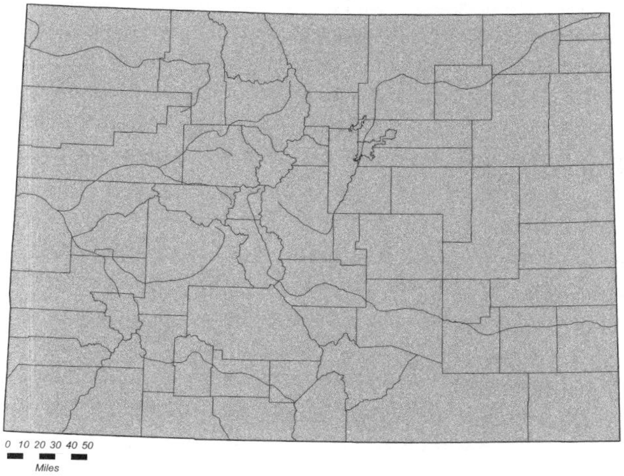

MAP 12-46. Distribution of the striped skunk (*Mephitis mephitis*) in Colorado.

the young in August. Male activity averaged 55 percent throughout the period. Adult skunks, including females with young, spend the daytime asleep in their dens, but the young often spend time aboveground at the den entrance. Diurnal activity increases in the fall as the animals feed intensively to gain weight for the metabolic demands of winter (Verts 1967; Larivière and Messier 1997b). When foraging, prey is located by its odor, as is apparent from watching the animals forage with their noses always to the ground. Muzzle-sized conical pits mark places where they have "rooted" while foraging for ground-dwelling arthropods. Striped skunks pounce cat-like on prey that is moving on the surface of the ground.

During the warmer months striped skunks often live aboveground, sleeping in dense vegetation, including croplands, hay meadows, and thickets. These bedding sites are seldom used more than 1 or 2 days. Natal dens are usually in burrows or under buildings that have a closed space; skunks are particularly attracted to old farmsteads in prairie country (Larivière and Messier 1998a; Larivière et al. 1999). During winter, 1 or 2 alternative dens are used. Burrows abandoned by other mammals, such as marmots, badgers, foxes, and coyotes, are often used as shelters (Storm 1972; Houseknecht and Tester 1978; Godin 1982). Dens usually have a single entrance and are most often built on sloping ground. Skunks are capable of digging their own burrows and will do so when no other shelter exists. During the winter in colder areas (including Colorado), solitary or communal dens (of 2 or more individuals) are used (Rosatte and Larivière 2003). Such groups are formed mostly of females, sometimes accompanied by 1 male (Verts 1967; Storm 1972; Houseknecht and Tester 1978; Wade-Smith and Verts 1982).

In cold areas striped skunks are inactive in the winter months but they do not actually hibernate. Winter foraging activity is greatly reduced and animals spend much time in winter dens, often for several months without emerging (Storm 1972; Sunquist 1974; Mutch and Aleksiuk 1977). When in the den, periodic arousal and movement occur. These bouts of activity usually last no more than 10 minutes, up to 2 or 3 times a day, but do not occur every day (Sunquist 1974). In Canada, body temperatures of skunks in winter dens were about 2–3°C lower than those of individuals active aboveground during the same season. Males tend to be more active in cold weather than are females.

Home ranges vary with season, age, and habitat. Estimates of home ranges vary from 0.5 km^2 in urban Toronto to 12.0 km^2 in prairie habitat, with most studies averaging 1.2 to 4.0 km^2; males typically have home ranges several times larger than females. On Bear River Refuge, Utah, striped skunk home ranges averaged 3.0 km^2 and tended to be linear along levees and roads (S. Frey and Conover 2006). There is extensive overlap of home ranges of females. Density estimates vary from 0.5 to 38.0 animals per square kilometer (Larivière and Messier 1998b, 2001a;

Rosatte and Larivière 2003). Length of winter, availability of winter den sites, use of communal dens, and food availability all influence density. Season of the year also affects population numbers; populations are low prior to emergence of young of the year (T. Bailey 1971; Wade-Smith and Verts 1982; Rosatte 1987).

Striped skunks are polygamous. Males increase their movements at the onset of the breeding season in search of mates. Males may form harems during the breeding season (Rosatte 1987). Skunks usually mate in February or March (Seton 1929; W. Hamilton 1937; Verts 1967; Greenwood and Sargeant 1998). Ovulation is induced by copulation. Females are monoestrous, although they will cycle again 1 month later if not bred during the first estrous period (Seton 1929; Verts 1967). Gestation is 59 to 77 days (Wade-Smith and Richmond 1978). Shorter gestation periods are associated with later matings, suggesting that delayed implantation occurs or is prolonged in early breeders. A litter of 5 to 8 young (range, 2 to 10) is born in May or early June (Wade-Smith and Verts 1982). Females actively defend the maternity den (Larivière and Messier 1998c). Striped skunks can breed at about 10 months of age. Sex ratios approximate 1:1.

Neonates weigh about 33 g, and pigmentation of the skin foreshadows the pattern of coloration. Eyes open at about 3 weeks of age, and ears open soon thereafter. Musk glands are developed at birth and the young can scent at a little over 1 week of age. Teeth begin to erupt at about 1 month, and weaning occurs at 8 weeks. Growth continues until about breeding age. Young skunks typically stay with the female until 2 or 4 months of age (Verts 1967). Young disperse from July to September, depending on location (Rosatte and Larivière 2003).

Striped skunks are well-known for their potential to spray unwary aggressors. Their graphic coloration serves as a warning to would-be predators who have experience with skunks. The anal glands are equipped with sphincter muscles that allow for forceful ejection of scent up to several meters (Godin 1982). Larivière and Messier (1996) found most skunks (69 percent occurrence) used the "tail-up" display when approached by an intruder, with foot-stomping occurring 17 percent of the time. Stomping was used more frequently in taller vegetation where the tail-up position was less readily visible. Until recently, a bath in tomato juice was the usual means of eliminating the odor. Effective commercial products are now available as well. The offensive chemical is a mercaptan, one of the class of sulfur-containing compounds familiar from their use in natural gas (which is itself odorless) to warn of dangerous leaks.

Mortality is 50 to 70 percent in juveniles, and most individuals do not live past 3 years of age. Great horned owls, eagles, mountain lions, bobcats, badgers, coyotes, and foxes prey on striped skunks. J. Hunter (2009) showed by field experiments that a variety of mammalian predators avoided striped skunks based on their body shape as well as their warning coloration. Skunks are a major vector of rabies, with about 20 percent of annual rabies cases in the United States and Canada associated with them. Most cases of skunk rabies are from the Midwest, Canadian prairie provinces, and northeastern parts of the United States and Canada (Rosatte and Larivière 2003). (Colorado typically has few cases of rabies in skunks.) Canine distemper and leptospirosis are also common in skunks. Vehicles and deliberate persecution account for many losses. In areas with a high incidence of rabies, skunks are often eliminated in control efforts during epizootics (Rosatte 1987).

Brinkerhoff, Ray, et al. (2008) found that skunks from foothills habitats near Boulder carried a richer assemblage of fleas than did skunks from adjacent grasslands; specifically, a number of species of fleas typical of rodents were found on skunks from the foothills but were absent from skunks in the grasslands. This suggests that striped skunks are associated with rock squirrels and/or woodrats (either as predators or as commensals). Further, it highlights the potential importance of mesocarnivores as potential vectors of flea-borne zoonotic diseases in complex landscapes.

Fur trappers take thousands of striped skunks annually even though the value of the pelt is usually no more than $3 to $6 (Rosatte and Larivière 2003). In Colorado, annual harvest in the late 1930s and early 1940s averaged more than 12,000 animals; more recently harvest has usually been several thousand animals per year, depending on value of furs (J. Fitzgerald 1993b). In the past decade and more, average harvest is estimated at about 1,150 (Table 4-3). Colorado has a 4-month season on the striped skunk as a furbearer and small game species. Literature on the species was reviewed by Godin (1982), Wade-Smith and Verts (1982), Rosatte (1987), and Rosatte and Larivière (2003).

Conepatus leuconotus

WHITE-BACKED HOG-NOSED SKUNK

Description

The white-backed hog-nosed skunk is a large skunk with a white back and black sides and venter. The muzzle and

PHOTOGRAPH 12-24. White-backed hog-nosed skunk (*Conepatus leuconotus*). Photograph by Joseph G. Hall.

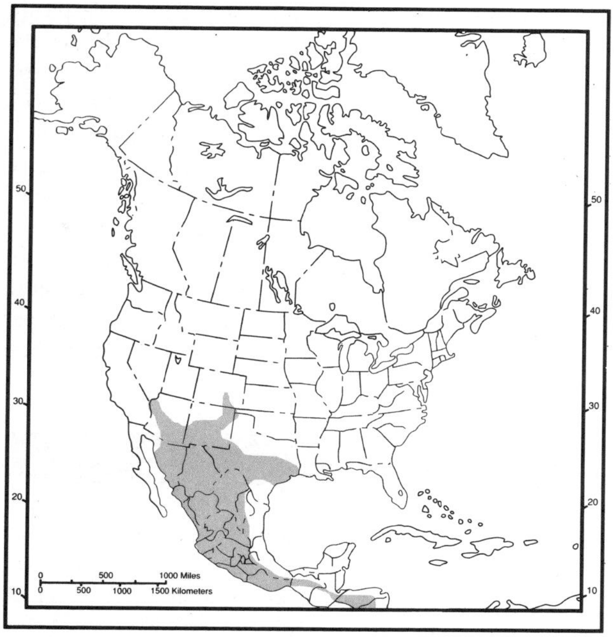

MAP 12-47. Distribution of the white-backed hog-nosed skunk (*Conepatus leuconotus*) in North America.

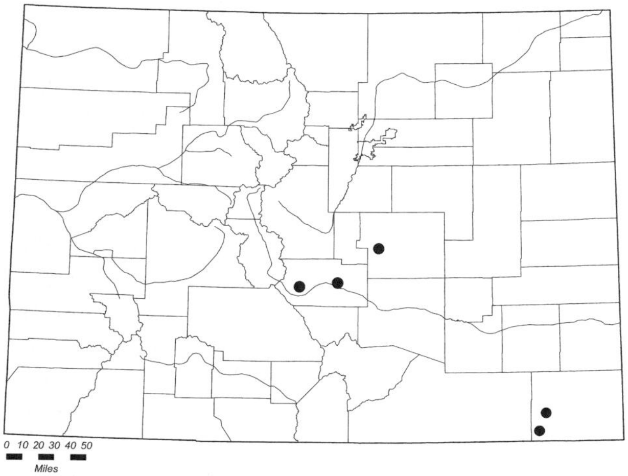

MAP 12-48. Distribution of the white-backed hog-nosed skunk (*Conepatus leuconotus*) in Colorado.

sides of the face are black and lack a white nose stripe. The nose is extended into a naked, flexible snout, hence the name "hog-nosed." The tail is usually completely white and proportionally shorter in length than that of the striped skunk. The fur is shorter and harsher than that of either the spotted or striped skunks. The claws on the front feet are long and stout. Measurements are: total length 450–900 mm; length of tail 190–290 mm; length of hindfoot 55–77 mm; length of ear 24–27; weight 1,500–4,500 g. The skull is highest in the parietal region, with the auditory bullae moderately inflated. The palate extends posteriorly past the plane of the molars and only 2 premolars are present on each side of the upper jaw. Females have 6 mammae.

Distribution

This skunk reaches its northern limits in extreme southeastern Colorado and ranges southward into Central America. The species is known from Colorado on the basis of 13 specimens and 1 clear track. The track and 2 skulls were recorded in 1996, 1997, and 2000 in Fremont, Baca, and Custer counties, respectively; all previous records were from the period 1922 to 1932 (Meaney, Ruggles, and Beauvais 2006). H. Donoho (in the early 1980s) and J. Fitzgerald (in 1991) sent questionnaires to Colorado Division of Wildlife personnel regarding the species. No reliable observations came from these inquiries, although one division biologist believed the species still occupied oakbrush-piñon habitats near Rye, Colorado (J. Fitzgerald 1993b). Chris Pague, chief conservation scientist with The Nature Conservancy in Colorado, photographed a road-killed hog-nosed skunk on Raton Pass, 1.3 km south of the Colorado state line on Interstate 25, in March 2003. Limited data from New Mexico (Meaney, Ruggles, and Beauvais 2006) showed slightly higher harvest of animals in recent years. It may be that the species is on a slight rebound in Colorado and New Mexico; however, significant effort will have to be expended to determine its status. The hog-nosed skunk in Colorado and the Oklahoma Panhandle (Caire et al. 1989) may represent a population disjunct by several hundred kilometers from their next nearest locality, in the Sandia Mountains of New Mexico (Findley et al. 1975). The present status of the species in Colorado is unknown. Two subspecies have been previously named from Colorado: *Conepatus mesoleucus fremonti* from El Paso and Fremont counties and *C. m. figginsi* from Baca County. D. Armstrong (1972) regarded the subspecific designations with skepticism but had inadequate data for a substantive conclusion. Dragoo et al. (2003) suggested that they represent 1 subspecies (*C. leuconotus figginsi*) and argued that the subspecies warrants special management.

Natural History

This is a species of rocky canyon country of the Southwest: piñon-juniper woodlands, oakbrush, shrublands with cactus, and montane shrublands; it also has been reported from desert and grassland environments (Dowler et al. 2005; Ebeling 2006; Meaney, Ruggles, and Beauvais 2006). In Colorado the few records are associated with oakbrush and piñon-juniper woodlands or oakbrush/ponderosa pine. Beauvais and Smith (2005) modeled potential habitat in Colorado. Hog-nosed skunks are thought not to thrive in contact with humans. This was once thought to be the commonest skunk species in Texas but it has declined drastically (Rosatte and Larivière 2003; Meaney, Ruggles, and Beauvais 2006).

Little information exists on the life history of the species. In Texas, they were observed to feed mostly on terrestrial insects, with beetles seeming to be of particular importance (Meaney, Ruggles, and Beauvais 2006). However, they also consumed carrion, small reptiles and mammals, and vegetable material, including prickly-pear fruit, berries, and nuts (V. Bailey 1932; W. B. Davis 1974; R. Patton 1974). They seemed to spend much of their time rooting for insects with the snout and long front claws. This rooting activity leaves large areas of disturbed litter and topsoil and is a good clue to their presence (F. Miller 1925). A difficulty in studying hog-nosed skunks is their apparent lack of interest in investigating the bait stations and baited traps commonly used in investigations of other carnivores (Meaney, Ruggles, and Beauvais 2006).

Hog-nosed skunks are thought to be solitary and mostly nocturnal (Meaney, Ruggles, and Beauvais 2006). They use rocky ledges, caves, abandoned mines, abandoned burrows, woodrat nests, and similar sites for denning. In Arizona they construct large, mounded grass nests up to a meter high in old mine shafts or caves, and they occupy woodrat dens (Hoffmeister 1986). It is not known whether they enter dormancy seasonally at their northern limits in Colorado. Most of their geographic range is far enough south that the animals can be active year-round. This is a species that might expand its range in Colorado with ongoing climate change.

Reproductive biology is not well-known. In Texas, mating occurs in late February (R. Patton 1974), with young born in April or May. Gestation takes 42 to 60 days, with litter size averaging 3. S. Ferguson et al. (1996) speculated that delayed implantation does not occur in the species. Young reach adult size by August and are thought to be sexually mature by 11 months (Meaney, Ruggles, and Beauvais 2006). Mortality factors and population dynamics are poorly understood, although roadkill appears to be significant in some areas and feral pigs may compete for foods in parts of the range. Literature on this species was reviewed by W. Howard and Marsh (1982); Rosatte (1987); Rosatte and Larivière (2003); Meaney, Ruggles, and Beauvais (2006); and Dragoo and Sheffield (2009). The species is considered a non-game mammal in Colorado (Colorado Division of Wildlife 2009c).

Family Procyonidae—Raccoons, Ringtails, and Kin

The family Procyonidae includes small to medium-sized carnivores with pointed snouts and, in many species, long tails ringed with contrasting colors and distinctive facial markings. The ears are small to medium-sized, and the face is typically short and broad. The feet have 5 digits with well-developed claws, variously non-retractile or retractile. The foot posture is plantigrade or semi-plantigrade. The number of teeth ranges from 36 to 40, with the loss of some premolars. The dental formula is 3/3, 1/1, 4/4, 2/2 = 40 teeth for Coloradan species. The incisors are unspecialized. Typical of carnivores, the canines are well developed. The carnassials, however, are poorly developed. The molars are often broad and somewhat triangular or rounded. The stomach is simple, and a cecum is absent.

Most procyonids are good climbers, typically sheltering in trees or rock crevices. They are crepuscular or nocturnal and omnivorous in their diets. The species are social to varying degrees; some are solitary, some form pairs, and others live in family groups. Females are monoestrous, having a single estrous cycle during a restricted breeding season. Males are typically about one-fifth larger than females and have a well-developed baculum.

The Procyonidae is a rather old lineage, dating from the Oligocene Epoch in North America, approximately 40 million years ago. *Procyon* and *Bassariscus* both are known from Miocene deposits (Savage and Russell 1983). Procyonids appear to be closely related to the Ursidae. There are 6 genera and 14 species in the Procyonidae, all restricted to the New World. In Colorado there are 2 genera, each represented by a single species. The Asian red panda (*Ailurus fulgens*) was included within the Procyonidae for many years. Flynn et al. (2000) suggested that the red panda is a "basic musteloid" and, as such, part of an unresolved trichotomous clade including the skunks and procyonids / mustelids. Wozencraft (2005) placed the red panda in its own family, the Ailuridae.

Key to the Species of the Family Procyonidae in Colorado

1. Animal slender; tail longer than head and body; rings on tail incomplete ventrally; posterior margin of bony palate not extending much beyond last molar . . . . Ringtail—*Bassariscus astutus*, p. 431

1' Animal robust; tail shorter than head and body; rings on tail complete ventrally; posterior margin of bony palate extending well beyond last molar . . . . Northern Raccoon—*Procyon lotor*, p. 433

Bassariscus astutus

RINGTAIL

Description

The ringtail—also called cacomistle, ringtail cat, miner's cat, rock cat, and civet cat—is a small, slender carnivore with a long tail. The dorsum is yellowish buff with black-tipped guard hairs and the venter is whitish. The tail is white marked with a black tip and 7 or 8 dark bands that are incomplete ventrally. The ears are conspicuous. The muzzle is pointed and the face is contrastingly marked with whitish areas around the eyes and below each ear. Measurements are: total length 615–850 mm; length of tail 310–440 mm; length of hindfoot 56–78 mm; length of ear 44–50 mm; weight 800–1,350 g, with males slightly larger than females. The claws are semi-retractile. The skull is slightly elongated with well-developed postorbital processes. The carnassial teeth are poorly developed. The posterior margin of the palate extends to the level of the last molars. Females have 4 mammae.

PHOTOGRAPH 12-25. Ringtail (*Bassariscus astutus*). Photograph by Joseph G. Hall.

Distribution

The ringtail inhabits arid and semiarid habitats throughout the Southwest, extending northward along the coast to central Oregon and in the Interior West to southern Idaho and northern Utah. In Colorado, most of our knowledge of its distribution is based on the work of Richard E. Richards while on the faculty at the University of Colorado at Colorado Springs. Ringtails occupy roughlands at moderate elevations (to about 2,800 m) on either side of the Continental Divide (Willey and Richards 1974; Gavin and Richards 1993), reaching northern limits in southwestern Wyoming (Crowe 1986). An individual was observed and photographed in 2008 in the town of Ouray at an elevation of about 7,790 ft. (2,375 m; B. Thomas 2008); D. and M. Beaver (personal communication) observed a ringtail near Owl Canyon, south of Livermore, Larimer County, in 2006. Presence of a ringtail in Cimarron County, in the Oklahoma Panhandle (Dalquest et al. 1990), suggests that the animals may be present in the roughlands of adjacent Baca County, Colorado. The species is probably most common in the canyon country of the southwestern part of the state. One subspecies, *Bassariscus astutus flavus*, occurs in Colorado.

MAP 12-49. Distribution of the ringtail (*Bassariscus astutus*) in North America.

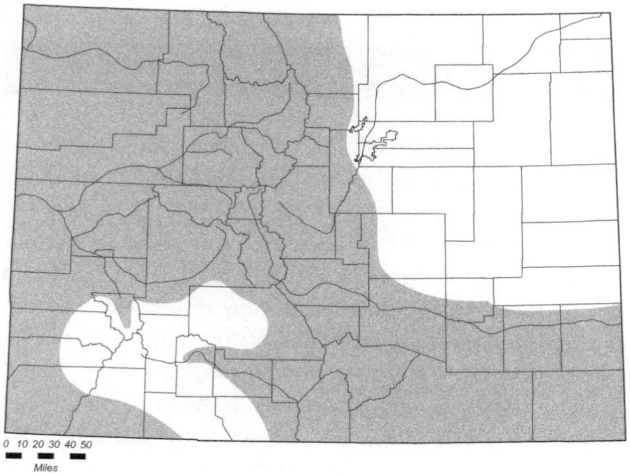

MAP 12-50. Distribution of the ringtail (*Bassariscus astutus*) in Colorado.

Natural History

In Colorado the ringtail is typically associated with rocky canyon country and foothills areas of piñon-juniper woodlands, montane shrublands, or mixed conifer-oakbrush. In California it has been reported to be common in riparian woodlands (Kaufmann 1987) and has usually been considered to remain close to surface water (Grinnell et al. 1937; Lechleitner 1969). However, studies of Coloradan animals suggest that the animals produce concentrated urine and probably do not require free water (Richards 1976).

Ringtail ecology is poorly known. Ringtails are omnivorous and their diet varies with food availability. They feed on various small mammals, including deer mice, ground squirrels, woodrats, lagomorphs, and bats. Birds, lizards, and insects may also be taken, the last being important seasonally. Fruits and arthropods may comprise over 80 percent of the diet (Kaufmann 1987; L. F. Alexander et al. 1994). Traces of carrion (deer) have also been reported. In Texas, plant material constituted more than 70 percent of the diet locally and seasonally; juniper "berries," cactus, and hackberry may be important (Toweill and Teer 1977).

Ringtails are agile, active carnivores and excellent climbers. They can move rapidly up rock faces using such techniques as chimney stemming, ricocheting, and power leaps. The hindfoot rotates 180 degrees during vertical descents (Trapp 1972). They appear to be mostly nocturnal, shy, and retiring animals and are seldom observed even in areas where they are relatively common. Ringtails den in rock crevices, under large boulders, in hollow logs and trees, or in old buildings.

Mating occurs in the spring, generally in March in Utah. Gestation takes 51–54 days. The young are born in late April, May, or early June. Captive animals can produce a second litter upon the death of the first. Litters average 3 to 4 young, with a range of 1 to 5 (E. Bailey 1974; Poglayen-Neuwall and Poglayen-Neuwall 1980). The young are altricial and weigh about 28 g at birth. The eyes open during the third and fourth weeks, and the teeth erupt during the fourth or fifth week. Trapp (1972) and Toweill and Toweill (1978) reported that only the female raises the young. The male may be totally excluded from the den (Kaufmann 1987). The young begin foraging with the female at about 2 months of age, and weaning occurs at 3 to 5 months. Both sexes are reproductively mature at about 10 months of age (E. Bailey 1974; Toweill and Toweill 1978; Poglayen-Neuwall and Poglayen-Neuwall 1980).

Densities range from about 2 animals per square kilometer in juniper and oak woodlands in Texas to 20 animals per square kilometer in riparian woodlands in central California (Kaufmann 1987). In Utah, densities were 1.5 to 2.9 animals per square kilometer in piñon-juniper and riparian woodlands (Trapp 1978). Populations in favorable areas in Colorado are probably at densities similar to or lower than those observed in Utah. Annual population peaks coincide with birth of young in June. Home ranges in Texas were linear and averaged 20 ha for females and 43 ha for males (Toweill and Teer 1980). In Utah, monthly home ranges averaged 136 ha (range, 49 to 233 ha), but individuals also showed indications of shifting on a seasonal basis (Trapp 1978).

The social behavior of ringtails is unknown but home ranges often overlap and some individuals may use common latrines, where scat piles accumulate (Trapp 1978). Males mark their home ranges with urine. Both sexes have anal glands whose secretions are emitted when the animal is alarmed. The animals have been reported to travel in pairs but there is no compelling evidence that permanent bonds are formed. The vocalizations include apparent contact calls, distress and alarm calls, and threat sounds (Poglayen-Neuwall and Poglayen-Neuwall 1980; Willey and Richards 1981).

Mortality factors are not well-known but great horned owls, snakes, and domestic cats and dogs have been reported to kill ringtails. Trapping and encounters with automobiles also take their toll. Until 1996, ringtails were listed as furbearers in Colorado, with harvests from 1974 to 1991 ranging from none to almost 600 annually (J. Fitzgerald 1993b). Season was closed on their take in 1997. Although we often think of the species as primarily an animal of the Western Slope, Fremont County had the highest estimated harvest from 1982 to 1991. The literature on the species was reviewed by Kaufmann (1987), Poglayen-Neuwall and Toweill (1988), and Gehrt (2003). The Colorado Division of Wildlife (2009f) includes the species (as "ring-tailed cat") on its list of small game and furbearers following several years of protection from harvest.

PHOTOGRAPH 12-26. Northern raccoon (*Procyon lotor*). Photograph by Walker Van Riper and R. J. Niedrach. All rights reserved. Photo Archives, Denver Museum of Nature and Science.

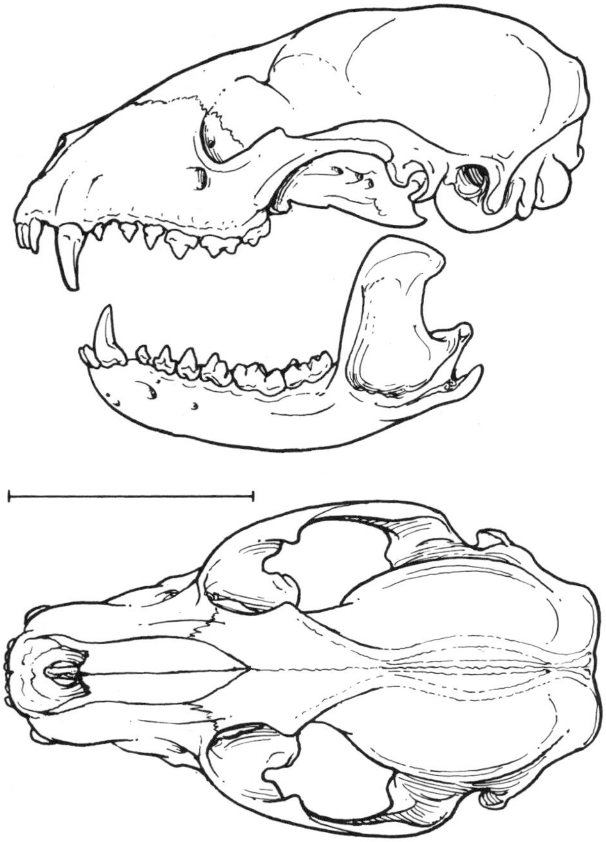

FIGURE 12-5. Lateral and dorsal views of the skull of a northern raccoon (*Procyon lotor*). Scale = 5 cm.

Procyon lotor

NORTHERN RACCOON

Description

Raccoons are stocky carnivores with bushy tails and relatively long legs. The forepaws have elongated digits adapted for grasping and manipulating food. The dorsal color is blackish to brownish gray and the underparts are paler grayish brown. The tail has 4 to 7 dark bands separated by paler bands of hair. The dark bands are usually complete ventrally. A blackish mask extends across the area of the eyes. The ears are conspicuous and rounded. The feet are plantigrade. Measurements are: total length 600–950 mm;

MAP 12-51. Distribution of the northern raccoon (*Procyon lotor*) in North America.

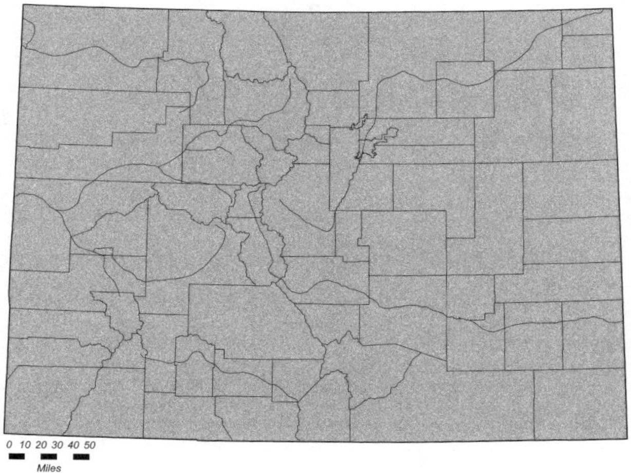

MAP 12-52. Distribution of the northern raccoon (*Procyon lotor*) in Colorado.

length of tail 190–405 mm; length of hindfoot 80–140 mm; weight 1.5–22.0 kg, with an average of 3–9 kg. Height at the shoulder is about 230–300 mm. Males are typically slightly larger than females. The skull is stout with prominent postorbital processes. The cheekteeth are robust, and the carnassials poorly developed. The posterior margin of the palate extends well beyond the last molars. The animals lack a cecum and the intestine is short. Females have 6 mammae and males have a well-developed baculum.

Distribution

Raccoons are widely distributed across North America from northern Mexico to much of southern Canada. Raccoons apparently have undergone considerable range extension since the early 1940s (G. Sanderson 1987). This extension is surely because of their adaptability and ability to benefit from anthropogenic changes; Larivière (2004) suggested that climatic warming has contributed to range expansion in Canada. Raccoons occur throughout Colorado along riparian corridors to elevations of about 3,050 m (10,000 ft.). One of us (JPF) routinely saw raccoon tracks and had reports of tracks from along the South Platte River in South Park at 2,900 m (9,500 ft.) in elevation during the late 1960s and 1970s. Raccoons are reported from Trappers Lake at an elevation of about 3,050 m (10,000 ft.) in northeastern Garfield County (McKean and Burkhard 1978). As D. Armstrong (1972) and R. Finley et al. (1976) have noted, the paucity of specimens in museum collections makes it difficult to assess taxonomic relationships of Coloradan populations. D. Armstrong (1972) mapped the subspecies *Procyon lotor hirtus* on the eastern plains, *P. l. pallidus* in the western third of the state, and *P. l. mexicanus* in the San Luis Valley. R. Finley (1995) discussed range expansion of *P. l. hirtus* through the mountains of Colorado and provided evidence that it (rather than *P. l. pallidus*) represents the subspecies along the Green and Colorado river drainages; he suggested that the extermination of the wolf may have allowed much of the western range expansion of the raccoon.

Natural History

The raccoon has been studied intensively, especially in eastern North America. Detailed studies have not been made in the Rocky Mountain region, however, where the animals have increased remarkably in recent decades. The raccoon is adaptable and occupies habitats ranging from hardwood swamps, marshlands, and upland mixed or deciduous forests in the East to riparian gallery forests, montane parks, and semidesert shrublands in the West. It is typically found near water and often in and near human settlements (C. A. Jones et al. 2003). In Colorado the animals are commonest in lowland riparian habitats, irrigated croplands, and urbanized areas of the eastern plains and foothills but are not uncommon along streams and reservoirs in mountain parklands.

In many situations, including wetlands and cottonwood river-bottom communities on the eastern plains and urbanizing areas along the Front Range of Colorado, raccoons, striped skunks, and red foxes (and opossums in areas farther east) form mesocarnivore assemblages where they may interact for resources, including den sites and food, or where anthropogenic food sources can allow for concentration of animals. In such situations these species may be selecting for the same general habitat configuration, including large- to medium-diameter trees, snags, proximity to water, and interspersion of habitat patches (creating productive edges) (Ladine 1997; Dion et al. 2000; Chamberlain et al. 2003; Gardner and Sunquist 2003; Prange et al. 2004; S. Frey and Conover 2006). They may also be searching for and using the same foods, for example ground-nesting waterfowl or passerines (Larivière and Messier 1998b; Larivière 1999a; Dion et al. 2000; S. Frey and Conover 2006).

Raccoons need suitable den sites, which may be hollow trees, brush piles, logs, rock crevices, caves, culverts, storm sewers, burrows excavated by other mammals, muskrat houses, or buildings (usually abandoned but sometimes even while occupied by humans). Henner et al. (2004) reported that female raccoons in mixed agricultural-prairie landscapes used tree-cavity dens when rearing young while males made more use of burrows and brush piles. Dens were selected for proximity to roads, habitat edges, and crops. They are opportunistic and make much use of abandoned burrows (Berner and Gysel 1967; Shirer and Fitch 1970). In south-central Wyoming, J. Fitzgerald (unpublished) recovered raccoon skulls up to 10 km from water and tree cover in white-tailed prairie dog towns and observed their tracks around playas in such country.

Raccoons are most active from sunset to sunrise, although at times they may forage in the daylight. Most activity occurs before midnight (Ellis 1964; Ladine 1997). During winter, they may sleep for extended periods, especially if snow cover accumulates. Basal metabolism and body temperature do not change appreciably during winter. Commensal denning and use of tree cavities for den sites can significantly reduce heat loss (Gehrt 2003). During warm spells they may arouse and become active, depending on stored fat reserves rather than feeding (W. Hamilton 1936; Stuewer 1943; Sharp and Sharp 1956). Late summer and fall weight gains may be up to 50 percent of the animals' lean body mass in colder climates (Gehrt 2003). In Colorado the length of winter inactivity varies from year to year, and in mild winters the animals are active practically year-round.

Literally hundreds of different food items have been reported in the literature, varying with season and locality. Except during spring, plant material is more important than animal foods. Raccoons are omnivorous opportunists, feeding on berries, garden and field crops, mast (acorns), and fruits, including wild plums, cherries, and grapes. Animal food consists mostly of arthropods, especially crayfish, but birds, eggs, small mammals, fish, snakes, lizards, and amphibians are also eaten. Carrion from such large mammals as horses, cattle, and deer is consumed occasionally. Along the South Platte River in Colorado during fall, plant material constituted 73 percent of the diet and animal matter comprised the remaining 27 percent (of which 13 percent was insects). More than half of the food volume was corn (Tester 1953).

Raccoons breed from December to June in Kansas (Stains 1956), and the cycle in Colorado, at least in eastern Colorado, probably is similar. The peak of breeding occurs in February, with young born in April or May. Mating systems range from polygyny to promiscuity, depending on local situations (Gehrt 2003). Most authors have reported a gestation period of 63 to 65 days (Kaufmann 1982). Ovulation is spontaneous. Copulation may last for an hour. Females may have a second estrus if the first litter is lost or if the female fails to become pregnant (Gehrt and Fritzell 1998; Gehrt 2003). Pregnant females typically move into a birthing den several days before parturition and may tear pieces of wood, bark, or similar materials to form a shallow bed. Litter size ranges from 1 to 8, with a mean of 3 to 4 (Hayssen et al. 1993; Gehrt 2003). Sex ratios of litters approximate 1:1, although sex ratios vary widely for adults.

The young are altricial, with eyes and ears opening at about 20 days. Teeth begin to erupt at about 1 month of age. Young raccoons begin to walk in about the fifth week and can run and climb by 7 weeks. After the eighth week the young are able to leave the den and follow the mother when she forages. Young are typically weaned by 3 months of age (W. Hamilton 1936; Stuewer 1943; Montgomery 1964, 1968, 1969). About 40 to 55 percent of juvenile females mate successfully, and the remainder breed as yearlings (Stuewer 1943; J. Wood 1955). Late litters may be the offspring of juvenile females (G. Sanderson and Nalbandov 1973). Males are sexually mature as juveniles but are not thought to contribute significantly to breeding until they are yearlings.

The typical social unit consists of a mother and her young of the year. Matrilineal assemblages of related females and their offspring also occur (Gehrt and Fritzell 1998). In some cases the young disperse in the fall and early winter, but in most instances they stay with the female through the winter and disperse in spring or summer (Sharp and Sharp 1956; D. Schneider et al. 1971; Fritzell 1977; Gehrt and Fritzell 1998). In North Dakota some yearling females were observed to stay with the mother and not disperse (Fritzell 1978a). Sometimes yearlings leave in pairs and stay together until late spring. Most adults seem to be solitary, although congregations of 2 to 2 dozen may share winter dens, and in Texas and Kansas, groups of adult males have been reported traveling and denning together (Gehrt et al. 1990; Gehrt and Fritzell 1998). Whereas pairs and small groups likely represent sibling associations or family groups, larger aggregations probably do not. Temporary feeding groups form in areas of abundant food resources. Generally, as the breeding season approaches, the incidence of fighting among adults increases and they become more solitary.

Dominance hierarchies form in certain situations. Raccoons appear to recognize their neighbors and form dominant-subordinate relations with them more quickly than with strangers (Barash 1974). Probably, dominance relationships come into play at concentrated food resources and during the breeding season and are facilitated by recognition of neighbors.

Mutual avoidance plays a major part in day-to-day activities. The degree to which raccoons actually are territorial is not clear (Lotze and Anderson 1979; Kaufmann 1982). Males in low-quality habitat or areas with patchy resources are territorial (Fritzell 1978b). On North Dakota prairies, home ranges of males rarely overlapped by more than 10 percent, and radio-tracked males rarely came closer to each other than 2 km (Fritzell 1978a). However, Gehrt and Fritzell (1998) found males in southern Texas often forming small social units. Home ranges of females overlapped extensively, as did male-female home ranges.

Ghert (2003) found most home range estimates to be from 50 to 300 ha. In colder areas, home range size decreases in winter. In optimal urban habitat in Ohio, home ranges were only 5 ha (C. Hoffmann and Gottschang 1977), whereas in prairie regions in North Dakota, home ranges averaged 2,560 ha for males and 806 ha for females (Fritzell 1978b). Raccoon home ranges on the Bear River Refuge in Utah averaged 360 ha (S. Frey and Conover 2006). In Illinois, home ranges were smallest in urban areas (21–37 ha) and largest in rural areas (71–182 ha), with the relatively predictable resources of urbanized areas resulting in the smaller, more stable home ranges (Prange et al. 2004). In Colorado, most home ranges in rural areas are probably linear because of dependence on riparian habitat. Densities of 0.5 to 1.0 animals per square kilometer and 1.5 to 3.2 animals per square kilometer have been found in North Dakota and Manitoba, respectively (W. Cowan 1973; Fritzell 1978b); similar densities can be expected for Colorado outside of human settlements (where dense populations are subsidized with artificial shelter and food resources, including garbage, pet food, and birdseed).

Most mortality in raccoons appears to be attributable to humans or to starvation. Raccoons are frequent traffic casualties. Thousands of raccoons are hunted and trapped annually in North America (Shieff and Baker 1987). In Colorado, raccoons are classified as small game and furbearers with a 4-month season (Colorado Division of Wildlife 2009f). Prior to the ban on trapping, several thousand were taken annually, with harvest increasing steeply from the 1970s to 1986 to about 4,400 animals (J. Fitzgerald 1993b). In recent years, annual harvest is estimated at about 1,800 (Table 4-3). Raccoons may live up to 16 years in the wild, but few live past their second year. In Missouri, only an estimated 1 raccoon in 100 lived to age 7 (G. Sanderson 1951). Estimated population turnover time was 7.4 years, with adult mortality averaging 56 percent. Similar figures were reported for Manitoba, where yearling mortality was 60 percent and mortality for all age classes combined was more than 50 percent (W. Cowan 1973). Mountain lions, bobcats, wolves, coyotes, gray and red foxes, and great horned owls are predators of raccoons. Raccoons harbor a wide variety of endo- and ectoparasites. Canine distemper is probably the most effective disease regulating populations (V. Robinson et al. 1957; Habermann et al. 1958), including populations in Colorado. The extensive literature on raccoons was reviewed by Lotze and Anderson (1979), Kaufmann (1982), G. Sanderson (1987), and Gehrt (2003).

13

Order Perissodactyla

Odd-toed Hoofed Mammals

Horses, tapirs, rhinos, asses, and zebras constitute the order Perissodactyla, the odd-toed ungulates. Perissodactyls were a diverse and dominant group during the early and mid-Tertiary, ranging across North America, Eurasia, and Africa. The fossil history was reviewed by Hooker (2005) and K. Rose (2006). Nine of the 12 recognized families are extinct and the natural distribution of the remaining wild species is now restricted to parts of Asia, southeastern Europe, Africa, the East Indies, and parts of South and Central America. Disappearance of ancient perissodactyls generally coincided with expansion of the even-toed ungulates, the artiodactyls. Domestic horses (*Equus caballus*) and asses (*E. asinus*) have been introduced locally in various parts of the world, including Colorado and other western states, where feral herds have become established.

Perissodactyls are called ungulates because they stand on hooves, or ungules (a stance termed unguligrade), or on digits (digitigrade), and they exhibit significant loss or modification of the metacarpal and metatarsal bones, most notably an increase in length. There has been reduction in the number of digits. Most members of the order have only 1 or 3 weight-bearing toes, and remaining toes are broader than those of artiodactyls. Tapirs are the exception to this "odd-toed" formula, as their forefeet have 4 digits, although the outermost is reduced in size; the hindfeet have 3 functional digits. In all perissodactyls the main axis of the foot passes through the third and longest digit, a condition termed mesaxonic. In equids, only the ancestral third (middle) digit is functional. The history of the evolution of the foot in the perissodactyls is well preserved in the fossil record.

The skull is elongate. The nasals are wide posteriorly. An alisphenoid canal is present. The dental formula totals 24–44, and the cheekteeth are lophodont. Perissodactyls vary considerably in size. Some tapirs and smaller equids weigh less than 300 kg and are less than 1 m high at the shoulder. At the other extreme, the white rhinoceros is one of the largest living terrestrial mammals, weighing up to 3,600 kg and standing 1.6 to 2.0 m high at the shoulder. Male perissodactyls lack a baculum. Females have inguinal mammae.

Modern perissodactyls are specialized to exploit grasslands and open brushy country (horses, rhinos, zebras) or dense tropical forests (tapirs). All species are grazers or browsers able to handle relatively coarse foods. Perissodactyls are "hindgut digesters" (in contrast to the ruminant artiodactyls, described in Chapter 14, which are foregut digesters). The stomach is simple and breakdown of cellulose occurs largely in the small intestine and cecum. Perissodactyls are slow to reach sexual maturity and often are long-lived, sometimes living more than 30 years.

There are 3 families, 6 genera, and 16 species of living perissodactyls (Grubb 2005a). In Colorado the only wild representative is the feral horse.

Family Equidae—Horses and Kin

The family Equidae evolved mostly in North America and secondarily in Asia. In North America many species arose from the Early Eocene to Pleistocene times but none survived to the Recent. The evolution of horses and their ancestors is complex in terms of dental and limb morphology as well as in ecological roles. Some were grazers and others were mostly browsers while the number of digits evolved toward the single hoof. S. Jenkins and Ashley (2003) provided a thorough summary of equid evolution and dispersal in the New World.

The family Equidae includes 7 Recent species, all in the genus *Equus*, represented by 3 species of African zebras (a fourth species of zebra, the South African quagga, went extinct in the nineteenth century; Grubb 2005a), 3 asses (the onager, the kiang, and the domestic ass, of which small-sized breeds are called donkeys or burros), and the horse (including the distinctive Przewalski's horse of Central Asia). All species of *Equus* have a single functional hooved digit on each foot. The radius and ulna are fused and weight is borne on the radius. In the hindleg, the tibia is enlarged and bears weight, but the fibula is reduced. Canines are present in mature males but reduced or absent in females. Cheekteeth are homodont and lophodont with high crowns. The skull is long, with the orbit completely enclosed by bone. The nasals are long and narrow, tapering to pointed ends anteriorly. Hair is well developed; all species have coarse manes and long, straight tail hairs.

Equids evolved on open hard ground where running speed was an advantage. They developed the most extreme alteration of the perissodactyl limb, which became long and slender. Only the third digit is functional. The calcaneus does not articulate with the fibula and the astragalus has a grooved, pulley-like surface for articulation with the tibia. The femur has a prominent third trochanter lacking in the artiodactyls.

Equids are highly social, forming herds of a few animals to a hundred or more during seasonal concentrations. Herds are family units, harems, or bachelor herds. Most equids are mobile and nomadic, moving in response to forage quality and availability and sources of free water. Some are territorial. Most Old World species are classified as endangered, vulnerable, or threatened because of loss of habitat and human hunting for trophies, hides, or meat. *Horses*, by the late preeminent American paleontologist G. G. Simpson (1951), is the classic study of horse evolution; MacFadden (1994) and J. Franzen (2009) provided more recent reviews.

Speculation about the cause of extinction of native North American horses ranges from hunting by early humans to climatic change and increasing competition from artiodactyls. Equids eventually were reestablished in North America from stock brought by the Spanish to Mexico as early as the mid-sixteenth century.

Equus caballus

FERAL HORSE

Description

Horses are highly variable in coat color, and a wonderful vocabulary exists to describe the many shades and patterns: bay, chestnut, roan, palomino, sorrel, buckskin, flea-bit gray, and paint, to name just a few. The following measurements apply to feral horses, which are usually smaller than domestic saddle horses and much smaller than most draft breeds. Adults range from less than 300 kg to more than 500 kg in weight, and males are heavier than females. Shoulder height is usually 1,300–1,400 mm. The dental formula is 3/3, 0–1/0–1, 3/3, 3/3 = 36 to 40 teeth. Age can be determined by tooth eruption and wear (Bone 1964).

It is sometimes impossible to distinguish feral horses from domestic herds ranging on public lands. Generally, small bands of nervous, small, scruffy-looking horses without apparent brands and living well away from ranch buildings may be feral or "wild" horses.

Distribution

Although many faunal works on mammals have tended to ignore horses or pay them only token attention as "intro-

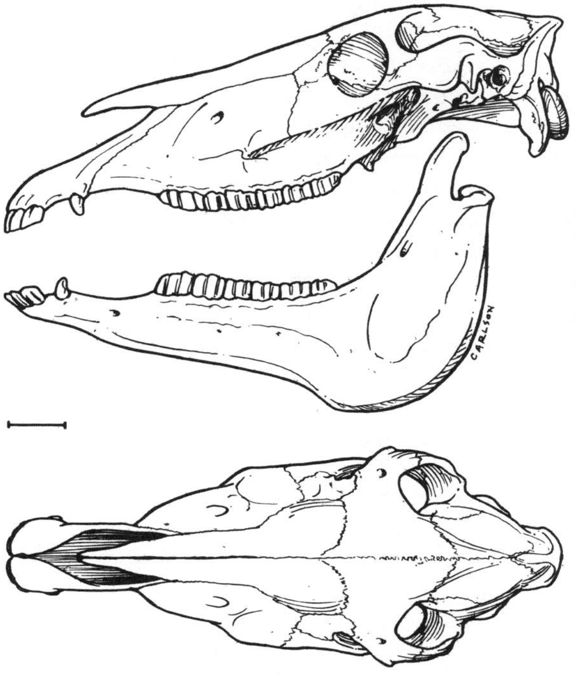

FIGURE 13-1. Skull of a horse (*Equus caballus*). The presence of a well-developed upper canine suggests that it is a male. Scale = 5 cm.

PHOTOGRAPH 13-1. Feral horses (*Equus caballus*). Photograph by Joseph Van Wormer. All rights reserved. Photo Archives, Denver Museum of Nature and Science.

ductions," they are important inhabitants of ecosystems in several western states and their impacts on the environment cannot be ignored as state and federal agencies attempt to manage public land in the West.

Domestic horses were influential in ecosystems of Colorado at least by the early eighteenth century, as indicated by their depiction in probable Comanche petroglyphs from along Two Buttes Creek in east-central Baca County (M. Mitchell 2004). In his classic monograph on the expansion of horses on the Great Plains and adjacent areas, Secoy (1953) mapped the southern San Luis Valley of Colorado as being within the "Horse Frontier" by 1615, and the zone with horses included most of southern Colorado by 1675. By 1710, the Horse Frontier encompassed most of Colorado, and by 1750 the southeastern part of the state was within the advancing "Gun Frontier" as well. By 1790, all of eastern Colorado had both horses and guns. Large populations of feral horses ranged parts of western North America in the 1700s and 1800s but they were exterminated as habitat declined and competition with domestic stock increased.

Today, feral horses occur in all of the western states except Washington, and about half of the estimated 42,000 animals are found in Nevada (S. Jenkins and Ashley 2003). In Colorado, populations are centered on BLM lands in 4 wild horse "Herd Management Areas": Piceance Basin / East Douglas Creek (west of Meeker), Little Book Cliffs (northeast of Grand Junction), Sandwash Basin (northwest of Maybell, Moffat County), and Spring Creek (southwest of Montrose).

Natural History

Feral horses are associated with semiarid grasslands and shrublands in western North America. In Colorado the animals inhabit shrublands and piñon-juniper woodlands with an understory of grasses. From 80 to more than 90 percent of the diet is grasses and sedges. During winter a variety of browse is consumed, including sagebrush, greasewood, saltbush, rabbitbrush, mountain mahogany, juniper, Douglas-fir, and spruce (Hubbard and Hansen 1976; R. Hansen and Clark 1977; R. Hansen et al. 1977). Aspen bark is also consumed when available.

Coprophagy (consuming feces) is not uncommon. Microbes in the small intestine and cecum process fibrous plant material, but not as effectively as the complex foregut (esophagus and stomach) of ruminants. Ruminants are more efficient than horses in deriving energy and nutrients from their foods, which are often broad-leafed plants with relatively low fiber content. Horses, on the other hand, harvest, digest, and eliminate their food faster, allowing them to consume large amounts of lower-quality forage (often grasses with high fiber) in a shorter period than

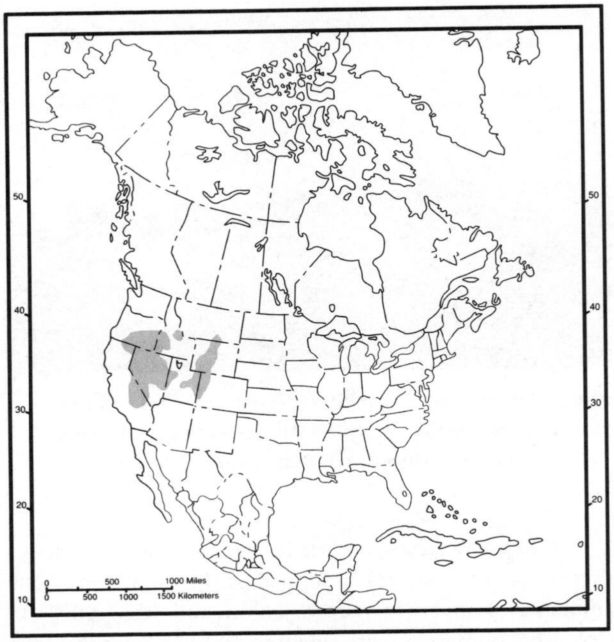

MAP 13-1. Distribution of the feral horse (*Equus caballus*) in North America.

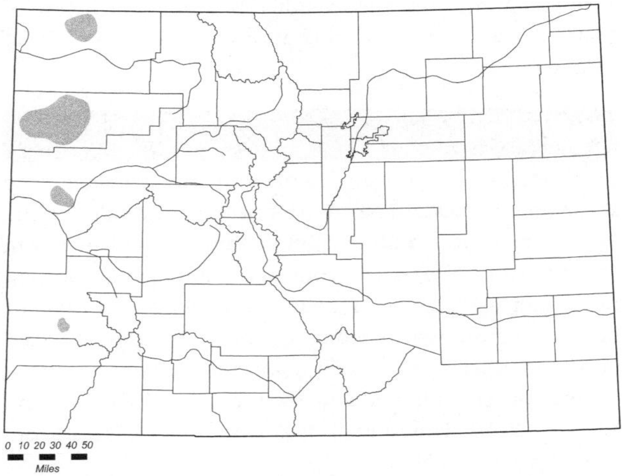

MAP 13-2. Distribution of the feral horse (*Equus caballus*) in Colorado.

most ruminants. In turn, these differences in food processing may force equids to spend more time foraging than ruminants do, possibly introducing them to greater risk of predation (S. Jenkins and Ashley 2003).

Feral horses are often blamed for deterioration of range conditions and/or competition with native wildlife or livestock for resources. Many studies—including Hobbs et al. (1996a, 1966b) in Colorado—have compared diets among horses, cattle, and wild ungulates to evaluate potential competition for resources. In the Douglas Mountain area northwest of Craig, dietary overlap of horses and deer was 1 percent, between cattle and deer was 4 percent, and between horses and cattle was 77 percent (R. Hansen et al. 1977). Wild horses and cattle selected food plants in significantly similar order. Most studies have not demonstrated significant resource competition (Beever 2003; S. Jenkins and Ashley 2003). Hubbard and Hansen (1976) compared diets of herbivores in 3 elevational vegetation zones in the Piceance Basin. Dietary overlap with cattle and horses versus mule deer was always less than 11 percent. Similarly, studies of horse impacts on vegetation are often inconclusive or contradictory.

Feral horses must have free water and typically visit water holes at least daily, most frequently in late afternoon. Berger (1985, 1986) reported that feral horses dominated native ungulates at water holes in the Great Basin, and in water-limited areas horses may impact native species like pronghorn and bighorn sheep negatively. Most research on wild horses has been done in the Great Basin; more work on impacts of the animals in the eastern part of their range—the Colorado Plateau and the Wyoming Basin—would be of interest.

Feral horses have complex social behaviors and lone individuals are seldom observed. Home ranges of bands frequently overlap and are associated with the distribution of available water. Herds usually remain within 6 to 8 km of a water source. Feral horses are generally not territorial and do not defend grazing areas or water holes (Berger 1977). Rather, social organization involves harems. Bands usually consist of a stallion, several mares, and their young. The mating system is polygynous and it had been thought that relatively few males breed. Recent use of microsatellite markers, however, suggests that subordinate males can contribute up to 52 percent of breeding (S. Jenkins and Ashley 2003)—in aggregate, more than the dominant stallion.

Mares are less aggressive than stallions and form complex associations with other mares in the band, establishing dominance hierarchies within the harem. Adult mares in a harem rarely move more than 300 m from other members of the herd. At parturition, females do move away from the herd, sometimes accompanied by non-pregnant mares. As young males reach 1–3 years of age, they are forced from the group by the dominant stallion and form small bachelor herds. Such herds are led by a young stallion, dominant in the bachelor herd but not old or strong enough to usurp a harem for himself. Breeding females are reported to expel younger females from some herds. These younger females are typically taken into harems of other males.

Dominance is maintained by a variety of displays and threat postures, including laying back of the ears, open-mouth displays, arching of the neck, and head shaking. When these displays escalate, actual fighting ensues, including biting and kicking. Flehmen is a characteristic behavior that involves curling the upper lip to facilitate passage of sexual odors through the incisive foramina to the vomeronasal organ. Flehmen is exhibited during pre-copulatory activity or during examination of urine, feces, or the fresh afterbirth.

Horses communicate through a variety of vocalizations, including nickers, squeals, neighs, snorts, and screams. Individual grooming, dusting, and rolling are common and mutual grooming is a daily activity that helps maintain herd integrity. Stallions do not groom or allow grooming by immature males. Use of common defecation sites may result in formation of "stud piles" of putative social value. Because males most commonly contribute to these piles, they were once thought to represent territorial markers, but because territoriality has not been observed, their function is not clear.

Over much of their range, feral horses can breed year-round but most breeding occurs during spring and summer. The average gestation is 340 days. Parturition (or "foaling") usually occurs in April, May, or June. Postpartum estrus follows about 1 week after foaling. However, in many wild herds, females only foal in alternate years. Reproductive success usually varies from 20 to 40 foals per 100 mares, with up to a 65 percent annual foaling rate for a population in Montana (Garrott and Taylor 1990). Sex ratios are close to even in foals. Young animals are protected by the mother and other herd members. Horses are long-lived, and domestic animals often live more than 30 years. This longevity is associated with a longer time to reach reproductive maturation compared with artiodactyls of similar size. Feral mares in many herds can foal as young as 2 years of age and may continue to bear young to 22 years of age (Garrott 1991b). Stallions seldom have an opportunity to breed before they are 6 years old (Garrott, Eagle, and Plotka 1991). Males displacing a harem stallion have been reported to cause recently conceived mares to abort through forced copulation. Re-insemination by the new stallion results in the mare foaling his progeny and not that of his predecessor (Berger 1983).

Mortality in wild horses is associated mostly with severe winter weather and starvation. In fact, adult survival rates of 95 percent have been documented in Nevada (Berger 1986) and 97 percent in Montana (Garrott and Taylor 1990; Garrott, Siniff, and Eberhardt 1991). Females have higher survival rates after age 5 than do males, and most mortality occurs in animals older than 15 (Garrott 1991b). M. Wolfe (1980) reported that the bands on Douglas Mountain had 21 percent foals and 7 percent yearlings in 1977. Few animals prey on feral horses, although mountain lions take some individuals, especially foals (J. Turner et al. 1992). Historically, feral horses were shot for pet food or simply to reduce competition with domestic cattle, sheep, horses, and big game.

Encouraged especially by animal rights groups, Congress enacted the Wild and Free-roaming Horse and Burro Protection Act in 1971, asserting federal ownership of feral horses on public lands. The act states that "wild free-roaming horses and burros are living symbols of the historic and pioneer spirit of the west; that they contribute to the diversity of life forms within the nation and enrich the lives of the American people." Details on the program (including adoption opportunities) are available on-line: http://www.blm.gov/co/st/en/BLM_Programs/wild_horse_and_burro.html. Presently, periodic roundups and sale of captured animals are used to control populations. However, research is now being conducted on the use of chemosterilants and other methods of birth control (Garrott 1991a).

The literature on feral horses was reviewed by Slade and Godfrey (1982), D. Bennett and Hoffmann (1999), and S. Jenkins and Ashley (2003). Stillman (2008) provided a literary, and broadly interdisciplinary, review of North American horses, including evolutionary diversification and local extinction, restoration by Spanish conquistadores in the sixteenth century, and eventual resumption of an important role, as mustangs, in native ecosystems in some parts of North America.

There is some debate as to whether the wild horses of the Intermountain West should be considered "feral" animals—escapees from domestication—or native wildlife. The majority view is that native North American horses went extinct as part of the broad (perhaps in part anthropogenic) megafaunal extinction at the end of the Pleistocene (for reviews, see Kurtén and Anderson 1980; Frison 1998; P. Martin 2005). Fossil mitochondrial DNA from Alaskan specimens of the Pleistocene species *E. lambi* is within the range of variation of modern *E. caballus* (Vilà et al. 2001). Ludwig et al. (2009) estimated the time of domestication of horses in eastern Europe and western Asia to the third millennium BC, so roughly 5,000 years ago, well after the apparent extinction of native horses in North America.

Depending on one's definition of "species" (see Mayr 1965 for a review of some of the options), that suggests to some that domestic horses are conspecific with some Pleistocene species.

Kirkpatrick and Fazio (2005) argued that the domestic horse is a North American native and therefore deserving of management as wildlife, rather than as a feral mammal (as is the assumption of the Federal Wild and Free-roaming Horse and Burro Protection Act). It is not certain, of course, whether recognition of horses as native wildlife would change management protocols. Wildlife species generally are managed under state laws and regulations, and in Colorado (as elsewhere in the United States) ungulate species are all subject to regulated hunting as game mammals.

14

Order Artiodactyla

Even-toed Hoofed Mammals

The Artiodactyla is one of several orders of hoofed mammals, or ungulates. Ungulates (which, in addition to artiodactyls, include the living horses, tapirs, and rhinos as well as a rich diversity of extinct forms) are mostly adapted to covering large distances quickly, allowing them to exploit the abundant but often diffuse plant resources of open country. Usually the limbs are elongate, toes are reduced in number, and the collarbone (clavicle) is lost, with accompanying reduction in lateral mobility of the limb, a trade-off for increased efficiency of fore-aft motion. Artiodactyls represent the zenith of these ungulate trends, and the order includes most of the living species of ungulates. In all artiodactyls the first digits ("thumb" in front, "big toe" behind) are missing. The second and fifth digits are reduced in more primitive living artiodactyls or lost completely in more advanced forms. The main weight of the body passes equally between the third and fourth digits in most species. One genus, *Tayassu*, the peccaries (family Tayassuidae), has 4 front toes per foot and 3 hind toes. In advanced artiodactyls the metacarpal bones of the front limbs and the metatarsal bones of the hind limbs are reduced in number and fused to form the cannon bones. The smallest of the artiodactyls is the mouse deer, *Tragulus*, which weighs about 8 kg, and the largest is *Hippopotamus*, which weighs up to 4,500 kg. For a technical appreciation of artiodactyls in particular, see Prothero and Foss (2007); Prothero and Schoch (2003) summarized ungulates in general, past and present. Some of the numerous taxonomic challenges within the artiodactyls were reviewed by Marcot (2007), synthesizing traditional "skin and skull" taxonomy with paleontology and molecular systematics.

The dental formula of artiodactyls varies, although in many groups the upper incisors and upper canines are reduced or absent. In some species the canines are retained and form tusks. The cheekteeth range from bunodont to selenodont and may be either high- or low-crowned. Molars usually are more complex than are the premolars. Many species have either horns or antlers that project from the skull. The mode of development of these cranial armaments (or adornments) helps with classification at the level of families. Emlen (2008) reviewed cranial armament of artiodactyls in the broad context of the zoology of animal weapons.

More primitive (plesiomorphic) artiodactyls have a simple stomach (as seen in pigs), but most living artiodactyls are ruminants, which have a complex "stomach" with 3 or 4 chambers (the anterior parts of which actually are elaborations of the esophagus). As it is harvested, forage enters the first compartment, the rumen (or "paunch"), a storage chamber whose bacteria help to digest some of the cellulose in the diet. In the reticulum, the moistened, pulpy food is formed into cud. From the reticulum the cud moves back to the mouth for further chewing. Then it is re-swallowed and shunted to the omasum, whence finally it moves to the abomasum, the true stomach. There, digestive juices subject it to further breakdown. This complex arrangement means that ruminants can gather large quantities of food rapidly and then retire to the relative safety of cover (or the herd) to ruminate, processing the food at leisure. The result is much more thorough processing of low-quality herbage than is possible for non-ruminants. The cecum is small. Because of the generally large size and the tendency of many species to live and move in herds, artiodactyls often are important in ecosystem function, influencing physiognomic structure and species composition, biogeochemical cycling (especially nitrogen), fire behavior, and other factors (Hobbs 1996).

Artiodactyls arose in the Eocene Epoch, approximately 60 million years ago, and reached their greatest diversity in the Miocene, 25 million years ago (see Theodor et al. 2005; K. Rose 2006; and Janis 2007). Today there are 10 families, 89 genera, and about 240 species (Grubb 2005b) distributed naturally throughout the world, except in the Antarctic, the Australian region, the West Indies, and most other oceanic islands. Various species have been introduced worldwide—as game mammals or livestock—except to the Antarctic. There are 3 suborders of Artiodactyla: the Suina, which includes pigs, peccaries, and hippopotamuses; the Tylopoda, including the Old World camels as well as the American guanaco (which gave rise to the domestic llama and alpaca; see Grubb 2005b:646 for review) and vicuña; and the Ruminantia (the largest group), including deer, giraffes, cattle, antelope, sheep, goats, and pronghorn. In present-day Colorado only the suborder Ruminantia is represented in the wild, with 3 families, 7 genera, and 8 species (2 of which—the moose and the mountain goat—were introduced).

Both fossil and molecular evidence suggests strongly that whales are closely related to artiodactyls (particularly to hippos among living groups). Therefore mammalogists increasingly consider artiodactyls and whales to be members of a single order, Cetartiodactyla (see D. W. Macdonald 2006; Bininda-Emonds et al. 2007). However, for convenience and for consistency with treatment of other orders of Coloradan mammals, we follow D. Wilson and Reeder (2005) in listing the Artiodactyla as an order separate from the Cetacea.

Because most of Colorado's big game mammals are artiodactyls, the group figures prominently in Chapter 4. Most artiodactyls are accessible, "watchable" wildlife—readily identifiable and active during daylight hours. For a guide to finding the animals, see Young (2000). Beidleman et al. (2000) compiled much of the early, non-technical literature on these animals in Colorado, which focused largely on artiodactyls as game mammals. Because skulls of domestic cattle, sheep, goats, pigs, and even llamas sometimes are found, they are included in keys here and later to facilitate identification of domestic as well as wild artiodactyls. The collared peccary (*Pecari tajacu*) has not been reported from Colorado but is included in this key for 2 reasons. First, some might confuse feral pigs with peccaries (or vice versa). Second, the collared peccary apparently is expanding its range in northwestern New Mexico (see Albert et al. 2004; Lamit and Hendrie 2009) and might eventually reach the semidesert shrublands of extreme southwestern Colorado.

Key to the Families of the Order Artiodactyla in Colorado

1. Postorbital bar incomplete, upper incisors present, canines present 2

1' Postorbital bar complete, upper incisors present or absent, canines present or absent 4

2. Upper canines curving sharply outward and enlarged as tusks; color variable, but lacking distinct white collar; hindfoot with 4 toes . . . . Family Suidae—Feral Pig—*Sus scrofa**

2' Upper canines straight, pointed downward; color "salt-and-pepper" gray, brown, or black, with distinct white collar; hindfoot with 3 toes . . . . Family Tayassuidae—Collared Peccary—*Pecari tajacu*†

3. Upper incisors present; hooves nail-like, feet conspicuously padded posterior to hoof . . . . Family Camelidae—Llama—*Lama glama**

* Domestic species.

† Species of possible occurrence.

3' Upper incisors absent; hooves encircle toe, feet not padded behind hoof 4

4. Nasal and lacrimal bones joined by sutures; horns (if present) permanent, not forked; horn sheath not deciduous; a single lacrimal foramen on or just within anterior rim of orbit . . . . Family Bovidae, p. 467

4' Nasal and lacrimal bones separated by ethmoid (prelacrimal) vacuity; deciduous bony antlers or horns present at least on males; horns, if present, with a deciduous horn sheath and forked in males; 2 lacrimal foramina present on or just within anterior rim of orbit 5

5. Males with deciduous antlers; dewclaws (vestigial hooves) present as reduced non-weight-bearing digits . . . . Family Cervidae, p. 445

5' Males with forked horns; females with unforked horns or lacking horns; horn sheaths deciduous; dewclaws absent . . . . Family Antilocapridae, p. 463

Family Cervidae—Deer and Kin

The family Cervidae includes a wide variety of mammals that range in size from the diminutive *Pudu* of the Andes to the familiar graceful deer and to the moose (*Alces*), which can weigh nearly a ton. Male cervids typically are larger than females. In most species males have branched, deciduous antlers that function in sexual recognition, courtship displays, male-male combat, and defense. Antlers are bone and grow from pedicels on the frontal bones. New antlers are grown each year during March to September and are covered with a highly vascular, finely haired skin (velvet) that is shed after the structures mature and harden. In temperate-dwelling species the antlers are shed in late winter or spring (mostly in February and March) until April or even early May in Colorado and mature in the fall (September and October). Two genera (*Moschus* and *Hydropotes*—the musk and water deer of Asia) lack antlers, and in the genus *Rangifer* (caribou or reindeer) both sexes have antlers.

There is a large vacuity (called the rostral fenestra, prelacrimal or lacrimal vacuity, or ethmoidal vacuity) at the junction of the frontal, nasal, lacrimal, and maxillary bones. A conspicuous depression, the antorbital pit, or lacrimal fossa, is located in front of the orbits and houses the antorbital, or preorbital, glands. The dental formula is 0/3, 0–1/1, 3/3, 3/3 = 32 to 34 teeth. The upper canines may be long and pointed or short and blunt. The lower canines are reduced and incisiform and are spatulate along with the lower incisors. The cheekteeth are brachydont and selenodont. The ulna and fibula are reduced. The foregut is 4-chambered and a cud is produced. A gall bladder is usually absent.

Breeding in the temperate zone typically occurs in the fall; tropical species often breed aseasonally and may have more than 1 estrous cycle per year. Most species have 1 or 2 young annually, but Chinese water deer may have up to 4. The placenta is cotyledonary, and in all but the musk deer the female has 2 pairs of mammae. Facial, tarsal, metatarsal, and interdigital skin glands are often well developed. The cervids are a relatively old group, dating to the Oligocene Epoch, approximately 40 million years ago (Groves 2009). Today there are 19 genera and 51 species of cervids distributed worldwide except in sub-Saharan Africa, Australia, and Antarctica. Species have been introduced into Australia as well as New Zealand and several other oceanic islands. In Colorado there are 3 genera and 4 species of cervids (1 of which is introduced). The New World genus *Odocoileus* appears in the fossil record about 3.5 million years ago (Kurtén in Geist 1998); *Cervus* probably reached North America about 250,000 years ago (Polziehn and Strobeck 1998); *Alces* is a relative newcomer to North America, with fossils in Alaska dating back only about 10,000 years (Guthrie 1990).

According to Presnall (1958), fallow deer (*Dama dama*) were released in the late 1920s or early 1930s east of La Jara, Conejos County, Colorado. Another small group was released in the Cherokee Park area of Larimer County in about 1935 and a third group was introduced in 1944 to Rio Blanco County, near Buford. In the late 1950s, a few fallow deer apparently persisted in Colorado, but we know of no reports in the last half century.

Key to the Species of the Family Cervidae in Colorado

1. Antlers palmate; both sexes with elongated premaxilla and an inflated bulbous nose; pendulous skin flap on throat; nasals short, less than one-half the length from their anterior border to the anterior border of the premaxillary . . . . Moose—*Alces alces*,* p. 459

* Introduced species.

1' Antlers not palmate; premaxilla not greatly elongated; nose not particularly inflated and bulbous; no pendulous skin growth on throat; nasals long, more than one-half the length from their anterior border to the anterior border of the premaxillary 2

2. Antlers large, directed posteriorly over shoulders; tail and rump patch yellowish; premaxillary bones reaching nasals; vomer not attached to median suture of palatine and not separating posterior narial cavity; knob-like upper canines present . . . . American Elk, or Wapiti—*Cervus canadensis*, p. 446

2' Antlers smaller, not directed posteriorly over shoulders; tail and rump patch white; premaxillary bones not reaching nasals; vomer attached to palatine suture and separating posterior narial cavity; no upper canines present 3

3. Antlers with single main beam and simple tines; tail broad, white on undersurface, often held vertically as a flag while running; face without contrasting color between muzzle and forehead; ears about one-half length of head . . . . White-tailed Deer—*Odocoileus virginianus*, p. 456

3' Antlers branching dichotomously from main beam; tail narrow, black-tipped, not held high when running; face contrastingly colored between muzzle and forehead; ears more than one-half length of head. . . . . Mule Deer—*Odocoileus hemionus*, p. 451

Cervus canadensis

AMERICAN ELK, OR WAPITI

In North America this animal is commonly called elk and occasionally wapiti, but in Europe the term "elk" refers to the animal that Americans call "moose," *Alces alces*. The American elk is presently recognized by many authorities (D. McCullough 1969; see also Grubb 2005b) as conspecific with the European red deer, *Cervus elaphus*. Differences in genetics, behavior, and morphology have led some authorities (e.g., Geist 1998) to assert that the name *C. canadensis* is valid for the North American elk and also the Siberian red deer (*C. e. sibiricus*). Molecular systematic research is as yet inconclusive (Polziehn and Strobeck 1998, 2002; Polziehn et al. 1998, 2001). We follow R. Baker et al. (2003) in use of the name *Cervus canadensis*.

Description

The elk is a large cervid whose general body color is pale tan or brown. There is a contrastingly darker mane of long hairs on the neck and a paler yellowish tan rump patch. The tail is short and blends in with the rump patch. The hair is relatively long and coarse. The legs are long and the ears are large and conspicuous. Males are larger than females and may weigh more than 450 kg although average weight is closer to 300 kg. There are 4 hooves on each foot but the 2 outermost are reduced to dewclaws, which are not weight-bearing. Measurements are: total length 2,100–2,800 mm; length of tail 100–220 mm; length of hindfoot 460–700 mm; length of ear 180–220 mm; weight 220–450 kg.

Adult males have large antlers, round in cross section, with a main beam extending backward over the neck and shoulders. Several tines or points arise from the main beam, with the tines typically not branching. Yearling males have only short "spikes," usually 30 to 45 cm in length, which are the main beams without tines. Older bulls may have up to 6 or 7 tines off of each main beam. The skull has a large antorbital vacuity. The upper jaw has short, rounded canines

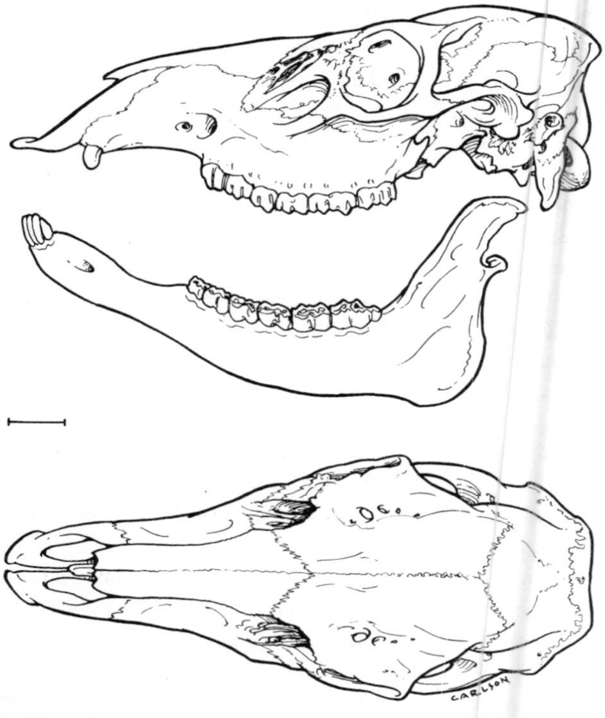

FIGURE 14-1. Lateral and dorsal views of the skull of a cow elk (*Cervus canadensis*). Scale = 5 cm.

PHOTOGRAPH 14-1. Elk, or wapiti (*Cervus canadensis*). © 1993 Wendy Shattil / Bob Rozinski.

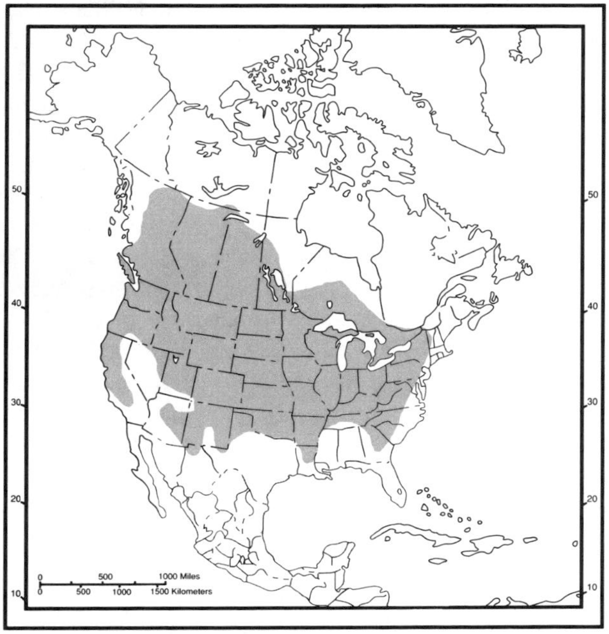

MAP 14-1. Distribution of the elk, or wapiti (*Cervus canadensis*) in North America.

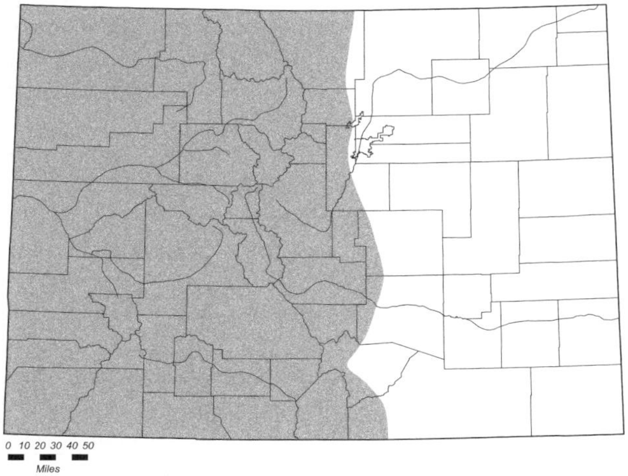

MAP 14-2. Distribution of the elk, or wapiti (*Cervus canadensis*) in Colorado.

and no incisors. Lower canines and incisors are spatulate and there is a diastema between them and the selenodont cheekteeth. The pattern of tooth eruption and wear can be used to age individuals (Quimby and Gaab 1957).

Distribution

Elk formerly occupied much of central and western North America from the southern Canadian provinces and Alaska south to the southern United States and eastward into the deciduous forests. This wide distribution encompassed prairie and eastern deciduous forest, as well as mountainous terrain in the West. Present populations are generally restricted to forested areas in rough country in western North America, but introductions as well as natural establishment have increased their distribution (Peek 2003). That heavy forests are not ideal habitat is suggested by the difficulty that large bulls have in moving through dense forests with their magnificent antlers. Elk have also been established or reestablished in North Dakota, Arkansas, Kentucky, Michigan, North Carolina, Oklahoma, Pennsylvania, Tennessee, and Wisconsin (Peek 2003). Elk were almost extirpated from Colorado in the early 1900s, when market hunting caused populations to decline to a mere 500 to 1,000 individuals (D. Armstrong 1972). Restoration, using elk from Wyoming, and careful management have led to the current high elk population in Colorado. The population estimate for 2007 was 292,000 animals (Colorado Division of Wildlife 2009g). Elk are big game animals under Colorado statute, and nearly a quarter million hunters harvest some 50,000 animals annually (Table 4-2). For details on the importance of elk to the big game program—and overall revenue—of the Colorado Division of Wildlife, see Chapter 4.

In Colorado the species ranges throughout the western two-thirds of the state generally at elevations above 1,800 m (6,000 ft.), although occasionally elk are reported in the South Platte river drainage on the eastern plains. Primeval patterns of geographic variation are not known, but *Cervus canadensis nelsoni* occurs over western Colorado whereas *C. c. canadensis* may have been the subspecies formerly inhabiting the eastern plains. *C. c. nelsoni* sometimes is called the Rocky Mountain elk to distinguish it from the Tule elk (*C. c. nannodes*) and Roosevelt elk (*C. c. roosevelti*) of the West Coast (Peek 2003).

Natural History

Elk are among the better-studied big game mammals of North America. Once the animals ranged well eastward on the Great Plains, but today, at least over much of western America, they are associated with semi-open forests or forest-edge situations adjacent to parks, meadows, and alpine tundra (R. Green 1982; Hoover and Wills 1987). However, some populations are capable of thriving in sagebrush shrub-grasslands (Strohmeyer and Peek 1996; Sawyer et al. 2007). Kie et al. (2003) contrasted the roles of western ungulates in forested ecosystems.

As generalist feeders, elk are both grazers and browsers, although they show a strong preference for grasses when available (Christianson and Creel 2007). In the northern and central Rocky Mountains, grasses and shrubs make up most of the winter diet, with grasses becoming prominent in the spring diet (Kufeld 1973). Forbs become increasingly important in late spring and summer whereas grasses again dominate in fall. However, on the White River Plateau in Colorado, grasses provided 77 to more than 90 percent of the diet in summer and fall (R. Boyd 1970). Browse contributed more than 56 percent of the winter diet. In that area, forbs were little utilized except in the summer and fall. In Rocky Mountain National Park, grasses and browse are the most frequently used forage (Hobbs 1979; Hobbs et al. 1979, 1981). Forbs tend to be favored on drier sites whereas browse is preferred in most mesic areas, including aspen groves, willow thickets, and moist meadows. In a study in Utah, wet meadows, dry meadows, clear-cuts, and revegetated roads were preferred feeding sites; wet meadows, revegetated roads, and mature lodgepole pine forests were preferred for resting and non-foraging activities (Collins et al. 1978). Ski areas—including recreational facilities, attendant commercial and residential development, and associated human activity—have a detrimental impact on local elk populations (an impact that may decrease over time; Morrison et al. 1995).

Elk have a considerable impact on aspen stands by browsing on twigs and new seedlings and feeding on the bark (Kaye et al. 2005). Such "barking" is generally done during the fall and winter months, and in heavily used stands all trees may be scarred to heights of about 2 m. Scarred bark is invaded by a fungus, so barking has serious negative impacts on vigor and regeneration of aspen in such places as Rocky Mountain National Park (Ratcliff 1941; Gysel 1960; Olmsted 1979). Elk also impact willow communities when their density levels exceed 15 elk per square kilometer. Examination of exclosures in Rocky Mountain National Park indicated that elk reduced annual growth of willows by 66 to 98 percent, creating a net loss of nitrogen in willow communities (Schoenecker et al. 2004). B. Baker et al. (2005) demonstrated that willows subjected to simulated beaver cutting recovered most (84 percent) of their pre-cut biomass within 2 growing seasons compared with willows subjected to both simulated beaver cutting and elk browsing. Elk were found to spend more time grazing in willow vegetation than in meadows, shrubland, and mixed conifer habitats. Zeigenfuss et al. (2002) reported a 20 percent decline in willow cover in the park over the past 50 years, along with a 94 percent decline in beaver populations. They concluded that elk browsing was primarily responsible for the situation but that lowered water tables resulting from a decline in beaver contributed to the problem. B. Baker (2003) suggested that the heavy browsing by elk or livestock disrupts beaver-willow mutualistic interactions that evolved under conditions with less browsing, which would have resulted when large predators controlled populations of browsing species such as elk. Kauffman et al. (2007) found that newly restored wolves in the Yellowstone area shaped landscape-level changes in habitat utilization by elk, with hunting grounds concentrated in open meadows and elk moving to cover in wooded areas.

Most studies of competition between elk and other species suggest that conflict and impacts are minimal. For example, mule deer, elk, and cattle may partition resources based on elevation, slope, or differences in vegetation (Stewart et al. 2002). Lindzey et al. (1997) could not demonstrate competition (a mutually detrimental symbiosis) between mule deer and elk. J. R. Nelson (1982) suggested that competition with cattle could be high and Hobbs et al. (1996a, 1996b) showed that elk grazing on winter and early spring range could reduce weight gain in cattle. In northwestern Colorado, considerable overlap was found in diets of elk, cattle, and wild horses (R. Hansen and Clark 1977). Elk appear to abandon areas being grazed by domestic sheep, and bighorn sheep seem to avoid areas being used by elk. Differences in diet tend to reduce competition between deer and elk.

Elk breed in the fall, with the peak of the rut in Colorado occurring during the last week of September and first week of October (R. Boyd and Ryland 1971). At least some bulls have completed antler growth and reached reproductive condition by late August and early September. Breeding is typically over by late October; however, in herds where younger bulls do most of the breeding the length of the rut may be prolonged by as much as a month (Noyes et al. 1996). During the rut, bulls have swollen necks and expend considerable energy in wallowing, bugling, thrashing, and digging, activities that attract other bulls, resulting in sparring encounters (Struhsaker 1967). These sparring encounters are frequent, although rarely do they escalate enough to cause serious damage. The bugle, most frequently given by bulls during the rut, is a loud, almost musical call that may serve as advertisement to cow elk, as a warning to potentially competing bulls, or as a herd-spacing mechanism. Cow elk also bugle but causes are not well understood (Feighny et al. 2006). Bulls typically compete for females and attempt to gather harems consisting of adult cows and calves. Other bulls continually attempt to usurp some of these cows or copulate with estrous females, forcing the herd bull to keep a continual vigil. At this time of the year bulls lose considerable weight and many go into the winter months in poor condition. Harem size is typically from 15 to 20 cows, although some exceed 30 animals (R. Boyd 1978; J. W. Thomas and Toweill 1982), and in northern Yellowstone, herd harems are replaced with rutting groups made up of mixed-sex and -age animals (Peek 2003). At times, congregations of elk in Moraine Park and Horseshoe Park in Rocky Mountain National Park appear to take on this same "rutting group" structure.

Females are seasonally polyestrous and may undergo up to 3 estrous cycles at approximately 21-day intervals if successful mating does not occur. Late-breeding animals may produce calves too late in the year for the offspring to survive the winter. Most calves are born in late May or early June following a 240- to 255-day gestation period. Yearling cows can breed, but only about 29 percent of them maintain calves into the fall in Colorado, compared with 76 percent for older females (Freddy 1987). Reduced breeding in yearling females is thought to result from weight and nutritional factors. Failure of yearling males to breed results mostly from an inability to compete with more mature bulls. Most breeding is done by males 3 years of age or older. Yearling bulls can breed, but pregnancy rates of cows bred by them are low. Calf/cow ratios fluctuate widely, from as low as 10–18 calves per 100 cows (G. Cole 1969; Dekker et al. 1995) to 71 per 100 cows on Colorado's White River Plateau (R. Boyd 1970). Calving grounds are carefully selected by the cows and are generally in locations where cover, forage, and water are in juxtaposition. In western Colorado most females calve within 200 m of water (J. W. Seidel 1977; Peek 2003). A single calf is typical; twins are known but rare. Calves weigh from 13 to 16 kg at birth and are precocial. They are covered with small white spots for their first few months. E. Thorne et al. (1976) and B. Smith et al. (1996) showed that low-weight calves have poor survival, as do those that are born late in the calving season.

Females with calves isolate themselves from the herd for the first 2 to 3 weeks. Then females with young rejoin the herd. During spring and summer, adult bulls usually segregate from cows, calves, and younger bulls and form small bands of their own. Younger bulls often stay with the cow-calf herds until the rut, at which time adult bulls usually force the younger animals to leave. The strong herding behavior in elk, as in other species, likely evolved as a mechanism for defense against predators (Geist 1982).

Overall sex ratios at birth may be biased toward males, but male survival is much lower than for females; adult bull/cow ratios can range from as low as 4:100 to more than 40:100 in herds subjected to relatively low hunting pressure (R. Boyd 1970; Flook 1970; B. Smith et al. 1996; Peek 2003). Ratios of 18 to 25 bulls per 100 cows are probably necessary to maintain early and synchronous breeding. In attempting to understand declines in calf-fawn recruitment in elk and mule deer, G. White, Freddy, et al. (2001) could not demonstrate that observed post-season adult female/male ratios had significant impacts on production of either elk calves or mule deer fawns. Variations in population structure in different herds mostly stem from hunting pressure and differential winter mortality, both of which favor cows over bulls. In Colorado, the structure of pre-season archery and muzzle-loader hunts may influence patterns of movement (M. Conner et al. 2001).

Elk tend to inhabit higher elevations during spring and summer and migrate to lower elevations for winter range. Lengths of seasonal migration can be as much as 80 to 100 km in the case of the Jackson Hole and northern Yellowstone herds (Boyce 1990; Peek 2003). Other herds, or even individuals within a population, may show hardly any movement, staying year-round on wintering grounds (R. Boyd 1970; Peek 2003). Migrating elk typically follow the melting snowpack upslope in spring, whereas fall migrations are tied to weather and availability of forage. Snow depth of about 40 cm triggers elk movement to winter ranges (J. M. Sweeney and Steinhoff 1976). Moving through snow more than a meter deep forces the animals to plow through snow in single file and to change leaders as they tire.

During winter, elk form large mixed herds on favored winter range. Except during the rut, when dominant bulls seem to dictate most activities, old cows typically are the leaders of such herds. These females lead the herd on migrations or movements to new feeding areas. They may also be the leaders when danger threatens.

Elk are generally nocturnal or crepuscular, although cloudy weather and freedom from disturbance may stimulate them to forage or move about during daylight hours. They favor relatively steep slopes (15 to 30 percent) over flats or steeper areas, although ridgetops are often used for bedding grounds. Generally elk do not move more than 1 km during their daily activities. Summer home ranges are usually fairly small, ranging from about 8 to 250 km^2 (Peek 2003). One can readily detect bedding sites by the distinctive odor of the animals and also by the trampled vegetation. R. Green (1982) investigated habitat selection and activity periods of elk in Rocky Mountain National Park.

Mortality is mostly caused by predation on calves, hunting, and winter starvation. Black bears and mountain lions may become skilled at locating and feeding on young calves as well as adult elk (Hornocker 1970; Schlegal 1977; Ruth 2004). Grizzly bears, wolves, coyotes, and mountain lions all feed on them in Yellowstone National Park and in Jasper National Park, Canada (French and French 1990; Dekker et al. 1995; Gese and Grothe 1995; Ruth 2004; D. W. Smith, Drummer, et al. 2004; Barber et al. 2005). In Colorado, mortality was attributed almost equally to starvation of calves (17 percent), hunting (13 percent), and predation (13 percent) (Bear and Green 1980). Freddy (2003) and Petersburg (1997) estimated that 70 to 94 percent of elk mortality is caused by human hunters.

Managed elk populations can fluctuate widely over time, with the northern Yellowstone elk herd estimated to have ranged from 6,000 to 23,000 animals (L. L. Eberhardt et al. 2007). Since the restoration of wolves in 1995, elk numbers decreased from about 17,000 to 8,335 (about 50 percent) by 2004, with the decline predicted to continue until human harvest decreases, wolf population stabilizes in response to fewer elk, and enough calves survive to reach prime breeding age (P. White and Garrott 2005). The initial, largely oblivious (and deadly) response of elk to restored wolf populations in Yellowstone figured prominently in Berger's (2008c) review of the natural history of fear. Although predation seems to be an important factor in the decline of the northern Yellowstone herd, wildlife managers are concerned about other poorly understood declines of elk populations, or calf recruitment, in parts of Colorado, Idaho, Washington, and Oregon (G. White, Freddy, et al. 2001; J. Cook et al. 2004). There is some concern that this could be a pattern following the decline in mule deer summarized by L. Carpenter (1997).

The complex behavioral and physiological ecology of the elk-wolf relationship in the Greater Yellowstone Ecosystem is being investigated in ongoing research by Scott Creel and colleagues from Montana State University (Creel, Christianson, et al. 2007; Christianson and Creel 2008; Creel and Christianson 2008, 2009; Liley and Creel 2008; Creel, Winnie, and Christianson 2009).

Recruitment and juvenile survival in elk are density dependent, so as populations grow, their productivity generally declines. For example, in Rocky Mountain National Park and the Estes Valley, 2 distinct subpopulations exist. As the park's population approaches carrying capacity of the range (estimated at about 1,070 animals), elk in the park are showing density-dependent reductions in recruitment and increased calf mortality. By contrast, the subpopulation living in the Estes Valley is still growing, with carrying capacity estimated at about 2,870 animals and a growth rate of 5 to 11 percent (Lubow et al. 2002). The close proximity of humans to concentrations of elk may have implications for recruitment. Disturbance of cow elk during the calving season may lead to lowered reproductive success (G. E. Phillips and Alldredge 2000).

In most of the West, including Colorado, elk numbers are managed through hunting. Although elk can live up to 20 years, the rate of population turnover in hunted populations is high. Males in the population on the White River Plateau survived an average of 1.2 years, and more than 85 percent of females suffered mortality by their fifth year (R. Boyd 1970). In less heavily hunted populations, one-half of all males born in a given year probably do not survive past 3 years of age and one-half of the females do not survive beyond age 5. Despite high turnover, elk populations can grow at a fast rate under favorable conditions, with the maximal sustainable growth rate estimated to be up to 28 percent (Peek 2003). Elk populations in and around Rocky Mountain National Park provide a good example of what happens when most elk are protected from hunting and have few effective natural predators. The total population has grown from an estimated 1,000 animals in 1944 to more than 3,000 today (Zeigenfuss et al. 2002; Schoenecker et al. 2004). Adult cow survival rate averages 0.91 and bull survival ranges from 0.42 to 0.79 (Lubow et al. 2002). Habitat deterioration and conflicts between elk and humans have led to a plethora of research projects and considerable controversy (see, e.g., Bear 1989; Hess 1993; F. Wagner et al. 1995; W. Baker et al. 1997; Larkins 1997; Barnett and Stohlgren 2001; Singer et al. 2002; Schoenecker et al. 2004). C. White et al. (1998) compared the ecology of aspen stands in 6 national parks from British Columbia south to Colorado, emphasizing the role of fire, browsers (especially elk), and wolves in maintaining the dynamics of these communities. Of those components, wolves are missing from Rocky Mountain National Park and fire is generally controlled. The National Park Service recently announced plans for shooting elk to control populations, a decision that has led to more controversy (Rocky Mountain National Park 2006). Some have objected to killing elk at all; others have been concerned that the shooting was to be done by Park Service sharpshooters rather than licensed hunters from the general public. Studies on fertility control in elk in Rocky Mountain National Park have yielded some positive results (M. Conner, Baker, et al. 2007).

Chronic wasting disease (CWD) is a concern to many wildlife agencies but the disease is poorly understood (E. Williams, Kirkwood, and Miller 2001). The potential for disease movement between farm-raised elk and wild populations has been examined in Colorado (Vercauteren et al. 2007). CWD has been reported in elk from nearly all game management units in the northwestern quarter of Colorado. For some details on this important emerging wildlife disease, see the account of the mule deer. Wild elk generally are not provided with supplemental feed in Colorado, avoiding the costs and untoward impacts on habitat, behavior, and disease seen in parts of other western states, especially Wyoming (B. Smith 2001).

For reviews of the vast literature on elk biology, consult O. Murie (1951), R. Boyd (1978), Boyce and Hayden-Wing (1979), Peek (1982, 2003), Thomas and Toweill (1982), Boyce (1990), and Wisdom and Cook (2000).

Genus *Odocoileus*

There are 2 species of *Odocoileus*, both of them indigenous to the New World—although both have been introduced elsewhere in the world as game animals. E. Hall (1981) listed North American deer as species of *Dama*, but the consensus is that this usage was in error (Grubb 2005b).

Deer are the most important big game mammals in the United States and second only to elk in Colorado. Historically, data on harvest in Colorado were not kept on individual species of deer, although the Division of Wildlife intends to rectify that situation in the future. Annually, some 100,000 hunters take an average of nearly 45,000 deer in Colorado (Table 4-2). Estimate of total statewide deer population (post-harvest) in 2007 was 539,000 (Colorado Division of Wildlife 2009g).

Nationwide, upwards of a half million deer are killed annually on US highways. Romin and Bissonette (1996) cited estimates ranging from 200,000 for 1980 and 500,000 for 1991. Schwabe and Schuhman (2002:609) cited the figure "700,000 per year and increasing." Such estimates are notoriously difficult because states differ in the extent of record-keeping and reporting. Numerous mitigation efforts have been employed, including signage directed at drivers, aversive signals for deer, fencing, habitat alteration, and wildlife underpasses and overpasses. Based on a composite score including frequency of impact, degree of damage, and effect on flight, deer were the most important wildlife hazard to aviation, although damage by a variety of kinds of birds (gull, geese, ducks, etc.) was more frequent (Dolbeer et al. 2000).

Odocoileus hemionus

MULE DEER

Description

Mule deer are medium-sized cervids with conspicuously long ears and a coarse coat. Individuals of the Coloradan subspecies, *Odocoileus hemionus hemionus*, average largest. Males are larger than females and can weigh up to 200 kg, but the average weight is closer to 70 kg (Hunter 1947; A. Anderson et al. 1974). Does are fully grown at 2 years of age, but bucks may continue to grow until 9 or 10 years old. The color in summer is reddish tan whereas the winter pelage is brownish gray. The rump and belly are white. The face is marked with a paler muzzle contrasting the gray forehead and brownish spots on either side of the rostrum. The tail is short and pale in color except for a black tip. There are 4 hooves on each foot, of which 2 are reduced to dewclaws. Metatarsal glands are well developed, usually more than 100 mm in length. Measurements are: total length 1,200–1,675 mm; length of tail 100–220 mm; length of hindfoot 380–530 mm; length of ear 180–230 mm. Mule deer stand 710–1,060 mm at the shoulder (A. Anderson et al. 1974). The skull has large vacuities and there are no upper canines or incisors. The lower incisors and canines are spatulate. The dentition can be used to age individuals

PHOTOGRAPH 14-2. Mule deer (*Odocoileus hemionus*). Photograph by Joseph Van Wormer. All rights reserved. Photo Archives, Denver Museum of Nature and Science.

PHOTOGRAPH 14-3. Hybrid of mule deer (*Odocoileus hemionus*) and white-tailed deer (*O. virginianus*). Note small ears and long tail with black stripe. Photograph by R. B. Gill.

based on eruption patterns and wear (W. Robinette et al. 1957, 1977); however, Hamlin et al. (2000) found tooth wear only 62 percent accurate compared with tooth sectioning (92 percent accurate). Genetic variability in mule deer in Colorado is about average for cervids and for mammals in general (heterozygosity, 3.6 percent), but less than in white-tailed deer (M. H. Smith et al. 1990). This difference may reflect the management history of local populations or differences in population structure and clearly deserves further study.

Males have antlers that are round in cross section and project forward and upward from the frontal bones. The antlers branch equally (dichotomously) to form 4 main tines, although many individuals have more than that number. Young males have either simple spikes or a single fork near the tips of the antlers. The number of tines cannot be used directly for aging an animal. The antlers are shed annually in late February or March (Hunter 1947; A. Anderson and Medin 1969, 1971). Occasional hybridization occurs between mule and white-tailed deer, the hybrid offspring showing intermediacy in appearance of such characters as tail and antlers (Photograph 14-3).

Distribution

Mule deer range in western North America from the central Yukon to north-central Mexico and eastward into the plains states. In Colorado, mule deer are found statewide in all ecosystems. About the turn of the twentieth century, populations in Colorado were greatly depleted because of market hunting. Not only was venison used by newly arrived settlers but it also was shipped east for sale. The advent of a conservation ethic and the Colorado Department of Fish and Game led to recovery of this species in the state (Barrows and Holmes 1990). Mule deer populations declined again over much of the western United States in the 1950s through mid-1970s (Workman and Low 1976; Connolly 1981; R. Gill et al. 2001; Mackie et al. 2003) because of overhunting, habitat loss, habitat alteration, and deterioration

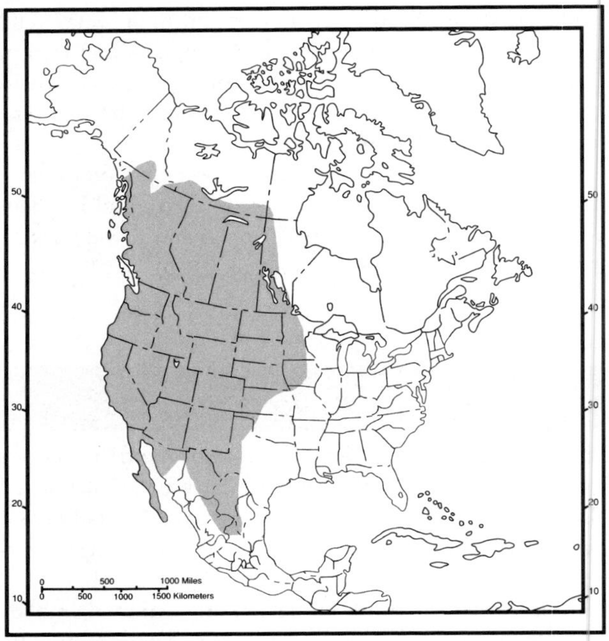

MAP 14-3. Distribution of the mule deer (*Odocoileus hemionus*) in North America.

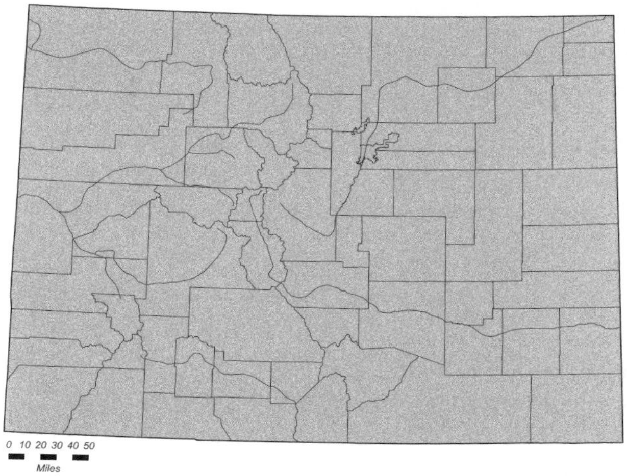

MAP 14-4. Distribution of the mule deer (*Odocoileus hemionus*) in Colorado.

of winter ranges. R. Gill (1999) estimated that the population had declined by more than 50 percent from numbers in the 1940s. Colorado still enjoys one of the highest mule deer populations in the United States but the decline has been sufficient to cause hunters and even the Colorado legislature to question methods of monitoring and management (R. Gill 1999; R. Gill et al. 2001; Freddy et al. 2004). In a number of urban localities herds are large enough to damage landscape plantings and to constitute a serious traffic hazard. Mule deer are hunted as big game in Colorado. Estimating populations of game animals is notoriously difficult and methods differ from one state to another. Rabe et al. (2002) reviewed survey methods in the western United States. As noted above, the Division of Wildlife does not identify deer to species for reporting purposes. From 2000 to 2005, an average of more than 44,000 deer (both mule and white-tailed) were harvested (Table 4-2). Highest densities are found in areas like the Piceance Basin in northwestern Colorado, the Uncompahgre Plateau and the Gunnison River drainage, and the foothills of the Front Range.

One subspecies, *Odocoileus hemionus hemionus*, occurs in Colorado. E. Hall (1981) used the generic name *Dama* for the mule and white-tailed deer; most authors apply *Dama* to the Old World fallow deer (*Dama dama*), a species in a different subfamily of deer.

Natural History

Mule deer occupy all ecosystems in Colorado, from grasslands to alpine tundra. They reach their greatest densities in shrublands on rough, broken terrain, which provides abundant browse and cover. A wide distribution and general adaptability make for broad diets; Kufeld et al. (1973) listed more than 788 plant species eaten by mule deer. However, Mackie et al. (2003) cited Hoffman (1985), who considered both mule deer and white-tailed deer to be "concentrate selectors" with a relatively small rumen and gut so that they have to eat small volumes of high-quality food. In contrast, moose, bison, horses, and cattle tend to be "bulk feeders," able to consume more low-quality materials. In the Rocky Mountains, winter diets consist of browse from a variety of trees and shrubs (74 percent) and forbs (15 percent). In spring, browse contributes 49 percent of the diet, and forbs and grasses make up about 25 percent each. Summer diets are 50 percent browse, and forb consumption increases to 46 percent. Browse use increases in the fall to 60 percent while forb use declines to 30 percent (Kufeld et al. 1973; L. Carpenter, Gill, et al. 1979). Several studies in Colorado have indicated that diets containing 30 percent or more sagebrush and/or juniper reduce rumen microbes and are therefore deleterious (Nagy et al. 1964; Nagy and Tengerdy 1967; L. Carpenter 1976; C. Schwartz et al. 1980). A. Alldredge et al. (1974) estimated that mule deer could consume no more than about 1 percent of available sagebrush forage on western rangelands. When heavy snows bury grasses and forbs on such rangelands and force mule deer to consume high amounts of sage and juniper, mortality rates increase because of malnutrition. Most studies indicate that mule deer use a considerable amount of browse, but when given the choice, succulent, herbaceous plants are much preferred (Mackie et al. 2003). Mule deer seem to be able to survive without free water except in arid environments. However, they do drink available water and also eat snow. Additional research in Colorado has explored chemical composition and digestibility (Dietz et al. 1962), age structure of shrubs on winter range (Roughton 1972), foraging on oak (Kufeld 1983), and forage use relative to logging in subalpine timber (Wallmo et al. 1972).

The animals are mostly nocturnal or crepuscular in the warmer months, becoming more diurnal in winter (Loveless 1967). Peaks of activity may occur around sunrise and sunset (L. Carpenter 1976). Activity depends on local conditions, including temperature, season, weather, and forage. As with most large mammals that do not hibernate, mule deer may be subjected to average temperature extremes that can range from less than –15°C in winter to more than 30°C in summer. They have a variety of mechanisms for accommodation, including panting, shivering, adjusting blood flow in the ears, erecting the hair, and increasing metabolic rate in winter and behaviorally seeking shade in hot weather and plant cover in cold weather (Loveless 1967; Mackie et al. 2003). Over much of Colorado the species is migratory, summering at higher elevations and moving downslope to winter range. Deer on the White River Plateau make annual migrations of about 80 to 90 km (Bartmann 1968; Bartmann and Steinert 1981), whereas on many other ranges seasonal movements may be only a few kilometers. Routes followed are often habitual, apparently based on years of learning. Snow depth of 15 to 30 cm appears to trigger fall movements and depths more than 50 cm prevent use of an area (Loveless 1967). However, Garrott et al. (1987) found that mule deer in northwestern Colorado migrated to winter range in October, before snow accumulation. They suggested that better-quality forage on winter range at that time of year triggers the movements. During mid-winter, deer moved to lower elevations and foraged on more protected south-facing exposures. This latter movement was timed with severity of weather.

Spring and summer ranges are most typically mosaics of meadows, aspen woodlands, alpine tundra–subalpine forest edge, or montane forest edge. Montane forests and piñon-juniper woodlands with good shrub understory are often favored winter ranges. Mule deer in cottonwood river-bottoms on the eastern plains tended to remain in the riparian vegetation about 80 percent of the time, although some individuals lived in cornfields when the crop was tall (Kufeld and Bowden 1995). Because of the mule deer's movements, their home ranges are difficult to measure. In areas where the animals do not migrate significant distances, annual home ranges are 7.0 to 22.0 km^2 (Mackie et al. 1982). However, seasonally the animals appear to be relatively sedentary, staying within areas of 40 to 900 ha. Kufeld and Bowden (1995) reported sedentary mule deer along the South Platte River on the eastern plains to have median home ranges of 3.92 km^2, compared with 7.7 km^2 for sympatric white-tailed deer. Gerlach (1987) reported mule deer home ranges averaging 1,220 ha on Fort Carson's Piñon Canyon Maneuver Site in Las Animas County. Mule deer expanded their range of movements in response to military training activities (T. Stephenson et al. 1996). On recreational and conservation lands near Boulder, S. G. Miller et al. (2001) found that deer were more alert to leashed dogs off-trail than on-trail, flushed at greater distance, and moved farther away. Mule deer activity was significantly lower within 100 m of trails where dogs were allowed (even on leash) than where dogs were prohibited (Lenth et al. 2008). Migrating individuals are philopatric, returning to the same areas year after year (Franzen 1968; L. Carpenter, Gill, et al. 1979). At the Rocky Mountain Arsenal, mule deer are sympatric with white-tailed deer, presenting ideal conditions for research on their interactions (D. G. Whittaker 1995; D. G. Whittaker and Lindzey 1999, 2001; D. G. Whittaker and F. G. Whittaker 2004), which are discussed in more detail in the account of the white-tailed deer.

In Colorado, mule deer breed in November and December. Females are in estrus 24 to 36 hours but will repeat estrous cycles every 3 to 4 weeks until bred. About 70 percent of breeding occurs in a 20-day span in some populations. The gestation period averages 203 days (A. Anderson and Medin 1967). Mule deer are sexually mature at about 18 months. Yearling females typically produce a single fawn while older females in good condition produce twins; pregnancy rates usually exceed 70 percent. During the rut, males become aggressive, their necks swell, and they reduce time spent feeding (Mackie et al. 2003). Precocial at birth, fawns weigh about 4 kg. They can consume vegetation at 2 to 3 weeks of age but are not weaned until fall. Sex ratios at birth favor males slightly, but with increasing age females commonly exceed males by ratios of 2:1, 5:1, or higher. Nutritional factors influence fawn sex ratios, and there is some evidence that does on poorer diets have a higher proportion of male fawns. Does are solitary during fawning. They form small groups with yearlings and fawns when the young are several months old. As winter approaches, the sizes of herds increase and large numbers may congregate on wintering grounds. When not in rut, adult males often form pairs or small groups of 3 to 5 individuals. Social behavior was summarized by Geist (1981).

Mortality in mule deer varies with age class and region. In fawns annual mortality varies from 27 to more than 75 percent (A. Anderson and Bowden 1977; Mackie et al. 2003). The decline in mule deer numbers in Colorado and elsewhere has led to increased research on causes, which potentially include predation, disease, hunting, competition, and habitat deterioration (R. Gill et al. 2001). The overall problem was reviewed by Unsworth et al. (1999), Kie and Czech (2000), R. Gill et al. (2001), and Mackie et al. (2003). Lindzey et al. (1997) reviewed research on competition and could find little evidence that it seriously reduced mule deer numbers.

Fawn to doe and buck to doe ratios have been investigated in several locations in Colorado. G. White, Freddy, et al. (2001) observed fawn to doe ratios declining from 79:100 in 1982 to 32:100 in 1997 and assessed buck to doe ratios (5-year average, 12:100), concluding that there was no evidence that adult sex ratios were affecting productivity on the Uncompahgre Plateau or across the rest of the state. Kufeld and Bowden (1995) reported fawn/doe ratios of 93:100 on the South Platte, with a buck/doe ratio of 26:100. Changes in pregnancy and/or fawn mortality have been investigated by Andelt et al. (2004), Pojar and Bowden (2004), and E. Myers (2001). Andelt et al. (2004) found no evidence that failure to breed or to maintain pregnancy was a major factor in mule deer decline, with observed pregnancy ranging from 90 to 93 percent.

Fawn mortality is primarily caused by predation and starvation. Pojar and Bowden (2004) found that 76 percent of mortality occurred before August 1 and mean survival averaged 50 percent, with most resulting from starvation or predation by coyotes. However, they could not conclude that disease, predation, or starvation was sufficient to cause observed declines. Preliminary studies using nutritional supplements during the winter on the Uncompahgre Plateau suggest that there was no increase in production or survival of neonates (Bishop et al. 2003). Larger fawns are more likely to survive, and smaller fawns are more likely to starve. Fawns taken by predators are highly variable in size, suggesting little selection (G. White, Garrott, et al. 1987). Studies in South Dakota indicated that fall populations must be at least 30 to 33 percent fawns to maintain stable numbers. Most mortality in older age classes results from hunting or, in winter, starvation (L. Carpenter 1976). Predators include coyotes, bobcats, golden eagles, mountain lions, black bears, brown bears, and domestic dogs. Locally, coyote, mountain lion, and wolf predation can account for significant mortality within populations, but in many cases such mortality may be compensatory rather than additive (Bartmann, White, and Carpenter 1992; Ballard et al. 2001). Predator control still is often promoted to increase numbers of deer for hunters (J. Harrington and Conover 2007); however, direct costs of predator reduction programs and public opposition to them mean that such programs are not justifiable under most conditions (Ballard et al. 2001).

Colorado is experiencing rapid human population growth nearly statewide and also intense energy development, especially on the Western Slope. Deer–motor vehicle accidents in Colorado are estimated at about 2,400 per year, not an insignificant number in terms of mortality and costs of insurance claims. Energy development may also prove to have significant impacts on mule deer, as studies in Wyoming have suggested (Sawyer et al. 2006). To date, there are no answers to the decline in mule deer.

Mule deer may survive up to 20 years in the wild, but such longevity is rare and population turnover is high. In Utah only 1 percent of bucks examined were classed as over 8 years of age (W. Robinette et al. 1977). Several studies suggest that annual turnovers of 28 to 43 percent of the population are not unusual in "stable" herds (Connolly 1981). In such areas, about half of the mortality is fawns, and adult bucks show about one-third higher mortality than do adult does. Excellent reviews of the extensive and diffuse research literature on mule deer were provided by W. Taylor (1956), Wallmo (1981), Mackie et al. (1982), A. Anderson and Wallmo (1984), Kie and Czech (2000), and Mackie et al. (2003).

Much research on mule deer has been done in Colorado, particularly by personnel of the Colorado Division of Wildlife and Colorado State University. For example, techniques have been developed for aerial and ground surveys, mark and recapture, stocking rates, and modeling population dynamics (P. Gilbert and Grieb 1957; McKean 1971; Medin and A. Anderson 1979; Kufeld et al. 1980; Bartmann et al. 1987; G. White and Bartmann 1998; Bowden et al. 2000). Studies of mule deer in the Piceance Basin revealed differences between subpopulations and change over the course of a 4-year study, suggesting rapid evolution (Scribner et al. 1991).

In recent years, chronic wasting disease (CWD) has become a major focus of research. CWD is an emerging disease of deer, elk, and moose, related to scrapie in sheep. It has been present in captive and free-ranging mule deer and elk in northeastern Colorado and adjacent Wyoming at least since the 1980s (E. Williams, Miller, et al. 2002; M. W. Miller et al. 2008). It now is reported from all Coloradan cervids, including moose. Like so-called mad cow disease and Creutzfeldt-Jakob disease, CWD is a transmissible spongiform encephalopathy (TSE) caused by a prion, a sort of "rogue protein." The evolutionary origin of prions has been linked to proteins that transport metallic ions across cell membranes (Schmitt-Ulms et al. 2009). Understanding the evolutionary history of prions holds some promise for prevention or treatment of prion-based disease. Infectious CWD prions have been transmitted within mule deer populations by contact with saliva and blood, but not urine or feces (Mathiason et al. 2006). In experimental situations, transmission was demonstrated from excreta and decomposed carcasses (M. W. Miller et al. 2004; Tamgüney et al 2009). To date there is no strong evidence for CWD transmission from wildlife to humans (Belay et al. 2004) or even to domestic cattle and sheep (Raymond et al. 2000). Mule deer on and near Table Mesa, immediately southwest of Boulder, have been studied for many years by city and state agency personnel and by private citizens (especially by CU-Boulder Professor Emeritus Charles Southwick and Heather Southwick). In a study in 2005 and 2006, annual survival of prion-infected adult deer (>2 years old) was 53 percent, whereas that for uninfected deer was 82 percent (M. W. Miller, Swanson, et al. 2008). About half of the infected deer that died (13/27) were killed by mountain lions; the other half apparently succumbed to "chronic wasting syndrome." An abundance of weakened prey animals may enhance mountain lion survival and reproduction.

Management of CWD in mule deer in Colorado includes attempting to prevent the spread of CWD beyond historically infected areas; culling animals to reduce the prevalence of CWD in infected areas (L. Wolfe, Miller, and Williams 2004); enforcing regulations against feeding and transportation of wildlife within and into Colorado; and continuing research, in cooperation with other agencies and entities, on the biology and management (detection, treatment) of CWD (Colorado Division of Wildlife 2009d).

The mule deer is Colorado's widest-ranging and most abundant cervid, so it is not surprising that this is the species in which CWD has been observed most often. Highest incidence is in northeastern Colorado, from Larimer County eastward along the South Platte Valley. CWD has been detected in most of the northern half of Colorado and southward on the Eastern Slope to the Wet Mountains and Sangre de Cristo Range north of La Veta Pass. For current status of CWD in Colorado, consult the Colorado Division of Wildlife (http://wildlife.state.co.us/Hunting/BigGame/CWD/). That excellent website includes an archive of technical papers on the disease in Colorado, available for download. The Chronic Wasting Disease Alliance (http://www.cwd-info.org/index.php) is a clearinghouse for information on CWD generally. M. Conner et al. (2007) provided an excellent synopsis of CWD in the context of a technical manual on monitoring the disease.

PHOTOGRAPH 14-4. White-tailed deer (*Odocoileus virginianus*). © 1993 Wendy Shattil / Bob Rozinski.

Odocoileus virginianus

WHITE-TAILED DEER

Description

White-tailed deer are medium-sized cervids with moderately long ears and wide, flat, bushy tails. The coat is coarse and rather short. The predominant color is bright reddish in the summer and grayish in the winter. The ventral color is white. The face is not contrastingly marked, but there may be a whitish spot on the throat, white eye rings, and a white ring around the muzzle. The tail is reddish brown on the dorsal surface and white ventrally. It is typically held high while running. Fawns are reddish brown in color with white dorsal spots, which are lost at 3 to 4 months of age. Metatarsal glands are conspicuous but usually much less than 100 mm in length. Measurements are: total length 1,340–2,060 mm; length of tail 150–330 mm; length of hindfoot 360–520 mm; length of ear 140–230 mm. Adult males are larger than females and may weigh more than 100 kg, although the average is closer to 80 kg. Adult white-tailed deer stand about 1 m at the shoulder.

Normally only males have antlers. The antlers of older bucks have a well-defined main beam from which arises a series of non-branching tines. Young bucks may have only simple spikes or single forks. Males typically shed their antlers in late February or March and the new set has completed its growth by late August or early September. The skull is similar to that of the mule deer, with a large antorbital vacuity and no canines or incisors on the upper jaw. The lower incisors and canines are spatulate and the cheekteeth are selenodont. Severinghaus (1949) discussed use of dental characteristics to age white-tailed deer. Hybridization with mule deer occurs occasionally (see Photograph 14-3).

Distribution

White-tailed deer are the widest-ranging cervid in North America. They exist in all the southern Canadian provinces, across the contiguous states except for large areas of California, Nevada, and Utah, and extend southward into South America (W. Smith 1991; K. Miller et al. 2003). White-tailed deer are expanding their range to the west while mule deer are more slowly spreading eastward (Whittaker and Lindzey 2001). There are 17 states with sympatric populations of the 2 species. In Colorado, white-tailed deer are rather common in river-bottoms of the eastern plains, particularly along the South Platte, Arkansas, and Republican rivers and their major tributaries. Individuals are also known from several isolated locations in the mountains, including above timberline in Rocky Mountain National Park, Middle Park, the White River drainage in Rio Blanco County, and the San Luis Valley in Rio Grande County. Almost extirpated by the 1920s, white-tails have recovered as a consequence of enforcement of game laws and deliberate restoration (Hunter 1948; D. Armstrong 1972). *Odocoileus virginianus dacotensis* is the subspecies ascribed a range in northeastern Colorado, and *O. v. texanus* occurs in the Arkansas watershed. These subspecies may be indistinct in Colorado because of artificial transplants, movements, and spread of populations. No rigorous analysis of geographic variation exists.

MAP 14-5. Distribution of the white-tailed deer (*Odocoileus virginianus*) in North America.

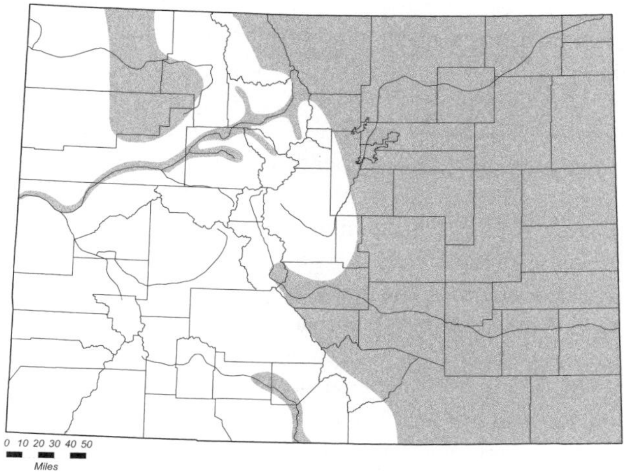

MAP 14-6. Distribution of the white-tailed deer (*Odocoileus virginianus*) in Colorado.

Natural History

One of the most adaptable of deer, white-tails are the most widely distributed cervids in North America, found from humid, tropical rainforest to the Arctic tree limit. In parts of the eastern United States they have become so common that Waller and Alverson (1997) considered them to be keystone herbivores. In our area, white-tailed deer occupy a variety of habitats, but they are typically associated with riparian woodlands and the associated irrigated agricultural lands of the eastern plains. They do not occupy dense coniferous forests or spend much time on open prairie. At the Rocky Mountain Arsenal, Whittaker and Lindzey (2001) found white-tailed deer to select wetlands with trees and shrubs, locust thickets, dryland trees, or shrubland-succulent communities during most of the year. Choice of habitats seemed to reflect needs for thermal cover and security. Kufeld (1992) and Kufeld and Bowden (1995) also found white-tailed deer closely tied to wooded and riparian communities, spending 70 to more than 90 percent of their time in such habitat.

The species has a catholic diet, selecting the most nutritious plant matter available at any particular time. In agricultural areas, white-tailed deer often prefer crops such as corn and wheat to native browse, forbs, and grasses. No detailed studies have been made on the diet of these deer in Colorado, but Whittaker and Lindzey (2001) showed relatively little use by white-tailed deer of browse, compared with forbs and grasses, from March to November. Studies in the eastern United States have suggested that browse provides only 3 to 17 percent of the diet and that grasses and forbs are much more important than in the diet of the mule deer (Hesselton and Hesselton 1982). However, Whittaker and Lindzey (2001) thought mule deer were much more selective toward forbs than were white-tailed deer at the Rocky Mountain Arsenal and were selectively using habitats with high percentages of forbs. Mushrooms have been reported as important foods, as have a variety of fruits, acorns (mast), and other nuts. In Colorado, mast is lacking in most white-tailed deer habitat. In situations of low forage availability, white-tailed does delay reproduction and have a lower incidence of twinning (Verme and Ullrey 1984).

White-tailed deer are secretive and often difficult to observe, even when they occur in large numbers. The animals are mostly crepuscular, although they also move and feed at night or during daylight. Unlike mule deer, white-tailed deer do not typically make significant seasonal migrations. However, Kufeld (1992) found that 25 percent of radio-collared white-tails along the South Platte and Arkansas rivers in eastern Colorado made seasonal movements, usually from the river-bottom to plains sites (often farmland) in late spring and summer, and returned to the bottomlands in the fall. Home ranges (measured as minimal convex polygons) of white-tails in that study averaged 7.7 km^2, compared with 3.9 km^2 for mule deer in the same habitats (Kufeld and Bowden 1995). At the Rocky Mountain Arsenal, seasonal home ranges for mule deer averaged 1,766 ha while white-tailed deer averaged 2,562 ha (Whittaker and Lindzey 2001). Brunjes et al. (2009) studied home ranges of mule and white-tailed deer in areas of sympatry in Texas, including the Panhandle. There was as much overlap between species as there was between individuals of the same species. Home ranges tended to be elongate, and adult bucks had larger home ranges than did does (Marchinton and Hirth 1984). White-tails are good swimmers and do not hesitate to cross bodies of water, even up to several miles across. During the winter on some northern ranges they may form relatively large herds in "yards," where they congregate for shelter from snow and cold in an area of good food reserves. In Colorado, white-tailed deer typically herd in groups of up to 20 animals in riparian woodlands during the winter months. Most groups of white-tailed deer appear to be composed of females and up to 2 generations of offspring. Such groups may commingle with other families and with small groups of bucks to form the winter herds (Kufeld 1992; Kufeld and Bowden 1995). Some studies of white-tailed deer have suggested that there is competition with mule deer for food and space, and Kufeld and Bowden (1995) proposed studies to investigate this potential in riparian areas in eastern Colorado. However, Whittaker and Lindzey (2001) saw little evidence of interactions between the species, and home ranges were mostly segregated.

White-tailed deer exhibit 2 conspicuous alarm signals, snorting and tail-flagging; alert deer may also stamp their front feet. Snorting is more frequent in family groups of does than in groups of males and is seen when the cause for alarm is very close or at some distance. Tail-flagging occurs in both male and doe groups but is not used when the cause for alarm is very close (Hirth and McCullough 1977; Bildstein 1983). Its function is disputed, but it seems both to signal to predators that they have been detected (so no longer have the advantage of surprise) and to alert group members and to facilitate group cohesion when the predator is at a safe distance.

White-tailed deer breed in fall, with a season similar to that of the mule deer. Kufeld and Bowden (1995) reported buck to doe ratios of 24:100 for white-tailed deer in January, suggesting that ample males were available for breeding. The peak of the rut is probably early November in Colorado. During the rut adult bucks become very active and spend much of their time searching for estrous females. Bucks typically make characteristic "scrapes" at this time by pawing patches of ground upon which they urinate and leave metatarsal gland scent. Trees near such scrapes often show signs of antler rubbing. Such marked areas are believed to represent breeding-season territories, defended against other males. Females during the rut typically become more solitary, often chasing yearling fawns away and increasing their range of movements. White-tailed deer can breed as fawns, with ovulation first occurring at about 6 or 7 months (Hesselton and Hesselton 1982; K. Miller et al. 2003). In some studies up to 60–70 percent of the female fawn crop has been shown to breed successfully. A small sample of adult deer collected on the Rocky Mountain Arsenal showed prepartum and postpartum averages of 1.89 and 1.04 for white-tailed deer and 1.77 and 1.31 for mule deer. One of 2 white-tail fawns was pregnant. Although male fawns are probably capable of breeding their first year, there is no evidence that they do so.

Does are polyestrous. Estrus lasts about 1 day and females who do not breed will recycle every 21–28 days. Females urinate more frequently during the onset of estrus (Verme and Ullrey 1984). The urine's chemistry alerts adult males, possibly during flehmen (lip-curling)—a stereotyped behavior in which fluid is suctioned into the vomeronasal organ for analysis. The gestation period averages 201 days. Male/female sex ratios approximate 112:100 in utero, with younger females having a significantly greater chance of having male offspring than do older females (Hesselton and Hesselton 1982). White-tails weigh about 3 kg at birth; twins or even triplets are not uncommon. Older does seem to protect their young better from predation and therefore contribute more offspring to the population than do younger deer (Mech and McRoberts 1990). Females typically become reclusive when fawning and stay away from other deer for the first month or so following parturition. Fawns begin to forage at about 2 to 3 weeks of age and are typically weaned by the fifth month. Growth is rapid and by 7 to 9 months fawns on good habitat may weigh 50–55 kg. Adult bucks reach full size at 4 or 5 years of age, whereas females are full-grown at 3 to 4 years. White-tailed bucks in riparian communities on Colorado's eastern plains grow especially fine antlers and are much sought by trophy hunters.

Mortality in white-tailed deer mostly is caused by hunting by humans, winter starvation, automobile accidents, and predation. Coyotes and mountain lions are important predators where their populations are high and ranges overlap with those of white-tails (Kunkel et al. 1999). Bobcats, bears, and eagles may also kill white-tailed deer on occasion. In the eastern United States it is estimated that domestic dogs may cause mortality equal to 10 percent of the legal harvest. Automobiles are estimated to kill 1.5 million deer a year in the United States (Conover et al. 1995); in Colorado most deer killed are mule deer. In most eastern populations the turnover rate is remarkably rapid. Rarely do bucks exceed 3.5 years of age, or females 5.5 years, although in captivity white-tailed deer have lived to almost 20 years of age (Hesselton and Hesselton 1982). Whittaker and Lindzey (2001) indicated that deer at the Rocky Mountain Arsenal National Wildlife Refuge were increasing in numbers at growth rates of 25 percent for mule deer and 8 percent for white-tailed deer. Better early fawn survival in mule deer in the first 30 days of life (66 percent) relative to white-tails (34 percent) may account for some of the differences in growth rate, because adult survivorship in both species was high (80 to 100 percent).

White-tailed deer are susceptible to chronic wasting disease, as are other cervids. CWD has been reported in white-tailed deer mostly in the South Platte watershed, from Larimer County eastward to Sedgwick County, generally north of Interstate 76. For some details on CWD, see the account of the mule deer.

Information specific to harvest of white-tailed deer in Colorado is unavailable, as data have been accumulated and compiled at the level of genus, *Odocoileus*, "deer." That should be rectified (see generic account of *Odocoileus* and also Table 4-2). In Colorado, where much of the hunting pressure (and much of the research effort) is concentrated on mule deer in mountain environments, long-term studies of white-tail demography would be of interest. Preliminary studies (such as Kufeld 1992; Kufeld and Bowden 1995; and Whittaker and Lindzey 2001) suggested differences in habitat requirements and demography of Coloradan populations relative to better-studied eastern populations. Reviews of the literature on the species are provided by W. Taylor (1956), Hesselton and Hesselton (1982), Halls (1984), W. Smith (1991), and K. Miller et al. (2003).

Alces alces

MOOSE

Description

Largest of extant cervids, moose are black, chocolate brown, or reddish brown with paler legs and belly. The winter pelage is grayer. Calves are reddish or rusty and lack the white spots characteristic of other young cervids. The long hair is coarse, brittle, and longer on the neck and shoulders than elsewhere. The front legs are longer than the hindlegs, creating a sloping back. There are 4 hooves on each foot; 2 are reduced in size and elevated as dewclaws. The large head has a long, broad muzzle and a heavy, bulbous nosepad. A fold of skin—the "bell" or dewlap—dangles from the throat region. Ears are large and erect. The tail is short and inconspicuous. The skull has a greatly elongated premaxillary region. Dentition can be used to age individuals (R. Peterson 1955; Sergeant and Pimlott 1959). Measurements are: total length 2,400–2,900 mm; length of tail 75–115 mm; length of hindfoot 750–850 mm; length of

PHOTOGRAPH 14-5. Moose (*Alces alces*). Photograph by J. W. Jackson. All rights reserved. Photo Archives, Denver Museum of Nature and Science.

ear 200–300 mm; weight 380–550 kg. (The upper weight limit applies to *Alces alces gigas*, the Alaskan subspecies.) Accurate weight and measurement data for *Alces a. shirasi* (the subspecies introduced to Colorado from the Middle Rockies) are lacking. An adult moose measures around 1.9 m tall at the shoulders. As with most cervids, tremendous changes in weight can occur between early spring and fall. Female moose may show a 48 percent increase in weight over this time span (Gasaway and Coady 1974).

Adult males have large palmate antlers that spread outward and backward from the skull. The total mass of the antlers can exceed 25 kg in mature bulls. Maximal antler development occurs between 8 and 13 years of age (Gasaway 1975; Bubenik 1998). Each antler has a number of points or tines that extend from the edges of the "palm" of the antlers. The shedding and growth pattern is similar to that of other deer. Bony outgrowths appear from the frontal bones in late winter. They grow through the summer and are relatively soft, covered with a highly vascularized, finely haired, thin skin, termed "velvet." In late summer and early fall the antlers harden and the velvet is rubbed off against bushes and trees. The hardened antlers remain on the animals through the rutting season into early winter, at which time they are shed (cast).

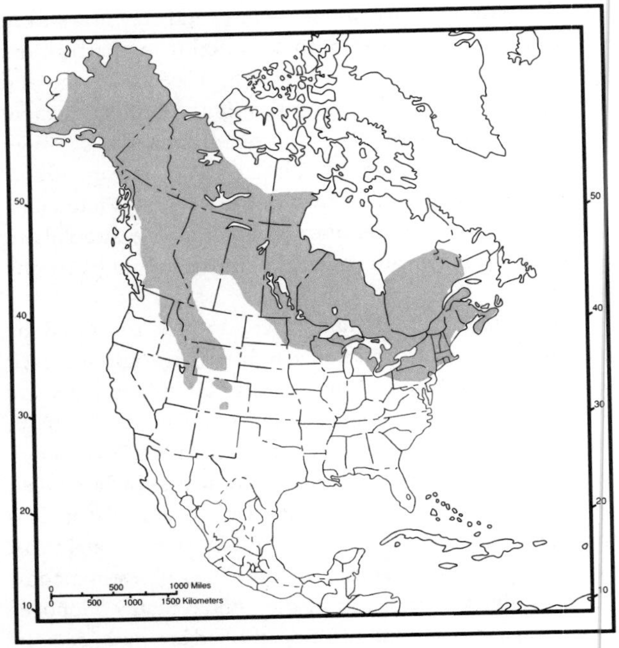

MAP 14-7. Distribution of the moose (*Alces alces*) in North America.

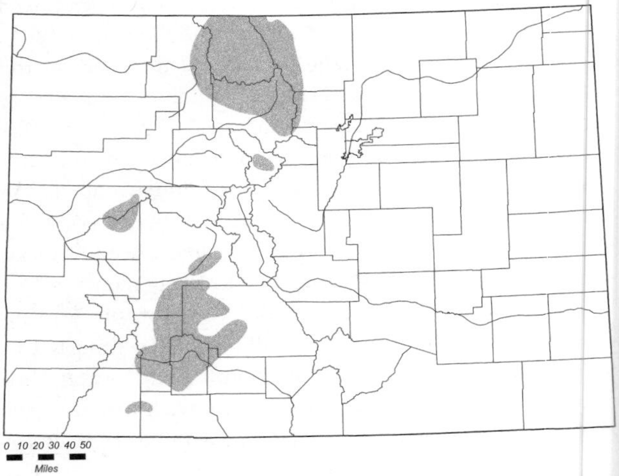

MAP 14-8. Distribution of the introduced moose (*Alces alces*) in Colorado.

Distribution

The moose of the New World is termed "elk" in the Old World, a Holarctic species distributed from northwestern Europe to northeastern North America. Moose are typically associated with areas with seasonal snow cover and forests. Moose wander widely, and there are several recent reports from the Central Great Plains (summarized by J. Hoffman et al. 2006). Similarly, in the past, moose were only occasional visitors to Colorado, with records of individuals from Routt, Larimer, and Rio Blanco counties. These animals were apparent stragglers that wandered into the northern part of the state from resident populations in Utah or Wyoming (D. Armstrong 1972). There is no documented record of breeding populations of moose in Colorado prior to their introduction by the Division of Wildlife beginning in 1978 (Nowlin et al. 1979), although moose have been expanding their range southward since the late 1800s (R. Peterson 1955; Duvall and Schoonveld 1988). The first release of moose (5 bulls and 19 cows and female calves) in Colorado occurred in 1978 and 1979 along the Illinois River in North Park (Nowlin et al. 1979). The habitat is willow and lodgepole pine at elevations of 2,700–2,850 m (8,850–9,350 ft.). A second release (2 bulls and 10 cows and female calves) was made 50 km to the northeast in 1987 (Duvall and Schoonveld 1988). Since then, animals have become established in several adjacent areas, including Middle Park, the upper reaches of the Laramie and Cache la Poudre rivers, and Rocky Mountain National Park. Other sightings have been reported in South Park, near Leadville, near Gunnison, near Yampa, and west of Denver. More recently, introductions were made in the area northwest of Creede in the early 1990s (Olterman et al. 1994; Olterman and Kenvin 1998), with 106 animals released to 12 different sites. In addition, 20 animals were introduced near Spring Creek Pass northwest of Creede in 1991 and an additional 45 animals were introduced there in 1992. Kufeld (1994) reviewed transplants and populations of moose in Colorado from 1978 to the 1990s. Stocks in Colorado came from the Uinta Mountains of northern Utah and from Grand Teton National Park, Wyoming. Moose have since been released on Grand Mesa, and one would assume that the species eventually will invade all suitable habitats in the state from the founding stocks (Kufeld and Bowden 1996a). Genetic variation in North American moose is rather low, suggesting bottlenecks in the population during the Pleistocene (Hundertmark and Bowyer 2004).

A. a. shirasi is the subspecies of the Rocky Mountain West, including animals transplanted to Colorado. North American moose have been called *Alces americanus* (see Grubb 2005b:653) but there is growing consensus that *Alces alces* is a single Holarctic species.

Natural History

Moose are inhabitants of boreal forest edge and openings in forests adjacent to water. Moose require a plentiful supply of browse, including stems, bark, buds, and leaves of deciduous or evergreen trees or shrubs for winter forage. Consequently, they are largely dependent on early successional vegetation in areas that have been recently burned, logged, or manipulated by beavers (M. Wolfe 1974). Daily forage intake (dry weight) is estimated to be 5 kg in winter and about 11 kg in warmer months. Typical moose habitat in the Rocky Mountains includes a mixture of willow, spruce, fir, aspen, alder, and birch. Willows are a winter staple on many western ranges (Peek 1974, 1997). Willow was the most commonly used community in North Park, followed by lodgepole pine stands. Aspen, spruce-fir, and grass meadows were used to lesser extents (Kufeld and Bowden 1996a); those authors recommended that clear-cuts in lodgepole pine forests be kept small so that no point was more than 100 m from cover and that lodgepole pine cover be left adjacent to willow bottoms.

In the Greys River Valley of western Wyoming, snowmobile traffic caused moose to move to less favorable habitat. The machines influenced movement of moose as much as 300 m from the trail (Colescott and Gillingham 1998). Even major habitat disturbance is not necessarily detrimental to moose. Fires and subsequent succession appear important in maintaining moose habitat over much of their range (Bowyer et al. 2003), but severe fire has been detrimental to moose in Yellowstone, at least in the short term. On the Tanana River Flats near Fairbanks, Alaska, Bowyer et al. (2001) found that bulls selected areas of willow thicket that had been treated by crushing with a bulldozer on frozen ground, apparently drawn by abundant new growth. Cows and calves favored untreated control sites.

During spring, summer, and fall, moose also utilize a variety of herbaceous vegetation, including grasses, sedges, aquatic emergents, and forbs. In Wyoming, principal foods are willows, algae, pondweed, and occasionally sagebrush (R. H. Denniston 1956). Summer diet of moose in Rocky Mountain National Park (Dungan and Wright 2005) included 20 species of plants, among them 6 kinds of willow that comprised 91 percent of the diet from June to mid-September (of which about half was contributed by Geyer willow [*Salix geyeriana*]). Other summer food plants included alder (2.5 percent), aspen (1.1 percent), birch (1.0 percent), aquatic plants (1.9 percent), forbs (1.1 percent), and grasses (0.9 percent). Working in the Grand Teton National Park, Wyoming, Berger et al. (2001) found that depressed populations of Neotropical migrant birds were associated with the high moose populations that resulted from the absence of hunting by humans, grizzlies, and wolves.

Competition for food between moose and elk usually is minimal (D. Stevens 1974) but may increase in severe winters (K. Jenkins and Wright 1987). Interspecific competition was discussed by Bowyer et al. (2003). In Colorado, the potential exists for competition with elk and beaver for willow browse, and willows can be seriously impacted by overuse (see Zeigenfuss et al. 2002). Therefore, decisions about management of moose can influence ecosystem dynamics (Naiman et al. 1994).

Moose are less social than other cervids (Altmann 1956; R. H. Denniston 1956) and sexual and spatial segregation is highly developed (Bowyer et al. 2001). Moose are reclusive and have strong attachments to particular home ranges, although some populations make seasonal migrations and many individuals will wander considerable distances in search of suitable new habitat. Yearling animals appear to be more mobile than adults and maintain larger home ranges (Houston 1968, 1974). Philopatry, a fidelity to specific ranges, may lengthen the time for colonization of suitable adjacent habitats. Most moose introduced in the vicinity of Creede moved less than 50 km from the release site (Olterman and Kenvin 1998). Mean areas occupied averaged 625 km^2 for males and 772 km^2 for females, with the authors indicating that the large size was related to animals either moving between seasonal home ranges or changing home ranges from one year to another. In North Park, home ranges (minimum convex polygons) ranged from 0.1 to 351.0 km^2, depending on sex and age of individuals, with seasonal areas up to 76 km^2 for bulls and 74 km^2 for cows. Subadult males showed the largest polygons, calves the smallest (Kufeld and Bowden 1996a). Males moved an average distance of 19 km and females 21 km between summer- and autumn-use areas. Elevational levels of ranges varied from 3,487 m to 2,451 m, with higher elevations often used in late summer and fall. Home ranges cited in other literature typically encompass no more than 5–10 km^2 (range, 3–92 km^2) and are usually smaller in winter than in summer. Moose calves have the same home range as the mother in their first year of life, and typically female calf moose tend to establish home ranges overlapping those of their mothers (Ballard et al. 1991; Bowyer et al. 2003). Density of moose at the Colorado release site in North Park did not exceed 0.38 individuals per square kilometer (Nowlin 1985).

Moose are uniquely adapted for survival in cold, snowy environments. Their long legs, large body size, and the insulative properties of their hair enable them to endure extreme cold in excess of –30°C without exceeding their thermal neutral zone. In fact, they may heat-stress at temperatures of 14 to 20°C (Renecker and Hudson 1986, 1990). Ongoing climate change may at some point influence the southern range for the species. Snow depth appears to trigger most movements in fall and winter, although moose can paw through up to 40 cm of snow in search of forage and can handle depths to 70 cm before their movements are severely hindered. During winter, moose may "yard up," or aggregate, in riparian areas. Snowmobile use in moose winter range may disturb animals, forcing them into less favorable areas (Colescott and Gillingham 1998). Moose are typically solitary and tend to ignore each other. In North Park, cows with calves maintained a spaced dispersion throughout the year, whereas bulls, cows without calves, and yearlings showed a clumped pattern during winter (Nowlin 1985). The only durable social bonds are those formed between cows and their calves, and they are typically broken just before birth of the next offspring.

Moose breed in fall, from mid-September to early November (R. H. Denniston 1956), with the peak in late September and early October. At that time bulls become aggressive toward each other and may display or fight for females. Bulls rub and thrash shrubs and small trees. Both males and females increase their vocalizations during the rut, using barks, croaks, and moans. Bulls respond to calls that sound like the grunt of a cow moose. As with other cervids, males typically show swelling of the neck and shoulders and forage very little, if at all. If not bred, females go through successive estrous cycles at 20- to 30-day intervals. Gestation lasts approximately 231 days, but females in a second estrus can shorten their gestation (C. Schwartz and Hundertmark 1993); most calving occurs in late May and early June (R. Peterson 1955). Some Alaskan moose form harems, but in Colorado a "tending-bond" mating system is typical, in which a dominant bull follows and protects a cow until she allows him to breed (Bowyer et al. 2003). However, small groups of bulls and cows may form at this time and agonistic interactions among males and among females may be exhibited (Altmann 1959). A single young is the mode, with twins occurring only in about 11 to 29 percent of births. Triplets are much rarer. Nowlin (1985) reported an initial calf/cow ratio of 77:100 and a 12 percent twinning rate in North Park, and Kufeld (1994) and Bowden and Kufeld (1995) reported ratios of 56:100 in later studies in the area. Olterman and Kenvin (1998) found calf/cow ratios of 52:100 in the Upper Rio Grande drainage of southwestern Colorado, recruitment comparable to increasing herds in Alaska. Moose calves weigh 12 to 13 kg at birth but may reach weights of around 175–180 kg by October, a gain of about 1 kg per day.

Both nutrition and population density appear to influence reproductive potential. With low populations and high forage availability, yearlings breed and adults have twins. In areas of high population density, yearlings often do not breed and females produce a single young (Blood 1974). Sex ratios usually approximate 1:1 in unhunted populations but may be as low as 40:100 bulls to cows in heavily hunted areas (although in the latter case reproductive success apparently is not significantly impaired; Bishop and Rausch 1974). An adult bull can service only 2 or 3 cows effectively, indicating that sex ratios of at least 50:100 bulls to cows are essential for good herd management (Vieira 2006).

Adult moose typically show high survival rates. Olterman and Kenvin (1998) reported survival of 0.94 in adult males and 0.83 in adult female moose near Creede. Kufeld and Bowden (1996b) also reported high rates of survival in North Park. Had it not been for illegal kills, the rates would have been close to 1.0 and 0.88. Despite such mortality, the population has expanded into the Laramie River drainage and has allowed controlled harvest starting in 1985, when 5 licenses for antlered animals were issued. In 5 reporting years between 1995 and 2007, an annual average of 191 hunters bagged an average of 116 moose (see Table 4-2).

As with other North American cervids, major mortality factors are hunting, malnutrition, and predation. In Colorado, efficient moose predators are absent. Wolves are the principal predator in northern parts of the range, and black bears and grizzly bears also take a toll, especially on calves (Hosley 1949; Franzmann et al. 1980), but in Colorado, moose populations do not occur in prime black bear habitat. Other predators implicated in moose kills are mountain lions, wolverines, coyotes, lynx, and domestic dogs, although mortality from such carnivores is low. Snow cover in excess of 70 cm severely impairs moose movement and may result in significant winter mortality from malnutrition. As with most cervids, winter mortality generally impacts calves the hardest, followed by older adults and adult males. Increasing use of snowmobiles across the West can also have impacts on moose (Colescott and Gillingham 1998). As with other cervids in Colorado, chronic wasting disease has been reported from moose, with records from Jackson and western Larimer counties. For details on CWD, see the account of the mule deer.

For reviews of the biology of moose, see R. Peterson (1955), Houston (1968), Franzmann (1978, 1981, 2000), Coady (1982), Franzmann and Schwartz (1998), Peek and Morris (1998), Bowyer et al. (2003), and Franzmann et al. (2007).

Family Antilocapridae—Pronghorn

The family Antilocapridae is an exclusively North American lineage. Only 1 species, the pronghorn, *Antilocapra americana*, survives today. The family is known as beginning in the Middle Miocene, with some 20 extinct genera known (E. Davis 2007). The modern pronghorn first appeared in the Early Pleistocene (Kurtén and Anderson 1980). The pronghorn and its fossil relatives are usually placed in a distinct family, although some authors (O'Gara and Matson 1975) place the group in a subfamily, Antilocaprinae, within the family Bovidae. However, the bone core of the pronghorn is an outgrowth from the frontal bone, as are pedicels in cervids. Antilocaprids and cervids also have 2 lacrimal foramina, in contrast to bovids, which have a single lacrimal foramen inside the anterior rim of the orbit of the eye. The pronghorn frequently is called "pronghorn antelope," or simply "antelope," but those names both are misnomers. True antelope are Old World mammals, members of the bovid subfamily Antilopinae, which includes the familiar gazelles of East Africa.

Antilocapra americana

PRONGHORN

Description

The pronghorn is a rather small, graceful ungulate with a decidedly large head and prominent, laterally positioned eyes. Males are larger than females. The general color is pale reddish brown to tan, with two broad white bands across the throat. The ventral surface and rump are white. In males the dorsal surface of the muzzle is often dark, and black jaw patches are visible on the side of the cheeks close to the neck. The guard hairs are moderately long, hollow, brittle, and coarse, with a longer, dark mane of hairs on the nape of the neck. The underfur is woolly. Hairs on the rump can be erected to form a conspicuous patch used to communicate potential danger. Fawns are similar to adults but paler in color with indistinct markings. Measurements are: total length 1,000–1,500 mm; length of tail 75–180 mm; length of hindfoot 400–432 mm; length of ear 140–150 mm; weight 36–70 kg. Adult pronghorn stand about 900 mm at the shoulder. The skull has an elongated antorbital vacuity and 2 lacrimal foramina at the anterior rim of the orbit. Lower incisors and canines are spatulate and cheekteeth are hypsodont and selenodont. Developmental changes in dentition allow aging (Dow and Wright 1962; McCutchen 1969).

PHOTOGRAPH 14-6. Pronghorn (*Antilocapra americana*). Photograph by Joseph Van Wormer. All rights reserved. Photo Archives, Denver Museum of Nature and Science.

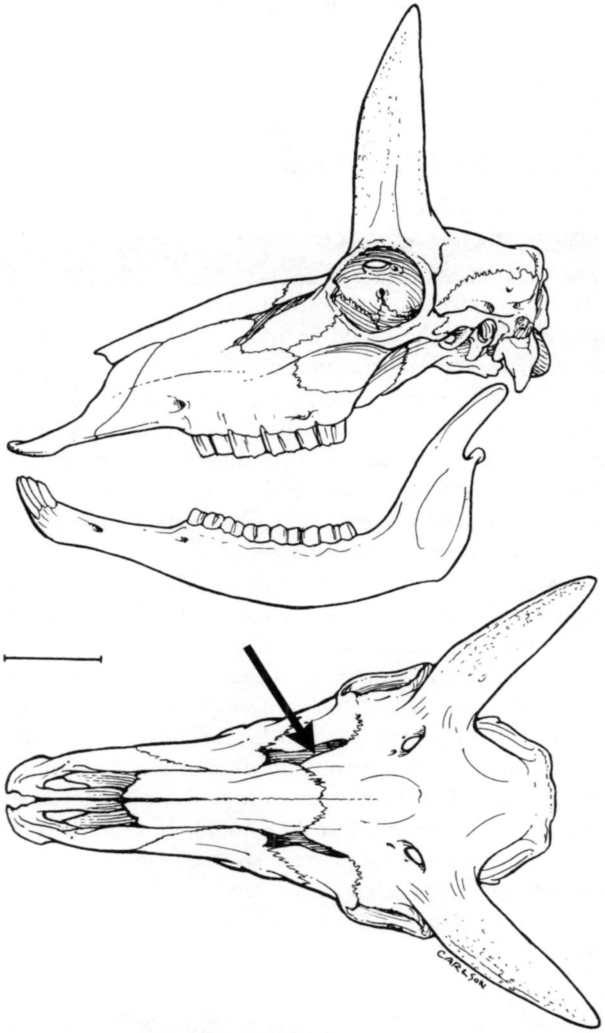

FIGURE 14-2. Lateral and dorsal views of the skull of a male pronghorn (*Antilocapra americana*). Note the prominent ethmoid vacuity (*arrow*). Scale = 5 cm.

Males and most females have horns that are composed of laterally flattened bony cores arising from the frontal bones, covered with a keratinous mass of fused hairs that form a sheath. The sheath is shed annually following the breeding season (O'Gara et al. 1971). Horns of females usually are very short, unforked nubs. Those of males are forked about one-third of the way from the tip and may exceed 250 mm in length; largest horn measurements may be reached in animals only 2 to 3 years old (C. Mitchell and Maher 2001). Min (1997) studied variation in horns and cheek patches of males in Middle Park and showed that these sexually dimorphic features are more variable than other morphological features, suggesting that they may be under sexual selection. Skin glands are well developed in the cheek area (the jaw patch), on the hock, between the hooves, and on the rump. Females have 4 mammae and a cotyledonary, epitheliochorial placenta.

Distribution

The pronghorn is an endemic North American mammal typically associated with high deserts and grasslands. Populations are scattered throughout most of the western United States, the prairie provinces of Canada, and northern Mexico. Almost half of the population is believed to be in Wyoming (J. Byers 2003b). In Colorado the species is found on the eastern plains, in the larger mountain parks and valleys, and on shrublands west of the mountains. Pronghorn were formerly very abundant throughout their range. Around 1800, more than 40 million animals were present, with about 2 million in Colorado (R. Hoover et al. 1959). Subsequently, the species was seriously threatened with extinction by early market hunters. By the early 1900s there were few pronghorn remaining and many states provided them complete protection (E. Nelson 1928). Under this

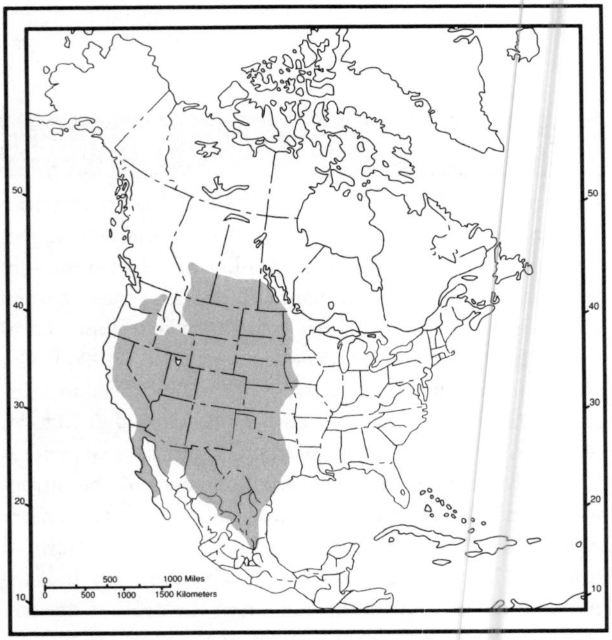

MAP 14-9. Distribution of the pronghorn (*Antilocapra americana*) in North America.

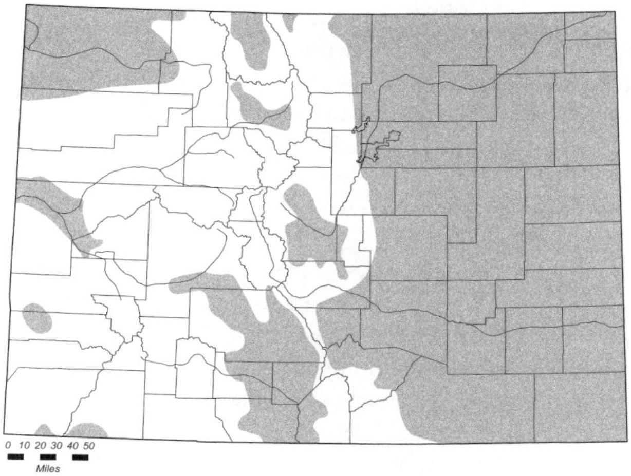

MAP 14-10. Distribution of the pronghorn (*Antilocapra americana*) in Colorado.

protection the animals began to increase and limited hunting seasons have since been allowed in most states within their range. The post-hunt population estimate of numbers of pronghorn in Colorado was 72,600 in 2007 (Colorado Division of Wildlife 2008g). Despite their secure status and abundance locally, 2 of the 5 subspecies of *Antilocapra americana* (the Sonoran pronghorn, *A. a. sonoriensis*, and *A. a. peninsularis* of Baja California) are listed as endangered under the Convention on International Trade in Endangered Species, although (based on mitochondrial DNA research) T. Lee et al. (1994) suggested that subspecific distinctions might not all be valid. One subspecies, *Antilocapra americana americana*, occurs in Colorado.

Natural History

Pronghorn inhabit grasslands and semidesert shrublands on rolling topography that affords good visibility. They are most abundant in shortgrass or mixed prairies and least common in xeric habitats. As an important big game mammal, pronghorn in Colorado have been the subject of considerable research. The average year-round diet in Colorado is approximately 43 percent forbs, 43 percent browse, 11 percent cactus, and 3 percent grass (Hoover et al. 1959). In the northern parts of the range, browse is the major food item, forming up to 64 percent of the annual diet and more than 70 percent during fall and winter; forbs and grasses constitute 24 percent of the annual diet and 7 percent of the fall and winter diet. In southern portions of their range, pronghorn are more dependent on forbs. On the Pawnee National Grassland in northeastern Colorado, grasses and forbs each represent 45–48 percent of the diet, and shrubs comprise 5 percent or less (C. Schwartz and Nagy 1976).

Delicate feeders, pronghorn are more selective than sheep, cattle, and bison (C. Schwartz et al. 1977). However, they do consume such plants as larkspur, locoweed, *Hymenoxys*, cocklebur, *Haplopappus*, yucca, and needle-and-thread, which are known to be poisonous or injurious to domestic stock (Hoover et al. 1959). In northwestern Colorado, shrubs make up more than 90 percent of the fall and winter diet on sagebrush and bitterbrush range, whereas forbs account for 64 to 80 percent of the spring and summer diet (Bear 1973). In Kansas, successful populations fed largely on forbs in late spring, summer, and early autumn; on forbs supplemented with wheat in late autumn and early spring; and on wheat and alfalfa in winter (Sexson et al. 1981). The use of cultivated crops during winter, when native foods are in short supply, varies with location and degree of agricultural activity. Although pronghorn are frequently observed in wheat fields, they do not appear to cause much if any impact on grain production (Liewer 1988; Torbit et al. 1993; Pojar et al. 1995), in part because they feed on winter wheat seedlings and then move out of wheat fields before "jointing" of stems and flowering of the wheat. Plant cover and structure are important for dietary needs and can also provide important hiding cover for neonates (Jacques et al. 2007). Although they are drought-tolerant, pronghorn like to drink daily during the warmer months and their distribution is often dictated by the location of water sources (Deblinger and Alldredge 1991).

Pronghorn may be active at any time but peaks of activity are crepuscular, especially when daytime temperatures are high. At night more time is spent bedded down than foraging. The size of home ranges occupied by pronghorn varies with season, habitat quality, population characteristics, and patterns of livestock use. Home ranges are from about 165 ha to more than 2,300 ha, with winter home ranges somewhat smaller than summer ones (D. Kitchen and O'Gara 1982). In certain areas adult males are territorial and maintain territories of 25 to 440 ha on good ranges. Normally, daily movements do not exceed 10 km. Pronghorn may make seasonal migrations between winter and summer ranges but, unlike those of most cervids, such movements appear to be tied more closely to succulence of vegetation than to weather conditions such as snow accumulation.

Pronghorn are rightly renowned for their extraordinary speed, estimates of which range beyond 60 mi. per hour. This is considerably faster, by the way, than any extant North American predator, so to understand pronghorn it is relevant to note that prior to the Holocene, cheetahs (*Acinonyx*) lived in the American West, including Colorado (Emslie 1986), so their extraordinary speed makes adaptive sense in historical context, the "ghost of predators past" (J. Byers 1997a). On fenced ranges, pronghorn prefer to crawl or slide under the barrier when possible rather than jumping over it. Thoughtful ranchers in pronghorn country often raise the lower wires of their fences to facilitate this behavior.

Pronghorn are highly social mammals with numerous stereotyped behavioral patterns and several vocalizations (Prenzlow et al. 1968; Waring 1969; D. Kitchen 1974). In spring and summer older, more dominant bucks are solitary whereas younger males form bachelor bands of up to a dozen or more individuals. Sparring and other low-level forms of aggression are often observed in these groups. After fawning, females form nursery bands that may include an occasional older male. J. Byers (2003b) reported that groups of female pronghorn show highly aggressive interactions. These lead to complex hierarchies of dominance (Fairbanks 1993). During winter large herds of mixed sex and age classes may form. Such concentrations facilitate census efforts (Bear 1969). Although conspicuous in the open landscapes that they inhabit, pronghorn are difficult to census. Pojar et al. (1995) suggested that aerial survey of quadrats is the least biased, most precise method.

Pronghorn breed in the fall, from mid-September to mid-October. At this time bachelor herds tend to break up, and older males from such herds attempt to mate with does attracted to mature bucks. The dominant males attempt to retain harems or to mate with does on their territories. Males do not start to breed until about 3 years of age and many never get an opportunity to mate. J. Byers (1997a) found females to control mating choice, mating with only 1 male during estrus. These sexual behaviors vary depending on a combination of range conditions and demographic factors, such as population size and sex ratios, and may even shift within a population (J. Byers 1997a). When succulent, palatable vegetation is clumped, such as in sagebrush habitats in the northern part of the range, mature bucks tend to be territorial. These territories are maintained from March through October. When sex ratios heavily favor females, when population densities are low, and in grassland areas, bucks typically gather harems and territories are not maintained (Hoover et al. 1959).

Females are diestrous, ovulation coincides with copulation, and a second estrus occurs 28 days later if females do not conceive (Pojar and Miller 1984). Females usually breed first at about 16 months of age, although some may enter estrus at 5 months (J. Byers 1997a). Typically they will then have young each year until they die (J. Byers 1997a). Gestation lasts about 9 months (36 weeks). Most fawns are dropped from late May to mid-June in Colorado (Hoover et al. 1959), although Pojar and Miller (1984) reported bimodal peaks of fawning in mid-June and mid-July for animals in southeastern Colorado. Twins are the rule in good habitat and fawns weigh 3 to 4 kg at birth. Birth weights of wild pronghorn fawns in Middle Park (Fairbanks 1993) were greater than those recorded for pen-reared animals (Wild et al. 1994). Sex ratios approximate 1:1 at birth, but differential mortality, including hunting of bucks, may lead to skewed ratios of 1 male to as many as 5 females. Females leave the herd to give birth and keep the young segregated for 3 to 6 weeks. In Wind Cave National Park, southwestern South Dakota, fawns were bedded in areas dominated by grasses rather than shrubs or forbs (Jacques et al. 2007); in south-central Wyoming, dense cover of sagebrush was selected (A. Alldredge et al. 1991).

Adult pronghorn mortality is mostly caused by hunting. Harvest of more than 40 percent of a herd in northwestern Colorado led to significant population decline, whereas 20 percent harvest rates allowed continued population growth (Bear 1968), so permitted harvest is tied closely to population size. In 5 reporting years between 1995 and 2007 (see Table 4-2), an estimated average of 11,830 license-holders took a mean of 7,825 pronghorn annually, a success rate of 66.1 percent. Accidental deaths also may be high from such causes as fence entanglement and suffocation against fences during blizzards. The severe winter of 2006 caused deaths of several hundred pronghorn on the plains when the animals were trapped by the deep snows on railroad tracks and then hit and killed by trains (T. Black, Colorado Division of Wildlife, personal communication). Great speed and keen eyes (set on the sides of the head, allowing remarkable peripheral vision but probably poor depth perception) protect adult pronghorn from most predators. Coyotes, bobcats, and golden eagles are among the most important predators (Hoover et al. 1959). Predation may cause localized losses of fawns of 12 to 99 percent (D. Kitchen and O'Gara 1982; J. Byers 1997b). Coyotes are implicated in most studies that show high fawn mortality (J. Byers 2003a; G. E. Phillips and White 2003; Jacques et al. 2007), with the latter authors showing condition models under which coyote control may be warranted. Very few pronghorn live more than 9 years in the wild but survivorship is typically high for adult males until about age 7 and females until age 10 (J. Byers 2003b). Lance and Pojar (1984) reviewed diseases and parasites, and general reviews of the biology of the pronghorn were provided by O'Gara (1978), Yoakum and Spalinger (1979), D. Kitchen and O'Gara (1982), Byers (1997a, 2003a, 2003b), and O'Gara et al. (2004). McCabe et al. (2004) provided an excellent summary of pronghorn-human interactions, focused particularly on the period before permanent Euro-American settlement of the West.

Family Bovidae—Cattle, Sheep, Goats, and Kin

The family Bovidae includes a remarkable array of browsing and grazing ungulates, from the slender, graceful antelopes of Asia and Africa to various stout, bulky cattle. Adult dik-diks (genus *Modoqua*) of Africa may stand only about 300 mm at the shoulder and weigh 3–6 kg, whereas some breeds of domestic cattle (*Bos taurus*) and the gaur (*Bos gaurus*) of southern Asia may weigh more than 1,000 kg and stand up to 2,200 mm at the shoulder. Most bovids inhabit grasslands, shrublands, or desert, but some have adapted to forests, mountainous terrain, and tundra. In keeping with habitats in open country, most species are gregarious and social, and many are territorial.

Permanent, unbranched horns consisting of a bony core (derived from outgrowths of the frontal bone merging with centers of dermal bone growth) and a horny sheath are present on males of all species and on females of most species. Certain domestic breeds lack horns. The dental formula is 0/3, 0/1, 3/2–3, 3/3 = 30–32 teeth. The lower incisors and canines are spatulate; the cheekteeth are selenodont and typically hypsodont. There is little or no antorbital vacuity and the lacrimal and nasal bones nearly meet. The third and fourth metapodials are fused to form the cannon bone. The ulna and fibula are reduced. Only 2 digits, the third and fourth, bear weight. The second and fifth digits may be absent or present as reduced dew hooves or dewclaws. The digestive system exhibits the 4-chambered ruminant "stomach," and a gall bladder is typically present. There are 2 to 4 mammae, usually merged into an inguinal udder. Scent glands are diverse and well developed in this group. Although 21 different glands have been reported (Gosling 1985), the most common are antorbital, interdigital, and inguinal glands. The placenta is cotyledonary.

The family Bovidae is not very old, dating from the Miocene of Europe, 30 million years ago. Salounias (2007) reviewed the rich fossil record. The rise of ruminant artiodactyls, including the bovids, may have contributed to the decline of the more primitive perissodactyls. The evolution of the bovids did create opportunities for rapid evolution of a number of large carnivores. The family has reached its greatest diversity in recent times, with 50 genera and about 143 species extant (D. Wilson and Reeder 2005), ranging (as natives or introductions) in all parts of the world except the Antarctic. The original distribution was limited to the Holarctic region, Africa, and some of the larger islands of the East Indies. Cattle, sheep, and goats were domesticated very early in the Neolithic Revolution and remain important sources of meat, milk, and fiber for humans. In Colorado there are 3 genera and 3 species of wild bovids, one of which—the mountain goat—is introduced.

Key to the Species of the Family Bovidae (Including Domestic Livestock) in Colorado

1\. Length of skull more than 350 mm; maxillary toothrow more than 120 mm; body large, more than 2,000 mm long; occipital-parietal region of skull at right angle to forehead at level of horns 2

1' Length of skull less than 350 mm; maxillary toothrow less than 120 mm; body less than 2,000 mm long; occipital-parietal region of skull at obtuse angle to forehead at level of horns 3

2\. Premaxillary not in contact with nasals; frontal region greatly expanded, laterally obscuring zygomatic bones in dorsal view; hair on head and front quarters conspicuously longer and more shaggy than hair on hindquarters; distinct hump on shoulder; head massive; both sexes with horns . . . . Bison—*Bison bison*, p. 470

2' Premaxillary touching nasals; frontal region narrower with zygomatic bones visible in dorsal view; hair on head and front quarters not conspicuously longer or shaggier than rest of body; no distinct hump on shoulder or, if present, hair not elongated or shaggy on front quarters; head less massive, more slender; sexes with or without horns . . . . Domestic Cattle—*Bos taurus**

3\. Color white to whitish yellow, hair long, soft, and shaggy; horns present on both sexes, relatively straight, short, slender, and black; horns round in cross section . . . . Mountain Goat—*Oreamnos americanus*,* p. 475

* Domestic species.

3' Color not uniformly white or, if whitish, the hairs typically not long, soft, and shaggy; horns present or absent, and if present not straight, slender, or black; cross section not round 4

4. Horns, if present, not highly pediceled, curling outward and downward; antorbital pits present; premaxillae barely or not touching nasals; premolars with prominent vertical enamel ridges on labial side; beard absent 5

4' Horns, if present, highly pediceled, never curling outward and downward; antorbital pits absent; premaxillae broadly contacting nasals; premolars without prominent vertical enamel ridges on labial side; beard well developed . . . . Domestic Goat—*Capra hircus**

5. Horns present on both sexes, massive at base on adult males, and strongly curling posteriorly, laterally, and downward; longer, straighter guard hairs mask woolly underfur; color uniform grayish brown with paler rump patch . . . . Mountain, or Bighorn, Sheep—*Ovis canadensis*, p. 478

5' Horns variable, present or absent, if present, not massive at base on adult males and not strongly curled; pelage conspicuously woolly, color variable but usually white to pale gray, paler-colored rump patch not typically present . . . . Domestic Sheep—*Ovis aries**

Bison bison

BISON, OR AMERICAN BUFFALO

PHOTOGRAPH 14-7. American bison (*Bison bison*). All rights reserved. Photo Archives, Denver Museum of Nature and Science.

Description

Heavy-bodied and powerfully built, bison are the largest of North American artiodactyls and can weigh up to 1,300 kg. Bison are characterized by a massive head and neck and a stout body that tapers from the heavy front quarters and pronounced shoulder hump to leaner flanks and hindquarters. Hair on the front quarters, neck, and most of the head is brownish black, relatively long, dense, and woolly. Hair on the hindquarters is much shorter and varies seasonally in color from chocolate brown to a paler brownish tan. A distinct beard hangs from the chin. The tail is moderately long with a tufted tip. The broad forehead has short, curved, relatively smooth horns. Males have thicker, longer horns and larger, heavier builds than females. Measurements are: total length 2,000–3,800 mm; length of tail 400–600 mm; length of hindfoot 530–680 mm; height at shoulder 1.5–1.8 m; weight 725–910 kg. The skull has a relatively narrow muzzle and an extremely broad forehead. The nasal bones are long and do not contact the premaxillary bones. Ethmoidal vacuities are lacking. Skulls of plains specimens measured 490–600 mm in greatest length, and greatest width may exceed 240 mm. The cheekteeth are hypsodont and selenodont; upper incisors are lacking. Upper canines are absent although there are a few reports of vestigial canines. Tooth replacement and wear are age indicators (W. Fuller 1959). A number of authors (J. K. Jones, Hoffmann, et al. 1992; Van Zyll de Jong et al. 1995; R. Baker et al. 2003) have placed the bison in the genus *Bos*, whereas other authorities (J. McDonald 1981; Meagher 1986; Grubb 1993, 2005b; Novak 1999; H. W. Reynolds et al. 2003) have retained use of the generic name *Bison*. In this case, contrary to our usual reliance on R. Baker et al. (2003) and instead following Grubb (2005b), we have chosen to retain *Bison*. The modern bison is a relatively young species, having originated only about 10,000 years ago (H. W. Reynolds et al. 2003).

Distribution

The plains bison once ranged over much of southern Canada, the prairie and plains states of the United States eastward to the coastal piedmont, and southward into northeastern Mexico. Numbers were estimated to range from 30 to 60 million. Shaw (1998) discussed problems with these estimates and provided insight into relative abundance

* Introduced species.

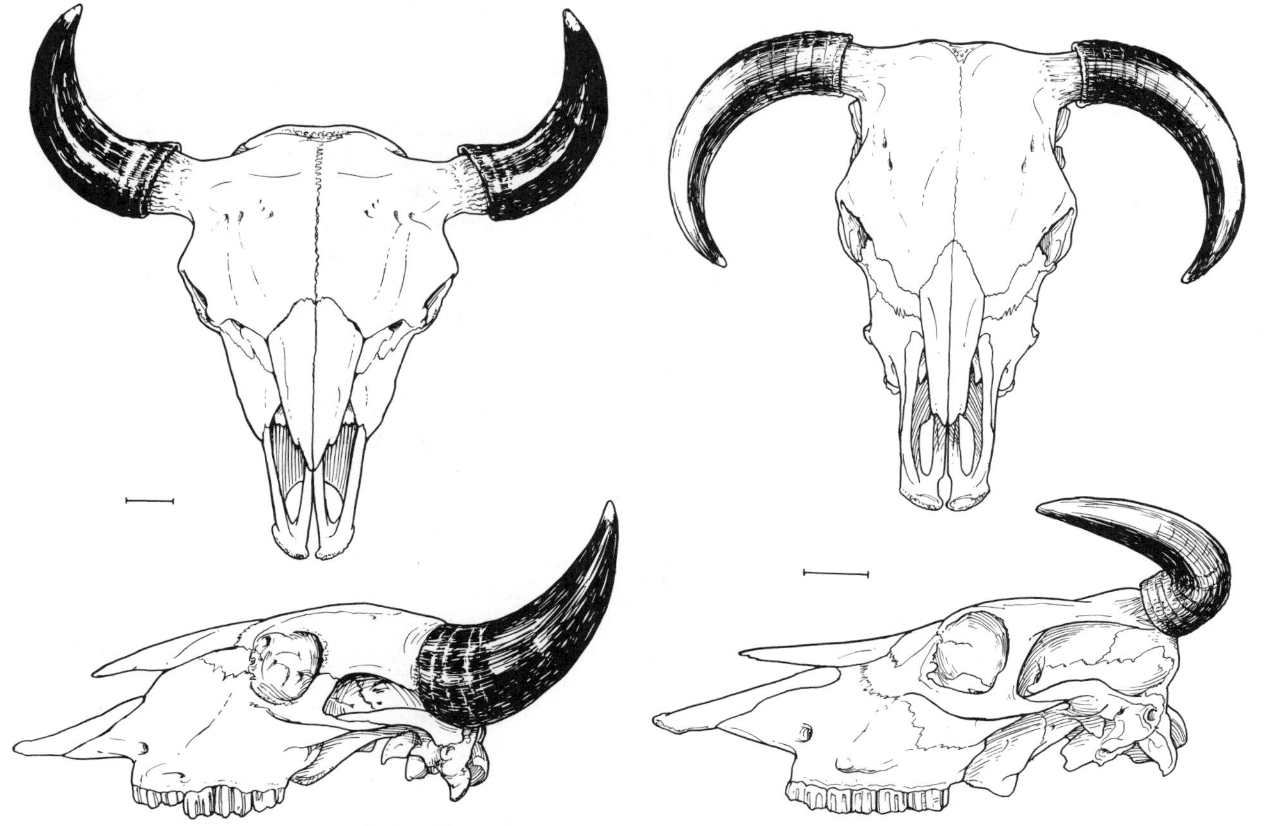

FIGURE 14-3. Dorsal and lateral views of skulls of bison (*Bison bison, left*) and domestic cow (*Bos Taurus, right*). Note that the premaxillary bone contacts the nasal bone in the skull of the domestic cow but not that of the bison. Scale = 5 cm.

and spatial distribution of bison in the early nineteenth century. The historic distribution of bison appears to have been limited by the deserts of western New Mexico, Arizona, and Nevada. The species did range into the northern Great Basin of Oregon, extreme northeastern California, and northwestern Nevada. Bison occupied most of Colorado except for the Uncompahgre Plateau and the San Juan Mountains in the southwest. Meaney and Van Vuren (1993) documented previously unpublished records of bison in the western two-thirds of the state, more clearly elucidating their distribution.

With ongoing climate change in Colorado, the remnant glaciers and ice fields in the Southern Rockies are melting toward their headwalls, sometimes revealing evidence of mammals of the high country. C. Lee et al. (2006) reported bison remains ranging from about 200 to more than 2,000 years old from Buchanan Pass Glacier and 2 smaller ice patches in the Indian Peaks west of Boulder. Remains of elk, mule deer, and bighorn sheep were found as well. There was no direct association of these remains with human hunters, although Native American use of such high-elevation sites is known in considerable detail (see J. Benedict 1992a, 1992b, 2005 for reviews).

Early Coloradan mammalogists (reviewed by D. Armstrong 1972) generally thought that *Bison bison bison*, the plains bison, occupied eastern Colorado, and *B. b. athabascae*, the wood bison or mountain bison, occupied portions of the mountains and western Colorado. However, most recent researchers (H. W. Reynolds et al. 2003) now believe that the wood bison is an animal of northwestern Canada and Alaska far removed from Colorado, which had only *B. b. bison*. Meagher (1986) pointed out that convincing evidence for subspecies is lacking in studies of blood chemistry and chromosomes; however, van Zyll de Jong (1986) pointed out significant cranial and morphological differences, so the status of the subspecies of *Bison bison* remains

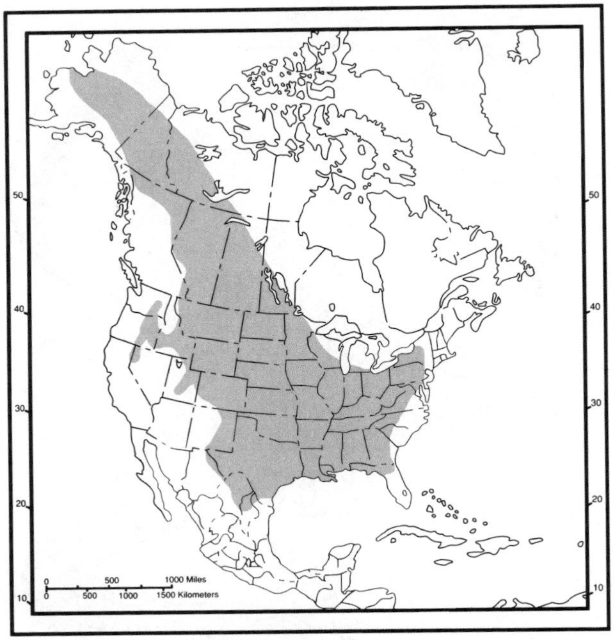

MAP 14-11. Historic distribution of the American bison (*Bison bison*) in North America.

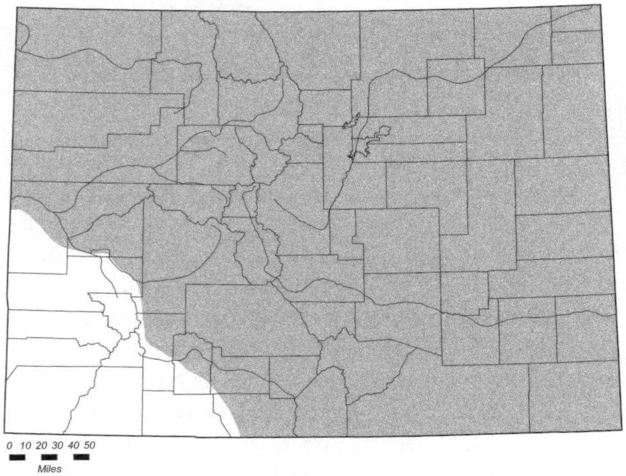

MAP 14-12. Historic distribution of the American bison (*Bison bison*) in Colorado.

open to debate. Based on examination of historical illustrations, Krumbiegel and Sehm (1989) argued that bison of the Northern Rockies and adjacent plains were subspecifically distinct from *Bison bison bison*, the subspecies of the central and southern plains. That work generally has not been accepted by zoologists.

E. Sanderson et al. (2008) estimated that the half million bison in North America today occupy less than 1 percent of their historical geographical range, so their historical ecological role is greatly compromised. Free-ranging herds of bison can still be seen in Yellowstone National Park and in Canada's Wood Buffalo National Park (in northern Alberta and adjacent Northwest Territories). Large, but more closely regulated, populations exist in Wind Cave and Badlands national parks, South Dakota, and on the National Bison Range in Montana. In Colorado, the bison living closest to natural conditions may be those on the Great Sand Dunes National Park and Preserve and the adjacent Medano-Zapata Ranch (owned and managed by The Nature Conservancy of Colorado). Some ranches on the eastern plains maintain relatively large herds, but they are carefully managed and generally closely confined. A small herd of fewer than 20 semi-wild bison existed in Colorado National Monument for several decades (Capp 1964; Wasser 1977). That canyon country probably was not usual habitat for bison under pre-industrial conditions. The herd was started in 1926 from 2 cows and a bull provided by Denver Mountain Parks. Because of detrimental impacts on the vegetation, the animals were removed from the monument in the late 1970s. The source for the Denver Mountain Park herd is thought to have been Yellowstone National Park, sometime between 1914 and 1923 (P. Miller 1964).

Natural History

Historically, no other mammal was as important to the survival of people in western North America as the bison. Native Americans of the plains and mountain parks relied extensively on bison for food, shelter, and clothing (Stiger 2001). Interaction of indigenous Coloradans with bison differed among various groups, from occasional, fortuitous hunting in the Southwest to strong dependence on the Great Plains, especially after the introduction of horses in the eighteenth century (Crum 2009). The arrival of European settlers, who saw bison as a resource to be used and perhaps plundered, marked the beginning of the end. Slaughtered for their hides, meat, and sometimes only their tongues; decimated as a tactic in the military attempt to subdue the Plains Indians; and sometimes shot for mere sport, bison were virtually eliminated from North America in the half century between 1830 and about 1880. Perhaps the most enduring symbol of the vast grasslands they roamed, bison have generated much interest, and their history is both fascinating and sobering (F. Roe 1970; McHugh 1972). Doubtless many of the fascinating and revealing observations of pioneer observers in Kansas and Nebraska collected by Fleharty (1995) reflect late nineteenth-century conditions and attitudes in eastern Colorado as well. Isenberg (2000) integrated the complex history of cultural evolution of both Native Americans and Euro-Americans and the changing ecology of the Great Plains in the demise of the bison. There are significant, ongoing efforts by American Indian groups to restore bison in the West, and hence to reclaim a part of their heritage (Garrett 2007; Zontek 2007). Danz (1997) provided a thorough and interesting interdisciplinary study of the American bison, detailing the natural history and ethnography, the history of its demise as the keystone species of the Great Plains, and the effects (and importance) of its restoration as livestock to small parts of its ancestral range.

Generally a mammal of grasslands, including mountain valleys and parks, bison also occupied semidesert shrublands and piñon-juniper woodlands and even ranged onto the alpine tundra. Bison were a keystone species of the North American tallgrass prairie, where (in conjunction with fire) they had an important impact on shaping species diversity (richness and evenness) of the vegetation (Knapp et al. 1999; Johnsgard 2005; Schuler et al. 2006). The vast herds of bison that roamed the Great Plains were a factor (along with fire, prairie dogs, and recurrent drought) in maintaining shortgrass prairie (J. W. Weaver and Clements 1938; Larson 1940).

The extent to which these movements were cyclic is a matter of contention; close study of reports of early travelers suggests that movements were erratic rather than regular, as bison were encountered more or less continually where long-term observations were possible (R. Hart 2001). Movements of the heavy-bodied, gregarious bison caused tremendous localized impacts, including scarification of soils, elimination of much of the shallow-rooted vegetation by trampling and foraging, and enrichment of soils by defecation and urination. Trampling, coupled with the animals' habits of dusting and mud-wallowing, facilitated the dispersal of seeds of a variety of plants and produced favored habitat for such animals as prairie dogs (and their specialized predator, the black-footed ferret), 13-lined ground squirrels, grasshoppers (and hence grasshopper mice), mound-builder ants (and hence horned lizards), mountain plovers, burrowing owls, and rattlesnakes. The tendency of bison to favor prairie dog colonies and burned areas also contributed to the dynamics of grassland vegetation as well as to prairie dog distribution (Coppock et al. 1983a, 1983b; Coppock and Detling 1986; Detling 1998; Shaw 1998). Edges of prairie dog towns provide optimal foraging habitat for bison in South Dakota (Krueger 1986). The biology and distribution of the brown-headed cowbird (an important brood parasite of several songbirds) were greatly influenced by the bison herds (Chace and Cruz 1998). "Horning" and rubbing of woody vegetation often lead to the death of trees, suggesting that in the past the large herds of bison had an impact on distribution of woody vegetation on the fringes of grasslands and along waterways (Shaw 1998).

Adult bison require about 7.5 kg of food per day, roughly 1.5 percent of their total body mass (A. Hawley et al. 1981). They may range 2 to 3 km per day to meet these dietary demands. Bison are grazers, so grasses, sedges, and rushes constitute the bulk of the diet. In shrublands, however, the species turns to higher percentages of browse, especially in fall and winter. Studies on the Pawnee National Grassland and in Colorado National Monument found bison to rely most heavily on grasses and shrubs at all times of the year (Peden 1976; Wasser 1977). On the Pawnee National Grassland in northeastern Colorado, bison fed on a total of 36 plant species, but 11 species made up the bulk of the diet. A similar selectivity was seen in semidesert shrublands and piñon-juniper woodlands of western Colorado. Saltbush, needle-and-thread, sand dropseed, galleta-grass, and prickly-pear were taken over most other species, and some common plants, including big sagebrush and cheatgrass, were virtually ignored. F. Hein and Preston (1998) reported that bison used different foraging sites at night than in the day and that nocturnal grazing accounted for about 15 percent of total daily grazing time. Post et al. (2001) demonstrated that use of cool-season (C_3) grasses was highest for all sex and age groups in spring and fall, while warm-season, drought-adapted (C_4) grasses, of lower nutritional value, were most often eaten by bulls.

Bison are less selective foragers than are domestic cattle on similar ranges (Peden et al. 1974). Although reasons are not clear, bison are more effective in utilizing low-protein diets during late fall, winter, and early spring than are cattle. By contrast, studies in the Henry Mountains of southeastern Utah found that bison and cattle had a 91 percent dietary overlap in an area seeded with crested wheatgrass and alfalfa. Cattle fed on shrubs more than bison did (Van Vuren and Bray 1983). In a shrub-steppe community, cattle fed on forbs more than did bison (Van Vuren 1984). Bison responded to forage availability, whereas cattle were more constrained by slope and vertical distance to water (Van Vuren 2001).

Bison are highly gregarious, with well-developed herd behaviors. The size of herds may differ with habitat and predation risk (Fortin et al. 2009). They make a number of different vocalizations during the breeding season, with the roaring of bulls a common sound (Gunderson and Mahan 1980). Bison breed in Colorado from July to September. Breeding in Wind Cave National Park in South Dakota occurs from late June to mid-September, reaching its peak between July 21 and August 15. Similar time spans are reported for Yellowstone National Park herds. During the rut, herds increase in size and activity. Bulls increase the frequency of sexual investigation–following behaviors, such as vulval exploration, flehmen (lip curls and head-lifting behaviors associated with olfactory investigation of females), vocalizations, threat postures, horning and thrashing of shrubs, wallowing, and fighting. As females approach estrus, bulls tend them, preventing them from engaging in normal herd routine and segregating them to the periphery of the group. Bonds that form during the rut are transitory, leading to some debate over whether females are polygamous or temporary monogamy occurs. Most females breed first when 2 to 4 years old, although in some instances yearlings breed successfully (Meagher 1973). Percentages of yearlings that breed vary from 6 to 13; by contrast, the proportion of 2-year-olds breeding ranges from 60 to 90 percent. Male bison are sexually mature by their third year, but most breeding is done by animals several years older.

The gestation period is about 285 days, similar to that for domestic cattle. Females are at their highest reproductive peak from 3 to 11 years of age. During that span they can be expected to produce 2 calves every 3 years, with some calves still nursing as yearlings. Twinning is rare. Birthrates in Yellowstone for bison 3 years of age or older varied from 0.40 calves per female in animals infected with brucellosis to 0.81 in older, non-infected females (J. Fuller et al. 2007). Birthrates in brucellosis-free wild herds probably averaged between 60 and 80 percent of reproductively mature females. Most calving occurs from April to June. Sex ratios at birth tend to favor males, averaging about 53 to 56 percent males. Calf crops in extant herds average about 18 to 20 percent of the population; similar numbers were probable in historic times (H. W. Reynolds et al. 1982).

In the Henry Mountains of Utah, characterized by piñon-juniper woodlands, montane forest, and openings of sagebrush and grasses, bison range over a 155,000 ha area (R. Stevens and Walker 1998). Bison social structure on the area is very fluid. Groups of cows, calves, yearlings, and young bulls did not form stable units. Most such groups persisted for only 1 to 4 days before encountering another group and combining and separating, thus forming new groups (Van Vuren 1983). Isolated groups persisted longer. Summer home ranges averaged 52 km^2 with large amounts of overlap. This relatively closed habitat is probably the most significant factor affecting group size. Also in this area females had low calf productivity. The average number of calves per adult cow was 0.52, and suckling by yearlings was frequent, whereas it is infrequent elsewhere (Van Vuren and Bray 1986). The low forage productivity is thought to be the cause of large home ranges and low calf productivity. These conditions may be comparable to what montane or Western Slope bison experienced in Colorado prior to their extirpation.

Free-ranging bison are generally migratory, active animals. It is likely that herds that occupied eastern Colorado tended to move in an east-west direction in late fall and winter so that they could seek refuge from winter storms along the Eastern Slope of the Rockies. This pattern was probably reversed in spring and summer, as open, windswept prairies were sought as a refuge from insect pests. Bison often use well-developed trails during long-distance migrations and are not hesitant to swim rivers. In inclement weather the animals typically "turn tail" and head into the storm, unlike domestic stock, which usually face away from the wind. This trait of bison would be valuable to breed into domestic cattle, which often are driven into fences by prairie blizzards, where they suffocate beneath snowdrifts. Bison obtain forage under the snow by sweeping it away with their broad, well-haired heads. Bison are typically diurnal, with the night spent resting or, more rarely, feeding and traveling.

Predation on bison, other than by humans, probably was limited to some losses to wolves and, to a lesser extent, grizzly bears. Predation probably was highest on calves or older solitary bulls. When wolves were restored to Yellowstone, they had minimal impact on bison for more than 2 years, but they eventually learned to kill bison, especially the young or injured or those in poor condition in late winter (D. W. Smith, Mech, et al. 2000). Historically, predation pressure on bison (and the ecology of the Great Plains generally) changed dramatically with the arrival of Europeans and their guns and horses in the late seventeenth and early eighteenth centuries. Other causes of mortality include anthrax and possibly brucellosis and tuberculosis, although the latter two are difficult to isolate as specific mortality factors (H. W. Reynolds et al. 1982).

In Yellowstone—even in the presence of wolves, grizzly bears, and brucellosis—annual survival of adult females is high, averaging 92 percent (J. Fuller et al. 2007), with an estimated population growth rate of 7 percent, similar to rates reported from Utah and Canada. The incidence of brucellosis in bison in the Yellowstone area has been a matter of contention among cattlemen, environmentalists, and state and federal politicians for years (Meyer and Meagher 1995; National Park Service 2000). J. Fuller et al. (2007) suggested that eradication of brucellosis from the herd might increase population size by 29 percent. Such a change in numbers might lead to even more movement from the national park onto adjacent national forests and private lands. High incidences of intestinal parasites are also thought to lead to some mortality. Drowning is a known mortality factor in Yellowstone and it has been suggested that it was once an important localized factor in free-ranging herds on the Great Plains. Evidence of high mortality associated with weather is lacking unless snowfall is excessive or combined with crusting and ice formation. Bison are long-lived animals, with some surviving 20 to 40 years (Soper 1941).

The literature on the biology of bison was reviewed by H. W. Reynolds et al. (1982), Meagher (1986), and H. W. Reynolds et al. (2003). L. Irby and Knight (1998) edited a major symposium volume on bison management and ecology. J. McDonald (1981) and Lott (2002) wrote readable books on bison biology, and D. Fitzgerald and Hasselstrom (1998) provided a beautiful and moving appreciation in photographs and text. Callanbach (1996) summarized some of the extensive literature on schemes to restore bison to the Great Plains—in their coevolved prehistoric role as a keystone species—as wild but managed herds.

PHOTOGRAPH 14-8. Mountain goat (*Oreamnos americanus*). Photograph by William E. Ervin.

Oreamnos americanus

MOUNTAIN GOAT

Description

The mountain goat has a sturdy build with a slight shoulder hump. The pelage is white to yellowish white with long guard hairs, woolly underfur, and a prominent mane, beard, and chaps. The black horns, hooves, and nosepad contrast sharply with the white pelage. The horns, present on both sexes, are of modest length (190–300 mm), relatively thin, conical, and unbranched. Well-developed horn (postcornual) glands are present at the base of the horns. The legs are short and the hooves have a pliable, elastic, slightly convex pad that extends beyond the rim of the outer hoof wall. This pad allows for excellent traction on steep, rocky cliff faces. Dewclaws are present. Females are smaller than males, and sex and age can be determined in the field (B. Smith 1988), albeit with difficulty, especially if herds are large (Hopkins et al. 1992). Côté and Festa-Bianchet (2003) indicated that the base of the horn is about the width of the eye in females while it is broader than the eye in males. Measurements are: total length 950–1,700 mm; length of tail 80–200 mm; length of hindfoot 300–370 mm; weight 40–140 kg. The skull lacks ethmoidal vacuities and the premaxillae do not contact the nasals. The bony cores of the horns are nearly straight and round in cross section. The posterior palate ends opposite the last upper molar. The lower incisors and canines are spatulate; the cheekteeth are selenodont and hypsodont. Aging techniques for mountain goats have been developed (Brandborg 1955; Lentfer 1955; B. Smith 1988), mostly using dental traits, horn annuli, and length of horns.

Distribution

British Columbia, the southwestern Yukon, and Alaska have the largest concentrations of native mountain goats. They also occur naturally in parts of Washington, Montana, Idaho, and Alberta; introductions have been made in Montana, South Dakota, Nevada, Utah, and Colorado (Côté and Festa-Bianchet 2003). Populations of mountain goats were introduced to Colorado in 1948, 1950, 1961, 1964, 1968, 1970, and 1971. Animals were brought from Idaho (the nearest native population), South Dakota (itself an introduced population), and British Columbia (Rutherford 1972a; Denny 1977). Mountain goats now exist in portions of the San Juan Mountains, West Elk Mountains, Gore Range, and Collegiate Peaks (J. Bailey and Johnson 1977) and on Mount Evans.

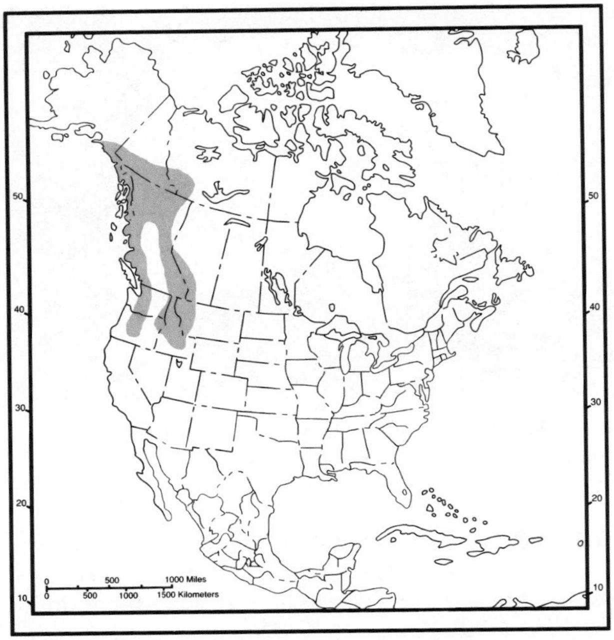

MAP 14-13. Historic distribution of the mountain goat (*Oreamnos americanus*) in North America.

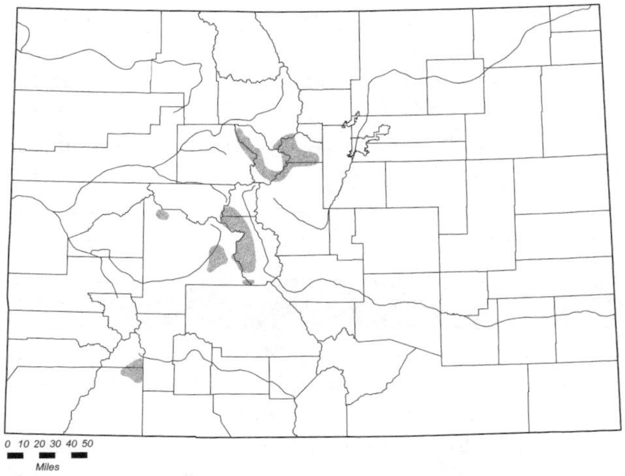

MAP 14-14. Distribution of the introduced mountain goat (*Oreamnos americanus*) in Colorado.

In March 1993, the Colorado Wildlife Commission, at the request of the International Order of Rocky Mountain Goats, and without significant input from Colorado Division of Wildlife biologists or other scientists, declared the mountain goat a native species (*Rocky Mountain News*, March 12, 1993). In part, the decision to list the mountain goat as native was an effort to preclude Rocky Mountain National Park from taking any action against goats invading bighorn sheep range within the park. M. Irby and Chappell (1994) reviewed an abundance of literature, primarily from historical accounts, to make the case that the mountain goat was indeed native to Colorado. Beidleman et al. (2000) listed some additional early references to mountain goats in Colorado, mostly in nineteenth-century popular literature. John Gross et al. (2000) reviewed the subject in detail, in the context of concerns about competition with native species (especially bighorn sheep) in Rocky Mountain National Park. Their conclusion (consistent with D. Armstrong 1972; J. Fitzgerald et al. 1994; among others) is that mountain goats are not native to the Southern Rockies. Park Service policy is to remove non-native species from the lands that they manage (D. Armstrong 2008). Houston and Schreiner (1995) published a general review of policies on alien species in US national parks.

In summary, despite the declaration of the Wildlife Commission, there are no authoritative scientific data to indicate that the modern mountain goat is a native species in the Southern Rockies, so we continue to consider the mountain goat as non-native to Colorado. Late Pleistocene remains of *Oreamnus americanus* were reported from Little Box Elder Cave at the northern end of the Laramie Mountains in southern Wyoming (Kurtén and Anderson 1980). Remains of an extinct species of mountain goat, *O. harringtoni*, were reported from deposits aged at about 600,000–850,000 years old from Porcupine Cave, in Park County, Colorado (Barnosky and Bell 2004).

I. Cowan and McCrory (1970) studied geographic variation and concluded that *Oreamnos americanus* is monotypic; previously, 4 subspecies had been recognized, with the name *O. a. missoulae* being applied to the population from the Middle Rockies introduced into Colorado. The species first appears in the fossil record about 300,000 years ago in British Columbia.

Natural History

Mountain goats are mammals of glaciated subalpine and alpine tundra and typically do not descend much below the level of the tree line, although they may temporarily use trees for shelter from wind and severe cold or snow. They normally also do not venture far from talus or rock faces. The best habitat appears to be a mixture of talus, cliffs, alpine meadows, ridgetops, and subalpine ecotones (J. Saunders 1955; John Gross et al. 2002), although in South

Dakota, introduced animals have thrived in montane forests on the Black Hills.

Summer forage consists of graminoids (grasses and sedges, 50–95 percent of the diet) and forbs (broad-leafed herbs, 4–14 percent of the diet) (J. Saunders 1955; Hibbs 1967; B. Johnson et al. 1978). Winter diets are also predominantly graminoids (88–90 percent) and browse (10–12 percent). Summer diets of Coloradan mountain sheep and mountain goats are similar, but in winter, goats eat fewer graminoids and more forbs than do sheep (Dailey et al. 1984). Mountain goats need free water or snow and typically select ranges that have abundant supplies of salts; they are known to travel 24 km or more to visit mineral licks (Brandborg 1955; Hopkins 1992; Hopkins et al. 1992).

Depending on local topographic and climatic conditions, some populations winter at high elevations on windblown slopes, while others migrate to tree line or even lower elevations during the winter (Hopkins et al. 1992). Migrations usually involve moves of only 4–6 km, but some populations may move as far as 24 km. Spring migrations are slower than fall movements; older males reach the summering grounds first and nannies with kids arrive later.

The daily activity pattern consists of foraging from dawn through most of the morning, resting at midday, and foraging again during late afternoon and evening. Generally sedentary, the animals typically do not move more than 0.5 km except during seasonal migrations. However, Hopkins et al. (1992) noted regular movements in excess of 12 km for herds using salt licks in the Gore Range. They bed on rocky shelves or vegetation and on hot days may lie on snow patches. Caves and overhanging rocks are used for shelter if available. John Gross et al. (2002) used GIS models to identify suitable habitat for goats on Mount Evans. There goats used moderate slopes at mid-elevations, southerly exposures, and areas near escape cover more than expected by chance. Considerable time is spent wallowing and dusting, especially in the warmer months. Home ranges of mountain goats are generally between 21 and 48 km^2 (Rideout and Hoffmann 1975). Goats in the Gore Range had home ranges of 4.9 to 48.0 km^2 (Hopkins et al. 1992), the largest range being that of a nanny with kid.

Mountain goats congregate on winter ranges, especially at salt licks and during storms. In late spring and summer, males are solitary whereas females, yearlings, and kids form herds. Although herds usually are small, summer herds of 30–50 animals are not unusual in the Gore Range. Females and kids remain separated from billies until late summer to early autumn (Hopkins et al. 1992; M. Irby and Fitzgerald 1994). Goats visiting a salt lick area in the Gore Range had a well-developed dominance hierarchy, with nannies with kids being dominant even over billies (M. Irby and Fitzgerald 1994; M. Irby 1996; Côté 2000); Masteller and Bailey (1988b) found similar patterns at bait stations. The breeding season is November and early December. Male rutting behavior includes increased wandering from 1 band of females to another, pawing shallow pits (which results in a soiled belly and hindquarters), and an increase in agonistic behavior among males. Various threat postures, often involving the horns, are used. Unlike the ritualized head-butting of mountain sheep, fighting is rare. However, when fighting does occur, serious injuries may result (Geist 1964; M. Irby and Fitzgerald 1994).

Mountain goats are polygamous. Estrus in females lasts 48 to 72 hours and most females first breed at about 2.5 years of age. Yearling females do not breed, although yearling males have been observed in rutting behavior. Gestation takes 178 days (Brandborg 1955) and kids are born in late May and early June. The incidence of twins ranges from 8 to 30 percent. Kids are precocious, often eating forage within a week after birth. They nurse until late August or early September. Survival of kids ranges from 38 to 92 percent (Côté and Festa-Bianchet 2003). L. Adams and Bailey (1982) estimated a 57 percent survival of kids in a Colorado population. Kid to adult ratios were 30:100 for the Gore Range population and tied closely to depth of snow in May (Hopkins et al. 1992). In the Sawatch Range, ratios of kids to older animals ranged from 18:100 to 71:100, lower reproductive success being correlated with high spring snowpack (L. Adams and Bailey 1982).

Mountain goats generally do not show high fluctuations in populations; most studies show moderate growth or stability, although introduced populations in Olympic National Park, Washington, have increased to the point that they are considered by many to be detrimental to native biotic communities (Houston et al. 1994; Houston and Schreiner 1995). Status and management of mountain goats in Colorado were originally studied in the context of increasing the herds to reach numbers suitable for harvest (Hibbs et al. 1969; Denny 1977). That was followed by investigations of goat biology (e.g., Thompson and Guenzel 1978; L. Adams et al. 1982a, 1982b; Risenhoover and Bailey 1982; Hopkins 1992; Hopkins et al. 1992; M. Irby and Fitzgerald 1994). More recently, concerns about habitat destruction and competition with native bighorn sheep predominate (Adams et al. 1982b; Dailey et al. 1984; Hobbs et al. 1990; D. Reed and Green 1994; John Gross et al. 2000, 2002; Jack Gross 2001; D. Reed 2001). Similar concerns about effects of introduced mountain goats on vegetation or on native ungulates have also been raised in Olympic National Park and Yellowstone (Lemke 2004).

Most mountain goat mortality occurs from starvation in winter and accidental deaths from avalanches and rock slides. Mountain lions are the most significant predator on mountain goats. Bobcats, coyotes, black bears, brown bears, and golden eagles also prey on them, mostly on young and infirm individuals and only occasionally on adults. Hamel and Côté (2009) reported maternal defense of kids against predatory attempts by eagles. Coyotes feed on winter-killed goats. Reviews of mountain goat biology were provided by Rideout and Hoffmann (1975), Rideout (1978), Wigal and Coggins (1982), Peek (2000), Côté and Festa-Bianchet (2003), and Festa-Bianchet and Côté (2008).

Colorado has a hunting season on mountain goats. There are 17 mountain goat management units scattered in the higher mountains of the state. Licenses are issued on a carefully controlled basis, with a drawing within each management unit. Successful hunters must wait 5 years before again entering a drawing for a license (Colorado Division of Wildlife 2009g). Over 5 reporting years between 1995 and 2007, an annual average of 186.6 license-holders took an average of 156 mountain goats, representing 83.9 percent success (Table 4-2).

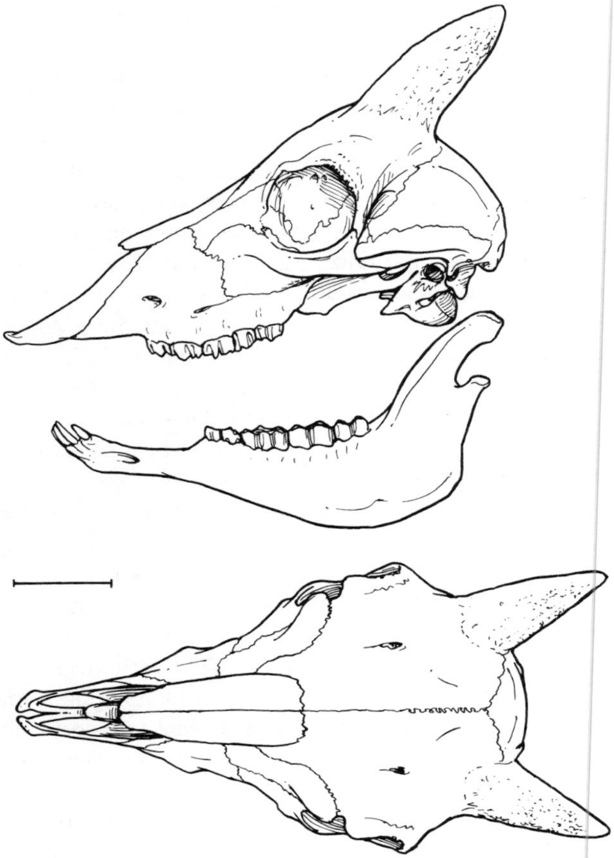

FIGURE 14-4. Lateral and dorsal views of the skull of a female (ewe) mountain, or bighorn, sheep (*Ovis canadensis*). Scale = 5 cm.

Ovis canadensis

MOUNTAIN, OR BIGHORN, SHEEP

Description

Mountain sheep, also called bighorn sheep or simply bighorns, are blocky, heavily built mammals. Measurements are: total length 1,250–1,950 mm; length of tail 70–130 mm; length of hindfoot 310–440 mm; length of ear 90–135 mm; weight 50–125 kg. Skulls of adult males may measure up to 320 mm in length and the horns and head may weigh more than 18 kg. The skull has antorbital pits; the premaxillae either barely reach or do not touch the nasals. The premolars have prominent vertical enamel ridges on the labial side. The incisors are spatulate and the molars are long and well developed. Permanent dentition is not fully in place until 4 years of age (Deming 1952).

Adult males have thick, massive horns that are heavily ridged, a characteristic useful in aging the animals (Geist 1966). On adult males the horns sweep sharply outward, backward, and downward, with the tips then curving upward, eventually forming "full curls." The horns on a

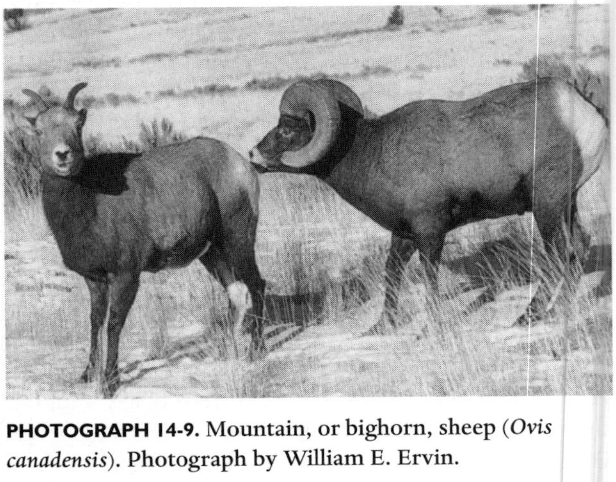

PHOTOGRAPH 14-9. Mountain, or bighorn, sheep (*Ovis canadensis*). Photograph by William E. Ervin.

mature ram may measure more than 46 cm around their base and 112 cm in total length. The tips of the horns are frequently worn or broken, a condition referred to as "brooming." Horns on subadults and females are shorter and more slender. Larger horn size is positively correlated with mating success in Rocky Mountain (but not desert) bighorns (Singer and Zeigenfuss 2002). Color varies seasonally and geographically from grayish brown to medium brown. The muzzle is grayish white and there is a paler gray rump patch, underbelly, and edging down the rear legs.

Distribution

Bighorn sheep are widely scattered in generally small and isolated populations throughout the Rocky Mountains, the Sierra Nevada, and other ranges from west-central Alberta and southeastern British Columbia south into northern Mexico (including most of Baja California). Transplants of individuals across ranges of various supposed subspecies have muddied their distributions and make it difficult to sort out historic patterns of geographic variation (see Wehausen and Ramey 2000). *Ovis canadensis canadensis*, the Rocky Mountain bighorn, is the native mountain sheep of Colorado. So-called desert bighorns are scattered across Nevada, Utah, Arizona, New Mexico, California, and northern and western Mexico.

Transplants of desert bighorns to Colorado began in 1979 on Black Ridge near Colorado National Monument (Creeden 1986; Creeden and Graham 1997; J. George et al. 2009). Translocations have included animals from Nevada, Arizona, and Utah and now include animals from both of the putative desert subspecies, *O. c. nelsoni* and *O. c. mexicana*. Desert bighorn populations now include the Black Ridge, Upper and Middle Dolores River, and Uncompahgre/Dominguez herds.

There is no strong evidence that desert bighorn were ever native to Colorado, although the Division of Wildlife and the Bureau of Land Management have suggested their presence (see J. George et al. 2009). C. McCarty and Bailey (1994) reviewed literature on habitat requirements of desert bighorns in the context of the introduction of the animals to southwestern Colorado.

In general, morphological differences between desert and Rocky Mountain bighorns are slight, and some of the differences may be environmental rather than genetic. Horns of desert bighorns are more slender and flare outward more than those of the Rocky Mountain bighorns, and usually they are shorter and have less basal circumference (Krausman and Bowyer 2003). Generally, desert sheep are paler in color and typically slightly smaller in overall size than Rocky Mountain bighorns. Bunch et al. (1999) discussed cytogenetics of native North American sheep.

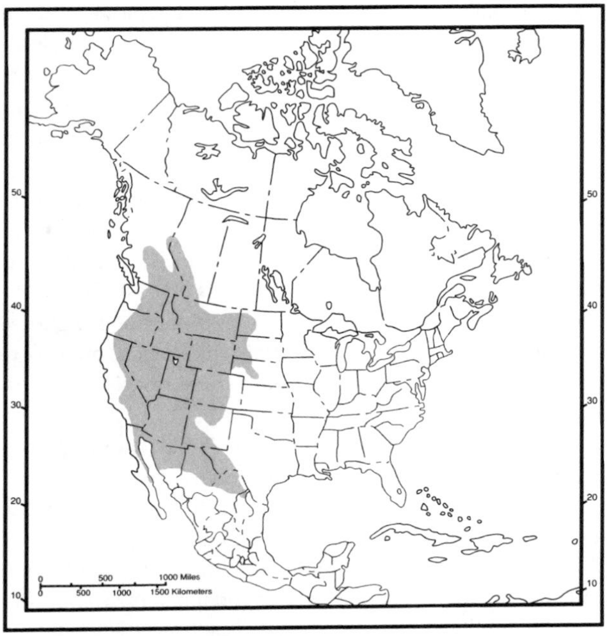

MAP 14-15. Distribution of the mountain, or bighorn, sheep (*Ovis canadensis*) in North America.

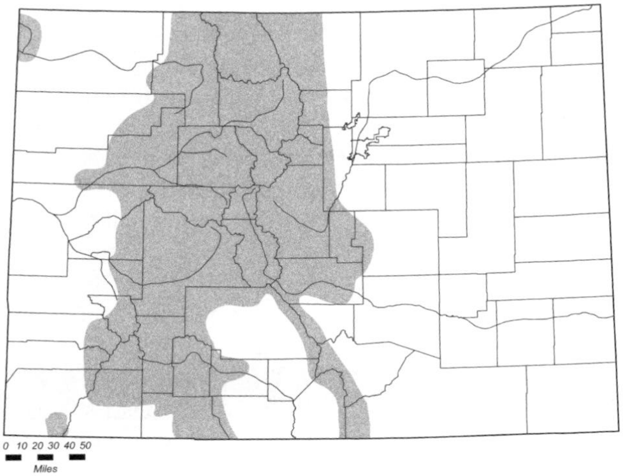

MAP 14-16. Distribution of the mountain, or bighorn, sheep (*Ovis canadensis*) in Colorado.

Colorado is thought to have the largest number of bighorn sheep of any state of the United States (Beecham et al. 2007), including an estimated 79 herds of Rocky Mountain bighorn (with an estimated 7,040 animals) and 4 herds of introduced desert bighorn (totaling about 325 animals). J. George et al. (2009) suggested that prior to Euro-American settlement and habitat disturbance by mining and the growth of the livestock industry, Rocky Mountain bighorns occurred as a large metapopulation, with local bands interbreeding over large geographical areas. Today bighorns occur mostly in fragmented herds with little connectivity, except perhaps in parts of the San Juan, Collegiate, and Sawatch ranges. Luikart and Allendorf (1996) studied variation in mitochondrial DNA in Rocky Mountain bighorns and found that regional gene flow in the Rockies appears to have occurred in the past, but today there is little gene flow among the semi-isolated subpopulations.

For many years, populations of Rocky Mountain bighorn sheep declined in Colorado. Estimates of total numbers in the state ranged from about 7,300 animals in 1915 to around 3,000 in the late 1950s and about 2,200 in 1970, and then rose to 6,045 in 1988 and an estimated 7,040 in 2007 (Buechner 1960; Moser 1962; Bear and Jones 1973; J. George et al. 2009). The accuracy of early estimates is uncertain. For example, in Rocky Mountain National Park alone, populations once may have been close to 4,000 but now may be just over 350 animals (Goodson 1978; McClintock and White 2007).

The history of Coloradan herds and their present status were reviewed by J. George et al. (2009). Increased populations in recent years were attributed to numerous translocations intended to augment existing herds or to start new ones, with greatest efforts in the 1980s. In 2007, translocated herds accounted for some 54 percent of all Colorado sheep herds and 48 percent of the total population. Some 78 percent of these herds had more than 100 individuals but most of them are not showing viable growth.

Natural History

Bighorn sheep show a tremendous range of elevational (and therefore temperature) tolerance, from 78 m below sea level in Death Valley to more than 4,000 m in the mountains of Colorado and California (Krausman and Bowyer 2003). Mountain sheep conjure images of pristine wilderness conditions because of their association with the high mountains and steep canyons. In part because of impacts imposed by humans, they typically occur only on steep, precipitous terrain, although a number of herds in the state (e.g., along Interstate 70 near Georgetown and in the Big Thompson Canyon west of Loveland) have habituated to areas adjacent to busy highways. Historical evidence suggests that at one time mountain sheep were much more widely distributed, even extending onto the eastern plains in areas close to the foothills. In Colorado, mountain sheep prefer open habitat with grass, low shrubs, rock cover, and topographic relief; this provides good visibility and escape terrain (L. Adams et al. 1982a; Risenhoover and Bailey 1985). Vegetational succession, as encroachment of shrubland and forest, has led to declines in sheep in recent years on some ranges (Wakelyn 1987). J. George et al. (2009) generally did not consider habitat and habitat conditions to be an especially important limiting factor, except for winter range in some cases and the ever-increasing fragmentation of habitat with human development. They considered southwestern Colorado to have a considerable amount of unoccupied quality habitat for desert bighorns.

The bulk of the diet is grasses and grasslike plants, browse, and some forbs (D. R. Smith 1954; Moser 1962; J. Todd 1972). Grasses and sedges (46 percent) and shrubs (45 percent) constitute the bulk of the yearly diet (J. Todd 1975). At lower elevations browse appears to be the staple in winter. At higher elevations grasses and grasslike plants may dominate both summer and winter diets (Woodward 1980), although B. Johnson and Smith (1980) suggested that in alpine summer ranges in New Mexico, the use of forbs and graminoids was about equal. In Colorado, winter diets of bighorns included more graminoids and fewer forbs than did the diet of mountain goats, whereas summer diets were more similar (Dailey et al. 1984). Some 80 to 90 percent of the diet of desert bighorns (*O. c. nelsoni*) was roughly equal amounts of browse and grass or grasslike materials (L. Wilson et al. 1980). Spowart and Hobbs (1985) investigated effects of burning on competition for forage between deer and mountain sheep. They concluded that the greatest degree of competition was in the spring in situations where the 2 species were crowded onto limited range; otherwise, sufficient forage was available to meet the needs of both species. Capp (1968) reported little competition among elk, deer, and mountain sheep on summer ranges in Rocky Mountain National Park because of little range overlap. Bighorn sheep, like many other ungulates, may seek out mineral salts, including road salt along highways as well as at natural "licks." For years, bighorns from the Mummy herd in Rocky Mountain National Park have used the Sheep Lake lick in Horseshoe Park. Increasing numbers of visitors and increasing traffic probably are having negative impacts on herd health and population, as may disease and low reproductive success (McClintock 2004; B. J. Keller and Bender 2007; McClintock and White 2007). Experiments on improving bighorn ranges in Colorado with fertilizer or herbicide application were inconclusive (Bear 1978).

Mountain sheep are gregarious mammals. They are diurnal, with 2 to 5 foraging bouts per day interspersed with periods of rest, play (generally among lambs or between lamb and mother), and maintenance behaviors such as rubbing, dusting, and scratching. They have a high degree of philopatry, or site fidelity, which ties them closely to areas that are familiar and leads to slow rates of expansion. Such fidelity renders them vulnerable to increased stress levels when disturbances to their ranges occur. During spring and summer, mountain sheep segregate by sex and age. Rams older than 3 or 4 form small bachelor herds, while females, lambs, and younger rams form larger units. As the breeding season approaches in fall, males gather and fight with repeated head-butting. Geist (1971) detailed the various social behaviors and interplays among individuals. Cooperative defense by bighorn ewes against potential predation by coyotes in Rocky Mountain National Park was reported by Goodson and Stevens (1994).

Seasonally, mountain sheep may make relatively short migrations from summer to winter ranges. Snow depth of more than 30 cm hampers foraging and movements. Many populations effect this migration through a series of deliberate, short-distance moves using favored habitat along the way. These movements have been interpreted as seasonal drift (Moser 1962) or as short-term use of seasonal home ranges (Geist 1971), with up to 4 or 5 such areas used, depending on the herd and the terrain. Movements associated with seasonal changes can cover distances of up to 60 km, although distances of 5 to 15 km are more typical. A movement of 5 to 8 km in the mountains of Colorado may lead to an elevational shift of hundreds of meters. Daily movements on a particular seasonal range average 0.5 to 1.5 km (D. R. Smith 1954; N. M. Simmons 1961; Oldemeyer 1966), although Hopkins (1992) noted regular movements in excess of 12 km for herds visiting salt licks in the Gore Range. In fall, adult rams move onto the breeding/winter range several weeks before ewes, lambs, and younger rams. Barriers to movement include large expanses of timber or dense brush (which restrict the view) and large rivers and wide valley floors.

Mountain sheep breed in November and December in our area, although desert bighorns may initiate breeding as early as July in parts of the Southwest. Breeding grounds are usually on the home ranges of females (Krausman and Shackleton 2000). Similar to moose and bison, a dominant male and a female approaching estrus will form "tending pairs," with males showing lip curls (flehmen), guarding and nosing behaviors, and frequent kicks with the foreleg while attempting to mount. Breeding attempts by mature rams decrease rapidly by January but younger rams may exhibit reproductive behaviors into April and May (Moser 1962). The species is polygamous, with dominant males typically doing most of the breeding. Young males can breed with females in the absence of dominant rams, but unless population structure demands it, most do not contribute significantly to breeding until 7 or 8 years of age. Most females breed at 2.5 years of age although both sexes may be mature as yearlings. Females are monoestrous. Within a herd usually only 1 female is in estrus at any one time, leading to several rams attempting to follow and copulate with her. Gestation takes approximately 175 to 180 days. Lambs are born in May or June in Colorado, with a peak in mid-June (Moser 1962), although desert bighorns may lamb as early as January in other states. There is some evidence that females can adjust gestation to time their lambing around inclement weather (or some other environmental condition) (Krausman and Bowyer 2003). Ewes segregate from the herd for about a week when lambing, and most populations have specific lambing grounds that are used year after year. A single young is the rule. Lambs at birth weigh about 3 to 5 kg. They are precocial and start to forage several weeks after birth, although they may not be weaned for 5 or 6 months.

Bighorn sheep can live up to 17 years, although individuals in the wild probably do not live much more than 10 to 12 years (Streeter 1970). The sex ratio at birth approximates 1:1, but differential mortality leads to adult ram/ewe ratios that vary widely depending on effects of hunting and other factors. Female reproductive success also varies widely. Lamb/ewe ratios for the Pikes Peak and Georgetown herds varied from 7:100 to 95:100, based on July counts over a 7-year period; average ratios were about 59:100 (Moser 1962). Streeter (1969) reported average ratios of 59:100 for herds on Mount Evans and the Buffalo Peaks from 1966 to 1968. Woodward et al. (1974), working with a declining population in the Sangre de Cristo Range, reported ratios of 83:100 and 72:100 in June counts.

For many years Colorado researchers have studied declining populations of bighorns. J. George et al. (2009) indicated that a major threat to Colorado bighorn populations (and populations in other western states) lies in the potential for transmission of "novel respiratory pathogens" from domestic sheep. They mapped existing domestic sheep grazing allotments and bighorn herd boundaries to indicate how many of these areas overlap. Over the years many studies have established bighorn sheep susceptibility to pasteurellosis (associated with a number of bacteria in the family Pasteurellaceae) (M. W. Miller 2001; J. George et al. 2008). These diseases can produce a variety of impacts on bighorns, ranging from large-scale die-off of all age groups to individual mortality and reduced recruitment of lambs.

Studies of declining bighorn populations in Colorado are numerous. For a number of years, Colorado wildlife personnel treated sheep for lungworm and pursued a vigorous program to capture and transplant excess individuals from healthy herds (Rutherford 1972b, 1972c; Bear 1979). J. Bailey (1990) summarized efforts to manage Colorado's bighorn sheep to that date.

Streeter (1969) and Woodward et al. (1974) found high levels of mortality in lambs (18 and 25 percent lamb survival) during late summer, fall, and winter. Streeter found significant adult mortality (about 30 percent) also occurred but no evidence of disease contributing to mortality in the Buffalo Peaks herd. He attributed the decrease to an experimental either-sex hunting season conducted for 3 years and a shift in behavioral patterns of the herd, leading to year-round use of their alpine range when historically they had utilized both lower elevations and alpine range.

Sheep die-offs from pneumonia, thought at one time to be induced by lungworm infections, affecting either lambs or all age classes, have been reported (Moser 1962; Bear and Jones 1973; Woodward et al. 1974; J. Bailey 1986; Singer et al 2000; McClintock and White 2007; J. George et al. 2009). In Hells Canyon, Idaho, Cassirer and Sinclair (2007) documented pneumonia as causing 43 percent of adult mortality and 86 percent of lamb mortality in bighorns, with the disease being the principal factor in population growth. This is in an area where most domestic sheep grazing had ended on federal lands by 1999. Singer et al. (2000) suggested that buffers of at least 20 km between domestic and wild sheep were needed to reduce chances of pathogenic disease transmission.

High mortality in the first year of life is caused by disease, nutrition, and weather (C. L. Douglas 2001). Coyotes, bobcats, mountain lions, and golden eagles are known predators of sheep, especially the young of the year. In certain populations mountain lions can be especially effective predators (Ross et al. 1997; Kamler et al. 2002; Cassirer and Sinclair 2007). A number of Division of Wildlife biologists working with radio-collared desert bighorns in Colorado suggest that mountain lion predation is an important source of mortality (J. George et al. 2009). Competition from domestic sheep and goats has led to extirpation of numerous populations of desert bighorns (Krausman and Bowyer 2003). In a number of Coloradan locations the impacts of introduced mountain goats on bighorn sheep is a matter of concern (B. Wunder 2000; Jack Gross 2001). J. George et al. (2009) suggested ways to manage both species to reduce conflicts, specifically urging careful monitoring and management of both species within bighorn sheep data analysis units.

Colorado populations of bighorn sheep were heavily exploited by early settlers and market hunters, leading to a complete closure of hunting in 1887 (Bear and Jones 1973). Hunting was reestablished in 1953 (Moser 1962) and limited harvest has been permitted since, mostly directed toward mature rams. Hunting is an important factor in shaping population structure. Hunting of trophy rams in herds of fewer than 100 animals may be deleterious because of impacts on the gene pool partly through learned behaviors (Geist 1975). Singer and Zeigenfuss (2002) found that young rams showed more rutting activity and lower survival in populations subject to heavy trophy hunting; however, most state wildlife agencies have continued to place emphasis on harvest of trophy rams. Based on studies in Alberta, Jorgenson et al. (1998) identified parameters of density and age and sex structure of bands that increased horn size and thus valuable "trophy rams." A number of studies have estimated and modeled Coloradan populations (Neal et al. 1993; J. George et al. 1996; C. McCarty and Miller 1998; McClintock and White 2007).

Bighorn sheep are an important game mammal in Colorado. Bighorn licenses are of limited availability and so are allocated by drawing for each of 71 bighorn sheep management units in central and western Colorado and in the roughlands of the southeastern part of the state. Licenses are issued by management unit, with strict limits on harvest of rams and ewes specified per unit. Hunters who harvest a bighorn sheep must wait 5 years before applying again for a license. License rules differ for Rocky Mountain and desert bighorn sheep (Colorado Division of Wildlife 2009g), and eventually reports of harvest will be maintained at the level of subspecies (see Table 4-2). In 5 reporting years from 1995 to 2007, an annual average of 295 license-holders took a mean of 156 bighorn, a success rate of 53.9 percent (Table 4-2).

General reviews of the abundant and scattered literature on mountain sheep were provided by Buechner (1960), Geist (1971), Wishart (1978), Monson and Sumner (1980), Lawson and Johnson (1982), Shackleton (1985), R. Valdez and Krausman (1999), Krausman and Shackleton (2000), Krausman and Bowyer (2003), and Beecham et al. (2007). The paper by D. R. Smith (1954) on bighorns in Idaho is still a useful work on general biology and management of sheep in the Rocky Mountains, and Welles and Welles's book on desert bighorn (1961) remains a classic.

The Rocky Mountain bighorn sheep was adopted as the official state animal on May 1, 1961, by an act of the Colorado General Assembly (Senate Bill 294, Colorado Revised Statutes 24-80-991). The Colorado Division of Wildlife later adopted the animal as its logo.

Family Suidae—Swine

Of living artiodactyls, pigs and peccaries are closest to the base of the family tree. This account of the pig family is presented out of the usual phylogenetic sequence followed in this book (based on D. Wilson and Reeder 2005), so as not to distract from accounts of native artiodactyls. The family Suidae is a relatively small group, including 5 genera and 19 species primarily living in Eurasia, Africa, and major offshore islands (Nowak 1999; D. Wilson and Reeder 2005). The fossil record dates from the Early Oligocene. Domesticated pigs are all descendants from *Sus scrofa*, the wild pig of Eurasia, and have been introduced to all parts of the world except extreme polar regions. Domesticated hogs may reach weights in excess of 450 kg, representing the largest members of the family; warthogs (*Phacochoerus*) of Africa and the bush pigs and river hogs of Africa (*Potamochoerus*) are the smallest, with some adults weighing as little as 40–50 kg. Most species occupy woodlands or brushlands, not infrequently using burrows they excavate or take over from other species. Most suids are social, occurring in herds or small family units. In most species (although not in *Sus scrofa*) the young are striped. The diet is typically omnivorous, varying from insects and fungi to fruit, small mammals, and carrion. The cheekteeth are bunodont, in keeping with this varied diet.

Most species of pigs look like pigs, with their long, relatively pointed heads; blocky bodies; and short necks. The snout is typically flat and broad, taking on a disclike shape, formed from cartilage and a prenasal bone—a bone not found in most mammals. The snout with its terminal nostrils is used in rooting for food materials. Pig skulls have a typical steeply sloping profile sharply truncated behind the orbits and displaying in most species elongated, flaring canines as tusks on both upper and lower jaws. The canines are best developed in males. Lower incisors tend to flare almost horizontally from the lower jaw. Dental formulas vary from 34 to 44 teeth. The eyes tend to be small whereas the ears are well developed. Most pigs have thick skin with sparse hair or bristles, and the hide is often prized as leather. There is no fusion of the bones of the feet; both the pollex and hallux are missing, so only 4 toes are present. The third and fourth digits have well-developed hooves and are the prime weight-bearers. Smaller hooves are present on the outer digits. Pigs have a relatively simple 2-chambered foregut and do not produce a cud.

Sus scrofa

FERAL PIG

Description

Feral pigs are escaped domestic pigs; they may appear physically to be intermediate between domestic pigs and European wild hogs, depending on how long they have been in the wild (J. R. Sweeney et al. 2003). Feral pigs can vary widely in color from black to red/brown, roan, or white. Spotted patterns are common. Depending on location and length of time that populations have been feral, the density and coarseness of the pelage may be greater than those normally observed in domestic animals. Likewise, body weight and size may vary considerably between populations. Studies in the eastern United States suggest average weights of males of 35 to 115 kg and females of 30 to slightly more than 90 kg. Hog skulls, with their steeply sloping profile, prominent tusks, and bunodont cheekteeth, are easy to distinguish from any other Colorado mammal. Pigs are the only mammals in Colorado that have the full ancestral placental number of 44 teeth.

Distribution

Feral swine are reported to be the most abundant introduced ungulate in the United States, with the total population estimated at around 4 million animals. They have occupied southeastern North America since the arrival of the earliest European explorers in the late 1500s, with introductions in California in the mid-1700s. The range of the species has increased since the 1980s to now include 28 states (T. A. Campbell et al. 2006). Some of the western states, including Texas and California, have large populations of wild pigs that increasingly impact the environment. In Colorado they extend northward from the Oklahoma border to Kiowa County south of Eads in the Arkansas River drainage (Minutes, Colorado Wildlife Commission, March 8, 2007).

Natural History

Feral pigs are able to live in many different habitats, provided cover and food are available. J. R. Sweeney et al. (2003) reviewed the literature on the species and provided the information in this account. In the West, feral pigs are usually associated with semiarid riparian woodlands and oak habitats. Much of southern Colorado at lower elevations would appear to provide suitable habitat. Winter cold may not be a major limiting factor, as populations of feral pigs have established in Canada. Lacking sweat glands, hogs have difficulty dealing with high temperatures, so they seek shaded, usually moist habitats in the summer months. Daily activity patterns often shift in hot weather from mostly crepuscular or diurnal to mostly nocturnal. Size of reported home ranges varies widely, with those in the West usually between 300 and 5,000 ha. Feral pigs are opportunistic in their diet, feeding on green herbaceous materials or rooting for plant materials, with mast (acorns) being a preferred food when available. Animal matter is eaten when encountered but does not seem to be actively sought. Competition for food may occur with wild animals that also rely heavily on mast or forage. Rooting by pigs may disturb large areas, resulting in significant microhabitat changes and destruction of plant cover.

A major concern with feral swine is their high reproductive potential, estimated to be 4 times that of native ungulates (R. Taylor et al. 1998). The species is polyestrous, with a gestation of about 113 days, and litter sizes average 3 to 9 young. Although biologically capable of having 2 litters a year, most feral pigs have a single litter annually. Adult males are often territorial, whereas females and their young may form large multigenerational units (called "sounders"). If populations of feral pigs increase as expected, competition with native wildlife species—white-tailed and mule deer, turkey, black bear, and even elk—is certainly possible in Colorado.

Appendix A

The Metric System

Throughout this book we use the metric system of measurement. You doubtless have some familiarity with the metric system already. International commerce and international athletic competition use the metric system almost exclusively. However, you may not yet "think" in metric units. (A late, great mammalogist—Professor J. K. Jones Jr., of the University of Kansas and then Texas Tech University—once observed, quite seriously, "mice weigh grams but bears weigh pounds.") And many of us have trouble with temperatures in Celsius, even though we have been reading them for years. Some of us still have to think hard before we decide to put on a jacket when the weather report says "20°C." (The answer is no, by the way—68°F is comfortable for most folks.)

The metric system is both more logical and far easier to use than the so-called English system (which even the notoriously traditional English have mostly abandoned). It is more logical because it is based—at least to some extent—on physical features of Earth rather than on the length of some forgotten monarch's appendages. The *meter* first was defined as 1/10,000,000 the distance from the equator to the North Pole, as measured along the line of longitude running through Paris. The *gram* is the mass of 1 cubic centimeter of water. Hence, a liter of water, 1,000 cc, weighs 1,000 grams, or 1 *kilogram*.

The metric system is easy to use because it is a *decimal* system, based on multiples of 10, like most currencies. That makes it much easier to manipulate with our everyday counting number system, which also is based on 10. (How people with 10 fingers and 10 toes ever managed to invent a measuring system in which a "foot" is subdivided into 12 inches is difficult to understand.)

Probably the whole world eventually will "go metric," even the United States. However, most of us—readers and writers—belong to generations in transition from the old system to the "new" (the "new" international system is more than 200 years old—a product of the Enlightenment, by the way). Hence, we provide a conversion table for reference and also a table of prefixes that indicate powers of 10. With those prefixes in mind, one can readily interpret new units to suit particular uses. We rate power plants in *mega*watts, computer memory chips and hard drives in *giga*bytes, and electronic pulses in *nano*seconds.

APPENDIX A

These terms are part of our intellectual and commercial environment, so they had better be part of our working vocabulary. (At present, the United States, Liberia, and Myanmar [Burma] are the last remaining holdouts for the "English" system.)

TABLE A-1. Some "English"-Metric and Metric-"English" conversion factors (rounded to 3 significant digits)

To convert	*to*	*Multiply by*
acres	hectares	0.405
° Celsius	° Fahrenheit	(° C × 9/5) + 32
° Fahrenheit	° Celsius	(° F – 32) × 5/9
centimeters	inches	0.394
feet	meters	0.305
gallons	liters	3.785
grams	ounces	0.035
hectares	acres	2.471
inches	centimeters	2.540
kilograms	pounds	2.205
kilometers	miles	0.621
liters	gallons	0.264
meters	feet	3.281
meters	yards	1.094
miles	kilometers	1.609
ounces	grams	28.350
pounds	kilograms	0.454
square kilometers	square miles	0.386
square miles	square kilometers	2.590
ton ("English")	tonne (metric)	0.908
tonne (metric)	ton ("English")	1.103
yards	meters	0.914

TABLE A-2. Prefixes indicating some powers of 10

Prefix	*Power of 10*	*Example*
mega-	10^{6}	megaton, megawatt
kilo-	10^{3}	kilowatt, kilogram
deci-	10^{-1}	decimeter, decibel
centi-	10^{-2}	centimeter
milli-	10^{-3}	milligram, millimeter
micro-	10^{-6}	micrometer
nano-	10^{-9}	nanosecond

Appendix B

Glossary

This glossary is not intended to be comprehensive. Rather, it lists terms that are used repeatedly in this book but are not in general English usage and therefore may not appear in abridged dictionaries. Also, terms in general English usage that have distinctive definitions in the context of mammalogy (or in zoology more broadly) are included. Adjectives formed from nouns (such as "alveolar" from "alveolus") generally are not included if the noun is defined, and vice versa. Terms defined or illustrated in Chapter 2 mostly are absent from this glossary.

abiotic—non-living; especially physical factors and processes of ecosystems: mineral soil, climate, and so on.

abomasum—the most posterior compartment of ruminant "stomach": the only chamber that actually is stomach (the 3 anterior chambers being modified segments of esophagus).

accessory tubercle—small, cusp-like structure on occlusal surface of tooth in addition to usual larger, higher cusps.

aestivation—summer dormancy; regulation in avoidance of hot and/or dry weather.

agonistic—contesting behavior, generally between individuals of the same species.

alisphenoid—paired lateral parts of composite bony structure forming base of braincase and inner wall of orbit.

allantois—an extra-embryonic membrane of higher vertebrates (amniotes); functions as waste repository in reptilian egg (and eggs of birds and monotremes) and furnishes blood vessels and connective tissue to placenta of therians.

allopatric—descriptive of geographic distributions that are geographically disjunct and do not overlap.

alluvium—sediment deposited by flowing water (contrast with *colluvium*).

Altithermal—time interval after recession of late major Pleistocene glaciation characterized by climate warmer and/or drier than present; also called Hypsithermal.

altricial—born at relatively undeveloped and helpless stage of development (compare *precocial*).

alveolus—socket in jaw in which tooth is rooted.

ambulatory—walking locomotion.

analogous—pertaining to similarity between organisms or structures not due to common ancestry; wings of bats and of butterflies are analogous structures (contrast with *homologous*).

androgenic—literally "male-forming"; descriptive of hormones that control development of male sexual characteristics.

anterior—pertaining to front of organism or structure.

anterior palatal spine—slender, forward-projecting process of maxillary bones that extends anteriorly between incisive foramina.

anterointernal fold—fold in enamel wall of tooth, located in medial (labial), anterior portion of crown.

antitragus—small, fleshy projection on posteroventral margin of pinna of some bats.

antler—deciduous, usually branched, bony growth from frontal bones of (especially male) cervids.

antorbital—located in front of orbit (eye socket).

appendicular—pertaining to appendages (contrast with *axial*).

apposable—capable of being brought into contact, as apposable thumb and forefinger of human hand; sometimes spelled *opposable*.

arboreal—tree-dwelling.

articular—pertaining to point of contact between 2 adjacent bones.

auditory bulla—bony capsule surrounding structure of middle and inner ear; called *tympanic bulla* if derived wholly from tympanic bone.

autecology—the ecology of single species: life history, habitat selection, population growth, and so forth (contrast with *synecology*).

axial—pertaining to axis (midline) of body, such as vertebral column (contrast with *appendicular*).

baculum—bone present in penis of many male mammals; also called os penis (also see *baubellum*).

basal length—distance from posterior margins of alveoli of upper incisors to most anterior point on lower margin of foramen magnum.

basioccipital—bone at base of occiput; forming ventral margin of foramen magnum.

basisphenoid—most posterior of several bones forming base of braincase.

baubellum—bone in clitoris of females of certain mammalian species; also called os clitoridis (also see *baculum*).

bicolored—of 2 distinct colors.

biconcave—shape indented from both sides or ends.

bicornuate—2-horned, as in bicornuate uterus.

bicuspid—generic term for tooth with 2 cusps; especially applied to premolars in humans.

biomass—total mass ("weight") of living material of an area or volume of biotic community; figures in measures of ecological productivity.

biome—major habitat types of Earth, usually described by structure (rather than taxonomy) of vegetation: grassland, temperate deciduous forest, savannah, and so forth; need not be geographically continuous.

biota—inclusive term for living organisms of particular place and time (fauna, flora, and microbiota).

biotic—pertaining to living organisms of site (contrast with *abiotic*).

blastocyst—mammalian blastula; hollow ball of embryonic cells; stage at which embryo of placental mammal implants in uterine lining.

bolus—discrete mass of food moving through anterior organs of digestive system.

boreal—northern.

brachydont—descriptive of low-crowned tooth (contrast with *hypsodont*).

braincase—posterior portion of skull, which houses brain; behind rostrum.

bristle—short, stiff hair.

buccal—pertaining to cheek cavity.

bulla—literally, "ball"; see *auditory bulla*.

bunodont—descriptive of low-crowned, generally rectangular tooth specialized for grinding.

calcaneum—heel bone; also calcaneus.

calcar—cartilaginous or bony spur projecting medially from ankle of many species of bats; helps to support uropatagium.

canine—most anterior tooth on maxillary and corresponding tooth of dentary (Figures 2-1 and 2-2); never numbering more than 1 per quadrant.

carapace—general term for "shell" of vertebrates, as in turtles or armadillos.

carnassials—specialized, sectorial (shearing) cheekteeth of carnivores; in members of order Carnivora, always fourth upper premolar over first lower molar (P^4/M_1).

carpals—bones of wrist (contrast with *tarsals*).

carrion—remains of dead animals.

caudal—pertaining to tail.

cecotrophy—consumption of specialized, nutritive "fecal" pellets (also called coprophagy, reingestion).

cecum—pouch off junction of small and large intestines; especially well developed in herbivores and often site of symbiotic microbial activity.

cementum—bony matrix that affixes tooth in alveolus.

Cenozoic—geologic era following Mesozoic ("Age of Mammals"); the past 65 million years.

cheekpouch—distended or expandable area in buccal region of many rodents, usually functioning to carry food from point of harvest to point of storage; may be fur-lined (as in geomyoids, heteromyids) or not (as in sciurids).

cheekteeth—collective term for premolars and molars; also called postcanine teeth or (where appropriate) molariform teeth.

chemosterilants—chemical compounds used to prevent reproduction.

circumboreal—occurring around the Northern Hemisphere.

cladogram—a kind of phylogenetic tree, illustrating the evolutionary branching sequence of lineages.

class—taxonomic category composed of 1 or more orders; for example, class Mammalia.

cloaca—common chamber for products of urogenital and digestive tracts; from the Latin for *sewer*.

coevolution—process of genetic change through time by which 2 or more species respond reciprocally to the presence of each other in the biotic community; often observed in pollination symbioses, seed dispersal, and so forth.

colluvium—sediment deposited by force of gravity (contrast with *alluvium*).

commensalism—symbiotic relationship in which 1 species is befitted and a second is essentially unaffected.

condylar fossa—depression in squamosal bone in which condyloid process of dentary articulates (Figure 2-1).

condyle—rounded prominence on bone, serving as point of articulation in hinged joints.

condylobasal length—measurement of skull taken along midline from posterior projections of occipital condyles to anterior border of sockets of incisors.

convergence—evolutionary phenomenon in which organisms of separate ancestry come to resemble each other in some way.

coprophagy—consumption of specialized, nutritive "fecal" pellets (also called cecotrophy, reingestion).

coronoid—literally, "crown-like"; process at top of ascending ramus of dentary (Figure 2-2).

corpora—plural of corpus.

corpus—literally, "body"; common descriptive term in anatomy, as in corpus luteum ("yellow body") on ovary.

countershading—pattern of coloration in which (usually darker) dorsum contrasts with venter; thought to function in crypsis.

cranial—pertaining to cranium or braincase.

cranial breadth—width of cranium taken at broadest point perpendicular to long axis of skull.

cranium—portion of skull containing brain.

crepuscular—active at dawn and/or dusk (contrast with *diurnal* and *nocturnal*).

Cretaceous—third and final geologic period of Mesozoic Era ("Age of Reptiles"), ending about 65 million years ago.

crown—exposed (usually enamel-covered) surface of tooth.

cursorial—pertaining to running locomotion.

cusp—projection (ridge, point, etc.) of crown of tooth.

deciduous—any structure that is shed or falls away, such as leaves, milk teeth, or antlers.

deciduous dentition—juvenal or milk teeth, shed and replaced by permanent dentition.

delayed fertilization—phenomenon (especially in some bats) wherein spermatozoa are stored in uterus and therefore fertilization does not immediately follow copulation and insemination.

delayed implantation—phenomenon wherein implantation of blastocyst in uterine lining does not immediately follow its formation.

demography—literally, "people mapping"; general term for population dynamics.

density—numbers of individuals per area.

dental—pertaining to teeth.

dental formula—numerical description of dentition of mammal (Table 2-1).

dentine—bone-like material that comprises bulk of typical mammalian tooth.

derived—trait (characteristic or condition) different from that of an ancestor; such traits once were termed *advanced*, a term to be avoided because it may connote evolution as "progress," which is a subjective judgment.

dermal—pertaining specifically to dermis, although sometimes applied to skin more generally.

dermis—inner layers of skin, beneath epidermis.

dewclaws—small, usually vestigial, hoofed or clawed digits on various (mostly cursorial) mammals with simplified feet.

dewlap—pendulous, often fatty flap of skin under neck, as in moose.

diagnostic—descriptive of characteristics or traits that define or unequivocally distinguish species or other taxa.

diastema—gap or space in toothrow, usually representing teeth lost in evolutionary reduction of dental formula; length of diastema is measured from posterior margin of alveolus of last incisor to anterior margin of alveolus of first cheektooth.

digitigrade—standing on digits or "tiptoes."

digits—inclusive term for toes and fingers.

diphyletic—artificial taxon including groups derived from separate ancestries.

dispersal—movement, especially one-way movement from place of birth to place of residence or reproduction.

dispersion—pattern of spacing of individuals within local population; may be uniform, contagious (clumped), or random.

distal—away from axis or body (or other specified point of reference) (contrast with *proximal*).

diurnal—active by day.

dormancy—extended period of inactivity; hibernation is an extreme form.

dorsal—referring to the back or upper surface (dorsum) (contrast with *ventral*).

dorsoventrally—from top to bottom (back to belly), as "dorsoventrally flattened."

dorsum—back, top (contrast with *venter*).

echolocation—process whereby mammals (especially bats) form images and orient themselves by means of emitting sounds (usually of high frequency) and then processing the echoes to form mental images of objects in the environment.

ecoregion—extensive geographic area of continent with ecological integrity and distinctiveness; examples include Central Shortgrass Steppe, Colorado Plateau, Southern Rocky Mountains.

ecosphere—more or less continuous global system of interaction between physical Earth and life; sum of Earth's ecosystems.

ecosystem—volume of environment in which biotic and abiotic components interact in cycles of materials and flow of energy.

ecotone—area of overlap or interaction between adjacent, distinctive ecological communities or ecosystems.

ectoparasite—parasite living outside body of host; often arthropods (ticks, mites, lice, fleas, etc.)

emigration—permanent movement of an individual or population out of an area (contrast with *immigration*).

enamel—mineral substance that covers crown of teeth in many mammals; hardest substance in vertebrate body.

endemic—species (or other taxonomic group) unique to a particular place.

endogenous—literally, "internally born"; descriptive of processes triggered from inside the individual organism, as an "endogenous rhythm."

endoparasite—parasite living inside body of host; often "worms" (flukes, tapeworms, nematodes, etc.) or microbes (protists, bacteria).

endothermy—process of maintaining body temperature by retaining waste heat from metabolic processes; "warm-bloodedness."

enzootic—descriptive of a disease continually present in particular wildlife population.

Eocene—second epoch of Cenozoic, following Paleocene and prior to Oligocene; several modern orders of mammals arose (Tables 3-1 and 3-2).

epizootic—descriptive of disease temporarily prevalent in wildlife population.

erythropoietic—tissue that produces red blood cells, such as bone marrow.

estrous—adjective describing cycle of hormones regulating reproductive periodicity in (especially nonhuman) female mammals.

estrus—interval of estrous cycle corresponding with maximal sexual receptivity of female mammal; "heat."

ethmoid vacuity—hollow of nasal chamber, containing olfactory membranes. In certain artiodactyls represented by opening in rostrum anterior to orbits, at junction of nasal, frontal, and maxillary sutures.

ever-growing—see *rootless*.

exoccipitals—lateral bones of occiput, forming sides of foramen magnum.

exogenous—literally, "externally born"; descriptive of processes triggered from outside the individual organism, as "exogenous rhythm."

exotic—literally, "from elsewhere"; descriptive of species not native to a particular place; introduced.

external auditory meatus—bony entrance to auditory bulla (Figure 2-1).

extirpation—local extinction.

family—taxonomic category above genus and below order; familial names of animals end in suffix *-idae*.

feces—solid wastes of digestive processes.

fellfield—stone-strewn ground.

femur—bone of proximal segment of tetrapod limb; articulates with pelvic girdle to form hip joint.

fenestrate—penetrated by window-like openings.

feral—pertaining to domestic animal reverted to wild state, or at least escaped from domestication into native ecosystems.

fertilization—process of producing a zygote (fertilized egg) from fusion of gametes (sex cells: egg and sperm); "conception."

foramen—opening or hole through a bone; passage for nerves and/or blood vessels.

foramen magnum—large opening for passage of spinal cord from skull, at posterior of cranium, surrounded by occipital bones (Figure 2-1).

foramina—plural of *foramen*.

forb—neologism contracted from "forest herb"; broad-leafed herbaceous plant (in contrast to graminoid, pertaining to grasses and grasslike plants).

form—shallow depression, usually beneath shrub or other cover, occupied by rabbits and hares.

fossa—literally, "ditch"; depression in bone into which muscles and/or other bones fit.

fossorial—descriptive of subterranean locomotion of moles and pocket gophers, for example.

frontal—paired bones at anterior end of braincase (Figure 2-1); point of growth of antlers, horns of artiodactyls.

fur—near-synonym of *pelage*, especially commercially valuable pelage.

furbearer—management term for mammals with commercially valuable pelage.

game—management term for mammals (and animals more generally) pursued for meat or "sport."

generic—in biology, of or pertaining to a genus.

genitalia—male or female sexual structures, usually qualified as external or internal.

genus—taxonomic category composed of 1 or more species.

gestation period—duration of period of internal development in placental mammals, from fertilization (or implantation) to parturition (or birth).

girdle—generic term for points of attachment of limbs (appendages) to body: hips, shoulders.

glenoid fossa—shallow depression in scapula that accommodates head of humerus in formation on shoulder joint.

glissant—gliding (gravity-powered "flight," as in "flying" squirrels); opposed to volancy (powered flight, as in bats).

graminoids—grasslike plants: grasses, sedges, rushes, and so forth.

grazer—herbivore specialized to feed (graze) on graminoids.

greatest length of skull—overall length of bones of skull (excluding any forward projection of anterior teeth).

guard hair—outer, generally longer and coarse, and often colored, hairs of pelage.

guild—functional subdivision of a biotic community defined ecologically, on the basis of foraging habits from example (such as grazers, browsers, gleaners). Intended to transcend taxonomic limits; guild of diurnal seedeaters includes chipmunks, ants, and sparrows, for example.

habitat—place where an organism occurs; see *niche*.

habituation—process by which individual organisms learn to ignore particular stimulus (such as human presence).

hair—complex structure of keratin extruded from epidermal follicle in mammalian skin.

hallux—first digit of hindfoot (e.g., human "big toe") (see *pollex*).

halophyte—plant adapted to salt tolerance.

harem—group of 2 or more females more-or-less controlled for breeding by single male.

hectare—metric unit of land area; a square 100 meters on a side, 10,000 square meters; there are 100 hectares to the square kilometer; hectare equals about 2.47 acres.

herbivory—feeding on plant material.

heterodont—teeth differentiated by size and/or shape in the toothrow.

hibernaculum—particular location of structure where hibernation is passed.

hibernation—regulation of physiology to minimum, especially in winter.

high-crowned—descriptive of teeth generally taller than broad; extreme case is ever-growing (rootless) teeth; see *hypsodont*.

Holarctic—biogeographic term; describes a taxon occurring in Northern Hemisphere, in both New and Old worlds (Nearctic plus Palearctic regions).

holotype—particular museum specimen to which scientific name is attached by original published description of species or subspecies; imprecisely called type or type specimen.

homeostasis—sum of processes by which organism maintains dynamic equilibrium of internal environment in face of continually changing external environment.

home range—area covered by an individual in its daily round of activities (compare *territory*).

homodont—teeth undifferentiated by size and/or shape in toothrow (as in cheekteeth of armadillo; Figure 6-1).

homologous—pertaining to structures (which may or may not have same function) with common evolutionary origin; human hand and wing of bat are homologous structures (contrast with *analogous*).

horizontal ramus—ventral portion (usually long axis) of dentary in which teeth are rooted.

horn—covering of keratin (the structural protein of hair and nails) over bony growth of skull; typical of family Bovidae (compare *antler*).

hypoglossal foramen—hole passing hypoglossal nerve (cranial nerve XII) from braincase to tongue.

hypsodont—descriptive of high-crowned teeth.

imbricate—overlapping arrangement, as in shingles on a roof.

immigration—permanent movement of individual or population into an area (contrast with *emigration*).

implantation—process by which blastocyst becomes embedded in uterine lining, preliminary to formation of placenta and remainder of gestation.

incisive foramen—holes in anterior palate, between premaxillary and maxillary bones, by which nasal and oral cavities communicate (Figure 2-1).

incisors—teeth (often adapted for nipping or gnawing) arising from premaxillary bone of upper jaw and corresponding teeth on anterior of mandible (Figures 2-1, 2-2).

incus—"anvil"; 1 of 3 bones of mammalian middle ear (derived from reptilian quadrate bone).

infraorbital foramen—opening ventral to anterior border of orbit, penetrating zygomatic portion of maxilla (Figure 2-1).

inguinal—pertaining to groin region.

interfemoral membrane—web of skin between legs of bat, forming part of flight surface (also called uropatagium).

interglacial—interval of time between successive advances of glacial ice during Pleistocene Epoch.

interorbital breadth—least distance across skull as measured between orbits.

interparietal bone—unpaired bone situated between parietal bones and anterior to supraoccipital (Figure 9-2).

jugal bone—central bone of zygomatic arch, bounded anteriorly by zygomatic (malar) process of maxillary and posteriorly by zygomatic process of squamosal (Figure 2-1).

juvenal—adjectival form of *juvenile*.

juvenile—general (and rather loosely defined) term for young mammal, beyond neonate, prior to subadult.

keel—a conspicuous ridge on calcar of some bats, shaped like keel of boat; presence or absence is important diagnostic feature in some species.

keratin—protein of which hair, nails (claws), and horns are made.

keystone species—species critical to natural function and maintenance of a biotic community, such as beaver in riparian systems of mountain parks, or bison on shortgrass steppe.

krummholz—"crooked wood"; twisted, stunted trees of upper tree line.

labial—pertaining to lips (used as term of orientation) (contrast with *lingual* or *buccal*).

lacrimal—pertaining to tears, as in "lachrymal glands" (also spelled *lachrimal*); as orientational term, ventromedial area of orbit; bone at that place (Figure 2-1).

lactation—production and delivery of milk by mammary glands.

lambdoidal ridge—ridge on skull (shaped like Greek letter *lambda*—inverted V shape) where occipital bone joins parietal and squamosal bones.

lateral—pertaining to side; away from midline.

lingual—pertaining to tongue; as term of orientation (contrast with *labial*).

loph—longitudinal or transverse ridge on occlusal surface of tooth formed by fusion and elongation of cusps.

lophodont—tooth characterized by well-developed lophs.

malar process—extension of maxillary bone that forms anterior base of zygomatic arch; articulates with jugal bone.

malleus—"hammer"; 1 of 3 bones of mammalian middle ear derived from reptilian articulare bone.

mammae—see *mammary glands*.

mammary glands—milk-producing glands of female mammals (and source of name of class).

mandible—composite structure comprising 2 dentary bones; length of mandible is measured on the bone itself, not including any forward-projecting incisor teeth.

mandibular toothrow—teeth of dentary; length measured from anterior edge of alveolus of most anterior mandibular tooth to posterior edge of alveolus of most posterior cheektooth.

marsupium—pouch of marsupial mammal in which mammae are located and externally developing young are carried.

masseteric tubercle—small projection of maxillary bone that provides additional surface area for attachment of masseteric muscle.

mastication—process of chewing.

mastoid bone—bone bounded by tympanic, squamosal, and exoccipital bones; often relatively massive and protuberant and marking posterolateral corner of skull.

mastoid breadth—breadth of posterior end of skull, measured at most lateral extension of mastoid bones.

maxilla—paired bones comprising upper jaw and bearing upper teeth (Figure 2-1).

maxillary toothrow—collective term for teeth of maxilla (upper jaw posterior to premaxilla); length is measured as distance from anterior margin of alveolus (socket) of canine to posterior margin of alveolus of last molar.

mean—in statistics, the average.

meatus—see *external auditory meatus*.

medial—pertaining to midline of body (contrast with *lateral*).

mesaxonic—pertaining to foot structure in which axis of symmetry passes through middle (third) toe, as in the horse.

metabolism—sum of chemical processes in an organism.

metacarpal—bones of forefoot, distal to wrist and proximal to phalanges.

metapodials—collective term for metacarpals and metatarsals.

metatarsal—bones of hindfoot, distal to ankle and proximal to phalanges.

midden—accumulation of food wastes, generally plant material, as produced by pine squirrels and woodrats.

migration—movement of individuals, mostly to access new feeding grounds or hibernacula, usually seasonal, cyclic (compare *dispersal*).

mode—in a series of values for a particular variable, the most common value.

molar—cheekteeth with no deciduous precursor, located posterior to premolars (Figures 2-1, 2-2).

molt—process of replacement of hairs, typically maturational or seasonal, and often precisely patterned.

monoestrous—having 1 estrous cycle (and hence 1 breeding period) annually (contrast with *polyestrous*).

monogamous—breeding system characterized by mating as pairs, 1 female per male.

monomorphic—literally, "one form"; little or no external difference in size or shape between sexes.

monophyletic—group of species derived from single common ancestor; in modern taxonomic practice, a taxon at any particular level in hierarchy is supposed to be monophyletic.

monotypic—descriptive of a species without discernable geographic variation.

multiparous—reproductive pattern in which female has plural litters in a lifetime.

nares—nasal passages.

nasal septum—bony, longitudinal plate that divides nasal chamber into right and left sides.

natality—pattern of births in a population.

Nearctic—biogeographic term for northern part of Western Hemisphere ("New World") (contrast with *Palearctic*).

neonate—newborn.

Neotropical—biogeographic term for New World (Western Hemisphere) tropics (contrast with *Paleotropical*).

niche—sum of resource requirements of a species population; a species' multidimensional "resource space"; see *habitat*.

nocturnal—active at night.

nomenclature—naming; in biology, the technical procedures for scientific naming.

nulliparous—descriptive of a female that has not borne offspring.

occipital—pertaining to occiput; the composite bone in that region.

occipital condyles—paired bony knobs of occiput that articulate with most anterior cervical (neck) vertebra (atlas).

occipitonasal length—length of skull from posterior end of occipital condyles to anterior end of nasal bones.

occiput—posteroventral region of skull, surrounding foramen magnum and providing point of insertion for cervical musculature.

occlusal surface—surface of tooth that contacts corresponding tooth in opposing jaw in process of mastication (chewing, grinding).

occlusion—functional contact between upper and lower teeth.

omasum—third compartment of ruminant "stomach"; actually modified section of esophagus.

omnivory—generalist food habits; feeding on both plant and animal matter (and perhaps fungi).

opposable—see *apposable*.

optic—pertaining to eye.

oral—pertaining to mouth.

orbits—bony sockets housing eyeballs (Figure 2-1).

order—taxonomic category above level of family and below level of class.

orogeny—mountain building.

os clitoridis—see *baubellum*.

os penis—see *baculum*.

ossicles—literally, "little bones"; especially bones of middle ear, the auditory ossicles.

ovary—female gonad; produces ova (eggs) and hormones.

oviducts—tube through which ova and then (after fertilization) zygote move from vicinity of ovary to uterus; also called Fallopian tubes.

ovulation—release of egg cell from follicle of ovary.

natatorial—locomotion by swimming.

palatal breadth—width of palate taken between any specified pair of teeth; typically excludes alveoli.

palatal length—measurement from most anterior point on premaxillary bone to posterior edge of palate.

palatine—paired medial bones at posterior end of palate (Figure 2-1).

papillae—any small, usually fleshy protuberance, as on tongue.

parapatric—descriptive of geographic distributions that abut but do not overlap.

parasite—consumer organism that derives its nourishment from another organism (the "host") but normally does not actually kill the host.

paraxonic—describes foot structure in which axis of symmetry passes between toes, as in deer, bison, and other artiodactyls.

parietal—paired bones of sides of braincase.

parous—pertaining to birth, bearing offspring; parous females are pregnant or have borne offspring previously.

partum—parturition.

parturition—process of giving birth.

patagium—wing membrane of bats (and gliding membrane of "flying" squirrels).

patella—kneecap.

pectoral—pertaining to shoulders.

pedicel—permanent prominence on frontal bone that serves as base and growing point of antler.

pelage—coat of hair and derivative structures (quills, bristles, vibrissae, etc.).

pelt—commercial term for pelage and underlying skin.

pelvic—pertaining to hips.

pendulous—hanging.

perianal—surrounding or in vicinity of the anus.

perineal—area between genitalia and anus.

pes—foot.

phalanges—plural of *phalanx*.

phalanx—individual bones of digits (fingers, toes).

phallus—alternative term for penis.

philopatry—tendency of individuals to remain as adults in the area of their birth.

phylogenetic tree—a diagram intended to illustrate evolutionary relationships of species or higher taxonomic groups.

phylogeny—pattern of historical, evolutionary relationships of species, often expressed as a "phylogenetic tree."

pinna—literally, "feather"; flap (typically cartilaginous and flexible) of ear

pistillate—of or pertaining to the female reproductive structures of seed plants (cones, flowers); see *staminate*.

placenta—composite structure produced by female mammal and developing embryo across which nutrients, gases, and wastes move between maternal and fetal bloodstreams.

plague—specifically, a contagious zoonotic bacterial disease; generically, a deadly, epidemic disease.

plantigrade—standing on sole of foot, with toes, foot bones, and distal parts of ankle in contact with ground.

podials—generic name for bones of foot.

pollex—first digit of forefoot; represented by human thumb; see *hallux*.

polyandrous—mating system in which female has more than 1 mate (compare *polygamous, polygynous*).

polyestrous—having more than 1 estrous cycle (hence the possibility of more than 1 breeding period) annually (contrast with *monoestrous*).

polygamous—mating system in which individuals have more than 1 mate; a general term in which gender is not specified (compare *monogamous, polyandrous, polygynous*).

polygynous—mating system in which 1 male mates with several females (compare *polyandrous, polygamous*).

polymorphic—descriptive of local species population with several distinctive colors or forms, as in color phases of red fox or Abert's squirrel.

population—individuals of same species in same general area; actual or potential reproductive unit.

postauricular—positioned behind ear.

postcornual—positioned behind horn.

postcranial—positioned behind the head, as in "postcranial skeleton."

postorbital breadth—smallest distance across skull as measured behind postorbital processes.

postorbital process—projection of temporal bone behind eye socket (orbit).

postpartum estrus—estrus immediately following parturition.

precocial—born in relatively well-developed and independent state (contrast with *altricial*).

prehensile—grasping, as in thumb of humans or tail of many New World monkeys.

premaxillary bone—anterior lateral bone of upper jaw, bearing upper incisor teeth (Figure 2-1).

premolar—cheekteeth of variable structure and function located ahead of molars; present in deciduous ("milk") dentition; in primitive mammals, 4 in each toothrow, above and below.

preorbital—positioned anterior to orbit, or eye socket.

preputial—pertaining to prepuce (foreskin of penis).

presphenoid—anteromedial bone of composite structure forming base of braincase beneath orbits (Figure 2-1).

prismatic—characterized by prisms; crystalline structure or shapes suggestive of crystals.

procumbent—anteroventrally directed.

proximal—near axis of body or specified point of reference (contrast with *distal*).

pterygoid—literally, "winglike"; paired bones lateral to sphenoid contributing to base of braincase.

rabies—infectious viral disease of nervous system.

ramus—literally, "branch"; divergent portions of bone or other structure, as in vertical or horizontal ramus of mandible.

raptor—bird of prey; inclusive (non-taxonomic) term for eagles, hawks, falcons, and owls.

recruitment—additions to population; sum of births and immigrants.

reentrant angle—sharply indented fold in side of hypsodont tooth; may be on lingual or labial side of tooth.

reingestion—consumption of specialized, nutritive "fecal" pellets (also called cecotrophy, coprophagy).

reticulum—second segment of ruminant gut, behind rumen and anterior to omasum; modified section of esophagus.

ricochetal—bipedal hopping locomotion, as in kangaroos and kangaroo rats.

riparian—river or streamside habitat.

rooted—descriptive of tooth in which pulp cavity closes at maturity, tooth fuses to alveolus, and dental growth ceases.

rootless—descriptive of tooth that continues to grow throughout life.

rostral breadth—breadth across rostrum, usually measured at suture between premaxillae and maxillae unless otherwise specified.

rostrum—portion of skull anterior to orbits; with lower jaw, comprises "muzzle."

rumen—most anterior compartment of ruminant "stomach"; actually highly modified segment of esophagus.

ruminant—member of suborder Ruminantia, advanced artiodactyls with 4-chambered "stomach" (first 3 chambers of which actually are modified sections of esophagus).

ruminate—process in which ruminant artiodactyls "chew cud," regurgitated material partially digested in rumen and reticulum.

saltatorial—locomotion by jumping.

scabies—contagious disease caused by burrowing of certain mites beneath skin.

scansorial—locomotion by scampering or climbing.

scapula—shoulder "blade" (not always blade-shaped); point of articulation of head of humerus (upper bone of forelimb).

scat—droppings, feces.

scrotum—sac in which testes of most mammals are carried during active spermatogenesis.

sebaceous glands—oil-secreting glands of hair follicles.

sebum—lubricant secreted by sebaceous glands.

secodont—describing cheekteeth with cusps adapted to shearing.

sectorial—descriptive of structures adapted to cutting, shearing.

selenodont—describing cheekteeth with crescent-shaped, longitudinal lophs.

species—group of actually or potentially interbreeding individuals reproductively isolated from other such groups; the different "kinds" or organisms.

spermatogenesis—sperm production.

sphenoidal fissure—vertical groove or elongate foramen in posteromedial area of orbit.

sphincter—muscles in circular array that constrict to close an opening (lips, anus).

squamosal—posterolateral bones of skull to which dentary articulates.

staminate—pertaining to male flowers or cones of seed plant (see *pistillate*).

stapes—"stirrup"; 1 of 3 ossicles of mammalian middle ear; homologue of reptilian columella auris (ear bone).

stochastic—describing events or processes characterized by randomness (contrast with *deterministic*).

subadult—developmental stage of mammal, usually with adult-like external appearance but sexually immature.

subnivean—descriptive of space beneath snow cover.

succession—in ecology, change in structure and floristic composition of vegetation (and dependent organisms) over time as biota changes conditions of site.

sudoriferous—sweat glands; also known as sudoriparous glands.

superciliary—pertaining to eyebrows.

supraorbital shield—bony projection of frontal bone above eye socket.

sympatric—descriptive of geographic distributions that overlap.

synecology—branch of ecology that studies interacting species; community ecology (contrast with *autecology*).

taiga—coniferous forest; from the Russian.

talus—slope of fragmented rock.

tarsals—bones of ankle (compare *carpals*).

taxon—a group of related populations at any level of the taxonomic hierarchy; plural *taxa*; the species *Canis latrans* (coyote) is a taxon, as are the genus *Canis* and the family Canidae.

taxonomic—pertaining to taxa or taxonomies, as a taxonomic category (species, genus, family, etc.)

taxonomy—scientific study of classifications.

temporal ridges—prominences on temporal bones serving as points of attachment for temporal muscles that close the jaw.

territory—portion of home range defended (actively or passively) by individual against other individuals of same species (see *home range*).

thecodont—teeth set in sockets (alveoli).

thoracic—pertaining to chest region, rib cage, and associated structures.

tibia—1 of 2 bones of distal segment of vertebrate hind limb.

torpor—partial suspension of physiologic activity; deep sleep.

tragus—flap of tissue appended to inner edge of pinna; especially prominent in bats.

tularemia—contagious bacterial disease typified by intermittent fever.

tympanic membrane—eardrum.

type—see *holotype*.

type locality—place at which holotype (type specimen) was collected.

type specimen—see *holotype*; museum specimen to which name of a species or subspecies is tied by reference.

underfur—short, often dense, insulating coat beneath guard hairs of many mammals.

ungulate—hoofed mammal.

ungule—hoof.

unguligrade—standing on the hooves.

unicuspid—tooth having single cusp or point.

urogenital tract—the common ducts and openings of the urinary and reproductive systems.

uropatagium—interfemoral membrane; flap of skin between hind limbs of many bats, including tail.

vacuity—space, usually in bone, typically accommodating glandular tissue.

vagility—capacity of a species to move, especially across barriers, to expand geographic range.

valvular—structure capable of closing, as a valve.

venter—lower (belly) surface (contrast with *dorsum*).

ventral—pertaining to venter (contrast with *dorsal*).

volant—capable of powered flight.

vomer—bone forming base of braincase; posterior roof of nasal passage (Figure 2-1).

vulva—external genitalia of female mammal.

zoonoses—general term for wildlife diseases transmissible to humans.

zygoma—cheekbone.

zygote—fertilized egg; product of syngamy (fusion of egg and sperm nuclei).

Literature Cited

Ables, E. D. 1969. Activity studies of red foxes in southern Wisconsin. J. Wildl. Mgmt. 33:145–153.

Ables, E. D. 1975. Ecology of the red fox in North America. Pp. 216–236, in The wild canids: their systematics, behavioral ecology and evolution (M. W. Fox., ed.). Van Nostrand Reinhold, New York, 508 pp.

Abramsky, Z. 1978. Small mammal community ecology, changes in species diversity in response to manipulated productivity. Oecologia 34:113–123.

Abramsky, Z., and C. R. Tracy. 1979. Population biology of a "noncycling" population of prairie voles and a hypothesis on the role of migration in regulating microtine cycles. Ecology 60:349–361.

Abramsky, Z., and G. M. Van Dyne. 1980. Field studies and a simulation model of small mammals inhabiting a patchy environment. Oikos 35:80–92.

Ackerman, B. B., F. G. Lindzey, and T. P. Hemker. 1984. Cougar food habits in southern Utah. J. Wildl. Mgmt. 48:147–155.

Ackers, S. H., and C. N. Slobodchikoff. 1999. Communication of stimulus size and shape in alarm calls of Gunnison's prairie dogs. Ethology 105:149–162.

Adams, C. 1976. Measurement and characteristics of fox squirrel, *Sciurus niger rufiventer*, home ranges. Amer. Midland Nat. 95:211–215.

Adams, L. G., and J. A. Bailey. 1982. Population dynamics of mountain goats in the Sawatch Range, Colorado. J. Wildl. Mgmt. 46:1003–1009.

Adams, L. G., and J. A. Bailey. 1983. Winter forages of mountain goats in central Colorado. J. Wildl. Mgmt. 47:1237–1243.

Adams, L. G., M. A. Masteller, and J. A. Bailey. 1982a. Movement and home range of mountain goats, Sheep Mountain–Gladstone Ridge, Colorado. Biennial Symp. Northern Wild Sheep and Goat Council 3:391–405.

Adams, L. G., K. L. Risenhoover, and J. A. Bailey. 1982b. Ecological relationships of mountain goats and Rocky Mountain bighorn sheep. Biennial Symp. Northern Wild Sheep and Goat Council 3:9–21.

Adams, R. A. 1988. Trends in reproductive biology of some bats in Colorado. Bat Research News 29:21–25.

Adams, R. A. 1990. Biogeography of bats in Colorado: ecological implications of species tolerances. Bat Research News 31:17–21.

Adams, R. A. 1992. Stages of development and sequence of bone formation in the little brown bat, *Myotis lucifugus*. J. Mamm. 73:160–167.

Adams, R. A. 1996. Size-specific resource use in juvenile little brown bats, *Myotis lucifugus* (Chiroptera: Vespertilionidae): is there an ontogenetic shift? Canadian J. Zool. 74:1204–1210.

LITERATURE CITED

Adams, R. A. 1997. Onset of juvenile volancy and foraging patterns of little brown bats, *Myotis lucifugus*. J. Mamm. 78:239–246.

Adams, R. A. 2000. Wing ontogeny, niche dimensions, and adaptive landscapes. Pp. 275–316, in Ontogeny, functional ecology and evolution of bats (R. A. Adams and S. C. Pedersen, eds.). Cambridge Univ. Press, Cambridge, UK.

Adams, R. A. 2003. Bats of the Rocky Mountain West: natural history, ecology, and conservation. Univ. Press Colorado, Boulder, 328 pp.

Adams, R. A. 2010. Bat reproduction declines when conditions mimic climate change projections for western North America. Ecology 91:2437–2445.

Adams, R. A., and M. A. Hayes. 2008. Water availability and successful lactation by bats as related to climate change in arid regions of western North America. J. Animal Ecol. 77:1115–1121.

Adams, R. A., B. J. Lengas, and M. Bekoff. 1987. Variations in avoidance responses to humans by black-tailed prairie dogs (*Cynomys ludovicianus*). J. Mamm. 58:686–689.

Adams, R. A., S. C. Pedersen, K. M. Thibault, J. Jadin, and B. Petru. 2003. Calcium as a limiting resource to insectivorous bats: can water holes provide a supplemental mineral source? J. Zoology London 260:189–194.

Adams, R. A., and J. A. Simmons. 2002. Directionality of drinking passes by bats at water holes: is there cooperation? Acta Chiropterologica 4:195–199.

Adams, R. A., and K. M. Thibault. 1999. Records of the Brazilian free-tailed bat, *Tadarida brasiliensis* (Chiroptera: Molossidae), in Colorado. Southwestern Nat. 44:542–543.

Adams, R. A., and K. M. Thibault. 2006. Temporal resource partitioning by bats at water holes. J. Zool. 270:466–472.

Addison, E. M., I. K. Barker, and D. B. Hunter. 1987. Diseases and parasites of furbearers. Pp. 893–909, in Wild furbearer management and conservation in North America (M. Novak, J. A. Baker, M. E. Obard, and B. Malloch, eds.). Ontario Trappers Association, Toronto, 1,150 pp.

Adler, P. M, and W. K. Lauenroth. 2000. Livestock exclusion increases the spatial heterogeneity of vegetation in Colorado shortgrass steppe. Applied Vegetation Sci. 3:213–222.

Adrian, W. J. ed., 1996. Wildlife forensic field manual, second ed. Colorado Division of Wildlife, Fort Collins.

Agnarsson, I., M. Kuntner, and L. H. May-Collado. 2009. Dogs, cats, and kin: a molecular species-level phylogeny of Carnivora. Molecular Phylogenetics Evol. 54:726–745.

Agricultural Statistics Board. 2005. Sheep and goats death loss. National Agricultural Statistics Service, USDA, 18 pp.

Albert, S., C. A. Ramotnik, and C. G. Schmitt. 2004. Collared peccary range expansion in northwestern New Mexico. Southwestern Nat. 49:524–528.

Alcoze, T. M., and E. G. Zimmerman. 1973. Food habits and dietary overlap of two heteromyid rodents from the mesquite plains of Texas. J. Mamm. 54:900–908.

Aldous, S. E., and J. Manweiler. 1941. The winter food habits of the short-tailed weasel in northern Minnesota. J. Mamm. 23: 250–255.

Aldridge, E. R. 1976. Prey selection by *Myotis lucifugus* (Chiroptera: Vespertilionidae). Amer. Nat. 110:619–628.

Aleksiuk, M. 1968. Scent-mound communication, territoriality, and population regulation in beaver (*Castor canadensis*). J. Mamm. 49:759–762.

Aleksiuk, M. 1970. The function of the tail as a fat storage depot in the beaver (*Castor canadensis*). J. Mamm. 51:145–148.

Alexander, L. 1977. Suitability of habitat for bobcats in Colorado. Unpubl. Report, Colorado Division Wildlife, Denver, 46 pp.

Alexander, L. F., B. J. Verts, and T. P. Farrell. 1994. Diets of ringtails (*Bassariscus astutus*) in Oregon. Northwestern Nat. 75:97–101.

Allan, P. F. 1946. Notes on *Dipodomys ordii richardsoni*. J. Mamm. 27:271–273.

Alldredge, A. W., R. D. Debliner, and J. Peterson. 1991. Birth and fawn bed site selection by pronghorns in a sagebrush-steppe community. J. Wildl. Mgmt. 55:222–227.

Alldredge, A. W., J. F. Lipscomb, and F. W. Whicker. 1974. Forage intake rates of mule deer estimated with fallout cesium-137. J. Wildl. Mgmt. 38:508–516.

Alldredge, M. W. 2007. Cougar demographics and human interactions along the urban-exurban Front Range of Colorado. Pp. 153–162, in Wildlife Research Reports, Predatory Mammals Conservation, Work Package 3003, Colorado Division of Wildlife, Fort Collins.

Alldredge, M. W. 2008. Cougar demographics and human interactions along the urban-exurban Front Range of Colorado. Pp. 155–166, in Wildlife Research Reports, Predatory Mammals Conservation, Work Package 3003, Colorado Division of Wildlife, Fort Collins.

Alldredge, M. W., E. J. Bergman, C. J. Bishop, K. A. Logan, and D. J. Freddy. 2008. Pilot evaluation of predator-prey dynamics on the Uncompahgre Plateau. Pp. 87–101, in Wildlife Research Reports, Deer Conservation, Work Package 3001, Colorado Division of Wildlife, Fort Collins.

Alldredge, M. W., and D. J. Freddy. 2008. Front-range cougar-human interaction pilot study: feasibility assessment of field techniques and protocols, Phase II. Enhancing assessment of aversive conditioning techniques for cougar-human interactions. Pp. 167–172, in Wildlife Research Reports, Predatory Mammals Conservation, Work Package 3003, Colorado Division of Wildlife, Fort Collins.

Allen, A. W. 1982. Habitat suitability index models: marten. U.S. Fish and Wildlife Service, FWS/OBS 82/10.11:1–9.

Allen, A. W. 1986. Habitat suitability index models: mink, revised. U.S. Fish and Wildlife Service, Biol. Rept. 82, Fort Collins, CO.

Allen, D. L. 1942. Populations and habits of the fox squirrel in Allegan County, Michigan. Amer. Midland Nat. 27:338–379.

Allen, D. L., and D. L. Otis. 1998. Relationship between deer mouse population parameters and Dieldrin contamination in the Rocky Mountain Arsenal National Wildlife Refuge. Canadian J. Zool. 76:243–250.

Allen, J., M. Bekoff, and R. Crabtree. 1999. An observational study of coyote (*Canis latrans*) scent-marking and territoriality in Yellowstone National Park. Ethology 105:289–302.

Allen, J. A. 1874. Notes on the mammals of portions of Kansas, Colorado, Wyoming, and Utah. Bull. Essex Inst. 5:43–66.

Allred, W. S., W. S. Gaud, and J. S. States. 1994. Effects of herbivory by Abert squirrels (*Sciurus aberti*) on cone crops of ponderosa pine. J. Mamm. 74:700–703.

Almasi-Klausz, E. E., and L. N. Carbyn. 1999. Winter abundance and distribution of small mammals in the Canadian mixed-grass prairies and implications for the swift fox. Pp. 206–209, in Proc. Fifth Prairie Conservation and Endangered Species Conference (J. Thorpe, T. A. Steeves, and M. Gollop, eds.). Provincial Mus. Alberta, Edmonton, 384 pp.

Althen, C. 1975. The interaction of circadian rhythms and thermal stress in controlling activity in the black-tailed prairie dog. Unpubl. doctoral dissert., Univ. Colorado, Boulder, 152 pp.

Altmann, M. 1956. Patterns of social behavior in big game. Trans. N. Amer. Wildl. and Nat. Resources Conf. 21:538–545.

Altmann, M. 1959. Group dynamics in Wyoming moose during the rutting season. J. Mamm. 40:420–424.

American Society of Mammalogists. 2008. Effects of wind-energy facilities on bats and other wildlife. J. Mamm. 89:1573–1575.

Amman, B. R., R. D. Owen, and R. D. Bradley. 2002. Utility of hair structure for taxonomic discrimination in bats, with an example from the bats of Colorado. Occas. Papers, Mus. Texas Tech Univ. 216:1–14.

Amstrup, S. C., and J. Beecham. 1976. Activity patterns of radio-collared black bears in Idaho. J. Wildl. Mgmt. 40:340–348.

Andelt, W. F. 1985. Behavioral ecology of coyotes in south Texas. Wildl. Monogr. 94:1–45.

Andelt, W. F. 1987. Coyote predation. Pp 128–140, in Wild furbearer management and conservation in North America (M. Novak, J. A. Baker, M. E. Obbard, and B. Malloch, eds.). Ontario Ministry of Naturalist Resources, 1,150 pp.

Andelt, W. F. 1996. Carnivores. Pp. 133–155, in Rangeland wildlife (P. R. Krausman, ed.). Soc. Range Mgmt., Denver, CO, 440 pp.

Andelt, W. F., D. P. Althoff, R. M. Case, and P. S. Gipson. 1980. Surplus killing by coyotes. J. Mamm. 51:377–378.

Andelt, W. F., and R. M. Case. 1995. Managing pocket gophers. Natural Resource Series, Colorado State Univ. Coop. Extension 6.515:1–5.

Andelt, W. F., and S. N. Hopper. 2000a. Livestock guard dogs reduce predation on domestic sheep in Colorado. J. Range Mgmt. 53:259–267.

Andelt, W. F., and S. N. Hopper. 2000b. Managing prairie dogs. Natural Resources Series, Colorado State Univ. Coop. Extension 6.506:1–5.

Andelt, W. F., R. L. Phillips, R. H. Schmidt, and R. B. Gill. 1999. Trapping furbearers: an overview of the biological and social issues surrounding a public policy controversy. Wildl. Soc. Bull. 27:53–64.

Andelt, W. F., T. M. Pojar, and L. W. Johnson. 2004. Long-term trends in mule deer pregnancy and fetal rates in Colorado. J. Wildl. Mgmt. 58:542–549.

Andelt, W. F., G. C. White, P. M. Schnurr, and K. W. Navo. 2009. Occupancy of random plots by white-tailed and Gunnison's prairie dogs. J. Wildl. Mgmt. 73:35–44.

Andersen, D. C. 1978. Observations on reproduction, growth, and behavior of the northern pocket gopher (*Thomomys talpoides*). J. Mamm. 59:418–422.

Andersen, D. C. 1987. Below-ground herbivory in natural communities: a review emphasizing fossorial mammals. Quart. Rev. Biol. 52:261–286.

Andersen, D. C., K. B. Armitage, and R. S. Hoffmann. 1976. Socioecology of marmots: female reproductive strategies. Ecology 57:552–560.

Andersen, D. C., and D. J. Cooper. 2000. Plant-herbivore-hydroperiod interactions: effects of native mammals on floodplain tree recruitment. Ecol. Applications 10:1384–1399.

Andersen, D. C., and D. W. Johns. 1977. Predation by badger on yellow-bellied marmot in Colorado. Southwestern Nat. 22: 283–284.

Andersen, D. C., J. A. MacMahon, and M. L. Wolfe. 1980. Herbivorous mammals along a montane sere: community structure and energetics. J. Mamm. 51:500–519.

Andersen, D. C., K. R. Wilson, M. S. Miller, and M. Falck. 2000. Movement patterns of riparian small mammals during predictable floodplain inundation. J. Mamm. 81:1087–1099.

Anderson, A. E. 1983. A critical review of literature on puma (*Felis concolor*). Special Rept., Colorado Division of Wildlife 54: 1–91.

Anderson, A. E., and D. C. Bowden. 1977. Mule deer-coyote interactions. Pp. 15–16, in Colorado Game Research Review, 1975–1976 (O. B. Cope, ed.). Colorado Division of Wildlife, Fort Collins, 73 pp.

Anderson, A. E., D. C. Bowden, and D. M. Kattner. 1989. Survival in an unhunted mountain lion (*Felis concolor hippolestes*) in southwestern Colorado. Proc. Mountain Lion Workshop 3: 57.

Anderson, A. E., D. C. Bowden, and D. M. Kattner. 1992. The puma on Uncompahgre Plateau, Colorado. Tech. Publ., Colorado Division of Wildlife 40:1–116.

Anderson, A. E., and D. E. Medin. 1967. The breeding season in migratory mule deer. Game Info. Leaflet, Colorado Game, Fish, and Parks Dept. 50:1–4.

Anderson, A. E., and D. E. Medin. 1969. Antler morphometry in a Colorado mule deer population. J. Wildl. Mgmt. 33:520–533.

Anderson, A. E., and D. E. Medin. 1971. Antler phenology in a Colorado mule deer population. Southwestern Nat. 15:485–494.

Anderson, A. E., D. E. Medin, and D. C. Bowden. 1974. Growth and morphometry of the carcass, selected bones, organs, and glands of mule deer. Wildl. Monogr. 39:1–122.

LITERATURE CITED

Anderson, A. E., and O. C. Wallmo. 1984. *Odocoileus hemionus*. Mammalian Species 219:1–9.

Anderson, C. R., Jr., and F. G. Lindzey. 1996. Moose sightability model developed from helicopter surveys. Wildl. Soc. Bull. 24:247–259.

Anderson, C. R., Jr., and F. G. Lindzey. 2003. Estimating cougar predation rates from GPS location clusters. J. Wildl. Mgmt. 57:307–316.

Anderson, C. R., Jr., and F. G. Lindzey. 2005. Experimental evaluation of population trend and harvest composition in a Wyoming cougar population. Wildl. Soc. Bull. 33:179–188.

Anderson, C. R., Jr., F. G. Lindzey, and D. B. McDonald. 2004. Genetic structure of cougar populations across the Wyoming Basin: metapopulation or megapopulation? J. Mamm. 85:1207–1214.

Anderson, D. R., K. P. Burnham, A. B. Franklin, R. J. Gutierrez, E. D. Foreman, R. G. Anthony, G. C. White, and T. M. Shenk. 1999. A protocol for conflict resolution in analyzing empirical data related to natural resource controversies. Wildl. Soc. Bull. 27:1050–1058.

Anderson, E. 1968. Fauna of the Little Box Elder Cave, Converse County, Wyoming: the Carnivora. Univ. Colorado Studies, Ser. Earth Sci. 5:1–59.

Anderson, E. 1994. Evolution, prehistoric distribution and systematics of *Martes*. Pp. 13–25 in Martens, sables, and fishers: biology and conservation (S. W. Buskirk, A. Harestad, M. Raphael, and R. A. Powell, eds.). Cornell Univ. Press, Ithaca, NY, 484 pp.

Anderson, E., S. C. Forrest, T. W. Clark, and L. Richardson. 1986. Paleobiology biogeography and systematics of the black-footed ferret, *Mustela nigripes* (Audubon and Bachman), 1851. Great Basin Naturalist Mem. 8:11–62.

Anderson, E. M. 1987a. Bobcat behavioral ecology in relation to resource use in southeastern Colorado. Unpubl. doctoral dissert., Colorado State Univ., Fort Collins, 107 pp.

Anderson, E. M. 1987b. A critical review and annotated bibliography of literature on the bobcat. Special Report, Colorado Division of Wildlife 62:1–61.

Anderson, E. M. 1990. Bobcat diurnal loafing sites in southeastern Colorado. J. Wildl. Mgmt. 54:600–602.

Anderson, E. M., and M. J. Lovallo. 2003. Bobcat and Lynx, *Lynx rufus* and *Lynx canadensis*. Pp. 758–786, in Wild mammals of North America, biology, management, and conservation, second ed. (G. A. Feldhamer, B. C. Thompson, and J. A. Chapman, eds.). Johns Hopkins Univ. Press, Baltimore, 1,216 pp.

Anderson, S. 1954. Subspeciation in the meadow mouse, *Microtus montanus*, in Wyoming and Colorado. Univ. Kansas Publ., Mus. Nat. Hist. 7:489–506.

Anderson, S. 1956. Subspeciation in the meadow mouse, *Microtus pennsylvanicus,* in Wyoming, Colorado, and adjacent areas. Univ. Kansas Publ., Mus. Nat. Hist. 9:85–104.

Anderson, S. 1959. Mammals of the Grand Mesa, Colorado. Univ. Kansas Publ., Mus. Nat. Hist. 9:405–414.

Anderson, S., and J. K. Jones, Jr., eds. 1984. Orders and families of mammals of the world. John Wiley and Sons, New York, 686 pp.

Anderson, S. H., and E. S. Williams. 1997. Plague in a complex of white-tailed prairie dogs and associated small mammals in Wyoming. J. Wildl. Dis. 33:720–732.

Andrews, R. D., and E. K. Boggess. 1978. Ecology of coyotes in Iowa. Pp. 249–265, in Coyotes: biology, behavior, and management (M. Bekoff, ed.). Academic Press, New York, 384 pp.

Animal Care and Use Committee. 1998. Guidelines for the capture, handling, and care of mammals as approved by the American Society of Mammalogists. J. Mamm. 79:1416–1431.

Anonymous. 1992. Fishing for fishers. Wyoming Wildl. 56:24–29.

Anonymous. 2006. "Most endangered mammal" making strides in Colorado. Newsletter, Great Plains Nat. Sci. Soc. 23(1):3–4.

Antevs, E. 1948. Climatic changes and pre–white man. Univ. Utah Bull. 38:168–191.

Antevs, E. 1954. Climate of New Mexico during the last glaciopluvial. J. Geology 62:182–191.

Anthony, A., and D. Foreman. 1951. Observations on the reproductive cycle of the black-tailed prairie dog (*Cynomys ludovicianus*). Physiol. Zool. 24:242–248.

Antolin, M. F., P. Gober, B. Luce, D. E. Biggins, W. E. Van Pelt, D. B. Seery, M. Lockhart, and M. Ball. 2002. The influence of sylvatic plague on North American wildlife at the landscape level, with special emphasis on black-footed ferret and prairie dog conservation. Trans. 57th North American Nat. Res. Conf., 104–127.

Antolin, M. F., L. T. Savage, and R. J. Eisen. 2006. Landscape features influence genetic structure of black-tailed prairie dogs (*Cynomys ludovicianus*). Landscape Ecol. 21:867–875.

Arbogast, B. S., R. A. Browne, and P. D. Weigl. 2001. Evolutionary genetics and Pleistocene biogeography of North American tree squirrels (*Tamiasciurus*). J. Mamm. 82:302–319.

Archer, S., M. G. Garrett, and J. K. Detling. 1987. Rates of vegetation change associated with prairie dog (*Cynomys ludovicianus*) grazing in North American mixed-grass prairie. Vegetatio 72:159–166.

Archibald, J. D. 2003. Timing and biogeography of the eutherian radiation: fossils and molecules compared. Molec. Phylogen. Evol. 28:350–359.

Archibald, J. D., and K. D. Rose. 2005. Womb with a view: the rise of placentals. Pp. 1–8, in The rise of placental mammals, origins and relationships of the major extant clades (K. D. Rose and J. D. Archibald, eds.). Johns Hopkins Univ. Press, Baltimore, 259 pp.

Archibald, W. S. 1963. A study of small mammal-habitat association in Weld County, Colorado. Unpubl. master's thesis, Colorado State College, Greeley, 63 pp.

Arjo, W. M., and D. H. Pletscher. 1999. Behavioral responses of coyotes to wolf recolonization in northwestern Montana. Canadian J. Zool. 77:1919–1927.

Arjo, W. M., D. H. Pletscher, and R. R. Ream. 2002. Dietary overlap between wolves and coyotes in northwestern Montana. J. Mamm. 83:754–766.

Arlton, A. V. 1936. An ecological study of the mole. J. Mamm. 17: 349–371.

Armitage, K. B. 1961a. Frequency of melanism in the golden-mantled marmot. J. Mamm. 42:100–101.

Armitage, K. B. 1961b. Frequency of melanism in the yellow-bellied marmot. J. Mamm. 42:100–101.

Armitage, K. B. 1962. Social behavior of a colony of the yellow-bellied marmot (*Marmota flaviventris*). Animal Behavior 10:319–331.

Armitage, K. B. 1973. Population changes and social behavior following colonization by the yellow-bellied marmot. J. Mamm. 54:842–854.

Armitage, K. B. 1974. Male behaviour and territoriality in the yellow-bellied marmot. J. Zool. 172:233–265.

Armitage, K. B. 1975. Social behavior and population dynamics of marmots. Oikos 26:341–354.

Armitage, K. B. 1976. Scent-marking by yellow-bellied marmots. J. Mamm. 57:583–584.

Armitage, K. B. 1979. Food selectivity by yellow-bellied marmots. J. Mamm. 50:628–629.

Armitage, K. B. 1991. Social and population dynamics of yellow-bellied marmots: results from long-term research. Ann. Rev. Ecol. and Systematics 22:379–407.

Armitage, K. B. 1998. Reproductive strategies of yellow-bellied marmots: energy conservation and differences between the sexes. J. Mamm. 79:385–393.

Armitage, K. B. 1999. Evolution of sociality in marmots. J. Mamm. 80:1–10.

Armitage, K. B. 2003. Marmots, *Marmota monax* and allies. Pp. 188–210, in Wild mammals of North America, biology, management, and economics, second ed. (G. A. Feldhamer, B. C. Thompson, and J. A. Chapman, eds.). Johns Hopkins Univ. Press, Baltimore, 1,216 pp.

Armitage, K. B. 2007. Evolution of sociality in marmots: it begins with hibernation. Pp. 356–367, in Rodent societies, an ecological & evolutionary perspective (J. O. Wolff and P. W. Sherman, eds.). Univ. Chicago Press, Chicago, 620 pp.

Armitage, K. B., and J. F. Downhower. 1974. Demography of yellow-bellied marmot populations. Ecology 55:1233–1245.

Armitage, K. B., J. F. Downhower, and G. E. Svendsen. 1976. Seasonal changes in weights of marmots. Amer. Midland Nat. 96:36–51.

Armitage, K. B., and D. Johns. 1982. Kinship, reproductive strategies, and social dynamics of yellow-bellied marmots. Behavioral Ecology and Sociobiology 11:55–63.

Armitage, K. B., D. Johns, and D. C. Andersen. 1979. Cannibalism among yellow-bellied marmots. J. Mamm. 50:205–207.

Armitage, K. B., and O. A. Schwartz. 2000. Social enhancement of fitness in yellow-bellied marmots. Proc. National Acad. Sci. 97:12149–12152.

Armstrong, D. M. 1971. Notes on variation in *Spermophilus tridecemlineatus* (Rodentia, Sciuridae) in Colorado and adjacent states, and description of a new subspecies. J. Mamm. 52:528–536.

Armstrong, D. M. 1972. Distribution of mammals in Colorado. Monogr., Univ. Kansas Mus. Nat. Hist. 3:1–415.

Armstrong, D. M. 1974. Second record of the Mexican big-eared bat in Utah. Southwestern Nat. 19:114–115.

Armstrong, D. M. 1977a. Distributional patterns of mammals in Utah. Great Basin Nat. 37:457–474.

Armstrong, D. M. 1977b. Ecological distribution of small mammals in the upper Williams Fork Basin, Grand County, Colorado. Southwestern Nat. 22:289–304.

Armstrong, D. M. 1979. Ecological distribution of rodents in Canyonlands National Park, Utah. Great Basin Nat. 39:199–205.

Armstrong, D. M. 1982. Mammals of the canyon country: a handbook of mammals of Canyonlands National Park and vicinity, Utah. Canyonlands Natural History Association, Moab, UT, 263 pp.

Armstrong, D. M. 1984. Mammalian associates of woodrats (*Neotoma)* on the Colorado Plateau, USA Program and Abstracts, Australian Mammal Society, American Society of Mammalogists, Joint Meeting, Sydney, unpaged.

Armstrong, D. M. 1986. Edward Royal Warren (1860–1942) and the development of Coloradan mammalogy. Amer. Zool. 26:363–370.

Armstrong, D. M. 1987. Rocky Mountain mammals, a handbook of mammals of Rocky Mountain National Park and vicinity, Colorado, revised ed. Colorado Associated Univ. Press, Boulder, 223 pp.

Armstrong, D. M. 1993. Effects of the Lawn Lake Flood on the local distribution of mammals. Pp. 170–191, in Ecological effects of the Lawn Lake flood of 1982, Rocky Mountain National Park (H. E. McCutchen, R. Heerman, and D. R. Stevens, eds.). Scientific Monograph, National Park Service, NPS/NRROMO/NRSM-93/21:1–214.

Armstrong, D. M. 1996. Northern limits of mammals of northern interior Mexico. Pp. 261–283, in Contributions in mammalogy, a memorial volume honoring Dr. J. Knox Jones, Jr. (H. H. Genoways and R. J. Baker, eds.). Texas Tech Univ. Press, Lubbock, 315 pp.

Armstrong, D. M. 2006. Lions, ferrets, & bears, a guide to the mammals of Colorado, second ed. Colorado Division of Wildlife, Denver, 65 pp.

Armstrong, D. M. 2008. Rocky Mountain mammals, a handbook of mammals of Rocky Mountain National Park and vicinity, third ed. Univ. Press Colorado, Boulder, 265 pp.

Armstrong, D. M. 2009. Hope in a world of wounds: sustainable stewardship in Colorado. Pp. 230–247, in Remedies for a new West, healing landscapes, histories, and cultures (P. N. Limerick, A. Cowell, and S. K. Collinge, eds.). Univ. Arizona Press, Tucson, 324 pp.

Armstrong, D. M., R. A. Adams, and J. Freeman. 1994. Distribution and ecology of bats in Colorado. Nat. Hist. Inventory, Univ. Colorado Mus. 15:1–82.

LITERATURE CITED

Armstrong, D. M., R. A. Adams, K. W. Navo, J. Freeman, and S. J. Bissell. 1995. Bats of Colorado, shadows in the night. Colorado Division of Wildlife, Denver, 29 pp.

Armstrong, D. M., R. A. Adams, and K. E. Taylor. 2006. New records of the eastern pipistrelle (*Pipistrellus subflavus*) in Colorado. Western North Amer. Nat. 56:268–269.

Armstrong, D. M., and J. Amoroso. 2002. Wolves in the Southern Rockies, principles, problems, and prospects. National Wildlife Federation, Boulder, and Colorado Wildlife Federation, Lakewood, 29 pp.

Armstrong, D. M., B. H. Banta, and E. J. Pokropus. 1973. Altitudinal distribution of small mammals along a cross-sectional transect through the Arkansas River watershed, Colorado. Southwestern Nat. 17:315–326.

Armstrong, D. M., J. C. Halfpenny, and C. H. Southwick. 2001. Vertebrates. Pp. 128–156, in Structure and function of an alpine ecosystem, Niwot Ridge, Colorado (W. D. Bowman and T. R. Seastedt, eds.). Oxford Univ. Press, New York, 337 pp.

Armstrong, D. M., and J. K. Jones, Jr. 1971. *Sorex merriami*. Mammalian Species, 2:1–2.

Armstrong, D. M., and J. K. Jones, Jr. 1972. *Notiosorex crawfordi*. Mammalian Species 17:1–5.

Armstrong, J. B., and A. N. Rossi. 2000. Status of avocational trapping based on the perspectives of state furbearer biologists. Wildl. Soc. Bull. 28:825–832.

Arnason, U., and B. Widegren. 1986. Pinniped phylogeny enlightened by molecular hybridizations using highly repetitive DNA. Molec. Biol. Evol. 3:356–365.

Arnett, E. B., W. K. Brown, W. P. Erickson, J. K. Fiedler, B. L. Hamilton, T. H. Henry, A. Jain, G. D. Johnson, K. Kerns, R. R. Koford, C. P. Nicholson, T. J. O'Connell, M. D. Piorkiowski, and R. D. Tankersley. 2008. Patterns of bat fatalities at wind energy facilities in North America. J. Wildl. Mgmt. 72:61–78.

Arnett, E. B., D. B. Inkley, D. H. Johnson, R. P. Larkin, S. Manes, A. M. Manville, R. Mason, M. Morrison, M. D. Strickland, and R. Thresher. 2007. Impacts of wind energy facilities on wildlife and wildlife habitat. Technical Review, The Wildlife Society 07-2:1–49.

Arnold, T. W., and E. K. Fritzell. 1987a. Food habits of prairie mink during the waterfowl breeding season. Canadian J. Zool. 55:2322–2324.

Arnold, T. W., and E. K. Fritzell. 1987b. Activity patterns, movements, and home ranges of prairie mink. Prairie Nat. 19: 25–32.

Asdell, S. A. 1964. Patterns of mammalian reproduction, second ed. Cornell Univ. Press, Ithaca, NY, 670 pp.

Asher, R. J. 2005. Insectivoran-grade placentals. Pp. 50–70, in The rise of placental mammals, origins and relationships of the major extant clades (K. D. Rose and J. D. Archibald, eds.). Johns Hopkins Univ. Press, Baltimore, MD, 259 pp.

Ashley, M. C. 2000. Feral horses in the desert: population genetics, demography, mating, and management. Unpubl. doctoral dissert., Univ. Nevada, Reno.

Asner, G. P., A. Elmore, L. Olander, R. E. Martin, and A. T. Harris. 2004. Grazing systems, ecosystem responses and global change. *Ann. Rev. Envir. and Resources* 29:261–299.

Attenborough, D. 2002. The life of mammals. Princeton Univ. Press, Princeton, NJ, 320 pp.

Aubry, K. B. 1983. The Cascade red fox: distribution, taxonomy, zoogeography and ecology. Unpubl. doctoral dissertation, Univ. Washington, Seattle, 151 pp.

Aubry, K. B. 1984. The recent history and present distribution of the red fox in Washington. Northwest Sci. 58:69–79.

Aubry, K. B. 1997. The Sierra Nevada red fox (*Vulpes vulpes necator*). Pp. 47–53 in Mesocarnivores of northern California: biology, management, and survey techniques, workshop manual. The Wildlife Society, California North Coast Chapter, Humboldt State. Univ., Arcata, 117 pp.

Aubry, K. B., K. S. McKelvey, and J. P. Copeland. 2007. Distribution and broadscale habitat relations of the wolverine in the contiguous United States. J. Wildl. Mgmt. 71:2.

Avery, S. R. 1989. Vocalization and behavior of the swift fox (*Vulpes velox*). Unpubl. master's thesis, Univ. Northern Colorado, Greeley, 104 pp.

Baerwald, E. F., G. H. D'Amours, B. J. Klug, and R.M.R. Barclay. 2008. Barotrauma is a significant cause of bat fatalities at wind turbines. Current Biol. 18:R695–R696.

Bai, Y., M. Y. Kosoy, C. Ray, R. J. Brinkerhoff, and S. K. Collinge. 2008. Temporal and spatial patterns of *Bartonella* infection in black-tailed prairie dogs (*Cynomys ludovicianus*). Microbial Ecol. 56:373–382.

Bailey, B. 1929. The mammals of Sherburne County, Minnesota. J. Mamm. 10:153–164.

Bailey, E. P. 1974. Notes on the development, mating behavior, and vocalization of captive ringtails. Southwestern Nat. 19:117–119.

Bailey, J. A. 1986. The increase and die-off of Waterton Canyon bighorn sheep: biology, management, and mismanagement. Biennial Symp. Northern Wild Sheep and Goat Council 5:325–340.

Bailey, J. A. 1990. Management of Rocky Mountain bighorn sheep herds in Colorado. Special Report, Colorado Division of Wildlife, 66.

Bailey, J. A., and B. K. Johnson. 1977. Status of introduced mountain goats in the Sawatch Range of Colorado. Pp. 54–63, in Proceedings of the First International Mountain Goat Symposium (W. Samuel and W. G. MacGregor, eds.). Fish and Wildlife Branch, British Columbia, 243 pp.

Bailey, R. G. 1978. Ecosystems of the United States. USDA Forest Service, RARE II, Map B, 1:7,500,000.

Bailey, T. N. 1971. Biology of striped skunks on a southwestern Lake Erie marsh. Amer. Midland Nat. 85:196–207.

Bailey, T. N. 1974. Social organization in a bobcat population. J. Wildl. Mgmt. 38:435–446.

Bailey, V. 1926. A biological survey of North Dakota. N. American Fauna 49:1–226.

Bailey, V. 1932. Mammals of New Mexico. N. American Fauna 53:1–412.

Baillie, J.E.M., C. Hilton-Taylor, and S. N. Stuart, eds. 2004. 2004 IUCN Red List of threatened species, a global species assessment. IUCN Species Survival Commission, Gland, Switzerland, 191 pp.

Bain, M. R., and T. M. Shenk. 2002. Nests of Preble's meadow jumping mouse (*Zapus hudsonius preblei*) in Douglas County, Colorado. Southwestern Nat. 47:630–633.

Baird, S. F. 1855. Characteristics of some new species of North American Mammalia, collected chiefly in connection with the U.S. surveys of a railroad route to the Pacific. Proc. Acad. Nat. Sci. Philadelphia 7:333–336.

Baird, S. F. 1858. Mammals, in Reports of explorations and surveys . . . from the Mississippi River to the Pacific Ocean . . . 8(1):1–757.

Baker, A.E.M. 1974. Interspecific aggressive behavior of pocket gophers *Thomomys bottae* and *T. talpoides* (Geomyidae: Rodentia). Ecology 55:671–673.

Baker, B. W. 2003. Beaver (*Castor canadensis*) in heavily browsed environments. Lutra 46:173–181.

Baker, B. W., and B. S. Cade. 1995. Predicting biomass of beaver food from willow stem diameters. J. Range Mgmt. 48:322–326.

Baker, B. W., H. C. Ducharme, D.C.S. Mitchell, T. R. Stanley, and H. R. Peinetti. 2005. Interaction of beaver and elk herbivory reduces standing crop of willow. Ecol. Applications 15:110–118.

Baker, B. W., D. L. Hawksworth, and J. D. Graham. 1992. Wildlife habitat response to riparian restoration on the Douglas Creek watershed. Proc. Annual Conf., Colorado Riparian Assoc. 4:62–80.

Baker, B. W., and E. P. Hill. 2003. Beaver, *Castor canadensis*. Pp. 288–310, in Wild mammals of North America, biology, management, and economics, second ed. (G. A. Feldhamer, B. C. Thompson, and J. A. Chapman, eds.). Johns Hopkins Univ. Press, Baltimore, 1,216 pp.

Baker, B. W., T. R. Stanley, and G. E. Plumb. 2000. Nest predation on black-tailed prairie dog colonies. J. Wildl. Mgmt. 54:776–784.

Baker, R. J., L. C. Bradley, R. D. Bradley, J. W. Dragoo, M. D. Engstrom, R. S. Hoffmann, C. A. Jones, F. Reid, D. W. Rice, and C. Jones. 2003. Revised checklist of North American mammals north of Mexico, 2003. Occas. Papers, Texas Tech Univ. 229:1–23.

Baker, R. J., R. D. Bradley, and L. R. McAliley, Jr. 2003. Gophers (Geomyidae). Pp. 276–287, in Wild mammals of North America, biology, management, and economics, second ed. (G. A. Feldhamer, B. C. Thompson, and J. A. Chapman, eds.). Johns Hopkins Univ. Press, Baltimore, 1,216 pp.

Baker, R. J., R. J. Gress, and D. L. Spencer. 1983. Mortality and population density of cottontail rabbits at Ross Natural History Reservation, Lyons County, Kansas. Emporia State Research Studies 31:1–49.

Baker, R. J., M. B. O'Neill, and L. R. McAliley. 2003. A new species of desert shrew, *Notiosorex*, based on nuclear and mitochondrial sequence data. Occas. Papers, Mus. Texas Tech Univ. 222:1–12.

Baker, R. J., J. C. Patton, H. H. Genoways, and J. W. Bickham. 1988. Genic studies of *Lasiurus* (Chiroptera: Vespertilionidae). Occas. Papers, Mus. Texas Tech Univ. 117:1–15.

Baker, R. J., and D. L. Spencer. 1965. Late fall reproduction in the desert shrew. J. Mamm. 46:330.

Baker, W. L. 2009. Fire ecology in Rocky Mountain landscapes. Island Press, Washington, DC, 632 pp.

Baker, W. L., J. A. Munroe, and E. E. Hessl. 1997. The effect of elk on aspen in the winter range of Rocky Mountain National Park, Colorado, USA. Ecography 20:155–165.

Bakken, A. A. 1959. Behavior of gray squirrels. Proc. Southeastern Assoc. Game Fish Commissioners 13:393–406.

Bakko, E. B., and L. N. Brown. 1967. Breeding biology of the white-tailed prairie dog, *Cynomys leucurus* in Wyoming. J. Mamm. 48:100–112.

Bakko, E. B., and J. Nahorniak. 1986. Torpor patterns in captive white-tailed prairie dogs (*Cynomys leucurus*). J. Mamm. 57: 576–578.

Balcombe, J. P. 1990. Vocal recognition of pups by mother Mexican free-tailed bats *Tadarida brasiliensis mexicana*. Animal Behavior 39:960–966.

Baldwin, R. A. 2008. Population demographics, habitat utilization, critical habitats, and condition of black bears in Rocky Mountain National Park. Unpubl. PhD dissert., New Mexico State Univ., Las Cruces, 391 pp.

Baldwin, R. A., and L. C. Bender. 2008a. Distribution, occupancy, and habitat correlates of American martens (*Martes americana*) in Rocky Mountain National Park, Colorado. J. Mamm. 89:419–427.

Baldwin, R. A., and L. C. Bender. 2008b. Den-site characteristics of black bears in Rocky Mountain National Park, Colorado. J. Wild. Mgmt. 72:1717–1724.

Baldwin, R. A., and L. C. Bender. 2009. Survival and productivity of a low-density black bear population in Rocky Mountain National Park, Colorado. Human-Wildlife Conflicts 3:271–281.

Baldwin, R. A., and L. C. Bender. 2010. Denning chronology of black bears in eastern Rocky Mountain National Park, Colorado. Western North American Nat. 70:48–54.

Baldwin, R. A., A. E. Houston, M. L. Kennedy, and P. S. Liu. 2004. An assessment of microhabitat variables and capture success of striped skunks (*Mephitis mephitis*). J. Mamm. 85:1068–1076.

Ball, L. C. 2002. A strategy for describing and monitoring bat habitat. J. Wildl. Mgmt. 56:148–1153.

Ballard, W. B., D. Lutz, T. W. Keegan, L. H. Carpenter, and J. C. deVos, Jr. 2001. Deer-predator relationships: a review of recent North American studies with emphasis on mule and black-tailed deer. Wildl. Soc. Bull. 29:99–115.

LITERATURE CITED

Ballard, W. B., J. S. Whitman, and D. J. Reed. 1991. Population dynamics of moose in south-central Alaska. Wildl. Monogr. 114:1–49.

Banci, V. A. 1994. Wolverine. Pp. 99–127, in The scientific basis for conserving forest carnivores: American marten, fisher, lynx, and wolverine in the western United States (L. F. Ruggiero, K. B. Aubry, S. W. Buskirk, L. J. Lyon, and W. J. Zielinski, eds.). USDA Forest Service Rocky Mountain Forest and Range Experiment Station, Gen. Tech. Report RM-254:1–184.

Bandoli, J. H. 1981. Factors influencing seasonal burrowing activity in the pocket gopher, *Thomomys bottae*. J. Mamm. 52:293–303.

Bandoli, J. H. 1987. Activity and plural occupancy of burrows in Botta's pocket gopher *Thomomys bottae*. Amer. Midland Nat. 118:10–14.

Banfield, A.W.F. 1974. The mammals of Canada. Univ. Toronto Press, Toronto, 438 pp.

Bangert, R., and C. N. Slobodchikoff. 2004. Prairie dog engineering indirectly affects beetle movement behavior. J. Arid Environ. 56:83–94.

Bangert, R., and C. N. Slobodchikoff. 2006. Conservation of prairie dog ecosystem engineering may support beta and gamma diversity. J. Arid Environ. 57:100–115.

Bangert, R. K., and C. N. Slobodchikoff. 2000. The Gunnison's prairie dog structures: a high desert grassland landscape as a keystone engineer. J. Arid Environ. 46:357–369.

Bangs, E., J. Fontaine, M. Jimenez, T. Meier, C Niemeyer, D. Smith, K. Murphy, D. Guernsey, L. Handegard, M. Collinge, R. Krischke, J. Shivik, C. Mack, I. Babcock, V. Asher, and D. Domenici. 2001. Gray wolf restoration in the northwestern United States. Endangered Species Update 18:147–152.

Bangs, E. E., S. H. Fritts, J. A. Fontaine, D. W. Smith, K. M. Murphy, C. M. Mack, and C. C. Niemeyer. 1998. Status of gray wolf restoration in Montana, Idaho, and Wyoming. Wildl. Soc. Bull. 26:785–798.

Banta, B. H., and T. M. Norris. 1968. The small mammal fauna sampled along a transect of prairie in El Paso, Colorado in 1963 and 1964. Wasmann J. Biol. 26:185–200.

Barash, D. P. 1971. Cooperative hunting in the lynx. J. Mamm. 52:480.

Barash, D. P. 1974. Neighbor recognition in two "solitary" carnivores: the raccoon (*Procyon lotor*) and the red fox (*Vulpes vulpes*). Science 185:794–796.

Barayshnikov, G. F., O.R.P. Bininda-Emonds, and A. V. Abramov. 2003. Morphological variability and evolution of the baculum (os penis) in Mustelidae (Carnivora). J. Mamm. 573–690.

Barber, S. M., L. D. Mech, and P. J. White. 2005. Yellowstone elk calf mortality following wolf restoration, bears remain top summer predators. Yellowstone Sci. 13(3):37–44.

Barber-Meyer, S. M. 2006. Elk calf mortality following wolf restoration to Yellowstone National Park. Unpubl. doctoral dissertation, Univ. Minnesota, 195 pp.

Barber-Meyer, S. M., L. D. Mech, and P. J. White. 2008. Elk calf survival and mortality following wolf restoration to Yellowstone National Park. Wildl. Monogr. 169:1–30.

Barbour, R. W., and W. H. Davis. 1969. Bats of America. Univ. Kentucky Press, Lexington, 286 pp.

Barbour, R. W., and W. H. Davis. 1970. The status of *Myotis occultus*. J. Mamm. 41:150–151.

Barclay, R.M.R. 1999. Bats are not birds—a cautionary note on using echolocation calls to identify bats: a comment. J. Mamm. 80:290–296.

Barnard, S. M. 1995. Bats in captivity. Wild Ones Animal Books, Springville, CA, 194 pp.

Barnes, A. M. 1982. Surveillance and control of bubonic plague in the United States. Symposium Zool. Soc. London 50:237–270.

Barnes, A. M. 1993. A review of plague and its relevance to prairie dog populations and the black-footed ferret. Pp. 28–37, in Proceedings of the Symposium on the Management of Prairie Dog Complexes for the Reintroduction of Black-footed Ferrets (J. L. Oldemeyer, D. E. Biggins, B. J. Miller, and R. Crete, eds.). Biol. Rept., U.S. Fish and Wildlife Service 93:1–95.

Barnett, D. T., and T. J. Stohlgren. 2001. Aspen persistence near the National Elk Refuge and Gros Ventre Valley elk feedgrounds of Wyoming, USA. Landscape Ecology 16:569–580.

Barnosky, A. D., ed. 2004. Biodiversity response to climate change in the Middle Pleistocene, the Porcupine Cave fauna from Colorado. Univ. California Press, Berkeley, 385 pp.

Barnosky, A. D., E. A. Hadly, and C. J. Bell. 2003. Mammalian response to global warming on varied temporal scales. J. Mamm. 84:354–368.

Barnosky, A. D., and C. J. Bell. 2004. Age and correlation of key fossil sites in Porcupine Cave. Pp. 318–326 in Biodiversity response to climate change in the Middle Pleistocene, the Porcupine Cave fauna from Colorado (A. D. Barnosky, ed.). Univ. California Press, Berkeley, 385 pp.

Baron, D. 2005. The beast in the garden: a modern parable of man and nature. W. W. Norton & Company, New York, 277 pp.

Baron, J. S. 2002. Rocky Mountain futures: forecasting a future we do not want. Pp. 301–305, in Rocky Mountain futures, an ecological perspective (J. S. Baron, ed.). Island Press, Washington, DC, 325 pp.

Barone, M. A., M. E. Roelke, J. Howard, J. L. Brown, A. E. Anderson, and D. E. Wildt. 1994. Reproductive characteristics of male Florida panthers, comparative studies from Florida, Texas, Colorado, Latin America, and North American zoos. J. Mamm. 75:150–162.

Barrows, P., and J. Holmes. 1990. Colorado's wildlife story. Colorado Division of Wildlife, Denver, 450 pp.

Bartels, M. A., and D. P. Thompson. 1993. *Spermophilus lateralis*. Mammalian Species 440:1–8.

Bartholomew, G. A., and H. H. Caswell. 1951. Locomotion in kangaroo rats and its adaptive significance. J. Mamm. 32: 155–169.

Bartholomew, G. A., and J. W. Hudson. 1959. Effects of sodium chloride on weight and drinking in the antelope ground squirrel. J. Mamm. 40:354–360.

Bartmann, R. M. 1968. Results from an 18-year deer tagging program in northwestern Colorado. Proc. Western Association of State Game and Fish Commissioners 48:166–172.

Bartmann, R. M., and S. F. Steinert. 1981. Distribution and movements of mule deer in the White River drainage, Colorado. Special Rept., Colorado Division of Wildlife 51:1–12.

Bartmann, R. M., G. C. White, and L. H. Carpenter. 1992. Compensatory mortality in a Colorado mule deer population. Wildl. Monogr. 121:3–39.

Bartmann, R. M., G. C. White, L. H. Carpenter, and R. A. Garrott. 1987. Aerial mark-recapture estimates of confined mule deer in pinyon-juniper woodland. J. Wildl. Mgmt. 51:41–46.

Baruch-Mordo, S., S. W. Breck, K. R. Wilson, D. M. Theobald. 2008. Spatiotemporal distribution of black bear–human conflicts in Colorado, USA. J. Wildl. Mgmt. 72:1853–1862.

Bass, R. 1995. The lost grizzlies: a search for survivors in the Colorado wilderness. Houghton Mifflin, Boston, 239 pp.

Bassett, J. E., and J. E. Wiebers. 1979. Subspecific differences in the urine concentrating ability of *Myotis lucifugus*. J. Mamm. 50:395–397.

Batcheller, G., and Furbearer Conservation Technical Work Group, Association of Fish and Wildlife Agencies. 2007. Summary of trapping regulations for fur harvesting in the United States. Publ. Wildl. Mgmt., Internet Center for Wildlife Damage Management, 55 pp.

Batcheller, G. R., T. A. Decker, D. A. Hamilton, and J. F. Organ. 2000. A vision for the future of furbearer management in the United States. Wildl. Soc. Bull. 28:833–840.

Bath, A. J. 1998. The role of human dimensions in wildlife resource research in wildlife management. Ursus 10:349–355.

Batzli, G. O., and F. O. Cole. 1979. Nutritional ecology of microtine rodents: digestibility of forage. J. Mamm. 58:583–591.

Baumgartner, L. L. 1940. The fox squirrel: its life history, habits, and management in Ohio. Wildl. Research Sta. Release, Ohio State Univ. 138:1–257.

Baumgartner, L. L. 1943. Fox squirrels in Ohio. J. Wildl. Mgmt. 7:193–202.

Beale, D. M., and A. D. Smith. 1973. Mortality of pronghorn antelope fawns in western Utah. J. Wildl. Mgmt. 37:343–352.

Bear, G., and R. Green. 1980. Elk investigations: elk population and ecological studies. Wildlife Research Rept., Colorado Division of Wildlife, July, 221–313.

Bear, G. D. 1968. Hunter harvest and population trend of a small herd of antelope located in Moffat County, Colorado. Proc. Pronghorn Antelope Workshop 3:85–91.

Bear, G. D. 1969. Evaluation of aerial antelope census technique. Game Information Leaflet, Colorado Division of Wildlife 69:1–3.

Bear, G. D. 1973. Antelope investigations: food habits of antelope. Game Research Rept., Colorado Division of Wildlife, January, 37–70.

Bear, G. D. 1978. Evaluation of fertilizer and herbicide applications on two Colorado bighorn sheep winter ranges. Division Rept., Colorado Division of Wildlife 10:1–75.

Bear, G. D. 1979. Evaluation of bighorn transplants in two Colorado localities. Special Rept., Colorado Division of Wildlife 45:1–12.

Bear, G. D. 1989. Seasonal distribution and population characteristics of elk in Estes Valley, Colorado. Colorado Division of Wildlife, Special Rept., 65:65–89.

Bear, G. D., and R. M. Hansen. 1966. Food habits, growth, and reproduction of white-tailed jackrabbits in southern Colorado. Tech. Bull., Agric. Exper. Sta., Colorado State Univ. 90:1–59.

Bear, G. D., and G. W. Jones. 1973. History and distribution of bighorn sheep in Colorado. Colorado Division of Wildlife, 231 pp.

Beattie, K. H., and T. A. Pierson. 1977a. For Colorado hunters ONLY, a questionnaire to help us find out what satisfactions you derive from hunting. Colorado Outdoors 26(2): unpaged insert.

Beattie, K. H., and T. A. Pierson. 1977b. What makes hunters happy? Colorado Outdoors 26(5):2–9.

Beauvais, G. P., and J. McCumber. 2006. Pygmy shrew (*Sorex hoyi*): a technical conservation assessment. Species Conservation Project, USDA Forest Service, Rocky Mountain Region, 34 pp.

Beauvais, G. P., and R. Smith. 2005. Predictive distribution maps for 54 species of management concern in the Rocky Mountain Region of the USDA Forest Service. Wyoming Natural Diversity Database, Univ. Wyoming, Laramie, 21 pp.

Beck, R. F., and R. M. Hansen. 1966. Estimating plains pocket gopher abundance on adjacent soil types by a revised technique. J. Range Mgmt. 19:224–225.

Beck, T.D.I. 1981. Black bear investigations. Job Progress Report, Colorado Division of Wildlife P-R Project W-126-R-4:305–316.

Beck, T.D.I. 1989. Development of river otter reintroduction procedures. Wildlife Research Job Progress Report, Colorado Division of Wildlife, Fort Collins, 199–209.

Beck, T.D.I. 1991. Black bears of west-central Colorado. Tech. Publ., Colorado Division of Wildlife 39:1–86.

Beck, T.D.I. 1995. Development of black bear inventory techniques. Wildlife Research Report. Project W-153-R-8, Colorado Division of Wildlife, Fort Collins.

Beck, T.D.I. 1996. Development of black bear inventory techniques. Wildlife Research Report. Project W-153-R-9, Colorado Division of Wildlife, Fort Collins.

Beck, T.D.I. 1997. Development of black bear inventory techniques. Wildlife Research Report. Project W-153-R-10, Colorado Division of Wildlife, Fort Collins.

Beck, T.D.I. 1999. Kit fox (*Vulpes macrotis*) status in Colorado. Wildlife Research Report. Project W-153-R-12, Colorado Division of Wildlife, Fort Collins.

Beck, T.D.I. 2000a. Colorado Status Report Survey. Pp. 58–62 in The Western Black Bear Workshop. Coos Bay, OR.

Beck, T.D.I. 2000b. Kit fox augmentation study. Wildlife Research Report. Project W-153-R-13, Colorado Division of Wildlife, Fort Collins.

LITERATURE CITED

Beckel-Kratz, A. 1977. Preliminary observations on the social behavior of the North American otter (*Lutra canadensis*). Otters 1977:28–32.

Becker, C. D., S. Boutin, and K. W. Larsen 1998. Constraints on first reproduction in North American red squirrels. Oikos 81:81–92.

Beckmann, J. P., and J. Berger. 2003. Using black bears to test ideal-free distribution models experimentally. J. Mamm. 84:594–606.

Bee, J. W., G. E. Glass, R. S. Hoffmann, and R. R. Patterson. 1981. Mammals in Kansas. Public Ed. Ser., Univ. Kansas Mus. Nat. Hist. 7:1–300.

Beecham, J. J. 1983. Population characteristics of black bears in west central Idaho. J. Wildl. Mgmt. 47:405–412.

Beecham, J. J., C. P. Collins, and T. D. Reynolds. 2007. Rocky Mountain bighorn sheep (*Ovis canadensis*): a technical conservation assessment. Species Conservation Project, Rocky Mountain Region, USDA Forest Service, 108 pp.

Beer, J. R. 1950. The reproductive cycle of the muskrat in Wisconsin. J. Wildl. Mgmt. 14:151–156.

Beer, J. R. 1961. Hibernation in *Perognathus flavescens*. J. Mamm. 42:103.

Beever, E. 2003. Management implications of the ecology of free-roaming horses in semi-arid ecosystems of the western United States. Wildl. Soc. Bull. 31:887–895.

Beever, E. A., P. F. Brussard, and J. Berger. 2003. Patterns of apparent extirpation among isolated populations of pikas (*Ochotona princeps*) in the Great Basin. J. Mamm. 84:37–54.

Beidleman, R. G. 1950. The cinereous shrew below 6000 feet in north central Colorado. J. Mamm. 31:459.

Beidleman, R. G. 1952. Possums and points west. Colorado Conservation 1:2–5.

Beidleman, R. G. 1954. October breeding of *Peromyscus* in north central Colorado. J. Mamm. 35:118.

Beidleman, R. G., R. R. Beidleman, and L. H. Beidleman. 2000. Annotated bibliography of Colorado vertebrate zoology, 1776–1995. Univ. Press Colorado, Boulder, 447 pp.

Beidleman, R. G., and J. D. Remington. 1955. Another record of the least shrew from northeastern Colorado. J. Mamm. 36:123.

Beidleman, R. G., and W. A. Weber. 1958. Analysis of a pika hay pile. J. Mamm. 39:599–600.

Beier, P. 1991. Cougar attacks on humans in the United States and Canada. Wildl. Soc. Bull. 19:403–412.

Beier, P., D. Choate, and R. H. Barrett. 1995. Movement patterns of mountain lions during different behaviors. J. Mamm. 76:1056–1070.

Beier, P., and J. E. Drennan. 1997. Forest structure and prey abundance in foraging areas of northern goshawks. Ecol. Appl. 7:564–571.

Bekoff, M. 1974. Social play and play soliciting by infant canids. Amer. Zool. 14:323–341.

Bekoff, M. 1977. *Canis latrans*. Mammalian Species 79:1–9.

Bekoff, M., ed. 1978. Coyotes: biology, behavior, and management. Academic Press, New York, 384 pp.

Bekoff, M. 1982. Coyote. Pp. 447–459, in Wild mammals of North America, biology, management, and economics (J. A. Chapman and G. A. Feldhamer, eds.). Johns Hopkins Univ. Press, Baltimore, 1,147 pp.

Bekoff, M. 2001. Cunning coyotes: tireless tricksters, protean predators. Pp. 381–407, in Model systems in behavioral ecology, integrating conceptual, theoretical, and empirical approaches (L. A. Dugatkin, ed.). Princeton Univ. Press, Princeton, NJ, 584 pp.

Bekoff, M., and S. M. Bexell. 2010. Ignoring nature: why we do it, the dire consequences, and the need for a paradigm shift to save animals, habitats, and ourselves. Human Ecol. Rev. 17:70–74.

Bekoff, M., and J. Diamond. 1976. Precopulatory and copulatory behavior in coyotes. J. Mamm. 57:372–375.

Bekoff, M., and E. M. Gese. 2003. Coyote, *Canis latrans*. Pp. 467–481, in Wild mammals of North America, biology, management, and economics, second ed. (G. A. Feldhamer, B. C. Thompson, and J. A. Chapman, eds.). Johns Hopkins Univ. Press, Baltimore, 1,216 pp.

Bekoff, M., and N. Hettinger. 1994. Animals, nature, and ethics. J. Mamm. 75:219–223.

Bekoff, M., and R. W. Ickes. 1999. Behavioral interactions and conflict among domestic dogs, black-tailed prairie dogs, and people in Boulder, Colorado. Anthrozoös 12:105–110.

Bekoff, M., and C. B. Lowe, eds. 2007. Listening to cougar. Univ. Press Colorado, Boulder. 228 pp.

Bekoff, M., and C. A. Meaney. 1997. Interactions among dogs, people, and the environment in Boulder, Colorado: a case study. Anthrozoös 10:23–29.

Bekoff, M., and M. C. Wells. 1980. The social ecology of coyotes. Sci. Amer. 242:130–148.

Bekoff, M., and M. C. Wells. 1982. Behavioral ecology of coyotes: social organization, rearing patterns, space use, and resource defense. Zeitschrift für Tierpsychologie 60:281–305.

Bekoff, M., and M. C. Wells. 1986. Social ecology and behavior of coyotes. Adv. Studies Behav. 16:251–338.

Belan, I., P. N. Lehner, and T. W. Clark. 1978. Vocalizations of the American pine marten, *Martes americana*. J. Mamm. 59:871–874.

Belay, E. D., R. A. Maddox, E. S. Williams, M. W. Miller, P. Gambetti, and L. B. Schoenberger. 2004. Chronic wasting disease and potential transmission to humans. Emerging Infectious Dis. 10:977–984.

Belk, M. C., C. L. Pritchett, and H. D. Smith. 1990. Patterns of microhabitat use by *Sorex monticolus* in summer. Great Basin Nat. 50:387–389.

Belk, M. C., and H. D. Smith. 1991. *Ammospermophilus leucurus*. Mammalian Species 368:1–8.

Belk, M. C., H. D. Smith, and J. Lawson. 1988. Use and partitioning of montane habitat by small mammals. J. Mamm. 59:688–695.

Belovsky, G. E. 1984. Summer diet optimization by beaver. Amer. Midland Nat. 111:209–222.

Benedict, A. D. 2008. The naturalist's guide to the Southern Rockies. Fulcrum Publishing, Golden, CO.

Benedict, J. B. 1979. Getting away from it all: a study of man, mountains and the two-drought Altithermal. Southwestern Lore 45:1–12.

Benedict, J. B. 1985. Arapaho Pass. Research Rept., Center for Mountain Archeology, Ward, Colorado 3:1–197.

Benedict, J. B. 1992a. Along the Great Divide: Paleoindian archaeology of the High Colorado Front Range. Pp. 343–359, in Ice Age hunters of the Rockies (D. J. Stanford and J. S. Day, eds.). Univ. Press Colorado, Niwot, 378 pp.

Benedict, J. B. 1992b. Footprints in the snow: high-altitude cultural ecology of the Colorado Front Range, USA Arctic and Alpine Research 24:1–16.

Benedict, J. B. 1996. The game drives of Rocky Mountain National Park. Research Rept., Center for Mountain Archaeology, Ward, Colorado 7:1–110.

Benedict, J. B. 1999. Effects of changing climate on game-animal and human use of the Colorado high country (USA) since 1000 BC. Arctic, Antarctic, and Alpine Research 31:1–15.

Benedict, J. B. 2005. Tundra game drives: an Arctic-alpine comparison. Arctic, Antarctic, and Alpine Research 37:425–434.

Benedict, J. B., and A. D. Benedict. 2001. Subnivean root caching by a montane vole (*Microtus montanus nanus*), Colorado Front Range, USA. Western N. Amer. Nat. 51:241–244.

Benedict, J. B., and B. L. Olson. 1978. The Mount Albion complex. Research Rept., Center for Mountain Archeology, Ward, Colorado 1:1–213.

Benedict, R. A. 1999. Characteristics of a hybrid zone between two species of short-tailed shrews (*Blarina*). J. Mamm. 80:135–141.

Benedict, R. A., P. W. Freeman, and H. H. Genoways. 1996. Prairie legacies—mammals. Pp. 149–166, in Prairie conservation, preserving North America's most endangered ecosystem (F. B. Samson and F. L. Knopf, eds.). Island Press, Washington, DC, 339 pp.

Benedict, R. A., H. H. Genoways, and P. W. Freeman. 2000. Shifting distributional patterns of mammals in Nebraska. Trans. Nebraska Acad. Sci. 26:55–84.

Beneski, J. T., Jr., and D. W. Stinson. 1987. *Sorex palustris*. Mammalian Species 296:1–6.

Benkman, C. W. 1995. The impact of tree squirrels (*Tamiasciurus*) on limber pine seed dispersal adaptations. Evolution 49:585–592.

Bennett, D., and R. S. Hoffmann. 1999. *Equus caballus*. Mammalian Species 628:1–14.

Bennett, L. E. 1994. Colorado gray wolf recovery: a biological feasibility study, Final Report, March 31. U.S. Fish and Wildlife Service and Univ. Wyoming Fish and Wildlife Cooperative Research Unit, Laramie, 318 pp.

Benson, J. F., M. J. Chamberlain, and B. D. Leopold. 2004. Land tenure and occupation of vacant home ranges by bobcats (*Lynx rufus*). J. Mamm. 85:983–988.

Benson, M. 1986. Martha Maxwell, Rocky Mountain naturalist. Univ. Nebraska Press, Lincoln, 335 pp.

Berg, J. K. 1999. River otter research project on the upper Colorado river basin in and adjacent to Rocky Mountain National Park, Colorado. Final Report, Rocky Mountain National Park, Grand Lake, CO, unpaged.

Berger, J. 1977. Organizational systems and dominance in feral horses in the Grand Canyon. Behav. Ecol. Sociobiol. 2:131–146.

Berger, J. 1983. Induced abortion and social factors in wild horses. Nature 303:59–61.

Berger, J. 1985. Interspecific interactions and dominance among wild Great Basin ungulates. J. Mamm. 56:571–573.

Berger, J. 1986. Wild horses of the Great Basin: social competition and population size. Univ. Chicago Press, Chicago, 326 pp.

Berger, J. 2008a. Undetected species losses, food webs, and ecological baselines: a cautionary tale from the Greater Yellowstone Ecosystem, USA. Oryx 42:139–142.

Berger, J. 2008b. Extant or extinct? White-tailed jack rabbits and Yellowstone's food web. Oryx 42:176.

Berger, J. 2008c. The better to eat you with: fear in the animal world. Univ. Chicago Press, Chicago, 292 pp.

Berger, J., P. B. Stacey, L. Bellis, and M. P. Johnson. 2001. A mammalian predator-prey imbalance: grizzly bear and wolf extinction affect avian Neotropical migrants. Ecol. Appl. 11:947–960.

Bergerud, A. T., and D. R. Miller. 1977. Population dynamics of Newfoundland beaver. Canadian J. Zool. 55:1480–1492.

Bergstrom, B. J. 1986. Ecological and behavioral relationships among three species of chipmunks (*Tamias*) in the Front Range of Colorado. Unpubl. doctoral dissert., Univ. Kansas, Lawrence, 111 pp.

Bergstrom, B. J. 1988. Home ranges of three species of chipmunks (*Tamias*) as assessed by radiotelemetry and grid trapping. J. Mamm. 59:190–193.

Bergstrom, B. J. 1992. Parapatry and encounter competition between chipmunk (*Tamias*) species and the hypothesized role of parasitism. Amer. Midland Nat. 128:168–179.

Bergstrom, B. J., and R. S. Hoffmann. 1991. Distribution and diagnosis of three species of chipmunks (*Tamias*) in the Front Range of Colorado. Southwestern Nat. 36:14–28.

Bernardos, D. A., C. L. Chambers, and M. J. Rabe. 2004. Selection of Gambel oak roosts by southwestern *Myotis* in ponderosa pine–dominated forests, northern Arizona. J. Wildl. Mgmt. 58:595–601.

Berner, A., and L. W. Gysel. 1967. Raccoon use of large tree cavities and ground burrows. J. Wildl. Mgmt. 31:706–714.

Berteaux, D., and S. Boutin. 2000. Breeding dispersal in female North American red squirrels. Ecology 81:1311–1326.

Berwyn. B. 2009. 10 lynx kittens found in 5 dens in Colorado. Aspen Times, June 28. http://www.aspentimes.com/article/20090624/NEWS/906249978/1002/NONE&parentprofile=1058.

Best, T. L. 1973. Ecological separation of three genera of pocket gophers (Geomyidae). Ecology 54:1311–1319.

Best, T. L. 1988. *Dipodomys spectabilis*. Mammalian Species 311:1–10.

LITERATURE CITED

Best, T. L. 1996. *Lepus californicus*. Mammalian Species 530:1–10.

Best, T. L., and B. Hoditschek. 1986. Relationships between environmental variation and the reproductive biology of Ord's kangaroo rat (*Dipodomys ordii*). Mammalia 50:173–183.

Best, T. L., and J. B. Jennings. 1997. *Myotis leibii*. Mammalian Species 547:1–6.

Best, T. L., and M. P. Skupski. 1994a. *Perognathus flavus*. Mammalian Species 471:1–10.

Best, T. L., and M. P. Skupski. 1994b. *Perognathus merriami*. Mammalian Species 473:1–7.

Betancourt, J. L., T. R. Van Devender, and P. S. Martin. 1990. Packrat middens, the last 40,000 years of biotic change. Univ. Arizona Press, Tucson, 467 pp.

Betts, B. J. 1997. Microclimate in Hell's Canyon mines used by maternity colonies of *Myotis yumanensis*. J. Mamm. 78:1240–1250.

Betts, B. J. 1998a. Effects of interindividual variation in echolocation calls on identification of big brown and silver-haired bats. J. Wildl. Mgmt. 52:1003–1010.

Betts, B. J. 1998b. Roosts used by maternity colonies of silver-haired bats in northeastern Oregon. J. Mamm. 79:643–650.

Bevers, M., J. Hof, D. W. Uresk, and G. L. Schenbeck. 1997. Spatial optimization of prairie dog colonies for black-footed ferret recovery. Operations Research 45:495–507.

Bezuidenhout, A. J., and H. E. Evans. 2005. The anatomy of the woodchuck (*Marmota monax*). Spec. Publ., Amer. Soc. Mammalogists 13, 180 pp.

Biggins, D. E., and D. M. Biggins. 2006. Bobcat attack on a cottontail rabbit. Southwestern Nat. 51:119–122.

Biggins, D. E., and M. Y. Kosoy. 2001. Influences of introduced plague on North American mammals: implications from ecology of plague in Asia. J. Mamm. 82:906–916.

Biggins, D. E., M. H. Schroeder, S. C. Forrest, and L. Richardson. 1986. Activity of radio-tagged black-footed ferrets. Great Basin Nat. Mem. 8:135–140.

Bildstein, K. L. 1983. Why white-tailed deer flag their tails. Amer. Nat. 121:709–715.

Bininda-Emonds, O.R.P., M. Cardillo, K. E. Jones, R.D.E. MacPhee, R.M.D. Beck, R. Grenyer, S. A. Price, R. A. Vos, J. L. Gittleman, and A. Purvis. 2007. The delayed rise of present-day mammals. Nature 446:507–512.

Birney, E. C. 1973. Systematics of three species of woodrats (genus *Neotoma*) in central North America. Misc. Publ. Mus. Nat. Hist., Univ. Kansas 58:1–173.

Birney, E. C. 1976. An assessment of relationships and effects of interbreeding among woodrats of the *Neotoma floridana* species-group. J. Mamm. 57:103–132.

Birney, E. C., W. E. Grant, and D. D. Baird. 1976. Importance of cover to cycles of *Microtus* populations. Ecology 57:1043–1051.

Birney, E. C., J. K. Jones, Jr., and D. M. Mortimer. 1971. The yellow-faced pocket gopher, *Pappogeomys castanops*, in Kansas. Trans. Kansas Acad. Sci. 73:368–375.

Bischoff-Mattson, Z., and D. Mattson. 2009. Effects of simulated mountain lion caching on decomposition of ungulate carcasses. Western N. American Nat. 69:343–350.

Bishop, C. J., G. C. White, D. J. Freddy, and B. E. Watkins. 2003. Effect of nutrition and habitat enhancements on mule deer recruitment and survival rates. Colorado Division of Wildlife, Job Progress Report W-185-R.

Bishop, R. H., and R. A. Rausch. 1974. Moose population fluctuations in Alaska, 1950–1972. Nat. Canadienne 101:559–593.

Bissell, S. J., and M. B. Dillon. 1982. Colorado Mammal Distribution Latilong Study. Nongame Section, Colorado Division of Wildlife, Denver, 24 pp.

Bissonette, T. H., and E. E. Bailey. 1944. Experimental modification and control of molts and changes of coat-color in weasels by controlled lighting. Ann. New York Acad. Sci. 45:221–260.

Bittner, S. L., and O. J. Rongstad. 1982. Snowshoe hare and allies (*Lepus americanus* and allies). Pp. 146–163, in Wild mammals of North America, biology, management, and economics (J. A. Chapman and G. A. Feldhamer, eds.). Johns Hopkins Univ. Press, Baltimore, 1,147 pp.

Black, H. L. 1970. Occurrence of the Mexican big-eared bat in Utah. J. Mamm. 51:190.

Black, H. L. 1974. A north temperate bat community: structure and prey populations. J. Mamm. 55:138–157.

Blair, W. F. 1937. Burrows and food of the prairie pocket mouse. J. Mamm. 18:284–288.

Blair, W. F. 1953. Population dynamics of rodents and other small mammals. Adv. Genetics 5:1–41.

Blake, B. H. 1972. The annual cycle and fat storage in two populations of golden-mantled ground squirrels. J. Mamm. 53:157–167.

Blake, B. H. 2002. Ultrasonic calling in isolated infant prairie voles (*Microtus ochrogaster*) and montane voles (*M. montanus*). J. Mamm. 83:536–545.

Blake, I. H., and A. K. Blake. 1969. An ecological study of timberline and alpine areas, Mount Lincoln, Park County, Colorado. Univ. Nebraska Studies, New Ser. 40:1–59.

Blehert, D. S., A. C. Hicks, M. Behr, C. U. Meteyer, B. M. Berlowski-Zier, E. L. Buckles, J.T.H. Coleman, S. R. Darling, A. Gargas, R. Niver, J. C. Okoniewski, R. J. Rudd, and W. B. Stone. 2008. Bat white-nose syndrome: an emerging fungal pathogen? Science On-line (Science DOI: 10.1126/science.1163874, October 30).

Blejwas, K. M., C. L. Williams, G. T. Shin, D. R. McCullough, and M. M. Jaeger. 2006. Salivary DNA evidence convicts breeding male coyotes of killing sheep. J. Wildl. Mgmt. 70:1087–1093.

Blood, D. A. 1974. Variation in reproduction and productivity of an enclosed herd of moose (*Alces alces*). Proc. International Congress of Game Biologists 11:59–66.

Blumhardt, M. 2009. Special report: a wolverine returns. Fort Collins Coloradoan, June 15. http://www.coloradoan.com/article/20090715/ENTERTAINMENT06/90714005/Special+report++A+wolverine+returns.

Blumstein, D. T. 1989. Food habits of red-tailed hawks in Boulder County, Colorado. J. Raptor Research 23:53–55.

Blumstein, D. T. 2008. Fourteen security lessons from antipredator behavior. Pp. 147–158, in Natural security: a Darwinian approach to a dangerous world (R. Sagarin and T. Taylor, eds.). Univ. California Press, Berkeley, 306 pp.

Blumstein, D. T. 2009. Social effects on emergence from hibernation in yellow-bellied marmots. J. Mamm. 90:1184–1187.

Blumstein, D. T., and K. B Armitage. 1997a. Does sociality drive the evolution of communicative complexity? A comparative test with ground-dwelling sciurid alarm calls. Amer. Nat. 150:179–200.

Blumstein, D. T., and K. B. Armitage. 1997b. Alarm calling in yellow-bellied marmots: I. The meaning of situationally variable alarm calls. Animal Behavior 53:143–147.

Blumstein, D. T., and K. B. Armitage. 1998a. Life history consequences of social complexity: a comparative study of ground-dwelling sciurids. Behavioral Ecol. 9:8–19.

Blumstein, D. T., and K. B. Armitage. 1998b. Why do yellow-bellied marmots call? Animal Behaviour 56:1053–1055.

Blumstein, D. T., L. Barrow, and M. Luterra. 2008. Olfactory predator discrimination in yellow-bellied marmots. Ethology 114:1135–1143.

Blumstein, D. T., L. Cooley, J. Winternitz, and J. C. Daniel. 2008. Do yellow-bellied marmots respond to predator vocalizations? Behav. Ecol. Sociobiol. 52:457–468.

Blumstein, D. T., S. Im, A. Nicodemus, and C. Zugmeyer. 2004. Yellow-bellied marmots (*Marmota flaviventris*) hibernate socially. J. Mamm. 85:25–29.

Blumstein, D. T., D. T. Richardson, L. Cooley, J. Winternitz, and J. C. Daniel. 2008. The structure, meaning and function of yellow-bellied marmot pup screams. Animal Behaviour 76: 1055–1064.

Blumstein, D. T., J. Steinmetz, K. B. Armitage, and J. C. Daniel. 1997. Alarm calling in yellow-bellied marmots: II. Kin selection of parental care? Animal Behavior 53:173–184.

Bock, C. E., K. T. Vierling, S. L. Haire, J. D. Boone, and W. W. Merkle. 2002. Patterns of rodent abundance on open-space grasslands in relation to suburban edges. Cons. Biol. 16:1653–1658.

Bodin, M. 2010. Bracing for white nose syndrome. High Country News 42 (10):8, 19.

Bogan, M. A. 1972. Observation on parturition and development in the hoary bat (*Lasiurus cinereus*). J. Mamm. 53:611–614.

Bogan, M. A. 1974. Identification of *Myotis californicus* and *M. leibii* in southwestern North America. Proc. Biol. Soc. Washington 87:49–56.

Bogan, M. A. 1999. Long-eared myotis/*Myotis evotis*. Pp 85–90, in The Smithsonian book of North American mammals (D. E. Wilson, and S. Ruff, eds.). Smithsonian Institution Press, Washington, DC, 750 pp.

Bogan, M. A. 2001. Western bats and mining. Pp. 41–50, in Bat conservation and mining: a technical interactive forum (K. Vories and T. Throgmorton, eds.). U.S. Department of Interior, Office of Surface Mining, Bat Conservation International, and Coal Research Center, Carbondale, IL. http://www.mcrcc.osmre.gov/PDF/Forums/Bat%20Conservation/1e.pdf.

Bogan, M. A., and P. M. Cryan. 2000. Bats of Wyoming. Pp 71–94, in Reflections of a naturalist: papers honoring Professor Eugene D. Fleharty (J. R. Choate, ed.). Fort Hays Studies, Special Issue, 1:1–241.

Bogan, M. A., P. M. Cryan, E. W. Valdez, L. E. Ellison, and T. J. O'Shea. 2003. Western crevice and cavity-roosting bats. Pp. 69–77, in Monitoring trends in bat populations in the United States and territories: problems and prospects (T. J. O'Shea and M. A. Bogan, eds.). Information and Tech. Rept., USGS/BRD/ITR-2003-003, 274 pp.

Bogan, M. A., R. B. Finley, Jr., and S. J. Petersburg. 1988. The importance of biological surveys in managing public lands in the western United States. Pp. 254–261, in Management of amphibians, reptiles, and small mammals in North America. Gen. Tech. Rept., Rocky Mountain Forest and Range Experiment Station, US Department of Agriculture, RM-166:1–458 (R. C. Szaro, K. E Severson, and D. R. Patton, technical coordinators).

Bogan, M. A., and P. Mehlhop. 1983. Systematic relationships of gray wolves (*Canis lupus*) in southwestern North America. Occas. Papers Mus. Southwestern Biol., Univ. New Mexico 1:1–20.

Bogan, M. A., T. J. O'Shea, and L. Ellison. 1996. Diversity and conservation of bats in North America. Endangered Species Update 13(4 & 5):1–4, 14.

Boggs, J. R. 1974. Social ecology of the white-throated woodrat (*Neotoma albigula*) in Arizona. Unpubl. doctoral dissert., Arizona State Univ., Tempe, 134 pp.

Bohn, K. M., B. Schmidt-French, C. Schwartz, M. Smotherman, and G. D. Pollack. 2009. Versatility and stereotypy of free-tailed bat songs. PLoS ONE 4(8):1–11.

Bonaccorso, F. J. 1998. Bats of Papua New Guinea. Conservation International and Univ. Chicago Press, Chicago, 489 pp.

Bonaccorso, F. J., and J. H. Brown. 1972. House construction of the desert woodrat, *N. lepida lepida*. J. Mamm. 53:283–288.

Bone, J. R. 1964. The age of the horse. Southwest Vet. 17:269–272.

Bonewell, L. R., and M. A. Hayes. 2009. Breaking news on Colorado bat conservation. The Chiropteran 18(2):1–3.

Bonham, C. D., and A. Lerwick. 1976. Vegetation changes induced by prairie dogs on shortgrass range. J. Range Mgmt. 29:221–225.

Borrego, N., A. Ozgul, K. B. Armitage, D. T. Blumstein, and M. K. Oli. 2008. Spatiotemporal variation in survival of male yellow-bellied marmots. J. Mamm. 89:365–373.

Bortolus, A. 2008. Error cascades in the biological sciences: the unwanted consequences of using bad taxonomy in ecology. Ambio 37:114–118.

Boulanger, J. G., and C. J. Krebs. 1994. Comparison of capture-recapture estimators of snowshoe hare populations. Canadian J. Zool. 72:1800–1807.

Boutin, S. 1979. Spacing behaviour of snowshoe hares in relation to their population dynamics. Unpubl. master's thesis, Univ. British Columbia, Vancouver, 141 pp.

Boutin, S., and D. E. Birkenholz. 1986. Muskrat and round-tailed muskrat. Pp. 315–325, in Wild furbearer management and conservation in North America (M. Novak, J. A. Baker, M. E. Obbard, and B. Malloch, eds.). Ontario Trappers Assoc., Toronto, 1,150 pp.

Boutin, S., B. S. Gilbert, C. J. Krebs, A.R.E. Sinclair, and J.N.M. Smith. 1985. The role of dispersal in the population dynamics of snowshoe hares. Canadian J. Zool. 53:106–115.

Bowden, D. C., and R. C. Kufeld. 1995. Generalized mark-sight population size estimation applied to Colorado moose. J. Wildl. Mgmt. 59:840–851.

Bowden, D. C., G. C. White, and R. M. Bartmann. 2000. Optimal allocation of sampling effort for monitoring a harvested mule deer population. J. Wildl. Mgmt. 54:1013–1024.

Bowen, G. S., R. G. McLean, R. B. Shriner, D. B. Francy, K. S. Pokorny, J. M. Trimble, R. A. Bolin, A. M. Barnes, C. H. Calisher, and D. J. Muth. 1981. The ecology of Colorado tick fever in Rocky Mountain National Park in 1974: II. Infection in small mammals. Amer. J. Trop. Med. Hygiene 310:490–496.

Bowen, W. D. 1982. Determining age of coyotes, *Canis latrans*, by tooth sections and tooth-wear patterns. Canadian Field-Nat. 96:339–341.

Bowers, M. A., and J. H. Brown. 1982. Body size and coexistence in desert rodents: chance or community structure? Ecology 563:392–400.

Bowker, J. M., D.B.K. English, and H. K. Cordell. 1999. Projections of outdoor recreation participation to 2050. Pp. 323–350, in Outdoor recreation in American life: a national assessment of demand and supply trends (H. K Cordell, principal investigator). Sagamore Publishing, Champaign, IL, 449 pp.

Bowman, W. D., D. M. Cairns, J. S. Baron, and T. R. Seastedt. 2002. Islands in the sky: alpine and treeline ecosystems of the Rockies. Pp. 183–202, in Rocky Mountain futures, an ecological perspective (J. S. Baron, ed.). Island Press, Washington, DC, 325 pp.

Bowman, W. D., and T. R. Seastedt, eds. 2001. Structure and function of an alpine ecosystem, Niwot Ridge, Colorado. Oxford Univ. Press, New York, 337 pp.

Bowyer, R. T. 1987. Coyote group size relative to predation on mule deer. Mammalia 51:515–526.

Bowyer, R. T., B. M. Pierce, L. K. Duffy, and D. A. Haggstrom. 2001. Sexual segregation in moose: effects of habitat manipulation. Alces 37:109–122.

Bowyer, R. T., V. Van Ballenberghe, and J. G. Kie. 2003. Moose, *Alces alces*. Pp. 931–964, in Wild mammals of North America, biology, management, and economics, second ed. (G. A. Feldhamer, B. C. Thompson, and J. A. Chapman, eds.). Johns Hopkins Univ. Press, Baltimore, 1,216 pp.

Boyce, M. S. 1981. Beaver life-history responses to exploitation. J. Appl. Ecol. 18:749–753.

Boyce, M. S. 1990. The Jackson elk herd: intensive wildlife management in North America. Cambridge Univ. Press, Cambridge, UK, 320 pp.

Boyce, M. S., and L. D. Hayden-Wing, eds. 1979. North American elk: ecology behavior and management. Univ. Wyoming, Laramie, 294 pp.

Boyce, M. S., and J. S. Waller. 2003. Grizzly bears for the Bitterroots: predicting potential abundance and distribution. Wildl. Soc. Bull. 31:670–683.

Boyd, D. K., S. H. Forbes, D. H. Pletscher, and F. W. Allendorf. 2001. Identification of Rocky Mountain gray wolves. Wildl. Soc. Bull. 29:78–85.

Boyd, D. K., and D. H. Pletscher. 1999. Characteristics of dispersal in a colonizing wolf population in the Central Rocky Mountains. J. Wildl. Mgmt. 53:1094–1108.

Boyd, D. K., D. H. Pletscher, R. R. Ream, and M. W. Fairchild. 1994. Prey characteristics of colonizing wolves and hunters in the Glacier National Park area. J. Wildl. Mgmt. 58:289–295.

Boyd, R. J. 1970. Elk of the White River Plateau, Colorado. Tech. Bull., Colorado Division of Game, Fish, and Parks 25:1–126.

Boyd, R. J. 1978. American elk. Pp. 11–29, in Big game of North America: ecology and management (J. L. Schmidt and D. L. Gilbert, eds.). Stackpole Books, Harrisburg, PA, 494 pp.

Boyd, R. J., and E. E. Ryland. 1971. Breeding dates of Colorado elk as estimated by fetal growth curves. Game Information Leaflet, Colorado Division of Game, Fish, and Parks 88:1–2.

Boyle, S. 2006. North American river otter (*Lontra canadensis*): a technical conservation assessment. Species Conservation Project, Rocky Mountain Region, USDA Forest Service, 55 pp.

Boyle, S., and S. Owens. 2007. North America beaver (*Castor canadensis*): a technical conservation assessment. Species Conservation Project, USDA Forest Service, Rocky Mountain Region, 50 pp.

Boyle, S. A., and D. R. Reeder. 2005. Colorado sagebrush: a conservation assessment and strategy. Colorado Division of Wildlife, Grand Junction. http://wildlife.state.co.us/WildlifeSpecies/SagebrushConservation/.

Brach, V. 1969. Some observations on a captive desert shrew, *Notiosorex crawfordi*. Bull. Southern California Acad. Sci. 58:119–120.

Bradley, B. A., R. A. Houghton, J. F. Mustard, and S. P. Hamburg. 2009. Regional analysis of the impacts of climate change on cheatgrass invasion shows potential risk and opportunity. Global Change Biol. 15:196–208.

Bradley, R. D., N. D. Durish, D. S. Rogers, J. R. Miller, M. D. Engstrom, and C. W. Kilpatrick. 2007. Toward a molecular phylogeny for *Peromyscus*: evidence from mitochondrial cytochrome-*b* sequences. J. Mamm. 88:1146–1159.

Bradley, R. D., D. D. Henson, and N. D. Durish. 2008. Re-evaluation of the geographic distribution and phylogeography of the *Sigmodon hispidus* complex based on mitochondrial DNA sequences. Southwestern Nat. 53:301–310.

Bradley, R. M. 1929. Habits and distribution of the rock squirrel in southern New Mexico. J. Mamm. 10:168–169.

Bradley, W. G. 1967. Home range, activity patterns, and ecology of the antelope ground squirrel in southern Nevada. Southwestern Nat. 12:231–252.

Bradley, W. G. 1968. Food habits of the antelope ground squirrel in southern Nevada. J. Mamm. 49:14–21.

Brand, C. J., ed. 2002. Landscape ecology of plague in the American Southwest. Proceedings of an American Southwest Workshop, Fort Collins, CO, September 19–20, 2000. USGS ITR 2002-0001, 24 pp.

Brand, C. J., and L. B. Keith. 1979. Lynx demography during a snowshoe hare decline in Alberta. J. Wildl. Mgmt. 43:827–849.

Brand, C. J., L. B. Keith, and C. A. Fischer. 1976. Lynx responses to changing snowshoe hare densities in central Alberta. J. Wildl. Mgmt. 40:416–428.

Brandborg, S. M. 1955. Life history and management of the mountain goat in Idaho. Wildlife Bull., Idaho Dept. Fish and Game 2:1–142.

Brassard, J. S., and R. Bernard. 1939. Observations on breeding and development of marten, *Martes a. americana* (Kerr). Canadian Field-Nat. 53:15–21.

Braun, C. E., ed. 1993. Mountain lion–human interaction symposium and workshop, Colorado Division of Wildlife, Denver, 114 pp.

Braun, C. E., and R. G. Streeter. 1968. Observations on the occurrence of white-tailed jackrabbits in the alpine zone. J. Mamm. 49:160–161.

Braun, J. K., and M. A. Mares. 1989. *Neotoma micropus*. Mammalian Species 330:1–9.

Breakey, D. R. 1963. The breeding season and age structure of feral house mouse populations near San Francisco Bay, California. J. Mamm. 44:153–168.

Breck, S. W. 2001. The effects of flow regulation on the population biology and ecology of beavers in northwestern Colorado. Unpubl. doctoral dissert., Colorado State Univ., Fort Collins, 132 pp.

Breck, S. W., K. R. Wilson, and D. C. Andersen. 2001. The demographic response of bank-dwelling beavers to flow regulation: a comparison on the Green and Yampa rivers. Canadian J. Zool. 79:1957–1964.

Breck, S. W., K. R. Wilson, and D. C. Andersen. 2003. Beaver herbivory and its effect on cottonwood trees: influence of flooding along matched regulated and unregulated rivers. River Research and Applications 19:43–58.

Brent, J. A. 1983. Colorado mountain lion investigations: Northwest Region. Unpubl. report, Colorado Division of Wildlife, Grand Junction, 14 pp.

Brewer, W. H. 1871. Animal life in the Rocky Mountains of Colorado. Amer. Nat. 5:220–223.

Bridgewater, D. D. 1966. Laboratory breeding, early growth, development and behavior of *Citellus tridecemlineatus* (Rodentia). Southwestern Nat. 11:325–337.

Briggs, J. M., K. A. Spielmann, H. Schaafsma, K. W. Kintigh, M. Kruse, K. Morehouse, and K. Schollmeyer. 2006. Why ecology needs archaeologists and archaeology needs ecologists. Frontiers Ecol. Environ. 4:180–188.

Briggs, W. 1976. Without noise of arms, the 1776 Dominguez-Escalante search for a route from Santa Fe to Monterrey. Northland Press, Flagstaff, AZ, 212 pp.

Brigham, R. M., H.D.J.N. Aldridge, and R. L. Mackey. 1992. Variation in habitat use and prey selection by Yuma bats, *Myotis yumanensis*. J. Mamm. 73:640–645.

Brigham, R. M., M. J. Vonhof, R.M.R. Barclay, and J. C. Gwilliam. 1997. Roosting behavior and roost site preferences of forest-dwelling California bats (*Myotis californicus*). J. Mamm. 78: 1231–1239.

Bright, A. D., M. J. Manfredo, and D. C. Fulton. 2000. Segmenting the public: an application of value orientations to wildlife planning in Colorado. Wildl. Soc. Bull. 28:218–226.

Bright, W. 1993. A coyote reader. Univ. California Press, Berkeley, 202 pp.

Brinkerhoff, R. J. 2008. Habitat-associated differences in flea assemblages of striped skunks (*Mephitis mephitis*). Comp. Parasitol. 75:127–131.

Brinkerhoff, R. J., S. K. Collinge, Y. Bai, and C. Ray. 2008. Are carnivores universally good sentinels of plague? Vector-borne and Zoonotic Dis. 9:1–7.

Brinkerhoff, R. J., A. B. Markeson, J. H. Knouft, K. L. Gage, and J. A. Montenieri. 2006. Abundance of two *Oropsylla* (Ceratophyllidae: Siphonaptera) species on black-tailed prairie dog (*Cynomys ludovicianus*) hosts. J. Vector Ecology 31:355–363.

Brinkerhoff, R. J., C. Ray, B. Thiagarajan, S. K. Collinge, J. F. Cully, Jr., B. Holmes, and K. L. Gage. 2008. Prairie dog presence affects occurrence patterns of disease vectors on small mammals. Ecography 31:654–662.

Britten, R. J. 2002. Divergence between samples of chimpanzee and human DNA sequences is 5%, counting indels. Proc. Nat. Acad. Sci. 99:13633–13635.

Bronson, M. T. 1980. Altitudinal variation in emergence time of golden-mantled ground squirrels (*Spermophilus lateralis*). J. Mamm. 51:124–126.

Brosi, B. J., and E. G. Biber. 2009. Statistical inference, Type II error, and decision making under the US Endangered Species Act. Frontiers Ecol. and Environ. 9:487–494.

Brown, D. J., W. A. Hubert, and S. H. Anderson. 1996. Beaver ponds create wetland habitat for birds in mountains of southwestern Wyoming. Wetlands 16:127–132.

Brown, H. L. 1946. Rodent activity in a mixed prairie near Hays, Kansas. Trans. Kansas Acad. Sci. 48:448–456.

Brown, H. L. 1947. Why has the white-tailed jack rabbit (*Lepus townsendii campanius* Hollister) become scarce in Kansas? Trans. Kansas Acad. Sci. 49:455–456.

Brown, J. H. 1987. Variation in desert rodent guilds: patterns, processes, and scales. Pp. 185–203, in Organization of communities, past and present (J.H.R. Gee and P. S. Giller, eds.). Blackwell Scientific Publications, Oxford, UK, 588 pp.

Brown, J. H., and M. Kurzius. 1989. Spatial and temporal variation in guilds of North American granivorous desert rodents. Pp. 71–90, in Patterns in the structure of mammalian communities (D. W. Morris, Z. Abramsky, B. J. Fox, and M. R. Willig, eds.). Spec. Publ. Museum, Texas Tech Univ. 28:1–266.

Brown, J. H., and R. C. Lasiewski. 1972. Metabolism of weasels: the cost of being long and thin. Ecology 53:939–943.

Brown, L. G., and L. E. Yeager. 1945. Fox squirrels and gray squirrels in Illinois. Bull. Illinois Nat. Hist. Surv. 23:449–536.

Brown, L. N. 1966. First record of the pygmy shrew in Wyoming and description of a new subspecies. Proc. Biol. Soc. Washington 79:49–52.

Brown, L. N. 1967a. Seasonal activity patterns and breeding of the western jumping mouse (*Zapus princeps*) in Wyoming. Amer. Midland Nat. 78:460–470.

Brown, L. N. 1967b. Ecological distribution of six species of shrews and comparison of sampling methods in the central Rocky Mountains. J. Mamm. 48:617–623.

Brown, L. N. 1968. Smallness of mean litter size in the Mexican vole. J. Mamm. 53:185–187.

Brown, L. N. 1969. Reproductive characteristics of the Mexican woodrat at the northern limit of its range in Colorado. J. Mamm. 50:536–541.

Brown, L. N. 1970. Population dynamics of the western jumping mouse (*Zapus princeps*) during a four year study. J. Mamm. 51:651–658.

Brown, R. N., C. H. Southwick, and S. C. Golian. 1989. Male-female spacing, territorial replacement, and the mating system of pikas (*Ochotona princeps*). J. Mamm. 70:622–627.

Browne-Nunez, C., and J. G. Taylor. 2002. Americans' attitudes toward wolves and wolf reintroduction: an annotated bibliography. Information Technology Report, USGS/BRD/ITR-2002-0002, 15 pp.

Brownfield, M. S., and B. A. Wunder. 1976. Relative medullary area: a new structural index for estimating urinary concentrating capacity of mammals. Comp. Biochem. Physiol. 55A:69–75.

Brunjes, K. J., W. B. Ballard, M. H. Humphrey, F. Harwell, N. E. McIntyre, P. R. Krausman, and M. C. Wallace. 2009. Home ranges of sympatric mule deer and white-tailed deer in Texas. Southwestern Nat. 54:253–260.

Bubenik, A. B. 1998. Evolution, taxonomy, and morphophysiology. Pp. 77–123 in Ecology and management of the North American moose (A. W. Franzmann and C. C. Schwartz, eds.). Smithsonian Institution Press, Washington, DC, 733 pp.

Buchanan, E. R. 1987. Timing of ovulation and early embryonic development in *Myotis lucifugus* (Chiroptera: Vespertilionidae) from northern central Ontario. Amer. J. Anat. 178:335–340.

Buech, R. R. 1984. Ontogeny and diurnal cycle of fecal reingestion in the North American beaver (*Castor canadensis*). J. Mamm. 55:347–350.

Buechner, H. K. 1960. The bighorn sheep in the United States, its past, present, and future. Wildl. Monogr. 4:1–174.

Bull, E. L., and T. W. Heater. 1995. Intraspecific predation on American marten. Northwestern Nat. 76:132–134.

Bull, E. L., and T. W. Heater. 2001. Survival, causes of mortality, and reproduction of the American marten in northeastern Oregon. Northwestern Nat. 82:1–6.

Bunch, T. D., R. S. Hoffmann, and C. F. Nadler. 1999. Cytology and cytogenetics. Pp. 263–276, in Mountain sheep of North America (R. Valdez and P. R. Krausman, eds.). Univ. Arizona Press, Tucson, 333 pp.

Bunnell, K. D., J. T. Flinders, and M. L. Wolfe. 2006. Potential impacts of coyotes and snowmobiles on lynx conservation in the intermountain West. Wildl. Soc. Bull. 34:828–838.

Burger, B. J., and J. G. Honey. 2008. Plesiadapidae (Mammalia, Primates) from the Late Paleocene Fort Union Formation of the Piceance Creek Basin, Colorado. J. Vert. Paleo. 28:816–825.

Burgess, S. A., and J. R. Bider. 1980. Effects of stream habitat improvements on invertebrates, trout populations and mink activity. J. Wildl. Mgmt. 44:871–880.

Burkot, T. R., B. S. Schneider, N. J. Pieniasek, C. M. Happ, J. S. Rutherford, S. B. Slemenda, E. Hoffmeister, G. O. Maupin, and N. S. Zeidner. 2000. *Babesia microti* and *Borrelia bissettii* transmission by *Ixodes spinipalpis* ticks among prairie voles, *Microtus ochrogaster*, in Colorado. Parasitology 121:6:595–599.

Burnett, W. L. 1925. Jack rabbits of Colorado with suggestions for their control. Circular Colorado State Entomologist 48: 1–11.

Burnett, W. L. 1931. Life history studies of the Wyoming ground squirrel (*Citellus elegans elegans*) in Colorado. Bull. Colorado Agric. Exper. Station 373:1–23.

Burnett, W. L., and S. C. McCampbell. 1926. The Zuni prairie dog in Montezuma County, Colorado. Circular, Colorado State Entomologist, Agricultural College 49:1–15.

Burnie, D., and D. E. Wilson, eds. 2001. Animal, the definitive visual guide to the world's wildlife. DK Publishing, New York, 624 pp.

Burns, J. A., D. L. Flath, and T. W. Clark. 1989. On the structure and function of white-tailed prairie dog burrows. Great Basin Nat. 49:517–524.

Burns, J. C., J. R. Choate, and E. G. Zimmerman. 1985. Systematic relationships of pocket gophers (genus *Geomys*) on the Central Great Plains. J. Mamm. 56:102–118.

Burns, S. F. 1979. The northern pocket gopher (*Thomomys talpoides*)—a major geomorphic agent on the alpine tundra. J. Colorado-Wyoming Acad. Sci. 11:86.

Burt, S. L., and T. L. Best. 1994. *Tamias rufus*. Mammalian Species 460:1–6.

Buskirk, S. W., S. C. Forrest, M. G. Raphael, and H. J. Harlow. 1989. Winter resting site ecology of marten in the Central Rocky Mountains. J. Wildl. Mgmt. 53:191–196.

Buskirk, S. W., A. S. Harestad, M. G. Raphael, and R. A. Powell, eds. 1994. Martens, sables, and fishers: biology and conservation. Cornell Univ. Press, Ithaca, NY, 496 pp.

Buskirk, S. W., H. J. Harlow, and S. C. Forrest. 1988. Temperature regulation in American marten (*Martes americana*) in winter. National Geog. Res. 4:208–218.

Buskirk, S. W., and L. F. Ruggiero. 1994. The American marten. Pp. 7–37, in The scientific basis for conserving forest carnivores, American marten, fisher, lynx and wolverine, in the western United States. (L. F. Ruggiero, K. B. Aubry, S. W. Buskirk, L. J. Lyon, and W. J. Zielinski, eds.). General Tech. Rept., USDA Forest Service, Rocky Mountain Forest and Range Experiment Station, RM-254:1–184.

Buskirk, S. W., L. F. Ruggiero, and C. J. Krebs. 2000. Habitat fragmentation and interspecific competition: implications for lynx conservation. Pp. 83–100 in L. F. Ruggiero, K. B. Aubry, S. W. Buskirk, G. M. Koehler, C. J. Krebs, K. S. McKelvey, and J. R. Squires, technical eds. Ecology and conservation of lynx in the United States. Univ. Press Colorado, Boulder, 350 pp.

Buskirk, S. W., and J. L. Zahratka. 2002. Ecology of snowshoe hares (*Lepus americanus*) in Colorado. Wildlife Research Report, Job Progress Report WP-0670, Colorado Division of Wildlife, Fort Collins.

Buskirk, S. W., and W. J. Zielinski. 2003. Small and mid-sized carnivores. Pp. 207–249, in Mammal community dynamics, management and conservation in the coniferous forests of western North America (C. J. Zabel and R. G. Anthony, eds.). Cambridge Univ. Press, Cambridge, UK, 709 pp.

Butler, D. R. 1995. Zoogeomorphology, animals as geomorphic agents. Cambridge Univ. Press, New York, 225 pp.

Butler, J. S., J. Shanahan, and D. J. Decker. 2003. Public attitudes toward wildlife are changing: a trend analysis of New York residents. Wildl. Soc. Bull. 31:1027–1036.

Byers, D. A., C. D. Smith, and J. M. Broughton. 2005. Holocene artiodactyl population histories and large game hunting in the Wyoming Basin, USA. J. Archaeol. Sci. 32:125–142.

Byers, E., and K. M. Ponte. 2005. The conservation easement handbook, second ed. Land Trust Alliance, Washington, DC, 555 pp.

Byers, J. A. 1997a. American pronghorn, social adaptations and the ghosts of predators past. Univ. Chicago Press, Chicago, 318 pp.

Byers, J. A. 1997b. Mortality risk to pronghorns from handling. J. Mamm. 78:894–899.

Byers, J. A. 2003a. Built for speed, a year in the life of pronghorn. Harvard Univ. Press, Cambridge, MA, 256 pp.

Byers, J. A. 2003b. Pronghorn, *Antilocapra americana*. Pp. 998–1008, in Wild mammals of North America, biology, management, and economics, second ed. (G. A. Feldhamer, B. C. Thompson, and J. A. Chapman, eds.). Johns Hopkins Univ. Press, Baltimore, 1,216 pp.

Byrne, A., L. L. Stebbins, and L. Delude. 1978. A new killing technique of the long-tailed weasel. Acta Theriol. 23:127–143.

Byrne, G. 1997. Fisher, lynx, wolverine observations and records for Colorado. Colorado Division of Wildlife, unpubl. report, 68 pp.

Byrne, G. 1998. A Colorado winter track survey for snowshoe hares and other species. Unpubl. report, Colorado Division of Wildlife, Glenwood Springs.

Byrne, G. and J. Copeland. 1997. An aerial survey for wolverine (*Gulo gulo*) in Colorado. Unpublished report, Colorado Division of Wildlife, 8 pp.

Caire, W., and R. B. Finley. 1977. The desert shrew *Notiosorex crawfordi* (Coues) from northwestern Colorado. Southwestern Nat. 22:284–285.

Caire, W., J. D. Tyler, B. P. Glass, and M. A. Mares. 1989. Mammals of Oklahoma. Univ. Oklahoma Press, Norman, 567 pp.

Cairns, D. M., D. R. Butler, and G. P. Malanson. 2002. Geomorphic and biogeographic setting of the Rocky Mountains. Pp. 27–39, in Rocky Mountain futures (J. S. Baron, ed.). Island Press, Washington, DC, 325 pp.

Calhoun, J. B. 1962. The ecology and sociology of the Norway rat. U.S. Dept. Health, Education, Welfare, Public Health Service, Bethesda, MD, 288 pp.

Calisher, C. H., J. E. Childs, W. P. Sweeney, K. M. Canestorp, and B. J. Beaty. 2000. Dual captures of Colorado rodents: implications for transmission of hantaviruses. Emerging Infect. Dis. 5:363–369.

Calisher, C. H., J. N. Mills, J. J. Root, and B. J. Beaty. 2003. Hantaviruses: etiologic agents of rare, but potentially life-threatening zoonotic diseases. J. Amer. Vet. Med. Assoc. 222:163–166.

Calisher, C. H., J. N. Mills, W. P. Sweeney, J. R. Choate, D. E. Sharp, K. M. Canestorp, and B. J. Beaty. 2001. Do unusual site-specific population dynamics of rodent reservoirs provide clues to the natural history of hantaviruses? J. Wildl. Dis. 37:280–288.

Calisher, C. H., J. N. Mills, W. P. Sweeney, J. J. Root, S. A. Reeder, E. S. Jentes, K. Wagoner, and B. J. Beaty. 2005. Population dynamics of a diverse rodent assemblage in mixed grass-shrub habitat, southeastern Colorado, 1995–2000. J. Wildl. Dis. 41:12–28.

Calisher, C. H., S. Nabity, J. J. Root, C. F. Fulhorst, and B. J. Beaty. 2001. Transmission of an arenavirus in white-throated woodrats (*Neotoma albigula*), southeastern Colorado, 1995–1999. Emerging Infect. Dis. 7:397–402.

Calisher, C. H., J. J. Root, J. N. Mills, J. E. Rowe, S. A. Reeder, E. S. Jentes, K. Wagoner, and B. J. Beaty. 2005. Epizootiology of Sin Nombre and El Moro Canyon hantaviruses, southeastern Colorado, 1995–2000. J. Wildl. Dis. 41:1–11.

Calisher, C. H., W. Sweeney, J. N. Mills, and B. J. Beaty. 1999. Natural history of Sin Nombre virus in western Colorado. Emerging Infect. Dis. 5:126–134.

Call, M. W. 1970. Beaver pond ecology and beaver-trout relationships in southeastern Wyoming. Unpubl. doctoral dissert., Univ. Wyoming, Laramie, 204 pp.

Callanbach, E. 1996. Bring back the buffalo! A sustainable future for America's Great Plains. Univ. California Press, Berkeley, 303 pp.

Camenzind, F. J. 1974. Territorial and social behavior of coyotes (*Canis latrans*) on the National Elk Refuge, northwestern Wyoming. J. Colorado-Wyoming Acad. Sci. 7(5):56.

Camenzind, F. J. 1978. Behavioral ecology of coyotes on the National Elk Refuge, Jackson, Wyoming. Pp 267–294, in Coyotes:

biology, behavior, and management (M. Bekoff, ed.). Academic Press, New York, 384 pp.

Cameron, G. N. 1973. Effect of litter size on postnatal growth and survival in the desert woodrat. J. Mamm. 54:489–493.

Cameron, G. N. 1995. Temporal use of home range by the hispid cotton rat. J. Mamm. 76:819–827.

Cameron, G. N., and D. Scheel. 2001. Getting warmer: effect of global climate change on distribution of rodents in Texas. J. Mamm. 82:652–680.

Cameron, G. N., and S. R. Spencer. 1981. *Sigmodon hispidus*. Mammalian Species 158:1–9.

Cameron, M. W. 1984. The swift fox (*Vulpes velox*) on the Pawnee National Grassland: its food habits, population dynamics and ecology. Unpubl. master's thesis, Univ. Northern Colorado, Greeley, 117 pp.

Campbell, L. A., J. G. Hallett, and M. A. O'Connell. 1996. Conservation of bats in managed forests: use of roosts by *Lasionycteris noctivagans*. J. Mamm. 77:976–985.

Campbell, T. A., S. J. Lapidge, and D. B. Long. 2006. Using baits to deliver pharmaceuticals to feral swine in southern Texas. Wildl. Soc. Bull. 34:1184–1189.

Campbell, T. M., III, and T. W. Clark. 1981. Colony characteristics and vertebrate associates of white-tailed and black-tailed prairie dogs in Wyoming. Amer. Midland Nat. 105:269–275.

Campbell, T. M., III, and T. W. Clark. 1983. Observation of badger copulatory and agonistic behavior. Southwestern Nat. 28: 107–108.

Campbell, T. M., III, T. W. Clark, L. Richardson, S. C. Forrest, and B. R. Houston. 1987. Food habits of Wyoming black-footed ferrets. Amer. Midland Nat. 117:208–210.

Capinera, J. L. 1987. An overview of the western grasslands. Pp. 1–8, in Integrated pest management on rangeland, a shortgrass prairie perspective (J. L. Capinera, ed.). Westview Press, Boulder, CO, 426 pp.

Capp, J. C. 1964. Ecology of the bison of Colorado National Monument. National Park Service, U.S. Dept. Interior, Washington, DC, 30 pp.

Capp, J. C. 1968. Bighorn sheep, elk, mule deer range relationships. Rocky Mountain Nature Assoc., Estes Park, 75 pp.

Capretta, P. J., R. C. Farentinos, V. M. Littlefield, and R. M. Potter. 1980. Feeding preferences of captive tassel-eared squirrels (*Sciurus aberti*) for ponderosa pine twigs. J. Mamm. 51:734–737.

Carbyn, L. N. 1983. Wolf predation on elk in Riding Mountain National Park, Manitoba. J. Wildl. Mgmt. 47:963–976.

Carbyn, L. N. 1987. Gray wolf and red wolf. Pp. 358–376, in Wild furbearer management and conservation in North America (M. Novak, J. A. Baker, M. E. Obard, and B. Malloch, eds.). Ontario Trappers Association, Toronto, 1,150 pp.

Carbyn, L. N., S. H. Fritts, and D. R. Seip, eds. 1995. Ecology and conservation of wolves in a changing world. Occas. Publ., Canadian Circumpolar Institute, Edmonton 35:1–620.

Carbyn, L. N., and D. Patriquin. 1983. Observations on home range sizes, movements and social organization of lynx, *Lynx canadensis*, in Riding Mountain National Park, Manitoba. Canadian Field-Nat. 97:262–267.

Carey, A. B. 1978. Distributional records for the prairie vole and hispid cotton rat in Colorado. J. Mamm. 59:624.

Carey, A. B., and J. E. Kershner. 1996. *Spilogale gracilis* in upland forests of western Washington and Oregon. Northwestern Nat. 77:29–34.

Carey, A. B., R. G. McLean, and G. O. Maupin. 1980. The structure of a Colorado tick fever ecosystem. Ecol. Monogr. 50:131–151.

Carey, C., G. L. Florant, B. A. Wunder, and B. Horwitz, eds. 1993. Life in the cold. Westview Press, Boulder, CO, 575 pp.

Carey, H. V., and P. Moore. 1986. Foraging and predation risk in yellow-bellied marmots. Amer. Midland Nat. 116:267–275.

Carleton, M. D. 1966. Food habits of two sympatric Colorado sciurids. J. Mamm. 47:91–103.

Carleton, M. D. 1984. Introduction to rodents. Pp. 255–265, in Orders and families of Recent mammals of the world (S. Anderson and J. K. Jones, Jr., eds.). Wiley, New York, 686 pp.

Carleton, M. D. 1989. Systematics and evolution. Pp. 7–141, in Advances in the study of *Peromyscus* (Rodentia) (G. L. Kirkland and J. N. Layne, eds.). Texas Tech Univ. Press, Lubbock, 367 pp.

Carleton, M. D., and G. G. Musser. 1984. Muroid rodents. Pp. 289–379 in Orders and families of Recent mammals of the world (S. Anderson and J. K. Jones, Jr., eds.). John Wiley and Sons, New York, 686 pp.

Carleton, M. D., and G. G. Musser. 2005. Order Rodentia. Pp. 745–751, in Mammal species of the world, a taxonomic and geographic reference, third ed. (D. E. Wilson and D. M. Reeder, eds.), Johns Hopkins Univ. Press, Baltimore, 2 vols.

Carpenter, J. W., M.J.G. Appel, R. C. Erickson, and M. N. Novilla. 1976. Fatal vaccine-induced canine distemper virus infection in black-footed ferrets. J. Amer. Vet. Med. Assoc. 169: 961–964.

Carpenter, J. W., and C. N. Hillman. 1978. Husbandry, reproduction, and veterinary care of captive ferrets. Ann. Proc. Amer. Assoc. Zoo Vet. 1978:36–47.

Carpenter, L. H. 1976. Nitrogen-herbicide effects on sagebrush deer range. Unpubl. doctoral dissert., Colorado State Univ., Fort Collins, 159 pp.

Carpenter, L. H., R. B. Gill, D. J. Freddy, and L. E. Sanders. 1979. Distribution and movements of mule deer in Middle Park, Colorado. Spec. Rept., Wildlife Research Section, Colorado Division of Wildlife 46:1–32.

Carpenter, L. H., O. C. Wallmo, and R. B. Gill. 1979. Forage diversity and dietary selection by wintering mule deer. J. Range Mgmt. 32:226–229.

Carraway, L. N. 1995. A key to Recent Soricidae of the western United States and Canada based primarily on dentaries. Occas. Papers, Univ. Kansas Mus. Nat. Hist. 175:1–49.

Carraway, L. N. 2007. Shrews (Eulypotyphla [*sic*]: Soricidae) of Mexico. Monogr., Western North Amer. Nat. 3:1–91.

Carraway, L. N., and R. M. Timm. 2000. Revision of the extant taxa of the genus *Notiosorex* (Mammalia: Insectivora: Soricidae). Proc. Biol. Soc. Washington 113:302–318.

Carraway, L. N., E. Yensen, B. J. Verts, and L. F. Alexander. 1993. Range extension and habitat of *Peromyscus truei* in eastern Oregon. Northwest Nat. 74:81–84.

Carrera, R., W. Ballard, P. Gipson, B. T. Kelly, P. R. Krausman, M. C. Wallace, C. Villalobos, and D. B. Wester. 2008. Comparison of Mexican wolf and coyote diets in Arizona and New Mexico. J. Wildl. Mgmt. 72:376–381.

Carroll, D., and L. L. Getz. 1976. Runway use and population density of *Microtus ochrogaster*. J. Mamm. 57:772–776.

Carroll, K. N. 2000. Macro- and microhabitat characteristics of the western spotted skunk, *Spilogale gracilis*, in the Sierra Nevada of northern California. Unpubl. master's thesis, California State Univ., Sacramento, 157 pp.

Carroll, L. E., and H. H. Genoways. 1980. *Lagurus curtatus*. Mammalian Species 124:1–6.

Carter, C. S., A. C. deVries, and L. L. Getz. 1995. Physiological substrates of mammalian monogamy: the prairie vole model. Neurosci. Biobehav. Rev. 19:303–314.

Carter, C. S., and L. L. Getz. 1985. Social and hormonal determinants of reproductive patterns in the prairie vole. Pp. 18–36, in Neurobiology: current comparative approaches (R. Gilles and J. Balthazart, eds.). Springer-Verlag, Berlin, 415 pp.

Cary, M. 1911. A biological survey of Colorado. N. Amer. Fauna 33:1–256.

Casey, D. E., J. DuWaldt, and T. W. Clark. 1986. Annotated bibliography of the black-footed ferret. Great Basin Nat. Mem. 8:185–208.

Cassells, E. S. 1997. The archaeology of Colorado, revised ed. Johnson Books, Boulder, CO, 409 pp.

Cassirer, E. F., and A.R.E. Sinclair. 2007. Dynamics of pneumonia in a bighorn sheep metapopulation. J. Wildl. Mgmt. 71: 1080–1088.

Catlett, R. H., and R. Z. Brown. 1961. Unusual abundance of *Peromyscus* at Gothic, Colorado. J. Mamm. 42:415.

Chace, J. F., and A. Cruz. 1998. Range of the brown-headed cowbird in Colorado: past and present. Great Basin Nat. 58:245–249.

Chamberlain, M. J., L. M. Conner, B. D. Leopold, and K. M. Hodges. 2003. Space use and multi-scale habitat selection of adult raccoons in central Mississippi. J. Wildl. Mgmt. 57:334–330.

Chamberlain, M. J., and B. D. Leopold. 2000. Spatial use patterns, seasonal habitat selection, and interactions among adult gray foxes in Mississippi. J. Wildl. Mgmt. 54:742–751.

Chambers, C. L., and R. R. Doucett. 2008. Diet of the Mogollon vole as indicated by stable-isotope analysis (δ^{13} C and δ^{15} C). Western N. Amer. Nat. 58:153–160.

Chambers, R. R., P. D. Sudman, and R. D. Bradley. 2009. A phylogenetic assessment of pocket gophers (*Geomys*): evidence from nuclear and mitochondrial genes. J. Mamm. 90:537–547.

Chapin, F. W., III, E. S. Zavaleta, V. T. Eviners, R. L. Naylor, P. M. Vitousek, H. L. Reynolds, D. E. Hooper, S. Lavorel, O. E. Sala, S. E. Hobbie, M. C. Mack, and S. Diaz. 2000. Consequences of changing biodiversity. Nature 405:234–242.

Chapman, B. R., and R. L. Packard. 1974. An ecological study of Merriam's pocket mouse in southeastern Texas. Southwestern Nat. 19:281–291.

Chapman, J. A. 1975. *Sylvilagus nuttallii*. Mammalian Species 56: 1–3.

Chapman, J. A., A. L. Harman, and D. E. Samuel. 1977. Reproductive and physiological cycles in the cottontail complex in western Maryland and nearby West Virginia. Wildl. Monogr. 56:1–73.

Chapman, J. A., J. G. Hockman, and W. R. Edwards. 1982. Cottontails. Pp. 83–123, in Wild mammals of North America, biology, management, and economics (J. A. Chapman and G. A. Feldhamer, eds.). Johns Hopkins Univ. Press, Baltimore, 1,147 pp.

Chapman, J. A., J. G. Hockman, M. M. Ojeda. 1980. *Sylvilagus floridanus*. Mammalian Species 136:1–8.

Chapman, J. A., and J. A. Litvaitis. 2003. Eastern cottontail, *Sylvilagus floridanus* and allies. Pp. 101–125, in Wild mammals of North America, biology, management, and economics, second ed. (G. A. Feldhamer, B. C. Thompson, and J. A. Chapman, eds.). Johns Hopkins Univ. Press, Baltimore, 1,216 pp.

Chapman, J. A., and G. R. Willner. 1978. *Sylvilagus audubonii*. Mammalian Species 106:1–4.

Chase, J. D., W. E. Howard, and J. T. Roseberry. 1982. Pocket gophers (Geomyidae). Pp. 239–255, in Wild mammals of North America (J. A. Chapman and G. A. Feldhammer, eds.). Johns Hopkins Univ. Press, Baltimore, 1,147 pp.

Childs, J. E. 1995. Special feature: zoonoses. J. Mamm. 76:663.

Childs, J. E., T. C. Kslazek, C. F. Spiropoulou, J. W. Krebs, S. Morzunov, G. O. Maupin, K. L. Gage, P. E. Rollin, J. Sarisky, R. E. Enscore, J. K. Frey, C. J. Peters, and S. T. Nichol. 1994. Serologic and genetic identification of *Peromyscus maniculatus* as the primary rodent reservoir for a new hantavirus in the southwestern United States. J. Infectious Dis. 169:1271–1280.

Chilelli, M., B. Griffith, and D. J. Harrison. 1996. Interstate comparisons of river otter harvest data. Wildl. Soc. Bull. 24:238–246.

Choate, J. R. 1970. Systematics and zoogeography of Middle American shrews of the genus *Cryptotis*. Univ. Kansas Publ., Mus. Nat. Hist. 19:195–317.

Choate, J. R., ed. 2000. Reflections of a naturalist: papers honoring Professor Eugene D. Fleharty. Fort Hays Studies, Special Issue 1:1–241.

Choate, J. R., and E. D. Fleharty. 1973. Habitat preference and spatial relations of shrews in a mixed grassland in Kansas. Southwestern Nat. 18:110–112.

Choate, J. R., E. D. Fleharty, and R. J. Little. 1974. Status of the spotted skunk, *Spilogale putorius*, in Kansas. Trans. Kansas Acad. Sci. 76:226–233.

Choate, J. R., and J. B. Pinkham. 1988. Armadillo in northeastern Colorado. Prairie Nat. 20:174.

Choate, J. R., and M. P. Reed. 1988. Least shrew, *Cryptotis parva*, in southwestern Kansas and southeastern Colorado. Southwestern Nat. 33:361–362.

Choate, J. R., and S. L. Williams. 1978. Biogeographic interpretation of variation within and among populations of the prairie vole, *Microtus ochrogaster*. Occas. Papers Mus., Texas Tech Univ. 49:1–25.

Choate, L. L., and C. Jones. 1998. Annotated checklist of Recent land mammals of Oklahoma. Occas. Papers, Mus. Texas Tech Univ. 181:1–13.

Christian, J. J. 1956. The natural history of a summer aggregation of the big brown bat, *Eptesicus fuscus fuscus*. Amer. Midland Nat. 55:66–95.

Christianson, D., and S. Creel. 2008. Risk effects in elk: sex-specific responses in grazing and browsing due to predation risk from wolves. Behav. Ecol. 19:1258–1266.

Christianson, D. A., and S. Creel. 2007. A review of environmental factors affecting elk winter diets. J. Wildl. Mgmt. 71:164–176.

Chronic, H., and F. Williams. 2002. Roadside geology of Colorado. Mountain Press Publishing Co., Missoula, MT, 398 pp.

Chronic, J., and H. Chronic. 1972. Prairie peak and plateau: a guide to the geology of Colorado. Colorado Geol. Surv. Bull. 32:1–126.

Chung-MacCoubrey, A. L. 2003. Monitoring long-term reuse of trees by bats in pinyon-juniper woodlands of New Mexico. Wildl. Soc. Bull. 31:73–79.

Chung-MacCoubrey, A. L., and M. A. Bogan. 2003. Bats of the piñon-juniper woodlands of southwestern Colorado. Pp. 131–149, in Ancient piñon-juniper woodlands, a natural history of Mesa Verde country (M. L. Floyd, ed.). Univ. Press Colorado, Boulder, 389 pp.

Churcher, C. S. 1959. The specific status of the New World red fox. J. Mamm. 40:513–520.

Churchill, J. 2009. Coyotes among us. Colorado Outdoors 58(3): 16–21.

Cid, M. S., J. K. Detling, A. D. Whicker, and M. A. Brizuela. 1991. Vegetation responses of a mixed-grass prairie site following exclusion of prairie dogs and bison. J. Range Mgmt. 44:100–105.

Ciesla, M. M. 2010. The health of Colorado's forests, special issue: threats to Colorado's current and future forest resources. Colorado State Forest Service, Fort Collins, and Division of Forestry, Colorado Department of Natural Resources, Denver, 37 pp.

Cincotta, R. P. 1989. Note on mound architecture of the black-tailed prairie dog. Great Basin Nat. 49:621–623.

Cincotta, R. P., D. W. Uresk, and R. M. Hansen. 1987. Demography of black-tailed prairie dog populations reoccupying sites treated with rodenticide. Great Basin Nat. 47:339–343.

Cinq-Mars, R. J., and L. N. Brown. 1969. Reproduction and ecological distribution of the rock mouse, *Peromyscus difficilis*, in northern Colorado. Amer. Midland Nat. 81:205–217.

Cinq-Mars, R. J., R. S. Hoffmann, and J. K. Jones, Jr. 1979. New records of the dwarf shrew (*Sorex nanus*) in South Dakota. Prairie Nat. 11:7–9.

Cisla, W. M. 2010. The health of Colorado's forests, 2009 Report, Colorado State Forest Service, Fort Collins, 37 pp.

Clark, B. K., and D. W. Kaufman. 1991. Effects of plant litter on foraging and nesting behavior of prairie rodents. J. Mamm. 72:502–512.

Clark, F. W. 1972. Influence of jackrabbit density on coyote population change. J. Wildl. Mgmt. 36:343–356.

Clark, T. W. 1968. Food uses of the Richardson ground squirrel (*Spermophilus richardsoni elegans*) in the Laramie Basin in Wyoming. Southwestern Nat. 13:248–249.

Clark, T. W. 1970. Richardson's ground squirrel (*Spermophilus richardsonii*) in the Laramie Basin, Wyoming. Great Basin Nat. 30:55–70.

Clark, T. W. 1971a. Towards a literature review of prairie dogs. J. Range Mgmt. 24:29–44.

Clark, T. W. 1971b. Ecology of the western jumping mouse in Grand Teton National Park. Northwest Sci. 45:229–238.

Clark, T. W. 1972. Influence of jackrabbit density on coyote population change. J. Wildl. Mgmt. 36:343–356.

Clark, T. W. 1973. Distribution and reproduction of shrews in Grand Teton National Park, Wyoming. Northwest Sci. 47: 128–131.

Clark, T. W. 1977. Ecology and ethology of the white-tailed prairie dog (*Cynomys leucurus*). Milwaukee Public Mus., Publ. Biol. Geol. 3:1–97.

Clark, T. W. 1986. Annotated prairie dog bibliography 1973–1985. Wildl. Tech. Bull., Montana Bureau of Land Management 1:1–32.

Clark, T. W. 1989. Conservation biology of the black-footed ferret *Mustela nigripes*. Spec. Sci. Rept., Wildlife Preservation Trust 3:1–175.

Clark, T. W., E. Anderson, C. Douglas, and M. Strickland. 1987. *Martes americana*. Mammalian Species 289:1–8.

Clark, T. W., M. Bekoff, T. M. Campbell, III, T. Hauptman, and B. D. Roberts. 1989. American marten, *Martes americana*, home ranges in Grand Teton National Park, Wyoming. Canadian Field-Nat. 103:423–425.

Clark, T. W., and T. M. Campbell, III. 1977. Short-term effects of timber harvest on pine marten behavior and ecology. Unpubl. Report, Idaho State Univ., Pocatello, 60 pp.

Clark, T. W., T. M. Campbell, III, and T. N. Hauptman. 1989. Demographic characteristics of American marten populations in Jackson Hole, Wyoming. Great Basin Nat. 49:587–596.

Clark, T. W., T. M. Campbell, III, M. H. Schroeder, and L. Richardson. 1988. Handbook of methods for locating black-footed ferrets. Wildl. Tech. Bull., Wyoming Bureau of Land Management 1:1–61.

Clark, T. W., T. M. Campbell, III, D. G. Socha, and D. E. Casey. 1982. Prairie dog colony attributes and associated vertebrate species. Great Basin Nat. 42:572–582.

Clark, T. W., and R. H. Denniston. 1970. On the descriptive ethology of Richardson's ground squirrel. Southwestern Nat. 15:193–200.

Clark, T. W., S. C. Forrest, L. Richardson, D. Casey, and T. M. Campbell, III. 1986. Descriptive ethology and activity patterns of black-footed ferrets. Great Basin Nat. Mem. 8:72–84.

Clark, T. W., D. Hinckley, and T. Rich. 1989. The prairie dog ecosystem: managing for biological diversity. Wildl. Tech. Bull., Montana Bureau of Land Management 2:1–55.

Clark, T. W., R. S. Hoffmann, and C. F. Nadler. 1971. *Cynomys leucurus*. Mammalian Species 7:1–4.

Clark, T. W., and M. R. Stromberg. 1987. Mammals in Wyoming. Publ. Educ. Ser., Univ. Kansas Mus. Nat. Hist. 10:1–314.

Clark, W. K. 1951. Ecological life history of the armadillo in the eastern plateau region. Amer. Midland Nat. 46:337–358.

Clark, W. R. 1973. Reproduction, survival, and density of snowshoe hares in northeastern Utah. Unpubl. master's thesis, Utah State Univ., Logan, 80 pp.

Clark, W. R., and G. S. Innis. 1982. Forage interactions and black-tailed jack rabbit population dynamics, a simulation model. J. Wildl. Mgmt. 46:1018–1035.

Cleveland, C. J., M. Betke, P. Federico, J. D. Frank, T. G. Hallam, J. Horn, J. D. López, Jr., G. F. McCracken, R. A. Medellín, A. Moreno-Valdez, C. G. Sansone, J. K. Westbrook, and T. H. Kunz. 2006. Economic value of the pest control service provided by Brazilian free-tailed bats in south-central Texas. Frontiers Ecol. and Environ. 5:238–243.

Clippinger, N. W. 2002. Biogeography, community ecology, and habitat of Preble's meadow jumping mouse (*Zapus hudsonius preblei*) in Colorado. Unpubl. doctoral dissert., Univ. Colorado, Boulder, 164 pp.

Clothier, R. R. 1955. Contribution to the life history of *Sorex vagrans* in Montana. J. Mamm. 36:214–221.

Coady, J. W. 1982. Moose. Pp. 902–922, in Wild mammals of North America, biology, management, and economics (J. A. Chapman and G. A. Feldhamer, eds.). Johns Hopkins Univ. Press, Baltimore, 1,147 pp.

Coates, K. P., and S. D. Schemnitz. 1994. Habitat use and foraging behavior of male mountain sheep in foraging associations with wild horses. Great Basin Nat. 54:86–90.

Cockerell, S. 1999. Crusader activists and the 1996 Colorado anti-trapping campaign. Wildl. Soc. Bull. 27:65–74.

Cockerell, T.D.A. 1927. Zoology of Colorado. Univ. Colorado, Boulder, 262 pp.

Cockrum, E. L. 1952. Mammals of Kansas. Univ. Kansas Publ., Mus. Nat. Hist. 7:1–303.

Cockrum, E. L. 1955. Reproduction in North American bats. Trans. Kansas Acad. Sci. 58:487–511.

Cockrum, E. L. 1960. The Recent mammals of Arizona: their taxonomy and distribution. Univ. Arizona Press, Tucson, 276 pp.

Cockrum, E. L., and H. S. Fitch 1952. Geographic variation in red-backed mice (genus *Clethrionomys*) of the Southern Rocky Mountain region. Univ. Kansas Publ., Mus. Nat. Hist. 5:281–292.

Cole, G. 1969. The elk of Grand Teton and southern Yellowstone National Parks. Research Rept., National Park Service, U.S. Dept. of Interior, GRTE-N-1:1–192.

Cole, S. J. 2008. Legacy in stone: rocky art of the Colorado Plateau and Four Corners Region, revised ed. Johnson Books, Boulder, CO.

Coleman, J. S., and S. A. Temple. 1993. Rural residents' free-ranging domestic cats: a survey. Wildl. Soc. Bull. 21:381–390.

Coleman, J. S., S. A. Temple, and S. R. Craven. 1997. Cats and wildlife, a conservation dilemma. Coop. Extension Publ., Univ. Wisconsin, 9 pp.

Colescott, J. H., and M. P. Gillingham. 1998. Reaction of moose (*Alces alces*) to snowmobile traffic in the Greys River Valley, Wyoming. Alces 34:329–338.

Collinge, S. K., W. C. Johnson, C. Ray, R. Matchett, J. Grensten, J. F. Cully, Jr., K. L. Gage, M. Y. Kosoy, J. E. Loye, and A. P. Martin. 2005. Landscape structure and plague occurrence in black-tailed prairie dogs on grasslands of the western USA. Landscape Ecol. 20:941–955.

Collins, W. B., P. J. Urness, and D. D. Austin. 1978. Elk diets and activities on different lodgepole pine habitat segments. J. Wildl. Mgmt. 42:799–810.

Colorado Department of Agriculture. 1990. Vertebrate rodent infestation survey. Spec. Publ., Colorado Department of Agriculture, 70 pp.

Colorado Department of Local Affairs. 2001. Colorado county profile system. Colorado Department of Local Affairs, Denver. http://dola.colorado.gov/demog/mule/Mule.cfm.

Colorado Division of Wildlife. 1990. A comparison of resident hunting participation and population trends 1960–1990. Unpubl. Internal Report, Colorado Division of Wildlife, Denver, 21 pp.

Colorado Division of Wildlife. 2003a. State of Colorado river otter recovery plan. Colorado Division of Wildlife, Denver, 51 pp.

Colorado Division of Wildlife. 2003b. Conservation Plan for Grassland Species in Colorado. Colorado Division of Wildlife, Denver, 205 pp.

Colorado Division of Wildlife. 2006a. Colorado's Comprehensive Wildlife Conservation Strategy and Wildlife Action Plans. Colorado Division of Wildlife, Denver, 328 pp.

Colorado Division of Wildlife. 2006b. North America's most endangered mammal making headway. http://wildlife.state.co.is/newsapp/press.asp?pressid=4081.

Colorado Division of Wildlife. 2007a. 2006 Annual Report. Colorado Outdoors 56(3):31–38.

Colorado Division of Wildlife. 2007b. Annual Report, Volunteer Program. http://wildlife.state.co.us/NR/rdonlyres/2B8AA361-FC15-40F6-BE32-9793ADC9BAB6/0/Annualreport2007Small.pdf.

Colorado Division of Wildlife. 2007c. Kit fox, endangered in Colorado. http://wildlife.state. co.us /WildlifeSpecies/SpeciesOfConcern/Mammals/KitFox.htm.

Colorado Division of Wildlife. 2007d. Living with wildlife in coyote country. http://wildlife.state.co.us/WildlifeSpecies/LivingWithWildlife/Mammals/CoyoteCountry.htm.

Colorado Division of Wildlife. 2007e. Living with wildlife in lion country. http://wildlife.state.co.us/WildlifeSpecies/LivingWithWildlife/Mammals/LionCountry1.htm.

Colorado Division of Wildlife. 2007f. Living with wildlife in red fox country. http://wildlife.state.co.us/WildlifeSpecies/LivingWithWildlife/Mammals/LivingWithRedFox.htm.

Colorado Division of Wildlife. 2007g. Mammals: Colorado endangered, threatened and species of special concern. http://wildlife.state.co.us/Wildlife Species/SpeciesofConcern/Mammals/.

Colorado Division of Wildlife. 2008a. Hunter Outreach Program, Youth Outreach and Women Afield, Report. Colorado Division of Wildlife, Denver, 18 pp. http://wildlife.state.co.us/NR/rdonlyres/D8DAC345-F649-4A89-A02B-32B93A483890/0/HunterOutreach ProgramReport2008.pdf.

Colorado Division of Wildlife. 2008b. Home on the range. Colorado Outdoors 57(1):28–30.

Colorado Division of Wildlife. 2008c. River otter. http://wildlife.state.co.us/WildlifeSpecies/SpeciesOfConcern/Mammals/RiverOtter.htm.

Colorado Division of Wildlife. 2008d. Lynx. http://wildlife.state.co.us/WildlifeSpecies/SpeciesOfConcern/Mammals/Lynx/.

Colorado Division of Wildlife. 2008e. Gray Wolf. http://wildlife.state.co.us/Wildlife Species/SpeciesOfConcern/Mammals/GrayWolf.htm.

Colorado Division of Wildlife. 2008f. Limited licenses for deer, elk, antelope, moose, and black bear. http://wildlife.state.co.us/NR/rdonlyres/86F0989E-76E8-4859-8292-6D9F80751804/0/Chapter2CoverLetter.pdf.

Colorado Division of Wildlife. 2008g. Private land habitat programs. http://wildlife.state.co.us/NR/rdonlyres/85E9F95F-FB3B-4F36-9AB1-C34BCAFBE33F/0/privatelandhandbook08.pdf.

Colorado Division of Wildlife. 2009a. Lynx kittens found in spring survey. http://wildlife.state.co.us/NewsMedia/PressReleases/Press.asp?PressId=6011.

Colorado Division of Wildlife. 2009b. Ranching for wildlife. http://wildlife.state.co.us/Hunting/BigGame/RanchingforWildlife/.

Colorado Division of Wildlife. 2009c. Chapter 10—nongame wildlife. http://wildlife.state.co.us/NR/rdonlyres/D9BADA66-8CBC-46DD-BE78-97C60EB1B813/0/Ch10.pdf.

Colorado Division of Wildlife. 2009d. Analysis of furbearer seasons. http://wildlife.state.co.us/NR/rdonlyres/54A2B43B-6CC8-4DED-A881-5A22C3E7D97/0/ANALYSISOFFURBEARERSEASONS2009final.pdf.

Colorado Division of Wildlife. 2009e. CWD info and testing. http://wildlife.state.co.us/Hunting/BigGame/CWD/.

Colorado Division of Wildlife. 2009f. Furbearers and small game, except migratory birds. http://wildlife.state.co.us/NR/rdonlyres/A348F16A-1B28-440E-9245-EB4E4630ACCE/0/Ch03.pdf.

Colorado Division of Wildlife. 2009g. Big game. http://wildlife.state.co.us/NR/rdonlyres/6E977561-C613-466D-BCFC-2CA9C9C91CD9/0/Ch02.pdf.

Colorado Division of Wildlife. 2010. Wolverine, *gulo gulo*. http://wildlife.state.co.us/WildlifeSpecies/SpeciesOfConcern/Mammals/Wolverine.htm.

Colorado Division of Wildlife and Colorado Department of Agriculture. 1997. Memorandum of understanding regarding Amendment 14 (prohibiting leghold and instant body-gripping traps, poison, or snares except under certain conditions). Spec. Rept., Colorado Division of Wildlife, Fort Collins, 57 pp.

Colorado Office of Economic Development and International Trade. 2007. Colorado Data Book. http://www.colorado.gov/cs/Satellite?c=Page&cid=1178305420531&pagename=OEDIT%2FOEDITLayout.

Colorado State Forest Service. 2005. Report on the Health of Colorado's Forests, Special Issue, Aspen Forests. Colorado State Forest Service, Fort Collins, 27 pp.

Colorado State Forest Service. 2007. Forest Challenges Today and Tomorrow. 2007 Report on the Health of Colorado's Forests. Colorado State Forest Service, Fort Collins, 30 pp.

Colorado Tourism Office. 2008. The benefits of tourism impact us all. Colorado Tourism Office, Denver, 2 pp. http://www.colorado.com/data/docs/ambassador/FY08TourismBenefitsBrochure.pdf.

Colorado Wildlife Federation. 2008. 2008 Colorado Conservation Summit: Colorado Wildlife at a Crossroads, Executive Summary. http://coloradowildlife.org/news/colorado-conservation-summit-executive-summary.html.

Colorado Wildlife Heritage Foundation. 2008. Annual Report 2008. http://www.cwhf.info/pdf/2008_ANNUALReport.pdf.

Colorado Wolf Management Working Group. 2004. Findings and recommendations for managing wolves that migrate into Colorado. Colorado Division of Wildlife, Denver, 69 pp.

Colvin, M. A., and D. V. Colvin. 1970. Breeding and fecundity of six species of voles (*Microtus*). J. Mamm. 51:417–419.

Compton, T. L. 1980. Coyote predation on an adult deer in southwestern Colorado. Southwestern Nat. 25:113–114.

Conaway, C. H. 1952. Life history of the water shrew *Sorex palustris navigator*. Amer. Midland Nat. 48:219–248.

Conaway, C. H. 1958. Maintenance, reproduction, and growth of the least shrew in captivity. J. Mamm. 39:507–512.

Conaway, C. H. 1959. The reproductive cycle of the eastern mole. J. Mamm. 40:180–194.

Conley, W. 1976. Competition between *Microtus*: a behavioral hypothesis. Ecology 57:224–237.

Conner, D. A. 1982. Geographic variation in short calls of pikas (*Ochotona princeps*). J. Mamm. 53:48–52.

Conner, D. A. 1983. Seasonal changes in activity patterns and the adaptive value of haying in pikas (*Ochotona princeps*). Canadian J. Zool. 51:411–416.

Conner, D. A. 1984. The role of an acoustic display in territorial maintenance in the pika. Canadian J. Zool. 52:1906–1909.

Conner, D. A. 1985a. Analysis of the vocal repertoire of adult pikas: ecological and evolutionary perspectives. Animal Behavior 33:124–134.

Conner, D. A. 1985b. The function of the pika short call in individual recognition. Zeitschrift für Tierpsychologie 67:131–143.

Conner, M. M., D. L. Baker, M. A. Wild, J. G. Powers, M. D. Hussain, R. L. Dunn, and T. M. Nett. 2007. Fertility control in free-ranging elk using gonadotropin-releasing hormone agonist leuprolide: effects on reproduction, behavior, and body condition. J. Wildl. Mgmt. 71:2346–2356.

Conner, M. M., J. E. Gross, P. C. Cross, M. R. Ebiner, R. R. Gillies, M. D. Samuel, and M. W. Miller. 2007. Scale-dependent approaches to modeling spatial epidemiology of chronic wasting disease. Special Rept., Utah Division of Wildlife Resources, 68 pp.

Conner, M. M., and T. M. Shenk. 2003. Distinguishing *Zapus hudsonius preblei* from *Zapus princeps princeps* by using repeated cranial measurements. J. Mamm. 84:1456–1463.

Conner, M. M., and T. M. Shenk. 2005. Use of morphometric measurements to differentiate *Zapus hudsonius preblei* from *Zapus princeps princeps* in Colorado and southeastern Wyoming. Spec. Rept., Colorado Division of Wildlife 78:1–24.

Conner, M. M., G. C. White, and D. J. Freddy. 2001. Elk movement in response to early-season hunting in northwest Colorado. J. Wildl. Mgmt. 55:926–940.

Connolly, G. E. 1981. Trends in populations and harvests. Pp. 225–243, in Mule and black-tailed deer of North America (O. C. Wallmo, ed.). Univ. Nebraska Press, Lincoln, 605 pp.

Conover, M. R., and D. O. Conover. 2001. For whom do we manage wildlife: the resource, society, or future generations. Wildl. Soc. Bull. 29:675–679.

Conover, M. R., W. C. Pitt, K. K. Kessler, T. J. DuBow, and W. A. Sanborn. 1995. Review of human injuries, illnesses, and economic losses caused by wildlife in the United States. Wildl. Soc. Bull. 23:407–414.

Conroy, C. J., and J. A. Cook. 2000a. Molecular systematics of a Holarctic rodent (Microtus: Muridae). J. Mamm. 81:344–359.

Conroy, C. J., and J. A. Cook. 2000b. Phylogeography of a post-glacial colonizer: *Microtus longicaudus* (Rodentia: Muridae). Molec. Ecol. 9:164–175.

Constantine, D. G. 1961. Gestation period in the spotted skunk. J. Mamm. 42:421–422.

Constantine, D. G. 1966. Ecological observations on lasiurine bats in Iowa. J. Mamm. 47:34–41.

Constantine, D. G. 1998. An overlooked external character to differentiate *Myotis californicus* and *Myotis ciliolabrum* (Vespertilionidae). J. Mamm. 79:624–630.

Converse, S. J., G. C. White, and W. M. Block. 2006. Small mammal responses to thinning and wildfire in ponderosa pine-dominated forests of the southwestern United States. J. Wildl. Mgmt. 70:1711–1722.

Cook, C. W. 1972. Energy budget for rabbits compared to cattle and sheep. Range Science Dept. Ser., Colorado State Univ. 13:1–17.

Cook, J. G., B. K. Johnson, R. C. Cook, R. A. Riggs, T. Delcurto, L. D. Bryant, and L. L. Irwin. 2004. Effects of summer-autumn nutrition and parturition date on reproduction and survival of elk. Wildl. Monogr. 155:1–61.

Cook, R. R., J.-L. E. Cartron, and P. J. Polechla, Jr. 2003. The importance of prairie dogs to nesting ferruginous hawks in grassland ecosystems. Wildl. Soc. Bull. 31:1073–1082.

Cook, R. S., M. White, D. O. Trainer, and W. C. Glazener. 1971. Mortality of young white-tailed deer fawns in South Texas. J. Wildl. Mgmt. 35:47–56.

Cooke, M. 1936. Report of the Great Plains Drought Area Committee. Hopkins Papers, Box 13, 17 pp. Franklin D. Roosevelt Library, Hyde Park, NY.

Cooley, H. S., R. B. Wielgus, G. M. Koehler, H. S. Robinson, and B. T. Maletzke. 2009. Does hunting regulate cougar populations? A test of the compensatory mortality hypothesis. Ecology 90:2913–2921.

Copeland, J., R. Yates, and L. Ruggiero. 2004. Wolverine population assessment in Glacier National Park, progress report. U.S. Forest Service, Rocky Mountain Research Station, Missoula, MT, 18 pp.

Copeland, J. P. 1996. Biology of the wolverine in central Idaho. Unpubl. master's thesis, Univ. Idaho, Moscow, 138 pp.

Copeland, J. P., and J. S. Whitman. 2003. Wolverine, *Gulo gulo*. Pp. 672–682, in Wild mammals of North America, biology, management, and economics, second ed. (G. A. Feldhamer, B. C. Thompson, and J. A. Chapman, eds.). Johns Hopkins Univ. Press, Baltimore, 1,216 pp.

Copeland, J. P., K. S. McKelvey, K. B. Aubry, A. Landa, J. Persson, R. M. Inman, J. Krebs, E. Lofroth, H. Golden, J. R. Squires, A. Magoun, M. K. Schwartz, J. Wilmot, C. L. Copeland, R. E. Yates, I. Kojola, and R. May. 2010. The bioclimatic envelope of the wolverine (*Gulo gulo*): do climatic constraints limit its geographic distribution? Canadian J. Zool. 88:233–246.

Copeland, J. P., J. M. Peek, C. R. Groves, W. E. Melquist, K. S. McKelvey, G. W. McDaniel, C. D. Long, and C. E. Harris. 2007. Seasonal habitat associations of the wolverine in central Idaho. J. Wildl. Mgmt. 71:2201–2212.

Coppock, D. L., and J. K. Detling. 1986. Alteration of bison and black-tailed prairie dog grazing interaction by prescribed burning. J. Wildl. Mgmt. 50:452–455.

Coppock, D. L., J. K. Detling, J. E. Ellis, and M. I. Dyer. 1983a. Plant herbivore interactions in a North American mixed-grass prairie: I. Effects of black-tailed prairie dogs on interseasonal above ground plant biomass and nutrient dynamics and plant species diversity. Oecologia 56:1–9.

Coppock, D. L., J. K. Detling, J. E. Ellis, and M. I. Dyer. 1983b. Plant herbivore interactions in a North American mixed-grass prairie: II. Responses of bison to modification of vegetation by prairie dogs. Oecologia 56:10–15.

Corcoran, A. J., J. R. Barber, and W. E. Conner. 2009. Tiger moth jams bat sonar. Science 325:325–327.

Corn, J. G., C. A Pague, A. R. Ellingson, M. Sherman, T. Zwiejacz, G. Kittel, and C. Flemming. 1995. Final report on the geographic extent of the Preble's meadow jumping mouse population on the United States Air Force Academy. Colorado Natural Heritage Program, Colorado State Univ., Fort Collins.

Cornely, J. E., and R. J. Baker. 1986. *Neotoma mexicana*. Mammalian Species 262:1–7.

Cornely, J. E., L. N. Carraway, and B. J. Verts. 1992. *Sorex preblei*. Mammalian Species 416:1–3.

Corona Research. 2006. Public opinions and perceptions of mountain lion issues. Colorado Division of Wildlife, Denver. http://wildlife.state.co.us/NR/rdonlyres/B3DE2DB6-AE25-4B8B-9676-B1A3007277F8/0/MountainLionSurveyResults.

Cortinas, M. R., and T. R. Seastedt. 1996. Short- and long-term effects of gophers (*Thomomys talpoides*) on soil organic matter dynamics in alpine tundra. Pedobiologia 40:162–170.

Costello, C. M. 2010. Estimates of dispersal and home-range fidelity in American black bears. J. Mamm. 91:116–121.

Costello, D. F. 1954. Vegetation zones in Colorado. Pp. iii–x, in Manual of the plants of Colorado (by H. D. Harrington). Sage Books, Denver, 666 pp.

Costello, D. F. 1966. The world of the porcupine. J. B. Lippincott Co., Philadelphia, 157 pp.

Côté, S. D. 2000. Dominance hierarchies in female mountain goats: stability, aggressiveness and determinants of rank. Behavior 137:1541–1566.

Côté, S. D., and M. Festa-Bianchet. 2003. Mountain goat, *Oreamnos americanus*. Pp. 1061–1075, in Wild mammals of North America, biology, management, and economics, second ed. (G. A. Feldhamer, B. C. Thompson, and J. A. Chapman, eds.). Johns Hopkins Univ. Press, Baltimore, 1,216 pp.

Coues, E., and J. A. Allen. 1877. Monographs of North American Rodentia. U.S. Geol. Surv. Terr. 11:1–1099.

Coues, E., and H. C. Yarrow. 1875. Report on the collections of mammals made in portions of Nevada, Utah, California, Colorado, New Mexico, and Arizona, during the years 1871, 1872, 1873, and 1874. . . . Explorations and surveys west of the one hundredth meridian . . . 5:35–129, 960–979.

Cougar Management Guidelines Working Group. 2005. Cougar management guidelines. WildFutures, Bainbridge Island, WA, xvi + 1,137 pp.

Covell, D. F. 1992. Ecology of the swift fox (*Vulpes velox*) in southeastern Colorado. Unpubl. master's thesis, Univ. Wisconsin–Madison, 111 pp.

Covell, D. F., D. S. Miller, and W. H. Karasov. 1996. Cost of locomotion and daily energy expenditure by free-living swift foxes (*Vulpes velox*): a seasonal comparison. Canadian J. Zool. 74:283–290.

Covell, D. F., and O. J. Rongstad. 1990. 1989 Annual Report, Ecology of swift fox on Pinon Canyon Maneuver Site. Environmental, Energy, and Natural Resources Division, Fort Carson, CO, 7 pp.

Cowan, I. McT., and G. J. Guiget. 1956. The mammals of British Columbia. Handbook, British Columbia Prov. Mus. 11:1–413.

Cowan, I. McT., and W. McCrory. 1970. Variation in the mountain goat, *Oreamnos americanus* (Blainville). J. Mamm. 51:60–73.

Cowan, W. F. 1973. Ecology and life history of the raccoon (*Procyon lotor hirtus* Nelson and Goldman) in the northern part of its range. Unpubl. doctoral dissert., Univ. North Dakota, Grand Forks, 161 pp.

Cowardin, L. M., D. S. Gilmer, and C. W. Shaiffer. 1985. Mallard recruitment in the agricultural environment of North Dakota. Wildl. Monogr. 92:1–37.

Cox, E. W., R. A. Garrott, and J. R. Cary. 1997. Effects of supplemental cover on survival of snowshoe hares and cottontail rabbits in patchy habitat. Canadian J. Zool. 75:1357–1363.

Coyner, B. S., T. E. Lee, Jr., D. S. Rogers, and R. A. Van den Bussche. 2010. Taxonomic status and species limits of *Perognathus* (Rodentia: Heteromyidae) in the Southern Great Plains. Southwestern Nat. 55:1–10.

Crabb, W. D. 1941. Food habits of the prairie spotted skunk in southeastern Iowa. J. Mamm. 22:349–364.

Crabb, W. D. 1944. Growth, development, and seasonal weights of spotted skunks. J. Mamm. 25:213–221.

Crabb, W. D. 1948. The ecology and management of the prairie spotted skunk in Iowa. Ecol. Monogr. 18:201–232.

Crabtree, R. L., and J. W. Sheldon. 1999a. The ecological role of coyotes on Yellowstone's northern range. Yellowstone Sci. 7:15–23.

Crabtree, R. L., and J. W. Sheldon. 1999b. Coyotes and canid coexistence in Yellowstone. Pp. 127–163, in Carnivores in ecosystems, the Yellowstone experience (T. W. Clark, A. P. Curlee, S. C. Minta, and P. M. Kareiva, eds.). Yale Univ. Press, New Haven, CT, 446 pp.

Craig, E. H., and B. L. Keller. 1986. Movements and home range of porcupines, *Erethizon dorsatum*, in Idaho shrub desert. Canadian Field-Nat. 100:168–173.

Craighead, D. J. 1998. An integrated satellite technique to evaluate grizzly bear habitat use. Ursus 10:187–201.

Craighead, F. C., Jr. 1979. Track of the grizzly. Sierra Club Books, San Francisco, 261 pp.

Craighead, F. C., Jr., and J. J. Craighead. 1972. Grizzly bear prehibernation and denning activities as determined by radiotracking. Wildl. Monogr. 32:1–35.

Craighead, J. J., and J. A. Mitchell. 1982. Grizzly bear. Pp. 515–556, in Wild mammals of North America, biology, management, and economics (J. A. Chapman and G. A. Feldhamer, eds.). Johns Hopkins Univ. Press, Baltimore, 1,147 pp.

Craighead, J. J., F. C. Craighead, Jr., and J. Sumner. 1976. Reproductive cycles and rates in the grizzly bear, *Ursus horribilis*, of the Yellowstone ecosystem. Internat. Conf. Bear Research Mgmt. 3:337–356.

Craighead, J. J., M. G. Hornocker, and F. C. Craighead, Jr. 1969. Reproductive biology of young female grizzly bears. J. Reprod. Fertil., Suppl. 5:447–475.

Craighead, J. J., J. S. Sumner, and J. A. Mitchell. 1995. The grizzly bears of Yellowstone: their ecology in the Yellowstone Ecosystem, 1959–1992. Island Press, Washington, DC, 556 pp.

Crampton, L. H., and R.M.R. Barclay. 1998. Selection of roosting and foraging habitat by bats in different-aged aspen mixed-wood stands. Cons. Biol. 12:1347–1358.

Cranford, J. A. 1978. Hibernation in the western jumping mouse (*Zapus princeps*). J. Mamm. 59:496–509.

Cranshaw, W., and R. Wilson. 2004. Fleas and plague. Insect Ser., Colorado State Univ. Coop. Extension 5.600:104.

Cranshaw, W. S., and F. B. Peairs. 2000. Colorado ticks and tick-borne diseases. Publ., Colorado State Univ. Extension 5.593: 1–5.

Crawford, D. L. 2003. Assessment of character displacement in two shrew species using geometric morphometrics and GIS. Unpubl. master's thesis, Univ. Colorado, Boulder, 60 pp.

Creeden, P. J. 1986. The ecology of desert bighorn sheep in Colorado. Unpubl. master's thesis, Colorado State Univ., Fort Collins, 72 pp.

Creeden, P. J., and V. K. Graham. 1997. Reproduction, survival, and lion predation in the Black Ridge Colorado National Monument desert bighorn herd. Trans. Desert Bighorn Council 41:37–43.

Creel, S., and D. Christianson. 2008. Relationships between direct and indirect predation and risk effects. Trends Ecol. and Evol. 23:194–201.

Creel, S., and D. Christianson. 2009. Wolf presence and increased willow consumption by Yellowstone elk: implications for trophic cascades. Ecology 90:2454–2466.

Creel, S., D. Christianson, S. Liley, and J. A. Winnie, Jr. 2007. Predation risk affects reproductive physiology and demography of elk. Science 315:960.

Creel, S., J. A. Winnie, Jr., and D. Christianson. 2009. Glucocorticoid stress hormones and the effect of predation risk on elk reproduction. Proc. Nat. Acad. Sci., Early Edition. www.pnas.org/cgi/doi/10.1073/pnas.0902235106.

Crete, M., and S. Larivière. 2003. Estimating the costs of locomotion in snow for coyotes. Canadian J. Zool. 81:1808–1814.

Criddle, S. 1943. The little northern chipmunk in southern Manitoba. Canadian Field-Nat. 57:81–86.

Crooks, K. 1994a. Den-site selection in the island spotted skunk of Santa Cruz Island, California. Southwestern Nat. 39:354–357.

Crooks, K. 1994b. Demography and status of the island fox and island spotted skunk on Santa Cruz Island, California. Southwestern Nat. 39:257–262.

Crooks, K. 1999. Western spotted skunk, *Spilogale gracilis*. Pp. 183–185, in The Smithsonian book of North American mammals (D. E. Wilson and S. Ruff, eds.). Smithsonian Institution Press, Washington, DC, 750 pp.

Crooks, K., and D. Van Vuren. 1995. Resource utilization by two insular endemic mammalian carnivores, the island fox and island spotted skunk. Oecologia 104:301–307.

Crowcroft, P., and F. P. Rowe. 1963. Social organization and territorial behavior in the wild house mouse (*Mus musculus* L.). Proc. Zool. Soc. London 140:517–531.

Crowe, D. M. 1975. Aspects of aging, growth, and reproduction of bobcats from Wyoming. J. Mamm. 56:177–198.

Crowe, D. M. 1986. Furbearers of Wyoming. Wyoming Game and Fish Department, Cheyenne, 74 pp.

Crowe, D. M., and D. Strickland. 1975. Population structures of some mammalian predators in southeastern Wyoming. J. Wildl. Mgmt. 39:449–450.

Crum, S. 2009. People of the Red Earth, American Indians of Colorado. Western Reflections Publishing, Lake City, CO.

Cruzan, J. 1968. Ecological distributions and interactions of four species of *Microtus* in Colorado. Unpubl. doctoral dissert., Univ. Colorado, Boulder, 129 pp.

Cryan, P. M. 2003. Seasonal distribution of migratory tree bats (*Lasiurus* and *Lasionycteris*) in North America. J. Mamm. 84:579–593.

Cryan, P. M., M. A. Bogan, and J. S. Altenbach. 2000. Effect of elevation on distribution of female bats in the Black Hills, South Dakota. J. Mamm. 81:719–725.

Cryan, P. M., M. A. Bogan, R. O. Rye, G. P. Landis, and C. L. Kester. 2004. Stable hydrogen isotope analysis of bat hair as evidence for seasonal molt and long-distance migration. J. Mamm. 85:996–1001.

Cryan, P. M., M. A. Bogan, and G. M. Yanega. 2001. Roosting habits of four bat species in the Black Hills of South Dakota. Acta Chiropterol. 3:43–52.

Cully, J. F. Jr. 1991. Response of raptors to reduction of a Gunnison's prairie dog population by plague. Amer. Midland Nat. 125:140–149.

Cully, J. F., Jr. 1993. Plague, prairie dogs, and black-footed ferrets. Pp. 38–49, in Proceedings of the Symposium on the Management of Prairie Dog Complexes for the Reintroduction of Black-Footed Ferrets (J. L. Oldemeyer, D. E. Biggins, B. J. Miller, and R. Crete, eds.). Biol. Rept., U.S. Fish and Wildlife Service 93:1–95.

Cully, J. F., Jr. 1997a. Growth and life-history change in Gunnison's prairie dog after a plague epizootic. J. Mamm. 78:156–157.

Cully, J. F., Jr. 1997b. Gunnison's prairie dog growth and life-history change after a plague epizootic. J. Mamm. 78:146–157.

Cully, J. F., Jr., A. M. Barnes, T. J. Quan, and G. Maupin. 1997. Dynamics of plague in a Gunnison's prairie dog colony complex from New Mexico. J. Wildl. Diseases 33:706–719.

Cully, J. F., Jr., and E. S. Williams. 2001. Interspecific comparisons of sylvatic plague in prairie dogs. J. Mamm. 82:894–905.

Culver, M. 2009. Lessons and insights from evolution, taxonomy, and conservation genetics. Pp. 27–40, in Cougar ecology and conservation (M. Hornocker and S. Negri, eds.). Univ. Chicago Press, Chicago, 306 pp.

Culver, R.C.E. 2004. A mitochondrial DNA phylogeny of *Thomomys talpoides* (the northern pocket gopher) in the Southern Rocky Mountains. Unpubl. master's thesis, Univ. Colorado, Boulder, 52 pp.

Cummins, T., and N. A. Slade. 2007. Summer captures of *Reithrodontomys megalotis* in elevated traps. Southwestern Nat. 52: 79–82.

Currie, P. O., and D. L. Goodwin. 1966. Consumption of forage by black-tailed jackrabbits on salt-desert ranges of Utah. J. Wildl. Mgmt. 30:304–311.

Currier, A., W. D. Kitts, and I. McT. Cowan. 1960. Cellulose digestion in the beaver (*Castor canadensis*). Canadian J. Zool. 38:1109–1116.

Currier, M.J.P. 1976. Characteristics of the mountain lion population near Cañon City, Colorado. Unpubl. master's thesis, Colorado State Univ., Fort Collins, 81 pp.

Currier, M.J.P. 1983. *Felis concolor*. Mammalian Species 200:1–7.

Currier, M.J.P., S. L. Sheriff, and K. R. Russell. 1977. Mountain lion population and harvest near Cañon City, Colorado, 1974–1977. Special Rept., Colorado Division of Wildlife and Cooperative Wildlife Research Unit 42:1–12.

Curtis, J. D. 1941. The sylvicultural significance of the porcupine. J. Forestry 39:583–594.

Curtis, J. D. 1944. Appraisal of porcupine damage. J. Wildl. Mgmt. 8:88–91.

Cutter, W. L. 1958a. Denning of the swift fox in northern Texas. J. Mamm. 39:70–74.

Cutter, W. L. 1958b. Food habits of the swift fox in northern Texas. J. Mamm. 39:527–532.

Cypher, B. L. 2003. Foxes, *Vulpes* species, *Urocyon* species, and *Alopex lagopus*. Pp. 511–546, in Wild mammals of North America, biology, management, and economics, second ed. (G. A. Feldhamer, B. C. Thompson, and J. A. Chapman, eds.). Johns Hopkins Univ. Press, Baltimore, 1,216 pp.

Cypher, B. L., and N. Frost. 1999. Condition of San Joaquin kit foxes in urban and exurban habitats. J. Wildl. Mgmt. 53: 930–938.

Cypher, B. L., and K. A. Spencer. 1998. Competitive interactions between coyotes and San Joaquin kit foxes. J. Mamm. 79: 204–214.

Cypher, B. L., G. D. Warrick, M.R.M. Otten, T. P. O'Farrell, W. H. Berry, C. E. Harris, T. T. Kato, P. M. McCue, J. H. Scrivner, and B. W. Zoellick. 2000. Population dynamics of San Joaquin kit foxes at the Naval Petroleum Reserves in California. Wildl. Monogr. 145:1–43.

Czaplewski, N. J. 1983. *Idionycteris phyllotis*. Mammalian Species 208:1–4.

Czech, B., P. K. Devers, and P. R. Krausman. 2001. The relationship of gender to species conservation attitudes. Wildl. Soc. Bull. 29:187–194.

Czelusniak, J., M. Goodman, B. F. Koob, D. A. Tagle, J. Shoshani, G. Braunitzer, T. K. Kleinschmidt, W. W. De Jong, and G. Matsuda. 1990. Perspectives from amino acid and nucleotide sequences on cladistic relationships among higher taxa of Eutheria. Current Mammalogy 2:545–572.

Dahlsted, K. J., S. Sather-Blair, B. K. Worcester, and R. Klukas. 1981. Application of remote sensing to prairie dog management. J. Range Mgmt. 34:218–223.

Dailey, T. V., N. T. Hobbs, and T. N. Woodward. 1984. Experimental comparisons of diet selection by mountain goats and mountain sheep in Colorado. J. Wildl. Mgmt. 48:799–806.

Dale, A. R. 1987. Ecology and behavior of bighorn sheep, Waterton Canyon, Colorado, 1981–1982. Unpubl. master's thesis, Colorado State Univ., Fort Collins, 169 pp.

Dall, W. H. 1915. Spencer Fullerton Baird, a biography. J. B. Lippincott, Philadelphia, 462 pp.

Dalquest, W. W. 1947. Notes on the natural history of the bat, *Myotis yumanensis*, in California, with a description of a new race. Amer. Midland Nat. 38:224–247.

Dalquest, W. W. 1975. The montane vole in northeastern New Mexico and adjacent Colorado. Southwestern Nat. 20:138–139.

Dalquest, W. W., F. B. Stangl, Jr., and J. K. Jones, Jr. 1990. Mammalian zoogeography of a Rocky Mountain–Great Plains interface in New Mexico, Oklahoma, and Texas. Spec. Publ., Mus., Texas Tech Univ. 24:1–78.

Daly, J. C., and J. L. Patton. 1986. Growth, reproduction, and sexual dimorphism in *Thomomys bottae* pocket gophers. J. Mamm. 57:256–265.

Danz, H. P. 1997. Of bison and man. Univ. Press Colorado, Boulder, 231 pp.

Darimont, C. T., S. M. Carlson, M. T. Kinnison, P. C. Paquet, T. E. Reimchen, and C. C. Wilmers. 2009. Human predators outpace other agents of trait change in the wild. Proc. Nat. Acad. Sci. 106:952–954.

Dartt, M. 1879. On the plains and among the peaks, or how Mrs. Maxwell made her natural history collection. Claxton, Remsen and Haffelfinger, Philadelphia, 225 pp.

Dasmann, R. F. 1966. Wildlife and the new conservation. Wildl. Soc. News 105:48–49.

David, E. B. 2007. Family Antilocapridae. Pp. 227–240, in The evolution of artiodactyls (D. R. Prothero and S. E. Foss, eds.). Johns Hopkins Univ. Press, Baltimore, 367 pp.

Davidow-Henry, B. R., J. K. Jones, Jr., and R. R. Hollander. 1989. *Cratogeomys castanops*. Mammalian Species 338:1–6.

Davidson, A. D., R. R. Parmenter, and J. R. Gosz. 1999. Responses of small mammals and vegetation to a reintroduction of Gunnison's prairie dogs. J. Mamm. 80:1311–1324.

Davis, A., M. Bunning, P. Gordy, N. Panella, B. Blitvich, and R. Bowen. 2005. Experimental and natural infection of North American bats with West Nile Virus. Amer. J. Trop. Med. and Hyg. 73:467–469.

Davis, A. H., Jr. 1966. Winter activity of the black-tailed prairie dog in north-central Colorado. Unpubl. master's thesis, Colorado State Univ., Fort Collins, 46 pp.

Davis, E. B. 2007. Family Antilocapridae. Pp. 227–240, in The evolution of artiodactyls (D. R. Prothero and S. E. Foss, eds.). Johns Hopkins University Press, Baltimore, xii + 367 pp.

Davis, F. W., and J. R. Choate. 1993. Morphologic variation and age structure in a population of the eastern mole, *Scalopus aquaticus*. J. Mamm. 74:1014–1025.

Davis, R., and S. J. Bissell. 1989. Distribution of Abert's squirrel (*Sciurus aberti*) in Colorado: evidence for a recent expansion of range. Southwestern Nat. 34:306–309.

Davis, R., and D. E. Brown. 1989. Role of post-Pleistocene dispersal in determining the modern distribution of Abert's squirrel. Great Basin Nat. 49:425–434.

Davis, R., and J. R. Callahan. 1992. Post-Pleistocene dispersal in the Mexican vole (*Microtus mexicanus*): an example of an apparent trend in the distribution of southwestern mammals. Great Basin Nat. 52:262–268.

Davis, R. B., C. F. Herreid, II, and H. L. Short. 1962. Mexican free-tailed bats in Texas. Ecol. Monogr. 32:311–326.

Davis, W. B. 1942. The moles of Texas. Amer. Midland Nat. 27: 380–386.

Davis, W. B. 1974. The mammals of Texas. Bull., Texas Parks and Wildl. Dept. 41:1294.

Davis, W. B., and D. J. Schmidly. 1994. The mammals of Texas. Texas Parks and Wildl. Dept., Austin, 338 pp.

Davis, W. H., and R. W. Barbour. 1970. Life history data on some southwestern *Myotis*. Southwestern Nat. 15:261–263.

Deardon, L. C. 1969. Burrows of the pallid vole, *Lagurus curtatus*, in Alberta, Canada. Canadian Field-Nat. 83:282.

Dearing, M. D. 1996. Disparate determinants of summer and winter diet selection in a generalist herbivore, *Ochotona princeps*. Oecologia 108:467–478.

Dearing, M. D. 1997a. Effects of *Acomastylus rossii* tannins on a mammalian herbivore, the North American pika, *Ochotona princeps*. Oecologia 108:467–478.

Dearing, M. D. 1997b. The manipulation of plant toxins by a food-hoarding herbivore, *Ochotona princeps*. Ecology 78:774–781.

Dearing, M. D. 1997c. The function of haypiles of pikas (*Ochotona princeps*). J. Mamm. 78:1156–1163.

Dearing, M. D. 2001. Plant-herbivore interactions. Pp. 266–282, in Structure and function of an alpine ecosystem, Niwot Ridge, Colorado (W. D. Bowman and T. R. Seastedt, eds.). Oxford Univ. Press, New York, 337 pp.

Dearing, M. D., A. M. Mangione, W. H. Karasov, S. Morzunov, E. Otterson, and S. St. Jeor. 1998. Prevalence of hantavirus in four species of *Neotoma* from Arizona and Utah. J. Mamm. 79:1254–1259.

DeBaca, R. S., and J. R. Choate. 2002. Biogeography of heteromyid rodents on the Central Great Plains. Occas. Papers Mus., Texas Tech Univ. 212:1–22.

DeBlase, A. F., and R. E. Martin. 1981. A manual of mammalogy with keys to families of the world. Wm. C. Brown, Dubuque, 436 pp.

Deblinger, R. D., and A. W. Alldredge. 1991. Influence of free water on pronghorn distribution in sagebrush/steppe grassland. Wildl. Soc. Bull. 19:321–326.

DeByle, N. V., and R. P. Winokur, eds. 1985. Aspen: ecology and management in the western United States. General Tech. Rept., USDA Forest Service, RM-119:1–283.

DeCalesta, D. S. 1971. Colorado cottontail foods. Unpubl. master's thesis, Colorado State Univ., Fort Collins, 71 pp.

Decker, D. J. 1989. Why manage for wildlife: an overview of wildlife values. Pp. 1–13, in Timber management and its effects on wildlife (J. C. Finley and M. C. Brittingham, eds.). School of Forestry Resources and Penn State Coop. Extension, Penn State Univ., University Park, 269 pp.

Decker, D. J., and L. C. Chase. 1997. Human dimensions of living with wildlife—a management challenge for the 21st century. Wildl. Soc. Bull. 25:788–795.

Decker, D. J., and L. C. Chase. 2001. Stakeholder involvement: seeking solutions in changing times. Pp. 133–152, in Human dimensions of wildlife management in North America (D. J. Decker, T. L. Brown, and W. F. Siemer, eds.). The Wildlife Society, Bethesda, MD, 447 pp.

Decker, D. J., and G. R. Goff, eds. 1987. Valuing wildlife: economic and social perspectives. Westview Press, Boulder, 424 pp.

Decker, D. J., and K. G. Purdy. 1988. Toward a concept of wildlife acceptance capacity in wildlife management. Wildl. Soc. Bull. 16:53–57.

Deems, E. F., Jr., and D. Pursley. 1983. North American furbearers, a contemporary reference. Internat. Assoc. Fish and Wildl. Agencies, 223 pp.

Dekker, D., W. Bradford, and J. R. Gunson. 1995. Elk and wolves in Jasper National Park, Alberta, from historical times to 1992. Pp. 85–94, in Ecology and conservation of wolves in a changing world (L. N. Carbyn, S. H. Fritts, and D. R. Seip, eds.). Occas. Publ., Canadian Circumpolar Institute, Edmonton, Alberta 35:1–642.

Dell'Amore, C. 2009. Ancient camels butchered in Colorado, stone tools show? National Geographic News, February 27.

Demboski, J. R., and J. A. Cook. 2003. Phylogenetic diversification within the *Sorex cinereus* group (Soricidae). J. Mamm. 84:144–158.

Deming, O. V. 1952. Tooth development of the Nelson bighorn sheep. California Fish and Game 38:523–529.

Deming, O. V. 1977. The status and management of mountain goats in Colorado. Pp. 29–36, in Proceedings of the First International Mountain Goat Symposium (W. Samuel and W. G. MacGregor, eds.). Fish and Wildlife Branch, Victoria, British Columbia, 243 pp.

Demott, S. L., and G. P. Lindsey. 1975. Pygmy shrew, *Microsorex hoyi*, in Gunnison County, Colorado. Southwestern Nat. 20:417–418.

DeNatale, C. E., T. R. Burkot, B. S. Schneider, and N. S. Zeidner. 2002. Novel potential reservoirs for *Borrelia* sp. and the agent of human granulocytic ehrlichiosis in Colorado. J. Wildl. Dis. 38:478–482.

Dennis, B., and M.R.M. Otten. 2000. Joint effects of density dependence and rainfall on abundance of San Joaquin kit fox. J. Wildl. Mgmt. 54:388–400.

Denniston, R. H. 1956. Ecology, behavior and population dynamics of the Wyoming or Rocky Mountain moose, *Alces alces shirasi*. Zoologica 41:105–118.

Denniston, R. M., II. 1957. Notes on breeding and size of young in the Richardson's ground squirrel. J. Mamm. 38:414–416.

Denny, R. N. 1952. A summary of North American beaver management, 1946–1948. Current Rept., Colorado Game and Fish Dept. 28:1–58.

Denny, R. N. 1975. The status of lynx in Colorado. Colorado Division of Wildlife, Denver, 2 pp.

Denny, R. N. 1977. Status and management of mountain goats in Colorado. Pp. 29–36, in Proc. First International Mountain Goat Symposium (W. Samuel and W. G. MacGregor, eds.). Ministry of Recreation and Conservation, Victoria, British Columbia, 136 pp.

DePue, J. E. 2007. Limited gene flow among reintroduced river otter populations in Colorado: evidence from DNA collected with a novel method. Unpubl. master's thesis, Univ. Wyoming, 53 pp.

DePue, J. E., and M. Ben-David. 2007. Hair sampling techniques for river otters. J. Wildl. Mgmt. 71:671–674.

DePue, J. E., and M. Ben-David. 2010. River otter latrine site selection in arid habitats of western Colorado, USA. J. Wild. Mgmt. 74:1763–1767.

Derner, J. D., J. K. Detling, and M. F. Antolin. 2006. Are livestock weight gains affected by black-tailed prairie dogs? Frontiers Ecol. and Environ. 4:459–464.

Desha, P. G. 1966. Observations on the burrow utilization of thirteen-lined ground squirrels. Southwestern Nat. 11:408–410.

Desmond, M. J., J. A. Savidge, and K. M. Eskridge. 2000. Correlations between burrowing owl and black-tailed prairie dog declines: a 7-year analysis. J. Wildl. Mgmt. 54:1067–1075.

Detling, J. K. 1998. Mammalian herbivores: ecosystem-level effects in two grassland national parks. Wildl. Soc. Bull. 26:438–448.

Detling, J. K. 2006. Black-tailed prairie dog interactions with other herbivores: mediation via alterations of vegetation. Pp. 111–118, in Recovery of the black-footed ferret: progress and continuing challenges (J. E. Roelle, B. J. Miller, J. L. Godbey, and D. E. Biggins, eds.). U.S. Geological Survey, Sci. Invest, Rept. 2005-5293, 288 pp.

Devenport, J. A. 1989. Social influences on foraging in black-tailed prairie dogs. J. Mamm. 70:166–168.

Dewey, T. A. 2006. Systematics and phylogeography of North American *Myotis* (Chiroptera: Vespertilionidae). Unpubl. PhD dissert., Univ. Michigan, Ann Arbor, 746 pp.

Dice, L. R. 1943. The biotic provinces of North America. Univ. Michigan Press, Ann Arbor, 78 pp.

Dieni, J. S., F. G. Lindzey, T. Wooley, and S. H. Anderson. 1996. Swift fox investigations in Wyoming: annual report. Pp 53–63, in Annual report of the Swift Fox Conservation Team, 1996 (B. Luce, and F. Lindzey, eds.). Wyoming Game and Fish Department, Lander, 110 pp.

Diersing, V. E. 1980. Systematics and evolution of the pygmy shrews (subgenus *Microsorex*) of North America. J. Mamm. 51:76–101.

Diersing, V. E., and D. F. Hoffmeister. 1977. Revision of the shrew *Sorex merriami* and a description of a new species of the subgenus *Sorex*. J. Mamm. 58:321–333.

Dieter, C. D., and T. R. McCabe. 1989. Factors influencing beaver lodge-site selection on a prairie river. Amer. Midland Nat. 122:408–411.

Dietz, D. R., R. H. Udall, and L. E. Yeager. 1962. Chemical composition and digestibility by mule deer of selected forage species, Cache la Poudre Range, Colorado. Tech. Publ., Colorado Game and Fish Dept. 14:1–89.

Dion, N., K. A. Hobson, and S. Larivière. 2000. Interactive effects of vegetation and predators on the success of natural and simulated nests of grassland songbirds. Condor 102:629–634.

Dixon, J. 1931. Pikas versus weasel. J. Mamm. 12:72.

Dixon, K. R. 1982. Mountain lion. Pp. 711–727, in Wild mammals of North America, biology, management, and economics (J. A. Chapman and G. A. Feldhamer, eds.). Johns Hopkins Univ. Press, Baltimore, 1,147 pp.

Dixon, K. R., and R. J. Boyd. 1967. Evaluation of the effects of mountain lion predation. Job Completion Report, Project W-38-R-21. Colorado Game, Fish and Parks Department, Fort Collins, 23 pp.

Dobie, J. F. 1961. The voice of the coyote. Univ. Nebraska Press, Lincoln, 386 pp.

Dodd, N. L., J. S. States, and S. S. Rosenstock. 2003. Tassel-eared squirrel population, habitat condition, and dietary relationships in north-central Arizona. J. Wildl. Mgmt. 57:622–633.

Dodge, W. E. 1982. Porcupine. Pp. 355–366, in Wild mammals of North America: biology, management, and economics (J. A. Chapman and G. A. Feldhamer, eds.). Johns Hopkins Univ. Press, Baltimore, 1,147 pp.

Dolbeer, R. A. 1973. Reproduction in the red squirrel (*Tamiasciurus hudsonicus*) in Colorado. J. Mamm. 54:536–540.

Dolbeer, R. A., and W. R. Clark. 1975. Population ecology of snowshoe hares in the central Rocky Mountains. J. Wildl. Mgmt. 39:535–549.

Dolbeer, R.A., S. E. Wright, and E. C. Cleary. 2000. Ranking the hazard level of wildlife species to aviation. Wildl. Soc. Bull. 28:372–378.

Dominguez, S. R., T. J. O'Shea, L. M. Oko, and K. V. Holmes. 2007. Detection of group 1 coronaviruses in bats in North America. Emerging Infectious Dis. 13:1295–1300.

Donlan, J., H. W. Greene, J. Berger, C. E. Bock, J. H. Bock, D. A. Burney, J. A. Estes, D. Foreman, P. S. Martin, G. W. Roemer, F. A. Smith, and M. E. Soulé. 2005. Re-wilding North America. Nature 436:913–914.

Donoho, H. S. 1972. Dispersion and dispersal of white-tailed and black-tailed jackrabbits, Pawnee National Grasslands. Unpubl. master's thesis, Colorado State University, Fort Collins, 83 pp.

Donoho, H. S. 1977. The status and management of the bobcat in Colorado. Unpubl. report, Colorado Division of Wildlife, Denver, 6 pp.

Dorrance, M. J. 1965. Behavior of mule deer in the Cache la Poudre drainage. Unpubl. master's thesis, Colorado State University, Fort Collins, 76 pp.

Doty, J. B., and R. C. Dowler. 2006. Denning ecology in sympatric populations of skunks (*Spilogale gracilis* and *Mephitis mephitis*) in west-central Texas. J. Mamm. 87:131–138.

Douglas, C. L. 1967. New records of mammals from Mesa Verde National Park, Colorado. J. Mamm. 48:322–323.

Douglas, C. L. 1969a. Ecology of pocket gophers in Mesa Verde, Colorado. Pp. 147–175, in Contributions in mammalogy (J. K. Jones, Jr., ed.). Misc. Publ., Mus. Nat. Hist., Univ. Kansas 51: 428.

Douglas, C. L. 1969b. Comparative ecology of pinyon mice and deer mice in Mesa Verde National Park, Colorado. Misc. Publ., Mus. Nat. Hist., Univ. Kansas 18:421–504.

Douglas, C. L. 2001. Weather, disease, and bighorn lamb survival during 23 years in Canyonlands National Park. Wildl. Soc. Bull. 29:297–305.

Douglas, C. W., and M. A. Strickland. 1987. Fisher. Pp. 510–529, in Wild furbearer management and conservation in North America (M. Novak, J. A. Baker, M. E. Obbard, and B. Malloch, eds.). Ontario Ministry of Natural Resources, Toronto, 1,150 pp.

Douglass, R. J. 1976. Spatial interactions and microhabitat selections of two locally sympatric voles, *Microtus montanus* and *Microtus pennsylvanicus*. Ecology 57:346–352.

Dow, S. A., Jr., and P. L. Wright. 1962. Changes in mandibular dentition associated with age in pronghorn antelope. J. Wildl. Mgmt. 26:1–18.

Dowler, R. C., J. B. Doty, S. A. Neiswenter, J. B. Coffey, and C. E. Ebeling. 2005. Ecology of three species of skunks in west Texas with emphasis on developing management recommendations for the hog-nosed skunk. Final report to Texas Parks and Wildlife Department, Austin, TX.

Downhower, J. F., and K. B. Armitage. 1971. The yellow-bellied marmot and the evolution of polygamy. Amer. Nat. 105: 355–370.

Downhower, J. F., and E. R. Hall. 1966. The pocket gopher in Kansas. Misc. Publ., Univ. Kansas Mus. Nat. Hist. 44:1–32.

Doyle, A. T. 1990. Use of riparian and upland habitats by small mammals. J. Mamm. 71:14–23.

Dragoo, J. W., J. R. Choate, T. L. Yates, and T. P. O'Farrell. 1990. Evolutionary and taxonomic relationships among North American arid-land foxes. J. Mamm. 71:318–332.

Dragoo, J. W., and R. L. Honeycutt. 1997. Systematics of mustelid-like carnivores. J. Mamm. 78:426–443.

Dragoo, J. W., and R. L. Honeycutt, and D. J. Schmidly. 2003. Taxonomic status of white-backed hog-nosed skunks, genus *Conepatus* (Carnivora: Mephitidae). J. Mamm. 84:159–176.

Dragoo, J. W., J. A. Lackey, K. E. Moore, E. P. Lessa, J. A. Cook, and T. L. Yates. 2006. Phylogeography of the deer mouse (*Peromyscus maniculatus*) provides a predictive framework for research on hantaviruses. J. General Virology 87:1997–2003.

Dragoo, J. W., and S. R. Sheffield. 2009. *Conepatus leuconotus*. (Carnivora: Mephitidae). Mammalian Species 827:1–8.

Dragoo, J. W., and R. K. Wayne. 2003. Systematics and population genetics of swift and kit foxes. Pp. 207–221, in The swift fox: ecology and conservation of swift foxes in a changing world (M. A. Sovada and L. Carbyn, eds.). Canadian Plains Research Center, Regina, Saskatchewan, 250 pp.

Drennan, J. E., and P. Beier. 2003. Forest structure and prey abundance in winter habitat of northern goshawks. J. Wildl. Mgmt. 57:177–185.

Drennan, J. E., P. Beier, and N. L. Dodd. 1998. Use of track stations to index abundance of sciurids. J. Mamm. 79:352–359.

Drewek, J. R. 1970. Population characteristics and behavior of introduced bighorn sheep in Owyhee County, Idaho. Unpubl. master's thesis, Univ. Idaho, Moscow, 46 pp.

Drickamer, L. C., and M. R. Capone. 1977. Weather parameters, trappability and niche separation in two sympatric species of *Peromyscus*. Amer. Midland Nat. 98:376–381.

Driver, J. C., and J. R. Woiderskia. 2007. Interpretation of the "lagomorph index" in the American Southwest. Quaternary Internat. 185:3–11.

Druecker, J. D. 1972. Aspects of reproduction in *Myotis volans*, *Lasionycteris noctivagans*, and *Lasiurus cinereus*. Unpubl. doctoral dissert., Univ. New Mexico, Albuquerque, 68 pp.

Drummond, A. 1995. Enos Mills, citizen of nature. Univ. Press Colorado, Boulder, 433 pp.

Duchamp, J. E., E. B. Arnett, M. A. Larson, and R. K. Swihart. 2007. Ecological considerations for landscape level management of bats. Pp. 237–261, in Bats in forests, conservation and management (M. J. Lacki, J. P. Hayes, and A. Kurta, eds.). Johns Hopkins Univ. Press, Baltimore, 352 pp.

Duda, M. D., S. J. Bissell, and C. Young. 1998. Wildlife and the American mind. Responsive Management, Harrisonburg, VA, 804 pp.

Duda, M. D., M. E. Jones, and A. Criscione. 2010. The sportsman's voice, hunting and fishing in America. Venture Publishing, State College, PA, xxiii, 259 pp.

Duerbrouck, J., and D. Miller. 2001. Cat attacks: true stories and hard lessons from cougar country. Sasquatch Books, Seattle, 256 pp.

Duffield, J. W., C. J. Neher, and D. A. Patterson. 2008. Wolf recovery in Yellowstone park visitor attitudes, expenditures, and economic impacts. Yellowstone Sci. 16:20–25.

Duke, K. L. 1944. The breeding season of two species of *Dipodomys*. J. Mamm. 25:155–160.

Duke, K. L. 1951. The external genitalia of the pika, *Ochotona princeps*. J. Mamm. 32:169–173.

Dunford, C. 1974. Annual cycle of cliff chipmunks in the Santa Catalina Mountains, Arizona. J. Mamm. 55:401–415.

Dunford, C., and R. Davis. 1975. Cliff chipmunk vocalizations and their relevance to the taxonomy of coastal Sonoran chipmunks. J. Mamm. 56:207–212.

Dungan, J. D., and R. G. Wright. 2005. Summer diet composition of moose in Rocky Mountain National Park, Colorado. Alces 41:139–146.

Dunigan, P.F.X., Jr., W. Lei, and W. H. Rickard. 1980. Pocket mouse population response to winter precipitation and drought. Northwest Sci. 54:289–295.

Dunkel, T. 2008. Wild idea. Nature Conservancy 58(3):48–55.

Dunn, J. P., J. A. Chapman, and R. E. Marsh. 1982. Jackrabbits. Pp. 124–145, in Wild mammals of North America, biology, management, and economics (J. A. Chapman and G. A. Feldhamer, eds.). Johns Hopkins Univ. Press, Baltimore, 1,147 pp.

Duran, J. C. 1973. Field investigations and energy determination of stomach contents of *Peromyscus boylii* in the Granite Basin Area, Yavapai County, Arizona. Unpubl. doctoral dissert., Univ. Northern Colorado, Greeley, 62 pp.

Durish, N. D., K. E. Halcomb, C. W. Kilpatrick, and R. D. Bradley. 2004. Molecular systematics of the *Peromyscus truei* species group. J. Mamm. 85:1160–1169.

Durrant, S. D. 1952. Mammals of Utah: taxonomy and distribution. Univ. Kansas Publ., Mus. Nat. Hist. 5:1–549.

Duvall, A. C., and G. S. Schoonveld. 1988. Colorado moose: reintroduction and management. Alces 24:188–194.

Eads, D. A., and E. E. Biggins. 2008. Aboveground predation by an American badger (*Taxidea taxus*) on black-tailed prairie dogs (*Cynomys ludovicianus*). Western N. Amer. Nat. 58:396–401.

Eads, D. A., J. G. Chipaualt, D. E. Biggins, T. M. Livieri, and J. J. Millspaugh. 2010. Nighttime aboveground movements by prairie dogs on colonies inhabited by black-footed ferrets. Western N. Amer. Nat. 70:261–265.

Eagle, T. C., and J. S. Whitman. 1987. Mink. Pp. 613–624, in Wild furbearer management and conservation in North America (M. Novak, J. A. Baker, M.E. Obbard, and B. Malloch, eds.). Ontario Trappers Association, Toronto, 1,150 pp.

Earle, R. D., and K. R. Kramm. 1980. Techniques for age determination in the Canadian porcupine. J. Wildl. Mgmt. 44:413–419.

Easterla, D. A. 1973. Ecology of the 18 species of Chiroptera at Big Bend National Park, Texas. Northwest Missouri State Univ. Studies 34:1–165.

Easterla, D. A., and J. O. Whitaker, Jr. 1972. Food habits of some bats from Big Bend National Park, Texas. J. Mamm. 53:887–890.

Ebeling, C. E. 2006. Comparison of detection methods for three sympatric species of skunk. Unpubl. master's thesis, Angelo State Univ., San Angelo, TX, 56 pp.

Eberhardt, L. E., and A. B. Sargeant. 1977. Mink predation on prairie marshes during the waterfowl breeding season. Pp. 32–43, in The 1975 predator symposium (R. L. Phillips and C. Jonkel, eds.). Montana Forest Conservation Experiment Station, 68 pp.

Eberhardt, L. L., P. J. White, R. A. Garrott, and D. B. Houston. 2007. A seventy-year history of trends in Yellowstone's northern elk herd. J. Wildl. Mgmt. 71:594–602.

Eberle, J. J. 2003. Puercan mammalian systematics and biostratigraphy in the Denver Formation, Denver Basin, Colorado. Rocky Mountain Geol. 38:143–169.

Ecke, D. H., and C. W. Johnson. 1952. Plague in Colorado, Part I. Plague in Colorado and Texas. Public Health Monogr., U.S. Public Health Service 6:1–54.

EDAW. 2000. Black-tailed prairie dog study of eastern Colorado. Executive Director's Office, Colorado Department of Natural Resources, 31 pp.

Edelman, A. J., J. L. Koprowski, and S. R. Bertelsen. 2009. Potential for nest site competition between native and exotic tree squirrels. J. Mamm. 90:167–174.

Edelmann, F., and J. Copeland. 1999. Wolverine distribution in the northwestern United States and a survey in the Seven Devils Mountains of Idaho. Northwest Sci. 73:295–300.

Edwards, C. W., and R. D. Bradley. 2002. Molecular systematics and historical phylobiogeography of the *Neotoma mexicana* species group. J. Mamm. 83:20–30.

Edwards, C. W., C. F. Fulhorst, and R. D. Bradley. 2001. Molecular phylogeny of the *Neotoma albigula* species group: further evidence of a paraphyletic assemblage. J. Mamm. 82:267–279.

Edwards, J., M. Ford, and D. Guynn. 2003. Fox and gray squirrels, *Sciurus niger* and *S. carolinensis*. Pp. 248–275, in Wild mammals of North America, biology, management, and economics, second ed. (G. A. Feldhamer, B. C. Thompson, and J. A. Chapman, eds.). Johns Hopkins Univ. Press, Baltimore, 1,216 pp.

Egoscue, H. J. 1956. Preliminary studies of the kit fox in Utah. J. Mamm. 37:351–357.

Egoscue, H. J. 1957. The desert wood rat: a laboratory colony. J. Mamm. 38:472–481.

Egoscue, H. J. 1960. Laboratory and field studies of the northern grasshopper mouse. J. Mamm. 41:99–110.

Egoscue, H. J. 1962a. Ecology and life history of the kit fox in Tooele County, Utah. Ecology 43:481–497.

Egoscue, H. J. 1962b. The bushy-tailed wood rat: a laboratory colony. J. Mamm. 43:328–337.

Egoscue, H. J. 1964a. The kit fox in southwestern Colorado. Southwestern Nat. 9:40.

Egoscue, H. J. 1964b. Ecological notes and laboratory life history of the canyon mouse. J. Mamm. 45:387–396.

Egoscue, H. J. 1965. Population dynamics of the kit fox in western Utah. Bull. Southern California Acad. Sci. 74:122–127.

Egoscue, H. J. 1979. *Vulpes velox*. Mammalian Species 122:1–5.

Egoscue, H. J., J. G. Bittmenn, and J. A. Petrovich. 1970. Some fecundity and longevity records for captive small mammals. J. Mamm. 51:622–623.

Ehrenfeld, D. W. 1974. The conservation of non-resources. Amer. Scientist 64:648–656.

Ehrlich, P. R., D. E. Breedlove, P. F. Brussard, and M. A. Sharp. 1972. Weather and the "regulation" of subalpine populations. Ecology 53:243–247.

Eiler, K. C., and S. A. Banack. 2004. Variability in the alarm call of golden-mantled ground squirrels (*Spermophilus lateralis* and *S. saturatus*). J. Mamm. 85:43–50.

Eisen, R. J., R. E. Enscore, B. J. Bigerstaff, P. J. Reynolds, P. Ettestad, T. Brown, J. Pape, D. Tanda, C. E. Levy, D. M. Engelthaler, J. Cheek, R. Bueno, Jr., J. Targhetta, J. A. Montenieri, and K. I. Gage. 2007. Human plague in the southwestern United States, 1957–2004: spatial models of elevated risk of human exposure to *Yersinia pestis*. J. Med. Entomol. 44:530–537.

Eisenberg, J. F. 1962. Studies on the social behavior of heteromyid rodents. Unpubl. doctoral dissert., Univ. California, Berkeley, 225 pp.

Eisenberg, J. F. 1964. Studies on the behavior of *Sorex vagrans*. Amer. Midland Nat. 72:417–425.

Eisenberg, J. F. 1981. The mammalian radiations. Univ. Chicago Press, Chicago, 610 pp.

Eisenberg, J. F., and D. E. Isaac. 1963. The reproduction of heteromyid rodents in captivity. J. Mamm. 44:61–67.

Elbroch, M. 2003. Mammal tracks & signs, a guide to North American species. Stackpole Books, Mechanicsburg, PA, 779 pp.

Elbroch, M. 2006. Animal skulls, a guide to North American species. Stackpole Books, Mechanicsburg, PA, 727 pp.

Eldridge, D. J. 2004. Mounds of the American badger (*Taxidea taxus*): significant features of North American shrub-steppe ecosystems. J. Mamm. 85:1060–1067.

Elias, S. A. 1995. Packrat middens, archives of desert biotic history. Encyclopedia of Environmental Biology 3:19–35.

Elias, S. A. 1996. The ice-age history of national parks in the Rocky Mountains. Smithsonian Institution Press, Washington, 150 pp.

Elias, S. A. 2001. Paleoecology and Late Quaternary environments of the Colorado Rockies. Pp. 285–303, in Structure and function of an alpine ecosystem, Niwot Ridge, Colorado (W. D. Bowman and T. R. Seastedt, eds.). Oxford Univ. Press, New York, 337 pp.

Elias, S. A. 2002. Rocky Mountains. Smithsonian Institution Press, Washington, DC, 164 pp.

Elias, S. A., and J. C. Halfpenny. 1991. Fox scat evidence of heavy predation on beetles on the alpine tundra, Front Range, Colorado. Coleopterists Bull. 45:189–190.

Elias, S. A., S. K. Short, and P. U. Clark. 1986. Paleoenvironmental interpretations of the late Holocene, Rocky Mountain National Park, Colorado. USA Rev. Paleobiol. 5:127–142.

Eliason, S. L. 2001. Structural foundations, triggering events, and ballot initiatives: the case of Proposition 5. Wildl. Soc. Bull. 29:207–210.

Ellerman, J. R. 1940. The families and genera of living rodents, Vol. I. British Museum (Natural History), London, 689 pp.

Ellinwood, S. R. 1978. A survey of bats of southeast Colorado. Unpubl. master's thesis, Univ. Northern Colorado, Greeley, 77 pp.

Elliott, P. F. 1988. Foraging behavior of a central-place forager: field tests of theoretical predictions. Amer. Nat. 131:159–174.

Ellis, R. J. 1964. Tracking raccoons by radio. J. Wildl. Mgmt. 28: 363–368.

Ellison, L. 1946. The pocket gopher in relation to soil erosion on mountain range. Ecology 27:101–114.

Ellison, L., and C. M. Aldous. 1952. Influence of pocket gophers on vegetation of subalpine grassland in central Utah. Ecology 33:177–186.

Ellison, L. E. 2008. Summary and Analysis of the U.S. Government Bat Banding Program. USGS Open-File Report 2008-1363, 117 pp.

Ellison, L. E., T. J. O'Shea, M. A. Bogan, A. L. Everette, and D. M. Schneider. 2003. Existing data on colonies of bats in the United States: summary and analysis of the U.S. Geological Survey's Bat Population Database. Pp. 127–237, in Monitoring trends in bat populations in the United States and territories: problems and prospects (T. J. O'Shea and M. A. Bogan, eds.). Information and Tech. Rept., USGS/BRD/ITR-2003-003, 274 pp.

Ellison, L. E., T. J. O'Shea, D. J. Neubaum, and R. A. Bowen. 2007. Factors influencing movement probabilities of big brown bats (*Eptesicus fuscus*) in buildings. Ecol. Applications 17:620–627.

Ellison, L. E., T. J. O'Shea, J. Wimsatt, R. D. Pearce, D. J. Neubaum, M. A. Neubaum, and R. A. Bowen. 2006. Sampling blood from big brown bats (*Eptesicus fuscus*) in the field with and without anesthesia: impacts on survival. J. Wildl. Dis. 42:849–852.

Ellison, L. E., and C. van Riper, III. 1998. A comparison of small-mammal communities in a desert riparian floodplain. J. Mamm. 79:972–985.

Ellison, L. E., M. B. Wunder, C. A. Jones, C. Mosch, K. W. Navo, K. Peckham, J. E. Burghardt, J. Annear, R. West, J. Siemers, R. A. Adams, and E. Brekke. 2003. Colorado bat conservation plan. Colorado Committee of the Western Bat Working Group, 107 pp. http://www.wbwg.org/colorado/colorado.htm.

Ellsworth, E., and T. D. Reynolds. 2006. Snowshoe hare (*Lepus americanus*): a technical conservation assessment. Species Conservation Project, Rocky Mountain Region, USDA Forest Service, 64 pp.

Elrod, D. A., E. G. Zimmerman, P. D. Sudman, and G. A. Heidt. 2000. A new subspecies of pocket gopher (genus *Geomys*) from the Ozark Mountains of Arkansas with comments on its historical biogeography. J. Mamm. 81:852–864.

Emlen, D. J. 2008. The evolution of animal weapons. Ann. Rev. Ecol., Evol., Syst. 39:387–413.

Emslie, S. D. 1986. Late Pleistocene vertebrates from Gunnison County, Colorado. J. Paleo. 50:170–176.

Emslie, S. D. 2002. Fossil shrews (Insectivora: Soricidae) from the Late Pleistocene of Colorado. Southwestern Nat. 47:62–69.

Emslie, S. D., M. Stiger, and E. Wambach. 2005. Packrat middens and Late Holocene environmental change in southwestern Colorado. Southwestern Nat. 50:209–215.

Enders, A. C. 1966. The reproductive cycle of the nine-banded armadillo (*Dasypus novemcinctus*). Pp. 295–310, in Comparative biology of reproduction in mammals (I. W. Rowlands, ed.). Academic Press, London, 559 pp.

Enders, R. K. 1952. Reproduction in the mink (*Mustela vison*). Proc. Amer. Phil. Soc. 96:691–755.

Environmental Protection Agency. 1997. Climate change and Colorado. EPA 230-F-97-0081:1–4. www.epa.gov/globalwarming impacts.

Erb, J., and H. R. Perry, Jr. 2003. Muskrats, *Ondatra zibethicus* and *Neofiber alleni*. Pp. 311–348, in Wild mammals of North America, biology, management, and economics (G. A. Feldhamer, B. C. Thompson, and J. A. Chapman, eds.). Johns Hopkins Univ. Press, Baltimore, 1,216 pp.

LITERATURE CITED

Erickson, K. A., and A. W. Smith. 1985. Atlas of Colorado. Colorado Associated Univ. Press, Boulder, 73 pp.

Erlinge, S. 1979. Adaptive significance of sexual dimorphism in weasels. Oikos 33:233–245.

Errington, P. L. 1940. Natural restocking of muskrat-vacant habitat. J. Wildl. Mgmt. 4:173–185.

Errington, P. L. 1943. An analysis of mink predation upon muskrats in north-central United States. Research Bull., Agric. Exp. Sta., Iowa State Coll. 320:798–924.

Errington, P. L. 1963. Muskrat populations. Iowa State Univ. Press, Ames, 665 pp.

Erwin, D. H. 2006. Extinction, how life nearly ended 250 million years ago. Princeton Univ. Press, Princeton, NJ, 296 pp.

Esch, G. W., R. G. Beidleman, and L. E. Long. 1959. Early breeding of the black-tailed jack rabbit in southeastern Colorado. J. Mamm. 40:442–443.

Etchberger, L. L., W. E. Stroh, B. D. Bibles, M. R. Dzialak, and R. C. Etchberger. 2006. Fleas and small mammal hosts within and adjacent to the Coyote Basin white-tailed prairie dog colony in northeastern Utah. Pp. 281–283, in Recovery of the black-footed ferret: progress and continuing challenges (J. E. Roelle, B. J. Miller, J. L. Godbey, and D. E. Biggins, eds.). Sci. Investigations Rept., USGS, 2005-5293, 288 pp.

Etling, K. 2004. Cougar attacks, encounters of the worst kind. Lyons Press, Guilford, CT, xxiv + 204 pp.

Eussen, J. T. 1999. Food habits of the kit fox (*Vulpes macrotis*) and swift fox (*Vulpes velox*) in Colorado. Unpubl. master's thesis, Univ. Northern Colorado, Greeley, 64 pp.

Evans, S. B., L. D. Mech, P. J. White, and G. A. Sargeant. 2006. Survival of adult female elk in Yellowstone following wolf restoration. J. Wildl. Mgmt. 70:1372–1378.

Everette, A. L., T. J. O'Shea, L. E. Ellison, L. A. Stone, and J. L. McCance. 2001. Bat use of a high-plains urban wildlife refuge. Wildl. Soc. Bull. 29:967–973.

Ewer, R. F. 1973. The carnivores. Cornell Univ. Press, Ithaca, 494 pp.

Facka, A. N., P. L. Ford, and G. W. Roemer. 2008. A novel approach for assessing density and range-wide abundance of prairie dogs. J. Mamm. 89:356–364.

Fagerstone, K. A. 1979. Food habits of the black-tailed prairie dog (*Cynomys ludovicianus*). Unpubl. master's thesis, Univ. Colorado, Boulder, 160 pp.

Fagerstone, K. A. 1982. Ethology and taxonomy of Richardson's ground squirrel (*Spermophilus richardsonii*). Unpubl. doctoral dissert., Univ. Colorado, Boulder, 298 pp.

Fagerstone, K. A. 1987a. Comparison of vocalizations between and within *Spermophilus elegans elegans* and *S. richardsoni*. J. Mamm. 58:853–857.

Fagerstone, K. A. 1987b. Black-footed ferret, long-tailed weasel, short-tailed weasel, and least weasel. Pp. 548–573, in Wild furbearer management and conservation in North America (M. Novak, J. A. Baker, M. E. Obbard, and B. Malloch, eds.). Ontario Trappers Association, Toronto, 1,150 pp.

Fagerstone, K. A. 1988. The annual cycle of Wyoming ground squirrels in Colorado. J. Mamm. 59:678–687.

Fagerstone, K. A., G. K. Lavoie, and R. E. Griffith, Jr. 1980. Black-tailed jackrabbit diet and density on rangeland and near agricultural crops. J. Range Mgmt. 33:229–233.

Fagerstone, K. A., and C. A. Ramey. 1996. Rodents and lagomorphs. Pp. 83–132, in Rangeland wildlife (P. R. Krausman, ed.). Soc. Range Mgmt., Denver, 440 pp.

Fairbanks, W. S. 1993. Birthdate, birthweight, and survival in pronghorn fawns. J. Mamm. 74:129–135.

Faith, J. T., and T. A. Surovell. 2009. Synchronous extinction of North America's Pleistocene mammals. Proc. Acad. Nat. Sci. 106:20641–20645.

Falck, M. 1996. Small mammal population dynamics in riparian zones of regulated versus unregulated rivers in northwestern Colorado. Unpubl. master's thesis. Colorado State Univ., Fort Collins, 67 pp.

Falck, M., K. R. Wilson, and D. C. Andersen. 2003. Small mammals within riparian habitats of a regulated and unregulated arid-land river. Western N. Amer. Nat. 53:35–42.

Falkenberg, J. C., and J. A. Clarke. 1998. Microhabitat use of deer mice: effects of interspecific interaction risks. J. Mamm. 79:558–565.

Fannin, J. W., and A. F. Fannin. 1982. The complete unabridged armadillo handbook. Eakin Press, Burnet, TX, 45 pp.

Farentinos, R. C. 1972a. Observations on the ecology of the tassel-eared squirrel. J. Wildl. Mgmt. 36:1234–1239.

Farentinos, R. C. 1972b. Social dominance and mating activity in the tassel-eared squirrel (*Sciurus aberti ferreus*). Animal Behav. 20:316–326.

Farentinos, R. C. 1972c. Nests of the tassel-eared squirrel. J. Mamm. 53:900–903.

Farentinos, R. C. 1974. Social communication of the tassel-eared squirrel (*Sciurus aberti*): a descriptive analysis. Zeitschrift für Tierpsychologie 34:441–458.

Farentinos, R. C. 1979. Seasonal changes in home range size of tassel-eared squirrels (*Sciurus aberti*). Southwestern Nat. 24: 49–62.

Farentinos, R. C. 1980. Sexual solicitation of subordinate males by female tassel-eared squirrels (*Sciurus aberti*). J. Mamm. 51:337–341.

FAUNMAP Working Group. 1996. Spatial response of mammals to Late Quaternary environmental fluctuations. Science 272:1601–1606.

Fedriani, J. M., T. K. Fuller, R. M. Sauvajot, and E. C. York. 2000. Competition and intraguild predation among three sympatric carnivores. Oecologia 125:258–270.

Feighny, J. A., K. E. Williamson, and J. A. Clarke. 2006. North American elk bugle vocalizations: male and female bugle call structure and context. J. Mamm. 87:1072–1077.

Feldhamer, G. A. 1979. Vegetative and edaphic factors influencing abundance and distribution of small mammals in southeast Oregon. Great Basin Nat. 39:207–218.

Feldhamer, G. A., L. C. Drickamer, S. H. Vessey, J. F. Merritt, and C. Krajewski. 2007. Mammalogy: adaptation, diversity, ecology, third ed. Johns Hopkins Univ. Press, Baltimore, 643 pp.

Feldhamer, G. A., R. S. Klann, A. S. Gerard, and A. C. Driskell. 1993. Habitat partitioning, body size, and timing of parturition in pygmy shrews and associated soricids. J. Mamm. 74:403–411.

Feldhamer, G. A., B. C. Thompson, and J. A. Chapman, eds. 2003. Wild mammals of North America, biology, management, and conservation. Johns Hopkins Univ. Press, Baltimore, 1,368 pp.

Fenneman, N. M. 1931. Physiography of western United States. McGraw-Hill, New York, 534 pp.

Fenton, M. B. 1983. Just bats. Univ. Toronto Press, Toronto, 165 pp.

Fenton, M. B. 1985. Communication in the Chiroptera. Indiana Univ. Press, Bloomington, 161 pp.

Fenton, M. B., and R.M.R. Barclay. 1980. *Myotis lucifugus*. Mammalian Species 142:1–8.

Fenton, M. B., and G. P. Bell. 1979. Echolocation and feeding in four species of *Myotis* (Chiroptera). Canadian J. Zool. 57:1271–1277.

Fenton, M. B., and G. P. Bell. 1981. Recognition of species of insectivorous bats by their echolocation calls. J. Mamm. 52: 233–243.

Fenton, M. B., and D. R. Griffin. 1997. High altitude pursuit of insects by echolocating bats. J. Mamm. 78:247–250.

Fenton, M. B., P. Racey, and J.M.V. Rayner, eds. 1987. Recent advances in the study of bats. Cambridge Univ. Press, Cambridge, UK, 470 pp.

Fenton, M. B., C. G. van Zyll de Jong, G. P. Bell, D. B. Campbell, and M. Laplante. 1980. Distribution, parturition dates, and feeding of bats in south-central British Columbia. Canadian Field-Nat. 94:416–420.

Ferguson, M.A.D., and H. G. Merriam. 1978. A winter feeding relationship between snowshoe hares and porcupines. J. Mamm. 59:878–880.

Ferguson, S. H., and S. Larivière. 2002. Can comparing life histories help conserve carnivores? Animal Conserv. 5:1–12.

Ferguson, S. H., and S. Larivière. 2004. Are long penis bones an adaptation to high latitude snowy environments? Oikos 105:255–267.

Ferguson, S. H., J. A. Virgl, and S. Larivière. 1996. Evolution of delayed implantation and associated grade shifts in life history traits of North American carnivores. Ecoscience 3:7–17.

Ferner, J. W. 1974. Habitat relationships of *Tamiasciurus hudsonicus* and *Sciurus aberti* in the Rocky Mountains. Southwestern Nat. 18:470–472.

Ferrell, C. S. 1995. Systematics and biogeography of the Great Basin pocket mouse, *Perognathus parvus*. Unpubl. master's thesis, Univ. Nevada–Las Vegas, 68 pp.

Festa-Bianchet, M., and S. D. Côté. 2008. Mountain goats: ecology, behavior, and conservation of an alpine ungulate. Island Press, Washington, DC, xii + 265 pp.

Feuerstein, V., R. L. Schmidt, C. P. Hibler, and W. H. Rutherford. 1980. Bighorn sheep mortality in the Taylor River–Almont Triangle area, 1978–1979:a case study. Special Rept., Colorado Division of Wildlife 48:1–19.

Field, R. J., and G. Feltner. 1974. Wolverine. Colorado Outdoors 23:1–6.

Finch, D. M., and L. F. Ruggiero. 1993. Wildlife habitats and biological diversity in the Rocky Mountains and Northern Great Plains. Nat. Areas J. 13:191–203.

Findlay, W. R. 1992. Ecological aspects and dietary habits of river otter in northeastern Utah. Unpubl. master's thesis, Brigham Young Univ., Provo, 80 pp.

Findley, J. S. 1955. Speciation of the wandering shrew. Univ. Kansas Publ., Mus. Nat. Hist. 9:1–68.

Findley, J. S. 1956. Comments on the winter food of red foxes in eastern South Dakota. J. Wildl. Mgmt. 20:216–217.

Findley, J. S. 1967. Insectivores and dermopterans. Pp. 87–103, in Recent mammals of the world (S. Anderson and J. K. Jones, Jr., eds.). Ronald Press Co., New York, 453 pp.

Findley, J. S. 1972. Phenetic relationships among bats of the genus *Myotis*. Syst. Zool. 21:31–52.

Findley, J. S. 1987. The natural history of New Mexican mammals. Univ. New Mexico Press, Albuquerque, 164 pp.

Findley, J. S. 1989. Morphological patterns in rodent communities of southwestern North America. Pp. 253–263, in Patterns in the structure of mammalian communities (D. W. Morris, Z. Abramsky, B. J. Fox, and M. R. Willig, eds.). Spec. Publ. Mus., Texas Tech Univ. 28:1–266.

Findley, J. S. 1993. Bats, a community perspective. Cambridge Univ. Press, New York, 167 pp.

Findley, J. S., and S. Anderson. 1956. Zoogeography of montane mammals of Colorado. J. Mamm. 37:80–82.

Findley, J. S., A. H. Harris, D. E. Wilson, and C. Jones. 1975. Mammals of New Mexico. Univ. New Mexico Press, Albuquerque, 360 pp.

Findley, J. S., and C. Jones. 1964. Seasonal distribution of the hoary bat. J. Mamm. 45:461–470.

Findley, J. S., and C. Jones. 1967. Taxonomic relationships of bats of the species *Myotis fortidens*, *M. lucifugus*, and *M. occultus*. J. Mammal. 48:429–444.

Finley, D. J. 1999. Distribution of the swift fox (*Vulpes velox*) on the eastern plains of Colorado. Unpubl. master's thesis, Univ. Northern Colorado, Greeley, 96 pp.

Finley, D. J., G. C. White, and J. P. Fitzgerald. 2005. Estimation of swift fox population size and occupancy rates in eastern Colorado. J. Wildl. Mgmt. 59:861–873.

Finley, R. B., Jr. 1954. *Notiosorex crawfordi* and *Antrozous pallidus* from southeastern Colorado. J. Mamm. 35:110–111.

Finley, R. B., Jr. 1958. The woodrats of Colorado: distribution and ecology. Univ. Kansas Publ., Mus. Nat. Hist. 10:213–552.

Finley, R. B., Jr. 1959. Observation of nocturnal animals by red light. J. Mamm. 40:591–594.

Finley, R. B., Jr. 1969. Cone caches and middens of *Tamiasciurus* in the Rocky Mountain region. Misc. Publ., Univ. Kansas Mus. Nat. Hist. 51:233–273.

Finley, R. B., Jr. 1990. Woodrat ecology and behavior and the interpretation of paleomiddens. Pp. 28–42, in Packrat middens, the last 40,000 years of biotic change (J. L. Betancourt,

T. R. Van Devender, and P. S. Martin, eds.). Univ. Arizona Press, Tucson, 467 pp.

Finley, R. B., Jr. 1995. The spread of raccoon (*Procyon lotor hirtus*) into the Colorado Plateau from the Northern Great Plains. Proc. Denver Mus. Nat. Hist. 3:1–6.

Finley, R. B., Jr., and M. A. Bogan. 1995. New records of terrestrial mammals in northwestern Colorado. Proc. Denver Mus. Nat. Hist. 3(10):1–6.

Finley, R. B., Jr., W. Caire, and D. E. Wilhelm. 1983. Bats of the Colorado oil shale region. Great Basin Nat. 43:554–560.

Finley, R. B., Jr., J. R. Choate, and D. F. Hoffmeister. 1986. Distributions and habitats of voles in southeastern Colorado and northeastern New Mexico. Southwestern Nat. 31:263–266.

Finley, R. B., Jr., and J. Creasy. 1982. First specimen of the spotted bat (*Euderma maculatum*) from Colorado. Great Basin Nat. 42:360.

Finley, R. B., Jr., D. E. Wilhelm, Jr., and W. Caire. 1976. Mammals of the Colorado oil shale region. Annual Progress Report, National Fish and Wildlife Laboratory, U.S. Fish and Wildlife Service, Fort Collins, 49 pp.

Finney, B. A. 1962. Re-examination of small mammal populations in Moon Gulch, Gilpin County, Colorado. J. Colorado-Wyoming Acad. Sci. 5(3):42.

Fitch, H. S., P. Goodrum, and C. Newman. 1952. The armadillo in the southeastern U.S. J. Mamm. 33:21–37.

Fitch, H. S., and D. G. Rainey. 1956. Ecological observations on the woodrat, *Neotoma floridana*. Univ. Kansas Publ., Mus. Nat. Hist. 8:499–533.

Fitch, H. S., and L. L. Sandidge. 1953. Ecology of the opossum on a natural area in northeastern Kansas. Univ. Kansas Publ., Mus. Nat. Hist. 7:305–338.

Fitch, H. S., and H. W. Shirer. 1970. A radiotelemetric study of spatial relationships in the opossum. Amer. Midland Nat. 84: 170–186.

Fitzgerald, B. M. 1977. Weasel predation on a cyclic population of the montane vole (*Microtus montanus*) in California. J. Animal Ecol. 46:367–397.

Fitzgerald, B. M., and D. C. Turner. 1988. Hunting behaviour of domestic cats and their impact on prey populations. Pp. 151–176, in The domestic cat: the biology of its behavior, second ed. (D. C. Turner and P. Bateson, eds.). Cambridge Univ. Press, Cambridge, UK, 244 pp.

Fitzgerald, D., and L. Hasseltrom. 1998. Bison, monarch of the plains. Graphic Arts Center Publishing, Portland, OR, 127 pp.

Fitzgerald, J. P. 1970. The ecology of plague in prairie dogs and associated small mammals in South Park, Colorado. Unpubl. doctoral dissert., Colorado State Univ., Fort Collins, 123 pp.

Fitzgerald, J. P. 1978. Vertebrate associations along the South Platte River in northeastern Colorado. Pp. 73–88, in Lowland river and stream habitat in Colorado: a symposium (W. D. Graul and S. Bissell, eds.). Colorado Chapter, Wildlife Soc., and Colorado Audubon, 195 pp.

Fitzgerald, J. P. 1993a. The ecology of plague in Gunnison's prairie dogs and suggestions for the recovery of black-footed ferrets. Pp. 50–59, in Proc. Symposium on the Management of Prairie Dog Complexes for the Reintroduction of Black-footed Ferrets (J. L. Oldemeyer, D. E. Biggins, B. J. Miller, and R. Crete, eds.). Biol. Rept., U.S. Fish and Wildlife Service 93:1–95.

Fitzgerald, J. P. 1993b. Furbearer management analysis: a report submitted to the Department of Natural Resources, Colorado Division of Wildlife, Denver, 115 pp.

Fitzgerald, J. P. 1996. Final report—status and distribution of the kit fox (*Vulpes macrotis*) in western Colorado. Job Progress Report, Colorado Division of Wildlife, Project W-153-R-7, 79 pp.

Fitzgerald, J. P., and R. R. Lechleitner. 1969. Sylvatic plague in Gunnison's prairie dogs and associated mammals in South Park, Colorado. J. Colorado-Wyoming Acad. Sci. 7:45.

Fitzgerald, J. P., and R. R. Lechleitner. 1974. Observations on the biology of Gunnison's prairie dog in central Colorado. Amer. Midland Nat. 92:146–163.

Fitzgerald, J. P., C. A. Meaney, and D. M. Armstrong. 1994. Mammals of Colorado. Denver Museum of Natural History and Univ. Press Colorado, Niwot, 467 pp.

Fitzgerald, J. P., D. Taylor, and M. Prendergast. 1989. New records of bats from northeastern Colorado. J. Colorado-Wyoming Acad. Sci. 21:22.

Fitzpatrick, F. L. 1925. The ecology and economic status of *Citellus tridecemlineatus*. Stud. Nat. Hist., Iowa State Univ. 11:1–40.

Flader, S. L. 1974. Thinking like a mountain, Aldo Leopold and the evolution of an ecological attitude toward deer, wolves, and forests. Univ. Wisconsin Press, Madison, 284 pp.

Flaherty, M., and R. Plakke. 1986. Response of the swift fox, *Vulpes velox*, to water stress. J. Colorado-Wyoming Acad. Sci. 18:51.

Flake, L. D. 1973. Food habits of four species of rodents on a short-grass prairie in Colorado. J. Mamm. 54:636–647.

Flake, L. D. 1974. Reproduction of four rodent species in a short-grass prairie of Colorado. J. Mamm. 55:213–216.

Flannery, T. 2001. The eternal frontier, an ecological history of North America and its peoples. Atlantic Monthly Press, New York.

Flather, C. H., L. A. Joyce, and C. A. Bloomgarden. 1994. General Technical Report, Rocky Mountain Forest and Range Experiment Station, Forest Service, USDA, RM-241:1–42.

Fleharty, E. D. 1995. Wild animals and settlers on the Great Plains. Univ. Oklahoma Press, Norman, 316 pp.

Fleharty, E. D., and J. R. Choate. 1973. Bioenergetic strategies of the cotton rat, *Sigmodon hispidus*. J. Mamm. 54:680–692.

Fleharty, E. D., J. R. Choate, and M. A. Mares. 1972. Fluctuations in population density of the hispid cotton rat: factors influencing a "crash." Bull. Southern California Acad. Sci. 71:132–138.

Fleharty, E. D., M. E. Krause, and D. P. Stinnett. 1973. Body composition, energy content, and lipid cycles of four species of rodents. J. Mamm. 54:426–438.

Fleharty, E. D., and M. A. Mares. 1973. Habitat preference and spatial relations of *Sigmodon hispidus* on a remnant prairie in west-central Kansas. Southwestern Nat. 18:21–29.

Fleharty, E. D., and L. E. Olson. 1969. Summer food habits of *Microtus ochrogaster* and *Sigmodon hispidus*. J. Mamm. 50:475–486.

Flinders, J. T., and J. A. Chapman. 2003. Black-tailed jackrabbit. Pp. 126–146, in Wild mammals of North America, biology, management, and conservation, second ed. (G. A. Feldhamer, B. C. Thompson, and J. A. Chapman, eds.). Johns Hopkins Univ. Press, Baltimore, 1,216 pp.

Flinders, J. T., and R. M. Hansen. 1972. Diets and habitats of jackrabbits in northeastern Colorado. Sci. Ser., Range Sci. Dept., Colorado State Univ. 12:1–29.

Flinders, J. T., and R. M. Hansen. 1973. Abundance and dispersion of leporids within a shortgrass ecosystem. J. Mamm. 54:287–291.

Flinders, J. T., and R. M. Hansen. 1975. Spring population responses of cottontails and jackrabbits to cattle grazing shortgrass prairie. J. Range Mgmt. 28:290–293.

Flook, P. R. 1970. Causes and implications of an observed sex differential in the survival of wapiti. Rept. Ser., Canadian Wildl. Serv. 11:1–71.

Florant, G. L., and M.R.C. Greenwood. 1986. Seasonal variation in pancreatic function in marmots: the role of pancreatic hormones and lipoprotein in fat deposition. Pp. 273–281 in Physiological and biochemical adaptations (H. C. Heller, X. J. Musacchia, and L.C.H. Wang, eds.). Elsevier Science, New York, 587 pp.

Florant, G. L., H. Porst, A. Peiffer, S. F. Hudachek, C. Pittman, S. A. Summers, M. W. Rajala, and P. E. Scherer. 2004. Fat-cell mass, serum leptin and adiponectin changes during weight gain and loss in yellow-bellied marmots (*Marmota flaviventris*). J. Comp. Physiol. B. 174:633–639.

Floyd, M. L., D. D. Hanna, W. H. Romme, and M. Colyer, eds. 2003. Ancient piñon-juniper woodlands, a natural history of Mesa Verde Country. Univ. Press Colorado, Boulder, 389 pp.

Flyger, V. F., and J. E. Gates. 1982. Pine squirrels: *Tamiasciurus hudsonicus* and *T. douglassi*. Pp. 230–238, in Wild mammals of North America, biology, management, and economics (J. A. Chapman and G. A. Feldhamer, eds.). Johns Hopkins Univ. Press, Baltimore, 1,147 pp.

Flyger, V. F., and E. Y. Levin. 1977. Congenital erythropoietic porphyria: normal porphyria of fox squirrels (*Sciurus niger*). Amer. J. Pathol. 87:269–272.

Flynn, J. J., M. A. Nedbal, J. W. Dragoo, and R. L. Honeycutt. 2000. Whence the red panda? Molec. Phylogenetics Evol. 17:190–199.

Flynn, J. J., and G. D. Wesley-Hunt. 2005. Carnivora. Pp. 175–214, in The rise of placental mammals, origins and relationships of the major extant clades (K. D. Rose and J. D. Archibald, eds.). Johns Hopkins Univ. Press, Baltimore, 259 pp.

Forbes, R. B. 1961. Notes on food of silky pocket mice. J. Mamm. 43:278–279.

Forbes, R. B. 1964. Some aspects of the life history of the silky pocket mouse *Perognathus flavus*. Amer. Midland Nat. 72:438–443.

Forbes, R. B. 1997. Subnivean foraging by Abert's squirrels. Spec. Publ., Mus. Southwestern Biol., Univ. New Mexico 3:287–290.

Foresman, K. R. 2001. The wild mammals of Montana. Spec. Publ., Amer. Soc. Mammal. 12:1–278.

Foresman, K. R., and R. A. Mead. 1973. Duration of post implantation in a western subspecies of the spotted skunk (*Spilogale putorius*). J. Mamm. 54:521–523.

Foresman, K. R., and D. E. Pearson. 1999. Activity patterns of American martens, *Martes americana*, snowshoe hares, *Lepus americanus*, and red squirrels, *Tamiasciurus hudsonicus*, in west-central Montana. Canadian Field-Nat. 113:386–389.

Formanowicz, D. R., Jr., P. J. Bradley, and E. D. Brodie, Jr. 1989. Food hoarding by the least shrew (*Cryptotis parva*): intersexual and prey type effects. Amer. Midland Nat. 122:26–33.

Forrest, S. C., D. E. Biggins, L. Richardson, T. W. Clark, T. M. Campbell, III, K. A. Fagerstone, and E. T. Thorne. 1988. Black-footed ferret (*Mustela nigripes*) population attributes at Meeteetse, Wyoming, 1981–1985. J. Mamm. 59:261–273.

Forrest, S. C., T. W. Clark, L. Richardson, D. Biggins, K. Fagerstone, and T. M. Campbell, III. 1985. Life history characteristics of the genus *Mustela*, with special reference to the black-footed ferret, *Mustela nigripes*. Pp. 23.1–23.14, in Black-footed ferret, workshop proceedings (S. H. Anderson and D. B. Inkley, eds.). Wyoming Game and Fish Dept., Laramie.

Forsyth, D. J. 1976. A field study of growth and development of nestling masked shrews (*Sorex cinereus*). J. Mamm. 57: 708–721.

Fortin, D., H. L. Beyer, M. S. Boyce, D. W. Smith, and T. Duchesne. 2005. Wolves influence elk movements: behavior shapes a trophic cascade in Yellowstone National Park. Ecology 86:1320–1330.

Fortin, D., M. Fortin, H. L. Beyer, T. Duschesne, S. Courant, and K. Dancome. 2009. Group-size-mediated habitat selection and group fusion-fission dynamics of bison under predation risk. Ecology 90:2480–2490.

Foster, C. N. 1976. What is a wolf? Colorado Outdoors 25(3): 40–41.

Foster, J. B. 1961. Life history of the *Phenacomys* vole. J. Mamm. 42:181–198.

Foster, M. A., and J. Stubbendieck. 1980. Effects of the plains pocket gopher (*Geomys bursarius*) on rangeland. J. Range Mgmt. 33:74–78.

Fox, J., S. Barthold, M. Davisson, C. Newcomer, F. Quimby, and A. Smith, eds. 2006. The muse in biomedical research. Academic Press, New York, 4 vols.

Fox, L. B., and C. C. Roy. 1995. Swift fox (*Vulpes velox*) management and research in Kansas: 1995. Pp. 39–47, in 1995 Report of the Swift Fox Conservation Team (S. H. Allen, J. W. Hoagland, and E. Dowd Stukel, eds.). North Dakota Game and Fish Dept., Bismarck, 170 pp.

Francis, C. M., E.L.P. Anthony, J. A. Brunton, and T. H. Kunz. 1994. Lactation in male fruit bats. Nature 367:691–692.

Franzen, J. L. 2009. The rise of horses, 55 million years of evolution. Johns Hopkins Univ. Press, Baltimore, 256 pp.

Franzen, R. W. 1968. The abundance, migration and management of mule deer in Dinosaur National Monument. Unpubl. master's thesis, Utah State Univ., Logan, 138 pp.

Franzmann, A. W. 1978. Moose. Pp. 67–82, in Big game of North America: ecology and management (J. L. Schmidt and D. L. Gilbert, eds.). Stackpole Books, Harrisburg, PA, 494 pp.

Franzmann, A. W. 1981. *Alces alces*. Mammalian Species 154:1–7.

Franzmann, A. W. 2000. Moose. Pp. 578–600, in Ecology and management of large mammals in North America (S. Demarais and P. R. Krausman, eds.). Prentice-Hall, Upper Saddle River, NJ, 778 pp.

Franzmann, A. W., and C. C. Schwartz. 1998. Ecology and management of the North American moose. Smithsonian Institution Press, Washington. 733 pp.

Franzmann, A. W., C. M. Schwartz, and R. E. McCabe, eds. 2007. Ecology and management of the North American moose, second ed. Univ. Press Colorado, Boulder, 776 pp.

Franzmann, A. W., C. C. Schwartz, and R. O. Peterson. 1980. Moose calf mortality in summer on the Kenai Peninsula. J. Wildl. Mgmt. 44:764–768.

Frase, B. A., and R. S. Hoffmann. 1980. *Marmota flaviventris*. Mammalian Species 135:1–8.

Frase, B. A., and W. E. Sera. 1993. Comparison between plant species in bushy-tailed woodrat middens and in the habitat. Great Basin Nat. 53:373–378.

Freddy, D. J. 1987. The White River elk herd: a perspective, 1960–85. Tech. Publ., Colorado Division of Wildlife 37:1–64.

Freddy, D. J. 2003. Estimating calf and adult survival rates and pregnancy rates of Gunnison Basin elk. Colorado Division of Wildlife Wildlife Research Report W-153-R-16, 71–132.

Freddy, D. J., G. C. White, M. C. Kneeland, R. H. Kahn, J. W. Unsworth, W. J. deVergie, V. K. Graham, J. H. Ellenberger, and C. H. Wagner. 2004. How many mule deer are there? Challenges of credibility in Colorado. Wildl. Soc. Bull. 32:916–927.

Frederiksen, J. K., and C. N. Slobodchikoff. 2007. Referential specificity in the alarm calls of the black-tailed prairie dog. Ethol., Ecol. and Evol. 19:87–99.

Freeman, G. E. 1981. Distributional records of bats of western Colorado. J. Colorado-Wyoming Acad. Sci. 13:50.

Freeman, G. E. 1984. Ecomorphological analysis of an assemblage of bats: resource partitioning and competition. Unpubl. doctoral dissert., Univ. Colorado, Boulder, 131 pp.

Freeman, G. E., and L. Wunder. 1988. Observations at a colony of the Brazilian free-tailed bat (*Tadarida brasiliensis*) in southern Colorado. Southwestern Nat. 33:102–103.

Freeman, P. W., J. D. Druecker, and S. Tvrz. 1993. *Sorex merriami* in Nebraska. Prairie Nat. 25:291–294.

Freeman, P. W., K. N. Geluso, and J. S. Altenbach. 1997. Nebraska's flying mammals. NEBRASKAland 75(6):38–45.

Freeman, P. W., and H. H. Genoways. 1998. Recent records of the nine-banded armadillo (Dasypodidae) in Nebraska. Southwestern Nat. 43:491–504.

French, N. R. 1971. Small mammal studies in the US/IBP Grassland Biome. Acta Zool. Fennici 8:438–53.

French, N. R., W. E. Grant, W. Grodzinski, and D. M. Swift. 1976. Small mammal energetics in grassland ecosystems. Ecol. Monogr. 46:201–220.

French, S. P., and M. G. French. 1990. Predatory behavior of grizzly bears feeding on elk calves in Yellowstone National Park, 1986–88. Internat. Conf. Bear Res. Mgmt. 8:335–341.

French, S. P., M. G. French, and R. R. Knight. 1994. Grizzly bear use of army cutworm moths in the Yellowstone Ecosystem. Internat. Conf. Bear Res. Mgmt. 9:389–399.

Frey, J. K. 1992. Response of a mammalian faunal element to climatic changes. J. Mamm. 73:43–50.

Frey, J. K. 2004. Taxonomy and distribution of the mammals of New Mexico: an annotated checklist. Occas. Papers, Mus. Texas Tech Univ. 240:1–32.

Frey, J. K. 2007. Morphology and genetics of the New Mexico meadow jumping mouse (*Zapus hudsonius luteus*). Progress Report, Conservation Services Division, New Mexico Dept. Game and Fish, Santa Fe, 15 pp.

Frey, J. K. 2009. Genetics of allopatric populations of the montane vole (*Microtus montanus*) and Mogollon vole (*Microtus mogollonensis*) in the American Southwest. Western N. Amer. Nat. 59:215–222.

Frey, J. K., and J. L. Malaney. 2006. Snowshoe hare (*Lepus americanus*) and mountain cottontail (*Sylvilagus nuttallii*) biogeography at their southern range limit. J. Mamm. 87:1175–1182.

Frey, J. K., and J. L. Malaney. 2009. Decline of the meadow jumping mouse (*Zapus hudsonius luteus*) in two mountain ranges in New Mexico. Southwestern Nat. 54:31–44.

Frey, J. K., and D. W. Moore. 1990. Nongeographic variation in the Mexican vole (*Microtus mexicanus*). Trans. Kansas Acad. Sci. 93:97–109.

Frey, J. K., J. J. Root, C. A. Jones, C. H. Calisher, and B. J. Beaty. 2002. New records of the Mogollon vole, *Microtus mogollonensis* (Mearns 1890), in southwestern Colorado. Western N. Amer. Nat. 52:120–123.

Frey, J. K., and Z. J. Schwenke. 2007. Mammals of Sugarite Canyon State Park, Colfax County, New Mexico. Final Report to New Mexico State Parks, 49 pp.

Frey, J. K., and T. L. Yates. 1996. Mammalian diversity in New Mexico. New Mexico J. Sci. 36:4–37.

Frey, S. N., and M. R. Conover. 2006. Habitat use by meso-predators in a corridor environment. J. Wildl. Mgmt. 70:1111–1118.

Friedrichsen, T. T. 1977. Responses of rodent populations to visitors in a national park. Unpubl. master's thesis, Colorado State Univ., Fort Collins, 98 pp.

Frison, G. C. 1998. Paleoindian large mammal hunters on the plains of North America. Proc. Nat. Acad. Sci. USA 95:14576–14583.

Fritzell, E. K. 1977. Dissolution of raccoon sibling bonds. J. Mamm. 58:427–428.

Fritzell, E. K. 1978a. Aspects of raccoon (*Procyon lotor*) social organization. Canadian J. Zool. 56:260–271.

Fritzell, E. K. 1978b. Habitat use by prairie raccoons during the waterfowl breeding season. J. Wildl. Mgmt. 42:118–127.

Fritzell, E. K. 1987. Gray fox and island gray fox. Pp. 408–420, in Wild furbearer management and conservation in North America (M. Novak, J. A. Baker, M. E. Obard, and B. Malloch, eds.). Ontario Trappers Association, Toronto, 1,150 pp.

Fritzell, E. K., and K. J. Haroldson. 1982. *Urocyon cinereoargenteus*. Mammalian Species 189:1–8.

Fujita, M. S., and T. H. Kunz. 1984. *Pipistrellus subflavus*. Mammalian Species 228:1–6.

Fuller, J. A., R. A. Garrott, P. J. White, K. E. Aune, T. J. Roffe, and J. C. Rhyan. 2007. Reproduction and survival of Yellowstone bison. J. Wildl. Mgmt. 71:2365–2372.

Fuller, T. K. 1978. Variable home range sizes of female gray foxes. J. Mamm. 59:446–449.

Fuller, W. A. 1959. The horns and teeth as indicators of age in bison. J. Wildl. Mgmt. 23:342–344.

Gage, K. L., R. S. Ostfeld, and J. G. Olson. 1995. Nonviral vector-born zoonoses associated with mammals in the United States. J. Mamm. 76:695–715.

Gaines, M. S. 1985. Genetics. Pp. 845–883, in Biology of New World *Microtus* (R. H. Tamarin, ed.). Spec. Publ., Amer. Soc. Mammalogists 8:1–893.

Gaines, M. S., and R. K. Rose. 1976. Population dynamics of *Microtus ochrogaster* in eastern Kansas. Ecology 57:1145–1161.

Gaines, M. S., N. C. Stenseth, M. L. Johnson, R. A. Ims, and S. Bondrup-Nielsen. A response to solving the enigma of population cycles with a multifactorial perspective. J. Mamm. 72:627–631.

Galatowitsch, S. M. 1990. Using the original land survey notes to reconstruct presettlement landscapes in the American West. Great Basin Nat. 50:181–191.

Galbreath, G. J. 1982. Armadillo. Pp. 71–79, in Wild mammals of North America, biology, management and economics (J. A. Chapman and G. A. Feldhamer, eds.). Johns Hopkins Univ. Press, Baltimore, 1,147 pp.

Galindo-Leal, C. 1997. Infestation of rock mice (*Peromyscus difficilis*) by botflies: ecological consequences of differences between sexes. J. Mamm. 78:900–907.

Galindo-Leal, C., and C. J. Krebs. 1998. Effects of food abundance on individuals and populations of the rock mouse (*Peromyscus difficilis*). J. Mamm. 79:1131–1142.

Gallie, J. A., and L. C. Drickamer. 2008. Ecological interactions between two ecosystem engineers: Gunnison's prairie dog and Botta's pocket gopher. Southwestern Nat. 53:51–60.

Gannon, W. L. 2003. Bats, Vespertilionidae, Molossidae, Phyllostomidae). Pp. 56–74, in Wild mammals of North America, biology, management, and economics, second ed. (G. A. Feldhamer, B. C. Thompson, and J. A. Chapman, eds.). Johns Hopkins Univ. Press, Baltimore, 1,216 pp.

Gannon, W. L., R. E. Sherwin, T. N. deCarvalho, and M. J. O'Farrell. 2000. Pinnae and echolocation call differences between *Myotis californicus* and *Myotis ciliolabrum* (Chiroptera: Vespertilionidae). Acta Chiropterol. 3:77–91.

Gannon, W. L., R. E. Sherwin, and S. Haymond. 2003. On the importance of articulating assumptions when conducting acoustic studies of habitat use by bats. Wildl. Soc. Bull. 31:45–61.

Gannon, W. L., R. S. Sikes, and Animal Care and Use Committee of the American Society of Mammalogists. 2007. Guidelines of the American Society of Mammalogists for the use of wild mammals in research. J. Mamm. 88:809–823.

Ganskopp, D., B. Myers, and S. Lambert. 1993. Black-tailed jackrabbit preferences for eight forages used for reclamation of Great Basin rangelands. Northwest Sci. 57:246–250.

Gardner, A. L. 1982. Virginia opossum. Pp. 3–36, in Wild mammals of North America, biology, management, and economics (J. A. Chapman and G. A. Feldhamer, eds.). Johns Hopkins Univ. Press, Baltimore, 1,147 pp.

Gardner, A. L. 2005a. Order Cingulata. Pp. 94–99 in Mammal species of the world, a taxonomic and geographic references (D. E. Wilson and D. M. Reeder, eds.). Johns Hopkins Univ. Press, Baltimore, 2 vols.

Gardner, A. L. 2005b. Order Didelphimorphia. Pp. 3–18 in Mammal species of the world, a taxonomic and geographic reference, third ed. (D. E. Wilson and D. M. Reeder, eds.). Johns Hopkins Univ. Press, Baltimore, 2 vols.

Gardner, A. L., and M. E. Sunquist. 2003. Opossum, *Didelphis virginiana*. Pp. 3–29, in Wild mammals of North America, biology, management, and economics, second ed. (G. A. Feldhamer, B. C. Thompson, and J. A. Chapman, eds.). Johns Hopkins Univ. Press, Baltimore, 1,216 pp.

Gardner, S. L., and G. D. Schmidt. 1986. Two new species of *Litomosoides* (Nematoda: Onchocercidae) from pocket gophers (Rodentia: Geomyidae) in Colorado. Syst. Parasit. 8:235–242.

Gardner, S. L., and G. D. Schmidt. 1988. Cestodes of the genus *Hymenolepis* Weinland, 1858 *sensu stricto* from pocket gophers *Geomys* and *Thomomys* spp. (Rodentia: Geomyidae) in Colorado and Oregon, with a discriminant analysis of four species of *Hymenolepis*. Canadian J. Zool. 56:896–903.

Garfield, B. 2001. Bear vs. man: recent attacks and how to avoid the increasing danger. Willow Creek Press, Minocqua, WI, 192 pp.

Gargas, A., M. T. Trest, M. Christiansen, T. J. Volk, and D. S. Belhert. 2009. *Geomyces destructans* sp. nov. associated with bat white-nose syndrome. Mycotaxon 108:147–154.

Garner, H. W. 1967. An ecological study of the brush mouse, *Peromyscus boylii*, in western Texas. Texas J. Sci. 19:285–291.

Garner, H. W. 1974. Population dynamics, reproduction, and activities of the kangaroo rat, *Dipodomys ordii*, in western Texas. Grad. Studies, Texas Tech Univ. 7:1–28.

Garrett, J. J. 2007. A triadic relationship on the Northern Great Plains: bison (*Bison bison*), native plants, and native people.

Unpubl. doctoral dissert., Colorado State Univ., Fort Collins, 143 pp.

Garrison, T. E., and T. L. Best. 1990. *Dipodomys ordii*. Mammalian Species 353:1–10.

Garrott, R. A. 1991a. Feral horse fertility control: potential and limitations. Wildl. Soc. Bull. 19:52–58.

Garrott, R. A. 1991b. Sex ratios and differential survival of feral horses. J. Animal Ecol. 60:929–936.

Garrott, R. A., T. C. Eagle, and E. D. Plotka. 1991. Age-specific reproduction in feral horses. Canadian J. Zool. 59:738–743.

Garrott, R. A., B. D. Siniff, and L. L. Eberhardt. 1991. Growth rates of feral horse populations. J. Wildl. Mgmt. 55:641–648.

Garrott, R. A., and L. Taylor. 1990. Dynamics of a feral horse population in Montana. J. Wildl. Mgmt. 54:603–612.

Garrott, R. A., G. C. White, R. M. Bartmann, L. H. Carpenter, and W. A. Alldredge. 1987. Movements of female mule deer in northwest Colorado. J. Wildl. Mgmt. 51:634–643.

Gasaway, W. C. 1975. Moose antlers: how fast do they grow? Misc. Publ., Alaska Department of Fish and Game, 2 pp.

Gasaway, W. C., and J. W. Coady. 1974. Review of energy requirements and rumen fermentation in moose and other ruminants. Naturaliste Canadienne 101:227–262.

Gashwiler, J. S., W. L. Robinette, and O. W. Morris. 1960. Foods of bobcats in Utah and eastern Nevada. J. Wildl. Mgmt. 24:226–229.

Gashwiler, J. S., W. L. Robinette, and O. W. Morris. 1961. Breeding habits of bobcats in Utah. J. Mamm. 42:76–84.

Gaston, K. J. 2009. Geographic range limits: achieving synthesis. Proc. Royal Soc. B. 276:1395–1406.

Gaston, R., M. G. Lockley, S. G. Lucas, and A. P. Hunt. 2003. *Grallator*-dominated fossil footprint assemblages and associated enigmatic footprints from the Chinle Group (Upper Triassic), Gateway area, Colorado. Ichnos 10:153–163.

Gavin, B. R., and R. E. Richards. 1993. Distribution update for Colorado ringtails (Carnivora: *Bassariscus astutus*): 1982–1993. J. Colorado-Wyoming Acad. Sci. 25(1):30.

Gay, S. W., and T. L. Best. 1995. Geographic variation in sexual dimorphism in the puma (*Puma concolor*) in North and South America. Southwestern Nat. 40:148–159.

Gehring, T. M., and R. K. Swihart. 2000. Field immobilization and use of radio collars on long-tailed weasels. Wildl. Soc. Bull. 28:579–585.

Gehring, T. M., and R. K. Swihart. 2003. Body size, niche breadth, and ecologically scaled responses to habitat fragmentation: mammalian predators in an agricultural landscape. Biol. Cons. 109:283–295.

Gehring, T. M., and R. K. Swihart. 2004. Home range and movements of long-tailed weasels in a landscape fragmented by agriculture. J. Mamm. 85:79–86.

Gehrt, S. D. 2003. Raccoon, *Procyon lotor* and allies. Pp. 611–634, in Wild mammals of North America, biology, management, and economics, second ed. (G. A. Feldhamer, B. C. Thompson, and J. A. Chapman, eds.). Johns Hopkins Univ. Press, Baltimore, 1,216 pp.

Gehrt, S. D., and E. K. Fritzell. 1996. Second estrus and late litters in raccoons. J. Mamm. 77:388–393.

Gehrt, S. D., and E. K. Fritzell. 1997. Sexual differences in home ranges of raccoons. J. Mamm. 78:921–931.

Gehrt, S. D., and E. K. Fritzell. 1998. Duration of familial bonds and dispersal patterns for raccoons in south Texas. J. Mamm. 79:859–872.

Gehrt, S. D., D. L. Spencer, and L. B. Fox. 1990. Raccoon denning behavior in eastern Kansas as determined from radio-telemetry. Trans. Kansas Acad. Sci. 93:71–78.

Geist, V. 1964. On the rutting behavior of the mountain goat. J. Mamm. 45:551–568.

Geist, V. 1966. Validity of horn segment counts in aging bighorn sheep. J. Wildl. Mgmt. 30:634–646.

Geist, V. 1971. Mountain sheep, a study in behavior and evolution. Univ. Chicago Press, Chicago, 283 pp.

Geist, V. 1975. Mountain sheep and man in the northern wilds. Cornell Univ. Press, Ithaca, NY, 248 pp.

Geist, V. 1981. Behavior: adaptive strategies in mule deer. Pp. 157–223, in Mule and black-tailed deer of North America (O. C. Wallmo, ed.). Univ. Nebraska Press, Lincoln, 605 pp.

Geist, V. 1982. Adaptive behavioral strategies. Pp. 219–278, in Elk of North America, ecology and management (J. W. Thomas and D. E. Toweill, eds.). Stackpole Books, Harrisburg, PA, 698 pp.

Geist, V. 1998. Deer of the world: their evolution, behavior and ecology. Stackpole, Mechanicsburg, PA, 456 pp.

Geluso, K. 2004. Westward expansion of the eastern fox squirrel (*Sciurus niger*) in northeastern New Mexico and southeastern Colorado. Southwestern Nat. 49:111–116.

Geluso, K., T. R. Mollhagen, J. T. Tigner, and M. A. Bogan. 2005. Westward expansion of the eastern pipistrelle (*Pipistrellus subflavus*) in the United States, including new records from New Mexico, South Dakota, and Texas. Western N. Amer. Nat. 56:405–409.

Geluso, K. N. 1971. Habitat distribution of *Peromyscus* in the Black Mesa region of Oklahoma. J. Mamm. 52:605–607.

Geluso, K. N. 1975. Urine concentration cycles of insectivorous bats in the laboratory. J. Comp. Physiol. 99:309–319.

Geluso, K. N. 1978. Urine concentrating ability and renal structure of insectivorous bats. J. Mamm. 59:312–323.

Genoways, H. H., and R. J. Baker, eds. 1996. Contributions in mammalogy: a memorial volume honoring Dr. J. Knox Jones, Jr. Museum of Texas Tech Univ., Lubbock, 315 pp.

Genoways, H. H., and J. H. Brown, eds. 1993. Biology of the Heteromyidae. Spec. Publ., Amer. Soc. Mammal. 10:1–719.

Genoways, H. H., and J. R. Choate. 1972. A multivariate analysis of systematic relationships among populations of the short-tailed shrew (genus *Blarina*) in Nebraska. Syst. Zool. 21:106–116.

Genoways, H. H., P. W. Freeman, and C. Grell. 2000. Extralimital records of the Mexican free-tailed bat (*Tadarida brasiliensis mexicana*) in the central United States and their biological significance. Trans. Nebraska Acad. Sci. 26:85–96.

Genoways, H. H., M. J. Hamilton, D. M. Bell, R. R. Chambers, and R. D. Bradley. 2008. Hybrid zones, genetic isolation, and systematics of pocket gophers (genus *Geomys*) in Nebraska. J. Mamm. 89:826–836.

Genoways, H. H., J. C. Patton III, and J. R. Choate. 1977. Karyotypes of shrews of the genera *Cryptotis* and *Blarina* (Mammalia: Soricidae). Experientia 33:1294–1295.

Geologic Names Committee, USGS. 2007. Divisions of geologic time—major chronostratigraphic and geochronologic units. http://pubs.usgs.gov/fs/2007/3015/fs2007-3015.pdf.

George, J. L., R. Kahn, M. W. Miller, and B. Watkins, eds. 2009. Colorado bighorn sheep management plan 2009–2019. Spec. Rept., Colorado Div. Wildl. 81:1–88.

George, J. L., D. J. Martin, P. M. Lukacs, and M. W. Miller. 2008. Epidemic pasteurellosis in a bighorn sheep population coinciding with the appearance of a domestic sheep. J. Wildl. Dis. 44:388–403.

George, J. L., M. W. Miller, G. C. White, and J. Vayhinger. 1996. Comparison of mark-resight population size estimators for bighorn sheep in alpine and timbered habitats. Biennial Symp. Northern Wild Sheep and Goat Council 10:20–25.

George, S. B. 1986a. *Blarina brevicauda*. Mammalian Species 261: 1–9.

George, S. B. 1986b. Evolution and historical biogeography of soricine shrews. Syst. Zool. 35:153–162.

George, S. B. 1988. Systematics, historical biogeography, and evolution of the genus *Sorex*. J. Mamm. 59:443–461.

George, S. B. 1990. Unusual records of shrews in New Mexico. Southwestern Nat. 35:464–465.

George, S. B., J. R. Choate, and H. H. Genoways. 1981. Distribution and taxonomic status of *Blarina hylophaga* Elliot (Insectivora: Soricidae). Ann. Carnegie Mus. Nat. Hist. 50:493–513.

George, S. B., J. R. Choate, and H. H. Genoways. 1986. *Blarina brevicauda*. Mammalian Species 261:1–9.

George, S. B., H. H. Genoways, J. R. Choate, and R. J. Baker. 1982. Karyotypic relationships within the short-tailed shrews, genus *Blarina*. J. Mamm. 53:639–645.

Gerber, J. D., and E. C. Birney. 1968. Immunological comparisons of four subgenera of ground squirrels. Syst. Zool. 17:413–416.

Gerell, R. 1970. Home ranges and movements of the mink, *Mustela vison* Schreber, in southern Sweden. Oikos 21:160–173.

Gerlach, T. P. 1987. Population ecology of mule deer on Piñon Canyon maneuver site, Colorado. Unpubl. master's thesis, Virginia Polytechnic Inst. and State Univ., Blacksburg, 61 pp.

Gese, E. M. 1990. Reproductive activity in an old-age coyote in southeastern Colorado. Southwestern Nat. 35:101–102.

Gese, E. M., and S. Grothe. 1995. Analysis of coyote predation on deer and elk during winter in Yellowstone National Park, Wyoming. Amer. Midland Nat. 133:36–43.

Gese, E. M., O. J. Rongstad, and W. R. Mytton. 1988a. Home range and habitat use of coyotes in southeastern Colorado. J. Wildl. Mgmt. 52:640–646.

Gese, E. M., O. J. Rongstad, and W. R. Mytton. 1988b. Relationship between coyote group size and diet in southeastern Colorado. J. Wildl. Mgmt. 52:647–653.

Gese, E. M., O. J. Rongstad, and W. R. Mytton. 1989a. Population dynamics of coyotes in southeastern Colorado. J. Wildl. Mgmt. 53:174–181.

Gese, E. M., O. J. Rongstad, and W. R. Mytton. 1989b. Changes in coyote movements due to military activity. J. Wildl. Mgmt. 53:334–339.

Gese, E. M., and R. L. Ruff. 1997. Scent-marking by coyotes, *Canis latrans*: the influence of social and ecological factors. Animal Behav. 54:1155–1166.

Gese, E. M., and R. L. Ruff. 1998. Howling by coyotes (*Canis latrans*): variation among social classes, seasons, and pack sizes. Canadian J. Zool. 76:1037–1043.

Gese, E. M., R. L. Ruff, and R. L. Crabtree. 1996a. Social and nutritional factors influencing dispersal of resident coyotes. Animal Behav. 52:1025–1043.

Gese, E. M., R. L. Ruff, and R. L. Crabtree. 1996b. Foraging ecology of coyotes (*Canis latrans*): the influence of extrinsic factors and a dominance hierarchy. Canadian J. Zool. 74:769–783.

Gese, E. M., R. L. Ruff, and R. L. Crabtree. 1996c. Intrinsic and extrinsic factors influencing coyote predation of small mammals in Yellowstone National Park. Canadian J. Zool. 74: 784–797.

Gese, E. M., R. D. Schlutz, M. R. Johnson, E. S. Williams, R. L. Crabtree, and R. L. Ruff. 1997. Serological survey for diseases in free-ranging coyotes (*Canis latrans*) in Yellowstone National Park, Wyoming. J. Wildl. Dis. 33:47–56.

Gese, E. M., R. D. Schlutz, O. J. Rongstad, and D. E. Anderson. 1991. Prevalence of antibodies against canine parvovirus and canine distemper virus in wild coyotes in southeastern Colorado. J. Wildl. Dis. 27:320–323.

Gese, E. M., T. E. Stotts, and S. Grothe. 1996. Interactions between coyotes and red foxes in Yellowstone National Park, Wyoming. J. Mamm. 77:377–382.

Gettinger, R. D. 1984. A field study of activity patterns of *Thomomys bottae*. J. Mamm. 55:76–84.

Gettinger, R. D., P. Arnold, B. A. Wunder, and C. L. Ralph. 1986. Seasonal effects of temperature and photoperiod on thermogenesis and body mass of the kangaroo rat (*Dipodomys ordii*). Pp. 505–509, in Living in the cold, physiological and biochemical adaptations (H. C. Heller, X. J. Musacchia, and L.C.H. Wang, eds.). Elsevier Science Publishers, New York, 587 pp.

Getz, L. L. 1960. A population study of the vole, *Microtus pennsylvanicus*. Amer. Midland Nat. 54:392–405.

Getz, L. L. 1961. Home ranges, territoriality, and movement of the meadow vole. J. Mamm. 42:24–36.

Getz, L. L. 1962. Aggressive behavior of the meadow and prairie voles. J. Mamm. 43:351–358.

Getz, L. L., and G. O. Batzli. 1979. Nutrition and population dynamics of the prairie vole, *Microtus ochrogaster*, in central Illinois. J. Animal Ecol. 48:455–470.

Getz, L. L., and C. S. Carter. 1980. Social organization in *Microtus ochrogaster* populations. The Biologist 62:56–69.

Getz, L. L., and C. S. Carter. 1996. Prairie-vole partnerships. Amer. Sci. 84(1):56–62.

Getz, L. L., J. E. Hofmann, and L. Jike. 1986. Relationship between social organization, mating system and habitats of Microtinae rodents. Acta Theriol. Sinica 6:273–284.

Getz, L. L., B. McGuire, and C. S. Carter. 2003. Social behavior, reproduction and demography of the prairie vole, *Microtus ochrogaster*. Ethol., Ecol. and Evol. 15:110–118.

Getz, L. L., N. G. Solomon, and T. M. Pizzuto. 1990. The effects of predation of snakes on social organization of the prairie vole, *Microtus ochrogaster*. Amer. Midland Nat. 123:365–371.

Gibbard, P. L., M. J. Head, M.J.C. Walker, and Subcommittee on Quaternary Stratigraphy. 2010. Formal ratification of the Quaternary System/Period and the Pleistocene Series/Epoch with a base of 2.58 Ma. J. Quaternary Sci. 25:96–102.

Gibbons, J. W. 1988. The management of amphibians, reptiles, and small mammals in North America: the need for an environmental attitude adjustment. Pp. 4–10, in Management of amphibians, reptiles, and small mammals in North America (R. C. Szaro, K. R. Severson, and D. R. Patton, tech. coord.). Gen. Tech. Rept., USDA Forest Service, RM-166:1–458.

Gier, H. T. 1968. Coyotes in Kansas. Agric. Exper. Station, Kansas State Univ., 118 pp.

Gier, H. T. 1975. Ecology and behavior of the coyote (*Canis latrans*). Pp. 247–262, in The wild canids: their systematics, behavioral ecology and evolution (M. W. Fox., ed.). Van Nostrand Reinhold, New York, 508 pp.

Gilbert, F. F., and E. G. Nancekivell. 1982. Food habits of mink (*Mustela vison*) and otter (*Lutra canadensis*) in northeastern Alberta. Canadian J. Zool. 50:1282–1288.

Gilbert, P. F., and J. R. Grieb. 1957. Comparison of air and ground deer counts in Colorado. J. Wildl. Mgmt. 21:33–37.

Gilin, C. L. 2002. Denning ecology of the swift fox (*Vulpes velox*) on the northeastern plains of Colorado. Unpubl. master's thesis, Univ. Northern Colorado, Greeley, 42 pp.

Gill, B. 2006. Dog talk. Colorado Outdoors 55(5):16–20.

Gill, R. B. 1991. Colorado fur trapping controversy preliminary analysis. Colorado Division of Wildlife, Denver, 21 pp.

Gill, R. B. 1999. Declining mule deer populations in Colorado: reasons and responses, a report to the Colorado legislature, November 1999. Colorado Division of Wildlife, Denver, 54 pp.

Gill, R. B., and T.D.I. Beck. 1990. Black bear management plan 1990–1995. Division Rept., Colorado Division of Wildlife 15:1–44.

Gill, R. B., T.D.I. Beck, C. J. Bishop, D. J. Freddy, N. T. Hobbs, R. H. Kahn, M. W. Miller, T. M. Pojar, and G. C. White. 2001. Declining mule deer populations in Colorado: reasons and responses. Spec. Rept., Colorado Division of Wildlife, Fort Collins 77:1–30.

Gill, R. B., and L. H. Carpenter. 1985. Winter feeding—a good idea? Proc. Western Assoc. Fish and Wildl. Agencies 65:57–66.

Gill, R. B., L. H. Carpenter, and D. C. Bowden. 1983. Monitoring large animal populations: the Colorado experience. Trans. North American Wildl. Conf. 48:330–341.

Gillette, L. N. 1943. The natural history and behavior of the western chipmunk and the mantled ground squirrel. Studies in Zool., Oregon State College 5:1–104.

Gillette, L. N. 1980. Movement patterns of radio-tagged opossums in Wisconsin. Amer. Midland Nat. 104:1–12.

Gillis, J. E. 1968. The activity of the big brown bat. Unpubl. master's thesis, Colorado State Univ., Fort Collins, 30 pp.

Gionfriddo, D. R., D. R. Culver, and J. Stevens. 2002. Biological Survey of Bent's Old Fort National Historic Site, Otero County, Colorado. Colorado Natural Heritage Program, Colorado State Univ., Fort Collins, 77 pp.

Gipson, P. S., and W. B. Ballard. 1998. Accounts of famous North American wolves, *Canis lupus*. Canadian Field-Nat. 112:724–739.

Gipson, P. S., I. K. Gipson, and J. A. Sealander. 1975. Reproductive biology of wild *Canis* in Arkansas. J. Mamm. 56:605–612.

Gittleman, J. L., ed. 1989. Carnivore behavior, ecology, and evolution. Cornell Univ. Press, Ithaca, NY, 620 pp.

Gittleman, J. L., ed. 1996. Carnivore behavior, ecology, and evolution, vol. 2. Cornell Univ. Press, Ithaca, NY, 644 pp.

Gittleman, J. L., S. M. Funk, D. W. MacDonald, and R. K. Wayne, eds. 2008. Carnivore Conservation. Cambridge Univ. Press, Cambridge, UK, 692 pp.

Glass, B. P. 1966. Some notes on reproduction in the red bat, *Lasiurus borealis*. Proc. Oklahoma Acad. Sci. 46:40–41.

Glass, G. E., T. M. Shields, R. R. Parmenter, D. Goade, J. N. Milles, J. Cheek, J. Cook, and T. L. Yates. 2006. Predicted hantavirus risk in 2006 for the southwestern U.S. Occas. Papers, Mus. Texas Tech Univ. 255:1–16.

Glazko, G. V., and M. Nei. 2003. Estimation of divergence times for major lineages of primate species. Molec. Biol. and Evol. 20:424–434.

Glick, D. 2006. Of lynx and men [scenes from a homecoming]. Nat. Geogr. 209:56–67.

Glover, F. A. 1943. Killing techniques of the New York weasel. Pennsylvania Game News 13:11–23.

Gober, P. 2009. A challenging future for the black-footed ferret. Endangered Species Bulletin. http://www.fws.gov/endangered/news/bulletin-spring2009/black-footed-ferret.html.

Godin, A. J. 1982. Striped and hooded skunks (*Mephitis mephitis* and allies). Pp. 674–687, in Wild mammals of North America, biology, management, and economics (J. A. Chapman and G. A. Feldhamer, eds.). Johns Hopkins Univ. Press, Baltimore, 1,147 pp.

Goehring, H. H. 1972. Twenty-year study of *Eptesicus fuscus* in Minnesota. J. Mamm. 53:201–207.

Goertz, J. W. 1963. Some biological notes on the plains harvest mouse. Proc. Oklahoma Acad. Sci. 43:123–125.

Goertz, J. W. 1970. An ecological study of *Neotoma floridana* in Oklahoma. J. Mamm. 51:94–104.

Gold, I. K. 1976. Effects of blacktail prairie dog mounds on shortgrass vegetation. Unpubl. master's thesis, Colorado State Univ., Fort Collins, 40 pp.

Goldman, E. A. 1944. Classification of wolves. Pp. 389–507 in The wolves of North America (S. P. Young and E. A. Goldman, eds.). American Wildlife Institute, Washington, DC, 636 pp.

Goldman, E. A. 1946. Classification of the races of the puma. Pp. 175–302, in The puma, mysterious American cat (S. P. Young and E. A. Goldman, eds.). American Wildl. Inst., Washington, DC, xiv + 358 pp.

Goldman, E. A., and M. C. Gardner. Two new cotton rats. Jour. Mamma. 28:57–59.

Golley, F. B., G. A. Petrides, E. L. Rauber, and J. H. Jenkins. 1965. Food intake and assimilation by bobcats under laboratory conditions. J. Wildl. Mgmt. 29:442–447.

Gompper, M. E., and H. M. Hackett. 2005. The long-term, range-wide decline of a once common carnivore: the eastern spotted skunk (*Spilogale putorius*). Animal Cons. 8:195–201.

Gonzalez-Voyer, A., M. Festa-Bianchet, and K. G. Smith. 2001. Efficiency of aerial surveys of mountain goats. Wildl. Soc. Bull. 29:140–144.

Goodman, P. 1984. River otter recovery plan for Colorado: draft. Colorado Division of Wildlife, Denver, 14 pp.

Goodrich, J. M. 1994. North American badgers (*Taxidea taxus*) and black-footed ferrets (*Mustela nigripes*): abundance, rarity and conservation in a white-tailed prairie dog (*Cynomys leucurus*)–based community. Unpubl. doctoral dissert., Univ. Wyoming, Laramie, 102 pp.

Goodrich, J. M., and S. W. Buskirk. 1998. Spacing and ecology of North American badgers (*Taxidea taxus*) in a prairie dog (*Cynomys leucurus*) complex. J. Mamm. 79:171–179.

Goodson, N. J. 1978. Status of bighorn sheep in Rocky Mountain National Park. Unpubl. master's thesis, Colorado State Univ., Fort Collins, 190 pp.

Goodson, N. J., and D. R. Stevens. 1994. Cooperative defense by female bighorn sheep. Northwestern Nat. 75:76–77.

Goodwin, H. T. 1995. Pliocene-Pleistocene biogeographic history of prairie dogs, genus *Cynomys* (Sciuridae). J. Mamm. 76:100–122.

Goodwin, H. T., and E. M. Ryckman. 2006. Lower incisors of prairie dogs (*Cynomys*) as biorecorders of hibernation and season of death. J. Mamm. 87:1002–1012.

Gordon, C. C. 1986. Winter food habits of the pine marten in Colorado. Great Basin Nat. 46:166–168.

Gordon, K. 1938. Observations on the behavior of *Callospermophilus* and *Eutamias*. J. Mamm. 19:78–84.

Gordon, K. 1943. The natural history and behavior of the western chipmunk and the mantled ground squirrel. Studies Zool., Oregon State College 5:1–104.

Gorman, T. A., J. D. Erb, B. R. McMillan, and D. J. Martin. 2006. Space use and sociality of river otters (*Lontra canadensis*) in Minnesota. J. Mamm. 87:740–747.

Gosling, L. M. 1985. The even-toed ungulates: order Artiodactyla. Pp. 550–618, in Social odours in mammals (R. E. Brown and D. W. Macdonald, eds.). Clarendon Press, Oxford, 882 pp.

Gosnell, H. 2009. Healing the howls, rewilding the Southern Rockies. Pp. 134–152, in Remedies for a new West, healing landscapes, histories, and cultures (P. N. Limerick, A. Cowell, and S. K. Collinge, eds.). Univ. Arizona Press, Tucson, 324 pp.

Gosselink, T. E., T. R. Van Deelen, R. E. Warner, and M. G. Joselyn. 2003. Temporal habitat partitioning and spatial use of coyotes and red foxes in east-central Illinois. J. Wildl. Mgmt. 57:90–103.

Gottfried, G. J., and D. R. Patton. 1984. Pocket gopher food habits on two disturbed forest sites in central Arizona. Research Paper, USDA Forest Service, RM-255:1–9.

Graber, K., T. France, and S. Miller. 1998. Petition for rule listing the black-tailed prairie dog (*Cynomys ludovicianus*) as threatened throughout its range. National Wildlife Federation. http://www.nwf.org/nwf/grasslands/petition.html.

Graf, R. P. 1985. Social organization of snowshoe hares. Canadian J. Zool. 53:468–474.

Graham, G. L., and F. R. Reid 1994. Bats of the world. St. Martin's Press, New York, 160 pp.

Graham, R. W. 1987. Late Quaternary mammalian faunas and paleoenvironments of the southwestern plains of the United States. Pp. 24–86, in Late Quaternary mammalian biogeography of the Great Plains and prairies (R. W. Graham, H. A. Semken, Jr., and M. A. Graham, eds.). Sci. Papers, Illinois State Mus. 22:1–491.

Graham, R. W., and E. L. Lundelius, Jr. 1994. FAUNMAP: a database documenting Late Quaternary distributions of mammal species in the United States. Sci. Papers, Illinois State Mus. 25:1–690.

Graham, S. J. 1977. The ecology and behavior of the western fox squirrel, *Sciurus niger rufiventer* (Geoffroy), on the South Platte bottomlands. Unpubl. honors thesis, Univ. Northern Colorado, Greeley, 75 pp.

Grant, W. E. 1972. Small mammal studies on the Pawnee Site during the 1971 field season. Tech. Rept., U.S. IBP Grassland Biome 163:1–51.

Grant, W. E., and E. C. Birney. 1979. Small mammal community structure in North American grasslands. J. Mamm. 50:23–36.

Grant, W. E., N. R. French, and L. J. Folse, Jr. 1980. Effects of pocket gopher *Thomomys talpoides* mounds on plant production in short grass prairie ecosystems. Southwestern Nat. 25:215–224.

Gray, G. G. 1993. Wildlife and people, the human dimensions of wildlife ecology. Univ. Illinois Press, Urbana, 260 pp.

Grayson, D. K., and D. B. Madsen. 2000. Biogeographic implications of recent low-elevation recolonization by *Neotoma cinerea* in the Great Basin. J. Mamm. 81:1100–1105.

Green, A. K., S. L. Haley, M. D. Dearing, D. M. Barnes, and W. H. Karasov. Intestinal capacity of P-glycoprotein is higher in the juniper specialist, *Neotoma stephensi*, than the sympatric generalist, *Neotoma albigula*. Comp. Biochem. Physiol. A. 139:325–333.

Green, G. I., D. J. Mattson, and J. M. Peek. 1997. Spring feeding on ungulate carcasses by grizzly bears in Yellowstone National Park. J. Wildl. Mgmt. 5:1040–1055.

Green, J. S., and J. T. Flinders. 1981. Diets of sympatric red foxes and coyotes in southeastern Idaho. Great Basin Nat. 41:251–254.

Green, N. E. 1969. Occurrence of small mammals on sandhill rangelands in eastern Colorado. Unpubl. master's thesis, Colorado State Univ., Fort Collins, 39 pp.

Green, R. A. 1982. Elk habitat selection and activity patterns in Rocky Mountain National Park. Unpubl. master's thesis, Colorado State Univ., Fort Collins, 165 pp.

Greene, E., and T. Meagher. 1998. Red squirrels, *Tamias hudsonicus*, produce predator-class specific alarm calls. Animal Behavior 55:511–518.

Greenland, D., J. Burbank, J. Key, L. Klinger, J. Moorhouse, S. Oaks, and D. Shankman. 1985. The bioclimates of the Colorado Front Range. Mountain Res. and Develop. 5:251–262.

Greenwood, R. J., and A. B. Sargeant. 1998. Age-related reproduction in striped skunks (*Mephitis mephitis*) in the Upper Midwest. J. Mamm. 75:657–662.

Greenwood, R. J., A. B. Sargeant, J. L. Peihl, D. Abuhl, and B. A. Hansen. 1999. Foods and foraging of prairie striped skunks during the avian nesting season. Wildl. Soc. Bull. 27:823–832.

Greer, K. R. 1955. Yearly food habits of the river otter in the Thompson Lakes region, northwestern Montana, as indicated by scat analysis. Amer. Midland Nat. 54:299–313.

Gregg, R. E. 1963. The ants of Colorado. Univ. Press Colorado, Boulder, 792 pp.

Griffin, D. G. 1958. Listening in the dark, the acoustic orientation of bats and men. Yale Univ. Press, New Haven, CT, 413 pp.

Grilliot, M. E., S. C. Burnett, and M. T. Mendoça. 2009. Sexual dimorphism in big brown bat (*Eptesicus fuscus*), ultrasonic vocalizations is context dependent. J. Mamm. 90:203–209.

Grinnell, J. J., J. S. Dixon, and J. M. Linsdale. 1937. Fur-bearing mammals of California 2 vols., Univ. California Press, Berkeley.

Grogan, R. G., and F. G. Lindzey. 1999. Estimating population size of a low density black bear population using capture-resight. Ursus 11:117–122.

Gross, Jack E. 2001. Evaluating effects of an expanding mountain goat population on native bighorn sheep: a simulation model of competition and disease. Biol. Cons. 101:171–185.

Gross, John E., M. C. Kneeland, D. F. Reed, and R. M. Reich. 2002. GIS-based habitat models for mountain goats. J. Mamm. 83:218–228.

Gross, John E., M. C. Kneeland, D. M. Swift, and B. A. Wunder (eds.). 2000. Scientific assessment of the potential effects of mountain goats on the ecosystems of Rocky Mountain National Park. Report to Rocky Mountain National Park, Estes Park, Colorado.

Gross, John E., and M. W. Miller. 2001. Chronic wasting disease in mule deer: disease dynamics and control. J. Wildl. Mgmt. 55:205–215.

Gross, John E., L. C. Stoddart, and F. H. Wagner. 1974. Demographic analysis of a northern Utah jackrabbit population. Wildl. Monogr. 40:1–68.

Groves, C. P. 2001. Primate taxonomy. Smithsonian Institution Press, Washington, DC, 550 pp.

Groves, C. P. 2005. Order Primates. Pp. 111–184, in Mammal species of the world, a taxonomic and geographic reference, third ed. (D. E. Wilson and D. M. Reeder, eds.), 2 vols. Johns Hopkins Univ. Press, Baltimore.

Groves, C. P. 2009. Family Cervidae. Pp. 249–256, in The evolution of artiodactyls (D. R. Prothero and S. E. Foss, eds.). Johns Hopkins Univ. Press, Baltimore, 367 pp.

Grubb, P. 1993. Order Artiodactyla. Pp. 377–414, in Mammal species of the world: a geographic and taxonomic reference, second ed. Smithsonian Institution Press, Washington, DC, 1,206 pp.

Grubb, P. 2005a. Order Perissodactyla. Pp. 629–636, in Mammal species of the world, a taxonomic and geographic reference, third ed. (D. E. Wilson and D. M. Reeder, eds.), 2 vols. Johns Hopkins Univ. Press, Baltimore.

Grubb, P. 2005b. Order Artiodactyla. Pp. 637–743, in Mammal species of the world, third ed. (D. E. Wilson and D. M. Reeder, eds.). Johns Hopkins Univ. Press, Baltimore, 2 vols.

Gruchy, D. F. 1950. Status of the opossum, *Didelphis virginiana*, in Colorado. J. Colorado-Wyoming Acad. Sci. 4:76.

Gruver, J. C., and D. A. Keinath. 2006. Townsend's big-eared bat (*Corynorhinus townsendii*): a technical conservation assessment. Species Conservation Project, Rocky Mountain Region, USDA Forest Service, 93 pp.

Guenther, S. E. 1948. Young beavers. J. Mamm. 29:419–420.

Gunderson, H. L., and B. R. Mahan. 1980. Analysis of sonograms of American bison (*Bison bison*). J. Mamm. 51:379–381.

Gunther, K. 2008. Yellowstone grizzly bears delisted but not forgotten. Yellowstone Sci. 16:30–34.

Guralnick, R. 2006a. The legacy of past climate and landscape change on species' current experienced climate and elevation ranges across latitude: a multispecies study utilizing mammals in western North America. Global Ecol. and Biogeogr. 16:14–23.

Guralnick, R. 2006b. Do flatland- and mountain-dwelling species show different structuring of their experienced environment over latitude? A western vs. central-eastern North America rodent multispecies comparison. Diversity and Distributions 12:731–741.

Gurnell, J. 1984. Home range, territoriality, caching behavior and food supply of the red squirrel (*Tamiasciurus hudsonicus fremonti*) in a subalpine lodgepole pine forest. Animal Behavior 32:1119–1131.

Gustafson, K. A. 1984. The winter metabolism and bioenergetics of the bobcat in New York. Unpubl. master's thesis, State Univ. New York, Syracuse, 112 pp.

Gustin, M. K., and G. F. McCracken. 1987. Scent recognition between females and pups in the bat *Tadarida brasiliensis mexicana*. Animal Behavior 35:13–19.

Guthrie, R. D. 1990. Frozen fauna of the Mammoth Steppe. Univ. Chicago Press, Chicago, 323 pp.

Gysel, L. W. 1960. An ecological study of the winter range of elk and mule deer in the Rocky Mountain National Park. J. Forestry 58:696–703.

Habeck, S. A. 1990. Winter feeding patterns by porcupines (*Erethizon dorsatum*) in the Colorado Front Range. Unpubl. master's thesis, Univ. of Colorado, Boulder, 99 pp.

Habermann, R. T., C. M. Herman, and F. P. Williams. 1958. Distemper in raccoons and foxes suspected of having rabies. J. Amer. Vet. Med. Assoc. 132:31–35.

Hadley, G. L., and K. R. Wilson. 2004a. Patterns of small mammal density and survival following ski-run development. J. Mamm. 85:97–104.

Hadley, G. L., and K. R. Wilson. 2004b. Patterns of density and survival in small mammals in ski runs and adjacent forest patches. J. Wildl. Mgmt. 58:288–298.

Hafner, D. J., K. E. Peterson, and T. L. Yates. 1981. Evolutionary relationships of jumping mice (genus *Zapus*) of the southwestern United States. J. Mamm. 52:501–512.

Hafner, D. J., and C. J. Shuster. 1996. Historical biogeography of western peripheral isolates of the least shrew, *Cryptotis parva*. J. Mamm. 77:536.

Hafner, D. J., and A. T. Smith. 2010. Revision of the subspecies of the America pika, *Ochotona princeps* (Lagomorpha, Ochotonidae). J. Mamm. 91:401–417.

Hafner, D. J., and D. W. Stahlecker. 2002. Distribution of Merriam's shrew (*Sorex merriami*) and the dwarf shrew (*Sorex nanus*), and new records for New Mexico. Southwestern Nat. 47:134–137.

Hafner, D. J., and R. M. Sullivan. 1995. Historical and ecological biogeography of Nearctic pikas (Lagomorpha: Ochotonidae). J. Mamm. 76:302–321.

Hafner, D. J., E. Yensen, and G. L. Kirkland, Jr., eds. 1998a. Status survey and conservation action plan, North American rodents. IUCN/SSC Rodent Specialist Group, Gland, Switzerland, 171 pp.

Hafner, D. J., E. Yensen, and G. L. Kirkland, Jr. 1998b. Summary descriptions of rodents of conservation concern. Pp. 23–124, in North American rodents (D. J. Hafner, E. Yensen, and G. L. Kirkland, Jr., eds.). IUCN, Gland, Switzerland, 171 pp.

Hafner, J. C., and M. S. Hafner. 1983. Evolutionary relationships of heteromyid rodents. Great Basin Nat. Memoirs 7:3–29.

Hafner, J. C., J. E. Light, D. J. Hafner, M. S. Hafner, E. Reddington, D. S. Rogers, and B. R. Riddle. 2007. Basal clades and molecular systematics of heteromyid rodents. J. Mamm. 88:1129–1145.

Hafner, M. S., and D. J. Hafner 1979. Vocalizations of grasshopper mice (genus *Onychomys*). J. Mamm. 50:85–94.

Hahn, D. E. 1966. The nine-banded armadillo, *Dasypus novemcinctus*, in Colorado. Southwestern Nat. 11:303.

Halfpenny, J. C. 1980. Reproductive strategies: intra- and interspecific comparison within the genus *Peromyscus*. Unpubl. doctoral dissert., Univ. Colorado, Boulder, 160 pp.

Halfpenny, J. C. 1986. A field guide to mammal tracking in North America. Johnson Books, Boulder, CO, 161 pp.

Halfpenny, J. C. 2001. Scats and tracks of the Rocky Mountains, second ed. Morris Book Publishing, Guilford, CT, 144 pp.

Halfpenny, J. C. 2003. Yellowstone wolves in the wild. Riverbend Publishing, Helena, MT, 103 pp.

Halfpenny, J. C. 2007a. Yellowstone bears in the wild. Riverbend Publishing, Helena, MT, 123 pp.

Halfpenny, J. C. 2007b. Tracking cougars, the basics. A Naturalist's World, Gardiner, MT, 35 pp.

Halfpenny, J. C., S. J. Bissell, and D. Nead. 1986. Status of the lynx (*Lynx canadensis*, Felidae) in Colorado with comments on its distribution in western North America. Unpublished manuscript, Institute of Arctic and Alpine Res., Boulder, 16 pp.

Halfpenny, J. C., and K. P. Ingraham. 1983. Growth and development of heather voles. Growth 47:437–445.

Halfpenny, J. C., K. P. Ingraham, J. Mattysse, and P. C. Lehr. 1986. Bibliography of alpine and subalpine areas of the Front Range, Colorado. Occas. Paper, Inst. Arctic and Alpine Res., Univ. of Colorado, Boulder, 43:xvi, 1–114.

Halfpenny, J. C., and G. C. Miller. 1981. Lynx and wolverine verification. Colorado Division of Wildlife, Wildlife Research Report, January, Part 1, pp. 53–82.

Halfpenny, J. C., and C. H. Southwick. 1982. Small mammal herbivores of the Colorado alpine tundra. Pp. 113–123, in Ecological studies in the Colorado alpine: a festchrift for John W. Marr (J. C. Halfpenny, ed.). Occas. Paper, Inst. Arctic and Alpine Res., Univ. Colorado, Boulder 37:113–123.

Halfpenny, J. C., and D. Thompson. 1996. Discovering Yellowstone wolves, watcher's guide. A Naturalist's World, Gardiner, MT, 60 pp.

Hall, E. R. 1951. American weasels. Univ. Kansas Publ., Mus. Nat. Hist. 4:1–466.

Hall, E. R. 1955. Handbook of mammals of Kansas. Misc. Publ., Univ. Kansas Mus. Nat. Hist. 7:1–303.

Hall, E. R. 1981. The mammals of North America, second ed. John Wiley & Sons, New York, 2 vols.

Hall, E. R. 1984. Geographic variation among brown and grizzly bears (*Ursus arctos*) in North America. Spec. Publ., Mus. Nat. Hist., Univ. Kansas 13:1–16.

Hall, J. G. 1997. Here today, gone tomorrow: an encounter with free-tailed bats. The Chiropteran 7:1, 6.

Hallam, T. 2004. Catastrophes and lesser calamities, the causes of mass extinctions. Oxford Univ. Press, Oxford, UK, 226 pp.

Hallberg, D. L., and G. R. Trapp. 1984. Gray fox temporal and spatial activity in a riparian-agricultural zone in California's Central Valley. Pp. 920–928, in California riparian systems: ecology, conservation, and productive management (R. W. Warner and K. M. Hendrix, eds.). Univ. California Press, Berkeley, 1,035 pp.

Hallett, J. G., M. A. O'Connell, and C. C. Maguire. 2003. Ecological relationships of terrestrial small mammals in western coniferous forests. Pp. 120–156, in Mammal community dynamics, management and conservation in the coniferous forests of western North America (C. J. Zabel and R. G. Anthony, eds.). Cambridge Univ. Press, Cambridge, UK, 709 pp.

Halls, L. K., ed. 1984. White-tailed deer: ecology and management. Stackpole Books, Harrisburg, PA, 870 pp.

Halse, A. 2007. Location and first appearance of rat incisor pigmentation. European J. Oral Sci. 80:428–433.

Hamel, S., and S. D. Côté. 2009. Maternal defensive behavior of mountain goats against predation by golden eagles. Western N. Amer. Nat. 59:115–118.

Hamilton, R. B., and D. T. Stalling. 1972. *Lasiurus borealis* with five young. J. Mamm. 53:190.

Hamilton, W. J., Jr. 1929. Breeding habits of the short-tailed shrew, *Blarina brevicauda*. J. Mamm. 10:125–134.

Hamilton, W. J., Jr. 1933. The weasels of New York. Amer. Midland Nat.,14:289–337.

Hamilton, W. J., Jr. 1936. The food and breeding habits of the raccoon. Ohio J. Sci. 36:131–140.

Hamilton, W. J., Jr. 1937. Winter activity of the skunk. Ecology 18:326–327.

Hamilton, W. J., Jr. 1953. Reproduction and young of the Florida wood rat, *Neotoma floridana* (Ord). J. Mamm. 34:180–189.

Hamilton, W. J., Jr., and W. R. Eadie. 1964. Reproduction in the otter, *Lutra canadensis*. J. Mamm. 45:242–252.

Hamlin, K. L., and J. A. Cunningham. 2009. Monitoring and assessment of wild ungulate interactions and population trends within the Greater Yellowstone area, southwestern Montana, and Montana statewide. Final Report, Montana Fish, Wildlife and Parks, Helena, 83 pp.

Hamlin, K. L., D. F. Pac, C. A. Sime, R. M. Desimone, and G. L. Dusek. 2000. Evaluating the accuracy of ages obtained by two methods for Montana ungulates. J. Wildl. Mgmt. 54: 441–449.

Hammitt, W. E., C. D. McDonald, and M. E. Patterson. 1990. Determinants of multiple satisfaction for deer hunting. Wildl. Soc. Bull. 18:331–337.

Hancock, D. C., Jr., and D. J. Nash. 1982. Dorsal hair length and coat color in Abert's squirrel (*Sciurus aberti*). Great Basin Nat. 42:597–598.

Handley, C. O., Jr. 1959. A revision of the American bats of the genera *Euderma* and *Plecotus*. Proc. U.S. Nat. Mus. 110:95–246.

Hansen, A. J., R. P. Neilson, V. H. Dale, C. H. Flather, L. R. Iverson, D. J. Currie, S. Shafer, R. Cook, and P. J. Bartlein. 2001. Global change in forests: responses of species, communities, and biomes. BioScience 51:765–779.

Hansen, K. 2006. Bobcat, master of survival. Oxford Univ. Press, New York, 248 pp.

Hansen, R. M. 1960. Age and reproductive characteristics of mountain pocket gophers in Colorado. J. Mamm. 41:323–335.

Hansen, R. M. 1962. Dispersal of Richardson ground squirrel in Colorado. Amer. Midland Nat. 58:58–66.

Hansen, R. M. 1963. Cotton rat from Kiowa County, Colorado. J. Mamm. 44:126.

Hansen, R. M. 1972. Estimation of herbage intake from jackrabbit feces. J. Range Mgmt. 25:468–471.

Hansen, R. M. 1975. Plant matter in the diet of *Onychomys*. J. Mamm. 56:530–531.

Hansen, R. M., and G. D. Bear. 1963. Winter coats of white-tailed jackrabbits in southwestern Colorado. J. Mamm. 44:420–422.

Hansen, R. M., and G. D. Bear. 1964. Comparison of pocket gophers from alpine, subalpine, and shrub-grassland habitats. J. Mamm. 45:638–640.

Hansen, R. M., and R. C. Clark. 1977. Foods of elk and other ungulates at low elevation in northwestern Colorado. J. Wildl. Mgmt. 41:76–80.

Hansen, R. M., R. C. Clark, and W. Lawhorn. 1977. Foods of wild horses, deer and cattle in the Douglas Mountain area, Colorado. J. Range Mgmt. 30:116–118.

Hansen, R. M., and J. T. Flinders. 1969. Food habits of North American hares. Sci. Ser., Range Sci. Dept., Colorado State Univ. 1:1–18.

Hansen, R. M., and I. K. Gold. 1977. Black-tailed prairie dogs, desert cottontails and cattle trophic relations on shortgrass range. J. Range Mgmt. 30:210–213.

Hansen, R. M., and M. K. Johnson. 1976. Stomach content weight and food selection by Richardson ground squirrels. J. Mamm. 57:749–751.

Hansen, R. M., and R. S. Miller. 1959. Observations on the plural occupancy of pocket gopher systems. J. Mamm. 40:577–584.

Hansen, R. M., and L. D. Reed. 1969. Energy assimilation in Richardson ground squirrels. Amer. Midland Nat. 82:290–292.

Hansen, R. M., and V. H. Reid. 1973. Distribution and adaptations of pocket gophers. Pp. 1–19, in Pocket gophers and Colorado mountain rangeland (G. T. Turner, R. M. Hansen, V. H. Reid, H. P. Tietjen, and A. L. Ward, eds.). Exper. Sta. Bull., Colorado State Univ. 2:1–554.

Hansen, R. M., and A. L. Ward. 1966. Some relations of pocket gophers to rangelands on Grand Mesa, Colorado. Tech. Bull., Colorado Agric. Exper. Sta. 88:1–22.

Hansson, A. 1947. The physiology of reproduction in mink (*Mustela vison*, Schreb.) with special reference to delayed implantation. Acta Zool. 28:1–136.

Harder, B. 2007. Perchance to hibernate, can we tap a dormant capacity to downshift our metabolism? Science News 171(4):56–58.

Hardin, G. 1972. Exploring new ethics for survival: the voyage of the Spaceship Beagle. Viking Press, New York, 273 pp.

Hargis, C. D., J. A. Bissonette, and D. L. Turner. 1999. The influence of forest fragmentation and landscape pattern on American martens. J. Applied Ecol. 36:157–172.

Hargis, C. D., and D. R. McCullough. 1984. Winter diet and habitat selection of marten in Yosemite National Park. J. Wildl. Mgmt. 48:140–146.

Harlow, H. J. 1981. Torpor and other physiological adaptations of the badger (*Taxidea taxus*) to cold environments. Physiol. Zool. 54:267–275.

Harlow, H. J., T. Lohuis, R. C. Anderson-Sprecher, and T.D.I. Beck. 2004. Body surface temperature of hibernating black bear may be related to periodic muscle activity. J. Mamm. 85:414–419.

Harlow, H. J., T. Lohuis, T.D.I. Beck, and P. A. Iaizzo. 2001. Muscle strength in overwintering bears. Nature 409:997.

Harlow, H. J., T. Lohuis, R. G. Grogan, and T.D.I. Beck. 2002. Body mass and lipid changes by hibernating reproductive and nonreproductive black bears (*Ursus americanus*). J. Mamm. 83:1020–1034.

Harlow, H. J., and G. E. Menkens, Jr. 1986. Comparison of hibernation in the black-tailed prairie dog, white-tailed prairie dog, and Wyoming ground squirrel. Canadian J. Zool. 54:793–796.

Harlow, H. J., and U. S. Seal. 1981. Changes in hematology and metabolism in the serum and urine of the badger, *Taxidea taxus*, during food deprivation. Canadian J. Zool. 59:2123–2128.

Haroldson, K. J., and E. K. Fritzell. 1984. Home ranges, activity, and habitat use by gray foxes in an oak-hickory forest. J. Wildl. Mgmt. 48:222–227.

Haroldson, M. A., C. C. Schwartz, S. Cherry, and D. S. Moody. 2004. Possible effects of elk harvest on fall distribution of grizzly bears in the Greater Yellowstone Ecosystem. J. Wildl. Mgmt. 68:129–137.

Harper, W. R. 1968. Chemosterilant assessment for beaver. Unpubl. master's thesis, Colorado State Univ., Fort Collins, 40 pp.

Harrington, F. H., and L. D. Mech. 1983. Wolf pack spacing: howling as a territory-independent spacing mechanism in a territorial population. Behav. Ecol. and Sociobiol. 12:161–183.

Harrington, F. H., and P. C. Paquet, eds. 1982. Wolves of the world: perspectives of behavior, ecology, and conservation. Noyes Publications, Park Ridge, NJ, 474 pp.

Harrington, J. L., and M. R. Conover. 2007. Does removing coyotes for livestock protection benefit free-ranging ungulates? J. Wildl. Mgmt. 71:1555–1560.

Harris, A. H. 1974. *Myotis yumanensis* in interior southwestern North America, with comments on *Myotis lucifugus*. J. Mamm. 55:589–607.

Harris, A. H., and L. N. Carraway. 1993. *Sorex preblei* from the Late Pleistocene of New Mexico. Southwestern Nat. 38:56–58.

Harrison, R. G., S. M. Bogdanowicz, R. S. Hoffmann, E. Yensen, and P. W. Sherman. 2003. Phylogeny and evolutionary history of the ground squirrels (Rodentia, Marmotinae). J. Molec. Evol. 10:249–276.

Harrison, R. L. 1993. A survey of anthropogenic ecological factors potentially affecting gray foxes (*Urocyon cinereoargenteus*) in a rural residential area. Southwestern Nat. 38:352–356.

Harrison, R. L. 1997. A comparison of gray fox ecology between residential and undeveloped rural landscapes. J. Wildl. Mgmt. 51:112–122.

Harrison, R. L. 1998. Bobcats in residential areas: distribution and homeowner attitudes. Southwestern Nat. 43:469–475.

Harrison, R. L. 2002. Estimating gray fox home-range size using half-night observation periods. Wildl. Soc. Bull. 30:1273–1275.

Harrison, R. L. 2003. Swift fox demography, movements, denning and diet in New Mexico. Southwestern Nat. 48:261–273.

Harrison, R. L. 2006. A comparison of survey methods for detecting bobcats. Wildl. Soc. Bull. 34:548–552.

Harrison, R. L., D. J. Barr, and J. W. Dragoo. 2002. A comparison of population survey techniques for swift foxes (*Vulpes velox*) in New Mexico. Amer. Midland Nat. 148:320–337.

Harrison, R. L., P.-G.S. Clarke, and C. M. Clarke. 2004. Indexing swift fox populations in New Mexico using scats. Amer. Midland Nat. 151:42–49.

Harrison, R. L., and C. G. Schmitt. 2003. Current swift fox distribution and habitat selection within area of historical occurrence in New Mexico. Pp. 71–77, in The swift fox: ecology and conservation of swift foxes in a changing world (M. A. Sovada and L. Carbyn, eds.). Canadian Plains Research Center, Regina, Saskatchewan, 250 pp.

Harrison, R. L., and J. Whitaker-Hoagland. 2003. A literature review of swift fox habitat and den-site selection. Pp. 79–89, in The swift fox: ecology and conservation of swift foxes in a changing world (M. A. Sovada and L. Carbyn, eds.). Canadian Plains Research Center, Regina, Saskatchewan, 250 pp.

Hart, E. B. 1971. Food preferences of the cliff chipmunk, *Eutamias dorsalis*, in northern Utah. Great Basin Nat. 31:182–188.

Hart, E. B. 1976. Life history notes on the cliff chipmunk, *Eutamias dorsalis*, in Utah. Southwestern Nat. 21:243–246.

Hart, E. B., M. C. Belk, E. Jordan, and M. W. Gonzalez. 2004. *Zapus princeps*. Mammalian Species 749:1–7.

Hart, R. H. 2001. Where the buffalo roamed—or did they? Great Plains Research 11:83–102.

Hartman, G. D., and T. L. Yates. 2003. Moles (Talpidae). Pp. 30–55, in Wild mammals of North America, biology, management, and economics, second ed. (G. A. Feldhamer, B. C. Thompson, and J. A. Chapman, eds.). Johns Hopkins Univ. Press, Baltimore, 1,216 pp.

Harvey, M. J. 1976. Home range, movements, and diel activity of the eastern mole, *Scalopus aquaticus*. Amer. Midland Nat. 95:436–445.

Harvey, M. J., J. S. Altenbach, and T. L. Best. 1999. Bats of the United States. Arkansas Game and Fish Commission, Little Rock, 64 pp.

Harwood, G. D. 1995. Restoration of small watersheds by natural beaver activity: a suitability study and field assessment method. Unpubl. master's thesis, Univ. Colorado, Boulder, 126 pp.

Hasenyager, R. N. 1980. Bats of Utah. Publ., Utah Division of Wildlife Resources 80-15:1–109.

Hash, H. S. 1987. Wolverine. Pp. 574–585, in Wild furbearer management and conservation in North America (M. Novak, J. A. Baker, M. E. Obbard, and B. Malloch, eds.). Ontario Trappers Association, Toronto, 1,150 pp.

Hatt, R. T. 1943. The pine squirrel in Colorado. J. Mamm. 24:311–345.

Haufler, J. B., and J. G. Nagy. 1984. Summer food habits of a small mammal community in the pinyon-juniper ecosystem. Great Basin Nat. 44:145–150.

Havlick, V. H. 1984. A population index and habitat relationships of three species of tree squirrels in the Boulder Mountain Parks. Unpubl. master's thesis, Univ. Colorado, Boulder, 40 pp.

Hawes, M. L. 1977. Home range, territoriality, and ecological separation in sympatric shrews, *Sorex vagrans* and *Sorex obscurus*. J. Mamm. 58:354–367.

Hawley, A.W. L., D. G. Peden, H. W. Reynolds, and W. R. Stricklin. 1981. Bison and cattle digestion of forages from the Slave River Lowlands, Northwest Territories, Canada. J. Range Mgmt. 34:126–130.

Hawley, V. D., and F. E. Newby. 1957. Marten home ranges and population fluctuations. J. Mamm. 38:174–184.

Hay, K. G. 1957. Record beaver litter for Colorado. J. Mamm. 38: 268–269.

Hay, K. G. 1958. Beaver census methods in the Rocky Mountain region. J. Wildl. Mgmt. 22:395–402.

Hay, K. G. 2010. Succession of beaver ponds in Colorado 60 years after beaver removal. J. Wildl. Mgmt. 74:1732–1736.

Hayes, J. P. 2003. Habitat ecology and conservation of bats in western coniferous forests. Pp. 81–119, in Mammal community dynamics, management and conservation in the coniferous forests of western North America (C. J. Zabel and R. G. Anthony, eds.). Cambridge Univ. Press, Cambridge, UK, 709 pp.

Hayes, M. A., K. W. Navo, L. R. Bonewell, C. J. Mosch, and R. A. Adams. 2009. Allen's big-eared bat (*Idionycteris phyllotis*) documented in Colorado based on recordings of its distinctive echolocation call. Southwestern Nat. 54:501–503.

Haynes, L. A. 1992. Mountain goat habitat of Wyoming's Beartooth Plateau: implications for management. Proc. of Biennial Symposium, Northern Wild Sheep and Goat Council 8: 325–339.

Haynie, M. L., R. A. Van Den Bussche, J. L. Hoogland, and D. A. Gilbert. 2003. Parentage, multiple paternity, and breeding success in Gunnison's and Utah prairie dogs. J. Mamm. 84:1244–1253.

Hayssen, V. 2008a. Reproductive effort in squirrels: ecological, phylogenetic, allometric, and latitudinal patterns. J. Mamm. 89:582–606.

Hayssen, V. 2008b. Reproduction within marmotine ground squirrels (Sciuridae, Xerinae, Marmotini): patterns among genera. J. Mamm. 89:607–616.

Hayssen, V., Ari Van Tiehoven, and Ans Van Tiehoven. 1993. Asdell's Patterns of Mammalian Reproduction, a compendium of species-specific information. Cornell Univ. Press, Ithaca, 1,023 pp.

Hayward, C. L. 1949. The short-tailed weasel in Utah and Colorado. J. Mamm. 30:436–437.

Hayward, C. L., and M. L. Killpack. 1956. Occurrence of *Perognathus fasciatus* in Utah. J. Mamm. 37:451.

Hayward, G. D., S. H. Henry, and L. F. Ruggiero. 1999. Response of red-backed voles to recent patch cutting in subalpine forest. Cons. Biol. 13:168–176.

Heaney, L. R., and R. M. Timm. 1983. Relationships of pocket gophers of the genus *Geomys* from the central and northern Great Plains. Misc. Publ., Univ. Kansas Mus. Nat. Hist. 74:1–59.

Heaney, L. R., and R. M. Timm. 1985. Morphology, genetics, and ecology of pocket gophers (genus *Geomys*) in a narrow hybrid zone. Biol. J. Linnean Soc. 25:301–317.

Heaney, L. R., and R. M. Timm. 2009. Morphology, genetics, and ecology of pocket gophers in a narrow hybrid zone. Biol. J. Linnean Soc. 25:301–317.

Heberlein, T. A. 1987. A profile of the American hunter. Environment 29(7):6–33.

Hecht, A., and P. R. Nickerson. 1999. The need for predator management in conservation of some vulnerable species. Endangered Species Update 16:114–118.

Hecker, K. R., and R. M. Brigham. 1999. Does moonlight change vertical stratification of activity of forest-dwelling insectivorous bats? J. Mamm. 80:1196–1201.

Hediger, H. 1970. The breeding behavior of the Canadian beaver (*Castor fiber canadensis*). Forma et Functio 2:336–351.

Hegdal, P. L., A. L. Ward, A. M. Johnson, and H. P. Tietjen. 1965. Notes on the life history of the Mexican pocket gopher (*Cratogeomys castanops*). J. Mamm. 46:334–335.

Heilbrun, R. D., N. J. Silvy, M. J. Peterson, and M. E. Tewes. 2006. Estimating bobcat abundance using automatically triggered cameras. Wildl. Soc. Bull. 34:69–73.

Heilbrun, R. D., N. J. Silvy, M. E. Tewes, and M J. Peterson. 2003. Using automatically triggered cameras to individually identify bobcats. Wildl. Soc. Bull. 31:748–755.

Hein, E. W., and W. F. Andelt. 1995. Evaluation of indices of abundance for an unexploited badger population. Southwestern Nat. 40:288–292.

Hein, F. J., and C. R. Preston. 1998. Summer nocturnal movements and habitat selection by *Bison bison* in Colorado. Pp. 96–102, in International Symposium on Bison Ecology and Management in North America (L. Irby and J. Knight, eds.). Montana State Univ., Bozeman, 395 pp.

Helgen, K. M., F. R. Cole, L. E. Helgen, and D. E. Wilson. 2009. Generic revision in the Holarctic ground squirrel genus *Spermophilus*. J. Mamm. 90:270–305.

Hemker, T. P., F. G. Lindzey, and B. B. Ackerman. 1984. Population characteristics and movement patterns of cougars in southern Utah. J. Wildl. Mgmt. 48:1275–1284.

Henderson, F. R. 1976. How to handle problem skunks. Pp. 35–38, in Proc. Second Great Plains Wildlife Damage Control Workshop, Manhattan, Kansas (available from Internet Center for Wildlife Damage Management, Univ. Nebraska–Lincoln, http://digitalcommons.unl.edu/gpwdcwp/191.

Henderson, F. R., P. F. Springer, and R. Adrian. 1969. The black-footed ferret in South Dakota. South Dakota Dept. of Game, Fish, and Parks Rept., Pierre, 37 pp.

Henke, S. E., and F. C. Bryant. 1999. Effects of coyote removal on the faunal community in western Texas. J. Wildl. Mgmt. 53:1066–1081.

Henner, C. M., M. J. Chamberlain, B. D. Leopold, and L. W. Burger, Jr. 2004. A multi-resolution assessment of raccoon den selection. J. Wildl. Mgmt. 58:179–187.

Hennings, D., and R. S. Hoffmann. 1977. A review of the taxonomy of the *Sorex vagrans* species complex from western North America. Occas. Papers, Univ. Kansas Mus. Nat. Hist. 58:1–35.

Henry, D. J. 1986. Red fox, the catlike canid. Smithsonian Institution Press, Washington, DC, 174 pp.

Henry, S. E., M. G. Raphael, and L. F. Ruggiero. 1990. Food caching and handling by marten. Great Basin Nat. 50:381–383.

Hermanson, J. W., and T. J. O'Shea. 1983. *Antrozous pallidus*. Mammalian Species 213:1–8.

Herrero, S. 2005. Bear attacks, their causes and avoidance. Lyons Press, Guilford, CT, 282 pp.

Herrero, S., and S. Fleck. 1990. Injury to people inflicted by black, grizzly or polar bears: recent trends and new insights. International Conf. Bear Research and Management 8:25–32.

Hershkovitz, P. 1962. Evolution of Neotropical cricetine rodents (Muridae), with special reference to the phyllotine group. Fieldiana Zool. 46:1–524.

Hershkovitz, P. 1971. Basic crown patterns and cusp homologies of mammalian teeth. Pp. 95–150, in Dental morphology and evolution (A. A. Dahlberg, ed.). Univ. Chicago Press, Chicago, 350 pp.

Hess, K., Jr. 1993. Rocky times in Rocky Mountain National Park. Univ. Press Colorado, Niwot, 167 pp.

Hesselton, W. T., and R. M. Hesselton. 1982. White-tailed deer. Pp. 878–901, in Wild mammals of North America, biology, management, and economics (J. A. Chapman and G. A. Feldhamer, eds.). Johns Hopkins Univ. Press, Baltimore, 1,147 pp.

Hetlet, L. A. 1968. Observations on a group of badgers in South Park, Colorado. Unpubl. master's thesis, Colorado State Univ., Fort Collins, 30 pp.

Hibbs, L. D. 1967. Food habits of the mountain goat in Colorado. J. Mamm. 48:242–248.

Hibbs, L. D., F. A. Glover, and D. L. Gilbert. 1969. The mountain goat in Colorado. Trans. N. American Wildlife and Natural Resources Conf. 34:409–418.

Hickman, G. C. 1975. The maternal behavior of a Mexican pocket gopher *Pappogeomys castanops*. Southwestern Nat. 20:142–144.

Hickman, G. C. 1977. Burrow system structure of *Pappogeomys castanops* (Geomyidae) in Lubbock County, Texas. Amer. Midland Nat. 97:50–58.

Hicks, E. A. 1949. Ecological factors affecting the activity of the western fox squirrel, *Sciurus niger rufiventer* (Geoffroy). Ecol. Monogr. 19:287–302.

Higginbotham, J. L., and L. K. Ammerman. 2002. Chiropteran community structure and seasonal dynamics in Big Bend National Park. Spec. Publ. Museum, Texas Tech Univ. 44:1–44.

Higgins, L. C., and P. Stapp. 1997. Abundance of thirteen-lined ground squirrels in shortgrass prairie. Prairie Nat. 29:25–37.

Hildebrand, M. 1961. Voice of the grasshopper mouse. J. Mamm. 42:263.

Hill, E. P. 1982. Beaver. Pp. 256–281, in Wild mammals of North America, biology, management, and economics (J. A. Chapman and G. A. Feldhamer, eds.). Johns Hopkins Univ. Press, Baltimore, 1,147 pp.

Hill, J. E., and J. D. Smith. 1984. Bats: a natural history. Univ. Texas Press, Austin, 243 pp.

Hillman, C. N. 1968. Field observations of black-footed ferrets in South Dakota. Trans. N. Amer. Wildl. Nat. Resources Conf. 33:433–443.

Hillman, C. N., and T. W. Clark. 1980. *Mustela nigripes*. Mammalian Species 126:1–3.

Hillman, C. N., and R. L. Linder. 1973. The black-footed ferret. Pp. 10–23, in Proceedings of the Black-footed Ferret and Prairie Dog Workshop (R. L. Linder and C. N. Hillman, eds.). South Dakota State Univ., Brookings, 208 pp.

Hillman, C. N., R. L. Linder, and R. B. Dahlgren. 1979. Prairie dog distributions in areas inhabited by black-footed ferrets. Amer. Midland Nat. 102:185–187.

Hillman, C. N., and J. C. Sharps. 1978. Return of the swift fox to northern Great Plains. Proc. South Dakota Acad. Sci. 57:154–162.

Hilton, B. L. 1992. Reproduction in the Mexican vole, *Microtus mexicanus*. J. Mamm. 73:586–590.

Hilton, H. 1978. Systematics and ecology of the eastern coyote. Pp. 209–228, in Coyotes: biology, behavior, and management (M. Bekoff, ed.). Academic Press, New York, 384 pp.

Hines, T. D. 1980. An ecological study of *Vulpes velox* in Nebraska. Unpubl. master's thesis, Univ. Nebraska, Lincoln, 131 pp.

Hines, T. D., and R. M. Case. 1991. Diet, home range, movements, and activity periods of swift fox in Nebraska. Prairie. Nat. 3: 131–138.

Hironaka, M., M. A. Fosberg, and A. H. Winward. 1983. Sagebrush-grass habitat types of southern Idaho. Bull., Univ. Idaho Forest, Wildl. and Range Exper. Station 35:1–44.

Hirth, D. H., and D. R. McCullough. 1977. Evolution of alarm signals in ungulates with special reference to white-tailed deer. Amer. Nat. 111:31–42.

Hobbs, N. T. 1979. Winter diet quality and nutritional status of elk in the upper montane zone, Colorado. Unpubl. doctoral dissert., Colorado State Univ., Fort Collins, 131 pp.

Hobbs, N. T. 1996. Modification of ecosystems by ungulates. J. Wildl. Mgmt. 50:695–713.

Hobbs, N. T., D. L. Baker, G. D. Bear, and D. C. Bowden. 1996a. Ungulate grazing in sagebrush grassland: effects of resource competition on secondary production. Ecol. Appl. 5:218–227.

Hobbs, N. T., D. L. Baker, G. D. Bear, and D. C. Bowden. 1996b. Ungulate grazing in sagebrush grassland: mechanisms of resource competition. Ecol. Appl. 5:200–217.

Hobbs, N. T., D. L. Baker, J. E. Ellis, and D. M. Swift. 1981. Composition and quality of elk winter diets in Colorado. J. Wildl. Mgmt. 45:156–171.

Hobbs, N. T., D. L. Baker, and R. B. Gill. 1983. Comparative nutritional ecology of montane ungulates during winter. J. Wildl. Mgmt. 47:1–16.

Hobbs, N. T., D. C. Bowden, and D. L. Baker. 2000. Effects of fertility control on populations of ungulates: general, stage-structured models. J. Wildl. Mgmt. 54:473–491.

Hobbs, N. T., J. E. Ellis, and D. M. Swift. 1979. Composition and quality of elk diets during winter and summer: a preliminary analysis. Pp. 47–53, in North American elk: ecology, behavior, and management (M. S. Boyce and L. D. Hayden-Wing, eds.). Univ. Wyoming, Laramie, 294 pp.

Hobbs, N. T., M. W. Miller, J. A. Bailey, D. F. Reed, and R. B. Gill. 1990. Biological criteria for introductions of large mammals: using simulation models to predict impacts of competition. Trans. North American Wildl. Nat. Res. Conf. 55:620–632.

Hodgdon, H. E., and J. S. Larson. 1973. Some sexual differences in behavior within a colony of marked beavers (*Castor canadensis*). Animal Behav. 21:147–152.

Hodges, K. E. 2000a. The ecology of snowshoe hares in northern boreal forests. Pp. 117–161, in Ecology and conservation of lynx in the United States (L. F. Ruggiero, K. B. Aubry, S. W. Buskirk, G. M. Koehler, C. J. Krebs, K. S. McKelvey, and J. R. Squires, eds.). Univ. Press Colorado, Boulder, 480 pp.

Hodges, K. E. 2000b. Ecology of snowshoe hares in southern boreal and montane forests. Pp 163–206, in Ecology and conservation of lynx in the United States (L. F. Ruggiero, K. B. Aubry, S. W. Buskirk, G. M. Koehler, C. J. Krebs, K. S. McKelvey, and J. R. Squires, eds.). Univ. Press Colorado, Boulder, 480 pp.

Hoditschek, B., and T. L. Best. 1983. Reproductive biology of Ord's kangaroo rat (*Dipodomys ordii*) in Oklahoma. J. Mamm. 54:121–127.

Hoehn, K. L., S. F. Hudachek, S. A. Summers, and G. L. Florant. 2004. Seasonal, tissue-specific regulation of Akt/protein kinase B and glycogen synthase in hibernators. Amer. J. Phys.—Reg., Integr., and Comp. Phys., 286:R498–R504.

Hoeman, J. V. 1964. High altitude winter records for white-tailed jackrabbits. J. Mamm. 45:495.

Hof, J., M. Bevers, D. W. Uresk, and G. L. Schenbeck. 2002. Optimizing habitat location for black-tailed prairie dogs in southwestern South Dakota. Ecol. Modelling 147:11–21.

Hoff, D. J. 1998. Integrated laboratory and field investigations assessing contaminant risk to American badgers (*Taxidea taxus*) on the Rocky Mountain Arsenal National Wildlife Refuge. Unpubl. doctoral dissert., Clemson Univ., Clemson, SC, 240 pp.

Hoffman, J. D., and J. R. Choate. 2008. Distribution and status of the yellow-faced pocket gopher in Kansas. Western N. Amer. Nat. 58:483–492.

Hoffman, J. D., J. R. Choate, and R. Channell. 2007. Effects of land use and soil texture on distributions of pocket gophers in Kansas. Southwestern Nat. 52:296–301.

Hoffman, J. D., and H. H. Genoways. 2005. Recent records of formerly extirpated carnivores in Nebraska. Prairie Nat. 37: 225–245.

Hoffman, J. D., H. H. Genoways, and J. R. Choate. 2006. Long-distance dispersal and population trends of moose in the central United States. Alces 42:115–131.

Hoffman, R. R. 1985. Digestive physiology of the deer: their morphophysiological specialisation and adaptation. Pp. 393–407 in Biology of deer production (P. F. Fennessey and K. R. Drew, eds.). Royal Society of New Zealand, Wellington, 482 pp.

Hoffmann, C. O., and J. L. Gottschang. 1977. Numbers, distribution, and movements of a raccoon population in a suburban residential community. J. Mamm. 58:623–636.

Hoffmann, L. A., E. F. Redente, and L. C. McEwen. 1995. Effects of selective seed predation by rodents on shortgrass establishment. Ecol. Appl. 5:200–208.

Hoffmann, R. S., and R. D. Fisher. 1978. Additional distributional records of Preble's shrew (*Sorex preblei*). J. Mamm. 59:883–884.

Hoffmann, R. S., and J. K. Jones, Jr. 1970. Influence of late-glacial and post-glacial events on the distribution of Recent mammals on the northern Great Plains. Pp. 355–394, in Pleistocene and Recent environments of the central Great Plains (W. Dort, Jr., and J. K. Jones, Jr., eds.). Special Publ., Dept. of Geology, Univ. Kansas 3:1–433.

Hoffmann, R. S., and J. G. Owen. 1980. *Sorex tenellus* and *Sorex nanus*. Mammalian Species 131:1–4.

Hoffmann, R. S., and A. T. Smith. 2005. Order Lagomorpha. Pp. 185–211, in Mammal species of the world, a taxonomic and geographic reference, third ed. (D. E. Wilson and D. M. Reeder, eds.), 2 vols. Johns Hopkins Univ. Press, Baltimore.

Hoffmann, R. S., P. L. Wright, and F. E. Newby. 1969. The distribution of some mammals in Montana, I. Mammals other than bats. J. Mamm. 50:579–604.

Hoffmeister, D. F. 1967. An unusual concentration of shrews. J. Mamm. 48:462–464.

Hoffmeister, D. F. 1970. The seasonal distribution of bats in Arizona: a case for improving mammalian range maps. Southwestern Nat. 15:11–22.

Hoffmeister, D. F. 1981. *Peromyscus truei*. Mammalian Species 161: 1–5.

Hoffmeister, D. F. 1986. Mammals of Arizona. Univ. Arizona Press, Tucson, 602 pp.

Hoffmeister, D. F., and V. E. Diersing. 1978. Review of the tassel-eared squirrels of the subgenus *Otosciurus*. J. Mamm. 59:402–413.

Hoffmeister, D. F., and L. S. Ellis. 1979. Geographic variation in *Eutamias quadrivittatus* with comments on the taxonomy of other Arizona chipmunks. Southwestern Nat. 24:655–666.

Hoffmeister, D. F., and W. W. Goodpaster. 1962. Life history of the desert shrew, *Notiosorex crawfordi*. Southwestern Nat. 7: 236–252.

Hoffmeister, D. F., and M. R. Lee. 1963. Revision of the desert cottontail, *Sylvilagus audubonii*, in the Southwest. J. Mamm. 44:501–518.

Hofmann, J. E., B. McGuire, and T. M. Pizzuto. 1989. Parental care in the sagebrush vole (*Lemmiscus curtatus*). J. Mamm. 70:162–165.

Hogdon, K. W., and J. S. Larson. 1980. A bibliography of the recent literature on beaver. Res. Bull., Univ. Massachusetts Agric. Exper. Sta. 565:1–128.

Hogue, J. E. 1955. *Taxidea taxus taxus*: the brawny and belligerent badger. Colorado Conservation 4:28–29.

Hogue, J. E. 1958. The red fox. Colorado Outdoors 7:12–14.

Hohn, B. M. 1966. Movement and activity patterns in a population of thirteen-lined ground squirrels, Itasca State Park, Minnesota. Unpubl. master's thesis, Univ. Minnesota, St. Paul, 78 pp.

Holbrook, S. J. 1978. Habitat relationships and coexistence of four sympatric species of *Peromyscus* in northwestern New Mexico. J. Mamm. 59:18–26.

Holcomb, L. C. 1965. Large litter size of red fox. J. Mamm. 46: 530.

Holden, M. E., and G. G. Musser. Family Dipodidae. Pp. 871–893, in Mammal species of the world, a taxonomic and geographic reference, third ed. (D. E. Wilson and D. M. Reeder, eds.), 2 vols. Johns Hopkins Univ. Press, Baltimore.

Holdenried, R. 1957. Natural history of the bannertail kangaroo rat in New Mexico. J. Mamm. 38:330–350.

Holdridge, L. R. 1967. Life zone ecology. Tropical Science Center, San José, Costa Rica, 203 pp.

Holgren, M., P. Stapp, C. R. Dickman, C. Gracia, S. Graham, J. R. Gutiérrez, C. Hice, F. Jaksic, D. A. Kelt, M. Letnic, M. Lima, B. C. Lopez, P. L. Meserve, W. B. Milstead, G. A. Polis, M. A. Previtali, M. Richter, S. Sabaté, and F. A. Squero. 2006. Extreme climatic events shape arid and semiarid ecosystems. Frontiers Ecol. Envir. 4:87–95.

Hollander, R. R. 1990. Biosystematics of the yellow-faced pocket gopher, *Cratogeomys castanops* (Rodentia: Geomyidae) in the United States. Spec. Publ., Museum, Texas Tech Univ. 33:1–62.

Hollister, N. 1909. Two new bats from the southwestern United States. Proc. Biol. Soc. Washington 22:43–44.

Hollister, N. 1916. A systematic account of the prairie dogs. N. Amer. Fauna 40:1–37.

Holloway, G. L., and R.M.R. Barclay. 2001. *Myotis ciliolabrum*. Mammalian Species 670:1–5.

Holmes, A.C.V., and G. C. Sanderson. 1965. Populations and movements of opossums in east-central Illinois. J. Wildl. Mgmt. 29:287–295.

Holmes, B. E. 2008. A review of black-footed ferret reintroduction in northwest Colorado, 2001–2006. Technical Note, White River Field Office, Bureau of Land Management 426:1–43.

Holst, V. D. 1985. The primitive eutherians, I. Orders Insectivora, Macroscelidea, and Scandentia. Pp. 105–154, in Social odours in mammals, vol. 1 (R. E. Brown and D. W. Macdonald, eds.). Clarendon Press, Oxford, UK, 506 pp.

Holter, J. B., G. Tyler, and T. Walski. 1974. Nutrition of the snowshoe hare (*Lepus americanus*). Canadian J. Zoology 52: 1553–1558.

Honacki, J. H., J. E. Kinman, and J. W. Koeppl. 1982. Mammal species of the world. Assoc. Systematics Collections, Lawrence, KS, 694 pp.

Honeycutt, R. L., L. J. Frabotta, and D. L. Rowe. 2007. Rodent evolution, phylogenetics, and biogeography. Pp. 8–23, in Rodent societies, an ecological & evolutionary perspective (J. O. Wolff and P. W. Sherman, eds.). Univ. Chicago Press, Chicago, 610 pp.

Honeycutt, R. L., and S. L. Williams. 1982. Genic differentiation in pocket gophers of the genus *Pappogeomys*, with comments on intergeneric relationships in the subfamily Geomyinae. J. Mamm. 53:208–217.

Hoofer, S. R., J. R. Choate, and N. E. Mandrak. 1999. Mensural discrimination between *Reithrodontomys megalotis* and *R. montanus* using cranial characteristics. J. Mamm. 80:91–101.

Hoofer, S. R., and R. A. Van Den Bussche. 2003. Molecular phylogenetics of the chiropteran family Vespertilionidae. Acta Chiropterol. 5 (supplement):1–63.

Hoofer, S. R., R. A. Van Den Bussche, and I. Horáček. 2006. Generic status of the American pipistrelles (Vespertilionidae) with description of a new genus. J. Mamm. 87:981–992.

Hoogland, J. L. 1979a. Aggression, ectoparasitism, and other possible costs of prairie dog (Sciuridae, *Cynomys* spp.) coloniality. Behaviour 69:1–35.

Hoogland, J. L. 1979b. The effect of colony size on individual alertness of prairie dogs (Sciuridae: *Cynomys* spp.) Animal Behavior 27:394–407.

Hoogland, J. L. 1981. The evolution of coloniality in white-tailed and black-tailed prairie dogs (Sciuridae: *Cynomys leucurus* and *C. ludovicianus*). Ecology 62:252–272.

Hoogland, J. L. 1983. Nepotism and alarm calling in the black-tailed prairie dog (*Cynomys ludovicianus*). Animal Behavior 31:472–479.

Hoogland, J. L. 1985. Infanticide in prairie dogs: lactating females kill offspring of close kin. Science 230:1037–1038.

Hoogland, J. L. 1987. Using molar attrition to age live prairie dogs. J. Wildl. Mgmt. 51:393–394.

Hoogland, J. L. 1995. The black-tailed prairie dog: social life of a burrowing mammal. Univ. Chicago Press, Chicago, 557 pp.

Hoogland, J. L. 1996a. *Cynomys ludovicianus*. Mammalian Species 535:1–10.

Hoogland, J. L. 1996b. Why do Gunnison's prairie dogs give anti-predator calls? Animal Behavior 51:871–880.

Hoogland, J. L. 1997. Duration of gestation and lactation for Gunnison's prairie dogs. J. Mamm. 78:173–180.

Hoogland, J. L. 1998. Estrus and copulation for Gunnison's prairie dogs. J. Mamm. 79:887–897.

Hoogland, J. L. 1999. Philopatry, dispersal, and social organization of Gunnison's prairie dogs. J. Mamm. 80:243–251.

Hoogland, J. L. 2001. Black-tailed, Gunnison's, and Utah prairie dogs all reproduce slowly. J. Mamm. 82:917–927.

Hoogland, J. L. 2003a. Sexual dimorphism of prairie dogs. J. Mamm. 84:1254–1266.

Hoogland, J. L. 2003b. Black-tailed prairie dog, *Cynomys ludovicianus* and allies. Pp. 232–247, in Wild mammals of North America, biology, management, and economics, second ed. (G. A. Feldhamer, B. C. Thompson, and J. A. Chapman, eds.). Johns Hopkins Univ. Press, Baltimore, 1,216 pp.

Hoogland, J. L. 2007a. Alarm calling, multiple mating, and infanticide among black-tailed, Gunnison's, and Utah prairie dogs. Pp. 438–450, in Rodent societies, an ecological & evolutionary perspective (J. O. Wolff and P. W. Sherman, eds.). Univ. Chicago Press, Chicago, 610 pp.

Hoogland, J. L. 2007b. Conservation of prairie dogs. Pp. 472–477, in Rodent societies: an ecological & evolutionary perspective (J. O. Wolff and P. W. Sherman, eds.). Univ. Chicago Press, Chicago, 610 pp.

Hooker, J. J. 2005. Perissodactyla. Pp. 199–214, in The rise of placental mammals, origins and relationships of the major extant clades (K. D. Rose and J. D. Archibald, eds.). Johns Hopkins Univ. Press, Baltimore, 259 pp.

Hooper, E. T. 1952. A systematic review of harvest mice (genus *Reithrodontomys*) in Latin America. Misc. Publ., Univ. Michigan Mus. Zool. 77:1–255.

Hooper, E. T., and G. G. Musser. 1964. The glans penis in Neotropical cricetines (family Muridae) with comments on classification of muroid rodents. Misc. Publ., Univ. Michigan Mus. Zool. 123:1–57.

Hoover, R. L., C. E. Till, and S. Ogilvie. 1959. The antelope of Colorado. Tech. Bull., Colorado Division of Game and Fish 4:1–110.

Hoover, R. L., and D. L. Wills, eds. 1987. Managing forested lands for wildlife. Colorado Division of Wildlife and Rocky Mountain Region, USDA Forest Service, Denver, 459 pp.

Hoover, R. L., and L. E. Yeager. 1953. Status of the fox squirrel in northeastern Colorado. J. Mamm. 34:359–365.

Hope, A. G., and R. R. Parmenter. 2007. Food habits of rodents inhabiting arid and semi-arid ecosystems of central New Mexico. Spec. Publ., Mus. Southwestern Biology, Univ. New Mexico 9:1–75.

Hopkins, A. L. 1992. Behavior and population dynamics of mountain goats in the Gore Range of Colorado. Unpubl. master's thesis, Univ. Northern Colorado, Greeley, 168 pp.

Hopkins, A., J. P. Fitzgerald, A. Chappell, and G. Byrne. 1992. Population dynamics and behavior of mountain goats using Elliott Ridge, Gore Range, Colorado. Proc. Biennial Symp. Northern Wild Sheep and Goat Council 8:340–356.

Hornocker, M. G. 1969. Winter territoriality in mountain lions. J. Wildl. Mgmt. 33:457–464.

Hornocker, M. G. 1970. An analysis of mountain lion predation upon mule deer and elk in the Idaho Primitive Area. Wildl. Monogr. 21:1–39.

Hornocker, M. G., and H. S. Hash. 1981. Ecology of the wolverine in northwestern Montana. Canadian J. Zool. 59:1286–1301.

Hornocker, M., and S. Negri, eds. 2009. Cougar ecology and conservation. Univ. Chicago Press, Chicago, 306 pp.

Hosken, D. J., K. E. Jones, K. Chipperfield, and A. Dixson. 2001. Is the bat os penis sexually selected? Behav. Ecol. Sociobiol. 50:450–460.

Hosley, N. W. 1949. The moose and its ecology. Leaflet, U.S. Fish and Wildlife Service 317:1–51.

House, W. A. 1964. Food habits of Richardson's ground squirrel in south-central Wyoming. Unpubl. master's thesis, Colorado State Univ., Fort Collins, 57 pp.

Houseknecht, C. R., and J. R. Tester. 1978. Denning habits of striped skunks (*Mephitis mephitis*). Amer. Midland Nat. 100: 424–430.

Houston, D. B. 1968. The Shiras moose in Jackson Hole, Wyoming. Tech. Bull., Grand Teton Natural History Assoc. 1:1–110.

Houston, D. B. 1974. Aspects of the social organization of moose. Pp. 690–696, in The behavior of ungulates and its relation to management (V. Geist and F. Walther, eds.). IUCN Publ. 24(2):1–941.

Houston, D. B., and E. G. Schreiner. 1995. Alien species in national parks: drawing lines in space and time. Cons. Biol. 9: 204–209.

Houston, D. B., E. G. Schreiner, and B. B. Moorhead. 1994. Mountain goats in Olympic National Park: biology and management of an introduced species. Sci. Monogr., National Park Service, NPS/NROLYM/NRSM-94/95, unpaged. http://www.nps.gov/history/history/online_books/science/25/index.htm.

Howard, J. A. 1967. Variation in the big brown bat, *Eptesicus fuscus*, in Kansas. Unpubl. master's thesis, Univ. Kansas, Lawrence, 37 pp.

Howard, W. E. 1961. A pocket gopher population crash. J. Mamm. 42:258–260.

Howard, W. E., and R. E. Marsh. 1982. Spotted and hog-nosed skunks. Pp. 664–673, in Wild mammals of North America, biology, management, and economics (J. A. Chapman and G. A. Feldhamer, eds.). Johns Hopkins Univ. Press, Baltimore, 1,147 pp.

Howe, R. J. 1977. Scent marking behavior in three species of woodrats (*Neotoma*) in captivity. J. Mamm. 58:685–688.

Howe, R. J. 1978. Agonistic behavior of three sympatric species of woodrats (*Neotoma mexicana*, *N. albigula*, and *N. stephensi*). J. Mamm. 59:780–786.

Howell, A. H. 1915. Revision of the American marmots. N. Amer. Fauna 37:1–80.

Hubbard, R. E., and R. M. Hansen. 1976. Diets of wild horses, cattle, and mule deer in the Piceance Basin, Colorado. J. Range Mgmt. 29:389–392.

Huckaby, L. S., and W. H. Moir. 1998. Forest communities at Fraser Experimental Forest, Colorado. Southwestern Nat. 43:204–218.

Hudson, B. W., et al. 1971. Serological and bacteriological investigations of an outbreak of plague in an urban tree squirrel population. Amer. J. Trop. Med. Hyg. 20:255–263.

Hudson, J. W. 1962. The role of water in the biology of the antelope ground squirrel *Citellus leucurus*. Univ. California Publ. Zool. 54:1–56.

Huebschman, J. J., P. W. Freeman, H. H. Genoways, and J. A. Gubanyi. 2000. Observations on small mammals recovered from owl pellets from Nebraska. Prairie Nat. 32:209–215.

Hughes, J. M., C. J. Peters, M. L. Cohen, and B.W.J. Mahy. 1993. Hantavirus Pulmonary Syndrome: an emerging infectious disease. Science 262:850–851.

Huheey, C. C. 1972. Sympatric hybridization of *Neotoma albigula* and *Neotoma micropus* in southeastern Colorado: a study of karyology, blood proteins, morphology, and ecology. Unpubl. doctoral dissert., Univ. Illinois, Urbana, 66 pp.

Humes, M. L., J. P. Hayes, and M. W. Collopy. 1999. Bat activity in thinned, unthinned, and old-growth forests in western Oregon. J. Wildl. Mgmt. 53:553–561.

Humphrey, S. R. 1974. Zoogeography of the nine-banded armadillo (*Dasypus novemcinctus*) in the United States. BioScience 24:457–462.

Humphrey, S. R. 1975. Nursery roosts and community diversity of Nearctic bats. J. Mamm. 56:321–346.

Humphrey, S. R., and J. B. Cope. 1976. Population ecology of the little brown bat, *Myotis lucifugus*, in Indiana and north-central Kentucky. Spec. Publ., Amer. Soc. Mammal. 4:1–81.

Humphrey, S. R., and T. H. Kunz. 1976. Ecology of a Pleistocene relict, the western big-eared bat (*Plecotus townsendii*), in the southern Great Plains. J. Mamm. 57:470–494.

Hundertmark, K. J., and R. T. Bowyer. 2004. Genetics, evolution, and phylogeography of moose. Alces 40:103–122.

Hunter, G. N. 1947. Physical characteristics of Colorado mule deer in relation to their age classes. Colorado Game and Fish Dept., 38 pp.

Hunter, G. N. 1948. History of white-tailed deer in Colorado. Colorado Game and Fish Dept., 10 pp.

Hunter, J. S. 2009. Familiarity breeds contempt: effects of striped skunk color, shape, and abundance on wild carnivore behavior. Behavioral Ecology 20:1315–1322.

Huntley, N., and R. Inouye. 1988. Pocket gophers in ecosystems: patterns and mechanisms. BioScience 38:786–793.

Huntley, N., and O. J. Reichman. 1994. Effects of subterranean mammalian herbivores on vegetation. J. Mamm. 75:852–859.

Hutterer, R. 2005. Order Soricomorpha. Pp. 220–300, in Mammal species of the world, a taxonomic and geographic reference, third ed. (D. E. Wilson and D. M. Reeder, eds.), 2 vols. Johns Hopkins Univ. Press, Baltimore.

Huxley, J. S. 1953. Evolution in action. Harper and Brothers, New York, 182 pp.

Hygnstrom, S. E., R. M. Timm, and G. E. Larson, eds. 1994. Prevention and control of wildlife damage. Univ. Nebraska Coop. Extension, Lincoln. http://digitalcommons.unl.edu/cgi/viewcontent.cgi?article=1000&context=icwdmhandbook.

Indeck, J. 1987. Sediment analysis and mammalian faunal remains from Little Box Elder Cave, Wyoming. Unpubl. doctoral dissert., Univ. Colorado, Boulder, 197 pp.

Ingersoll, T. E., K. W. Navo, and P. de Valpine. 2010. Microclimate preferences during swarming and hibernation in the Townsend's big-eared bat. J. Mamm. 91:1242–1250.

Ingles, L. G. 1941. Natural history observations on the Audubon cottontail. J. Mamm. 22:227–250.

Ingles, L. G. 1960. A quantitative study of the activity of the dusky shrew (*Sorex vagrans obscurus*). Ecology 41:656–660.

Ingles, L. G. 1961. Home range and habitats of the wandering shrew. J. Mamm. 42:455–462.

Inman, K. H., R. M. Inman, R. R. Wigglesworth, A. J. McCue, B. L. Brock, J. D. Rieck, and W. Harrower. 2003. Greater Yellowstone Wolverine Study, Wildlife Conservation Society, North America Program, Cumulative Progress Report, 17 pp.

Inman, R. M., C. M. Costello, D. E. Jones, K. H. Inman, B. C. Thompson, and H. B. Quigley. 2007. Denning chronology and design of effective bear management units. J. Wildl. Mgmt. 71:1476–1483.

Innes, D.G.L. 1994. Life histories of the Soricidae: a review. Pp. 111–136, in Advances in the biology of shrews (J. F. Merritt, G. L. Kirkland, Jr., and R. K. Rose, eds.). Spec. Publ., Carnegie Mus. Nat. Hist. 18:11–458.

Innes, D.G.L., and J. S. Millar. 1994. Life histories of *Clethrionomys* and *Microtus* (Microtinae). Mammal Review 24:179–207.

Inouye, D. W., B. Barr, K. B. Armitage, and B. D. Inouye. 2000. Climate change is affecting altitudinal migrants and hibernating species. Proc. Nat. Acad. Sci. 97:1630–1633.

Inouye, R. S., N. Huntley, and G. A. Wasley. 1997. Effects of pocket gophers (*Geomys bursarius*) on microtopographic variation. J. Mamm. 78:1144–1148.

Irby, L., and J. Knight, eds. 1998. International Symposium on Bison Ecology and Management in North America. Montana State Univ., Bozeman, 395 pp.

Irby, M. L. 1996. The social structure of the Rocky Mountain goat (*Oreamnos americanus*). Unpubl. master's thesis, Univ. Northern Colorado, Greeley, 131 pp.

Irby, M. L., and A. Chappell. 1993. Literature review of the historic distribution of the Rocky Mountain goat (*Oreamnos americanus*) in Colorado. Colorado Division of Wildlife, Denver, 96 pp.

Irby, M. L., and A. F. Chappell. 1994. Review of the historical literature regarding the distribution of the Rocky Mountain goat (*Oreamnos americanus*). Proc. Biennial Symposium, North American Wild Sheep and Goat Council 9:75–80.

Irby, M. L., and J. P. Fitzgerald. 1994. Social status and nanny-kid separation in Rocky Mountain goats. Proc. Biennial Symposium Northern Wild Sheep and Goat Council 9:121–130.

Isenberg, A. C. 2000. The destruction of the bison. Princeton Univ. Press, Princeton, NJ, 206 pp.

Ivan, J. S. 2008. Density, demography, and seasonal movements of snowshoe hare in Colorado. Wildlife Research Report, Lynx Conservation, Colorado Division of Wildlife, Fort Collins. Work Package 0670:26–38.

Jachowski, D. S., J. J. Millspaugh, D. E. Biggins, T. M. Livieri, and M. R. Matchett. 2008. Implications of black-tailed prairie dog spatial dynamics to black-footed ferrets. Nat. Areas J. 28:14–25.

Jackson, D. H. 1986. Ecology of bobcats in east-central Colorado. Unpubl. doctoral dissert., Colorado State Univ., Fort Collins, 116 pp.

Jackson, H.H.T. 1915. A review of the American moles. North American Fauna 38:1–100.

Jackson, L. S. 1985. Bobcat diets and small mammal populations in south-central Colorado. Unpubl. master's thesis, Colorado State Univ., Fort Collins, 82 pp.

Jackson, V. L., and J. R. Choate. 2000. Dens and den sites of the swift fox, *Vulpes velox*. Southwestern Nat. 45:212–220.

Jackson, W. B. 1982. Norway rat and allies. Pp. 1077–1088, in Wild mammals of North America, biology, management, and economics (J. A. Chapman and G. A. Feldhamer, eds.). Johns Hopkins Univ. Press, Baltimore, 1,147 pp.

Jacob, F. 1984. The possible and the actual. Pantheon Books, New York.

Jacobson, S. K., and M. D. McDuff. 1998. Training idiot savants: the lack of human dimensions in conservation biology. Cons. Biol. 12:263–267.

Jacques, C. N., J. A. Jenks, J. D. Sievers, and D. E. Roddy. 2007. Vegetative characteristics of pronghorn bed sites in Wind Cave National Park, South Dakota. Prairie Nat. 39:49–53.

Jacques, C. N., J. A. Jenks, J. D. Sievers, D. E. Roddy, and F. G. Lindzey. 2007. Survival of pronghorns in western South Dakota. J. Wildl. Mgmt. 71:737–743.

James, T. R., and R. W. Seabloom. 1969. Reproductive biology of the white-tailed jack rabbit in North Dakota. J. Wildl. Mgmt. 33:558–568.

James, W. B., and E. S. Booth. 1952. Biology and life history of the sagebrush vole. Walla Walla College Publ., Dept. Biol. Sci. 1:23–43.

Jameson, E. W., Jr. 1952. Food of deer mice, *Peromyscus maniculatus* and *P. boylei*, in the northern Sierra Nevada, California. J. Mamm. 33:50–60.

Jameson, E. W., Jr. 1953. Reproduction of deer mice (*Peromyscus maniculatus* and *P. boylei*) in the Sierra Nevada, California. J. Mamm. 34:44–58.

Jameson, E. W., Jr. 1964. Patterns of hibernation of captive *Citellus lateralis* and *Eutamias speciosus*. J. Mamm. 45:455–460.

Jameson, E. W., Jr. 1999. Host-ectoparasite relationships among North American chipmunks. Acta Theriol. 44:225–231.

Janacek, L. L. 1990. Genic variation in the *Peromyscus truei* group (Rodentia: Cricetidae). J. Mamm. 71:301–308.

Janes, D. W. 1959. Home range and movements of the eastern cottontail in Kansas. Univ. Kansas Publ., Mus. Nat. Hist. 10:553–572.

Janetos, A. C., L. Hansen, D. Inouye, B. P. Kelly, L. Meyerson, W. Peterson, and R. Shaw. 2008. Biodiversity. Pp. 151–181, in The effects of climate change on agriculture, land resources, and biodiversity. US Environmental Protection Agency, Washington, DC, 362 pp.

Janis, C. M. 2007. Artiodactyl paleoecology and evolutionary trends. Pp. 292–302, in The evolution of artiodactyls (D. R. Prothero and S. E. Foss, eds.). Johns Hopkins Univ. Press, Baltimore, 367 pp.

Jannett, F. J., Jr. 1980. Social dynamics of the montane vole, *Microtus montanus*, as a paradigm. The Biologist 62:3–19.

Jannett, F. J., Jr. 1982. Nesting patterns of adult voles, *Microtus montanus*, in field populations. J. Mamm. 53:495–498.

Jannett, F. J., Jr. 1984. Reproduction of the montane vole, *Microtus montanus*, in subnivean populations. Spec. Publ., Carnegie Mus. Nat. Hist. 10:215–224.

Jenkins, H. O. 1948. A study of the meadow mice of three Sierra Nevada meadows. Proc. California Acad. Sci. 26:43–67.

Jenkins, K. J., and R. G. Wright. 1987. Dietary niche relationships among cervids relative to winter snowpack in northwestern Montana. Canadian J. Zool. 55:1397–1401.

Jenkins, S. H., and M. C. Ashley. 2003. Wild horse, *Equus caballus* and allies. Pp. 1148–1163, in Wild mammals of North America, biology, management, and economics, second ed. (G. A. Feldhamer, B. C. Thompson, and J. A. Chapman, eds.). Johns Hopkins Univ. Press, Baltimore, 1,216 pp.

Jenkins, S. H., and S. W. Breck. 1998. Differences in food hoarding among six species of heteromyid rodents. J. Mamm. 79:1221–1233.

Jenkins, S. H., and P. E. Busher. 1979. *Castor canadensis*. Mammalian Species 120:1–8.

Jenkins, S. H., and P. E. Busher. 1980. Problems, progress, and prospects in studies of food selection by beavers. Pp. 559–579, in Worldwide Furbearer Conference Proceedings (J. A. Chapman and D. Pursley, eds.) 1:1–651.

Jepsen, G. L. 1966. Early Eocene bat from Wyoming. Science 154:1333–1339.

Johnsgard, P. A. 2005. Prairie dog empire, a saga of the shortgrass prairie. Univ. Nebraska Press, Lincoln, 243 pp.

Johnson, B. K., and D. R. Smith. 1980. Food habits and forage preferences of bighorn sheep in alpine and subalpine communities. Proc. Biennial Symposium, Northern Wild Sheep and Goat Council 1980:1–17.

Johnson, B. K., R. D. Schultz, and J. A. Bailey. 1978. Summer forages of mountain goats in the Sawatch Range, Colorado. J. Wildl. Mgmt. 42:636–639.

Johnson, C. E. 1921. The "hand-stand" habit of the spotted skunk. J. Mamm. 2:87–89.

Johnson, D. R. 1967. Diet and reproduction of Colorado pika. J. Mamm. 48:311–315.

Johnson, D. W. 1981. Ecology of small mammals on two isolated buttes in Canyonlands National Park, Utah. Southwestern Nat. 26:395–407.

Johnson, D. W., and D. M. Armstrong. 1987. *Peromyscus crinitus*. Mammalian Species 287:1–8.

Johnson, G. E. 1917. The habits of the thirteen-lined ground squirrel (*Citellus tridecemlineatus*) with especial reference to burrows. Quart. Rev., Univ. North Dakota 7:261–271.

Johnson, G. E. 1927. Observations on young prairie dogs (*Cynomys ludovicianus*) born in the laboratory. J. Mamm. 8:110–115.

Johnson, G. E. 1928. Hibernation of the thirteen-lined ground squirrel *Citellus tridecemlineatus* (Mitchell), I. A comparison of the normal and hibernating states. J. Exper. Zool. 50:15–30.

Johnson, G. E., M. A. Foster, and R. M. Coco. 1933. The sexual cycle of the thirteen-lined ground squirrel in the laboratory. Trans. Kansas Acad. Sci. 36:250–269.

Johnson, K. 1979. Ecology, behavior, and social organization of the rock squirrel, *Spermophilus variegatus*. Unpubl. master's thesis, Trinity Univ., San Antonio, TX, 107 pp.

Johnson, K. 1981. Social organization in a colony of rock squirrels (*Spermophilus variegatus*, Sciuridae). Southwestern Nat. 26:237–242.

Johnson, K. R., and R. G. Raynolds. 2006. Ancient Denvers. Denver Museum of Nature and Science, Denver, CO, 34 pp.

Johnson, K. R., and R. K. Stucky. 1995. Prehistoric journey, a history of life on Earth. Roberts Rinehart Publishers, Boulder, CO, 144 pp.

Johnson, M. K., and R. M. Hansen. 1979. Foods of cottontails and woodrats in south-central Idaho. J. Mamm. 50:213–215.

Johnson, M. L., and C. W. Clanton. 1954. Natural history of *Sorex merriami* in Washington State. Murrelet 35:1–4.

Johnson, M. L., and S. Johnson. 1982. Voles. Pp. 326–354, in Wild mammals of North America, biology, management, and economics (J. A. Chapman and G. A. Feldhamer, eds.). Johns Hopkins Univ. Press, Baltimore, 1,147 pp.

Johnson, W. C., and S. K. Collinge. 2004. Landscape effects on black-tailed prairie dog colonies. Biol. Cons. 115:487–497.

Johnson, W. E., T. K. Fuller, and W. L. Franklin. 1996. Sympatry in canids: a review and assessment. Pp. 189–218, in Carnivore behavior, ecology, and evolution, vol. 2 (J. L. Gittleman, ed.). Cornell Univ. Press, Ithaca, NY, 644 pp.

Jolley, T. W., R. L. Honeycutt, and R. D. Bradley. 2000. Phylogenetic relationships of pocket gophers (genus *Geomys*) based on the mitochondrial 12S mRNA gene. J. Mamm. 81:1025–1034.

Jones, C. 1965. Ecological distributions and activity periods of bats of the Mogollon Mountains area of New Mexico and adjacent Arizona. Tulane Studies Zool. 12:93–100.

Jones, C., and N. J. Hildreth. 1989. *Neotoma stephensi*. Mammalian Species 328:1–3.

Jones, C., R. S. Hoffmann, D. W. Rice, R. J. Baker, M. D. Engstrom, R. D. Bradley, D. J. Schmidly, and C. A. Jones. 1997. Revised checklist of North American mammals north of Mexico, 1997. Occas. Papers, Mus., Texas Tech Univ. 173:1–19.

Jones, C., and R. D. Suttkus. 1972. Notes on netting bats for eleven years in western New Mexico. Southwestern Nat. 16:261–266.

Jones, C. A. 1999. *Zapus hudsonius* in southern Colorado. Occas. Papers Mus., Texas Tech Univ. 191:1–7.

Jones, C. A. 2002. Mammals of the James M. John and Lake Dorothey State Wildlife Areas, Las Animas County, Colorado. Proc. Denver Mus. Nature & Sci. 4(3):1–22.

Jones, C. A., and C. N. Baxter. 2004. *Thomomys bottae*. Mammalian Species 742:1–14.

Jones, C. A., R. D. Beane, and E. A. Dickerson. 2003. Habitat use by birds and mammals along the urban South Platte River in Denver, Colorado. Occas. Papers, Mus., Texas Tech. Univ. 221:1–16.

Jones, C. G., J. H. Lawton, and M. Shacek. 1997. Positive and negative effects of organisms as physical ecosystem engineers. Ecology 78:1946–1957.

Jones, G. S., and D. B. Jones. 1985. Observations of intraspecific behavior of meadow jumping mice, *Zapus hudsonius*, and escape behavior of a western jumping mouse, *Zapus princeps*, in the wild. Canadian Field-Naturalist 99:378–380.

Jones, J. H., and N. S. Smith. 1979. Bobcat density and prey selection in central Arizona. J. Wildl. Mgmt. 43:666–672.

Jones, J. K., Jr. 1953. Geographic distribution of the pocket mouse, *Perognathus fasciatus*. Misc. Publ., Mus. Nat. Hist., Univ. Kansas 5:515–526.

Jones, J. K., Jr. 1958. A new bog lemming (genus *Synaptomys*) from Nebraska. Univ. Kansas Publ., Mus. Nat. Hist. 9:385–388.

Jones, J. K., Jr. 1964. Distribution and taxonomy of mammals in Nebraska. Univ. Kansas Publ., Mus. Nat. Hist. 16:1–356.

Jones, J. K., Jr., D. M. Armstrong, and J. R. Choate. 1985. Guide to mammals of the plains states. Univ. Nebraska Press, Lincoln, 371 pp.

Jones, J. K., Jr., D. M. Armstrong, R. S. Hoffmann, and C. Jones. 1983. Mammals of the Northern Great Plains. Univ. Nebraska Press, Lincoln, 379 pp.

Jones, J. K., Jr., E. D. Fleharty, and P. B. Dunnigan. 1967. The distributional status of bats in Kansas. Misc. Publ., Univ. Kansas Mus. Nat. Hist. 46:1–33.

Jones, J. K., Jr., R. S. Hoffmann, D. W. Rice, C. Jones, R. J. Baker, and M. D. Engstrom. 1992. Revised checklist of North American mammals north of Mexico, 1991. Occas. Papers, Mus., Texas Tech. Univ. 146:1–23.

Jones, J. K., Jr., and R. B. Loomis. 1954. Records of the short-tailed shrew and least shrew in Colorado. J. Mamm. 35:110.

Jones, J. K., Jr., and R. W. Manning. 1990. Additional records of bats from the Black Mesa region of Oklahoma. Texas J. Science 42:210–212.

Jones, J. K., Jr., R. W. Manning, C. Jones, and R. R. Hollander. 1988. Mammals of the northern Texas Panhandle. Occas. Papers, Mus., Texas Tech Univ. 126:1–54.

Jones, K. L., D. H. Van Vuren, and K. R. Crooks. 2008. Sudden increase in a rare endemic carnivore: ecology of the island spotted skunk. J. Mamm. 89:75–86.

Jones, W. T. 1985. Body size and life-history variables in heteromyids. J. Mamm. 56:128–132.

Jonkel, C. J. 1987. Brown bear. Pp. 456–473, in Wild furbearer management and conservation in North America (M. Novak, J. A. Baker, M. E. Obbard, and B. Malloch, eds.). Ontario Trappers Association, Toronto, 1,150 pp.

Jonkel, C. J., and I. McT. Cowan. 1971. The black bear in the spruce-fir forest. Wildlife Monogr. 27:1–57.

Jonkel, C. J., and R. P. Weckwerth. 1963. Sexual maturity and implantation of blastocysts in the pine marten. J. Wildl. Mgmt. 27:93–98.

Jorgenson, J. T., M. Festa-Bianchet, and W. D. Wishart. 1998. Effects of population density on horn development in bighorn rams. J. Wildl. Mgmt. 52:1011–1020.

Joyce, L. A., and R. Birdsey, eds. 2000. The impact of climate change on America's forests: a technical document supporting the 2000 USDA Forest Service RPA Assessment. Gen. Tech. Rept., Rocky Mountain Research Station, USDA Forest Service, RMS-GTR-59:1–133.

Judd, S. R., and S. P. Cross. 1980. Chromosomal variation in *Microtus longicaudus* (Merriam). Murrelet 61:2–5.

Juelson, T. C. 1970. A study of the ecology and ethology of the rock squirrel, *Spermophilus variegatus* (Erxleban), in northern Utah. Unpubl. doctoral dissert., Univ. Utah, Salt Lake City, 173 pp.

Junge J. A., and R. S. Hoffmann. 1981. An annotated key to the long-tailed shrews (genus *Sorex*) of the United States and Canada, with notes on Middle American *Sorex*. Occas. Papers, Mus. Nat. Hist., Univ. Kansas 94:1–48.

Justice, K. E., and F. A. Smith. 1992. A model of dietary fiber utilization by small mammalian herbivores, with empirical results for *Neotoma*. Amer. Nat. 139:398–416.

Kahn, R., T. Beck, J. Fitzgerald, D. Finley, and B. Roell. 1996. Swift fox investigations in Colorado, 1996. Pp. 10–15, in Annual report of the Swift Fox Conservation Team, 1996 (B. Luce and F. Lindzey, eds.). Wyoming Game and Fish Department, Lander, 110 pp.

Kahn, R., L. Fox, P. Horner, B Giddings, and C. Roy, tech. eds. 1997. Conservation assessment and conservation strategy for swift fox in the United States. Colorado Division of Wildlife, Denver, 54 pp.

Kalcounis, M. C., and R. M. Brigham. 1998. Secondary use of aspen cavities by tree-roosting big brown bats. J. Wildl. Mgmt. 52:603–611.

Kalcounis-Rueppell, M. C., and R. R. Spoon. 2009. *Peromyscus boylii* (Rodentia: Cricetidae). Mammalian Species 838:1–14.

Kalmbach, E. R. 1943. The armadillo: its relation to agriculture and game. Texas Game, Fish and Oyster Comm., Austin, 60 pp.

Kamler, J. F. 2002. Relationships of swift foxes and coyotes in northwest Texas. Unpubl. doctoral dissert., Texas Tech Univ., Lubbock, 107 pp.

Kamler, J. F., and W. B. Ballard. 2002. A review of native and nonnative red foxes in North America. Wildl. Soc. Bull. 30: 370–379.

Kamler, J. F., W. B. Ballard, E. B. Fish, P. R. Lemons, K. Mote, and C. C. Perchellet. 2003. Habitat use, home ranges, and survival of swift foxes in a fragmented landscape: conservation implications. J. Mamm. 84:989–995.

Kamler, J. F., W. B. Ballard, E. M. Gese, R. L. Harrison, S. Karki, and K. Mote. 2004. Adult male emigration and a female-based social organization in swift foxes, *Vulpes velox*. Animal Behav. 57:699–702.

Kamler, J. F., W. B. Ballard, E. M Gese, R. L. Harrison, and S. M. Karki. 2004. Dispersal characteristics of swift foxes. Canadian J. Zool. 82:1837–1842.

Kamler, J. F., W. B. Ballard, R. L. Gilliland, P. R. Lemmons, and K. Mote. 2003. Impacts of coyotes on swift foxes in northwestern Texas. J. Wildl. Mgmt. 57:317–323.

Kamler, J. F., W. B. Ballard, R. L. Gilliland, and K. Mote. 2002. Improved trapping methods for swift foxes and sympatric coyotes. Wildl. Soc. Bull. 30:1262–1266.

Kamler, J. F., W. B. Ballard, R. L. Harrison, and C. G. Schmitt. 2005. Range expansion of red foxes in northwestern Texas and northeastern New Mexico. Southwestern Nat. 50:100–101.

Kamler, J. F., W. B. Ballard, P. R. Lemons, and K. Mote. 2003. Variation in mating system and group structure in two populations of swift foxes, *Vulpes velox*. Animal Behaviour 68:83–88.

Kamler, J. F., and P. S. Gipson. 2000. Home range, habitat selection, and survival of bobcats, *Lynx rufus*, in a prairie ecosystem in Kansas. Canadian Field-Nat. 114:388–394.

Kamler, J. F., L. A. Green, and W. B. Ballard. 2003. Recent occurrence of black bears in the southwestern Great Plains. Southwestern Nat. 48:303–306.

Kamler, J. F., R. M. Lee, J. C. deVos, Jr., W. B. Ballard, and H. A. Whitlaw. 2002. Survival and cougar predation of translocated bighorn sheep in Arizona. J. Wildl. Mgmt. 56:1267–1272.

Kaprowski, J. L. 2007. Alternative reproductive tactics and strategies of tree squirrels. Pp. 856–895, in Rodent societies, an ecological and evolutionary perspective (J. O. Wolff and P. W. Sherman, eds.). Univ. Chicago Press, Chicago, xv + 610 pp.

Kareiva, P. 2008. Ominous trends in nature recreation. Proc. Nat. Acad. Sci. 105:2757–2758.

Kashian, D. M., W. H. Romme, and C. M. Regan. 2007. Reconciling divergent interpretations of quaking aspen decline on the northern Colorado Front Range. Ecol. Appl. 17:1296–1311.

Kauffman, M. J., J. F. Brodie, and E. S. Jules. 2010. Are wolves saving Yellowstone's aspen? A landscape-level test of a behaviorally mediated trophic cascade. Ecology 91:2742–2755.

Kauffman, M. J., N. Varley, D. W. Smith, D. R. Stahler, D. R. MacNulty, and M. S. Boyce. 2007. Landscape heterogeneity shapes predation in a newly restored predator-prey system. Ecology Letters 10:690–700.

Kaufman, D. M., and D. W. Kaufman. 1992. Geographic variation in length of tail of white-footed mice (*Peromyscus leucopus*) in Kansas. J. Mamm. 73:789–796.

Kaufman, D. W., and E. D. Fleharty. 1974. Habitat selection by nine species of rodents in north-central Kansas. Southwestern Nat. 18:443–452.

Kaufman, D. W., and G. A. Kaufman. 1990. House mice (*Mus musculus*) in natural and disturbed habitats in Kansas. J. Mamm. 71:428–432.

Kaufmann, J. H. 1982. Raccoon and allies. Pp. 567–585, in Wild mammals of North America, biology, management, and economics (J. A. Chapman and G. A. Feldhamer, eds.). Johns Hopkins Univ. Press, Baltimore, 1,147 pp.

Kaufmann, J. H. 1987. Ringtail and coati. Pp. 500–508, in Wild furbearer management and conservation in North America (M. Novak, J. A. Baker, M. E. Obbard, and B. Malloch, eds.). Ontario Trappers Association, Toronto, 1,150 pp.

Kavanau, J. L., and C. E. Rischer. 1972. Influences of ambient temperature on ground squirrel activity. Ecology 53:158–164.

Kawamichi, T. 1976. Hay territoriality and dominance rank of pikas (*Ochotona princeps*). J. Mamm. 57:133–148.

Kay, C. E., and D. L. Bartos. 2000. Ungulate herbivory on Utah aspen: assessment of long-term exclosures. J. Range Mgmt. 53:145–153.

Kaye, M. W., D. Binkley, and T. J. Stohlgren. 2005. Effects of conifers and elk browsing on quaking aspen forests in the central Rocky Mountains, USA. Ecol. Appl. 15:1284–1295.

Kays, R. W., and D. E. Wilson. 2009. Mammals of North America, second ed. Princeton Univ. Press, Princeton, NJ, 248 pp.

Keane, R. E., K. C. Ryan, T. T. Veblen, C. D. Allen, J. A. Logan, and B. Hawkes. 2002. The cascading effects of fire exclusion in Rocky Mountain ecosystems. Pp. 133–152, in Rocky Mountain futures (J. S. Baron, ed.). Island Press, Washington, DC, 325 pp.

Keefover-Ring, W. 2004a. The state of pumas in the West. Sinapu, Boulder, CO, 21 pp.

Keefover-Ring, W. 2004b. The state of *Puma concolor* in Colorado. Sinapu, Boulder, CO, 3 pp.

Keefover-Ring, W. 2009. War on wildlife, the U.S. Department of Agriculture's "Wildlife Services." WildEarth Guardians, Santa Fe, NM, 98 pp.

Keen, J. 2008. Donations decline from taxpayer refunds. USA Today, April 9.

Keinath, D. A. 2000. Habitat use by red-backed voles (*Clethrionomys gapperi*) in the Rocky Mountains: issues of movement, scale and habitat affinity. Unpubl. master's thesis, Univ. Wyoming, Laramie, 90 pp.

Keinath, D. A. 2004. Fringed myotis (*Myotis thysanodes*): a technical conservation assessment. Species Conservation Project, Rocky Mountain Region, USDA Forest Service, 63 pp.

Keinath, D. A., and G. D. Hayward. 2003. Red-backed vole (*Clethrionomys gapperi*) response to disturbance in subalpine forests: use of regenerating patches. J. Mamm. 84:956–966.

Keith, J. O. 1965. The Abert squirrel and its dependence on ponderosa pine. Ecology 46:150–163.

Keith, J. O. 2003. The Abert squirrel (*Sciurus aberti*): a technical conservation assessment. Species Conservation Project, USDA Forest Service, Rocky Mountain Region, Denver, CO, 63 pp.

Keith, J. O., R. M. Hansen, and A. L. Ward. 1959. Effect of 2,4-D on abundance of foods of pocket gophers. J. Wildl. Mgmt. 23:137–145.

Keith, L. B. 1974. Some features of population dynamics in mammals. Proc. International Congress Game Biologists 11:17–58.

Keith, L. B. 1990. Dynamics of snowshoe hare populations. Pp. 119–195, in Current mammalogy (H. H. Genoways, ed.). Plenum Press, New York.

Keith, L. B., and S.E.M. Bloomer. 1993. Differential mortality of sympatric snowshoe hares and cottontail rabbits in central Wisconsin. Canadian J. Zool. 71:1694–1697.

Keith, L. B., and L. A. Windberg. 1978. A demographic analysis of the snowshoe hare cycle. Wildl. Monogr. 58:1–70.

Kelker, G. H. 1943. A winter wildlife census in northeastern Wisconsin. J. Wildl. Mgmt. 7:133–141.

Keller, B. J., and L. C. Bender. 2007. Bighorn sheep response to road-related disturbances in Rocky Mountain National Park, Colorado. J. Wildl. Mgmt. 71:2329–2337.

Keller, B. L. 1985. Reproductive patterns. Pp. 725–778, in Biology of New World *Microtus* (R. H. Tamarin, ed.). Spec. Publ., Amer. Soc. Mammalogists 8:1–593.

Kellert, S. R. 1977. Policy implications of a national study of American attitudes and behavioral relations to animals. U.S. Fish and Wildlife Service, Washington, DC, 124 pp.

Kellert, S. R. 1980. American attitudes toward and knowledge of animals: an update. Internat. J. Studies Animal Problems 1:87–119.

Kellert, S. R. 1987. Social and psychological dimensions of an environmental ethic. Proc. Internat. Conf. Outdoor Ethics, Lake of the Ozarks, MO, 18–19.

Kellert, S. R. 1988. Human-animal interactions: a review of American attitudes to wild and domestic animals in the twentieth century. Pp. 137–175, in Animals and people sharing the world (A. N. Rowan, ed.). Univ. Press New England, Hanover, NH, 206 pp.

Kellert, S. R., and J. K. Berry. 1987. Attitudes, knowledge, and behaviors toward wildlife as affected by gender. Wildl. Soc. Bull. 15:363–371.

Kelly, B. T. 1991. Carnivore scat analysis: an evaluation of techniques and the development of predictive models of prey consumed. Unpubl. master's thesis, Univ. Idaho, Moscow, 200 pp.

Kelt, D. A., M. S. Hafner, and American Society of Mammalogists' Ad Hoc Committee for Guidelines on Handling Rodents in the Field. 2010. Updated guidelines for protection of mammalogists and wildlife researchers from Hantavirus Pulmonary Syndrome (HPS). J. Mamm. 91:1525–1527.

Kemp, G. A., and L. B. Keith. 1970. Dynamics and regulation of red squirrel (*Tamiasciurus hudsonicus*) populations. Ecology 51:763–779.

Kennelly, J. J., and B. E. Johns. 1976. The estrous cycle of coyotes. J. Wildl. Mgmt. 40:272–277.

Kennerly, T. E., Jr. 1958. Comparisons of morphology and life history of two species of pocket gophers. Texas J. Sci. 10: 133–146.

Kennerly, T. E., Jr. 1964. Microenvironmental conditions of the pocket gopher burrow. Texas J. Sci. 16:395–441.

Kessler, R. 1998. Old Spanish Trail North Branch and its travelers. Sunstone Press, Santa Fe, NM, 384 pp.

Kevan, P. G., and D. M. Kendall. 1997. Liquid assets for fat bankers: summer nectarivory by migratory moths in the Rocky Mountains, Colorado, USA. Arctic and Alpine Research 29: 478–482.

Keystone Center. 1991. Final consensus report of the Keystone Policy Dialogue on Biological Diversity on Federal Lands. Keystone Center, Keystone, CO, 91 pp.

Kie, J. G., R. T. Bowyer, and K. M. Stewart. 2003. Ungulates in western coniferous forests: habitat relationships, population dynamics, and ecosystem processes. Pp. 296–340, in Mammal community dynamics, management and conservation in the coniferous forests of western North America (C. J. Zabel and R. G. Anthony, eds.). Cambridge Univ. Press, Cambridge, UK, 709 pp.

Kie, J. G., and B. Czech. 2000. Mule and black-tailed deer. Pp. 629–657, in Ecology and management of large mammals in North America. (S. Demarais and P. R. Krausman, eds.). Prentice-Hall, Upper Saddle River, NJ.

Kielan-Jaworowska, K., R. L. Cifelli, and Z.-X. Luo. 2004. Mammals from the age of dinosaurs. Columbia Univ. Press, New York, 630 pp.

Kilgore, D. L., Jr. 1969. An ecological study of the swift fox (*Vulpes velox*) in the Oklahoma Panhandle. Amer. Midland Nat. 81: 512–534.

Kilgore, D. L., Jr. 1970. The effect of northward dispersal on growth rate of young, size of young at birth, and litter size in *Sigmodon hispidus*. Amer. Midland Nat. 84:510–520.

Kilgore, D. L., Jr., and K. B. Armitage. 1978. Energetics of yellow-bellied marmot populations. J. Mamm. 50:628–629.

Kimball, J. W. 1948. Pheasant population characteristics and trends in the Dakotas. Trans. N. American Wildl. Conf. 13:291–311.

King, C. M. 1983. Mustela erminea. Mammalian Species 195:1–8.

King, C. M, and R. A. Powell. 2006. The natural history of weasels and stoats, ecology, behavior, and management, second ed. Oxford Univ. Press, New York, 464 pp.

King, J. A. 1955. Social behavior, social organization, and population dynamics in a black-tailed prairie dog town in the Black Hills of South Dakota. Contrib. Lab. Vert. Biology, Univ. Michigan 67:1–123.

King, J. A., ed. 1968. Biology of *Peromyscus* (Rodentia). Spec. Publ., Amer. Soc. Mammalogists 2:1–593.

King, M.-C., and A. C. Wilson. 1975. Evolution at two levels in humans and chimpanzees. Science 188:107–116.

King, R. H. 2005. Microclimate effects from closing abandoned mines with culvert bat gates. US Bureau of Land Management Papers, U.S. Dept. Interior, Tech. Note 416:i–iii + 1–13.

King, T. L., J. F. Switzer, C. Morrison, M. S. Eackles, C. C. Young, B. A. Lubinsi, and P. Cryan. 2006. Comprehensive genetic analyses reveal evolutionary distinction of a mouse (*Zapus hudsonius preblei*) proposed for delisting from the US Endangered Species Act. Molec. Ecol. 15:4331–4359.

Kinlaw, A. 1995. *Spilogale putorius*. Mammalian Species 511:1–7.

Kinlaw, A. 1999. A review of burrowing by semi-fossorial vertebrates in arid environments. J. Arid Environ. 41:127–145.

Kintigh, K. M. 1999. A den-centered analysis of swift fox habitat characteristics on the Kiowa National Grassland, New Mexico. Final report, USDA Forest Service, 15 pp.

Kiriazis, J., and C. N. Slobodchikoff. 2006. Perceptual specificity in the alarm calls of Gunnison's prairie dogs. Behav. Proc. 73:29–35.

Kirkland, G. L., Jr., and J. S. Findley. 1996. First Holocene record for Preble's shrew (*Sorex preblei*) in New Mexico. Southwestern Nat. 41:320–322.

Kirkland, G. L., Jr., and J. N. Layne, eds. 1989. Advances in the study of *Peromyscus* (Rodentia). Texas Tech Univ. Press, Lubbock, 366 pp.

Kirkland, G. L., Jr., R. R. Parmenter, and R. E. Skoog. 1997. A five-species assemblage of shrews from the sagebrush-steppe of Wyoming. J. Mamm. 28:83–89.

Kirkpatrick, J. F., and P. M. Fazio. 2005. Wild horses as native North American wildlife. Unpubl. Statement in support of H. R. 291, U.S. House of Representatives. http://www.awionline.org/legislation/pdf/Wild_Horses_Native_NA_WildlifeFINAL.pdf.

Kirsch, J.A.W. 1977. The classification of marsupials. Pp. 1–50, in The biology of marsupials (D. Hunsaker, II, ed.). Academic Press, New York, 537 pp.

Kirsch, J.A.W., and J. H. Calaby. 1977. The species of living marsupials: an annotated list. Pp. 9–26, in The biology of marsupials (B. Stonehouse and D. Gilmore, eds.). Macmillan, London, 486 pp.

Kisiel, D. S. 1971. October birth by *Peromyscus difficilis nasutus* in north central Colorado. Southwestern Nat. 16:213–214.

Kitchen, A. M. 1999. Resource partitioning between coyotes and swift foxes: Space, time, and diet. Unpubl. master's thesis, Utah State Univ., 47 pp.

Kitchen, A. M., E. M. Gese, S. M. Karki, and E. R. Schauster. 2005. Spatial ecology of swift fox social groups: from group formation to mate loss. J. Mamm. 86:547–554.

Kitchen, A. M., E. M. Gese, and E. R. Schauster. 1999. Resource partitioning between coyotes and swift foxes: space, time, and diet. Canadian J. Zool. 77:1645–1656.

Kitchen, A. M., E. M. Gese, and E. R. Schauster. 2000a. Changes in coyote activity patterns due to reduced exposure to human persecution. Canadian J. Zool. 78:853–857.

Kitchen, A. M., E. M. Gese, and E. R. Schauster. 2000b. Long-term spatial stability of coyote (*Canis latrans*) home ranges in southeastern Colorado. Canadian J. Zool. 78:458–464.

Kitchen, D. W. 1974. Social behavior and ecology of the pronghorn. Wildlife Monogr. 38:1–96.

Kitchen, D. W., and B. W. O'Gara. Pronghorn. 1982. Pp. 960–971, in Wild mammals of North America, biology, management, and economics (J. A. Chapman and G. A. Feldhamer, eds.). Johns Hopkins Univ. Press, Baltimore, 1,147 pp.

Kittell, T.G.F., P. E. Thornton, J. A. Royle, and T. N. Chase. 2002. Climates of the Rocky Mountains: historical and future patterns. Pp. 59–82, in Rocky Mountain futures (J. S. Baron, ed.). Island Press, Washington, DC, 325 pp.

Kivett, V. K., and O. B. Mock. 1980. Reproductive behavior in the least shrew (*Cryptotis parva*) with special reference to the aural glandular region of the female. Amer. Midland Nat. 103:339–345.

Klatt, L. E. 1971. A comparison of the ecology of active and abandoned black-tailed prairie dog towns. Unpubl. master's thesis, Colorado State Univ., Fort Collins, 52 pp.

Klatt, L. E., and D. Hein. 1978. Vegetative differences among active and abandoned towns of black-tailed prairie dogs (*Cynomys ludovicianus*). J. Range Mgmt. 31:315–317.

Klingener, D. 1963. Dental evolution of *Zapus*. J. Mamm. 44:248–260.

Klingener, D. 1984. Gliroid and dipodoid rodents. Pp. 381–388, in Orders and families of Recent mammals of the World. (S. Anderson and J. K. Jones, Jr., eds.). John Wiley and Sons, New York, 686 pp.

Knapp, A. K., J. M. Blair, J. M. Briggs, S. L. Collins, D. C. Hartnett, L. C. Johnson, and E. G. Towne. 1999. The keystone role of bison in the North American tallgrass prairie. BioScience 49:39–50.

Knick, S. T. 1990. Ecology of bobcats relative to exploitation and a prey decline in southeastern Idaho. Wildl. Monogr. 108:1–42.

Knick, S. T., and D. L. Dyer. 1997. Distribution of black-tailed jackrabbit habitat determined by GIS in southwestern Idaho. J. Wildl. Mgmt. 51:75–85.

Knight, D. H. 1994. Dynamics of subalpine forests. Pp 128–138, in Flammulated, boreal, and great gray owls in the United States: a technical conservation assessment (G. D. Hayward and J. Verner, eds.). Gen. Tech. Rept., Rocky Mountain Forest and Range Experiment Station, USDA, Forest Service, Fort Collins, CO, RM-253:1–213.

Knight, R. L., and K. J. Gutzwiller, eds. 1995. Wildlife and recreationists: coexistence through research and management. Island Press, Covelo, CA, 372 pp.

Knight, R. L., F. W. Smith, S. W. Buskirk, W. H. Romme, and W. L. Baker, eds. 2000. Forest fragmentation in the Southern Rocky Mountains. Univ. Press Colorado, Boulder, 474 pp.

Knopf, F. L. 1986. Changing landscapes and the cosmopolitanism of the eastern Colorado avifauna. Wildl. Soc. Bull. 14:132–142.

Knopf, F. L., and M. L. Scott. 1990. Altered flows and created landscapes in the Platte River headwaters, 1840–1990. Pp. 47–70, in Management of dynamic ecosystems (J. M. Sweeney, ed.). North-Central Section, The Wildlife Society, West Lafayette, IN, 180 pp.

Knowles, C. 2002. Status of white-tailed and Gunnison's prairie dogs. National Wildlife Federation, Missoula, MT, and Environmental Defense, Washington, DC, 30 pp.

Knowles, C. J. 1986. Some relationships of black-tailed prairie dogs to livestock grazing. Great Basin Nat. 46:198–203.

Knowles, P. R. 1985. Home range size and habitat selection of bobcats, *Lynx rufus*, in north-central Montana. Canadian Field-Nat. 99:6–12.

Knowlton, F. E., E. M. Gese, and M. M. Jaeger. 1999. Coyote depredation control: an interface between biology and management. J. Range Mgmt. 52:398–412.

Knowlton, F. F. 1972. Preliminary interpretations of coyote population mechanics with some management implications. J. Wildl. Mgmt. 36:369–382.

Knowlton, F. F., and E. M. Gese. 1995. Coyote population processes revisited. Pp. 1–6, in Coyotes in the Southwest: a compendium of our knowledge (D. Rollins, C. Richardson, T. Blankenship, K. Canon, and S. Henke, eds.). Texas Parks and Wildlife Dept., Austin, 174 pp.

Koch, P. L., and A. D. Barnosky. 2006. Late Quaternary extinctions: state of the debate. Ann. Rev. Ecol., Evol., and Syst. 37:215–250.

Koehler, D. A., and A. E. Thomas. 2000. Managing for enhancement of riparian and wetland areas of the western United States: an annotated bibliography. General Technical Report, USDA Forest Service, RMRS-GTR-54:1–369.

Koehler, G. M. 1990. Population and habitat characteristics of lynx and snowshoe hares in north-central Washington. Canadian J. Zool. 58:845–851.

Koehler, G. M., and K. B. Aubry. 1994. Lynx. Pp. 74–98, in American marten, fisher, lynx, and wolverine, the scientific basis for conserving forest carnivores in the western United States. United States Department of Agriculture, Forest Service. General Technical Report RM-254, Fort Collins, CO, 184 pp.

Koehler, G. M., and J. D. Brittell. 1990. Managing spruce-fir habitat for lynx and snowshoe hares. J. Forestry 88:10–14.

Koehler, G. M., and M. G. Hornocker. 1977. Fire effects on marten habitat in the Selway-Bitterroot Wilderness. J. Wild. Mgmt. 41:500–505.

Koehler, G. M., and M. G. Hornocker. 1989. Influences of seasons on bobcats in Idaho. J. Wildl. Mgmt. 53:197–202.

Koehler, G. M., and M. G. Hornocker. 1991. Seasonal resource use among mountain lions, bobcats, and coyotes. J. Mamm. 72:391–396.

Koehler, G. M., M. G. Hornocker, and H. S. Hash. 1980. Wolverine marking behavior. Canadian Field-Nat. 94:339–341.

Koehler, G. M., and D. J. Pierce. 2003. Black bear home-range sizes in Washington: climatic, vegetative, and social influences. J. Mamm. 84:81–91.

Koehler, G. M., and D. J. Pierce. 2005. Survival, cause-specific mortality, sex, and ages of American black bears in Washington State, USA. Ursus 16:157–166.

Koford, C. B. 1958. Prairie dogs, whitefaces, and blue grama. Wildl. Monogr. 3:1–78.

Kolenosky, G. B., and S. M. Strathearn. 1987. Black bear. Pp. 442–454, in Wild furbearer management and conservation in North America (M. Novak, J. A. Baker, M. E. Obbard, and B. Malloch, eds.). Ontario Trappers Association, Toronto, 1,150 pp.

Koloski, J. H. 2002. Mountain lion ecology and management on the Southern Ute Indian Reservation. Unpubl. master's thesis, Univ. Wyoming, Laramie, 121 pp.

Koopman, M. E. 2002. Movements and home ranges of San Joaquin kit foxes relative to oil-field development. Western N. Amer. Nat. 52:151–159.

Koopman, M. E., B. L. Cypher, and J. H. Scrivner. 2000. Dispersal patterns of San Joaquin kit foxes (*Vulpes macrotis macrotis*). J. Mamm. 81:213–222.

Koopman, M. E., J. H. Scrivner, and T. T. Kato. 1998. Patterns of den use by San Joaquin kit foxes. J. Wildl. Mgmt. 52: 373–379.

Koplin, J. R., and R. S. Hoffmann. 1968. Habitat overlap and competitive exclusion in voles (*Microtus*). Amer. Midland Nat. 80:494–507.

Koprowski, J. L. 1994. *Sciurus niger*. Mammalian Species 479:1–9.

Koprowski, J. L. 2002. Handling tree squirrels with a safe and efficient restraint. Wildl. Soc. Bull. 30:101–103.

Koprowski, J. L. 2007. Alternative reproductive strategies of tree squirrels. Pp. 86–95, in Rodent societies, an ecological & evolutionary perspective (J. O. Wolff and P. W. Sherman, eds.). Univ. Chicago Press, Chicago, 620 pp.

Koprowski, J. L., J. L. Roseberry, and W. D. Klimstra. 1988. Longevity records for the fox squirrel. J. Mamm. 59:383–384.

Korb, J. E., and T. A. Ranker. 2001. Changes in stand composition and structure between 1981 and 1996 in four Front Range plant communities in Colorado. Plant Ecology 157:1–11.

Korschgen, L. J. 1959. Food habits of the red fox in Missouri. J.Wildl. Mgmt. 23:168–176.

Korschgen, L. J. 1981. Foods of fox and gray squirrels in Missouri. J. Wildl. Mgmt. 45:260–266.

Kotler, B. P., J. S. Brown, and M. Hickey. 1999. Food storability and the foraging behavior of fox squirrels (*Sciurus niger*). Amer. Midland Nat. 142:77–87.

Kotliar, N. B., B. W. Baker, A. D. Whicker, and G. Plumb. 1999. A critical review of assumptions about the prairie dog as a keystone species. Environmental Mgmt. 24:177–192.

Kozawa, Y., T. Sakae, H. Mishima, R. H. Barckhaus, E.-R. Krefting, P. F. Schmidt, and H. J. Höhling. 1988. Electron-microscopic and microprobe analyses of the pigmented and unpigmented enamel of *Sorex* (Insectivora). Histochemistry 90:61–65.

Kozlowski, A. J., T. J. Bennett, E. M. Gese, and W. M. Arjo. 2003. Live capture of denning mammals using an improved box-trap enclosure: kit foxes as a test case. Wildl. Soc. Bull. 31:630–633.

Krausman, P. R., V. C. Bleich, J. W. Cain III, T. R. Stephenson, D. W. DeYoung, P. W. McGrath, P. K. Swift, B. M. Pierce, and Brian D. Jansen. 2004. From the field: neck lesions in ungulates from collars incorporating satellite technology. Wildl. Soc. Bull. 32:987–991.

Krausman, P. R., and R. T. Bowyer. 2003. Mountain sheep, *Ovis canadensis* and *O. dalli*. Pp. 1095–1115, in Wild mammals of North America, biology, management, and economics, second ed. (G. A. Feldhamer, B. C. Thompson, and J. A. Chapman, eds.). Johns Hopkins Univ. Press, Baltimore, 1,216 pp.

Krausman, P. R., and D. M. Shackleton. 2000. Bighorn sheep. Pp. 517–544, in Ecology and management of large mammals in North America (S. Demarais and P. R. Krausman, eds.). Prentice-Hall, Upper Saddle River, NJ, 778 pp.

Krebs, C. J. 1970. *Microtus* population biology: behavioral changes associated with the population cycle in *M. ochrogaster* and *M. pennsylvanicus*. Ecology 51:34–52.

Krebs, C. J., and J. H. Myers. 1974. Population cycles in small mammals. Adv. Ecol. Research 8:267–399.

Krebs, J., E. Lofroth, J. Copeland, V. Banci, D. Cooley, H. Golden, A. Magoun, R. Mulders, and B. Shults. 2004. Synthesis of survival rates and causes of mortality in North American wolverines. J. Wildl. Mgmt. 58:493–502.

Krebs, J. W., M. L. Wilson, and J. E. Childs. 1995. Rabies—epidemiology, prevention, and future research. J. Mamm. 76:681–694.

Krenz, M. C. 1977. Vocalization of the rock squirrel *Spermophilus variegatus*. Unpubl. master's thesis, Texas Tech Univ., Lubbock, 46 pp.

Kritzman, E. B. 1974. Ecological relationships of *Peromyscus maniculatus* and *Perognathus parvus* in eastern Washington. J. Mamm. 55:172–188.

Krueger, K. 1986. Feeding relationships among bison, pronghorn, and prairie dogs: an experimental analysis. Ecology 67:760–770.

Kruger, F. A., J. Fielder, and C. A. Meaney. 1995. Explore Colorado, a naturalist's notebook. Westcliffe Publishers, Boulder, CO.

Krumbiegel, L., and G. G. Sehm. 1989. The geographic variability of the plains bison: a reconstruction using the earliest European illustrations of both subspecies. Archives Nat. Hist. 16:169–190.

Krutzsch, P. H. 1954. North American jumping mice (genus *Zapus*), Univ. Kansas Publ., Mus. Nat. Hist. 7:349–472.

Krutzsch, P. H. 1975. Reproduction of the canyon bat, *Pipistrellus hesperus*, in the southwestern United States. Amer. J. Anat. 143:163–200.

Kruuk, H. 2006. Otters, ecology, behaviour and conservation. Oxford Univ. Press, 280 pp.

Küchler, A. W. 1964. The potential natural vegetation of the conterminous United States, 1:3,168,000. Spec. Publ., Amer. Geogr. Soc. 36:1–37.

Kufeld, R. C. 1973. Foods eaten by the Rocky Mountain elk. J. Range Mgmt. 26:106–113.

Kufeld, R. C. 1983. Responses of elk, mule deer, cattle, and vegetation to burning, spraying, and chaining of Gambel oak rangeland. Tech. Publ., Colorado Division of Wildlife 34:1–47.

Kufeld, R. C. 1992. Development of census methods for deer in plains riverbottom habitats. Job Progress Report, Project W-153-R-5, Research Center, Colorado Division of Wildlife, Fort Collins, 13 pp.

Kufeld, R. C. 1994. Status and management of moose in Colorado. Alces 30:41–44.

Kufeld, R. C., and D. C. Bowden. 1995. Mule deer and white-tailed deer inhabiting eastern Colorado Plains River Bottoms. Tech. Publ., Colorado Division of Wildlife, 41 pp.

Kufeld, R. C., and D. C. Bowden. 1996a. Survival rates of Shiras moose (*Alces alces shirasi*) in Colorado. Alces 32:9–14.

Kufeld, R. C., and D. C. Bowden. 1996b. Movements and habitat selection of Shiras moose (*Alces alces shirasi*) in Colorado. Alces 32:85–99.

Kufeld, R. C., J. H. Olterman, and D. C. Bowden. 1980. A helicopter quadrat census for mule deer on Uncompahgre Plateau, Colorado. J. Wildl. Mgmt. 44:632–639.

Kufeld, R. C., O. C. Wallmo, and C. Feddema. 1973. Foods of the Rocky Mountain mule deer. Research Paper, USDA Forest Service, RM-111:1–31.

Kugler, K. A., and K. Geluso. 2009. Distribution of the eastern woodrat (*Neotoma floridana campestris*) in southern Nebraska. Western N. Amer. Nat. 59:175–179.

Kumar, S., A. Fillipski, V. Swarna, A. Walker, and S. B. Hedges. 2005. Placing confidence limits on the molecular age of the human-chimpanzee divergence. Proc. Nat. Acad. Sci. 102:18842–18847.

Kundaeli, J. N., and H. G. Reynolds. 1972. Desert cottontail use of natural and modified pinyon-juniper woodlands. J. Range Mgmt. 25:116–118.

Kunkel, K. E. 2003. Ecology, conservation, and restoration of large carnivores in western North America. Pp. 250–295, in Mammal community dynamics, management and conservation in the coniferous forests of western North America (C. J. Zabel and R. G. Anthony, eds.). Cambridge Univ. Press, Cambridge, UK, 709 pp.

Kunkel, K. E., and D. H. Pletscher. 1999. Species-specific population dynamics of cervids in a multipredator ecosystem. J. Wildl. Mgmt. 53:1082–1093.

Kunkel, K. E., T. K. Ruth, D. H. Pletscher, and M. G. Hornocker. 1999. Winter prey selection by wolves and cougars in and near Glacier National Park, Montana. J. Wildl. Mgmt. 53: 901–910.

Kuntz, D. W., H. J. Armstrong, and F. J. Athearn. 1989. Faults, fossils, and canyons, significant geologic features on public lands in Colorado. Cultural Resource Ser., Colorado Office, Bureau of Land Management 25:1–61.

Kunz, T. H. 1973. Resource utilization temporal and spatial components of bat activity in central Iowa. J. Mamm. 54:14–32.

Kunz, T. H. 1974. Reproduction, growth, and mortality of the vespertilionid bat, *Eptesicus fuscus*, in Kansas. J. Mamm. 55:1–13.

Kunz, T. H. 1982a. *Lasionycteris noctivagans*. Mammalian Species 172:1–5.

Kunz, T. H., ed. 1982b. Ecology of bats. Plenum Press, New York, 425 pp.

Kunz, T. H. 2008. Field guide to the bats of North America. Oxford Univ. Press, New York, 224 pp.

Kunz, T. H., E. B. Arnett, B. M. Cooper, W. P. Erickson, R. P. Larkin, T. Mabee, M. L. Morrison, M. D. Strickland, and J. M. Szewczak. 2007. Assessing impacts of wind-energy development on nocturnally active birds and bats: a guidance document. J. Wildl. Mgmt. 71:2449–2486.

Kunz, T. H., E. B. Arnett, W. P. Erickson, A. R. Hoar, G. D. Johnson, R. P. Larkin, M. D. Strickland, R. W. Thresher, and M. D. Tuttle. 2007. Ecological impacts of wind energy development on bats: questions, research needs, and hypotheses. Frontiers in Ecol. and Envir. 5:315–324.

Kunz, T. H., and M. B. Fenton, eds. 2003. Bat ecology. Univ. Chicago Press, Chicago, 779 pp.

Kunz, T. H., and D. J. Hosken. 2008. Male lactation: why, why not, and is it care? Trends in Ecol. and Evol. 24:80–85.

Kunz, T. H., and R. A. Martin. 1982. *Plecotus townsendii*. Mammalian Species 175:1–6.

Kunz, T. H., and S. Parsons. 2009. Ecological and behavioral methods for the study of bats. Johns Hopkins Univ. Press, Baltimore, 944 pp.

Kunz, T. H., and P. A. Racey, eds. 1998. Bat biology and conservation. Smithsonian Institution Press, Washington, DC, 365 pp.

Kunz, T. H., and D. S. Reynolds. 2003. Bat colonies in buildings. Pp. 91–102, in Monitoring trends in bat populations in the United States and territories: problems and prospects (T. J. O'Shea and M. A. Bogan, eds.). Information and Technology Report, USGS/BRD/ITR-2003-003, 274 pp.

Kunz, T. H., and S. K. Robson. 1995. Postnatal growth and development in the Mexican free-tailed bat (*Tadarida brasiliensis mexicana*): birth size, growth rates, and age estimation. J. Mamm. 76:769–783.

Kurose, N., A. V. Abaramov, and R. Masuda. 2008. Molecular phylogeny and taxonomy of the genus *Mustela* (Mustelidae, Carnivora), inferred from mitochondrial DNA sequences: new perspectives on phylogenetic status of the back-striped weasel and American mink. Mammal Study 33:25–33.

Kurtén, B. 1971. The Age of Mammals. Columbia Univ. Press, New York, 250 pp.

Kurtén, B., and E. Anderson. 1980. Pleistocene mammals of North America. Columbia Univ. Press, New York, 442 pp.

Kwiecinski, G. G. 1998. *Marmota monax*. Mammalian Species 591:1–8.

Kyle, C. J., and C. Strobeck. 2002. Connectivity of peripheral and core populations of North American wolverines. J. Mamm. 83:1141–1150.

Kyle, C. J., R. D. Weir, N. J. Newhouse, H. Davis, and C. Strobeck. 2004. Genetic structure of sensitive and endangered northwestern badger populations (*Taxidea taxus taxus* and *T. t. jeffersonii*). J. Mamm. 85:633–639.

Lackey, J. A., D. G. Huckaby, and B. G. Ormiston. 1985. *Peromyscus leucopus*. Mammalian Species 247:1–10.

Lacki, M. J., and M. D. Baker. 2007. Day roosts of female fringed myotis (*Myotis thysanodes*) in xeric forests of the Pacific Northwest. J. Mamm. 88:967–973.

Lacki, M. J., J. P. Hayes, and A. Kurta, eds. 2007. Bats in forests, conservation and management. Johns Hopkins Univ. Press, Baltimore, 352 pp.

Ladine, T. A. 1997. Activity patterns of co-occurring populations of the Virginia opossum (*Didelphis virginiana*) and raccoons (*Procyon lotor*). Mammalia 61:345–354.

Laing, S. P., and F. G. Lindzey. 1991. Cougar habitat selection in south-central Utah. Pp. 27–37, in Mountain Lion–Human

Interaction Symposium and Workshop (C. Braun, ed.), Colorado Division of Wildlife, Denver, 114 pp.

Lair, H. 1985a. Mating seasons and fertility of red squirrels in southern Quebec. Canadian J. Zool. 53:2323–2327.

Lair, H. 1985b. Length of gestation in the red squirrel, *Tamiasciurus hudsonicus*. J. Mamm. 56:809–810.

Lamb, T., T. R. Jones, and P. J. Wettstein. 1997. Evolutionary genetics and phylogeography of tassel-eared squirrels (*Sciurus aberti*). J. Mamm. 78:117–133.

Lambert, C.M.S., R. B. Wielgus, H. S. Robinson, D. D. Katnik, H. S. Cruickshank, R. Clarke, and J. Almack. 2006. Cougar population dynamics and viability in the Pacific Northwest. J. Wildl. Mgmt. 70:246–254.

Lamit, L. J., and M. N. Hendrie. 2009. Range expansion of the collared peccary in New Mexico: potential for interactions between historically separate subspecies. Western North Amer. Nat. 59:253–256.

Lance, W. R., and T. M. Pojar. 1984. Diseases and parasites of pronghorn: a review. Special Rept., Wildlife Research Sec., Colorado Division of Wildlife 57:1–14.

Landholt, L.M., and H. H. Genoways. 2000. Population trends in furbearers in Nebraska. Trans. Nebraska Acad. Sci. 26:97–110.

Landstrom, R. E. 1971. Longevity of white-throated woodrat. J. Mamm. 52:623.

Langenau, E. E., Jr., R. J. Moran, J. R. Terry, and D. C. Cue. 1981. Relationship between deer kill and ratings of the hunt. J. Wildl. Mgmt. 45:959–964.

Langford, A. 1983. Pattern of nocturnal activity of male *Dipodomys ordii* (Heteromyidae). Southwestern Nat. 28:341–346.

Langlois, J. P., L. Fahrig, G. Merriam, and H. Artsob. 2001. Landscape structure influences continental distribution of hantavirus in deer mice. Landscape Ecol. 16:255–266.

Larivière, S. 1996. The American mink, *Mustela vison* (Carnivora, Mustelidae) can climb trees. Mammalia 60:485–486.

Larivière, S. 1999a. Reasons why predators cannot be inferred from nest remains. Condor 101:718–721.

Larivière, S. 1999b. *Mustela vison*. Mammalian Species 608:1–9.

Larivière, S. 2001. *Ursus americanus*. Mammalian Species 647:1–11.

Larivière, S. 2003. Mink, *Mustela vison*. Pp. 662–671, in Wild mammals of North America, biology, management, and conservation, second ed. (G. A. Feldhamer, B. C. Thompson, and J. A. Chapman, eds.). Johns Hopkins Univ. Press, Baltimore, 1,216 pp.

Larivière, S. 2004. Range expansion of raccoons in the Canadian prairies: review of hypotheses. Wildl. Soc. Bull. 32:955–963.

Larivière, S., and S. H. Ferguson. 2002. On the evolution of the mammalian baculum: vaginal friction, prolonged intromission or induced ovulation? Mammal Rev. 32:283–294.

Larivière, S., and S. H. Ferguson. 2003. Evolution of induced ovulation in North American carnivores. J. Mamm. 84:937–947.

Larivière, S., J. Huot, and C. Samson. 1994. Daily activity patterns of female black bears in a northern mixed-forest environment. J. Mamm. 75:613–620.

Larivière, S., and F. Messier. 1996. Aposematic behavior in the striped skunk, *Mephitis mephitis*. Ethology 102:986–992.

Larivière, S., and F. Messier. 1997a. Characteristics of waterfowl nest predation by striped skunk (*Mephitis mephitis*): can predators be identified from nest remains? Amer. Midland Nat. 137:393–396.

Larivière, S., and F. Messier. 1997b. Seasonal and daily activity patterns of striped skunks (Mephitis mephitis) in the Canadian prairies. J. Zool., London 243:255–262.

Larivière, S., and F. Messier. 1998a. Effect of density and nearest neighbours on simulated waterfowl nests: can predators recognize high-density nesting patches? Oikos 83:12–20.

Larivière, S., and F. Messier. 1998b. Spatial organization of a prairie striped skunk population during waterfowl nesting season. J. Wildl. Mgmt. 52:199–204.

Larivière, S., and F. Messier. 1998c. Denning ecology of the striped skunk in the Canadian prairies: implications for waterfowl nest predation. J. Applied Ecology 35:207–213.

Larivière, S., and F. Messier. 2001a. Space-use patterns by female striped skunks exposed to aggregations of simulated duck nests. Canadian J. Zool. 79:1604–1608.

Larivière, S., and F. Messier. 2001b. Temporal patterns of predation of duck nests in the Canadian prairies. Amer. Midland Nat. 146:339–344.

Larivière, S., and M. Pasitschniak-Arts. 1996. *Vulpes vulpes*. Mammalian Species 537:1–11.

Larivière, S., and L. R. Walton. 1997. *Lynx rufus*. Mammalian Species 563:1–8.

Larivière, S., and L. R. Walton. 1998. *Lontra canadensis*. Mammalian Species 587:1–8.

Larivière, S., L. R. Walton, and F. Messier. 1999. Selection by striped skunks (*Mephitis mephitis*) of farmsteads and buildings as denning sites. Amer. Midland Nat. 142:96–101.

Larkins, K. F. 1997. Patterns of elk movement and distribution in and adjacent to the eastern boundary of Rocky Mountain National Park. Unpubl. master's thesis, Univ. Northern Colorado, Greeley, 118 pp.

Larsen, K. W., C. D. Becker, S. Boutin, and M. Blower. 1997. Effects of hoard manipulation on life history and reproductive success of female red squirrels (*Tamiasciurus hudsonicus*). J. Mamm. 78:192–203.

Larsen, K. W., and S. Boutin. 1998. Sex-unbiased philopatry in the North American red squirrel (*Tamiasciurus hudsonicus*). Pp. 21–32, in Ecology and evolutionary biology of tree squirrels (M. A. Steele, J. F. Merritt, and D. A. Zegers, eds.). Spec. Publ., Virginia Mus. Nat. Hist. 5:1–310.

Larson, F. 1940. The role of the bison in maintaining the short grass plains. Ecology 21:113–121.

Lashnits, D. 2008. Habitat partnership. Colorado Outdoors 57(5): 16–19.

Lauenroth, W. K. 1979. Grassland primary production: North American grasslands in perspective. Pp. 3–24, in Perspectives in grassland ecology (N. R. French, ed.). Springer-Verlag, New York, 204 pp.

Lauenroth, W. K., and I. C. Burke. 2008. Ecology of the shortgrass steppe, a long-term perspective. Oxford Univ. Press, New York, 528 pp.

Laundré, J. W. 1989. Burrows of least chipmunks in southeastern Idaho. Northwestern Nat. 70:18–20.

Laundré, J. W. 1994. Resource overlap between mountain goats and bighorn sheep. Great Basin Nat. 54:114–121.

Laundré, J. W., L. Hernandez, D. Streubel, K. Altendorf, and C. L. Gonzalez. 2000. Aging mountain lions using gum-line recession. Wildl. Soc. Bull. 28:963–966.

Laundré, J. W., and T. D. Reynolds. 1993. Effects of soil structure on burrow characteristics of five small mammal species. Great Basin Nat. 53:358–366.

Lausen, C. 2009. When is a species not a species? Genetic techniques complicate taxonomy. Bats 27(1):11–13.

Lausen, C. L., I. Delisle, R.M.R. Barclay, and C. Strobeck. 2008. Beyond mtDNA: nuclear gene flow suggests taxonomic oversplitting in the little brown bat. Canadian J. Zoology 86: 700–713.

LaVal, R. K., and M. L. LaVal. 1979. Notes on reproduction, behavior, and abundance of the red bat, *Lasiurus borealis*. J. Mamm. 50:209–212.

LaVoie, G. K., G. K. Tietjen, and M. W. Fall. 1971. Albinism in *Thomomys talpoides* from Colorado. Great Basin Nat. 31:181.

Lawlor, T. E. 1979. Handbook of the orders and families of living mammals, second ed. Mad River Press, Eureka, CA, 327 pp.

Lawlor, T. E. 1998. Biogeography of Great Basin mammals: paradigm lost? J. Mamm. 79:1111–1130.

Lawlor, T. E. 2003. Faunal composition and distribution of mammals in western coniferous forests. Pp. 41–80, in Mammal community dynamics, management and conservation in the coniferous forests of western North America (C. J. Zabel and R. G. Anthony, eds.). Cambridge Univ. Press, Cambridge, UK, 709 pp.

Lawson, B., and R. Johnson. 1982. Mountain sheep. Pp. 1036–1055, in Wild mammals of North America, biology, management, and economics (J. A. Chapman and G. A. Feldhamer, eds.). Johns Hopkins Univ. Press, Baltimore, 1,147 pp.

Lay, D. W. 1942. Ecology of the opossum in eastern Texas. J. Mamm. 23:147–159.

Layden, P. C., M. J. Manfredo, and P. Tucker. 2003. Integrating public values towards wildlife into land use planning: a case study in La Plata County, Colorado. Wildl. Soc. Bull. 31: 174–184.

Layne, J. N. 1968. Ontogeny. Pp. 148–253, in Biology of *Peromyscus* (Rodentia) (J. A. King, ed.). Spec. Publ., Amer. Soc. Mammalogists 2:1–593.

Layne, J. N. 2003. Armadillo, *Dasypus novemcinctus*. Pp. 75–97, in Wild mammals of North America, biology, management, and economics, second ed. (G. A. Feldhamer, B. C. Thompson, and J. A. Chapman, eds.). Johns Hopkins Univ. Press, Baltimore, 1,216 pp.

Layne, J. N., and D. Glover. 1977. Home range of the armadillo in Florida. J. Mamm. 58:411–413.

Lechleitner, R. R. 1954. Age criteria in mink, *Mustela vison*. J. Mamm. 35:496–503.

Lechleitner, R. R. 1957. Reingestion in the black-tailed jack rabbit. J. Mamm. 38:481–485.

Lechleitner, R. R. 1958. Movements, density, and mortality in a black-tailed jack rabbit population. J. Wildl. Mgmt. 22:371–384.

Lechleitner, R. R. 1959. Sex ratio, age classes, and reproduction of the black-tailed jack rabbit. J. Mamm. 40:63–81.

Lechleitner, R. R. 1964. Another record of the least shrew from Colorado. J. Mamm. 45:298.

Lechleitner, R. R. 1969. Wild mammals of Colorado: their appearance, habits, distribution, and abundance. Pruett Publishing Co., Boulder, 254 pp.

Lechleitner, R. R., L. Kartman, M. I. Goldenberg, and B. W. Hudson. 1968. An epizootic of plague in Gunnison's prairie dogs (*Cynomys gunnisoni*) in southcentral Colorado. Ecology 49:734–743.

Lechleitner, R. R., J. V. Tileston, and L. Kartman. 1962. Die-off of a Gunnison's prairie dog colony in central Colorado, I. Ecological observations and description of the epizootic. Zoonoses Res. 1:185–199.

LeCount, A. 1977. Some aspects of black bear ecology in the Arizona chaparral. Proc. Internat. Conf. Bear Res. Mgmt. 4: 175–180.

Lee, C. M., J. B. Benedict, and J. B. Lee. 2006. Ice patches and remnant glaciers: paleontological and archeological possibilities in the Colorado high country. Southwestern Lore 72:26–41.

Lee, T. E., Jr., J. W. Bickham, and M. D. Scott. 1994. Mitochondrial DNA and allozyme analysis of North American pronghorn populations. J. Wildl. Mgmt. 58:307–318.

Leege, T. A. 1968. Natural movements of beavers in southeastern Idaho. J. Wildl. Mgmt. 32:973–976.

Lehmer, E. M., B. Van Horne, B. Kulbartz, and G. L. Florant. 2001. Facultative torpor in free-ranging black-tailed prairie dogs (*Cynomys ludovicianus*). J. Mamm. 82:551–557.

Lehner, P. N. 1976. Coyote behavior: implications for management. Wildl. Soc. Bull. 4:120–126.

Lehner, P. N. 1978a. Coyote communication. Pp. 127–162, in Coyotes: biology, behavior, and management (M. Bekoff, ed.). Academic Press, New York, 384 pp.

Lehner, P. N. 1978b. Coyote vocalizations: a lexicon and comparison with other canids. Animal Behavior 26:712–722.

Lehner, P. N., R. Krumm, and A. T. Cringan. 1976. Tests for olfactory repellents for coyotes and dogs. J. Wild. Mgmt. 40:145–150.

Lemke, T. O. 2004. Origin, expansion, and status of mountain goats in Yellowstone National Park. Wildl. Soc. Bull. 32:532–541.

Lemons, P. R., II. 2001. Ecology of swift fox in northwest Texas: dens and den site activity. Unpubl. master's thesis, Texas Tech Univ., Lubbock, 71 pp.

Lenihan, C., and D. Van Vuren. 1996. Growth and survival of juvenile yellow-bellied marmots. Canadian J. Zoology 74:297–302.

Lentfer, J. W. 1955. A two-year study of the Rocky Mountain goat in the Crazy Mountains, Montana. J. Wildl. Mgmt. 19:417–429.

Lenth, B. E., R. L. Knight, and M.E. Brennan. 2008. The effects of dogs on wildlife communities. Natural Areas J. 28:218–227.

Leonard, J. A., C. Vilà, K. Fox-Dobbs, P. L. Koch, R. K. Wayne, and B. Van Valkenburgh. 2007. Megafaunal extinctions and the disappearance of a specialized wolf ecomorph. Current Biol. 17:1146–1150.

Leonard, M. L., and M. B. Fenton. 1984. Echolocation calls of *Euderma maculatum* (Chiroptera: Vespertilionidae): use in orientation and communication. J. Mamm. 55:122–126.

Leopold, A. 1949. A Sand County almanac, and sketches here and there. Oxford Univ. Press, New York, 226 pp.

Lerass, H. J. 1938. Observations on the growth and behavior of harvest mice. J. Mamm. 19:441–444.

Lesmeister, D. B., M. E. Gompper, and J. J. Millspaugh. 2008. Summer resting and den site selection by eastern spotted skunks (*Spilogale putorius*) in Arkansas. J. Mamm. 89:1512–1520.

Lessa, E. P., and C. S. Thaeler, Jr. 1989. A reassessment of morphological specializations for digging in pocket gophers. J. Mamm. 70:689–700.

Levenson, H. 1985. Systematics of the Holarctic chipmunks (*Tamias*). J. Mamm. 56:219–242.

Lewandowski, J. 2006. Black-footed ferrets are back. Colorado Outdoors 55(3):20–23.

Lewandowski, J. 2007. Bats and abandoned mines. Colorado Outdoors 56(3):10–13.

Lewis, S. E. 1994. Night roosting ecology of pallid bats (*Antrozous pallidus*) in Oregon. Amer. Midland Nat. 132:219–226.

Lewis, S. E. 1995. Roost fidelity of bats: a review. J. Mamm. 76:481–496.

Lewis, W. D. 2009. Another Yellowstone wolf confirmed in Colorado. Colorado Outdoors 58(2):14.

Lewis, W. D. 2010. DOW declares Colorado lynx reintroduction program a success. Colorado Outdoors 59(5):14–15.

Li, C.-K., and S.-Y. Ting. 1985. Possible phylogenetic relationships: eurymylid-rodent and mimotonid-lagomorph. Pp. 35–58, in Evolutionary relationships among rodents (W. P. Luckett and J.-L. Hartenberger, eds.). NATO ASI, Series A: Life Sci. 92:1–721.

Licht, D. S. 1997. Ecology and economics of the Great Plains. Univ. Nebraska Press, Lincoln, 225 pp.

Licht, D. S. 2009. Observations of badgers preying on black-tailed prairie dogs. Prairie Nat. 41:129–130.

Lidicker, W. Z., Jr. 1988. Solving the enigma of microtine "cycles." J. Mamm. 59:225–235.

Liers, E. E. 1951. Notes on the river otter (*Lutra canadensis*). J. Mamm. 32:1–9.

Liers, E. E. 1958. Early breeding in the river otter. J. Mamm. 39: 438–439.

Liewer, J. A. 1988. Pronghorn grazing impacts on winter wheat. Unpubl. master's thesis, Colorado State Univ., Fort Collins, 32 pp.

Liley, S., and S. Creel. 2008. What best explains vigilance in elk: characteristics of prey, predators, or the environment? Behav. Ecol. 19:245–254.

Lim, B. K. 1987. *Lepus townsendii*. Mammalian Species 288:1–6.

Linder, R., B. Dahlgren, and C. N. Hillman. 1972. Black-footed ferret-prairie dog interrelationships. Pp. 22–37, in Proc. Symposium on Rare and Endangered Wildlife of the Southwestern United States. New Mexico Department of Game and Fish, Santa Fe, 167 pp.

Lindzey, F. G. 1971. Ecology of badgers in Curlew Valley, Utah and Idaho with emphasis on movement and activity patterns. Unpubl. master's thesis, Utah State Univ., Logan, 55 pp.

Lindzey, F. G. 1978. Movement patterns of badgers in northwestern Utah. J. Wildl. Mgmt. 42:418–422.

Lindzey, F. G. 1982. Badger. Pp. 653–663, in Wild mammals of North America, biology, management, and economics (J. A. Chapman and G. A. Feldhamer, eds.). Johns Hopkins Univ. Press, Baltimore, 1,147 pp.

Lindzey, F. G. 1987. Mountain lion. Pp. 656–668, in Wild furbearer management and conservation in North America (M. Novak, J. A. Baker, M. E. Obbard, and B. Malloch, eds.). Ontario Trappers Association, Toronto, 1,150 pp.

Lindzey, F. G. 2003. Badger, *Taxidea taxus*. Pp. 683–691, in Wild mammals of North America, biology, management, and economics, second ed. (G. A. Feldhamer, B. C. Thompson, and A. Chapman, eds.). Johns Hopkins Univ. Press, Baltimore, 1,216 pp.

Lindzey, F. G., W. G. Hepworth, T. A. Mattson, and A. F. Reeves. 1997. Potential for competitive interactions between mule deer and elk in the western United States and Canada: a review. Wyoming Coop. Fish and Wildl. Res. Unit, Laramie, 82 pp.

Lindzey, F. G., W. D. Van Sickle, B. B. Ackerman, D. Barnhurst, T. P. Hemker, and S. P. Laing. 1994. Cougar population dynamics in southern Utah. J. Wildl. Mgmt. 58:619–624.

Linhart, S. B., and W. B. Robinson. 1972. Some relative carnivore densities in areas under sustained coyote control. J. Mamm. 53:880–884.

Link, M. A. 1995. Kit fox (*Vulpes macrotis*) distribution in western Colorado. Unpubl. master's thesis, Univ. Northern Colorado, Greeley, 115 pp.

Linnell, J.D.C., J. Odden, M. E. Smith, R. Aanes, and J. E. Swenson. 1999. Large carnivores that kill livestock: do "problem individuals" really exist? Wildl. Soc. Bull. 27:698–705.

Linscombe, G., N. Kinler, and R. J. Aulerich. 1982. Mink. Pp. 629–643, in Wild mammals of North America, biology, management, and economics (J. A. Chapman and G. A. Feldhamer, eds.). Johns Hopkins Univ. Press, Baltimore, 1,147 pp.

Linzey, A. V. 1983. *Synaptomys cooperi*. Mammalian Species 210: 1–5.

Lipscomb, J., H. Riffel, H. Funk, and C. Gardner. 1983. Colorado small game, furbearer and varmint harvest, 1982. Federal Aid Wildlife Restoration Project, Colorado Division of Wildlife, W-121-R:1–186.

Liskop, K. S., R.M.F.S. Sadlier, and B. P. Saunders. 1981. Reproduction and harvest of wolverine (*Gulo gulo*) in British Columbia. Pp. 469–477, in Proc. Worldwide Furbearer Conference (J. A. Chapman and D. Pursley, eds.). Frostburg, MD, 2,059 pp.

Litaor, M. I., R. Mancinelli, and J. C. Halfpenny. 1996. The influence of pocket gophers on the status of nutrients in alpine soils. Geoderma 70:37–48.

Livo, L. 1992. The piñon and the packrat. Colorado Outdoors 41(5): 20–23.

Llewellyn, J. B. 1981. Habitat selection by the desert woodrat (*Neotoma lepida*) inhabiting a piñon-juniper woodland in western Nevada. Southwestern Nat. 26:76–78.

Lloyd, H. G. 1975. The red fox in Britain. Pp. 207–215, in The wild canids: their systematics, behavioral ecology and evolution (M. W. Fox, ed.). Van Nostrand Reinhold Co., New York, 508 pp.

Lloyd, K. J., and J. J. Eberle. 2008. A new talpid from the Late Eocene of North America. Acta Palaeontologica Polonica 53: 539–543.

Lloyd, K. J., M. P. Worley-Georg, and J. J. Eberle. 2008. The Chadronian mammalian fauna of the Florissant Formation, Florissant Fossil Beds National Monument, Colorado. Spec. Paper, Geol. Soc. America 435:117–126.

Lockley, M. G. 1998. The vertebrate track record. Nature. 396:429–432.

Lockley, M. G., and J. R. Foster. 2003. Late Cretaceous mammal tracks from North America. Ichnos 10:269–203.

Lockley, M. G., S. G. Lucas, A. P. Hunt, and R. Gaston. 2004. Ichnofaunas from the Triassic-Jurassic boundary sequences of the Gateway area, western Colorado: implications for faunal composition and correlations with other areas. Ichnos 11:89–102.

Logan, K. A. 2005. Puma population structure and vital rates on the Uncompahgre Plateau, Colorado. Wildlife research report, Work Package-3003. Colorado Division of Wildlife, Fort Collins.

Logan, K. A. 2008. Puma population structure and vital rates on the Uncompahgre Plateau. Wildlife Research Reports, Predatory Mammals Conservation, Colorado Division of Wildlife, Work Package 3003:105–150.

Logan, K. A., and L. L. Sweanor. 2000. Puma. Pp. 347–377, in Ecology and management of large mammals in North America (S. Demarais and P. R. Krausman, eds.). Prentice-Hall, Upper Saddle River, NJ, 778 pp.

Logan, K. A., and L. Sweanor. 2001. Desert puma: evolutionary ecology and conservation of an enduring carnivore. Island Press, Washington, DC, 390 pp.

Logan, K. A., L. Sweanor, T. K. Ruth, and M. G. Hornocker. 1996. Cougars of the San Andreas Mountains, New Mexico. Final report by Hornocker Wildlife Institute, Moscow, Idaho, to New Mexico Department of Game and Fish, Santa Fe, 280 pp.

Loker, C. A., and D. J. Decker. 1995. Colorado black bear hunting referendum: what was behind the vote? Wildl. Soc. Bull. 23:370–376.

Loker, C. A., D. J. Decker, R. B. Gill, T.D.I. Beck, and L. H. Carpenter. 1994. The Colorado black bear hunting controversy: a case study of human dimensions in contemporary wildlife management. HDRU Series No. 94-4. Human Dimensions Research Unit, Cornell Univ., Ithaca, NY, 56 pp.

Loker, C. A., D. J. Decker, and S. J. Schwager. 1999. Social acceptability of wildlife management actions in suburban areas: 3 cases from New York. Wildl. Soc. Bull. 27:152–159.

Lomolino, M. V., J. H. Brown, and R. Davis. 1989. Island biogeography of montane forest mammals in the American Southwest. Ecology 70:180–194.

Lomolino, M. V., and G. A. Smith. 2004. Terrestrial vertebrate communities at black-tailed prairie dog (*Cynomys ludovicianus*) towns. Biol. Cons. 115:89–100.

Long, C. A. 1965. The mammals of Wyoming. Univ. Kansas Publ., Mus. Nat. Hist. 14:493–758.

Long, C. A. 1972. Notes on habitat preference and reproduction in pygmy shrews, *Microsorex*. Canadian Field-Nat. 86:155–160.

Long, C. A. 1973. *Taxidea taxus*. Mammalian Species 26:1–4.

Long, C. A. 1974. *Microsorex hoyi* and *Microsorex thompsoni*. Mammalian Species 33:1–4.

Long, C. A., and D. Cronkite. 1970. Taxonomy and ecology of sibling chipmunks in central Colorado. Southwestern Nat. 14:283–291.

Long, C. A., and R. S. Hoffmann. 1992. *Sorex preblei* from the Black Canyon, first record for Colorado. Southwestern Nat. 37:318–319.

Long, C. A., and C. A. Killingley. 1983. The badgers of the world. Charles C. Thomas, Springfield, IL, 404 pp.

Longhurst, W. 1944. Observations on the ecology of the Gunnison prairie dog in Colorado. J. Mamm. 25:24–36.

Lott, D. F. 2002. American bison, a natural history. Univ. California Press, Berkeley, 245 pp.

Lotze, J.-H., and S. Anderson. 1979. *Procyon lotor*. Mammalian Species 119:1–8.

Loughry, W. J., and G. F. McCracken. 1991. Factors influencing female-pup scent recognition in Mexican free-tailed bats. J. Mamm. 72:624–626.

Loukmas, J. J., and R. S. Halbrook. 2001. A test of the mink habitat suitability index model for riverine systems. Wildl. Soc. Bull. 29:821–826.

Louv, R. 2005. Last child in the woods, saving our children from nature-deficit disorder. Algonquin Books, Chapel Hill, NC, 334 pp.

Lovallo, M. J., and E. M. Anderson. 1995. Range shift by a female bobcat (*Lynx rufus*) after removal of neighboring female. Amer. Midland Nat. 134:409–412.

Lovallo, M. J., and E. M. Anderson. 1996. Bobcat (*Lynx rufus*) home range size and habitat use in northwest Wisconsin. Amer. Midland Nat. 135:241–252.

Loveless, C. M. 1967. Ecological characteristics of a mule deer winter range. Tech. Bull., Colorado Division of Game, Fish, and Parks 20:1–124.

Lovell, D. C., J. R. Choate, and S. J. Bissell. 1985. Succession of mammals in a disturbed area of the Great Plains. Southwestern Nat. 30:335–342.

Lovell, D. C., W. R. Whitworth, J. R. Choate, S. J. Bissell, M. P. Moulton, and J. D. Hoffman. 2004. Geographic relationships of pocket gophers in southeastern Colorado. Trans. Nebraska Acad. Sci. 29:45–55.

Loy, R. R. 1981. An ecological investigation of the swift fox, *Vulpes velox*, on the Pawnee National Grassland, Colorado. Unpubl. master's thesis, Univ. Northern Colorado, Greeley, 64 pp.

Lozier, J. D., P. Aniello, and M. J. Hickerson. 2009. Predicting the distribution of Sasquatch in western North America: anything goes with ecological niche modelling. J. Biogeography 36:1623–1627.

Lubow, B. C., F. J. Singer, T. L. Johnson, and D. C. Bowden. 2002. Dynamics of interacting elk populations within and adjacent to Rocky Mountain National Park. J. Wildl. Mgmt. 56: 757–775.

Luce, B. 1998. Wyoming's bats, wings in the night. Wyoming Wildlife 57(8):17–32.

Luce, B. 2002. A multi-state conservation plan for the black-tailed prairie dog, *Cynomys ludovicianus*, in the United States. Wildlife Management Institute, Washington, DC, 48 pp.

Luce, D. G., et al. 1980. Food habits of the plains pocket gopher on western Nebraska rangeland. J. Range Mgmt. 33:129–131.

Luce, D. G., and J. L. Stubbendieck. 1981. Damage to alfalfa fields by plains pocket gophers. J. Wildl. Mgmt. 45:258–260.

Luce, R. J. 2002. A multi-state conservation plan for the black-tailed prairie dog, *Cynomys ludovicianus*, in the United States, addendum to the Black-tailed Prairie Dog Conservation Assessment and Strategy, November 3, 1999. Prairie Dog Conservation Team, Sierra Vista, AZ, 58 pp.

Luce, R. J., and Keinath. 2007. Spotted bat (*Euderma maculatum*): a technical conservation assessment. Species Conservation Project, Rocky Mountain Region, USDA Forest Service, 78 pp.

Ludwig, A., M. Pruvost, M. Reissmann, N. Benecke, G. A. Brockmann, P. Castaños, M. Cieslak, S. Lippold, L. Llorente, A.-S. Malaspinas, M. Slatkin, and M. Hofreiter. 2009. Coat color variation at the beginning of horse domestication. Science 324:485.

Luikart, G., and F. W. Allendorf. 1996. Mitochondrial-DNA variation and genetic population structure in Rocky Mountain bighorn sheep (*Ovis canadensis canadensis*). J. Mamm. 77:109–123.

Luo, Z.-X., and J. R. Wible. 2005. A Late Jurassic digging mammal and early mammalian diversification. Science 308:103–107.

Lusby, G. C., V. H. Reid, and O. D. Knipe. 1971. Effects of grazing on hydrology and biology of the Badger Wash Basin in western Colorado, 1953–1966. Water Supply Papers, USGS 1532-D:1–90.

Lyons, S. K. 2003. A quantitative assessment of the range shifts of Pleistocene mammals. J. Mamm. 84:385–402.

Lytle, T., J. Caufield, and D. Hanna. 1981. River otter restoration and monitoring. Job Progress Report. Project SE-3-3, unpaged.

MacArthur, R. A. 1978. Winter movements and home range of the muskrat. Canadian Field-Nat. 92:345–349.

MacArthur, R. H., and E. O. Wilson. 1967. The theory of island biogeography. Princeton Univ. Press, Princeton, NJ, 203 pp.

MacDonald, D. 1956. Beaver carrying capacity of certain mountain streams in North Park, Colorado. Unpubl. master's thesis, Colorado A&M College, Fort Collins, 136 pp.

Macdonald, D. W., ed. 2006. The encyclopedia of mammals. Facts-on-File, New York, 936 pp.

Macdonald, D. W. 2009. The Princeton encyclopedia of mammals. Princeton Univ. Press, Princeton, NJ, 976 pp.

Macdonald, D. W., and P. J. Bacon. 1982. Fox society, contact rate and rabies epizootiology. Comp. Immunol., Microbiol., and Infect. Dis. 5:247–256.

Macêdo, R. H., and M. A. Mares. 1988. *Neotoma albigula*. Mammalian Species 310:1–7.

MacFadden, B. J. 1994. Fossil horses: systematics, paleobiology, and evolution of the family Equidae. Cambridge Univ. Press, New York, 383 pp.

MacInnes, C. D. 1987. Rabies. Pp. 910–929, in Wild furbearer management and conservation in North America (M. Novak, J. A. Baker, M. E. Obbard, and B. Malloch, eds.). Ontario Trappers Association, Toronto, 1,150 pp.

Mack, C. M. 1985. River otter restoration in Grand County, Colorado. Unpubl. master's thesis, Colorado State Univ., Fort Collins, 133 pp.

Mackie, R. J., K. L. Hamlin, and D. F. Pac. 1982. Mule Deer. Pp. 862–877, in Wild mammals of North America, biology, management, and economics (J. A. Chapman and G. A. Feldhamer, eds.). Johns Hopkins Univ. Press, Baltimore, 1,147 pp.

Mackie, R. J., J. G. Kie, D. F. Pac, and K. L. Hamlin. 2003. Mule deer, *Odocoileus hemionus*. Pp. 889–905, in Wild mammals of North America, biology, management, and economics (G. A. Feldhamer, B. C. Thompson, and J. A. Chapman, eds.). Johns Hopkins Univ. Press, Baltimore, 1,216 pp.

MacLean, S. F., Jr., B. M. Fitzgerald, and F. A. Pitelka. 1974. Population cycles in Arctic lemmings: winter reproduction and predation by weasels. Arctic and Alpine Research 6:1–12.

MacMillen, R. E. 1983. Water regulation in *Peromyscus*. J. Mamm. 54:38–47.

Magle, S., J. Zhu, and K. Crooks. 2005. Behavioral responses to repeated human intrusion by black-tailed prairie dogs (*Cynomys ludovicianus*). J. Mamm. 86:524–530.

Magle, S. B. 2008. Observations on body mass of prairie dogs in urban habitats. Western N. Amer. Nat. 58:113–118.

Magle, S. B., E. W. Ruell, M. F. Antolin, and K. R. Crooks. 2010. Population genetic structure of black-tailed prairie dogs, a highly interactive species, in fragmented urban habitat. J. Mamm. 91:326–335.

Magoun, A. J., and J. P. Copeland. 1998. Characteristics of wolverine reproductive den sites. J. Wildl. Mgmt. 52:1313–1320.

Magoun, A. J., and P. Valkenburg. 1983. Breeding behavior of free-ranging wolverines (*Gulo gulo*). Acta Zool. Fennici 174: 175–177.

Magurran, A. E. 1988. Ecological diversity and its measurement. Princeton Univ. Press, Princeton, NJ, 179 pp.

Maier, T. J., and K. L. Doyle. 2006. Aggregations of masked shrews (*Sorex cinereus*): density-related mating behavior? Mammalia 70:86–89.

Maj, M., and E. O. Garton. 1994. Fisher, lynx, wolverine summary of distribution information. Pp. 169–175, in The scientific basis for conserving forest carnivores: American marten, fisher, lynx, and wolverine in the western United States (L. F. Ruggiero, K. B. Aubry, S. W. Buskirk, L. J. Lyon, and W. J. Zielinski, eds.). General Technical Report RM-254, U.S. Forest Service, 184 pp.

Makar, P. W. 1980. Bobcat and coyote food habits and habitat use in Rocky Mountain National Park. Unpubl. master's thesis, Colorado State Univ., Fort Collins, 32 pp.

Malaney, J. L., and J. K. Frey. 2006. Summer habitat use by snowshoe hare and mountain cottontail at their southern zone of sympatry. J. Wildl. Mgmt. 70:877–883.

Malville, L. E. 1988. River otter tracking in Larimer County. Report to Colorado Division of Wildlife, unpaged.

Malville, L. E. 1990. Movements, distribution, and habitat selection of river otters reintroduced into the Dolores River, southwestern Colorado. Unpubl. master's thesis, Univ. Colorado, Boulder, 67 pp.

Mandel, R. D., J. L. Hofman, S. Hoken, and J. M. Blackmar. 2004. Buried Paleo-Indian landscapes and sites on the High Plains of northwestern Kansas. Field Guide, Geol. Soc. America 5:69–88.

Manfredo, M. J. 1989. Human dimensions in wildlife management. Wildl. Soc. Bull. 17:447–449.

Manfredo, M. J., D. C. Fulton, and C. L. Pierce. 1997. Understanding voter behavior of wildlife ballot initiatives: Colorado's trapping amendment. Human Dimensions Wildl. 2:22–29.

Manfredo, M. J., C. L. Pierce, D. Fulton, J. Pate, and R. B. Gill. 1999. Public acceptance of wildlife trapping in Colorado. Wildl. Soc. Bull. 27:499–508.

Manfredo, M. J., T. L. Teel, and A. D. Bright. 2003. Why are public values toward wildlife changing? Human Dimensions Wildl. 8:282–306.

Manfredo, M., J. Vaske, P. Brown, D. Decker, and E. Duke. 2009. Wildlife and society, the science of human dimensions. Island Press, Washington, DC, 368 pp.

Manfredo, M. J., and H. C. Zinn. 1996. Population change and its implications for wildlife management in the New West: a case study of Colorado. Human Dimensions Wildl. 13:62–74.

Manfredo, M. J., H. C. Zinn, L. Sikorowski, and J. Jones. 1998. Public acceptance of mountain lion management: a case study of Denver, Colorado, and nearby foothills areas. Wildl. Soc. Bull. 26:964–970.

Mankin, P. C., and L. L. Getz. 1994. Burrow morphology as related to social organization of *Microtus ochrogaster*. J. Mamm. 75:492–499.

Mann, C. C. 2006. 1491, New revelations of the Americas before Columbus. Vintage Books, New York, 538 pp.

Manning, R. W. 1993. Systematic and evolutionary relationships of the long-eared myotis, *Myotis evotis* (Chiroptera: Vespertilionidae). Spec. Publ., Museum, Texas Tech Univ. 37:1–58.

Manning, R. W., and C. Jones. 1998. Annotated checklist of Recent land mammals of Texas, 1998. Occas. Papers, Mus. Texas Tech Univ. 182:1–20.

Manning, R. W., and J. K. Jones, Jr. 1988. *Perognathus fasciatus*. Mammalian Species 303:1–4.

Manning, R. W., and J. K. Jones, Jr. 1989. *Myotis evotis*. Mammalian Species 329:1–5.

Manno, T. G. 2007. Why are Utah prairie dogs vigilant? J. Mamm. 88:555–563.

Manville, R. H. 1949. A study of small mammal populations in northern Michigan. Misc. Publ., Mus. Zool., Univ. Michigan 73:1–83.

Marchinton, R. L., and D. H. Hirth. 1984. Behavior. Pp. 129–168, in White-tailed deer: ecology and management (L. K. Halls, ed.). Stackpole Books, Harrisburg, PA, 870 pp.

Marcot, J. D. 2007. Molecular phylogeny of terrestrial artiodactyls: conflicts and resolution. Pp. 4–18, in The evolution of artiodactyls (D. R. Prothero and S. E. Foss, eds.). Johns Hopkins Univ. Press, Baltimore, 367 pp.

Markley, M. H., and C. F. Bassett. 1942. Habits of captive marten. Amer. Midland Nat. 28:605–616.

Marks, R. 2005. Swift fox (*Vulpes velox*). Fish and Wildlife Habitat Mgmt. Leaflet, Natural Resources Conservation Service 33:1–8.

Marr, J. W. 1967. Ecosystems of the east slope of the Front Range in Colorado. Univ. Colorado Studies, Ser. Biology 8:1–134.

Marsden, H. M., and N. R. Holler. 1964. Social behavior in confined populations of the cottontail and the swamp rabbit. Wildlife Monogr. 13:5–39.

Marshall, W. H. 1936. A study of the winter activities of the mink. J. Mamm. 17:382–392.

Marshall, W. H., G. W. Gullion, and G. Schawb. 1962. Early summer activities of porcupines as determined by radio-positioning techniques. J. Wildl. Mgmt. 26:75–79.

Marti, C. D. 1972. Notes on the least shrew in Colorado. Southwestern Nat. 15:447–448.

Marti, C. D., and C. E. Braun. 1975. Use of tundra habitats by prairie falcons in Colorado. Condor 77:213–214.

Martin, D., and B. Holmes. 2007. Fit for ferrets. Colorado Outdoors 56(3):28–30.

Martin, D. J., G. C. White, and F. M. Pusateri. 2007. Occupancy rates by swift foxes (*Vulpes velox*) in eastern Colorado. Southwestern Nat. 52:541–551.

Martin, I. G. 1980. An ethogram of captive *Blarina brevicauda*. Amer. Midland Nat. 104:290–294.

Martin, I. G. 1981. Tolerance of conspecifics by short-tailed shrews (*Blarina brevicauda*) in simulated natural conditions. Amer. Midland Nat. 106:206–208.

Martin, I. G. 1983. Daily activity of short-tailed shrews (*Blarina brevicauda*) in simulated natural conditions. Amer. Midland Nat. 109:136–144.

Martin, L. D., and R. S. Hoffmann. 1987. Pleistocene faunal provinces and Holocene biomes of the central Great Plains. Guidebook Series, Kansas Geol. Surv. 5:159–165.

Martin, P. S. 2005. Twilight of the mammoths, Ice Age extinctions and the rewilding of America. Univ. California Press, Berkeley, 250 pp.

Martin, P. S., and R. G. Klein, eds. 1984. Quaternary extinctions, a prehistoric revolution. Univ. Arizona Press, Tucson, 892 pp.

Martin, R. D. 1986. Are fruit bats primates? Nature 320:482–483.

Martin, R. E., R. H. Pine, and A. F. DeBlase. 2001. A manual of mammalogy with keys to families of the world, third ed. McGraw-Hill, Boston, 333 pp.

Martin, S. K. 1994. Feeding ecology of American martens and fishers. Pp. 297–315, in Martens, sables, and fishers: biology and conservation (S. W. Buskirk, A. Harestad, and M. Raphael, eds.). Cornell Univ. Press, Ithaca, New York, 496 pp.

Martin, S. K., and R. H. Barrett. 1983. The importance of snags to pine marten habitat in the northern Sierra Nevada. Pp. 114–116, in Snag habitat management: proceedings of a symposium (J. W. Davis, G. A. Goodwin, and R. A. Ockenfils, tech. coord.). Technical Report, USDA Forest Service. RM-99, 226 pp.

Martinsen, D. L. 1968. Temporal patterns in the home ranges of chipmunks (*Eutamias*). J. Mamm. 49:83–91.

Martinsen, D. L. 1969. Energetics and activity patterns of short-tailed shrews (*Blarina*) on restricted diets. Ecology 50:505–510.

Martorello, D. A., T. H. Eason, and M. R. Pelton. 2001. A sighting technique using cameras to estimate population size of black bears. Wildl. Soc. Bull. 29:560–567.

Maser, C., B. R. Mate, J. F. Franklin, and C. T. Dyrness. 1981. Natural history of Oregon coast mammals. General Tech., Rept., USDA Forest Service, PNW-133:1–496.

Maser, C. E., E. W. Hammer, C. Brown, R. E. Lewis, R. L. Tausch, and M. L. Johnson. 1974. The sage vole, *Lagurus curtatus* (Cope 1868), in the Crooked River National Grassland, Jefferson County, Oregon, a contribution to its life history and ecology. Saugetierkundliche Mitteilungen 22:193–222.

Maser, C. E., J. M. Trappe, and R. A. Nussbaum. 1978. Fungal–small mammal interrelationships with emphasis on Oregon coniferous forests. Ecology 59:799–809.

Mason, C. F., and S. M. MacDonald. 1983. Some factors influencing the distribution of mink (*Mustela vison*). J. Appl. Ecol. 20:281–283.

Masteller, M. A., and J. A. Bailey. 1988a. Do persisting matrilineal groups partition resources on mountain goat winter ranges? Proc. Biennial Symp. Northern Wild Sheep and Goat Council 6:26–38.

Masteller, M. A., and J. A. Bailey. 1988b. Agonistic behavior among mountain goats foraging in winter. Canadian J. Zool. 56:2585–2588.

Masterson, L. 2006. Living with bears. PixyJack Press, Boulder, CO, 255 pp.

Matchett, M. R., D. E. Biggins, V. Carlson, B. Powell, and T. Rocke. 2009. Enzootic plague reduces black-footed ferret (*Mustela nigripes*) survival in Montana. Vector-Borne and Zoonotic Diseases 10:27–35.

Mathiason, C. K., et al. 2006. Infectious prions in the saliva and blood of deer with chronic wasting disease. Science 314:133–136.

Matlack, R. S., P. S. Gipson, and D. W. Kaufman. 2000. The swift fox on rangeland and cropland in western Kansas: relative abundance, mortality, and body size. Southwestern Nat. 45: 221–225.

Matocq, M. D., Q. R. Shurtliff, and C. R. Feldman. 2007. Phylogenetics of the woodrat genus *Neotoma* (Rodentia: Muridae): implications for the evolution of phenotypic variation in male external genitalia. Molec. Phylogen. Evol. 42:637–652.

Matthews, V., K. KellerLynn, and B. Fox. 2003. Messages in stone, Colorado's colorful geology. Colorado Geological Surv., Denver, 157 pp.

Mattson, D. J. 2004. Exploitation of pocket gophers and their food caches by grizzly bears. J. Mamm. 85:731–742.

Mattson, D. J., B. M. Blanchard, and R. R. Knight. 1991. Food habits of Yellowstone grizzly bears, 1977–1987. Canadian J. Zool. 59:1619–1629.

Mattson, D. J., and D. P. Reinhart. 1997. Excavation of red squirrel middens by grizzly bears in the whitebark pine zone. J. Applied Ecology 34:926–940.

Mattson, T. A., S. W. Buskirk, and N. L. Stanton. 1996. Roost sites of the silver-haired bat (*Lasionycteris noctivagans*) in the Black Hills, South Dakota. Great Basin Nat. 56:247–253.

Maupin, G. O., K. I. Gage, J. Piesman, J. Monteniere, S. L. Sviat, L. VanderZanden, C. M. Happ, M. Dolan, and B.J.B. Johnson. 1994. Discovery of an enzootic cycle of *Borrelia burgdorferi* in *Neotoma mexicana* and *Ixodes spinipalpus* from northern Colorado, an area where Lyme disease is nonendemic. J. Infectious Disease 170:636–643.

Maxell, M. H., and L. N. Brown. 1968. Ecological distribution of rodents on the High Plains of eastern Wyoming. Southwestern Nat. 13:143–158.

Mayr, E. 1965. Animal species and evolution. Belknap Press of Harvard Univ. Press, Cambridge, MA, 797 pp.

McAliley, L. R., M. B. O'Neill, and R. J. Baker. 2007. Molecular evidence for genetic subdivisions in the desert shrew, *Notiosorex crawfordi*. Southwestern Nat. 52:410–417.

McAllister, J. A., and R. S. Hoffmann. 1988. *Phenacomys intermedius*. Mammalian Species 305:1–8.

McBee, K., and R. J. Baker. 1982. *Dasypus novemcinctus*. Mammalian Species 162:1–9.

McCabe, R. A. 1949. Notes on live-trapping mink. J. Mamm. 30: 416–423.

McCabe, R. E., B. W. O'Gara, and H. M. Reeves. 2004. Prairie ghost, pronghorn and human interaction in early America. Wildlife Management Institute and Univ. Press Colorado, Boulder, xvii + 175 pp.

McCaffrey, R. E., M. C. Wallace, J. F. Kamler, and J. D. Ray. 2003. Noteworthy distributional records of the prairie vole in the Texas and Oklahoma panhandles. Southwestern Nat. 48:717–719.

McCain, C. M. 2005. Elevational gradients in diversity of small mammals. Ecology 86:366–372.

McCain, C. M. 2007. Area and mammalian diversity. Ecology 88: 76–86.

McCain, L. 2008. Report from the burrow, forecast of the prairie dog. WildEarth Guardians, Denver, CO, 20 pp.

McCarley, W. H. 1959. An unusually large nest of *Cryptotis parva*. J. Mamm. 40:243.

McCarley, W. H. 1966. Annual cycle, population dynamics, and adaptive behavior of *Citellus tridecemlineatus*. J. Mamm. 47: 294–316.

McCarty, C. W., and J. A. Bailey. 1994. Habitat requirements of desert bighorn sheep. Spec. Publ., Colorado Division of Wildlife. 59:1–36.

McCarty, C. W., and M. W. Miller. 1998. Modeling the population dynamics of bighorn sheep. Spec. Rept., Colorado Division of Wildlife. 73:1–35.

McCarty, R. 1978. *Onychomys leucogaster*. Mammalian Species 87:1–6.

McClintock, B. T. 2004. The mark-resight method: an application to bighorn sheep in Colorado and a simulation study evaluating estimators. Unpubl. master's thesis. Colorado State Univ., Fort Collins.

McClintock, B. T., and G. C. White. 2007. Bighorn sheep abundance following a suspected pneumonia epidemic in Rocky Mountain National Park. J. Wildl. Mgmt. 71:183–189.

McCloskey, R. J., and K. G. Shaw. 1977. Copulatory behavior of the fox squirrel. J. Mamm. 58:663–665.

McCord, C. M., and J. E. Cardoza. 1982. Bobcat and lynx. Pp. 728–766, in Wild mammals of North America, biology, management, and economics (J. A. Chapman and G. A. Feldhamer, eds.). Johns Hopkins Univ. Press, Baltimore, 1,147 pp.

McCoy, C. J., Jr., and P. H. Miller. 1964. Ecological distribution of the subspecies of *Ammospermophilus leucurus* in Colorado. Southwestern Nat. 9:89–93.

McCracken, G. F. 1984. Communal nursing in Mexican free-tailed bat maternity colonies. Science 223:1090–1091.

McCracken, G. F. 1996. Bats aloft: a study of high-altitude feeding. Bats 14(3):7–10.

McCracken, G. F. 2003. Estimates of population sizes in summer colonies of Brazilian free-tailed bats (*Tadarida brasiliensis*). Pp. 21–30, in Monitoring trends in bat populations in the United States and territories: problems and prospects (T. J. O'Shea and M. A. Bogan, eds.). Information and Technology Report, USGS/BRD/ITR-2003-003, 274 pp.

McCracken, G. F., and M. F. Gassel. 1997. Genetic structure in migratory and nonmigratory populations of Brazilian free-tailed bats. J. Mamm. 78:348–357.

McCullough, C. R., and E. K. Fritzell. 1984. Ecological observations of eastern spotted skunks on the Ozark Plateau. Trans. Missouri Acad. Sci. 18:25–32.

McCullough, D. R. 1969. The Tule elk: its history, behavior, and ecology. Univ. California Publ. Zool. 88:1–290.

McCutchen, H. E. 1969. Age determination of pronghorn by the incisor cementum. J. Wildl. Mgmt. 33:172–175.

McCutchen, H. E. 1987. Black bear species/area relationships studied at Rocky Mountain National Park. Park Sci. 7:18–19.

McCutchen, H. E. 1989. Observations of American black bear cryptic behavior in a national park. Proc. Intern. Conf. Bear Research and Mgmt. 8:20–25.

McDonald, J. N. 1981. North American bison: their classification and evolution. Univ. California Press, Berkeley, 316 pp.

McDonald, K. A., and J. H. Brown. 1992. Using montane mammals to model extinctions due to global change. Cons. Biol. 5:409–415.

McDonough, C. M. 1997. Pairing behavior of the nine-banded armadillo (*Dasypus novemcinctus*). Amer. Midland Nat. 138: 290–298.

McDonough, C. M. 2000. Social organization of nine-banded armadillos (*Dasypus novemcinctus*) in a riparian habitat. Amer. Midland Nat. 144:139–151.

McDonough, C. M., and W. J. Loughry. 1997a. Influences on activity patterns in a population of nine-banded armadillos. J. Mamm. 78:932–941.

McDonough, C. M., and W. J. Loughry. 1997b. Patterns of mortality in a population of nine-banded armadillos, *Dasypus novemcinctus*. Amer. Midland Nat. 138:299–305.

McGee, B. K., W. B. Ballard, K. L. Nicholson, B. L. Cypher, P. R. Lemmons, and J. F. Kamler. 2006. Effects of artificial escape dens on swift fox populations in northwest Texas. Wildl. Soc. Bull. 34:821–827.

McGinnies, W. J., H. L. Schantz, and W. G. McGinnies. 1991. Changes in vegetation and land use in eastern Colorado: a photographic study, 1904–1986. Agricultural Research Service, USDA, ARS-85:1–165.

McGrew, J. C. 1977. Distribution and habitat characteristics of the kit fox (*Vulpes macrotis*) in Utah. Unpubl. master's thesis, Utah State Univ., Logan, 92 pp.

McGrew, J. C. 1979. *Vulpes macrotis*. Mammalian Species 123:1–6.

McGuire, B., and M. Novak. 1986. Parental care and its relationship to social organization in the montane vole (*Microtus montanus*). J. Mamm. 57:305–311.

McHugh, T. 1972. The time of the buffalo. Alfred A. Knopf, New York, 339 pp.

McKay, D. O., and B. J. Verts. 1978. Estimates of some attributes of a population of Nuttall's cottontails. J. Wildl. Mgmt. 42: 159–168.

McKean, W. T. 1971. Stocking rates for mule deer and livestock on certain pinyon-juniper areas. Game Information Leafl., Colorado Division of Game, Fish, and Parks 87:1–2.

McKean, W. T., and W. T. Burkhard. 1978. Fish and wildlife analysis for the Yellow Jacket Project. Colorado Division of Wildlife, Denver, 119 pp.

McKechnie, A. M., A. T. Smith, and M. M. Peacock. 1994. Kleptoparasitism in pikas (*Ochotona princeps*): theft of hay. J. Mamm. 75:488–491.

McKeever, S. 1964. The biology of the golden-mantled ground squirrel. Ecol. Monogr. 34:383–401.

McKelvey, K. S., K. B. Aubry, and Y. K. Ortega. 2000. History and distribution of lynx in the contiguous United States. Pp. 207–264, in Ecology and conservation of lynx in the United States (L. F. Ruggiero, K. B. Aubry, S. W. Buskirk, G. M. Koehler, C. J. Krebs, K. S. McKelvey, and J. R. Squires, eds.). Univ. Press Colorado, Boulder, 480 pp.

McKelvey, K. S., J. V. Kienast, K. B. Aubry, G. M. Koehler, B. T. Maletzke, J. R. Squires, E. L. Lindquist, S. Loch, and M. K. Schwartz. 2006. DNA analysis of hair and scat collected along snow tracks to document the presence of Canada lynx. Wildl. Soc. Bull. 34:451–455.

McKelvey, K. S., G. W. McDaniel, L. Scott Mills, and P. C. Griffin. 2002. Effects of plot size and shape on pellet density estimates for snowshoe hares. Wildl. Soc. Bull. 30:751–755.

McKenna, M. C. 1975. Toward a phylogenetic classification of the Mammalia. Pp. 21–46, in Phylogeny of the primates (W. P. Luckett and F. S. Szalay, eds.). Plenum Publishing,. New York, 483 pp.

McKenna, M. C., and S. K. Bell. 1997. Classification of mammals above the species level. Columbia Univ. Press, New York, 631 pp.

McKinstry, M. C., and S. H. Anderson. 1999. Attitudes of private- and public-land managers in Wyoming, USA, toward beaver. Environmental Mgmt. 23:95–101.

McKinstry, M. C., R. R. Karhu, and S. H. Anderson. 1997. Use of active beaver, *Castor canadensis*, lodges by muskrats (*Ondatra zibethicus*) in Wyoming. Canadian Field-Nat. 111:310–311.

McLean, R. G. 2008. The introduction and emergence of wildlife diseases in North America. Pp. 261–278, in Wildlife science, linking ecological theory and management applications. (T. E. Fulbright and G. G. Hewitt, eds.). CRC, Boca Raton, FL, 384 pp.

McLean, R. G., A. B. Carey, L. J. Kirk, and D. B. Francy. 1993. Ecology of porcupines (*Erethizon dorsatum*) and Colorado Tick Fever virus in Rocky Mountain National Park, 1975–77. J. Med. Ent. 30:236–238.

McLean, R. G., D. B. Francy, G. S. Bowen, R. E. Bailey, C. H. Calisher, and A. M. Barnes. 1981. The ecology of Colorado tick fever in Rocky Mountain National Park in 1974, I. Objectives, study design, and summary of principal findings. American J. Trop. Med. Hyg. 30:483–489.

McLellan, B. N., and F. W. Hovey. 2001. Habitats selected by grizzly bears in a multiple use landscape. J. Wildl. Mgmt. 55:92–99.

McLellan, B. N., F. W. Hovey, R. D. Mace, J. G. Woods, D. W. Carney, M. L. Gibeau, W. L. Wakkinen, and W. F. Kasworm. 1999. Rates and causes of grizzly bear mortality in the interior mountains of British Columbia, Alberta, Montana, Washington, and Idaho. J. Wildl. Mgmt. 53:911–920.

McManus, J. J. 1970. Behavior of captive opossums, *Didelphis marsupialis virginiana*. Amer. Midland Nat. 84:144–169.

McManus, J. J. 1974. *Didelphis virginiana*. Mammalian Species 40: 1–6.

McNab, B. K. 1991. The energy expenditure of shrews. Pp. 35–45, in The biology of the soricidae (J. S. Findley and T. L. Yates, eds.). Spec. Publ., Mus. Southwestern Biol., Univ. New Mexico 1:1–91.

McPhee, J. 1998. Annals of the former world. Farrar, Straus and Giroux, New York, 696 pp.

Meacham, J. W. 1971. Entry. Bat Res. News 12:37.

Meacham, J. W. 1974. A Colorado colony of *Tadarida brasiliensis*. Bat Res. News 15:8–9.

Mead, R. A. 1967. Age determination in the spotted skunk. J. Mamm. 48:606–616.

Mead, R. A. 1968a. Reproduction in eastern forms of the spotted skunk (genus *Spilogale*). J. Zool. 156:119–136.

Mead, R. A. 1968b. Reproduction in western forms of the spotted skunk (genus *Spilogale*). J. Mamm. 49:373–390.

Mead, R. A. 1981. Delayed implantation in mustelids, with special emphasis on the spotted skunk. J. Repro. and Fertility, Supplement 29:11–24.

Mead, R. A. 1989. Reproduction in mustelids. Pp. 124–137, in Conservation biology and the black-footed ferret (U. S. Seal, E. T. Thorne, M. A. Bogan, and S. H. Anderson, eds.). Yale Univ. Press, New Haven, CT, 328 pp.

Mead, R. A., M. Rector, G. Starypan, S. Neirinckx, M. Jones, and M. N. Don-Carlos. 1991. Reproductive biology of captive wolverine. J. Mamm. 72:807–814.

Meadow, R., R. P. Reading, M. Phillips, M. Mehringer, and B. J. Miller. 2005. The influence of persuasive arguments on public attitudes toward a proposed wolf restoration in the southern Rockies. Wildl. Soc. Bull. 33:154–163.

Meadows, L. E., W. F. Andelt, and T.D.I. Beck. 1998. Managing bear damage to beehives. Natural Resources Series, Wildlife, Colorado State Univ. Coop. Extension 6.519:1–6.

Meagher, M. 1973. The bison of Yellowstone National Park. Science Monogr., National Park Service 1:1–161.

Meagher, M. 1986. *Bison bison*. Mammalian Species 266:1–8.

Mealy, W. V., and P. Friederici, eds. 1992. Value in American wildlife art. Roger Tory Peterson Institute of Natural History, Jamestown, NY, 145 pp.

Meaney, C., and G. P. Beauvais. 2004. Species assessment for gray wolf (*Canis lupus*) in Wyoming. Wyoming State Office, Bureau of Land Management, Cheyenne, 43 pp.

Meaney, C. A. 1986. Scent-marking in pikas (*Ochotona princeps*): test of a breeding-facilitation hypothesis. Pp. 571–577, in Chemical signals in vertebrates (D. Duvall, D. Muller-Schwarze, and R. M. Silverstein, eds.). Plenum Press, New York.

Meaney, C. A. 1987. Cheek-gland odors in pikas (*Ochotona princeps*): discrimination of individual and sex differences. J. Mamm. 58:391–395.

Meaney, C. A. 1990a. Distributional extensions of mammals in Colorado. J. Colorado-Wyoming Acad. Sci. 12(1):48.

Meaney, C. A. 1990b. Spatial utilization and scent-mark location in a territorial lagomorph. Pp. 388–393, in Chemical signals in vertebrates (D. W. Macdonald, D. Muller-Schwarze, and S. Natynczznk, eds.). Oxford Univ. Press, Oxford, UK.

Meaney, C. A., ed. 1991. Colorado mammal distribution latilong study. Colorado Division of Wildlife, Denver, 31 pp.

Meaney, C., M. Bakeman, M. Reed-Eckert, and E. Wostl. 2007. Effectiveness of ledges in culverts for small mammal passage. Research Branch, Colorado Dept. Transportation, Final Report, Report CDOT-2007-9:1–32.

Meaney, C. A., S. J. Bissell, and J. S. Slater. 1987. A nine-banded armadillo, *Dasypus novemcinctus* (Dasypodidae), in Colorado. Southwestern Nat. 32:507–508.

Meaney, C. A., M. Reed-Eckert, and G. P. Beauvais. 2006. Kit fox (*Vulpes macrotis*): a technical conservation assessment. Prepared for USDA Forest Service, Rocky Mountain Region, Species Conservation Project, 43 pp.

Meaney, C. A., A. K. Ruggles, and G. P. Beauvais. 2006. American hog-nosed skunk (*Conepatus leuconotus*): a technical conservation assessment. Species Conservation Project, USDA Forest Service, Rocky Mountain Region, 40 pp.

Meaney, C. A., A. K. Ruggles, N. W. Clippinger, and B. C. Lubow. 2002. The impact of recreational trails and grazing on small mammals in the Colorado Piedmont. Prairie Nat. 34:115–136.

Meaney, C. A., A. K. Ruggles, B. C. Lubow, and N. W. Clippinger. 2003. Abundance, survival, and hibernation in Preble's meadow jumping mice (*Zapus hudsonius preblei*) in Boulder County, Colorado. Southwestern Nat. 48:610–623.

Meaney, C. A., and D. Van Vuren. 1993. Recent distribution of bison in Colorado west of the Great Plains. Proc. Denver Mus. Nat. Hist. 4:1–10.

Mech, L. D. 1970. The wolf: the ecology and behavior of an endangered species. Natural History Press, Garden City, NY, 384 pp.

Mech, L. D. 1974. *Canis lupus*. Mammalian Species 37:1–6.

Mech, L. D. 1980. Age, sex, reproduction, and spatial organization of lynxes colonizing northeastern Minnesota. J. Mamm. 51:261–267.

Mech, L. D., and L. Boitani, eds. 2003. Wolves, behavior, ecology, and conservation. Univ. Chicago Press, Chicago, 448 pp.

Mech, L. D., and R. E. McRoberts. 1990. Survival of white-tailed deer fawns in relation to maternal age. J. Mamm. 71:465–467.

Mech, L. D., D. W. Smith, K. M. Murphy, and D. R. MacNulty. 2001. Winter severity and wolf predation on a formerly wolf-free elk herd. J. Wildl. Mgmt. 55:998–1003.

Medin, D. E., and A. E. Anderson. 1979. Modeling the dynamics of a Colorado mule deer population. Wildlife Monogr. 58:1–77.

Medin, D. E., and W. P. Clary. 1990. Bird and small mammal populations in a grazed and ungrazed riparian habitat in Idaho. USDA Forest Service, Intermountain Research Station, Ogden, UT, Research Paper, INT-425:1–6.

Medin, D. E., and W. P. Clary. 1991. Small mammals of a beaver pond ecosystem and adjacent riparian habitat in Idaho. USDA, Forest Service, Intermountain Research Station, Ogden, UT, Research Paper, INT-432:1–8.

Medin, D. E., and K. E. Torquemada. 1988. Beaver in western North America: an annotated bibliography, 1966–1986. General Technical Rept., USDA Forest Service, INT-242:1–18.

Mehrer, C. F. 1976. Gestation period in the wolverine, *Gulo gulo*. J. Mamm. 57:570.

Mellott, R. S., and J. R. Choate. 1984. *Sciurus aberti* and *Microtus montanus* on foothills of the Culebra Range in southern Colorado. Southwestern Nat. 29:135–137.

Mellott, R. S., J. R. Choate, and C. Loeffler. 1987. Mammals of the Spanish Peaks State Wildlife Areas, Colorado. Fort Hays Studies, Third Ser. (Science) 9:1–30.

Mellott, R. S., and E. D. Fleharty. 1986. Distribution status of the hispid cotton rat (*Sigmodon hispidus*) in Colorado. Trans. Kansas Acad. Sci. 89:75–77.

Melquist, W. E., and A. E. Dronkert. 1987. River otter. Pp. 626–641, in Wild furbearer management and conservation in North America (M. Novak, J. A. Baker, M. E. Obbard, and B. Malloch, eds.). Ontario Trappers Association, Toronto, 1,150 pp.

Melquist, W. E., and M. G. Hornocker. 1979. Methods and techniques for studying and censusing river otter populations. Tech. Rep., Univ. Idaho Forest, Wildlife and Range Exper. Sta. 8:1–17 pp.

Melquist, W. E., and M. G. Hornocker. 1983. Ecology of river otters in west central Idaho. Wildlife Monogr. 83:1–60.

Melquist, W. E., P. J. Polechla, Jr., and D. Toweill. 2003. River otter, *Lontra canadensis*. Pp. 708–734, in Wild mammals of North America, biology, management, and conservation, second ed. (G. A. Feldhamer, B. C. Thompson, and J. A. Chapman, eds.). Johns Hopkins Univ. Press, Baltimore, 1,216 pp.

Melquist, W. E., J. S. Whitman, and M. G. Hornocker. 1981. Resource partitioning and coexistence of sympatric mink and river otter populations. Pp. 187–220, in Proc. Worldwide Furbearer Conf. (J. A. Chapman and D. Pursley, eds.). Worldwide Furbearer Conf., Frostburg, MD, 2,059 pp.

Meng, J., and A. R. Wyss. 2005. Glires (Lagomorpha, Rodentia). Pp. 145–158, in The rise of placental mammals, origins and relationships of the major extant clades (K. D. Rose and J. D. Archibald, eds.). Johns Hopkins Univ. Press, Baltimore, 259 pp.

Menkens, G. E., Jr., and S. H. Anderson. 1989. Temporal-spatial variation in white-tailed prairie dog demography and life histories in Wyoming. Canadian J. Zool. 57:343–349.

Menkens, G. E., Jr., and S. H. Anderson. 1991. Population dynamics of white-tailed prairie dogs during an epizootic of sylvatic plague. J. Mamm. 72:328–331.

Mercure, A., K. Ralls, K. P. Koepeli, and R. K. Wayne. 1993. Genetic subdivisions among small canids: mitochondrial DNA differentiation of swift, kit, and arctic foxes. Evolution 47: 1313–1328.

Meredith, D. H. 1974. Long distance movements by two species of chipmunks (*Eutamias*) in southern Alberta. J. Mamm. 55: 466–469.

Merriam, C. H. 1895. Synopsis of the American shrews of the genus *Sorex*. N. American Fauna 10:57–100.

Merritt, J. F. 1981. *Clethrionomys gapperi*. Mammalian Species 146: 1–9.

Merritt, J. F. 1984. Growth patterns and seasonal thermogenesis of *Clethrionomys gapperi* inhabiting the Appalachian and Rocky Mountains of North America. Pp. 201–213, in Winter ecology of small mammals (J. F. Merritt, ed.). Spec. Publ., Carnegie Mus. Nat. Hist. 10:1–380.

Merritt, J. F. 1985. Influence of snowcover on survival of *Clethrionomys gapperi* inhabiting the Appalachian and Rocky Mountains of North America. Acta Zoologica Fennica 173:73–74.

Merritt, J. F. 1995. Seasonal thermogenesis and changes in body mass in masked shrews, *Sorex cinereus*. J. Mamm. 76:1020–1035.

Merritt, J. F., G. L. Kirkland, Jr., and R. K. Rose, eds. 1994. Advances in the biology of shrews. Spec. Publ., Carnegie Mus. Nat. Hist. 18:1–458.

Merritt, J. F., and J. M. Merritt. 1978a. Population ecology and energy relationships of *Clethrionomys gapperi* in a Colorado subalpine forest. J. Mamm. 59:576–598.

Merritt, J. F., and J. M. Merritt. 1978b. Seasonal home ranges and activity of small mammals of a Colorado subalpine forest. Acta Theriol. 23:195–202.

Merritt, J. F., and J. M. Merritt. 1980. Population ecology of the deer mouse (*Peromyscus maniculatus*) in the Front Range of Colorado. Ann. Carnegie Mus. Nat. Hist. 49:113–130.

Meserve, P. L. 1977. Three dimensional home ranges of cricetid rodents. J. Mamm. 58:549–558.

Messick, J. P. 1981. Ecology of the badger in southwestern Idaho. Unpubl. doctoral dissert., Univ. Idaho, Moscow, 52 pp.

Messick, J. P. 1987. North American badger. Pp. 586–597, in Wild furbearer management and conservation in North America (M. Novak, J. A. Baker, M. E. Obbard, and B. Malloch, eds.). Ontario Trappers Association, Toronto, 1,150 pp.

Messick, J. P., and M. G. Hornocker. 1981. Ecology of the badger in southwestern Idaho. Wildl. Monogr. 76:1–53.

Messick, J. P., G. W. Smith, and A. M. Barnes. 1983. Serologic testing of badgers to monitor plague in southwestern Idaho. J. Wildl. Diseases 19:1–6.

Messick, J. P., M. C. Todd, and M. G. Hornocker. 1981. Comparative ecology of two badger populations. Pp. 1290–1304, in Proc. Worldwide Furbearer Conf. (J. A. Chapman and D. Pursley, eds.). Worldwide Furbearer Conference, Frostburg, MD, 2,059 pp.

Messmer, T. A., M. W. Brunson, D. Reiter, and D. G. Hewitt. 1999. United States public attitudes regarding predators and their management to enhance avian recruitment. Wildl. Soc. Bull. 27:75–85.

Messmer, T. A., D. Reiter, and B. C. West. 2001. Enhancing wildlife sciences' linkage to public policy: lessons from the predator-control pendulum. Wildl. Soc. Bull. 29:1253–1259.

Meyer, B. J., and R. K. Meyer. 1944. Growth and reproduction of the cotton rat, *Sigmodon hispidus hispidus*, under laboratory conditions. J. Mamm. 25:107–129.

Meyer, M. E., and M. Meagher. 1995. Brucellosis in free-ranging bison (*Bison bison*) in Yellowstone, Grand Teton, and Wood Buffalo National Parks: a review. J. Wildl. Dis. 31:579–598.

Michener, G. R. 2000. Caching of Richardson's ground squirrels by North American badgers. J. Mamm. 81:1106–1117.

Michener, G. R. 2004. Hunting techniques and tool use by North American badgers preying on Richardson's ground squirrels. J. Mamm. 85:1019–1027.

Michener, G. R., and A. N. Iwaniuk. 2001. Killing techniques of North American badgers preying on Richardson's ground squirrels. Canadian J. Zool. 79:2109–2113.

Middleton, M. D. 1983. Early Paleocene vertebrates of the Denver Basin, Colorado. Unpubl. doctoral dissert., Univ. Colorado, Boulder, 403 pp.

Mielke, H. W. 1977. Mound building by pocket gophers (Geomyidae): their impact on soils and vegetation in North America. J. Biogeography 4:171–180.

Mighetto, L. 1991. Wild animals and American environmental ethics. Univ. Arizona Press, Tucson, 177 pp.

Mikesic, D. G., and C. T. LaRue. 2003. Recent status and distribution of red foxes (*Vulpes vulpes*) in northeastern Arizona and southeastern Utah. Southwestern Nat. 48:624–634.

Milchunas, D. G., W. K. Lauenroth, and I. C. Burke. 1998. Livestock grazing: animal and plant biodiversity of shortgrass steppe and the relationship to ecosystem function. Oikos 83:65–74.

Miller, B., G. Ceballos, and R. Reading. 1994. The prairie dog and biotic diversity. Cons. Biol. 8:677–681.

Miller, B., B. Dugelby, D. Foreman, C. Martinez del Rio, R. Noss, M. Phillips, R. Reading, M. E. Soulé, J. Terborgh, and L. Willcox. 2001. The importance of large carnivores to healthy ecosystems. Endangered Species Update 18:202–210.

Miller, B., D. Foreman, M. Fink, D. Shinneman, J. Smith, M. DeMarco, M. Soulé, and R. Howard. 2003. Southern Rockies Wildlands Network Vision, a science-based approach to rewilding the southern Rockies. Southern Rockies Ecosystem Project, Boulder, CO, 248 pp.

Miller, B., R. P. Reading, and S. Forrest. 1996. Prairie night: black-footed ferrets and the recovery of endangered species. Smithsonian Institution Press, Washington, DC, 254 pp.

Miller, B., R. Reading, J. Hoogland, T. Clark, G. Ceballos, R. List, S. Forrest, L. Hanebury, P. Manzano, J. Pacheco, and D. Uresk. 2000. The role of prairie dogs as keystone species: a response to Stapp. Cons. Biol. 14:318–321.

Miller, D. A., E. B. Arnett, and M. J. Lacki. 2003. Habitat management for forest-roosting bats of North America: a critical review of habitat studies. Wildl. Soc. Bull. 31:30–44.

Miller, D. S., B. G. Campbell, R. G. McLean, E. Campos, and D. F. Covell. 1998. Parasites of swift fox (*Vulpes velox*) from southeastern Colorado. Southwestern Nat. 43:476–479.

Miller, D. S., D. F. Covell, R. G. McLean, W. J. Adrian, M. Niezgoda, J. M. Gustafson, O. J. Rongstad, R. D. Schulz, L. J. Kirk, and T. J. Quan. 2000. Serologic survey for selected infectious disease agents in swift and kit foxes from the western United States. J. Wildl. Diseases 36:798–805.

Miller, F. W. 1924. The range of *Cryptotis parva* (Say). J. Mamm. 5:199.

Miller, F. W. 1925. A new hog-nosed skunk. J. Mamm. 5:50–51.

Miller, F. W. 1930. A note on the pygmy vole in Colorado. J. Mamm. 11:83–84.

Miller, G. S., Jr., and G. M. Allen. 1928. The American bats of the genera *Myotis* and *Pizonyx*. Bulletin U.S. Nat. Mus. 144:1–218.

Miller, I. 2010. A day in the life at the Snowmass Ice Age dig site. Catalyst, Denver Museum of Nature and Science, December, pp. 6–7.

Miller, K. V., L. I. Muller, and S. Demarais. 2003. White-tailed deer, *Odocoileus virginianus*. Pp. 906–930, in Wild mammals of North America, biology, management, and economics, second ed. (G. A. Feldhamer, B. C. Thompson, and J. A. Chapman, eds.). Johns Hopkins Univ. Press, Baltimore, 1,216 pp.

Miller, M. S. 1998. Ecology of deer mice (*Peromyscus maniculatus*) and Ord's kangaroo rat (*Dipodomys ordii*) in riparian zones of regulated versus unregulated rivers in northwestern Colorado. Unpubl. master's thesis, Colorado State Univ., Fort Collins, 68 pp.

Miller, M. S., K. W. Wilson, and D. C. Andersen. 2003. Ord's kangaroo rats living in floodplain habitats: factors contributing to habitat attraction. Southwestern Nat. 48:411–418.

Miller, M. W. 2001. Pasteurellosis. Pp. 330–339, in Infectious diseases of wild mammals, third ed. (E. S. Williams and I. K. Barker, eds.). Iowa State Univ. Press, Ames, 558 pp.

Miller, M. W., H. M. Swanson, L. L. Wolfe, F. G. Quartarone, S. L. Huwer, C. H. Southwick, and P. M. Lukacs. 2008. Lions and prions and deer demise. PLoS ONE 3(12):1–7.

Miller, M. W., E. S. Williams, N. T. Hobbs, and L. L. Wolfe. 2004. Environmental sources of prion transmission in mule deer. EMBO Journal 10(6):1003–1006.

Miller, M. W., E. S. Williams, C. W. McCarty, T. R. Spraker, T. J. Kreeger, C. T. Larsen, and E. T. Thorne. 2000. Epizootiology of chronic wasting disease in free-ranging cervids in Colorado and Wyoming. J. Wildl. Diseases 36:676–690.

Miller, P. H. 1964. The ecological distribution of mammals in Colorado National Monument, Mesa County, Colorado. Unpubl. master's thesis, Oklahoma State Univ., Stillwater, 133 pp.

Miller, P. H., and C. J. McCoy. 1965. Kit fox in Colorado. J. Mamm. 46:342–343.

Miller, R. S. 1964. Ecology and distribution of pocket gophers (Geomyidae) in Colorado. Ecology 42:256–272.

Miller, R. S., and R. A. Ward. 1960. Ectoparasites of pocket gophers from Colorado. Amer. Midland Nat. 54:382–391.

Miller, S. D., and J. F. Cully, Jr. 2001. Conservation of black-tailed prairie dogs (*Cynomys ludovicianus*). J. Mamm. 82:889–893.

Miller, S. G., R. L. Knight, and C. K. Miller. 2001. Wildlife responses to pedestrians and dogs. Wildl. Soc. Bull. 29:124–136.

Mills, E. A. 1909. Wildlife on the Rockies. Houghton Mifflin, Boston, 270 pp.

Mills, E. A. 1913. In beaver world. Houghton Mifflin, Boston, 227 pp.

Mills, E. A. 1915. The Rocky Mountain wonderland. Houghton Mifflin, Boston, 362 pp.

Mills, E. A. 1919. The grizzly, our greatest wild mammal. Riverside Press, Cambridge, MA, 284 pp.

Mills, E. A. 1922. Watched by wild animals. Houghton Mifflin, Boston, 155 pp.

Mills, J. N., T. L. Yates, J. E. Childs, R. R. Parmenter, T. G. Ksiazek, P. E. Rollin, and C. J. Peters. 1995. Guidelines for working with rodents potentially infected with hantavirus. J. Mamm. 76:716–722.

Mills, J. N., T. L. Yates, T. G. Ksiazek, C. J. Peters, and J. E. Childs. 1999. Long-term studies of hantavirus reservoir populations in the southwestern United States: rationale, potential, and methods. Emerging Infect. Dis. 5:95–101.

Milner, J., C. Jones, and J. K. Jones, Jr. 1990. *Nyctinomops macrotis*. Mammalian Species 351:1–4.

Min, S. E. 1997. Variation in sexually dimorphic traits of male pronghorns. J. Mamm. 78:31–47.

Minnis, D. L. 1998. Wildlife policy-making by the electorate: an overview of citizen-sponsored ballot measures on hunting and trapping. Wildl. Soc. Bull. 57:75–83.

Minta, S. C. 1993. Sexual differences in spatio-temporal interaction among badgers. Oecologia 96:402–409.

Minta, S. C., P. M. Kareiva, and A. P. Curlee. 1999. Carnivore research and conservation: learning from history and theory. Pp. 323–404, in Carnivores in ecosystems (T. W. Clark, A. P. Curlee, S. C. Minta, and P. M. Kareiva, eds.). Yale Univ. Press, New Haven, CT, 429 pp.

Minta, S. C., and M. Mangel. 1989. A simple population estimate based on simulation for capture-recapture and capture-resight data. Ecology 70:1738–1751.

Minta, S. C., K. A. Minta, and D. F. Lott. 1992. Hunting associations between badgers (*Taxidea taxus*) and coyotes (*Canis latrans*). J. Mamm. 73:814–820.

Mitchell, C. D., and C. H. Maher. 2001. Are horn characteristics related to age in male pronghorns? Wildl. Soc. Bull. 29:908–916.

Mitchell, J. L. 1961. Mink movements and populations on a Montana river. J. Wildl. Mgmt. 25:48–54.

Mitchell, M. D. 2004. Tracing Comanche history: Eighteenth century rock art depictions of leather-armoured horses from the Arkansas River basin, south-eastern Colorado, USA. Antiquity 78:115–126.

Mitchell, R. S. 1972. Small rodents of the flood plain of the South Platte River at the proposed Narrows Reservoir site. Unpubl. master's thesis, Univ. Northern Colorado, Greeley, 50 pp.

Mohamed, R. M. 1989. Ecology and biology of *Perognathus* species in a grassland ecosystem in northeastern Colorado. Unpubl. doctoral dissert., Univ. Northern Colorado, Greeley, 177 pp.

Mollhagen, T. R., and M. A. Bogan. 1997. Bats of the Henry Mountains region of southeastern Utah. Occas. Papers, Mus. Texas Tech Univ. 170:1–13.

Monk, R. R., and J. K. Jones, Jr. 1996. *Perognathus flavescens*. Mammalian Species 525:1–4.

Monroe, M. C., S. P. Morzunov, A. M. Johnson, M. D. Bowen, H. Artsob, T. Yates, C. J. Peters, P. E. Rollin, T. G. Ksiasek, and S. T. Nichol. 1999. Genetic diversity and distribution of *Peromyscus*-borne hantaviruses in North America. Emerging Infect. Dis. 5:75–86.

Monson, G., and L. Sumner, eds. 1980. The desert bighorn. Univ. Arizona Press, Tucson, 370 pp.

Montgomery, G. G. 1964. Tooth eruption in preweaned raccoons. J. Wildl. Mgmt. 28:582–584.

Montgomery, G. G. 1968. Pelage development of young raccoons. J. Mamm. 49:142–145.

Montgomery, G. G. 1969. Weaning of captive raccoons. J. Wildl. Mgmt. 33:154–159.

Monty, A.-M., and R. E. Emerson. 2003. Eastern woodrat, *Neotoma floridana* and allies. Pp. 381–393, in Wild mammals of North America, biology, management, and economics, second ed. (G. A. Feldhamer, B. C. Thompson, and J. A. Chapman, eds.). Johns Hopkins Univ. Press, Baltimore, 1,216 pp.

Moore, J. C. 1959. Relationships among the living squirrels of the Sciurinae. Bull. Amer. Mus. Nat. Hist. 118:157–206.

Moore, T. D., L. E. Spence, and C. E. Dugnolle. 1974. Identification of the dorsal guard hairs of some mammals of Wyoming. Wyoming Game and Fish Dept., Cheyenne, 174 pp.

Mooring, M. S. 1989. Ontogeny of allogrooming in mule deer (*Odocoileus hemionus*). J. Mamm. 70:434–437.

Morales, J. C., and J. W. Bickham. 1995. Molecular systematics of the genus *Lasiurus* (Chiroptera: Vespertilionidae) based on restriction-site maps of the mitochondrial ribosomal genes. J. Mamm. 76:730–749.

More, G. 1976. Some winter food habits of lynx in the southern MacKenzie district, NWT. Canadian Field-Nat. 90:499–500.

Morgart, J. R. 1985. Carnivorous behavior by a white-tailed antelope ground squirrel, *Ammospermophilus leucurus*. Southwestern Nat. 30:304–305.

Morrell, S. H. 1972. Life history of the San Joaquin kit fox. California Fish and Game 58:162–174.

Morrell, S. H. 1975. San Joaquin kit fox distribution and abundance in 1975. Admin. Rept., Wildlife Management Branch, California Dept. Fish and Game 75–3:1–27.

Morrell, T. E., M. J. Rabe, J. C. deVos, H. Green, and C. R. Miller. 1999. Bats captured in two ponderosa pine habitats in north-central Arizona. Southwestern Nat. 44:501–506.

Morrison, J. R., W. J. De Verge, A. W. Alldredge, and W. W. Andree. 1995. The effects of ski area expansion on elk. Wildl. Soc. Bull. 23:481–489.

Morton, P., C. Weller, J. Thompson, M. Haefele, and N. Culver. 2004. Drilling in the Rocky Mountains, how much and at what cost? The Wilderness Society, Washington, DC, 33 pp.

Moser, D. A. 1962. The bighorn sheep of Colorado. Tech. Publ., Colorado Game and Fish Dept. 10:1–49.

Moses, R. A., G. J. Hickling, and J. S. Millar. 1995. Variation in sex ratios of offspring in wild bushy-tailed woodrats. J. Mamm. 76:1047–1055.

Moulton, M. P. 1978. Small mammal associations in grazed versus ungrazed cottonwood riparian woodlands in eastern Colorado. Pp. 133–140, in Lowland river and stream habitat in Colorado: a symposium (W. D. Graul and S. J. Bissell, tech. coords.). Colorado Chapter, Wildlife Society and Colorado Audubon Council, Greeley, 195 pp.

Moulton, M. P., J. R. Choate, and S. J. Bissell. 1979. Sympatry of pocket gophers on Mesa de Maya, Colorado. Trans. Kansas Acad. Sci. 82:194–195.

Moulton, M. P., J. R. Choate, and S. J. Bissell. 1981. Small mammals on revegetated agricultural land in eastern Colorado. Prairie Nat. 13:99–104.

Moulton, M. P., J. R. Choate, and S. J. Bissell. 1983. Biogeographic relationships of pocket gophers in southeastern Colorado. Southwestern Nat. 28:53–60.

Moulton, M. P., J. R. Choate, S. J. Bissell, and R. A. Nicholson. 1981. Associations of small mammals on the central High Plains of eastern Colorado. Southwestern Nat. 26:53–57.

Mowat, G. K., G. Poole, and M. O'Donoghue. 2000. Ecology of lynx in northern Canada and Alaska. Pp. 265–306, in Ecology and conservation of lynx in the United States (L. F. Ruggiero, K. B. Aubry, S. W. Buskirk, G. M. Koehler, C. J. Krebs, K. S. McKelvey, and J. R. Squires, eds.). Univ. Press Colorado, Boulder, 480 pp.

Muir, J. 1911. My first summer in the Sierra. Houghton Mifflin, Boston, 268 pp.

Mulhern, D. W., and C. J. Knowles. 1997. Black-tailed prairie dog status and future conservation planning. Pp. 19–29, in Conserving biodiversity on native rangelands: symposium proceedings, August 17, 1995, Fort Robinson State Park, Nebraska (D. Uresk, G. Schenbeck, and J. O'Rourke, eds.). General Technical Report, USDA Forest Service, RM-GR-298:1–38.

Müller, B., M. Glösmann, L. Peichl, G. C. Knop, C. Hageman, and J. Ammermüller. 2009. Bat eyes have ultraviolet-sensitive cone photoreceptors. PLoS ONE 4(7):1–7.

Müller-Schwarze, D., and L. Sun. 2003. The beaver: natural history of a wetlands engineer. Cornell Univ. Press, Ithaca, NY, 208 pp.

Mullican, T. R., and B. L. Keller. 1986. Ecology of the sagebrush vole (*Lemmiscus curtatus*) in southeastern Idaho. Canadian J. Zool. 54:1218–1223.

Mumford, R. E. 1973. Natural history of the red bat (*Lasiurus borealis*) in Indiana. Period. Biol. 75:155–158.

Munn, L. C. 1993. Effects of prairie dogs on physical and chemical properties of soils. Pp. 11–17, in Proc. Symposium on the Management of Prairie Dog Complexes for the Reintroduction of Black-footed Ferrets (J. L. Oldemeyer, D. E. Biggins, B. J. Miller, and R. Crete, eds.). Biol. Rept., U.S. Fish and Wildlife Service 93:1–95.

Murie, A. 1940. Ecology of the coyote in the Yellowstone. Fauna Series, U.S. Nat. Park Serv. 4:1–206.

Murie, O. J. 1935. Food habits of the coyote in Jackson Hole, Wyoming. Circular, USDA 362:1–24.

Murie, O. J. 1951. The elk of North America. The Stackpole Co., Harrisburg, PA, 376 pp.

Murphy, S. M., and Y. B. Linhart. 1999. Comparative morphology of the gastrointestinal tract of the feeding specialist *Sciurus aberti* and several generalist congeners. J. Mamm. 80:1325–1330.

Murray, D. L. 2003. Snowshoe hare and other hares, *Lepus americanus* and allies. Pp. 147–175, in Wild mammals of North America, biology, management, and economics, second ed. (G. A. Feldhamer, B. C. Thompson, and J. A. Chapman, eds.). Johns Hopkins Univ. Press, Baltimore, 1,216 pp.

Murray, J. A. 1987. Wildlife in peril: the endangered mammals of Colorado: river otter, black-footed ferret, wolverine, lynx, grizzly bear, gray wolf. Roberts Rinehart, Boulder, 226 pp.

Musgrove, B. F. 1951. Weasel foraging patterns in the Robinson Lake area, Idaho. Murrelet 32:8–11.

Musser, G. G., and M. D. Carleton. 2005. Superfamily Muroidea. Pp. 894–1531, in Mammal species of the world, a taxonomic and geographic reference, third ed. (D. E. Wilson and D. M. Reeder, eds.), 2 vols. Johns Hopkins Univ. Press, Baltimore.

Mutch, G.R.P., and M. Aleksiuk. 1977. Ecological aspects of winter dormancy in the striped skunk (*Mephitis mephitis*). Canadian J. Zool. 55:607–615.

Mutel, C. F., and J. C. Emerick. 1992. From grassland to glacier, the natural history of Colorado and the surrounding region, second ed. Johnson Books, Boulder, CO, 290 pp.

Muth, R. M., R. R. Zwick, M. E. Mather, J. F. Organ, J. J. Daigle, and S. A. Jonker. 2006. Unnecessary source of pain and suffering or necessary management tool: attitudes of conservation professionals toward outlawing leghold traps. Wildl. Soc. Bull. 34:706–715.

Muths, E. 1999. Dwarf shrew found in Rocky Mountain National Park. Park Sci. 19(1):1–2.

Myers, E. P. 2001. Assessing the role of selected infectious disease agents in neonatal mule deer fawn mortality on the Uncompahgre Plateau of western Colorado. Unpubl. master's thesis, Colorado State Univ., Fort Collins, 61 pp.

Myers, G. T., and T. A. Vaughan. 1964. Food habits of the plains pocket gopher in eastern Colorado. J. Mamm. 45:588–597.

Myers, L. G. 1969. Home range and longevity in *Zapus princeps* in Colorado. Amer. Midland Nat. 82:628–629.

Nadler, C. F., R. S. Hoffmann, and K. R. Greer. 1971. Chromosomal divergence during evolution of ground squirrel populations (Rodentia: *Spermophilus*). Syst. Zool. 20:298–305.

Nagy, J. G., H. W. Steinhoff, and G. M. Ward. 1964. Effects of essential oils of sagebrush on deer rumen microbial function. J. Wildl. Mgmt. 28:785–790.

Nagy, J. G., and R. P. Tengerdy. 1967. Antibacterial action of essential oils of *Artemisia* as an ecological factor, II. Antibacterial action of the volatile oils of *Artemisia tridentata* (big sagebrush) on bacteria from the rumen of mule deer. Applied Microbiol. 16:441–444.

Naiman, R. J. 1988. Animal influences on ecosystem dynamics. BioScience 38:750–753.

Naiman, R. J., C. A. Johnston, and J. C. Kelley. 1988. Alteration of North American streams by beaver. BioScience 38:753–762.

Naiman, R. J., G. Pinay, C. A. Johnson, and J. Pastor. 1994. Beaver influences on the long-term biogeochemical characteristics of boreal forest drainage networks. Ecology 75:905–921.

Nams, V. 1981. Prey selection mechanisms of the ermine (*Mustela erminea*). Pp. 861–882, in Proc. Worldwide Furbearer Conference (J. A. Chapman and D. Pursley, eds.). Worldwide Furbearer Conference, Frostburg, MD, 2,059 pp.

Nams, V., and S. S. Beare. 1982. Use of trees by ermine, *Mustela erminea*. Canadian Field-Nat. 96:89–90.

Nash, D. J., and C. A. Ramey. 1970. The tassel-eared squirrel in Colorado. Occas. Publ., Dept. Zool., Colorado State Univ. 2:1–6.

Nash, D. J., and R. N. Seaman. 1977. *Sciurus aberti*. Mammalian Species 80:1–5.

National Assessment Synthesis Team. 2000. Climate change impacts on the United States, the potential consequences of climate variability and change. Cambridge Univ. Press, Cambridge, UK, 154 pp.

National Park Service. 2000. Bison management plan for the state of Montana and Yellowstone National Park, Executive Summary, National Park Service, Washington, DC, 97 pp.

Nava, J. A. 1970. The reproductive biology of the Alaska lynx (*Lynx canadensis*). Unpubl. master's thesis, Univ. Alaska, Fairbanks, 141 pp.

Navo, K. W., J. A. Gore, and G. T. Skiba. 1992. Observations of the spotted bat, *Euderma maculatum*, in northwestern Colorado. J. Mamm. 73:547–551.

Navo, K. W., S. G. Henry, T. E. Ingersoll. 2002. Observations of swarming by bats and band recoveries in Colorado. Western N. Amer. Nat. 52:124–126.

Navo, K. W., and P. Krabacher. 2005. The use of bat gates at abandoned mines in Colorado. Bat Research News 46:1–8.

Nead, D. M., J. C. Halfpenny, and S. Bissell. 1984. The status of wolverines in Colorado. Northwest Sci. 58:286–289.

Neal, A. K., G. C. White, R. B. Gill, D. F. Reed, and J. H. Olterman. 1993. Evaluation of mark-resight model assumptions for estimating mountain sheep numbers. J. Wildl. Mgmt. 57:436–450.

Neff, D. J. 1957. Ecological effects of beaver habitat abandonment in the Colorado Rockies. J. Wildl. Mgmt. 21:80–84.

Neff, D. J. 1959. A seventy-year history of a Colorado beaver colony. J. Mamm. 40:381–387.

Negus, N. C. 1950. Habitat adaptability of *Phenacomys* in Wyoming. J. Mamm. 31:351.

Negus, N. C., P. J. Berger, and B. W. Brown. 1986. Microtine population dynamics in a predictable environment. Canadian J. Zool. 54:785–792.

Neiswenter, S. A., and R. C. Dowler. 2007. Habitat use of western spotted skunks and striped skunks in Texas. J. Wildl. Mgmt. 71:583–586.

Neiswenter, S. A., and B. R. Riddle. 2010. Diversification of the *Perognathus flavus* species group in emerging arid grasslands of North America. J. Mamm. 91:348–362.

Nellis, C. H., and L. B. Keith. 1968. Hunting activities and success of lynxes in Alberta. J. Wildl. Mgmt. 32:718–722.

Nellis, C. H., S. P. Wetmore, and L. B. Keith. 1972. Lynx-prey interactions in central Alberta. J. Wildl. Mgmt. 36:320–329.

Nelson, E. W. 1928. Status of the pronghorned antelope, 1922–1924. Bull., USDA 1346:1–64.

Nelson, J. L., B. L. Cypher, C. D. Bjurlin, and S. Creel. 2007. Effect of habitat on competition between kit foxes and coyotes. J. Wildl. Mgmt. 71:1467–1475.

Nelson, J. R. 1982. Relationships of elk and other large herbivores. Pp. 443–478, in Elk of North America, ecology and management (J. W. Thomas and D. E. Toweill, eds.). Stackpole Books, Harrisburg, PA, 698 pp.

Nelson, R. A., and T.D.I. Beck. 1984. Hibernation adaptation in the black bear: implications for management. Proc. Eastern Workshop Bear Mgmt., Research 7:48–53.

Nelson, R. A., H. W. Wahner, J. D. Jones, R. D. Ellefson, and P. E. Zollman. 1973. Metabolism of bears before, during, and after winter sleep. Amer. J. Physiol. 224:491–496.

Neubaum, D. J. 2005. Records of the eastern red bat on the northern Front Range of Colorado. Prairie Nat. 37:41–42.

Neubaum, D. J., M. A. Neubaum, L. E. Ellison, and T. J. O'Shea. 2005. Survival and condition of big brown bats (*Eptesicus fuscus*) after radiotagging. J. Mamm. 86:95–98.

Neubaum, D. J., T. J. O'Shea, and K. R. Wilson. 2006. Autumn migration and selection of rock crevices as hibernacula by big brown bats in Colorado. J. Mamm. 87:470–479.

Neubaum, D. J., K. R. Wilson, and T. J. O'Shea. 2007. Urban maternity-roost selection by big brown bats in Colorado. J. Wildl. Mgmt. 72:728–736.

Neubaum, M. A., M. R. Douglas, M. E. Douglas, and T. J. O'Shea. 2007. Molecular ecology of the big brown bat (*Eptesicus fuscus*): genetic and natural history variation in a hybrid zone. J. Mamm. 88:1230–1238.

Neuweiler, G. 2000. The biology of bats. Oxford Univ. Press, New York, 310 pp.

Nevo, E. 1979. Adaptive convergence and divergence of subterranean mammals. Ann. Rev. Ecol. Syst. 10:269–308.

Newmark, W. D. 1986. Species-area relationship and its determinants for mammals in western North American national parks. Biol. J. Linnean Soc. 28:83–98.

Newmark, W. D. 1987. A land-bridge island perspective on mammalian extinctions in western North American parks. Nature 325:430–432.

Newmark, W. D. 1995. Extinction of mammal populations in western national parks. Cons. Biol. 9:512–526.

Nicholls, T. H., F. G. Hawksworth, L. M. Merrill. 1984. Birds of the Fraser Experimental Forest, Colorado, and their role in dispersing lodgepole pine dwarf mistletoe. Colorado Field Ornith. 23:3–12.

Nie, M. A. 2003. Beyond wolves, the politics of wolf recovery and management. Univ. Minnesota Press, Minneapolis, 253 pp.

Nixon, C. M., D. M. Worley, and M. W. McClain. 1968. Food habits of squirrels in southeast Ohio. J. Wildl. Mgmt. 32:294–305.

Noel, D., and T. B. Johnson. 1993. Bats of Arizona. Arizona Wildlife Views 36(8)1–37.

Nordyke, K. A., and S. W. Buskirk. 1988. Evaluation of small mammals as ecological indicators of old-growth conditions. Pp. 353–358, in Management of amphibians, reptiles, and small mammals in North America (R. C. Szaro, K. E. Severson, and D. R. Patton, tech. coords.). Gen. Tech. Rept., Rocky Mountain Forest and Range Experiment Station, USDA, RM-166:1–458.

Nordyke, K. A., and S. W. Buskirk. 1991. Southern red-back vole, *Clethrionomys gapperi*, populations in relation to stand succession and old-growth character in the central Rocky Mountains. Canadian Field-Nat. 105:330–334.

Novacek, M. J. 1985. Cranial evidence for rodent affinities. Pp. 59–81, in Evolutionary relationships among rodents (W. P. Luckett and J.-L. Hartenberger, eds.). NATO ASI Series, Series A: Life Sci. 92:1–721.

Novacek, M. J. 1990. Morphology, paleontology, and the higher clades of mammals. Current Mammal. 2:507–543.

Novak, M. 1987. Beaver. Pp. 283–312, in Wild furbearer management and conservation in North America (M. Novak, J. A. Baker, M. E. Obbard, and B. Malloch, eds.). Ontario Ministry of Natural Resources, Toronto, 1,150 pp.

Novak, M., J. A. Baker, M. E. Obbard, and B. Malloch, eds. 1987. Wild furbearer management and conservation in North America. Ontario Trappers Association, Toronto, 1,150 pp.

Nowak, R. 1978. Evolution and taxonomy of coyotes and related *Canis*. Pp. 3–16 in Coyotes: biology, behavior, and management (M. Bekoff, ed.). Academic Press, New York, 384 pp.

Nowak, R. M. 1973. Return of the wolverine. National Parks Cons. Mag. 47:20–23.

Nowak, R. M. 1994. Walker's bats of the world. Johns Hopkins Univ. Press, Baltimore, 287 pp.

Nowak, R. M. 1995. Another look at wolf taxonomy. Pp. 375–397, in Ecology and conservation of wolves in a changing world (L. N. Carbyn, S. H. Fritts, and D. R. Seip, eds.). Occas. Publ., Canadian Circumpolar Inst., Univ. Alberta, Edmonton 35:1–642.

Nowak, R. M., ed. 1999. Walker's mammals of the world, sixth ed. Johns Hopkins Univ. Press, Baltimore, 2 vols.

Nowak, R. M. 2002. The original status of wolves in eastern North America. Southeast. Nat. 1:95–130.

Nowlin, R. A. 1985. Distribution of moose during occupation of vacant habitat in north-central Colorado. Unpubl. master's thesis, Colorado State Univ., Fort Collins, 60 pp.

Nowlin, R. A., W. K. Seitz, and R. N. Denney. 1979. Initial progress of the Colorado moose reintroduction. Proc. North American Moose Conf. and Workshop 15:187–212.

Noyes, J. H., B. K. Johnson, L. D. Bryant, S. L. Findholt, and J. W. Thomas. 1996. Effects of bull age on conception dates and pregnancy rates of cow elk. J. Wildl. Mgmt. 50:508–517.

Nudds, J. R., and P. A. Selden. 2008. Fossil ecosystems of North America, a guide to the sites and their extraordinary biotas. Univ. Chicago Press, Chicago, 288 pp.

Nydegger, N. C., and G. W. Smith. 1986. Prey populations in relation to *Artemisia* vegetation types in southwestern Idaho. Pp. 152–156, in Proc. Symp. Biology of *Artemisia* and *Chrysothamnus* (J. F. Eisenberg and D. G. Kleiman, eds.). USDA Forest Service Research Station, Ogden, Utah, 398 pp.

Oakleaf, J. K., C. Mack, and D. L. Murray. 2003. Effects of wolves on livestock calf survival and movements in central Idaho. J. Wildl. Mgmt. 57:299–306.

Oakleaf, J. K., D. L. Murray, J. R. Oakleaf, E. E. Bangs, C. M. Mack, D. W. Smith, J. A. Fontaine, M. D. Jimenez, T. J. Meier, and C. C. Niemeyer. 2006. Habitat selection by recolonizing wolves in the northwestern United States. J. Wildl. Mgmt. 70:554–563.

Oaks, E. C., P. J. Young, G. L. Kirkland, Jr., and D. F. Schmidt. 1987. *Spermophilus variegatus*. Mammalian Species 272:1–8.

Obbard, M. E. 1987. Red squirrel. Pp. 265–281, in Wild furbearer management and conservation in North America (M. Novak, J. A. Baker, M. E. Obbard, and B. Malloch, eds.). Ontario Ministry of Natural Resources, Toronto, 1,150 pp.

O'Donoghue, M., S. Boutin, C. J. Krebs, and E. J. Hofer. 1997. Numerical responses of coyotes and lynx to the snowshoe hare cycle. Oikos 80:150–162.

O'Farrell, J. J. 1974. Seasonal activity patterns of rodents in a sagebrush community. J. Mamm. 55:809–823.

O'Farrell, M. J., and W. G. Bradley. 1970. Activity patterns of bats over a desert spring. J. Mamm. 51:18–26.

O'Farrell, M. J., W. J. Bradley, and G. W. Jones. 1967. Fall and winter bat activity at a desert spring in southern Nevada. Southwestern Nat. 12:163–171.

O'Farrell, M. J., C. Corben, and W. L. Gannon. 2000. Geographic variation in the echolocation calls of the hoary bat (*Lasiurus cinereus*). Acta Chiropterologica 2:75–83.

O'Farrell, M. J., and W. L. Gannon. 1999. A comparison of acoustic versus capture techniques for the inventory of bats. J. Mamm. 80:24–30.

O'Farrell, M. J., B. W. Miller, and W. L. Gannon. 1999. Qualitative identification of free-flying bats using the Anabat detector. J. Mamm. 80:11–23.

O'Farrell, M. J., and E. H. Studier. 1973. Reproduction, growth, and development in *Myotis thysanodes* and *M. lucifugus* (Chiroptera: Vespertilionidae). Ecology 54:18–30.

O'Farrell, M. J., and E. H. Studier. 1980. *Myotis thysanodes*. Mammalian Species 137:1–5.

O'Farrell, T. P. 1987. Kit fox. Pp. 422–431, in Wild furbearer management and conservation in North America (M. Novak, J. A. Baker, M. E. Obbard, and B. Malloch, eds.). Ontario Trappers Association, Toronto, 1,150 pp.

O'Farrell, T. P., R. J. Olson, R. O. Gilbert, and J. D. Hedlund. 1975. A population of Great Basin pocket mice, *Perognathus parvus*, in the shrub-steppe of south-central Washington. Ecol. Monogr. 45:1–28.

O'Gara, B. W. 1978. *Antilocapra americana*. Mammalian Species 90:1–7.

O'Gara, B. W., and G. Matson. 1975. Growth and casting of horns by pronghorns and exfoliation of horns by bovids. J. Mamm. 56:829–846.

O'Gara, B. W., R. F. Moy, and G. D. Bear. 1971. The annual testicular cycle and horn casting in the pronghorn (*Antilocapra americana*). J. Mamm. 52:537–544.

O'Gara, B. W., J. D. Yoakum, and R. E. McCabe, eds. 2004. Pronghorn: ecology and management. Univ. Press Colorado, Boulder, 904 pp.

Oldemeyer, J. L. 1966. Winter ecology of bighorn sheep in Yellowstone National Park. Unpubl. master's thesis, Colorado State Univ., Fort Collins, 107 pp.

Oli, M. K., and K. B. Armitage. 2003. Sociality and individual fitness in yellow-bellied marmots: insights from a long-term study (1962–2001). Oecologia 136:543–550.

Oli, M. K., and K. B. Armitage. 2008. Indirect fitness benefits do not compensate for the loss of direct fitness in yellow-bellied marmots. J. Mamm. 89:874–881.

Oliver, G. V., and A. L. Wright. 2011. The banner-tailed kangaroo rat (*Dipodomys spectabilis*) (Rodentia: Heteromyidae), in Utah. Western N. Amer. Nat. 70:562–566.

Olmsted, C. E., Jr. 1979. The ecology of aspen with reference to utilization by large herbivores in Rocky Mountain National Park. Pp. 89–97, in North American elk: ecology, behavior, and management (M. S. Boyce and L. D. Hayden-Wing, eds.). Univ. Wyoming, Laramie, 294 pp.

Olsen, A., and P. N. Lehner. 1978. Conditioned avoidance of prey in coyotes. J. Wildl. Mgmt. 42:676–679.

Olson, R., and W. A. Hubert. 1994. Beaver: water resources and riparian habitat manager. Univ. Wyoming, Laramie, 48 pp.

Olson, T. E., and F. L. Knopf. 1988. Patterns of relative diversity within riparian small mammal communities, Platte River watershed, Colorado. Pp. 379–386, in Management of amphibians, reptiles, and small mammals in North America (R. C. Szaro, K. R. Severson, and D. R. Patton, tech. coords.). General Technical Report, USDA Forest Service, RM-166:1–458.

Olson, T. L., and F. G. Lindzey. 2002a. Swift fox survival and production in southeastern Wyoming. J. Mamm. 83:199–206.

Olson, T. L., and F. G. Lindzey. 2002b. Swift fox (*Vulpes velox*) home-range dispersion patterns in southeastern Wyoming. Canadian J. Zool. 80:2024–2029.

Olterman, J. H., and D. W. Kenvin. 1998. Reproduction, survival, and occupied ranges of Shiras moose transplanted to southwestern Colorado. Alces 34:41–46.

Olterman, J. H., D. W. Kenvin, and R. C. Kufeld. 1994. Moose transplant to southwestern Colorado. Alces 30:1–8.

O'Meara, T. E., J. B. Haufler, L. H. Stetter, and J. G. Nagy. 1981. Nongame wildlife responses to chaining of pinyon-juniper woodlands. J. Wildl. Mgmt. 45:381–389.

O'Meilia, M. E., F. L. Knopf, and J. C. Lewis. 1982. Some consequences of competition between prairie dogs and beef cattle. J. Range Mgmt. 35:580–585.

O'Neal, G. T., J. T. Flinders, and W. P. Clary. 1986. Behavioral ecology of the Nevada kit fox (*Vulpes macrotis nevadensis*) on a managed desert rangeland. Current Mammalogy 1:443–481.

Onorato, D., C. White, P. Zager, and L. P. Waits. 2006. Detection of predator presence at elk mortality sites using mtDNA analysis of hair and scat samples. Wildl. Soc. Bull. 34:815–820.

Organ, J. E., and E. R. Fritzell. 2000. Trends in consumptive recreation and the profession. Wildl. Soc. Bull. 28:780–787.

Ormsbee, P. C., and W. C. McComb. 1998. Selection of day roosts by female long-legged myotis in the central Oregon Cascade Range. J. Wildl. Mgmt. 52:596–603.

Orr, R. T. 1940. The rabbits of California. Occas. Papers, California Acad. Sci. 19:1–227.

Orr, R. T. 1950. Unusual behavior and occurrence of a hoary bat. J. Mamm. 31:456–457.

Orr, R. T. 1954. Natural history of the pallid bat, *Antrozous pallidus*. Proc. California Acad. Sci. 28:165–264.

Ortega, J. C. 1990a. Home-range size of adult rock squirrels (*Spermophilus variegatus*) in southeastern Arizona. J. Mamm. 71:171–176.

Ortega, J. C. 1990b. Reproductive biology of the rock squirrel (*Spermophilus variegatus*) in southeastern Arizona. J. Mamm. 71:448–457.

O'Shea, T. J., and M. A. Bogan. 2003a. Introduction. Pp. 1–7, in Monitoring trends in bat populations in the United States and territories: problems and prospects (T. J. O'Shea and M. A. Bogan, eds.). Information and Technology Report, USGS/BRD/ITR-2003-003, 274 pp.

O'Shea, T. J., and M. A. Bogan, eds. 2003b. Monitoring trends in bat populations of the United States and territories: problems and prospects. USGS, Biological Resource Discipline, Information and Technology Report, USGS/BRD/ITR-2003-003.

O'Shea, T. J., M. A. Bogan, and L. E. Ellison. 2003. Monitoring trends in bat populations in the United States and territories: status of the science and recommendations for the future. Wildl. Soc. Bull. 31:16–29.

O'Shea, T. J., P. M. Cryan, E. A. Snider, E. W. Valdez, L. E. Ellison, and D. J. Neubaum. 2011. Bats of Mesa Verde National Park, Colorado: composition, reproduction, and roosting habits. Monogr., Western N. Amer. Nat. 5:1–19.

O'Shea, T. J., L. E. Ellison, D. J. Neubaum, M. A. Neubaum, C. A. Reynolds, and R. A. Bowen. 2010. Recruitment in a Colorado population of big brown bats: breeding probabilities, litter size, and first-year survival. J. Mamm. 91:418–428.

O'Shea, T. J., A. L. Everette, and L. E. Ellison. 2001. Cyclodiene insecticide, DDE, DDT, arsenic, and mercury contamination of big brown bats (*Eptesicus fuscus*) foraging at a Colorado Superfund site. Archives Envir. Contamination and Toxicol. 40:112–120.

O'Shea, T. J., and T. A. Vaughan. 1977. Nocturnal and seasonal activities of the pallid bat, *Antrozous pallidus*. J. Mamm. 58: 269–284.

O'Shea, T. J., and T. A. Vaughan, 1999. Population changes in bats from central Arizona: 1972–1997. Southwestern Nat. 44:495–500.

Osmundson, C. L., and S. W. Buskirk. 1993. Size of food caches as a predictor of beaver colony size. Wildl. Soc. Bull. 21:64–69.

Ostfeld, R. S., and J. N. Mills. 2007. Social behavior, demography, and rodent-borne pathogens. Pp. 478–486, in Rodent societies: an ecological and evolutionary perspective (J. O. Wolff and P. W. Sherman, eds.). Univ. Chicago Press, Chicago, 610 pp.

Ostrander, E. A. 2007. Genetics and the shape of dogs. Amer. Sci. 95:406–413.

Ostroff, A. C., and E. J. Finck. 2003. *Spermophilus franklinii*. Mammalian Species 724:1–5.

Ostrow, D. G., N. Huntley, and R. S. Inouye. 2002. Plant-mediated interactions between the northern pocket gopher, *Thomomys talpoides*, and aboveground herbivorous insects. J. Mamm. 83:991–998.

Otterman, J. H., and D. W. Kenvin. 1998. Reproduction, survival, and occupied ranges of Shiras moose transplanted to southwestern Colorado. Alces 34:41–46.

Owen, J. G. 2001. On a possible fractal boundary dimension for mammalian geographical ranges at regional scales: a case study in Texas. Occas. Papers, Museum of Texas Tech University 208:1–4.

Ozgul, A., D. Z. Childs, M. K. Oli, K. B. Armitage, D. T. Blumstein, L. E. Olson, S. Tuljapurkar, and T. Coulson. 2010. Coupled dynamics of body mass and population growth in response to environmental change. Nature 466:482–485.

Packard, F. M. 1947. A survey of the beaver population of Rocky Mountain National Park, Colorado. J. Mamm. 28:219–227.

Packard, J. M., L. D. Mech, and U. S. Seal. 1983. Social influences on reproduction in wolves. Pp. 78–85, in Wolves in Canada and Alaska: their status, biology, and management (L. N. Carbyn, ed.). Rept. Ser., Canadian Wildl. Serv. 45:1–135.

Packard, R. L. 1956. The tree squirrels of Kansas. Misc. Publ., Univ. Kansas Mus. Nat. Hist. 11:1–67.

Packer, C., M. Kosmala, H. S. Cooley, H. Brink, L. Pintea, D. Garshells, G. Purchase, M. Strauss, A. Swanson, G. Balme, L. Hunter, and K. Nowell. 2009. Sport hunting, predator control and conservation of large carnivores. PLoS ONE 4(6): 1–8.

Pang, J.-F., C. Kluetsch, X.-J. Zou, A. Zhang, L.-Y. Luo, H. Angleby, A. Ardalan, C. Ekström, A. Sköllermo, J. Lundeberg, S. Matsumura, T. Leitner, Y.-P. Zhang, P. Savolainen. In press. mtDNA data indicates a single origin for dogs south of Yangtze River, less than 16,300 years ago, from numerous wolves. Molec. Biol. and Evolution.

Pankratz, H. 2009. Young wolverine makes 500-mile trip to Colorado. Denver Post, June 19.

Pape, W. J., T. D. Fitzsimmons, and R. E. Hoffman. 1999. Risk for rabies transmission from encounters with bats, Colorado, 1977–1996. Emerging Infect. Dis. 5:433–437.

Paquet, P. C., and L. N. Carbyn. 2003. Gray wolf, *Canis lupus* and allies. Pp. 482–510, in Wild mammals of North America, biology, management, and economics, second ed. (G. A. Feldhamer, B. C. Thompson, and J. A. Chapman, eds.). Johns Hopkins Univ. Press, Baltimore, 1,216 pp.

Paquet, P. C., J. A. Vucetich, M. K. Phillips, and L. M. Vucetich. 2001. Mexican wolf recovery: three-year program review and assessment. Prepared by Conservation Breeding Specialist Group, Apple Valley, MN, for U.S. Fish and Wildlife Service, Albuquerque, NM. 94 pp.

Paradiso, J. L., and R. M. Nowak. 1982. Wolves. Pp. 460–474, in Wild mammals of North America, biology, management, and economics (J. A. Chapman and G. A. Feldhammer, eds.). Johns Hopkins Univ. Press, Baltimore, 1,147 pp.

Parker, G. R., J. W. Maxwell, L. D. Morton, and G.E.J. Smith. 1983. The ecology of the lynx (*Lynx canadensis*) on Cape Breton Island. Canadian J. Zool. 51:770–786.

Parker, M. 1986. Beaver, water quality, and riparian systems. Pp. 88–94, in Proc. Wyoming Water 1986 and Streamside Zone Conference (D. J. Brosz and J. D. Rodgers, eds.). Wyoming Water Research Center, Univ. Wyoming, Laramie, 181 pp.

Parker, M., F. J. Wood, Jr., B. H. Smith, and R. G. Elder. 1985. Erosional downcutting in lower order riparian systems: have historical changes been caused by removal of beaver? Riparian ecosystems and their management: reconciling conflicting uses. General Technical Report, USDA Forest Service, Rocky Mountain Forest and Range Experiment Station, RM-120:1–523 pp.

Parmesan, C. 2006. Ecological and evolutionary responses to Recent climate change. Ann. Rev. Ecol., Evol., Syst. 37:637–669.

Parsons, D. R. 1998. "Green fire" returns to the Southwest: reintroduction of the Mexican wolf. Wildl. Soc. Bull. 26:799–807.

Pasitschniak-Arts, M. 1993. *Ursus arctos*. Mammalian Species 439: 1–10.

Pasitschniak-Arts, M., and S. Larivière. 1995. *Gulo gulo*. Mammalian Species 499:1–10.

Pate, J., M. J. Manfredo, A. D. Bight, and G. Tischbein. 1996. Coloradans' attitudes toward reintroducing the gray wolf into Colorado. Wildl. Soc. Bull. 24:421–428.

Patterson, B. D. 1984. Geographic variation and taxonomy of Colorado and Hopi chipmunks (genus *Eutamias*). J. Mamm. 55:442–456.

Patterson, B. D. 1995. Local extinctions and the biogeographic dynamics of boreal mammals in the Southwest. Pp. 151–176, in Storm over a mountain island: conservation biology and the Mount Graham Affair (C. A. Istock and R. S. Hoffmann, eds.). Univ. Arizona Press, Tucson, 291 pp.

Patterson, B. D., and L. R. Heaney. 1987. Preliminary analysis of geographic variation in red-tailed chipmunks (*Eutamias ruficaudus*). J. Mamm. 58:782–791.

Patton, D. R. 1977. Managing southwestern ponderosa pine for Abert squirrel. J. Forestry, 75(5):264–267.

Patton, D. R. 1984. A model to evaluate Abert squirrel habitat in uneven-aged stands of ponderosa pine. Wildl. Soc. Bull. 12:408–414.

Patton, J. L. 1990. Geomyid evolution: the historical, selective, and random bass for patterns within and among species. Pp. 49–69, in Evolution of subterranean mammals at the organismal and molecular levels (O. Reig, ed.). Alan R. Liss, New York, 434 pp.

Patton, J. L. 2005a. Family Heteromyidae. Pp. 844–858, in Mammal species of the world, a taxonomic and geographic reference, third ed. (D. E. Wilson and D. M. Reeder, eds.), 2 vols. Johns Hopkins Univ. Press, Baltimore.

Patton, J. L. 2005b. Family Geomyidae. Pp. 859–870, in Mammal species of the world, a taxonomic and geographic reference, third ed. (D. E. Wilson and D. M. Reeder, eds.), 2 vols. Johns Hopkins Univ. Press, Baltimore.

Patton, J. L., G. G. Huckaby, and S. T. Álvarez-Castañeda. 2008. The evolutionary history and a systematic revision of woodrats of the *Neotoma lepida* group. Univ. California Publ., Zoology 135:1–412 + appendices.

Patton, R. F. 1974. Ecological and behavioral relationships of the skunks of Trans-Pecos Texas. Unpubl. doctoral dissert., Texas A&M Univ., College Station, 199 pp.

Pauli, J. N., R. M. Stephens, and S. H. Anderson. 2006. White-tailed prairie dog (*Cynomys leucurus*): a technical conservation assessment. Species Conservation Project, Rocky Mountain Region, USDA Forest Service, Denver, CO, 43 pp.

Pauls, R. W. 1978. Behavioural strategies relevant to the energy economy of the red squirrel (*Tamiasciurus hudsonicus*). Canadian J. Zool. 56:1519–1525.

Pearce, R. D., and T. J. O'Shea. 2007. Ectoparasites in an urban population of big brown bats (*Eptesicus fuscus*) in Colorado. J. Parasit. 93:518–530.

Pearson, D. E., and R. M. Callaway. 2006. Biological control agents elevate hantavirus by subsidizing deer mouse populations. Ecology Letters 9:443–450.

Pearson, D. E., and L. F. Ruggiero. 2003. Transect versus grid trapping arrangements for sampling small-mammal communities. Wildl. Soc. Bull. 31:454–459.

Pearson, O. P. 1942. On the cause and nature of a poisonous action produced by the bite of a shrew (*Blarina brevicauda*). J. Mamm. 23:159–166.

Pearson, O. P. 1944. Reproduction in the shrew (*Blarina brevicauda* Say). American J. Anat. 75:39–93.

Pearson, O. P. 1946. Scent glands of the short-tailed shrew. Anat. Record 94:615–629.

Pearson, P. G. 1952. Observations concerning the life history and ecology of the wood rat *Neotoma floridana floridana* (Ord). J. Mamm. 33:459–463.

Pechacek, P., F. G. Lindzey, and S. H. Anderson. 2000. Home range size and spatial organization of swift fox *Vulpes velox* (Say, 1823) in southeastern Wyoming. Mammal. Biol. 55:209–215.

Peden, D. G. 1976. Botanical composition of bison diets on shortgrass plains. Amer. Midland Nat. 96:225–229.

Peden, D. G., G. M. Van Dyne, R. W. Rice, and R. M. Hansen. 1974. The trophic ecology of *Bison bison* L. on shortgrass plains. J. Appl. Ecol. 11:489–498.

Peek, J. M. 1974. On the nature of winter habitats of Shiras moose. Naturaliste Canadienne 101:131–141.

Peek, J. M. 1982. Elk. Pp. 851–861, in Wild mammals of North America, biology, management, and economics (J. A. Chapman and G. A. Feldhamer, eds.). Johns Hopkins Univ. Press, Baltimore, 1,147 pp.

Peek, J. M. 1997. Habitat relationships. Pp. 351–375, in Ecology and management of the North American moose (A. W. Franzmann and C. C. Schwartz, eds.). Smithsonian Institution Press, Washington, DC, 733 pp.

Peek, J. M. 2000. Mountain goat. Pp. 467–490, in Ecology and management of large mammals in North America (S. Demarais and P. R. Krausman, eds.). Prentice-Hall, Upper Saddle River, NJ, 778 pp.

Peek, J. M. 2003. Wapiti, *Cervus elaphus*. Pp. 877–888, in Wild mammals of North America, biology, management, and economics, second ed. (G. A. Feldhamer, B. C. Thompson, and J. A. Chapman, eds.). Johns Hopkins Univ. Press, Baltimore, 1,216 pp.

Peek, J. M., D. E. Brown, S. R. Kellert, L. D. Mech, J. H. Shaw, V. V. Ballenburghe, and J. D. Gill. 1991. Restoration of wolves in North America. Technical Review, The Wildlife Society 91:1–21.

Peek, J. M., and K. I. Morris. 1998. Status of moose in the contiguous United States. Alces 34:423–434.

Pefaur, J. E., and R. S. Hoffmann. 1974. Notes on the biology of the olive-backed pocket mouse *Perognathus fasciatus* on the Northern Great Plains. Prairie Nat. 5:7–15.

Pefaur, J. E., and R. S. Hoffmann. 1975. Studies of small mammal populations at three sites on the Northern Great Plains. Occas. Papers, Mus. Nat. Hist., Univ. Kansas 37:1–27.

Peixoto, I. D., and G. Abramson. 2006. The effect of biodiversity on the hantavirus epizootic. Ecology 87:873–879.

Pelton, M. R. 1982. Black bear. Pp. 504–514, in Wild mammals of North America, biology, management, and economics (J. A. Chapman and G. A. Feldhamer, eds.). Johns Hopkins Univ. Press, Baltimore, 1,147 pp.

Pelton, M. R. 2003. Black bear, *Ursus americanus*. Pp. 547–555, in Wild mammals of North America, biology, management, and economics, second ed. (G. A. Feldhamer, B. C. Thompson, and J. A. Chapman, eds.). Johns Hopkins Univ. Press, Baltimore, 1,216 pp.

Pelton, M. R., and F. T. Vanmanen. 1994. Distribution of black bears in North America. Proc. Eastern Workshop on Black Bear Research and Management 12:133–138.

Pence, D. B., and J. W. Custer. 1981. Host-parasite relationships in the wild Canidae in North America, II. Pathology of infectious diseases in the genus *Canis*. Pp. 760–785, in Proc. Worldwide Furbearer Conference (J. A. Chapman and D. Pursley, eds.). Worldwide Furbearer Conference, Inc., Frostburg, MD, 2,059 pp.

Pennisi, E. 2009. Western U.S. forests suffer death by degrees. Science 323:447.

Perault, D. R., P. G. Wolf, and T. C. Edwards, Jr. 1997. Hierarchical analysis of genetic partitioning by *Tamias minimus* and *T. umbrinus*. J. Mamm. 78:134–145.

Pergams, O.R.W., and P. A. Zaradic. 2008. Evidence for a fundamental and pervasive shift away from nature-based recreation. Proc. Nat. Acad. Sci. 105:2295–2300.

Perla, B., and C. N. Slobodchikoff. 2002. Habitat structure and alarm call dialects in the Gunnison's prairie dog (*Cynomys gunnisoni*). Behav. Ecol. 13:844–850.

Perrine, J. D. 2005. Ecology of red fox (*Vulpes vulpes*) in the Lassen Peak region of California, USA. Unpubl. doctoral dissert., Univ. California, Berkeley, 251 pp.

Perry, H. R., Jr. 1982. Muskrats. Pp. 282–325, in Wild mammals of North America, biology, management, and economics (J. A. Chapman and G. A. Feldhamer, eds.). Johns Hopkins Univ. Press, Baltimore, 1,147 pp.

Peters, R. P., and L. D. Mech. 1975. Scent-marking in wolves. Amer. Sci. 53:628–637.

Petersburg, M. L. 1997. Emigration, fidelity, distribution and survival of elk on a northwestern Colorado winter range. Unpubl. master's thesis, Colorado State Univ., Fort Collins.

Peterson, A. T. 2001. Predicting species' geographic distributions based on ecological niche modeling. Condor 103:599–605.

Peterson, D. 1998. Ghost grizzlies: does the great bear still haunt Colorado?, revised ed. Johnson Books, Boulder, CO, 280 pp.

Peterson, R. L. 1955. North American moose. Univ. Toronto Press, Toronto, 280 pp.

Pettigrew, J. D. 1986. Flying primates? Megabats have the advanced pathway from eye to mid-brain. Science 231:1304–1306.

Pettus, D., and R. R. Lechleitner. 1963. *Microsorex* in Colorado. J. Mamm. 44:119.

Peyton, R. D. 2008. Multiple scale habitat affinities of small mammal assemblages on the Niobrara chalk barrens at Fort Carson Military Reservation in Pueblo County, Colorado. Unpubl. master's thesis, Univ. Colorado, Colorado Springs, 69 pp.

Pfeifer, S. 1980. Aerial predation on Wyoming ground squirrels. J. Mammalogy 61:368–371.

Phelps, K. L., C. J. Schmidt, and J. R. Choate. 2008. Presence of the evening bat (*Nycticeius humeralis*) in westernmost Kansas. Trans. Kansas Acad. Sci. 111:159–160.

Phillips, G. E., and A. W. Alldredge. 2000. Reproductive success of elk following disturbance by humans during calving season. J. Wildl. Mgmt. 54:521–530.

Phillips, G. E., and G. C. White. 2003. Pronghorn population response to coyote control: modeling and management. Wildl. Soc. Bull. 31:1162–1175.

Phillips, G. L. 1966. Ecology of the big brown bat (Chiroptera: Vespertilionidae) in northeastern Kansas. Amer. Midland Nat. 75:168–198.

Phillips, M. K., N. Fascione, P. Miller, and O. Byers. 2000. Wolves in the Southern Rockies, a Population and Habitat Viability Assessment: Final Report. IUCN/SSC Conservation Specialist Group, Apple Valley, MN, 111 pp.

Phillips, M. L., W. R. Clark, S. M. Nusser, M. A. Sovada, and R. J. Greenwood. 2004. Analysis of predator movement in prairie landscapes with contrasting grassland composition. J. Mamm. 85:187–195.

Phillips, M. L., W. R. Clark, M. A. Sovada, D. J. Horn, R. R. Koford, and R. J. Greenwood. 2003. Predator selection of prairie landscape features and its relation to duck nest success. J. Wildl. Mgmt. 57:104–115.

Phillips, R. L., R. D. Andrews, G. L. Storm, and R. A. Bishop. 1972. Dispersal and mortality of red foxes. J. Wildl. Mgmt. 36:237–248.

Piaggio, A. J., K.E.G. Miller, M. D. Matocq, and S. L. Perkins. 2009. Eight polymorphic microsatellite loci developed and characterized from Townsend's big-eared bat, *Corynorhinus townsendii*. Molec. Ecol. Res. 9:258–260.

Piaggio, A. J., K. W. Navo, and C. W. Stihler. 2009. Intraspecific comparison of population structure, genetic diversity, and dispersal among three subspecies of Townsend's big-eared bats, *Corynorhinus townsendii townsendii*, *C. t. pallescens*, and the endangered *C. t. virginianus*. Cons. Genetics 10:143–159.

Piaggio, A. J., and S. L. Perkins. 2005. Molecular phylogeny of North American long-eared bats (Vespertilionidae: *Corynorhinus*): inter- and intraspecific relationships inferred from mitochondrial and nuclear DNA sequences. Molec. Phylogen. Evol. 37:762–775.

Piaggio, A. J., and G. S. Spicer. 2001. Molecular phylogeny of the chipmunks inferred from mitochondrial cytochrome *b* and cytochrome oxidase II gene sequences. Molec. Phylog. Evol. 20:335–350.

Piaggio, A. J., E. W. Valdez, M. A. Bogan, and G. S. Spicer. 2002. Systematics of *Myotis occultus* (Chiroptera: Vespertilionidae) inferred from sequences of two mitochondrial genes. J. Mamm. 83:386–395.

Pickton, T., and L. Sikorowski. 2004. The economic impacts of hunting, fishing, and wildlife watching in Colorado. Final Report for Colorado Division of Wildlife. BBC Research & Consulting, 21 pp. [revised 2008].

Pierce, B. M., and V. C. Bleich. 2003. Mountain lion, *Puma concolor*. Pp. 744–757, in Wild mammals of North America, biology, management, and conservation, second ed. (G. A. Feldhamer, B. C. Thompson, and J. A. Chapman, eds.). Johns Hopkins Univ. Press, Baltimore, 1,216 pp.

Pierce, B. M., V. C. Bleich, and R. T. Bowyer. 2000a. Selection of mule deer by mountain lions and coyotes: effects of hunting style, body size, and reproductive status. J. Mamm. 81:462–472.

Pierce, B. M., V. C. Bleich, and R. T. Bowyer. 2000b. Social organization of mountain lions: does a land-tenure system regulate population size? Ecology 81:1533–1543.

Pierce, B. M., V. C. Bleich, C.L.B. Chetkiewicz, and J. D. Wehausen. 1998. Timing of feeding bouts of mountain lions. J. Mamm. 79:222–226.

Pierson, E. D. 1998. Tall trees, deep holes, and scarred landscapes. Conservation biology of North American bats. Pp. 309–325, in Bat biology and conservation (T. H. Kunz and P. A. Racey, eds.). Smithsonian Institution Press, Washington, DC, 365 pp.

Pigage, H. K., J. C. Pigage, and J. F. Tillman. 2005, Fleas associated with the northern pocket gopher (*Thomomys talpoides*) in Elbert County, Colorado. Western N. Amer. Nat. 55:210–214.

Pilgrim, K. L., D. K. Boyd, and S. H. Forbes. 1998. Testing for wolf-coyote hybridization in the Rocky Mountains using mitochondrial DNA. J. Wildl. Mgmt. 52:683–689.

Pizzimenti, J. J. 1975. Evolution of the prairie dog genus *Cynomys*. Occas. Papers, Mus. Nat. Hist., Univ. Kansas 39:1–73.

Pizzimenti, J. J. 1981. Increasing sexual dimorphism in prairie dogs: evidence for changes during the past century. Southwestern Nat. 26:43–47.

Pizzimenti, J. J., and R. S. Hoffmann. 1973. *Cynomys gunnisoni*. Mammalian Species 25:1–4.

Placer, J., and C. N. Slobodchikoff. 2000. A fuzzy-neural system for identification of species-specific alarm calls of Gunnison's prairie dogs. Behav. Proc. 52:1–9.

Planz, J. V., E. G. Zimmerman, T. A. Spradling, and D. R. Akins. 1996. Molecular phylogeny of the *Neotoma floridana* species group. J. Mamm. 77:519–535.

Plumpton, D. L., and R. S. Lutz. 1993. Nesting habitat use by burrowing owls in Colorado. J. Raptor Res. 27:175–179.

Poché, R. M., and G. L. Bailey. 1974. Notes on the spotted bat (*Euderma maculatum*) from southwest Utah. Great Basin Nat. 34:254–256.

Podlutsky, A. J., A. M. Khritankov, N. D. Ovodov, and S. N. Austad. 2005. A new field record for bat longevity. J. Gerontology, Series A 60:1366–1368.

Pogany, G. C., W. S. Allred, and T. Barnes. 1998. The reproductive cycle of Abert's squirrel. Pp. 53–59, in Ecology and Evolutionary Biology of Tree Squirrels (M. A. Steele, J. F. Merritt, and D. A. Zegers, eds.). Spec. Publ. Virginia Mus. Nat. Hist., 6:1–310.

Poglayen-Neuwall, I., and I. Poglayen-Neuwall. 1980. Gestation period and parturition of the ringtail *Bassariscus astutus* (Lichtenstein, 1830). Zeitschrift für Saugetierkunde 45:73–81.

Poglayen-Neuwall, I., and D. E. Toweill. 1988. *Bassariscus astutus*. Mammalian Species 327:1–8.

Pojar, T. M., and D. C. Bowden. 2004. Neonatal mule deer fawn survival in west-central Colorado. J. Wildl. Mgmt. 58:550–560.

Pojar, T. M., D. C. Bowden, and R. B. Gill. 1995. Aerial counting experiments to estimate pronghorn density and herd structure. J. Wildl. Mgmt. 59:117–128.

Pojar, T. M., and L. W. Miller. 1984. Recurrent estrus and cycle length in pronghorn. J. Wildl. Mgmt. 48:973–979.

Pokropus, E. J., and B. H. Banta. 1966. Observations on two Colorado shrews in captivity. Wasmann J. Biology 24:75–81.

Polder, E. 1968. Spotted skunk and weasel populations den and cover usage in northeast Iowa. Proc. Iowa Acad. Sci. 75:142–146.

Polderboer, E. B., L. W. Kuhn, and G. O. Hendrickson. 1941. Winter and spring habits of weasels in central Iowa. J. Wildl. Mgmt. 5:115–119.

Polechla, P. J. 2000. Ecology of the river otter and other wetland furbearers in the upper Rio Grande. Final report to the Bureau of Land Management. Mus. Southwestern Biology, Univ. New Mexico, Albuquerque.

Polechla, P. J. 2002a. A review of the natural history of the river otter (*Lontra canadensis*) in the southwestern United States with special reference to New Mexico. Final Report, North American Wilderness Recovery, Richmond, VT, 48 pp.

Polechla, P. J. 2002b. River otter (*Lontra canadensis*) and riparian survey of the Los Pinos, Piedra, and San Juan Rivers in Archuleta, Hinsdale, and La Plata Counties, Colorado. Final Report to Colorado Division of Wildlife, Denver, CO, 97 pp.

Polechla, P. J. 2003. Spring diet of the river otter (*Lontra canadensis*) in the Piedra and San Juan Rivers, Southwestern Colorado. Report to Colorado Division of Wildlife, 25 pp.

Polly, P. D. 2003. Paleophylogeography: the tempo of geographic differentiation in marmots (*Marmota*). J. Mamm. 84:369–384.

Polziehn, R. O., J. Hamr, F. F. Mallory, and C. Strobeck. 1998. Phylogenetic status of North American wapiti (*Cervus elaphus* subspecies). Can. J. Zool. 76:998–1010.

Polziehn, R. O., J. Hamr, F. F. Mallory, and C. Strobeck. 2001. Microsatellite analysis of North American wapiti (*Cervus elaphus*) populations. Molec. Ecol. 9:1561–1576.

Polziehn, R. O., and C. Strobeck. 1998. Phylogeny of wapiti, red deer, sika deer, and other North American cervids as determined from mitochondrial DNA. Molec. Phylog. Evol. 10:249–290.

Polziehn, R. O., and Strobeck. 2002. A phylogenetic comparison of red deer and wapiti using mitochondrial DNA. Molec. Phylog. Evol. 22:342–356.

Poole, K. G., and R. P. Graf. 1996. Winter diet of marten during a snowshoe hare decline. Canadian J. Zool. 74:456–466.

Population Reference Bureau. 2009. 2009 World Population Data Sheet. Population Reference Bureau, New York, 19 pp.

Porth, A. T. 1995. Movements of black-tailed jackrabbits (*Lepus californicus*) and effects of high population density on the nitrogen budget of sage-brush steppe. Unpubl. master's thesis, Idaho State Univ., Pocatello, 111 pp.

Post, D. M., T. S. Armbrust, E. A. Horne, and J. R. Goheen. 2001. Sexual segregation results in differences in content and quality of bison (*Bos bison*) diets. J. Mamm. 82:407–413.

Pottinger, R. 2005. Hantavirus in Indian Country: the first decade in review. Amer. Indian Culture and Res. J. 29(20):35–56.

Pough, F. H., C. M. Janis, and J. B. Heiser. 2008. Vertebrate life, eighth ed. Prentice-Hall, Englewood Cliffs, NJ, 752 pp.

Poulson, D. D. 1988. *Chaetodipus hispidus*. Mammalian Species 320:1–4.

Powell, R. A. 1973. A model for raptor predation on weasels. J. Mamm. 54:259–263.

Powell, R. A. 1979. Mustelid spacing patterns: variations on a theme by *Mustela*. Zeitschrift für Tierpsychologie 50:153–165.

Powell, R. A. 1981. *Martes pennanti*. Mammalian Species 156:1–6.

Powell, R. A. 1993. The fisher: life history, ecology and behavior, second ed. Univ. Minnesota Press, Minneapolis, 237 pp.

Powell, R. A., and G. Proulz. 2003. Trapping and marking terrestrial mammals for research: integrating ethics, performance criteria, techniques, and common sense. Institutional Laboratory Animal Research J. 44:259–276.

Powell, R. A., S. W. Buskirk, and W. J. Zielinski. 2003. Fisher and marten, *Martes pennanti* and *Martes americana*. Pp. 635–649, in Wild mammals of North America, biology, management, and conservation, second ed. (G. A. Feldhamer, B. C. Thompson, and J. A. Chapman, eds.). Johns Hopkins Univ. Press, Baltimore, 1,216 pp.

Powell, R. A., and W. J. Zielinski. 1989. Mink response to ultrasound in the range emitted by prey. J. Mamm. 70:637–638.

Powell, R. A., and W. J. Zielinski. 1994. Fisher. Pp. 38–73, in The scientific basis for conserving forest carnivores, American marten, fisher, lynx and wolverine, in the western United States (L. F. Ruggiero, K. B. Aubry, S. W. Buskirk, L. J. Lyon, and W. J. Zielinski, eds.). General Technical Report, Rocky Mountain Forest and Range Experiment Station, USDA Forest Service, RM-254:1–184.

Power, M. E., D. Tilman, J. A. Estes, B. A. Menge, W. J. Bond, L. S. Mills, G. Daily, J. C. Castilla, J. Lubchenko, and R. T. Paine. 1996. Challenges in the quest for keystones. BioScience. 46:609–620.

Powers, R. A., and B. J. Verts. 1971. Reproduction in the mountain cottontail rabbit in Oregon. J. Wildl. Mgmt. 35:605–612.

Prange, S., S. D. Gehrt, and E. P. Wiggers. 2004. Influences of anthropogenic resources on raccoon (*Procyon lotor*) movements and spatial distribution. J. Mamm. 85:483–490.

Prenzlow, E. J., D. L. Gilbert, and F. A. Glover. 1968. Some behavior patterns of the pronghorn. Special Rept., Colorado Division of Game, Fish, and Parks 17:1–16.

Presnall, C. C. 1958. The present status of exotic mammals in the United States. J. Wildl. Mgmt. 22:45–50.

Preston, J. R., and R. E. Martin. 1963. A gray shrew population in Harmon County, Oklahoma. J. Mamm. 44:268–270.

Pritchett, L., R. L. Knight, and J. Lee. 2007. Home land: ranching and a West that works. Johnson Press, Boulder, CO, 217 pp.

Prothero, D. R. 2006. After the dinosaurs, the age of mammals. Indiana Univ. Press, Bloomington, 362 pp.

Prothero, D. R., and S. E. Foss, eds. 2007. The evolution of artiodactyls. Johns Hopkins Univ. Press, Baltimore, 367 pp.

Prothero, D. R., and R. M. Schoch. 2003. Horns, tusks, and flippers, the evolution of hoofed mammals. Johns Hopkins Univ. Press, Baltimore, 384 pp.

Proulx, G., K. Aubry, J. Birks, S. Buskirk, C. Fortin, H. Frost, W. Krohn, L. Mayo, V. Monakhoc, D. Payer, M. Saeki, M. Santos-Reis, R. Weir, and W. Zielinski. 2004. World distribution and status of the genus *Martes* in 2000. Pp. 21–76, in Martens and fishers in human-altered environments, an international perspective (A. K. Fuller, G. Proulx, and D. J. Harrison, eds.). Springer Science, New York, 279 pp.

Pruitt, W. O., Jr. 1953. An analysis of some physical factors affecting the local distribution of the shorttail shrew (*Blarina brevicauda*) in the northern part of the Lower Peninsula of Michigan. Misc. Publ., Mus. Zool., Univ. Michigan 79:1–39.

Pruitt, W. O., Jr. 1954. Notes on Colorado *Phenacomys* and pikas. J. Mamm. 35:450–452.

Pugh, S. R., S. Johnson, and R. H. Tamarin. 2003. Voles, *Microtus* species. Pp. 349–370, in Wild mammals of North America, biology, management, and economics, second ed. (G. A. Feldhamer, B. C. Thompson, and J. A. Chapman, eds.). Johns Hopkins Univ. Press, Baltimore, 1,216 pp.

Pulawa, L. K., and G. L. Florant. 2000. The effects of caloric restriction on the body composition and hibernation of the golden-mantled ground squirrel (*Spermophilus lateralis*). Physiol. and Biochem. Zool. 73:538–546.

Pulteney, R. 1781. A general view of the writings of Linnaeus. T. Payne, London, 425 pp.

Quick, H. F. 1951. Notes on the ecology of weasels in Gunnison County, Colorado. J. Mamm. 32:281–290.

Quimby, D. C. 1951. The life history and ecology of the jumping mouse, *Zapus hudsonius*. Ecol. Monogr. 21:61–95.

Quimby, D. C., and J. E. Gaab. 1957. Mandibular dentition as an age indicator in Rocky Mountain elk. J. Wildl. Mgmt. 21:435–451.

Quinn, N.W.S., and G. Parker. 1987. Lynx. Pp. 682–694, in Wild furbearer management and conservation in North America (M. Novak, J. A. Baker, M. E. Obbard, and B. Malloch, eds.). Ontario Trappers Association, Toronto, 1,150 pp.

Quinones, B. E. 1988. The potential for human plague acquired from rock squirrels in the Fort Collins area. Unpubl. master's thesis, Colorado State Univ., Fort Collins, 56 pp.

Rabb, G. B. 1959. Reproductive and vocal behavior in captive pumas. J. Mamm. 40:616–617.

Rabe, M. J., T. M. Morrell, H. Green, J. C. deVos, Jr., and C. R. Miller. 1998. Characteristics of ponderosa pine snag roosts used by reproductive bats in northern Arizona. J. Wildl. Mgmt. 52:612–621.

Rabe, M. J., S. S. Rosenstock, and J. C. deVos, Jr. 2002. Review of big-game survey methods used by wildlife agencies of the western United States. Wildl. Soc. Bull. 30:46–52.

Raesly, E. J. 2001. Progress and status of river otter reintroduction projects in the United States. Wildl. Soc. Bull. 29:856–862.

Raesly, R. L., and J. E. Gates. 1987. Winter habitat selection by north temperate cave bats. Amer. Midland Nat. 118:15–31.

Rafiti, R. 2009. Wolverine encounter. Colorado Outdoors 58(4):15.

Ragan, T. 2002. Taxes help save species. Colorado Springs Gazette, January 2.

Rainey, D. G. 1956. Eastern woodrat: life history and ecology. Misc. Publ., Mus. Nat. Hist., Univ. Kansas 8:535–646.

Ralls, K., and L. L. Eberhardt. 1997. Assessment of abundance of San Joaquin kit foxes by spotlight surveys. J. Mamm. 78:65–73.

Ralls, K., K. L. Pilgrim, P. J. White, E. E. Paxinos, M. K. Schwartz, and R. C. Fleisher. 2001. Kinship, social relationships, and den sharing in kit foxes. J. Mamm. 82:858–866.

Ralls, K., and P. J. White. 1995. Predation on San Joaquin kit foxes by larger canids. J. Mamm. 76:723–729.

Rambaldini, D. A., and R. M. Brigham. 2008. Torpor use by free-ranging pallid bats (*Antrozous pallidus*) at the northern extent of their range. J. Mamm. 89:933–941.

Ramey, C. A., and D. J. Nash. 1971. Abert's squirrel in Colorado. Southwestern Nat. 16:125–126.

Ramey, C. A., and D. J. Nash. 1976a. Geographic variation in Abert's squirrels (*Sciurus aberti*). Southwestern Nat. 21:135–139.

Ramey, C. A., and D. J. Nash. 1976b. Coat color polymorphism of Abert's squirrel, *Sciurus aberti*, in Colorado. Southwestern Nat. 21:209–217.

Ramey, R. R., II, H.-P. Liu, W. E. Clinton, L. M. Carpenter, and J. D. Wehausen. 2005. Genetic relatedness of the Preble's meadow jumping mouse (*Zapus hudsonius preblei*) to nearby subspecies of *Z. hudsonius* as inferred from variation in cranial morphology, mitochondrial DNA, and microsatellite DNA: implications for taxonomy and conservation. Animal Cons. 8:329–346.

Ramey, R. R., II, J. D. Wehausen, H.-P. Liu, C. W. Epps, and L. M. Carpenter. 2006. Response to Vignieri *et al.* (2006): should hypothesis testing or selective post hoc interpretation of results guide the allocation of conservation effort? Animal Cons. 9:244–247.

Ramey, R. R., II, J. D. Wehausen, H.-P. Liu, C. W. Epps, and L. M. Carpenter. 2007. How King et al. (2006) define an "evolutionary distinction" of a mouse subspecies: a response. Molec. Ecol. 16:3518–3521.

Ramm, S. A. 2007. Sexual selection and genital evolution in mammals: a phylogenetic analysis of baculum length. Amer. Nat. 169:360–369.

Ramos, C. N. 1998. Evolution and biogeography of North American Leporidae. Unpubl. doctoral dissert., Univ. Colorado, Boulder, 192 pp.

Ramos, C. N. 1999. Morphometric variation among some leporids (Mammalia: Lagomorpha) of North America. Proc. Denver Mus. Nat. Hist. 16:1–12.

Randa, L. A., and J. A. Yunger. 2006. Carnivore occurrence along an urban-rural gradient: a landscape-level analysis. J. Mamm. 87:1154–1164.

Randall, J. A., and R. E. Johnson. 1979. Population densities and habitat occupancy by *Microtus longicaudus* and *M. montanus*. J. Mamm. 50:217–219.

Randolph, J. C. 1973. Ecological energetics of a homeothermic predator, the short-tailed shrew. Ecology 54:1166–1187.

Randolph, J. C., G. N. Cameron, and J. A. Wrazen. 1991. Dietary choice of a generalist grassland herbivore, *Sigmodon hispidus*. J. Mamm. 72:300–311.

Ransome, D. B., and T. P. Sullivan. 1997. Food limitation and habitat preference of *Glaucomys sabrinus* and *Tamiasciurus hudsonicus*. J. Mamm. 78:538–549.

Raphael, M. G. 1987. Nongame wildlife research in subalpine forests of the central Rocky Mountains. Pp. 113–122, in Management of subalpine forests: building on 50 years of research (C. A. Troendle, M. R. Kaufmann, R. H. Hamre, and R. P. Winokur, eds.). Gen. Tech. Rept., USDA Forest Service, RM-149:1–253.

Raphael, M. R. 1988. Habitat associations of small mammals in a subalpine forest, southeastern Wyoming. Pp. 359–367, in Management of amphibians, reptiles, and small mammals in North America (R. C. Szaro, K. E Severson, and D. R. Patton, tech. coords.). Gen. Tech. Rept., Rocky Mountain Forest and Range Experiment Station, USDA, RM-166:1–458.

Rasmussen, T. K., and G. Callison. 1981. A new species of triconodont mammal from the Upper Jurassic of Colorado. J. Paleo. 55:678–634.

Ratcliff, H. M. 1941. Winter range conditions in Rocky Mountain National Park. Trans. N. Amer. Wildl. Conf. 5:132–139.

Rathbun, A. P., M. C. Wells, and M. Bekoff. 1980. Cooperative predation by coyotes on badgers. J. Mamm. 51:375–376.

Rausch, R. L. 1953. On the status of some Arctic mammals. Arctic 6:91–148.

Rausch, R. L. 1963. Geographic variation in size in North American brown bears, *Ursus arctos* L., as indicated by condylobasal length. Canadian J. Zool. 41:33–45.

Rausch, R. A. 1967. Some aspects of the population ecology of wolves, Alaska. Amer. Zool. 7:253–265.

Rausch, R. A., and A. M. Pearson. 1972. Notes on the wolverine in Alaska and the Yukon Territory. J. Wildl. Mgmt. 36:249–268.

Raymond, G. J., A. Bossers, L. D. Raymond, K. I. O'Rourke, L. E. McHolland, P. K. Bryant III, M. W. Miller, E. S. Williams, M. Smits, and B. Caughey. 2000. Evidence of a molecular barrier limiting susceptibility of humans, cattle and sheep to chronic wasting disease. EMBO Journal 19:4425–4430.

Raymond, M., J.-F. Robitaiile, P. Lauzon, and R. Vaudry. 1990. Prey-dependent profitability of foraging behaviour of male and female ermine, *Mustela erminea*. Oikos 58:323–328.

Raynor, L. S. 1985a. Dynamics of a plague outbreak in Gunnison's prairie dog. J. Mamm. 56:194–196.

Raynor, L. S. 1985b. Effects of habitat quality on growth, age of first reproduction and dispersal in Gunnison's prairie dogs (*Cynomys gunnisoni*). Canadian J. Zool. 53:2835–2840.

Raynor, L. S., A. K. Brody, and C. Gilbert. 1987. Hibernation in the Gunnison's prairie dog. J. Mamm. 58:147–150.

Reading, R. P., and T. W. Clark. 1990. Black-footed ferret annotated bibliography, 1986–1990. Tech. Bull., Montana Bureau Land Mgmt. 3:1–22.

Reading, R. P., and R. Matcett. 1997. Attributes of black-tailed prairie dog colonies in northcentral Montana. J. Wildl. Mgmt. 51:664–673.

Reed, A. W., G. A. Kaufman, and D. W. Kaufman. 2006. Species richness–productivity relationship for small mammals along a desert-grassland continuum: differential responses of functional groups. J. Mamm. 87:777–783.

Reed, D. F. 2001. A conceptual interference competition model for introduced mountain goats. J. Wildl. Mgmt. 55:125–128.

Reed, D. F., and K. A. Green. 1994. Mountain goats on Mount Evans, Colorado—conflicts and the importance of accurate population estimates. Biennial Symposium Northern Wild Sheep and Goat Council 9:139–143.

Reed, E. B. 1955. January breeding of *Peromyscus* in north central Colorado. J. Mamm. 36:462–463.

Reed, J. E., R. J. Baker, W. B. Ballard, and B. T. Kelly. 2004. Differentiating Mexican gray wolf and coyote scats using DNA analysis. Wildl. Soc. Bull. 32:685–692.

Reed, K. M., and J. R. Choate. 1986a. Natural history of the plains pocket mouse in agriculturally disturbed sandsage prairie. Prairie Nat. 18:79–90.

Reed, K. M., and J. R. Choate. 1986b. Geographic variation in the plains pocket mouse (*Perognathus flavescens*) on the Great Plains. Texas J. Sci. 38:227–240.

Reed, M. P., and J. R. Choate. 1988. Noteworthy southwestern records of the prairie vole. Southwestern Nat. 33:495–496.

Reed-Eckert, M., C. Meaney, and G. P. Beauvais. 2004. Species assessment for grizzly (brown) bear (*Ursus arctos*) in Wyoming. Wyoming State Office, Bureau of Land Management, U.S. Department of Interior, Cheyenne, 54 pp.

Reed-Eckert, M. L. 2010. Teetering on the edge of suitable climate: kit fox (*Vulpes macrotis*) range limit dynamics in east-central Utah and west-central Colorado, 1983 to 2009. Unpublished master's thesis, Univ. of Colorado, Boulder, vii + 66 pp.

Reeve, A. F., and T. C. Vosburgh. 2006. Shooting prairie dogs. Pp. 119–128, in Recovery of the black-footed ferret: progress and continuing challenges (J. E. Roelle, B. J. Miller, J. L. Godbey, and D. E. Biggins, eds.). Scientific Investigations Report, USGS, 2005-5293, 288 pp.

Reeves, H. M., B. W. O'Gara, and R. E. McCabe. 2009. Prairie ghost: pronghorn and human interaction in early America. Univ. Press Colorado, Boulder, 208 pp.

Reeves, H. M., and R. M. Williams. 1956. Reproduction, size, and mortality in the Rocky Mountain muskrat. J. Mamm. 37:494–500.

Reich, L. M. 1981. *Microtus pennsylvanicus*. Mammalian Species 159:1–8.

Reichman, O. J., J. H. Benedix, Jr., and T. R. Seastedt. 1993. Distinct animal-generated edge effects in a tallgrass prairie community. Ecology 74:1281–1285.

Reichman, O. J., and E. W. Seabloom. 2002. The role of pocket gophers as subterranean ecosystem engineers. Trends Ecol. Evol. 17:44–49.

Reid, D. G., T. E. Code, A.C.H. Reid, and S. M. Herrero. 1994. Spacing, movements, and habitat selection of the river otter in boreal Alberta. Canadian J. Zool. 72:1314–1324.

Reid, D. G., S. M. Herrero, and T. E. Code. 1988. River otters as agents of water loss from beaver ponds. J. Mamm. 59:100–107.

Reid, V. H. 1973. Population biology of the northern pocket gopher. Pp. 21–41, in Pocket gophers and Colorado mountain rangeland (G. T. Turner, R. M. Hansen, V. H. Reid, H. P. Tietjen, and A. L. Ward, eds.). Exper. Sta. Bull., Colorado State Univ. 2:1–554.

Reig, O. A. 1977. A proposed unified nomenclature for the enameled components of the molar teeth of the Cricetidae (Rodentia). J. Zool., London 181:227–241.

Reiter, E. K., M. W. Brunson, and R. H. Schmidt. 1999. Public attitudes toward wildlife damage management and policy. Wildl. Soc. Bull. 27:746–758.

Remington, J. D. 1952. Food habits, growth, and behavior of two captive pine marten. J. Mamm. 33:66–70.

Renecker, L. A., and R. J. Hudson. 1986. Seasonal energy expenditures and thermoregulatory responses of moose. Canadian J. Zool. 54:322–327.

Renecker, L. A., and R. J. Hudson. 1990. Behavioral and thermoregulatory responses of moose to high ambient temperatures and insect harassment in aspen-dominated boreal forests. Alces 26:66–72.

Rennicke, J. 1990. Colorado wildlife. Falcon Press Publishing Co., Helena, MT, 138 pp.

Responsive Management/National Shooting Sports Foundation. 2008. The future of hunting and the shooting sports: research-based recruitment and retention strategies. Report to U.S. Fish and Wildlife Service, 261 pp.

Retzer, J. L., H. M. Swope, J. D. Remington, and W. H. Rutherford. 1956. Suitability of physical factors for beaver management in the Rocky Mountains of Colorado. Tech. Bull., Colorado Department of Fish and Game 2:1–32.

Reynolds, H. C. 1952. Studies on reproduction in the opossum (*Didelphis virginiana*). Univ. California Publ. Zool. 52:223–284.

Reynolds, H. W., C. C. Gates, and R. D. Glaholt. 2003. Bison, *Bison bison*. Pp. 1009–1060, in Wild mammals of North America, biology, management, and economics, second ed. (G. A. Feldhamer, B. C. Thompson, and J. A. Chapman, eds.). Johns Hopkins Univ. Press, Baltimore, 1,216 pp.

Reynolds, H. W., R. D. Glaholt, and A. L. Hawley. 1982. Bison. Pp. 972–1007, in Wild mammals of North America, biology, management, and economics (J. A. Chapman and G. A. Feldhamer, eds.). Johns Hopkins Univ., Press, Baltimore, 1,147 pp.

Reynolds, J. L., T. N. Feinstein, and J. J. Ebersole, 2006. Sexual reproduction of Gambel oak (*Quercus gambelii*) near its northeastern limit. Western N. Amer. Nat. 50:225–227.

Ribble, D. O., and F. B. Samson. 1987. Microhabitat associations of small mammals in southeastern Colorado, with special emphasis on *Peromyscus* (Rodentia). Southwestern Nat. 32:291–303.

Ribble, D. O., and S. Stanley. 1998. Home ranges and social organization of syntopic *Peromyscus boylii* and *P. truei*. J. Mamm. 79:932–941.

Ribble, D. O., A. E. Wurtz, E. K. McConnell, J. J. Buegge, and K. C. Welch, Jr. 2002. A comparison of home ranges of two species of *Peromyscus* using trapping and radiotelemetry data. J. Mamm. 83:260–266.

Rice, D. W. 1957. Sexual behavior of tassel-eared squirrels. J. Mamm. 38:129.

Rich, S. M., C. W. Kilpatrick, J. L. Shippee, and K. L. Crowell. 1996. Morphological differentiation and identification of *Peromyscus leucopus* and *P. maniculatus* in northeastern North America. J. Mamm. 77:985–991.

Richards, R. E. 1976. The distribution, water balance, and vocalization of the ringtail, *Bassariscus astutus*. Unpubl. doctoral dissert., Univ. Northern Colorado, Greeley, 68 pp.

Richardson, L., T. W. Clark, S. C. Forrest, and T. M. Campbell, III. 1987. Winter ecology of black-footed ferrets (*Mustela nigripes*) at Meeteetse, Wyoming. Amer. Midland Nat. 117:225–239.

Richens, V. B. 1966. Notes on the digging activity of a northern pocket gopher. J. Mamm. 47:531–533.

Richins, G. H., H. D. Smith, and C. D. Jorgensen. 1974. Growth and development of the western harvest mouse, *Reithrodontomys megalotis megalotis*. Great Basin Nat. 34:105–120.

Ricketts, T. H., E. Dinerstein, D. M. Olson, C. J. Loucks, W. Eichbaum, D. Della Sala, K. Kavanagh, P. Hedao, P. T. Hurley, K. M. Carney, R. Abell, and S. Walters. 1999. Terrestrial ecoregions of North America, a conservation assessment. Island Press, Washington, DC, 485 pp.

Riddle, B. R. 1995. Molecular biogeography in the pocket mice (*Perognathus* and *Chaetodipus*) and grasshopper mice (*Onychomys*): the late Cenozoic development of a North American aridlands rodent guild. J. Mamm. 76:283–301.

Riddle, B. R., and J. R. Choate. 1986. Systematics and biogeography of *Onychomys leucogaster* in western North America. J. Mamm. 567:233–255.

Riddle, B. R., and R. L. Honeycutt. 1990. Historical biogeography in North American arid regions: an approach using mitochondrial-DNA phylogeny in grasshopper mice (genus *Onychomys*). Evolution 44:1–15.

Ride, W.E.L. 1964. A review of Australian fossil marsupials. J. Royal Soc. Western Australia 47:97–131.

Ride, W.E.L. 1970. A guide to the native mammals of Australia. Oxford Univ. Press, Melbourne, 249 pp.

Rideout, C. B. 1978. Mountain goat. Pp. 149–159, in Big game of North America, ecology and management (J. L. Schmidt and D. L. Gilbert, eds.). Stackpole Books, Harrisburg, PA, 494 pp.

Rideout, C. B., and R. S. Hoffmann. 1975. *Oreamnos americanus*. Mammalian Species 63:1–6.

Riebsame, W. E., and J. J. Robb, eds. 1997. Atlas of the New West: portrait of a changing region. W. W. Norton, New York, 192 pp.

Riley, S. 2001. Spatial and resource overlap of bobcats and gray foxes in urban and rural zones of a national park. Pp. 32–39, in Proc. Symposium on Current Bobcat Research and Implications for Management (A. Woolf, C. K. Nielsen, and R. D. Bluett, eds.). The Wildlife Society 2000 Conference, Nashville, TN, 83 pp.

Riley, S. 2006. Spatial ecology of bobcats and gray foxes in urban and rural zones of a national park. J. Wildl. Mgmt. 70:1425–1435.

Riley, S. J., D. J. Decker, L. H. Carpenter, J. F. Organ, W. F. Siemer, G. F. Mattfeld, and G. Parsons. 2002. The essence of wildlife management. Wildl. Soc. Bull. 30:585–593.

Riley, S. J., and R. A. Malecki. 2001. A landscape analysis of cougar distribution and abundance in Montana, USA. Environ. Mgmt. 28:317–323.

Riley, S. J., W. F. Siemer, D. J. Decker, L. H. Carpenter, J. F. Organ, and L. T. Berchielli. 2003. Adaptive impact management: an integrative approach to wildlife management. Human Dimensions Wildl. 8:81–95.

Ripple, W. J., and R. L. Beschta. 2004. Wolves, elk, willows, and trophic cascades in the upper Gallatin Range of southwestern Montana, USA. Forest Ecol. Mgmt. 200:164–181.

Ripple, W. J., and E. J. Larsen. 2000. Historic aspen recruitment, elk, and wolves in northern Yellowstone National Park. Biol. Conserv. 95:361–370.

Risenhoover, K. L., and J. A. Bailey. 1982. Social dynamics of mountain goats in summer: implications for age ratios. Biennial Symp. Northern Wild Sheep and Goat Council 3:364–373.

Risenhoover, K. L., and J. A. Bailey. 1985. Foraging ecology of mountain sheep: implications for habitat management. J. Wildl. Mgmt. 49:797–804.

Rissman, A. R., L. Lozier, T. Comendant, P. Kareiva, J. M. Kiesecker, M. R. Shaw, and A. M. Merenlender. 2007. Conservation easements: biodiversity protection and private use. Cons. Biology 21:709–718.

Ritzli, C. M., B. C. Bartels, and D. W. Sparks. 2005. Ectoparasites and food habits of Elliot's short-tailed shrew, *Blarina hylophaga*. Southwestern Nat. 50:88–93.

Rivinus, E. F., and E. M. Youssef. 1992. Spencer Baird of the Smithsonian. Smithsonian Institution Press, Washington, DC, 228 pp.

Roach, J. L., P. Stapp, B. Van Horne, and M. F. Antolin. 2001. Genetic structure of a metapopulation of black-tailed prairie dogs. J. Mamm. 82:946–959.

Robinette, K. W., W. F. Andelt, and K. P. Burnham. 1995. Effect of group size on survival of relocated prairie dogs. J. Wildl. Mgmt. 59:867–874.

Robinette, W. L., J. S. Gashwiler, and O. W. Morris. 1959. Food habits of the cougar in Utah and Nevada. J. Wildl. Mgmt. 23:261–273.

Robinette, W. L., J. S. Gashwiler, and O. W. Morris. 1961. Notes on cougar productivity and life history. J. Mamm. 42:204–217.

Robinette, W. L., N. V. Hancock, and D. A. Jones. 1977. The Oak Creek mule deer herd in Utah. Resource Publ., Utah Division of Wildlife 77-15:1–148.

Robinette, W. L., D. A. Jones, G. Rogers, and J. S. Gashwiler. 1957. Notes on tooth development and wear for Rocky Mountain mule deer. J. Wildl. Mgmt. 21:134–153.

Robinson, J. W., and R. S. Hoffmann. 1975. Geographical and interspecific cranial variation in big-eared ground squirrels (*Spermophilus*): a multivariate study. Syst. Zool. 24:79–88.

Robinson, M. J. 2005. Predatory bureaucracy, the extermination of wolves and the transformation of the West. Univ. Press Colorado, Boulder, 473 pp.

Robinson, T. J., and C. A. Matthee. 2005. Phylogeny and evolutionary origins of the Leporidae: a review of cytogenetics, molecular analyses and a supermatrix analysis. Mammal Rev. 55:231–247.

Robinson, V. B., J. W. Newberne, and D. M. Brooks. 1957. Distemper in the American raccoon (*Procyon lotor*). J. Amer. Vet. Med. Assoc. 131:276–278.

Robinson, W. B. 1953. Population trends of predators and fur animals in 1080 station areas. J. Mamm. 34:220–227.

Rocke, T. E., S. R. Smith, D. T. Stinchcomb, and J. E. Osorio. 2008. Immunization of black-tailed prairie dog against plague through consumption of vaccine-laden baits. J. Wildl. Dis. 44:930–937.

Rocky Mountain National Park. 2006. Elk and Vegetation Management Plan., 2 vols. Rocky Mountain National Park, Estes Park, CO. http://www.nps.gov/romo/parkmgmt/elkvegetation.htm.

Rodeck, H. G., and S. Anderson. 1956. *Sorex merriami* and *Microtus mexicanus* in Colorado. J. Mamm. 37:436.

Rodhouse, T. J., S. A. Scott, P. C. Ormsbee, and J. M. Zinck. 2008. Field identification of *Myotis yumanensis* and *Myotis lucifugus*: a morphological evaluation. Western N. Amer. Nat. 58:437–443.

Rodriguez, R. M., and L. K. Ammerman. 2004. Mitochondrial DNA divergence does not reflect morphological difference between *Myotis californicus* and *Myotis ciliolabrum*. J. Mamm. 85:842–851.

Roe, F. G. 1970. The North American buffalo, second ed. Univ. Toronto Press, Toronto, 991 pp.

Roe, K. A., and C. M. Roe. 2003. Habitat selection guidelines for black-tailed prairie dog relocations. Wildl. Soc. Bull. 31:1246–1253.

Roell, B. J. 1999. Demography and spatial use of swift fox (*Vulpes velox*) in northeastern Colorado. Unpubl. master's thesis, Univ. Northern Colorado, Greeley, 145 pp.

Roelle, J. E., B. J. Miller, J. L. Godbey, and D. E. Biggins, eds. 2006. Recovery of the black-footed ferret: progress and continuing challenges. Sci. Investigations Rept., USGS, 2005-5293:1–288.

Rogers, D. S., D. J. Shurtleff, and C. L. Pritchett. 2000. Records of mammals from the East Tavaputs Plateau, Utah. Western N. Amer. Nat. 50:221–224.

Rogers, J. G., Jr., and G. K. Beauchamp. 1976. Influence of stimuli from populations of *Peromyscus leucopus* on maturation of young. J. Mamm. 57:320–330.

Rogowitz, G. L. 1990. Seasonal energetics of the white-tailed jackrabbit (*Lepus townsendii*). J. Mamm. 71:277–285.

Rogowitz, G. L. 1992. Reproduction of white-tailed jackrabbits on semi-arid range. J. Wildl. Mgmt. 56:676–684.

Rogowitz, G. L. 1997. Locomotor and foraging activities of the white-tailed jackrabbit (*Lepus townsendii*). J. Mamm. 78:1172–1181.

Rogowitz, G. L., and M. L. Wolfe. 1991. Intraspecific variation in life-history traits of the white-tailed jackrabbit (*Lepus townsendii*). J. Mamm. 72:796–806.

Rohwer, S. A., and D. L. Kilgore, Jr. 1973. Interbreeding in the arid-land foxes, *Vulpes velox* and *V. macrotis*. Systematic Zoology 22:157–165.

Rolley, R. E. 1987. Bobcat. Pp. 670–681, in Wild furbearer management and conservation in North America (M. Novak, J. A. Baker, M. E. Obbard, and B. Malloch, eds.). Ontario Trappers Association, Toronto, 1,150 pp.

Rolston, H., III. 1986. Philosophy gone wild: essays in environmental ethics. Prometheus Books, Buffalo, NY, 269 pp.

Romin, L. A., and J. A. Bissonette. 1996. Deer-vehicle collisions: status of state monitoring activities and mitigation efforts. Wildl. Soc. Bull. 24:276–283.

Rominge, E. M., H. A. Whitlaw, D. L. Weybright, W. C. Dunn, and W. B. Ballard. 2004. The influence of mountain lion predation on bighorn sheep translocations. J. Wildl. Mgmt. 58: 993–999.

Romme, W. H., J. Clement, J. Hicke, D. Kulakowski, L. H. MacDonald, T. L. Schoennagel, and T. T. Veblen. 2006. Recent forest insect outbreaks and fire risk in Colorado forests: a brief synthesis of relevant research. Colorado Forest Restoration Institute, Colorado State Univ., Colorado State Forest Service, Fort Collins, and Univ. Idaho, Moscow, 24 pp.

Rongstad, O. J. 1965. A life history study of thirteen-lined ground squirrels in southern Wisconsin. J. Mamm. 46:76–87.

Rongstad, O. J., T. R. Laurion, and D. E. Andersen. 1989. Ecology of swift fox on the Piñon Canyon Maneuver Site, Colorado. Final Rept. to Environmental, Energy, and Natural Resources Division, Fort Carson, CO, 52 pp.

Root, J. J., W. C. Black IV, C. H. Calisher, K. R. Wilson, and B. J. Beaty. 2004. Genetic relatedness of deer mice (*Peromyscus maniculatus*), infected with Sin Nombre virus. Vector-Borne and Zoonotic Diseases 4:149–157.

Root, J. J., W. C. Black, IV, C. H. Calisher, K. R. Wilson, R. S. Mackie, J. N. Mills, and B. J. Beaty. 2003. Analyses of gene flow among populations of deer mice (*Peromyscus maniculatus*) at sites near Hantavirus Pulmonary Syndrome case-patient residences. J. Wildl. Dis. 39:287–298.

Root, J. J., C. H. Calisher, and B. J. Beaty. 2001. Microhabitat partitioning by two chipmunk species (*Tamias*) in western Colorado. Western N. Amer. Nat. 51:114–118.

Root, J. J., J. S. Hall, R. G McLean, N. L. Marlenee, B. J. Beaty, J. Gansowski, and L. Clark. 2005. Serologic evidence of exposure of wild mammals to flaviviruses in the central and eastern United States. Amer. J. Tropical Medicine and Hygiene 72:622–630.

Root, J. J., P. T. Oesterle, H. J. Sullivan, J. S. Hall, N. L. Marlenee, R. G. McLean, J. A. Montenieri, and L. Clark. 2007. Short report: fox squirrel (*Sciurus niger*) associations with West Nile Virus. Amer. J. Tropical Medicine and Hygiene 76:782–784.

Root, J. J., P. T. Oesterle, N. M. Nemeth, K. Klenk, D. H. Gould, R. G. McLean, L. Clark, and J. S. Hall. 2006. Experimental infection of fox squirrels (*Sciurus niger*) with West Nile Virus. Amer. J. Tropical Medicine and Hygiene 75:697–701.

Root, J. J., K. R. Wilson, C. H. Calisher, K. D. Wagoner, K. D. Abbott, T. L. Yates, A. J. Kuenzi, M. L. Morrison, J. N. Mills, and B. J. Beaty. 2005. Spatial clustering of murid rodents infected with hantaviruses: implications from meta-analyses. Ecol. Appl. 15:565–574.

Root, T. L., and L. Hughes. 2005. Present and future phonological changes in wild plants and animals. Pp. 61–69, in Climate change and biodiversity (T. Lovejoy and L. Hannah, eds.). Yale Univ. Press, New Haven, CT, 440 pp.

Root, T. L., J. T. Price, K. R. Hall, S. H. Schneider, C. Rosenzweig, and J. A. Pounds. 2003. Fingerprints of global warming on wild animals and plants. Nature 421:57–60.

Root, T. L., and S. H. Schneider. 2002. Climate change: overview and implications for wildlife. Pp. 1–56, in Wildlife responses to climate change, North American case studies (S. H. Schneider and T. L. Root, eds.). Island Press, Washington, DC, 437 pp.

Roppe, J. R., and D. Hein. 1978. Effects of fire on wildlife in a lodgepole pine forest. Southwestern Nat. 23:279–288.

Rosatte, R. C. 1987. Striped, spotted, hooded, and hog-nosed skunk. Pp. 598–613, in Wild furbearer management and conservation in North America (M. Novak, J. A. Baker, M. E. Obbard, and B. Malloch, eds.). Ontario Trappers Association, Toronto, 1,150 pp.

Rosatte, R. C., and S. Larivière. 2003. Skunks, genera *Mephitis, Spilogale*, and *Conepatus*. Pp. 692–707, in Wild mammals of North America, biology, management, and economics, second ed. (G. A. Feldhamer, B. C. Thompson, and J. A. Chapman, eds.). Johns Hopkins Univ. Press, Baltimore, 1,216 pp.

Rosatte, R. C., M. J. Power, and C. D. MacInnes. 1991. Ecology of urban skunks, raccoons and foxes in metropolitan Toronto. Pp. 31–38, in Wildlife conservation in metropolitan environments (L. W. Adams and D. L. Leedy, eds.). Nat. Inst. Urban Wildl., Columbia, MD, 264 pp.

Rose, G. B. 1977. Mortality rates of tagged adult cottontail rabbits. J. Wildl. Mgmt. 41:511–514.

Rose, K. D. 2006. The beginning of the age of mammals. Johns Hopkins Univ. Press, Baltimore, 428 pp.

Rose, K. D., and J. D. Archibald. 2005. The rise of placental mammals, origins and relationships of the major extant clades. Johns Hopkins Univ. Press, Baltimore, 259 pp.

Rose, K. D., R. J. Emry, T. J. Gaudin, and G. Storch. Xenarthra and Pholidota. Pp. 106–126, in The rise of placental mammals, origins and relationships of the major extant clades (K. D. Rose and J. D. Archibald, eds.). Johns Hopkins Univ. Press, Baltimore, 259 pp.

Rosenstock, S. S. 1996. Shrub-grassland small mammal and vegetation responses to rest from grazing. J. Range Mgmt. 49: 199–203.

Rosenzweig, M. L. 1989. Habitat selection, community organization, and small mammal studies. Pp. 5–21, in Patterns in the structure of mammalian communities (D. W. Morris, Z. Abramsky, B. J. Fox, and M. R. Willig, eds.). Spec. Publ., Mus. Texas Tech Univ. 28:1–266.

Ross, P. I., M. G. Jalkotzy, and M. Festa-Bianchet. 1997. Cougar predation on bighorn sheep in southwestern Alberta during winter. Canadian J. Zool. 74:771–775.

Rothwell, R. 1979. Nest sites of red squirrels (*Tamiasciurus hudsonicus*) in the Laramie Range of southeastern Wyoming. J. Mamm. 50:404–405.

Roughton, R. D. 1972. Shrub age structures on a mule deer winter range in Colorado. Ecology 53:615–625.

Rowland, M. M., M. J. Wisdom, D. H. Johnson, B. C. Wales, J. P. Copeland, and F. B. Edelmann. 2003. Evaluation of landscape models for wolverines in the interior northwest, United States of America. J. Mamm. 84:92–105.

Rowley, W. D. 1985. U.S. Forest Service grazing and rangelands, a history. Texas A&M Univ. Press, College Station, 270 pp.

Roze, U. 1989. The North American porcupine. Smithsonian Institution Press, Washington, DC, 261 pp.

Roze, U. 2002. A facilitated release mechanism for quills of the North American porcupine (*Erethizon dorsatum*). J. Mamm. 83:381–385.

Roze, U., and L. M. Ilse. 2003. Porcupine, *Erethizon dorsatum*. Pp. 371–380, in Wild mammals of North America, biology, management, and economics, second ed. (G. A. Feldhamer, B. C. Thompson, and J. A. Chapman, eds.). Johns Hopkins Univ. Press, Baltimore, 1,216 pp.

Rozinski, B., W. Shattil, and A. D. Benedict. 2005. Valley of the Dunes, Great Sand Dunes National Park and Preserve. Fulcrum Publishing, Golden, CO, 150 pp.

Rue, L. L. 1964. The world of the beaver. J. B. Lippincott, Philadelphia, 155 pp.

Ruedas, L. A. 1998. Systematics of *Sylvilagus* Gray, 1867 (Lagomorpha: Leporidae) from southwestern North America. J. Mamm. 79:1355–1378.

Ruedi, M., and F. Mayer. 2001. Molecular systematics of bats of the genus *Myotis* (Vespertilionidae) suggests deterministic ecomorphological convergences. Molec. Phylog. and Evol. 21:436–448.

Ruffer, D. G. 1965a. Burrows and burrowing behavior of *Onychomys leucogaster*. J. Mamm. 46:241–247.

Ruffer, D. G. 1965b. Sexual behavior of the northern grasshopper mouse (*Onychomys leucogaster*). Animal Behav. 13:447–452.

Ruffer, D. G. 1968. Agonistic behavior of the northern grasshopper mouse (*Onychomys leucogaster breviauritus*). J. Mamm. 49:481–487.

Ruffner, G. A., R. M. Poché, M. Meierkord, and J. A. Neal. 1979. Winter bat activity over a desert wash in southwestern Utah. Southwestern Nat. 24:447–453.

Ruggiero, L. F., K. B. Aubry, S. W. Buskirk, G. M. Koehler, C. J. Krebs, K. S. McKelvey, and J. R. Squires, eds. 2000. Ecology and conservation of lynx in the United States. Univ. Press Colorado, Boulder, 480 pp.

Ruggiero, L. F., K. F. McKelvey, K. B. Aubrey, J. P. Copeland, D. H. Pletscher, and M. G. Hornocker. 2007. Wolverine conservation and management. J. Wildl. Mgmt. 71:2145–2146.

Ruggiero, L. F., D. E. Pearson, and S. E. Henry. 1998. Characteristics of American marten den sites in Wyoming. J. Wildl. Mgmt. 52:663–673.

Runyan, A. M., and D. T. Blumstein. 2004. Do individual differences influence flight initiation distance? J. Wildl. Mgmt. 58:1124–1129.

Rusch, D. A., and W. G. Reeder. 1978. Population ecology of Alberta red squirrels. Ecology 59:400–420.

Russell, J. C., N. Hasler, R. Klette, and B. Rosenhahn. 2009. Automatic track recognition of footprints for identifying cryptic species. Ecology 90:2007–2013.

Russell, K. R. 1978. Mountain lion. Pp. 207–225, in Big game of North America: ecology and management (J. L. Schmidt and D. L. Gilbert, eds.). Stackpole Books, Harrisburg, PA, 494 pp.

Russell, R. J. 1968. Evolution and classification of the pocket gophers of the subfamily Geomyinae. Univ. Kansas Publ., Mus. Nat. Hist. 16:473–579.

Rust, C. C. 1962. Temperature as a modifying factor in the spring pelage change of short-tailed weasels. J. Mamm. 43:323–328.

Ruth, T. K. 2004. Ghost of the Rockies, the Yellowstone Cougar Project. Yellowstone Sci. 12:13–24.

Ruth, T. K., D. W. Smith, M. A. Haroldson, P. C. Buotte, C. C. Schwartz, H. B. Quigley, S. Cherry, K. M. Murphy, D. Tyers, and K. Frey. 2003. Large-carnivore response to recreational big-game hunting along the Yellowstone National Park and Absaroka-Beartooth Wilderness boundary. Wildl. Soc. Bull. 31:1150–1161.

Rutherford, W. H. 1952. Effects of summer flash flood upon a beaver population. J. Mamm. 34:261–262.

Rutherford, W. H. 1955. Wildlife and environmental relationships of beaver in Colorado forests. J. Forestry 53:803–806.

Rutherford, W. H. 1956. Productivity rates, age classes and sex ratios of spring-caught beavers in Colorado. Outdoor Facts, Colorado Dept. Nat. Resources, Division of Game, Fish, and Parks 4:1.

Rutherford, W. H. 1964. The beaver in Colorado: its biology, ecology, management, and economics. Tech. Publ., Colorado Division of Game, Fish, and Parks 17:1–49.

Rutherford, W. H. 1972a. Status of mountain goats in Colorado. Game Information Leaflet, Colorado Division of Game, Fish, and Parks 90:1–4.

Rutherford, W. H. 1972b. Status of transplanted bighorn sheep in Colorado. Game Information Leaflet, Colorado Division of Game, Fish, and Parks 92:1–3.

Rutherford, W. H. 1972c. Guidelines for evaluating bighorn sheep transplanting sites in Colorado. Game Information Leaflet, Colorado Division of Game, Fish, and Parks 93:1–3.

Ryon, T. R. 1996. Evaluation of historical capture sites of the Preble's meadow jumping mouse in Colorado. Unpubl. master's thesis, Univ. Colorado–Denver, 67 pp.

Ryon, T. R. 2001. Summer nests of Preble's meadow jumping mouse. Southwestern Nat. 46:376–378.

Saariko, J., and I. Hanski. 1990. Timing of rest and sleep in foraging shrews. Animal Behavior 40:861–869.

Sacks, B. N., M. M. Jaeger, J.C.C. Neale, and D. R. McCullough. 1999. Territoriality and breeding status of coyotes relative to sheep predation. J. Wildl. Mgmt. 53:593–605.

Saldaña-DeLeon, J. L., and C. A. Jones. 1998. Annotated checklist of the Recent mammals of Colorado. Occas. Papers, Mus. Texas Tech Univ. 79:1–14.

Salkeld, D. J., R. J. Eisen, P. Stapp, A. P. Wilder, J. Lowell, D. W. Tripp, D. Albertson, and M. F. Antolin. 2007. The potential role of swift foxes (*Vulpes velox*) and their fleas in plague outbreaks in prairie dogs. J. Wildl. Diseases 43:425–431.

Salkeld, D. J., M. Salathé, P. Stapp, and J. H. Holland. 2010. Plague outbreaks in prairie dog populations explained by percolation thresholds of alternate host abundance. Proc. Nat. Acad. Sci. 107:14247–14250.

Salkeld, D. J., and P. Stapp. 2006. Seroprevalence rates and transmission of plague (*Yersinia pestis*) in mammalian carnivores. Vector-Borne and Zoonotic Dis. 5:231–239.

Salkeld, D. J., and P. Stapp. 2008. Prevalence and abundance of fleas in black-tailed prairie dog burrows: implications for the transmission of plague (*Yersinia pestis*). J. Parasitol. 94:616–621.

Salmon, A. B., S. Leonard, V. Masamsetti, A. Pierce, A. J. Podlutsky, N. Podlutskaya, A. Richardson, S. N. Austad, and A. R. Chaudburi. 2009. The long lifespan of two bat species is correlated to protein oxidation and enhanced protein homeostasis. Fed. Amer. Soc. Exper. Biol. J. 23:2317–2326.

Salounias, N. 2007. Family Bovidae. Pp. 278–291, in The evolution of artiodactyls (D. R. Prothero and S. E. Foss, eds.). Johns Hopkins Univ. Press, Baltimore, 367 pp.

Salsbury, C. M., and K. B. Armitage. 1994. Home range size and exploratory excursions of adult, male yellow-bellied marmots. J. Mamm. 75:648–656.

Samson, C., and M. Raymond. 1998. Movement and habitat preference of radio-tracked stoats, *Mustela erminea*, during summer in southern Quebec. Mammalia 62:165–174.

Samson, F. B., F. L. Knopf, and L. B. Hass. 1988. Small mammal response to the introduction of cattle into a cottonwood floodplain. Pp. 432–438, in Management of amphibians, reptiles, and small mammals in North America (R. C. Szaro, K. R. Severson, and D. R. Patton, tech. coords.). Gen. Tech. Rept., Rocky Mountain Forest and Range Experiment Station, USDA, RM-166:1–458.

Samuel, D. E., and B. B. Nelson. 1982. Foxes. Pp. 475–490, in Wild mammals of North America, biology, management, and economics (J. A. Chapman and G. A. Feldhamer, eds.). Johns Hopkins Univ. Press, Baltimore, 1,147 pp.

Samuel, W. M., M. J. Pybus, and A. A. Kocan. 2001. Parasitic diseases of wild animals, second ed. Iowa State Univ. Press, Ames, 559 pp.

Sanderson, E. W., K. H. Redford, B. Weber, K. Aune, D. Baldes, J. Berger, D. Carter, C. Curtin, J. Derr, S. Dobrott, E. Fearn, C. Fleener, S. Forrest, C. Gerlach, C. C. Gates, J. E. Gross, P. Gogan, S. Grassel, J. A. Hiltiy, M. Jensen, K. Kunkel, D. Lammers, R. List, K. Miowski, T. Olson, C. Pague, P. B. Robertson, and B. Stephenson. 2008. The ecological future of the North American bison: conceiving long-term, large-scale conservation of wildlife. Conservation Biol. 22:252–266.

Sanderson, G. C. 1951. Breeding habits and a history of the Missouri raccoon population from 1941 to 1948. Trans. North American Wildl. Conf. 16:445–460.

Sanderson, G. C. 1987. Raccoon. Pp. 486–499, in Wild furbearer management and conservation in North America (M. Novak, J. A. Baker, M. E. Obbard, and B. Malloch, eds.). Ontario Trappers Association, Toronto, 1,150 pp.

Sanderson, G. C., and A. V. Nalbandov. 1973. The reproductive cycles of the raccoon in Illinois. Bull., Illinois Nat. Hist. Surv. 31:25–85.

Sandidge, L. L. 1953. Food and dens of the opossum (*Didelphis virginiana*) in northeastern Kansas. Trans. Kansas Acad. Sci. 56:97–106.

Sargeant, A. B. 1972. Red fox spatial characteristics in relation to water fowl predation. J. Wildl. Mgmt. 36:225–236.

Sargeant, A. B. 1978. Red fox prey demands and implications to prairie duck production. J. Wildl. Mgmt. 42:520–527.

Sargeant, A. B. 1982. A case history of a dynamic resource—the red fox. Pp. 121–137, in Midwest furbearer management (G. C. Sanderson, ed.). Proc. Symposium 43rd Midwest Fish and Wildlife Conference, Wichita, 195 pp.

Sargeant, A. B., and S. H. Allen. 1989. Observed interactions between coyotes and red foxes. J. Mamm. 70:631–633.

Sargeant, A. B., S. H. Allen, and J. O. Hastings. 1987. Spatial relations between sympatric coyotes and red foxes in North Dakota. J. Wildl. Mgmt. 51:285–293.

Sargeant, G. A., D. H. Johnson, and W. E. Berg. 1998. Interpreting carnivore scent-station surveys. J. Wildl. Mgmt. 52:1235–1245.

Sargeant, G. A., D. H. Johnson, and W. E. Berg. 2003. Sampling designs for carnivore scent-station surveys. J. Wildl. Mgmt. 57:289–298.

Sargeant, G. A., P. J. White, M. A. Sovada, and B. L. Cypher. 2003. Scent-station survey techniques for swift and kit foxes. Pp 99–105, in The swift fox: ecology and conservation of swift foxes in a changing world (M. A. Sovada and L. Carbyn, eds.). Canadian Plains Research Center, Regina, Saskatchewan, 250 pp.

Sasse, D. B. 2003. Job-related mortality of wildlife workers in the United States, 1937–2000. Wildl. Soc. Bull. 31:1015–1020.

Saunders, J. K., Jr. 1955. Food habits and range use of the Rocky Mountain goat in the Crazy Mountains, Montana. J. Wildl. Mgmt. 19:429–437.

Saunders, J. K., Jr. 1963a. Movements and activities of the lynx in Newfoundland. J. Wildl. Mgmt. 27:390–400.

Saunders, J. K., Jr. 1963b. Food habits of the lynx in Newfoundland. J. Wildl. Mgmt. 27:384–390.

Saunders, J. K., Jr. 1964. Physical characteristics of the Newfoundland lynx. J. Mamm. 45:36–47.

Saunders, S., and T. Easley. 2006. Losing ground, western national parks endangered by climate disruption. Rocky Mountain Climate Organization, Louisville, CO, and Natural Resources Defense Council, Washington, DC, 29 pp.

Saunders, S., T. Easeley, and S. Farver. 2009. National parks in peril: the threats of climate disruption. Rocky Mountain Climate Organization, Louisville, CO, and Natural Resources Defense Council, Washington, DC, 54 pp.

Saunders, S., and M. Maxwell. 2005. Less snow, less water: climate disruption in the West. Rocky Mountain Climate Organization, Louisville, CO, 30 pp.

Saunders, S., C. Montgomery, and T. Easley. 2008. Hotter and drier, the West's changed climate. Rocky Mountain Climate Organization, Louisville, CO, and Natural Resources Defense Council, Washington, DC, 54 pp.

Savage, D. E., and D. E. Russell. 1983. Mammalian paleofaunas of the world. Addison Wesley Publishing Co., Reading, MA, 432 pp.

Savage, R.J.G., and M. R. Long. 1986. Mammal evolution: an illustrated guide. Facts on File, New York, 259 pp.

Sawyer, H., R. M. Nielson, F. G. Lindzey, L. Keith, J. K. Powell, and A. A. Abraham. 2007. Habitat selection of Rocky Mountain elk in a nonforested environment. J. Wildl. Mgmt. 71:868–874.

Sawyer, H., R. M. Nielson, F. Lindzey, and L. L. McDonald. 2006. Winter habitat selection of mule deer before and during development of a natural gas field. J. Wildl. Mgmt. 70:396–403.

Schauster, E. R., E. M. Gese, and A. M. Kitchen. 2002. An evaluation of survey methods for monitoring swift fox abundance. Wildl. Soc. Bull. 30:464–477.

Scheck, S. H., and E. D. Fleharty. 1980. Subterranean behavior of the adult thirteen-lined ground squirrel (*Spermophilus tridecemlineatus*). Amer. Midland Nat. 103:191–195.

Scheel, D., T. L. Vincent, and G. N. Cameron. 1996. Global warming and the species richness of bats in Texas. Cons. Biology 10:452–464.

Scheffer, T. H. 1947. Ecological comparisons of the plains prairie dog and the Zuni species. Trans. Kansas Acad. Sci. 49:401–406.

Scheibe, J. S., and M. J. O'Farrell. 1995. Habitat dynamics in *Peromyscus truei*: eclectic females, density dependence, or reproductive constraints? J. Mamm. 76:368–375.

Scheiber, L. L. 2006. Late Prehistoric bison hide production and hunter gatherer identities on the North American plains. Pp. 57–75, in Gender and hide production (L. Frink and K. Weedman, eds.). AltaMira Press, Walnut Creek, CA, 296 pp.

Scheiber, L. L. 2007. Bison economies on the Late Prehistoric North American High Plains. J. Field Archaeol. 32:297–313.

Scheiber, L. L. 2008. Intersecting landscapes in northeastern Colorado: a case study from the Donovan Site. Pp. 17–40, in Archaeological landscapes on the High Plains (L. L. Scheiber and B. J. Clark, eds.). Univ. Press Colorado, Boulder, 296 pp.

Scheiber, L. L., and C. A. Reher. 2007. The Donovan Site (5LO204): an Upper Republican animal processing camp on the High Plains. Plains Anthropologist 52:337–364.

Schladweiler, J. L., and G. L. Storm. 1969. Den use by mink. J. Wildl. Mgmt. 33:1025–1026.

Schladweiler, J. L., and J. R. Tester. 1972. Survival and behavior of hand-reared mallards released in the wild. J. Wildl. Mgmt. 36:1118–1127.

Schlegel, M. W. 1977. Factors affecting calf elk survival on Coolwater Ridge in north central Idaho. Pp. 35–39, in Proc. Western States Elk Workshop, Colorado Division of Wildlife, Denver, 64 pp.

Schlegel, M. W. 1976. Factors affecting calf elk survival in north central Idaho: a progress report. Western Assoc. State Game and Fish Comm. 56:342–355.

Schmidly, D. J. 1973. Geographic variation and taxonomy of *Peromyscus boylii* from Mexico and the southern United States. J. Mamm. 54:111–130.

Schmidly, D. J. 1977. The mammals of trans-Pecos Texas. Texas A&M Univ. Press, College Station, 225 pp.

Schmidly, D. J. 1983. Texan mammals east of the Balcones Fault Zone. Texas A&M Univ. Press, College Station, 400 pp.

Schmidt, C. J., J. R. Choate, and K. L. Phelps. 2008. Wandering Canada lynx in Kansas. Trans. Kansas Acad. Sci. 111:161–162.

Schmidt, E., A. J. Piaggio, C. E. Bock, and D. M. Armstrong. 2003. Part II: Bat use and fatalities at the National Wind Technology Center, June 2001–June 2002. National Wind Technology Center Site Environmental Assessment: bird and bat use and fatalities—final report. NREL/SR-500-32981:15–21.

Schmitt-Ulms, G., S. Ehsani, J. C. Watts, D. Westaway, and H. Wille. 2009. Evolutionary descent of prion genes from the ZIP family of metal ion transporters. PLoS ONE 4(9):1–13.

Schneider, D. G., L. D. Mech, and J. R. Tester. 1971. Movements of female raccoons and their young as determined by radiotracking. Animal Behav. Monogr. 4:1–43.

Schneider, S. H., and T. L. Root, eds. 2001. Wildlife responses to climate change: North American case studies. Island Press, Washington, DC, 368 pp.

Schoenecker, K. A., F. J. Singer, L. C. Zeigenfuss, D. Binkley, and R.S.C. Menezes. 2004. Effects of elk herbivory on vegetation and nitrogen processes. J. Wildl. Mgmt. 58:837–849.

Schoennagel, T. T. Veblen, D. Kulakowski, and A. Holz. 2007. Multidecadal climate variability and climate interactions affect subalpine fire occurrence, western Colorado (USA). Ecology 88:2891–2902.

Schorr, R. A. 2001. Meadow jumping mice (*Zapus hudsonius preblei*) on the U.S. Air Force Academy, El Paso County, Colorado. Colorado Natural Heritage Program, Colorado State Univ., Fort Collins, 53 pp.

Schorr, R. A. 2006. Survey for bats in Jackson County, Colorado. Colorado Natural Heritage Program, Colorado State Univ., Fort Collins, 15 pp.

Schorr, R. A., P. M. Lukacs, and G. L. Florant. 2009. Body mass and winter severity as predictors of overwinter survival in Preble's meadow jumping mouse. J. Mamm. 90:17–24.

Schorr, R. A., J. L. Siemers, P. M. Lukas, J. P. Gionfriddo, J. R. Sovell, R. J. Rondeau, and M. B. Wunder. 2007. Using survival of rodents to assess quality of prairie habitats. Southwestern Nat. 52:552–563.

Schowalter, D. B. 1980. Swarming, reproduction, and early hibernation of *Myotis lucifugus* and *Myotis volans* in Alberta, Canada. J. Mamm. 51:350–354.

Schramm, P. 1951. Laboratory copulations and gestations of porcupine, *Erethizon dorsatum*. J. Mamm. 32:219–221.

Schramm, P. 1952. Sexual maturity and first recorded copulation of a 16-month male porcupine, *Erethizon dorsatum dorsatum*. J. Mamm. 33:329–331.

Schramm, P. 1961. Copulation and gestation in the pocket gopher. J. Mamm. 42:167–170.

Schuler, K. L., D. M. Leslie, Jr., J. H. Shaw, and E. J. Maichak. 2006. Temporal-spatial distribution of American bison (*Bison bison*) in a tallgrass prairie fire mosaic. J. Mamm. 87:539–544.

Schullery, P. 1986. The bears of Yellowstone. Roberts Rinehart Publishers, Boulder, CO, 263 pp.

Schulz, T. T., and L. A Joyce. 1992. A spatial application of a marten habitat model. Wildl. Soc. Bull. 20:74–83.

Schulz, T. T., and W. C. Leininger. 1991. Nongame wildlife communities in grazed and ungrazed montane riparian sites. Great Basin Nat. 51:286–292.

Schwabe, K. A., and P. W. Schuhmann. 2002. Deer-vehicle collisions and deer value: an analysis of competing literatures. Wildl. Soc. Bull. 30:609–615.

Schwartz, C. C., M. A. Haroldson, G. C. White, R. B. Harris, S. Cherry, K. A. Keating, D. Moody, and C. Servheen. 2006. Temporal, spatial, and environmental influences on the demographics of grizzly bears in the Greater Yellowstone Ecosystem. Wildl. Monogr. 161:1–68.

Schwartz, C. C., and K. J. Hundertmark. 1993. Reproductive characteristics of Alaskan moose. J. Wildl. Mgmt. 57:454–468.

Schwartz, C. C., S. D. Miller, and M. A. Haroldson. 2003. Grizzly bear, *Ursus arctos*. Pp. 556–586, in Wild mammals of North America, biology, management, and economics, second ed. (G. A. Feldhamer, B. C. Thompson, and J. A. Chapman, eds.). Johns Hopkins Univ. Press, Baltimore, 1,216 pp.

Schwartz, C. C., and J. G. Nagy. 1976. Pronghorn diets relative to forage availability in northeastern Colorado. J. Wildl. Mgmt. 40:469–478.

Schwartz, C. C., J. G. Nagy, and W. L. Regelin. 1980. Juniper oil yield, terpenoid concentration, and antimicrobial effects on deer. J. Wildl. Mgmt. 44:107–113.

Schwartz, C. C., J. G. Nagy, and R. W. Rice. 1977. Pronghorn dietary quality relative to forage availability and other ruminants in Colorado. J. Wildl. Mgmt. 41:161–168.

Schwartz, M. W. 2008. The performance of the Endangered Species Act. Ann. Rev. Ecol., Evol. Syst. 39:179–199.

Schwartz, O. A., and K. B. Armitage. 2003. Population biology of yellow-bellied marmots: a 40 year perspective. Pp. 245–250, in Adaptive strategies and diversity in marmots (R. Ramousse, D. Allaine, and M. Le Berre, eds.). International Network on Marmots, Lyon, France, 203 pp.

Schwartz, O. A., K. B. Armitage, and D. Van Vuren. 1998. A 32-year demography of yellow-bellied marmots (*Marmota flaviventris*). J. Zool. 246:337–346.

Scott, T. G. 1943. Some food coactions of the northern plains red fox. Ecol. Monogr. 13:427–479.

Scott, V. E., and G. L. Crouch. 1988. Summer birds and mammals of aspen-conifer forests in west-central Colorado. Research Paper, USDA Forest Service, RM-280:1–6.

Scott-Brown, J. M., S. Herrero, and J. Reynolds. 1987. Swift fox. Pp. 433–441, in Wild furbearer management and conservation in North America (M. Novak, J. A. Baker, M. E. Obbard, and B. Malloch, eds.). Ontario Trappers Association and Ontario Ministry of Natural Resources, Toronto, 1,150 pp.

Scribner, K. T., M. H. Smith, R. A. Garrott, and L. H. Carpenter. 1991. Temporal, spatial, and age-specific changes in genotypic composition of mule deer. J. Mamm. 72:126–137.

Scribner, K. T., and R. J. Warren. 1986. Electrophoretic and morphologic comparisons of *Sylvilagus floridanus* and *S. audubonii* in Texas. Southwestern Nat. 31:65–71.

Seal, U. S., E. T. Thorne, M. A. Bogan, and S. H. Anderson, eds. 1989. Conservation biology and the black-footed ferret. Yale Univ. Press, New Haven, CT, 328 pp.

Seamon, J. O., and G. H. Alder. 1996. Population performance of generalist and specialist rodents along habitat gradients. Canadian J. Zool. 74:1130–1139.

Seastedt, T. R. 2002. Base camps of the Rockies: the intermountain grasslands. Pp. 219–236, in Rocky Mountain futures (J. S. Baron, ed.). Island Press, Washington, DC, 325 pp.

Seastedt, T. R., and P. J. Murray. 2008. Belowground herbivory in grasslands. Pp. 54–67, in Root feeders: an ecosystem perspective (S. N. Johnson and P. J. Murray, eds.). CAB International, Wallingford, Oxfordshire, UK.

Secoy, F. R. 1953. Changing military patterns on the Great Plains. Monogr., Amer. Ethnol. Soc. 21:1–112.

Seery, D. B., and D. J. Matiatos. 2000. Response of wintering buteos to plague epizootics in prairie dogs. Western N. Amer. Nat. 50:420–425.

Seidel, J., B. Andree, S. Berlinger, K. Buell, G. Byrne, B. Gill, D. Kenvin, and D. Reed. 1998. Draft strategy for the conservation and reestablishment of lynx and wolverine in the southern Rocky Mountains. Colorado Division of Wildlife, Fort Collins, 116 pp.

Seidel, J. W. 1977. Elk calving behavior in west central Colorado. Pp. 38–40, in Proc. Western States Elk Workshop, Colorado Division of Wildlife, Denver, 64 pp.

Seidensticker, J. C., IV, M. A. O'Connell, and A.J.T. Johnsingh. 1987. Virginia opossum. Pp. 247–263, in Wild furbearer management and conservation in North America (M. Novak, J. A. Baker, M. E. Obbard, and B. Malloch, eds.). Ontario Ministry of Natural Resources, Toronto, 1,150 pp.

Seidensticker, J. C., IV, M. G. Hornocker, W. V. Wiles, and J. P. Messick. 1973. Mountain lion social organization in the Idaho Primitive Area. Wildlife Monogr. 35:1–60.

Seidman, V. M., and C. J. Zabel. 2001. Bat activity along intermittent streams in northwestern California. J. Mamm. 82:738–747.

Selko, L. F. 1937. Food habits of Iowa skunks in the fall of 1936. J. Wildl. Mgmt. 1:70–76.

Selvig, K. A., and A. Halse. 1975. The ultrastructural localization of iron in rat incisor enamel. European J. Oral Sci. 83:88–95.

Sera, W. E., and C. N. Early. 2003. *Microtus montanus*. Mammalian Species 716:1–10.

Serbousek, M. R., and K. Geluso. 2009. Bats along the Republican River and its tributaries in southwestern Nebraska: distribution, abundance, and reproduction. Western N. Amer. Nat. 59:180–185.

Serfass, T. L., R. P. Brooks, J. M. Novak, P. E. Johns, and O. E. Rhodes, Jr. 1998. Genetic variation among populations of river otter in North America: considerations for reintroduction projects. J. Mamm. 79:736–746.

Sergeant, D. E., and D. H. Pimlott. 1959. Age determination in moose from sectioned incisor teeth. J. Wildl. Mgmt. 23:315–321.

Sergio, F., T. Caro, D. Brown, B. Clucas, J. Hunter, J. Ketchum, K. McHugh, and F. Hiraldo. 2008. Top predators as conservation tools: ecological rationale, assumptions, and efficacy. Annual Review of Ecol., Evol., and Syst. 39:1–19.

Servheen, C. 1999. Status and management of the grizzly bear in the lower 48 United States. Pp. 50–54, in Bears: status survey and conservation action plan (C. Servheen, S. Herrero, and B. Peyton, comps.). International Union for the Conservation of Nature/Species Survival Commission, Bear and Polar Bear Specialist Groups, Cambridge, UK, 319 pp.

Servheen, C., S. Herrero, and B. Peyton. 1999. Bears, status survey and conservation action plan. International Union for the Conservation of Nature, Gland, Switzerland, 310 pp.

Servheen, C., and R. Shoemaker. 2008. Delisting the Yellowstone grizzly bear, a lesson in cooperation, conservation, and monitoring. Yellowstone Sci. 16:25–29.

Seton, E. T. 1929. Lives of game animals. Doubleday, Doran and Co., Garden City, NY, 949 pp.

Severinghaus, C. W. 1949. Tooth development and wear as criteria of age in white-tailed deer. J. Wildl. Mgmt. 13:195–216.

Severson, K. E., and G. E. Plumb. 1998. Comparison of methods to estimate population densities of black-tailed prairie dogs. Wildlife Soc. Bull. 26:859–866.

Sexson, M. L., J. R. Choate, and R. A. Nicholson. 1981. Diet of pronghorn in western Kansas. J. Range Mgmt. 34:489–433.

Sexton, N. R., and S. C. Stewart. 2007. Understanding knowledge and perceptions of bats among residents of Fort Collins, Colorado. Open-File Report, USGS, 2007-1245:22 pp.

Shackleton, D. M. 1985. *Ovis canadensis*. Mammalian Species 230: 1–9.

Shadle, A. R. 1951. Laboratory copulations and gestations of porcupine, *Erethizon dorsatum*. J. Mamm. 32:219–221.

Shadle, A. R. 1952. Sexual maturity and first recorded copulation of a 16-month male porcupine, *Erethizon dorsatum epixanthum*. J. Mamm. 33:329–331.

Shadle, A. R., M. Smelzer, and M. Metz. 1946. The sex reactions of porcupines (*Erethizon d. dorsatum*) before and after copulation. J. Mamm. 27:116–121.

Shalaway, S., and C. N. Slobodchikoff. 1988. Seasonal change in the diet of prairie dogs. J. Mamm. 59:835–841.

Shankar, V., R. A. Bowen, A. D. Davis, C. E. Rupprecht, and T. J. O'Shea. 2004. Rabies in a captive colony of big brown bats (*Eptesicus fuscus*). J. Wildlife Diseases 40:403–413.

Shankar, V., L. A. Orciari, C. de Mattos, I. V. Kuzmin, W. J. Pape, T. J. O'Shea, and C. E. Rupprecht. 2005. Genetic divergence of rabies viruses from bat species of Colorado, USA. Vector-borne and Zoonotic Diseases 5:330–341.

Sharp, W. M., and L. H. Sharp. 1956. Nocturnal movements and behavior of wild raccoons at a winter feeding station. J. Mamm. 37:170–177.

Sharpe, V. A., B. Norton, and S. Donnelley, eds. 2001. Wolves and human communities: biology, politics, and ethics. Island Press, Washington, DC, 321 pp.

Shattil, W., and R. Rozinsky. 1990. Close to home: Colorado's urban wildlife. (F. R. Rhinehart and E. A. Webb, eds.). Denver Museum of Natural History and Colorado Urban Wildlife Partnership, Denver, 200 pp.

Shaw, J. H. 1998. Bison ecology: what we do and do not know. Pp. 113–120, in International Symposium on Bison Ecology and Management in North America (L. Irby and J. Knight, eds.). Montana State Univ., Bozeman, 395 pp.

Sheets, R. G., R. L. Linder, and R. B. Dahlgren. 1971. Burrow systems of prairie dogs in South Dakota. J. Mamm. 52:451–453.

Sheets, R. G., R. L. Linder, and R. B. Dahlgren. 1972. Food habits of two litters of black-footed ferrets in South Dakota. Amer. Midland Nat. 87:249–251.

Sheffield, S. R., and H. H. Thomas. 1997. *Mustela frenata*. Mammalian Species 570:1–9.

Shenk, T. 2001. Post-release monitoring of lynx: July 1, 2000–June 30, 2001. Job Progress Report, Colorado Division of Wildlife, Fort Collins, W-153-R-13:7–34.

Shenk, T. M. 2000. Post-release monitoring of reintroduced lynx. Wildlife Research Annual Report, Job Progress Report, Colorado Division of Wildlife, Fort Collins, W-153-R-13:29–46.

Shenk, T. M. 2002. Post-release monitoring of lynx reintroduced to Colorado. Wildlife Research Report, Job Progress Report, Colorado Division of Wildlife, Ft. Collins, WP-0670:7–34.

Shenk, T. M. 2003. Post-release monitoring of lynx reintroduced to Colorado. Wildlife Research Report, Interim Report—Preliminary results, Job Progress Report, Colorado Division of Wildlife, Fort Collins, WP-0670:21–29.

Shenk, T. M. 2004. Post-release monitoring of lynx reintroduced to Colorado. Wildlife Research Report, Job Progress Report, Colorado Division of Wildlife, Fort Collins, WP-0670:5–13.

Shenk, T. M. 2005. Post-release monitoring of lynx reintroduced to Colorado. Wildlife Research Report, Job Progress Report, Colorado Division of Wildlife, Fort Collins, WP-0670:1–22.

Shenk, T. M. 2007. Post-release monitoring of lynx reintroduced to Colorado. Wildlife Research Reports, Lynx Conservation. Colorado Division of Wildlife, Fort Collins, WP-0670:1–37.

Shenk, T. M. 2008. Post-release monitoring of lynx reintroduced to Colorado. Colorado Division of Wildlife, Wildlife Research Reports, 1–38.

Shenk, T. M., G. C. White, and K. P. Burnham. 1998. Sampling-variance effects on detecting density dependence from temporal trends in natural populations. Ecol. Monogr. 68: 445–463.

Sherburne, S. S., and J. A. Bissonette. 1993. Squirrel middens influence marten (*Martes americana*) use of subnivean access points. Amer. Midland Nat. 129:204–207.

Sherrod, S. K., and T. R. Seastedt. 2001. Effects of the northern pocket gopher (*Thomomys talpoides*) on alpine soil characteristics, Niwot Ridge, CO. Biogeochemistry 55:195–218.

Sherrod, S. K., T. R. Seastedt, and M. D. Walker. 2005. Northern pocket gopher (*Thomomys talpoides*) control of alpine plant community structure. Arctic, Antarctic, and Alpine Research 37:4:585–590.

Sherwin, R. E., and J. S. Altenbach. 2001. Success of bat gates. Pp. 165–173, in Proc. Bat Conservation and Mining: A Technical Interactive Forum (K. C. Vories and D. Throgmorton, eds.). U.S. Department of Interior, Office of Surface Mining, Alton, IL.

Sherwin, R. E., and W. L. Gannon. 2005. Documentation of an urban winter roost of the spotted bat (*Euderma maculatum*). Southwestern Nat. 50:402–407.

Sherwin, R. E., W. L. Gannon, and J. S. Altenbach. 2003. Managing complex systems simply: understanding inherent variation in the use of roosts by Townsend's big-eared bat. Wildl. Soc. Bull. 31:62–72.

Sherwin, R. E., W. L. Gannon, and S. Haymond. 2000. The efficacy of acoustic techniques to infer differential use of habitat by bats. Acta Chiropterologica 2:145–153.

Sherwin, R. E., D. Stricklan, and D. S. Rogers. 2000. Roosting affinities of Townsend's big-eared bat (*Corynorhinus townsendii*) in northern Utah. J. Mamm. 81:939–947.

Shick, K. R., D. E. Pearson, and L. F. Ruggiero. 2006. Forest habitat associations of the golden-mantled ground squirrel: implications for fuels management. Northwest Sci. 80:133–139.

Shieff, A., and J. A. Baker. 1987. Marketing and international fur markets. Pp. 862–877, in Wild furbearer management and conservation in North America (M. Novak, J. A. Baker, M. E. Obbard, and B. Malloch, eds.). Ontario Trappers Association, Toronto, 1,150 pp.

Shinneman, D., R. McClellan, and R. Smith. 2000. The state of the Southern Rockies ecoregion. Southern Rockies Ecosystem Project, Nederland, CO, 137 pp.

Shipley, B. K., and R. P. Reading. 2006. A comparison of herpetofauna and small mammal diversity on black-tailed prairie dog (*Cynomys ludovicianus*) colonies and non-colonized grasslands in Colorado. J. Arid Environments 66:27–41.

Shipley, B. K., R. P. Reading, and B. J. Miller. 2008. Capture rates of reptiles and amphibians on black-tailed prairie dog (*Cynomys ludovicianus*) colonies and on uncolonized prairie in Colorado. Western N. Amer. Nat. 58:245–248.

Shipman, P. 2009. The woof at the door. Amer. Sci. 97:286–289.

Shirer, H. W., and H. S. Fitch. 1970. Comparison from radiotracking of movements and denning habits of the raccoon, striped skunk, and opossum in northeastern Kansas. J. Mamm. 51:491–503.

Shivik, J. A., M. M. Jaeger, and R. H. Barrett. 1996. Coyote movements in relation to the spatial distribution of sheep. J. Wildl. Mgmt. 50:422–430.

Shriner, W. M. 1998. Yellow-bellied marmot and golden-mantled ground squirrel responses to heterospecific alarm calls. Animal Behavior 55:529–536.

Shriner, W. M., and P. B. Stacey. 1991. Spatial relationships and dispersal patterns in the rock squirrel, *Spermophilus variegatus*. J. Mamm. 72:601–606.

Shubin, N. 2008. Your inner fish, a journey into the 3.5-billion-year history of the human body. Pantheon Books, New York, 220 pp.

Shump, K. A., Jr. 1978. Ecological importance of nest construction in the hispid cotton rat (*Sigmodon hispidus*). Amer. Midland Nat. 100:103–115.

Shump, K. A., Jr., and D. P. Christian. 1978. Differential burrowing by hispid cotton rats (*Sigmodon hispidus*: Rodentia). Southwestern Nat. 23:681–709.

Shump, K. A., Jr., and A. U. Shump. 1982a. *Lasiurus cinereus*. Mammalian Species 185:1–5.

Shump, K. A., Jr., and A. U. Shump. 1982b. *Lasiurus borealis*. Mammalian Species 183:1–6.

Siders, M. S., and W. Jolley. 2009. Roost sites of Allen's lappet-browed bats (*Idionycteris phyllotis*). Southwestern Nat. 54: 201–203.

Siemers, J. L. 2002. A survey of Colorado's caves for bats. Colorado Natural Heritage Program, Colorado State Univ., Fort Collins, 18 pp.

Siemers, J. L., Y. R. Chen, K. M. Canestorp, J. R. Sovell, and K. L. Cornelisse. 2006. Range expansion of the least shrew (*Cryptotis parva*) in Colorado. Southwestern Nat. 551:267–269.

Siemers, J. L., and R. A. Schorr. 2006. Distributional survey of rare small mammals (orders Insectivora, Chiroptera, and Rodentia) in Colorado: year two. Colorado Natural Heritage Program, Colorado State Univ., Fort Collins, 28 pp.

Siemers, J. L., and R. A. Schorr. 2007a. Distributional survey of rare small mammals (orders Insectivora, Chiroptera, and Rodentia) in Colorado: year three. Colorado Natural Heritage Program, Colorado State Univ., Fort Collins, 30 pp.

Siemers, J. L., and R. A. Schorr. 2007b. Small mammal atlas project (2002–2007): review and recommendations. Colorado Natural Heritage Program, Colorado State Univ., Fort Collins, 25 pp.

Siemers, J. L., R. A. Schorr, and A. C. Rinker. 2003. Distributional survey of rare small mammals (orders Insectivora, Chiroptera, and Rodentia) in Colorado: year one. Colorado Natural Heritage Program, Colorado State Univ., Fort Collins, 21 pp.

Sikes, R. S. 1995. Costs of lactation and optimal litter size in northern grasshopper mice (*Onychomys leucogaster*). J. Mamm. 76: 348–357.

Sikes, R. S. 1996. Tactics of maternal investment of northern grasshopper mice in response to postnatal restriction of food. J. Mamm. 77:1092–1101.

Sikorowski, L., J. Smeltzer, and M. J. Manfredo. 1998. Wildlife management in Colorado: the past, the present, and predictions of the future. Trans. North American Wildl. and Nat. Resources Conf. 53:257–267.

Silver, J., and A. W. Moore. 1941. Mole control. Fish and Wildlife Bulletin, U.S. Dept. of Interior 16:1–17.

Silver, L. M. 1995. Mouse genetics: concepts and applications. Oxford Univ. Press, New York, 376 pp.

Simmons, N. B. 2005a. Chiroptera. Pp. 159–174, in The rise of placental mammals, origins and relationships of the major extant clades (K. D. Rose and J. D. Archibald, eds.). Johns Hopkins Univ. Press, Baltimore, 259 pp.

Simmons, N. B. 2005b. Order Chiroptera. Pp. 312–529, in Mammal species of the world, a taxonomic and geographic reference, third ed. (D. E. Wilson and D. M. Reeder, eds.), 2 vols. Johns Hopkins Univ. Press, Baltimore.

Simmons, N. B., K. L. Seymour, J. Haberstetzer, and G. F. Gunnell. 2008. Primitive Early Eocene bat from Wyoming and the evolution of flight and echolocation. Nature 451:818–821.

Simmons, N. M. 1961. Daily and seasonal movements of Poudre River bighorn sheep. Unpubl. master's thesis, Colorado State Univ., Fort Collins, 180 pp.

Simms, D. A. 1979a. North American weasels: resource utilization and distribution. Canadian J. Zool. 57:504–520.

Simms, D. A. 1979b. Studies on an ermine population in southern Ontario. Canadian J. Zool. 57:824–832.

Simons, L. H., R. C. Szaro, and S. C. Belfit. 1990. Distribution of *Notiosorex crawfordi* and *Sorex arizonae* along an elevational gradient. J. Mamm. 71:634–640.

Simpson, G. G. 1945. The principles of classification and a classification of mammals. Bull. Amer. Mus. Nat. Hist. 85:1–350.

Simpson, G. G. 1951. Horses: the story of the horse family in the modern world and through sixty million years of history. Oxford Univ. Press, Oxford, UK.

Simpson, M. R. 1993. *Myotis californicus*. Mammalian Species 428: 1–4.

Singer, F. J., A. Harting, K. K. Symonds, and M. B. Coughenaur. 1997. Density dependence, compensation, and environmental effects on elk calf mortality in Yellowstone National Park. J. Wildl. Mgmt. 51:12–25.

Singer, F. J., E. S. Williams, M. W. Miller, and L. C. Zeigenfuss. 2000. Population growth, fecundity, and survivorship in recovering populations of bighorn sheep. Restoration Ecology 8:75–84.

Singer, F. J., and L. C. Zeigenfuss. 2002. Influence of trophy hunting and horn size on mating behavior and survivorship of mountain sheep. J. Mamm. 83:682–698.

Singer, F. J., L. C. Zeigenfuss, B. Lubow, and M. J. Rock. 2002. Ecological evaluation of ungulate overabundance in U.S. national parks: a case study. Pp. 205–248, in Ecological evaluation of the abundance and effects of elk herbivory in Rocky Mountain National Park, Colorado, 1994–1999. Open File Report 02-208. Final report to the National Park Service, Rocky Mountain National Park, Estes Park, CO.

Sinha, A. A., and R. A. Mead. 1976. Morphological changes in the trophoblast, uterus and corpus luteum during delayed implantation and implantation in the western spotted skunk. Amer. J. Anat. 145:331–356.

Skryja, D. D. 1974. Reproductive biology of the least chipmunk (*Eutamias minimus operarius*) in southeastern Wyoming. J. Mamm. 55:221–224.

Skryja, D. D., and T. W. Clark. 1970. Reproduction, seasonal changes in body weight, fat deposition, spleen and adrenal gland weight of the golden-mantled ground squirrel *Spermophilus lateralis lateralis* in the Laramie Mountains, Wyoming. Southwestern Nat. 15:201–208.

Skupski, M. P. 1995. Population ecology of the western harvest mouse, *Reithrodontomys megalotis*: a long-term perspective. J. Mamm. 76:358–367.

Slade, L. M., and E. B. Godfrey. 1982. Wild horses. Pp. 1089–1098, in Wild mammals of North America, biology, management, and economics (J. A. Chapman and G. A. Feldhamer, eds.). Johns Hopkins Univ. Press, Baltimore, 1,147 pp.

Sleeper, R. A., A. A. Spencer, and H. W. Steinhoff. 1976. Effects of varying snowpack on small mammals. Pp. 437–489, in Ecological impacts of snowpack augmentation in the San Juan Mountains, Colorado (H. W. Steinhoff and J. D. Ives, eds.). Colorado State Univ. Publ., Fort Collins, 487 pp.

Slobodchikoff, C. N. 2002. The language of prairie dogs. Plateau 6:30–38.

Slobodchikoff, C. N., S. H. Ackers, and M. Van Ert. 1998. Geographical variation in prairie dog alarm calls. J. Mamm. 79:1265–1272.

Slobodchikoff, C. N., J. Kiriazis, C. Fischer, and E. Creef. 1991. Semantic information distinguishing individual predators in the alarm calls of Gunnison's prairie dogs. Animal Behav. 42:713–719.

Slobodchikoff, C. N., and J. Placer. 2006. Acoustic structures in the alarm calls of Gunnison's prairie dogs. J. Acoustic. Soc. Amer. 119:3153–3160.

Slobodchikoff, C. N., A. Robinson, and C. Schaack. 1988. Habitat use by Gunnison's prairie dogs. Pp. 403–408, in Management of amphibians, reptiles, and small mammals in North America (R. C. Szaro, K. E. Severson, and D. R. Patton, tech. coords.). Gen, Tech. Rept., U.S. Forest Service, RM-166:1–458.

Slobodchikoff, C. N., T. A. Vaughan, and R. Warner. 1987. How prey defenses affect a predator's net energetic profit. J. Mamm. 58:668–671.

Slough, B. G. 1978. Beaver food cache structure and utilization. J. Wildl. Mgmt. 42:644–646.

Smallwood, K. S., and M. L. Morrison. 1999a. Spatial scaling of pocket gopher (Geomyidae) density. Southwestern Nat. 44: 73–82.

Smallwood, K. S., and M. L. Morrison. 1999b. Estimating burrow volume and excavation rate of pocket gophers (Geomyidae). Southwestern Nat. 44:173–182.

Smartt, R. A. 1978. A comparison of ecological and morphological overlap in a *Peromyscus* community. Ecology 59:216–220.

Smith, A. T., N. A. Formozov, R. S. Hoffmann, Z. Changlin, and M. A. Erbajeva. 1990. The pikas. Pp. 14–60, in Rabbits, hares and pikas, status survey and conservation action plan (J. A. Chapman and J.E.C. Flux, eds.). IUNC/SSC Lagomorph Specialist Group, Gland, Switzerland, 168 pp.

Smith, A. T., and B. L. Ivins. 1983. Colonization in a pika population: dispersal versus philopatry. Behavioral Ecology and Sociobiology 13:37–47.

Smith, A. T., and B. L. Ivins. 1984. Spatial relationships and social organization in adult pikas: a facultatively monogamous mammal. Zeitschrift für Tierpsychologie 66:289–308.

Smith, A. T., and M. L. Weston. 1990. *Ochotona princeps*. Mammalian Species 352:1–8.

Smith, B. L. 1988. Criteria for determining age and sex of American mountain goats in the field. J. Mamm. 59:395–402.

Smith, B. L. 2001. Winter feeding of elk in North America. J. Wildl. Mgmt. 55:173–190.

Smith, B. L., R. L. Robbins, and S. H. Anderson. 1996. Adaptive sex ratios: another example? J. Mamm. 77:818–825.

Smith, C. C. 1968. The adaptive nature of social organization in the genus of three (*sic*) squirrels *Tamiasciurus*. Ecol. Monogr. 38:31–63.

Smith, C. C. 1970. The coevolution of pine squirrels (*Tamiasciurus*) and conifers. Ecological Monogr. 40:349–371.

Smith, D. R. 1954. The bighorn sheep in Idaho, its status, life history, and management. Wildl. Bull., Idaho Dept. Fish and Game 1:1–154.

Smith, D. W. 2005. Ten years of Yellowstone wolves, 1995–2005. Yellowstone Sci. 13:7–33.

Smith, D. W., and E. Almberg. 2007. Wolf diseases in Yellowstone National Park. Yellowstone Sci. 15:17–19.

Smith, D. W., T. D. Drummer, K. M. Murphy, D. S. Guernsey, and S. B. Evans. 2004. Winter prey selection and estimation of wolf kill rates in Yellowstone National Park, 1995–2000. J. Wildl. Mgmt. 58:153–166.

Smith, D. W., and G. Ferguson. 2005. Decade of the wolf: Returning the wild to Yellowstone. Lyons Press, Guilford, CT, 256 pp.

Smith, D. W., L. D. Mech, M. Meagher, W. E. Clark, R. Jaffe, M. K. Phillips, and J. A. Mack. 2000. Wolf-bison interactions in Yellowstone National Park. J. Mamm. 81:1128–1135.

Smith, D. W., R. O. Peterson, and D. B. Houston. 2003. Yellowstone after wolves. BioScience 53:330–340.

Smith, F. A. 1995. Den characteristics and survivorship of woodrats (*Neotoma lepida*) in the eastern Mojave Desert. Southwestern Nat. 40:366–372.

Smith, F. A. 1997. *Neotoma cinerea*. Mammalian Species 564:1–8.

Smith, F. A., J. L. Betancourt, and J. H. Brown. 1995. Evolution of body size in the woodrat over the past 25,000 years of climate change. Science 270:2012–2014.

Smith, F. A., H. Browning, and U. L. Shepherd. 1998. The influence of climate change on the body mass of woodrats (*Neotoma*) in an arid region of New Mexico, USA. Ecography 21:140–148.

Smith, G. W. 1990. Home range and activity patterns of black-tailed jackrabbits. Great Basin Nat. 50:249–256.

Smith, H. D., and C. D. Jorgensen. 1975. Reproductive biology of North American desert rodents. Pp. 305–330, in Rodents in desert environments (I. Prakash and P. K. Ghosh, eds.). Dr. W. Junk, The Hague, Netherlands, 640 pp.

Smith, L. 1941. An observation on the nest-building behavior of the opossum. J. Mamm. 22:201–202.

Smith, M. E., and M. C. Belk. 1996. *Sorex monticolus*. Mammalian Species 528:1–5.

Smith, M. F. 1998. Phylogenetic relationships and geographic structure in pocket gophers of the genus *Thomomys*. Molecular Phylogenetics and Evol. 9:1–14.

Smith, M. F., J. L. Patton, J. C. Hafner, and D. J. Hafner. 1983. *Thomomys bottae* pocket gophers of the central Rio Grande Valley, New Mexico: local differentiation, gene flow, and historical biogeography. Occas. Papers Mus. Southwestern Biol. 2:1–16.

Smith, M. H., K. T. Scribner, L. H. Carpenter, and R. A. Garrott. 1990. Genetic characteristics of Colorado mule deer (*Odocoileus hemionus*) and comparisons with other cervids. Southwestern Nat. 35:1–8.

Smith, R. E. 1958. Natural history of the prairie dog in Kansas. Misc. Publ., Univ. Kansas Mus. Nat. Hist. 16:1–36.

Smith, R. J. 1995. Harvest rates and escape speeds in two coexisting species of montane ground squirrels. J. Mamm. 76:189–195.

Smith, R. L., D. J. Hubartt, and R. L. Shoemaker. 1980. Seasonal changes in weight, cecal length, and pancreatic function in snowshoe hares. J. Wildl. Mgmt. 44:719–724.

Smith, S. J., D. M. Leslie, Jr., M. J. Hamilton, J. B. Lack, and R. A. Van Den Bussche. 2008. Subspecific affinities and conservation genetics of western big-eared bats (*Corynorhinus townsendii pallescens*) at the edge of their distributional range. J. Mamm. 89:799–814.

Smith, W. P. 1991. *Odocoileus virginianus*. Mammalian Species 388: 1–13.

Smith, W. P. 2007. The northern flying squirrel: biological portrait of a forest specialist in post–European settlement North America. J. Mamm. 88:837–839.

Smith, W. P., R. G. Anthony, J. R. Waters, Norris L. Dodd, and C. J. Zabel. 2003. Ecology and conservation of arboreal rodents in western coniferous forests. Pp. 157–206, in Mammal community dynamics, management and conservation in the coniferous forests of western North America (C. J. Zabel and R. G. Anthony, eds.). Cambridge Univ. Press, Cambridge, UK, 709 pp.

Smolen, M. J., H. H. Genoways, and R. J. Baker. 1980. Demographic and reproductive parameters of the yellow-cheeked pocket gopher (*Pappogeomys castanops*). J. Mamm. 51:224–226.

Smolen, M. J., and B. L. Keller. 1987. *Microtus longicaudus*. Mammalian Species 271:1–7.

Snyder, D. P. 1956. Survival rate, longevity, and population fluctuation in the white footed mouse, *Peromyscus leucopus*, in southwestern Michigan. Misc. Publ. Mus. Zool., Univ. Michigan 95:1–33.

Snyder, M. A. 1992. Selective herbivory by Abert's squirrel mediated by chemical variability in ponderosa pine. Ecology 73:1730–1741.

Snyder, M. A. 1998. Abert's squirrels (*Sciurus aberti*) in ponderosa pine (*Pinus ponderosa*) forests: directional selection, diversifying selection. Pp. 195–201, in Ecology and evolutionary biology of tree squirrels (M. A. Steele, J. F. Merritt, and D. A. Zegers, eds.). Spec. Publ. Virginia Mus. Nat. Hist. 5:1–310.

Snyder, M. A., and Y. B. Linhart. 1994. Nest-site selection by Abert's squirrel: chemical characteristics of nest trees. J. Mamm. 75:136–141.

Snyder, M. A., and Y. B. Linhart. 1997. Porcupine feeding patterns: selectivity by a generalist herbivore? Canadian J. Zool. 75:2107–2111.

Solounias, N. 2007. Family Bovidae. Pp. 278–291, in The evolution of artiodactyls (D. R. Prothero and S. E. Foss, eds.). Johns Hopkins Univ. Press, Baltimore, 367 pp.

Somers, P. 1973. Dialects in southern Rocky Mountain pikas, *Ochotona princeps* (Lagomorpha). Animal Behavior 21:124–137.

Somers, P., D. D. Hanna, M. Colyer, and M. K. Floyd. 2003. Mammals of the old-growth piñon-juniper, Pp. 111–130, in Ancient piñon-juniper woodlands, a natural history of Mesa Verde Country (Floyd, M. L., D. D. Hanna, W. H. Romme, and M. Colyer, eds.). Univ. Press Colorado, Boulder, 389 pp.

Soper, J. D. 1919. Notes on Canadian weasels. Canadian Field-Nat. 33:43–47.

Soper, J. D. 1941. History, range, and home life of the northern bison. Ecol. Monogr. 11:349–412.

Sorenson, M. W. 1962. Some aspects of water shrew behavior. Amer. Midland Nat. 58:445–462.

Southwick, C. H., S. C. Golian, M. R. Whitworth, J. C. Halfpenny, and R. Brown. 1986. Population density and fluctuations of pikas (*Ochotona princeps*) in Colorado. J. Mamm. 57:149–153.

Sovada, M. A., and L. Carbyn, eds. 2003. The swift fox: ecology and conservation of swift foxes in a changing world. Canadian Plains Research Center, Regina, Saskatchewan, 250 pp.

Sovada, M. A., C. C. Roy, J. B. Bright, and J. R. Gillis. 1998. Causes and rates of mortality of swift foxes in western Kansas. J. Wildl. Mgmt. 52:1300–1306.

Sovada, M. A., C. C. Roy, and D. J. Telesco. 2001. Seasonal food habits of swift fox (*Vulpes velox*) in cropland and rangeland landscapes in western Kansas. Amer. Midland Nat. 145:101–111.

Sovell, J. R., B. A. Wunder, P. M. Lukacs, J. P. Gionfriddo, and J. L. Siemers. 2004. Population parameters and fat composition of small mammals on Pueblo Chemical Depot (2000–2003). Colorado Natural Heritage Program, Colorado State Univ., Fort Collins.

Sparks, D. R. 1968. Diet of black-tailed jackrabbits on sandhill rangeland in Colorado. J. Range Mgmt. 21:203–208.

Sparks, D. W., and J. R. Choate. 2000. Distribution, natural history, conservation status, and biogeography of bats in Kansas. Pp. 173–228, in Reflections of a naturalist: papers honoring Professor Eugene D. Fleharty (J. Choate, ed.). Fort Hays Studies, Spec. Issue 1:1–241.

Sparks, D. W., K. J. Roberts, and C. Jones. 2000. Vertebrate predators on bats in North America north of Mexico. Pp. 229–441, in Reflections of a naturalist: papers honoring Professor Eugene D. Fleharty (J. Choate, ed.). Fort Hays Studies, Spec. Issue 1, 241 pp.

Spector, S. 2002. Biogeographic crossroads as priority areas for biodiversity conservation. Cons. Biol. 16:1480–1487.

Spencer, A. W. 1966. Identification of the dwarf shrew, *Sorex nanus*. J. Colorado-Wyoming Acad. Sci. 5:89.

Spencer, A. W. 1975. Additional records of *Sorex nanus* and *Sorex merriami* in Colorado. J. Colorado-Wyoming Acad. Sci. 7:48.

Spencer, A. W., and D. Pettus. 1966. Habitat preferences of five sympatric species of long-tailed shrews. Ecology 47:677–683.

Spencer, A. W., and H. W. Steinhoff. 1968. An explanation of geographic variation in litter size. J. Mamm. 49:281–286.

Spencer, D. L. 1968. Sympatry and hybridization of the eastern and southern plains wood rats. Unpubl. doctoral dissert., Oklahoma State Univ., Stillwater, 85 pp.

Spencer, W. D., R. H. Barrett, and W. J. Zielinski. 1983. Marten habitat preferences in the northern Sierra Nevada. J. Wildl. Mgmt. 47:1181–1186.

Spowart, R. A., and N. T. Hobbs. 1985. Effects of fire on diet overlap between mule deer and mountain sheep. J. Wildl. Mgmt. 49:942–946.

Spraker, T. R., M. W. Miller, E. S. Williams, D. M. Getzy, W. J. Adrian, G. G. Schoonveld, R. A. Spowart, K. I. O'Rourke, J. M. Miller, and P. A. Merz. 1997. Spongiform encephalopathy in free ranging mule deer (*Odocoileus hemionus*), white-tailed deer (*Odocoileus virginianus*), and Rocky Mountain elk (*Cervus elaphus nelsoni*) in northcentral Colorado. J. Wildl. Dis. 33:1–6.

Squires, J. R., J. P. Copeland, T. J. Ulizio, M. K. Schwartz, and L. F. Ruggiero. 2007. Sources and patterns of wolverine mortality in western Montana. J. Wildl. Mgmt. 71:2213–2220.

Squires, J. R., and T. Laurion. 2000. Lynx home range and movements in Montana and Wyoming: preliminary results. Pp. 337–349, in Ecology and conservation of lynx in the United States (L. F. Ruggiero, K. B. Aubry, S. W. Buskirk, G. M. Koehler, C. J. Krebs, K. S. McKelvey, and J. R. Squires, eds.). Univ. Press Colorado, Boulder, 480 pp.

Stadelmann, B., L. G. Herrera, J. Arroyo-Cabrales, J. J. Flores-Martínez, B. P. May, and M. Ruedi. 2004. Molecular systematics of the fishing bat *Myotis (Pizonyx) vivesi*. J. Mamm. 85:133–139.

Stains, H. J. 1956. The raccoon in Kansas: natural history, management, and economic importance. Misc. Publ. Mus. Nat. Hist., Univ. Kansas 10:1–76.

Stalheim, W. 1965. Some aspects of the natural history of the rock squirrel, *Citellus variegatus*. Unpubl. master's thesis, Univ. New Mexico, Albuquerque, 55 pp.

Stalling, D. T. 1990. *Microtus ochrogaster*. Mammalian Species 355: 1–9.

Stanford, D. 1974. Preliminary report of the excavations of the Jones-Miller Hell Gap Site, Yuma County, Colorado. Southwestern Lore 40(3–4):29–36.

Stanford, D. 1975. The 1975 excavations at the Jones-Miller Site, Yuma County, Colorado. Southwestern Lore 41(4):34–38.

Stanford, D. J., and J. S. Day, eds. 1992. Ice Age hunters of the Rockies. Denver Mus. Nat. Hist., Denver, and Univ. Press Colorado, Niwot, 378 pp.

Stangl, F. B., Jr., and R. J. Baker. 1984. A chromosomal subdivision of *Peromyscus leucopus*: implication for the subspecies concept as applied to mammals. Pp. 139–1245, in Festschrift for Walter W. Dalquest in honor of his sixty-sixth birthday (N. V. Horner, ed.). Dept. Biology, Midwestern State Univ., Wichita Falls, TX, 163 pp.

Stangl, F. B., Jr., R. D. Owen, and D. E. Morris-Fuller. 1991. Cranial variation and asymmetry in southern populations of the porcupine, *Erethizon dorsatum*. Texas J. Sci. 32:237–259.

Stanley, W. C. 1963. Habits of the red fox in northeastern Kansas. Misc. Publ., Univ. Kansas Mus. Nat. Hist. 34:1–31.

Stapp. P. 1997a. Community structure of shortgrass-prairie rodents: competition or risk of intraguild predation? Ecology 78:1519–1530.

Stapp, P. 1997b. Habitat selection by an insectivorous rodent: patterns and mechanisms across multiple scales. J. Mamm. 78:1128–1143.

Stapp, P. 1998. A reevaluation of the role of prairie dogs in Great Plains grasslands. Cons. Biol. 12:1253–1259.

Stapp, P. 1999. Size and habitat characteristics of home ranges of northern grasshopper mice (*Onychomys leucogaster*). Southwestern Nat. 44:101–105.

Stapp, P. 2007. Rodent communities in active and inactive colonies of black-tailed prairie dogs in shortgrass steppe. J. Mamm. 88:241–249.

Stapp, P., and M. F. Antolin, and M. Ball. 2004. Patterns of extinction in prairie dog metapopulations: plague outbreaks follow El Niño events. Frontiers Ecol. Environ. 2:235–240.

Stapp, P., and M. D. Lindquist. 2007. Roadside foraging by kangaroo rats in a grazed short-grass prairie landscape. Western N. Amer. Nat. 57:368–377.

Stapp, P., D. J. Salkeld, R. J. Eisen, R. Pappert, J. Young, L. G. Carter, K. L. Gage, D. W. Tripp, and M. F. Antolin. 2008. Exposure of small rodents to plague during epizootics in black-tailed prairie dogs. J. Wildl. Dis. 44:724–740.

Stapp, P., and B. Van Horne. 1997. Response of deer mice (*Peromyscus maniculatus*) to shrubs in shortgrass prairie: linking small-scale movements and the spatial distribution of individuals. Functional Ecol. 11:644–651.

Stapp, P., B. Van Horne, and M. D. Lindquist. 2008. Ecology of mammals of the shortgrass steppe. Pp. 132–180, in Ecology of the shortgrass steppe, a long-term perspective (W. K. Lauenroth and I. C. Burke, eds.). Oxford Univ. Press, New York. 528 pp.

Stapp, P., J. K. Young, S. VandeWoude, and B. Van Horne. 1994. An evaluation of the pathological effects of fluorescent powder on deer mice (*Peromyscus maniculatus*). J. Mamm. 75:704–709.

Stapp, P. T. 1996. Determinants of habitat use and community structure of rodents in northern shortgrass steppe. Unpubl. doctoral dissert., Colorado State Univ., Fort Collins, 145 pp.

Starrett, A., and P. Starrett. 1956. Merriam shrew, *Sorex merriami*, in Colorado. J. Mamm. 37:276.

States, J. S., W. S. Gaud, W. S. Allred, and W. J. Austin. 1988. Foraging patterns of tassel-eared squirrels in selected ponderosa pine stands. Pp. 425–431, in Management of amphibians, reptiles, and small mammals in North America (R. C. Szaro, K. E. Severson, and D. R. Patton, tech. coords.). General Tech. Rept., Rocky Mountain Forest and Range Experiment Station, USDA, RM-166:1–458.

States, J. S., and P. J. Wettstein. 1998. Food habits and evolutionary relationships of the tassel-eared squirrel (*Sciurus aberti*). Pp. 185–194, in Ecology and evolutionary biology of tree squirrels (M. A. Steele, J. F. Merritt, and D. A. Zegers, eds.). Virginia Museum of Natural History Special Publication 6, Martinsville.

Steele, M. A. 1998. Tamiasciurus hudsonicus. Mammalian Species 586:1–9.

Steele, M. A., J. F. Merritt, and D. A. Zegers, eds. 1998. Ecology and evolutionary biology of tree squirrels. Spec. Publ., Virginia Mus. Nat. Hist. 5:1–320.

Steiner, A. L. 1975. Bedding and nesting material gathering in rock squirrels, *Spermophilus (Otospermophilus) variegatus grammurus* (Say) (Sciuridae) in the Chiricahua Mountains of Arizona. Southwestern Nat. 20:363–370.

Steinert, S. F., H. D. Riffel, and G. C. White. 1994. Comparisons of big game harvest estimates from check station and telephone surveys. J. Wildl. Mgmt. 58:335–340.

Stephens, R. M., and S. H. Anderson. 2005. Swift fox (*Vulpes velox*): a technical conservation assessment. Species Conservation Project, Rocky Mountain Region, USDA Forest Service, 45 pp.

Stephenson, A. B. 1969. Temperatures within a beaver lodge in winter. J. Mamm. 50:134–136.

Stephenson, R. L., and D. E. Brown. 1980. Snow cover as a factor influencing mortality of Abert's squirrels. J. Wildl. Mgmt. 44:951–955.

Stephenson, T. R., M. R. Vaughan, and D. Andersen. 1996. Mule deer movements in response to military activity in southeast Colorado. J. Wildl. Mgmt. 50:777–787.

Sterling, K. B. 1974. The last of the naturalists: the career of C. Hart Merriam. Arno Press, New York, 488 pp.

Sterner, R. T., and S. A. Shumake. 1978. Coyote damage-control research: a review and analysis. Pp. 297–325, in Coyotes: biology, behavior, and management (M. Bekoff, ed.). Academic Press, New York, 384 pp.

Sterner, R. T., B. E. Petersen, S. E. Gaddis, K. L. Tope, and D. J. Poss. 2003. Impacts of small mammals and birds on low-tillage, dryland crops. Crop Protection 22:595–602.

Steuter, A. A., E. M. Steinauer, G. L. Hill, P. A. Bowers, and L. L. Tieszen. 1995. Distribution and diet of bison and pocket gophers in a sandhills prairie. Ecol. Appl. 5:756–766.

Stevens, D. R. 1974. Rocky Mountain elk–Shiras moose range relationships. Naturaliste Canadienne 101:505–516.

Stevens, G. C., and J. F. Fox. 1991. The causes of treeline. Ann. Rev. Ecol. and Syst. 22:177–191.

Stevens, R., and S. C. Walker. 1998. Species establishment and community changes on bison range restoration projects, Henry Mountains, Utah. Pp. 121–129, in International Symposium on Bison Ecology and Management in North America (L. Irby and J. Knight, eds.). Montana State Univ., Bozeman, 395 pp.

Stevens, R. T., T. L. Ashwood, and J. M. Sleeman. 1997. Fall-early winter home ranges, movements, and den use of male mink, *Mustela vison,* in eastern Tennessee. Canadian Field-Nat. 111:312–314.

Stevens, R. T., and M. L. Kennedy. 2006. Geographic variation in body size of American mink (*Mustela vison*). Mammalia 70:145–152.

Stewart, K. M., R. T. Bowyer, J. G. Kie, N. J. Cimon, and B. K. Johnson. 2002. Temporospatial distributions of elk, mule deer, and cattle: resource partitioning and competitive displacement. J. Mamm. 83:229–244.

Stickel, L. F. 1968. Home range and travels. Pp. 373–411, in Biology of *Peromyscus* (Rodentia) (J. H. King, ed.). Spec. Publ., Amer. Soc. Mammalogists 2:1–593.

Stiger, M. 2001. Hunter-gatherer archaeology of the Colorado high country. Univ. Press Colorado, 317 pp.

Stillman, D. 2008. Mustang, the saga of the wild horse in the American West. Houghton Mifflin, New York, 348 pp.

Stinson, N., Jr. 1977a. Species diversity, resource partitioning, and demography of small mammals in a subalpine deciduous forest. Unpubl. doctoral dissert., Univ. Colorado, Boulder, 238 pp.

Stinson, N., Jr. 1977b. Home range of the western jumping mouse, *Zapus princeps*, in the Colorado Rocky Mountains. Great Basin Nat. 37:87–90.

Stinson, N., Jr. 1978. Habitat structure and rodent species diversity on north- and south-facing slopes in the Colorado lower montane zone. Southwestern Nat. 23:77–84.

Stockrahm, D.M.B., and R. W. Seabloom. 1988. Comparative reproductive performance of black-tailed prairie dog populations in North Dakota. J. Mamm. 59:160–164.

Stoddard, J. L. 1920. Nests of the western fox squirrel. J. Mamm. 1:122–123.

Stoddart, L. C. 1985. Severe weather related mortality of black-tailed jack rabbits. J. Wildl. Mgmt. 49:696–698.

Stoecker, R. 1976. Pocket gopher distribution in relation to snow in the alpine tundra. Pp. 281–287, in Ecological impacts of snowpack augmentation in the San Juan Mountains, Colorado (H. W. Steinhoff and J. D. Ives, eds.). Colorado State Univ. Publ., Fort Collins, 487 pp.

Stoecker, R. E. 1970. An analysis of sympatry in two species of *Microtus*. Unpubl. doctoral dissert., Univ. Colorado, Boulder, 58 pp.

Stohlgren, T. J., T. T. Veblen, K. C. Kendall, W. L. Baker, C. D. Allen, J. A. Logan, and K. C. Ryan. 2002. The heart of the Rockies: montane and subalpine ecosystems. Pp. 203–218, in Rocky Mountain futures, an ecological perspective (J. S. Baron, ed.). Island Press, Washington, DC, 325 pp.

Stone, R. 1993. The mouse–piñon nut connection. Science 262: 833.

Stone, S. A., N. Fascione, C. Miller J. Pissot, G. Schrader, and J. Timberlake. 2008. Livestock and wolves, a guide to nonlethal tools and methods to reduce conflicts. Defenders of Wildlife, Washington, DC, 23 pp.

Stones, R. C., and C. L. Hayward. 1968. Natural history of the desert woodrat *Neotoma lepida*. Amer. Midland Nat. 80:458–476.

Storch, G., and G. Richter. 1988. Der Ameisenbär *Eurotamandua,* ein "Sudamerikaner" in Europa. Pp. 211–215, in Messel—ein Schaufenster in die Geschichte der Erde und des Lebens (S. Schaal and E. Ziegler, eds.). Waldemar Kramer, Frankfurt am Main, 315 pp.

Storm, G. L. 1965. Movements and activities of foxes as determined by radio tracking. J. Wildl. Mgmt. 29:1–12.

Storm, G. L. 1972. Daytime retreats and movements of skunks on farmlands in Illinois. J. Wildl. Mgmt. 36:31–45.

Storm, G. L., R. D. Andrews, R. L. Phillips, R. A. Bishop, D. B. Siniff, and J. R. Tester. 1976. Morphology, reproduction, dispersal, and mortality of midwestern red fox populations. Wildl. Monogr. 49:1–82.

Storz, J. F. 1995. Local distribution and foraging behavior of the spotted bat (*Euderma maculatum*) in northwestern Colorado and adjacent Utah. Great Basin Nat. 55:78–83.

Storz, J. F. 2002. Contrasting patterns of divergence between quantitative traits and neutral DNA markers: analysis of clinal variation. Molec. Ecol. 11:2537–2551.

Storz, J. F., and J. M. Dubach. 2004. Natural selection drives altitudinal divergence at the albumin locus in deer mice, *Peromyscus maniculatus*. Evolution 58:1342–1352.

Storz, J. F., and M. W. Nachman. 2003. Natural selection on protein polymorphism in the rodent genus *Peromyscus*: evidence from interlocus contrasts. Evolution 57:2628–2635.

Storz, J. F., and C. F. Williams. 1996. Summer population structure of subalpine bats in Colorado. Southwestern Nat. 41:322–324.

Strait, S. G., and S. C. Smith. 2006. Elemental analysis of soricine enamel: pigmentation variation and distribution in molars of *Blarina brevicauda*. J. Mamm. 87:700–705.

Streeter, R. G. 1969. Demography of two Rocky Mountain bighorn sheep populations in Colorado. Unpubl. doctoral dissert., Colorado State Univ., Fort Collins, 96 pp.

Streeter, R. G. 1970. A literature review on bighorn sheep population dynamics. Spec. Rept., Colorado Division of Game, Fish, and Parks 24:8–11.

Streeter, R. G., and C. E. Braun. 1968. Occurrence of pine marten, *Martes americana* (Carnivora: Mustelidae), in Colorado alpine areas. Southwestern Nat. 13:449–451.

Streubel, D. P. 1975. Behavioral features of sympatry of *Spermophilus spilosoma* and *Spermophilus tridecemlineatus* and some life history aspects of *S. spilosoma*. Unpubl. D.A. dissert., Univ. Northern Colorado, Greeley, 130 pp.

Streubel, D. P., and J. P. Fitzgerald. 1978a. *Spermophilus spilosoma*. Mammalian Species 101:1–4.

Streubel, D. P., and J. P. Fitzgerald. 1978b. *Spermophilus tridecemlineatus*. Mammalian Species 103:1–5.

Stricklan, D., J. T. Flinders, and R. G. Cates. 1995. Factors affecting selection of winter food and roosting resources for porcupines in Utah. Great Basin Nat. 55:29–36.

Strickland, M. A., and C. W. Douglas. 1987. Marten. Pp. 530–546, in Wild furbearer management and conservation in North America (M. Novak, J. A. Baker, M. E. Obbard, and B. Malloch, eds.). Ontario Trappers Association, Toronto, 1,150 pp.

Strickland, M. A., C. W. Douglas, M. Novak, and N. P. Hunziger. 1982. Marten. Pp. 599–612, in Wild mammals of North America, biology, management, and economics (J. A. Chapman and G. A. Feldhamer, eds.). Johns Hopkins Univ. Press, Baltimore, 1,147 pp.

Strohmeyer, D. C., and J. M. Peek. 1996. Wapiti home range and movement patterns in a sagebrush desert. Northwest Sci. 70:79–87.

Stromberg, M. R. 1982. New records of Wyoming bats. Bat Research News 23:42–44.

Struhsaker, T. T. 1967. Behavior of elk (*Cervus canadensis*) during the rut. Zeitschrift für Tierpsychologie. 24:80–114.

Stuart, G. E. 2001. Ancient pioneers, the first Americans. National Geographic Soc., Washington, DC, 199 pp.

Stuart, J. N., J. K. Frey, Z. J. Schwenke, and J. S. Sherman. 2007. Status of the nine-banded armadillo in New Mexico. Prairie Nat. 39:163–169.

Stucky, R. K. 1990. Evolution of land mammal diversity in North America during the Cenozoic. Current Mamm. 2:375–432.

Stucky, R. K., and M. C. McKenna. 1993. Mammalia. Pp. 739–771, in The fossil record 2 (M. Benton and M. Whyte, eds.). Chapman and Hall, London, 845 pp.

Studier, E. H., and M. J. O'Farrell. 1972. Biology of *Myotis thysanodes* and *M. lucifugus* (Chiroptera: Vespertilionidae), 1. Thermoregulation. Comp. Biochem. Physiol. 38:567–596.

Stuewer, F. W. 1943. Reproduction of raccoons in Michigan. J. Wildl. Mgmt. 7:60–73.

Sudman, P. D., J. C. Burns, and J. R. Choate. 1986. Gestation and postnatal development of the plains pocket gopher. Texas J. Sci. 38:91–94.

Sudman, P. D., J. R. Choate, and E. G. Zimmerman. 1987. Taxonomy of chromosomal races of *Geomys bursarius lutescens* Merriam. J. Mamm. 58:526–543.

Sudman, P. D., J. K. Wickliffe, P. Horner, M. J. Smolen, J. W. Bickham, and R. D. Bradley. 2006. Molecular systematics of pocket gophers of the genus *Geomys*. J. Mamm. 87:668–676.

Sullivan, R. M. 1985. Phyletic, biogeographic, and ecologic relationships among montane populations of least chipmunks (*Eutamias minimus*) in the Southwest. Syst. Zool. 34:419–448.

Sullivan, R. M., and K. E. Peterson. 1988. Systematics of southwestern populations of least chipmunks (*Tamias minimus*) reexamined: a synthetic approach. Occas. Papers, Mus. Southwestern Biology 5:1–27.

Sullivan, T. P., B. Jones, and D. S. Sullivan. 1989. Population ecology and conservation of the mountain cottontail, *Sylvilagus nuttallii*, in southern British Columbia. Canadian Field-Nat. 103:335–340.

Summerlin, C. T., and J. L. Wolfe. 1973. Social influences on trap response of the cotton rat *Sigmodon hispidus*. Ecology 54:1156–1159.

Sumrell, F. 1949. A life history study of the ground squirrel *Citellus spilosoma major* (Merriam). Unpubl. master's thesis, Univ. New Mexico, Albuquerque, 100 pp.

Sun, C. 1997. Dispersal of young in red squirrels (*Tamiasciurus hudsonicus*). Amer. Midland Nat. 138:252–259.

Sunquist, M. E. 1974. Winter activity of striped skunks (*Mephitis mephitis*) in east-central Minnesota. Amer. Midland Nat. 92:434–446.

Sureda, M., and M. L. Morrison. 1999. Habitat characteristics of small mammals in southeastern Utah. Great Basin Nat. 59: 323–330.

Sutton, D. A. 1953. A systematic review of Colorado chipmunks (genus *Eutamias*). Unpubl. doctoral dissert., Univ. Colorado, Boulder, 208 pp.

Sutton, D. A. 1995. Problems of taxonomy and distribution in four species of chipmunks. J. Mamm. 76:843–850.

Svendsen, G. E. 1974. Behavioral and environmental factors in the spatial distribution and population dynamics of a yellow-bellied marmot population. Ecology 55:760–771.

Svendsen, G. E. 1976a. Structure and location of burrows of yellow-bellied marmot. Southwestern Nat. 20:487–494.

Svendsen, G. E. 1976b. Vocalizations of the long-tailed weasel (*Mustela frenata*). J. Mamm. 57:398–399.

Svendsen, G. E. 1978. Castor and anal glands of the beaver (*Castor canadensis*). J. Mamm. 59:618–620.

Svendsen, G. E. 1979. Territoriality and behaviors in a population of pikas (*Ochotona princeps*). J. Mamm. 50:324–330.

Svendsen, G. E. 1982. Weasels. Pp. 613–628, in Wild mammals of North America, biology, management, and economics (J. A. Chapman and G. A. Feldhamer, eds.). Johns Hopkins Univ. Press, Baltimore, 1,147 pp.

Svendsen, G. E. 1989. Pair formation, duration of pair-bonds, and mate replacement in a population of beavers (*Castor canadensis*). Canadian J. Zool. 57:336–340.

Svendsen, G. E. 2003. Weasels and black-footed ferret, *Mustela* species. Pp. 650–661, in Wild mammals of North America, biology, management, and economics, second ed. (G. A. Feldhamer, B. C. Thompson, and J. A. Chapman, eds.). Johns Hopkins Univ. Press, Baltimore, 1,216 pp.

Svihla, A. 1929. Life history notes on *Sigmodon hispidus hispidus*. J. Mamm. 10:352–353.

Svihla, A. 1932. A comparative life history study of the mice of the genus *Peromyscus*. Misc. Publ. Mus. Zoology, Univ. Michigan 24:1–39.

Svihla, A. 1936. Breeding and young of the grasshopper mouse. J. Mamm. 17:172–173.

Svoboda, P. L., and J. R. Choate. 1987. Natural history of the Brazilian free-tailed bat in the San Luis Valley of Colorado. J. Mamm. 58:224–234.

Svoboda, P. L., D. K. Tolliver, and J. R. Choate. 1988. *Peromyscus boylii* in the San Luis Valley, Colorado. Southwestern Nat. 33:239–240.

Swann, D. E., C. C. Hass, D. C. Dalton, and S. A. Wolf. 2004. Infrared-triggered cameras for detecting wildlife: an evaluation and review. Wildl. Soc. Bull. 32:357–365.

Sweanor, L. L. 1990. Mountain lion social organization in a desert environment. Unpubl. master's thesis, Univ. Idaho, Moscow, 172 pp.

Sweanor, L. L., K. A. Logan, and M. Hornocker. 2000. Cougar dispersal patterns, metapopulation dynamics, and conservation. Cons. Biology 14:798–808.

Sweeney, J. M., and H. W. Steinhoff. 1976. Ecological impacts of snowpack augmentation in the San Juan Mountain, Colorado. Pp. 415–435, in Ecological impacts of snowpack augmentation in the San Juan Mountains, Colorado (H. W. Steinhoff and J. D. Ives, eds.). Colorado State Univ. Publ., Fort Collins, 487 pp.

Sweeney, J. R., J. M. Sweeney, and S. W. Sweeney. 2003. Feral hog, *Sus scrofa*. Pp. 1164–1179, in Wild mammals of North America, biology, management, and conservation, second ed. (G. A. Feldhamer, B. C. Thompson, and J. A. Chapman, eds.). Johns Hopkins Univ. Press, Baltimore, 1,216 pp.

Sweitzer, R. A. 1993. Predation or starvation: consequences of foraging decisions by porcupines (*Erethizon dorsatum*). J. Mamm. 77:1068–1077.

Sweitzer, R. A. 2003. Breeding movements and reproductive activities of porcupines in the Great Basin Desert. Western N. Amer. Nat. 53:1–11.

Sweitzer, R. A., and J. Berger. 1998. Evidence for female-biased dispersal in North American porcupines (*Erethizon dorsatum*). J. Zool. (London) 244:159–166.

Sweitzer, R. A., S. H. Jenkins, and J. Berger. 1997. Near-extinction of porcupines by mountain lions and consequences of ecosystem change in the Great Basin Desert. Conservation Biol. 11:1407–1417.

Swenk, M. H. 1926. Notes on *Mustela campestris* Jackson, and on the American forms of least weasels. J. Mamm. 7:313–330.

Swihart, R. K., and N. A. Slade. 1989. Differences in home-range size between sexes of *Microtus ochrogaster*. J. Mamm. 70: 816–820.

Taber, R. D., and N. F. Payne. 2003. Wildlife, conservation, and human welfare: a United States and Canadian perspective. Krieger Publishing Company, Melbourne, Victoria, Australia, 218 pp.

Tabor, J. E. 1974. Productivity, survival, and population status of river otter in western Oregon. Unpubl. master's thesis, Oregon State Univ., Corvallis, 62 pp.

Tabor, J. E., and H. M. Wight. 1977. Population status of river otter in western Oregon. J. Wildl. Mgmt. 41:692–699.

Taitt, M. J., and C. J. Krebs. 1985. Population dynamics and cycles. Pp. 567–620, in Biology of New World *Microtus* (R. H. Tamarin, ed.). Special Publ., Amer. Soc. Mammalogists 8:1–893.

Tamarin, R. H., ed. 1985. Biology of New World *Microtus*. Spec. Publ., Amer. Soc. Mammalogists 8:1–893.

Tamgüney, G., M. W. Miller, L. L. Wolfe, T. M. Sirochman, D. V. Glidden, C. Palmer, A. Lemus, S. J. DeArmond, and S. B. Prusiner. 2009. Asymptomatic deer excrete infectious prions in faeces. Nature, doi:10.1038/nature08289.

Tardiff, S. E., and J. A. Stanford. 1998. Grizzly bear digging: effects on subalpine meadow plants in relation to mineral nitrogen availability. Ecology 29:2219–2228.

Taulman, J. F. 1994. Observations of nest construction and bathing behaviors in the nine-banded armadillo, *Dasypus novemcinctus*. Southwestern Nat. 39:378–380.

Taulman, J. F., and L. W. Robbins. 1996. Recent range expansion and distributional limits of the nine-banded armadillo (*Dasypus novemcinctus*) in the United States. J. Biogeography 23:635–648.

Taylor, K. 2009. Voyage of the dammed, beaver experts gather to chart a path to a wetter West. High Country News 41(10):12–13, 24.

Taylor, R. B., E. C. Hellgren, T. M. Gabor, and L. M. Ilse. 1998. Reproduction of feral pigs in southern Texas. J. Mamm. 79:1325–1331.

Taylor, S. L., and S. W. Buskirk. 1994. Forest microenvironments and resting energetics of the American marten *Martes americana*. Ecography 17:249–256.

Taylor, W. P. 1935. Ecology and life history of the porcupine (*Erethizon epixanthum*) as related to the forests of Arizona and the southwestern United States. Univ. Arizona Bull. 6:1–177.

Taylor, W. P., ed. 1956. The deer of North America. The Stackpole Company, Harrisburg, PA, 668 pp.

Tazik, D. J., and L. L. Getz. 2007. Intraspecific and interspecific territoriality in *Microtus ochrogaster* and *M. pennsylvanicus*. Prairie Nat. 39:41–48.

Tedford, R. N. 1976. Relationships of pinnipeds to other carnivores (Mammalia). Syst. Zool. 25:363–374.

Teipner, C. L., E. O. Garton, and L. Nelson, Jr. 1983. Pocket gophers in forest ecosystems. Gen. Tech. Rept., Intermountain Forest and Range Exper. Sta., USDA Forest Service, INT-154:1–53.

Tekiela, S. 2007. Mammals of Colorado field guide. Adventure Publications, Cambridge, MN, 373 pp.

Telleen, S. L. 1976. Identification of live Colorado chipmunks. Unpubl. master's thesis, Univ. Colorado, Boulder, 56 pp.

Telleen, S. L. 1978. Structural niches of *Eutamias minimus* and *E. umbrinus* in Rocky Mountain National Park. Unpubl. doctoral dissert., Univ. Colorado, Boulder, 141 pp.

Tester, J. R. 1953. Fall food habits of the raccoon in the South Platte Valley of northeastern Colorado. J. Mamm. 34:500–502.

Tevis, L., Jr. 1950. Summer behavior of a family of beavers in New York State. J. Mamm. 31:40–65.

Tevis, L., Jr. 1952. Autumn foods of chipmunks and golden-mantled ground squirrels in the northern Sierra Nevada. J. Mamm. 33:198–205.

Tevis, L., Jr. 1955. Observations on chipmunks and mantled squirrels in northeastern California. Amer. Midland Nat. 53: 71–78.

Thaeler, C. S., Jr. 1968. Karyotypes of sixteen populations of the *Thomomys talpoides* complex of pocket gophers (Rodentia—Geomyidae). Chromosoma 25:172–183.

Theobald, D. M., J. R. Miller, and N. T. Hobbs. 1997. Estimating the cumulative effects of development on wildlife habitat. Landscape and Urban Planning 39:25–36.

Theodor, J. M., K. D. Rose, and J. Erfurt. 2005. Artiodactyla. Pp. 215–233, in The rise of placental mammals, origins and relationships of the major extant clades (K. D. Rose and J. D. Archibald, eds.). Johns Hopkins Univ. Press, Baltimore, 259 pp.

Thies, K. M., M. L. Thies, and W. Caire. 1996. House construction by the southern plains woodrat (*Neotoma micropus*) in southwestern Oklahoma. Southwestern Nat. 41:116–122.

Thogmartin, W. E., A. L. Gallant, M. G. Knutson, T. J. Fox, and M. J. Suarez. 2004. Commentary: a cautionary tale regarding use of the National Land Cover Dataset 1992. Wildl. Soc. Bulletin 32:970–978.

Thomas, B. 2008. [Photograph]. Ouray County Plaindealer, May, 2–8, p. 1.

Thomas, C. D., A. Cameron, R. E. Green, M. Bakkenes, L. J. Beaumont, Y. C. Collingham, B.F.N. Erasmus, M. F. de Siqueira, A. Grainger, L. Hannah, L. Hughes, B. Huntley, A. S. van Jaarsveld, G. F. Midgley, L. Miles, M. A. Ortega-Huerta, A. T. Peterson, O. D. Phillips, S. E. Williams. 2004. Extinction risk from climate change. Nature 427:145–148.

Thomas, D. W., M. B. Fenton, and R.M.R. Barclay. 1979. Social behavior of the little brown bat, *Myotis lucifugus*, I. Mating behavior. Behav. Ecol. Sociobiol. 5:129–136.

Thomas, J. A., and E. C. Birney. 1979. Parental care and mating system of the prairie vole, *Microtus ochrogaster*. Behav. Ecol. Sociobiol. 5:171–186.

Thomas, J. W., L. F. Ruggiero, R. W. Mannan, J. W. Schoen, and R. A. Lancia. 1988. Management and conservation of old-growth forests in the United States. Wildl. Soc. Bull. 16:252–262.

Thomas, J. W., and D. E. Toweill, eds. 1982. Elk of North America, ecology and management. Stackpole Books, Harrisburg, PA, 698 pp.

Thomas, R. E. 1988. A review of flea collection records from *Onychomys leucogaster* with observations on the role of grasshopper mice in the epizoology of wild rodent plague. Great Basin Nat. 48:83–95.

Thomas, R. E., M. L. Beard, T. J. Quan, L. G. Carter, A. M. Barnes, and C. E. Hopla. 1989. Experimentally induced plague infection in the northern grasshopper mouse (*Onychomys leucogaster*) acquired by consumption of infected prey. J. Wildl. Dis. 25:477–480.

Thompson, C. M., D. J. Augustine, and D. M. Mayers. 2008. Swift fox response to prescribed fire in shortgrass steppe. Western N. Amer. Nat. 58:251–256.

Thompson, I. D., and P. W. Colgan. 1994. Marten activity in uncut and logged boreal forests in Ontario. J. Wildl. Mgmt. 58:280–288.

Thompson, J. N., Jr., and S. D. Barrett. 1969. The nest complex of *Perognathus hispidus* (Rodentia: Heteromyidae) in Oklahoma. Proc. Oklahoma Acad. Sci. 48:105–108.

Thompson, R. W., and J. C. Halfpenny. 1989. Canada lynx presence on the Vail ski area and proposed expansion area. Western Ecosystems, unpubl., 29 pp.

Thompson, T. G., and W. Conley. 1983. Discrimination of coexisting species of *Peromyscus* in south-central New Mexico. Southwestern Nat. 28:199–209.

Thorington, R. W., and R. S. Hoffmann. 2005. Family Sciuridae. Pp. 754–818, in Mammal species of the world, a taxonomic and geographic reference, third ed. (D. E. Wilson and D. M. Reeder, eds.), 2 vols. Johns Hopkins Univ. Press, Baltimore.

Thorn, C. E. 1978. A preliminary assessment of the geomorphic role of pocket gophers in the alpine zone of the Colorado Front Range. Geografiska Annaler 50A:181–187.

Thorn, C. E. 1982. Gopher disturbance: its variability by Braun-Blanquet vegetation units in the Niwot Ridge alpine tundra zone, Colorado Front Range, USA. Arctic and Alpine Res. 14:45–51.

Thorne, D. H., and D. C. Anderson. 1990. Long-term soil-disturbance pattern by a pocket gopher, *Geomys bursarius*. J. Mamm. 71:84–89.

Thorne, E. T., R. E. Dean, and W. G. Hepworth. 1976. Nutrition during gestation in relation to successful reproduction in elk. J. Wildl. Mgmt. 40:330–335.

Thorne, E. T., N. Kingston, W. R. Jolley, and R. C. Bergstrom, eds. 1982. Diseases of wildlife in Wyoming, second ed. Wyoming Game and Fish Dept., Cheyenne, 353 pp.

Thorne, E. T., and E. Williams. 1988. Diseases and endangered species: the black-footed ferret as a recent example. Cons. Biol. 2:66–73.

Thornton, W. A., G. C. Creel, and R. E. Trimble. 1971. Hybridization in the fox genus, *Vulpes*, in West Texas. Southwestern Nat. 15:473–484.

Tiemeier, O. W. 1965. Bionomics. Pp. 5–37, in The black-tailed jackrabbit in Kansas. Tech. Bull., Kansas Agric. Exper. Sta. 140:1–75.

Tileston, J. V., and R. R. Lechleitner. 1966. Some comparisons of the black-tailed and white-tailed prairie dogs in north-central Colorado. Amer. Midland Nat. 75:292–316.

Timm, R. M., and R. D. Price. 1980. The taxonomy of *Geomydoecus* (Mallophaga: Trichodectidae) from the *Geomys bursarius* complex (Rodentia: Geomyidae). J. Med. Entomol. 17:126–145.

Tinker, D. B., H. J. Harlow, and T.D.I. Beck. 1998. Protein use and muscle-fiber changes in free-ranging, hibernating black bears. Physiol. Zool. 71:414–424.

Tischbein, G. 1980. Are there grizzlies in Colorado? Colorado Outdoors 29(1):12–14.

Tischendorf, J. W., D. J. Scott, S. D. Scott, and B. Heicher. 1995. A sighting of a large group of pumas (*Puma concolor*). Southwestern Nat. 40:226–227.

Todd, A. W., and L. B. Keith. 1983. Coyote demography during snowshoe hare decline in Alberta. J. Wildl. Mgmt. 47:394–404.

Todd, J. W. 1972. A literature review on bighorn sheep food habits. Spec. Rept., Colorado Game, Fish, and Parks Dept. 27:1–21.

Todd, J. W. 1975. Foods of Rocky Mountain bighorn sheep in southern Colorado. J. Wildl. Mgmt. 39:108–111.

Todd, M. 1980. Ecology of badgers in southcentral Idaho, with additional notes on raptors. Unpubl. master's thesis, Univ. Idaho, Moscow, 164 pp.

Tolliver, K. K., M. H. Smith, P. E. Jones, and M. W. Smith. 1985. Low levels of genetic variability in pikas from Colorado. Canadian J. Zool. 53:1735–1737.

Tomasi, T. E. 1978. Function of venom in the short-tailed shrew (*Blarina brevicauda*). J. Mamm. 59:852–854.

Tomasi, T. E. 1979. Echolocation by the short-tailed shrew (*Blarina brevicauda*). J. Mamm. 50:751–759.

Tomasi, T. E., and R. S. Hoffmann. 1984. *Sorex preblei* in Utah and Wyoming. J. Mamm. 55:708.

Tomasik, E., and J. A. Cook. 2005. Mitochondrial phylogeography and conservation genetics of wolverine (*Gulo gulo*) of northwestern North America. J. Mamm. 86:386–396.

Tomback, D. F., and K. C. Kendall. 2002. Rocky road in the Rockies: challenges to biodiversity. Pp. 153–181, in Rocky Mountain futures (J. S. Baron, ed.). Island Press, Washington, DC, 325 pp.

Tomback, D. F., A. W. Schoettle, K. E. Chevalier, and C. A. Jones. 2005. Life on the edge for limber pine: seed dispersal within a peripheral population. Ecoscience 12:519–529.

Tomberlin, D. R. 1969. Population ecology of two chipmunk populations in southern central Colorado. J. Colorado-Wyoming Acad. Sci. 5:63.

Topping, M. G., and J. S. Millar. 1998. Mating patterns and reproductive success in the bushy-tailed woodrat (*Neotoma cinerea*) as revealed by DNA fingerprinting. Behav. Ecol. Sociobiol. 43:115–124.

Torbit, S. C., R. B. Gill, A. W. Alldredge, and J. C. Liewer. 1993. Impacts of pronghorn grazing on winter wheat in Colorado. J. Wildl. Mgmt. 57:173–181.

Torres, J. R. 1973. The future of the black-footed ferret of Colorado. Pp. 27–33, in Proc. Black-footed Ferret and Prairie Dog Workshop (R. L. Linder and C. N. Hillman, eds.). South Dakota State Univ., Brookings, 208 pp.

Torres, S. 2005. Lion sense, traveling and living safely in mountain lion country, second ed. Globe Pequot Press, Guilford, CT, xv + 77 pp.

Toweill, D. E. 1974. Winter food habits of river otters in western Oregon. J. Wildl. Mgmt. 38:107–111.

Toweill, D. E., and J. E. Tabor. 1982. River otter. Pp. 688–703, in Wild mammals of North America, biology, management, and economics (J. A. Chapman and G. A. Feldhamer, eds.). Johns Hopkins Univ. Press, Baltimore, 1,147 pp.

Toweill, D. E., and J. G. Teer. 1977. Food habits of ringtails in the Edwards Plateau region of Texas. J. Mamm. 58:660–663.

Toweill, D. E., and J. G. Teer. 1980. Home range and den habits of Texas ringtails (*Bassariscus astutus flavus*). Pp. 1103–1120, in Proc. Worldwide Furbearer Conference (J. A. Chapman and D. Pursley, eds.). Worldwide Furbearer Conference, Frostburg, MD, 2,059 pp.

Toweill, D. E., and D. B. Toweill. 1978. Growth and development of captive ringtails (*Bassariscus astutus flavus*). Carnivore 1:46–53.

Trainer, C. E. 1975. Direct causes of mortality in mule deer fawns during summer and winter periods on Steens Mountain, Oregon. Proc. Western Assoc. State Game and Fish Commissions 55:163–170.

Trainor, A. M., T. M. Shenk, and K. R. Wilson. 2007. Microhabitat characteristics of Preble's meadow jumping mouse high-use areas. J. Wildl. Mgmt. 71:469–477.

Trapp, G. R. 1972. Some anatomical and behavioral adaptations of ringtails, *Bassariscus astutus*. J. Mamm. 53:547–557.

Trapp, G. R. 1978. Comparative behavioral ecology of the ringtail (*Bassariscus astutus*) and gray fox (*Urocyon cinereoargenteus*) in southwestern Utah. Carnivore 1:3–32.

Trapp, G. R., and D. L. Hallberg. 1975. Ecology of the gray fox (*Urocyon cinereoargenteus*): a review. Pp. 164–178, in The wild canids: their systematics, behavioral ecology and evolution (M. W. Fox, ed.). Van Nostrand Reinhold, New York, 508 pp.

Travis, S. E., and C. N. Slobodchikoff. 1993. Effects of food resource distribution on the social system of Gunnison's prairie dogs. Canadian J. Zoology 71:186–1192.

Travis, S. E., C. N. Slobodchikoff, and P. Keim. 1995. Ecological and demographic effects on intraspecific variation in the social system of prairie dogs. Ecology 76:1794–1803.

Travis, S. E., C. N. Slobodchikoff, and P. Keim. 1996. Social assemblages and mating relationships in prairie dogs: a DNA fingerprint analysis. Behav. Ecology 7:95–100.

Travis, S. E., C. N. Slobodchikoff, and P. Keim. 1997. DNA fingerprinting reveals low genetic diversity in Gunnison's prairie dog. J. Mamm. 78:725–732.

Travis, W. R. 2007. New geographies of the American West, land use and the changing patterns of place. Island Press, Washington, DC, 291 pp.

Travis, W. R., D. M. Theobald, and D. B. Fagre. 2002. Transforming the Rockies: human forces, settlement patterns, and ecosystem effects. Pp. 1–24, in Rocky Mountain futures (J. S. Baron, ed.). Island Press, Washington, DC, 325 pp.

Trent, T. T., and O. S. Rongstad. 1974. Home range and survival of cottontail rabbits in southwestern Wisconsin. J. Wildl. Mgmt. 38:459–472.

Trethewey, D.E.C., and B. J. Verts. 1971. Reproduction in eastern cottontail rabbits in western Oregon. Amer. Midland Nat. 86:463–476.

Trippe, T. M. 1874. Appendix to Oscines, A. Pp. 223–233, in E. Coues, Birds of the Northwest: a hand-book of the ornithology of the region drained by the Missouri River and its tributaries. Misc. Publ., U.S. Geol. Surv. of the Territories 3:1–791.

Troendle, C. A., M. R. Kaufmann, R. H. Hamre, and R. P. Winokur, eds. 1987. Management of subalpine forests: building on 50 years of research. Gen. Tech. Rept., USDA Forest Service, RM-149:1–253.

Truett, J. C., J.A.L.D. Dullum, M. R. Matchett, E. Owens, and D. Seery. 2001. Translocating prairie dogs: a review. Wildl. Soc. Bull. 29:863–872.

Tubbs, A. A. 1977. Ecology and population biology of the spotted ground squirrel, *Spermophilus spilosoma obsoletus*. Unpubl. D.A. dissert., Univ. Northern Colorado, Greeley, 64 pp.

Tumlison, R. 1987. *Felis lynx*. Mammalian Species 269:1–8.

Tumlison, R. 1993. Geographic variation in the lappet-eared bat, *Idionycteris phyllotis*, with descriptions of subspecies. J. Mamm. 74:412–421.

Turkowski, F. J. 1969. Food habits and behavior of the gray fox (*Urocyon cinereoargenteus*) in the lower and upper Sonoran life zones of southwestern United States. Unpubl. doctoral dissert., Arizona State Univ., 136 pp.

Turkowski, F. J. 1975. Dietary adaptability of the desert cottontail. J. Wildl. Mgmt. 39:748–756.

Turkowski, F. J., and C. K. Brown. 1969. Notes on distribution of the desert shrew. Southwestern Nat. 14:128.

Turner, A. 1997. The big cats and their fossil relatives. Columbia Univ. Press, New York, 256 pp.

Turner, A. 2004. Prehistoric mammals. National Geographic Society, Washington, DC, 192 pp.

Turner, G. T. 1973. Effects of pocket gophers on the range. Pp. 51–61, in Pocket gophers and Colorado mountain rangeland (G. T. Turner, R. M. Hansen, V. H. Reid, H. P. Tietjen, and A. L. Ward, eds.). Exper. Station Bull., Colorado State Univ. 2:1–554.

Turner, G. T., R. M. Hansen, V. H. Reid, H. P. Tietjen, and A. L. Ward. 1973. Pocket gophers and Colorado mountain rangeland. Exper. Station Bull., Colorado State Univ. 554S:1–90.

Turner, J. W., Jr., M. L. Wolfe, and J. F. Kirkpatrick. 1992. Seasonal mountain lion predation on a feral horse population. Canadian J. Zool. 70:929–934.

Turner, R. W., and J. B. Bowles. 1967. Comments on reproduction and food habits of the olive-backed pocket mouse in western North Dakota. Trans. Kansas Acad. Sci. 70:266–267.

Tuttle, M. D. 1981. Bats and public health. Contrib. Biol. and Geol., Milwaukee Public Mus. 48:1–9.

Tuttle, M. D. 1988. America's neighborhood bats. Univ. Texas Press, Austin, 96 pp.

Tuttle, M. D. 2004. The bat house builder's handbook. Bat Cons. Internat., Austin, TX, 34 pp.

Tuttle, M. D. 2005. Battered by harsh winds: must bats pay the price for wind energy? Bats 23(3):1–6.

Tuttle, M. D., and D.A.R. Taylor. 1994. Bats and mines. Resource Publ., Bat Cons. Internat. 3:1–31.

Tyron, C. A., Jr. 1947. Behavior and post-natal development of a porcupine. J. Wildl. Mgmt. 11:282–283.

Ubico, S. R., G. O. Maupin, K. A. Fagerstone, and R. G. McLean. 1988. A plague outbreak in white-tailed prairie dogs (*Cynomys leucurus*) of Meeteetse, Wyoming. J. Wildl. Dis. 24:399–406.

Ucitel, D., D. P. Christian, and J. M. Graham. 2003. Vole use of coarse woody debris and implications for habitat and fuel management. J. Wildl. Mgmt. 57:65–72.

U.S. Department of Agriculture, Forest Service. 2006. Black-tailed prairie dog management, decision notice, finding of no significant impact, USDA Forest Service, Pawnee National Grassland. http://www.fs.fed.us/r2/arnf/projects/ea-projects/png/pdog/dn.pdf.

U.S. Department of Commerce. 2000. State and county quick facts, Colorado. United States Census Bureau, Washington, DC. http://quickfacts.census.gov/qfd/states/08/08067.html.

U.S. Department of Commerce. 2001. Statistical abstract of the United States, 2001. Administrative and Customer Services Division, Bureau of the Census. United States Government Printing Office, Washington, DC.

U.S. Fish and Wildlife Service. 1998. Final rule to list Preble's meadow jumping mouse as a threatened species. United States Fish and Wildlife Service Final Report, Part 17. Federal Register 63:26517–26530.

U.S. Fish and Wildlife Service. 1999. Endangered and threatened wildlife and plants: 90-day finding for a petition to list the black-tailed prairie dog as threatened. Federal Register, March 25, 64:14424–14428.

U.S. Fish and Wildlife Service. 2000. 12-month administrative finding for a petition to list the black-tailed prairie dog as threatened. Federal Register, February 4, 65:5476–5488.

U.S. Fish and Wildlife Service. 2003. Endangered and threatened wildlife and plants: Final Rule to Reclassify and Remove the Gray Wolf From the List of Endangered and Threatened Wildlife in Portions of the Conterminous United States;

Establishment of Two Special Regulations for Threatened Gray Wolves. Final Rule. Federal Register 68(62):15804–15875, April 1.

U.S. Fish and Wildlife Service. 2008a. Colorado. http://ecos.fws.gov/tess_public//pub/state Listing.jsp?state=CO&status=listed.

U.S. Fish and Wildlife Service. 2008b. Threatened and Endangered Species System, Colorado. http://ecos.fws.gov/tess_public//pub/stateListing.jsp?state=CO &status=listed.

U.S. Fish and Wildlife Service. 2009. Black-tailed prairie dog. http://www.fws.gov/mountain-prairie/species/mammals/btprairiedog/.

U.S. Fish and Wildlife Service. 2010. White-Nose Syndrome: Something is killing our bats. http://www.fws.gov/whitenose syndrome/#map, revised November 10.

U.S. Fish and Wildlife Service and U.S. Bureau of Census. 2006. National Survey of Fishing, Hunting, and Wildlife-Associated Recreation, U.S. Fish and Wildlife Service and U.S. Census Bureau, 168 pp. http://library.fws.gov/pubs/nat_survey 2006_final.pdf.

U.S. Geological Survey. 1992. National Land Cover Dataset http://landscape cover.usgs. gov/natllandcover.html.

Unsworth, J. W., J. J. Beecham, and L. R. Irby. 1989. Female black bear habitat use in west central Idaho. J. Wildl. Mgmt. 53:668–673.

Unsworth, J. W., D. F. Pac, G. C. White, and R. M. Bartmann. 1999. Mule deer survival in Colorado, Idaho, and Montana. J. Wildl. Mgmt. 53:315–326.

Urbigkit, C. 2008. Yellowstone wolves, a chronicle of the animal, the people, and the politics. McDonald and Woodward, Blacksburg, VA, 350 pp.

Uresk, D. W. 1984. Black-tailed prairie dog food habits and forage relationships in western South Dakota. J. Range Mgmt. 37:325–329.

Uresk, D. W. 1987. Relation of black-tailed prairie dogs and control programs to vegetation, livestock, and wildlife. Pp. 312–323, in Integrated pest management on rangeland, a shortgrass prairie perspective (J. L. Capinera, ed.). Westview Press, Boulder, CO, 426 pp.

Uresk, D. W., K. E. Severson, and J. Javersak. 2003a. Vegetative characteristics of swift fox denning and foraging sites. Research Paper, Rocky Mountain Research Station, USDA Forest Service, RMRS-RP-38:1–4.

Uresk, D. W., K. E. Severson, and J. Javersak. 2003b. Detecting swift fox: smoked-plate scent stations versus spotlighting. USDA Forest Service, Rocky Mountain Research Station, RMRS-RP-39:1–5.

Valdez, E. W. 1998. Noteworthy records of bats from southern Colorado. Prairie Nat. 30:181–182.

Valdez, E. W. 2006. Geographic variation in morphology, diet, and ectoparasites of *Myotis occultus* in New Mexico and southern Colorado. Unpubl. doctoral dissert., Univ. New Mexico, Albuquerque, 99 pp.

Valdez, E. W., J. R. Choate, M. A. Bogan, and T. L. Yates. 1999. Taxonomic status of *Myotis occultus*. J. Mamm. 80:545–552.

Valdez, E. W., and P. M. Cryan. 2009. Food habits of the hoary bat (*Lasiurus cinereus*) during spring migration through New Mexico. Southwestern Nat. 54:195–200.

Valdez, E. W., C. M. Ritzi, and J. O. Whitaker, Jr. 2009. Ectoparasites of the occult bat, *Myotis occultus* (Chiroptera: Vespertilionidae). Western N. Amer. Nat. 59:364–370).

Valdez, E. W., J. N. Stuart, and M. A. Bogan. 1999. Additional records of bats from the Middle Rio Grande Valley, New Mexico. Southwestern Nat. 44:398–400.

Valdez, R., and P. R. Krausman. 1999. Mountain sheep of North America. Univ. Arizona Press, Tucson, 353 pp.

Van Deusen, J. L., and C. A. Myers. 1962. Porcupine damage in immature stands of ponderosa pine in the Black Hills. J. Forestry 811–813.

Van Dyke, F. G., R. H. Brocke, H. G. Shaw, B. B. Ackerman, T. P. Hemker, and F. G. Lindzey. 1986. Reactions of mountain lions to logging and human activity. J. Wildl. Mgmt. 50:95–102.

Van Dyke, F. G., W. C. Klein, and S. T. Stewart. 1998. Long-term range fidelity in Rocky Mountain elk. J. Wildl. Mgmt. 52:1020–1035.

Van Etten, K. W., K. R. Wilson, and R. L. Crabtree. 2007. Habitat use of red foxes in Yellowstone National Park based on snow tracking and telemetry. J. Mamm. 88:1498–1507.

Van Gelder, R. G. 1959. A taxonomic revision of the spotted skunks (genus *Spilogale*). Bull. Amer. Mus. Nat. Hist. 117:229–392.

Van Horne, B. 1982. Demography of the longtail vole *Microtus longicaudus* in seral stages of coastal coniferous forest, southeast Alaska. Canadian J. Zool. 50:1690–1709.

Van Horne, B. 2007. Conservation of ground squirrels. Pp. 463–471, in Rodent societies: an ecological and evolutionary perspective (J. O. Wolff and P. W. Sherman, eds.). Univ. Chicago Press, Chicago, 610 pp.

Van Mantgem, P. J., N. L. Stephenson, J. C. Byrne, L. D. Daniels, J. F. Franklin, P. Z. Fulé, M. E. Harmon, A. J. Larson, J. M. Smith, A. H. Taylor, and T. T. Veblen. 2009. Widespread increase of tree mortality rates in the western United States. Science 2323:521–524.

Van Nimwegen, R. E., J. Kretzer, and J. F. Cully, Jr. 2008. Ecosystem engineering by a colonial mammal: how prairie dogs structure rodent communities. Ecology 89:3298–3305.

Van Pelt, W. E. 1999. The black-tailed prairie dog conservation assessment and strategy, fifth draft. Nongame and Endangered Wildlife Program. Arizona Game and Fish Dept., Phoenix, 61 pp.

Van Vleck, D. B. 1969. Standardization of *Microtus* home range calculations. J. Mamm. 50:69–80.

Van Vuren, D. H. 2001. Spatial relations of American bison (*Bison bison*) and domestic cattle in a montane environment. Animal Biodiversity and Cons. 24:117–124.

Van Vuren, D. V. 1983. Group dynamics and summer home range of bison in southern Utah. J. Mamm. 54:329–332.

Van Vuren, D. V. 1984. Summer diets of bison and cattle in southern Utah. J. Range Mgmt. 37:260–261.

Van Vuren, D. V. 1990. Yellow-bellied marmots as prey of coyotes. Amer. Midland Nat. 125:135–139.

Van Vuren, D. V., and K. B. Armitage. 1991. Duration of snow cover and its influence on life-history variation in yellow-bellied marmots. Canadian J. Zool. 59:1755–1758.

Van Vuren, D., and K. B. Armitage. 1994a. Survival of dispersing and philopatric yellow-bellied marmots: what is the cost of dispersal? Oikos 69:179–181.

Van Vuren, D., and K. B. Armitage. 1994b. Reproductive success of colonial and noncolonial female yellow-bellied marmots (*Marmota flaviventris*). J. Mamm. 75:950–955.

Van Vuren, D., and M. P. Bray. 1983. Diets of bison and cattle on a seeded range in southern Utah. J. Range Mgmt. 36:499–500.

Van Vuren, D., and M. P. Bray. 1986. Population dynamics of bison in the Henry Mountains, Utah. J. Mamm. 57:503–511.

van Zyll de Jong, C. G. 1972. A systematic review of the Nearctic and Neotropical river otters (genus *Lutra*, Mustelidae, Carnivora). Life Sci. Contrib., Royal Ontario Mus. 80:1–104.

van Zyll de Jong, C. G. 1975. The distribution and abundance of the wolverine (*Gulo gulo*) in Canada. Canadian Field-Nat. 89:431–437.

van Zyll de Jong, C. G. 1984. Taxonomic relationships of Nearctic small-footed bats of the *Myotis leibii* group (Chiroptera: Vespertilionidae). Canadian J. Zool. 52:2519–2526.

van Zyll de Jong, C. G. 1986. A systematic study of Recent bison, with particular consideration of the wood bison (*Bison bison athabascae* Rhoads 1898). Publ. Nat. Sci., Nat. Mus. Canada 6:1–69.

van Zyll de Jong, C. G. 1987. A phylogenetic study of the Lutrinae (Carnivora: Mustelidae) using morphological data. Canadian J. Zool. 55:2536–2544.

van Zyll de Jong, C. G. 1991. Speciation in the *Sorex cinereus* group. Pp. 65–73, in The biology of the Soricidae (J. S. Findley and T. L. Yates, eds.). Spec. Publ., Mus. Southwestern Biol., Univ. New Mexico 1:1–91.

van Zyll de Jong, C. G., C. Gates, H. Reynolds, and W. Olson. 1995. Phenotypic variation in remnant populations of North American bison. J. Mamm. 76:391–405.

Vander Haegen, W. M., S. M. McCorquodale, C. R. Peterson, G. A. Green, and E. Yensen. 2001. Wildlife communities of eastside shrubland and grassland habitats. Pp. 349–377, in Wildlife-habitat relationships in Oregon and Washington (D. H. Johnson and T. A. O'Neil, eds.). Oregon State Univ. Press, Corvallis, 736 pp.

Vander Wall, S. B. 1997. Dispersal of single-leaf piñon pine (*Pinus monophylla*) by seed-caching rodents. J. Mamm. 78:181–191.

Vaughan, M. R., and L. B. Keith. 1981. Demographic response of experimental snowshoe hare populations to overwinter food shortage. J. Wildl. Mgmt. 45:354–380.

Vaughan, T. A. 1959. Functional morphology of three bats: *Eumops*, *Myotis*, *Macrotus*. Univ. Kansas Publ., Mus. Nat. Hist. 12:1–153.

Vaughan, T. A. 1961a. Vertebrates inhabiting pocket gopher burrows in Colorado. J. Mamm. 42:171–174.

Vaughan, T. A. 1961b. Cranial asymmetry in the pocket gopher. J. Mamm. 42:412–413.

Vaughan, T. A. 1962. Reproduction in the plains pocket gopher in Colorado. J. Mamm. 43:1–13.

Vaughan, T. A. 1967a. Food habits of the northern pocket gophers on shortgrass prairie. Amer. Midland Nat. 77:176–189.

Vaughan, T. A. 1967b. Two parapatric species of pocket gophers. Evolution 21:148–158.

Vaughan, T. A. 1969. Reproduction and population densities in a montane small mammal fauna. Pp. 51–74, in Contributions in mammalogy (J. K. Jones, Jr., ed.). Misc. Publ. Mus. Nat. Hist., Univ. Kansas 51:1–428.

Vaughan, T. A. 1974. Resource allocation in some sympatric subalpine rodents. J. Mamm. 55:764–795.

Vaughan, T. A. 1980. Woodrats and picturesque junipers. Pp. 387–401, in Aspects of vertebrate history (L. L. Jacobs, ed.). Mus. Northern Arizona Press, Flagstaff, 407 pp.

Vaughan, T. A. 1982. Stephens' woodrat, a dietary specialist. J. Mamm. 53:53–62.

Vaughan, T. A. 1990. Ecology of living packrats. Pp. 14–27, in Packrat middens, the last 40,000 years of biotic change (J. L. Betancourt, T. R. Van Devender, and P. S. Martin, eds.). Univ. Arizona Press, Tucson, 467 pp.

Vaughan, T. A., and R. M. Hansen. 1961. Activity rhythm of the plains pocket gopher. J. Mamm. 42:541–543.

Vaughan, T. A., and R. M. Hansen. 1964. Experiments on interspecific competition between two species of pocket gophers. Amer. Midland Nat. 72:444–452.

Vaughan, T. A., and T. J. O'Shea. 1976. Roosting ecology of the pallid bat, *Antrozous pallidus*. J. Mamm. 57:19–42.

Vaughan, T. A., J. M. Ryan, and N. J. Czaplewski. 2011. Mammalogy, fifth ed. Jones and Bartlett, Sudbury, MA, 750 pp.

Vaughan, T. A., and W. P. Weil. 1980. The importance of arthropods in the diet of *Zapus princeps* in a subalpine habitat. J. Mamm. 51:122–124.

Vavra, M., W. A. Laycock, and R. D. Pieper, eds. 1994. Ecological implications of livestock herbivory in the West. Soc. Range Mgmt., Denver, 297 pp.

Veilleux, J. P. 2008. Current status of White-nose Syndrome in the northeastern United States. Bat Research News 49:15–17.

Venge, O. 1959. Reproduction in the fox and mink. Animal Breed. Abstr. 27:129–145.

Vercauteren, K. C., M. J. Lavelle, N. W. Seward, J. W. Fischer, G. E. Phillips. 2007. Fence-line contact between wild and farmed cervids in Colorado: potential for disease transmission. J. Wildl. Mgmt. 71:1594–1602.

Verdolin, J., and C. N. Slobodchikoff. 2002. Vigilance and predation risk in Gunnison's prairie dogs. Canadian J. Zoology 80:1197–1203.

Verdolin, J. L., K. Lewis, and C. N. Slobodchikoff. 2008. Morphology of burrow systems: a comparison of Gunnison's (*Cynomys gunnisoni*), white-tailed (*C. leucurus*), black-tailed (*C. ludovicianus*), and Utah (*C. parvidens*) prairie dogs. Southwestern Nat. 53:201–207.

Verme, L. J., and D. E. Ullrey. 1984. Physiology and nutrition. Pp. 91–118, in White-tailed deer ecology and management (L. K. Halls, ed.). Stackpole Books, Harrisburg, PA, 870 pp.

Verts, B. J. 1967. The biology of the striped skunk. Univ. Illinois Press, Urbana, 218 pp.

Verts, B. J., and L. N. Carraway. 1998. Land mammals of Oregon. Univ. California Press, Berkeley, 668 pp.

Verts, B. J., and L. N. Carraway. 1999. *Thomomys talpoides*. Mammalian Species 618:1–11.

Verts, B. J., and L. N. Carraway. 2001. *Tamias minimus*. Mammalian Species 653:1–10.

Verts, B. J., and L. N. Carraway. 2002. *Neotoma lepida*. Mammalian Species 699:1–12.

Verts, B. J., L. N. Carraway, and A. Kinlaw. 2001. *Spilogale gracilis*. Mammalian Species 674:1–10.

Verts, B. J., and G. L. Kirkland, Jr. 1988. *Perognathus parvus*. Mammalian Species 318:1–8.

Vickery, P. D., M. L. Hunter, Jr., and J. V. Wells. 1992. Evidence of incidental nest predation and its effects on nests of threatened grassland birds. Oikos 63:281–288.

Vieira, M. 2006. Moose management plan, Data Analysis Unit M-2, Laramie River Herd. Colorado Division of Wildlife, Fort Collins, 23 pp.

Vignieri, S. N., E. M. Hallerman, B. J. Bergstrom, D. J. Hafner, A. P. Martin, P. Devers, P. Grobler, and N. Hitt. 2006. Mistaken view of taxonomic validity undermines conservation of an evolutionarily distinct mouse: a response to Ramey *et al.* 2005. Animal Cons. 9:237–243.

Vilà, C., J. A. Leonard, A. Götherström, S. Marklund, K. Sandberg, K. Lidén, R. K. Wayne, and H. Ellegren. 2001. Widespread origins of domestic horse lineages. Science 291:474–477.

Virgl, J. A., and F. Messier. 1996. Population structure, distribution, and demography of muskrats during the ice-free period under contrasting water fluctuations. Ecoscience 3:54–62.

Vogtsberger, L. M., and G. W. Barrett. 1973. Bioenergetics of captive red foxes. J. Wildl. Mgmt. 37:495–500.

Voigt, D. R. 1987. Red fox. Pp. 378–392, in Wild furbearer management and conservation in North America (M. Novak, J. A. Baker, M. E. Obbard, and B. Malloch, eds.). Ontario Trappers Association, Toronto, 1,150 pp.

Voigt, D. R., and W. E. Berg. 1987. Coyote. Pp. 344–357, in Wild furbearer management and conservation in North America (M. Novak, J. A. Baker, M. E. Obbard, and B. Malloch, eds.). Ontario Trappers Association, Toronto, 1,150 pp.

Voltura, M. B., and B. A. Wunder. 1994. Physiological responses of the Mexican woodrat (*Neotoma mexicana*) to condensed tannins. Amer. Midland Nat. 132:405–409.

Voltura, M. B., and B. A. Wunder. 1998. Electrical conductivity to predict body composition of mammals and the effect of gastrointestinal contents. J. Mamm. 79:279–286.

Vorhies, C. T., and W. P. Taylor. 1940. Life history and ecology of the white-throated wood rat, *Neotoma albigula albigula,* in relation to grazing in Arizona. Tech. Bull., College of Agriculture, Univ. Arizona 86:454–529.

Vosburgh, T. C., and L. R. Irby. 1998. Effects of recreational shooting on prairie dogs. J. Wildl. Mgmt. 52:362–372.

Wade, O. 1935. Notes on the northern tuft-eared squirrel, *Sciurus aberti ferreus* True, in Colorado. Amer. Midland Nat. 16:201–202.

Wade-Smith, J., and M. E. Richmond. 1978. Induced ovulation, development of the corpus luteum, and tubal transport in the striped skunk (*Mephitis mephitis*). Amer. J. Anat. 153:123–142.

Wade-Smith, J., and B. J. Verts. 1982. *Mephitis mephitis*. Mammalian Species 173:1–7.

Wadsworth, C. E. 1969. Reproduction and growth of *Eutamias quadrivittatus* in southeastern Utah. J. Mamm. 50:256–261.

Wadsworth, C. E. 1972. Observations of the Colorado chipmunk in southeastern Utah. Southwestern Nat. 16:451–454.

Wagner, D. M. 2002. Current status and habitat use of Gunnison's prairie dog (*Cynomys gunnisoni*) in Arizona. Unpubl. doctoral dissert., Northern Arizona Univ., Flagstaff, 77 pp.

Wagner, F. H., R. Foresta, R. B. Gill, D. R. McCullough, M. R. Pelton, W. F. Porter, and H. Salwasser. 1995. Wildlife policies in the U.S. national parks. Island Press, Washington, DC, 251 pp.

Wagner, F. H., and L. C. Stoddart. 1972. Influence of coyote predation on black-tailed jackrabbit populations in Utah. J. Wildl. Mgmt. 36:329–342.

Wagner, K. K., R. H. Schmidt, and M. R. Conover. 1997. Compensation programs for wildlife damage in North America. Wildlife Soc. Bull. 25:312–319.

Wainwright, L. C. 1968. Cottontail reproduction in Colorado. Unpubl. master's thesis, Colorado State Univ., Fort Collins, 57 pp.

Wakelyn, L. A. 1987. Changing habitat conditions on bighorn sheep ranges in Colorado. J. Wildl. Mgmt. 51:904–912.

Waldien, D. L., J. P. Hayes, and E. B. Arnett. 2000. Day-roosts of female long-eared myotis in western Oregon. J. Wildl. Mgmt. 54:785–796.

Wallace, D. R. 2004. Beasts of Eden, walking whales, dawn horses, and other enigmas of mammal evolution. Univ. California Press, Berkeley, 340 pp.

Wallace, G. N., D. M. Theobald, T. Ernst, and K. King. 2008. Assessing the ecological and social benefits of private land conservation in Colorado. Cons. Biol. 22:284–296.

Waller, D. M., and W. S. Alverson. 1997. The white-tailed deer: a keystone herbivore. Wildl. Soc. Bull. 25:217–226.

Wallmo, O. C., ed. 1981. Mule and black-tailed deer of North America. Univ. Nebraska Press, Lincoln, 605 pp.

Wallmo, O. C., W. L. Regelin, and D. W. Reichert. 1972. Forage use by mule deer relative to logging in Colorado. J. Wildl. Mgmt. 36:1025–1033.

Waltari, E., R. J. Hijmans, A. T. Peterson, A. S. Nyári, S. L. Perkins, and R. L. Guralnick. 2007. Locating Pleistocene refugia: comparing phylogeographic and ecological niche model predictions. PLoS ONE 7:1–7.

Wang, Z., and M. A. Novak. 1994. Parental care and litter development in primiparous and multiparous prairie voles (*Microtus ochrogaster*). J. Mamm. 75:18–23.

Ward, A. L. 1960. Mountain pocket gopher food habits in Colorado. J. Wildl. Mgmt. 24:89–92.

Ward, A. L., P. L. Hegdal, V. B. Richens, and H. P. Tietjen. 1967. Gophacide, a new pocket gopher control agent. J. Wildl. Mgmt. 31:332–338.

Ward, A. L., and J. O. Keith. 1962. Feeding habits of pocket gophers on mountain grasslands, Black Mesa, Colorado. Ecology 43:744–749.

Waring, G. H. 1966. Sounds and communications of the yellow-bellied marmot (*Marmota flaviventris*). Animal Behavior 14: 177–183.

Waring, G. H. 1969. The blow sound of pronghorns (*Antilocapra americana*). J. Mamm. 50:647–648.

Waring, G. H. 1970. Sound communications of black-tailed, white-tailed and Gunnison's prairie dog. Amer. Midland Nat. 83:167–185.

Warner, R. M., and N. J. Czaplewski. 1984. *Myotis volans*. Mammalian Species 224:1–4.

Warner, T. J., ed. 1976. The Domínguez-Escalante Journal: their expedition through Colorado, Utah, Arizona, and New Mexico in 1776 (A. Chavez, trans.). Brigham Young Univ. Press, Provo, UT, 203 pp.

Warren, E. R. 1908. Further notes on the mammals of Colorado. Colorado College Publ., Gen. Ser. 33:59–90.

Warren, E. R. 1910. The mammals of Colorado. G. P. Putnam's Sons, New York, 300 pp.

Warren, E. R. 1911. The history of Colorado mammalogy. Colorado College Publ., Gen. Ser. 54:312–328.

Warren, E. R. 1927. The beaver, its work and its ways. Monogr. Amer. Soc. Mammal. 2:1–177.

Warren, E. R. 1942. The mammals of Colorado, second ed. Univ. Oklahoma Press, Norman, 330 pp.

Warren, E. R., and E. R. Hall. 1939. A new subspecies of beaver from Colorado. J. Mamm. 20:358–362.

Warrick, G. D., and B. L. Cypher. 1998. Factors affecting the spatial distribution of a kit fox population. J. Wildl. Mgmt. 52:707–717.

Warrick, G. D., and C. E. Harris. 2001. Evaluation of spotlight and scent-station surveys to monitor kit fox abundance. Wildl. Soc. Bull. 29:827–832.

Wasser, C. H. 1977. Bison-induced stresses in Colorado National Monument. Unpubl. report, National Park Service, 8 pp.

Wasserman, D., and D. J. Nash. 1979. Variation in hemoglobin types in the deer mouse (*Peromyscus maniculatus*) along an altitudinal gradient. Great Basin Nat. 39:192–194.

Watermolen, D. J. 2001. Catalog of state and provincial mammal publications for the United States and Canada, 1980–1999. Bureau Integrated Sci. Svc., Wisconsin Dept. Nat. Resources, Madison, Publ. SS-960:1–50.

Waters, D. A., and W. L. Gannon. 2004. Bat call libraries: management and potential use. Pp. 150–157, in Bat echolocation research: tools, techniques and analysis (R. M. Brigham, E.K.V. Kalko, G. Jones, S. Parsons, and H.J.G.A. Limpens, eds.). Bat Conservation International, Austin, Texas, 157 pp.

Waters, M. R., and T. W. Stafford, Jr. 2007. Redefining the age of Clovis: implications for the peopling of the Americas. Science 315:1122–1126.

Watkins, L. C. 1972. *Nycticeius humeralis*. Mammalian Species 23: 1–4.

Watkins, L. C. 1977. *Euderma maculatum*. Mammalian Species 77: 1–4.

Wayne, R. K., N. Lehman, and T. K. Fuller. 1995. Conservation genetics of the gray wolf. Pp. 399–408, in Ecology and conservation of wolves in a changing world (L. N. Carbyn, S. H. Fritts, and D. R. Seip, eds.). Occas. Publ., Canadian Circumpolar Institute, Edmonton, Alberta 35:1–642.

Weaver, J. L., P. C. Paquet, and L. E. Ruggiero. 1996. Resilience and conservation of large carnivores in the Rocky Mountains. Cons. Biol. 10:964–976.

Weaver, J. W., and F. E. Clements. 1938. Plant ecology. McGraw-Hill Book Co., New York, 601 pp.

Weaver, T., E. M. Payson, and D. L. Gustafson. 1996. Prairie ecology—the shortgrass prairie. Pp. 67–75, in Prairie conservation, preserving North America's most endangered ecosystem (F. B. Samson and F. L. Knopf, eds.). Island Press, Washington, DC, 339 pp.

Webb, C. T., C. P. Brooks, K. L. Gage, and M. F. Antolin. 2006. Classic flea-borne transmission does not drive plague epizootics in prairie dogs. Proc. Nat. Acad. Sci. USA 103:6236–6241.

Webb, E. A. 1990. Introduction. Pp. 1–13, in Close to home: Colorado's urban wildlife (F. R. Rinehart and E. A. Webb, eds.). Denver Mus. Nat. Hist. and Colorado Urban Wildlife Partnership, Denver, 200 pp.

Webb, E. A., and S. Q. Foster, eds. 1991. Perspectives in urban ecology. Denver Mus. Nat. Hist., Denver, 89 pp.

Webb, S. D. 1989. The fourth dimension in North American terrestrial mammal communities. Pp. 181–203, in Patterns in the structure of mammalian communities (D. W. Morris, Z. Abramsky, B. J. Fox, and M. R. Willig, eds.). Spec. Publ., Mus. Texas Tech Univ. 28:1–266.

Webber, P. J., and D. E. May. 1977. The magnitude and distribution of belowground plant structure in the alpine tundra of Niwot Ridge, Colorado. Arctic and Alpine Research 9:157–174.

Weber, W. A. 1965. Theodore Dru Alison Cockerell, 1866–1948. Univ. Colorado Studies, Series in Bibliography 1:1–124.

Weber, W. A. 1976. Rocky Mountain flora. Colorado Assoc. Univ. Press, Boulder, 479 pp.

Weber, W. A., and R. C. Wittman. 2001. Colorado flora: Western Slope, third ed. Univ. Press of Colorado, Boulder, 488 pp.

Webster, W. D., and J. Knox Jones, Jr. 1982. *Reithrodontomys megalotis*. Mammalian Species 167:1–5.

Weckwerth, R. P., and V. D. Hawley. 1962. Marten food habits and population fluctuations in Montana. J. Wildl. Mgmt. 26:55–74.

Wehausen, J. D. 1996. Effects of mountain lion predation on bighorn sheep in the Sierra Nevada and Granite Mountains of California. Wildl. Soc. Bull. 24:471–479.

Wehausen, J. D., and R. R. Ramey II. 2000. Cranial morphometric and evolutionary relationships in the northern range of *Ovis canadensis*. J. Mamm. 81:145–161.

Weller, T. J., and C. J. Zabel. 2001. Characteristics of fringed myotis day roosts in northern California. J. Wildl. Mgmt. 55:489–497.

Welles, R. E., and F. B. Welles. 1961. The bighorn of Death Valley. Fauna Ser., Nat. Park Service 6:1–242.

Wells, M. C., and M. Bekoff. 1981. An observational study of scent marking by wild coyotes. Animal Behavior 26:251–258.

Wells, P. V., and C. D. Jorgensen. 1964. Pleistocene wood rat middens and climatic change in Mohave Desert: a record of juniper woodlands. Science 143:1171–1173.

Wells-Gosling, N., and L. R. Heaney. 1984. *Glaucomys sabrinus*. Mammalian Species 229:1–8.

Werdelin, L. 1981. Evolution of lynxes (*Lynx* spp.). Ann. Zool. Fennici 18:37–71.

Werner, R. M., and J. A. Vick. 1977. Resistance of the opossum (*Didelphis virginiana*) to envenomization by snakes of the family Crotalidae. Toxicon 15:29–33.

Westoby, M., and F. H. Wagner. 1973. Use of a crested wheatgrass seeding by black-tailed jackrabbits. J. Range Mgmt. 26:349–352.

Weston, F. 2008. Colorado State Parks & Natural Areas. Westcliffe Publishers, Boulder, CO, 160 pp.

Weston, J. L., and I. L. Brisbin, Jr. 2003. Demographics of a protected population of gray foxes (*Urocyon cinereoargenteus*) in South Carolina. J. Mamm. 84:996–1005.

Wettstein, P. J., M. Strausbauch, T. Lamb, J. States, R. Chakraborty, L. Jin, and R. Riblet. 1995. Phylogeny of six *Sciurus aberti* subspecies based on nucleotide sequences of cytochrome b. Molecular Phylog. Evol. 4:150–162.

Wheat, J. B. 1967. A Paleo-Indian bison kill. Scientific American 216:44–52.

Wheatley, M., K. W. Larsen, and S. Boutin. 2002. Does density reflect habitat quality for North American red squirrels during a spruce-cone failure. J. Mamm. 83:716–727.

Whicker, A. D., and J. K. Detling. 1988. Ecological consequences of prairie dog disturbances. BioScience 38:778–785.

Whicker, A. D., and J. K. Detling. 1993. Control of grassland ecosystem processes by prairie dogs. Pp. 18–27, in Proc. Symposium on the Management of Prairie Dog Complexes for the Reintroduction of Black-footed Ferrets (J. L. Oldemeyer, D. E. Biggins, B. J. Miller, and R. Crete, eds.). Biol. Rept., U.S. Fish and Wildlife Service 93:1–95.

Whisenant, S. G. 1990. Changing fire frequencies on Idaho's Snake River Plains: ecological and management implications. Pp. 4–10, in Proc. Symposium on Cheatgrass Invasion, Shrub Die-off, and Other Aspects of Shrub Biology and Management (E. D. Mc Arthur, E. M. Romney, S. D. Smith, and P. T. Tueller, comps.). USDA Forest Service, Ogden, UT. General Technical Report, INT-276:1–351.

Whitaker, J. O., Jr. 1963. A study of the meadow jumping mouse, *Zapus hudsonius* (Zimmermann), in central New York. Ecol. Monogr. 33:215–254.

Whitaker, J. O., Jr. 1972. *Zapus hudsonius*. Mammalian Species 11: 1–7.

Whitaker, J. O., Jr. 1974. *Cryptotis parva*. Mammalian Species 43: 1–8.

Whitaker, J. O., Jr. 2004. *Sorex cinereus*. Mammalian Species 743:1–9.

Whitaker, J. O., Jr., H. K. Dannelly, and D. A. Prentice. 2004. Chitinase in insectivorous bats. J. Mamm. 85:15–18.

Whitaker, J. O., Jr., C. Maser, and L. E. Keller. 1977. Food habits of bats of western Oregon. Northwest Sci. 51:46–55.

Whitaker, J. O., Jr., C. Neefus, and T. H. Kunz. 1996. Dietary variation in the Mexican free-tailed bat (*Tadarida brasiliensis mexicana*). J. Mamm. 77:716–724.

White House Council on Environmental Quality. 2008. White House Conference on North American Wildlife Policy, facilitation of hunting heritage and wildlife conservation. The Recreational Hunting and Wildlife Conservation Plan as directed by Executive Order 13442, 53 pp. http://wildlifeconservation.gov/documents/RecHuntingActionPlan11009dp.pdf.

White, C. A., C. E. Olmsted, and C. E. Kay. 1998. Aspen, elk and fire in the Rocky Mountain national parks of North America. Wildl. Soc. Bull. 26:449–462.

White, D., Jr., K. C. Kendall, and H. D. Picton. 1998. Grizzly bear feeding activity at alpine army cutworm moth aggregation sites in northwest Montana. Canadian J. Zool. 76:221–227.

White, D., Jr., K. C. Kendall, and H. D. Picton. 1999. Potential energetic effects of mountain climbers on foraging grizzly bears. Wildl. Soc. Bull. 27:146–151.

White, E. M., and D. C. Carlson. 1984. Estimating soil mixing by rodents. Proc. South Dakota Acad. Sci. 53:34–37.

White, E. P. 2004. Factors affecting bat house occupancy in Colorado. Southwestern Nat. 49:344–349.

White, G. C. 2005. Consulting services for mark-recapture analyses. Wildlife Research Report, WP 3001. Colorado Division of Wildlife, Fort Collins.

White, G. C., and R. M. Bartmann. 1998. Mule deer management—what should be monitored? Pp. 104–118, in Proc. 1997 Deer and Elk Workshop, Rio Rico, AZ (J. C. deVos, Jr., ed.). Arizona Game and Fish Dept., Phoenix, 356 pp.

White, G. C., J. R. Dennis, and F. M. Pusateri. 2005. Area of black-tailed prairie dog colonies in eastern Colorado. Wildl. Soc. Bull. 33:265–272.

White, G. C., D. F. Freddy, R. B. Gill, and J. H. Ellenberger. 2001. Effect of adult sex ratio on mule deer and elk productivity in Colorado. J. Wildl. Mgmt. 55:543–551.

White, G. C., R. A. Garrott, R. M. Bartmann, L. H. Carpenter, and A. W. Alldredge. 1987. Survival of mule deer in northwest Colorado. J. Wildl. Mgmt. 51:852–859.

White, J. A. 1953a. Taxonomy of the chipmunks, *Eutamias quadrivittatus* and *Eutamias umbrinus*. Univ. Kansas Publ., Mus. Nat. Hist. 5:563–582.

White, J. A. 1953b. The baculum in the chipmunks of western North America. Univ. Kansas Publ., Mus. Nat. Hist. 5:611–631.

White, P. J., W. H. Berry, J. J. Eliason, and M. T. Hanson. 2000. Catastrophic decrease in an isolated population of kit foxes. Southwestern Nat. 45:204–211.

White, P. J., and T. Davis. 2007. Chronic wasting disease, planning for an inevitable dilemma. Yellowstone Sci. 15:8–10.

White, P. J., and R. A. Garrott. 1997. Factors regulating kit fox populations. Canadian J. Zool. 75:1982–1988.

White, P. J., and R. A. Garrott. 2005. Northern Yellowstone elk after wolf restoration. Wildl. Soc. Bull. 33:942–955.

White, P. J., T. J. Kreeger, J. R. Tester, and U. S. Seal. 1989. Anal-sac secretions deposited with feces by captive red foxes (*Vulpes vulpes*). J. Mamm. 70:814–816.

White, P. J., K. Ralls, and R. A. Garrott. 1994. Coyote–kit fox interactions as revealed by telemetry. Canadian J. Zool. 72:1831–1836.

White, P. J., K. Ralls, and C.A.V. White. 1995. Overlap in habitat and food use between coyotes and San Joaquin kit foxes. Southwestern Nat. 40:342–349.

White, P. J., D. W. Smith, J. W. Duffield, M. Jimenez, T. McEneanry, and G. Plumb. 2005. Yellowstone after wolves—environmental impact statement predictions and ten-year appraisals. Yellowstone Sci. 13:34–41.

White, P. J., C.A.V. White, and K. Ralls. 1996. Functional and numerical responses of kit foxes to a short-term decline in mammalian prey. J. Mamm. 77:370–376.

White, R., S. Murray, and M. Rohweder. 2000. Pilot analyses of global ecosystems: grassland ecosystems. World Resources Inst., Washington, DC, 100 pp.

Whitford, W. G. 1976. Temporal fluctuations in density and diversity of desert rodent populations. J. Mamm. 57:351–369.

Whitlock, C., M. A. Reasoner, and C. H. Key. 2002. Paleoenvironmental history of the Rocky Mountain region during the past 20,000 years. Pp. 41–57, in Rocky Mountain futures (J. S. Baron, ed.). Island Press, Washington, DC, 325 pp.

Whitman, J. S. 1981. Ecology of the mink (*Mustela vison*) in west-central Idaho. Unpubl. master's thesis, Univ. Idaho, Moscow, 101 pp.

Whittaker, D., and R. L. Knight. 1998. Understanding wildlife responses to humans. Wildl. Soc. Bull. 26:312–317.

Whittaker, D. G. 1995. Patterns of coexistence for sympatric mule and white-tailed deer on Rocky Mountain Arsenal, Colorado. Unpubl. doctoral dissert., Univ. Wyoming, Laramie.

Whittaker, D. G., and F. G. Lindzey. 1999. Effects of coyote predation on early fawn survival in sympatric deer species. Wildl. Soc. Bull. 27:256–262.

Whittaker, D. G., and F. G. Lindzey. 2001. Population characteristics of sympatric mule and white-tailed deer on Rocky Mountain Arsenal, Colorado. J. Wildl. Mgmt. 55:946–952.

Whittaker, D. G., and F. G. Whittaker. 2004. Habitat use patterns of sympatric deer species on Rocky Mountain Arsenal, Colorado. Wildl. Soc. Bull. 32:1114–1123.

Whitworth, M. R., and C. H. Southwick. 1980. Growth of pika in laboratory confinement. Growth 45:66–72.

Whitworth, M. R., and C. H. Southwick. 1984. Sex differences in the ontogeny of social behavior in pikas: possible relationships to dispersal and territoriality. Behav. Ecol. Sociobiol. 15:175–182.

Wiedorn, W. S. 1954. A new experimental animal for psychiatric research: the opossum *Didelphis virginiana*. Science 119:360–361.

Wigal, R. A., and V. L. Coggins. 1982. Mountain goat. Pp. 1008–1020, in Wild mammals of North America, biology, management, and economics (J. A. Chapman and G. A. Feldhamer, eds.). Johns Hopkins Univ. Press, Baltimore, 1,147 pp.

Wigley, T. B., D. A. Miller, and G. K. Yarrow. 2008. Planning for bats on forest industry lands in North America. Pp. 293–318, in Bats in forests, conservation and management (M. J. Lacki, J. P. Hayes, and A. Kurta, eds.). Johns Hopkins Univ. Press, Baltimore, 352 pp.

Wilbert, C. J., S. W. Buskirk, and K. G. Gerow. 2000. Effects of weather and snow on habitat selection by American martens (*Martes americana*). Canadian J. Zool. 78:1691–1696.

Wild, M., and M. Miller. 2005. Throw disease to the wolves? Denver Post, August 9.

Wild, M. A., M. W. Miller, D. L. Baker, N. T. Hobbs, R. B. Gill, and B. J. Maynard. 1994. Comparing growth rates of dam- and hand-raised bighorn sheep, pronghorn, and elk neonates. J. Wildl. Mgmt. 58:340–347.

Wild, M. A., T. M. Shenk, and T. R. Spraker. 2006. Plague as a mortality factor in Canada lynx (*Lynx canadensis*) reintroduced to Colorado. J. Wildlife Diseases 42:646–650.

Wildlife Management Institute. 2008. Season's end, global warming's threat to hunting and fishing. Bipartisan Policy Center, Washington, DC, 109 pp.

Wildlife Services. 2002. A producer's guide to preventing predation of livestock. Program Aid, Animal and Plant Health Inspection Service, USDA 1722:1–10.

Wiley, R. W. 1971. Activity periods and movements of the eastern woodrat. Southwestern Nat. 16:43–54.

Wiley, R. W. 1980. *Neotoma floridana*. Mammalian Species 139: 1–7.

Wiley, R. W. 1984. Reproduction in the southern plains woodrat (*Neotoma micropus*) in western Texas. Spec. Publ. Mus., Texas Tech Univ. 22:137–164.

Wilkins, K. T. 1986. *Reithrodontomys montanus*. Mammalian Species 257:1–5.

Wilkins, K. T. 1989. *Tadarida brasiliensis*. Mammalian Species 331: 1–10.

Wilkinson, J. A., and J. F. Douglass. 2002. Mule deer group kills coyote. Western N. Amer. Nat. 52:253.

Willems, N. J., and K. B. Armitage. 1975a. Thermoregulation and water requirements in semiarid and montane populations of the least chipmunk, *Eutamias minimus*, I. Metabolic rate and body temperature. Comp. Biochem. Physiol. 51A:717–722.

Willems, N. J., and K. B. Armitage. 1975b. Thermoregulation and water requirements in semiarid and montane populations of the least chipmunk, *Eutamias minimus*, II. Water balance. Comp. Biochem. Physiol. 52A:109–120.

Willems, N. J., and K. B. Armitage. 1975c. Thermoregulation and water requirements in semiarid and montane populations of the least chipmunk, *Eutamias minimus*, III. Acclimatization at a high ambient temperature. Comp. Biochem. Physiol. 52A:121–128.

Willey, R. B., and R. E. Richards. 1974. The ringtail (*Bassariscus astutus*): vocal repertoire and Colorado distribution. J. Colorado-Wyoming Acad. Sci. 7(5):58.

Willey, R. B., and R. E. Richards. 1981. Vocalizations of the ringtail (*Bassariscus astutus*). Southwestern Nat. 26:23–30.

Williams, D. F. 1978. The systematics and ecogeographic variation of the Apache pocket mouse (Rodentia: Heteromyidae). Bull. Carnegie Mus. Nat. Hist. 10:1–57.

Williams, D. F., and J. S. Findley. 1979. Sexual size dimorphism in vespertilionid bats. Amer. Midland Nat. 102:113–126.

Williams, D. F., and H. H. Genoways. 1979. A systematic review of the olive-backed pocket mouse, *Perognathus fasciatus* (Rodentia, Heteromyidae). Ann. Carnegie Mus. 48:73–102.

Williams, E. S., and I. K. Barker, eds. 2001. Infectious diseases of wild animals, third ed. Iowa State Univ. Press, Ames, 558 pp.

Williams, E. S., J. K. Kirkwood, and M. W. Miller. 2001. Transmissible spongiform encephalopathies. Pp. 292–301, in Infectious diseases of wild mammals, third ed. (E. S. Williams and I. K. Barker, eds.). Iowa State Univ. Press, Ames, 446 pp.

Williams, E. S., M. W. Miller, T. J. Kreeger, R. H. Kahn, and E. T. Thorne. 2002. Chronic wasting disease of deer and elk: a review with recommendations for management. J. Wildl. Mgmt. 56:551–563.

Williams, G. P. 1978. Historical perspective of the Platte Rivers in Nebraska and Colorado. Pp. 11–41, in Lowland River and Stream Habitat in Colorado: a symposium (W. D. Graul and S. J. Bissell, eds.). Colorado Chapter, Wildlife Society, and Colorado Audubon Council, 195 pp.

Williams, O. 1952. New *Phenacomys* records from Colorado. J. Mamm. 33:399.

Williams, O. 1955a. The distribution of mice and shrews in a Colorado montane forest. J. Mamm. 36:221–231.

Williams, O. 1955b. Home range of *Peromyscus maniculatus rufinus* in a Colorado ponderosa pine community. J. Mamm. 36: 42–45.

Williams, O. 1955c. The food of mice and shrews in a Colorado montane forest. Univ. Colorado Studies, Ser. Biol. 3:109–114.

Williams, O. 1959. Food habits of the deer mouse. J. Mamm. 40: 415–419.

Williams, O., and B. A. Finney. 1964. *Endogone*—food for mice. J. Mamm. 45:265–271.

Williams, O., and G. S. McArthur. 1972. New information on the least shrew in northern Colorado. Southwestern Nat. 15:448–449.

Williams, P. K. 1968. Social tendencies of *Perognathus hispidus*. Texas J. Sci. 20:95–96.

Williams, S. L., and R. J. Baker. 1976. Vagility and local movements of pocket gophers (Geomyidae: Rodentia). Amer. Midland Nat. 96:303–316.

Williams, T. R. 1957. Marten and hawk harass snowshoe hare. J. Mamm. 38:517–518.

Williamson, S. M., R. K. Ross, and D. Irani. 2008. Economic impacts of climate change on Colorado. Center for Integrative Environ. Research, Univ. Maryland, College Park, 16 pp.

Willig, M. R., and K. W. Selcer. 1989. Bat species density gradients in the New World: a statistical assessment. J. Biogeography 16:189–195.

Willner, G. R., G. A. Feldhamer, E. E. Zucker, and J. A. Chapman. 1980. *Ondatra zibethicus*. Mammalian Species 141:1–8.

Wilshire, H. G., J. E. Neilson, and R. W. Hazlett. 2008. The American West at work, science, myth, and politics of land abuse and recovery. Oxford Univ. Press, New York, 640 pp.

Wilson, A. C., and V. M. Sarich. 1969. A molecular time scale for human evolution. Proc. Nat. Acad. Sci. 53:1088–1093.

Wilson, D. E. 1968. Ecological distribution of the genus *Peromyscus*. Southwestern Nat. 13:267–274.

Wilson, D. E. 1973. Systematic status of *Perognathus merriami*. Proc. Biol. Soc. Washington 86:175–192.

Wilson, D. E. 1982. Wolverine. Pp. 644–652, in Wild mammals of North America, biology, management, and economics (J. A. Chapman and G. A. Feldhamer, eds.). Johns Hopkins Univ. Press, Baltimore, 1,147 pp.

Wilson, D. E. 1997. Bats in question: the Smithsonian answer book. Smithsonian Institution Press, Washington, DC, 168 pp.

Wilson, D. E., and F. R. Cole. 2000. Common names of mammals of the world. Smithsonian Institution Press, Washington, DC, 204 pp.

Wilson, D. E., and J. F. Eisenberg. 1990. Origin and applications of mammalogy in North America. Current Mammal. 2:1–35.

Wilson, D. E., and D. Reeder. 1993. Mammals species of the world: a taxonomic and geographic reference, second ed. Smithsonian Institution Press, Washington, DC, 1,206 pp.

Wilson, D. E., and D. M. Reeder. 2005. Mammal species of the world, a taxonomic and geographic reference, third ed., 2 vols. Smithsonian Institution Press, Washington, DC.

Wilson, D. E., and S. Ruff, eds. 1999. The Smithsonian book of North American mammals. Smithsonian Institution Press, Washington, DC, 750 pp.

Wilson, E. O. 1992. The diversity of life. Belknap Press of Harvard Univ. Press, Cambridge, MA, 424 pp.

Wilson, G. M., and J. R. Choate. 1997. Taxonomic status and biogeography of the southern bog lemming, *Synaptomys cooperi*, on the central Great Plains. J. Mamm. 78:444–458.

Wilson, L. O., J. Blaidsell, G. Welsh, R. Weaver, R. Brigham, W. Kelly, J. Yoakum, M. Hinks, J. Turner, and J. De Forge. 1980. Desert bighorn habitat requirements and management recommendations. Trans. Desert Bighorn Council 24:1–7.

Wilson, P. J. 2003. Mitochondrial DNA extracted from eastern North American wolves killed in the 1800s is not of gray wolf origin. Canadian J. Zool. 81:936–940.

Wilson, P. J., S. Grewal, I. D. Lawford, J.N.M. Heal, A. G. Granacki, D. Pennock, J. B. Theberge, M. T. Theberge, D. R. Voigt, W. Waddell, R. E. Chambers, P. C. Paquet, G. Goulet, D. Cluff, and B. N. White. 2000. DNA profiles of the eastern Canadian wolf and the red wolf provide evidence for a common evolutionary history independent of the gray wolf. Canadian J. Zool. 78:1–11.

Wilson, S. M., and A. B. Carey. 1996. Observations of weasels in second-growth Douglas-fir forests in the Puget Trough, Washington. Northwest Nat. 77:35–39.

Wimsatt, J., T. J. O'Shea, L. E. Ellison, R. D. Pearce, and V. R. Price. 2005. Anesthesia and blood sampling of wild big brown bats (*Eptesicus fuscus*) with an assessment of impacts on survival. J. Wildl. Dis. 41:87–95.

Winter, S. L., and J. F. Cully, Jr. 2007. Burrowing owl associations with black-tailed prairie dog colonies in southwestern Kansas and southeastern Colorado. Prairie Nat. 39:69–73.

Winternitz, B. L., and D. W. Crumpacker. 1985. Species of special concern—Colorado Wildlife Workshop. Colorado Division of Wildlife, Denver, 92 pp.

Winterrowd, M. F., F. S. Dobson, J. L. Hoogland, and D. W. Foltz. 2009. Social subdivision influences effective population size in the colonial-breeding black-tailed prairie dog. J. Mamm. 90:380–387.

Wirsing, A. J., and D. L. Murray. 2002. Patterns of consumption of woody plants by snowshoe hares in the northwestern United States. Ecoscience 9:440–449.

Wirsing, A. J., T. D. Steury, and D. L. Murray. 2002. Relationship between body condition and vulnerability to predation in red squirrels and snowshoe hares. J. Mamm. 83:707–715.

Wisdom, M. J., and J. G. Cook. 2000. North American elk. Pp. 694–735, in Ecology and management of large mammals in North America (S. Demarais and P. R. Krausman, eds.). Prentice Hall, Upper Saddle River, NJ, 778 pp.

Wisely, S. M., R. M. Santymire, T. M. Livieri, P. E. Marinari, J. S. Kreeger, D. E. Wildt, and J. Howard. 2005. Environment influences morphology and development for in situ and ex situ populations of the black-footed ferret (*Mustela nigripes*). Animal Conservation 8:321–328.

Wisely, S. M., M. J. Statham, and R. C. Fleischer. 2008. Pleistocene refugia and Holocene expansion of a grassland-dependent species, the black-footed ferret (*Mustela nigripes*). J. Mamm. 89:87–96.

Wishart, W. D. 1978. Bighorn sheep. Pp. 161–172, in Big game of North America: ecology and management (J. L. Schmidt and D. L. Gilbert, eds.). Stackpole Books, Harrisburg, PA, 494 pp.

Wisz, M. S. 1999. Islands in the big sky: equilibrium biogeography of isolated mountain ranges in Montana. Unpubl. master's thesis, Univ. Colorado, Boulder.

Wockner, G., G. McNamee, and S. Campbell. 2005. Comeback wolves, western writers welcome the wolf home. Johnson Books, Boulder, CO. 207 pp.

Wolfe, L. L., M. W. Miller, and E. S. Williams. 2004. Feasibility of "test-and-cull" for managing chronic wasting disease in urban mule deer. Wildl. Soc. Bull. 32:500–505.

Wolfe, M. L. 1974. An overview of moose coactions with other animals. Naturaliste Canadienne 101:437–456.

Wolfe, M. L. 1980. Feral horse demography: a preliminary report. J. Range Mgmt. 33:354–359.

Wolfe, M. L., N. V. Debyle, C. S. Winchell, and T. R. McCabe. 1982. Snowshoe hare cover relationships in northern Utah. J. Wildl. Mgmt. 46:662–670.

Wolff, J. O., and G. C. Bateman. 1978. Effects of food availability and ambient temperature on torpor cycles of *Perognathus flavus* (Heteromyidae). J. Mamm. 59:707–716.

Wood, D. L., and A. D. Barnosky. 1994. Middle Pleistocene climate change in the Colorado Rocky Mountains indicated by fossil mammals from Porcupine Cave. Quaternary Res. 41:366–375.

Wood, J. E. 1955. Notes on reproduction and rate of increase of raccoons in the Post Oak Region of Texas. J. Wildl. Mgmt. 19:409–410.

Wood, J. E. 1958. Age structure and productivity of a gray fox population. J. Mamm. 39:74–86.

Woodburne, M. O., G. F. Gunnell, and R. K. Stucky. 2009a. Climate directly influences Eocene mammal faunal dynamics in North America. Proc. Nat. Acad. Sci. 106:13399–13403.

Woodburne, M. O., G. F. Gunnell, and R. K. Stucky. 2009b. Land mammal faunas of North America rise and fall during the Early Eocene Climatic Optimum. Annals, Denver Museum of Nature & Science 1:1–78.

Woods, C. A. 1973. *Erethizon dorsatum*. Mammalian Species 29:1–6.

Woods, C. A., and C. W. Kilpatrick. 2005. Infraorder Hystricognathi. Pp. 1538–1600, in Mammal species of the world, a taxonomic and geographic reference (D. E. Wilson and D. M. Reeder, eds.). Johns Hopkins University Press, Baltimore, 2 vols.

Woodward, T. N. 1980. Seasonal dietary preferences of bighorn sheep. Job Progress Rept., Colorado Division of Wildlife 2:330–336.

Woodward, T. N., R. J. Gutierrez, and W. H. Rutherford. 1974. Bighorn lamb production, survival, and mortality in south-central Colorado. J. Wildl. Mgmt. 38:771–774.

Woolley, T. P., and F. G. Lindzey. 1997. Relative precision and sources of bias in pronghorn sex and age composition surveys. J. Wildl. Mgmt. 51:57–63.

Workman, G. W., and J. B. Low, eds. 1976. Mule deer decline in the West: a symposium. Agric. Exp. Sta., College Nat. Resources, Utah State Univ., Logan, 134 pp.

Worley-Georg, M. P., and J. J. Eberle. 2006. Additions to the Chadronian mammalian fauna, Florissant Formation, Florissant Fossil Beds National Monument, Colorado. J. Paleo. 26:685–696.

Worthen, G. L., and D. L. Kilgore, Jr. 1981. Metabolic rate of pine marten in relation to air temperature. J. Mamm. 52:624–628.

Wostl, E., K. Navo, and N. LaMantia-Olson. 2009. Additional observations of the eastern pipistrelle (*Perimyotis subflavus*) in Colorado. Bat Research News 50:55–56.

Wozencraft, W. C. 1989. The phylogeny of the recent Carnivora. Pp. 495–535, in Carnivore behavior, ecology, and evolution (J. L. Gittleman, ed.). Comstock Publishing, Ithaca, NY, 620 pp.

Wozencraft, W. C. 1993. Order Carnivora. Pp. 279–348, in Mammal species of the world: a taxonomic and geographic reference, second ed. (D. W. Wilson and D. Reeder, eds.). Smithsonian Institution Press, Washington, DC, 1,206 pp.

Wozencraft, W. C. 2005. Order Carnivora. Pp. 532–628, in Mammal species of the world: a taxonomic and geographic reference, third ed. (D. E. Wilson and D. M. Reeder, eds.). Smithsonian Institution Press, Washington, DC, 2 vols.

Wright, G. J., R. O. Peterson, D. W. Smith, and T. O. Lemke. 2006. Selection of northern Yellowstone elk by gray wolves and hunters. J. Wildl. Mgmt. 70:1070–1078.

Wright, P. L. 1942. Delayed implantation in the long-tailed weasel (*Mustela frenata*), the short-tailed weasel (*Mustela cicognani*) and the marten (*Martes americana*). Anat. Record 83:341–353.

Wright, P. L. 1947. The sexual cycle of the male long-tailed weasel (*Mustela frenata*). J. Mamm. 28:343–352.

Wright, P. L. 1948a. Breeding habits of captive long-tailed weasels (*Mustela frenata*). Amer. Midland Nat. 39:338–344.

Wright, P. L. 1948b. Preimplantation stages in the long-tailed weasel (*Mustela frenata*). Anat. Record 100:595–607.

Wright, P. L. 1966. Observations on the reproductive cycles of the American badger (*Taxidea taxus*). Symp. Zool. Soc. London 15:27–45.

Wright, P. L. 1969. The reproductive cycle of the male American badger, *Taxidea taxus*. J. Reproductive Fert., Suppl. 5:435–445.

Wunder, B. A. 1974. The effect of activity on body temperature of Ord's kangaroo rat (*Dipodomys ordii*). Physiol. Zool. 47: 29–36.

Wunder, B. A. 1984. Strategies for, and environmental cueing mechanisms of, seasonal changes in thermoregulatory parameters of small mammals. Pp. 165–172, in Winter ecology of small mammals (J. F. Merritt, ed.). Spec. Publ., Carnegie Mus. Nat. Hist. 10:1–380.

Wunder, B. A. 1985. Energetics and thermoregulation. Pp. 812–844, in Biology of New World *Microtus* (R. H. Tamarin, ed.). Spec. Publ., Amer. Soc. Mammalogists 8:1–893.

Wunder, B. A. 2000. Mountain goats in Colorado: native or not? Pp. 11–26, in Scientific assessment of the potential effects of mountain goats on the ecosystems of Rocky Mountain National Park (J. E. Gross, M. C. Kneeland, D. M. Swift, and B. A. Wunder eds.). Report to Rocky Mountain National Park, Estes Park, CO.

Wunder, L. A. 1987. Behavior and activity pattern of a maternity colony of *Myotis lucifugus*. Unpubl. doctoral dissert., Colorado State Univ., 127 pp.

Wunder, L. A., and D. J. Nash. 1981. Behavior of juvenile *Myotis lucifugus* in a summer nursery colony. J. Colorado-Wyoming Acad. Sci. 13:50–51.

Wyss, A. R. 1987. The walrus auditory region and the monophyly of pinnipeds. Amer. Mus. Novitates 2871:1–31.

Wyss, A. R. 1988. Evidence from flipper structure for a single origin of pinnipeds. Nature 334:427–428.

Wyss, A. R. 1989. Flippers and pinniped phylogenies: has the problem of convergence been overrated? Marine Mamm. Sci. 5:343–360.

Wywialowski, A. P., and G. W. Smith. 1988. Selection of microhabitat by the red-backed vole, *Clethrionomys gapperi*. Great Basin Nat. 48:216–223.

Yahner, R. H. 2003. Pine squirrels, *Tamiasciurus hudsonicus* and *T. douglasii*. Pp. 268–275, in Wild mammals of North America, biology, management, and economics, second ed. (G. A. Feldhamer, B. C. Thompson, and J. A. Chapman, eds.). Johns Hopkins Univ. Press, Baltimore, 1,216 pp.

Yamaguchi, N., and D. W. Macdonald. 2003. The burden of cooccupancy: intraspecific resource competition and spacing patterns in American mink, *Mustela vison*. J. Mamm. 84:1341–1355.

Yates, T. L., et al. 2002. The ecology and evolutionary history of an emergent disease: Hantavirus Pulmonary Syndrome. BioScience 52:989–998.

Yates, T. L., W. L. Gannon, and D. E. Wilson, eds. 1996. Life among the muses: papers in honor of J. S. Findley. Spec. Publ., Mus. Southwestern Biol. 3:1–302.

Yates, T. L., and R. J. Pedersen. 1982. Moles. Pp. 37–51, in Wild mammals of North America, biology, management, and economics (J. A. Chapman and G. A. Feldhamer, eds.). Johns Hopkins Univ. Press, Baltimore, 1,147 pp.

Yates, T. L., and D. J. Schmidly. 1978. *Scalopus aquaticus*. Mammalian Species 105:1–4.

Yeager, L. E. 1950. Implications of some harvest and habitat factors on pine marten management. Trans. N. Amer. Wildl. Conf. 15:319–335.

Yeager, L. E. 1959. Status and population trend of fox squirrels on fringe range, Colorado. J. Wildl. Mgmt. 23:102–107.

Yeager, L. E., and K. G. Hay. 1955. A contribution toward a bibliography on the beaver. Tech. Bull., Colorado Dept. Game and Fish 1:1–103.

Yeager, L. E., and J. D. Remington. 1956. Sight observations of Colorado martens, 1950–1955. J. Mamm. 37:521–524.

Yeager, L. E., and W. H. Rutherford. 1957. An ecological basis for beaver management in the Rocky Mountain region. Trans. N. Amer. Wildl. Nat. Resources Conf. 22:269–300.

Yensen, E., D. L. Quinney, K. Johnson, K. Timmerman, and K. Steenhof. 1992. Fire, vegetation changes and population fluctuations of Townsend's ground squirrels. Amer. Midland Nat. 128:299–312.

Yensen, E., and P. W. Sherman. 2003. Ground squirrels, *Spermophilus* and *Ammospermophilus* species. Pp. 211–223, in Wild mammals of North America, biology, management, and economics, second ed. (G. A. Feldhamer, B. C. Thompson, and J. A. Chapman, eds.). Johns Hopkins Univ. Press, Baltimore, 1,216 pp.

Yoakum, J. D., and D. E. Spalinger, comps. 1979. American pronghorn antelope. Wildlife Society, Washington, DC, 244 pp.

York, C. L. 1949. Notes on home ranges and population density of two species of heteromyid rodents in southwestern Texas. Texas J. Sci. 1:42–46.

Young, M. T. 2000. Colorado wildlife viewing guide, second ed. Falcon Publishing, Helena, MT, 216 pp.

Young, R. T. 1908. Notes on the distribution of Colorado mammals, with description of a new species of bat (*Eptesicus pallidus*) from Boulder. Proc. Acad. Nat. Sci. Philadelphia 60:403–409.

Young, S. P., and E. A. Goldman. 1944. The wolves of North America. American Wildlife Institute, Washington, DC, 385 pp.

Young, S. P., and E. A. Goldman. 1946. The puma, mysterious American cat. American Wildlife Institute, Washington, DC, 358 pp.

Young, S. P., and H.H.T. Jackson. 1951. The clever coyote. Wildlife Management Institute, Washington, DC, 411 pp.

Youngman, P. M. 1958. Geographic variation in the pocket gopher, *Thomomys bottae*, in Colorado. Misc. Publ. Mus. Nat. Hist., Univ. Kansas 9:363–384.

Zabel, C. J., and R. G. Anthony. 2003. Mammal community dynamics: management and conservation in the coniferous forests of western North America. Cambridge Univ. Press, Cambridge, UK, 709 pp.

Zackheim, H. 1982. Ecology and population status of the river otter in southwestern Montana. Unpubl. master's thesis, Univ. Montana, Missoula, 100 pp.

Zahratka, J. L. 2004. The population and habitat ecology of snowshoe hares (*Lepus americanus*) in the Southern Rocky Mountains. Unpubl. master's thesis, Univ. Wyoming, Laramie, 88 pp.

Zahratka, J. L., and S. W. Buskirk. 2007. Is size of fecal pellets a reliable indicator of species of leporids in the Southern Rocky Mountains? J. Wildl. Mgmt. 71:2081–2083.

Zahratka, J. L., and T. M. Shenk. 2008. Population estimates of snowshoe hares in the Southern Rocky Mountains. J. Wildl. Mgmt. 72:906–912.

Zaradic, P. A., O.R.W. Pergams, and P. Kareiva. 2009. The impact of nature experience on willingness to support conservation. PLoS ONE 4(10):1–5.

Zegers, D. A. 1977. Energy dynamics and role of Richardson's ground squirrel (*Spermophilus richardsonii elegans*) in a montane meadow ecosystem. Unpubl. doctoral dissert., Univ. Colorado, Boulder, 177 pp.

Zegers, D. A. 1981. Time budgets of Wyoming ground squirrels, *Spermophilus elegans*. Great Basin Nat. 41:222–228.

Zegers, D. A. 1984. *Spermophilus elegans*. Mammalian Species 214: 1–7.

Zegers, D. A., and O. Williams. 1979. Energy flow through a population of Richardson's ground squirrels. Acta Theriol. 24: 221–235.

Zeigenfuss, L. C., F. J. Singer, S. A. Williams, and T. L. Johnson. 2002. Influences of herbivory and water on willow in elk winter range. J. Wildl. Mgmt. 66:788–795.

Zelley, R. A. 1971. The sounds of the fox squirrel, *Sciurus niger rufiventer*. J. Mamm. 52:597–604.

Zielinski, W. J., and N. P. Duncan. 2004. Diets of sympatric populations of American martens (*Martes americana*) and fishers (*Martes pennanti*) in California. J. Mamm. 85:470–477.

Zimmerman, E. G., C. W. Kilpatrick, and B. J. Hart. 1978. The genetics of speciation in the rodent genus *Peromyscus*. Evolution 32:565–579.

Zimmerman, E. G., and M. E. Nejtek. 1977. Genetics and speciation of three semispecies of *Neotoma*. J. Mamm. 58:391–402.

Zimmerman, G., P. Stapp, and B. Van Horne. 1996. Seasonal variation in the diet of great horned owls (*Bubo virginianus*) of shortgrass prairie. Amer. Midland Nat. 136:149–156.

Zinn, H. C. 2003. Hunting and sociodemographic trends: older hunters from Pennsylvania and Colorado. Wildl. Soc. Bull. 31:1004–1014.

Zinn, H. C., and W. F. Andelt. 1999. Attitudes of Fort Collins, Colorado, residents toward prairie dogs. Wildl. Soc. Bull. 27: 1098–1106.

Zinn, H. C., and M. J. Manfredo. 1996. Societal preferences for mountain lion management along Colorado's Front Range. Human Dimensions Perspectives, Occas. Paper Series, Colorado Division of Wildlife 29:1–5.

Zoellick, B. W., C. E. Harris, R. T. Kelly, T. P. O'Farrell, T. T. Kato, and M. E. Koopman. 2002. Movements and home ranges of San Joaquin kit foxes (*Vulpes macrotis mutica*) relative to oilfield development. Western N. Amer. Nat. 52:151–159.

Zoellick, B. W., H. M. Ulmschneider, B. S. Cade, and A. W. Stanley. 2004. Isolation of Snake River islands and mammalian predation of waterfowl nests. J. Wildl. Mgmt. 58:650–662.

Zontek, K. 2007. Buffalo nation: American Indian efforts to restore the bison. Bison Books, Lincoln, NE, 256 pp.

Zubaid, A., G. F. McCracken, and T. H. Kunz. 2006. Functional and evolutionary ecology of bats. Oxford Univ. Press, New York, 360 pp.

Zumbaugh, D. M., J. R. Choate, and L. B. Fox. 1985. Winter food habits of the swift fox on the central High Plains. Prairie Nat. 17:41–47.

Zwinger, A. H., and B. E. Willard. 1972. Land above the trees, a guide to American alpine tundra. Harper and Row, New York, 487 pp.

Index

Page numbers in *italics* indicate illustrations.

INDEX

INDEX

INDEX